## Mileage Chart

**New York City**

| 10 = Distance in miles |
|---|
| 10 = Distance in kilometers |

| | | | | | | | | | |
|---|---|---|---|---|---|---|---|---|---|
| **233** / 375 | **Washington, DC** | | | | | | | | |
| **779** / 1253 | **688** / 1107 | **Chicago** | | | | | | | |
| **1286** / 2069 | **1050** / 1689 | **1371** / 2206 | **Miami** | | | | | | |
| **1300** / 2092 | **1073** / 1726 | **922** / 1483 | **856** / 1377 | **New Orleans** | | | | | |
| **1541** / 2479 | **1315** / 2116 | **921** / 1482 | **1349** / 2171 | **515** / 829 | **Dallas** | | | | |
| **1793** / 2885 | **1669** / 2685 | **994** / 1599 | **2079** / 3345 | **1390** / 2237 | **878** / 1413 | **Denver** | | | |
| **2816** / 4531 | **2725** / 4385 | **2030** / 3266 | **3329** / 5356 | **2690** / 4328 | **2178** / 3504 | **1306** / 2101 | **Seattle** | | |
| **2873** / 4623 | **2782** / 4476 | **2106** / 3389 | **3106** / 4998 | **2272** / 3656 | **1729** / 2782 | **1248** / 2008 | **801** / 1289 | **San Francisco** | |
| **2763** / 4444 | **2640** / 4248 | **1989** / 3200 | **2736** / 4402 | **1902** / 3060 | **1445** / 2325 | **998** / 1606 | **1131** / 1820 | **382** / 614 | **Los Angeles** |

EYEWITNESS TRAVEL

# USA

EYEWITNESS TRAVEL

# USA

DK

LONDON, NEW YORK,
MELBOURNE, MUNICH AND DELHI
www.dk.com

MANAGING EDITOR  Aruna Ghose
ART EDITOR  Benu Joshi
PROJECT EDITOR  Vandana Mohindra
EDITORS  Kajori Aikat, Rimli Borooah,
Nandini Mehta, Manjari Rathi
DESIGNERS  Pallavi Narain, Supriya Sahai, Priyanka Thakur
SENIOR CARTOGRAPHER  Uma Bhattacharya
CARTOGRAPHER  Alok Pathak
PICTURE RESEARCHER  Taiyaba Khatoon
ADDITIONAL PICTURE RESEARCH  Kiran K. Mohan
DTP COORDINATOR  Shailesh Sharma
DTP DESIGNER  Vinod Harish
US EDITOR  Mary Sutherland

MAIN CONTRIBUTORS
Jackie Finch, Andrew Hempstead, Jamie Jensen, Nancy Mikula, Joanne Miller,
Eric Peterson, Kevin Roe, Kap Stann

MAIN PHOTOGRAPHERS
Andy Holligan, Jon Spaull, Peter Wilson

MAIN ILLUSTRATORS
Arun P, Gautam Trivedi

Printed and bound by South China Printing Co. Ltd. (China)

First American Edition, 2004

14 15 16 17 10 9 8 7 6 5 4 3 2 1

Published in the United States by DK Publishing,
375 Hudson Street, New York, New York 10014

**Reprinted with revisions 2006, 2008, 2010, 2012, 2015**

ISSN 5668-5834
ISBN 978-1-46541-206-5

MIX
Paper from
responsible sources
FSC
www.fsc.org  FSC™ C018179

Front cover main image: View over Monument Valley from the top of Hunt's Mesa, Arizona

◀ Beautiful mountain terrain of Yosemite National Park, California

Bronze bull, symbol of Wall Street, near the
US Custom House, New York City

# Contents

View of Dallas from the Reunion Tower Observation area

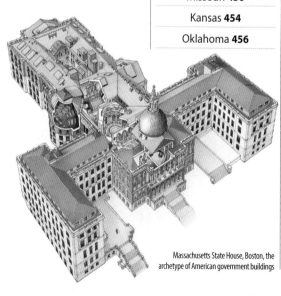

Massachusetts State House, Boston, the archetype of American government buildings

# HOW TO USE THIS GUIDE

This guide helps you to get the most from your visit to the United States. *Visiting the USA* maps the country and gives tips on practical considerations and travel. *USA at a Glance* gives an overview of some of the main attractions and a brief history of the country. The book is divided into 14 regional sections, each covering from one to seven states. The chapter on each region starts with a historical portrait and a map of the area. The main sightseeing section then follows and includes maps of the major cities. For each region there is a section of practical and travel information, followed by listings of recommended hotels and restaurants.

## USA MAP

The colored areas shown on the map on the inside front cover indicate the 14 regional chapters in this guide. **For each region** there is an index of the practical and listings pages at the end of the chapter.

**1 At a Glance**
The map here highlights the different states in each section as well as the most interesting cities, towns, and regions.

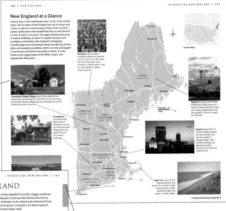

**Each region chapter** has color-coded thumb tabs.

**2 Introduction to a Region**
This section gives the reader an insight into the region's geography, historical background, politics, and the character of the people. A chart lists the key dates and events in the region's history.

**3 Regional Map**
For easy reference, sights in each region are numbered and plotted on a map. The black bullet numbers (eg. ❸) also indicate the order in which the sights are covered in the chapter.

**Sights at a Glance** lists the numbered sights in sequential order.

**4 City Map**
This plots individual sights within the most important cities. The sights within a city such as Boston are indicated with clear bullet numbers (eg. ⑫), in contrast to the black bullets used on the regional maps.

**Visitors' Checklist** gives all the practical information needed to plan your visit.

**Sights at a Glance** lists the numbered sights within the city.

**5 Major Sights**
Historic buildings are dissected to reveal their interiors, while museums and galleries have color-coded floor plans to help you find the most important exhibits.

**Stars indicate** the features that no visitor should miss.

**6 Detailed Information**
Cities, towns, and other sights are described individually. Their entries appear in the same order as the numbering on the regional map at the beginning of the section.

**Each entry** begins with essential practical information, including the address and telephone number of the local tourist information office. Opening times are given for major sights and museums.

**7 Practical Information**
This section covers subjects such as travel, security, shopping, and entertainment. Some cities, such as New York, are covered separately.

**Directory boxes** give contact information for the services and venues mentioned in the text.

**Climate charts** are also provided for each region.

# VISITING
# THE USA

# DISCOVERING THE USA

The following tours have been designed to take in as many of the country's highlights as possible, while keeping long-distance travel to a minimum. First come five two-day tours of some of the USA's most notable cities: New York City, Washington DC, Boston, Chicago, and San Francisco. With abundant attractions, inviting neighborhoods, and thriving cultural scenes, these metropolises are consistently ranked among North America's most popular cities for visitors. These itineraries can be followed individually or combined to form longer tours. Next come six five-day tours, covering historic New England, sunny Southern Florida, the atmospheric South and Texas, the breathtaking Southwest and Rockies, iconic California, and the spectacular Pacific Northwest. These regions are filled with countless activities and attractions, including some of the world's most decorated wine regions. The routes can be combined to make a superb multi-week trip through the whole country. Pick, combine, and follow your favorite tours, or simply dip in and out and be inspired.

**Golden Gate Bridge**
San Francisco's Golden Gate Bridge, stretching 1.7 miles (2.7 km) across San Francisco Bay, links the city with Marin County and offers breathtaking views.

## Five Days in the Pacific Northwest

- Explore the inviting shops, design studios, and cafés that populate **Portland's** trendy **Pearl District**.
- Dodge the flying fish found at **Seattle's** famous **Pike Place Market**.
- Feel humbled by the magisterial beauty of **Mount Rainier National Park** and **Mount St. Helens National Volcanic Monument**.

## Five Days in California

- Treat yourself to samples at the world-class wineries found in the **Napa** and **Sonoma Valleys**.
- Snap a photo at the base of **San Francisco's** one and only **Golden Gate Bridge**.
- Pretend you're a movie star while strolling along **Los Angeles's** iconic **Sunset** and **Hollywood Boulevards**.

## Five Days in the Southwest and Rockies

- Take in the glitz and glamour that line the **Las Vegas Strip**.
- Peer into the vast expanse of the **Grand Canyon** and marvel at one of nature's great wonders.
- Enjoy the unique adobe architecture that makes **Santa Fe** one of the country's most breathtaking cities.

**New England**
Picturesque historic villages, such as this Shaker-style settlement with a classic New England steepled church, abound in New England.

## Five Days in New England

- Visit **Newport** to stroll the **Cliff Walk**, stopping to take in historic mansions such as the **Breakers**.
- Enjoy stunning natural scenes by driving the famous **27-mile Loop Road** in **Acadia National Park**.
- Experience **Portland's** atmospheric **Old Port** neighborhood.

## Five Days in the Deep South, Southeast, and Texas

- Give yourself a history lesson at **Atlanta's Martin Luther King Jr. National Historic Site** and the **Jimmy Carter Library & Museum**.
- Let the good times roll by shopping, dining, and drinking the day away on **New Orleans's** famous **Royal** and **Bourbon Streets**.
- Channel your inner cowboy (or cowgirl) with a visit to the **Fort Worth Stockyards National Historic District**.

**Key**

— Five Days in the Pacific Northwest
— Five Days in California
— Five Days in the Southwest and Rockies
— Five Days in New England
— Five Days in the Deep South, Southeast, and Texas
— Five Days in South Florida

**Florida Keys**
This chain of fossilized coral islands protected by a coral reef draws visitors to fish, snorkel, dive, and enjoy the sandy beaches.

## Five Days in South Florida

- Snorkel or swim the coral reefs of the **Florida Keys**.
- Indulge in **Miami Beach's** world-class nightlife and **Art Deco** architecture.
- Be amazed by the vast landscapes of the **Everglades National Park**.

## Two Days in New York City

*With careful planning, many of the city's most famous sites and unique experiences can be enjoyed during a two-day visit.*

### Day 1
**Morning** Start with a 1-hour guided tour of the city's vast **Metropolitan Museum of Art** *(p90)*, known as the Met, offered every 15 minutes daily from 10:15am. Art lovers should make the short walk across Fifth Avenue to Frank Lloyd Wright's amazing **Solomon R. Guggenheim Museum** *(p92)*, home to one of the world's most acclaimed modern art collections. Follow this with a walk through neighboring **Central Park** *(pp88–9)*.

**Afternoon** Hop on the Fifth Avenue bus to 59th Street and Grand Army Plaza, then walk on down **Fifth Avenue** *(p87)* to the **Rockefeller Center** *(p86)* at 49th Street, passing shopping meccas such as Bergdorf Goodman, Tiffany, Trump Tower, and Saks Fifth Avenue, as well as the striking **St. Patrick's Cathedral** *(p87)*. Visit the 89th-floor observatory at the **Empire State Building** *(p83)* for the legendary panorama of the city. For souvenir shopping, **Macy's** *(p83)* is a block west, or continue on to the bright lights of **Times Square** *(p84)*.

### Day 2
**Morning** To avoid long lines, head to **Battery Park City** *(p77)* early to catch the boat to the **Statue of Liberty** *(p77)* and **Ellis Island** *(p77)*, the symbol of America's immigrant heritage. There will be time on your return to visit the moving **World Trade Center Site and 9/11 Memorial** *(p76)*, in Lower Manhattan (book in advance). If time allows, take a quick walk down **Wall Street** *(p76)*.

**Afternoon** Stroll around the leafy lanes of trendy **Greenwich Village** *(pp80–81)* and browse

Washington's colonnaded Jefferson Memorial on the banks of the Tidal Basin

its many world-class boutiques selling everything from books and clothes to gourmet culinary treats. Give your feet a break by sampling the lively cafés and coffee shops of **SoHo** *(p80)*.

## Two Days in Washington DC

*The USA's capital is full of breathtaking monuments, attractive neighborhoods, and historic sites.*

### Day 1
**Morning** Start the day with a roam around the nation's legislative heart, the Neo-Classical **United States Capitol** *(pp202–203)*. Then stroll the grand mile-long **Mall** *(pp204–205)*, lined on either side with an amazing choice of museums. Stop at the **National Museum of American History** *(p207)* to see the First Ladies exhibition, the flag that inspired the national anthem, and Abraham Lincoln's top hat. Afterward, join the line for the elevator taking you to the top of the city's tallest landmark, the **Washington Monument** *(p208)*.

**Afternoon** Take in one of the world's most recognizable homes, the **White House** *(pp210–11)*, residence of the US president, then take a virtual tour at the **White House Visitor Center** *(p211)*. End the day with a show at the **Kennedy Center** *(p212)*, renowned for its music, theater, and ballet productions.

### Day 2
**Morning** While away a few hours exploring the trove of great paintings at the **National Gallery of Art** *(p206)*. Then head to the **National Air & Space Museum** *(p205)*, which showcases exhibits ranging from the Wright brothers' first airplane to the latest space rockets.

**Afternoon** Walk along **Tidal Basin** *(p208)*, which is particularly pretty when the cherry trees are in blossom. Take in the striking monuments honoring past presidents, including the **Jefferson Memorial** *(p208)* and **Franklin D. Roosevelt Memorial** *(p209)*. A short distance from here is the awe-inspiring **Lincoln Memorial** *(p209)*, which looms large over the Reflecting Pool. Make your way to the **Smithsonian American Art Museum & National Portrait Gallery** *(p207)*, which houses portraits of all the American presidents.

## Two Days in Boston

*Boston's importance in American history has left it with a unique architectural heritage. It has a wealth of sights, parks, and gardens.*

### Day 1
**Morning** Compact and walkable, **Boston** can be easily explored on foot. Begin your day at **Boston Common** and the **Public Gardens** *(p141)*. Grab a coffee and stroll the Back Bay's *(p151)* world-class shops before the crowds arrive.

Boston Common, one of the city's green spaces, surrounded by high-rise buildings

**Afternoon** Continue your culture crawl of the city with a relaxing afternoon at one of the nearby museums – the **Museum of Fine Arts** *(p152)* or the **Isabella Stewart Gardner Museum** *(p152)*.

**Day 2**
**Morning** Explore some of New England's priciest real estate in the historic **Beacon Hill** *(pp140–41)* neighborhood. Grab a jolt of caffeine at a stylish coffee shop and then peruse the high-end boutiques and antique shops lining the neighborhood's primary artery, beautiful **Charles Street** *(p140)*.

**Afternoon** Head toward the waterfront to enjoy the city's major attraction, the **New England Aquarium** *(p149)*. Join the steady stream of locals, international visitors, and student groups who fill **Quincy Market** *(p147)* to shop, dine, and watch street performers. Check out neighboring **Faneuil Hall** *(p142)*, one of the city's most historic sights. In the evening, stroll through the atmospheric **North End** *(pp142–3)*. Stop by the **Paul Revere House** *(p148)*, and the atmospheric **Old North Church** *(p148)*; both are particularly photogenic at night.

## Two Days in Chicago

*The Midwest's largest city is a labyrinth of historic neighborhoods. Chicago is famous for its imposing architecture and vibrant cultural institutions.*

**Day 1**
**Morning** Explore the impressive collections at the **Art Institute of Chicago** *(p388)*. Highlights include the impressionist collection and the modern art wing. Afterward, check out the contemporary art in **Millennium Park** *(p388)*, including the Pritzker Pavilion with Frank Gehry's sweeping bandshell and Juan Plensa's "Crown Fountain."

Navy Pier, a bustling recreational and cultural center in Chicago

**Afternoon** Window shop on the **Magnificent Mile** *(p386)*. Look out for the castle-like Water Tower and Pumping Station. North of here, the Fourth Presbyterian Church is the second-oldest surviving building on Michigan Avenue. Across the street, visit the **John Hancock Center** *(p387)* for panoramic views.

**Day 2**
**Morning** Start out at **Navy Pier** *(p387)*, browsing shops before enjoying the fun at the **Chicago Children's Museum** *(p387)*. Those without kids can take in a state-of-the-art IMAX movie.

**Afternoon** The museum campus houses three cultural gems: the **Field Museum**, the **John G. Shedd Aquarium**, and the **Adler Planetarium and Astronomy Museum** *(p391)*. Afterward, enjoy the gorgeous harbor views from the campus lawn. At sunset, catch the sound and light show at **Buckingham Fountain** *(p390)*.

## Two Days in San Francisco

*Set on steep, wooded hills, this jewel of a city has historic sights, cultural treasures, and distinct, characterful neighborhoods.*

**Day 1**
**Morning** Fit in with the healthy California types and do some pedal-powered sightseeing by renting a bike *(p698)*. Start out

from the colorful **Fisherman's Wharf** *(p690)* and cycle over the magnificent **Golden Gate Bridge** *(p695)* to the pretty former fishing town of **Sausalito** *(p697)*. Then catch a ferry back and have lunch at a café in the **Ferry Building** *(p686)*. After lunch, take a quick look at the Gandhi Monument and its inscription *(p686)* on the building's east side.

**Afternoon** Visit **North Beach** *(p690)*, stopping off at some of the historic businesses that have made the neighborhood famous: **City Lights Bookstore**, **Vesuvio**, and **Caffè Trieste** *(p690)*. Make the climb to snap scenic photos from the top of **Coit Tower** *(p690)*. End the day with a ferry trip to visit **Alcatraz Island** *(p691)*, site of the notorious, historic prison (tickets are limited, so book ahead).

**Day 2**
**Morning** Stroll around the former "Flower Power" district of **Haight Ashbury** *(p693)*, stopping to check out the iconic **Red Victorian B&B** *(p693)*. Work your way east-by-northeast until you reach the city's **Chinatown** *(p688)*, stopping for lunch in one of the many award-winning eateries.

**Afternoon** Take in the spectacular **California Academy of Sciences** *(p694)*, which covers virtually every aspect of the natural world. Then, take a bus across town until you reach historic **Mission Dolores** *(p693)*, in the heart of one of the city's trendiest neighborhoods, the Mission District.

Typical Victorian houses in San Francisco's Haight Ashbury district

## Five Days in New England

- **Arriving** Fly into T.F. Green Airport, located just south of Providence, and fly out of Portland International Jetport. As an alternative, visitors can fly in and out of Boston's Logan International Airport.

- **Transport** Eastern Massachusetts can pose parking and traffic problems, so consider whether the area's transport options – notably the MBTA – satisfy your needs. There are bus and rail options linking most of New England's major cities, but to best explore the region a car is needed.

### Day 1: Providence and Newport

**Providence** (pp160–61), Rhode Island's largest city, is full of visitor attractions. Head downtown to admire the imposing **Rhode Island State House** with its white marble dome. Then stroll through the **Waterplace Park and Riverwalk** (p160) before heading uphill to peruse the eclectic neighborhood shops and ethnic eateries near the **Brown University** (p160) campus. From there take in **Benefit Street's "Mile of History"** (p160), which includes houses ranging in style from Colonial and Federal to Greek Revival and Victorian. Grab a bite at one of the city's hot-dog stands, then cross the tiny state

Rhode Island State House, Providence, with its marble dome and bronze statue

to reach the small city of **Newport** (p162). Later, walk some (or all) of the 3.5-mile (5.5-km) **Cliff Walk** (p163), stopping to admire historic mansions such as the **Breakers** (p163).

### Days 2 and 3: Boston

*Make the quick trip north to Boston, then follow the "Two Days in Boston" itinerary on pp12–13.*

### Day 4: Acadia National Park to Bar Harbor

Get an early start and drive to Maine's **Acadia National Park** (p180), being sure to take the **27-mile (43-km) Loop Road**, the park's stunning main attraction. Once darkness nears, make the short trip to **Bar Harbor** (p180). The area's busiest port is popular for its restaurants, shops, and lodging options.

### Day 5: Portland

Head south to Maine's primary hub. Though it has burned down four times since its establishment in 1633, **Portland** (p178) remains one of America's most inviting small cities. Take a stroll along Congress Street and through the restored **Old Port District**. Spend the afternoon viewing the Winslow Homer collections at the **Portland Museum of Art** (p178), or visit the historical **Victoria Mansion** or the **Wadsworth-Longfellow House** (p178).

## Five Days in South Florida

- **Arriving** Miami International Airport, west of downtown, and the smaller Fort Lauderdale International Airport, about 30 minutes north of Miami, have direct flights to and from international major cities.

- **Transport** There are some bus lines and private tour companies, but most visitors to South Florida rent a car.

### Day 1: Miami

Start your visit downtown at **Bayside Marketplace** (p294), the launch point for numerous boat-trip operators. Enjoy a

morning coffee at this fun complex, then take a 90-minute cruise to see the mansions of the rich and famous and the Miami skyline. Stop at HistoryMiami in the **Miami-Dade Cultural Center** (p294) to appreciate the dynamic history of the region, its Latin influences, and the rate at which it has grown. Enjoy the rest of the day relaxing and people-watching on the hedonistic playground that is **South Beach** (p292) before sampling its famed nightlife.

### Day 2: Miami Beach

Relax on **Miami Beach** (pp292–3). A walk down Ocean Drive between 6th and 13th Streets provides the most concentrated collection of tropical-motif **Art Deco** (pp292–3) buildings in the world. Stroll the shops of the **Lincoln Road Mall** (p292) before settling on a sidewalk café. If time allows, learn about the region's Jewish heritage with a visit to the moving **Holocaust Memorial** (p293), where the centerpiece is an enormous arm and hand reaching upward.

### Day 3: Florida Keys

Drive down the Overseas Highway (US 1) into the Florida Keys. At **Key Largo** (p322), head for **John Pennekamp Coral Reef State Park** (p322) to arrange a visit to the coral reef. Plan on 3 hours for snorkel or glass-bottom boat tours. After lunch, continue along US 1 toward **Key West** (p323) for a walk along **Duval Street** (p323), capped off with sunset at **Mallory Square** (p323).

### Day 4: Florida Keys

Start your day by hopping aboard the **Conch Train** (p323) for a narrated overview of the city. Stop at **Wreckers' Museum** (p323), which illustrates the Keys' long maritime history. Then head to the Spanish-colonial-style **Hemingway Home** (p323), where the writer Ernest Hemingway lived from 1931 to 1940. Browse the city's many colorful shops, then enjoy a margarita at a lively bar or café.

*For practical information on traveling around the USA, see pp30–35*

Miami Beach, stretching for 10 miles (16 km) along the Florida coast

## Day 5: Everglades National Park

Finally, head deep into the heart of the massive **Everglades National Park** (p321). Enter the park via Main Park Road for a 39-mile (63-km) scenic drive. Visit the **Pa-hay-okee Overlook** (p321) for a panorama of the vast "river of grass." At **Flamingo** (p321), manatees and American crocodiles may be spotted near the marina. On the return trip, a stroll down the **Mahogany Hammock Trail** (p321) takes you through one of the Everglades' tree islands.

### Five Days in the Deep South, Southeast, and Texas

- **Arriving** Fly into Hartsfield–Jackson Atlanta International Airport. Depart from Austin's Bergstrom International Airport.

- **Transport** While there are some bus and rail options linking major cities, a car is the easiest way to get around.

## Day 1: Atlanta

**Atlanta** (p262) is a booming metropolis generally considered to be the capital of the South, and an ideal introduction to the region. Learn about the city's role in hosting the 1996 Summer Olympics with a visit to downtown's **Centennial Olympic Park** (p262). Nearby are two of the city's most popular attractions: the modern **Georgia Aquarium** (p262) and the

impressive **World of Coca-Cola** (p262). The world headquarters of CNN are here, and visitors can channel their inner newscaster with a visit to the **CNN Studio** (p262). Historical attractions include the **Martin Luther King Jr. National Historic Site** (p262) and the **Jimmy Carter Library & Museum** (p263).

## Day 2: Alabama to New Orleans

Drive southwest through **Alabama** (p364), cutting through the heart of the Deep South. Cities such as **Montgomery** (p364), the state capital, **Selma** (p364), and **Mobile** (p364) are all worthy of a quick pit stop. Stay on course and you'll arrive at **New Orleans** (pp342–51) before sundown. Spend the evening sampling the city's dining and live music scenes.

## Day 3: New Orleans

Get to know 18th-century New Orleans with historical exhibitions in the **Cabildo** (p346). Then proceed past street musicians and fortune-tellers to the **Presbytère** (p346) for some colorful carnival culture at the Mardi Gras museum. Stroll through the gardens in lively **Jackson Square** (p345) towards the restored **Old US Mint** (p344). Take a shopping break to the **French Market** (p344), which is filled with open-air produce stalls and souvenir stands. Then stroll down **Royal Street** (p349), which is lined with art galleries and antique shops, before ducking around the corner

onto infamous **Bourbon Street** (p348), home to countless lively bars serving lethal cocktails and music clubs.

## Day 4: Dallas

If an all-day drive through swamp-filled Louisiana and dusty East Texas doesn't inspire, take one of the numerous daily flights from New Orleans to the Dallas-Fort Worth region. Any visit to **Dallas** (p472) must include a stop at the **Sixth Floor Museum** (p472), which provides a chilling look back at the 1963 assassination of President John F. Kennedy. Other worthy cultural sites include the **Dallas Museum of Art** (pp472–3) and **Nasher Sculpture Center** (p473). End the day by feasting on some authentic Texas barbecue.

## Day 5: Fort Worth

The neighboring city of **Fort Worth** (p474) shows off more of the state's roots. The **Amon Carter Museum** (p475) features the American art of the Wild West, and lively **Sundance Square** (p474) is filled with historic markers and shops selling classic cowboy hats and gaudy belt buckles. Spend the afternoon at the **Fort Worth Stockyards National Historic District** (p474), which features daily cattle processions of massive longhorns, while **Billy Bob's Texas** (p475), the "world's largest honky-tonk," is a must-see. If you're lucky, a Texas icon such as Willie Nelson or George Strait will be taking the stage during your visit.

St. Louis Cathedral, on garden-filled Jackson Square, New Orleans

## Five Days in the Southwest and Rockies

- **Arriving** Fly into Las Vegas's McCarran International Airport, located right on the Strip. Depart from Albuquerque International Sunport or Santa Fe Municipal Airport.

- **Transport** A rental car is a necessity for making the most of the region.

### Day 1: Las Vegas, Central Strip

Start by visiting **Bellagio** casino (p503) and its showpiece conservatory. Then catch the monorail to **CityCenter** (p503) for the stylish Crystals shopping mall. Now head north across the Strip to **Paris** (p503), and enjoy the view from atop the Eiffel Tower. Eat lunch outdoors beside the Strip, or in one of the legendary all-you-can-eat buffets. Next, visit **Caesars Palace** (p503), admiring its version of Michelangelo's *David* and browsing beneath the artificial sky of its Forum Shops, then move on to the **Venetian** (p504) and cruise along the Grand Canal in a gondola. Later on, as well as dining in a gourmet restaurant and taking in a show, join the after-dark crowds on the Strip sidewalk, to see free attractions like the volcano outside the **Mirage** (p504) and the fountains at **Bellagio** (p503).

### Day 2: Las Vegas, South Strip

Tour the mega-casinos at the southern end of the Strip. Enter the **Luxor** (p502) pyramid between the paws of the giant Sphinx, and visit its exhibitions of artifacts from the sunken *Titanic* and "plastinated" human bodies. Then walk through **Excalibur** (p502) castle to reach **New York-New York** (p502); to see its Manhattan skyline close up, take a ride on its roller coaster. Drive to the city's original downtown core and visit a casino along the **Fremont Street Experience** (p506); at sundown, watch the sound-and-light shows on the overarching canopy.

### Day 3: Grand Canyon

Set off early for a full day at the South Rim of the **Grand Canyon** (p532). Begin with the views from **Grand Canyon Village** (p532), then tour the canyon overlooks along **Desert View Drive** (p532). Spend the night in the park itself, either in fine accommodations or rustic camp-style lodging.

### Day 4: Grand Canyon to Santa Fe

Drive east toward New Mexico, stopping to take the 28-mile (45-km) scenic route through the **Petrified Forest National Park** (p526). Arrive in breath-taking **Santa Fe** (pp540–41) in time to watch the sunset change the colors of the adobe buildings that populate North America's oldest state capital.

### Day 5: Santa Fe

Spend a full day in Santa Fe, visiting the **Palace of the Governors** (p540) and the **Georgia O'Keeffe Museum** (p541) downtown, and the **Museum of International Folk Art** (p541) on the periphery. Sample New Mexico's chilies, served in any number of ways. While the afternoon away on the art gallery-packed **Canyon Road** (p541).

## Five Days in California

- **Arriving** Fly into San Francisco International Airport or Oakland International Airport. Depart from San Diego International Airport.

- **Transport** California does have a decent rail network, but a car is necessary to get the most out of a visit to the state. Prepare for some of America's worst traffic; avoid rush hours at all costs.

### Day 1: Wine Country

After a short drive north from the Bay Area, explore the world-class wineries that dot the **Napa** (pp700–701) and **Sonoma Valleys** (p700). **Clos Pegase, Rutherford Hill**, and **Mumm** (p700) are among the most popular. Take a break from the bacchanalia with a visit to the region's historic sites, such as the **Mission San Francisco Solano de Sonoma** (p700) and the **Petrified Forest** (p701).

### Day 2: San Francisco

*Select a day from the "Two Days in San Francsico" itinerary on p13.*

### Day 3: San Francisco to Hearst Castle®

Drive south along the stunning California coastline. First comes the beautiful **17-Mile Drive** (p680), followed by the rugged **Big Sur** (pp678–9). Consider a pit stop in two of the region's loveliest destinations: **Carmel** (p680) and **Monterey** (pp680–81), the latter home to the world-class **Monterey Bay Aquarium** (pp680–81). If time allows, take a guided tour of **Hearst Castle®**

A nighttime view of the colorful Strip, Las Vegas

*For practical information on traveling around the USA, see pp30–35*

Boats moored at the Embarcadero, San Diego

(pp676–7), the astonishing mountaintop home of media tycoon William Randolph Hearst. Spend the night in either **Santa Barbara** (p674) or **San Luis Obispo** (p675), both filled with charming shops and inviting restaurants serving local wines.

## Day 4: Los Angeles

Continue south to **Los Angeles** (pp646–59). The entertainment capital of the world is a sprawling mass of humanity linked by seemingly endless freeways, some of which terminate at the attractive oceanfront cities of **Venice** (p649) and **Santa Monica** (pp648–9). The iconic **Sunset Boulevard** (pp652–3) and **Hollywood Boulevard** (p654) are must-sees for first-time visitors. Art lovers should make a beeline to the **Getty Center** (p648) and **Museum of Contemporary Art** (p657).

## Day 5: San Diego

Head south, stopping just short of the Mexican border in San Diego (p666). Get your fill of culture with a visit to the **Museum of Contemporary Art** (p666) or the waterfront **Embarcadero** (p666), home to the city's **Maritime Museum** (p666), where you can board historic sailing ships. Head across town to immerse yourself in **Old Town San Diego Historical Park** (p666). Next, make for **Balboa Park** (pp668–9), with its many museums. If time allows, squeeze in a visit to the **San Diego Zoo** (p669). End your day with sunset cocktails and dinner at the **Hotel del Coronado** (p710), on exclusive Coronado Island.

## Five Days in the Pacific Northwest

- **Arriving** Fly into Portland International Airport, 12 miles (19 km) northeast of downtown, and depart from Seattle-Tacoma International Airport, south of downtown Seattle.

- **Transport** Hiring a car is essential for this itinerary. Budget-minded travelers can use bus and rail connections for some longer journeys, then hire rental cars when needed.

## Day 1: Seattle

Begin by exploring Seattle's most famous historic neighborhood, **Pioneer Square** (p604), wandering its cobblestone streets. Grab lunch at the city's most popular attraction, **Pike Place Market** (p604), then cross the city by **Monorail** (p606) to **Seattle Center** (p606), home to the **EMP Museum** (p606) – a must for music fans – and the **Space Needle** (p606), which offers breathtaking views of the city, Mount Rainier, and beyond. Trend-seekers can cap off the day in the funky **Ballard** (p607) and **Fremont** (p606) neighborhoods.

## Day 2: Seattle to Astoria

Head south from Seattle via two of the region's most famous sights. **Mount Rainier National Park** (pp614–15) offers several days' worth of attractions; depending on the season, choose from the likes of **Nisqually Glacier** (p614) and **Narada Falls** (p614). Continue on to **Mount St. Helens National Volcanic Monument** (p617), a popular attraction since it erupted in 1980. Once darkness approaches, make the short drive to **Astoria, Oregon** (p620) for dinner and a good night's rest.

## Day 3: Astoria to Cannon Beach

**Astoria** (p620) offers numerous historic attractions such as the **Captain George Flavel House Museum** (p620). Climb atop the **Astoria Column** (p620) for

scenic views of the region, then head south towards **Cannon Beach** (p621). Take in the natural beauty at **Ecola State Park** (p621), visiting the beach to dip your toes in the chilly Pacific waters. Enjoy dinner in one of the town's inviting bistros.

## Day 4: Oregon Dunes to Portland

Continue south to the **Oregon Dunes National Recreation Area** (p621). Take it all in from the scenic overlook point, or if time allows you can see the tallest dunes by following the **Umpqua Scenic Dunes Trail** (p621). Continue south, stopping to check out the craggy rock formations and imposing dunes near the small town of **Bandon** (p621). Head north towards the state's largest city, **Portland** (p618), arriving in time for a drink at one of the award-winning microbreweries.

## Day 5: Portland

Start the day in one of the hip **Pearl District** (p619) coffee shops. Continue on foot through the city's port, known as **Old Town** (p619). The neighborhood's diverse history can be seen in the breathtaking **Lan Su Chinese Garden** (p619). If it's the weekend, check out the **Portland Saturday Market** (p619), one of the oldest and most decorated of its kind in the US. Spend the afternoon at the **Portland Art Museum** (p618), then head over to **Pioneer Courthouse Square** (p618) to people-watch.

Narada Falls, one of many cascades within Mount Rainier National Park

# Putting the USA on the Map

Spreading over 3,000 miles (4,800 km) east to west between the Atlantic and Pacific Oceans, the United States covers the heart of the North American continent and has a population of 317 million people. Bordered by Mexico to the south and Canada to the north, it extends for over 1,500 miles (2,414 km), covering more than 3.5 million sq miles (9 million sq km), and includes climates from the tropics to the Arctic Circle. The continental US is divided into 48 states. These, together with the two states, Alaska in the extreme northwest, and the islands of Hawai'i in the Pacific Ocean, compose the 50 United States of America. The national capital is Washington, DC, a small federal district located between the states of Maryland and Virginia.

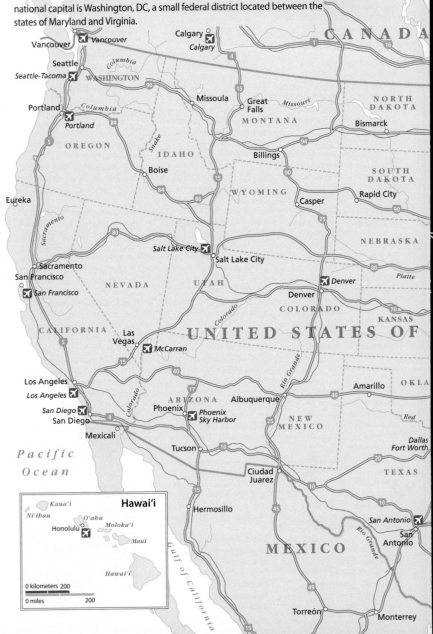

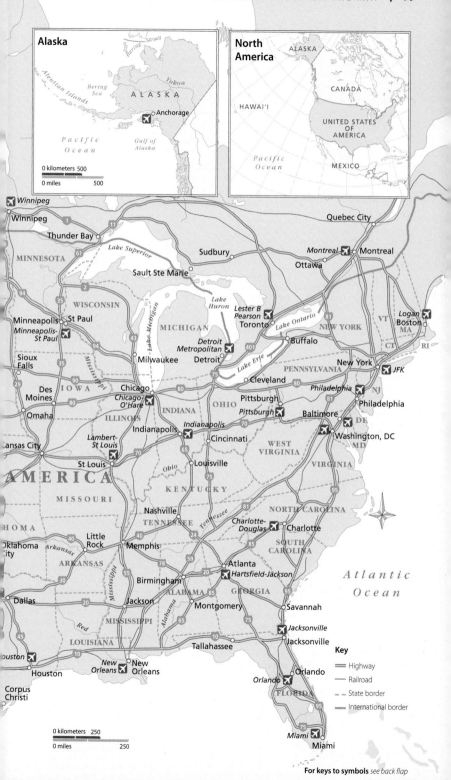

**Alaska**

Bering Strait
Yukon
Aleutian Islands
Bering Sea
ALASKA
✈ Anchorage
Pacific Ocean
Gulf of Alaska

0 kilometers 500
0 miles 500

**North America**

ALASKA
CANADA
HAWAI'I
UNITED STATES OF AMERICA
Pacific Ocean
MEXICO

✈ Winnipeg
Winnipeg
1
11
Thunder Bay
61
Quebec City
MINNESOTA
Lake Superior
Sudbury
Montreal ✈ Montreal
Ottawa
2
Sault Ste Marie
94
35
WISCONSIN
Lake Huron
Lester B Pearson ✈
Toronto
Lake Ontario
VT
Logan ✈
Boston
MA
NEW YORK
81
Minneapolis ✈ St Paul
Minneapolis-St Paul
43
MICHIGAN
Lake Michigan
Buffalo
CT
RI
94
Detroit Metropolitan ✈
Detroit
401
Lake Erie
75
New York ✈ JFK
PENNSYLVANIA
Sioux Falls
35
Mississippi
Milwaukee
Cleveland
80
90
Chicago
Chicago O'Hare ✈
80
Pittsburgh
Philadelphia ✈
NJ
81
Des Moines
IOWA
INDIANA
OHIO
Pittsburgh ✈
Philadelphia
29
80
ILLINOIS
Indianapolis ✈
Baltimore ✈
DE
Omaha
Lambert-St Louis ✈
Indianapolis
Cincinnati
65
✈
Washington, DC
ansas City
70
St Louis
Ohio
Louisville
WEST VIRGINIA
MD
AMERICA
75
VIRGINIA
MISSOURI
KENTUCKY
95
HOMA
Nashville
Tennessee
NORTH CAROLINA
Oklahoma City
40
Little Rock
TENNESSEE
24
Charlotte-Douglas ✈ Charlotte
klahoma city
Arkansas
Memphis
85
SOUTH CAROLINA
ARKANSAS
59
Atlanta ✈
78
Hartsfield-Jackson
20
Atlantic
55
Birmingham
Ocean
30
Jackson
ALABAMA
GEORGIA
95
Dallas
20
Montgomery
Savannah
Mississippi
Alabama
75
Red
MISSISSIPPI
65
45
LOUISIANA
10
Jacksonville ✈
Tallahassee
Jacksonville
uston ✈
10
New Orleans ✈ New Orleans
Houston
Orlando
Corpus Christi
Orlando ✈
FLORIDA

**Key**

═══ Highway
─── Railroad
- - - State border
───── International border

Miami ✈
75
Miami

*For keys to symbols see back flap*

# PRACTICAL INFORMATION

Millions of visitors travel to the US from around the world every year, and millions of Americans also spend their leisure time exploring and enjoying their country. The nation's richly diverse history, culture, art, and landscape, as well as its tradition of hospitality and service, makes traveling in the US both enjoyable and stress-free. In all parts of the country, tourist facilities are generally of a very high standard.

This section gives some basic information on the various transportation and accommodation options available. It deals with issues such as passport and visa formalities, travel insurance, banking, communications, and health care. This section covers the country as a whole, but more specific information is provided in subsequent *Practical Information* sections at the end of each regional chapter.

## When to Go

The best time to visit the US depends on a visitor's interests and itinerary. It is important to time your visit carefully, because the country's geography and weather patterns vary greatly from region to region, even at the same time of the year. Summer is generally the warmest and most popular time to travel, especially to the northern areas. Summer in the southern parts, especially in the deserts of the Southwest, can be unbearably hot, while in New England they are generally cool and pleasant. All over the country, the summer months are when children are out of school and on vacation, so most resort areas and national parks are full to capacity during these times. Summer is also the time when numerous outdoor cultural events, fairs, and festivals take place.

Spring can be the best time to visit the Rockies and the Deep South; the crowds are fewer, and discounts are often available. April and May in particular are ideal times to experience the wildflowers and gardens of the southern US. Fall is another good time to travel, since the leaves on the trees in the mountain forests, particularly in the northeast, are at their peak of color, and the high humidity of summer has decreased to more pleasant levels. Winter brings on the greatest diversity of weather, ranging from heavy snows in the winter sports capitals of New England and the Rocky Mountains, to tropical sunshine on the beaches of Florida and Hawai'i.

## Passport & Visas

All travelers to the US, including returning Americans, are required to hold a valid passport with an electronic chip in it, regardless of their age. Passports should be valid for at least six months longer than you expect to remain in the country. Holders of Canadian, Australian, New Zealand, EU, or UK passports with a round-trip ticket do not need a visa for a visit of up to 90 days. Some form of government-issued photo ID, though, is required.

Citizens of many countries may take part in the "visa waiver" plan, using the ESTA form, which must be completed online at least 72 hours before travel at https://esta.cbp. dhs.gov. However, due to increased security measures, it is wise to confirm visa requirements with the US embassy before traveling, or with a travel agent.

Visitors from countries that need a visa must apply to a US embassy well in advance.

Travelers interested in studying, working, or staying for a longer period than the stated 90 days should request special visas from the nearest US embassy. If you are in the US and need to extend your stay,

## The Climate of the USA

Given the sheer vastness of its size, the United States is characterized by a diversity of climates. In addition to the many regional variations, the country also experiences dramatically shifting weather patterns, produced mostly by the Pacific westerlies that sweep across the entire continent. The *Practical Information* section for each region contains a panel like the one below.

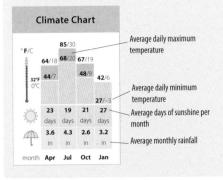

**Climate Chart**

°F/C
85/30 — Average daily maximum temperature
64/18  68/20  67/19
48/9
32°F / 0°C  44/7  42/6
27/−3 — Average daily minimum temperature

23 days   19 days   21 days   27 days — Average days of sunshine per month

3.6 in   4.3 in   2.6 in   3.2 in — Average monthly rainfall

month   **Apr**   **Jul**   **Oct**   **Jan**

you should contact the nearest office of the **Bureau of Citizenship and Immigration Services** *(see p25)* in the US, and apply for an extension. Failure to do so may result in a fine or deportation.

## Customs Allowances & Duty-free

All visitors to the US are required to complete a Customs Declaration before entering the country. On this form, which is available from airlines and customs officials upon arrival, you must state the value of any goods being brought into the US, and you may be charged duty on especially valuable items. Travelers are allowed to bring small quantities of tobacco and alcohol along with them, but certain goods are forbidden. These include meat products, plants or seeds, Cuban cigars, and ancient cultural artifacts. When you leave the US, make sure that you are aware of the duty-free allowances for tobacco products (200 cigarettes for each person over 18 years old), and for alcoholic beverages (0.2 gallons or one liter of spirits for each person over 21). No meat products, plants, seeds, fruits, or firearms may be taken out of the US.

## Planning a Trip

Since the country is so large and diverse, it is essential to plan ahead in order to make the

### Public Holidays

**New Year's Day** (Jan 1)
**Martin Luther King Jr. Day** (3rd Mon in Jan)
**Presidents' Day** (3rd Mon in Feb)
**Memorial Day** (last weekend in May)
**Independence Day** (Jul 4)
**Labor Day** (1st Mon in Sep)
**Columbus Day** (2nd weekend in Oct)
**Veterans' Day** (Nov 11)
**Thanksgiving** (4th Thu in Nov)
**Christmas Day** (Dec 25)

most of your time in the US. Following a logical, efficient itinerary, and allowing enough time to get between places to enjoy them are two of the most important concerns. Some suggested tours can be found on pages 10–17 of this book. Bear in mind that the US is split into six time zones *(see p30)*. All of the states and major cities offer a variety of information which can be ordered in advance over the telephone or accessed via websites. Local bookstores are also a valuable source of travel information, as are municipal libraries, travel agencies, and local and regional tourism bureaus across the country.

## Children

Children are welcomed everywhere, and an amazing number of attractions exist primarily for the enjoyment of young people. From amusement parks and aquariums to national parks and children's museums, their enjoyment is catered to all over the US.

Most restaurants have special children's menus, with simple foods, smaller portions, and lower prices. For a small charge, most lodgings will provide an extra bed or crib *(see p27)*, and many hotels or motels have adjoining or connecting rooms available especially for families. The main exceptions to kid-friendly status are some bed-and-breakfast accommodations, certain gourmet restaurants in the larger cities, as well as those deluxe resorts that focus on providing relaxing escapes or luxurious spa-like pampering to their guests.

## Senior Citizens

Older travelers, or "seniors," make up a fairly large proportion of the traveling public, and most hotels and other establishments offer discounts and special services to attract them. Visitors over

### Conversion Chart

**US Standard to Metric**
1 inch = 2.54 centimeters
1 foot = 30 centimeters
1 mile = 1.6 kilometers
1 ounce = 28 grams
1 pound = 454 grams
1 US pint = 0.5 liter
1 US quart = 0.947 liter
1 US gallon = 3.8 liters

**Metric to US Standard**
1 centimeter = 0.4 inch
1 meter = 3 feet 3 inches
1 kilometer = 0.6 miles
1 gram = 0.04 ounce
1 kilogram = 2.2 pounds
1 liter = 1.1 US quarts

the age of 50 can contact the **American Association of Retired Persons** or AARP *(see p25)* to request a membership, which costs about $16 per year and offers good travel discounts. A few organizations cater to seniors who enjoy traveling both in and outside the US, including **Road Scholar** (800-454-5768/ www.roadscholar.org), which arranges educational trips for those over the age of 55. These include inexpensive accommodations, activities, lectures, and meals.

## Disabled Travelers

Disabled travelers will find traveling easy in the US, because the country has initiatives aimed at providing "barrier-free" access throughout. The Americans with Disabilities Act (ADA) requires most public buildings, including museums, hotels, and restaurants, to make their services and facilities accessible to all people, including those using wheelchairs *(see p27)*. Trains, buses, and taxis are designed to accommodate wheelchairs. Two of the many organizations in the country that will help disabled visitors plan and enjoy their trips are **The Guided Tour Inc** (215-782- 1370/www.guidedtour.com) and **Care Vacations** (780-986- 6404/www.carevacations.com).

# Communications & Banking

Most banks in the US can accept transfer of funds from foreign banks. Many travelers already use credit cards or "automated teller" (ATM) cash/debit cards, so getting money from a bank or ATM should be relatively simple. It's best to buy traveler's checks in US dollar amounts before entering the country in order to avoid delays and extra charges. The country offers excellent telephone and mail services; cell phones and public Internet cafés have made keeping in touch easier and less expensive than ever, and most hotels also offer Internet hookups.

## Telephones

Many companies offer telephone services in the US at varying rates. Most public pay phones accept coins, but calls can also be charged to a credit card. Local calls cost between 50 cents and $1, with additional charges for longer calls. Some hotels offer guests free local calls, but some levy hefty charges per call, so check ahead. Making international calls is very expensive. Consider using a prepaid calling card for lowest rates on overseas calls. Tri-band and quad-band cell

phones may work in the US, with best rates available by buying a SIM chip for a US carrier. Prepaid cell phones are also an option. Many car rental companies also rent cell phones for customers.

## Postal Services

Post offices are open from 9am to 5pm (weekdays) with some open on Saturday mornings. Postcards and letters can be dropped into big blue mailboxes on street corners. Domestic mail should include the five-digit zip code. Rates for international mail vary, so buy stamps from a local post office. To receive mail, General Delivery service is available, whereby letters are held for you at a specific post office for 30 days. Mail forwarding services also exist for a fee.

## Internet Access

Local libraries, shopping malls, hotels, and university hangouts are perhaps the least expensive and easiest places to access the Internet. Most library computers will let you send e-mail and surf the web. Many large cities have designated stores that offer Internet access for a small fee.

## Banking

Banks can be found in all US cities and towns, and many have service centers in supermarkets and malls. Other financial institutions such as savings-and-loans and credit unions also offer banking services. Traveler's checks can be cashed as long as you have your passport. Banks

## Reaching the Right Number

- The international code for the US is 1.
- For long-distance calls within the US or to Canada: dial 1, the 3-digit area code, and the 7-digit local number.
- For local calls: dial the 7- or 10-digit local number.
- International direct-dial call: dial **011** followed by country code (UK: **44**; Australia: **61**; New Zealand: **64**; South Africa: **27**) then the city or area code (omit the first 0) and then the local number.
- International call via the operator: dial **01**, followed by country code, then city code (without the first 0), and then the local number.
- For operator assistance: dial **0**.
- An **800**, **888**, **877**, or **866** prefix indicates a free call.
- Directory inquiries: dial **411**.
- **For emergencies: dial 911**.

also give cash advances against credit cards, but card companies charge a high fee for this service. Most banks will not exchange foreign currency. Banking hours are 9am to 4pm, weekdays, but some banks remain open till 6pm on Fridays, and some open on Saturday mornings as well.

## Automated Teller Machines

Almost all banks have 24-hour ATMs, as do most train stations, airports, and malls. ATMs are connected to a number of bank-card networks and can dispense cash from accounts held in other states or countries. The primary US bank-card networks are **Visa Plus, Cirrus/ Mastercard, Star**, and **Interlink**. Be sure that your bank permits international cash withdrawals, and that your card and personal identification number (PIN) are compatible with US machines. Many ATMs charge a fee of $1 to $2.50 per transaction. Exchange rates, however, are better than those for traveler's checks or foreign currency.

## Credit Cards

The most commonly accepted credit cards are VISA, MasterCard, American Express, Japanese Credit Bureau (JCB), Discover, and Diners Club (DC). Credit cards can be used in hotels, restaurants, stores, and to pay for such services as medical care or car rental. Having a credit card will make your stay much easier, and the exchange rates on cards are often better than those for traveler's checks or currency.

## Traveler's Checks

Some visitors prefer to carry traveler's checks rather than cash as they can be replaced if lost or stolen. The most widely accepted traveler's checks are those issued by American Express in US dollars. It is easier to pay for purchases with traveler's checks and get cash as change, than go to the trouble of cashing the checks at a bank. Buy checks in a variety of denominations, with $10, $20, and $50 bills. It can be difficult to cash $100 bills except at a bank. Foreign currency checks are not accepted, and out-of-state checks are difficult to cash. Contact the **American Express Helpline** for lost, stolen, or destroyed traveler's checks.

## Foreign Exchange

Try to change your money into US denominations before traveling to the US. You may find it difficult to exchange foreign currency except in international airport terminals in major cities. The main foreign exchange companies in the US are American Express and **Travelex**. If you are in the need of ready cash, you can always visit a duty-free shop and buy something so that you can cash a traveler's check.

10-cent coin
(a dime)

5-cent coin
(a nickel)

1-dollar
coin

25-cent coin
(a quarter)

## Coins

*American coins come in 1-dollar, and 50-, 25-, 10-, 5-, and 1-cent pieces. 1-cent pieces are popularly called pennies, 5-cent are nickels, 10-cent are dimes, and 25-cent pieces are quarters.*

## Bank Notes

*Units of currency are dollars and cents; 100 cents make a dollar. Notes (bills) come in $1, $5, $10, $20, $50, and $100s. All bills were once green, which made it hard to differentiate between them; now only the $1 bill is completely green.*

# Health & Security

The United States does not have a national health service, and health care, though excellent, is operated for the most part by the private sector, making it extremely expensive. Medical travel insurance is highly recommended in order to defer some of the costs related to an accident or sudden illness. In terms of safety, some of the larger urban areas have a higher crime rate than rural locations, so a few basic precautions are necessary for a trouble-free visit. Be sure to check with friends or hotel staff about which parts of town are best avoided.

## Personal Safety

While most places on the tourist trail are reasonably safe to travel, visitors should nonetheless take safety precautions to avoid being a victim of crime. Generally speaking, most crimes occur in neighborhoods or areas not frequented by travelers. It is always a good idea to steer clear of neighborhoods that are off the beaten track. Avoid wearing expensive jewelry, carry only small amounts of cash, wear a money belt under clothing, and always carry cameras or camcorders securely.

## Money

Carry only small amounts of cash, and keep credit cards in a money belt rather than a backpack or trouser pocket. The safest way of carrying money is in the form of traveler's checks, which allow you to keep your hard cash to a minimum. Always use ATM machines during the day or on busy, well-lit streets.

## Hotel Safety

Theft from hotel rooms is uncommon, but it is best not to leave valuables out when you leave the room. Consider placing them, and any large amounts of cash, in the hotel or in-room safe, a service that is usually free of charge. While in your room, use the deadbolt lock for additional safety, and take time to familiarize yourself with the nearest emergency exits and fire escape routes. Never allow strangers into your hotel room or give them details of where you are staying.

## Security in Your Car

A rental car can serve as a convenient place to store your new purchases. However, it is also a magnet for criminals, especially in parking areas at major sites or hiking trails. Always lock your car when you leave it, and place suitcases and valuables in the trunk. Expensive items such as cameras left out in the open or in an unlocked car are easy targets for smash-and-grab thieves. Use hotel parking garages for overnight.

## Keeping Valuables & Documents Safe

Before you leave home, make photocopies of important documents such as passport and visa, and bring one copy with you and leave another in a safe place or with a friend. Do the same for the serial numbers of your traveler's checks and credit cards, in the event they are stolen or lost. All important documents and your wallet should be kept in a money belt.

## Outdoor Safety

Participating in outdoor recreational activities can entail certain risks, which can be minimized by taking proper precautions. For activities such as mountain biking, rock-climbing, whitewater river-rafting, or motorcycling, wearing helmets and other protective devices are essential. Always wear a life jacket when canoeing or sailing. Desert and high-altitude travelers should wear hats and sunscreen, and drink plenty of water to avoid dehydration. In desert areas, be sure to take a first-aid kit, extra gasoline, and a tool kit for your vehicle, and always carry a cell phone.

Hikers should always be prepared for sudden weather changes, especially at higher elevations. Stay on marked trails, and if camping or hiking alone, it's best to notify someone of your plans, destination, and estimated time of arrival. Many trails have sign-in sheets where you mark the start and completion of your hike or campout. In forested areas, hikers should wear bright-colored clothes and avoid off-trail forests and fields during hunting season.

## Insects & Animals

Outdoor enthusiasts should be wary of dangerous animals in wilderness areas. Be especially careful in bear country, as attacks have become more frequent. A wise precaution is never to feed animals, or interfere with any wildlife. Insect stings and bites are an annoyance but are not usually life-threatening. Black flies, mosquitoes, and deer flies are a nuisance, so be sure to carry insect repellant. Also, carry a snakebite or first-aid kit if going into snake country. If bitten by a snake or scorpion, seek medical help immediately.

Try to avoid contact with allergenic plants such as poison ivy or poison oak. In the wild, drinking water should always be treated or boiled to combat waterborne bacteria.

## Safety in Water

If possible, surfers and ocean swimmers should stay in areas with lifeguards on duty. If you are not used to dangerous currents, avoid unguarded beaches. Whether or not you are an experienced swimmer, pay attention to the lifeguards and the overall condition of the lake or ocean water. Never swim alone, and watch out for surfers, waterskiers, motorboats, and jet skis. Keep an especially close eye on children at all times.

## Preventing Forest Fires

While hiking in wilderness areas, be very careful lighting campfires. Since firewood is scarce, and forest fires start very quickly, always check whether campfires are allowed where you are camping. Make sure to extinguish all fires carefully and completely. A fire that still smokes is not out.

## Reporting Lost & Stolen Property

Although the chances of recovering lost or stolen property are very slim, it is a good idea to report all missing items (including your car) to the police. Most public transportation companies, such as taxi firms, buses, subways, and airlines, operate Lost and Found departments, which can be reached by phoning their general access number. It is useful to have a record of your valuables' serial numbers and a receipt of purchase. Be sure to ask for a copy of the police report for your insurance claim. For lost or stolen credit cards or traveler's checks, contact the company that issued them.

## Police

Most law enforcement in the US is handled at the state and local government level. State troopers and the State Highway Patrol deal with traffic accidents and offenses outside city boundaries. County police and sheriffs patrol rural areas, small towns, and villages.

Law enforcement officers carry handguns and other weapons, and should always be treated with respect and courtesy. The officers are usually friendly, helpful, and interested in your safety. In the wake of the 2001 terrorist attacks, National Transportation Security Administration officials are stationed in all US airports, train stations, bus terminals, and large, crowded venues. They provide passenger screening, crowd control, and other services.

On federal lands, including national parks and forests, park rangers are there to protect the visitors. Wilderness areas are, for the most part, free of crime.

## Legal Assistance

Travelers from outside the US who are in need of legal assistance should contact their nearest consulate or the embassy in Washington, DC. If arrested, you have the right to remain silent, to have legal counsel, and to make at least one phone call. The police will provide you with any necessary phone numbers, and should treat you with respect and courtesy.

## Insurance & Medical Treatment

Comprehensive travel insurance is highly recommended to anyone intending to visit the US. Any emergency medical or dental care can be very expensive, so having proof of insurance coverage is essential to help defray some of the costs related to an unscheduled hospital visit. Bring a backup prescription if you take any medication.

A good insurance policy will also pay for the replacement of stolen or damaged property. If you need to cancel or change your travel plans, many policies will refund your costs.

## Emergencies

If you need emergency help from the fire, police, or medical services then dial 911. The call is free from any public phone, and emergency phone boxes are located along major highways and Interstates. All US medical facilities will provide emergency care to injured people, regardless of means. The **Travelers' Aid Society** specializes in giving assistance to those travelers who find themselves stranded or in need of emergency help.

# DIRECTORY

## Emergencies

**All Emergencies**
Tel 911
for police, fire, or medical emergency.

**Travelers' Aid Society**
w travelersaid.org

## Hospitals & Medical Facilities

Tel 411
for directory assistance.

## Lost/Stolen Credit Cards & Traveler's Checks

**American Express**
Tel (800) 528-4800 (credit cards).
Tel (800) 221-7282 (checks).
w americanexpress.com

**Mastercard**
Tel (800) 826-2181.
w mastercard.us

**VISA**
Tel (800) 336-8472.
w visa.com

## Embassies

**Australia**
w usa.embassy.gov.au

**Canada**
w can-am.gc.ca/washington

**New Zealand**
w nzembassy.com

**South Africa**
w saembassy.org

**United Kingdom**
w gov.uk/government/world/usa

**US Bureau of Citizenship and Immigration Services**
w uscis.gov

**US Embassy**
w travel.state.gov

## Senior Citizens

**American Association of Retired Persons**
601 E St NW Washington D.C., 20049.
Tel (888) 687-2277.
w aarp.org

# Where to Stay

The US offers a variety of accommodations to suit all tastes and budgets. At the high end of the comfort scale, visitors can choose from luxury hotels and resorts, found in most major cities. Country inns and bed-and-breakfasts (B&Bs), usually located in large, refurbished historic houses, offer a more personal atmosphere. If you're traveling on a budget, there are several convenient inexpensive motels all along the highways. Hotels, motels, and inns generally offer clean surroundings. For those who wish to experience wide open spaces, there are more than enough campgrounds in parks and forests.

## Hotels and Resorts

There is no better place to experience the comfort of the US than to stay in one of the country's chain hotels, such as the **Hilton**, **Marriott**, and **Starwood** groups. Historic and modern hotels as well as resorts are usually located in downtown areas. Most resort hotels focus on relaxation and offer spa facilities or access to golf courses, tennis, and other activities. The best hotels, in major cities, often have the finest restaurants and cocktail bars. These hotels offer a full range of guest services, including swimming pools and health clubs, and their concierge can provide guests with shopping and tourist information, and even preferential seating at restaurants as well as theaters.

There are also a number of classic older hotels in traditional vacation spots, notably the early 20th-century rustic lodges that are found in state and national parks. Some of these parks' famous hotels, such as Yellowstone's Old Faithful Inn (see p593), are located in unforgettably scenic locations.

An alternative to the chain or resort properties are the boutique hotels. These all have their own distinctive atmosphere and stress service over amenities. They can be expensive, so ask for special rates or promotions.

## Business Travelers

Many downtown hotels cater to business people, and some offer "club-level" accommodations with extra-large rooms. These suites usually provide breakfast, snacks, and evening cocktails.

## Motels

Most motels provide overnight accommodations. Usually located along the highways, they offer parking for your car right next to your room. Motels tend to have fewer amenities than hotels, and are less expensive. Services may include swimming pools and children's play areas as well as a restaurant. The rooms typically have one large or two smaller beds, a bathroom, a TV, and a phone.

Many motels are run as part of national franchises, but some of the more pleasant ones are locally owned. The most popular motel chains include **Holiday Inn** and **Motel 6**.

## Bed-and-Breakfast and Historic Inns

Historic inns usually offer a classier, more enriching experience. Generally located in beautifully restored historic homes or mansions, they are often decorated with heirlooms and antiques. B&Bs, on the other hand, offer a wider choice, from rooms in private homes, where you may have to share a bathroom, to luxurious private accommodations that differ from historic inns in name only. Most of these establishments are run as full-time businesses by professional staff.

Many inns and B&Bs rent out rooms on a nightly basis, though some offer discounts for week-long stays. B&Bs also offer breakfast, often served communally. These are usually fairly lavish, multi-course affairs, with eggs, savory treats, and pastries. Some B&Bs, especially in rural areas near popular tourist sites, may also serve gourmet dinners featuring regional specialties.

## Hostels

For solo travelers, one of the best ways to meet others and save money is to take advantage of the clean hostels run by **Hostelling International** (HI), the American affiliate of the International Youth Hostels Association (IYHA). These can be found in the centers of nearly all major cities and near popular destinations. They offer affordable beds in dormitory-style shared rooms, segregated by gender, and many also have a few private rooms for couples or families. Some hostels are housed in unique buildings, such as lighthouses or renovated army barracks.

All hostels have kitchen facilities, bathrooms, and common rooms. HI Hostels have several rules, including no alcohol and occasionally a curfew; guests are sometimes expected to bring their own bed linen or pay rental charges. HI Hostels are open to travelers of all ages, although non-members are asked to pay a nominal surcharge in addition to nightly rates, which is usually $15–50 for a dormitory room. In many urban areas, there are also a number of privately run hostels that offer basic rooms or dormitory beds.

## Campgrounds

Most local, state, and national parks, national forests, and other public lands provide parking and a single or double campsite for tents. The sites are equipped with a picnic table, a campfire pit, toilet facilities, and sometimes hot showers (see p47). Some are fancier, with electrical and water "hook-ups" for self-contained recreational vehicles (RVs). Overnight fees vary with location, facilities, and season but generally run from $20 to $50 a night. Many campgrounds accept advance reservations, however, some operate on a "first-come, first-served" basis. Services such as Woodall's and Good Sam carry listings of campsites.

Privately operated campgrounds, such as those run by **Kampgrounds of America** (KOA) offer several features, including game rooms, swimming pools, and grocery stores. Some also offer log cabins, suitable for families. The most popular campgrounds fill up early during weekends and in the summer. It is also a good idea to set up camp well before sunset. Overnight camping in highway rest areas or along public roads is not only illegal but dangerous as well.

## Rustic or Basic Accommodations

There are several basic "walk-in" campgrounds in forest areas, used primarily by backpackers. These are generally free, but check with park rangers about wilderness permits and other regulations. Vast portions of the West have such areas, managed by US government departments such as the National Park Service, the US Forest Service, and the Bureau of Land Management *(see p47)*.

## Prices

Room rates for overnight stays vary quite a bit, from under $20 a night for a campground or hostel, to over $500 a night in a deluxe downtown hotel. Most places quote the rate per room, but in some destinations, such as Las Vegas and Miami, rates are often quoted per person, should two people share a room.

Room rates at all levels of comfort vary with demand. It is, therefore, worthwhile to ask for discounts or special packages, especially on weekends in urban areas, weekdays in rural areas, or in the off-season.

## Reservations

Some lodgings offer discounts for online and advance bookings. It is also better to check for last-minute booking discounts. Many hotels offer package deals in conjunction with a special event, such as theater or concert tickets with overnight accommodations.

A number of lodgings will request a credit card number when you make a reservation. If you choose to cancel, you may be charged for a night's stay, depending on the time. For example, if you don't cancel by 6pm or earlier, you may be charged for one night. At the most popular places in peak season, many hotels and resorts may insist on a two-night minimum stay.

Most of the large lodging companies operate toll-free telephone lines for reservations. These lines give up-to-date information about room rates, availability, and are also a good means to compare prices. Companies also publish free directories of all their properties, with maps and other details.

## Children

Many hotels welcome children and provide extra supplies such as cots; babysitting services may also be available. Some also offer activities and other fun programs. Children up to the age of 12, and sometimes up to 16 or 18, can stay free of charge in their parents' room. Rooms often have sofas that unfold into beds; or extra beds may be set up for an additional fee. For more information see page 21.

## Disabled Travelers

US law requires that all businesses provide facilities for the disabled *(see p21)*. However, lodgings do their best to accommodate all guests. If you have specific needs, give advance notice. Most places have wheelchair accessibility, wide doorways, handicap-accessible bathrooms, and support bars near toilets, as well as in showers.

## Recommended Hotels

The lodging options featured in this guide have been selected across a wide price range for their excellent facilities, good location, and value. Luxury options abound, offering the very best in service and facilities. The style-conscious will feel most at home in the larger cities' boutique hotels. For a more intimate experience, consider staying in a cozy historic inn or B&B. Budget establishments – from hostels to clean motels and motor lodges – help to keep vacation costs down. If traveling with a family, consider the world-class resorts, several of which also include activity packages.

For the best of the best, look out for options that feature the DK Choice label. These have been highlighted in recognition of an exceptional feature, such as a stunning location, a notable history, or inviting atmosphere. Most of these are popular, so be sure to reserve ahead.

# Where to Eat and Drink

In addition to offering top-class regional cuisines, many of which are rapidly gaining international recognition, the US offers a diverse range of eating experiences, especially in its larger cities. New York, Los Angeles, San Francisco, and Chicago rival any global city for the quality of ingredients and variety of cuisines available, with ambiences ranging from rustic to romantic. The best of each region can often be found in the spirit of the immigrant communities that have helped to shape the local culture. Mexican food is often excellent at local restaurants in Southwestern states such as New Mexico and Arizona; top-quality Asian fare can be enjoyed in the bustling expat conclaves found in most coastal cities. When it comes to smaller towns with limited dining options, hotel restaurants are often the best option.

## Eating Hours

In the US, breakfast is often a banquet: restaurants offer extensive breakfast menus to choose from, while hotels usually have large buffets. Bacon, eggs, hash brown potatoes, pancakes, waffles, cereals, toast, and muffins appear on most menus. Sunday brunch is a feast to be lingered over, with seafood, meat, and poultry dishes served as well. Breakfast times range from 6 or 6:30am to 10:30 or 11am, though "all-day breakfasts" are increasingly popular at many cafés. Brunch is frequently available until 2pm.

Lunch is generally from around 11:30am until 2:30pm or 3pm. Many of the pricier restaurants offer scaled-down versions of their evening menu for lunch, which can be good value. Evening meals are served from 5:30pm or 6pm, and the last seating is seldom later than 9pm. In small towns, many restaurants are closed in the evening, so call ahead to check. At the other extreme, around-the-clock cities such as New York, Las Vegas, and Miami feature a bevy of around-the-clock options – from inviting eateries to casual diners – offering a variety of meals at any time of the day or night.

## Prices and Tipping

Although finding dining bargains in the country's popular cities can be a challenge, eating out in most parts of the country is a very affordable pastime, and even the most expensive restaurants in nearly all areas offer good value.

Light meals in cafés and diners usually cost between $10 and $15, while many chain restaurants serve complete dinners such as chicken or steak with potatoes and vegetables or salad for under $15. Ethnic restaurants, such as Mexican, Chinese, and Thai, often offer wonderful deals in the form of hearty combination plates for $8–$12. At finer restaurants and upscale cafés, dinner entrées can range from $20 to more than $50, and many offer wallet-friendly prix-fixe meals, excluding drinks, for less than $50.

Most regions offer their own particular form of a dining deal: New York's popular diners, for instance, offer complete meals for under $20, and Las Vegas's iconic casino buffets serve myriad dishes, such as roasts, salads, pasta, and fish, to a high standard at reasonable prices (usually all-you-can-eat deals are priced between $15 and $50).

Waiters are generally paid fairly low wages, meaning they earn the bulk of their income through tips. This means that all restaurants with table service expect some sort of gratuity at the end of the meal. It is standard practice to leave between 15 and 20 percent of the bill as the tip. If the service is good or bad, adjust the tip rate accordingly. If you are paying by credit card, you may include the tip in the charged amount on the space provided on the receipt. Some fast-food restaurants have optional tip-jars next to the cashier. Bartenders expect to be tipped accordingly (usually $1–$2 per drink, or 20 percent, whichever is greater) for each round of drinks.

Sales tax will not be shown on menu prices, but is applicable to each item of food and drink. Although they vary from state to state and from city to city, these usually add around 5–10 percent to the cost of a meal.

## Types of Food and Restaurants

Dining establishments in the US come in a wide variety of shapes and sizes – from small and friendly diners offering hearty burgers and snacks to gourmet restaurants serving the latest global-minded cuisine; some even feature molecular gastronomy. Top-rated hotels and resorts are guaranteed to feature classy in-house dining options.

Starting at the lower end of the scale, fast food is a way of life throughout the country, and a string of outlets such as McDonald's, Burger King, Wendy's, KFC, and Taco Bell can be found along the main strips of most towns. They serve the usual inexpensive variations on burgers, sandwiches, fries, and soft drinks. Chains such as Applebee's and Denny's have more variety, with soups, salads, sandwiches, meals, and desserts. These are generally good value, but the quality varies from one establishment to the next. Pizza chains are also ubiquitous around the country.

Mid-range restaurants can include a range of ethnic cuisines, such as Italian, Greek, Chinese, Japanese, and Indian. Many dependable restaurants of this type can be found in shopping malls and commercial establishments. Those feeling adventurous should keep an eye out for roadside stands and snack bars; if there is a queue, chances are that you have found a hidden gem serving restaurant-quality fare at reasonably affordable prices, albeit without waiter service and other frills.

Foodies across the country are keen to enjoy the best of what is fresh and locally sourced. In response, thousands of restaurants have placed a heavy emphasis on filling their menus with dishes composed of seasonal specialties and farm-fresh ingredients. Regional highlights include world-class seafood in the Pacific Northwest and New England, hearty steaks and chops in the Midwest, and stunning year-round produce in California and Florida.

## Coffeehouses and Cafés

Coffeehouses are popular throughout the country, with one seemingly on every other corner in major cities. Along with specialty coffees, they generally serve pastries, bagels, desserts, and sandwiches. Cafés range from simple establishments serving snacks to trendy eateries offering a variety of dining options.

## Vegetarian Options

Classic American cuisine is largely meat-based, which means that vegetarians may not find much variety outside the larger cities and resorts. However, salads can be found everywhere, from fine-dining restaurants to fast-food chains, and could constitute a meal in themselves; they generally come topped with meat or seafood, but vegetarian orders are often accommodated. Many fast-food chains also now serve salads, soups, or baked potatoes to cater to the more health-conscious among their customers. Additionally, ethnic restaurants can usually be counted on to offer a few meatless options such as veggie stir-fries and rice dishes.

## Alcohol

Beer and wine can be found just about anywhere food is served; basic mixed drinks are also common. Visitors need to be 21 years or older to buy alcohol. Be sure to carry a form of identification as it is often requested before you are served. Some regions still prohibit restaurants from serving alcohol, so look for a "BYOB" ("bring your own bottle") sign in the window and consider picking up a bottle of wine before settling in for a meal. Alcohol is forbidden on all Native American reservations.

## Disabled Facilities

Federal and state legislation has made most restaurants in the US at least partially accessible by wheelchair, and many more are accessible to people with other disabilities. Historic structures are sometimes exempted from the accessibility requirements. Entrances are generally ramped, doors may be fitted with an automatic opener, and restrooms usually include the appropriate stalls and sinks.

## Children

Restaurants across the country are generally very child-friendly. Most establishments serve children's portions and will provide a high chair upon request. Many bars, lounges, and restaurants with a focus on nightlife prohibit guests under 18 or 21 years in the evening. Also, some of the nation's finest restaurants dissuade customers from bringing babies and small children to ensure comfort and quiet for other customers. When in doubt, call ahead to check.

## Dress Codes

Dining is usually a casual pastime throughout the US. Even in high-end restaurants, there is seldom a need for a jacket and tie; only the finest and most traditional upscale establishments enforce a dress code. Make enquiries while reserving a table.

## Reservations

Reservations are recommended for the best and most popular restaurants in any given city, and many establishments will only accept reservations for large groups or parties of six or more. However, the majority of restaurants do not require reservations, and most high-profile restaurants allow space for walk-in guests who do not book in advance. For those booking more than a day in advance, it would be wise to confirm the booking on the day of your reservation.

## Smoking

Smoking laws vary from state to state and city to city. Almost all restaurants that allow smoking have non-smoking sections. Smokers are often completely out of luck when looking to light up while dining in key destinations such as New York and Los Angeles; their best bet is to hope for a smoker-friendly patio, or to have a smoke pre- or post-meal out front on the sidewalk.

## Recommended Restaurants

The restaurants featured in this guide have been selected across a wide price range for their value, good food, atmosphere, and location. From authentic, no-frills snack shacks to pricey temples of gastronomy, these restaurants run the gamut across all price levels and cuisine types.

For the best of the best, look out for restaurants featuring the DK Choice label. These establishments have been highlighted in recognition of their exceptional qualities – a celebrity chef, exquisite food, a beautiful setting, an inviting ambience – or a combination of these. Most of these venues are exceptionally popular among local residents and visitors, so be sure to inquire regarding reservations or you may end up facing a lengthy wait for a table.

# Travel by Air

The United States is a nation on the move, with a huge number of airlines that fly both within the country and all around the world. While international travel is offered by US airlines as well as by hundreds of airlines in other countries, domestic travel is limited to airlines based in the United States. Because the country is so enormous, and competition has reduced prices considerably, air travel has become an integral part of life. Today, most long-distance and medium-distance domestic travel is by plane.

### Flying to the US

Most large foreign cities have several daily flights to a number of US cities, especially primary gateways to the East Coast, the West Coast, and throughout the Midwest. The main East Coast cities include New York, Boston, Washington, DC, Atlanta, and Miami; Chicago, St. Louis, Houston, Dallas, and Denver serve as main cities in the central region; and the West Coast is served by Los Angeles, San Francisco, and Seattle.

Most international flights from Europe travel across the Atlantic to New York, Washington, DC, Miami, Boston, and Chicago, taking roughly seven hours. Flights from Asia arrive at the West Coast airports, often stopping in Hawai'i on the way. These flights, as well as flights from Australia, take between 11 and 12 hours.

### Keeping Costs Down

Air fares fluctuate in the US depending on the season, sometimes doubling during the peak holiday periods, especially in summer, and around Thanksgiving and Christmas. Fares are usually less expensive between February and March, when round-trip transatlantic flights can cost significantly less. You often get a better deal, too, by flying mid week.

The least expensive fares are the APEX (Advance Purchase Excursion) tickets for scheduled airlines. These must be bought 21 days in advance and are valid for a 7- to 30-day period. However, any changes that need to be made can cost an additional fee. Some airlines also offer cheaper fares if you limit your stay to a certain period of time. Senior citizens and children may receive discounts on certain flights.

These tickets are not always available, though. Another option is the short-term Internet fares advertised by airlines if there are any available seats. These are valid within a few days of the announcement (fares may be announced on a Wednesday for traveling that weekend and returning the next weekend).

### Arrival at the Airport

All international and US visitors must go through customs and immigration when they arrive in the US *(see p21)*. All major airports have multilingual information booths to answer your questions and give details on transportation into the city.

Most international airports are well connected to the nearest city either by public transportation or the vast array of rental car facilities. Many rentals supply shuttle buses to car pickup points, usually located just outside the airport. Major airlines are connected to countless domestic airline services, and all have facilities for disabled passengers. Still, it is a good idea to prearrange any necessary services through your airline or agent.

### Security

After the September 11, 2001 terrorist attacks, airport authorities tightened their pre-flight security checks (especially for domestic flights). International visitors should expect to be frisked thoroughly and have their hand luggage examined. Items such as battery cells, scissors, nail files, knitting needles, sharp objects, and containers holding more than

### Time Zones across the United States

The United States covers six different times zones – the "Lower 48" states are divided into Eastern, Central, Mountain, and Pacific time, while Alaska and Hawai'i have their own zones. The zones are divided into one-hour increments. For instance, when it is 8pm in New York, it is 7pm in Chicago, 6pm in Denver, 5pm in Los Angeles, 4pm in Anchorage, and 3pm in Honolulu.

Eastern Time is five hours behind Greenwich Mean Time, and Hawai'i is 11 hours behind Greenwich Mean Time. With a few variations, the United States observes Daylight Savings Time between mid-March and early November.

Pacific Time

Mountain Time

Central Time

Eastern Time

3 oz (100 ml) of liquid are prohibited. Signs throughout the Customs areas explain which items are prohibited in checked luggage. Visitors with visas are photographed and fingerprinted on arrival, for details to be checked against a national security database. In light of increased security, expect a long wait to check in.

## Flying within the United States

Visitors interested in seeing the entire country may want to take advantage of domestic flights. These are operated by around a dozen different major airlines, many of which fly internationally too. An extensive domestic flight network serves most cities.

The major US airlines operate a "hub-and-spoke" network – long-distance flights travel between regional airports, from where shorter flights continue on to your destination. Most **Delta Airlines** flights converge on their hubs in Atlanta and Minneapolis; **United Airlines** flights converge in Chicago and Denver; while **American Airlines** usually flies first to Dallas or Chicago.

## Booking a Domestic Flight

For foreign visitors, the easiest way to book a domestic flight is to have it agree with your itinerary. This way you have to buy only one set of tickets and often get a better deal. Another money-saving option is to take advantage of "Visit USA" (VUSA) coupons, which are good for numerous domestic flights (between three and ten flights), for a prepaid fee. However, these coupons must be bought before you arrive and must be redeemed with the same airline alliance with which you flew internationally.

The Internet and the deregulation of the airline industry have made planning trips and purchasing tickets much easier. The best prices now are on airlines' websites.

## Domestic Airlines

Most international airlines have formed alliances with domestic flights, for instance, **British Airways** is partnered with American Airlines, and Air France/KLM with Delta Airlines, making flight networks effectively interlinked. Beside the major international US airlines, there are a large number of domestic airlines that offer inexpensive flights. The most popular of these are **Southwest Airlines** and **Jet Blue** which connect to and from smaller airports rather than from major ones. These airlines are a less expensive but reliable means of travel. They offer basic snacks, and do not transfer to or

from other carriers, which can make connecting flights a hassle, but their fares are low, and there are fewer restrictions.

## Fly-Drive

Many airlines, in addition to travel companies and agents, offer fly-drive packages for tourists, which combine air fares and car rentals. These deals are well worth considering, since they give you flexibility and usually save you more money than if you were to book plane and car travel separately.

## DIRECTORY

### Airline Carriers

**American Airlines**
Tel (800) 433-7300.
W aa.com

**British Airways**
Tel (800) 247-9297.
W britishairways.com

**Delta Airlines**
Tel (800) 241-4141.
W delta.com

**Jet Blue**
Tel (800) 538-2583.
W jetblue.com

**Southwest Airlines**
Tel (800) 435-9792.
W southwest.com

**United Airlines**
Tel (800) 241-6522.
W united.com

| Airport | Information | Distance from City | Taxi Fare to City | Average Travel Time |
|---|---|---|---|---|
| Chicago (O'Hare) | (800) 832-6352 | 17 miles (27 km) from downtown | $45–50 to downtown | Road: 30 mins to downtown |
| Dallas–Fort Worth (International) | (972) 574-8888 | 18 miles (29 km) from Dallas | $50–55 to downtown Dallas | Road: 25 mins to downtown Dallas |
| Los Angeles (LAX) | (310) 646-5252 | 15 miles (24 km) from downtown | $60–65 to downtown | Road: 30 mins to downtown |
| Miami (International) | (305) 876-7000 | 10 miles (16 km) from Miami Beach | $35 to Miami Beach | Road: 20 mins to Miami Beach |
| New York City (JFK) | (718) 244-4444 | 15 miles (24 km) from Manhattan | $50–55 to downtown Manhattan | Road: 1 hr to downtown Manhattan |
| San Francisco (SFO) | (650) 821-8211 | 14 miles (22 km) from downtown | $50–55 to downtown | Road: 25 mins to downtown |
| Seattle (Sea-Tac) | (206) 431-4444 | 14 miles (22 km) from downtown | $40–45 to downtown | Road: 25 mins to downtown |
| Washington, DC (Dulles International) | (703) 572-2700 | 26 miles (42 km) from downtown | $55–60 to downtown | Road: 40 mins to downtown |

# Travel by Road

Away from major cities, where traffic can be frustrating, driving in the United States is a delightful experience. Driving is a favorite American pastime, and to see the country in all its glory, you have to drive a car. Major roads and most highways are rarely crowded, and drivers are generally courteous and safe. Gasoline in the US is comparatively inexpensive, and car rental rates are also reasonable. You can get by without a car in a few larger towns, and in cities like New York, Boston, or San Francisco you will probably be better off without one. However, in most of the country, if you want to explore the wide open spaces of the western US, you will need a car since public transportation there is limited.

## Types of Road

The US has an excellent network of roads, with over 4 million miles (6 million km) of paved roads open to the public. For long-distance travelers, the fastest and most convenient part of the US highway system is the Interstate Highway, a high-speed, limited-access highway. Some have between 6 and 12 lanes running both directions, while rural areas generally have 2 or 3 lanes.

Stretching all across the country in an east-to-west and north-to-south grid, Interstate Highways are abbreviated on signs with a capital "I," followed by a number. The main Interstates start with I-5 on the West Coast and end with I-95, the busy main route along the East Coast. Transcontinental Interstates run east-to-west and range from I-10 between Florida and California to I-90 between Boston and Seattle.

In and around cities, a complicated system of ring roads, link roads, and spur roads are also part of the Interstate system. These roads are often better known by name than number, for instance I-405 in Southern California is referred to as the "San Diego Freeway."

Most Interstates are free, but some states charge tolls. These sections, known as "turnpikes," have the same numbers as sections without toll booths.

Before the Interstate Highway System came into use, the primary long-distance highways were federal ones. Today, these are the main routes in rural areas and are officially signed as "US" and a number, ranging from US-1 along the East Coast to US-101 along the West Coast. Lined by neon-lit motels, and other classic landmarks of roadside America, these roads are slower but more enjoyable to drive on, and along with many other state

## Rules of the Road

- All traffic drives on the right.
- All distances are measured in miles.
- Seat belts are compulsory, and children under the age of 4 are required to have special car seats.
- At traffic signals, green lights mean you can proceed safely; amber lights mean prepare to stop; and red lights mean stop. A flashing red light means stop before proceeding; and a flashing yellow light means proceed with caution.
- At a red octagonal stop sign, traffic must come to a complete halt before proceeding. When two or more cars reach a stop sign simultaneously from different sides of the intersection, drivers must yield to traffic on the right.
- A yellow triangular yield sign directs you to give way to other traffic.
- In towns and cities, roads are usually divided by a painted center line (usually white). Smaller streets may have no dividing line.
- On all roads, a double yellow line means do not pass or cross the lines.
- Some roads have a central lane, protected by painted single lines; this is a designated turning area for making left-hand turns.
- "U" turns are legal only where posted.
- On multi-lane highways, the fastest traffic travels in the left-hand lanes; slower traffic occupies the right-hand lane.

- Cargo-carrying heavy trucks generally stay in the slow lane. Keep your distance from these vehicles, because they have poor visibility and enormous weight and size.
- On multi-lane highways traffic can pass only on the left-hand side. On smaller roads safe passing places are indicated with a broken yellow line on your side of the double yellow line.
- Speed limits vary from state to state, but range from 25 mph (40 km/h) in residential areas to 65–75 mph (105–120 km/h) on highways.
- There is a minimum speed of 45 mph (72 km/h) on highways and Interstate Highways. Farm traffic and pedestrians are not permitted on Interstates.
- Parking is allowed on most streets, subject to posted rules, but any restrictions are posted at the site. Park only in the direction of travel. If you receive a ticket, pay it immediately or it will be charged (with a penalty) to the rental car company, who will collect it from your credit card.
- Visitors should be aware of regional exceptions to the standard US driving laws. Some of these are pointed out in the "Practical Information" section of each chapter.
- Most foreign licenses are valid, but if your license is not in English, or does not have a photo ID, you must get an International Driver's License.
- Drunk driving is a serious offense and can result in a heavy fine or jail term.

and country roads, provide the country's most scenic routes *(see pp50–51)*.

Road names vary from state to state. In the northeast, for example, highways are called "routes" while in Texas, roads are labeled "FM," farm to market or "RM," ranch to market.

## Tips for Renting a Car

Most rental cars are relatively new and low on mileage, and rates are approximately $300 a week. The best rates are generally offered for cars rented for full-week time periods, and for returning cars to the same location they were rented from. A more economical option is the fly-drive *(see p31)*.

Small economy or sub-compact cars have the lowest rates. Many companies also offer upgrades to larger or more luxurious vehicles for very modest rates. Most rental cars have automatic transmissions, power steering, and air-conditioning, but you should confirm this in advance. Also, check for any pre-existing damage to the car and note this on your contract.

To rent a car, you must be at least 25 years old, have a valid driving license, a clean driving record, and a major credit card. The car company will "authorize" an amount ranging between $250–1,000, to assure payment and return of the vehicle. Depending on your existing car insurance policy, you may want to accept the "damage waiver" and liability insurance that the rental company will offer you, and this will add $20–30 per day to the rental cost.

## Driveaways

An inexpensive option for a long-distance road trip is a driveaway car. Driveaways let you take a private car to a predetermined place in a specified amount of time. Most driveaways are offered to private members, but some ads may appear in magazines or newspapers.

Flexiblity is essential for a driveaway deal since the destination is beyond your control. You have to choose an efficient route and average about 400 miles (644 km) a day. However, since you have to pay only for the gas, the price is quite good. To use a driveaway car, you must have a clean driving record, and most companies require a minimum deposit to cover the insurance deductible.

One of the biggest drive-away companies, **Auto Driveaway**, has offices all over the US. Other firms are listed in phone books under "Automobile Transporters."

## RV Rentals

Recreational vehicles (RVs) or mobile homes, are great for families or groups, as they are equipped with beds, kitchens, and bathroom facilities. Costs run between $900–1,400 for seven nights plus a per-mile charge, but lodging is free and you have some flexibility, despite the vehicles' slow, stocky designs. Although rental RVs are usually older, conditions are similar to those for cars.

It is illegal in most places to pull over to the side of the road and camp. Many chain retail outlets, notably WalMart, allow one night's free stay in their parking lots, with approval of the manager or front desk. Even with an RV, it costs about $20 a night to park in a campground *(see p26–7)*. For more details contact **Recreational Vehicle Association of America** or **Cruise America**.

## Insurance

It is extremely important that you have adequate insurance if you plan on driving around in the US. Rental agencies generally include insurance in the cost, but if you bring a car into the country, you must make absolutely sure that you are adequately covered by car and life insurance.

## Gas Stations

Except in the most remote areas, gas stations are easy to find and conveniently located. Many stations require advance payment, either by cash or credit/debit card. Most gas stations also have attached convenience stores, where you can buy food, beverages, and newspapers.

## Rest Areas

Conveniently located immediately adjacent to Interstates and major highways, rest areas are easily accessible and provide restrooms, telephones, picnic tables, dog-walking areas, and sometimes free coffee. Some even allow overnight stays, but be wary of strangers. It is a good idea to make stops to take a rest when driving long distances.

# Travel by Motorcycle or Bike

For visitors with time on their hands as well as a sense of adventure, touring the United States by motorcycle or bicycle can be a rewarding experience. Ride the open road with a Harley-Davidson, or mountain bike throughout the beautiful and peaceful American wilderness for the adventure of a lifetime. Good planning, familiarizing yourself with the rules and regulations, and using the right equipment can make this an enjoyable way of seeing the country.

## Motorcycles

Fans of Marlon Brando's famous movie *The Wild One* (1953) or Jack Nicholson's classic *Easy Rider* (1969) may dream of exploring the United States on a motorcycle. Today, there are several motorcycle rental companies, especially in bike-friendly areas, where licensed riders drive classic motorcycles such as Harley-Davidsons or BMWs.

An American motorcycle license or an International Driving Permit for motorcycles is necessary. Also, the law in most states requires that you wear a helmet.

## Motorcycle Rentals & Tours

Renting is expensive, since the rates and liability insurance can add up to well over $100 a day. Moreover, you have to pay extra for collision insurance. If you plan to stay for a long period, it might be less expensive to buy a bike for a few months, then resell it. **Eagle Rider Motorcyle Rentals & Tours** rents Harley-Davidson and other motorcycles in more than 25 states for pickup and returns to the same location, and offers both guided and self-guided tours. **Blue Sky Motorcycle Rentals** has locations in about 10 states, primarily in California and the western US.

Riders may be interested in taking part in one of the many motorcycle rallies, when thousands of riders get together for annual gatherings held in places like Daytona Beach, Florida (early March); Laconia, New Hampshire (mid-June); or Sturgis, South Dakota (August).

## Bicycles

Bicycles are another great way to see the country. Unlike motorcycles, bicycles can be brought on to airplanes as luggage. Check the requirements first with your airline – many carriers require that you disassemble and pack the bike into a special box, which is available in most good bike shops.

In a great many cities, there are extensive networks of bike paths, which are often separated from car traffic. In some larger cities, bikes can be strapped onto the outside of local buses or carried on the subway.

For serious long-distance biking, it's important to equip yourself with a good bike, tools and spares, maps, and preferably a helmet. Cyclists must obey all traffic laws and should be careful to lock up their bikes and gear.

In the US, bikes are not as common as they are in many other countries. Car and truck drivers are not used to sharing the road with bikes, which can make cycling hazardous. Be aware of RV drivers in particular, because it is easy for them to misjudge the size of their vehicles. Bikes are prohibited on restricted-access highways and freeways.

## Bicycle Rentals & Tours

Bikes are available for rent in all major US cities for around $25 a day, or you can buy used bikes from flea markets or garage sales. Notices of secondhand sales appear in newspaper ads or hostel notices. Look in the Yellow Pages for local bike-rental companies. **Backroads** organizes a variety of guided bike tours, following some of the most spectacular scenic routes, with overnight stays in country inns or national park campsites. If interested in long-distance cycling, be sure to contact the **Adventure Cycling Association**, which has developed a network of bike-friendly routes on quiet and scenic roads and also offers a wide range of guided tours, as well as advice. .

## Recreational Biking

In country areas, many bike paths have been reclaimed from unused railroad lines. Known as "rail trails," these are some of the best long-distance bicycling and walking routes in the country, often running alongside rivers and having moderate grades. In addition, there are miles and miles of country roads everywhere you go. Areas such as California's Wine Country and New England's river valleys are among the most popular. The more athletic or daredevil traveler may also want to try off-road mountain biking, which is encouraged in many recreational areas such as downhill ski resorts in summer.

---

# Travel by Bus or Train

Although more time-consuming than flying, you can enjoy long-distance bus and train trips that let you see the beauty of the US. Greyhound – the major long-distance buses – offers clean, modern travel conditions with on-board movies and restroom facilities. Amtrak trains are spacious and comfortable. Amtrak provides restaurant cars, observation cars, and great social atmospheres. If you want to meet fellow travelers, buses and trains are the transportation options for you.

## Traveling by Bus

The nationwide carrier **Greyhound Lines** serves all the major cities that airlines do, plus many smaller towns along the way, but the travel times are much longer. On long journeys, be sure to take something to eat and drink as meals are determined by where the bus stops.

Buses are also a good option for urban or suburban transportation, but because service can be limited in rural areas, you should plan your route carefully when visiting the countryside. Greyhound buses also provide links with major airports as well as Amtrak services.

## Tickets & Reservations

Many bus stations are located in low-rent parts of town, so it is usually a good idea to take a taxi home from the station at night.

Ask about discounts and special fares including online booking discounts. Most major bus lines offer discounts for children under 12, students, and senior citizens (with proper ID), as well as unlimited travel within a set period. Tickets can be bought on the day of travel, although fares may be less expensive if they are bought in advance. For advance tickets, contact Greyhound directly or ask a travel agent.

International visitors should know that Greyhound tickets are cheaper if bought from an agent outside the US. If you plan to interrupt your trip to explore on your own, or tour the US on an extended trip, there may be a travel package just for you.

## Bus Tours

In most states, bus companies offer short package trips in deluxe air-conditioned buses that tour major attractions. These guided tours provide a comfortable way of seeing the sights, without having to worry about time schedules, admission tickets, and opening hours. Meals and accommodation are included.

For passengers with more time to spare, you may want to try certain bus companies, such as **Green Tortoise**, that offer leisurely trips between major cities. Passengers on these buses can take breaks to camp out, prepare meals, and explore the countryside. Unlike other buses, there are foam mattresses for sleeping. These tours are not for everyone, nevertheless they can provide an enjoyable, relaxed, and memorable tour of the country.

## Traveling by Train

The use of railroads in the US is dwindling. Still, there is a small and enjoyable network of long-distance passenger train routes, operated by **Amtrak**, the national rail system. In spite of its limited network and sometimes inconvenient schedules, a scenic train ride can be an unforgettable experience.

## Train Tickets & Reservations

In general, Amtrak tickets should be booked in advance. To make the most of an Amtrak trip, consider paying the extra money to get a sleeping compartment, which costs around $150 a night on a twin-sharing basis. Meal service is included in the price. Amtrak travel is especially good value for international visitors, who can take advantage of a number of rail tickets for 15, 30, or 45 days of train travel for a fee of $450–880, depending on the dates and regions of travel.

## Historic Railroads

Many pioneer railroads that braved the Wild West frontier are now back in business as tourist attractions, running short trips (often under coal-fired steam) through some spectacular scenery. Many trains, running along narrow-gauge tracks, were constructed by mining or logging companies over a century ago.

Among the most popular railroads are the **Durango & Silverton Narrow Gauge** in southwestern Colorado (see p588), the **Cumbres & Toltec** line in New Mexico, and the **Grand Canyon Railway** in Williams, Arizona, which goes to the rim of the Grand Canyon.

(see p588)

## DIRECTORY

### Long-distance Buses

**Greyhound Lines**
Tel (800) 231-2222 (24 hrs).
W greyhound.com

### Bus Tours

**Green Tortoise**
Tel (800) 867-8647.
W greentortoise.com

### Railroads

**Amtrak**
Tel (800) 872-7245.
W amtrak.com

**Cumbres & Toltec Railroad**
Tel (888) 286-2737.
W cumbrestoltec.com

**Durango & Silverton Narrow Gauge**
Tel (888) 872-4607.
W durangotrain.com

**Grand Canyon Railway**
Tel (800) 843-8724.
W thetrain.com

# USA AT A GLANCE

# USA THROUGH THE YEAR

The size and scope of the United States means that at almost any time of year you can find the right weather to suit any activity. In the middle of winter, for example, while skiers are enjoying the deep snows of the Rockies and New England, sun-seekers flock to Florida or the Arizona deserts. Both the weather and the calendar of events heat up in the summer with a proliferation of county fairs, arts and music festivals, and other events, many celebrating the nation's diverse history and culture. October and November are prime time for harvest festivals, especially near Thanksgiving. The year ends with a variety of religious holidays, including Christmas, Hanukkah, Ramadan, and the African-American celebration Kwanzaa, while the college and professional football seasons climax with a series of New Year's Day championship games and the Super Bowl finale.

## Spring

Spring inspires a definite sense of renewal all over the country. Wildflowers carpet the deserts, the magnolias and cherry trees burst into bloom, and melting snows fill streams and waterfalls to their annual peak. Among the events that celebrate the season, the most symbolic are the first games of the baseball season, which begins in April.

### March
**Academy Awards** (late Feb–mid-Mar), Hollywood, CA. The movie industry honors its stars with golden Oscars.
**Lahaina Ocean Arts Festival** (early Mar), Lahaina, HI. Lectures, dives, and whale-watching celebrating the humpback whale that winters off the Hawaiian coast.
**Bike Week** (early Mar), Daytona, FL. Motorcycle racers and enthusiasts congregate in one of the US's largest gatherings of bikers.
**St. Patrick's Day Parade** (weekend nearest Mar 17), Boston, MA; New York City, NY; Chicago, IL; San Francisco, CA. Parades celebrating Irish heritage are held in these major cities. Towns such as Butte, MT, and Savannah, GA, also hold parties.
**South by Southwest Festival** (mid-Mar), Austin, TX. An independent pop-music and film festival.
**National Cherry Blossom Festival** (late Mar–early Apr), Washington, DC. More than 200 events, such as exhibitions, free guided walking tours, a firework display, and concerts, celebrate the blossoming of the city's famous cherry trees and the arrival of spring.

### April
**Easter** (date varies). This spring holiday is a study in contrasts. Early-morning outdoor " Easter Sunrise" services are held all over the country, while in New York City, outrageously dressed characters join in the Easter Parade down Fifth Avenue. At this time, college kids flock to warm climes in Florida, Texas, and California for their annual "Spring Break."
**Patriot's Day** (Mon nearest Apr 18), Lexington and Concord, MA. Early-morning re-enactments of the first battles of the American Revolution are followed by the country's most famous race, the Boston Marathon.
**New Orleans Jazz & Heritage Festival** (late Apr), New Orleans, LA. Performances by top and emerging talents.

## May
**Cinco de Mayo** (May 5). Celebrations of Mexican culture featuring folk dancing and mariachi music, take place all over the US to mark the anniversary of the Battle of Puebla.
**Kentucky Derby** (first Sat in May), Louisville, KY. The country's biggest horse race and the start of the "Triple Crown" championship takes place at the end of a two-week-long public party.
**Wright Plus** (mid- or late May), Chicago, IL. You can tour architect Frank Lloyd Wright's buildings and residences during this annual housewalk at Oak Park.
**Spoleto Festival USA** (late May–early Jun), Charleston, SC. The largest arts festival in the United States.
**Indianapolis 500** (Sun before Memorial Day), Indianapolis, IN. The most famous auto race in the US draws over 100,000 fans.
**Kinetic Sculpture Race** (Memorial Day weekend), Arcata,

Jockeys at Churchill Downs for the Kentucky Derby, Louisville

◀ View of the San Remo apartments building from Central Park, New York City

CA. Northern California's good-natured culture is evident at this three-day event, in which human-powered sculptures are raced over land and sea.

## Summer

The Memorial Day holiday, at the end of May, marks the unofficial beginning of summertime. This is prime vacation and travel time for students and families. It is also a good time to enjoy music festivals, usually held in idyllic rural locations. The weather is hot and frequently humid, with afternoon storms in much of the country.

Independence Day fireworks light up the sky in Houston, Texas

The flamboyant Lesbian and Gay Pride Parade, New York City

### June
**B.B. King Homecoming Festival** (late May/early Jun), Indianola, MS. One of the oldest and most popular of the many Deep South summer blues festivals.
**Harvard-Yale Regatta** (early Jun), New London, CT. This series of collegiate rowing races offers visitors a chance to observe the Ivy League elite at play.
**Red Earth Native American Festival** (early–mid-Jun), Oklahoma City, OK. One of the largest gatherings of Native American dancers and musicians is held at what was the last vestige of "Indian Territory."
**Lesbian and Gay Pride Day** (Sun in late Jun), New York City, NY; San Francisco, California. Major parades featuring elaborate floats and festivities fill the streets of both these cities.

**Taste of Chicago**, (late Jun–early Jul), Chicago, IL. The city's best food and music can be experienced at an open-air party, held on the Lake Michigan waterfront.

### July
**Independence Day** (Jul 4), Bristol, RI; Boston, MA; Independence, MO; Stone Mountain near Atlanta, GA. Although the entire country celebrates the Fourth of July with parades and fireworks displays, these cities put on particularly good shows.
**Ernest Hemingway Days** (mid-Jul), Key West, FL. The city where the famous writer lived offers a week of theatrical productions, short-story contests, and a Hemingway look-alike competition.
**Tanglewood Music Festival** (Jul–Aug), Lenox, MA. The Boston Symphony and Boston Pops give outdoor concerts in a beautiful Berkshire Mountains estate.
**Hawaiian International Billfish Tournament** (late Jul–mid-Aug), Kailua-Kona, HI. An annual event since 1959, this international fishing tournament draws teams of anglers from far and wide in search of record-sized marlin.

### August
**Sunflower River Blues & Gospel Festival** (early Aug), Clarksdale, MS. One of the country's most enjoyable blues festivals takes place in the home of the blues, the Mississippi Delta.

**Newport Jazz Festival** (early–mid-Aug), Newport, RI. Founded in 1954, this popular festival draws the very best jazz musicians from all over the country and the world.
**Elvis Week** (mid-Aug), Memphis, TN. Also called "Deathweek," a series of events are held to celebrate the life and times of Elvis Presley, leading up to the anniversary of his death on August 16.
**Alaska State Fair** (late Aug–Sep), Palmer, AK. This fair is especially famous for its super-sized vegetables, with pumpkins and cabbages grown to world-record sizes due to the state's 24-hour summer sunshine.
**US Open Tennis Championships** (Aug–Sep), New York City, NY. Professional tennis players from the world over compete in this Grand Slam tournament.

Opening ceremony of the annual US Open Tennis Championships

The famous fiery colors of New England's fall foliage

## Fall

During fall in New England, the leaves of the hardwood trees turn stunning shades of red and gold, drawing appreciative tourists from all over the world. In the West, wine-growing regions celebrate the annual harvest, and in the Great Lakes and Midwest, beer lovers join the Oktoberfest celebrations in the nation's many German enclaves. The approach of winter and the start of the Christmas shopping season is kicked off by the nationally televised Macy's Thanksgiving Day parade down Broadway in New York City.

### September

**Mississippi Delta Blues and Heritage Festival** *(mid-Sep)*, Greenville, MS. A blues and African-American culture festival in the heart of the Mississippi Delta.

**Norwalk Seaport Oyster Festival** *(mid-Sep)*, Norwalk, CT. Fireworks, antique boats, and lots of local oysters to sample.

**Northeast Kingdom Fall Foliage Festival** *(mid-Sep–early Oct)*, VT. Celebrating the change of seasons, as well as the brilliantly colored fall foliage, several tours and events are held in small towns all over northern Vermont.

**Major League Baseball Championships** *(Sep–Oct)*. The nation's top professional teams face off, with the winners competing in October's World Series.

**Texas State Fair** *(late Sep–mid-Oct)*, Dallas, TX. One of the country's largest state fairs, with a focus on Texas.

**Fall Pilgrimage** *(late Sep–mid-Oct)*, Natchez, MS. A three-week-long series of events celebrate antebellum architecture and culture.

### October

**King Biscuit Blues Festival** *(early Oct)*, Helena, AR. Sponsored by the King Biscuit flour company, the small Mississippi River town of Helena has been celebrating the blues since the 1920s.

**Festivals Acadiens** *(early Oct)*, Lafayette, LA. Over 100,000 people flock to this Cajun Country capital to enjoy the unique sights, sounds, and tastes of Louisiana life.

**Ironman Triathlon** *(Sat nearest to full moon)*, Kailua-Kona, HI. More than 1,000 of the world's fittest athletes take part in a highly challenging series of trials,

Giant cowboy balloon at the Texas State Fair in Dallas

combining a 2.4-mile (3.8-km) swim, a 112-mile (180-km) bike ride, and a 26-mile (42-km) marathon run.

**American Royal Rodeo** *(date varies, mid-Oct to early Nov)*, Kansas City, MO. One of the country's largest and most prominent professional rodeo competitions. Also features livestock shows.

**Italian Heritage Parade** *(mid-Oct)*, San Francisco, CA. Columbus Avenue, winding through the city's Italian-American North Beach district, comes alive with a parade celebrating Italian pride. Other such parades are held throughout the country.

**Oktoberfest** *(late Oct)*. Modeled on the famous one in Munich, beer-flavored festivals are held in German neighborhoods of most large cities in the US, as well as small German towns like New Braunfels TX, Hermann MO, and Leavenworth, WA.

**Haunted Happenings** *(throughout Oct)*, Salem, MA. Leading up to Halloween, the historic home of the Salem Witch Trials stages a series of supernatural-themed events and activities.

**Halloween** *(Oct 31)*. While children dress up in scary costumes and beg for candy, many adults flock to raucous public parties in places like Key West, FL, and New York's Greenwich Village.

### November

**Dia de los Muertos (Day of the Dead)** *(Nov 1)*, San Francisco, CA. Festivities in San Francisco's Mission District highlight this Catholic festival, when the souls of the dead are said to visit the living. Similar festivities take place in Mexican neighborhoods across the country.

**Thanksgiving** *(4th Thu in Nov)*. Celebrating the survival of the pilgrims who landed at Plymouth, MA, in 1620, this holiday sees families coming together from all over the country to share in a massive meal of roast turkey, stuffing, cranberry sauce, and

Turkey Float in Macy's Thanksgiving Day Parade, New York City

pumpkin pie. Many restaurants serve special Thanksgiving meals, and the town of Plymouth, MA recreates a pilgrim Thanksgiving worship service.

**Macy's Thanksgiving Day Parade** *(Thanksgiving Day)*, New York City, NY. Giant inflatable figures march down New York's Broadway to celebrate Thanksgiving and the start of the Christmas holiday season.

## Winter

Perhaps best known for the shopping mania that leads up to Christmas, winter in American cities is a time of twinkling lights, ringing cash registers, and occasional snowstorms. Department stores along New York's Fifth Avenue, Chicago's State Street, and other shopping districts attract shoppers with exuberant displays in their store windows. Many ski resorts stage special winter activities, such as sleigh rides and visits from Santa Claus. Winter is also the best time to watch the gray whale migration along the Pacific Ocean, or to observe the humpback whales on the way to their winter breeding grounds in Hawai'i. February also sees a number of public parades and parties, which range from the Chinese New Year celebrations to the wild fun and festivity of Mardi Gras in New Orleans.

## December
**Triple Crown of Surfing** *(late Nov to mid-Dec)*, North Shore O'ahu, HI. The world's most prestigious surfing competition usually spans three weeks, waves and weather permitting.

**Boston Tea Party Re-enactment** *(mid-Dec)*, Boston, MA. Costumed performers and interpreters bring to life the famous Boston Tea Party, a protest that played an important role in precipitating the famous American Revolution.

**New Year's Eve** *(Dec 31)*, New York City, NY. The country's foremost New Year celebration starts with the countdown in New York's Times Square, which is televised live across Eastern US and repeated (on tape) for viewers elsewhere in the country. Major New Year's Eve parties occur in most major cities, with great public celebrations in Las Vegas and San Francisco.

## January
**New Year's Day** *(Jan 1)*. Parades and festivities are held all around the country and are often connected with a championship college football game such as the Orange Bowl in Miami, the Cotton Bowl in Dallas, the Sugar Bowl in New Orleans, and the Rose Bowl in Pasadena, CA, which is usually preceded by a nationally televised parade.

**Martin Luther King Jr. Day** *(3rd Mon)*. Events are held around the country to honor the birth and life of the Civil Rights leader.

**Riverwalk Mud Festival** *(mid-Jan)*, San Antonio, TX. While workers drain the water to clear out downtown's River Walk, musicians and artists celebrate.

**Cowboy Poetry Gathering** *(late Jan)*, Elko, NV. Cowboys come to this town to narrate tales, quote their very own poems, and sing songs about the heroic American West.

## February
**Groundhog Day** *(Feb 2)*, Punxsutawney, PA. The star of this festival is a small rodent who forecasts the beginning of spring.

**Mardi Gras** *(date varies, Feb–Mar)*, New Orleans, LA. Colorful parades, lavish parties, and masked balls are held. Many smaller cities hold similar celebrations.

Lion dance during Chinese New Year, Chinatown, San Francisco

**Chinese New Year** *(date varies, late Jan to mid-Feb)*, San Francisco, CA. To celebrate Chinese New Year, colorful parades are held here, in New York City, and several other cities.

**Iditarod Trail Sled Dog Race** *(late Feb–early Mar)*, Anchorage, AK. This test of endurance takes packs of dogs and their drivers two grueling weeks.

# Climate of the USA

Much of the US enjoys temperate weather, but the country is so vast that many regions experience climatic extremes. Alaska has the harshest winter, while the warmest temperatures are in Hawai'i and Florida. Even within the "Lower 48" states, the weather varies tremendously, from the heavy snows of the Rocky Mountains to the intense heat of Death Valley in the California desert. Besides the four main seasons, the US also sees some unusual weather, including destructive tornadoes that may form in spring and summer across the Great Plains; thunderstorms that burst over the South during summer; and powerful hurricanes that strike coastal areas in the Southeast in autumn.

**Subarctic (Alaska)**
Though temperatures drop well below freezing for most of the year, the warm summers are extended by the non-stop daylight of the "midnight sun."

**Temperate (California)**
The West Coast's mild climate is much like that of the Mediterranean regions, with mild winters and long, sunny summers.

Seattle
Portland
THE PACIFIC NORTHWEST
Boise
Helena
THE ROCKIES
Sioux Falls
Salt Lake City
Cheyenne
Omaha
San Francisco
CALIFORNIA
THE SOUTHWEST
Denver
THE GREAT PLAINS
Las Vegas
Los Angeles
Albuquerque
Oklahoma City
San Diego
Phoenix
Dallas
TEXAS
San Antonio

**Tropical (Hawai'i)**
This island paradise is warm and pleasant year-round. Significant rain falls in winter, usually on the northeastern or windward coasts.

**Arid (Southwest)**
The hot, dry climate of the Southwestern desert draws millions of visitors. Winter snows can fall at higher elevations, but sunshine is guaranteed throughout the year.

**Cool Continental (Great Lakes)**
The Great Lakes states are famous for their frigid winters, when the region receives the country's heaviest snowfall.

**Cool Temperate (New England)**
Bright, sunny days followed by frosty nights cause the most intense color in New England's famous autumn foliage. The region experiences warm summers and cold winters with high snowfalls in certain areas.

| 0 kilometers | 500 | |
| 0 miles | | 500 |

NEW ENGLAND

Minneapolis

Milwaukee

Buffalo

Detroit

Chicago

NYC & THE MID-ATLANTIC REGION

Boston

New York

Philadelphia

THE GREAT LAKES

Indianapolis

Washington, DC

Kansas City

St. Louis

DC & THE CAPITAL REGION

Charlotte

Memphis

THE SOUTHEAST

THE DEEP SOUTH

Atlanta

Savannah

Jacksonville

Houston

New Orleans

FLORIDA

Miami

**Cool Temperate (Great Plains)**
Chilled by arctic winds in winter, and hit by fierce tornadoes in spring, the Midwest states usually enjoy long, hot summers.

**Warm Tropical (Florida)**
The sultry climate of Florida and the Gulf of Mexico is usually warm and frequently very humid. Hurricanes can hit the coast between June and late November, making December to April the most popular time to visit the region.

# National Parks

For many visitors, the highlight of a visit to the US is to experience the country's sublime scenery and abundant wildlife. Some 84 million acres (34 million hectares) of pristine splendor have been preserved as national parks, found in all of the 50 states. From Acadia National Park on the rugged coast of Maine to the deserts of Death Valley in California, the parks encompass a variety of terrain, as well as the habitats of several endangered species. Most have a full range of facilities, including delightful rustic lodges, and offer a variety of outdoor activities.

**Yellowstone National Park** (*see pp576–7*) in Wyoming is the country's first and oldest national park. Highlights include geysers and the country's largest bison herd.

**Grand Teton National Park's** (*see p575*) peaks make it one of Wyoming's top sights.

**Badlands National Park** (*see p440*), South Dakota's most important park, combines craggy sandstone formations with mixed grass prairie.

Olympic NP
North Cascades NP
Mt. Rainier NP
Glacier NP

THE PACIFIC NORTHWEST
THE ROCKIES

Crater Lake NP
Yellowstone NP
Badland NP

Redwood NP
Grand Teton NP

Lassen Volcanic NP
Great Basin NP
Rocky Mountain NP

CALIFORNIA

Yosemite NP
Bryce Canyon NP
Arches NP
THE GREA PLAIN

Kings Canyon NP
Mesa Verde NP

Sequoia NP
Death Valley NP
Grand Canyon NP
THE SOUTH-WEST

Joshua Tree NP
Petrified Forest NP

Saguaro NP
Carlsbad Caverns NP
TEXAS

Guadalupe Mountains NP

Big Bend NP

**Olympic National Park** (*see p608*), a UNESCO biosphere reserve, preserves Washington's lush forests.

**Death Valley National Park** (*see pp672–3*) in California's Mojave Desert, is one of the world's hottest places.

**Mesa Verde National Park's** (*see p588*) great cliff dwellings offer glimpses of Colorado's early inhabitants.

**Yosemite National Park** (*see p706*), a wilderness of forests, meadows, and granite rocks, is California's prime destination.

**Grand Canyon National Park** (*see pp530–33*), perhaps the most-visited park in both Arizona and the US, is an awe-inspiring spectacle of magnificent rock formations.

**Voyageurs National Park** *(see p419)*, an area of staggering natural beauty, was named after French-Canadian fur trappers. Although most visitors traverse the park's network of lakes and streams by boat, there are numerous hiking trails as well.

Caribou in Denali National Park, Alaska

## Alaska

Kobuk Valley NP
Gates of the Arctic NP
Denali NP *(see pp728–9)*
Wrangell St. Elias NP
Lake Clark NP
Glacier Bay NP Katmai NP
Kenai Fjords NP
*(see p725)*

## Hawai'i

Haleakalā NP
Hawai'i Volcanoes NP
*(see pp738–9)*

0 kilometers 500
0 miles 500

Voyageurs NP

Acadia NP

NEW ENGLAND

NYC & MID-ATLANTIC REGION

THE GREAT LAKES

Cuyahoga Valley NP

Shenandoah NP

DC & THE CAPITAL REGION

Mammoth Cave NP

Great Smoky Mountains NP

Hot Springs NP

THE SOUTHEAST

**Great Smoky Mountains National Park** *(see p264)*, in Tennessee and North Carolina, supports an incredible diversity of plant life.

THE DEEP SOUTH

FLORIDA

Biscayne NP

Everglades NP

**Acadia National Park** *(see p180)*, a wild, unspoiled island paradise in Maine, is crisscrossed by hiking trails that offer breathtaking coastal views. Its main attraction, however, is the scenic 27-mile (43-km) Loop Road.

**Everglades National Park** *(see p321)* covers a vast expanse of low-lying wetlands at the southern tip of Florida. This unique ecosystem is characterized by tree islands or hammocks that support a fantastic variety of flora and fauna. Alligators are the park's best-known and most-feared residents.

# Exploring the National Parks

It is no exaggeration to claim that one could spend a lifetime exploring the sprawling expanses of national parks such as the Grand Canyon or Yosemite. Most people visit parks simply because they happen to be near one, or to see specific sights such as the geysers of Yellowstone. To make their trip more worthwhile and enjoyable, visitors should restrict the number of parks they intend to visit, and instead explore a couple of the most appealing ones at leisure. Plan for a minimum of one full day per park.

## Background

The world's first national park was established in 1872 to protect the geothermal wonders and wild creatures of Yellowstone, on the crest of the Rocky Mountains. In the years since, a staggering 401 places of scenic or historical interest in the US have been given federal protection, including 59 parks within the National Park system.

America's national parks offer visitors some of the most unforgettable wilderness experiences anywhere in the world, from stunning glacial lakes and lush forests to arid expanses of desert.

The **National Park Service**, a unit of the US Department of the Interior, also manages national seashores, battlefields, and national historic sites (such as Independence Hall in Philadelphia, Pennsylvania) and national memorials (such as Mount Rushmore in South Dakota).

## Planning your Visit

The national parks draw millions of visitors each year. In fact, the immensely popular Great Smoky Mountains National Park sees over 10 million visitors, while more than 3 million people visit comparatively remote parks such as Yellowstone and Yosemite. To avoid the crowds, aim to visit the parks outside the peak summer season (June–August), when they are full to capacity.

While the most popular parks are the jewels in the crown of US public lands, there are many quieter parks where you can enjoy nature without the crowds. Also try to take advantage of the many well-maintained trails to enable you to get away from the crowds and the traffic, and to really enjoy the parks at close range.

## Passports, Fees & Permits

To help maintain their facilities, most parks charge admission fees, valid for seven days, which range from nominal amounts ($1–5) at the smaller sites to upwards of $20 at prime attractions. Some parks don't charge a fee but do collect charges for specific activities.

If planning to visit more than two or three parks, visitors should consider an **America the Beautiful – National Parks and Federal Recreational Lands Pass**. Valid for one year, these cost approximately $80, and give admission to the bearer and passengers in the same private vehicle to all national parks and federal recreational lands, including national forests and **Bureau of Land Management (BLM)** properties. In parks where a per-person fee is charged, the pass admits the pass holder and three adults (children under 16 are free). This pass can be bought at

## Top National Parks

Listed below, are some of the most popular national parks in the United States (in alphabetical order), including the top parks on the previous pages. This chart depicts the various types of landscape and geological formations that are found within each park.

| | Volcanic/Geothermal | Mountainous | Glaciers | Climatic Extremes | Dramatic Erosion | Coral Reefs & Islands | Coastal Marshlands |
|---|---|---|---|---|---|---|---|
| **Acadia NP, ME** (see pp180) | | ● | | | | | |
| **Arches NP, UT** (see pp512–13) | | | | | ● | | |
| **Badlands NP, SD** (see p440) | | | | | ● | | |
| **Biscayne NP, FL** (see p322) | | | | | | ■ | |
| **Bryce Canyon NP, UT** (see pp518–19) | | | | | ● | | |
| **Canyonlands NP, UT** (see p514) | | | | | ● | | |
| **Death Valley NP, CA** (see pp672–3) | | | | ■ | | | |
| **Denali NP, AK** (see pp728–9) | | ■ | | | | | |
| **Everglades NP, FL** (see p321) | | | | | | | ■ |
| **Glacier NP, MT** (see p571) | | | ● | | | | |
| **Glen Canyon & Lake Powell, AZ** (see p515) | | | | | ● | | |
| **Grand Canyon NP, AZ** (see pp530–33) | | | | | ● | | |
| **Grand Teton NP, WY** (see p575) | | ■ | | | | | |
| **Great Smoky Mts. NP, TN, NC** (see p264) | | ■ | | | | | |
| **Hawai'i Volcanoes NP, HI** (see p738) | ● | | | | | | |
| **Mesa Verde NP, CO** (see p588) | | | | | ■ | | |
| **Mount Rainer NP, WA** (see pp614–15) | ● | | | | | | |
| **Olympic NP, WA** (see p608) | | | | | ■ | | |
| **Rocky Mountain NP, CO** (see p583) | | ■ | | | | | |
| **Sequoia & Kings Canyon NP, CA** (see p707) | | | | | ■ | | |
| **Shenandoah NP, VA** (see p223) | | ■ | | | | | |
| **Voyageurs NP, MN** (see p419) | | | | ● | | | |
| **Yellowstone NP, WY** (see pp576–7) | ● | | | | | | |
| **Yosemite NP, CA** (see p706) | | | ● | | | | |
| **Zion NP, UT** (see p517) | | | | | ● | | |

Visitors overlooking Thunder Hole, Acadia National Park, Maine

any park entrance, or in advance via the Internet (www.store.usgs.gov/pass). US citizens or permanent residents over the age of 62 are eligible for the **Senior Pass** (for a one-time $10 fee), a lifetime pass to national parks, monuments, historic sites, recreation areas, and wildlife refuges. It admits the pass holder and accompanying passengers in a private vehicle (if there is a per-vehicle fee), or up to four adults (at sites with per-person fees). It also provides a 50 percent discount on federal fees charged for various facilities and can be obtained in person from a federal area, such as a national park or monument. The **Access Pass**, which has the same lifetime privileges as the Senior Pass, is issued free to US citizens or permanent residents with permanent disabilities. Documentation of disability is required.

**ELK CROSSING NEXT 2 MILES**
Wildlife warning sign

## Types of Accommodation

Visitor facilities vary from park to park. Some provide very basic amenities, while others, especially the popular ones, have deluxe hotels close by. It is advisable to make reservations for overnight accommodation well in advance of your visit. Some parks make reservations on a first-come-first-served basis only, so the sooner you arrive at your destination, the better.

Most parks have campsites for both tents and RVs but these are often "unserviced," with no RV hookups for electricity, water, or sewage. Campsites usually cost $10–50 a night. The **US Forest Service** and Bureau of Land Management campsites are less expensive and more readily available.

Shark Valley Visitor Center, Everglades National Park

## Practical Tips for Visiting the Parks

- Wear appropriate clothing – sturdy boots, a protective hat, plus waterproof or warm clothing, depending on the conditions.
- Carry plenty of drinking water, a pair of binoculars, a first-aid kit, sun screen, and insect repellant.
- Do not litter. Use the litter bins provided, or carry your waste out of the park.
- Do not play loud music or blow car horns within park limits, as this disturbs everyone, including the wildlife.
- Do not interfere, provoke, or try to feed any wildlife.
- Hunting is prohibited and visitors found in violation will face heavy penalties.
- Do not approach bears or other wild animals; they can be extremely dangerous.

- Talk softly when on park trails to improve your chances of spotting wildlife.
- Do not wander off on your own, and do not venture off marked park trails; it is not only hazardous if you encounter dangerous animals but it is also easy to get lost in the wilderness.
- Be sure to tell a friend or fellow traveler your itinerary; in case you don't return on time they can inform the park ranger.
- Observe and obey all signs throughout the individual park regarding speed limits, food, animals, water, and all other safety precautions. Following these rules and regulations will enhance your enjoyment of the park and keep both you and the wildlife safe.

# Great American Cities

One of the main attractions of visiting the US is the chance of enjoying its many great cities. They vary from Colonial-era, pedestrian-friendly places such as Boston, with its distinctly European ambience, to the frenzied modern metropolis of Los Angeles, where no one walks, except to and from the car. In between, there is a wide range of cities, each with its own history and culture. Washington, DC, the capital, is known for its political focus and national galleries; Miami offers a spicy taste of Latin America; New Orleans is packed with multicultural music, food, and fun; and New York and Chicago are famous for their architecture and exciting nightlife. On the West Coast, San Francisco and Seattle have picturesque settings and vibrant arts scenes. All in all, cities here have something for everyone.

**Seattle** *(see pp604–7)* has risen from the ashes of the Great Fire of 1889 to become a prosperous city of gleaming skyscrapers, upscale shops, and sophisticated hotels.

**San Francisco's** *(see pp682–99)* many hills, ocean views, and rich ethnic mix give it a distinctive character, in keeping with its status as the West Coast's cultural capital.

Seattle

Portland

THE
PACIFIC
NORTHWEST   Boise

Helena

THE
ROCKIES

Sioux Fall:

Salt Lake City   Cheyenne

Omah

San
Francisco

CALIFORNIA   THE
SOUTHWEST

Denver

THE
GREA'
PLAIN

Las Vegas

Los
Angeles

Albuquerque

Oklahoma
City

San Diego   Phoenix

El Paso

Dallas

TEXAS

San
Antonio

0 km   250

0 miles   250

**Dallas** *(see pp472–3)* in many ways is synonymous with the wealth of Texan oil fields and cattle. Today, it is both the state's financial and entertainment center.

**Los Angeles** *(see pp646–65)* is often associated with movies, the glamor of Hollywood, the luxury of residential Beverly Hills, and the excitement of Sunset Boulevard. Yet this vibrant city is also home to some of the country's finest museums and galleries as well as the most popular beaches along the Pacific Ocean.

**Chicago** *(see pp384–95)*, located on the southwestern edge of Lake Michigan, is famous throughout the world for its magnificent, innovative architecture. New building techniques were perfected here, and it was here too that architects, such as Frank Lloyd Wright and others, created masterpieces of modern design.

**Philadelphia** *(see pp108–15)*, where the Declaration of Independence was signed on July 4, 1776, is the birthplace of America. Today, this "City of Brotherly Love" is one of the country's most popular destinations.

**Boston** *(see pp138–55)* is justly proud of its past. While its Colonial heritage is reflected in its buildings, the city also includes numerous important sites directly related to America's fight for freedom.

NEW ENGLAND

NYC & THE MID-ATLANTIC REGION

Boston

New York

THE GREAT LAKES

Minneapolis

Milwaukee

Detroit

Chicago

Philadelphia

Washington, DC

Indianapolis

Kansas City

St. Louis

DC & THE CAPITAL REGION

Nashville

Charlotte

THE SOUTHEAST

Memphis

THE DEEP SOUTH

Atlanta

Savannah

Houston

New Orleans

Jacksonville

FLORIDA

Miami

**New York** *(see pp74–99)*, the "Big Apple," is one of the world's great cities. One aspect of its character lies in its striking modern architecture. Others revolve around its many outstanding museums, its ethnic neighborhoods, and the choice of entertainment.

**New Orleans** *(see pp342–51)* is a fun city of bars, restaurants, and the always lively Mardi Gras celebrations.

**Miami's** *(see pp290–99)* focus of action concentrates on South Beach, with its Art Deco hotels and trendy shops.

**Washington, DC** *(see pp200–15)*, the nation's capital, is an impressive city of classical architecture and grand, tree-lined avenues. Beside its political focus, the city also has a cultural heart, with museums located along the Mall.

# Best Scenic Routes

One of the great pleasures of traveling in the US is the chance to explore its many scenic highways and byways. From quiet rural lanes to breathtaking coastal drives, they offer glimpses of the land's abundant natural beauty, and provide an opportunity to get to know its many inviting small towns. Many of the best-known routes are also historic and follow in the footsteps of the pioneer wagon trains, the Pony Express, or along trails taken by Civil War soldiers. For additional information on scenic routes, visit www.fhwa.dot.gov/byways.

**Going-to-the-Sun Road** *(see p571)* cuts across Glacier National Park, following the steep Rocky Mountain cliffs. The route offers breathtaking mountain views.

**Historic Columbia River Highway** *(see p620)* offers incomparable views of Oregon's diverse landscape, including Mount Hood's snowcapped summit. It also passes several waterfalls and lush orchards.

**Pacific Coast Highway** (Highway 1) was named California's first scenic highway in 1966. One of the world's most stunning drives, its most beautiful stretch is through Big Sur.

**Route 66** *(see p457)*, from Chicago to Los Angeles, is perhaps America's best-loved highway. Much of the original route remains intact, offering a nostalgic cruise across the country's heartland.

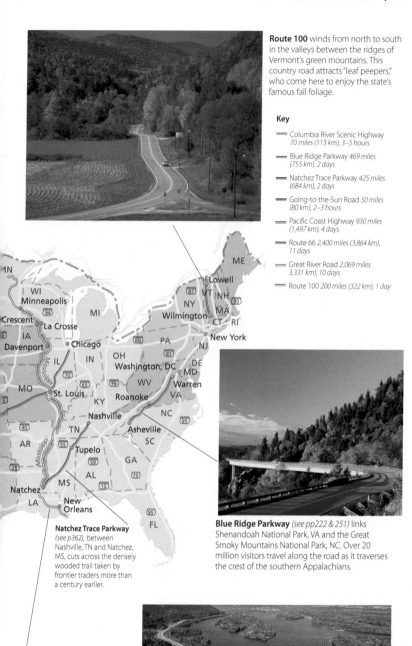

**Route 100** winds from north to south in the valleys between the ridges of Vermont's green mountains. This country road attracts "leaf peepers," who come here to enjoy the state's famous fall foliage.

**Key**

Columbia River Scenic Highway *70 miles (113 km), 3–5 hours*

Blue Ridge Parkway *469 miles (755 km), 2 days*

Natchez Trace Parkway *425 miles (684 km), 2 days*

Going-to-the-Sun Road *50 miles (80 km), 2–3 hours*

Pacific Coast Highway *930 miles (1,497 km), 4 days*

Route 66 *2,400 miles (3,864 km), 11 days*

Great River Road *2,069 miles 3,331 km), 10 days*

Route 100 *200 miles (322 km), 1 day*

**Natchez Trace Parkway** *(see p362)*, between Nashville, TN and Natchez, MS, cuts across the densely wooded trail taken by frontier traders more than a century earlier.

**Blue Ridge Parkway** *(see pp222 & 251)* links Shenandoah National Park, VA and the Great Smoky Mountains National Park, NC. Over 20 million visitors travel along the road as it traverses the crest of the southern Appalachians.

**Great River Road** follows most of the course of the Mississippi, from its source in Minnesota to the Gulf of Mexico. Running along both banks of the river, the route takes in areas of great scenic beauty and many historic sites as well as large towns, such as St. Louis and New Orleans.

# HISTORY OF THE USA

Man first entered North America from Siberia some 13,000 and 30,000 years ago, migrating over the Bering Strait land bridge to Alaska. As the ice receded, they moved south into the rich gamelands of the Great Plains. Isolated from Eurasia by melting ice and rising sea levels, those early settlers were mainly hunter-gatherers, as agricultural life evolved sporadically.

During this period of isolation, unique ecological, genetic, and social patterns emerged that proved disastrously fragile when confronted by the first Europeans in the late 15th century.

### Early European Explorers

European exploration began in earnest when improvements in shipping made the longer voyages of Columbus (1492) and Cabot (1497) viable. Early explorers were astonished by the quantity of natural resources they encountered here. Fur-bearing animals such as beavers were quickly exploited for their pelts. Once Europeans began to investigate further, they were able to draw heavily on the indigenous peoples' detailed knowledge, and use their pre-existing trails to explore the continent. An early map of 1507 displays the name "America," taken from one of the New World's early explorers, Amerigo Vespucci.

### Competing Colonies

The long rivalry between Spain, France, and Great Britain continued with the discovery of the New World in 1492. Spain founded the first successful North American colonies, in Florida in 1565 and New Mexico in 1598, combining commercial and religious interests. France's first permanent settlement was at Quebec (1608), while the Dutch set up a trading post (1624) at the mouth of the Hudson River. However, it was the English who gained control, with colonies in Virginia (1607), New England (1620), and Pennsylvania (1681). Many early colonists died of disease and malnutrition. Virginia eventually became the most lucrative New World colony, thanks to the production of tobacco. By 1700, these English colonies' population was 250,000, excluding Native Americans, while only some 1,000 non-Natives lived in Spanish or French regions.

Christopher Columbus sets foot in the New World on October 12, 1492

◄ George Washington before Yorktown, painted by Rembrandt Peale between 1824 and 1825

John Trumbull's 1786 painting of the Battle of Bunker Hill

## The American Revolution

The 18th century was a period of significant change throughout the world, and this was especially true in the New World. Colonists expanded their domain, displacing or killing the native tribes through a combination of land purchases, warfare, and disease. In the southern colonies of Virginia and Carolina, where the lack of available land discouraged new

immigrants, African slaves were imported in great numbers, reaching a total of 150,000, 40 percent of the population, by 1750.

The American Revolution began swiftly, and transformed the face of the world in a few short years. The removal of a potential French threat, following Britain's conquest of Canada in the Seven Years' War, led to American complaints about British abuse, epitomized by the phrase "No Taxation without Representation." In 1770, British troops opened fire on a group of unruly workers, killing five in what became known as the Boston Massacre. In 1773, some colonial merchants disguised as Indians dumped a boatload of tea into Boston Harbor, to protest Britain's monopoly of the tea trade.

War broke out in April 1775, when British "Redcoats" marched on the town of Concord in an attempt to seize a stockpile of weapons from the American "Minutemen." As the British fought their way back to Boston, more than 75 Redcoats and over 90 Americans were killed. The British occupied New York City and Philadelphia, while the ill-equipped Americans struggled through a harsh winter. The war moved south, and frontier fighters under Daniel Boone and George Rogers Clark captured British outposts in Kentucky and Illinois. The Americans eventually succeeded, largely due to French support, and the war officially ended in 1783.

### KEY DATES IN HISTORY

**1763** The Seven Years' War ends, France surrenders its Great Lakes lands to Great Britain

**1773** Boston Tea Party

**April 19, 1775** The Revolutionary War begins

**1776** The Declaration of Independence is adopted in Philadelphia

**1783** Treaty of Paris puts an end to the Revolutionary War

**1790** A 100-mile (160-km) square on the Maryland/ Virginia border, Washington, the District of Columbia, is set aside as the new capital

**1793** Samuel Slater's water-powered mill at Pawtucket, Rhode Island, brings the Industrial Revolution to the US

**1803** Ohio is the first of the Northwest Territories to become a state

**1803** The Louisiana Purchase

**1814** Francis Scott Key composes "The Star-Spangled Banner"

**1824** The Bureau of Indian Affairs, a division of the US War Department, is formed to handle relations with Indian tribes

**1832** Resisting attempts to remove his people from their traditional homelands, Chief Black Hawk leads a militant band of 1,000 Fox-Sauk Indians but is destroyed by the US Army

The Boston Tea Party: patriots disguised as Indians dumping tea into Boston Harbor

George Washington holding a copy of the US Constitution, surrounded by Founding Fathers, 1787

## Birth of a Nation

By 1783, the newly formed United States of America had a draft constitution and a border that extended as far west as the Mississippi River. The new Constitution was officially adopted in 1788, and in 1791 the ten amendments of the "Bill of Rights" were added, enumerating each citizen's freedom of speech, press, religion, and public assembly. In 1800, the capital moved from Philadelphia to the newly created city of Washington, DC, which by now had a population of 3,200 people.

## Manifest Destiny

America expanded greatly in its early years, first opening the "Northwest Territory" lands along the Great Lakes in 1787. The Louisiana Purchase of 1803 added a huge area of western lands formerly controlled by France. This rapid expansion created the need to survey the new territories. Lewis and Clark's famed cross-continental expedition between 1803 and 1806 was funded by Congress at the express request of President Thomas Jefferson.

The first test of strength for this new independent country came in 1812, when the US found itself caught in the middle of an ongoing war between France and Great Britain. Though both countries agreed to stop interfering with American ships, US forces attacked British interests in Canada, and in retaliation the British burned the Capitol and White House in Washington,

DC. Ironically, the war was ended by a peace treaty that was signed two weeks before its biggest skirmish – the Battle of New Orleans – took place in January 1815.

After the War of 1812, the US abandoned hopes of annexing Canada, and so began its great push westward. Settlers poured into the Great Plains, Oregon, and eventually the northern periphery of the Republic of Mexico, including Texas and California. The Santa Fe Trail, open for trade by 1823, brought New Mexico under US influence. By 1850, there was an extensive communications network. Steamboat traffic dominated the rivers, augmented by canals and cross-country railroads.

The consolidation of western lands encouraged millions of pioneers to migrate west and forge new lives for themselves. By the mid-19th century, people had grown accustomed to the idea that the country would stretch undivided across the continent, from ocean to ocean. This idea, in the words of populist journalist John L. O'Sullivan, was the country's "Manifest Destiny." Orderly settlement was made possible by the official survey and division of these lands into rectangular sections, each one square mile in area. Overland trails were opened leading west to the gold fields of California, which itself became a state in 1850. By 1860, more than half the population lived west of the Appalachian Mountains, compared to less than 10 percent in 1800.

An 1891 illustration depicting Indians fighting US soldiers

## Territorial Conflict

Although involved in conflicts with Britain over Canada, the US managed to resolve these issues peacefully. However, this was not so with Mexico, which feared US territorial ambitions, especially after President Andrew Jackson offered to purchase Texas. The crisis accelerated after Texas declared independence from Mexico in 1835. Turning a blind eye to Native American tribes (and the legal ownership of much of the land by Spain), the United

States took over Texas in 1845, a move that set off war with Mexico. This war in turn led to the US confiscation of California and much of the Southwest. In 1848, Mexico yielded nearly half of its territory; the cession of the northern Oregon territory by Britain in 1846, and James Gadsden's 1853 purchase of 30,000 sq miles (78,000 sq km) in the Southwest completed the westward expansion. Thus, in less than 50 years, the country had more than tripled in size.

### KEY DATES IN HISTORY

**1838** US Government forcibly expels native Cherokee Indians westward along the "Trail of Tears"

**1846–1848** Mexican War. US acquires Arizona, California, Utah, Nevada, and New Mexico

**1859** Abolitionist John Brown raids the Federal Armory at Harpers Ferry

**1861** Confederates attack Fort Sumter in South Carolina

**1861** The Battle of Bull Run (Manassas), the first major land battle of the Civil War

**Jan 1, 1863** President Abraham Lincoln issues the Emancipation Proclamation, freeing slaves in areas controlled by the Confederate army

**July, 1863** Union forces defeat General Robert E. Lee and the Confederacy at Gettysburg

**April 9, 1865** Robert E. Lee surrenders to Union General Ulysses Grant at Appomattox Court House, Virginia

**April 14, 1865** President Lincoln assassinated by a Confederate sympathizer, John Wilkes Booth, in Washington, DC

**Dec 18, 1865** The 13th amendment to the US Constitution is adopted, effectively putting an end to slavery in the US

**1870** African-Americans granted full citizenship

## The Destruction of the Indians

Since the 1500s, diseases such as small pox and syphilis had wiped out almost 90 percent of some tribes. As European settlement increased, forced relocation of tribes became frequent. It reached its peak with the forced march of most of the Cherokee Nation from the southeast to Oklahoma along the "Trail of Tears." As Europeans spread westward, tribes were forced onto reservations, often the poorest and most desolate lands, where many remain even today. The building of the transcontinental railroads in the late 19th century opened the West to hunters who eventually killed millions of buffalo. Within a few hundred years, North America's indigenous cultures had been destroyed or marginalized by Europeans, who transformed the continent into a world economic, industrial, and political power.

## Civil War

Between independence in 1783 and 1860, two very different societies developed within the US. In the North, there emerged an industrialized society, committed to liberal banking and credit systems, and protective tariffs, whereas the South was a less populous, agrarian society opposed to the sale of public land in the Midwest, high duties, and restrictions on slavery.

The causes of the Civil War are still up for debate. Though slavery was clearly the divisive issue, the war was not fought to free the slaves. Instead, the battle lines were drawn over the question of extending slavery into the newly forming western states. The South, resisting the federal government's growing power, wanted each new state to decide this question independently. The northern states wanted to keep slavery within its current limits, in part to protect their own manual labor. The federal government left the decision to the new states, and riots between pro- and anti-slave campaigners raged across the west. In 1856, pro-slave guerrillas burned the city of Lawrence, Kansas, and 200 people were killed in retaliation. Three years later, 22 abolitionists led by John Brown attacked the Federal Armory at Harpers Ferry, Virginia, hoping to incite a slave rebellion. He and his forces were killed, but his efforts further polarized the already divided nation. By 1860, the country was composed of 18 "free states" – mainly in the North, and 15 "slave states" – mainly in the South. When Abraham Lincoln was elected president in 1860, South Carolina seceded from the Union, followed by six other southern states, which joined together to form the Confederate States of America.

The first shots of the Civil War were fired in April, 1861, when the Confederates attacked Fort Sumter in South Carolina.

President Lincoln mobilized US soldiers to quell the rebellion, and soon four other slave-holding states, including Virginia, seceded from the Union. Richmond became the new Confederate capital, and Virginia provided most of the Confederate military leadership. Four slave states remained in the Union, and the western counties of Virginia separated to form West Virginia, which joined the Union in 1863.

The Confederates won the first major land battle at Manassas, Virginia, in July 1861, and for the next two years battles raged across Virginia and Maryland. With their defeat at Gettysburg in 1863, the Confederates were finally turned back. In the same year, Union forces gained control of the Mississippi River. Union forces destroyed Atlanta in 1864 and marched across Georgia, cutting off supply lines and virtually encircling the remaining Confederate army. By April 1865, the Civil War was over.

The destruction caused by the war was immense. Nearly three million soldiers (some 10 percent of the total population at the time) fought in the war, and 620,000 of them died. Entire cities lay in ruins, and it would be years before the nation recovered from the ravages of war.

Confederate forces occupy Fort Sumter, South Carolina, on April 15, 1861

## The Wild West

The end of the 19th century was a time of radical change across the country. The conquered South and the newly freed slaves suffered the ravages of the Reconstruction, while in the West, Native Americans saw their lands taken away and their lifestyles destroyed. Their culture's death knell was sounded in 1862, when the Homestead Act granted 160 acres (65 ha) of land to any white settler, freed slave, or single woman. The Army battled Indian tribes across the Great Plains in the 1870s and 1880s, and Indian resistance in the Southwest desert came to an end with the surrender of Apache chief Geronimo in 1886.

Buffalo Bill's Wild West poster, 1900

In the East and Midwest, massive mills and factories replaced local producers, as the population shifted from self-sufficient farms to chaotic city life. In a relatively brief period, the pace of life was altered by the growth of railroads, the telegraph, the telephone, the airplane, and the automobile. Railroads brought the once-distant West within reach of eastern markets, and the frontier towns that appeared along the railroads were often lawless places. During this post-Civil War period, the US became an international power, buying Alaska from Russia in 1867, then taking over Hawai'i in 1893, the Philippines in 1899, and Panama in 1903.

## Immigration, Urbanization & Industrialization

While stories of the Wild West captivated people's imagination, the most significant development was the increasing importance of industrialization. The rapid demographic shift from small towns and farms to big cities and factories was inevitable. This change was made possible in part by waves of immigration that doubled the population in a few decades.

In the 1880s, over six million immigrants arrived, and by the first decade of the 20th century a million people were arriving every year. By World War I, the population reached 100 million, 15 percent of whom were foreign born. The majority settled in East Coast cities, and for the first time in US history the population was predominantly urban.

The consolidation of the population was mirrored by a consolidation in industry and business. By 1882, John D. Rockefeller's Standard Oil Company had a monopoly in the petroleum industry, followed by other effective monopolies, legally organized as "trusts," in tobacco products, banking, and steel. These corporations' abuse of monopoly power was exposed by such writers as Upton Sinclair and Frank Norris. Political movements too resisted the rise of corporations, finding an ally in "trust-busting" President Theodore Roosevelt, who also made significant steps toward

### KEY DATES IN HISTORY

**1867** Russia sells Alaska for $7.2 million

**1869** First transcontinental railroad is completed when the Union Pacific and Central Pacific meet at Promontory, Utah

**1876** The Battle of Little Big Horn, Montana

**1876** The US Supreme Court legalizes "separate but equal" facilities for whites and non-whites, sanctioning racial segregation

**1884** New York and Boston telephone link

**1886** The Statue of Liberty erected in New York

**1898** USS *Maine* explodes in Havana, sparking Spanish-American War

**1915** The Lincoln Highway from New York City to San Francisco is the first trans-continental highway

**1915** The "Great Migration" of African-Americans to northern cities begins

**April 6, 1917** US declares war on Germany

**1925** Fundamentalist Christians ban the teaching of the theory of evolution in many states

**1929** The US stock market crash

**1934** Benny Goodman's orchestra popularizes "Swing" jazz

**1939** The first regular commercial TV broadcasts begin

Cartoon of Uncle Sam welcoming immigrants into the "US Ark of Refuge"

protecting the natural environment from the ravages of unrestrained industrial development.

The early 20th century also saw the growth of labor unions, which staged successful and sometimes violent strikes to improve pay and conditions, and helped protect children from working in factories.

### Boom & Bust

Involvement in World War I confirmed America's position as a world power, drawing the nation away from its long-cherished isolationism. But, after the war, soldiers returned home from Europe to severe unrest, with labor strikes and race riots. This economic depression caused enormous suffering and changed the domestic role of the government forever.

The 1920s, known as the "Jazz Age," saw an explosion of artistic creativity, especially in popular music. Architectural and engineering landmarks were constructed, and the rising popularity of the automobile encouraged the building of the first transcontinental highways, which linked the nation and gave rise to the first suburbs.

This creativity coincided with Prohibition, when the sale of alcohol was made illegal. Ironically, it was Prohibition itself that led to the freewheeling, drug-and alcohol-fuelled lifestyles of the Roaring Twenties.

### The Great Depression & the "New Deal"

The Wall Street Crash of 1929 shattered millions of dreams and left many Americans destitute. Farmers and black people in cities and rural areas were particularly hard hit, as banks withdrew funding. Unemployment and the gross domestic product dropped to half of what it was in the 1920s. Extended drought and sustained winds caused such destruction that the Great Plains was dubbed the "Dust Bowl," forcing some 200,000 Great Plains farmers to migrate west to California.

The Republican government, which had promoted the boom and was blamed for the crash, was rejected by the electorate, leading to the 1932 election of Democrat Franklin Delano Roosevelt. In his first 100 days in office, Roosevelt established federal government relief programs (the "New Deal") to revitalize the economy, provide jobs, and aid those who were hurt by the economic downturn. Roosevelt also set up regulatory bodies to help prevent economic turmoil in the future. Although millions of dollars of federal funding were spent on relief, 20 percent of Americans still continued to be unemployed in 1939.

Duke Ellington, celebrated icon of the Jazz Age

The battleships USS *West Virginia* and *Tennessee* burning after the Japanese attack on Pearl Harbor

## The Cold War

The Japanese attack on Pearl Harbor in 1941 and the subsequent US entry into World War II marked the beginning of America's new role in international politics. With the onset of the Cold War, the numerous US military bases, established during World War II, gained renewed importance. The Cold War also encouraged

### KEY DATES IN HISTORY

**Dec 7, 1941** Japanese attack on Pearl Harbor

**1945** The UN established in San Francisco

**Aug 14, 1945** After US bombing of Hiroshima and Nagasaki, Japan surrenders, ending WW II

**1961** Alan Shepard is the first American in outer space; the Soviets erect the Berlin Wall

**1962** Naval blockade against Soviet missile bases in Cuba

**1963** Assassination of John F. Kennedy, Dallas

**1968** Martin Luther King Jr. assassinated

**1969** Neil Armstrong walks on the moon

**1974** Richard Nixon resigns after Watergate

**1989** Fall of Berlin Wall; end of Cold War

**1990–91** The Gulf War

**Sept 11, 2001** Terrorist attacks on New York City & Washington, DC

**2003** Space shuttle *Columbia* explodes, killing all on board

**2003** George W. Bush declares war on Iraq

**2005** Hurricane Katrina wreaks havoc in New Orleans and other cities of Louisiana and Mississippi, displacing more than 500,000 people

**2008** Banking collapse triggers recession

**2012** Barack Obama is re-elected to a second term as president of the United States

**2014** One World Trade Center opens in Manhattan, New York City, at the site of the 2001 terrorist attack

alliances with other nations. America's powerful influence, and investment overseas was seen as a way to bind other nations to the capitalist sphere. The Marshall Plan of 1948 provided $13 billion to aid reconstruction of postwar western Europe and reduce Communist influence.

Economic and social developments were often overshadowed by the specter of nuclear war. The Korean War was the first of many fought to stop the spread of Communism. Fear on the domestic front inspired years of anti-Communist "Witch Trials," such as those conducted by Senator Joseph McCarthy. Cold War fears also led to numerous military operations around the world, including the takeover of Guatemala in 1954, an ill-fated invasion of Cuba in 1961, and the Vietnam War of the 1960s and 1970s, the longest and most costly of attempts to contain the perceived Communist threat.

After Vietnam, the US retreated from an active international role. The Soviet invasion of Afghanistan in 1979 revived the Cold War for another decade. With the collapse of the Soviet Union in 1991, the United States became the world's only superpower.

### Postwar Prosperity

Unlike much of the rest of the world, this was one of the most prosperous periods in US history. The economy, stimulated by mobilization of industry during World War II, and the arms race with the Soviet Union were key factors in creating unprecedented affluence. As manufacturing switched to a peacetime mode, consumer durables flowed into the marketplace. America's position at the hub of the international trading system gave her access to crucial foreign markets. Home ownership was brought within reach of middle-class Americans, thanks to government supports and mass-production construction techniques. Most adults owned a car, and consumer products, such as refrigerators, washers, dryers, and dishwashers, multiplied within the home.

## Civil Rights Movement

As black Americans migrated from the rural south to urban centers in the 1940s and 1950s, whites abandoned city life for the suburbs, taking their tax dollars with them. The financial crisis was made worse by the decline of traditional industries, and many cities during the 1960s and 1970s suffered as well. Housing deteriorated, roads went unrepaired, and poverty, crime, and racial tension were common features of many urban areas. Poverty was not confined to the inner cities; people in rural areas in the Deep South and the Appalachians were some of the most deprived in the country.

The new postwar opportunities were denied to many African-Americans, particularly in the still-segregated South. Aided by a 1954 Supreme Court judgment that ruled segregation unconstitutional, African-Americans fought for an end to discrimination. In 1955, a bus boycott in Montgomery, Alabama, forced the company to end segregation. The success inspired similar protests throughout the South. In 1964 and 1965, Congress passed legislation banning racial discrimination.

The 1960s also saw a rise in political consciousness among other groups; protests against the Vietnam War grew in number, and in the 1970s, the women's movement made some progress towards achieving an end to sexual discrimination. A tide of environmentalism also swept the country, culminating in 1970 with the creation of the US Environmental Protection Agency. During the AIDS crisis of the late 1980s, homosexuality became an increasingly accepted aspect of life, with gay and lesbian couples earning greater legal protections. During his second term, President Obama has supported same-sex marriage and by 2014, same-sex marriage was legalized in 16 states and the District of Columbia.

## The Modern Era

The postwar boom ended in the early 1970s, with the Vietnam War and the energy crisis producing prolonged inflation

Reverend Martin Luther King Jr. delivering a sermon at the Ebenezer Baptist Church, Atlanta

and recession. In the 1980s, computers and other digital devices began to change the way Americans communicated. The Internet opened new ways of working and generated large amounts of wealth. By the turn of the millennium, the Internet-fueled boom went bust, causing the economy to fall into recession. The controversial election of George W. Bush in 2001 dominated the news and showed that the American public was deeply divided over crucial issues.

The terrorist attacks on New York and Washington, DC in September 2001 instigated the launch of the "war against terrorism" by President Bush. This resulted in a war against the Taliban in Afghanistan in 2002 and another one to oust Saddam Hussein in Iraq in 2003. Economic stress from five years of warfare combined with deregulation of the financial sector resulted in crisis for the economy in late 2008, from which the country is slowly recovering. The presidential election campaigns of 2008 spelled a new direction in US politics, with greater representation of minorities. Barack Obama won, becoming the 44th president and the first African-American president. He was re-elected in 2012.

# The American Presidents

The presidents of the United States have come from all walks of life; at least two were born in a log cabin – Abraham Lincoln and Andrew Jackson. Others, such as Franklin D. Roosevelt and John F. Kennedy, came from privileged backgrounds. Millard Fillmore attended a one-room schoolroom, and Jimmy Carter raised peanuts. Many, including Ulysses S. Grant and Dwight D. Eisenhower, were military men, who won public popularity for their great achievements in battle.

**Key to Timeline**

- Federalist
- Democratic Republican
- Whig
- Republican
- Democrat

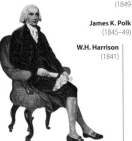

**Millard Fillmore**
(1850–53)

**William McKinley**
(1897–1901)

**Zachary Taylor**
(1849–50)

**Franklin Pierce**
(1853–57)

**James K. Polk**
(1845–49)

**Benjamin Harrison**
(1889–93)

**W.H. Harrison**
(1841)

**Chester A. Arthur**
(1881–85)

**Rutherford B. Hayes**
(1877–81)

**George Washington**
(1789–97) was a Revolutionary War general. He was unanimously chosen to be the first president of the United States.

**James Madison** (1809–17), known as the Father of the Constitution, was co-author of the Federalist Papers.

**Andrew Johnson**
(1865–69)

| 1775 | 1800 | 1825 | 1850 | 1875 |
|------|------|------|------|------|
| 1775 | 1800 | 1825 | 1850 | 1875 |

**John Adams**
(1797–1801), a lawyer and historian, was the first president to live in the White House.

**James Monroe**
(1817–25)

**John Quincy Adams**
(1825–29)

**John Tyler**
(1841–45)

**James A. Garfield**
(1881)

**Ulysses S. Grant**
(1869–77)

**Martin Van Buren**
(1837-41)

**Grover Cleveland**
(1885–89)

**James Buchanan**
(1857–61)

**Thomas Jefferson**
(1801–1809), architect, inventor, landscape designer, diplomat, and historian, was the quintessential Renaissance man.

**Andrew Jackson**
(1829–37) defeated the British at the Battle of New Orleans in the War of 1812.

**Abraham Lincoln**
(1861–65) won the epithet, "the Great Emancipator", for his role in the abolition of slavery. He led the Union through the Civil War.

**Grover Cleveland**
(1893–97)

**Harry S. Truman** (1945–53) made the decision to drop the atomic bombs on Hiroshima and Nagasaki in 1945.

**Woodrow Wilson** (1913–21) led the country through World War I and paved the way for the League of Nations.

**John F. Kennedy** (1961–63) was one of the most popular presidents. He sent the first astronaut into space, started the Peace Corps, and created the Arms Control and Disarmament Agency. His assassination rocked the nation.

**Richard Nixon** (1969–74) opened up China and sent the first men to the moon. He resigned after the Watergate scandal.

**Franklin D. Roosevelt** (1933–45) started the "New Deal", a reform and relief program, during the Great Depression. He was elected to four terms.

**Jimmy Carter** (1977–81), who brokered the peace accord between Israel and Egypt, won the 2002 Nobel Peace prize.

**Barack Obama** (2009– ) becomes the first African-American president.

**George Bush** (1989–93)

| 900 | 1925 | 1950 | 1975 | 2000 | 2025 |
|-----|------|------|------|------|------|

| 900 | 1925 | 1950 | 1975 | 2000 | 2025 |
|-----|------|------|------|------|------|

**William H. Taft** (1909–13)

**Dwight D. Eisenhower** (1953–61)

**Gerald Ford** (1974–77)

**George W. Bush** (2001–09)

**Herbert Hoover** (1929–33)

**Warren Harding** (1921–23)

**Calvin Coolidge** (1923–29)

**Ronald Reagan** (1981–89), a one-time movie actor and popular president, cut taxes, increased military spending, and reduced government programs.

**William J. Clinton's** (1993–2001) two-term presidency saw unprecedented prosperity.

**Lyndon B. Johnson** (1963–69) escalated the Vietnam conflict, resulting in widespread protests.

**Theodore Roosevelt** (1901–9) created many national parks and oversaw the construction of the Panama Canal.

## The Role of the First Lady

In the 19th century, the First Lady acted primarily as hostess and "behind-the-scenes" adviser. Dolley Madison was known as the "Toast of Washington." Later, when Eleanor Roosevelt held her own press conferences, the role of First Lady changed greatly. Jackie Kennedy gave unprecedented support to the arts, Rosalynn Carter attended Cabinet meetings, Nancy Reagan told the world to "Just Say No" to drugs, Barbara Bush promoted literacy, and Hillary Clinton ran her own political campaign.

First Lady & Senator Hillary Clinton in New York, 1999

# NEW YORK CITY & THE MID-ATLANTIC REGION

# New York City & the Mid-Atlantic Region at a Glance

The three-state region surrounding New York City is one of the most fascinating areas in the US. New Jersey, the region's smallest but most densely populated state, extends between New York and Philadelphia. To its west, the idyllic pastoral landscape of Pennsylvania stretches almost all the way to the Great Lakes, with towns, green farm valleys, and the rolling folds of the Allegheny Mountains. Farther north, New York State has cities, towns, and rural hamlets spreading between the Hudson River Valley and Niagara Falls. Of the two main cities, New York City is a vibrant, cosmopolitan city and the financial capital of the world, while Philadelphia is more historic, in keeping with its status as the capital of Colonial America.

**Niagara Falls** *(see p105)*, located on the border between Canada and the US, is one of New York State's prime attractions, drawing more than 10 million visitors a year.

**Pittsburgh** *(see p118)*, in Pennsylvania, has rebuilt itself from the ashes of an industrial past to become one of the country's most appealing cities. The Andy Warhol Museum and the Carnegie Museum of Art are popular tourist attractions here.

Lake Ontario

Rochester     Syracuse

Buffalo

*Lake Erie*

Jamestown     Elmira

Erie

Meadville

Williamsport

**PENNSYLVANIA**
*(See pp108–19)*

Pittsburgh     Altoona

Harrisburg

Gettysburg

0 kilometers    100
0 miles    100

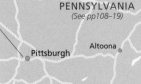

**Gettysburg** *(see p116)* is one of Pennsylvania's most significant historic sites. In July 1863, this peaceful town was the scene of a devastating Civil War battle. It was here, four months later, that President Abraham Lincoln delivered his moving Gettysburg Address.

◄ Scenic fall landscape of Allegheny River, Pittsburgh, Pennsylvania

**New York State** *(see p100–105)* offers a diversity of landscapes, from the beauty of the Hudson Valley, to the craggy Adirondack Mountains and the lush wine country of the Finger Lakes. Other highlights include Albany, the state capital, and the awesome Niagara Falls.

**Locator Map**

Plattsburgh

Glens Falls

Utica

**NEW YORK**
*(See pp74–105)*

Albany

Binghamton

Poughkeepsie

Scranton

Newark   New York City

Brookhaven

Allentown

Trenton

Philadelphia

**NEW JERSEY**
*(See pp106–107)*

Atlantic City

Cape May

**New York City** *(see pp74–99)*, with its world-class museums and wide variety of shopping, dining, and entertainment options, is one of the most frequently visited cities in the United States. Its distinctive skyline features a varied collection of skyscrapers, including the iconic Empire State Building.

**Philadelphia** *(see pp108–15)*, the "City of Brotherly Love," was the focus of the revolutionary movement for American independence. Its historic Independence National Historic Park preserves structures and artifacts relating to those stirring times.

**Cape May** *(see p107)*, at the southern tip of New Jersey, is a Victorian-period resort that draws many visitors. The state's other attractions include the opulent casinos of Atlantic City and the picturesque wilds of the Delaware Gap.

*For hotels and restaurants see pp122–7*

# NEW YORK CITY & THE MID-ATLANTIC REGION

The tri-state region around New York City truly embodies American diversity and dynamism. The vitality of New York City and Philadelphia is balanced by a surprisingly calm, almost pastoral hinterland. The Mid-Atlantic landscape is spectacular and ranges from dramatic mountain scenery, superb river valleys, and forests, interspersed with rolling farmlands.

New York City, or the "Big Apple," dominates northeastern US, and to a large extent controls the country's economy and culture. It is, without exaggeration, one of the world's great cities, and it is hard to imagine visiting the region without spending some time here. Philadelphia, the other major city, was the nation's leading city during Colonial times, and its wealth of history offers unforgettable insights into early American ideals.

Fascinating as these cities are, the broader region around them paints a much fuller picture of the nation. New Jersey, despite its reputation for heavy industry and sprawling suburbia, has much to offer, from the Victorian-era coastal resort of Cape May to Ivy League Princeton University. Pennsylvania, to the west, juxtaposes peaceful scenes of rural farmland in the "Pennsylvania Dutch" country where Amish and Mennonite communities still speak German (Deutsch), with the industrial cities of Pittsburgh and Reading. Farther north, the state of New York has majestic mountains, picturesque lakes, and the scenic Hudson River Valley.

## History

The Mid-Atlantic Region's natural wealth supported some of early America's most powerful and accomplished Native peoples. The first main groups were the Algonquian tribes, including the Lenni Lenape, who lived in what is now New Jersey and Pennsylvania. In the early 16th century, the Algonquian Indians were ousted by incoming tribes of Iroquois Indians. Settling in the Finger Lakes area in central New York State, the Iroquois, one of North America's most socially sophisticated tribes, formed a powerful alliance among their five constituent tribes – the Senecas, Cayugas, Oneidas, Mohawks, and Onondagas.

Amish farmers harvesting corn in Lancaster County, Pennsylvania

◀ Brooklyn Bridge over the Hudson River in Manhattan, New York City

Around this time, the first Europeans were making efforts to forge trade relations. Although Giovanni da Verrazano visited New York as early as 1524, it was not until 1609, when the Dutch West India Company sent Henry Hudson to explore the river that now bears his name, that the first settlements were established. In the same year, a French explorer, Samuel de Champlain, laid claim to northeastern New York State, having ventured there by way of Quebec.

In 1624 the Dutch founded the region's first colony, Fort Orange, at present-day Albany, began another at New Amsterdam (later New York) the following year, and later expanded to make footholds in New Jersey and Pennsylvania. Relations between the Dutch and the Indians were mutually beneficial, in that the Dutch supplied guns and other metal products to the

**Giovanni da Verrazano**

Detail from Benjamin West's monumental *Penn's Treaty with the Indians*, circa 1770

Indians, who paid for them with valuable beaver and other pelts. However, contact with foreigners led to the spread of diseases, including smallpox and measles, which soon decimated Native populations.

From the 1660s onward, as England wrestled for power in the New World, upstate New York evolved into a battleground for distant European wars. To consolidate their control over trans-Atlantic trade, the English first acquired the Dutch colonies and established a new one of their own – Pennsylvania. This colony, which developed on land granted by King Charles II to wealthy Quaker William Penn in 1680, thrived, thanks to fertile soil, a healthy climate, and a group of comparatively wealthy and industrious colonists. Its capital, Philadelphia, flourished and became the key center of the nascent movement for American independence.

## Independence & Industry

Throughout the first half of the 18th century, the English and their American colonists fought a series of frontier battles against the French and their Indian allies. The cost of these wars in loss of life and property was high, and to pay for them the English Crown raised a series of taxes, many of which were especially onerous for the merchants of New York and Philadelphia. In 1774, and again in 1776, delegates to Philadelphia's Continental Congress debated the issues and eventually declared independence from England. Soon after, the English

### KEY DATES IN HISTORY

**1524** Italian sailor Giovanni da Verrazano sails into New York harbor

**1609** Henry Hudson explores and maps the Hudson River and New Jersey shore

**1624** The Dutch establish Fort Orange

**1664** England takes over New Netherland. The city of New Amsterdam is renamed New York

**1731** Benjamin Franklin establishes the nation's first public library in Philadelphia

**1776** The Declaration of Independence is adopted in Philadelphia

**1825** The 363-mile (588-km) Erie Canal opens

**1863** Union forces defeat Robert E. Lee and the Confederacy at Gettysburg

**1929** Stock Market crash triggers the Great Depression

**1933** New York Governor Franklin Delano Roosevelt is elected president

**1978** Gambling legalized in Atlantic City

**1987** Stock Market crash

**2001** World Trade Center (WTC) destroyed in terrorist attack

**2004** Cornerstone laid for new tower at WTC site

**2011** The National September 11 Memorial opened on the 10-year anniversary of 9/11

military occupied New York and Philadelphia and held them until the end of the Revolutionary War in 1783.

Perhaps the most significant early battle took place in the summer of 1777 at Saratoga Springs, where patriots defeated the English under General John Burgoyne. Although this success earned the Americans the vital support of France, the revolutionary forces, organized into the Continental Army under George Washington, still suffered tremendous hardships. More than 3,000 soldiers died of disease at Valley Forge, outside Philadelphia, in the winter of 1777–8. After the British abandoned their American colonies in 1783, New York City served as the capital of the new nation until 1790, followed by Philadelphia from 1790 to 1800.

Although the battle for independence was fought and won by farmers and tradesmen, the following century saw the region emerge as a major industrial powerhouse. The Erie Canal was cut across upstate New York between 1817 and 1825, and Pennsylvania became the nation's biggest producer of coal and steel. Railroads crisscrossed the region by the mid-19th century, and it was this industrial might that enabled the North to withstand the divisive Civil War. The region sent more than 600,000 men to fight for the Union, but the main battle fought here was in July 1863, at the small town of Gettysburg in southeastern Pennsylvania. Known as the "high tide" of the war, this battle was the northern limit of Confederate success, the only time southern forces crossed the Mason-Dixon Line, the Pennsylvania–Maryland border that marked the divide between free and slave states.

**War memorial in Congress Park, Saratoga Springs**

## People & Culture

For nearly a century after the Civil War, the mines, mills, and factories of New York, New Jersey, and Pennsylvania attracted a huge influx of European immigrants. Between 1880 and 1910, some 12 million immigrants passed through New York City's port. During the World War years more people, including African-Americans from the Deep South, came here to work in the several arms-related factories. Today, as much as one-third of the present population counts itself as ethnic minorities, and in many cities these "minorities" often comprise a large majority of the residents. Thus some neighborhoods are identified by their ethnic makeup – Chinatown or Little Italy in New York City, the Italian Market in South Philadelphia, or the Polish areas of Pittsburgh's South Side.

Years of labor strife, and many economic upheavals led to many industries closing down in the 1960s and 1970s. New York City, the financial center of world capitalism, flirted with bankruptcy in the 1970s.

Today, however, things are different. "Heritage tourism" of battlefields, former industrial sites, historic canals, and railroads is a significant business, drawing almost as many millions of visitors as the natural wonders of Niagara Falls.

San Gennaro Festival in Manhattan's Little Italy

# Exploring New York City & the Mid-Atlantic Region

The two major cities of New York and Philadelphia naturally dominate travel in the Mid-Atlantic Region. However, the region's other attractions include the exclusive summer retreats of the Hamptons, the collegian environs of Princeton, and industrial Pittsburgh, today a vibrant cultural center. Equally attractive are its scenic wonders, ranging from the broad beaches of New Jersey and the tranquil beauty of Pennsylvania's Amish Country to the wilderness of New York State's Adirondacks. A car is essential to explore the region's vast interior. All roads tend to lead through both New York City and Philadelphia, especially the New Jersey Turnpike (I-95), the main north–south artery. Heading west from the coast, the two main roads are I-80 across Pennsylvania and I-90, the New York Thruway. Many state and country roads connect the rural areas, while the major cities have good Amtrak and commuter train services.

Taughannock Falls surrounded by trees in fall foliage, Taughannock Falls State Park

## Sights at a Glance

**❶** *New York City pp74–99*

**New York State**

**❷** Jones Beach State Park
**❸** The Hamptons & Montauk
**❹** Hudson River Valley
**❺** Albany
**❻** Saratoga Springs
**❼** Adirondack Mountains
**❽** Cooperstown
**❾** Finger Lakes
**❿** Syracuse
**⓫** Rochester
**⓬** Chautauqua
**⓭** Buffalo
**⓮** Niagara Falls

**New Jersey**

**⓯** Princeton
**⓰** Atlantic City
**⓱** Cape May

**Pennsylvania**

**⓲** *Philadelphia pp108–15*
**⓳** Gettysburg
**⓴** Lancaster
**㉑** Hershey
**㉒** York
**㉓** Reading
**㉔** Longwood Gardens
**㉕** Pittsburgh
**㉖** Laurel Highlands
**㉗** Western Amish Country

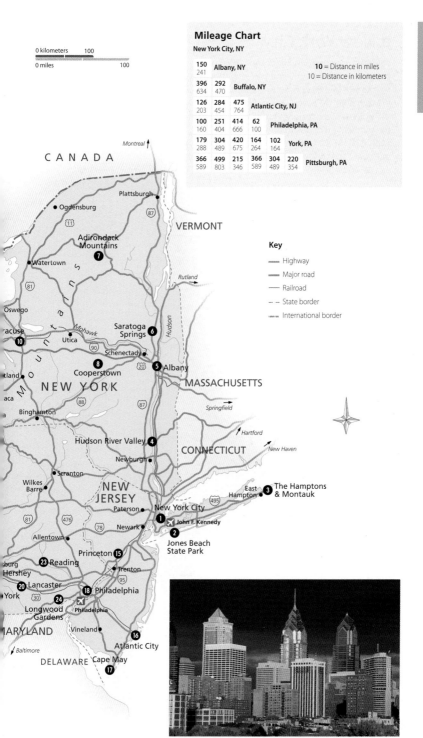

0 kilometers    100
0 miles         100

## Mileage Chart

**New York City, NY**

| | | | | | | |
|---|---|---|---|---|---|---|
| **150**<br>241 | **Albany, NY** | | | | **10** = Distance in miles | |
| **396**<br>634 | **292**<br>470 | **Buffalo, NY** | | | 10 = Distance in kilometers | |
| **126**<br>203 | **284**<br>454 | **475**<br>764 | **Atlantic City, NJ** | | | |
| **100**<br>160 | **251**<br>404 | **414**<br>666 | **62**<br>100 | **Philadelphia, PA** | | |
| **179**<br>288 | **304**<br>489 | **420**<br>675 | **164**<br>264 | **102**<br>164 | **York, PA** | |
| **366**<br>589 | **499**<br>803 | **215**<br>346 | **366**<br>589 | **304**<br>489 | **220**<br>354 | **Pittsburgh, PA** |

Montreal ↑

C A N A D A

• Ogdensburg

Plattsburgh •

VERMONT

(87)

Adirondack
Mountains ❼

Watertown •

Rutland ↗

(81)

Oswego •

acuse •

❿

Utica •

Mohawk

Saratoga
Springs ❻

Hudson

(90)

Schenectady •

Cooperstown ❽

(20)

❺ Albany

land •

N E W   Y O R K

MASSACHUSETTS

aca •

(88)

(87)

Springfield ↗

Binghamton •

a

Hartford ↗

Hudson River Valley ❹

Newburgh •

CONNECTICUT

New Haven ↗

Scranton •

Wilkes
Barre •

N E W
J E R S E Y

Paterson •

East
Hampton • ❸

The Hamptons
& Montauk

(495)

(81)

(476)

(78)

New York City

❶

✈ John F. Kennedy

Allentown •

Newark •

❷

Princeton ❿⓯

Jones Beach
State Park

burg

❷⓷ Reading

Trenton •

Hershey

(95)

❷⓪ Lancaster

(30)

❿⓲ Philadelphia

York •

❷⓸

✈ Philadelphia

Longwood
Gardens

ARYLAND

Vineland •

❿⓺

Baltimore ↙

DELAWARE  Cape May •

Atlantic City

⓱

### Key

── Highway
── Major road
── Railroad
– – State border
━━ International border

A view of Philadelphia's impressive modern architecture

# ❶ New York City

With its skyscrapers and bright lights, this is a city of superlatives. It covers an area of 301 sq miles (780 sq km), and comprises the five distinct boroughs of Manhattan, the Bronx, Queens, Brooklyn, and Staten Island. Most of the major sights lie within Manhattan, the southern tip of which was the target of the September 11, 2001 terrorist attack. Glittering shops, museums, and theaters are located in Midtown and along Central Park.

**Key**

░ Place of interest

═ Highway

## Sights at a Glance

① Wall Street
② World Trade Center Site and 9/11 Memorial
③ Battery Park City
④ Statue of Liberty
⑤ Ellis Island
⑥ South Street Seaport
⑦ *Brooklyn Bridge p78*
⑧ Civic Center
⑨ Eldridge Street Synagogue
⑩ Chinatown
⑪ Little Italy
⑫ TriBeCa
⑬ SoHo Historic District
⑭ Washington Square
⑮ Greenwich Village
⑯ East Village
⑰ Union Square
⑱ Flatiron Building
⑲ Madison Square
⑳ *Empire State Building p83*
㉑ Herald Square
㉒ Times Square
㉓ The New York Public Library
㉔ Morgan Library & Museum
㉕ Grand Central Terminal
㉖ United Nations
㉗ Rockefeller Center
㉘ *St. Patrick's Cathedral p87*
㉙ Museum of Modern Art
㉚ Fifth Avenue
㉛ *A Tour of Central Park pp88–9*
㉜ Whitney Museum of American Art
㉝ Frick Collection
㉞ Metropolitan Museum of Art
㉟ *The Solomon R. Guggenheim Museum p92*
㊱ American Museum of Natural History
㊲ Lincoln Center

## Greater New York
*(see inset map)*

㊳ Columbia University
㊴ Riverside Church
㊵ St. Nicholas Historic District
㊶ Studio Museum in Harlem
㊷ *The Cloisters p96*
㊸ The Bronx
㊹ Brooklyn

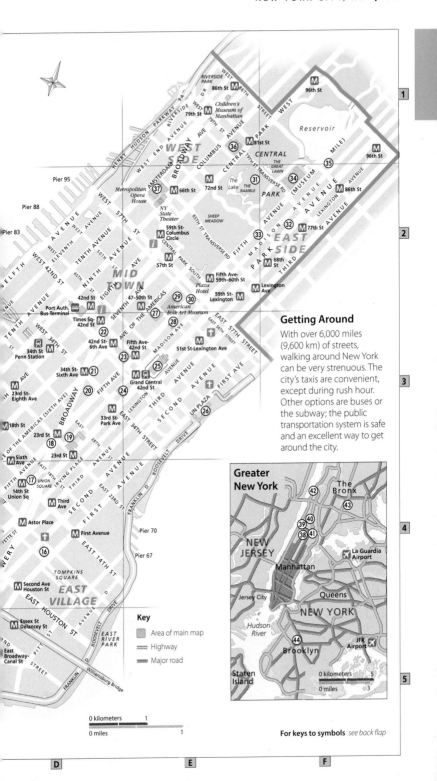

**1**

**2**

## Getting Around

With over 6,000 miles (9,600 km) of streets, walking around New York can be very strenuous. The city's taxis are convenient, except during rush hour. Other options are buses or the subway; the public transportation system is safe and an excellent way to get around the city.

**3**

### Greater New York

**4**

**5**

### Key

Area of main map

Highway

Major road

0 kilometers 1

0 miles 1

**For keys to symbols** *see back flap*

D    E    F

Trinity Church at the foot of Wall Street

## ① **Wall Street**

**Map** B5. M 2, 3, 4, 5 to Wall St, I, R, W to Rector St. M1, M6, M15.

Named for the wall that kept enemies and warring Indians out of Manhattan, Wall Street is now the heart of the city's financial district. One of the prominent sites here is the **Federal Reserve Bank** on Liberty Street. Inspired by the Italian Renaissance, this is a government bank for banks, where US currency is issued. Five stories below ground is a large storehouse for inter-national gold. Each nation's hoard is stored in its own compartment within the subterranean vault, guarded by 90-ton doors.

Farther away is the **Federal Hall National Monument**, where a bronze statue of George Washington on the steps marks the site where the nation's first president took his oath of office in 1789 *(see p71)*. The imposing structure was built between 1834 and 1842 as the US Custom House, and is one of the finest Classical designs in the city.

At the head of Wall Street is **Trinity Church**. Built in 1846, this square-towered Episcopal church is the third one on this site in one of America's oldest Anglican parishes, founded in 1697. Designed by Richard

Upjohn, it was one of the grandest churches of its day, marking the beginning of the best period of Gothic Revival architecture in America. The sculpted brass doors were inspired by Ghiberti's *Doors of Paradise* in Florence. Its 280-ft (85-m) steeple was New York's tallest structure until the 1860s. Many famous New Yorkers are buried here.

The hub of the world's financial markets, the **New York Stock Exchange** (NYSE) is housed in a 17-story building built in 1903. Initially, trading in stocks and shares took place haphazardly in the area, but 24 brokers signed an agreement in 1792 to deal only with one another. This formed the basis of the NYSE. Membership was strictly limited and a "seat" that cost $25 in 1817 can now cost as much as several million dollars. The NYSE became a for-profit public company in 2006. The NYSE has weathered slumps ("bear markets") and booms ("bull markets") and has seen advances in technology, from ticker tape to electronic trading, turn a local market into a global one.

Bronze bull, symbol of Wall Street, near Custom House

🔼 **Trinity Church**
Broadway at Wall St. **Tel** (212) 602-0800. **Open** 7am–6pm Mon–Fri, 8am–4pm Sat, 7am–4pm Sun. 🔼 12:05pm Mon–Fri, 9am, 11:15am Sun. Concerts: 1pm Thu & occasionally 5pm Sun. W **trinitywallstreet.org**

New York Stock Exchange
20 Broad St. **Tel** (212) 656-3000. **Closed** visitors' gallery closed for security reasons. W **nyse.com**

## ② **World Trade Center Site and 9/11 Memorial**

**Map** B5. Viewing wall on Church St. M Cortlandt St, Rector St, WTC Station. **Memorial Tel** (212) 266-5211. **Open** hours may vary but are usually 10am–8pm daily. Tickets must be reserved online or by phone.
W **911memorial.org**

Immortalized by countless filmmakers and photographers, the twin towers of the World Trade Center dominated the Manhattan skyline from 1973 until the September 2001 terrorist attack.

"Ground Zero" continues to evolve as the area is redeveloped and offices are reoccupied. Most notably, on the tenth anniversary of 9/11, the National September 11 Memorial was opened. The beautiful memorial is marked by twin reflecting pools, shimmering in the "footprints" of where the Twin Towers once stood. The pools feature the largest man-made waterfalls in North America and around them, etched in bronze, are the names of all 2,983 victims. An accompanying museum features collections relating to the history of the World Trade Center and the 9/11 attacks, including tributes of remembrance.

Battery Park City's World Financial Center from the Hudson River

*For hotels and restaurants see pp122–7*

### ③ Battery Park City

**Map** B5. **M** 1 to Rector St. 🚹 🖉 🏠 **W** batteryparkcity.org World Financial Center: West St. **Tel** (212) 945-2600. **M** 1, 2, 3, A, C, & J, M, Z to Chambers St; 4, 5, 6 to Brooklyn Bridge/City Hall Station; E to WTC Station; W, R to City Hall. 🚹 🖉 🖥 🏠 **W** worldfinancialcenter.com; **W** skyscraper.org

New York's youngest neighborhood is an ambitious development on 92 reclaimed acres (37 ha) along the Hudson River. This huge commercial and residential complex can house more than 25,000 people, at an estimated cost of $4 billion. A 2-mile (3-km) esplanade offers grand views of the Statue of Liberty.

The most visible part is the **World Financial Center**. A model of urban design by Cesar Pelli & Associates, this development is a vital part of the revival of Lower Manhattan, and its damage in the World Trade Center attack was attended to as a matter of urgency. At the heart of the complex lies the dazzling Winter Garden, a vast glass-and-steel public space often used for concerts and arts events. It is flanked by restaurants and shops, and opens onto a lively piazza and marina on the Hudson River.

The Skyscraper Museum is located at 39 Battery Park at the Ritz Carlton hotel.

### ④ Statue of Liberty

**Map** A5. Liberty Island. **M** 1, W, R to S Ferry; 4, 5 to Bowling Green. 🚌 M6, M15 to S Ferry, then Circle Line–Statue of Liberty Ferry from the Battery every 30–45 mins, 9:30am–3:30pm summer (winter hours vary). 🚢 time pass required. **Tel** (201) 604-2800 for reservation or book online **W** statue reservations.com **Open** Jul–Aug: 9am– 6pm daily; Sep–Jun: 9:30am–5pm daily. **Closed** Dec 25. Ferry fare includes entry to Ellis & Liberty Is. 🚹 elevator to the top of the pedestal; interior of pedestal accessible. 🖥 🏠 **W** nps.gov/stli

The figure presiding over New York harbor, titled "Liberty Enlightening the World," has

Statue of Liberty, an enduring symbol of New York

been the symbol of freedom for millions since her inauguration by President Grover Cleveland in 1886. A gift from the French to the American people to mark the US centennial in 1876, the statue was the brainchild of sculptor Frédéric-Auguste Bartholdi. In Emma Lazarus's poem, which is engraved on the base, Lady Liberty says: "Give me your tired, your poor, / Your huddled masses yearning to breathe free."

The 305-ft- (93-m-) high statue stands on a pedestal set within the walls of an old army fort. In one hand Liberty holds the new torch, with a 24-carat gold-leaf flame, while in the other is a book inscribed July 4, 1776, in Latin. The rays of her crown represent the seven seas and seven continents. The crown was closed to the public following the September 11 attacks, but reopened in 2009. Groups of 10 people at a time can now climb up the 377 steps from the main lobby to this level.

After a $100 million restoration in time for its bicentennial, the statue was unveiled on July 3, 1986.

### ⑤ Ellis Island

**Map** A5. **M** 4, 5 to Bowling Green; 1, W, R to White-hall/South Ferry, then Circle Line/Statue of Liberty Ferry from the Battery. **Departures:** every 30–45 mins 9:30am–3:30pm summer (winter hours vary). **Tel** (877) 523-9849 or (201) 604-2800. **Open** Jul–Aug: 9am–6pm daily; Sep–Jun: 9:30am–5:15pm daily. **Closed** Dec 25. 🚢 ferry fare includes entry to Ellis and Liberty Is. 🚹 🍴 🏛 🖥 🏠 **W** nps.gov/elis; **W** statuecruises.com

More than half of America's population can trace its roots to Ellis Island, which served as the country's immigration depot from 1892 until 1954. Nearly 17 million people passed through its gates in the greatest wave of immigration the world has ever known. First- and second-class passengers were processed on board, but steerage passengers were ferried from arrival vessels and taken to the crowded island for medical and legal examinations. Immigrants with contagious diseases could be sent back. Ellis Island lay in ruins until 1990, when a $189 million project by the Statue of Liberty– Ellis Island Foundation, Inc., renewed the buildings.

Centered on the Great Hall or Registry Room, the site today houses the three-story **Ellis Island Immigration Museum** with permanent exhibits. Much of its story is told with photos and the voices of immigrants, and an electronic database traces ancestors. Outside, the American Immigrant Wall of Honor is the largest wall of names in the world. No other place explains so well the "melting pot" that formed the character of the nation.

Main building, Ellis Island, viewed from the water

## ⑥ South Street Seaport

**Map** C5. Fulton St. **Tel** (212) 732-7678.
Ⓜ Fulton St. **Open** Nov–Mar:
10am–7pm Mon–Sat, 11am–6pm
Sun; Apr–Oct: 10am–9pm Mon–Sat,
11am–8pm Sun. ♿ 🎫 Concerts.
🖊 📷 🌐 southstreetseaport.com
South Street Seaport Museum: 12
Fulton St. **Open** Jan–Mar: 10am–5pm
Fri–Sun; Apr–Dec: 10am–5pm Tue–
Sun. **Closed** Tue; Jan 1, Thanksgiving,
Dec 25. 🖼 ♿ 🎫 Exhibits, films:
🖊 📷 southstreetseaport
museum.org

Called the "street of sails" in the
19th century, the heart of New
York's port in the historic South
Street Seaport district has been
imaginatively restored as a
tourist center. Glitzy stores
and restaurants sit harmoniously
beside seafaring craft, historic
19th-century commercial
buildings, and museum exhibits,

The Ambrose lightship at a South Street
Seaport pier on the East River

with spectacular views of
Brooklyn Bridge and the East
River from the cobblestone
streets. The historic ships
docked here range from the
little tugboat *W.O. Decker* to the
grand four-masted bark *Peking*,

the second-largest sailing
ship in existence. Mini-trips on
the schooner *Pioneer* are a
great way to see the river.
    **South Street Seaport
Museum** covers the 12 blocks
of what was America's leading
port. In addition to the six
historic ships, it has more than
10,000 artifacts, artworks, and
documents from the 19th- and
early 20th-century maritime
world. In the **Maritime Crafts
Center**, at Pier 15, see ornate
objects such as ships'
figureheads being made
using traditional woodcarving
and model-making skills.
    **Schermerhorn Row**, on
Fulton and South Streets, was
built as warehouses in 1813,
combining Federal style and
Greek Revival elements. The Row
has been restored and houses a
visitor center, shops, restaurants,
and an ice-skating rink.

## ⑦ Brooklyn Bridge

**Map** C5. Ⓜ J, M, Z to Chambers St;
4, 5, 6 to Brooklyn Bridge–City Hall
(Manhattan side); A, C to High St,
Brooklyn Bridge (Brooklyn side).
🚌 M9, M15, M22, M103. ♿

An engineering wonder when
it was built in 1883, the Brooklyn
Bridge linked Manhattan and
Brooklyn, then two separate
cities. At that time it was the
world's largest suspension bridge
and the first to be constructed
of steel. The German-born
engineer John A. Roebling
conceived of a bridge

spanning the East River while
ice-bound on a ferry to
Brooklyn. The bridge took
16 years to build, required
600 workers, and claimed over
20 lives, including Roebling's.
Most died of caisson disease

(known as "the bends") after
coming up from the under-
water excavation chambers.
From the pedestrian walkway
there are fabulous views of the
city towers, seen through the
artistic cablework.

Brooklyn Bridge, the first ever steel suspension bridge

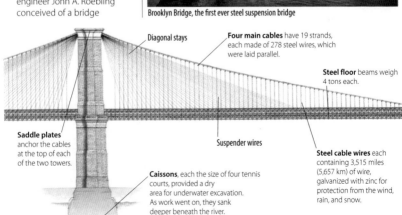

**Diagonal stays**

**Four main cables** have 19 strands,
each made of 278 steel wires, which
were laid parallel.

**Steel floor** beams weigh
4 tons each.

**Saddle plates**
anchor the cables
at the top of each
of the two towers.

**Suspender wires**

**Steel cable wires** each
containing 3,515 miles
(5,657 km) of wire,
galvanized with zinc for
protection from the wind,
rain, and snow.

**Caissons**, each the size of four tennis
courts, provided a dry
area for underwater excavation.
As work went on, they sank
deeper beneath the river.

*For hotels and restaurants see pp122–7*

City Hall's stately 19th-century Georgian façade

## ⑧ Civic Center

**Map** C5. Ⓜ 2 & 3 to Park Pl; A, C to Chambers St; W, R to City Hall. Woolworth Building: 233 Broadway. Ⓜ City Hall, Park Place. **Open** office hours. City Hall: City Hall Park. **Tel** (212) 331. Ⓜ Brooklyn Bridge–City Hall. **Open** for prearranged tours only. ♿ 🏛 Municipal Building: 1 Center St. Ⓜ Brooklyn Br–City Hall. ♿

Manhattan's busy Civic Center is the hub of the city, state, and federal government court systems and the city's police department. The 1926 New York County Courthouse is adjacent to the 31-story, pyramid-topped 1933 US Courthouse. The Tweed Courthouse, constructed by the infamous Boss Tweed, a corrupt politician, is being restored to house the Museum of the City of New York.

The monumental buildings here include the 1913 Gothic **Woolworth Building**, headquarters of Five-and-Dime mogul Frank W. Woolworth. Designed by architect Cass Gilbert, it was the city's tallest building until 1930 and set the standard for future skyscrapers. In contrast is the historic **City Hall**, the seat of government since 1812. This Georgian building with French Renaissance influences is considered one of the finest examples of early 19th-century American architecture. The City Hall Park was New York's village green 250 years ago. To its northeast, the **Municipal Building** is a wedding-cake fantasy of towers and spires, topped by the statue *Civic Fame*.

## ⑨ Eldridge Street Synagogue

**Map** C5. 12 Eldridge St. **Tel** (212) 219-0888. Ⓜ E Broadway. **Open** 10am–5pm Sun–Thu, 10am–3pm Fri. ✡ Fri at sundown, Sat 10am onward. 📷 ♿ 🎧 half-hourly 10am–3pm. 🏛 🌐 **eldridgestreet.org**

This Moorish-style house of worship was the first large temple built in the US by Jewish immigrants from Eastern Europe, from where 80 percent of American Jews came. At the turn of the century, it was the most flamboyant temple in the neighborhood, and as many as 1,000 people attended services here. As congregants left the area, attendance waned and the temple closed in the 1950s.

Three decades later a group of citizens raised funds to restore the magnificent sanctuary. The synagogue is now a National Historic Landmark.

## ⑩ Chinatown

**Map** C5. Streets around Mott St. Ⓜ Canal St. Eastern States Buddhist Temple: 64b Mott St. **Open** 9am–6pm daily. 🌐 **explorechinatown.com**

New York's largest and most colorful ethnic neighborhood is Chinatown. In the early 20th century this was primarily a male community, made up of immigrant workers. Wages were sent to families back in China, who were prevented from joining them by strict immigration laws. Today, more than 200,000 Chinese Americans live here. The shops and sidewalks overflow with exotic foods and herbs, and gifts ranging from backscratchers to fine antiques. Most people, however, visit Chinatown to eat in one of the more than 200 restaurants or shop for Asian delicacies.

Other sights here include the **Eastern States Buddhist Temple**, with its incense-scented interior and more than 100 golden Buddhas; and tiny, crooked Doyers Street, called "Bloody Angle," reminiscent of the Tong wars between the 1920s and 1940s. The Tongs were social clubs or rival criminal fraternities who gave the old locale its dangerous reputation.

## ⑪ Little Italy

**Map** C4. Streets around Mulberry St. Ⓜ Canal St. 🌐 **littleitalynyc.com**

The Lower East Side's other ethnic neighborhood is Little Italy, home to southern Italian immigrants in the late 19th century. The immigrants preserved their language, customs, and food, making Mulberry Street lively with the colors, flavors, and atmosphere of Italy. Today, although Little Italy has shrunk to a few blocks, the 10-day Feast of San Gennaro in September draws crowds of joyful celebrants. Also on Mulberry Street is the Gothic-Revival style **Old St. Patrick's Cathedral**. It became a local parish church when the cathedral moved uptown *(see p87)*.

NoLita, north of Little Italy, is filled with boutiques, and the city's fashionable flock here for the coolest small labels.

Little Italy, once home to thousands of immigrants

## ⑫ TriBeCa

**Map** C4. S of Houston St, N of Chambers St, & W of Lafayette St to Hudson River. Ⓜ Spring St, Canal St, Franklin St, Chambers St.

The neighborhood named for its geographic shape, TRIangle BElow CAnal, once consisted mostly of abandoned warehouses. Then Robert de Niro set up his TriBeCa Film Center in a converted coffee warehouse, and TriBeCa became the center of the city's movie industry. Known as Hollywood East, many screenings and events take place here. The annual TriBeCa Film Festival in the spring draws celebrities and crowds, and features a superb range of films, from foreign flicks to blockbusters. There are also musical concerts, street fairs, and premiere parties.

TriBeCa is now one of New York's most elite neighborhoods, with stylish restaurants, hip hotels, art galleries, cafés, and big lofts occupied by celebrity residents.

## ⑬ SoHo Historic District

**Map** C4. S of Houston St. Greene Street: Ⓜ Canal St, Spring St, Prince St.

The largest concentration of cast-iron architecture in the world survives in SoHo, a former industrial district.

The region comprises nearly 150 buildings and roughly covers the area from Houston Street south to Spring Street and from West Broadway to the east, around Crosby Street. Its heart is **Greene Street**; 50 cast-iron buildings are stretched out over a five-block area. The finest are those at 72–76, the "King" and 28–30, the "Queen." A 19th-century American innovation, cast iron was cheaper than either stone or brick and allowed decorative elements to be prefabricated in foundries from molds and used as building façades. The area was threatened with demolition in the 1960s, but was saved by the protests of the many artists living and working in its then low-rent former warehouses.

The **Singer Building** on Broadway was built by Ernest Flagg in 1904, at a time when steel-framed brick and terracotta were replacing cast iron. This ornate 12-story building, adorned with wrought-iron balconies and graceful arches painted in striking dark green, was an office and warehouse for the Singer sewing machine company. The original Singer name is cast in iron above the entrance to the store on Prince Street.

Plush stores may have replaced many of SoHo's experimental galleries, but you'll still find vestiges of the neighborhood's artistic past, including the **Morrison Hotel Gallery**, which features fine art, music, and photography since the 1940s as well as book signings and other events. SoHo's streets are lined with trendy cafés, restaurants, shops, and chic designer boutiques. It is also the city's favorite Sunday brunch-and-browse neighborhood.

🏛 **Morrison Hotel Gallery**
24 Prince St. **Tel** (212) 941-8770. **Open** 11am–6pm Mon–Thu, 11am–7pm Fri & Sat, noon–6pm Sun. 🔲 **morrisonhotel gallery.com**

Window on the corner of West 4th Street and Washington Square

## ⑭ Washington Square

Greenwich Vil. **Map** C4. Ⓜ W 4th St.

Now one of the city's most vibrant open spaces, Washington Square was once a marshland that was filled to form a park. Stanford White's magnificent marble arch, completed in 1895, replaced a wooden version that marked the centenary of George Washington's inauguration. In 1916, a group of artists led by John Sloan and Marcel Duchamp broke in, climbed atop the arch, and declared the "free and independent republic of Washington Square, the state of New Bohemia." Decades later, Bob Dylan sang his first folk songs near the fountain in the small park's center.

## ⑮ Greenwich Village

**Map** C4. N of Houston St & S of 14th St. Ⓜ W 4th St–Washington Square, Christopher St–Sheridan Square, 8th St.

Simply known as "the Village," this crazy-quilt pattern of streets is a natural enclave that has been a bohemian haven and home to many celebrated writers, artists, and jazz musicians. Later, it became a popular gay district, which comes alive at night, when cafés, theaters, and clubs beckon at every turn. A stroll through its narrow old-fashioned lanes reveal charming

The "Queen," SoHo Historic District

row houses, hidden alleys, and leafy courtyards. The 15 Italianate row houses, lining the north side of **St. Luke's Place**, date from the 1850s. Poet Marianne Moore lived here, and Theodore Dreiser wrote his *An American Tragedy* at No. 16.

The heart of the Village is **Sheridan Square**, where seven streets meet in a maze once known as "the mousetrap." The Stonewall Inn, a gay bar on Christopher Street, was where a riot took place against police harassment on June 27, 1969 – a landmark in the Gay Rights Movement.

**Jefferson Market Courthouse**, "Old Jeff," is perhaps the area's most treasured landmark. It was built as a courthouse in 1877 and turned into a public library in 1967. Opposite is Patchin Place, a group of 19th-century houses where playwright Eugene O'Neill and poets John Masefield and e. e. cummings lived. Northwest of Greenwich Village lies the fashionable Meatpacking District, crammed with clubs, bars, and restaurants. This neighborhood is also the starting point for the popular High Line, an urban park built on disused elevated tram lines.

🚇 **Jefferson Market Courthouse**
425 Ave of the Americas. Ⓜ W 4th St–Washington Sq. **Tel** (212) 243-4334. **Open** noon–8pm Mon & Wed, 10am–6pm Tue, noon–6pm Thu, 1–6pm Fri, 10am–5pm Sat. **Closed** public hols. ♿ 🌐 nypl.org

Original furnishings in East Village's Merchant's House Museum

## ⑯ East Village

**Map** D4. 14th St to Houston St. Ⓜ Astor Place.

Prominent New Yorkers, such as Peter Stuyvesant, the Astors, and the Vanderbilts, lived in this former Dutch enclave until 1900, when they moved uptown. Thereafter, it was home to German, Jewish, Irish, and Ukrainian immigrants. In the 1960s the East Village became a haven for hippies, and this is the place where punk rock was born. Today, the East Village is home to numerous bohemian cafés and lively restaurants, vintage boutiques and independent movie houses.

The six-story **Cooper Union**

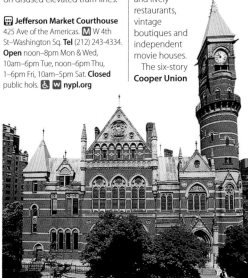
Pointed tower of "Old Jeff," Greenwich Village

was set up in 1859 by Peter Cooper, a wealthy industrialist who built the first US steam locomotive and founded New York's first free, non-sectarian and coeducational college. Its Great Hall was inaugurated in 1859 by Mark Twain, and Abraham Lincoln delivered his "Right Makes Might" speech there in 1860.

The 1832 **Merchant's House Museum**, a remarkable Greek Revival brick townhouse, is a time capsule of a vanished way of life. It was bought by Seabury Tredwell, a wealthy merchant, and remained in the family until 1933.

One of New York's oldest churches, the 1799 **St. Mark's-in-the-Bowery** is located on East 10th Street. Governor Peter Stuyvesant and his descendants are buried here.

The English-style **Tompkin Square** was the site of America's first organized labor demonstration in 1874, the main gathering place during the neighborhood's hippie era and, in 1991, an arena for violent riots when the police tried to evict the homeless who had occupied the grounds. A small statue of a boy and a girl commemorates the more than 1,000 local residents who died in the *General Slocum* steamer disaster on June 15, 1904.

🏛 **Merchant's House Museum**
29 E 4th St. **Tel** (212) 777-1089. **Open** noon–5pm Thu–Mon & by appt. 📷 🚫 Photography without flashes allowed. 🌐 **merchantshouse.com**

## ⑰ Union Square

**Map** D4. Ⓜ 14th St–Union Square. Greenmarket: 8am–6pm Mon, Wed, Fri, Sat.

Opened in 1839, this park was once the hangout for drug dealers and soapbox orators. Renovations have transformed this area into a flourishing section of Manhattan. A market fills the square, where more than 200 farmers from all over New York State sell fresh produce, including herbs, berries, vegetables, flowers, home-baked pastries, honey, and woven yarns. The square is also ringed by a wide variety of shops, from discount department stores to gourmet supermarkets.

## ⑱ Flatiron Building

**Map** D3. 175 5th Ave. Ⓜ 23rd St. **Open** office hours.

This unusual building, its shape conforming to a triangular plot of land, has intrigued New Yorkers since it was built by Chicago architect David Burnham in 1902. One of the first buildings to use a steel frame, it heralded the era of the skyscrapers.

It soon became known as the Flatiron for its triangular shape, but some called it "Burnham's folly," predicting that

Flatiron Building, New York's most famous early skyscraper

Appellate Court, said to be the world's busiest courthouse, Madison Square

the winds created by the building's shape would knock it down. It has, however, withstood the test of time.

The stretch of Fifth Avenue to the south of the building was once rather run-down, but has come to life with chic shops such as Emporio Armani and Paul Smith, giving the area new cachet and a new name, "the Flatiron District."

## ⑲ Madison Square

**Map** D3. Ⓜ 23rd St.

Quiet Madison Square opened in 1847 at the center of a fashionable residential district where politican Theodore Roosevelt and writer Edith Wharton were born. It was bordered by the elegant Fifth Avenue Hotel, the Madison Square Theater, and Stanford White's Madison Square Garden. The torch-bearing arm of the Statue of Liberty was exhibited here in 1884. Nicely landscaped, this statue-filled park borders some of the city's hottest restaurants. Area residents stroll and walk their dogs at all hours.

Just off Madison Square is the spectacular **New York Life Insurance Company** building, designed in 1928 by Cass Gilbert of Woolworth Building fame *(see p79)*. The building has Gilbert's trademark pyramid-shaped tower, modeled on the Giralda in Seville. Its interior is adorned with hanging lamps, bronze doors and paneling, and a grand staircase leading to a subway station. One block

south is the **Appellate Division of the Supreme Court of the State of New York**, a small marble palace designed by James Brown Lord in 1900. Considered to be the busiest courthouse in the world, appeals relating to civil and criminal cases for New York and the Bronx are heard here. During the week, the public can admire the fine interior, designed by the Herter brothers, including the courtroom when it is not in session. Displays in the lobby often feature some of the court's more famous and infamous cases. Among the celebrities whose appeals were settled here are Babe Ruth, Charlie Chaplin, Fred Astaire, Harry Houdini, Theodore Dreiser, and Edgar Allan Poe.

Also on the east side of Madison Square is the 54-story **Metropolitan Life Tower**. Built in 1909, this was the world's tallest building at that time, an appropriate corporate symbol for the largest insurance company in the world. The huge four-sided clock has minute hands said to weigh 1,000 lb (454 kg) each. A series of historical murals by N.C. Wyeth, the famed illustrator of such classics as *Robin Hood*, *Treasure Island*, and *Robinson Crusoe* (and the father of painter Andrew Wyeth), are now on display in the lobby.

🏛 **Appellate Division of the Supreme Court of the State of New York**
E 25th St at Madison Ave. **Open** 9am–5pm Mon–Fri. **Closed** public hols. ✉

## ⑳ Empire State Building

**Map** D3. 350 5th Ave. **Tel** (212) 736-3100. Ⓜ B, D, F, N, Q, R, W, 1, 2, 3 to 34th St; 6 to 33rd St. 🚌 Q32, M1–M5, M16, M34. Observatories: **Open** 8am–2am. Last elevators at 1:15am. 🅿 ♿ 📷 ⚡ 🅦 esbnyc.com

The Empire State Building is New York's tallest and most impressive skyscraper. Construction began in March 1930, not long after the stock market crash, and, by the time it opened in 1931, space was so difficult to rent that it was nicknamed "the Empty State Building." Only the immediate popularity of the observatories saved the building from bankruptcy – to date, they have attracted more than 120 million visitors – but the building soon became a symbol of the city the world over. It only took 410 days to build this 102-story limestone and brick skyscraper, with an average of four and a half stories added every week. The 102nd floor can be visited for an additional fee. Each February, the annual Empire State Run-Up is held, when 150 runners race up the 1,576 steps from the lobby to the 86th floor (known for its outdoor observation decks), in 10 minutes.

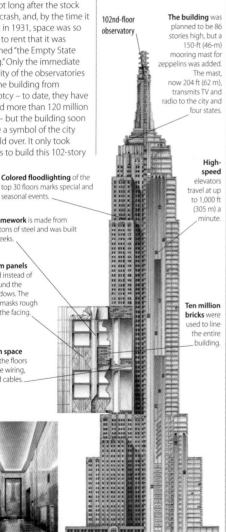

**102nd-floor observatory**

**The building** was planned to be 86 stories high, but a 150-ft (46-m) mooring mast for zeppelins was added. The mast, now 204 ft (62 m), transmits TV and radio to the city and four states.

**High-speed** elevators travel at up to 1,000 ft (305 m) a minute.

**Colored floodlighting** of the top 30 floors marks special and seasonal events.

**The framework** is made from 60,000 tons of steel and was built in 23 weeks.

**Aluminum panels** were used instead of stone around the 6,500 windows. The steel trim masks rough edges on the facing.

**Ten million bricks** were used to line the entire building.

**Sandwich space** between the floors houses the wiring, pipes, and cables.

Fifth Avenue Entrance Lobby, Empire State Building

Macy's 34th Street entrance

## ㉑ Herald Square

**Map** D3. 6th Ave. Ⓜ 34th St- Penn Station.

Named after the *New York Herald*, which had its offices here from 1893 to 1921, the square was the hub of the rowdy, mid-19th-century theater district known as the Tenderloin District. Theaters, dance halls, hotels, and restaurants kept the area humming with life until reformers clamped down on sleaze in the 1890s. The ornamental clock, on an island where Broadway meets 6th Avenue, is all that survives of the Herald Building.

Herald Square became a mecca for shoppers after the Manhattan Opera House was razed in 1901 to make way for **Macy's**. The "world's largest store" began modestly. It was founded by former whaler Rowland Hussey Macy in 1857; the red star logo was from his tattoo, a souvenir of his sailing days. The store was sold in 1888 and moved to its present premises in 1902. The 34th Street façade still has its original clock, canopy, and lettering.

Macy's sponsors New York's famous Thanksgiving Day parade *(see p41)* and the Fourth of July fireworks. Its annual Spring Flower Show draws thousands of visitors.

🏬 **Macy's**
151 W 34th St. **Tel** (212) 695-4400. **Open** 9am–9:30pm Mon–Thu, 9am–10pm Fri, 9am–11pm Sat, 11am–8:30pm Sun. **Closed** public hols. 🅦 macys.com

## ㉒ Times Square

**Map** D3. Ⓜ 42nd St–Times Square.
ℹ 1560 Broadway (46th St),
8am–8pm daily. Ⓖ noon Fri.
Ⓦ timessquarenyc.org

Named for the New York Times
Tower, Times Square is the city's
most famous intersection.
Although the *New York Times*
has moved from its original
headquarters at the square's
southern end, the crystal ball still
drops at midnight on New Year's
Eve, as it has since the building
opened with fanfare in 1906.

Since 1899, when Oscar
Hammerstein built the Victoria
and Republic theaters, this has
also been the heart of the city's
theater district. The district's
transformation in the 1990s led
to the renovation of many
theaters, such as the New Victory
and the New Amsterdam. Their
productions, as well as the area's
bars and restaurants, attract
theatergoers each evening.

Old-world Broadway glamor
rubs shoulders with modern
entertainment in Times Square
*(see p98)*. MTV has its studios
here, and E-Walk is a vast
entertainment and retail
complex. Exciting structures,
such as the Bertelsmann
building and the minimalist
Condé Nast offices, sit alongside
the classic establishments, such
as Sardi's, the Paramount Hotel,
and the Baroque Lyceum Theater.
A lovely addition to Times
Square are the pedestrian plazas,
dotted with tables and chairs.

The New York Public Library's atmospheric
Main Reading Room

## ㉓ The New York Public Library

**Map** E3. 5th Ave & 42nd St. **Tel** (212)
930-0803. Ⓜ 42nd St–Grand Central.
**Open** daily, hours vary. **Closed** public
hols. ♿ Ⓖ Lectures, workshops,
readings: 🅿 Ⓦ nypl.org

Architects Carrère and Hastings
won the coveted job of
designing New York's main
public library in 1897. The white
marble Beaux Arts edifice they
designed fulfilled the library's
first director's vision of a light,
quiet, airy place, where millions
of books could be stored and
yet be available to readers as
promptly as possible. Built on
the site of the former Croton
Reservoir, it opened in 1911 to
immediate acclaim, despite
having cost the city $9 million.
The architects' genius is best
seen in the Main Reading Room,
a vast paneled space as majestic
as a cathedral, extending almost
two city blocks. Below it are 88
miles (140 km) of shelves,
holding over seven million
volumes. It takes only minutes
for the staff or a computerized
dumbwaiter to supply any
book. The Periodicals Room
holds 10,000 current periodicals
from 128 countries. On
its walls are murals by Richard
Haas, honoring New York's great
publishing houses. The original
library combined the
collections of John Jacob Astor
and James Lenox. Its collections
today range from Thomas
Jefferson's handwritten copy
of the Declaration of
Independence to T.S. Eliot's
typed copy of "The Waste Land."
More than 1,000 queries are
answered daily, using the vast
database of the CATNYP and
LEO computer catalogs.

This library is the hub of a
network of 82 branches, with
nearly seven million users. Other
well-known branches include
the New York Public Library for
the Performing Arts at the
Lincoln Center *(see p93)* and the
Schomburg Center in Harlem.
The latter is recognized as one
of the leading institutions
focusing exclusively on African-
American, African Diaspora, and
African experiences. It hosts panel
events and movie screenings.

### Midtown Manhattan

Midtown Manhattan's skyline is
graced with some of the city's
most spectacular towers and
spires – from the familiar beauty of
the Empire State Building's Art
Deco pinnacle to the dramatic
wedge shape of Citigroup's
modern headquarters. As the
shoreline progresses uptown, so
the architecture becomes more
varied; the United Nations
complex dominates a long stretch,
and then Beekman Place begins a
strand of exclusive residential
enclaves that offer the rich and
famous some seclusion.

Elevator door at the
Chrysler Building

**United Nations**, founded in 1945, has its
impressive headquaters on an 18-acre
(7-ha) site on the East River *(see p86)*.

Empire State Building
*(see p83)*

The
Highpoint    Tudor
City

The skylit Garden Court, Morgan Library & Museum

## ㉔ Morgan Library & Museum

**Map** E3. 225 Madison Ave. **Tel** (212) 685-0008. Ⓜ 6 to 33rd St, 7 to 5th Ave, 4, 5, 6, 7, S to Grand Central Terminal & Museum. **Open** 10:30am–5pm Tue–Thu, 10:30am–9pm Fri, 10am–6pm Sat, 11am–6pm Sun. **Closed** Mon, Jan 1, Thanksgiving, Dec 25. 🎟 free 7–9pm Fri. ♿ 🎧 ▢ 🗓 ✉ 🌐 themorgan.org

This magnificent palazzo-style building was designed in 1902 to house the private collection of banker Pierpont Morgan (1837–1913), one of the great collectors of his time. Established in 1924 as a public institution by Morgan's son, J.P. Morgan Jr., it has a splendid collection of rare manuscripts, prints, books, and bindings.

The complex includes the original library and J.P. Morgan Jr.'s home. Pierpont Morgan's opulent study and his original library contain some of his favorite paintings, objets d'art, and a wide variety of cultural artifacts. Prominent among the exhibits are one of the 11 surviving copies of the Gutenberg Bible (1455), printed on vellum, and six surviving leaves of the score for Mozart's Horn Concerto in E-flat Major, written in different-colored inks.

The Garden Court, a three-story skylit garden area, links the library with the house. Exhibits are changed regularly.

## ㉕ Grand Central Terminal

**Map** E3. E 42nd St at Park Ave. **Tel** (212) 532-4900. Ⓜ 4, 5, 6, 7, S to Grand Central. 🚌 M42 , M101–104. **Open** 5:30am–1:30am daily. ♿ 🎧 Wed 12:30pm (free), call (212) 935-3960 & Fri 12:30pm (free), call (212) 883-2420. Baggage check; lost & found: (212) 340-2555. 🌐 grandcentralterminal.com

One of the world's great train terminals, this outstanding Beaux Arts building is New York's most visited, with 500,000 people passing through it daily. The present building, dating from 1913, remains an impressive sight. Its glory is the main concourse, dominated by three great arched windows that fill the space with natural light. The high-vaulted ceiling of this vast pedestrian area is decorated with twinkling constellations. The information booth here is surmounted by a wonderful four-faced clock. The Grand Staircase, styled after the staircase in Paris's Opera House, is a reminder of the glamorous days of early rail travel. Adjacent to the main concourse is the Vanderbilt Hall.

Today, Grand Central is no longer limited to the city's commuters. It has become an attraction in its own right, with a museum, over 40 shops, a gourmet food market, and fine restaurants, including the famed Oyster Bar (see p125). Also worth visiting is the The Campbell Apartment bar, in a beautiful space that was formerly the private office of tycoon John W. Campbell (smart attire must be worn here).

Tiffany glass clock surrounded by sculptures on top of the Grand Central Terminal building

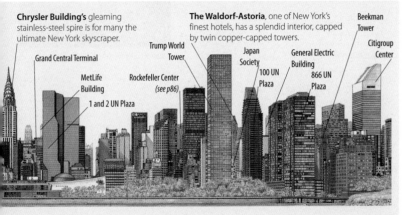

**Chrysler Building's** gleaming stainless-steel spire is for many the ultimate New York skyscraper.

Grand Central Terminal

MetLife Building

1 and 2 UN Plaza

Rockefeller Center (see p86)

Trump World Tower

**The Waldorf-Astoria**, one of New York's finest hotels, has a splendid interior, capped by twin copper-capped towers.

Japan Society

100 UN Plaza

General Electric Building

866 UN Plaza

Beekman Tower

Citigroup Center

The UN Buildings seen from the garden

## ㉖ United Nations

**Map** E3. 1st Ave at 46th St. **Tel** (212) 963-8687. Ⓜ 4, 5, 6, 7, S to 42nd St–Grand Central Station. 🚌 M15, M27, M42, M50, M104. **Open** Jan–Feb: Mon–Fri only; Mar–Dec: 9:30am–4:45pm daily. **Closed** Jan 1, Presidents' Day, Memorial Day, Jul 4, Labor Day, Eid, Thanksgiving, Dec 25 (limited schedule during year-end hols). 🎟 for tours. ♿ 🎧 Mon–Fri in 20 languages. Lectures, films. 📷 📱 🅦 un.org

When New York was chosen as the UN headquarters, philanthropist and multi-millionaire John D. Rockefeller Jr. donated $8.5 million for the purchase of the East River site. This complex was the creation of American architect Wallace Harrison and a team of international consultants.

The United Nations was formed near the end of World War II to preserve world peace, promote self-determination, and to aid economic and social well-being around the globe. Currently 189 members meet regularly each year from mid-September to mid-December in the General Assembly, the closest thing to a world parliament.

The most powerful body is the Security Council, housed in the Conference Building. Here, delegates and their assistants meet to confer on issues related to international peace and security. In 1988, the UN Peacekeeping Forces were awarded the Nobel Peace Prize. The Trusteeship Council and the Economic and Social Council are in the same building.

Daily hour-long guided tours show visitors the various council chambers and General Assembly hall, offering a behind-the-scenes view of the organization at work.

## ㉗ Rockefeller Center

**Map** E3. 630 5th Ave between 49th & 52nd Sts. ℹ (212) 332-6868. Ⓜ 47th–50th Sts. ♿ 🎧 📱 📷 (212) 664-7174 (reservations advised). Top of the Rock observatory: **Tel** 877-NYC-ROCK. **Open** 8am–11pm daily. 🅦 rockefellercenter.com

A city within a city, and a National Historic Landmark, this urban wonder is the world's largest privately owned complex. Begun in the 1930s, it was built on a site leased by John D. Rockefeller Jr. for a new opera house he had planned. When the 1929 Depression scuttled the plans, Rockefeller, stuck with a long-term lease, went ahead with his own

development. This was the first commercial project to integrate gardens, dining, and shopping with office space. The number of buildings has now grown to 19, though the more modern structures do not match the Art Deco elegance of the original 14. The center's Channel Gardens, named after the English Channel because they separate the French and British buildings, change with the calendar.

The centerpiece of the center is the 70-story G.E. Building, headquarters of NBC studios. Backstage tours of the network's studios are a popular attraction. The TV show *Today* can also be viewed live every weekday morning from the sidewalk in front of the studio. A favorite attraction is the **Top of the Rock** observatory on the 67th–70th floors. Another draw is the 1932 Radio City Music Hall. Once a movie palace, it now hosts dazzling events, including the annual Christmas and Easter shows. The center houses a skating rink in winter.

A view of Rockefeller Center

## Works of Art at the UN

The UN Building has acquired numerous works of art and reproductions by major artists; many have been gifts from member nations. Most of them have either a peace or international friendship theme. The legend on Norman Rockwell's *The Golden Rule* reads "Do unto others as you would have them do unto you." Marc Chagall designed a large stained-glass window as a memorial to former Secretary General Dag Hammarskjöld, who was accidentally killed while on a peace mission in 1961. A Henry Moore sculpture, *Reclining Figure: Hand* (1979), graces the grounds. There are many other sculptures and paintings by the artists of many nations.

*Reclining Figure: Hand* (1979), a gift from the Henry Moore Foundation

*For hotels and restaurants see pp122–7*

The Great Bronze Doors in St. Patrick's Church

## ㉘ St. Patrick's Cathedral

**Map** E3. 5th Ave & 50th St. **Tel** (212) 753-2261. Ⓜ 6 to 51st St; E, V to Fifth Ave. 🚌 M1, M2, M3, M4, M27, M50. **Open** 7:30am–8:30pm daily. 🔔 frequent Mon–Sat, 7, 8, 9, 10:15am & noon, 1, 4 (Spanish), 5:30pm Sun. ♿ Mon–Fri 🕗 8:30am–8pm Concerts & lectures.

New York's finest Gothic Revival building was designed by James Renwick Jr. and completed in 1878. This is also the largest Catholic cathedral in the US and seats more than 2,500 people every Sunday. When Archbishop John Hughes decided to build a cathedral here in 1850, many criticized his choice of a site so far from the city's center at the time. Today, the church rises over the heart of bustling midtown Manhattan.

## ㉙ Museum of Modern Art

**Map** E2. 11 W 53rd St. **Tel** (212) 708-9400. Ⓜ 5th Ave–53rd St. 🚌 M1, M2, M3, M4, M27, M50. **Open** 10:30am–5:30pm Sat–Thu, 10:30am–8pm Fri. **Closed** Thanksgiving, Dec 25. 🎫 free for under 16s; free entry for all 4–8pm Fri. 🔊 🎧 groups. 📷 🚫 ♿ 🌐 **moma.org**

One of the world's most comprehensive collections of modern art is on view at the Museum of Modern Art (MoMA). Founded in 1929, it set the standard for other museums of its kind. It was also the first art museum to include utilitarian objects in its collection, from ball bearings and silicon chips to household appliances.

Following a $650 million expansion project, MoMA reopened in 2004. The building provides gallery space over six floors, almost twice that of the old museum. Expanses of glass allow abundant natural light into the building. MoMA's collection includes more than 150,000 works of art, ranging from Impressionist classics to an unrivaled collection of modern and contemporary art, including paintings, sculptures, prints, drawings, photographs, and graphic designs. Some of the highlights of the collection include well-known works, such as Picasso's *Les Demoiselles d'Avignon* (1907), Van Gogh's *Starry Night* (1889), and Monet's *Water Lilies* (c.1920).

## ㉚ Fifth Avenue

**Map** E2. Ⓜ 5th Ave–53rd St, 5th Ave–59th St.

From its inception in the early 1800s, Fifth Avenue has been the territory of New York's rich and famous. Then, it was lined with palatial mansions built by the Astors, Vanderbilts, Belmonts, and Goulds, giving it the sobriquet Millionaires' Row. But, as retail and commercial ventures set up outlets here in the 1900s, society moved farther north.

Today, the heart of New York's best-known avenue extends from the Empire State Building *(see p83)* to the Grand Army Plaza, presided over by the 1907 Plaza Hotel. Along this stretch are a range of famous stores that have made Fifth Avenue synonymous with luxury goods throughout the world.

The Cartier store, at 52nd Street, is housed in a 1905 Beaux Arts mansion, originally the home of banker Morton F. Plant, who supposedly traded it for a perfectly matched string of pearls. Other well-known jewelry and accessory stores include Tiffany's, made famous by Truman Capote's 1958 *Breakfast at Tiffany's*, Harry Winston, and Henri Bendel. Among the high-quality department stores are Saks Fifth Avenue, Bergdorf Goodman, and the wonderful FAO Schwarz toy store.

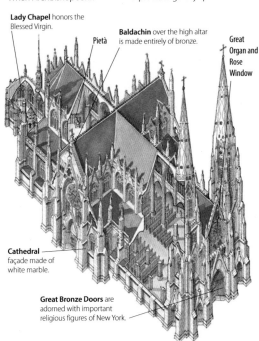

**Lady Chapel** honors the Blessed Virgin.

**Pietà**

**Baldachin** over the high altar is made entirely of bronze.

**Great Organ and Rose Window**

**Cathedral** façade made of white marble.

**Great Bronze Doors** are adorned with important religious figures of New York.

# ③ A Tour of Central Park

New York's "backyard," an 843-acre (340-ha) swath of green, provides recreation and beauty for residents and visitors. Designed by Frederick Law Olmsted and Calvert Vaux in 1858, the park took 16 years to create and involved the planting of over 500,000 trees and shrubs. A short walking tour from 59th to 79th Streets takes in some of Central Park's most picturesque features, from the dense wooded Ramble to the open formal spaces of Bethesda Terrace.

**★ Strawberry Fields**
This peaceful area was created by Yoko Ono in memory of John Lennon, who lived in the nearby Dakota apartments.

**★ Bethesda Fountain**
The richly ornamented formal terrace overlooks the Lake and the wooded shores of the Ramble.

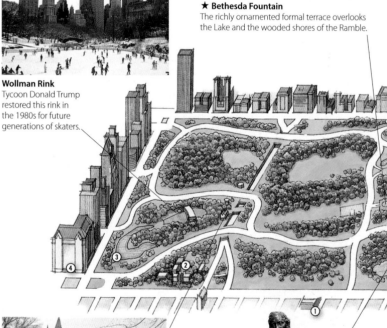

**Wollman Rink**
Tycoon Donald Trump restored this rink in the 1980s for future generations of skaters.

**★ The Dairy**
This Victorian Gothic building houses the visitor center. Make it your first stop and pick up a calendar of park events.

**Hans Christian Andersen's Statue**
A favorite Central Park landmark for children, this is a popular site for storytelling in summer.

**Bow Bridge**
This cast-iron bridge links the Ramble with Cherry Hill by a graceful arch, 60 ft (18 m) above the Lake.

**Locator Map**

**San Remo Apartments**
This is one of the five twin-towered apartments on Central Park West, famed for their grace and architectural detail.

**★ Belvedere Castle**
From the terraces there are unequaled views of the city and surrounding park. Within the stone walls is the Central Park Learning Center.

## KEY

① **Frick Collection** *(see p90)*

② **Wildlife Conservation Center** has three climate zones that are home to over 130 species of animals.

③ **The Pond**

④ **Plaza Hotel**

⑤ **The Dakota Apartment Building**

⑥ **American Museum of Natural History** *(see p93)*

⑦ **The Ramble** is a wooded area of 37 acres (15 ha), crisscrossed by paths and streams. It is a paradise for bird-watchers – over 250 species have been spotted in the park, which is on the Atlantic migration flyway.

⑧ **Obelisk**

⑨ **Reservoir**

⑩ **Guggenheim Museum** *(see p92)*

⑪ **Metropolitan Museum** *(see p90)*

⑫ **Alice in Wonderland** is immortalized in bronze at the northern end of Conservatory Water, along with the Cheshire Cat, the Mad Hatter, and the Dormouse.

**★ Conservatory Water**
From March to November, this is the scene of model boat races each Saturday. Many of the tiny craft are stored in the boathouse that adjoins the Lake.

## ㉜ Whitney Museum of American Art

**Map** F2. 945 Madison Ave. **Tel** (212) 570-3600, (800) WHITNEY. **Ⓜ** 6 to 77th St. 🚌 M1, M2, M3, M4, 30, 72. **Open** 11am–6pm Wed, Thu, Sat & Sun, 1–9pm Fri. **Closed** public hols. 🐾 by donation 6–9pm Fri. ♿ 🛍 Lectures, film & video presentations: ✏️ 📷 **Ⓦ** whitney.org

An entire range of 20th- and 21st-century American art is showcased in the Whitney Museum. Sculptor Gertrude Vanderbilt Whitney founded the museum in 1930 after the Metropolitan Museum of Art rejected her personal collection of works by living artists, such as George Bellows and Edward Hopper. Initially, the museum was set up behind Whitney's studio in Greenwich Village (*see pp80–81*) and moved to its present inverted pyramid building designed by Marcel Breuer in 1966. A Midtown branch is now housed in the Philip Morris Building. The Leonard and Evelyn Lauder galleries on the fifth floor have permanent collections, showing works by Calder, O'Keeffe, and Hopper. Changing exhibitions occupy the lobby, and the second, third, and fourth floors. Highlights include Alexander

James Whistler's second portrait of *Lady Meux* (1881), Frick Collection

Calder's fanciful sculpture *Circus* (1926–31), and works by Edward Hopper, whose *Early Sunday Morning* (1930) depicts the emptiness of American city life. Other artists represented here include Roy Lichtenstein. The Whitney Biennial takes place in even-numbered years and is the most significant survey of new trends in American art.

## ㉝ Frick Collection

**Map** F2. 1 E 70th St. **Tel** (212) 288-0700. **Ⓜ** 6 to 68th St. 🚌 M1, M2, M3, M4, 30, M72, M79. **Open** 10am– 6pm Tue–Sat, 11am–5pm Sun. **Closed** most public hols. 🐾 children under 10 not admitted. ✉️ ♿ 📷 Concerts, lectures, film & video: **Ⓦ** frick.org

The priceless art collection of steel magnate Henry Clay Frick (1849–1919) is exhibited in a residential setting amid the furnishings of his opulent mansion, providing a rare glimpse of how the extremely wealthy lived in New York's gilded age. Frick intended the collection to be a memorial to himself and bequeathed the entire house to the nation on his death.

The collection includes a superb display of Old Master paintings, French furniture, and Limoges enamel. Of special interest is the skylit West Gallery offering oils by Hals, Rembrandt, and Vermeer, whose *Officer and the Laughing Girl* (1655–60) is a fine example of the Dutch painter's use of light and shadow. The Oval Room features Whistler, while the Library and Dining Room are devoted to English works. In the Living Hall are works by Titian, Bellini, and Holbein.

The grand entrance of the Metropolitan Museum of Art

## ㉞ Metropolitan Museum of Art

**Map** F2. 1000 Fifth Ave. ✖️ (212) 535-7710. **Ⓜ** 4, 5, 6 to 86th St. 🚌 M1, M2, M3, M4. **Open** 9:30am–5:15pm Sun & Tue–Thu, 9:30am–8:45pm Fri & Sat. **Closed** Jan 1, 1st Mon in May, Thanksg., Dec 25. 🐾 ♿ 🛍 📷 ✏️ 📺 📷 Concerts, lectures, film & video presentations: **Ⓦ** metmuseum.org

One of the world's great museums, the Metropolitan houses treasures that span 5,000 years of culture from all over the world. Founded in 1870 by a group of artists and philanthropists who visualized an American art institution to rival those of Europe, it began with three private European collections and 174 paintings. Today, its holdings number over two million, and the original 1880 Gothic Revival building by Calvert Vaux and Jacob Wrey has been expanded many times. Additions include inviting courts with huge windows overlooking Central Park, and the breathtaking **Byzantine Galleries**, located under the Grand Staircase.

Most of the collections are housed on the two main floors. On the first floor are the **Costume Institute** and part of the **Robert Lehman Collection**. This extraordinary private collection, acquired in 1969, includes Old Masters, Dutch, Spanish, and French artists, Post-Impressionists, and Fauvists, as well as ceramics and furniture. The state-of-the-art Costume Institute covers fashion trends from the 17th century to the present day. On view are Napoleonic and Victorian ballgowns, Elsa Schiaparelli's shocking-pink

*Cypresses* (1889), painting by Vincent van Gogh

evening dresses, creations by Worth and Quant, and the costumes of the Ballets Russes.

The second floor includes the **American Wing**, **European Sculpture and Decorative Arts**, **Egyptian Art**, and the **Michael C. Rockefeller Wing**. Built by Nelson Rockefeller in memory of his son, who lost his life on an art-finding expedition in New Guinea, the wing showcases a superb collection of over 1,600 primitive artworks from Africa, the islands of the Pacific, and the Americas. Among the African works are outstanding ivory and bronze sculptures from the royal kingdom of Benin (Nigeria). Also on view are pre-Columbian gold, ceramics, and stonework from Mexico and Central and South America. The American Wing has one of the world's finest collections of American paintings, including several by Edward Hopper. Prize exhibits include Gilbert Stuart's first portrait of George Washington, John Singer Sargent's notorious portrait of *Madame X*, and the monumental *Washington Crossing the Delaware* by Emanuel Leutze. There are also period rooms, including one designed by Frank Lloyd Wright, and Tiffany glass.

The Metropolitan has one of the largest collections of Egyptian art outside Cairo. Objects range from the fragmented jasper lips of a 15th-century BC queen to the massive Temple of Dendur. Many of the objects were discovered during museum-sponsored expeditions during the early 20th century.

The **Lila Wallace Wing** holds the museum's growing contemporary art collection. Some great works include Picasso's portrait of *Gertrude Stein* (1905) and Jackson Pollock's *Autumn Rhythm* (1950).

The heart of the museum, however, is its awe-inspiring collection of 3,000 **European Paintings**. Its highlights are masterpieces by Dutch and Flemish painters, specifically Brueghel's *The Harvesters* (1551) and Rembrandt's *Self-Portrait* (1660), painted when he was 54. Among the finest Impressionist and Post-Impressionist paintings is *Cypresses* (1889), painted by Vincent van Gogh the year before he died.

The third floor has a comprehensive collection of **Asian Art**, featuring textiles, sculpture, and ceramics from China, Japan, Korea, Southeast Asia, and India. The full-size Ming-style Chinese scholar's garden in the Astor Court was built by craftspeople from Souzhou. The **Cantor Roof Garden** has superb annual shows of 20th-century sculpture, displayed against the dramatic backdrop of the city's skyline. Guests can also visit the museum shops, located on the main floor and mezzanine.

## Floor Plan of the Metropolitan Museum of Art

1 Byzantine Galleries
2 Costume Institute
3 Robert Lehman Collection
4 American Wing
5 European Sculpture and Decorative Arts
6 Egyptian Art
7 Michael C. Rockefeller Wing
8 Lila Wallace Wing
9 European Paintings
10 Asian Art
11 Access to Cantor Roof Garden

### Key to Floor Plan

First Floor

Second Floor

Third Floor

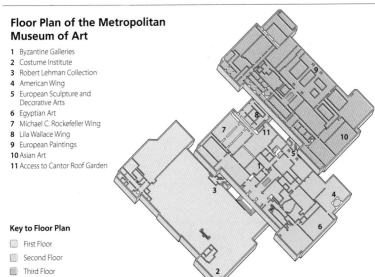

## ㉟ The Solomon R. Guggenheim Museum

1071 5th Ave at 89th St. **Tel** (212) 423-3500. **M** 4, 5, 6 to 86th St. M1, M2, M3, M4. **Open** 10am–5:45pm Sun–Wed & Fri, 10am–7:45pm Sat. **Closed** Thu, Jan 1, Dec 25. "Pay What You Wish" 5:45–7:45pm Sat. Concerts, lectures, performing art series. **W** guggenheim.org

One of the world's finest collections of modern and contemporary art is housed in a building that is considered one of the great architectural achievements of the 20th century. The only New York building to be designed by the celebrated American architect Frank Lloyd Wright (see p394), it was completed after his death in 1959. Its shell-like façade is a New York landmark, while the interior is dominated by a spiral ramp that curves down and inward from the dome, passing works

by major 19th- and 20th-century artists.

Over the years, Solomon Guggenheim's core collection of Abstract Expressionist art has been added to by donations of several important collections, from Willem de Kooning to Jackson Pollock and Robert Motherwell. The museum now owns a large body of work by famous artists such as Kandinsky, and major holdings of Brancusi, Calder, Klee, Chagall, Miró, Léger, Mondrian, Picasso, Oldenburg, and Rauschenberg.

Not all of the permanent collection is on display at any one time. Only a small portion is on view because the main gallery, the Great Rotunda, usually features special exhibitions. The Small Rotunda shows some of the museum's famous Impressionist and Post-Impressionist holdings. The Tower galleries feature exhibitions of work from the permanent collection and contemporary pieces. A fifth-floor sculpture terrace overlooks the scenic

Cézanne's *Man with Arms Crossed* (1895–1900), Guggenheim Museum

Central Park. Three important acquisitions by the museum are the Justin Thannhauser collection, with over 30 works by Picasso, more than 100 photographs and unique objects from the Robert Mapplethorpe Foundation, and Minimalist, Post-Minimalist, and Conceptual art from Giuseppe Panza's collection.

## The Solomon R. Guggenheim Museum

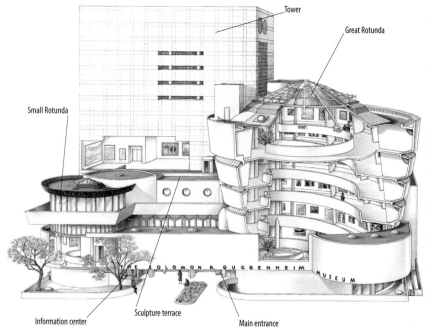

Tower

Great Rotunda

Small Rotunda

Information center

Sculpture terrace

Main entrance

THE SOLOMON R. GUGGENHEIM MUSEUM

## ㊱ American Museum of Natural History

Central Park West at 79th St. **Tel** (212) 769-5100. 🅜 B, C to 81st St. 🚌 M7, M10, M11, M79. **Open** 10am–5:45pm daily. 🚫 **Closed** Thanksgiving, Dec 25. ♿ 🎫 Donation. 📷 📱 🏛 🆆 **amnh.org**

This is one of the largest natural history museums in the world, attracting more than 4.5 million visitors each year. Since the original building opened in 1877, the complex has grown to cover four city blocks, and today holds more than 30 million specimens and artifacts. The most popular areas are the dinosaurs, and the Milstein Family Hall of Ocean Life.

Enter at Central Park West onto the second floor to view the Barosaurus exhibit, African, Asian, Central and South American peoples, and animals. First-floor exhibits include ocean life, meteors, minerals and gems, and the Hall of Biodiversity. North American Indians, birds, and reptiles occupy the third floor. Dinosaurs, fossil fishes, and early mammals are on the fourth floor.

The **Rose Center** for Earth and Space has as its centerpiece the Hayden Planetarium. The planetarium contains a technologically advanced Space Theater, the famous Cosmic Pathway, and a Big Bang Theater.

Barosaurus, American Museum of Natural History

The Lincoln Center for the Performing Arts complex

## ㊲ Lincoln Center

Broadway between W 62nd & W 65th Sts. 🅜 1 to 66th St. 🚌 M5, M7, M10, M11, M66, M104.

A giant cultural complex, built in the 1950s, Lincoln Center was conceived when both the Metropolitan Opera House and the New York Philharmonic needed homes. At that time, the notion of a single complex where different performing arts could exist side by side was considered both daring and risky. Today, the Lincoln Center draws audiences of over five million each year.

The **Lincoln Center for the Performing Arts** was born in May 1959, when President Eisenhower traveled to New York to turn a shovelful of earth, composer Leonard Bernstein lifted his baton, and the New York Philharmonic and the Juilliard Choir broke into the *Hallelujah Chorus*. The center soon covered 15 acres (6 ha) on the site of the slums that had once been the setting for Bernstein's classic musical *West Side Story*.

Lincoln Center includes the **New York State Theater**, home to the highly acclaimed New York City Ballet and the New York City Opera, a troupe devoted to presenting opera at popular prices; and the **Metropolitan Opera House**, the focal point of the plaza. This fine building has five great arched windows, which offer views of the opulent foyer and two radiant murals by Marc Chagall. All the greats have sung here, including Maria Callas, Jessye Norman, and Luciano Pavarotti. The other two significant

institutions here are the Lincoln Center Theater and Avery Fisher Hall, home to the New York Philharmonic, America's oldest orchestra. The best way to see the complex is by guided tour.

The **American Folk Art Museum** features an excellent and extensive collection of traditional folk art, including quilts, carvings, and paintings, dating from the 18th century to the present. The gallery is home to work by self-taught artists from the US and abroad. Many pieces, from decorative arts to detailed needlepoints, celebrate US history and culture, and reveal a strong national identity. The museum's Contemporary Center, established in 1997, is dedicated to folk art from the 20th and 21st centuries, and includes everything from abstract paintings and poignant self-portraits, to embroidered pillowcases and unique dolls.

The **Hotel des Artistes**, nearby at 1 West 67th Street, was built in 1918 as working artists' studios. Past residents have included Alexander Woollcott, Isadora Duncan, Noël Coward, Rudolph Valentino, and Norman Rockwell. The Café des Artistes is well-known for its misty, romantic Howard Chandler Christy murals and fine cuisine.

🎭 **Lincoln Center for the Performing Arts**
**Tel** (212) 546-2656. ♿ 🎫 (212) 875-5350. 📷 🏛 🆆 **lincolncenter.org**

🏛 **American Folk Art Museum**
2 Lincoln Square. **Tel** (212) 595-9533. **Open** noon–7:30pm Tue–Sat, noon–6pm Sun. 🎫 ♿ 🎫 📷 📱 🏛
🆆 **folkartmuseum.org**

# Greater New York

Though officially part of New York City, upper Manhattan and the boroughs outside Manhattan are very different in feel and spirit. Away from the bustle of the inner city, they are residential and do not have the famous skyscrapers of New York. The difference is evident even in the way residents describe a trip to Manhattan as "going into the city." Yet these areas feature such attractions as Columbia University, the city's largest zoo, botanical gardens, museums, churches, beaches, and huge sports arenas.

Classical-style library building on the main campus of Columbia University, Manhattan

## ㊳ Columbia University

**Map** F4. Main entrance at W 116th St & Broadway. **Tel** (212) 854-1754. Ⓜ 1 to 116th St-Columbia University. Visitors' Center: **Tel** (212) 854-4900. **Open** 9am–5pm Mon–Fri. 🕐 1pm Mon–Fri. 🆆 columbia.edu

One of America's oldest and finest universities, Columbia was founded as King's College under a charter granted by King George II of Great Britain, in 1754. Originally situated in lower Manhattan, the present campus was built in Morningside Heights. Architects McKim, Mead & White, who designed its first buildings around a central quadrangle, placed the university on a terrace, serenely above street level. A Classical, columned building, the **Low Library**, dominates the quadrangle. Daniel Chester French's statue *Alma Mater*, (1903) in front of it, became familiar as the backdrop to the 1968 anti-Vietnam War student demonstrations. The building now houses offices, and the rotunda is used for a variety of academic and ceremonial purposes. Its books were moved to Butler Library, across the quadrangle, in 1932. To the

right, the 1904 **St. Paul's Chapel** is known for its fine woodwork and vaulted interior, and has fine acoustics.

Columbia, part of the Ivy League, is noted for its law, medicine, and journalism schools. Founded in 1912 by publisher Joseph Pulitzer, the School of Journalism is home of the Pulitzer Prize awarded for the best in letters and music. Columbia's distinguished faculty and alumni, past and present, include over 50 Nobel laureates. Famous alumni include Isaac Asimov, J.D. Salinger, and James Cagney.

Visitors to the campus can stroll along the central quadrangle, where jeans-clad future leaders of America meet and mingle between classes. Across from the campus are the cafés where students engage in lengthy philosophical arguments, debate in the topics of the day, or simply unwind.

Also across the campus to the east on Amsterdam Avenue lies the **Cathedral of St. John the Divine**. Begun in 1892 and only two-thirds finished, with its

600-ft- (180-m-) long and 146-ft- (45-m-) wide interior, this Neo-Gothic cathedral, with its hand-carved gargoyles, is slated to be the largest in the world. Medieval construction methods, such as stone on stone with supporting buttresses, continue to be used to complete the structure.

The cathedral hosts popular cultural events.

🔼 **St. Paul's Chapel**
Columbia University. **Tel** (212) 854-1487 concert info. Ⓜ 116th St-Columbia Univ. **Open** 10am–11pm Mon–Sat (term time), 10am–4pm (breaks). 🕐 Sun. ♿

🔼 **Cathedral of St. John the Divine**
Amsterdam Ave at W 112th St. **Tel** (212) 316-7490. Ⓜ 1 to Cathedral Pkwy (110th St). 🚌 M4, M5, M7, M11, M104. **Open** 7am–6pm Mon–Sat, 7am–7pm Sun. 🕐 Choral Evensong 4pm Sun. ♿ 🕐 🎧 Concerts, plays, exhibitions, gardens. 🆆 stjohndivine.org

## ㊴ Riverside Church

**Map** F4. 490 Riverside Dr at 122nd St. **Tel** (212) 870-6700. Ⓜ 116th St-Columbia Univ. **Open** 10:30am–5pm Tue–Sun. 🕐 10:45am Sun with prior permission. ♿ 🕐 free tour 12:15pm Sun; Carillon Bell Concerts: 12:30, 3pm Sun. **Tel** (212) 870-6784. Theater: **Tel** (212) 870-6784. 🆆 theriversidechurchny.org

The design of Riverside Church was inspired by the cathedral at Chartres in France. This Gothic church with a 21-story steel frame was lavishly funded by John D. Rockefeller Jr., in 1930. The Laura Spelman Rockefeller Memorial Carillon (in honor of Rockefeller's mother) is the largest in the world, with 74 bells. The 20-ton Bourdon, or hour bell, is the largest and heaviest tuned carillon bell ever cast. The organ, with its 22,000 pipes, is among the world's largest. The second gallery features a figure by Jacob Epstein, *Christ in Majesty* (1954–5), cast in plaster and covered in gold leaf. Another Epstein statue, *Madonna and Child*

Carved stonework at the Cathedral of St. John the Divine

The 21-story Riverside Church, from the north

(1950), stands in the court next to the cloister. The screen panels honor eight men and women, including Socrates, Michelangelo, Florence Nightingale, and Booker T. Washington, whose lives exemplified the teachings of Christ.

For quiet reflection, enter the small, secluded Christ Chapel, patterned after an 11th-century Romanesque church in France. It was possible for visitors to take the elevator to the 20th floor and then walk the 140 steps to the top of the 392-ft (120-m) bell tower, but the observation deck has been closed indefinitely. There is no access to the bell tower during carillon concerts.

## ⑩ St. Nicholas Historic District

**Map** F4. 202–250 W 138th & W 139th St. Ⓜ 135th St (B, C).

A startling contrast to the run-down surroundings, the two blocks here, known as the King Model Houses, were built in 1891 when Harlem was considered a neighborhood for New York's gentry. They still comprise one of the city's most distinctive examples of row townhouses. A distinct feature of these houses is the provision of a central service alley that can be accessed from the avenue ends and at different points along the block. The alley serves a very useful feature in concealing garbage cans and service deliveries.

The developer, David King, chose three leading architects, who succeeded in blending their different styles to create a harmonious whole. The most famous of these was the firm of McKim, Mead & White, who were responsible for the northernmost row of solid brick Renaissance palaces. Their homes featured ground-floor entrances rather than the typical New York brownstone stoops. The parlor floors have ornate wrought-iron balconies below, as well as carved decorative medallions above their windows.

The Georgian buildings designed by Price and Luce are built of buff brick with white stone trim. James Brown Lord's Georgian-style buildings feel much closer to Victorian, with outstanding red-brick façades and brownstone foundations. Over the years, many distinguished professional and civic leaders made their homes here. Among them were celebrated musicians W.C. Handy and Eubie Blake, and one of the founders of the American Negro Theater, Abram Hill. He collaborated in the production of a play set in the historic district and called it *On Striver's Row*, a name by which the district is now commonly known.

## ⑪ Studio Museum in Harlem

**Map** F4. 144 W 125th St. **Tel** (212) 864-4500. Ⓜ 125th St (2, 3). **Open** noon–9pm Thu & Fri, 10am–6pm Sat, noon–6pm Sun. **Closed** public hols. 🅿 donation. 🎫 ♿ 📷 Lectures, children's programs, films. 📷 🖥
Ⓦ **studiomuseum.org**

The museum was founded in 1967 in a loft on upper Fifth Avenue with the mission of becoming the premier center for the collection and exhibition of the art and artifacts of African Americans.

The present premises, a five-story building on Harlem's main commercial street, was donated to the museum by the New York Bank for Savings in 1979. There are galleries on two levels for changing exhibitions featuring artists and cultural themes, and three galleries are devoted to the permanent collection of works by major black artists, such as Romare Bearden and Elizabeth Catlett.

The photographic archives comprise one of the most complete records in existence of Harlem in its heyday. From the main floor a side door opens onto a small sculpture garden. In addition to its excellent exhibitions, the museum also maintains a national artist-in-residence program and offers regular lectures, a variety of children's programs, and film festivals. A range of books, T-shirts, and African crafts are available in the small shop.

Exhibition space at the Studio Museum in Harlem

## ㊷ The Cloisters

**Map** F4. Fort Tryon Park.**Tel** (212) 923-3700. **M** A to 190th St (exit via elevator). **🚌** M4. **Open** Mar–Oct: 10am–5:15pm daily; Nov–Feb: 10am–4:45pm daily. **Closed** Jan 1, Thanksg., Dec 25. 🎟 donations. No videos. **♿ 📷** book in advance. **📱** Concerts, lectures. **w** metmuseum.org/cloisters

This world-famous branch of the Metropolitan Museum *(see pp90–91)*, devoted to medieval art, resides in a building that incorporates medieval cloisters, chapels, and halls. The museum, organized in chronological order, starts with the Romanesque period (AD 1000) and moves to the Gothic (1150 to 1520). It is noted for its

Vaulted ceiling of the Pontaut Chapter House at the Cloisters

exquisite illuminated manuscripts, stained glass, metalwork, enamels, ivories, and beautifully preserved tapestries. Perhaps the most interesting exhibits in the Cloisters are the gardens, planted according to horticultural information found in medieval treatises and poetry. Early music concerts are performed regularly here and are extremely popular. Call in advance for tickets.

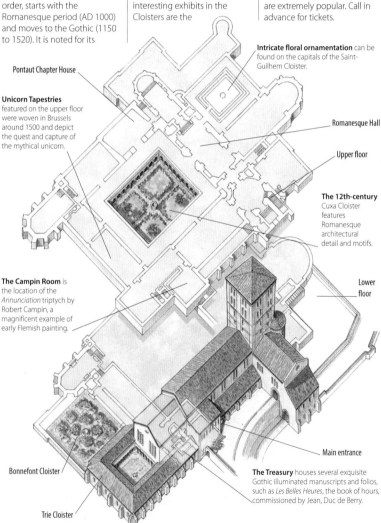

**Pontaut Chapter House**

**Unicorn Tapestries** featured on the upper floor were woven in Brussels around 1500 and depict the quest and capture of the mythical unicorn.

**The Campin Room** is the location of the *Annunciation* triptych by Robert Campin, a magnificent example of early Flemish painting.

**Bonnefont Cloister**

**Trie Cloister**

**Intricate floral ornamentation** can be found on the capitals of the Saint-Guilhem Cloister.

**Romanesque Hall**

**Upper floor**

**The 12th-century** Cuxa Cloister features Romanesque architectural detail and motifs.

**Lower floor**

**Main entrance**

**The Treasury** houses several exquisite Gothic illuminated manuscripts and folios, such as *Les Belles Heures*, the book of hours, commissioned by Jean, Duc de Berry.

Jungle World, a climate-controlled tropical rainforest at the Bronx Zoo

## ㊸ The Bronx

**Map** F4. Ⓜ B, D, 4 to 161st St (Yankee Std); 2, 5 to Tremont Ave (Bronx Zoo); 4, B, D to Bedford Park Blvd (NY Bot. Garden).

Once a prosperous suburb with a famous Grand Concourse lined with apartment buildings for the wealthy, parts of the Bronx have now become a symbol of urban decay. However, visitors still frequent the area to escape the overwhelming city concrete for some beauty and quiet, while New Yorkers flock to the **Yankee Stadium**, home of the New York Yankees baseball team. Don't miss a side-trip to one of the city's wealthiest and most beautiful parts – Riverdale – located between W 242 and Broadway.

But the most outstanding attraction of the Bronx is the **Bronx Zoo**. Opened in 1899, this is the largest urban zoo in the US, home to more than 4,000 animals of 500 species, living in realistic representations of their natural habitats. The park is a leader in the perpetuation of endangered species, such as the Indian rhinoceros and the snow leopard. Its 265 acres (107 ha) of woods, streams, and parklands include a children's zoo, camel safaris, and a shuttle train that takes visitors around the sprawling park.

Across the road from the Zoo's main entrance, visitors can experience 250 acres (101 ha) of beauty and hands-on enjoyment at the **New York Botanical Garden**. One of the oldest and largest botanical gardens in the world, it has 48 specialty gardens and plant collections, 50 acres (20 ha) of virgin forest, and a vast Children's Adventure Garden. The Enid A. Haupt conservatory, with its interconnected glass galleries, features the lovely exhibit "A World of Plants."

### 🐾 Bronx Zoo
Fordham Rd /Bronx River Pkwy. **Tel** (718) 367-1010. **Open** Apr–Oct: 10am–5pm daily (5:30pm Sat & Sun); Nov–Mar: 10am–4:30pm daily. 🏛 donation. ♿ 🚻 ♨ 🏛 Children's zoo: Ⓦ **bronxzoo.com;** Ⓦ **nybg.org**

## ㊹ Brooklyn

**Map** F5. Ⓜ Prospect Pk (Brooklyn Bot. Gardens); 2, 3 to Eastern Pkwy (Brooklyn Mus); C, 3 to Kingston (Brooklyn Children's Mus); D, F, N, Q to Stillwell Ave (Coney Is).

One of the most ethnically diverse boroughs in New York, Brooklyn, if it were a separate city, would be the country's fourth largest. Many entertainment greats, such as Mel Brooks, Phil Silvers, Woody Allen, and Neil Simon, celebrate their birthplace with great affection and humor. Among the diverse neighborhoods are the historic residential districts of Park Slope and Brooklyn Heights, beautiful tree-lined enclaves that offer a wonderful

Ibis Coffin (332–330 BC) in gold leaf and silver, Brooklyn Museum of Art

stroll past Victorian houses and cafés. An oval gateway in the Grand Army Plaza, designed by Frederick Law Olmsted and Calvert Vaux, leads to the lush, green Prospect Park.

The adjacent **Brooklyn Botanic Gardens** feature a traditional Elizabethan-style "knot" herb garden, one of the largest bonsai and rose collections in the country, and some rare rainforest trees.

To its southeast, lies the 1897 **Brooklyn Museum of Art**, designed by McKim, Mead & White. Though only one-fifth completed, the museum is one of the most impressive cultural institutions in the US, with a permanent collection of some 1 million objects, housed in a grand five-story structure spanning 560,000 sq ft (41,805 sq m). Highlights include African, Oceanic, and New World art; a collection of classic Egyptian and ancient Middle Eastern artifacts; and some works of American and European contemporary art.

To the north on Brooklyn Avenue lies the imaginative **Brooklyn Children's Museum**, the world's first designed especially for young people. Programs and displays are based on a remarkable collection of 20,000 cultural artifacts and natural history specimens, plants and animals, and interactive exhibits.

Brooklyn poet Walt Whitman composed many of his works on the borough's farthest point, **Coney Island**. It was billed as the "World's Largest Playground" in the 1920s, with its combination of rides and lovely beaches. Today, Coney Island is a bit run-down but holds historical memorabilia. A short trip to the **New York Aquarium** is a must.

### 🏛 Brooklyn Museum of Art
200 Eastern Pkwy, Brooklyn. **Tel** (718) 638-5000. **Open** 10am– 5pm Wed–Fri, 11am–6pm Sat, 11am–11pm first Sat in month, 11am–6pm Sun. **Closed** Jan 1, Thanksgiving, Dec 25. 🏛 Contribution expected. ♿ 🚻 🏛 ⬛ 🏛 Concerts, lectures: Ⓦ **brooklynmuseum.org**

# New York City Practical Information

Visitors to New York are treated very much the same as anyone else and as long as you follow a few guidelines on personal security you'll be able to explore the city as freely as any native New Yorker. Buses and subway trains are reliable and inexpensive. Beside, the wide range of prices offered by the many hotels, restaurants, and entertainment venues means your New York trip can be both fun and affordable.

## Tourist Information

Advice on any aspect of life in New York City is available from the **New York Convention and Visitors' Bureau (NYC & Co.)**. Their 24-hour touch-tone phone service offers help outside office hours. Brochures and information kiosks are also found at the walk-in office of the **Times Square Visitors Bureau**.

## Personal Security

Though New York is rated among the safest large US cities with around-the-clock foot, horse, bike, and car patrols by the police in tourist areas, it is always good to be cautious. At night, if you can't afford a taxi, try to travel with a group. Walk as if you know where you're going. Avoid making eye contact and getting into confrontations with down-and-outs. If someone asks you for money, do not get drawn into conversation. Always keep some change handy for bus fares; carry your Metrocard in your pocket. Never carry too much cash, and lock your valuables in the hotel safe. Do not allow anyone except hotel or airport personnel to carry your luggage.

Public toilets in bus stations should be avoided at all times of the day. It is best to find a hotel or store if you want to use a restroom. Since parks are sometimes used for drug dealing, they are safest when there is a crowd, for example, for a rally or concert. If you want to go for a jog in a park, always make sure you avoid lonely areas and pathways, and follow a map that shows safe routes.

## Getting Around

Rush hours extend from 8am to 10am, 11:30am to 1:30pm and 4:30pm to 6:30pm, Mon–Fri. At these times, most forms of public transportation are crowded.

Buses are a comfortable way to get around, but they often tend to be slow. Subways are quick, reliable, and inexpensive, and make stops throughout central Manhattan. The vast system extends over 233 miles (375 km) and most routes operate throughout the year. You can buy a Metrocard for the $2.50 subway and bus single fares. Cards come in $2.75 to $80 amounts depending on the number of trips you intend to take. If $5 or more is put on the card, you get a 5 percent bonus; discounts increase as you put more money on the card. Other options are $30 for an unlimited 7-day pass. Taxis are best for door-to-door service, but can be held up in traffic jams. You should hail only yellow taxis, as they are the only ones with licences. If their roof numbers are lit up, they are available.

Heavy traffic and expensive rentals make driving in New York a frustrating experience. The speed limit is 30 mph (48 km/h). Parking in Manhattan is difficult and costly. Many hotels include parking charges in their room rates. New York's tow-away crews are active, and one-third of cars towed suffer damage. If you cannot find your car at its parking place, first call the traffic department's tow-away office. For specific details call the **Department of Transportation** (Tel: 311). If you receive a parking ticket, you have 7 days to pay the hefty fine. If the car is not at the pound, contact the police.

## Etiquette

It is illegal to smoke in *any* public place or building in New York. Bars all over the city also ban smoking.

Tipping is part of New York life. In general, 10 to 15 percent of your bill is enough – 20 percent for outstanding service. For bartenders and coat check, $1–2 is typical.

## Entertainment

New York City is a non-stop entertainment extravaganza, every day, all year round. Whatever your taste, you can be sure the city will satisfy it on both a grand and an intimate scale.

New York is famous for its extravagant musicals and its ferocious critics. The Times Square area hosts the "power productions" of Broadway – the big, highly publicized dramas, musicals, and revivals starring many Hollywood luminaries in sure-fire money earners, in theaters such as the **Ambassador** and the **Lyceum** (1903), the oldest theater still in operation. Off-Broadway and Off-Off-Broadway stages such as **Actors' Playhouse**, host experimental shows, ranging from the well-appointed to the improvised, in lofts, churches, or even outside at the open-air **Delacorte Theater** in Central Park.

The city is also a great center of traditional ballet and modern dance. The New York City Ballet, founded by the legendary choreographer George Balanchine, performs in the **New York State Theater**. The **Dance Theater of Harlem** is world famous for its modern, and ethnic productions, as is the esteemed **Alvin Ailey American Dance Theater**.

There's every imaginable form of music in New York, from international stadium rock to the sounds of the 1960s, from Dixieland jazz or country blues, soul, and world music to street musicians. The city's music scene changes at a dizzying pace, so there's no way to predict what you may find when you arrive. The top performers such as Elton John, Bruce Springsteen, and the Stones perform in the huge arenas at Shea Stadium and

Madison Square Garden. **Webster Hall** features live music, from punk to rock.

New York's nightlife and club scene is legendary. Whatever your preference – disco, stand-up comedy, or the soothing melodies of a Harry Connick Jr. – you'll be amazed at the choice. New Yorkers thrive on dancing. Dance floors available all over the city range from the ever-popular **SOB's** – for reggae, soul, jazz, and salsa – to huge places, such as **Roseland Ballroom**. The historic **Copacabana** alternates live bands with a disco. **Cielo** is a popular, strobe-lit bar and nightclub, as is the 1980s-themed **Culture Club**.

The city is also a film buff's paradise. Apart from new US releases, which show months in advance of other countries, many classic and foreign films are screened in this hotbed for new and innovative talent.

New Yorkers are sports crazy, and there are activities to suit every taste. Visitors can choose from health clubs and horseback riding to playing tennis or jogging. Spectator sports are provided by professional baseball (**Yankee Stadium**), ice hockey and basketball (**Madison Square Garden**), and football (Giants Stadium), while for tennis fans there is the US Open and Virginia Slims tournaments.

## Shopping

New York is the consumer capital of the world: a shopper's paradise, with dazzling displays and a staggering variety of goods for sale. Everything is available here, from high fashion to rare books, state-of-the-art electronics, and an array of exotic food. Keep in mind that the city's sales tax is a hefty 8.625 percent.

Known as the fashion capital of America, New York boasts such names as **Polo/Ralph Lauren** and Calvin Klein. There are fashion stores such as **Brooks Brothers** (menswear) and **Ann Taylor** (women's wear), and shops of international names such as **Yves St. Laurent** and **Giorgio Armani**. Manhattan is also known for its world-class jewelry shops, including **Cartier** and **Tiffany & Co**. The city is a bargain hunter's dream, with huge discounts on anything from household goods to designer clothes.

As the publishing capital of the US, New York has the country's best bookstores. Don't miss the **Barnes & Noble** stores, the **Strand Book Store** for rare and used books, and **Shakespeare & Co**.

Dozens of tiny shops specialize in unusual merchandise, from butterflies and bones to toy firefighting equipment and occult potions. Don't miss a trip to the legendary **FAO Schwarz** for toys of all kinds. Some of New York's best souvenirs can be found in the city's many museum shops, including the **Museum of Modern Art** and the **American Museum of Natural History**.

# DIRECTORY

## Tourist Offices

**NYC & Co.**
ⓦ nycgo.com

**Times Square Visitors' Bureau**
ⓦ timessquarenyc. org

## Transportation

**Department of Transportation**
55 Water St,
9th Floor.
**Tel** 311.

## Entertainment

**Actors' Playhouse**
100 Seventh Ave S.
**Tel** (212) 463-0060.

**Alvin Ailey American Dance Theater**
405 W 55th St.
**Tel** (212) 405-9000.

**Ambassador**
219 W 49th St.
**Tel** (212) 239-6200.

**Dance Theater of Harlem**
466 W 152nd St.
**Tel** (212) 690-2800.

**Delacorte Theater**
Central Park, 81st St.
**Tel** (212) 535-4284
(summertime only).

**Lyceum**
149 W 45th St,
New York City.
**Tel** (212) 239-6200.

**Madison Square Garden**
7th Ave at 33rd St.
**Tel** (212) 465-6741.
ⓦ thegarden.com

**New York State Theater**
Lincoln Center,
Broadway at 65th St.
**Tel** (212) 870-5570.

**Webster Hall**
125 E 11th St.
**Tel** (212) 353-1600.

**Yankee Stadium**
1 E 161st St, Bronx.
**Tel** (718) 293-4300.

## Bars & Clubs

**Cielo**
18 Little W 12th St.
**Tel** (212) 645-5700.

**Copacabana**
560 W 34th St.
**Tel** (212) 239-2672.

**Culture Club**
20 W 39th St.
**Tel** (212) 921-1999.

**Roseland Ballroom**
239 W 52nd St.
**Tel** (212) 247-0200.

**SOB's (Sounds of Brazil)**
204 Varick St.
**Tel** (212) 243-4940.

## Shopping

**American Museum of Natural History**
W 79th St,
Central Park W.
**Tel** (212) 769-5100.

**Ann Taylor**
645 Madison Ave.
**Tel** (212) 832-2010.

**Barnes & Noble**
105 5th Ave.
**Tel** (212) 807-0099.

**Brooks Brothers**
346 Madison Ave.
**Tel** (212) 682-8800.

**Cartier**
653 5th Ave.
**Tel** (212) 753-0111.

**FAO Schwarz**
767 5th Ave.
**Tel** (212) 644-9400.

**Giorgio Armani**
760 Madison Ave.
**Tel** (212) 988-9191.

**Museum of Modern Art**
11 W 53rd St.
**Tel** (212) 708-9400.

**Polo/Ralph Lauren**
Madison Ave at 72nd St.
**Tel** (212) 606-2100.

**Shakespeare & Co.**
716 Broadway.
**Tel** (212) 529-1330.

**Strand Book Store**
828 Broadway.
**Tel** (212) 473-1452.

**Tiffany & Co**
5th Ave at 57th St.
**Tel** (212) 755-8000.

**Yves St. Laurent**
3 E 57th St.
**Tel** (212) 980-2970.

# New York State

Stretching north for over 200 miles (322 km) to the Canadian border, and 400 miles (644 km) west to the Great Lakes, the "Empire State" is a world away from New York City. Due east of Manhattan, Long Island is the largest island adjoining the continental US, with miles and miles of suburbs, farmland, and beaches jutting out into the Atlantic Ocean. To the north, the Hudson River is an area of opulent mansions and small towns. The state capital, Albany, marks the start of the vast Upstate area, comprising the Adirondacks, rural farmland, and vibrant cities.

The octagonal Montauk Point Lighthouse, completed in 1796

## ❷ Jones Beach State Park

Wantagh. 🚊 Long Island Railroad from Penn Station to Jones Beach. Operates Jun–Labor Day, (718) 217-5477. 🚌 ℹ️ (516) 785-1600. **Open** Jun–Labor Day: sunrise–midnight. 🏊 ♿ Jones Beach Theater. 🌐 jonesbeach.com

Located on Long Island, Jones Beach State Park is only 33 miles (53 km) from Midtown Manhattan. A popular destination since it was created in 1929, this barrier island resort features more than 4 square miles (10 square km) of parkland, beaches, and a wide variety of outdoor and cultural activities.

The park's oceanside beaches are complemented by a stillwater bayside beach and several swimming, diving, and wading pools, and surf facilities. The park's other recreational options include golf courses, restaurants, fishing docks, and a 2-mile (3-km) boardwalk.

The 11,200-seat **Jones Beach Theater** is a popular venue for

rock and pop concerts in summer. Another landmark, the 200-ft (61-m), brick-and-stone structure, the **Jones Beach Tower**, is modeled on the campanile of St. Mark's Cathedral in Venice.

## ❸ The Hamptons & Montauk

🏖️ 15,000. 🚁 🚊 🚌 ℹ️ (877) 386-6654. 🌐 hamptonstravelguide.com

At Riverhead, Long Island splits into two peninsulas – the mostly pastoral North Fork and the more urban South Fork. Most of South Fork's beaches and cultural attractions are concentrated in the expensive and trendy summer retreats of The Hamptons and Montauk.

Most New Yorkers tend to associate The Hamptons (from west to east, Westhampton Beach, Hampton Bays, Southampton, Bridgehampton, East Hampton, and Amagansett) with its celebrity residents and fashionistas who migrate here from Manhattan during the

summer. However, the area also has a rich historical heritage. In the 19th-century whaling community of Sag Harbor, to the north of Bridgehampton, the **Custom House**, built in 1789, commemorates the town's post-Revolutionary War heyday as one of the first official ports of entry into the US. On the Village Green in East Hampton, the **Home Sweet Home Museum** houses a variety of early Colonial, rough-shingled structures, including a classic saltbox house built in 1750, and the still-operational Old Hook Mill, constructed in 1806.

The easternmost Long Island community, Montauk is a busy summer resort, serving as a jumping-off point for the area's nature trails and beaches. Other activities are golf, horseback riding, cycling, surfing, and fishing. Montauk State Park contains the **Montauk Point Lighthouse**, commissioned by George Washington in 1792. Still in operation, the octagonal stone structure is an important landmark for oceangoing vessels.

🏛️ **Custom House**
Main St & Garden Sq, Sag Harbor. **Tel** (631) 692-4664. **Open** hours vary; call ahead. 🏊 🌐 splia.org/hist_ custom.htm

🏛️ **Home Sweet Home Museum**
14 James Lane, East Hampton. **Tel** (631) 324-0713. **Open** May–Sep; 10am–4pm Mon–Sat, 2–4pm Sun; Oct & Nov: weekends only; Dec–Apr: by appointment only. **Closed** public hols. ♿ 🌐 easthampton.com/ homesweethome

One of the many swimming pools at Jones Beach State Park

# ❹ Hudson River Valley

🚊 🚌 📷 ℹ️ 3 Neptune Rd, Poughkeepsie. **Tel** (845) 463-4000.
Ⓦ dutchesstourism.com

From its source high in the Adirondack Mountains, the Hudson courses past bustling riverport towns and the dramatic Catskill and Taconic mountain ranges for nearly 315 miles (507 km) to its mouth at New York harbor. Strikingly beautiful and strategically located, the valley has played a pivotal role in North American military, economic, and cultural history.

Settled by the Dutch in the 1620s *(see p53)*, it was soon dotted with trading posts that grew up around the thriving fur trade with local Iroquois tribes. The area's Dutch heritage survives in names of places such as Catskill, Kinderhook, and Claverack, as well as in the early 19th-century fictional writings of Washington Irving (1783–1859), whose tales of *Rip Van Winkle* and *The Legend of Sleepy Hollow* made him America's first internationally recognized author. Irving's modest but whimsically eclectic Hudson River home, **Sunnyside**, is now a tourist attraction.

The Hudson's economic and transportation advantages also made it a key strategic objective of both British and American forces during the Revolutionary War, resulting in many pitched battles. Fort Putnam, one of the forts built along the river in 1778 to defend the colonies from British attacks, has been restored and is now part of the

The imposing exterior of the lavishly furnished Vanderbilt Mansion

**United States Military Academy** at West Point. Established in 1802, the academy has trained the nation's leading military officers, including opposing Civil War generals Ulysses S. Grant and Robert E. Lee, and World War II commanders Douglas MacArthur and Dwight D. Eisenhower. The Military Academy Museum provides a comprehensive introduction to a tour of the fortress-like grounds.

In the 19th century, many of New York's emerging elite constructed seasonal retreats along the Hudson. The largest of these is the **Vanderbilt Mansion** in Hyde Park. Completed in 1899, this Italian-Renaissance-style palace was built by the architecture firm of McKim, Mead & White, for railroad baron Frederick W. Vanderbilt. The magnificent home offers a spectacular view of the river, and is laden with French furniture, art, tapestries, housewares, and architectural details taken from a Parisian château once occupied by Napoleon. An older and less ostentatious mansion is Springwood, the home of Franklin D.

Statue of George Washington at the US Military Academy

Roosevelt (FDR), America's 32nd president *(see p59)*. Roosevelt was born here in 1882, and it was used as a summer White House during his 1933–45 term. The house is now part of the **Home of Franklin D. Roosevelt National Historic Site**, which also includes an extensive museum and library detailing Roosevelt's leadership during the Great Depression and World War II. Both FDR and Eleanor are buried here. The nearby Eleanor Roosevelt National Historic Site preserves Val-Kill, the First Lady's weekend and holiday cottage retreat.

### 🏛 Sunnyside
W Sunnyside Lane, off Rte 9, Tarrytown. **Tel** (914) 591-8763.
**Open** Apr–Oct: for timed tours only at 10:30am, noon, 1:30pm, 3pm Wed–Sun (also 3:30pm Sat & Sun). 🎫 ♿
Ⓦ hudsonvalley.org

### 🏛 US Military Academy
W Sunnyside Lane, Rte 9 W, West Point. **Tel** (845) 938-2638. **Open** by tour only. 9:45am–3:30pm Mon–Sat: every half hr, photo IDs required; Dec–Feb: only 2 tours per day. 🎫 for tours only. **Closed** Jan 1, Thanksg., Dec 25. ♿ Ⓦ usma.edu

### 🏛 Home of Franklin D. Roosevelt National Historic Site
4097 Albany Post Rd, Rte 9, Hyde Park. **Tel** (845) 229-5320. **Open** 9am– 5pm daily. **Closed** Jan 1, Thanksgiving, Dec 25. 🎫 grounds free. ♿ 📷 📱
Ⓦ nps.gov/hofr

Sunnyside, Washington Irving's home

New York State Capitol in Albany, a blend of architectural styles

## ❺ Albany

🏙 101,000. ✈ 🚌 🚆 𝒊 25 Quackenbush Square, (518) 434-1217. **W** albany.org

Albany has been a central force in New York State since 1614, when the explorer Henry Hudson *(see p70)* established a fur-trading post, Fort Orange, at the northernmost navigable point on the Hudson River. When the British took over the settlement in 1664, they changed its name to Albany. In 1797 Albany was selected as the New York State capital, and the town's political future was secured. The city expanded dramatically in the 1830s with the completion of the Erie Canal, which linked the Hudson River to the Great Lakes. When canal traffic declined in the 1850s, Albany retained its commercial dominance, rapidly evolving into a New York Central railroad terminus and manufacturing center.

While transportation and industry are still important components of the local economy, government is the main concern in today's Albany. The majestic **New York State Capitol**, built over 30 years and completed in 1898, occupies a central location near the city's downtown. The massive stone building is a curious amalgam of Italian and French Renaissance and Romanesque, replete with ornamented stairways, soaring arches, and an ornate Senate chamber embellished with red granite, yellow and pink marble, stained glass, onyx, and mahogany.

The **New York State Museum** chronicles the state's rich heritage, beginning with its first Native American occupants and incorporating the stories of New York's many immigrants, early settlers, and business elite. A reconstructed Iroquois longhouse and a restored 1940s subway car from New York City's legendary A-train are highlights here.

🏛 **New York State Capitol**
Empire State Plaza. **Tel** (518) 474-2418. **Open** tours Mon–Sat; call ahead for times. **Closed** Jan 1, Easter, Thanksgiving, Dec 25, public hols. ♿ 🏠

🏛 **New York State Museum**
Empire State Plaza. **Tel** (518) 474-5877. **Open** 9:30am–5pm Tue–Sun. **Closed** Jan 1, Thanksgiving, Dec 25. ♿ 📄 📷 **W** nysm.nysed.gov

Sprawling Saratoga National Historical Park

## ❻ Saratoga Springs

🏙 25,000. 🚌 🚆 𝒊 297 Broadway, (518) 587-3241. **W** saratoga.org

This town has been known for its horseracing, gambling, and high society since it emerged as a resort in the 19th century. The therapeutic waters from the town springs at **Saratoga Spa State Park** sparked an annual influx of wealthy tourists seeking relief from various ailments. Other more enjoyable distractions were offered by the lavish casinos and horseracing facilities. One of Saratoga's original gambling establishments, the elegant Canfield Casino, is now part of **Congress Park**. The gabled grandstand of the Saratoga Race Track, built during the Civil War, is still in use, attracting large crowds during the racing season in August. For a glimpse of the area's more tempestuous Revolutionary War past, **Saratoga National Historical Park**, 15 miles (24 km) southeast, was the site of the 1777 Battle of Saratoga. Here, American commander Horatio Gates led Colonial forces to a decisive victory over 9,000 British regulars, Hessians, and Native Americans commanded by General John Burgoyne. The victory ensured American control of the Hudson River shipping corridor, and prompted the French King Louis XVI to send troops to the colonists' aid later that year.

Saratoga Race Track

🏛 **Saratoga Spa State Park**
I-87, exit 13N. **Tel** (518) 584-2535. **Open** 8am–sunset daily. 🅿 ♿ **W** saratoga spastatepark.org

🏛 **Saratoga National Historical Park**
Rte 4, 8 miles (13 km) S of Schuylerville. **Tel** (518) 664-9821. **Open** 9am–5pm daily. **Closed** Jan 1, Thanksgiving, Dec 25. 🅿 ♿ 📷 **W** nps.gov/sara

The tranquil waters of Otsego Lake, Cooperstown

# ❼ Adirondack Mountains

🚌 ℹ️ 216 Main St, Lake Placid.
**Tel** (518) 523-2445.

Spanning almost one-fourth of the state, the Adirondack Mountains encompass various ecosystems and hundreds of lakes and rivers, with only 1,100 miles (1,770 km) of road. Rugged peaks such as the 5,344-ft (1,629-m) Mount Marcy are some of the scenic highlights. Two visitor centers serve as gateways to **Adirondack Park** and provide information about the conservation movement that led to the park's creation in 1894 as part of the nation's first forest preserve.

The picturesque village of **Lake Placid** straddles Mirror Lake and Lake Placid in the north-central section of the park. Home to the 1932 and 1980 Winter Olympic Games, it is both a summer resort and winter sports training and competitive center.

🏕️ **Adirondack Park**
1 mile N of Rte 86/Rte 30, & 14 miles (22 km) E of Long Lake, Rte 28N.
**Tel** (518) 327-3000. **Open** 9am–5pm daily. **Closed** Thanksgiving, Dec 25. ♿

# ❽ Cooperstown

🏙️ 2,200. 🚌 ℹ️ 31 Chestnut St.
**Tel** (607) 547-9983.

Overlooking Otsego Lake, this neat little village is the legendary birthplace of baseball and home of the **National Baseball Hall of Fame**. This engaging shrine and museum pays homage to baseball greats from the last 150 years, with a colorful array of gear, uniforms, photographs, audio-video features, and special exhibits. Founded in 1786, Cooperstown also has a superb collection of Native American artifacts, folk art, and Hudson River School paintings in the **Fenimore Art Museum**. The adjacent Farmer's Museum features exhibits on 19th-century rural life. Glimmerglass Opera, on the shores of Lake Otsego, is nationally renowned.

🏛️ **National Baseball Hall of Fame**
25 Main St. **Tel** (888) 425-5633.
**Open** Memorial Day–Labor Day: 9am– 9pm daily; Labor Day–Memorial Day: 9am–5pm daily. **Closed** Jan 1, Thanksgiving, Dec 25. 🏛️ ♿
🌐 **baseballhalloffame.org**

### Baseball

"America's Pastime," the country's first nationwide spectator sport, evolved from the British games of cricket and rounders, as well as town ball, a New England variant. The first recorded amateur game took place in 1845 in New York City. Since the 1870s, when professional play matured, baseball has seen many superstars, such as Babe Ruth, Ty Cobb, and Ted Williams.

Babe Ruth

# ❾ Finger Lakes

🚆 🚌 🚐 ℹ️ 904 E Shore Dr, Ithaca.
**Tel** (607) 272-1313. 🅦 **visitithaca. com**

According to the Iroquois tribes of west-central New York, the Finger Lakes were created when the Great Spirit placed his hand on the region, leaving behind a series of slender lakes. Seneca Lake is the deepest of these water bodies, at 630 ft (192 m), while Cayuga Lake is the longest, stretching 40 miles (64 km) between the lively town of **Ithaca** – containing the picturesque Cornell University campus – and historic **Seneca Falls**.

Downtown Ithaca, which has a diverse array of art galleries, bookstores, and excellent restaurants, is a pleasant place to start a tour of the Finger Lakes region. **Taughannock Falls State Park**, north of Ithaca, is a wooded oasis, with the 215-ft (65-m) falls tumbling gracefully into a cool, green pool, where swimming is permitted in season. At the top of Cayuga Lake, the quiet Seneca Falls is the spot where 19th-century feminists Elizabeth Cady Stanton and Susan B. Anthony held the first American women's rights convention in 1848, laying the foundation for the Suffrage Movement some 70 years later.

🏕️ **Taughannock Falls State Park**
10 miles (16 km) N of Ithaca, Rte 89.
**Tel** (607) 387-6739. **Open** 8am–sunset daily (some trails closed in winter).
🌲 🅦 **nysparks.state.ny.us/parks**

Taughannock Falls State Park in the Finger Lakes region

## ⑩ Syracuse

🅰 163,900. ✈ 🚉 🚌 ℹ 572 S Salina St, (315) 470-1910.
**w** visitsyracuse.org

Like many upstate New York cities, Syracuse prospered after the arrival of the Erie Canal in the 1820s. The **Erie Canal Museum**, housed in a restored canal-side building just east of downtown, has a full-size canal boat replica and a multimedia overview of the canal's role in the city's history. The downtown Armory Square historic and entertainment district preserves many brick and cast-iron commercial and warehouse buildings from Syracuse's late 19th-century boom period, as well as the 3,000-seat **Landmark Theatre**, built in 1928.

A downtown surprise is the **Everson Museum of Arts**, which has a remarkable permanent collection of more than 11,000 items that range from Ming dynasty porcelains to works by American painters from Gilbert Stuart to Jackson Pollock and Andrew Wyeth, as well as New York State landscapes by local artists. The building is the first museum designed by architect I.M. Pei.

🏛 **Erie Canal Museum**
318 Erie Blvd E. **Tel** (315) 471-0593. **Open** 10am–5pm Mon–Sat, 10am–3pm Sun. **Closed** public hols.
♿ 📷 **w** eriecanalmuseum.org

🏛 **Everson Museum of Arts**
401 Harrison St. **Tel** (315) 474-6064. **Open** noon–5pm Wed–Sun (to 8pm Thu). ♿ ⬛ 📷 **w** everson.org

Old lithograph showing the inauguration of the Erie Canal

The Kodak Company's office building in Rochester

## ⑪ Rochester

🅰 231,600. ✈ 🚉 🚌 ℹ 45 East Ave, (800) 677-7282.
**w** visitrochester.com

This lovely city, with its abundant parkland and fine museums, evolved out of an industrial past, rooted in the milling industries that developed around the Genesee River's High Falls. The Center for High Falls includes a pedestrian bridge with scenic views of the still-roaring falls, an art gallery, a local history display, and a tour of an 1816 factory that lies three stories below street level.

One of the city's most popular attractions is the **Strong National Museum of Play**, a hands-on, interactive center dedicated to the study of play, particularly in relation to American culture. **George Eastman House** is where the eccentric founder of the city's Eastman Kodak Company lived until his death in 1932. It is now the superb International Museum of Photography and Film, containing massive still, film, and video holdings, and cameras, as well as a collection of books on photography.

🏛 **Strong National Museum of Play**
1 Manhattan Square. **Tel** (585) 263-2700. **Open** 10am–5pm Mon–Thu, 10am–8pm Fri & Sat, noon–5pm Sun. **Closed** Jan 1, Thanksgiving, Dec 25. 🎨 ♿ ⬛ 📷 **w** museumofplay.org

🏠 **George Eastman House**
900 East Ave. **Tel** (585) 271-3361. **Open** 10am–5pm Tue–Sat (to 8pm Thu), 1–5pm Sun. **Closed** Mon, Jan 1, Thanksgiving, Dec 25. 🎨 ♿ 🔲 ⬛ 📷 **w** eastmanhouse.org

## ⑫ Chautauqua

🅰 4,600. 🚌 ℹ Chautauqua Institution, Chautauqua, (800) 836-2787.

A secluded community located on Chautauqua Lake in western New York State, this town doubles in population in summer, when its Victorian cottages and tree-lined streets are crowded with people attending the town's famous **Chautauqua Institution**. Founded in 1874 as an instructional center for Methodist Sunday-school teachers, it spawned the Chautauqua Movement, sponsoring correspondence courses and lecture tours in an effort to make the liberal arts more accessible. The town is now one of the nation's premier venues for theater, classical music, and opera. The shady, open-air amphitheater on the timeless Chautauqua campus holds lectures, performances, and religious services from late June to late August.

Renoir's *Little Blue Nude* (1879), Albright-Knox Art Gallery, Buffalo

## ⑬ Buffalo

🅰 328,100. ✈ 🚉 🚌 ℹ 617 Main St, (800) 283-3256.
**w** buffalocvb.org

Burned by the British during the War of 1812, the fortunes of the frontier outpost of Buffalo revived some 13 years later, when it became the western terminus of the Erie Canal. This secured its economic future as the gateway to the prosperous Great Lakes trade. The **Buffalo and Erie County Historical**

Buffalo's skyline on a sunny morning from the city harbor

**Society** is housed in what was originally the New York State Pavilion, the only building to survive from the 1901 Pan-American Exposition. Its numerous exhibits focus on the town's rich ethnic and industrial heritage.

The nearby **Albright-Knox Art Gallery** overlooks bucolic Delaware Park, designed by Frederick Law Olmsted (see p88). On display are works by Picasso and de Kooning, and a large collection of North American paintings by Jackson Pollock, Frida Kahlo, and others. Also worth a side-trip to LeRoy is the **Jell-O Museum**, on Main Street, containing displays and trivia relating to "America's favorite dessert."

**Albright-Knox Art Gallery**
Elmwood Ave, off Rte 198. **Tel** (716) 882-8700. **Open** 10am–5pm Tue–Sun (to 10pm first Fri of month). **Closed** Jan 1, Thanksgiving, Dec 25. **albrightknox.org**

## ⓲ Niagara Falls

61,800. Prospect St, (716) 282-8992. **niagara-usa.com**

Louis Hennepin, the French priest who was one of the first Europeans to gaze upon Niagara Falls in 1678, wrote that "the Universe does not afford its parallel." Even today the three Niagara Falls waterfalls, which plunge nearly 200 ft (61 m) into a rocky gorge, are as awe-inspiring as they were over 300 years ago. Despite the rampant development on both the US and Canadian sides of the Niagara River (which separates the Canadian province of Ontario from New York State), the spectacle still provides enough drama, mist, and romance to lure more than 10 million tourists a year.

Visitors on the American side often start their exploration with a visit to **Niagara Falls State Park**, where the 240-ft (73-m) Prospect Point

Observation Tower provides a scenic overview of the falls. For a closer exploration, there are a number of paid excursions, such as the **Cave of the Winds** elevator ride to the base of the falls, and the **Maid of the Mist** boat ride, which departs from Prospect Park and passes directly in front of the Falls and into the river's Horseshoe Basin, for a view of the more dramatic Canadian Falls.

The pedestrian-friendly Rainbow Bridge provides quick passage from downtown Niagara Falls to the Canadian side, where most of the area's commercial attractions are located. At night, the Falls are dramatically illuminated by electricity generated by the **Niagara Power Project**. Its visitor center traces the development of hydroelectricity in the area and features an operating model of a hydropower turbine.

**Niagara Falls State Park**
Prospect St. **Tel** (716) 278-1796. **Open** sunrise–sunset daily. Visitor Center: 8am–10pm in summer; 8am–6pm in winter. **niagarafallsstatepark.com** Cave of the Winds: Goat Island. **Open** May 1–Jun 23: 9am–5pm Sun–Thu, 9am–9pm Fri & Sat; Jun 24–Sep 4: 9am–9pm Sun–Thu, 9am–10pm Fri & Sat; Sep 5–Oct 9: 9am–7pm Sun–Thu, 9am–9pm Fri & Sat, Oct 10–23: 9am–5pm daily. Maid of the Mist Ride: Prospect Park. **Open** 9am–7:45pm in summer; check at office for details.

The majestic Niagara Falls, one of the most dramatic spectacles the country offers

# New Jersey

Despite the industrial image earned by New Jersey's manufacturing and railroad towns such as Newark and Hoboken, the "Garden State" really does live up to its moniker. Outside the urban, industrial corridor that lies across the Hudson River from New York City and extends all the way into Philadelphia, New Jersey is a gentle country of green and orderly small towns, dairy farms, rolling hills, pine forests, and miles and miles of white sandy beaches along the Atlantic Ocean.

Strolling on the peaceful campus of Princeton University

## ⓯ Princeton

🏙 12,000. 🚉 🚌 ℹ Princeton Chamber of Commerce, 216 Rockingham Row, Princeton Forrestal Village, (609) 924-1776.
Ⓦ **visitprinceton.org**

The central New Jersey village of Princeton witnessed considerable activity during the Revolutionary War period, changing hands between British forces under General Charles Cornwallis and the Continental Army, led by General George Washington. The once-sleepy agricultural village is now a pleasant tree-lined town, combining sophisticated shops, lodgings, and a variety of restaurants, with one of America's most prestigious universities.

The center of Princeton's shopping and dining area is Nassau Street. Located here is Bainbridge House, built in 1766, which now accommodates **The Historical Society of Princeton**. The Society offers local history

Princeton's tiger mascot

exhibits and free walking tours, highlighting the town's fine 18th-century architecture. The popular Palmer Square, on Nassau Street, is home to Nassau Inn, Princetown's premier hotel since 1756.

The College of New Jersey, one of the 14 original Colonial colleges, moved to Princeton in 1756 and was renamed **Princeton University** in 1896. Nassau Hall, a landmark building on campus, was the site of the initial meeting of the New Jersey State Legislature in 1776. Renowned physicist Albert Einstein spent his final years here at the Institute for Advanced Study. Today, the campus covers 2.5 sq miles (6.5 sq km), and the university enrolls 6,000 students annually. The grounds include sculptures by Picasso, Henry Moore, Louise Nevelson, and Alexander Calder. The Art Museum in McCormick Hall displays paintings and sculptures that range from

ancient pre-Columbian, Asian, and African art to modern works. The University Chapel is one of the world's largest – of special interest are the Gothic architecture, stained-glass windows, and the superb 16th-century French pulpit and lectern. About 30 gargoyles in different styles decorate buildings on the campus, including the Firestone Library. Inside this building, the Cotsen Children's Library features a small museum with works by Beatrix Potter, the Brothers Grimm, and Hans Christian Andersen.

### 🏛 Princeton University Visitors' Center
Welcome Desk, First Campus Center. **Tel** (609) 258-1766. **Open** daily. 📷 11:15am, 1pm, 3:30pm Mon–Sat, 1pm, 3:30pm Sun. **Closed** public hols. ♿ Ⓦ **princeton.edu**

## ⓰ Atlantic City

🏙 38,000. ✈ 🚉 🚌 ℹ Greater Atlantic City Convention & Visitors Bureau, 2314 Pacific Ave, (609) 449-7130. Ⓦ **atlanticcitynj.com**

Called the "Queen of the Coast" by generations of beachgoers, Atlantic City has been a favored vacation spot since the mid-1800s. The first casino opened on the boardwalk in 1978, and since then the town has become one of the most popular destinations on the eastern seaboard.

All gambling – euphemistically referred to as "gaming" – takes place in the large, ostentatious, casino-hotels that lie within a

Tourists in a rolling chair on the boardwalk at Atlantic City

Lucy, the Margate Elephant, near Atlantic City

block of the boardwalk and beach. Although the casinos are justly famous for their nightlife, families will find plenty of other entertainment during the day. Atlantic City's boardwalk, lined with shops and amusement arcades, is always busy with people enjoying a stroll at any time of day or night. Another way to see the boardwalk is in a "**Rolling Chair**," a rickshaw-like wicker chair on wheels that seats up to three people. Beyond the boardwalk, white-sand beaches beckon sunbathers and swimmers.

Until 2006, Atlantic City hosted the prestigious Miss America Pageant, which had been held here since 1928. In nearby Margate City, **Lucy, the Margate Elephant** stands tall in celebration of American marketing ingenuity. Built by a real-estate developer in 1881 to draw prospects to his holdings, "Lucy" has served as a residence and a tavern over the years. Today, guided tours take visitors into the 90-ton (90,000-kg) structure that has become instantly recognizable as part of the Jersey Shore and Atlantic City.

### 🏛 Rolling Chair
Atlantic City Famous Rolling Chair Co., 1605 Boardwalk. **Tel** (609) 347-7148.

### 🏛 Lucy, the Margate Elephant
9200 Atlantic Ave, Margate City. **Tel** (609) 823-6473. **Open** mid-Jun–Labor Day: 10am–8pm Mon–Sat, 10am–5pm Sun; Apr–mid-Jun & after Labor Day–last weekend in Oct: 11am–4pm Mon–Fri, 10am–5pm Sat & Sun; Nov–Mar: hours vary. 🅿

## ⑰ Cape May

🏛 4,400. 🚉 🚌 ℹ Cape May Welcome Center, Lafayette & Elmira Sts, Cape May, (609) 884-9562. 🌐 **capemaychamber.com**

First explored by Cornelius Mey for the Dutch West India Company in 1621, Cape May is one of the oldest seashore resorts on the Atlantic Coast. Visited by a number of US presidents including James Buchanan, Ulysses S. Grant, Benjamin Harrison, and Franklin Pierce, it was popular with socialites from New York and Philadelphia during the late 1800s. Since then, this resort at the southernmost point of New Jersey, has continued to enjoy a fine reputation among beach lovers. A small boardwalk and sandy beach afford a lovely view of sunrise over the Atlantic Ocean.

Today, the area is characterized by the great Victorian building boom that took place in the 19th century. The central district is made up of so-called "cottages," two- and three-story buildings intended as summer homes for large families. They have been built in styles popular at the turn of the 20th century, ranging from lacy Queen Anne to Italianate. Most of the historic homes have been lovingly restored to period condition, and some are open to the public. Many others have been converted into B&B (bed-and-breakfast) lodgings. There are several tours of the Victorian homes, including a special trolley tour.

The **Historic Cold Spring Village** is a living history museum consisting of 25 authentically restored buildings set on a 20-acre (8-ha) site. Costumed interpreters portray 19th-century lifestyles that would have been common in a southern New Jersey rural community. Trades and crafts such as pottery making, bookbinding, and blacksmithing are also demonstrated.

Nearby, the **Cape May County Park and Zoo** is home to 200 species of animals; some, such as Brazilian golden lion tamarins, are rare or endangered. The park, which is free, also features a 35-acre (14-ha) African savanna habitat accessed by an 800-ft-(244-m-) long boardwalk.

### 🏛 Historic Cold Spring Village
720 US 9, Cape May. **Tel** (609) 898-2300. **Open** late Jun–Labor Day: 10am–4:30pm Tue–Sun; after Labor Day–Sep 30 & Memorial Day–late Jun: 10am–4:30pm Mon–Fri. 🅿 ♿ ▯ 🅿 🌐 hcsv.org

One of Cape May's charming bed-and-breakfast lodgings

# ⑱ Philadelphia

Pennsylvania's largest city, Philadelphia or the "City of Brotherly Love," is also the birthplace of the nation. In 1776, representatives from the 13 British colonies signed the Declaration of Independence here, and the city served as an early capital of the fledgling United States. Since its founding by English Quaker William Penn in the late 17th century, Philadelphia's port on the Delaware River has welcomed thousands of immigrants from all over the world. Their labor strengthened the expanding city through two centuries of industrial growth, wars, and economic reversals. Even today, the city's neighborhoods and restaurants reflect this ethnic mix. Philadelphia's rich history, world-class art collections, special-interest museums, fine restaurants and hotels, and the nation's largest landscaped public park combine to make the city one of America's most popular destinations.

William Penn's statue on Philadelphia City Hall

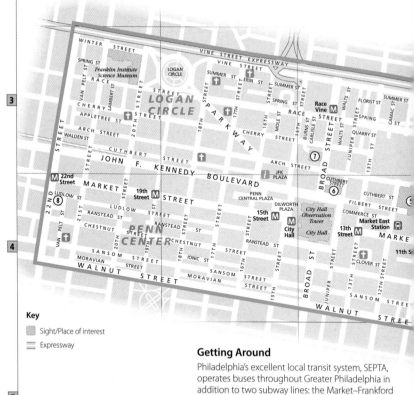

## Key

▨ Sight/Place of interest

▨ Expressway

## Getting Around

Philadelphia's excellent local transit system, SEPTA, operates buses throughout Greater Philadelphia in addition to two subway lines: the Market–Frankford line (east–west, under Market St) and the Broadway Street line (north–south). Purple-painted, tourist-oriented "Philly Phlash" shuttles travel in a loop through downtown to all major attractions (May to December; weekends only from September). Taxis are plentiful and moderately priced.

**For keys to symbols** *see back flap*

## Sights at a Glance

① Independence Hall
② Second Bank of the United States
③ US Mint
④ Independence Seaport Museum
⑤ Reading Terminal Market
⑥ Masonic Temple
⑦ Pennsylvania Academy of Fine Arts
⑧ College of Physicians of Philadelphia/Mütter Museum

**Greater Philadephia**
*(see inset map)*

⑨ Eastern State Penitentiary
⑩ Philadelphia Zoo
⑪ Fairmount Park
⑫ Philadelphia Museum of Art
⑬ The Barnes Foundation

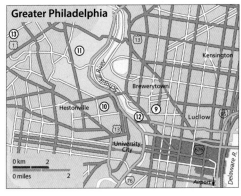

Greater Philadelphia

**Key**

▨ Area of main map
━ Highway
━ Major road
═ Other road

0 meters    250
0 yards     250

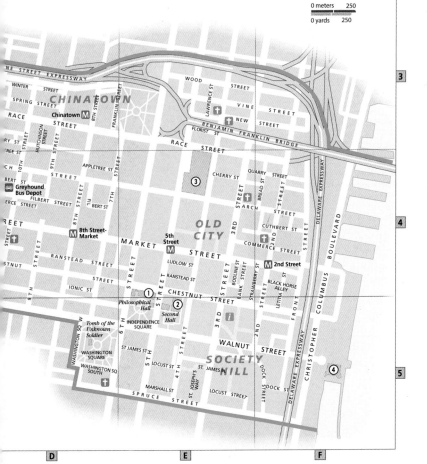

# Independence National Historic Park

Known locally as Independence Mall, this 45-acre (18-ha) urban park encompasses several well-preserved 18th-century structures associated with the American Revolution. The Declaration of Independence that heralded the birth of a new nation was signed in this historic area. Dominated by the tall brick tower of Independence Hall, the park includes the oldest street in Philadelphia, the US Mint, and several special-interest museums exploring Philadelphia's Colonial and seafaring past as well as its ethnic heritage. Around 20 of the buildings are now open to the public.

Plaque commemorating Independence Hall

Arch St. Friends Meeting House

**African American Museum**
Inspirational stories of Philadelphia's famous African-American citizens are displayed alongside exhibits of contemporary works.

**Christ Church Cemetery,** where Ben Franklin and other notables are buried.

Constitution Center

RACE STREET

ARCH S

6TH STREET

MARKET ST

6TH ST

★ **National Museum of American Jewish History**
This unique museum celebrates the history of Jews in America through artifacts such as this Torah scroll and ark (mid-1700s) from the collection of Congregation Mikveh Israel.

7TH STREET

**Independence Visitor Center**

**The Atwater-Kent Museum** traces Philadelphia's history, from its infancy as a small country town to current times.

**Key**

 Suggested route

**The Liberty Bell**
Inscribed with the words, "Proclaim Liberty throughout all the Land," the Liberty Bell was rung when the Declaration of Independence was adopted. It is now located in the new Liberty Bell Center *(see p112)*.

| 0 meters | | 500 |
| 0 yards | | 500 |

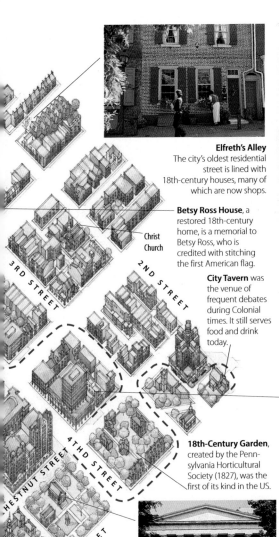

**Elfreth's Alley**
The city's oldest residential street is lined with 18th-century houses, many of which are now shops.

**Betsy Ross House**, a restored 18th-century home, is a memorial to Betsy Ross, who is credited with stitching the first American flag.

Christ Church

**City Tavern** was the venue of frequent debates during Colonial times. It still serves food and drink today.

3RD STREET

2ND STREET

4THD STREET

CHESTNUT STREET

STREET

WALNUT STREET

**18th-Century Garden**, created by the Pennsylvania Horticultural Society (1827), was the first of its kind in the US.

Washington Square Park

★ ① **Independence Hall**
The centerpiece of the park, this World Heritage Site was the place where the Declaration of Independence was signed on July 4, 1776 (see p112).

**Franklin Court**
Benjamin Franklin lived and worked in these buildings, which include the B. Free Franklin post office and museum.

★ ② **Second Bank of the US**
An extensive collection of portraits of luminaries involved in the military, diplomatic, and political events of 1776 is on display at this Grecian style building (see p112).

## ① Independence Hall

Chestnut St between 5th & 6th Sts. **Tel** (800) 967-2283 for timed tickets in Mar–Dec. **M** 5th St. **🚌** Philly Phlash. **Open** 9am–5pm Mon–Fri, 9am–6pm Sat & Sun. **&** **📷** **W** nps.gov/inde

Just west of the Delaware River, this unadorned brick building is the most important structure in the Independence Hall National Park. Previously designated the State House of Pennsylvania, it is the site of the drafting of the Declaration of Independence, the document that declared America's freedom from the British Empire.

The Liberty Bell on display near Independence Hall

Independence Hall, completed in 1748, was designed by master carpenter Edmund Woolley and lawyer Andrew Hamilton. The chambers of the meeting rooms are furnished simply, as they were during the late 1700s. Today, park personnel re-create history by pointing out the Windsor-style chairs from which Colonial leaders debated the contents of the Declaration. Although the Continental Congress rejected two passages in the first draft – an ill-tempered reference to the English people, and a bitter denunciation of the slave trade – the document was adopted without significant change and approved by Congress on July 4, 1776. The US Constitution was drafted in the same room in 1787.

The large, brass **Liberty Bell** that once hung in the tower has now been placed in the new Liberty Bell Center near Independence Hall. In 1846, a small crack developed and the bell could no longer be sounded. However, it remains the best-known symbol of the Colonial struggle for self-governance. The center incorporates displays that highlight Liberty Bell's importance to the story of America's independence.

## ② Second Bank of the United States

420 Chestnut St. **Tel** (215) 965-2305. **Open** call for times. **W** nps.gov/inde/second-bank.htm

Built between the years 1819 and 1824, this is one of America's finest examples of Greek Revival architecture. Once a repository that provided credit for federal government and private businesses, it now houses a collection of late 18th- and early 19th-century portraits. On view are 185 paintings of Colonial and federal leaders, military officers, explorers, and scientists.

Many of the portraits are by Charles Willson Peale (1741–1827), his brother James, and their respective sons and daughters, who together form America's most distinguished family of artists. After the Revolutionary War, Peale began collecting portraits, and today, 94 of his original paintings, including likenesses of the American Founding Fathers George Washington and Alexander Hamilton, and the Continental Army's French ally, the Marquis de Lafayette, are on display along with the portraiture of other artists.

## ③ US Mint

5th & Arch Sts. **Tel** (215) 408-0114. **M** 5th St. **Open** 9am–4:30pm Mon–Sat in summer; limited hours in winter; call ahead. **Closed** public hols. **&** **📷** **📷** **W** usmint.gov

The Philadelphia mint, the oldest in the US, makes most of the coins that Americans use every day, and also produces gold bullion coins and national medals. The first US coins, minted in 1793, were copper pennies and half pennies intended solely for local commerce in the colonies. Today, 24 hours a day, 5 days a week, hundreds of machines and operators in a room the size of a football field blank, anneal, count, and bag millions of dollars' worth of quarters, dimes, and pennies. Commemorative coins are available in the gift shop.

## ④ Independence Seaport Museum

211 S Columbus Blvd. **Tel** (215) 925-5439. **M** 2nd St. **🚌** Philly Phlash. **Open** 10am–5pm daily. **Closed** Jan 1, Thanksgiving, Dec 25. **📷** free 10am–noon Sun. **&** **W** phillyseaport.org

Quartered in a stunning modern building on the waterfront, this 100,000-sq-ft (9,290-sq-m) museum's mandate is to preserve US maritime history and traditions, with special focus on the Chesapeake Bay, and the Delaware River and its tributaries. Displays combine art and artifacts with hands-on computer games, large-scale models, and audiovisuals.

Aerial view of Independence Hall

*For hotels and restaurants see pp122–7*

The Ben Franklin Bridge, which connects Pennsylvania with New Jersey, is re-created in the museum as a three-and-a-half story replica that straddles a working model of the Delaware River.

Other highlights include "Divers of the Deep," featuring underwater technology through the ages, and "Workshop on the Water," an active boat shop and gallery where visitors can watch as artisans craft traditional wooden 19th-century boats. The World War II submarine USS *Becuna*, commissioned in 1943, and the USS *Olympia*, Admiral George Dewey's flagship in the Battle of Manila (1898), are berthed next to the museum.

Coffee shop in Philadelphia's Reading Terminal Market

## ⑤ Reading Terminal Market

12th & Filbert Sts. **Tel** (215) 922-2317. Ⓜ City Hall, 13th St, Juniper St. 🚌 Philly Phlash, SPREE bus. **Open** 8am–6pm Mon–Sat, 9am–5pm Sun. **Closed** Jan 1, Dec 25. ♿ 🆆 readingterminalmarket.org

This market was created underneath a train shed after two farmers' markets were leveled to make space for a new terminal in 1892. So modern was the market that people came from as far as the New Jersey shore to buy fresh Lancaster County produce. Reading Terminal Market declined over the years and was nearly destroyed in the 1970s. Today, however, it has been revitalized, and fishmongers, butchers, bakers, florists, and greengrocers vie for space with dairy and baked goods stands run by Amish women.

Equestrian statue in the Masonic Temple courtyard

## ⑥ Masonic Temple

1 N Broad St. **Tel** (215) 988-1917. Ⓜ City Hall. 🚌 Philly Phlash. **Open** tours at 10am, 11am, 1, 2, 3pm Tue–Fri, 10am, 11am, noon Sat. **Closed** Jan 1, Easter, Jul–Aug: Sat; Thanksg., Dec 25. ♿ 🅿 📷 🆆 pagrandlodge.org

An architectural jewel dedicated in 1873 as the Grand Lodge of Free and Accepted Masons of Pennsylvania, this remarkable building contains a number of meeting halls in various decorative styles. Among them, the Oriental Hall's (1896) coloring and ornamentation has been copied from the Alhambra in Granada, Spain, the Renaissance Hall (1908) follows an Italian Renaissance motif, while the Egyptian Hall (1889) takes its inspiration from the Temples of Luxor, Karnak, and Philae. High arches, pinnacles, and spires form the Gothic Hall, and the cross-and-crown emblem of Sir Knights – "Under this sign you will conquer" – hangs over a replica of the Archbishop's throne in Canterbury Cathedral.

The halls, still in use, were created to honor the building trades, and much of the stone and tilework are imperceptibly faux-finished – an attestation to the skill of the men who made them. President George Washington wore his Masonic apron when he laid the cornerstone of the Capitol building in Washington, DC. The apron is on display in the museum on the first floor.

## ⑦ Pennsylvania Academy of Fine Arts

118 N Broad S at Cherry St. **Tel** (215) 972-7600. Ⓜ 15th St, Rocelvine. 🚌 Philly Phlash. **Open** 10am–5pm Tue–Sat, 11am–5pm Sun. **Closed** public hols. 🅿 ♿ 💻 📷 🆆 pafa.org

The collection of this museum and school, founded in 1805, spans the history of American painting. Galleries display works by some of the art world's best-known denizens. One of them, the Classical stylist Benjamin West (1738–1820), a Quaker from Philadelphia, helped organize the British Royal Academy in 1768, and four years later was named Historical Painter to the King. Impressionist and former Academy of Fine Arts student Mary Cassatt (1844–1926), and modern abstractionist Richard Diebenkorn (1922–93), among others, share wall space. This distinctive building is considered one of the finest examples of Victorian-Gothic architecture in America.

*The Foxhunt* by Winslow Homer, Pennsylvania Academy of Fine Arts

Displays of medical curiosities at Mütter Museum

## ⑧ College of Physicians of Philadelphia/ Mütter Museum

19 S 22nd St. **Tel** (215) 563-3737.
Ⓜ 22nd St. 🚌 17, 21. **Open**
10am–5pm daily. **Closed** Jan 1,
Thanksgiving, Dec 24 & 25. 🅿 ♿
🆆 **muttermuseum.org**

Founded in 1787 for the "advancement of the science of medicine," the still-active college is a major source of health information. This is provided by the institute's C. Everett Koop Community Health Information Center, through the library, videotapes, and searchable computer system.

Mütter Museum, on the first floor of one of the buildings, is a fascinating collection of preserved specimens, skeletal constructions, and wax figures. These were originally used for educational purposes in the mid-19th century, when diseases and genetic defects were identifiable only by their physical manifestations. Some afflictions are quite grotesque, and may not be suitable for small children or those who are queasy.

The museum also contains medical instruments, exhibits on the history of medicine over the last 100 years, a re-creation of an early 20th-century doctor's office, and a medicinal plant garden. As well as this, it also holds shows displaying contemporary art, photography, and other subjects.

## ⑨ Eastern State Penitentiary

Fairmount Ave at 22nd St. **Tel** (215)
236-3300. 🚌 7, 32, 33, 43, 48. **Open**
10am–5pm daily. **Closed** Jan 1,
Thanksgiving, Dec 25. 🅿 ♿ 🅿 🔍
🆆 **easternstate.org**

Named the "house" by inmates and guards, the Eastern State Penitentiary, established in 1829, was a revolutionary concept in criminal justice. Prior to this, criminals were thrown together in despicable conditions and punished by physical brutality. The Philadelphia Quakers proposed an alternative – a place where a criminal could be alone to ponder and become penitent for his actions. During incarceration, with sentences seldom less than five years in length, prisoners literally never heard or saw another human being for the entire duration of their stay. The prison had a single entrance and 30-ft-

Corridor inside the Eastern State Penitentiary

(9-m-) high boundary walls. Each solitary cell had a private outdoor exercise yard contained by a 10-ft (3-m) wall. Eastern State's many "guests" included bootlegger and crime lord Al Capone. The prison was officially closed in 1971.

## ⑩ Philadelphia Zoo

3400 W Girard Ave. **Tel** (215) 243-1100.
🚋 Philly Phlash. **Open** Mar–Oct:
9:30am–5pm daily; Nov–Feb: 9:30am–
4pm daily. **Closed** Jan 1, Thanksg., Dec
24, 25 & 31. 🅿 🅿 🅿 🅿 🅿
🆆 **philadelphiazoo.org**

This zoo, the oldest in America, was founded in 1859. Set within verdant grounds, interspersed with statuary, the zoo is home to over 2,000 animals, including rare species such as naked mole rats and bamboo-eating lemurs. A walk-through giant otter habitat shows the animals at their playful best. The big cats – lions, clouded leopards, tigers (including rare white tigers), and jaguars – are kept in near-natural habitats or inside the Carnivora House, in weather-protected cages that provide close-up views. Other features are an open birdhouse with uncaged finches and hummingbirds, a reptile house, where alligators bask in a tropical paradise, and a 3-acre (1-ha) reserve for 11 primate species, including the nation's only blue-eyed lemurs. A large zoo balloon offers a panoramic view of the city.

## ⑪ Fairmount Park

ℹ John F. Kennedy Blvd & N 16th St,
(215) 683-0200. 🚋 Philly Phlash.
Ⓜ Market-Frankford line. **Open** daily.
🆆 **fairmontpark.org**

Designed by Frederick Law Olmsted (1822–1903), America's preeminent landscape architect who also designed Central Park, Fairmount Park is a 14-sq-mile (36-sq-km-) greenway. It encompasses seven historic manor houses decorated in period style, dozens of sculptures, a horticultural center, and

Downtown Philadelphia rising above Fairmount Park

Japanese house and gardens among other features. A waterworks, innovative in 1840, was designed and built to pump water from the Schuylkill River, which divides the park into east and west. The grounds are interspered with roads, hiking, biking, and bridle trails. Visitors can also rent rowboats and canoes.

A handful of rowing clubs occupy Victorian boathouses along the river. The boathouses are turreted, gabled, and decorated with coats of arms. At night, when viewed from the West Fairmount Park shore, the houses are outlined with tiny lights.

In 1894, wealthy manufacturer Richard Smith donated Smith Playground to the children of Philadelphia in memory of his son. Among the attractions are merry-go-rounds, a giant slide, and a mansion and playhouse.

Also in Fairmount Park is the 99-acre (40-ha) **Laurel Hill Cemetery**. This vast "park within a park" is dotted with obelisks, statuary, and classic Greek mausoleums. It was such a popular picnic and walking area during the late Victorian period that admission was by ticket only.

## ⑫ Philadelphia Museum of Art

26th St & Benjamin Franklin Pkwy. **Tel** (215) 763-8100. Philly Phlash, 7, 32, 38, 43, 48. **Open** 10am–5pm Tue–Sun; select galleries are open on Wed & Fri evenings. **Closed** Mon, legal hols. Sun donation. **W** philamuseum.org

This museum attracts major exhibitions to supplement its superlative permanent collection ranging from 15th-century illuminated manuscripts to modern sculpture by Constantin Brancusi. The full-scale medieval cloister courtyard and fountain on the second floor is a favorite, as are the French Gothic chapel and a pillared temple from Madurai, India. Throughout the museum are computerized stations with information on the exhibits. A collection of Pennsylvania Dutch and American decorative arts adjoins galleries that feature paintings by American artists.

Medieval diptych, Philadelphia Museum of Art

## ⑬ The Barnes Foundation

Philadelphia Campus, 2025 Benjamin Franklin Parkway. **Tel** (610) 667-0290. 44. **Open** reservation only: Jul–Aug: 9:30am–5pm Wed–Fri; Sep–Jun: 9:30am–5pm Fri–Sun. **Closed** public hols. **W** barnesfoundation.org

Established in the year 1922 to share the private collection of pharmaceutical magnate Albert C. Barnes with "people of all socioeconomic levels," this museum has one of the world's premier displays of French modern and Post-Impressionist paintings. Among the more than 800 works on view, there are 180 by Auguste Renoir, 69 by Paul Cézanne, 60 by Henri Matisse, and more by Picasso, Seurat, Modigliani, van Gogh, Rousseau, and almost every other noteworthy artist of that era. Other exhibits include ancient Greek and Egyptian art, medieval manuscripts, African sculpture, American furniture, ceramics, and handwrought ironwork. The art is displayed to highlight artistic affinities between diverse works. For instance, the Barnes Collection is displayed in accordance with Dr. Barnes' unique specifications – paintings, sculpture, and craft pieces are grouped into 96 distinct ensembles, without labels and with very little regard to chronology.

The glittering silhouettes of Victorian boathouses along Schuylkill River, Fairmount Park

# Pennsylvania

Pennsylvania has it all – American history, beautiful scenery, varied recreation, lodging, and dining, ranging from the refined to the simple. Of its two main cities, Philadelphia *(see pp108–15)*, the birthplace of America, is a complex, stunning city, while Pittsburgh re-created itself from a grimy, industrial center to a sparkling gem on the forks of the Ohio River. Most of the state, however, is rural and bucolic, a green patchwork of dairy and produce farms, embroidered with forests and streams, tidy fields, and small towns.

Memorial at Gettysburg National Military Park

## ⓭ Gettysburg

⛰ 7,000. 🚉 🚌 ℹ 102 Carlisle St, (800) 337-5015. 🌐 gettysburg.org

A pivotal confrontation of the Civil War *(see p57)* took place near the small farming community of Gettysburg in early July 1863. Nearly 100,000 Union soldiers fought 75,000 Confederates led by Robert E. Lee. After three days of fighting, a staggering 50,000 soldiers lay dead or wounded, and the Confederates were turned back.

Though the war raged for another two years, Gettysburg was recognized as a turning point. To commemorate the site, a burial ground was purchased, and President Lincoln dedicated the **Gettysburg National Cemetery** with his Gettysburg Address. Several impressive monuments have been placed throughout the fields and forests of the battlefield, now the **Gettysburg National Military Park**. The Cyclorama, a giant circular mural painted in 1884, dramatizes a crucial battle scene – Picket's Charge, where over 6,000 Confederate soldiers were killed or wounded.

🏛 **Gettysburg National Military Park**
Tel (717) 334-1124. Park: **Open** Apr–Oct: 6am–10pm daily; Nov–Mar: 6am–7pm daily. Visitor Center: 8am–5pm daily (to 6pm summer). **Closed** Jan 1, Thanksgiving, Dec 25. ♿ 🎁 🌐 nps.gov/gett

## ⓴ Lancaster

⛰ 55,600. 🚉 🚌 ℹ 501 Greenfield Rd, Lancaster, (800) 723-8824. 🌐 padutch.com; 🌐 cityoflancasterpa.com

This market town at the heart of the Pennsylvania Dutch Country *(see p69)* is surrounded by almost 5,000 small farms. The region is famous for the German-immigrant "Old Order Amish" Christians, who live and work without modern conveniences like electricity. The **Landis Valley Museum's** large outdoor collection focuses on the state's German rural heritage. Among the exhibits are a crossroads village and an adjoining farmstead with traditional breeds of animals and heirloom plants. Visitors can see demonstrations of skills such as sheepshearing.

Ephrata Cloister, northeast of town in the village of Ephrata, is a collection of medieval-style buildings, founded in 1732. It was home to one of America's earliest communal societies, semi-monastics who practiced an austere lifestyle emphasizing spirituality, and the artistic use of music and the written word. In 1745, the colony set up one of the country's earliest printing presses. This tradition continues today; Ephrata is the home of the world-famous Rodale Press.

🏛 **Landis Valley Museum**
2451 Kissel Hill Rd. **Tel** (717) 569-0401. **Open** call ahead, as hours vary. ♿ 🎁 🌐 landisvalleymuseum.org

## ㉑ Hershey

⛰ 7,400. 🚉 🚌 ℹ 1255A Harrisburg Pike, Harrisburg, (800) 995-0969. 🌐 hersheypa.com

This factory town, now a popular tourist destination, revolves around chocolate, so much so that even its streetlights are shaped like silver-foil-wrapped Hershey Kisses. The town's main attraction is **Chocolate World**, which features a 15-minute ride through a series of animated tableaux revealing Hershey's chocolate-making process. A free sample awaits at the end of the tour, while a series of shops sell souvenirs and every Hershey product made. Nearby is **Hershey Park**, a 90-acre (36-ha) amusement park. Hershey Park offers 80 rides, including five water slides, four roller

"Sisters House" and "Meeting House" in Ephrata Cloister

coasters, and one of the finest Philadelphia Toboggan Company four-row carousels in existence today.

### Chocolate World

SR 743 & US 422, Hershey. **Tel** (717) 534-4900. **Open** 9am–5pm daily, hours may vary, so call for details.

**w** hersheyschocolateworld.com

## ❷ York

 42,200. 1425 Eden Rd, York, (717) 852-9675. **w** yorkpa.org

The first Pennsylvania settlement west of the Susquehanna River, York was laid out in 1741. At that time, its inhabitants were mainly tavernkeepers and craftspeople, catering to pioneers heading west. Since then, manufacturing has become the prime economic force. York's many covered public markets include the 1888 **Central Market**, the best place in town for local fresh produce, flowers, meats, baked goods, and inexpensive restaurants.

East of historic York, at the **Harley-Davidson Vehicle Operations Plant**, giant presses form steel sheets into fenders while gleaming motorcycles fly overhead. A small museum shows Harley-Davidson's history from its days as a motorized bike company in 1903 to the present.

### Harley-Davidson Final Assembly Plant

1425 Eden Rd. **Tel** (877) 883-1450. **Open** schedule varies, so phone ahead (children under 12 not allowed on factory floor). **Closed** public hols. hourly 9am–2pm Mon–Fri.

**w** harley-davidson.com

Last checks at the Harley-Davidson Vehicle Operations Plant in York

A lush greenhouse in Longwood Gardens

## ❷ Reading

78,400. 352 Penn St, Reading, (800) 443-6610.

**w** readingberkspa.com

Once a center of industry, Reading has reinvented itself as a discount-outlet capital, with clusters of buildings housing more than 80 name-brand stores from Brooks Brothers to Mikasa and Wedgwood. The **Reading Pagoda**, on the town's outskirts, is modeled after a Shogun Dynasty castle that was built as part of an early 1900s resort. Today, cherry trees encircle the building, and there are walking trails throughout the adjacent park.

## ❷ Longwood Gardens

US 1, Kennett Square. **Tel** (610) 388-1000. **Open** 9am–5pm daily; longer hrs in summer.

**w** longwoodgardens.org

Pierre du Pont, millionaire financier and industrialist, acquired the 1,000-acre (405-ha) Longwood Gardens in the wooded Brandywine Valley in

1906. His aim was to preserve the property's unusual trees, and to provide a place of entertainment for his family and friends.

More than 11,000 varieties of plants including spectacular year-round seasonal displays, whimsical topiaries, and a children's garden are open to the public. The massive main greenhouse and conservatory are engineering marvels. But the real star of Longwood are the fabulous fountains, whose choreographed eruptions rise above the treetops and are highlighted at night by colored lights, creating dazzling displays that are often the backdrop for musical events. Shows and festivals range from the annual Wine & Jazz Festival, which takes place in May, to Longwood Carillon concerts, where musicians play 62 cast bells that ring out throughout the foliage. The gardens are also the setting for many kid-friendly events, including colorful kite-flying weekends, summer camp programs, storytelling sessions, and lively explorations of treehouses.

### Harley-Davidson

What began as a tinkering project for 21-year-old William Harley and 20-year-old Arthur Davidson, grew into a company that has dominated racing since 1914. After World War I, the first American entered

15th Anniversary Fat Boy

Germany on a Harley-Davidson. In 1956, Elvis Presley posed on a model KH. Today, Harley Owners Group has more than 900,000 members.

Pittsburgh's Golden Triangle, with its downtown skyscrapers

# ㉕ Pittsburgh

🏙 369,900. ✈ 🚌 🚆 🚍 ℹ 425 6th
Ave, 30th Floor, (800) 359-0758.
🌐 visitpittsburgh.com

Located at the point where the
Allegheny and Monongahela
rivers come together to form
the Ohio River, Pittsburgh is an
American success story. It grew
from a frontier outpost to
become an industrial giant,
home to the huge mills of the
US Steel conglomerate as well
as the food-processing company
Heinz and the Westinghouse
electric company. From the Civil
War through World War II,
Pittsburgh was a thriving
metropolis, but in the 1950s and
1960s its fortunes faded.

Endowed by steel magnate
Andrew Carnegie, the **Carnegie
Museum of Art** offers a
brilliantly lit suite of galleries
with collections ranging from
ancient Egyptian sculpture to
Impressionist, Post-Impressionist, and modern American
art by Roy Lichtenstein and
Alexander Calder. The Hall of
Sculpture is a two-storied
columned hall that replicates
the interior of the Temple of
Athena in Athens. It is adorned
with casts from the Greek
classical era. Next door, the Hall
of Architecture is filled with
reproductions of some of the
best examples of classical,
medieval, and Renaissance
architectural details. The
Carnegie Museum of Natural
History, in the same complex,
opens out on a central gallery
and relies on filtered natural
light as a part of its architectural

charm. Exhibits change from
time to time, but most of the
displays consist of dioramas that
feature taxidermy specimens.

At the **Carnegie Science
Center** on Allegheny Avenue,
the idea is to make science
accessible through play. More
than 40,000 sq ft
(3,716 sq m) of the
186,000-sq-ft
(17,280-sq-m)
center is devoted
to numerous
interactive exhibits.
The Miniature
Railroad and Village
displays the rich
historical,
architectural, and
cultural heritage
of western
Pennsylvania. In the four-story
Rangos Omnimax® Theater,
audience members recline
while images are projected onto

Students relaxing at Pittsburgh
University

Hall of Sculpture at Carnegie Museum of
Art, Pittsburgh

a 79-ft (24-m) domed ceiling.
The 42-story **Cathedral of
Learning** houses the University
of Pittsburgh's Nationality
Classrooms, which seek to
reflect the different ethnic
groups that contribute to the
city's heritage. Started in the
1930s, each of the 26 rooms, the
last of which were completed in
2000, has authentic decor and
furnishings depicting a unique
time and place from 5th-
century BC Greece to
16th-century Poland.

In the city's north side, the
tile-clad exterior of the **Andy
Warhol Museum** reflects the
workaday character of the
neighborhood. Appearances
are deceptive here, and this
former warehouse conceals a
brightly illuminated,
ultramodern interior. The
museum celebrates the
Pittsburgh-born
founder of
American Pop Art,
Andy Warhol
(1928–87), through
selections of works
from its archives.
These include
paintings, and
video and film
clips. Works of
related artists are
also on display.

Located 5 miles
(8 km) southeast of Pittsburgh is
**Kennywood Amusement Park**.
It was built in 1905 as a Luna
Park, a popular name for
amusement parks that
showcased the new electric
light bulb. The park offers thrill
rides, a stunt show, and a 1926
carousel made by the Dentzel
Company – premier hand-
carvers of carousel animals.

🏛 **Carnegie Museum of Art**
4,400 Forbes Ave. **Tel** (412) 622-3131.
**Open** Jul–Aug: 10am–5pm Mon–Sat
(to 8pm Thu), noon–5pm Sun; Sep–
Jun: 10am–5pm Tue–Sat (to 8pm Thu);
noon–5pm Sun. **Closed** public hols.
🅿 ♿ 🖥 🏛 🌐 cmoa.org;
🌐 carnegiemnh.org

🏛 **Andy Warhol Museum**
117 Sandusky St. **Tel** (412) 237-8300.
**Open** 10am–5pm Tue–Sun.
**Closed** public hols. 🅿 🖥 🏛
🌐 warhol.org

*For hotels and restaurants see pp122–7*

# ㉖ Laurel Highlands

🛈 120 E Main St Ligonier, (800) 333-5661. Ⓦ **laurelhighlands.org**

To the south of Pittsburgh, ridges gather together, valleys become canyons, and mountain laurel covers the slopes, giving the region its name. The splendid 1,700-ft- (518-m) deep Youghiogheny Gorge cuts through the scenic Laurel Ridge Mountains, where an area of nearly 30 sq miles (77 sq km) forms the **Ohiopyle State Park**. The park includes more than 28 miles (45 km) of the Youghiogheny River. White-water rafting is popular here, as are hiking, jogging, biking, and cross-country skiing on the 43-mile (69-km) Youghiogheny River Trail.

**Fallingwater**, an architectural tour de force by renowned architect Frank Lloyd Wright, lies north of the park. Built in 1936, the house reflects Wright's interest in structures that were an integral part of the landscape.

**Laurel Ridge State Park** stretches from the village of Ohiopyle in the west to the Conemaugh River in the east. The 70-mile (113-km) Laurel Highlands Hiking Trail is open all year round. The Johnstown Flood Museum chronicles the Conemaugh River disaster that killed more than 2,000 people and destroyed Johnstown in 1889.

🏕 **Ohiopyle State Park**
7 Sheridan St, Ohiopyle. **Tel** (724) 329-8591. **Open** daily.

## The Amish

All Amish trace their roots to the Swiss Anabaptist ("New Birth") movement of 1525, an offshoot of the Protestant Reformation, whose creed rejected the formality of established churches. Today's Old Order Amish are the most conservative of the sect, disdaining any device that would connect them to the larger world, including electricity, phones, and cars. Conspicuous because of their plain, dark attire – with white prayer caps for the women and straw hats for the men – and their horse-and-buggy mode of transportation, the Amish in America are little changed from their 17th-century ancestors who came seeking religious freedom.

Amish buggy on a rural highway

🏠 **Fallingwater**
SR 381, Mill Run. **Tel** (724) 329-8501. **Open** mid-Mar–end-Nov: 10am–4pm Thu–Tue (11am–3pm Fri–Sun in winter). **Closed** Jan, Feb, Easter, Thanksgiving, Dec 25. 🅿 🖼 Ⓦ **paconserve.org**

# ㉗ Western Amish Country

🛈 229 S Jefferson St, New Castle, (888) 284-7599.

The scenic territory around the town of New Castle, 56 miles (145 km) from Pittsburgh, is a hand-stitched quilt of agricultural acreage, parks, and villages. Like the residents of the Pennsylvania Dutch Country near Lancaster (see p116), a large population of Old Order Amish and Mennonites have plowed and planted farms in the Enon Valley, near New Castle. **Montgomery Locks and Dam**, completed in 1936, is one of 20 huge locks and dams on the Ohio River from Pittsburgh to Cairo, Illinois. The dam creates a pool more than 18 miles (29 km) long for recreational and commercial use.

**McConnell's Mill State Park** follows the path of Slippery Rock Creek and contains a former water-driven gristmill, now a museum. The untamed beauty of Slippery Rock Gorge is very popular with rock climbers and rappellers.

**Moraine State Park**, about 5 miles (8 km) east of McConnell's Park, is a small paradise reborn from an industrial wasteland where mining flourished until the 1950s. Mines were then sealed, gas and oil wells plugged, and the 5-sq-mile (13-sq-km) Lake Arthur was constructed.

🏕 **McConnell's Mill State Park**
Portersville. **Tel** (724) 368-8091. **Open** sunrise–sunset daily.

The Youghiogheny River looping through Ohiopyle State Park, Laurel Highlands

# Practical Information

Successful traveling around New York, New Jersey, and Pennsylvania benefits from advance planning, simply because there is so much to see and do in such a concentrated area. The major cities are packed with attractions, hotels, and restaurants, while the expansive and diverse areas in between often double as resort areas, catering to city-dwellers in need of a change of pace. Depending upon the time, you can explore significant historical sights, appreciate stunning scenery, take in a local celebration, or simply relax along the coast.

## Tourist Information

New York, New Jersey, and Pennsylvania each publishes a wide variety of informative, richly illustrated travel brochures. All of this information can be ordered by telephone or accessed via websites, and further information is available from the multitude of local and regional tourism bureaus across the three states. The wealth of available information covers climate, transportation, attractions, accommodations, restaurants, recreation, festivals, regional history, and much more.

## Natural Hazards

Thunderstorms occur frequently across the Mid-Atlantic Region. A basic precaution that visitors should take, if they find themselves in the middle of a sudden storm, is never to stand under a tree, as they are perfect targets for lightning strikes.

Also, there is danger of the tree toppling due to strong winds. Western New York State and Pennsylvania experience extreme winter conditions; the Adirondacks face severe winter storms and sub-zero temperatures, while sudden heavy snowfalls often cause chaos in New York City. Visitors should listen for weather warnings and broadcasts on the radio and TV.

## Getting Around

Unlike much of the US, the Mid-Atlantic is a region where you can get around without a car. Some of the faster train services in the US link New York and Washington, DC with Philadelphia, bringing the two cities within an hour of each other. Other lines run across Pennsylvania, up the Hudson Valley between New York City and Albany, then across to Buffalo and Niagara Falls, and

between Philadelphia and Atlantic City. Seat belts are required for drivers and front-seat passengers in the entire Mid-Atlantic Region. Most states also require seat belts for back-seat passengers, and child seats are required for all automobile occupants age 4 and under. Speed limits vary but are usually 70 to 75 mph (113 to 121 km/h) on Interstate Highways outside of densely populated urban areas, weather permitting. Talking on a cell phone while driving is dangerous and against the law.

## Events & Festivals

New York City and the Mid-Atlantic states stage a diverse range of annual community, regional, and national festivals. One of the nation's most unusual annual events takes place in central Pennsylvania on February 2, when a chubby rodent named "Punxsutawney Phil" wakes up from his winter hibernation on **Groundhog Day**. "Phil" forecasts the advent of spring, which in US folklore is related to whether he can see his shadow. In March, as an expression of New York City's strong Irish heritage, the city politicians and other characters march through the city as part of a boisterous **St. Patrick's Day** celebration. Summer brings a deluge of outdoor events, fireworks, and concerts in city parks. Street festivals are the norm for community celebrations of the July 4 Independence Day holiday. County and state fairs crop up in the Mid-Atlantic countryside in July and August, as do music festivals like the **Glimmerglass Opera Festival** in Cooperstown. The Christmas shopping season kicks off with the annual extravaganza of massive inflatable figures in the **Macy's Thanksgiving Day** parade in New York City.

## Sports

With high-quality professional teams in every major sport, the New York and Mid-Atlantic

---

### The Climate of the Mid-Atlantic Region

Weather across the vast Mid-Atlantic Region can be as varied as the scenery. New York's Adirondack Mountains are famed for the extremities of climate, while in Long Island and the coastal areas of New Jersey the climate is milder. Western New York and Pennsylvania see some of the nation's heaviest snowfalls in winter. By late spring, the snows melt and the foliage returns to the gardens. Summer brings warm weather and high humidity, and thunderstorms that can put a sudden end to a pleasant day. Late summer and fall have comparatively stable weather.

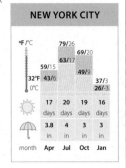

**NEW YORK CITY**

| °F /°C | Apr | Jul | Oct | Jan |
|---|---|---|---|---|
| | | 79/26 | | |
| | | | 69/20 | |
| | 59/15 | 63/17 | | |
| 32°F 43/6 | | | 49/9 | |
| 0°C | | | | 37/3 |
| | | | | 26/-3 |
| ☀ | 17 days | 20 days | 19 days | 16 days |
| ☂ | 3.8 in | 4 in | 3 in | 3 in |
| month | Apr | Jul | Oct | Jan |

Region is a great place to watch some of the world's greatest athletes perform. The cities here host a wide array of professional and amateur sports teams, with major pro baseball, football, and basketball franchises operating in New Jersey, New York City, Philadelphia, and Pittsburgh. Another extremely popular spectator sport is ice hockey.

There are also many "minor league" teams in smaller cities, and hundreds of high-quality sports teams fielded by the various public and private universities across the region.

The baseball season lasts from April to September, football from September through January, and basketball from winter through mid-spring.

However, an extremely popular sports event is the **US Open Tennis Championships**, which is held annually in the borough of Queens in August. Horse-racing's **Belmont Stakes** in early June is the last leg of the "Triple Crown" championship, while throughout the months of July and August racing continues at historic Saratoga Springs. Participant sports are also prominent, with the New York Marathon in November being one of the more popular events.

## Outdoor Activities

New York State is also home to one of the country's prime winter sports resorts – Lake Placid in the Adirondack Mountains, where the 1932 and 1980 Winter Olympics were held. There are also ski areas in the Pocono Mountains of Pennsylvania and New Jersey, as well as Camelback Mountain and Hidden Valley in Western Pennsylvania, and Hunter Mountain and Catamount in Catskills, in New York State. For the best skiing, however, the most avid skiers head to the resorts of Vermont and New Hampshire.

## Entertainment

The world capital of the entertainment industry, New York City is a showcase for just about any form of performance. A quick read of the many local newspapers, like the *New York Times* or the *Village Voice*, and magazines such as *Time Out New York*, *New York Magazine*, and the *New Yorker* will point you toward hundreds of events and activities. **Lincoln Center** is home to many ballet, opera, and orchestral performances, as is legendary **Carnegie Hall**. The region's other large cities, Philadelphia, Pittsburgh, and Newark, also host numerous cultural and entertainment events. Newark's **New Jersey Performing Arts Center** hosts a superb array of music and art events.

## Shopping

New York City is without a doubt one of the world's greatest marketplaces, and it is safe to say that if you cannot buy a certain thing here, it probably does not exist at all. Everything ranging from fashionable boutiques to cut-price computers can be found in Manhattan, and some neighborhoods of New York City cater especially to the interest of shoppers and bargain hunters. Don't miss the opportunity to take a trip to at least one of the city's exceptional and world-famous department stores, such as **Bloomingdale's**, **Macy's**, **Tiffany & Co.**, or **Barney's**.

# DIRECTORY

# Where to Stay

## New York City

### DK Choice

**DOWNTOWN: East Village
Bed & Coffee** $
B&B                    Map D4
*110 Ave C, 10009*
**Tel** *(917) 816-0071*
W bedandcoffee.com
A quirky inn whose themed
rooms range from soothing Zen
and bright Mexican, to earth-
toned beach decor. Each floor
has shared bathrooms and fully
equipped kitchens. Rooms
feature iPod docking stations.

**DOWNTOWN: Off Soho Suites** $
Value                    Map C5
*11 Rivington St, 10002*
**Tel** *(212) 979-9808*
W offsoho.com
Well-maintained budget suites,
with either private or shared
kitchens, and a fitness center.

**DOWNTOWN: Marriott New
York City Financial Center** $$
Business                Map C5
*85 W St, 10006*
**Tel** *(212) 385-4900*
W marriott.com
This modern, grand hotel offers
an indoor pool and views of
the Statue of Liberty.

**DOWNTOWN: Crosby
Street Hotel** $$$
Boutique                Map D4
*79 Crosby St, 10012*
**Tel** *(212) 226-6400*
W firmdalehotels.com
A slice of upscale London,
featuring cheerful rooms,
afternoon tea, and a plush
restaurant.

**DOWNTOWN: Inn at
Irving Place** $$$
B&B                    Map D4
*56 Irving Place, 10003*
**Tel** *(212) 533-4600*
W innatirving.com
This exclusive guesthouse in
two magnificent adjoining
brownstones offers elegant
rooms with upscale amenities.

**DOWNTOWN: The James** $$$
Boutique                Map C4
*27 Grand St, 10013*
**Tel** *(212) 465-2000*
W jameshotels.com
Elegant rooms feature rain
showers and natural linens,
while the rooftop bar offers
skyline views.

**DOWNTOWN: SoHo
Grand Hotel** $$$
Boutique                Map C4
*301 W Broadway, 10013*
**Tel** *(212) 965-3000*
W sohogrand.com
A sophisticated hotel with tasteful
rooms, a lively bar, and great
views of downtown Manhattan.

**MIDTOWN: Chelsea Star Hotel** $
Value                    Map D3
*300 W 30th St, 10011*
**Tel** *(212) 244-7827*
W starhotelny.com
A life-size statue of Betty Boop
greets guests at this colorful
hotel. Dorms and private rooms.

**MIDTOWN: La Quinta
Manhattan** $
Value                    Map D3
*17 W 32nd St, 10001*
**Tel** *(212) 736-1600*
W lq.com
Guests here enjoy comfortable
rooms, a lovely rooftop bar, and
complimentary breakfast.

### DK Choice

**MIDTOWN: POD 51** $
Value                    Map E3
*230 E 51st St, 10022*
**Tel** *(212) 355-0300*
W podhotel.com
One of New York City's best
budget hotels – the rooms
are small and "pod-like" but
shrewdly outfitted with colorful
furnishings, comfortable
beds, and flat-screen TVs. The
lobby features bright murals,
communal tables, a friendly
concierge, and a café/bar
with a daily happy hour. Relax
on the rooftop, with views of
the skyscrapers of Midtown.

**MIDTOWN: Ace Hotel** $$
Boutique                Map D3
*20 W 29th St, 10001*
**Tel** *(212) 679-2222*
W acehotel.com
A chic rock 'n' roll hotel with
more than 200 rooms, most
featuring art by local and
international artists.

**MIDTOWN: Andaz
5th Avenue** $$
Boutique                Map D3
*485 5th Ave, 10017*
**Tel** *(212) 601-1234*
W newyork.5thavenue.andaz.
hyatt.com
This sleek hotel offers loft-style,
hypoallergenic rooms with state-
of-the-art air purification systems.

**MIDTOWN: Library Hotel** $$
Boutique                Map D3
*299 Madison Ave, 10017*
**Tel** *(212) 983-4500*
W libraryhotel.com
A library theme drives the decor
of this charming hotel. There are
books in all the elegant rooms,
plus a poetry garden.

**MIDTOWN:
The London NYC** $$$
Luxury                  Map E2
*151 W 54th St, 10019*
**Tel** *(212) 307-5000*
W thelondonnyc.com
A mural of London's Hyde
Park defines this grand hotel.
Enjoy creative cuisine at Gordon
Ramsay's on-site restaurant.

**MIDTOWN: The Standard** $$$
Boutique                Map C3
*848 Washington St, 10014*
**Tel** *(212) 645-4646*
W standardhotels.com
This trendy hotel soaring over the
Meatpacking District has amazing
river or city views. The rooftop bar
is a magnet for celebrities.

**UPPER EAST SIDE:
Bentley Hotel** $$
Boutique                Map E3
*500 E 62nd St, 10065*
**Tel** *(212) 644-6000*
W bentleyhotelnyc.com
A towering hotel with stellar
views of the East River. Spacious
rooms feature designer amenities
and marble bathrooms.

The sumptuous London NYC, Manhattan's
tallest hotel

Room with Asian-style decor at the Mandarin Oriental

**UPPER EAST SIDE:**
**The Pierre** $$$
Luxury          Map E2
2 E 61st St, 10021
**Tel** (212) 838-8000
W tajhotels.com
A grand lobby gives way to
impeccable rooms, some with
Central Park views. Sophisticated
amenities include a special
room-service menu for pets.

**UPPER EAST SIDE:**
**Sherry-Netherland** $$$
Luxury          Map E3
781 5th Ave, 10022
**Tel** (212) 355-2800
W sherrynetherland.com
This old-world hotel with huge,
well-appointed suites offers luxury
living and top-of-the-line service.

**UPPER WEST SIDE: Hostelling**
**International New York** $
Value
891 Amsterdam Ave, 10025
**Tel** (212) 932-2300
W hinewyork.org
A vast hostel resembling a
campus dorm, with a cafeteria,
a games room, and picnic tables.

**UPPER WEST SIDE:**
**Mandarin Oriental** $$$
Luxury
80 Columbus Circle, 10023
**Tel** (212) 805-8800
W mandarinoriental.com
This dramatic hotel with Asian-
inspired opulence offers over 200
luxuriously appointed rooms, a
trendy bar, and a superlative spa.

## New York State

**ALBANY: Morgan State House** $$
B&B
393 State St, 12210
**Tel** (518) 427-6063
W statehouse.com
This elegant, European-style
urban inn in a historic
neighborhood has an English

garden. Spacious rooms feature
luxurious bedding and amenities.
No children under 16.

**BUFFALO: Hyatt Regency** $$
Boutique
2 Fountain Plaza, 14202
**Tel** (716) 856-1234
W buffalo.hyatt.com
Located in the heart of the theater
and financial districts, this hotel
offers spacious rooms and
panoramic views.

### DK Choice

**EAST HAMPTON:**
**The Maidstone** $$$
Luxury
207 Main St, 11937
**Tel** (631) 324-5006
W themaidstone.com
This plush B&B in the storied
East End of Long Island opened
to guests in the 1870s. The
stylish decor does not preclude
a warm, friendly atmosphere
with gracious service. The cozy
rooms are ultra-comfortable
and packed with modern
amenities. It has glorious
gardens and a chic lounge.

**LAKE GEORGE:**
**The Georgian Resort** $$
Value
384 Canada St, 12845
**Tel** (518) 668-5401
W georgianresort.com
A lakeside resort hotel offering
comfortable rooms, a relaxing
private beach, on-site restaurant,
and a heated outdoor pool.

**LAKE PLACID:**
**Lake Placid Lodge** $$$
Luxury
144 Lodge Way, 12946
**Tel** (518) 523-2700
W lakeplacidlodge.com
At this legendary property on
Lake Placid, choose from lakeside
suites, private cabins, and lodge
rooms. No children under 12.

**NIAGARA FALLS: The Red**
**Coach Inn** $$$
Historic
2 Buffalo Ave, 14303
**Tel** (716) 282-1459
W redcoach.com
An English Tudor-style property
located just minutes from the
Falls. Comfortable rooms are
fitted with antiques and a
complimentary breakfast is served.

**ROCHESTER:**
**Strathallan Hotel** $$
Boutique
550 E Ave, 14607
**Tel** (585) 461-5010
W strathallan.com
Elegant property with charming
European-style decor. The rooms
are stylish and comfortable, with
upscale amenities, and service is
friendly and efficient.

**SARATOGA SPRINGS:**
**Saratoga Arms** $$$
Luxury
497 Broadway, 12866
**Tel** (518) 584-1775
W saratogaarms.com
An elegant hotel combining
historic charm with modern
amenities. Romantic rooms have
fireplaces. Breakfast is included.

**SOUTHAMPTON: 1708 House** $$
B&B
126 Main St, 11968
**Tel** (631) 287-1708
W 1708house.com
Historic inn near the heart of
town, with cozy rooms, a parlor
with a fireplace, and a wood-
paneled reading room. Free
parking pass for local beaches.

**SYRACUSE: Jefferson**
**Clinton Hotel** $$
Historic
416 South Clinton St, 13202
**Tel** (315) 425-0500
W jeffersonclintonhotel.com
Rooms are comfortable and well-
appointed at this 1927 hotel in
downtown Armory Square.
Complimentary buffet breakfast.

## New Jersey

**ATLANTIC CITY: Borgata Hotel**
**Casino & Spa** $$$
Luxury
1 Borgata Way, 08401
**Tel** (609) 317-1000
W theborgata.com
Located off the lively Boardwalk,
this hotel offers dramatic archi-
tecture, a lovely pool and gardens,
two spas, and top-notch dining.
The spacious rooms have large
windows and plush amenities.

**For more information on types of hotels** see pages 26–7

**DK Choice**

**CAPE MAY: The Queen Victoria Bed and Breakfast** $$
B&B
*102 Ocean St, 08204*
**Tel** *(609) 884-8702*
W queenvictoria.com
This restored Victorian property is Cape May's premier B&B. In the heart of the historic district, it is close to the beach and the town's attractions. The individually styled rooms are spacious and comfortable, with a mix of modern and antique decor. Relax in the parlors and porches, or explore the area on a complimentary bike.

**HOBOKEN: W Hoboken** $$$
Boutique
*225 River St, 07030*
**Tel** *(201) 253-2400*
W whoboken.com
A chic hotel offering stylish decor, stunning views of New York City's skyline, a trendy cocktail bar, and a luxurious spa.

**NEWARK: Courtyard Newark Downtown** $
Value
*858 Broad St, 07102*
**Tel** *(973) 848-0070*
W marriott.com
This modern hotel combines plush, spacious rooms with friendly service. The comfortable lobby and communal areas are great for working or relaxing.

**PRINCETON: Inn at Glencairn** $$
B&B
*3301 Lawrenceville Rd, 08540*
**Tel** *(609) 497-1737*
W innatglencairn.com
A renovated Georgian manor set in lush grounds. Rooms come with comfortable four-poster beds and antique furnishings.

# Pennsylvania

**GETTYSBURG: The Inn at Herr Ridge** $$
B&B
*900 Chambersburg Rd, 17325*
**Tel** *(717) 334-4332*
W innatherrridge.com
Once a Confederate hospital, this is now a welcoming adults-only inn offering cozy, flamboyantly decorated rooms. Conveniently located close to the historic battlefields.

**DK Choice**

**HERSHEY: The Hotel Hershey** $$$
Luxury
*100 Hotel Rd, 17033*
**Tel** *(717) 533-2171*
W thehotelhershey.com
This sprawling retreat, hugely popular with families, offers reflecting pools, fountains, and lush gardens. Delicious chocolate is present throughout, from a chocolate kiss on the pillow to a decadent chocolate bath at the spa. The elegant rooms and guest cottages boast panoramic views of the grounds and Hershey Valley. Activities on offer include golf, basketball, volleyball, tennis, and hiking.

**LANCASTER: Fulton Steamboat Inn** $$
Historic
*Routes 30 and 896, 17602*
**Tel** *(717) 299-9999*
W fultonsteamboatinn.com
This charming property resembles a 19th-century steamboat, with nautical- and Victorian-themed guest rooms. The lovely patio has a fire pit and koi pond. Activities for children are on offer.

**LANCASTER: Lancaster Arts Hotel** $$
Boutique
*300 Harrisburg Ave, 17602*
**Tel** *(717) 299-3000*
W lancasterartshotel.com
Deluxe accommodations in the heart of downtown, with original artwork displayed throughout. The guest rooms feature modern comforts alongside exposed brick and wooden beams.

**PHILADELPHIA: Four Points by Sheraton Philadelphia City Center** $$
Chain
*1201 Race St, 19107*
**Tel** *(215) 496-2700*
W fourpointsphiladelphia citycenter.com
The stylish, comfortable rooms at this conveniently located hotel offer complimentary perks, such as bottled water, Wi-Fi, and coffee. Good business amenities.

**PHILADELPHIA: Rittenhouse 1715** $$
Luxury
*1715 Rittenhouse Square St, 19103*
**Tel** *(215) 546-6500*
W rittenhouse1715.com
An exclusive hotel known for its impeccable service. It offers a tranquil atmosphere in a cosmopolitan location and elegant, well-appointed rooms.

**PHILADELPHIA: Spruce Hill Manor** $$
B&B
*3709 Baring St, 19104*
**Tel** *(215) 472-2213*
W sprucehillmanor.com
This Victorian mansion surrounded by lush gardens is in a quiet residential location. Handsome rooms have antique furnishings and kitchenettes.

**PITTSBURGH: DoubleTree by Hilton Pittsburgh Downtown** $$
Value
*1 Bigelow Sq, 15219*
**Tel** *(412) 281-5800*
W doubletree3.hilton.com
Modern, stylish hotel with a wealth of on-site amenities, comfortable rooms, and a complimentary shuttle service.

**PITTSBURGH: The Priory** $$
Boutique
*614 Pressley St, 15212*
**Tel** *(412) 231-3338*
W thepriory.com
The Priory is a charming European-style property that was once home to Benedictine monks. Plush rooms have all the amenities. There is a cozy sitting room and a lovely courtyard.

The Hotel Hershey, set in beautiful grounds

# Where to Eat and Drink

## New York City

**DOWNTOWN: Corner Bistro** $
American **Map** C3
*331 W 4th St, 10014*
**Tel** *(212) 242-9502*
Some of the best burgers in the city make this dive bar a cult favorite. Choose from the extensive menu of local beers.

**DOWNTOWN: Katz's Delicatessen** $
Deli **Map** D4
*205 E Houston St, 10002*
**Tel** *(212) 254-2246*
A New York institution, this Jewish deli serves towering pastrami or corned-beef sandwiches and other local delicacies. Vegetarians can relish the fat *knishes* (potato and cabbage dumplings) and *matzoh* ball soup.

**DOWNTOWN: Shake Shack** $
American **Map** D4
*SE cnr of Madison Square Park, near Madison Ave and E 23rd St, 10010*
**Tel** *(212) 889-6600*
Relish the juicy burgers and crinkle-cut fries served at this perennially popular shack, while sitting under the cool shade of trees. Delicious shakes.

**DOWNTOWN: Balthazar** $$
French **Map** D4
*80 Spring St, 10012*
**Tel** *(212) 965-1414*
Atmospheric bistro with large picture windows overlooking Spring Street. Restaurateur Keith McNally's crown jewel serves all the French favorites – *steak-frites*, oysters, and Bordeaux wine.

**DOWNTOWN: Blue Hill** $$
New American **Map** D4
*75 Washington Place, 10011*
**Tel** *(212) 539-1776*
This restaurant uses the freshest seasonal ingredients sourced from local farms in its dishes. The elaborate "Farmer's Feast" five-course tasting menu is based on the week's harvest.

**DOWNTOWN: Momofuku Noodle Bar** $$
Asian **Map** D4
*171 1st Ave, 10003*
**Tel** *(212) 475-7899*
Celebrated Korean-American chef David Chang offers innovative ramen and other Japanese classics. Try the pork buns or the fried chicken, which comes with pancakes. Delectable desserts.

Pure Food and Wine, a vegan restaurant serving food in its natural and purest state

**DOWNTOWN: Otto** $$
Italian **Map** D4
*15th Ave, 10003*
**Tel** *(212) 995-9559*
Buzzing, upscale pizzeria from chef Mario Batali – do not miss the lardo pizza. The wine list has excellent vintages from Italy.

**DOWNTOWN: Pure Food and Wine** $$
Vegetarian **Map** D4
*54 Irving Place, 10003*
**Tel** *(212) 477-1010*
Unique and upscale restaurant dedicated to raw vegan cuisine, without the use of processed ingredients. Try the coconut noodles and zucchini lasagne.

**DOWNTOWN: The Spotted Pig** $$
British **Map** C3
*314 W 11th St, 10014*
**Tel** *(212) 620-0393*
Britons will feel at home in this upscale pub. Excellent wine list and plenty of stouts and ales. Try the five-course vegetarian platter.

**DOWNTOWN: Eleven Madison Park** $$$
American/French **Map** C3
*11 Madison Ave, 10010*
**Tel** *(212) 889-0905* **Closed** *Sun*
Contemporary cuisine is served in this Art Deco restaurant. The food is exquisite, but it comes at a price. Payment by credit card.

**MIDTOWN: Burger Joint at Le Parker Meridien** $
American **Map** E2
*119 W 57th St, 10019*
**Tel** *(212) 708-7414*
Mouthwatering burgers, shakes, and beers are served in the lobby of Le Parker Meridien hotel.

**Price Guide**
The following prices are for a three-course meal per person, with a glass of house wine, including tax and service.

| | |
|---|---|
| $ | up to $30 |
| $$ | $30 to $60 |
| $$$ | over $60 |

**MIDTOWN: Carnegie Deli** $
Deli **Map** E2
*854 7th Ave, 10019*
**Tel** *800-334-5606*
Huge pastrami or corned beef sandwiches are on offer at this classic New York deli. Also worth trying are the delicious *knishes* (dumplings).

**MIDTOWN: Empire Diner** $$
American **Map** C3
*210 10th Ave, 10011*
**Tel** *(212) 596-7523*
This chrome Art Deco diner takes comfort food to a high art, from *matzoh* ball bone marrow soup to a juicy burger on a brioche bun. This is a great place to stop off and refuel halfway along the Highline.

**MIDTOWN: Grand Central Oyster Bar** $$
Seafood **Map** E3
*Grand Central, Lower Level, 42nd St, 10017*
**Tel** *(212) 490-6650*
Sample fresh oysters at this seafood palace. The simple preparation – a squirt of lemon or a hand-plucked garnish – allows the delicious fresh fish and shellfish to shine on their own merit.

**MIDTOWN: Le Bernardin** $$$
French **Map** E2
*155 W 51st St, 10019*
**Tel** *(212) 554-1515*
Chef Eric Ripert turns out French masterpieces at this elegant restaurants. Creative dishes include red snapper with charred green tomatoes. Great for seafood lovers.

### DK Choice

**UPPER EAST SIDE: Daniel** $$$
French **Map** E2
*60 E 65th St, 10021*
**Tel** *(212) 288-0033* **Closed** *Sun*
The opulent restaurant of acclaimed chef Daniel Boulud offers a superlative sensory experience, from the first step into the grand dining room and the rich forkful of foie gras to the sinful bite of the sinful chocolate mousse. Excellent wine list and seamless service.

**For more information on types of restaurants** *see pages 28–9*

**UPPER WEST SIDE: Per Se** $$$
American                    Map E2
*10 Columbus Circle, 10019*
**Tel** *(212) 823-9335*
Famed chef Thomas Keller brings superlative Californian cuisine to New York, served as nine-course tasting menus. Excellent selection of wines. Spectacular views of Central Park.

**FARTHER AFIELD: Sripraphai** $
Thai
*64-13 39th Ave, Queens, 11377*
**Tel** *(718) 899-9599*    **Closed** *Wed*
Locals swear by this hole-in-the-wall place, said to serve the best Thai in the city. There is an elaborate menu dedicated to vegetarian food – try the sautéed drunken noodles with tofu, vegetables, chili, and basil leaves.

## DK Choice

**FARTHER AFIELD: Peter Luger Steak House** $$$
American
*178 Broadway, Brooklyn, 11211*
**Tel** *(718) 387-7400*
For over 125 years, this New York institution has been satisfying carnivores with massive juicy slabs, from porterhouse to prime rib and pot roast. Their delectable steak sauce is also sold in bottles.

# New York State

**ALBANY: Scrimshaw** $$
Seafood/Steak House
*660 Albany Shaker Rd, 12211*
**Tel** *(518) 869-8100*  **Closed** *Sun–Tue*
This popular restaurant in the Desmond Hotel has a broad selection of dishes. Choose from classics like seared swordfish to more innovative fare such as Atlantic salmon with a tangerine-ginger glaze. Reserve ahead.

**BINGHAMTON: Number 5** $$$
Steak House
*33 S Washington St, 13903*
**Tel** *(607) 723-0555*
Housed in an antique-filled fire station built in 1897, Number 5 is a great setting for an intimate meal or a large gathering. Traditional favorites include seared salmon and filet mignon.

**BUFFALO: Anchor Bar** $
American
*1047 Main St, 14209*
**Tel** *(716) 886-8920*
Visitors and locals alike flock to this old-school spot, home of the city's iconic namesake chicken wings. Spicy buffalo wings, burgers, sandwiches, and other bar favorites are on offer.

**COOPERSTOWN: Nicoletta's Italian Café** $
Italian
*96 Main St, 13326*
**Tel** *(607) 547-7499*
This family-owned spot offers traditional Italian specialties such as sausage with roasted peppers and clam linguine. Reservations recommended in summer.

## DK Choice

**EAST HAMPTON: The 1770 House Restaurant & Inn** $$$
New American
*143 Main St, 11937*
**Tel** *(631) 324-1770*   **Closed** *Sun*
A quintessential Hamptons dining spot, dotted with antique furnishings and historical memorabilia. The seasonal menu has innovative dishes that feature fresh ingredients. An award-winning wine list and tasty dessert menu round out the experience. The downstairs tavern offers casual pub fare.

**ITHACA: Moosewood** $$
Vegetarian
*215 N Cayuga St, 14850*
**Tel** *(607) 273-9610*
Set in a historic school building, Moosewood has been serving organic, vegetarian fare since 1973. The daily-changing menu depends on what's fresh. Guests can also purchase Moosewood's best-selling cookbooks.

**LAKE GEORGE: The Log Jam Restaurant** $$
American
*1484 State Route 9, Site 1, 12845*
**Tel** *(518) 798-1155*
The log cabin offers breathtaking views, while fireplaces and a pot-belly stove provide warmth. The seafood, prime rib, and lamb chops are all superb.

**LAKE PLACID: Paradox Lodge** $$$
French
*2169 Saranac Ave, 12946*
**Tel** *(518) 523-9078*    **Closed** *Mon–Wed*
Paradox Lodge is a family-owned gem with a warm and inviting atmosphere, offering a range of fresh steak and seafood dishes. Friendly service. Reservations recommended.

**NIAGARA FALLS: Donatello's Restaurant** $
American
*466 3rd St, 14301*
**Tel** *(716) 282-2069*    **Closed** *Sun*
Close to the Falls, Donatello's is popular for its doughy pizza, hot sandwiches, and tangy wings, all at reasonable prices. Friendly service. Great for kids.

**ROCHESTER: Nick Tahou Hots** $
American
*320 W Main St, 14608*
**Tel** *(585) 436-0184*    **Closed** *Sun*
This local institution is home of the original Garbage Plate – a combination of several diner favorites all on one plate. An unmissable tourist destination.

# New Jersey

## DK Choice

**ATLANTIC CITY: Atlantic City Bar and Grill** $$
Seafood
*1219 Pacific Ave, 08401*
**Tel** *(609) 348-8080*
This family-owned restaurant has long been a favorite with locals, visitors, and celebrities. Steaks, crabs, shrimp cocktails, lobsters, mussels, home-made pastas, burgers, sandwiches, and pizzas are served in a friendly environment. Sports memorabilia adorn the walls.

Steak dish at Peter Luger Steak House, Brooklyn

### CAPE MAY: Cabanas Beach Bar & Grill $
American
429 Beach Ave, 08204
Tel (609) 884-4800 Closed Mon–Wed
Family-friendly oceanfront spot serving sandwiches, seafood, and more. Choose from oysters, shrimp, shellfish specialties, chicken, tacos, burgers, and prime ribs. Pool tables, large-screen TVs, and live music entertain.

### HOBOKEN: Amanda's $$
New American
908 Washington St, 07030
Tel (201) 798-0101
Beautifully restored brownstone with an elegant but comfortable dining room. The sophisticated menu features roasted meats, seared fish, and fresh vegetables. Popular brunch spot.

### NEWARK: Hobby's Delicatessen & Restaurant $
Deli
32 Branford Pl, 07102
Tel (973) 623-0410 Closed Sun
This family-owned Jewish deli is a downtown staple serving legendary corned beef, hearty soups, tender pastrami, house-made pickles, and other Eastern European delicacies. The friendly service and atmosphere attract a loyal clientele.

### TRENTON: Delorenzo's Pizza $
Pizzeria
147 Sloan Ave, 08619
Tel (609) 393-2952 Closed Mon
This family-run restaurant draws fans of the Trenton Tomato Pie. The menu features thin-crust pizzas with a variety of toppings, as well as salads and soups.

# Pennsylvania

### GETTYSBURG: Dobbin House Tavern/Alexander Dobbin Dining Room $$
American
89 Steinwehr Ave, 17325
Tel (717) 334-2100
In a building dating from 1776, this intimate restaurant offers historic meals in a historic setting with original fireplaces. Colonial dishes include roast duck and pork tenderloin with raspberry. Reservations are recommended.

### HERSHEY: Hershey Pantry $
American
801 E Chocolate Ave, 17033
Tel (717) 533-7505 Closed Sun
Locals and visitors alike crowd here for the region's best breakfast. Home-made baked

Colonial decor and a waitress in period costume at City Tavern, Philadelphia

goods, French toast, and hearty plates please all appetites. The lunch and dinner menu includes seafood, pasta, hearty salads, sandwiches, steaks, and home-made desserts.

### LANCASTER: Silver Spring Family Restaurant $
American
3653 Marietta Ave, 17601
Tel (717) 285-5974
This casual, family-style reastaurant serves breakfast, lunch, and dinner. The expansive menu has everything from salads and burgers to meatloaf and pasta with meatballs. Friendly service keeps the regulars coming back.

### LANCASTER: The Greenfield Restaurant $$
American
595 Greenfield Rd, 17601
Tel (717) 393-0668
Located in a restored stone farmhouse, the menu here features classics such as lamb chops, filet mignon, and crab cakes. Enjoy a drink in the wine cellar or lounge. Live jazz weekly.

### PHILADELPHIA: Jim's Steaks $
Steak House
400 South St, 19147
Tel (215) 928-1911
Long lines are ever-present outside this popular eatery's distinctive Art Deco storefront. The authentic Philly cheese steaks topped with mounds of onions and dripping hot cheese keep the crowds coming back for more.

### PHILADELPHIA: Monk's Café $
Belgian
264 S 16th St, 19146
Tel (215) 545-7005
At this popular gastropub with an incredible selection of fine beers, the kitchen produces mussels served a variety of ways,

as well as burgers, sandwiches, steaks, and seafood. Do try the award-winning pommes frites.

## DK Choice

### PHILADELPHIA: City Tavern $$
American
138 S 2nd St, 19106
Tel (215) 413-1443
This unique restaurant is a historically accurate reconstruction of the original 1773 tavern. The kitchen re-creates 18th-century Colonial-style cuisine with dishes like turkey pot pie and braised rabbit. Ales brewed according to George Washington's and Thomas Jefferson's original recipes are also served. The Colonial decor is complemented by staff in period costume.

### PHILADELPHIA: Zahav $$
Middle Eastern
237 St James Pl, 19106
Tel (215) 625-8800
An eclectic, one-of-a-kind eatery in Society Hill offering refined dining in a casual atmosphere. Traditional Israeli cuisine blends with modern techniques. Hummus and laffa bread is an essential starter, though the entire adventurous menu impresses.

### PITTSBURGH: Primanti Brothers $
Sandwich deli
46 18th St, 15222
Tel (412) 263-2142
This 24-hour eatery is a beloved fixture with multiple locations. Giant sandwiches satisfy, especially the infamous cheese steak stuffed with meat, cheese, tomatoes, coleslaw, and French fries. Friendly service and a homey atmosphere.

For more information on types of restaurants see pages 28–9

# NEW ENGLAND

# New England at a Glance

Tucked away in the northeasternmost corner of the United States, the six states of New England are rich in history and culture as well as in natural beauty. Many of the country's earliest settlements were established here, as were the first centers of higher education. The region therefore abounds in historic buildings, as well as in superb museums and prestigious universities. New England's topography includes large tracts of farmland, dense woodlands, pristine lakes, and sweeping coastlines, which are rocky and jagged in some areas and serene and sandy in others. It is also home to the rugged peaks of the White, Green, and Appalachian Mountains.

**Vermont** is an enclave of unspoiled wilderness. Vermont is at its scenic best in fall, when the Green Mountain State changes its verdant green cloak for a rich palette of yellow, orange, and red.

**Canterbury Shaker Village** *(see p176)*, located in New Hampshire, was founded in 1792. This is one of the many picturesque historic villages that are scattered around the rolling farmlands of the state.

**Connecticut** is quintessential New England. Steepled churches around immaculate village greens are typical features of its serene landscape.

Burlington

Brettc Wood

**VERMONT** *(See pp170–73)*

**NEW HAMPSH** *(See pp174–*

Rutland

Concord

Manchester

Bennington

**MASSACHUSE** *(See pp138–59)*

Springfield

Provid

Hartford

**RH ISL** *(See pp1*

**CONNECTICUT** *(See pp164–67)*

New Haven

Stamford

**Block Island** *(see p163)* in Rhode Island is one of the many tranquil havens situated along the pristine shoreline of this tiny state. Great Salt Pond has three marinas and is an excellent spot for kayaking and fishing.

◄ Portland Head Lighthouse in Cape Elizabeth, Fort Williams Park, Maine

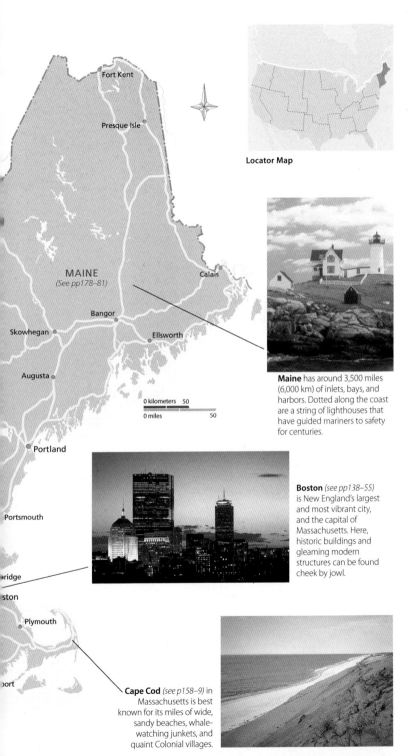

**Locator Map**

**Maine** has around 3,500 miles (6,000 km) of inlets, bays, and harbors. Dotted along the coast are a string of lighthouses that have guided mariners to safety for centuries.

MAINE
*(See pp178–81)*

Fort Kent

Presque Isle

Calais

Bangor

Skowhegan

Ellsworth

Augusta

0 kilometers 50

0 miles 50

Portland

Portsmouth

**Boston** *(see pp138–55)* is New England's largest and most vibrant city, and the capital of Massachusetts. Here, historic buildings and gleaming modern structures can be found cheek by jowl.

ridge

ston

Plymouth

ort

**Cape Cod** *(see p158–9)* in Massachusetts is best known for its miles of wide, sandy beaches, whale-watching junkets, and quaint Colonial villages.

# NEW ENGLAND

For many people, New England is white-steepled churches, craggy coastlines, historic villages, and timeless landscapes of tranquil farmlands and country roads, with the sophisticated city of Boston as its cultural and commercial hub. Many also regard it as the cradle of American civilization, for New England's early history is the history of the United States itself.

From the beginning, the region has been shaped by both geography and climate. Early explorers charted its coastline, and communities soon sprang up by the coast, where goods and people could be ferried more easily from the Old World to the New. Early commerce depended heavily on the ocean, from shipping and whaling to fishing and boat-building.

The harsh, unpredictable climate, poor soil, hilly terrain, and dense virgin forests also helped shape the character of its people. To survive in this area required toughness, ingenuity, and a spirit of independence – all traits that became ingrained in the New England psyche. The slogan "Live free or die" on New Hampshire license plates is a reminder that the same spirit lives on. Indeed, New England today is as much a state of mind as it is a physical space. Despite this, New England is also home to the opulence of Newport, Rhode Island, the beautiful surburban communities of Connecticut, and the self-assured sophistication of Boston.

## History

New England's historical connections are far richer than any other area in America, for it was here that much of the drama of forming a new country was played out. In 1614, the English explorer John Smith sailed along the coast of Massachusetts, named it New England, and declared that it was the best place to set up a new colony. On December 26, 1620, a group of 102 Puritans, who had left England to escape religious persecution, landed at Plymouth Rock after a grueling 66-day voyage on the *Mayflower* and established one of America's first permanent English settlements. Soon, large settlements had also grown up in Boston, Rhode Island, Connecticut, New Hampshire, and Maine.

Stonington, a scenic town on Deer Isle, Penobscot Bay, Maine

◀ A farm surrounded by fall foliage in picturesque Woodstock, Vermont

As the colonists became more prosperous and self-sufficient, their resentment of British control and British taxes increased. The turning point came with the "Boston Tea Party" in 1773, when three British ships arrived at Boston Harbor laden with tea. About 60 local leaders, disguised as Indians, boarded the ships and dumped 342 tea chests, worth about $1,700,000 in today's money, into the harbor as an act of defiance against an oppressive regime.

Meanwhile, locals had begun stockpiling arms in the countryside. In 1775, when British soldiers were sent to Concord to destroy these caches, American patriots (known as "Minutemen," for their ability to muster at a moment's notice) repelled them at Concord and nearby Lexington. They had been tipped off by a dramatic "midnight" horseback ride from Boston by Paul

*Minute Man* statue in Concord

Revere. The American Revolution had begun, with the first major battle at Bunker Hill in Boston on June 17, 1775. The Declaration of Independence, signed by Colonial leaders in Philadephia on July 4, 1776, announced the birth of a new nation.

In the 19th century, New England's maritime trade grew more lucrative, as ships plied between the region's harbors and the West Indies, Europe, and the Far East. The whaling industry reached its zenith at this time, and cotton and wool manufacturing also flourished. New England's role in 19th-century America was not merely one of economic powerhouse. It was the cultural heart of the nation as well. Boston was the center of a strong protest against slavery. Instigated by a newspaper called *The Liberator*, the so-called abolitionist movement set up what came to be known as the Underground Railroad, which provided escape routes for fleeing slaves.

## People & Culture

New England has continued to play an important role in the life of the nation. It was this region that produced the first flowering of American culture, with influential 19th-century literary giants such as Henry David Thoreau, Herman Melville, Nathaniel Hawthorne, and Mark Twain. All these writers won international

### KEY DATES IN HISTORY

**1614** John Smith explores the Northeast coast

**1620** The Pilgrims land at Plymouth

**1630** Group of Puritans settle in Boston

**1636** Harvard, America's first college, founded

**1692** Salem witch trials begin

**1770** British soldiers kill five in Boston Massacre

**1773** New taxes spur Boston Tea Party

**1775** Battles at Concord and Lexington mark beginning of Revolutionary War

**1776** Continental Congress ratifies Declaration of Independence

**1783** Treaty of Paris ends Revolutionary War

**1820** Maine breaks away from Massachusetts and becomes 20th state

**1831** Abolitionist William Lloyd Garrison publishes first edition of anti-slavery newspaper

**1851** Herman Melville publishes *Moby Dick*

**1884** Mark Twain publishes *The Adventures of Huckleberry Finn*

**1897** Country's first subway opens in Boston

**1961** John F. Kennedy becomes president

**2004** Massachusetts becomes first US state to legally recognize gay marriage

**2012** Oldest field in Major League Baseball, Fenway Park, celebrates centenary

**2013** Terrorist bombs set off at the Boston Marathon

Harvard University's Widener Library, the third-largest library in the United States

The New England shoreline, great for sailing

recognition and acclaim. The literary tradition still lives on in New England, led by such outstanding contemporary talents as Anita Shreve, John Irving, and Stephen King, who are all residents of this region. The beauty and majesty of the landscape, which inspired some of America's best-known creative spirits, such as the poet Robert Frost and the painters Winslow Homer and Grandma Moses, still continues to exert its charm on contemporary artists, such as Sabra Field and photographer Abelardo Morell.

In 1636, Harvard College was founded in Boston, making it the birthplace of higher education in America. Today, the region's concentration of educational institutions, including famous Ivy League universities such as Yale and Brown, is a magnet for some of America's best and brightest.

By the mid-19th century, New England's population, which had earlier been quite homogenous, changed dramatically as waves of Irish immigrants arrived, driven from their homeland by the potato famines in the 1840s. Immigrants from Italy, Portugal, and Eastern Europe also arrived, flocking to the textile mills which had boomed in New England just after the Industrial

Revolution. They have left a lasting impact on the region's social life and politics, many of them ascending to the top of New England's social hierarchy – a fact that became evident to the country with the election of the Boston-born Democrat John F. Kennedy (1917–63) in 1960 as the very first Roman Catholic president of the US. Nevertheless, even today there is a special cachet in New England's society for people known as "Boston Brahmins" popularly called WASPs (White Anglo-Saxon Protestants) – descendants of the earliest British settlers.

While industrialization and urbanization have left their stamp on the region, New England's stunning physical beauty still remains. The craggy coastline of Maine, the beautiful beaches located in Cape Cod, the picturesque Vermont villages, the magnificent mountains and forests of New Hampshire, and the places of historic interest found across the region attract thousands of visitors. In recent years, the growth of hi-tech industries in the area has brought a new dynamism and prosperity to New England. This seems fitting, since it was the area's natural beauty that convinced the early settlers of New England's viable future.

National Monument of Forefathers, Plymouth

# Exploring New England

The six states of New England offer a diverse
array of attractions. Vermont is famous for
its ski resorts and rolling farmland, New
Hampshire for its dense forests and spectacular
passes through the White Mountains, and
Maine for its rugged coastline and vast tracts
of wilderness. Farther south, Massachusetts
is rich in history, culture, and scenic beaches,
Connecticut in picture-postcard villages,
and Rhode Island in opulent mansions. The
entire New England region boasts a dazzling
display of fall foliage.

**Key**

— Highway

— Major road

— Railroad

– – State border

–·–·– International border

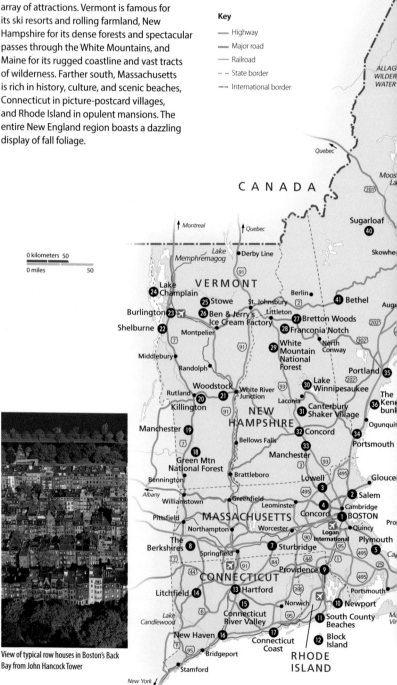

View of typical row houses in Boston's Back
Bay from John Hancock Tower

0 kilometers 50

0 miles 50

ALLAG
WILDER
WATER

Quebec

Moos
La

CANADA

↑ Montreal    ↑ Quebec

Sugarloaf
**40**

Lake
Memphremagog • Derby Line    Skowhe

**VERMONT**    Berlin •    **41** Bethel

Lake
**24** Champlain    **25** Stowe    St. Johnsbury    Aug

Burlington **23**    **26** Ben & Jerry's    Littleton    **27** Bretton Woods

Shelburne **22**    Ice Cream Factory    **28** Franconia Notch

Montpelier    **29** White    North    Portland **35**

Middlebury    Mountain    Conway

Randolph    National
Forest

Woodstock    Lake    The
**30** Winnipesaukee    Ken

Rutland    **21** White River    **36** bun

**20**    Junction    Laconia

Killington    **31** Canterbury
Shaker Village    Ogunqui

**NEW**
HAMPSHIRE    **32** Concord    **34**

Manchester **19**    Bellows Falls    Portsmouth

**18**    **33**

Green Mtn    Manchester
National Forest    Brattleboro    Lowell    Glouce

Bennington    **3**

Albany →    Williamstown    Greenfield    **2** Salem

Pittsfield    Leominster    **4** Cambridge

**MASSACHUSETTS**    Concord    **1** BOSTON

Northampton    Worcester    Logan    Quincy    Pro

The    International
Berkshires **8**    Springfield    **7** Sturbridge    Plymouth

**CONNECTICUT**    Providence    **5** Ca

**9**

Litchfield **14**    **13** Hartford    Portsmouth

**15**    Norwich    **10** Newport

Lake
Candlewood    Connecticut    **11** South County
River Valley    Beaches

New Haven **16**    **17**    **12** Block
Connecticut    Island    M
Coast    Vir
Bridgeport    **RHODE**
ISLAND

Stamford

New York ↙

## Mileage Chart

| | | | | | | | | |
|---|---|---|---|---|---|---|---|---|
| **Boston, MA** | | | | | | | | |
| 40<br>64 | **Plymouth, MA** | | | | | | | |
| 51<br>82 | 54<br>87 | **Providence, RI** | | | | | | |
| 101<br>163 | 134<br>216 | 86<br>138 | **Hartford, CT** | | | | | |
| 137<br>220 | 162<br>261 | 103<br>166 | 39<br>63 | **New Haven, CT** | | | | |
| 216<br>348 | 255<br>410 | 276<br>444 | 235<br>378 | 273<br>439 | **Burlington, VT** | | | |
| 68<br>109 | 106<br>171 | 127<br>204 | 157<br>253 | 193<br>311 | 151<br>243 | **Concord, NH** | | |
| 107<br>172 | 147<br>237 | 156<br>251 | 203<br>327 | 239<br>384 | 208<br>335 | 96<br>154 | **Portland, ME** | |
| 171<br>275 | 211<br>340 | 237<br>381 | 264<br>425 | 302<br>486 | 151<br>243 | 158<br>254 | 73<br>117 | **Bethel, ME** |

**10** = Distance in miles
10 = Distance in kilometers

Busy street of Cape Cod's Provincetown in the summertime

## Sights at a Glance

1 *Boston pp138–55*

### Massachusetts

2 Salem
3 Lowell
4 Concord
5 *Plymouth p157*
6 Cape Cod
7 Sturbridge
8 The Berkshires

### Rhode Island

9 *Providence pp160–61*
10 *Newport pp162–3*
11 South County Beaches
12 Block Island

### Connecticut

13 *Hartford pp164–5*
14 Litchfield
15 Connecticut River Valley
16 New Haven
17 Connecticut Coast

### Vermont

18 Green Mountain National Forest
19 Manchester
20 Killington
21 Woodstock

22 Shelburne Museum & Farms
23 Burlington
24 Lake Champlain
25 Stowe
26 Ben & Jerry's Ice Cream Factory

### New Hampshire

27 Bretton Woods
28 Franconia Notch
29 White Mountain National Forest
30 Lake Winnipesaukee
31 *Canterbury Shaker Village p176*
32 Concord
33 Manchester
34 Portsmouth

### Maine

35 *Portland p178*
36 The Kennebunks
37 Penobscot Bay
38 Acadia National Park
39 Campobello Island
40 Sugarloaf
41 Bethel

# ❶ Boston

Boston is located on the northeastern Atlantic Coast on Massachusetts Bay. Founded in the early 17th century around a large natural harbor at the mouth of the Charles River, the capital of Massachusetts today covers an area of 49 sq miles (127 sq km) and has a population of 630,000. It is a major center of American history, culture, and learning. The central city is focused around the harbor on the Shawmut Peninsula, while Greater Boston encompasses the surrounding area.

Massachusetts State House with its gilded dome, designed by Charles Bulfinch

## Sights at a Glance

① *Beacon Hill pp140–41*
② Black Heritage Trail
③ Boston Common & Public Garden
④ Boston Athenaeum
⑤ *The Freedom Trail pp142–3*
⑥ *Massachusetts State House pp144–5*
⑦ Park Street Church
⑧ Downtown Crossing
⑨ Theater District
⑩ Chinatown
⑪ Post Office Square
⑫ Old South Meeting House
⑬ King's Chapel & Burying Ground
⑭ *Old State House p147*
⑮ Quincy Market
⑯ Copp's Hill Burying Ground
⑰ Old North Church
⑱ Paul Revere Mall
⑲ Paul Revere House
⑳ Waterfront
㉑ *Trinity Church p150*

㉒ Copley Square
㉓ Newbury Street
㉔ Commonwealth Avenue

**Greater Boston**
*(see inset map)*
㉕ John F. Kennedy Library & Museum
㉖ Isabella Stewart Gardner Museum
㉗ Museum of Fine Arts
㉘ Cambridge
㉙ Charlestown

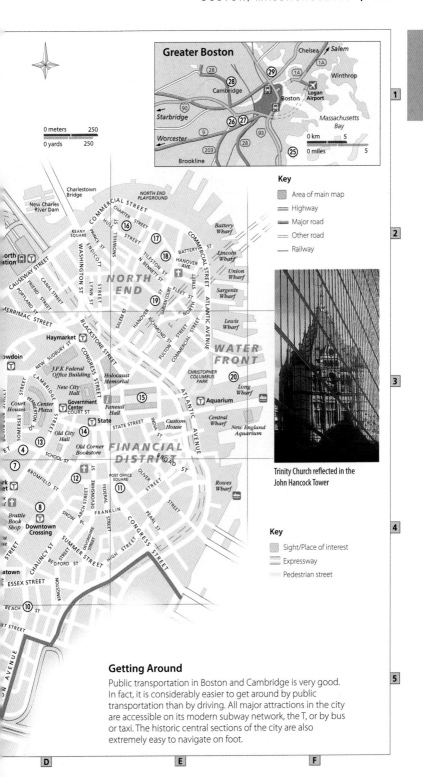

**Greater Boston**

Chelsea · Salem
Winthrop
Cambridge
Logan Airport
Boston
Starbridge
Worcester
Massachusetts Bay
Brookline

0 km 5
0 miles 5

0 meters 250
0 yards 250

**Key**

- Area of main map
- Highway
- Major road
- Other road
- Railway

Charlestown Bridge
New Charles River Dam
NORTH END PLAYGROUND
COMMERCIAL STREET
KEANY SQUARE
CHARTER STREET
HULL ST
PRINCE ST
TILESTON STREET
TILLMONS
WASHINGTON ST
ENDICOTT ST
CANAL STREET
FRIEND STREET
PORTLAND STREET
LYNN ST
BATTERY STREET
N. BENNETT ST
HANOVER AVE
COMMERCIAL STREET
Battery Wharf
Lincoln Wharf
Union Wharf
Sargents Wharf
Lewis Wharf
ATLANTIC AVENUE
NORTH END
North Station
CAUSEWAY STREET
MERRIMAC STREET
BLACKSTONE STREET
SALEM ST
HANOVER ST
RICHMOND ST
FLEET ST
GARDEN COURT
NORTH ST
FULTON ST
COMMERCIAL STREET
WATER FRONT
Haymarket
Bowdoin
NEW SUDBURY STREET
CAMBRIDGE STREET
CONGRESS STREET
J.F.K Federal Office Building
New City Hall
Holocaust Memorial
CHRISTOPHER COLUMBUS PARK
Long Wharf
Aquarium
Court Houses
SOMERSET STREET
PEMBERTON
Center Plaza
Government Center
COURT ST
Faneuil Hall
Old City Hall
STATE STREET
State
INDIA ST
Custom House
Central Wharf
New England Aquarium
Old Corner Bookstore
SCHOOL ST
FINANCIAL DISTRICT
BROAD ST
ATLANTIC AVENUE
BROMFIELD ST
TREMONT ST
POST OFFICE SQUARE
DEVONSHIRE
ARCH STREET
FEDERAL STREET
OLIVER STREET
Rowes Wharf
Brattle Book Shop
Downtown Crossing
SNOW PL
DEVONSHIRE STREET
FRANKLIN STREET
PEARL ST
CONGRESS STREET
Chinatown
CHAUNCY ST
SUMMER STREET
BEDFORD ST
HIGH STREET
ESSEX STREET
KINGSTON ST
BEACH ST
AVENUE

Trinity Church reflected in the John Hancock Tower

**Key**

- Sight/Place of interest
- Expressway
- Pedestrian street

## Getting Around

Public transportation in Boston and Cambridge is very good. In fact, it is considerably easier to get around by public transportation than by driving. All major attractions in the city are accessible on its modern subway network, the T, or by bus or taxi. The historic central sections of the city are also extremely easy to navigate on foot.

# ① Beacon Hill

The south slope of Beacon Hill was, from the 1790s to the 1870s, Boston's most sought-after neighborhood, until its wealthy elite decamped to the more exclusive Back Bay. Many of the district's houses were designed by the influential architect Charles Bulfinch (1763–1844) and his disciples, and the south slope evolved as a textbook example of Federal architecture. The finest houses are either on Boston Common or perched on top of the hill, offering fine views. Though the earlier houses were set well back from the street, the economic depression of 1807–12 resulted in row houses being built right out to the street.

**Beacon Street**
The fine Federal-style mansions here, some with ornate reliefs, overlook the beautiful green expanse of Boston Common.

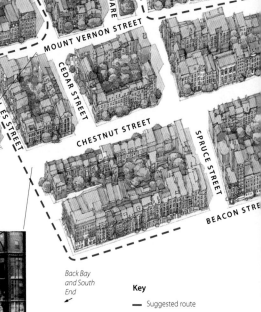

**Louisburg Square**
The crowning glory of the Beacon Hill district, this square was developed in the 1830s. Today, it is still Boston's most desirable address.

**Charles Street Meeting House**
was built in the early 19th century to house a congregation of Baptists.

**Mount Vernon Street**,
with its gracious mansions, was described by novelist Henry James in the 1890s as "the most civilized street in America."

*Back Bay and South End*

**Key**

— Suggested route

| 0 meters | 50 |
|---|---|
| 0 yards | 50 |

**★ Charles Street**
This elegant street is lined with antique stores, fine restaurants, and gourmet groceries. At its top end are two groups of striking Greek-Revival row houses.

★ **Nichols House Museum**
This small museum offers an insight into the life and times of Beacon Hill resident Rose Nichols, who lived here from 1885 to 1960.

WALNUT STREET

→ *Massachusetts State House*

**Hepzibah Swan Houses**
Charles Bulfinch designed these three elegant houses for the daughters of a wealthy Beacon Hill proprietress.

## ② Black Heritage Trail

**Map** C3. tours by National Park Service Rangers, (617) 742-5415. nps.gov/boaf

In the first US census in 1790, Massachusetts was the only state to record no slaves. During the 1800s, Boston's large free African-American community lived principally on the north slope of Beacon Hill and in the adjacent West End. Free walking tours of the Black Heritage Trail are led by the National Park Service Rangers from spring to fall, departing from the Robert Gould Shaw Memorial on Boston Common. The sights include safe houses for escaped slaves, and the **Museum of African American History**, which traces Boston's black history and preserves the African Meeting House, the country's oldest black church. Dedicated in 1806, the building's restored interior once rang with the passionate oratory of abolitionists. The site also includes the Abiel Smith School, the first school built solely for African-American children.

**Museum of African American History**
46 Joy St. **Tel** (617) 720-2991. **Open** 10am–4pm Mon–Sat. **Closed** public hols. afroammuseum.org

## ③ Boston Common & Public Garden

**Map** C4. Park St, Boylston St, Arlington. **Open** 24 hrs. Visitor Center: 139 Tremont St, (617) 426-3115. **Open** 8:30am–5pm Mon–Fri, 9am–5pm Sat & Sun (times vary in winter). bostonusa.com

The city's most beautiful green space, Boston Common was established in 1634. For two centuries it served as a common pasture, gallows site, and a military camp and drill ground. By the 19th century, it had become a center for open-air civic activity and remains so to this day. At the northeastern edge of the Common is the **Robert Shaw Memorial**, with a magnificent relief depicting the

first free black regiment in the Union Army during the Civil War, and their white colonel, Robert Shaw. In the southeastern corner is the Central Burying Ground, dating from 1756, with graves of British and American casualties from the historic Battle of Bunker Hill in 1775 *(see p155)*.

Southwest of the Common is the more formal 24-acre (10-ha) Public Garden, designed in English style in 1869. Amid its beautifully tended lawns and flowerbeds is a superb bronze equestrian statue of George Washington. A path leads from the statue to a serene lagoon, spanned by the miniature, ornamental Lagoon Bridge. Visitors can explore the lagoon on the delightful Swan Boats.

Bronze statue of George Washington in the Public Garden

## ④ Boston Athenaeum

**Map** D3. 10½ Beacon St. **Tel** (617) 227-0270. Park St. **Open** 9am–8pm Mon–Wed, 9am–5:30pm Thu–Fri, 9am–4pm Sat. boston athenaeum.org

Housed in an elegant Palladian-style building, this library's treasures include George Washington's personal library and the theological library given by King William III of England to the King's Chapel *(see p146)*. The Athenaeum's collection, first organized in 1807, originally included many fine paintings. These were later donated to the Museum of Fine Arts *(see pp152–3)* when that was set up.

# ⑤ The Freedom Trail

Boston has more sites directly related to the American Revolution than any other city. The most important of these sites, as well as some associated with the city's history, have been linked together as "The Freedom Trail." This 2.5-mile (4-km) walking route, marked in red on the sidewalks, starts at Boston Common, weaves through the central city and Old Boston, and ends at Bunker Hill in Charlestown.

Faneuil Hall, popularly known as the "Cradle of Liberty"

## Central City

The Freedom Trail starts at the Visitor Information Center on Boston Common ① *(see p141)*. This is where angry colonials rallied against their British masters and where the British forces were encamped during the 1775–76 military occupation. Political speakers still expound from their soapboxes here. Walking toward the northwest

Continuing along Tremont Street you will come to King's Chapel and Burying Ground ⑤ *(see p146)*. The tiny cemetery is Boston's oldest, while King's Chapel was the principal Anglican church in Puritan Boston. The box pew on the right, just inside the front entrance, was reserved for condemned prisoners to hear their last sermons before going to the gallows on Boston Common.

### Heart of Old Boston

Head back along Tremont Street and turn down School

*(see p147)* presides over the head of State Street. The Colonial government building, it also served as the first state legislature, and the merchants' exchange in the basement was where Boston's Colonial shipping fortunes were made. The square in front of the Old State House is the Boston Massacre Site ⑩, where British soldiers opened fire on a taunting mob in 1770, killing five. Follow State Street down to Congress Street and turn left to reach Faneuil Hall ⑪, with its distinctive grasshopper weathervane. Though built

*[Map of the Freedom Trail area showing Boston Common, Beacon St, Park Street, Old Granary Burying Ground, Tremont Street, Pemberton Square, Government Center, Haymarket, School Street, Court Square, Washington St, Milk Street, Devonshire Street, State St, Congress Street, Union Street, North Street, with numbered markers ① through ⑫]*

Steeple of Park Street Church

corner of the Common provides a wonderful view of the Massachusetts State House ② *(see pp144–5)*, located on Beacon Street. It was built as the new center of state governance after the Revolution. Along Park Street, at the end of the Common, is Park Street Church ③ *(see p145)*, built in 1810 and a bulwark of the anti-slavery movement. Adjacent to it, the Old Granary Burying Ground ④ is the final resting place of patriots John Hancock and Paul Revere.

Street, where a hopscotch-like mosaic embedded in the sidewalk marks the site of the First Public School ⑥, established in 1635. At the bottom of the street is the former Old Corner Bookstore ⑦, a landmark which is more associated with Boston's literary flowering than with the Revolution. To its south on Washington Street is the Old South Meeting House ⑧ *(see p146)*, a graceful, white-spired brick church, modeled on Sir Christopher Wren's English country churches. A few blocks along, the Old State House ⑨

primarily as Boston's first central marketplace, it was also known as "Cradle of Liberty." The red stripe of the Freedom Trail points the way to the North End and the Paul Revere House ⑫. This is Boston's oldest house, home to the man known for his "midnight ride" *(see p148)*.

## The North End

Following the Freedom Trail through the North End, allow time to try some of the Italian cafés and bakeries along Hanover Street. Cross through the Paul Revere Mall to reach Old

North Church ⑬ *(see p148)*, whose spire is instantly visible over the shoulder of the equestrian statue of Paul Revere. In 1775, two lanterns hung in the belfry signaled the advance of British troops on Lexington and Concord. The crest of Copp's Hill lies close by on Hull Street. Some of Boston's earliest gallows were here, and people would gather below to watch the hangings of heretics and pirates. Much of the hilltop is covered by Copp's Hill Burying Ground ⑭, established in 1660 *(see p148)*.

## Charlestown

Cross the iron bridge over the Charles River, which links the North End in Boston with City Square in Charlestown, and turn right, following the

## Key

···· Walk route

0 meters 250
0 yards 250

*Boston Inner Harbor*

Freedom Trail along Water Street to the Charlestown Navy Yard ⑮. Berthed along-side Pier 1 is the USS *Constitution (see p155)*. In the War of 1812, she earned the nickname "Old Ironsides" for the resilience of her live oak hull against cannon fire. The granite obelisk that towers above the Charlestown waterfront is Bunker Hill Monument ⑯ *(see p155)*. This landmark commemorates the battle of June 17, 1775, which ended with a costly victory for British forces. As a monument to the first large-scale battle of the Revolution, the obelisk, based on those of ancient Egypt, remains a prototype for others across the US.

View of Bunker Hill Monument from Charlestown harbor

## Tips for Walkers

**Map C4. Starting point:** Boston Common Visitor Center. Free Park Ranger tours leave from Faneuil Hall. **Length:** 2.5 miles (4 km). **Getting there:** Park Street Station (Ⓣ Green and Red lines) to start. State (Orange and Blue lines) and Haymarket (Orange and Green lines). Ⓣ stations can be found on route. Visitors should follow red stripe on sidewalk for the full route.

## Walk

① Boston Common
② Massachusetts State House
③ Park Street Church
④ Old Granary Burying Ground
⑤ King's Chapel & Burying Ground
⑥ First Public School
⑦ Old Corner Bookstore
⑧ Old South Meeting House
⑨ Old State House
⑩ Boston Massacre Site
⑪ Faneuil Hall
⑫ Paul Revere House
⑬ Old North Church
⑭ Copp's Hill Burying Ground
⑮ Charlestown Navy Yard & the USS *Constitution*
⑯ Bunker Hill Monument

# ⑥ Massachusetts State House

The cornerstone of the Massachusetts State House was laid in 1795 by Paul Revere and Samuel Adams. Completed in 1798, the Charles Bulfinch-designed center of state government served as a model for the US Capitol building in Washington and as an inspiration for many other state capitols. Later additions were made, but the original building remains the archetype of American government buildings. Its gilded dome serves as the zero-mile marker for Massachusetts.

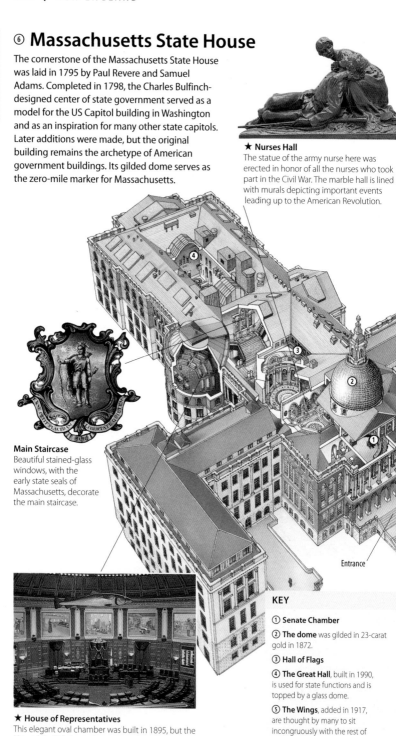

**★ Nurses Hall**
The statue of the army nurse here was erected in honor of all the nurses who took part in the Civil War. The marble hall is lined with murals depicting important events leading up to the American Revolution.

**Main Staircase**
Beautiful stained-glass windows, with the early state seals of Massachusetts, decorate the main staircase.

Entrance

**KEY**

① **Senate Chamber**

② **The dome** was gilded in 23-carat gold in 1872.

③ **Hall of Flags**

④ **The Great Hall**, built in 1990, is used for state functions and is topped by a glass dome.

⑤ **The Wings**, added in 1917, are thought by many to sit incongruously with the rest of the structure.

**★ House of Representatives**
This elegant oval chamber was built in 1895, but the "Sacred Cod" that now hangs over the gallery came to the State House when it first opened in 1798.

## VISITORS' CHECKLIST

**Map** D3. Beacon Hill.
**Tel** (617) 727-3676. **Open**
10am–3:30pm Mon–Fri. Booking
advised. ♿ 🎫
**w** sec.state.ma.us/trs

**Transport**
Ⓣ Park St.

**Senate Chamber**
Situated directly beneath
the dome, this chamber
features a beautiful
sunburst ceiling.

⑤

**Hall of Flags**
Flags carried into battle by
regiments from the state of
Massachusetts are displayed
here beneath a stained-glass
skylight, depicting seals of the
original 13 colonies.

# ⑦ Park Street Church

**Map** D4. 1 Park St. **Tel** (617) 523-3383.
Ⓣ Park St. **Open** Jul–Aug: 9am–4pm
Tue–Fri, 9am–3pm Sat; Sep–Jun: call
for hours. ♿ **w** parkstreet.org

Since its dedication in 1810,
the Park Street Church has
been one of Boston's most
influential pulpits. In 1829,
the firebrand crusader for the
abolition of slavery, William
Lloyd Garrison, gave his first
abolition speech here; and in
1893 the anthem "America the
Beautiful" debuted at Sunday
service in this church. The
church, with its 217-ft (65-m)
steeple was designed by the
English architect Peter Banner,
who actually adapted a design
by the earlier English architect,
Christopher Wren.

Adjacent to the church, on
Tremont Street, is the mid-
17th-century **Old Granary
Burying Ground**, which was
once the site of a grain storage
facility. Among those buried in
this historic cemetery are three
important signatories to the
Declaration of Independence –
Samuel Adams, John Hancock,
and Robert Paine – as well as
one of the city's most famous
sons, the patriot Paul Revere.

**🎫 Old Granary Burying
Ground**
Tremont St. **Open** 9am–5pm daily.

# ⑧ Downtown Crossing

**Map** D4. Washington, Winter, &
Summer Sts. Ⓣ Downtown Crossing.

This pedestrian shopping
district features sidewalk
vendors and food carts. The
major department store is
Macy's, part of a nationwide
chain. Farther down Washington
Street is Boston's jewelry district,
while more unique shops can
be found on the side streets.
The Brattle Book Shop, for
example, was founded in 1825
and stocks more than 250,000
rare, used, and out-of-print
books and magazines.

# ⑨ Theater District

**Map** C4. Ⓣ Boylston, Tufts Medical
Center.

Boston's first theater opened in
1793 on Federal Street. Fifty
years later, with patronage from
the city's elite, Boston had
become a major tryout town
and boasted several lavish
theaters. Many major US
premieres were held here,
among them Handel's *Messiah*,
and Tennessee Williams'
*A Streetcar Named Desire*.
Among the grandest theaters
are the opulent **Colonial
Theater**, decorated with
frescoes and friezes; the 1,650-
seat **Shubert Theater**, with its
imposing Neo-Classical façade;
and the **Wang Theater**,
with a glittering seven-
story auditorium.

**🎭 Colonial Theater**
106 Boylston St. **Tel** (617) 482-9393.
**Open** phone to check. ♿
**w** colonial-theater.com

# ⑩ Chinatown

**Map** D5. Bounded by Kingston,
Kneeland, Washington, & Essex Sts.
Ⓣ Chinatown.

This is the third largest
Chinatown in the US, after
those in San Francisco and
New York. Pagoda-topped
telephone booths set the tone
of the neighborhood, which is
full of restaurants, and stores
selling garments and Chinese
medicine. Boston's Chinese
colony was fully established
by the turn of the 19th century,
and the area's population has
since swelled with new
arrivals from Korea, Vietnam,
and Cambodia.

Typical store and restaurant façades in
Boston's Chinatown

Sculptural fountain in Boston's Post Office Square

## ⑪ Post Office Square

**Map** E4. Cnr of Congress and Milk Sts. Ⓣ State, Downtown. 🖥

Enclosed on the west side by the impressive Art Deco former post office building, Post Office Square is the nerve center of Boston's financial district. The east side of the square faces the Renaissance-style former Federal Reserve Bank, now the Langham Boston Hotel (see p184). The graceful 1947 Art Moderne structure on the south side was headquarters for the New England Telephone Company, and the laboratory of telephone pioneer Alexander Graham Bell was located on nearby Court Street. A public park provides an oasis of green among the high-rise buildings of the city. Local workers and tourists are able to relax on the lawns to the sound of water in the sculptural fountain, and in summer a kiosk sells luncheon fare.

## ⑫ Old South Meeting House

**Map** D4. 310 Washington St. **Tel** (617) 482-6439. Ⓣ Park St, State, Government Center (closed until 2016). **Open** Apr–Oct: 9:30am–5pm daily; Nov–Mar: 10am–4pm daily. 🚻 ♿ 🆆 oldsouthmeetinghouse.org

Built for Puritan religious services in 1729, this edifice, with a tall octagonal steeple, had Colonial Boston's biggest capacity for town meetings. From 1765 on, it became the venue for large and vociferous crowds, led by a group of merchants called "the Sons of Liberty" to gather in protest against British taxation and the hated Stamp Act. During a protest rally on December 16, 1773, the fiery speechmaker Samuel Adams flashed the signal that led to the Boston Tea Party (see p149) at Griffin's Wharf several hours later. The British retaliated by turning Old South into an officers' tavern and a stable for army horses. Today, the Meeting House holds lectures and exhibitions, and has a multimedia show, which relives the events. The shop sells "Boston Tea Party" tea and books on the history of Boston and New England.

*Alexander Graham Bell*

## ⑬ King's Chapel & Burying Ground

**Map** D3. 58 Tremont St. **Tel** (617) 227-2155. Ⓣ Park St, State, Government Center (closed until 2016). **Open** late May–mid-Sep: 10am–5pm Mon, Thu, Fr & Sat, 10–11:15am, 1:30–5pm Tue & Wed, 1:30–5pm Sun; mid-Sep–late May: call for hours. Music recitals: 12:15pm Tue. 🆆 **kings-chapel.org**

The first chapel on this site was built in 1689, but when the Governor of New England decided that a larger church was needed, the present granite edifice was begun in 1749. It was constructed around the original wooden chapel, which was then dismantled and heaved out of the windows of its replacement. High ceilings and open arches enhance the sense of spaciousness and light inside the chapel. Its other notable features include a pulpit shaped like a wine glass, which dates back to 1717, and a huge bell that was recast by the foundry of Revolutionary hero Paul Revere (see p148). The adjacent cemetery, Boston's oldest, contains the graves of 12-time Colonial governor John Winthrop, and Mary Chilton, the first woman to step off the *Mayflower*.

The simply decorated interior of King's Chapel on Tremont Street

## ⑭ Old State House

**Map** D3. Washington & State Sts.
**Tel** (617) 720-1313. ⓣ State.
**Open** 9am–5pm daily (until 6pm
Jun–Aug). ♿ ♿ ♿
🌐 bostonhistory.org

Now dwarfed by the towers of the Financial District, the Old State House was the seat of the British Colonial government

Old State House amid the skyscrapers of the Financial District

between 1713 and 1776. The royal lion and unicorn still decorate the eastern façade. After independence, the Massachusetts legislature took possession of the building, and it has had many uses since, including a produce market, Masonic Lodge, and Boston City Hall. Its wine cellars now function as a subway station.

In 1776, the Declaration of Independence was read from the balcony on the East Façade. A circle of cobblestones below the balcony marks the site of the Boston Massacre. On March 5, 1770, British guardsmen opened fire on taunting Colonists, killing five. After the Boston Tea Party, this was one of the most inflammatory events leading up to the American Revolution (see p54). Inside, exhibits include a multimedia presentation about the Boston Massacre and the restored Royal Council Chamber, where visitors can sit in the Royal Governor's chair.

Greek-Revival Custom House tower, one of Boston's most striking sights

## ⑮ Quincy Market

**Map** E3. Between Chatham & Clinton Sts. **Tel** (617) 523-1300.
ⓣ Haymarket, State. **Open** 10am–9pm Mon–Sat, noon–6pm Sun.
♿ 🌐 faneuilhallmarketplace.com

This immensely popular shopping and dining complex attracts nearly 14 million people every year. It was developed from the old buildings of the city's meat, fish, and produce markets, which were beautifully restored in the 1970s. The 535-ft-(163-m-) long Greek-Revival-style colonnaded hall is now filled with fast-food stands and tables beneath the spectacular central rotunda. Completing the ensemble are the twin North and South Market buildings, refurbished to house boutiques, restaurants, and business offices.

A short distance southeast of Quincy Market is the **Custom House** with its Greek-Revival tower. The 495-ft (150m) tower with a four-sided clock was built in 1915 and for much of the 20th century was Boston's only skyscraper until it was exceeded by the Prudential Tower. There is a display of local history in the rotunda. Call for the schedule of tours of the tower, which offer spectacular city and harbor views.

🏛 **Custom House**
3 McKinley Square. **Tel** (617) 310-6300.
Tower: ♿ 🌐 marriott.com/vacationclub

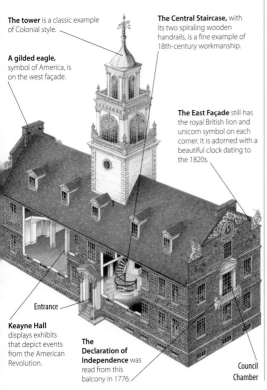

**The tower** is a classic example of Colonial style.

**A gilded eagle,** symbol of America, is on the west façade.

**The Central Staircase,** with its two spiraling wooden handrails, is a fine example of 18th-century workmanship.

**The East Façade** still has the royal British lion and unicorn symbol on each corner. It is adorned with a beautiful clock dating to the 1820s.

Entrance

**Keayne Hall** displays exhibits that depict events from the American Revolution.

**The Declaration of Independence** was read from this balcony in 1776.

Council Chamber

Slate tombstones of Boston's early settlers, Copp's Hill Burying Ground

## ⑯ Copp's Hill Burying Ground

**Map** E2. Entrances at Charter & Hull Sts. **Tel** (617) 635-4505. Ⓣ N Station. **Open** 9am–5pm daily.

Existing since 1659, this is Boston's second-oldest cemetery, after the one by King's Chapel (see p146). Among those buried here are Robert Newman, the sexton who hung Paul Revere's signal lanterns in the belfry of the Old North Church, influential Colonial period Puritan ministers, as well as hundreds of black slaves and freedmen.

During the British occupation of Boston, King George lll's troops were said to have used the slate headstones for target practice, and pockmarks from their musket balls are still visible. Copp's Hill Terrace, directly across Charter Street, is the site where, in 1919, a 2.3-million-gallon tank of molasses exploded, drowning 21 people in a huge, syrupy tidal wave.

## ⑰ Old North Church

**Map** E2. 193 Salem St. **Tel** (617) 523-6676. Ⓣ Haymarket, Aquarium, N Station. **Open** 9am–5pm daily (reduced hours Jan & Feb, extended hours Jun–Oct). 🕐 9am, 11am Sun (also 5pm Jul–Aug). ♿ 🅿 donation. 📷 Mar–Dec: "Behind the Scenes Tour" (fee charged). Ⓦ **oldnorth.com**

Officially named Christ Episcopal Church, the Old North Church, which dates from 1723,

is Boston's oldest surviving religious edifice. It is built of brick in the Georgian style, similar to that of St. Andrew's-by-the-Wardrobe in Blackfriars, London, designed by Sir Christopher Wren. The church was made famous on April 18, 1775, when sexton Robert Newman, aiding Paul Revere, hung a pair of lanterns in the belfry. These were to warn the patriots in Charlestown of the westward departure of British troops, on their way to engage the revolutionaries.

An imposing marble bust of George Washington, dating from 1815, adorns the church interior, which has unusual high-sided box pews. These were designed to enclose footwarmers, which were filled with hot coals or bricks during wintry weather. The tower contains the first set of church bells made in North America, cast in 1745. One of the first bellringers was a teenage Paul Revere.

## ⑱ Paul Revere Mall

**Map** E2. Hanover St. Ⓣ Haymarket, Aquarium. ♿

This brick-paved plaza, between Hanover and Unity Streets, provides a precious stretch of open space in the crowded neighborhood of the North End, populated largely by people of Italian descent. Laid out in 1933, its focal point is an equestrian statue of Paul Revere (1735–1818). Benches, a fountain, and

twin rows of linden trees give the space, much used by local people, a distinctly European feel. South of the Mall is busy Hanover Street, which is lined with Italian eateries.

## ⑲ Paul Revere House

**Map** E2. 19 N Square. **Tel** (617) 523-2338. Ⓣ Haymarket, Aquarium. **Open** mid-Apr–Oct: 9:30am–5:15pm daily; Nov–mid-Apr: 9:30am–4:15pm daily. **Closed** Jan–Mar: Mon. 🎧 ♿ Ⓦ **paulreverehouse.org**

Boston's oldest surviving clapboard frame house is historically significant, for it was here in 1775 that Paul Revere began his legendary horseback ride to warn his compatriots in Lexington (see p155) of the impending arrival of British troops. This historic event was later immortalized by Henry Wadsworth Longfellow (see p154) in his epic poem which begins, "Listen, my children, and you shall hear of the midnight ride of Paul Revere."

A versatile gold- and silversmith, and maker of church bells and cannons, Revere lived here from 1770 to 1800. Small leaded casement windows, an overhanging upper story, and nail-studded front door make the house a fine example of 18th-century Early American architecture. Two rooms in the house contain artifacts and furniture from the Revere family. In the courtyard is a large bronze bell cast by Revere, who is known to have made nearly 200 church bells.

Paul Revere House, where the patriot began his midnight ride

## ⑳ **Waterfront**

**Map** E3. Atlantic Ave. New England Aquarium: Central Wharf. **Tel** (617) 973-5200. Ⓣ Aquarium. **Open** Jul–Aug: 9am–6pm Sun–Thu, 9am–7pm Fri & Sat; Sep–Jun: 9am–5pm Mon–Fri, 9am–6pm Sat & Sun. 🅿️ ♿ 🅰️ 🅰️ 🖥️ Ⓦ **neaq.org** Boston Tea Party Ships and Museum: Congress St Bridge. **Tel** (617) 338-1773. Ⓣ South Station. **Open** call for hours. 🅿️ Ⓦ **bostonteapartyship.com** Institute of Contemporary Art: 100 Northern Ave. **Tel** (617) 478-3100. Ⓣ Courthouse. **Open** 10am–5pm Tue, Wed, Sat & Sun, 10am–9pm Thu & Fri. 🅿️ ♿ Ⓦ **icaboston.org** Children's Museum: 300 Congress St. **Tel** (617) 426-6500. Ⓣ S Station. **Open** 10am–5pm daily (to 9pm Fri). 🅿️ ♿ Ⓦ **bostonkids.org**

Boston's waterfront is one of the city's most fascinating areas. Fringed by wharves and warehouses – a reminder of the city's past as a key trading port – its attractions include a famous aquarium and two fine museums.

One of the largest wharves is **Long Wharf**, established in 1710. Once extending 2,000 ft (610 m) into Boston Harbor and lined with shops and warehouses, it provided secure mooring for the largest ships of the time.

Harbor Walk connects Long Wharf with other adjacent wharves, dating from the early 1800s. Most of them have now been converted to fashionable harborside apartments. **Rowes Wharf**, to the south of the waterfront, is a particularly fine example of such revitalization. This modern red-brick development, with condominiums, a hotel, and offices, features a large archway that links the city to the harbor.

The waterfront's prime attraction is the **New England Aquarium**, which dominates Central Wharf. Designed in 1969, the aquarium's core encloses a vast four-story ocean tank, which houses a Caribbean coral reef and contains a wide array of marine creatures such as sharks, moray eels, barracudas, and sea turtles, as well as exotic, brightly colored tropical fish. A curving walkway runs around the outside of the tank from the top to the bottom, and provides different viewpoints of the interior at many levels.

Lionfish, New England Aquarium

A particularly popular section of the aquarium is the Penguin Pool, which runs around the base of the ocean tank, while the west wing has an outdoor tank with a lively colony of harbor seals. In 2001, the Simons IMAX® Theater was opened on the wharf, which presents changing programs of 3-D films on a giant screen. A highlight of the aquarium's programs are the boat trips from Boston Harbor, which take visitors to the whale feeding grounds far offshore. The aquarium also has a gift shop and a café with a beautiful view of the harbor. Griffin's Wharf, where the Boston Tea Party took place on December 16, 1773, was long ago buried beneath landfill. Anchored nearby on Fort Point Channel, the **Boston Tea Party Ships** replicate the British East India Company ships involved in the Tea Party protest *(see p54)*. At Fan Pier, the light-flooded galleries, performance space open to harbor views, and cutting-edge media center highlight the landmark building of the **Institute of Contemporary Art**, where exhibitions place strong emphasis on electronic media and performance art.

Overlooking Fort Point Channel is a rejuvenated 19th-century wool warehouse that houses the **Children's Museum**, one of the best in the country. Its many attractions and interactive exhibits include a climbing wall, a hands-on art studio, and a "construction zone" with child-scaled trucks and blocks. They can also follow a giant maze or act in KidStage plays. An international flavor is added by a visit to the silk merchant's house, transplanted from Kyoto in Japan.

View down Long Wharf toward the waterfront and Custom House

# ㉑ Trinity Church

Routinely voted one of America's ten finest buildings, this masterpiece by Henry Hobson Richardson dates from 1877. The church is a beautiful granite and sandstone Romanesque structure, standing on wooden piles driven through mud into bedrock, surmounted by granite pyramids. John LaFarge designed the interior, while some of the windows were designed by Edward Burne-Jones and executed by William Morris.

**VISITORS' CHECKLIST**

**Practical Information**
Map B5. Copley Sq. **Tel** (617) 536-0944. Ⓣ Copley. **Open** daily.
🕇 7:45am, 9am, 11:15am, 6pm
Sun. Concerts: Sep–Jun: 12:15pm
Fri. 📷 call for hours. ♿ ♿
ⓦ trinitychurchboston.org

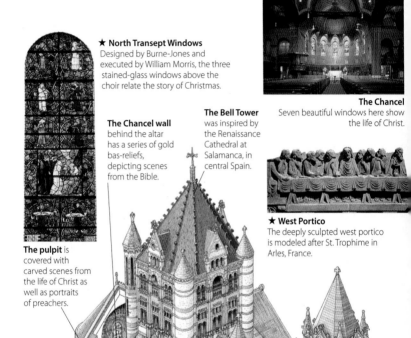

★ **North Transept Windows**
Designed by Burne-Jones and executed by William Morris, the three stained-glass windows above the choir relate the story of Christmas.

**The Chelsea**

**The Chancel**
Seven beautiful windows here show the life of Christ.

**The Chancel wall**
behind the altar has a series of gold bas-reliefs, depicting scenes from the Bible.

**The Bell Tower**
was inspired by the Renaissance Cathedral at Salamanca, in central Spain.

★ **West Portico**
The deeply sculpted west portico is modeled after St. Trophime in Arles, France.

**The pulpit** is covered with carved scenes from the life of Christ as well as portraits of preachers.

West Porti

North Transept Windows

Main Entrance

View over Back Bay and Charles River from the John Hancock Tower

## ㉒ Copley Square

**Map** B5. ⓣ Copley.

Named after the famous painter John Singleton Copley *(see p153)*, Copley Square was a marsh until 1870 and took on its present form only in the late 20th century. Today, this inviting plaza is an open space of trees and fountains, and a hive of civic activity with weekly farmers' markets and concerts in summer.

The **John Hancock Tower**, constructed in 1975, anchors the southeastern side of the Square. The tallest building in New England, the 740-ft (226-m) tower's mirrored façade reflects the beautiful Trinity Church and the original (1947) Hancock Building, with its rooftop beacon that forecasts the weather. Flashing red indicates rain ahead – or that the Boston Red Sox game has been postponed.

West of the Hancock Tower, across Copley Square, is the Italian palazzo-style **Boston Public Library**, built 1887–95. A marvel of fine wood and marble, the library has huge bronze doors, and murals by John Singer Sargent in a third-floor gallery. The vast Bates Hall on the second

floor of this library is notable for its soaring barrel-vaulted ceiling. Close by, on the corner of Boylston and Dartmouth Streets, is the fabulous Italian-Gothic-style **New Old South Church**, built in 1874–5.

**🏛 John Hancock Tower**
200 Clarendon St. **Closed** to the public.

**🏛 Boston Public Library**
Copley Square. **Tel** (617) 536-5400. **Open** 9am–9pm Mon–Thu, 9am–5pm Fri & Sat; Oct–May: 1–5pm Sun. **Closed** public hols. ♿ 🅿 2:30pm Mon, 6pm Tue & Thu, 11am Wed, Fri & Sat. 🆆 bpl.org

## ㉓ Newbury Street

**Map** B5. ⓣ Arlington, Copley, Hynes Convention Center/ICA.

Newbury Street is a Boston synonym for "stylish." Lined with high-fashion outlets, art galleries, and chic restaurants, this is a great place for people-watching. Lower Newbury near the Public Garden is posh and elegant, while upper Newbury buzzes with youth-oriented shops and services. Churches provide vestiges of a more decorous era. Most notable is

the **Church of the Covenant**, which contains the world's largest collection of Louis Comfort Tiffany stained-glass windows and an elaborate Tiffany lantern.

**🏛 Church of the Covenant**
67 Newbury St. **Tel** (617) 266-7480. **Open** 10:30am Sun. 🅿 ♿ 🅿 📷
🆆 cotcbos.org

## ㉔ Commonwealth Avenue

**Map** B4. ⓣ Arlington, Copley, Hynes Convention Center/ ICA.

Envisioned as Boston's Champs Elysées, this avenue, 200-ft (61-m) wide, is lined with beautiful townhouses. In the second half of the 19th century, it became an arena for America's leading domestic architects, and a walk along it is like flicking through a catalog of architectural styles. Bronze statues of historic figures line the central mall. Abolitionist William Lloyd Garrison's statue, located between Exeter and Dartmouth Streets, is said to capture his air of moral superiority, while the best-loved memorial features sailor and historian Samuel Eliot Morison. In his statue, found between Exeter and Fairfield Streets, Morison strikes an informal pose, dangling his feet from a rock.

The Romanesque-style **First Baptist Church**, on the corner of Commonwealth Avenue and Clarendon Street, is one of the most distinctive buildings of the city skyline. Completed in 1872, its free-standing square bell tower, modeled on Italian campaniles, is topped with a decorative frieze by Bartholdi, the sculptor who created the Statue of Liberty. The faces in the frieze, which depict the sacraments, are likenesses of prominent Bostonians of the time, among them Henry Wadsworth Longfellow and Ralph Waldo Emerson.

**🏛 First Baptist Church**
110 Commonwealth Ave. **Tel** (617) 267-3148. **Open** for Sun worship. ♿

# Greater Boston

Southwest of central Boston, what were once the marshlands of the Fenway now house two superb art museums – the Museum of Fine Arts and the Isabella Stewart Gardner Museum. West of the city, across the Charles River, is the college town of Cambridge, dominated by Harvard University. To its east is historic Charlestown, which forms a major part of Boston's Freedom Trail *(see pp142–3)*.

The dramatic structure of the John F. Kennedy Library and Museum

## ㉕ John F. Kennedy Library & Museum

Columbia Point, Dorchester.
**Tel** (617) 514-1600. Ⓣ JFK/U Mass.
**Open** 9am–5pm daily. **Closed** Jan 1,
Thanksgiving, Dec 25. 🅿 ♿ 🎁 🏛
🆆 jfklibrary.org

Housed in a dramatic white concrete and black glass building designed by architect I.M. Pei, this museum chronicles the 1,000 days of the Kennedy presidency. The combination of video and film footage, papers, and memorabilia evoke the euphoria of "Camelot" as well as the numb horror of the assassination with an immediacy that is uncommon in historical museums. Some of the key chambers in the White House, including the Oval Office, are re-created here.

The house at 83 Beals Street in Brookline, where the late president was born in 1917, is now the **John F. Kennedy National Historic Site**. The Kennedy family moved to a larger house in 1921; in 1966 they repurchased this house, and restored it to how it would have looked in 1917. It is open during the summer and fall.

## ㉖ Isabella Stewart Gardner Museum

280 The Fenway. **Tel** (617) 566-1401.
Ⓣ MFA. **Open** 11am–5pm Wed–Mon
(until 9pm Thu). **Closed** Jan 1, Thanksg.,
Dec 25. 🅿 🎁 🏛 call for concert
schedule. 🆆 gardnermuseum.org

This Venetian-style palazzo, completed in 1903, houses a remarkable collection of over 2,500 works of art, including Old Masters and Italian Renaissance pieces. Advised by art scholar Bernard Berenson, the wealthy and strong-willed Isabella Stewart Gardner began collecting art in the late 19th century and acquired masterpieces by Titian,

Rembrandt, and Matisse as well as the American painters James McNeill Whistler and John Singer Sargent. The paintings, sculptures, and tapestries are still displayed as Mrs. Gardner arranged them, in galleries around a flower-filled central courtyard.

A striking modern wing designed by architect Renzo Piano opened in 2012, adding galleries, a café, and an intimate performance space for the acclaimed concert series.

## ㉗ Museum of Fine Arts

Avenue of the Arts, 465 Huntington
Ave. **Tel** (617) 267-9300. Ⓣ MFA.
**Open** 10am–4:45pm Sat–Tue,
10am–9:45pm Wed–Fri (selected
collections Thu & Fri). **Closed** Jan 1,
3rd Mon in Apr, Jul 4, Thanksgiving,
Dec 25. 🅿 ♿ 🎁 🏛 Lectures,
concerts, & films. 🎁 💻 📷
🆆 mfa.org

The largest art museum in New England, and one of the five largest in the US, the Museum of Fine Arts (MFA) has a

Central courtyard of the palazzo-style Isabella Stewart Gardner Museum

Japanese Temple Room, Museum of Fine Arts

permanent collection of approximately 450,000 objects, ranging from Egyptian artifacts to modern American paintings. Though founded in 1876, the MFA's original Beaux Arts-style building dates from 1909. It was augmented in 2010 by the 53 galleries of the Art of Americas Wing. In 2011, the museum transformed its west-facing wing, designed in 1981 by I.M. Pei, into the Linde Family Wing for Contemporary Art.

The Museum of Fine Art's excellent collection of ancient **Egyptian and Nubian Art** is unparalleled outside of Africa and derives primarily from the MFA–Harvard University excavations along the Nile, which began in 1905. It also includes a wonderful collection of mummies that is located on the first floor. The adjacent gallery of Ancient Near Eastern Art exhibits Babylonian, Assyrian, and Sumerian reliefs. On the second floor are several monumental sculptures of Nubian kings, dating from the 7th to 6th centuries BC.

The MFA boasts one of America's top holdings of **Classical Art** as well. Among the highlights of this collection are Greek figured vases, carved Etruscan sarcophagi, and Roman portrait busts. Also on display are a series of wall-paintings unearthed in Pompeii in 1901. The **Asian Art** collections are said to be the most extensive under one roof anywhere in the world. They include Indian sculpture and narrative paintings, and exhibitions of Islamic miniature paintings that keep changing.

A beautiful stairway with carved lions leads to the Chinese and Japanese galleries on the second floor. Outstanding exhibits here include scroll and screen paintings. A highlight of the museum is the serene **Japanese Temple Room**, on the first floor, known for its exquisite examples of Buddhist art.

The **European Art** collections date from the 7th to the 20th centuries and feature Dutch paintings, including portraits by Rembrandt. The Koch Gallery, with its magnificent wooden coffered ceiling, displays masterpieces by El Greco, Titian, and Rubens.

Egyptian sarcophagi

Boston's 19th-century collectors enriched the MFA with wonderful French art: the museum features several paintings by Jean-François Millet as well as by 19th-century French artists such as Edouard Manet, Pierre-Auguste Renoir, and Edgar Degas. It also has several paintings by van Gogh, and holds the most important Monet collection outside of Paris. One of the most popular galleries displays *La Japonaise* by Monet and *Dance at Bougival* by Renoir.

The **American Painting** collection includes more than 1,600 works. Among the highlights are portraits by the Boston artist John Singleton Copley, perhaps America's most talented 18th-century painter, and sumptuous portraits by John Singer Sargent (1856– 1925), who also painted murals on the museum's domed rotunda. Other works include 19th-century landscapes by early Luminist painter Fitz Henry Lane, and seascapes by Winslow Homer. Twentieth-century American masters represented include Stuart Davis, Jackson Pollock, and Georgia O'Keeffe.

The **Decorative Arts** exhibit displays silver tea services made by Paul Revere *(see p148)*; 18th-century Boston-style clocks; numerous ship models; and outstanding examples of contemporary crafts. Period rooms present decorative arts in a historical context. They include furnishings and reproduced decor of the three circa-1800 rooms from a Peabody mansion designed by Federal-period architect Samuel McIntire.

In addition to these major collections, the Museum of Fine Arts also has important holdings in the multifarious arts of Africa, Oceania, and the ancient Americas, and collections of musical instruments and manuscripts. A pioneer in collecting photography, the MFA holds archival work by Yousuf Karsh and Bradford Washburn.

John Singer Sargent's murals on the domed rotunda, MFA

The simple interior of Christ Church in Cambridge

## ㉘ Cambridge

ⓣ Harvard. 🚊 1, 69. ℹ️ Harvard Square Information Booth: (617) 441-2884. Cambridge Office of Tourism: (800) 862-5678. 🛏 Sun. 🚣 River Festival (late Jun). 🆆 **harvard.edu** 🆆 **cambridge-usa.org**

Though part of the Greater Boston metropolitan area, Cambridge is a town in its own right, dominated by two world-famous universities, the **Massachusetts Institute of Technology** (MIT) and **Harvard**. It also has a number of sights associated with the American Revolution.

Among them is the historic house on Brattle Street, now known as the **Longfellow House – Washington's Head-quarters National Historic Site**. Built by Colonial-era merchants loyal to the British Crown during the Revolution, it was seized by American revolutionaries, and served as George Washington's headquarters during the Siege of Boston. From 1843 until his death in 1888, it was also the home of the famous poet Henry Wadsworth Longfellow, who wrote his most famous poems, including *The Song of Hiawatha*, here.

**Harvard Square** is the area's main shopping and entertainment district, full of cafés, inexpensive restaurants, trendy boutiques, and street performers. Harvard's large student population is much in evidence here, adding to the square's lively character.

**Cambridge Common**, north of Harvard Square, was set aside as a common pasture and military drill ground in the

1630s. It has served as a center for social, religious, and political activity ever since. The Common was used as an army encampment from 1775 to 1776, and a stone here marks the spot where George Washington took command of the Continental Army on July 3, 1775, beneath the Washington Elm. Today, its tree-shaded lawns and playgrounds are popular with families and students.

**Christ Church**, a short distance south of the Common, was designed in 1761 by Peter Harrison, the architect of Boston's King's Chapel *(see p146)*. In 1775, it served as a barracks for Continental Army troops, who melted down the organ pipes to cast musket balls. The church was restored for services on New Year's Eve, 1775, when George Washington and his wife were among the worshipers.

The 135-acre (55-ha) campus of the Massachusetts Institute of Technology (MIT), one of the world's leading universities in engineering and the sciences, stretches along the Charles River. Among the masterpieces of modern architecture that dot its campus are Eero Saarinen's Kresge Auditorium and Kresge Chapel, and the Wiesner Building designed by I.M. Pei, which houses a noted collection of avant-garde art in the List Visual Art Center. Art and Science are blended in the MIT

Museum, with exhibits such as Harold Edgerton's stroboscopic flash photographs and the latest holographic art.

An altogether more old-world atmosphere prevails at the campus of Harvard University, with its red-brick, ivy-covered walls. Founded in 1636, Harvard is the oldest university in the US and one of the world's most prestigious centers of learning. At the heart of the campus, which encompasses more than 400 buildings, is the leafy **Old Harvard Yard**, dotted with student dormitories. Its focal point is the statue of its most famous benefactor, the cleric John Harvard. To the right of the statue is the imposing Widener Library, which, with over 3 million volumes, is the third largest in the US. Another impressive building in the Yard is the Memorial Church, built in 1931, whose steeple is modeled on that of the Old North Church *(see p148)*. Standing out amid Harvard's Georgian-style buildings is the Carpenter Center for Visual Arts, designed by the avant-garde French architect Le Corbusier.

The **Harvard Art Museums** are a major draw for visitors. In November 2014, the university's main art museum building, which was originally completed in 1927, reopened after a six-year project of renovation and expansion designed by architect

Students strolling through Harvard Yard

Renzo Piano. The facility brings the collections of the university's three major art museums under one roof. The Italianate courtyard, a favorite feature of the 1927 building, remains at the heart of the museum. A glass roof illuminates the space and a café is located just off the courtyard. The three museum collections span the continents and centuries.

The **Fogg Art Museum** focuses on European art from the late Middle Ages to the present, with particular strengths in pre-Renaissance and Renaissance painting, as well as the Wertheim Collection of Impressionist and Post-Impressionist art.

The **Busch-Reisinger Museum** concentrates on Germanic art, particularly of the 20th century, and contains works by such masters as Wassily Kandinsky, Paul Klee, Emil Nolde, and Oskar Kokoschka. Late medieval sculpture and 18th-century art are also strongly represented.

The **Sackler Museum** houses a rich collection of ancient Greek and Roman, Asian, Indian, and Near Eastern art, and some of the finest Chinese bronzes outside China.

The **Harvard Museum of Natural History** is the public face of three Harvard institutions: the Botanical Museum, the Museum of Comparative Zoology, and the Mineralogical and Geological Museum. Highlights include fascinating exhibits, from dinosaurs to whales to ants, and the "glass flowers" – 3,000 botanically correct, exquisite models of 850 plant species in handblown glass, created between 1887 and 1936 by father and son artisans Leopold and Rudolph Blaschka. Don't miss the spectacular geodes or the collections of mysterious meteorites.

The **Peabody Museum of Archaeology and Ethnology**, entered at the opposite side of the building from the Natural History Museum, has impressive collections of Egyptian, North American Indian, and Central American artifacts as well as objects from the South Pacific Islands. Outstanding exhibits

Chinese statues from the Sackler Museum's collection

include totem carvings by Pacific Northwest tribes, Navajo weavings, artifacts from the Lewis & Clark Expedition, and casts of objects unearthed at Chichén Itzá in Mexico and Copán in Honduras.

🏛 **Harvard Art Museums**
32 Quincy St. **Tel** (617) 495-9400. **Open** 10am–5pm Tue–Sat, 1–5pm Sun. **Closed** public hols. 🔲 ♿ 📷
W **harvardartmuseums.org**

🏛 **Peabody Museum of Archaeology & Ethnology**
11 Divinity Ave. **Tel** (617) 496-1027. **Open** 9am–5pm daily. **Closed** Jan 1, Jul 4, Thanksgiving, Dec 24 & 25. 🔲 ♿ 📷 W **peabody.harvard.edu**

🏛 **Harvard Museum of Natural History**
26 Oxford St. **Tel** (617) 495-3045. **Open** 9am–5pm daily. **Closed** Jul 4, Thanksgiving, Dec 24 & 25. 🔲 ♿ 📷
W **hmnh.harvard.edu**

## ㉙ Charlestown

Ⓣ Community College. 🚌 93. ⛴ from Long Wharf. 🎪 Wed. 🎉 Jun 24.

Historic Charlestown, its picturesque streets lined with Colonial houses, is the site of the pivotal Battle of Bunker Hill, which took place on June 17, 1775. This was the Revolution's first pitched battle between British and Colonial troops, and, though the latter lost, they made a courageous stand, inflicting huge losses on the much larger British force. The **Bunker Hill Monument**, a 221-ft (67-m) granite obelisk, dedicated in 1843, commemorates this event. The building has no elevator, but 294 stone

steps lead to the top where climbers are rewarded with spectacular views of Boston Harbor and the new Zakim Bridge, the new northern gateway to Boston (staircase closes at 4:30pm). Exhibits in the base of the monument explain the history and significance of the battle, which bought time for Continental Army forces to assemble to keep the British occupying forces penned up on the Boston peninsula.

**Charlestown Navy Yard**, established in 1800, is the home of America's most famous warship, the USS *Constitution*. Built in 1797, and nicknamed "Old Ironsides" *(see p143)*, she is the oldest commissioned warship afloat and a veteran of 42 victorious battles at sea. Thoroughly overhauled for the 1997 bicentennial, she is taken out into the harbor on July 4 each year for a turnaround that reverses her position at the pier. Visitors must pass a security check.

### Environs
The Colonial town of **Lexington**, 16 miles (26 km) northwest of Boston, is the site of the first bloody skirmish between armed colonists, called Minutemen, and British troops. This battle, on April 19, 1775, acted as a catalyst for the Revolutionary War *(see p54)*. The Lexington Battle Green, with its Minute Man statue, is the focal point of the town. Three historic buildings associated with the battle and maintained by the local Historical Society are open to visitors seasonally.

Granite obelisk of the Bunker Hill Monument in Charlestown

# Massachusetts

Of all the New England states, Massachusetts may have the most diverse mix of natural and man-made attractions. Scenic seascapes and picturesque villages beckon along the eastern seaboard and Cape Cod. Venturing inland, visitors will find historic towns where America's early architecture has been well preserved. In the west, green mountains and valleys, and rich culture, characterize the Berkshire Hills.

## ❷ Salem

🏙 38,000. ✈ 🚢 From Boston's Long Wharf. 🛈 2 New Liberty St, (978) 740-1650. 🎭 Haunted Halloween (Oct). 🅦 salem.org

This coastal town, founded in 1626, is best known for the infamous witch trials of 1692, which resulted in the execution of 20 innocent people. The **Salem Witch Museum** traces the history of witchcraft and evolving perceptions of witches to the present day.

In the 18th and 19th centuries, Salem was one of New England's busiest ports, its harbor filled with ships carrying treasures from around the globe. The **Peabody Essex Museum** contains some of the world's deepest holdings of Asian art and artifacts. Many of the museum's exhibits, such as jewelry, porcelain figures, costumes, and scrimshaw objects, were brought back from distant shores by Salem's sea captains. The town's historic waterfront has been preserved as the **Salem Maritime National Historic Site**. It offers tours and maintains the 1819 Custom House and a re-created 1797 East Indiaman sailing ship, the *Friendship*, which is moored at a historic wharf.

### 🏛 Peabody Essex Museum
East India Sq. **Tel** (978) 745-9500, (866) 745-1876. **Open** 10am–5pm Tue–Sun. 🎨 🎫 🛒 ♿ 🅦 pem.org

### Environs
Marblehead, just 4 miles (6 km) from Salem, is a picturesque and historic seaport village, with historic buildings, mansions, and cottages, most notable of which are Abbot Hall and the Jeremiah Lee Mansion.

## ❸ Lowell

🏙 103,000. ✈ 🚌 🛈 40 French St, 2nd Floor (978) 459-6150.

Lowell has the distinction of being the country's first industrial city. In the early 19th century, the first cloth mill equipped with a power loom opened here, and the town soon had a number of giant mill complexes. But after the Great Depression *(see p59)* the mills closed down, leaving Lowell a ghost town. Since 1978, many downtown buildings have been restored and the Lowell National Historical Park traces the history of the town's textile industry. Lowell is also home to the **New England Quilt Museum**, which has a varied collection of displays of beautiful antique, as well as contemporary, quilts.

Concord's Old Manse, home to 19th-century literary giants

## ❹ Concord

🏙 17,750. ✈ 🛈 58 Main St, (978) 369-3120. 🎭 Battle of Concord Re-enactment (Apr). 🅦 concord machamberofcommerce.org

This peaceful, prosperous town has an eventful past. It was here that the Battle of Concord took place on April 19, 1775 which, together with the battle at nearby Lexington *(see p155)*, signaled the beginning of the Revolutionary War. The 900-acre (400-ha) **Minute Man National Historical Park** preserves the site of the battle, where a group of ordinary citizens and colonist farmers, known as Minutemen *(see p54)*, fought against British troops, driving them back from the park's North Bridge and chasing them back to Boston.

In the 19th century, Concord blossomed into the literary heart and soul of the country, with many writers establishing homes here. Both Ralph Waldo Emerson and Nathaniel Hawthorne lived briefly in **The Old Manse**; Emerson lived for nearly 50 years, until his death in 1882, at **Emerson House**, where his furniture, books, and memorabilia are on display.

Also in Concord is **Walden Pond**, immortalized in the writings of the essayist Henry David Thoreau (1817–62). In his influential work *Walden; or Life in the Woods*, Thoreau called for a return to simplicity in everyday life and a respect for nature. Walden is widely considered to be the birthplace of the conservationist movement. The pond and its

---

### Salem Witch Trials

In 1692, Salem was swept by a wave of hysteria in which 200 citizens were accused of practicing witchcraft. In all, 150 people were jailed and 19 were hanged as witches, while another man was crushed to death with stones. No one was safe: two dogs were executed on the gallows for being witches. Not surprisingly, when the governor's wife became a suspect, the trials came to an abrupt and officially sanctioned end.

Early accused: Rebecca Nurse

surrounding 333 acres (135 ha) of undeveloped woodland are ideal for walks, swimming, and fishing.

### ◆ Walden Pond State Reservation

915 Walden St. **Tel** (978) 369-3254. **Open** call for hours. 🏛 🅿 ♿

## ❺ Plymouth

🏔 52,000. ✈ 🚢 to Provincetown (seasonal). 🛈 130 Water St, (508) 747-7525, (800) USA-1620. 🌐 seeplymouth.com

The ship *Mayflower*, with 102 Pilgrims aboard, sailed into Plymouth Harbor in 1620 and established the first permanent European settlement in New England. Today the town bustles with visitors exploring the sites of America's earliest days, including **Plimoth Plantation**. Plymouth itself is a popular seaside resort, with a 3.5-mile (6-km) beach, offering harbor cruises and fishing excursions. In the fall, the surrounding bogs turn ruby red as the annual cranberry harvest gets underway.

*Mayflower II*, replica of the original Pilgrim ship, in Plymouth

Most of the historic sights can be accessed on foot by the Pilgrim Path that stretches along the waterfront and downtown areas. A sightseeing trolley also connects points of interest. At the Harbor is **Plymouth Rock**, a boulder marking the spot where the Pilgrims are said to have first stepped ashore. Moored by it is the *Mayflower II*, a replica of the 17th-century sailing ship that carried the Pilgrims over from England. Many of those

who survived the brutal crossing on this small, cramped ship succumbed to illness and malnutrition during their first winter in Plymouth. They are buried across the street on **Coles Hill**, where there is a statue of the Indian chief Massasoit, who became an ally of the survivors. There is a panoramic view of the harbor from here.

The **Pilgrim Hall Museum**, opened in 1824, has the largest existing collection of Pilgrim-era furniture, armor, and decorative arts. There are also several historic homes, including the 1677 **Harlow Old Fort House**, one of the few remaining 17th-century buildings in the town. It is operated by the Plymouth Antiquarian Society, which offers seasonal tours and special events, including an annual Pilgrim breakfast.

### 🏛 Plimoth Plantation

Rte 3A. 🛈 137 Warren Ave, (508) 746-1622. **Open** late Mar–Nov: 9am–5pm daily. 🅿 ♿ limited access to parts of site; wheelchairs available on request. 📷 🌐 plimoth.org

## Plimoth Plantation

Encircled by a palisade, Plimoth Plantation is a re-creation of the Pilgrims' 1627 village, complete with costumed interpreters, portraying actual colonists, each with a story to tell. The Wampanoag Village depicts Native American life before settlers arrived.

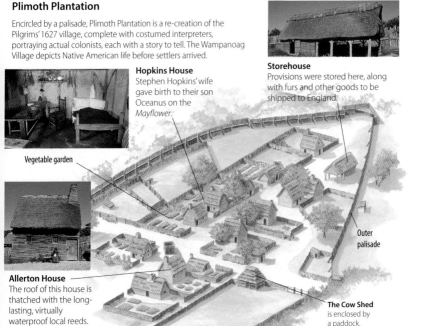

**Hopkins House**
Stephen Hopkins' wife gave birth to their son Oceanus on the *Mayflower.*

**Storehouse**
Provisions were stored here, along with furs and other goods to be shipped to England.

Vegetable garden

Outer palisade

**Allerton House**
The roof of this house is thatched with the long-lasting, virtually waterproof local reeds.

**The Cow Shed**
is enclosed by a paddock.

Cape Cod's Old Harbor Life-Saving Station, built in 1897

# ❻ Cape Cod

🚗 🚄 215 Iyannough Rd, Hyannis. 🚢 Ocean St, Hyannis; Railroad Ave, Woods Hole. *i* Jct Rtes 132 & 6, Hyannis, Rte 3, Plymouth, (508) 362-3225. 🎭 Cape Cod Maritime Week (May), Annual Bourne Scallop Festival (Sep).

More than 13 million people arrive each summer to enjoy the boundless beaches, natural beauty, and quaint Colonial villages of Cape Cod, and the neighboring islands of Martha's Vineyard and Nantucket. A special attraction for visitors are whale-watching cruises, offered from April to mid-October. The Cape, shaped like an upraised arm bent at the elbow, extends some 70 miles (113 km) into the sea.

**Cape Cod National Seashore**, stretching more than 40 miles (64 km) along the northernmost section of the Cape, from Provincetown to Chatham, is famous for its horseshoe-shaped dunes, white sand beaches, salt marshes, glacial cliffs, and woodlands. Historical structures, such as the **Old Harbor Life-Saving Station** and the 18th-century Atwood Higgins House, are interspersed among the area's beautiful natural features.

One of the most popular destinations on the Cape is **Provincetown**. This picturesque town has a historic past – the Pilgrims first landed here in 1620 and stayed for five weeks before pushing on to the mainland. The 252-ft (77-m) **Pilgrim Monument**, the tallest granite structure in the US, commemorates this event. Today, Provincetown is especially vibrant during the

Pilgrim Monument

summer months, when its population swells and it is a leading gay resort. Busy MacMillan Wharf is the jumping-off point for whale-watching cruises. Since the early 20th century, the town has also had a bustling artists' colony, counting among its famous residents the painters Mark Rothko and Jackson Pollock, and the writers Eugene O'Neill and Tennessee Williams. The work of local artists is also displayed in the Provincetown Art Association and Museum. **Chatham**, an attractive, upscale community, offers fine inns, attractive shops, and a popular summer playhouse. Fishing boats stop and unload their catch at the pier, and the surrounding waters offer good opportunities for seasonal anglers. The Railroad Museum, housed in an 1887 Victorian train station, has photos, memorabilia, and vintage railroad cars.

**Hyannis**, the largest village in Cape Cod, is a busy shopping center and the main transportation hub for the region. It is also famous as the summer home of the country's most celebrated political dynasty, the Kennedys. The heavily screened Kennedy compound is best seen from the water aboard a sightseeing cruise. At its center is the

"cottage" that multi-millionaire Joseph Kennedy (1888–1969) bought in 1926, expanding it into a sprawling vacation retreat for his nine children and their families. The **John F. Kennedy Hyannis Museum** recalls those happy times. After Kennedy's assassination in 1963, a simple memorial was erected in his honor: a pool and fountain, and a circular wall bearing Kennedy's profile.

One of Hyannis' most popular forms of transportation is the **Cape Cod Central Railroad**, which offers a scenic 2-hour round trip to the Cape Cod canal.

Hiking trails, salt marshes, tidal pools, and 12 miles (19 km) of beaches attract visitors to **Falmouth**, with its picturesque village green. It also has the 3.3-mile (5-km) Shining Sea Bike Path, with vistas of beach, harbor, and woodland. The path leads to the world's largest independent marine science research center, the Woods Hole Oceanographic Institute.

**Sandwich**, the oldest town in the Cape, is straight off a postcard: a church overlooking a picturesque pond, fed by a brook that powers the waterwheel of a Colonial-era gristmill. The church bell, dating to 1675, is said to be the oldest in the US. The town's most unusual attraction is **Heritage Museums & Gardens**, a 75-acre (30-ha) garden and museum housing the eclectic collection of the pharmaceutical tycoon Josiah K. Lilly Jr. (1893–1966). Exhibits include 37 antique cars, Native American relics, and a 1912 carousel. The gardens are famous for their lovely rhododendrons. Just a 45-minute boat ride away from the mainland lies **Martha's Vineyard**. This 108-sq mile (280-sq km) island combines

Popular sightseeing trip on the Cape Cod Central Railroad

*For hotels and restaurants see pp184–9*

Fishing boat moored outside a fishing shack, Martha's Vineyard

mesmerizing scenic beauty with the charms of a beach resort and abounds in opportunities for outdoor activities. Each town has its own distinctive atmosphere and architectural style.

Most visitors arrive by ferry at the island's commercial hub, Vineyard Haven. On the eastern shore is Edgartown, with the gracious 19th-century homes of the town's wealthy sea captains and merchants. The **Martha's Vineyard Museum** is housed in one of them – the Thomas Cooke House (c.1730), filled with family possessions and other exhibits. From here, a short ferry ride goes to Chappaquiddick Island, where, in 1969, a car driven by Senator Edward Kennedy (1932–2009) went off the bridge, killing a woman passenger.

North of Edgartown is Oak Bluff, with its gingerbread cottages, while the Western Shoreline is tranquil and rural with pristine beaches.

**Nantucket Island**, a 14-mile- (22-km-) long enclave of tranquillity with only one town, remains a largely untamed world of kettle ponds, quiet beaches, cranberry bogs, and fields of wild grapes and blueberries, punctuated by occasional houses. Nantucket was a prosperous center of the whaling industry in the early 1800s, and the mansions of sea captains and merchants reflect those glory days. The **Nantucket Historical Association** (NHA) operates 11 historical buildings in the town, one of which houses a fascinating Whaling Museum. A popular spot, 8 miles (13 km) from town, is Siasconset village, famous for its rose-colored bluffs and lanes with tiny cottages.

**Cape Cod National Seashore**
Rte 6, Cape Cod. *i* Salt Pond Visitor Center, Rte 6, Eastham, (508) 255-3421. **Open** year-round. late Jun–early Sep only. **W** nps.gov/caco

**John F. Kennedy Hyannis Museum**
397 Main St, Hyannis. **Tel** (508) 970-3077. **Open** mid-Apr–May & Nov: 10am–4pm Mon–Sat, noon–4pm Sun; Jun–Oct: 9am–5pm Mon–Sat, noon–5pm Sun. **W** jfkhyannis museum.org

**Heritage Museums & Gardens**
67 Grove St, Sandwich. **Tel** (508) 888-3300. **Open** mid-Apr–Oct: 10am–5pm daily. **W** heritagemuseumsandgardens.org

**Martha's Vineyard Museum**
59 School St, Edgartown. **Tel** (508) 627-4441. **Open** mid-May–mid-Oct: 10am–5pm Mon–Sat, noon–5pm Sun.

**Nantucket Historical Association (NHA)**
15 Broad St, Nantucket Island. **Tel** (508) 228-1894. Historic buildings: **Open** call for hours. Whaling Museum only. **W** nha.org

## 🅐 Sturbridge

Old Sturbridge Village: Rte 20, Sturbridge. **Tel** (508) 347-3362. **Open** early Apr–late Oct: 9:30am–5pm daily; late Oct–early Apr: 9:30am–4pm Tue–Sun. **Closed** Dec. **W** osv.org

This small town is home to **Old Sturbridge Village**, an open-air museum in the form of an early 19th-century village. At the heart of the museum are about 40 vintage buildings that have been restored and relocated from all over New England. They include the Federal-style Towne House, a meetinghouse, a tavern, and a store.

## 🅑 The Berkshires

🛫 🚉 Pittsfield. *i* 66 Allen St, Pittsfield, (413) 743-4500. **W** berkshires.org

Wooded hills, green valleys, rippling rivers, and waterfalls have long attracted visitors to this western corner of Massachusetts, which is rich in opportunities for outdoor as well as cultural activity. The area is speckled with scenic small towns and villages. **Pittsfield**, in the shadow of Mount Greylock, is famous as the home of Herman Melville (1819–91), where he wrote his masterpiece, *Moby Dick*. **Lenox** has the grand estates of prominent families such as the Carnegies. Each summer, it also hosts the prestigious Tanglewood Musical Festival, featuring performances from a wide variety of musical genres. The main street of **Stockbridge** has been immortalized in the paintings of one of America's most beloved illustrators, Norman Rockwell (1894–1978), who lived here for 25 years. His works can be seen in the town's **Norman Rockwell Museum**.

Especially attractive to nature lovers is the **Mount Washington State Forest** and the nearby **Bash Bish State Park**.

**Norman Rockwell Museum**
Rte 183. **Tel** (413) 298-4100. **Open** May–Oct: 10am–5pm daily; Nov–Apr: 10am–4pm Mon–Fri, 10am–5pm Sat & Sun. **Closed** Jan 1, Thanksgiving, Dec 25. **W** nrm.org

Bash Bish Falls, near Mount Washington State Forest in the Berkshires

# Rhode Island

The smallest state in America, Rhode Island is not an island at all but has a shoreline dotted with lovely islets and beaches. Although known as the Ocean State, half of Rhode Island is woodland, ideal for nature walks and camping. The state's two major cities are Providence, the lively capital, and Newport, which has some of New England's most opulent mansions.

Stately buildings along Benefit Street's Mile of History in Providence

## ❾ Providence

🏙 174,000. ✈ 🚇 Providence Station, 100 Gaspee St. 🚌 Kennedy Plaza. 🚢 Point St (to Newport). ℹ 1 Sabin St, (401) 751-1177 or (800) 233-1636. 🎭 Festival of Historic Houses (Jun–Dec); International Film Festival (Aug). 🌐 goprovidence.com

Perched on seven hills on the banks of Narragansett Bay, Providence is an interesting blend of the historic and the modern. It started life as a farming community, established in 1636 by the clergyman Roger Williams, who was driven from the Massachusetts Bay colony for his outspoken beliefs on religious freedom. It soon became a flourishing seaport, and then evolved into a hub of industry in the 19th century, with immigrants from Europe pouring in to work in its textile mills.

Providence is bisected by the Providence River. On its west bank is the downtown district, with a lively dining and entertainment scene and a revitalized waterfront, largely due to Waterfire Providence®'s art installations and bonfires. To the east is the campus of Brown University and several historic streets. The most outstanding of these is **Benefit Street's Mile of History**. This lovely tree-lined street has more than 100 houses ranging in style from Colonial and Federal to Greek Revival and Victorian. Its architectural gems include the **Providence Athenaeum**, a Greek-Revival-style library, whose collection dates back to 1753 and the First Unitarian Church. Its 2,500-lb (1,130-kg) bell was one of the largest cast by Paul Revere's foundry. Also on Benefit Street is the Rhode Island School of Design's **RISD Museum of Art**, whose comprehensive collection ranges from Ancient Egyptian to contemporary American art. A short distance to the north, on Main Street, is the **First Baptist Church in America**. Built in 1774–5, it has an intricately carved wooden interior and a Waterford crystal chandelier.

Founded in 1764, **Brown University** is the seventh-oldest college in the US and one of the prestigious Ivy League schools. Its beautiful campus, a rich blend of Gothic and Beaux Arts styles, is worth exploring. Notable buildings here include the John Hay Library with its collection of memorabilia relating to President Abraham Lincoln, the John Carter Brown Library with a fascinating collection of Americana, and the List Art Center, a striking building designed by Philip Johnson, which features Classical and contemporary art.

**John Brown House**, a Georgian mansion, built in 1786 for a wealthy merchant and shipowner, has been impeccably restored. Its interior is decorated with ornate plaster-ornamented ceilings, a grand staircase with twisted balusters, and wallpapers from France. Its 12 rooms are a repository for some of the finest furniture and antiques of that period. Nearby, another house with fine 18th-century furnishings is the 1707 **Governor Stephen Hopkins House**.

One of the brightest additions to downtown Providence is **Waterplace Park and Riverwalk**, a 4-acre (1.6-ha) walkway located at the junction of three rivers – the Moshassuck, Providence, and Woona-squatucket. Visitors can also stroll along the park's cobblestone paths, float under footbridges in canoes or gondolas, and enjoy free concerts at the amphitheater during the summer season.

Roger Williams Park and Zoo, a highlight of downtown Providence

*For hotels and restaurants see pp184–9*

Known as the "Temple of Trade", **The Arcade**, an 1828 Greek-Revival building, covers an entire block in the city's old financial district. The first indoor shopping mall in the US, this massive three-story stone complex, with its high Ionic granite columns, has a skylight extending the entire length of the building, providing light even on rainy days. Renovated in 2013, the building has shops and restaurants on the first level, with apartments above.

Downtown Providence is dominated by the imposing **Rhode Island State House**, constructed in 1904. Its magnificent white marble dome is topped by a bronze statue called *Independent Man*, a symbol of Rhode Island's free spirit. Among the displays inside are the original state charter of 1663 and a full-length portrait of President George Washington by Gilbert Stuart.

The city's largest green space is the **Roger Williams Park and Zoo**. Once farmland, this 422-acre (171-ha) park now holds gardens, greenhouses, and ponds, a lake with paddleboats and rowboats, as well as jogging and cycling tracks and a tennis center. Children especially love the carousel rides and train, the planetarium, and the Museum of Natural History. The highlight of the park, however, is the zoo, which has more than 900 animals, including mammals such as zebras, giraffes, and cheetahs. An underwater window allows visitors to look at the penguins and polar bears as they cavort playfully in the water.

**RISD Museum of Art**
224 Benefit St. **Tel** (401) 454-6500.
**Open** 10am–5pm Tue–Sun, 10am–9pm Thu. **Closed** public hols.
**w risd.edu**

Rhode Island State House with its marble dome

**John Brown House**
52 Power St. **Tel** (401) 273-7507.
Apr–Nov: 1:30–3pm Tue–Fri, 10:30am–3pm Sat; Dec–Mar: 10:30am–3pm Fri & Sat.

**Rhode Island State House**
82 Smith St. **Tel** (401) 222-3983.
**Open** 8:30am–4:30pm Mon–Fri.
**Closed** public hols.
9am, 10am, 11am, 1pm, 2pm.

## Downtown Providence

1. Benefit Street's Mile of History
2. Providence Athenaeum
3. RISD Museum of Art
4. First Baptist Church in America
5. Brown University
6. John Brown House
7. Governor Stephen Hopkins House
8. Waterplace Park and Riverwalk
9. The Arcade
10. Rhode Island State House

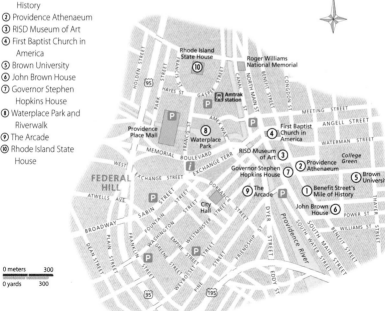

0 meters 300
0 yards 300

Roger Williams Park and Zoo
TF Green State Airport
12 miles (19 km)

For keys to symbols *see back flap*

Scores of yachts in the harbor at Newport

## ⑩ Newport

28,000. Gateway Center, 23 America's Cup Ave. Perrotti Park (to Providence). 23 America's Cup Ave, (401) 845-9123, (800) 326-6030. Newport Tennis Week (Jul), JVC Jazz Festival (Aug).
**discovernewport.org**

A center of trade, culture, wealth, and military activity for more than 300 years, Newport is a true sightseeing mecca. The town's main attractions are its mansions, most of them located on Bellevue Avenue on the southeastern side of the city. Built between 1748 and 1902, when the rich and famous flocked here each summer to beat New York's heat, these summer "cottage" retreats of the country's wealthiest families, such as the Vanderbilts and the Astors, are some of America's grandest private homes. Modeled on European palaces and decorated with the finest artworks, the mansions were used for only 10 weeks of the year. **The Breakers** is one of the finest examples.

Newport is also home to the oldest synagogue in USA. Built in 1763 by Sephardic Jews who had fled Spain and Portugal in search of religious tolerance, the **Touro Synagogue** is an outstanding example of 18th-century architecture. It is located just east of Washington Square, where a number of historic Colonial buildings have been preserved. Among them is the seasonal Brick Market Museum and Shop housed in the market, which was the center of commerce in Colonial times. Also on the Square is the White Horse Tavern *(see p188)*, which claims to be the oldest continuously operating tavern in America; it was granted its liquor license in 1673.

Apart from its mansions and historic sites, Newport also has numerous outdoor attractions. South of Washington Square is

### The Breakers

The architecture and ostentation of the Gilded Age of the late 1800s reached its pinnacle with The Breakers, the summer home of the railroad magnate Cornelius Vanderbilt II (1843–99). Completed in 1895, the four-story, 70-room limestone mansion was modeled after 16th-century palaces in Turin and Genoa. Its interior is adorned with marble, stained glass, gilt, and crystal.

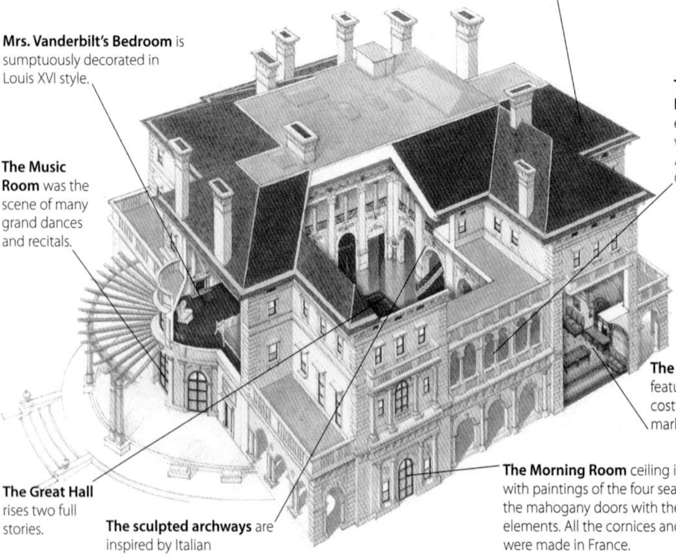
**The Dining Room**, a two-story room, has a stunning arched ceiling and two huge crystal chandeliers.
**Mrs. Vanderbilt's Bedroom** is sumptuously decorated in Louis XVI style.
**The Upper Loggia** has enchanting views of the Atlantic Ocean.
**The Music Room** was the scene of many grand dances and recitals.
**The Billiard Room** features several costly wall marbles.
**The Morning Room** ceiling is adorned with paintings of the four seasons, the mahogany doors with the four elements. All the cornices and panels were made in France.
**The Great Hall** rises two full stories.
**The sculpted archways** are inspired by Italian Renaissance-style palazzos.

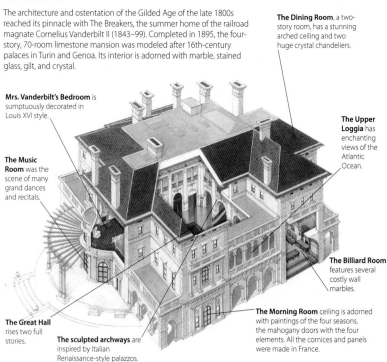

The breathtaking Cliff Walk, popular with visitors in Newport

**Fort Adams State Park**, with Fort Adams, built in 1853, as its centerpiece. No longer in use as a garrison, the fort is surrounded with facilities for swimming and other sports. Each year, Newport's famous Jazz Festival is held here. The park also has the Museum of Yachting, with a collection of luxury yachts.

Another popular site is the 3.5-mile- (5.5-km-) long **Cliff Walk**, southwest of downtown. The trail, along the city's ragged cliffs, offers some fine views of the Gilded-Age mansions and has been designated a National Recreation Trail. The Forty Steps, each named for someone lost at sea, lead to the ocean.

### The Breakers
Ochre Point Ave. **Tel** (401) 847-1000. **Open** Apr–mid-Nov: 9am–5pm daily. Call for winter hours. **Closed** Thanksg., Dec 24 & 25. every 15 minutes. newportmansions.org

### Touro Synagogue
85 Touro St. **Tel** (401) 847-4794. **Open** call for times. Services: Shabbat & all Jewish hols. every half-hr.

### Fort Adams State Park
Harrison Ave. **Tel** (401) 847-2400. **Open** sunrise to sunset daily. Museum of Yachting: **Tel** (401) 847-1018. **Open** Jun–Oct: 11am–4:30pm Wed–Mon; Nov–May: by appt.

## ❶ South County Beaches

Narragansett: 36 Ocean Rd, (401) 783-7121. Charlestown: 4945 Old Post Rd, (401) 364-3878.

Southwest of Newport, between **Narragansett** and Watch Hill, are some 100 miles (161 km) of pristine white sand beaches and a series of tidal salt ponds. The ponds are big lures for bird-watchers hoping to study the egrets, sandpipers, and herons that swim and wade in the salty marshes. Many of the beaches are free to the public, except for parking fees. **Scarborough State Beach** is excellent for bodysurfing and surfboarding, while the sheltered, cove-protected **Roger Wheeler State Beach** is a favorite for families. **East Matunuck State Beach** is popular with surfers on windy days. The beautiful sandy stretch of **Charlestown Town Beach** has a boat ramp with access to the coastal ponds of the Ninigret National Wildlife Refuge.

Farther west along the coast is **Misquamicut State Beach**. The largest beach in the state, it has gentle surf and an old-time amusement park with rides and many diversions for children.

## ❷ Block Island

State Pier, Galilee. Ferries carry cars by advance bookings, (401) 783-7996. blockislandferry.com

Lying just 13 miles (21 km) off the coast, Block Island is a great destination for outdoor enthusiasts who enjoy such activities as swimming, fishing, sailing, bird-watching, canoeing, and horseback riding. Some 30 miles (48 km) of natural trails entice hikers and cyclists to experience the island's natural beauty. The village of Old

Harbor is the island's main hub of activity. Victorian houses, hotels, and shops line the streets, and anglers can charter boats to fish for striped bass, bluefish, flounder, and cod. South of the village are the dramatic 200-ft- (61-m-) high red clay cliffs of **Mohegan Bluffs**, and the Southeast Lighthouse, which was once the most powerful in New England.

A favorite with hikers is **Rodman's Hollow Natural Area**. This glacial depression, well marked with nature trails, is a refuge for hawks and white-tailed deer. On Block Island's northwestern coast is **Great Salt Pond**, which is completely protected from the ocean. It is an excellent spot for kayaking and fishing. Nearby New Harbor is the island's prime marina and boating center. **Clayhead**, on the island's northeastern coast, offers wonderful views of the Atlantic Ocean, and is the starting point for a nature trail that goes all the way north to **Settler's Rock**. A plaque here honors the 16 Englishmen who landed here in 1661. The rock is at the edge of Sachem Pond, a favorite for swimming and kayaking. An 18-mile (29-km) driving tour of Block Island is a comfortable way to take in all these sites.

Plaque to early English pioneers, Settler's Rock, Block Island

The dramatic red clay cliffs at Mohegan Bluffs, Block Island

# Connecticut

Although compact enough to drive across in a few hours, Connecticut has treasures that entice visitors to stay for days. Along its magnificent shoreline are beaches, marinas, and the remarkable maritime museum at Mystic Seaport. Inland, the Connecticut River Valley and the Litchfield Hills are dotted with scenic and historic villages. Hartford, the bustling capital, and New Haven, home of Yale University, are its main cities.

## ⓭ Hartford

🏙 139,000. ✈ 🚌 🚉 1 Union Place.
ℹ 1 Constitution Plaza, (888) 288-
4748. 🎭 Mark Twain Days (summer).
ⓦ **ctvisit.com**

Founded in 1636 by a group of English settlers from the Massachusetts Bay Colony, Hartford's golden age was in the 19th century, when it became a flourishing center of the insurance industry. It also became a vibrant cultural center, thanks to resident authors such as Mark Twain. In recent years, an ambitious revitalization program has breathed new life into the city.

Dominating the cityscape is the gleaming gold-leaf dome of the **State Capitol**, a Victorian-Gothic building perched on a hilltop. Many of Hartford's attractions are accessible on foot from here. The Capitol overlooks the 40-acre (16-ha) **Bushnell Park**, the creation of Hartford native Frederick Law Olmsted (1822–1903), who also laid out New York's Central Park. There are 100 varieties of trees, and a 1914 carousel with 48 hand-carved horses.

The 1796 **Old State House**, designed by Charles Bulfinch (*see p140*), is the country's oldest Capitol building. With its grand center hall and staircase, and ornate cupola, it is a superb example of Federal architecture. Nearby, the **Center Church** has five stained-glass windows designed by the US artist Louis Comfort Tiffany (1848–1933). To its south is the **Wadsworth Atheneum**, the oldest continuously operating public art museum in the country. Its collection includes Renaissance, Baroque, and Impressionist art, as well as works by American artists.

West of downtown is the 1874 **Mark Twain House and Museum**, a Gothic-style masterpiece with peaked gables, expansive upper balconies, and towering turrets. Constructed at the height of Twain's career, the 19-room home was based on a floor plan drawn up by his wife Olivia. Of special interest are

The Connecticut State Capitol, overlooking Bushnell Park

---

## Downtown Hartford

① State Capitol
② Bushnell Park
③ Old State House
④ Center Church
⑤ Wadsworth Atheneum

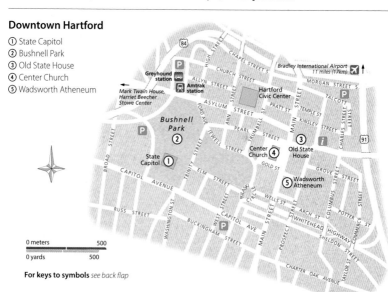

0 meters 500
0 yards 500

**For keys to symbols** *see back flap*

The Billiard Room, Mark Twain House, Hartford

the library with its ornate wooden fireplace mantel; the tranquil Billiard Room where Twain wrote some of his best-known works, including *The Adventures of Tom Sawyer*; and the Master Bedroom with its beautifully carved bed. An informative visitor center illuminates Twain's life and work.

Next door is the **Harriet Beecher Stowe Center**, where the famous author of the anti-slavery novel *Uncle Tom's Cabin* (1852) lived until her death in 1896. The house is adorned with gingerbread ornamentation typical of late 19th-century Victorian design, while the elegance of its interior displays Harriet's less well-known talent as a decorator.

🏛 **Mark Twain House and Museum**
351 Farmington Ave. **Tel** (860) 247-0998. **Open** 9:30am–5:30pm Mon–Sat, noon–5:30pm Sun. **Closed** Tue (Jan–Mar), public hols. 📷 🎫 obligatory.
♿ 1st floor only.
🌐 **marktwainhouse.org**

## ⑭ Litchfield

🏠 8,850. ℹ Litchfield Hills Visitors' Bureau, PO Box 968, (860) 567-4506.
🌐 **northwestct.com**

This picturesque and historic town is at the center of the Litchfield Hills region in northwestern Connecticut, which many people consider the most scenic part of the state. Anchored by the Housatonic River, the bucolic landscape of lovely woods, valleys, lakes, and wildlife offers great opportunities for sports such as canoeing, kayaking, whitewater rafting, tubing, fly-fishing, and hiking. In fall, the brilliant foliage along the region's roads entrances sightseers.

Litchfield's many historic houses include the 1784 **Tapping Reeve House and Law School**, the country's first law school. On the outskirts of the town, on Route 202, **Mount Tom State Park** has trails leading to the 1,325-ft (404-m) summit. The lake is ideal for activities such as scuba diving, swimming, boating, and fishing.

## ⑮ Connecticut River Valley

Windsor: 🏠 27,800. ℹ (860) 787-9640. Old Lyme: 🏠 6,800.
ℹ 27 Greenmanville Ave, Mystic, (860) 536-8822, (860) 701-9113.
🌐 **mystic.org**

The Connecticut River Valley is dotted with picture-postcard perfect little towns and villages. **Windsor**, settled in the early 1630s by Pilgrims from Plymouth (*see p157*), has a number of historic houses, open to visitors, such as the 1758 **John & Sarah Strong House** (undergoing renovations until late 2015). Nearby is the Palisade Green, where nervous settlers built a walled stockade in their 1637 war with the Pequot Indians.

**Wethersfield**, settled in 1634, stands as a primer of American architecture from the 18th to the 20th centuries. Especially worth visiting is the Webb-Deane-Stevens Museum, which is a trio of dwellings that depict the lifestyles of three different 18th-century Americans – a diplomat, a wealthy merchant, and a leather tanner. The **Dinosaur State Park**, farther south, preserves some 500 prehistoric dinosaur tracks beneath a geodesic dome. It also has a display of a life-size model of an 8-ft- (2-m-) tall Dilophosaurus.

Just outside the town of East Haddam is the bizarre and ostentatious **Gillette Castle**, built in 1919 by the actor William Gillette. This 24-room granite mansion is built like a medieval castle, complete with battlements and turrets, and is rife with oddities such as Gillette's home-made trick locks and furniture set on wheels and tracks.

Picturesque Old Lyme boasts several 18th- and 19th-century houses built for sea captains. It is also renowned for the **Florence Griswold Museum**, housed in an 1817 mansion. Paintings by some of America's leading artists, such as Childe Hassam and Clark Voorhees, adorn the walls of this museum, together with superb works by other artists who lived in art patron Florence Griswold's house and painted on its wall panels to repay her generosity.

🏛 **Wethersfield**
ℹ Greater Hartford Tourism District, 1 Constitution Plaza, Hartford, (888) 288-4748. 🌐 **ctvisit.com**

🏛 **Gillette Castle**
67 River Rd, off Rte 82, Hadlyme. **Tel** (860) 526-2336. **Open** late May–Columbus Day: 10am–5pm daily. 📷
🎫 ♿

🏛 **Florence Griswold Museum**
96 Lyme St, Old Lyme. **Tel** (860) 434-5542. **Open** 10am–5pm Tue–Sat, 1–5pm Sun. 📷 🎫 ♿ 🌐 **flogris.org**

*The Harpist* by Alphonse Jongers at the Florence Griswold Museum

# ⑯ New Haven

🗺 123, 626. ✈ ℹ 195 Church St, (203) 777-8550. 🌐 **visitnewhaven. com** Yale University: ℹ 149 Elm St, (203) 432-2300. 🚻 ♿
🎭 International Festival of Arts and Ideas (Jun). 🌐 **yale.edu**

Founded in 1638, New Haven is located on the coast, where three rivers flow into Long Island Sound. Although this has helped make it a major manufacturing center, the city is better known as the home of **Yale University**, one of the world's most prestigious institutions of higher learning. Its alumni include no fewer than four American presidents, including the Bushes Sr. and Jr, and Bill Clinton. Yale, founded in 1701, has made New Haven a leading center for education, research, and technology, and has enriched its cultural life as well.

The main area of the town is the 16-acre (6-ha) **New Haven Green**, serving as the setting for many of New Haven's activities and festivals. Three beautiful early 19th-century churches are located on the Green, of which the **First Church of Christ**, with a Tiffany stained-glass window, is regarded as a masterpiece of American Georgian style. Much of the core of downtown New

Tiffany stained-glass window, First Church of Christ

Haven is covered by the Yale University campus, dotted with Georgian and Neo-Gothic buildings, as well as modern structures designed by Eero Saarinen and Philip Johnson. Major landmarks on the campus are the beautiful Gothic-style Memorial Quadrangle and the Harkness Tower, whose carillon rings out at intervals through the day.

Yale's outstanding museums are a prime attraction for visitors. The **Yale Center for British Art**, whose collection was donated by the philanthropist Paul Mellon (1907–99), has the largest collection of British art outside the UK and includes paintings by Gainsborough, Hogarth, and Turner. The treasures of the **Beinecke Rare Book and Manuscript Libraries** include one of the world's few remaining Gutenberg Bibles. The **Yale University Art Gallery**, reflecting the generosity and taste of the Yale alumni, houses works by artists such as Picasso, van Gogh, Manet, and Monet, while the **Peabody Museum of Natural History** is famous for its collection of dinosaurs. A must for the musically inclined is the **Yale Collection of Musical Instruments**. Its stunning exhibits consist of violins and harpsichords dating back

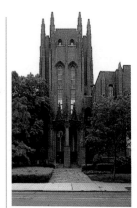

Entrance to the Peabody Museum of Natural History, Yale University

centuries. These historical instruments are still played at concerts held here today.

The most popular park in New Haven is the 84-acre (34-ha) Lighthouse Point Park on Long Island Sound. It has nature trails, a bird sanctuary, as well as an 1840 lighthouse.

🏛 **Yale Center for British Art**
1080 Chapel St. **Tel** (203) 432-2800. **Open** 10am–5pm Tue–Sat, noon–5pm Sun. **Closed** public hols. 🚻 ♿ 🎁

🏛 **Beinecke Rare Book & Manuscript Libraries**
121 Wall St. **Tel** (203) 432-2977. **Open** 9am–7pm Mon–Thu, 9am–5pm Fri, noon–5pm Sat. **Closed** Sat in Aug & public hols.

🏛 **Yale University Art Gallery**
1111 Chapel St. **Tel** (203) 432-0600. **Open** 10am–5pm Tue–Fri (to 8pm Thu), 11am–5pm Sat & Sun. **Closed** public hols. 🚻 ♿ 🎁 🌐 **artgallery. yale.edu**

Church spires around New Haven Green, the focal point of the town

*For hotels and restaurants in this region see pp184–9*

The *Charles W. Morgan*, the last wooden whaling ship, in Mystic Seaport

# ⑰ Connecticut Coast

Mystic: 🏔 2,600. ℹ️ 27 Greenmanville Ave, (860) 536-8822. Madison: 🏔 16,000. ℹ️ 1 Constitution Plaza, Hartford, (888) 288-4748. Stamford: Fairfield County. 🏔 117,083.
🌐 **visitwesternct.com**

Connecticut's magnificent 105-mile- (170-km-) long shoreline, is scalloped by coves, inlets, and harbors, dotted with beaches, marinas, and state parks. Historic towns and villages also lie along the coast.

One of the most popular tourist destinations along the Connecticut Coast is **Mystic Seaport**. This re-created 18th- and 19th-century seafaring village, where nearly every home sports a nautical motif, also has the world's largest maritime museum. Mystic's main attraction is its preservation shipyard and its fleet of antique ships, including the restored whaling ship *Charles W. Morgan*, built in 1841. Another highlight is the Mystic River Scale Model, with more than 250 detailed buildings. The impressive Mystic Aquarium has a huge gallery of penguins, stingrays, and sharks, while seals and sea lions can be seen cavorting in the outdoor Seal Island.

A short distance west of Mystic Seaport is **New London**. This historic town was torched by British forces during the American Revolution, but, remarkably, many of the houses survived. Among them is the Joshua Hempsted House, built in 1678, which is insulated with seaweed. By the 19th century

New London had recovered to become a prosperous center of the whaling industry – the row of colonnaded Greek-Revival mansions on Whale Oil Row attest to the affluence of that era.

The resort town of **Madison**, full of antique stores and boutiques, also has several historic homes open for viewing. Among the fascinating artifacts on display at the **Deacon John Grave House** is the family bookkeeping ledger, with entries from 1678 to 1895. Also in Madison is **Hammonasset Beach State Park**, the largest shoreline park in the state, with a 2-mile- (3-km-) long beach that attracts swimmers, sailors, sunbathers, and divers. Neighboring **Guilford** has a Tudor-Gothic-style granite fort. This three-story stronghold, built in 1640 by a group of Puritan settlers to protect themselves against attacks by the local Indians, is the oldest stone dwelling of its kind in New England.

From Guilford's Stony Creek Dock, travelers can cruise to the **Thimble Islands** aboard tour boats that operate in the area, watching seals or taking in the

The Thimbles, home to seals, whales, and colorful legends

glorious fall colors. Many of the 365 islands are little more than large boulders, but some privately owned islands have small communities. Legend has it that the privateer Captain Kidd (1645–1701) hid plundered treasure on Money Island while being pursued by the British fleet.

**Coastal Fairfield County**, in the southernmost corner of the state, has attractions for every taste. The shoreline is dusted with beaches offering a variety of summer recreation opportunities, while naturalists are drawn to its nature preserves and zoo. The area also has numerous art galleries and museums.

**Bridgeport** is home to the Beardsley Zoo, the Barnum Museum, and the Discovery Museum. The Barnum Museum is currently closed for repairs.

The charming town of **Westport** on the banks of the Saugatuck River has the Sherwood Island State Park. **Norwalk** has historic buildings, shops, and cafés along its waterfront, as well as a Maritime Aquarium. **New Canaan**, set in a landscape of woods, streams, and rolling fields, is spectacular in fall. **Stamford** has a unique First Presbyterian Church, shaped like a fish, and a lively downtown area.

**Greenwich**, blessed with a stunning coastline, is home to an art colony, the Bush-Holley Historic Site. A 44-mile (71-km) drive through Fairfield County gives a good overview of the Connecticut coast.

🏛 **Mystic Seaport**
75 Greenmanville Ave (Rte 7).
**Tel** (860) 572-0711. Ships and exhibits:
**Open** Apr–Oct: 9am–5pm; Nov–Mar:
call for hours. **Closed** Dec 24 & 25. 🅿️
🌐 **mysticseaport.org**

🏠 **Deacon John Grave House**
Madison, 581 Boston Post Rd.
**Tel** (203) 245-4798. **Open** call to
arrange tour. 🅿️ 📷

🏖 **Hammonasset Beach State Park**
I-95, exit 62. Park: **Tel** (203) 245-2785.
**Open** 8am–dusk daily. 🅿️ 📷 ♿
Campground reservations: **Tel** (877)
668-2267.

Federal-style rowhouses in the historic Beacon Hill neighborhood, Boston ▶

# Vermont

Vermont's varied attractions are scattered throughout the state. Historic villages and the natural splendors of the Green Mountain National Forest grace the south, while in the northwest Lake Champlain provides a backdrop for the lively college town of Burlington. Famous ski resorts such as Stowe are perched amid the mountains that run the length of the state. In fall, Vermont's display of leaf colors is spectacular.

Woodward Reservoir in the Green Mountain National Forest

## ⑱ Green Mountain National Forest

ℹ️ Forest Supervisor, Green Mountain National Forest, 231 N Main St, Rutland. **Tel** (802) 747-6700. 🌐 **fs.usda.gov/greenmountain**

This huge spine of greenery and mountains runs for 550 sq miles (1,400 sq km) – almost the entire length of Vermont – along two-thirds of the Green Mountain Range. The mountains, many of them over 4,000 ft (1,200 m) high, have some of the best ski centers in the US, including Sugarbush and Mount Snow.

The National Forest is divided into northern and southern sectors, and encompasses six wilderness areas, many of them with no roads, electricity, or clearly marked trails. Less primitive areas of the forest, however, have picnic sites, camping grounds, and more than 500 miles (805 km) of hiking paths, including the famous Long and Appalachian Trails. The area's lakes, rivers, and reservoirs offer excellent boating and fishing, and there are designated paths for horseback riders as well as bikers.

In the southwest corner of the Green Mountain National Forest is **Bennington**, Vermont's third-largest city. An important manufacturing center, Bennington is also home to the small but prestigious Bennington College. Three 19th-century wooden covered bridges (just off Route 67) herald the approach to the town, which was established in 1749. A few decades later, Ethan Allen arrived on the scene to lead the Green Mountain Boys, a citizen's militia that scored several decisive victories against British forces during the Revolutionary War.

The town's most prominent landmark is the 306-ft- (93-m-) high **Bennington Battle Monument**, a granite obelisk commemorating a 1777 battle, when Colonial forces defeated the British. The monument looms over the Old Bennington Historic District, which has a village green ringed by Federal-style brick buildings. The 1806 First Congregational Church is particularly striking, with its vaulted plaster and wood ceilings. Next to the church is the Old Burying Ground where one of America's most loved poets, Robert Frost, is buried.

The 1891 Bennington Battle Monument

A major attraction for visitors is the **Bennington Museum and Grandma Moses Gallery**. Apart from an impressive collection of Americana, the museum has a gallery devoted to folk artist Anna Mary "Grandma" Moses, who lived in the Bennington area. A farmer's wife with no formal art training, Grandma Moses (1860–1961) started painting landscapes as a hobby when she was in her mid-seventies. "Discovered" by critics in 1940, her distinctive primitive paintings soon won international renown.

🏛️ **Bennington Museum & Grandma Moses Gallery**
75 Main St. **Tel** (802) 447-1571. **Open** 10am–5pm Thu–Tue (daily Jul–Oct). **Closed** Jan, Thanksgiving, Dec 25. 🅿️ ♿ 📷 🌐 **benningtonmuseum.org**

## ⑲ Manchester

🏔️ 3,860. ✈️ 🚌 ℹ️ 39 Bonnet St, (802) 362-2100.

This scenic town, ringed by mountains, is a favorite destination for both shoppers and skiers. Manchester Depot and Manchester Center are major outlet centers in New England, offering brand-name goods in their designer outlets and factory stores. Visitors also enjoy following the Equinox Skyline Drive, with its panoramic views from the crest of Mount Equinox.

The town has two major ski areas – **Stratton**, with more than 90 trails and a hillside ski village with shops and restaurants, and **Bromley**, a busy, family-oriented ski area.

Manchester has been a vacation resort since the 19th century, and its gracious mansions evoke that era. One of the most elegant is **Hildene**, a 24-room Georgian manor built by Robert Todd Lincoln, son of President Abraham Lincoln. Among its notable features are a 1,000-pipe Aeolian organ.

🏛️ **Hildene**
Rte 7A. **Tel** (802) 362-1788. **Open** 9:30am–4:30pm daily. 🅿️ 📷 every 30 mins. ♿ 🌐 **hildene.org**

# ⑳ Killington

🏔 1,000. 🚍 ℹ️ Rte 4, West Killington, (802) 422-3333, (800) 621-6867.

Sporty types who like outdoor adventure and a lively social life head for this year-round resort. Killington operates the largest ski center in the eastern United States, with 191 runs for alpine skiing and snowboarding spread across seven peaks, including nearby Pico Mountain. It also has cross-country ski areas at Mountain Top Inn and Mountain Meadows.

Killington itself is the second highest peak in Vermont, at 4,240 ft (1,295 m). The ski season here lasts eight months, longer than anywhere else in Vermont.

In summer as well as fall, a gondola ferries visitors up to the peaks from where, on clear day, there are views of five states and distant Canada.

# ㉑ Woodstock

🏔 1,000. 🚍 🚌 ℹ️ Mechanic St, (802) 432-1100, (888) 496-6378.
**w** woodstockvt.com

Even in Vermont, where historic, picturesque villages are commonplace, Woodstock stands out. Founded in 1761, the town is an enclave of renovated brick and clapboard Georgian houses, many of them beautifully restored, thanks to the generosity of philanthropists such as the Rockefeller family, and the railroad magnate Frederick Billings (1823–90), who also financed the planting of 10,000 trees here. **Billings Farm and Museum** is still a working entity. The 1890 farmhouse has

The *Ticonderoga*, at Shelburne Museum

been restored, and visitors can attend seasonal events such as apple-cider pressing in the fall and plowing competitions in the spring. The museum's exhibits include vintage farm implements, butter churns, and ice cutters.

Nearby Quechee is home to the **Vermont Institute of Natural Science**, a reserve where injured birds of prey are cared for until they can be returned to the wild.

### 🏛 Billings Farm & Museum
River Rd. **Tel** (802) 457-2355.
**Open** May–Oct: 10am–5pm daily.
Call for winter hours. 🅿️ ♿ 🚻

### 🦅 Vermont Institute of Natural Science
Woodstock Rd, Quechee. **Tel** (802) 359-5000. **Open** mid-Apr–Oct: 10am–5pm daily; Nov–Apr: call for hours. 🅿️ 🚫 ♿ **w** vinsweb.org

### Environs
Six miles (10 km) east of town is the stunningly beautiful **Quechee Gorge**. The best view of the chasm is on Route 4, which crosses the gorge via a steel bridge. A short hiking trail leads from the parking lot on the east side to the Ottauquechee River below.

# ㉒ Shelburne Museum & Farms

Rte 7, 7 miles (11 km) S of Burlington. **Tel** (802) 985-3346. **Open** mid-May–late Oct: 10am–5pm daily (Pizzagalli Center open year-round).
**Closed** late Oct–May, Thanksgiving, Dec 25. 🅿️ 🚫 🚻 💻 📷
**w** shelburnemuseum.org

Established in 1947 by collector Electra Webb, Shelburne Museum's 39 exhibition buildings and their contents constitute one of America's finest museums. Its eclectic collection, which celebrates three centuries of American ingenuity, includes folk art, antique tools, and circus memorabilia, along with scrimshaw, duck decoys, and paintings by artists such as Winslow Homer and Grandma Moses.

Among the relocated or replicated historic buildings on view are a horseshoe-shaped **Circus Building**, housing a 500-ft- (152-m-) long miniature circus parade, and an 1890 **Railroad Station**. Visitors can also explore an 1871 Lake Champlain lighthouse and the *Ticonderoga*, a former Lake Champlain steamship. The Pizzagalli Center for Art and Education is open all year for art workshops, lectures, film screenings, and musical performances.

Shelburne is home to a historic 2-sq-mile (6-sq-km) estate, Shelburne Farms, with its beautiful green rolling pastures and woodlands. There are tours of the dairy, and there are also special areas where children can pet and play with the animals.

One of the many beautiful homes in the village of Woodstock

First Unitarian Church, Burlington

## ㉓ Burlington

🏙 39,000. ✈ 🚌 1200 Airport Dr.
🚢 King St Dock. 🛈 Suite 100, 60
Main St, (802) 863-3489, (877) 686-5253. 🎷 Discover Jazz Festival (Jun).
🌐 vermont.org

Vermont's largest city, Burlington is one of the most popular tourist destinations in the state. Half of the population of this lively town is made up of students from the University of Vermont and the city's four colleges. Rich in interesting shops and restaurants as well as grand old mansions and historic landmarks, Burlington is also Vermont's center of commerce and industry. It is scenically located on the shores of Lake Champlain.

The center of Burlington is compact and easy to explore on foot. It includes the historic district, at the core of which is the four-block section known as the **Church Street Marketplace**.

The neighborhood has been converted into a pedestrian mall, complete with trendy boutiques, patio restaurants, and crafts shops. Many of them are housed in Queen Anne-style buildings from the late 1800s. The historical attractions in this neighborhood include the 1861 **First Unitarian Church**, the oldest house of worship in Burlington, and the **City Hall**, which marks the southern boundary of the marketplace. This graceful building, built of local brick, marble, and granite, dates to 1928. The City Hall Park is a popular outdoor concert venue, and in summer street performers and musicians add color and action to the area.

On the waterfront is **Battery Park**, the site of a battle between US soldiers and the British Royal Navy in 1812. Today, the park is a peaceful place, from where there are lovely views of Burlington Bay and the backdrop of the Adirondack Mountains on the other side of Lake Champlain. South of the park is the **Burlington Boat House**; here a three-decker cruise ship, *Spirit of Ethan Allen III*, takes visitors on a 90-minute trip, which gives a good historical overview, as the captain narrates tales of the Revolutionary War.

The **Robert Hull Fleming Museum**, on the campus of the University of Vermont, is on a hillside overlooking the city. The artifacts in this elegant 1931 Colonial-Revival building range from ancient Mesopotamian objects to European paintings and sculptures and Native American crafts. Visitors can enjoy a coffee while browsing in the bookshop.

🏛 **Robert Hull Fleming Museum**
61 Colchester Ave. **Tel** (802) 656-0750.
**Open** 10am–4pm Tue–Fri (to 7pm Wed), noon–4pm Sat & Sun. ♿ ♿
📷 📷 🌐 uvm.edu/~fleming

## ㉔ Lake Champlain

Vermont–New York border from Whitehall to Alburg. ✈ 🚌 🛈 60 Main St, Burlington, (802) 863-3489, (877) 686-5253.

Sometimes called the sixth Great Lake because of its size, Lake Champlain is 120 miles (190 km) long, 12 miles (19 km) wide, and has 500 miles (800 km) of shoreline. Said to be the home of "Champ," a water serpent that could be a distant cousin of the Loch Ness Monster, the lake is sprinkled with about 70 islands. At the northern end of the lake is **Isle La Motte**, which has a statue of Samuel de Champlain, the French explorer who discovered and explored much of the surrounding region. On nearby **Grand Isle** is America's oldest log cabin (1783). The lake has its western shore in New York State, and seasonal hour-long ferry rides run between Burlington and Port Kent, New York.

Some of Lake Champlain's treasures are underwater, preserved in a marine park where scuba divers can explore

Statue in Burlington's Battery Park

Sailing and boating, popular on beautiful Lake Champlain

shipwrecks resting on sandbars and at the bottom of this clear-water lake.

The **Lake Champlain Maritime Museum** at Basin Harbor gives a complete overview of the region's marine history through fascinating displays of ship models, old divers' suits, and photographs of vintage Lake Champlain steamers.

 **Lake Champlain Maritime Museum**
4472 Basin Harbor Rd, Vergennes. **Tel** (802) 475-2022. **Open** late May–mid-Oct: 10am–5pm. 🅿️ ♿
**w** lcmm.org

## ㉕ Stowe

🏔️ 3,500. ✈️ ℹ️ 51 Main St, (802) 253-7321, (877) 467-8693.
**w** gostowe.com

This mountain-ringed village is the skiing capital of New England and draws hordes of visitors in winter. Mountain Road begins in the village and is lined with chalets, motels, restaurants, and pubs; it leads to the area's highest peak, **Mount Mansfield** (4,393 ft/1,339 m).

In summer, too, there are plenty of outdoor activities on offer. Visitors can hike, rock-climb, fish, canoe, bike, or inline-skate along the paved, meandering 5.5-mile (8.5-km) **Stowe Recreational Path**, which winds from the village church across the West Branch River, then through green woodlands.

Stowe's other claim to fame is as the home of the musical Von Trapp family, who were the

The Austrian-style Trapp Family Lodge in Stowe

inspiration behind the 1965 movie *The Sound of Music*. After their daring escape from Austria during World War II, they chose Stowe as their new home. Their **Trapp Family Lodge** is set in a 4-sq-mile (11-sq-km) estate. This giant wooden chalet is now one of the most popular hotels in the area *(see p186)*.

## ㉖ Ben & Jerry's Ice Cream Factory

Rte 100, Waterbury. **Tel** (866) BJTOURS. **Open** Jul–mid-Aug: 9am–9pm daily; mid-Aug–Oct: 9am–7pm daily; Nov–Jun: 10am–6pm daily. 🅿️ ♿ 🚫 📷

Although Ben Cohen and Jerry Greenfield hail from Long Island, New York, they have done more than any other "flatlanders" to put Vermont's dairy industry on the map. In 1978, these childhood friends paid $5 for a correspondence course on making ice cream, and soon parlayed their knowledge into what became an enormously successful ice-cream franchise.

No longer privately owned, the factory uses the richest dairy products to produce their ice cream and frozen yogurt. The Ben & Jerry trademark is the black and white Holstein cow, which embellishes everything on sale in the gift shop.

Tours of the factory start every 15 minutes and run for 30 minutes. Visitors learn all there is to know about making ice cream. They are given a bird's-eye view of the factory floor, and at the end of the tour they get a chance to sample the products and sometimes taste new flavors.

Ben & Jerry's bus, gaily decorated with dairy cows

A skilift in Vermont, one of the best skiing areas of the US

## Skiing in New England

In New England, top-notch slopes and cross-country ski trails are never far away. The best skiing is concentrated in the three northern states. Vermont has the most high-quality peaks, and the world-famous resorts of Killington and Stowe. Two great trails in Vermont for skiers and snowshoers are the Catamount Trail and the Trapp Family Lodge Ski Center. New Hampshire's White Mountains have some of the best downhill, alpine, and cross-country ski trails in the Northeast. In Maine, Sugarloaf/USA and Sunday River are considered the best hills in the state. Downhill ski trails are rated by a standard code: Easier = green circle; more difficult = blue square; most difficult = black diamond; and expert = double diamond. Equipment, and lessons for all levels are available at all the resorts.

# New Hampshire

New Hampshire's natural beauty is evident all over the state. The northern part is rippled by the tall peaks of the White Mountain Range and the spectacular chasm of Franconia Notch. Ponds and lakes, such as the pristine Lake Winnipesaukee, dot central New Hampshire. The main cities – historic Concord and lively Portsmouth, with its scenic Atlantic coastline – nestle amid the tranquil farmlands of the south.

The striking exterior of the Omni Mount Washington Hotel

## ㉗ Bretton Woods

🏔 550. ✈ 🛈 (800) 346-3687. 📧 🌐 **visitwhitemountains.com**

This tiny enclave in the Mount Washington Valley has an unusual claim to fame. In 1944, with the need for currency stability after the economic upheavals of World War II, it hosted the United Nations conference that led to the establishment of the International Monetary Fund and, later, the World Bank. The setting for this historic meeting was the magnificent **Omni Mount Washington Hotel** *(see p186)*. Opened in 1902, the hotel's white exterior and crimson roof stand out in contrast to Mount Washington, looming behind it. The hotel has entertained several distinguished guests, including the British Prime Minister Winston Churchill, and three US presidents. Surrounded by 27 sq miles (70 sq km) of parkland, its facilities include a 27-hole golf course. Nearby, Bretton Woods ski area offers alpine skiing and 62 miles (100 km) of cross-country trails.

### 🏨 Omni Mount Washington Hotel
Rte 302, Bretton Woods. **Tel** (603) 278-1000, (800) 314-1752. ♿ 📷

### Environs
Dominating the Mount Washington Valley is the 6,288-ft (1,917-m) peak of **Mount Washington**, the highest in the northeastern United States. The peak has the dubious distinction of having the worst weather in the world, and in April 1934 clocked the second-highest wind ever recorded on earth: 230 mph (370 km/h). On clear days there are panoramic views from the top. There are hiking trails and an auto road to the summit, but the most exciting way up is by the **Mount Washington Cog Railway**. This steam-powered train chugs the 3.5-mile (5.6-km) route to the top along a heart-stoppingly steep track. Some of the best alpine skiing is in Tuckerman Ravine on Mount Washington.

## ㉘ Franconia Notch

I-93, Franconia Notch Pkwy. 🛈 (603) 823-8800. Park: **Open** daily. Flume Gorge Visitor Center: **Tel** (603) 745-8391. **Open** May–Oct: 9am–5pm daily. 📷 for Flume Gorge, Visitor Center, & campgrounds. 🌐 **nh.stateparks.org**

This spectacular mountain pass, carved between the Kinsman and Franconia ranges, and designated as the Franconia Notch State Park, has some of the state's most stunning natural wonders. Foremost among them was the **Old Man of the Mountain**, a rocky outcrop on the side of a cliff that resembled a man's profile until the nose and forehead crashed down in May 2003. Other attractions compensate for the loss. The trout-filled **Profile Lake** reflects the brilliant colors of fall foliage on the slopes of **Cannon Mountain**. A boardwalk and stairways lead visitors through the **Flume Gorge**, a narrow, chasm whose granite walls tower more than 90 ft (27 m) above the boardwalk, while an aerial

## Fall Foliage in New England

Thousands of visitors head for New England in the fall, to gaze in wonder at the annual changing of leaf colors. The color change is not just a capricious act of Nature. As daylight hours diminish, the leaves of deciduous trees stop producing the green pigment chlorophyll, and other pigments hidden behind the chlorophyll's color now burst into view. More pigments are produced by sugars that remain trapped in the leaves. The result is a riotous display of shades of yellow, orange, crimson, and maroon. The peak period for "leaf-peeping" varies from early October in northern New England to late October in the southern section, but this can differ, depending on the weather *(see Fall Foliage Hotlines, p183 and www.yankeemagazine.com)*.

Glorious colors lighting up the New England landscape in fall

Narrow Flume Gorge in Franconia Notch State Park

tramway speeds passengers to the 4,180-ft (1,254-m) summit of Cannon Mountain in just 8 minutes.

Robert Frost (1874–1963), one of America's best-loved poets, settled in the Franconia Notch region in 1915. The majestic setting inspired him to pen many of his greatest works here, including the famous poem "Stopping By Woods on a Snowy Evening".

# 🌀 White Mountain National Forest

ℹ️ 71 White Mountain Dr, Campton (603) 536-6100. Camping: **Tel** (877) 444-6777. Call for availability & reservations. 🌀 ⛷️

New Hampshire's most beautiful wilderness area, the White Mountain National Forest, sprawls over 1,203 sq miles (3,116 sq km). The area has an abundance of wildlife, including a large population of moose, which can often be seen from the road.

Outdoor activities offered in this region range from bird-watching and rock climbing to skiing and kayaking. But even less sporty travelers will revel in the spectacular scenery visible from their car – valleys flanked by tall pine forests, waterfalls that tumble over rocky outcrops, and more than 20 summits that soar to over 4,000 ft (1,200 m). An especially scenic stretch of road is the 100-mile- (161-km-) long **White Mountains Trail** that loops across Mount Washington Valley through Crawford Notch and Franconia Notch. In autumn, brilliant fall foliage

colors transform the rugged countryside into a palette of flaming red maples, golden birch, and maroon northern red oaks, interspersed with evergreens.

Another popular route is the **Kancamagus Highway**, touted by many as the most beautiful road in New England. This 34-mile (55-km) road, which runs through the White Mountain National Forest between Lincoln and Conway, offers exceptional vistas as it climbs 3,000 ft (914 m) through the Kancamagus Pass. The road descends into the Saco Valley and joins up with the trout-filled Swift River. There is easy access for fishermen from the highway to the river, and there are campgrounds and picnic areas along the entire length of the highway. Well-marked trails allow drivers to stretch their legs amid the beautiful scenery – a popular one is the short loop that leads to the lovely Sabbaday Falls.

🚣 **Kancamagus Hwy**

Rte 112 between Lincoln & Conway. ℹ️ Saco District Ranger Station, 33 Kancamagus Hwy, (603) 447-5448.

## Environs

Close to the White Mountains is the **Lincoln/Woodstock** region, whose main attraction is **Clark's Trading Post**. This curious combination of circus acts, amusement park rides, and museums makes a welcome change for children after a leaf-peeping drive. Lincoln is a base camp for both backwoods adventurers and stick-to-the-road sightseers. Nearby **Loon Mountain** is one of the state's

premier ski resorts. In summer, it offers activities such as nature walks, tours of caves, mountain biking, and horseback riding.

🚠 **Loon Mountain**

E of I-93, near Lincoln. **Tel** (603) 745-8111, (800) 229-5666. 🌀 ⛷️ 🚴

# 🌀 Lake Winnipesaukee

ℹ️ Lakes Region Association, (800) 605-2537. 🌐 lakesregion.org

With a shoreline that meanders for 240 miles (386 km), and a surface area of 72 sq miles (187 sq km), this stunning lake has New Hampshire's largest stretch of waterfront. Ringed by mountains and scattered with 274 islands, Lake Winnipesaukee has sheltered bays, harbors, and resort towns around its shores. The largest and prettiest of these is **Wolfeboro**. Leaving from Weirs Beach, the MS *Mount Washington* offers the best scenic cruise in all New England. To its north is upscale **Meredith**, with lovely lakeside homes.

North of Meredith is pristine **Squam Lake**, ideal for boating and fishing, where the movie *On Golden Pond* (1981) was filmed. The town of **Center Sandwich** is on Winnipesaukee's north shore. Surrounded by woodland, it is a favorite destination during fall foliage season. On the eastern shore, the Castle in the Clouds mansion crowns the crest of a hill that rises some 750 ft (229 m) above the lake. A 70-mile (113-km) drive around Lake Winnipesaukee takes in all these sights.

The beautiful scenery to be found in White Mountain National Forest

## ㉛ Canterbury Shaker Village

288 Shaker Rd, Canterbury. **Tel** (603) 783-9511, (866) 783-9511. **Open** late May–Oct: 10am–5pm daily; call for winter hours. 🅿 📷 ♿ 🛍 🏠
**w** shakers.org

Founded in 1792, this village was occupied by Shakers for 200 years. The Shakers were a sect that broke away from the Quakers, who fled to America to escape religious persecution in Britain in the mid-18th century. Their belief in celibacy and strict separation from the rest of the world eventually led to their demise. The 690-acre (280-ha) site, which has several buildings open to visitors, is punctuated by millponds, nature trails, and traditional gardens. Skilled artisans can be seen re-creating Shaker crafts, known for their simple lines and beautiful workmanship.

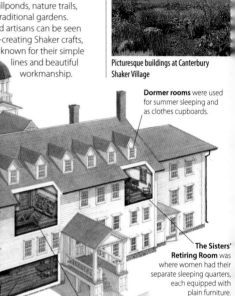

Picturesque buildings at Canterbury Shaker Village

**The belfry** contains a bell made by the Revolutionary War hero Paul Revere.

**Dormer rooms** were used for summer sleeping and as clothes cupboards.

**Brethren's Retiring Room**

**The Sisters' Retiring Room** was where women had their separate sleeping quarters, each equipped with plain furniture.

**The Dining Room** could hold as many as 60 Shakers per sitting.

**The Old Library and Archives** contains 1,500 Shaker books and documents, and is open by appointment.

## ㉜ Concord

🏠 37,500. ✈ 🚌 🛈 49 S Main St, (603) 224-2508.

New Hampshire's capital is a quiet little town, dominated by its impressive **State House**. Built in 1819 from granite and marble, it is one of the oldest state houses in America. Another landmark is the giant glass pyramid of the **McAuliffe-Shepard Discovery Center**. A Concord schoolteacher, McAuliffe (1948–86) was tragically killed when the *Challenger* Space Shuttle (*see p302*), launched by NASA on January 28, 1986, exploded and crashed 73 seconds after liftoff. The astronomy and space exploration exhibits in the planetarium also include multimedia shows such as "Destination Mars."

**🏛 McAuliffe-Shepard Discovery Center**
2 Institute Dr. **Tel** (603) 271-7827. **Open** 10am–5pm Thu–Sat, 11:30am–5pm Sun. 🅿 ♿ 🏠
**w** starhop.com

## ㉝ Manchester

🏠 105,250. ✈ 🚌 🛈 54 Hanover St, (603) 666-6600. 📷

Once a major center of the textile industry, with its mills powered by waterpower from the Merrimack River, today

The Currier Museum of Art in Manchester

Manchester is famous as the home of New Hampshire's premier art museum, the **Currier Museum of Art**. The gallery opened a major extension in 2008 to better display its collection of works by such European masters as Claude Monet and Henri Matisse, as well as works of 20th-century American painters

*For hotels and restaurants see pp184–9*

Portsmouth's Market Street, a favorite with tourists

such as Andrew Wyeth (1917–2009) and Georgia O'Keeffe (1887–1986). Also part of the museum is the Zimmerman House. The single-story home with its elegant exterior was built in 1950 by the pioneering American architect Frank Lloyd Wright. He also designed the furniture now displayed within the house.

The only indoor mall in the state is the Mall of New Hampshire in Manchester.

**Ⅲ Currier Museum of Art**
150 Ash St. **Tel** (603) 669-6144.
**Open** 11am–5pm Mon, Wed–Fri & Sun, 10am–5pm Sat. 🔊 📷 🔊 📷
📷 ⓦ currier.org

## ❸❹ Portsmouth

🏔 26,000. ✈ 🚌 10 Ladd St. ⓘ 500 Market St or Market Sq, (603) 610-5510. 🏠 mid-May–Oct: 8:30am–1pm daily. 🎭 Market Square Day (Jun), Prescott Park Arts Festival (Jul–Aug daily).
ⓦ portsmouthchamber.org

Girded by the Piscataqua River and North and South Mill ponds, Portsmouth is a historic town, compact enough to be explored on foot. Established in 1623, it became a prosperous hub of maritime commerce by the 18th century. It was also a hotbed of revolutionary fervor, and the place where the Colonial naval hero John Paul Jones (1747–92) took command of the warship *Ranger*. During the American Revolution, Jones led several raids along the British coast, for which he was awarded a gold medal by Congress.

A number of Portsmouth's historic buildings, many of which have been turned into boutiques and restaurants, are in the downtown core, especially along **Market Street**. Historic houses and gardens can also be found along the **Portsmouth Harbor Trail**, a walking tour of the Historic District. Especially worth visiting is the elegant 1763 Moffatt-Ladd House on Market Street, one of the earliest examples of the Federal style of architecture. The Wentworth-Gardner House on Mechanic Street, is regarded as one of the finest examples of Georgian architecture in the country. Both houses have beautiful interiors and are open to visitors in summer and fall.

A popular destination in summer is Water Country, which has a huge wave pool, a pirate ship, and a man-made lagoon. Interactive exhibits are the highlight of the **Children's Museum of New Hampshire**, where children can interact with a sound sculpture or command a submarine. Visitors can explore the real thing at Albacore Park where a sleek submarine, the USS *Albacore*, is on display. When it was built in 1953, it was the fastest underwater vessel of its kind.

Portsmouth's most popular attraction is **Strawbery Banke**, a 10-acre (4-ha) site near the waterfront located at the very spot at which Portsmouth was founded. This outdoor museum contains more than 40 buildings that depict life from 1695 to 1954. Many buildings are set amid gardens cultivated according to their eras, from early pioneer herb gardens to formal Victorian flowerbeds. The houses open to the public are furnished in period style and contain interesting collections of decorative arts and ceramics.

The **Jones House**, a 1790 structure, has activities for children. The elegant 1760s Chase House is furnished with sumptuous pieces from several periods, while the Sherburne House, built in 1695, now serves as an exhibit on 17th-century house design and construction. In the Dinsmore Shop, built in 1800, visitors can watch a cooper making barrels and casks.

Strawbery Banke also has a Colonial Revival Garden, the Aldrich Garden, planted with flowers mentioned in the poetry of Portsmouth native Thomas Bailey Aldrich. On Sundays from June through October an open market is held on Puddle Dock.

**Ⅲ Children's Museum of New Hampshire**
6 Washington St, Dover. **Tel** (603) 742-2002. **Open** 10am–5pm Tue–Sat (also Mon in summer), noon–5pm Sun. 🔊 🔊 ⓦ childrens-museum.org

**Ⅲ Strawbery Banke**
Marcy St. **Tel** (603) 433-1100.
**Open** check for hours. 🔊 🔊 limited access to some buildings. 📷 📷 📷
ⓦ strawberybanke.org

Inside lavishly furnished Chase House, Strawbery Banke, in Portsmouth

# Maine

The largest state in New England, Maine is truly the Great Outdoors. Its most popular attractions are found along the spectacular coastline, beginning in the southeast with its largest and liveliest city, Portland, and the resort towns of the Kennebunks. Farther north, yachts and windjammers ply the waters of Penobscot Bay, while Acadia National Park stands as Maine's coastal jewel. World-class skiing, hiking, and boating opportunities are found inland, at Bethel and Sugarloaf.

## ㉟ Portland

65,000. ✈ ▦ 950 Congress St & 100 Thompson's Point Rd. ▦ Commercial & Franklin Sts. ℹ 14 Ocean Gateway Pier, (207) 772-5800. ▦ Wed & Sat. ▦ Old Port Festival (Jun 4), Victorian Holiday (Nov 24–Dec 23). **W visitportland.com**

This historic city has a beautiful location on the crest of a peninsula, with expansive views of Casco Bay and the Calendar Islands. Once a flourishing port, Portland was devastated by no fewer than four major fires, the last one in 1866. Nevertheless, the city still has a number of sturdy stone Victorian buildings.

The West End has fine mansions and a splendid promenade overlooking the water. Portland's liveliest area, however, is around the **Old Port**, near the harbor. This restored neighborhood's narrow streets are filled with shops, restaurants, and art galleries. Dominating the area is the regal **United States Custom House**, with its gilded ceilings, marble staircases, and chandeliers. It was built after the Civil War (1861–65). From the docks, ships offer cruises to the Calendar Islands, harbor tours, and deep-sea fishing trips.

West of the Old Port, the **Portland Museum of Art**, displays works by the area's most famous artist, Winslow Homer (1836–1910), as well as by European masters such as Gauguin and Picasso. The **Children's Museum and Theatre of Maine** has three floors of interactive exhibits, plus dressing up and crafts. The **Maine Narrow Gauge Railroad Co. & Museum** displays vintage locomotives and offers scenic trips along the waterfront.

Several of Portland's fine historic houses are open to visitors. They include the **Wadsworth-Longfellow House** (1785), where poet Henry Wadsworth Longfellow grew up; and the **Victoria Mansion** with its painted trompe l'oeil walls. Portland's signature landmark is the **Portland Head Light** at Fort Williams Park. First illuminated in 1791, the lighthouse is surrounded by beach and picnic areas, and the keeper's house is now a museum.

Children's Museum banner

---

🏛 **Portland Museum of Art**
7 Congress Sq. **Tel** (207) 775-6148. **Open** late May–Oct: 10am–5pm daily (to 9pm Fri); Oct–late May: 10am–5pm Tue–Sun (to 9pm Fri). ♿ ▦ **W portlandmuseum.org**

🏛 **Children's Museum and Theatre of Maine**
142 Free St. **Tel** (207) 828-1234. **Open** year-round: 10am–5pm Tue–Sat, noon–5pm Sun. **Closed** public hols. ♿ ▦ **W kitetails.org**

---

## Downtown Portland

① United States Custom House
② Portland Museum of Art
③ Children's Museum and Theatre of Maine
④ Wadsworth-Longfellow House
⑤ Victoria Mansion

Greyhound Station 5 miles (8 km)
Portland International Airport 4 miles (7 km)

0 meters 400
0 yards 400

## ⊕ The Kennebunks

✈ ℹ 16 Water St, Kennebunk, (207) 967-0857. W **visitthe kennebunks.com**

First a thriving shipbuilding center and port, then a summer retreat for the rich, the Kennebunks are made up of two villages, Kennebunk and Kennebunkport.

Kennebunkport's historic village is graced by several Federal and Greek-Revival structures, and the striking 1824 **South Congregational Church**, with its soaring white steeple. History of a different sort can be found at the **Seashore Trolley Museum**, where some 200 antique streetcars are housed, including one called "Desire." Tours of the countryside are offered on one of the restored trolleys. The scenic drive along Route 9 offers views of surf along rocky Cape Arundel. At **Cape Porpoise**, travelers can sample lobster pulled fresh from the Atlantic. Kennebunk is famous for its beaches, notably **Kennebunk Beach**, and for one of the most romantic houses in New England, the 1826 **Wedding Cake House**. According to local lore, George Bourne was unexpectedly called to sea before his marriage. Although a very hastily arranged wedding took place, there was no time to bake the traditional wedding cake. So the shipbuilder vowed to his bride that on his return he would remodel their home to look like a wedding cake. Today the ornate latticework offers proof that Bourne was a man of his word. Seasonal architectural walking tours of Kennebunk's historic area are offered by the **Brick Store Museum**, housed in four restored 19th-century buildings.

🏛 **Seashore Trolley Museum**
195 Log Cabin Rd, Kennebunkport. **Tel** (207) 967-2712. **Open** call for times. 🅿 ♿ W **trolleymuseum.org**

🏛 **Brick Store Museum**
117 Main St, Kennebunk. **Tel** (207) 985-4802. **Open** 10am–4:30pm Tue–Fri, 10am–1pm Sat. **Closed** Sun, public hols. 🅿 W **brickstoremuseum.org**

Boats on the waters of Penobscot Bay's Stonington village, Deer Isle

## ⊕ Penobscot Bay

🚢 Rockland: ℹ 1 Park Dr, (207) 596-0376. Camden: ℹ 2 Public Landing, (207) 236-4404. Searsport: ℹ Main & Steamboat, (207) 548-6510. Castine: ℹ Emerson Hall, Court St, (207) 326-4502. Deer Isle: ℹ Rte 15 at Eggemoggin Rd, (207) 348-6124.

Penobscot Bay is picture-book Maine, with hills sloping down into the ocean, wave-pounded cliffs, sheltered harbors bobbing with boats, and lobster traps piled on the docks. Penobscot Bay is also famous for its islands, which can be visited on boat tours from the mainland.

Penobscot Bay's commercial center is the fishing town of **Rockland**, whose biggest event is the lobster festival on the first full weekend of August. A prime attraction is the Farnsworth Art Museum, displaying the works of leading American painters such as Edward Hopper and Andrew Wyeth.

A favorite destination for tourists is **Camden**, with its spired churches, elegant homes, and shops along the waterfront.

Sailboats moored in Penobscot Bay's Camden Harbor

A short distance from the village is Camden Hills State Park, which offers breathtaking views of the bay from the summit of Mount Battie. Standing on this point, the poet Edna St. Vincent Millay (1892–1950) was inspired to write her first volume of poetry. Nearby **Searsport** is regarded as the antiques capital of Maine and has large and busy flea markets on weekends in the summer.

The more remote eastern shore leads to serene, perfectly preserved villages such as **Castine** and Blue Hill. In Castine is the historic Fort George, built by the British in 1799, and witness to the American Navy's worst defeat during the Revolutionary War. Blue Hill is a living postcard, surrounded by fields of blueberries, and with many of its clapboard buildings listed on the National Historic Register.

**Deer Isle**, reached from the mainland via a graceful suspension bridge, is actually a series of small islands linked by causeways. Island highlights include the scenic towns of Stonington and Deer Isle. From Stonington, it is an 8-mile (13-km) boat ride to the thickly wooded Isle au Haut, much of which belongs to Acadia National Park (*see p180*). Monhegan Island, with its dramatic cliffs and hiking trails, is an artists' colony. North Haven Island is a summer colony, covered with meadows of wildflowers. Vinalhaven, with its granite shoreline and inland moors, is a perfect place for a swim or a hike.

*For hotels and restaurants see pp184–9*

Bass Harbor Head, which exemplifies Maine's rock-bound shoreline

## ❸ Acadia National Park

ℹ️ Hulls Cove Visitor Center, off Rte 3 in Hulls Cove, (207) 288-3338. **Open** mid-Apr–Oct: daily. 🚌 Bangor–Bar Harbor. 🅿️ 📷 at Hulls Cove. ♿ 🌐 **nps.gov/acad**

An unspoiled paradise, heavily visited in summer, the 55-sq-mile (142-sq-km) Acadia National Park covers much of Mount Desert Island, off the southeast Maine coast.

The scenic Loop Road, a 27-mile (43-km) drive (closed Dec–mid-Apr), climbs and dips with the pink granite mountains of the east coast of the island and takes in its main sights. Among these is the 1,527-ft- (465-m-) high **Cadillac Mountain**, the highest point on the Atlantic Coast. Hiking trails and an auto road lead to spectacular panoramas at the summit. The road continues south to the idyllic **Sand Beach**, but the icy water discourages many swimmers. Farther south there is a unique natural phenomenon known locally as **Thunder Hole** – when the tide

rises during heavy winds, air trapped in this crevice is compressed and then expelled with a resounding boom. The Loop Road continues inland, swinging past Jordan Pond, Bubble Pond, and Eagle Lake.

On the southern shore of the park is the quaint village of **Bass Harbor**, where an 1858 lighthouse is perched on the rocky coastline, offering magnificent views of the ocean. The park is home to numerous animals, including woodchucks, white-tailed deer, and red foxes. Visitors who want a closer, more intimate look at the park's flora and fauna can do so on foot, bike, or horseback along the 45 miles (72 km) of old broken-stone carriage roads, which wind through the park.

Cutting through the center of Mount Desert Island is **Somes Sound**, a finger-shaped natural fjord that juts 5 miles (8 km) inland. It separates the quiet village of Southwest Harbor from Northeast Harbor, which is the center of Mount Desert Island's social scene, with its upscale shops and handsome mansions.

The elegant resort town of **Bar Harbor** is a lively tourist center and a good base from which to explore the Acadia National Park. More than 5 million visitors each year pass through Bar Harbor on their way to the wilds of the park. Located on Mount Desert Island's northeastern shore, it was the 19th century summer haven for some of America's richest people, including the Astors and the Vanderbilts. In 1947, a fire destroyed a third of the town's lavish homes, thus ending its reign as a high-society enclave. Attractions include the **Abbe Museum**, which celebrates Maine's Native American heritage with displays of tools, crafts, art, artifacts, and archaeology. A seasonal branch of the museum is located at Sieur de Monts Spring in Acadia National Park next to the Wild Gardens of Acadia, which has some 300 species of local plants. The museum sponsors a Native American Festival and Basketmakers Market each summer.

**Mount Desert Oceanarium**, situated 8.5 miles (14 km) northwest of the town, is an inviting spot for families to walk along a salt marsh and to learn about marine life. The facility includes a touch tank Discovery Pool, the Maine Lobster Museum, and a lobster hatchery, where eggs grow until the lobsters are large enough to be released. Retired lobstermen recount the gritty work of harvesting Maine's signature shellfish.

🚌 **Bar Harbor**
ℹ️ 1201 Bar Harbor Rd, Trenton, (207) 288-5103.

Cadillac Mountain, the highest point on the Atlantic coast, with striking panoramas at the summit

*For hotels and restaurants see pp184–9*

Roosevelt Cottage, built in 1897, on Campobello Island

# ❸❾ Campobello Island

Roosevelt Campobello International Park: **i** (506) 752-2922. **Open** Island: dawn–dusk; Park: late May–mid-Oct. 🚌 every 15 mins (ID required for international border crossing). ♿
**W** fdr.net

Located on Campobello Island is the **Roosevelt Campobello International Park**, established in 1964 as a memorial to President Franklin D. Roosevelt (see p59). The island's main settlement of Welshpool was where the future president spent most of his summers until 1921, when he contracted polio. Despite his disability, Roosevelt was elected to four terms, leading the US through the Great Depression and World War II.

The highlight of the 44-sq-mile (113-sq-km) park – which actually lies in Canada and is the only international park in the world – is **Roosevelt Cottage**. Built in 1897, this sprawling, 34-room, two-and-a-half-story wood-frame summer home displays furnishings and mementos that had belonged to President F.D. Roosevelt and his family.

At the island's southern tip is **Liberty Point**, where a pair of observation decks perched on the rugged cliffs offer far-ranging views of the Atlantic.

A short distance inland from here is **Lower Duck Pond Bog**, a prime habitat for the great blue heron, killdeer, and the American black duck.

On the island's western shore is **Mulholland Point**, with an 1885 lighthouse and a picnic site offering views of the FDR Memorial Bridge.

# ❹❶ Sugarloaf

**i** (207) 237-2000, (800) 843-5623.

Maine's highest ski mountain, Sugarloaf is the center of this touristy village packed with hotels, restaurants, and condominiums. Downhill skiers, in particular, are attracted to **Sugarloaf/USA** ski center with its more than 130 trails and a vertical drop of 2,820 ft (860 m). The center also offers cross-country skiing, ice skating, and snowshoeing.

In summer, the emphasis shifts to the resort's 18-hole golf course, boating on the lakes and rivers, and hiking in the nearby Carrabassett Valley. The resort is also famous for its network of more than 50 miles (80 km) of mountain-biking trails, through flat as well as steep and challenging terrain. Canoeing, kayaking, and paddle-boarding are also available.

**⬢ Sugarloaf/USA**
Carrabassett Valley. **Tel** (207) 237-2000, (800) 843-5623. **Open** daily. 🎿 🚌 ⬛ in lodge. ⬛
**W** sugarloaf.com

# ❹❶ Bethel

🏔 2,500. ✈ **i** 8 Station Place, (207) 824-2282, (800) 442-5826.
**W** bethelmaine.com

A picturesque historic district, a major ski resort, and proximity to the White Mountains give Bethel year-round appeal. First settled in 1796, the town was a farming and lumbering center until the coming of the railroad in 1851 made it a popular resort. The lineup of classic clapboard mansions on the town green includes the Federal-style **Moses Mason House** (c.1813), restored and furnished with period pieces.

There are scenic drives in all directions, taking in unspoiled Colonial hamlets such as Waterford to the south, and beautiful mountain terrain to the north. **Sunday River Ski Resort**, 6 miles (10 km) north of town in Newry, has more than 130 ski trails. **Grafton Notch State Park** has spectacular scenery along its drives and hiking trails. The park's special spots include waterfalls and sweeping views of the scenic surroundings from Table Rock and Old Speck Mountain.

**🏛 Moses Mason House**
10–14 Broad St. **Tel** (207) 824-2908. **Open** Jul–Aug: 1–4pm Tue–Sun; Sep–Jun: by appt. 🎿 ⬛ ♿

**⬢ Sunday River Ski Resort**
Off Rte 2 in Newry. **Tel** (800) 543-2754. **Open** daily. 🎿
**W** sundayriver.com

**⬛ Grafton Notch State Park**
Rte 26 NW of Newry. **Tel** (207) 824-2912. **Open** daily. 🎿

Screw Auger Falls in Grafton Notch State Park, Bethel

# Practical Information

Although particularly popular during summer and fall, New England is a four-season vacation destination. The superb skiing facilities attract tourists during winter, which often lasts from mid-November to April. The region offers a wide variety of recreational activities within a relatively small area. On any weekend, vacationers can hike the White Mountains of New Hampshire, swim at Maine's Ogunquit Beach, and take in the Boston Symphony Orchestra. Outside of Boston, where public transportation is excellent, you definitely need a car for sightseeing.

## Tourist Information

State tourism offices are great sources of information and are happy to send road maps, brochures, and listings of attractions, accommodations, and events, free of charge. Some places also offer discount vouchers for lodgings, restaurants, and entry fees. Many towns have a visitors' bureau that offers information on local lodgings, events, and restaurants.

## Personal Security

New England's comparatively low crime rate makes it a safe holiday destination. But it is good to take precautions. Since pickpockets tend to frequent popular tourist sights, use a money belt for cash and documents and keep cameras out of sight. Avoid wearing expensive jewelry and leave your valuables in the hotel safe.

## Natural Hazards

The risks involved in taking part in outdoor activities can be minimized with proper precautions. Be prepared for sudden changes in the weather, especially in higher elevations. Wear protective gear for adventure sports and never try to interfere with wildlife. When hiking, wear insect repellent to avoid tick bites, which can cause Lyme disease.

## Getting Around

Many bus companies serve particular sections of New England, making it relatively simple to get from state to state. In Boston and Cambridge, it is easier to get around by public transportation than by driving. Once outside the city you will need a car. In fact, much of New England's charm lies along

scenic jaunts down the coast and driving tours during the fall foliage season. Several books list the best driving tours of the region. Yankee Magazine (www.yankeemagazine.com) details recommended routes, historic stops, and places to eat and stay.

## Safety for Drivers

Large areas of New England are wild, so be prepared for any eventuality. This is doubly true in winter, when sudden blizzards and white-outs caused by blowing snow can leave motorists stranded. Stock salt, a snow brush, an ice scraper, and a small shovel. If you do get stuck in an out-of-the-way place, stay inside your car. Keep the motor running for warmth, but open your window slightly and keep the tailpipe clear to prevent carbon monoxide buildup. **American Automobile Association (AAA)** provides roadside assistance.

## Laws

The legal drinking age in New England is 21, and young people can be asked to produce a proof of age in order to buy alcohol or enter a bar. You can lose your driver's license if caught driving under the influence of alcohol or drugs. Cigarettes can be sold only to people 18 years of age or older. Smoking and drinking in public spaces is illegal.

## Sports & Outdoor Activities

With miles of coastline, mountain ranges, forests, and rivers, the region has much to offer to sports lovers. The choice of camping areas in national forests ranges from primitive sites to ones with various facilities. Hiking trails crisscross almost the entire region, with the most popular being the New England section of the Appalachian Trail and Vermont's Long Trail. The **Appalachian Trail Conservancy** runs various information and

---

## The Climate of New England

New England's weather can vary greatly from year to year. Generally, the short spring is cloudy and wet, with rainy skies and melting snow. Summer can be unpredictable, but is generally dry – July and August are usually the sunniest months. Bright fall days out among the colorful foliage are spectacular – the peak fall foliage period usually lasts from mid-September to late October. Snow usually starts in December; the temperature can dip to 0° F (−18° C) or lower in winter. In general, it is warmer along the coast and in the southern section of New England.

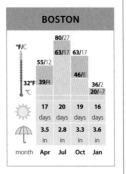

**BOSTON**

| °F/C | | | |
|---|---|---|---|
| | 80/27 | | |
| 63/17 | 63/17 | | |
| 55/12 | | 46/8 | |
| 32°F 39/4 | | | 36/2 |
| °C | | | 20/−7 |

| | | | |
|---|---|---|---|
| 17 days | 20 days | 19 days | 16 days |
| 3.5 in | 2.8 in | 3.3 in | 3.6 in |
| month Apr | Jul | Oct | Jan |

education programs on the Appalachian Trail. Miles of quiet back roads in the region are a cyclist's paradise. Mountain bikers also have plenty to choose from. Some ski areas let bikers use their lifts and slopes in summer.

New England's Green and White Mountains offer superb rock climbing, hang gliding, and paragliding sites.

Anglers will love New England. Deep-sea fishing is best at Point Judith in Rhode Island. Brook trout and bass are plentiful in the inland streams and lakes, especially in Maine. The state's latticework of rivers is ideal for canoeing, kayaking, and whitewater rafting.

Penobscot Bay, Maine, and Newport, Rhode Island, are both considered sailing meccas. For those who want something calmer than the Atlantic Ocean, New England has countless lakes, and boats can be rented at many seaside and lakeside resorts. Whale-watching cruises have become a very popular activity. Take the cruise on a calm day, as choppy water can cause seasickness.

The region's northernmost reaches, with a thick annual blanket of snow, offer great skiing, skating, and snowmobiling opportunities. Stowe, located in Vermont, can claim the title of New England's ski capital. The world-famous **Stowe Mountain Resort** offers excellent trails for skiers of all levels.

## Entertainment

New England is a traveler's dream, as it offers a wide range of entertainment. Free concerts and festivals abound in fall, spring, and summer, and there is no shortage of bars and nightclubs in which to slake, or build, your thirst. Boston's Harvard Square is famous for its street performers who entertain crowds in summer and fall. Mellow jazz lounges and smoky blues bars attract a devoted clientele, as do nightclubs.

Classical music, theater, and dance have long been the mainstays of the region's cultural identity. The larger towns and cities have good symphony orchestras, dance, and drama companies. But the hub of the region's performing arts is Boston. The **Boston Symphony Orchestra (BSO)** and its popular music doppelgänger, the Boston Pops, are the city's cherished institutions. The BSO performs a full schedule of concerts at Symphony Hall from October to April. The Pops move in for performances in May and June.

Theater is alive and well across New England's six states, but the epicenter of this dynamic world is, again, Boston. The most avant-garde contemporary theater found in Boston is at the **American Repertory Theater (ART)**.

## Shopping

New England's well-known factory outlets offer brand name clothing at huge discounts. Freeport, Maine, has the famous outdoor equipment outlet **L.L. Bean**. The interconnected **Copley Place** and **Shops at Prudential Center** are Boston's leading upscale indoor shopping malls. The region is an antique hunter's dream, with stores and barns offering a wide array of objects from the past. The Charles Street section of Boston's Beacon Hill is one of the prime antiquing areas. Look for shops run by New Hampshire craftsmen, Vermont-made products, and Maine crafts. Tourists looking for gifts with a regional flavor should sample the maple syrup and maple sugar candy.

# DIRECTORY

## Tourist Information

**Connecticut**
w ctvisit.com

**Greater Boston**
w bostonusa.com

**Maine**
w visitmaine.com

**Massachusetts**
w massvacation.com

**New Hampshire**
w visitnh.gov

**Rhode Island**
w visitrhodeisland.com

**Vermont**
w 1-800-vermont.com

## Fall Foliage Hotlines

**Connecticut**
Tel (888) 288-4748.

**Maine**
Tel (800) 777-0317.

**Massachusetts**
Tel (800) 227-6277.

**New Hampshire**
Tel (800) 258-3608.

**Rhode Island**
Tel (800) 556-2484.

**Vermont**
Tel (800) 837-6668.

## Road Emergency

**American Automobile Assn. (AAA)**
Tel (800) 222-4357.

## Hiking

**Appalachian Trail Conservancy**
799 Washington St, Harpers Ferry, WV 25425-0807. Tel (304) 535-6331.
w appalachiantrail.org

## Skiing

**Stowe Mountain Resort**
5781 Mountain Rd, Stowe, VT 05672. Tel (800) 253-3000. w stowe.com

## Entertainment

**American Repertory Theater**
64 Brattle St, Cambridge, MA. Tel (617) 547-8300.
w amrep.org

**Boston Symphony Orchestra**
301 Massachusetts Ave, Boston, MA.
Tel (617) 266-1492.
w bso.org

## Shopping

**Copley Place**
100 Huntington Ave, Boston, MA. Tel (617) 262-6600. w simon.com

**L.L. Bean**
95 Main Street, Freeport, ME. Tel (877) 755-2326.
w llbean.com

**Shops at Prudential Center**
800 Boylston St, Boston, MA. Tel (800) 746-7778.
w prudentialcenter.com

# Where to Stay

## Boston

**BACK BAY AND SOUTH END:**
**Midtown Hotel**                    $
Value
*220 Huntington Ave, 02115*
**Tel** *(617) 262-1000*
🅦 midtownhotel.com
This 1960s-style motor inn offers
connecting rooms that are perfect
for big families. Outdoor pool.

**BACK BAY AND SOUTH END:**
**Hotel 140**                        $$
Value                          **Map** 5B
*140 Clarendon St, 02116*
**Tel** *(617) 585-5600*
🅦 hotel140.com
Well-furnished, minimalist rooms
near Copley Square.

**BACK BAY AND SOUTH END:**
**Newbury Guest House**              $$
B&B                            **Map** 5B
*261 Newbury St, 02116*
**Tel** *(617) 670-6000*
🅦 newburyguesthouse.com
Cozy rooms with eclectic
furnishings are located in the city's
most famous shopping street.

**BACK BAY AND SOUTH END:**
**Mandarin Oriental**               $$$
Luxury                         **Map** 5B
*776 Boylston St, 2199*
**Tel** *(617) 535-8888*
🅦 mandarinoriental.com
Spacious rooms here feature
designer linens and modern
electronics. Spa and fine dining.

### DK Choice

**BACK BAY AND SOUTH END:**
**Taj Boston**                      $$$
Luxury                         **Map** 4C
*15 Arlington St, 02116*
**Tel** *(617) 536-5700*
🅦 tajhotels.com/boston
First opened in 1927 as the
original Ritz-Carlton, Taj Boston
is one of New England's most
inviting hotels, epitomizing
opulence and "Old Boston"
style. It enjoys a scenic location,
close to most major attractions.
The lobby bar is legendary.

**BEACON HILL AND THE**
**THEATER DISTRICT:**
**Boston Park Plaza**                $$
Historic                       **Map** 5C
*50 Park Plaza, 02116*
**Tel** *(617) 426-2000*
🅦 bostonparkplaza.com
Dating to 1927, this elegant hotel
is popular with business travelers
and conventioneers.

**BEACON HILL AND THE**
**THEATER DISTRICT:**
**John Jeffries House**              $$
B&B                            **Map** 3C
*14 David G Mugar Way, 02114*
**Tel** *(617) 367-1866*
🅦 johnjeffrieshouse.com
Located in former nurses' quarters
near the Charles River, rooms are
bright and most have kitchenettes.
Lovely Federal-style public areas.

**BEACON HILL AND THE**
**THEATER DISTRICT:**
**Liberty Hotel**                   $$$
Luxury                         **Map** 3C
*215 Charles St, 02114*
**Tel** *(617) 224-4000*
🅦 libertyhotel.com
Once the Charles Street Jail, this
hotel features beautiful archi-
tecture and a wealth of amenities,
from bicycle rentals and yoga
classes to guided walking tours.

**GREATER BOSTON:**
**The Charles Hotel**                $$
Luxury
*1 Bennett St, Cambridge, 02138*
**Tel** *(617) 864-1200*
🅦 charleshotel.com
This modern hotel with well-
appointed rooms has an
outstanding jazz club, the
Regattabar, and Rialto restaurant.

**GREATER BOSTON:**
**Constitution Inn**                 $$
B&B
*150 3rd Ave, Charlestown Navy Yard,*
*Charlestown, 02129*
**Tel** *(617) 241-8400*
🅦 constitutioninn.org
This inn caters mostly to military
personnel, but welcomes all
visitors to its modern rooms with
complimentary use of the fitness
center, pool, and sauna.

The historic, opulent Omni Parker
House, Boston

**GREATER BOSTON: Royal**
**Sonesta**                          $$
Business
*5 Cambridge Pkwy, Cambridge, 02142*
**Tel** *(617) 806-4200*
🅦 sonesta.com
A great art collection and
striking views of the skyline
from most rooms make this
landmark a top choice.
Bargain family packages are
often available in summer.

**NORTH END AND THE**
**WATERFRONT: The Langham**
**Boston**                          $$$
Luxury                         **Map** 4E
*250 Franklin St, 02110*
**Tel** *(617) 451-1900*
🅦 boston.langhamhotels.com
A sophisticated hotel in an Art
Nouveau building at the heart of
the Financial District, The
Langham offers spacious rooms
with Second Empire decor.

**OLD BOSTON AND THE**
**FINANCIAL DISTRICT:**
**Omni Parker House**                $$
Historic                       **Map** 3D
*60 School St, 02108*
**Tel** *(617) 227-8600*
🅦 omniparkerhouse.com
America's oldest continuously
operating hotel, this 1856
gem is where the Boston
cream pie was born.

**OLD BOSTON AND THE**
**FINANCIAL DISTRICT:**
**XV Beacon**                       $$$
Luxury                         **Map** 3D
*15 Beacon St, 02108*
**Tel** *(617) 670-1500*
🅦 xvbeacon.com
Chic, cozy boutique hotel popular
with business travelers. Rooms
feature plenty of high-tech extras.

## Massachusetts

**AMHERST: Allen House Inn**         $$
B&B
*599 Main St, 01002*
**Tel** *(413) 253-5000*
🅦 allenhouse.com
This Victorian property has
decor inspired by the English and
American Victorian Arts and
Crafts Movement.

## DK Choice

**CONCORD: Colonial Inn** $$
Historic
*48 Monument Sq, 01742*
**Tel** *(978) 369-9200*
W concordscolonialinn.com
One of the state's top choices
for historical lodging, this
landmark structure dates
back to 1716 and has operated
as an inn since 1889. Ask for
one of the 15 rooms in the
original inn. Lovely atmosphere
with Colonial Revival features
and period decor.

**GREAT BARRINGTON:**
**Monument Mountain Motel** $
Value
*247 Stockbridge Rd, 02130*
**Tel** *(413) 528-3272*
W monumentmountainmotel.com
Ideal spot for outdoor activities,
with stunning hiking trails nearby.
Excellent connecting family units.

**LENOX: Canyon Ranch** $$$
Luxury
*165 Kemble St, 01240*
**Tel** *(413) 637-4100*
W canyonranch.com
This deluxe spa resort – one of
New England's most expensive
options – offers all-inclusive
packages with access to several
health and wellness facilities.

**NANTUCKET: Century House** $$$
Luxury
*10 Cliff Rd, 02554*
**Tel** *(508) 228-0530*
W centuryhouse.com
Open since 1833, the island's
oldest family-run inn has a lovely
19th-century ambience.

## Rhode Island

**BLOCK ISLAND: 1661 Inn**
**and Hotel Manisses** $$
B&B
*5 Spring St, 02807*
**Tel** *(401) 466-2421*
W blockislandresorts.com
Offers cozy rooms across two
buildings. The hotel section
closes mid-October to March.

**NEWPORT: Castle Hill**
**Inn and Resort** $$$
Luxury
*590 Ocean Dr, 02840*
**Tel** *(401) 849-3800*
W castlehillinn.com
Set in a stunning waterfront
locale, Castle Hill offers scenic
private cottages along with
fine-dining options.

1661 Inn and Hotel Manisses on Block Island, Rhode Island

**PROVIDENCE: Courtyard**
**Providence Downtown** $$
Business
*32 Exchange Terrace, 02903*
**Tel** *(401) 272-1191*
W marriott.com
At this low-rise hotel connected to
Providence Place mall and the R.I.
Convention Center via a walkway,
most rooms offer city views.

## DK Choice

**PROVIDENCE: Hotel**
**Providence** $$
Luxury
*311 Westminster St, 02903*
**Tel** *(401) 861-8000*
W hotelprovidence.com
The best boutique hotel in
the state, Hotel Providence
combines modern design
with classic European flair.
The 16 suites are inspired by
and named after prominent
New England authors. Located
in the city's arts and theater
district, it has an award-winning
full-service restaurant on site.

## Connecticut

**HARTFORD: Hilton** $$
Business
*315 Trumbull St, 06103*
**Tel** *(860) 728-5151*
W hilton.com
This expansive downtown hotel
is just a short walk from key sites.
Fitness center and indoor pool.

**MASHANTUCKET:**
**Foxwoods Resort Casino** $$
Luxury
*350 Trolley Line Blvd, 06338*
**Tel** *(860) 312-3000*
W foxwoods.com
One of the world's largest casino
resorts features over 25 restau-
rants and many shopping options.

**MONTVILLE: Mohegan Sun** $$
Luxury
*1 Mohegan Sun Blvd, 06382*
**Tel** *(888) 226-7711*
W mohegansun.com
Entertainment haven with three
casinos, famous performers,
gourmet dining, and shopping.

**MYSTIC: Whaler's Inn** $$
B&B
*20 East Main St, 06355*
**Tel** *(860) 536-1506*
W whalersinnmystic.com
This centrally located, welcoming
inn requires a minimum two-
night stay on weekends and
holidays except in winter.

## DK Choice

**NEW HAVEN: Study at Yale** $$
Luxury
*1157 Chapel St, 06511*
**Tel** *(203) 503-3900*
W studyhotels.com
A sleek, contemporary hotel
located across the street from
Yale School of Art, Study at Yale
provides a hip base from which
to explore the city's various
cultural and culinary delights.
The luxurious rooms are fitted
with large flatscreen TVs, leather
reading chairs, seersucker robes,
and iPod docks. A farm-to-table
restaurant completes the
thoroughly modern atmosphere.

## Vermont

**BRATTLEBORO: Latchis Hotel** $
Historic
*50 Main St, 05301*
**Tel** *(802) 254-6300*
W latchis.com
An Art Deco hotel with a movie
theater and auditorium that often
has concerts. Modest rooms with
Continental breakfast included.

**For more information on types of hotels** *see pages 26–7*

Omni Mount Washington Hotel, Bretton Woods, New Hampshire

### BURLINGTON: Sheraton Burlington Hotel $$
Business
*870 Williston Rd, 05403*
**Tel** *(802) 865-6600*
W sheratonburlington.com
The state's largest hotel, set close to the University of Vermont, is perfect for business travelers.

### MANCHESTER: The Equinox Resort $$$
Luxury
*3567 Main St, 05254*
**Tel** *(802) 362-4700*
W equinoxresort.com
This historic 18th-century resort offers stunning public spaces and spacious rooms. Popular activities include boating, golf, falconry, fly-fishing, and shooting.

### MONTPELIER: The Inn at Montpelier $$
B&B
*147 Main St, 05602*
**Tel** *(802) 223-2727*
W innatmontpelier.com
Two stately Federal-era houses boast rooms with wood-burning fireplaces. A generous Continental breakfast is included.

## DK Choice

### STOWE: Trapp Family Lodge $$
Resort
*700 Trapp Hill Rd, 05672*
**Tel** *(802) 253-8511*
W trappfamily.com
This world-famous resort is run by the family that inspired *The Sound of Music*. The 96-room property includes an Austrian-style lodge and cozy chalets. Enjoy nightly live entertainment, sleigh rides, skiing, and exquisite cuisine that pairs nicely with beer from the on-site brewery.

**For key to prices** *see page 184*

# New Hampshire

## DK Choice

### BRETTON WOODS: Omni Mount Washington Hotel $$
Luxury
*310 Mt Washington Hotel Rd, 03585*
**Tel** *(603) 278-1000*
W omnihotels.com
A favorite with dignitaries since 1902, this elegant hotel is a prime example of Spanish Renaissance architecture. It boasts numerous public areas, dining facilities, a signature spa, a canopy tour and a golf course designed by Donald Ross. Guests enjoy high-quality service in a beautiful natural setting.

### CONCORD: The Centennial Inn $$
B&B
*96 Pleasant St, 03301*
**Tel** *(603) 227-9000*
W thecentennialhotel.com
A restored 1892 Victorian mansion, with rooms and suites handsomely furnished with antiques.

### KEENE: Lane Hotel $
Historic
*30 Main St, 03441*
**Tel** *(603) 357-7070*
W thelanehotel.com
Originally an upscale department store in 1891, this sophisticated hotel has reproduction furnishings.

### MANCHESTER: Hilton Garden Inn $
Business
*101 S Commercial St, 03101*
**Tel** *(603) 669-2222*
W hgi-manchester.com
Ideally located for both leisure and business travelers, the rooms here are well appointed.

### PORTSMOUTH: Sheraton Harborside Portsmouth $$
Business
*250 Market St, 03801*
**Tel** *(603) 431-2300*
W sheratonportsmouth.com
Modern hotel with a sauna, fitness room, and a large pool on site.

# Maine

### KENNEBUNKPORT: The Colony Hotel $$
B&B
*140 Ocean Ave, 04046*
**Tel** *(207) 967-3331*
W thecolonyhotel.com
Overlooking the ocean, this hotel has a heated saltwater pool, a surf beach, and extensive gardens. Closed late-October to mid-May.

## DK Choice

### KENNEBUNKPORT: White Barn Inn $$$
Historic
*37 Beach Ave, 04043*
**Tel** *(207) 967-2321*
W whitebarninn.com
Dating back to 1820, this restored inn offers a variety of lodging options. Rooms, suites, and cottages are filled with flowers and fruit, and equipped with modern amenities. A natural stone-heated swimming pool and spa provide relaxation. The acclaimed on-site restaurant, which has been featured on TV shows, serves excellent local, seasonal cuisine.

### OGUNQUIT: The Cliff House Resort & Spa $$
Historic
*591 Shore Rd, 03907*
**Tel** *(207) 361-1000*
W cliffhousemaine.com
Iconic spa resort offering rooms with balconies. Closed mid-December to March.

### PORTLAND: The Inn at St. John $
B&B
*939 Congress St, 04102*
**Tel** *(800) 636-9127*
W innatstjohn.com
Tastefully furnished rooms, some with shared baths. Dogs welcome.

### PORTLAND: Portland Regency Hotel $$
Business
*20 Milk St, 04101*
**Tel** *(207) 774-4200*
W theregency.com
This inviting hotel, in the heart of the Old Port, has rooms with Colonial-style furnishings.

# Where to Eat and Drink

## Boston

### BACK BAY AND SOUTH END:
**Flour Bakery** $
American
*1595 Washington St, 02118*
**Tel** *(617) 267-4300*
One of the neighborhood's most popular meeting spots, where both locals and tourists stop by for gourmet sandwiches, coffee, and freshly baked goods.

### BACK BAY AND SOUTH END:
**Mike's City Diner** $
American
*1714 Washington St, 02118*
**Tel** *(617) 267-9393*
This classic breakfast-and-lunch diner is often crowded, with a line of guests waiting outside to be seated. The menu features filling classics such as corned beef hash and home fries.

### BACK BAY AND SOUTH END:
**Joe's American Bar & Grill** $$
American      **Map** 5B
*181 Newbury St, 02116*
**Tel** *(617) 536-4200*
Joe's offers an extensive menu of favorites, from giant salads to prime burgers. The patio is great for people-watching. Kid-friendly staff.

### BACK BAY AND SOUTH END:
**Parish Café** $$
American      **Map** 4B
*361 Boylston St, 02116*
**Tel** *(617) 247-4777*
Parish Café is renowned for its innovative sandwiches created by some of Boston's best chefs. In summer, the sidewalk patio offers terrific views of the street.

### BACK BAY AND SOUTH END:
**Grill 23** $$$
Steak House      **Map** 5B
*161 Berkeley St, 02117*
**Tel** *(617) 542-2255*
This big-ticket steak house is reminiscent of the exclusive supper clubs of the Prohibition era. Prime aged beef with an inventive spin is served in a sumptuously classic interior.

### BACK BAY AND SOUTH END:
**Island Creek Oyster Bar** $$$
Seafood
*500 Commonwealth Ave, 02215*
**Tel** *(617) 532-5300*
Far more than an oyster bar, this large restaurant serves a plethora of exceptionally fresh and delicious seafood in casual surroundings.

## DK Choice

### BACK BAY AND SOUTH END:
**L'Espalier** $$$
French
*776 Boylston St, 02199*
**Tel** *(617) 262-3023*
A romantic destination, L'Espalier offers some of New England's most acclaimed contemporary French cuisine, seved by an impeccable waitstaff. Chef-owner Frank McClelland's vegetarian entrées, featuring produce from his own farm, are every bit as sophisticated as those with meat. Inventive desserts, an unrivaled cheese program, and a to-die-for wine list complete this gourmet experience.

### BACK BAY AND SOUTH END: Toro
$$$
Spanish
*1704 Washington St, 02118*
**Tel** *(617) 536-4300*
Book well in advance at Toro, the city's most popular spot for upscale tapas and Latin fare. The menu is filled with traditional and modern dishes made from locally sourced ingredients.

### BEACON HILL AND THE THEATER DISTRICT:
**Anna's Taqueria** $
Mexican      **Map** 3C
*242 Cambridge St, 02114*
**Tel** *(617) 227-8822*
Popular cafeteria-style chain serving delectable no-frills Mexican bites such as burritos, tacos, and quesadillas. A favorite of neighborhood students and the surrounding medical community.

The elegant interior of L'Espalier, a fine-dining restaurant in Boston

### Price Guide
Prices are based on a three-course meal per person, with a half-bottle of house wine, including tax and service.

| | |
|---|---|
| $ | up to $35 |
| $$ | $35 to $60 |
| $$$ | over $60 |

### BEACON HILL AND THE THEATER DISTRICT:
**No. 9 Park** $$$
New American      **Map** 4D
*9 Park St, 02108*
**Tel** *(617) 742-9991*
This bold bistro overlooking Boston Common serves inventive gourmet dishes that pair well with the imaginative wine list.

### GREATER BOSTON:
**Craigie on Main** $$$
New American
*853 Main St, 02138*
**Tel** *(617) 497-5511*      **Closed** *Mon*
Run by one of Boston's most lauded chefs Tony Maws, this bustling Cambridge gastropub offers a seasonal menu. The fried pigs' tails are legendary.

### NORTH END AND THE WATERFRONT:
**James Hook & Co.** $
Seafood      **Map** 4E
*15 Northern Ave, 02110*
**Tel** *(617) 423-5501*
Located on Fort Point Channel, this seafood joint serves fresh lobster, clams, crab, and fish to go.

### NORTH END AND THE WATERFRONT: Pizzeria Regina
$
Pizzeria      **Map** 2E
*11 1/2 Thacher St, 02113*
**Tel** *(617) 227-0765*
The city's best-known pizza spot since 1926 hasn't changed much. Expect good-value wine and amazing brick-oven pies.

### NORTH END AND THE WATERFRONT:
**Legal Sea Foods** $$$
Seafood      **Map** 3E
*255 State St, 02109*
**Tel** *(617) 742-5300*
Legendary local chain serving very fresh fish in a fine-dining setting. The clam chowder is unrivaled, while the raw clams and oysters are impeccable.

### OLD BOSTON AND THE FINANCIAL DISTRICT: O Ya
$$$
Japanese
*9 East St, 02111*
**Tel** *(617) 654-9900* **Closed** *Sun & Mon*
One of the city's most acclaimed restaurants, the hard-to-find O Ya serves delicious Japanese fare.

For more information on types of restaurants *see pages 28–9*

# Massachusetts

**ESSEX: Woodman's of Essex** $
Seafood
*121 Main St, 01929*
**Tel** *(978) 768-6057*
Casual no-frills restaurant famed for its fried clams, huge steamed lobsters, and clam cakes.

**LENOX: Bistro Zinc** $$
French
*56 Church St, 01240*
**Tel** *(413) 637-8800*
At this upscale bistro with a long zinc bar, modern dishes feature alongside familiar French favorites.

**MARTHA'S VINEYARD:**
**Net Result** $
Seafood
*79 Beach Rd, 02554*
**Tel** *(508) 693-6071*    **Closed** *Tue (except summer)*
Fish market and café run by the island's largest seafood distributor. Serves excellent sushi and lobster.

**PLYMOUTH: Lobster Hut** $$
Seafood
*25 Town Wharf, 02360*
**Tel** *(508) 746-2270*
Waterfront self-service restaurant just steps from the *Mayflower II* offering classic fish-shack dishes.

## DK Choice

**WALTHAM: La Campania** $$$
Italian    **Closed** *Sun*
*504 Main St, 02452*
**Tel** *(781) 894-4280*
The widely respected La Campania serves upscale Italian fare in a pleasant farmhouse setting. The menu features authentic Neapolitan dishes made in a wood-burning brick oven, including pasta made with fresh ingredients. Good wine list.

# Rhode Island

**BLOCK ISLAND:**
**Manisses Dining Room** $$$
American
*5 Spring St, 02807*
**Tel** *(401) 466-2836*    **Closed** *Oct–May*
Formal eatery popular for freshly caught seafood, home-made pastas, and elaborate desserts.

**NEWPORT: Crazy Dough's Pizza** $
Pizzeria
*446 Thames St, 02840*
**Tel** *(401) 619-3343*    **Closed** *Mon*
The top choice for a quick, good-value meal of award-winning pizzas and calzones.

**NEWPORT:**
**White Horse Tavern** $$$
American
*26 Marlborough St, 02840*
**Tel** *(401) 849-3600*
One of America's oldest taverns, White Horse serves upscale fare in candlelit environs, with low-beamed ceilings, hearth fires, and Colonial decor.

**PROVIDENCE: East Side**
**Pockets** $
Middle Eastern
*278 Thayer St, 02906*
**Tel** *(401) 453-1100*
This family-owned eatery is especially popular with students of Brown University. Serves savory Middle Eastern wraps and platters, with good vegetarian options.

## DK Choice

**PROVIDENCE: Al Forno** $$$
Italian
*577 S Main St, 02903*
**Tel** *(401) 273-9760*  **Closed** *Sun & Mon*
Diners come from far and wide to enjoy the nationally renowned Italian fare at Al Forno. The menu boasts delectable dishes including wood-fire grilled meats, thin-crust pizzas made in stone-floor ovens, and baked pasta dishes, all made using seasonal ingredients. Offers a comprehensive wine list. The kitchen's talents have spawned numerous cookbooks.

# Connecticut

**HARTFORD: Max Downtown** $$$
New American
*185 Asylum St, 06103*
**Tel** *(860) 522-2530*
The flagship restaurant of a local chain, Max Downtown serves modern American fare in smart, stylish environs. The menu and wine list are extensive.

**MONTVILLE:**
**Bobby Flay's Bar Americain** $$$
New American
*1 Mohegan Sun Blvd, 06382*
**Tel** *(860) 862-8000*
The popular TV chef treats locals and tourists to his interpretations of American classics and top-notch seafood in a French brasserie-style dining room that can get noisy.

**MYSTIC:**
**Flood Tide Restaurant** $$$
American
*3 Williams Ave, 06355*
**Tel** *(860) 536-8140*    **Closed** *Tue*
This restaurant is popular for its tasty local seafood and traditional fare. The casual environs and a great kids' menu make this a particularly family-friendly spot.

**NEW HAVEN:**
**Frank Pepe's Pizzeria** $
Pizzeria
*157 Wooster St, 06511*
**Tel** *(203) 865-5762*
Opened in 1925, this simple spot is known for its delicious thin-crust pizzas. Especially popular is their white clam pizza – a must-try.

## DK Choice

**NEW HAVEN: Louis' Lunch** $
American
*263 Crown St, 06511*
**Tel** *(203) 562-5507*  **Closed** *Sun & Mon*
It is widely considered that this famous lunch counter is where the hamburger originated. Louis' Lunch was the first eatery ever to serve a ground beef patty on toasted bread all the way back in 1895, when it opened. Today, it remains mostly unchanged, with an old-time ambience that matches its small menu and low prices. The delicious burgers are steamed in vintage broilers.

Al Forno, an acclaimed Italian restaurant in Providence, Rhode Island

# Vermont

**BURLINGTON: Leunig's Bistro $$$**
*French*
*115 Church St, 05401*
**Tel** *(802) 863-3759*
Located in a 1920s Art Deco building, this award-winning grill and bistro has a varied menu of French classics and Mediterranean-influenced American dishes.

**MIDDLEBURY:**
**American Flatbread $**
*Pizzeria*
*137 Maple St, 05753*
**Tel** *(802) 388-3300* **Closed** *Sun & Mon*
This local institution utilizes organic produce and cooks its pies in wood-fired clay ovens. Award-winning craft beers.

**MONTPELIER: Neci on Main $$**
*New American*
*118 Main St, 05602*
**Tel** *(802) 223-3188* **Closed** *Mon*
Employing students of the New England Culinary Institute, Neci on Main boasts dishes with French touches and local ingredients.

## DK Choice

**QUECHEE: Simon Pearce**
**Restaurant $$$**
*New American*
*1760 Quechee Main St, 05059*
**Tel** *(802) 295-1470*
Housed in a restored mill overlooking the Ottauquechee River, Simon Pearce enjoys a scenic location. After checking out the namesake glass-blowing studio, where the glassware and pottery used by the restaurant are produced, guests fill the romantic dining room to enjoy fresh, modern American cuisine and an award-winning wine list.

**STOWE: Pie in the Sky $**
*Italian*
*492 Mountain Rd, 05672*
**Tel** *(802) 253-5100*
This is where skiers fuel up with tasty pizzas, baked pastas, and big calzones. The weekday all-you-can-eat lunch is a good bargain.

# New Hampshire

**CONCORD: The Common Man $$**
*American*
*25 Water St, 03301*
**Tel** *(603) 228-3463*
American comfort food served in pleasant environs. Guests can choose to sit in the spacious dining room or the inviting pub.

The historic, Colonial-style White Horse Tavern, Newport, Massachusetts

**HANOVER: Lou's $**
*American*
*30 South Main St, 03755*
**Tel** *(603) 643-3321*
Popular for its comfort food, Lou's has served up breakfast and lunch fare to many generations of Dartmouth College students.

**MANCHESTER: Red**
**Arrow Diner $**
*American*
*61 Lowell St, 03101*
**Tel** *(603) 626-1118*
Dating back to 1922, this diner serves classic American dishes around the clock. Friendly service.

## DK Choice

**MEREDITH: Hart's Turkey**
**Farm Restaurant $**
*American*
*233 Daniel Webster Hwy, 03253*
**Tel** *(603) 279-6212*
Family-run restaurant specializing in serving country-style turkey dinners, including turkey pot pie, turkey livers, and even turkey tempura. A huge selection of non-turkey dishes is also available, such as prime rib, as well as a full line of seafood.

**PORTSMOUTH:**
**The Oar House $$$**
*New American*
*55 Ceres St, 03801*
**Tel** *(603) 436-4025*
Upscale cuisine, including local seafood, served in a restored 1803 warehouse with maritime-inspired decor, close to the harbor.

# Maine

**BAR HARBOR: West Street**
**Café $$**
*American*
*76 West St, 04609*
**Tel** *(207) 288-5242* **Closed** *Dec–May*
This welcoming eatery located near the downtown waterfront

serves an array of fresh seafood, steak, pasta dishes, and home-made pies.

**KENNEBUNKPORT:**
**The Clam Shack $**
*Seafood*
*2 Western St, 04046*
**Tel** *(207) 967-2560* **Closed** *Nov–Apr*
Seaside takeout stand serving fried and steamed seafood. Fresh-cut onion rings are a popular accompaniment.

**OGUNQUIT: Barnacle Billy's $$**
*Seafood*
*70 Perkins Cove Rd, 03907*
**Tel** *(207) 646-5575* **Closed** *Nov–Mar*
Classic, bare-bones Maine lobster house with a basic seafood menu. Enjoy your meal in casual, seaside surroundings.

**PORTLAND: Fore Street $$$**
*New American*
*288 Fore St, 04101*
**Tel** *(207) 775-2717*
The menu at Fore Street features fresh ingredients from Maine's community of farmers, fishermen, foragers, and cheese-makers. High-vaulted ceilings and a brick hearth add to the warm environs.

## DK Choice

**ROCKLAND:**
**Primo Restaurant $$$**
*New American*
*2 South Main St, 04841*
**Tel** *(207) 596-0770* **Closed** *Mon–Wed; Jan–Mar*
Primo is a welcoming, nationally acclaimed restaurant run by a talented chef, Melissa Kelly, who grows her own produce, and also raises pigs. The innovative cuisine is famous, and features seasonal, local seafood and vegetables freshly procured from their farm. It also offers an extensive international wine list and a range of desserts.

**For more information on types of restaurants** *see pages 28–9*

# WASHINGTON, DC & THE CAPITAL REGION

# Washington, DC & the Capital Region at a Glance

Washington, DC and the four states that make up the Capital Region lie in the northeastern United States. This area played an important role in America's history – the earliest colonies were established here, and many battles of the Revolutionary War and Civil War were fought on its fields. The region is, therefore, dotted with magnificent historic sites. Washington, DC is one of America's most visited cities and offers a great range of cultural attractions. The surrounding region's rich variety of landscapes includes Virginia's lush, rolling countryside, West Virginia's rugged mountains, Maryland's picturesque bays and harbors, and Delaware's parks, beaches, and opulent country mansions.

**New River Gorge National River** *(see p224),* in West Virginia, runs through dense forests. The dramatic gorge is a perfect white-water rafting destination.

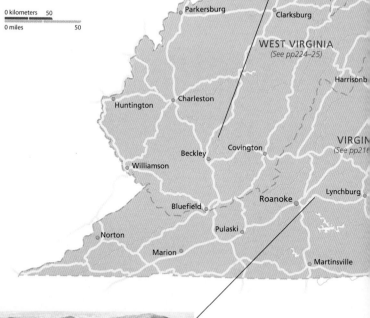

0 kilometers 50
0 miles 50

Wheeling

Cumberla

Parkersburg

Clarksburg

**WEST VIRGINIA**
*(See pp224–25)*

Harrisonb

Huntington

Charleston

Beckley

Covington

**VIRGIN**
*(See pp216*

Williamson

Lynchburg

Bluefield

Roanoke

Norton

Pulaski

Marion

Martinsville

**Blue Ridge Parkway** *(see p222),* stretching 215 miles (346 km) through Virginia, winds its way along the crest of the Appalachian Mountains all the way to North Carolina. This lovely route is at its best during spring and fall.

◀ The Neo-Classical Jefferson Memorial on the banks of the Tidal Basin, Washington, DC

**Baltimore** *(see p226)* epitomizes the rich maritime heritage of Maryland. This pleasant port city's redeveloped waterfront features many shops and restaurants, as well as the stunning National Aquarium.

**Locator Map**

**Rehoboth Beach** *(see p231),* along the Atlantic Ocean in Delaware, is one of the state's liveliest beach resorts, with restaurants and shopping malls, as well as a range of options for endless entertainment.

**Washington, DC** *(see pp200–215),* the nation's imposing capital, is dominated by the White House, the president's official residence since the 1820s. Each year, 1.5 million visitors take the tour of this elegantly decorated mansion, the city's signature landmark.

# WASHINGTON, DC & THE CAPITAL REGION

Center of government for the world's most powerful nation, Washington, DC is a stately, Neo-Classical city, with grand avenues and monumental public buildings that reflect the pride and ambitions that course through the corridors of power. Its surrounding region preserves important places where the young nation evolved from a Colonial outpost to an independent country.

Located midway along the Atlantic Coast, the nation's capital lies at the heart of the East Coast. This was also the heart of the Colonial landscape where the country began, and where many of its most significant events occurred. Besides its rich tapestry of historical events, this region also has one of the country's most beautiful and varied landscapes. Just 30 miles (48 km) east from the White House is Chesapeake Bay, the country's largest and most productive estuary, while to the west are the lush Appalachian hardwood forests. This wide variety of topography and scenery is paralleled by an equally wide range of social and economic situations; the area in and around the nation's capital is home to some of the wealthiest as well as the most deprived citizens in the United States.

## History

The first Europeans to this area were a small band of Spanish explorers and Jesuit priests who tried unsuccessfully to set up a colony around Chesapeake Bay in 1570. They were followed by the English, who in honor of the "Virgin Queen" Elizabeth I, named the entire region between Spanish Florida and French Canada, "Virginia." But it was not until 1607, under the reign of James I, that Virginia's first successful English settlement, Jamestown, was founded a few miles up the James River on Chesapeake Bay. Despite the initial hardships, the Colonists' prospects improved after they learned to cultivate tobacco and corn. By the 1630s, Virginia had become the world's leading producer of tobacco.

Natural chimney formations in the Shenandoah Valley at Front Royal, Virginia

◄ The Governor's Palace in Colonial Williamsburg, Virginia

Nighttime view of Lincoln Memorial and Washington Monument with the US Capitol in the distance

Jamestown's eventual success led to the establishment of the Catholic colony of Maryland, named in honor of King James's wife, Queen Mary. Governed by Lord Baltimore, the colony attracted Catholics from England as well as Puritan and Quaker settlers from Virginia. Every year, thousands of English immigrants came to the new colonies in search of opportunities impossible back home. By the mid-1660s,

### KEY DATES IN HISTORY

**1607** Establishment of the private English colony of Jamestown in Virginia

**1624** Virginia becomes a royal colony

**1632** King Charles I establishes Maryland

**1664** Delaware comes under British rule

**1699** Williamsburg becomes Virginia's capital

**1774** Virginia's Peyton Randolph leads the first Continental Congress to discuss freedom

**1775–81** The Revolutionary War

**1791** George Washington obtains land for the capital city

**1830** The Baltimore and Ohio Railroad (B&O) is the nation's first long-distance railroad

**1846** The Smithsonian Institution is established

**1865** Confederate General Robert E. Lee surrenders to the Union at Appomattox

**1932** During the Great Depression, a "Bonus Army" of WWI veterans camp around the Capitol to plead for government aid

**1935** US Supreme Court building is completed

**1963** Martin Luther King Jr. delivers his "I have a Dream" speech before Lincoln Memorial

**1989** L. Douglas Wilder is elected governor of Virginia, the first black person to hold such high office

**Sept 11, 2001** Terrorist attack on the Pentagon

**2009** The nation's first African-American president, Barack Obama, is inaugurated

both Virginia and Maryland had evolved into England's most profitable New World colonies. In 1664, the English took control of Delaware, founded and settled by the Dutch and the Swedish in the early 1600s. West Virginia, however, did not separate from Virginia until the Civil War.

By the 1670s, a simultaneous rise in taxes and a swift drop in tobacco prices caused widespread suffering and a short-lived rebellion. The situation stabilized in the early 1700s, when some of the tobacco farmers began to reap great fortunes. Much of their success was based on the shift from servant labor to that of African slaves, whose numbers grew from a few hundred in 1650 to over 150,000 in 1750, when blacks made up nearly half the total population.

### Independence & Civil War

Frustration over British rule eventually led to calls for independence. Although the Revolutionary War ended at Yorktown, Virginia, in 1781, it was only after the Treaty of Paris that American independence became a reality. Virginia, by far the largest and wealthiest of the American colonies, provided many of the "Founding Fathers," including George Washington, the military leader and first president; Thomas Jefferson, author of the Declaration of Independence and third president; and James Madison, author of the Constitution and two-term president.

In 1791, Washington, empowered by a Congressional act, selected the site for the nation's capital on land incorporated from

Maryland and Virginia, a choice determined by its location midway between north and south. This independent federal territory, termed the District of Columbia (DC) was merged with the city of Washington in 1878. When the government moved to Washington in 1800, the US Capitol and the president's home (later renamed the "White House") were still under construction. Both were burned by the British during the War of 1812.

Nothing has been more divisive in the region's history than the issue of slavery. Many residents were slaveholders; others became ardent abolitionists. As racial tensions escalated, war between the North and the South became inevitable. Over the course of the four-year Civil War (1861–65), many significant battles, including General Robert E. Lee's surrender at Appomattox Court House, took place here. The area was also home to the rival capitals – Washington, DC and Richmond, Virginia.

Cycling, a pleasant way to explore Washington, DC

Between the 1880s and the 1930s, Washington, DC evolved into the grand city intended by its planners. Wide avenues were opened up, tawdry railroads were removed from the National Mall, and many grand buildings were constructed to house the expanding bureaucracy. Even so, it

wasn't until the mid-1900s, with the advent of air conditioning, that the capital became a year-round, world-class city.

## People & Culture

Washington and the surrounding area reflect less stereotypical aspects of contemporary US. Its residents range from "blue-bloods" with roots reaching back to before the *Mayflower* landed at Plymouth Rock, to more recent immigrants and descendants of African-American slaves. This diversity is often surprising. Some of the most patrician communities are in northern Virginia's anglophile "Hunt Country" and among Annapolis' nautical millionaires. Alongside are outposts of blue-collar industry, and many anachronistic communities, such as the Chesapeake's traditional fisherman ("watermen") villages and the proud holdouts of Appalachian mountain culture, still visible in West Virginia.

Washington itself offers very revealing images of class and character, with its many poor, minority neighborhoods seemingly a world away from the wealthy, mainly white enclave of Georgetown. Many of these formerly all-black neighborhoods, including Shaw, Eckington, Petworth, Ledroit Park, and Columbia Heights, are rapidly gentrifying as young professionals buy homes there.

From these diverse social strata have emerged many remarkable people. Francis Scott Key composed the national anthem "The Star-Spangled Banner" in Baltimore, while Thurgood Marshall championed Civil Rights as an activist and later as a Supreme Court Justice. Writers include the poet and horror-story creator Edgar Allen Poe, the scholar, editor, and journalist H.L. Mencken, and contemporary novelist Anne Tyler. Singers include Patsy Cline and Ella Fitzgerald, from Virginia, and Baltimore's Billie Holliday and DC native Duke Ellington who made jazz and swing the nation's soundtrack.

Lee's surrender at Appomattox Court House

# Exploring Washington, DC & the Capital Region

Washington, DC, the nation's capital, with its magnificent monuments, superb museums, and cosmopolitan flavor, is a favorite destination for tourists. Within easy reach of the capital, the four states of Virginia, West Virginia, Maryland, and Delaware are equally rewarding to explore, offering a varied area of mountains, plains, beaches, and historic towns. Among the region's most popular attractions are the Colonial town of Williamsburg, the scenic splendours of the Shenandoah Valley and the Blue Ridge Parkway, and the unspoiled wilderness of West Virginia. The port city of Baltimore and the tranquil beaches of Delaware also draw many visitors.

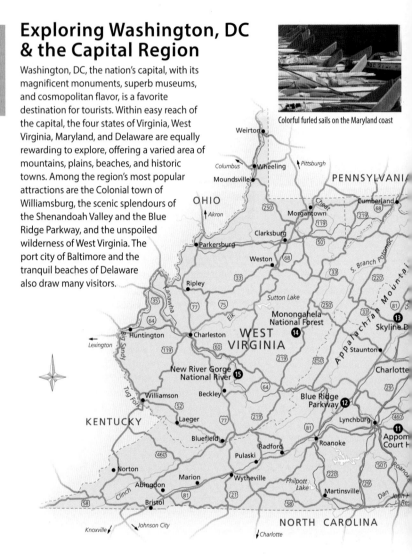

Colorful furled sails on the Maryland coast

John Brown's Fort, Harpers Ferry National Park in West Virginia

**Key**

— Highway
— Major road
— Railroad
--- State border

**For key to symbols** *see back flap*

The interior of the Oval Office in the White House, Washington, DC

## Sights at a Glance

**1** *Washington, DC pp200–215*

### Virginia

**2** Alexandria
**3** *Mount Vernon pp216–17*
**4** Fredericksburg
**5** *Colonial Williamsburg pp218–19*
**6** Jamestown & Yorktown
**7** Norfolk
**8** Richmond
**9** Chincoteague
**10** *Charlottesville p221*
**11** Appomattox Court House National Historical Park
**12** Blue Ridge Parkway
**13** *Skyline Drive p223*

### West Virginia

**14** Monongahela National Forest
**15** New River Gorge National River
**16** Harpers Ferry

### Maryland

**17** Antietam National Battlefield
**18** Frederick
**19** Baltimore
**20** Annapolis
**21** North Bay
**22** St. Michaels
**23** Easton
**24** Crisfield
**25** Salisbury
**26** Ocean City

### Delaware

**27** Wilmington
**28** Winterthur
**29** Hagley Museum/ Eleutherian Mills
**30** Nemours Mansion & Gardens
**31** New Castle
**32** Lewes
**33** Rehoboth Beach

## Mileage Chart

**Washington, DC**

| | | | | | | | |
|---|---|---|---|---|---|---|---|
| **7** / 11 | **Alexandria, VA** | | | | | | |
| **105** / 169 | **102** / 164 | **Richmond, VA** | | | | | |
| **69** / 111 | **73** / 118 | **167** / 269 | **Harpers Ferry, WV** | | | | |
| **45** / 72 | **51** / 82 | **150** / 241 | **67** / 108 | **Baltimore, MD** | | | |
| **32** / 51 | **41** / 66 | **137** / 220 | **89** / 143 | **31** / 50 | **Annapolis, MD** | | |
| **107** / 172 | **114** / 183 | **224** / 360 | **141** / 227 | **70** / 113 | **97** / 156 | **Wilmington, DE** | |
| **106** / 170 | **113** / 182 | **222** / 357 | **138** / 222 | **69** / 111 | **96** / 154 | **6** / 10 | **New Castle, DE** |

**10** = Distance in miles
**10** = Distance in kilometers

# ❶ Washington, DC

Washington, DC covers an area of 61 sq miles (158 sq km) and has a population of about 600,000. As the capital of the US and the seat of federal government, it is rich in grand monuments. It also has a vibrant cultural life, with superb museums, most of them free, and an array of entertainments. The city is made up of four quadrants, with the US Capitol at the central point. The northwest quadrant contains most of the tourist sights, with other sights and places of interest located round the Capitol and south of the Mall, in the southwest quadrant.

Tourists checking their routes at a tourist information kiosk

## Getting Around

Washington's excellent public transportation system is more convenient than driving a car. Traffic is heavy and parking spaces are limited. All the major tourist attractions in the city are accessible on foot, or by Metrorail, Metrobus, the Circulator bus, or taxi.

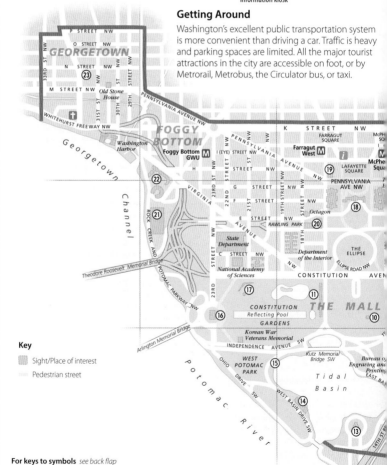

**Key**

▨ Sight/Place of interest

▨ Pedestrian street

**For keys to symbols** *see back flap*

## Sights at a Glance

① *United States Capitol pp202–203*
② Library of Congress
③ US Supreme Court
④ National Air & Space Museum
⑤ National Gallery of Art
⑥ National Museum of Natural History
⑦ National Museum of African Art
⑧ National Museum of American History
⑨ Smithsonian American Art Museum &
   National Portrait Gallery
⑩ Washington Monument
⑪ National World War II Memorial
⑫ United States Holocaust Memorial
   Museum
⑬ Jefferson Memorial
⑭ Franklin D. Roosevelt Memorial
⑮ Martin Luther King, Jr. Memorial
⑯ Lincoln Memorial
⑰ Vietnam Veterans Memorial
⑱ *The White House pp210–211*
⑲ Renwick Gallery
⑳ Corcoran Gallery of Art
㉑ The Kennedy Center
㉒ Watergate Complex
㉓ Georgetown

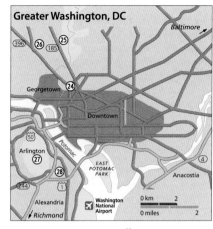

**Greater Washington, DC**
*(see inset map)*

㉔ Phillips Collection
㉕ National Zoological Park
㉖ Washington National
   Cathedral
㉗ Arlington National
   Cemetery
㉘ The Pentagon

**Key**

▨ Area of main map
═ Highway
━ Major road

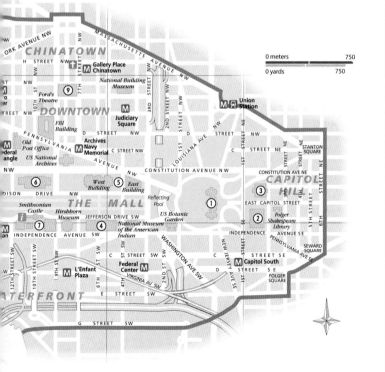

# ① United States Capitol

One of the world's best known symbols of democracy, the US Capitol has been the legislative heart of America for over 200 years. The cornerstone of this grand Neo-Classical building was laid by George Washington in 1793, and by 1800 it was occupied, though unfinished. The British burned the Capitol in the War of 1812, and in 1815 work began on its restoration. Many architectural and artistic features, such as Constantino Brumidi's murals and the Statue of Freedom, were added later.

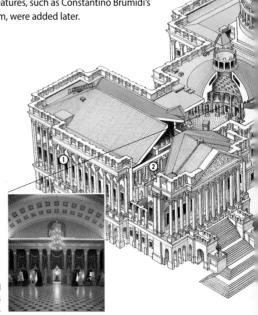

### KEY

① **The House Chambers**

② **The Hall of Columns** is lined with statues of notable Americans.

③ **The Crypt and "geographical center of Washington"**

④ **The Dome,** made of cast iron painted to look like marble, is one of the largest in the world.

⑤ **The Columbus Doors** are made of bronze and depict Christopher Columbus's life and explorations.

⑥ **The Senate Chamber** was completed in 1859.

⑦ **The Brumidi Corridors** are lined with frescoes, bronze works, and paintings by the Italian artist Constantino Brumidi (1805–80).

★ **National Statuary Hall**
Statues of prominent citizens from each state stand in this hall.

## ② Library of Congress

**Map** F4. 10 1st St, SE. **Tel** (202) 707-5000. Ⓜ Capitol S. 🚌 32, 34, 36, 96. **Open** 10am–5:30pm Mon–Sat. **Closed** federal hols. 📷 ♿ 🚫 For access to reading rooms, visitors must have a user card obtained from Room LM140 of the Madison Building. Photo I.D. is essential. 🌐 **loc.gov**

The Library of Congress holds the largest collection of books, manuscripts, microfilms, maps, and music in the world. First established in the US Capitol in 1800, the library was destroyed when the Capitol was burned in 1814. Thomas Jefferson then sold the library his personal collection as a replacement, and from this seed the collection continued to grow. Since 1897, it has been housed in a grand Italian Renaissance-style main building, now known as the Thomas Jefferson Building. In front of it is a fountain with a striking bronze statue of the Roman sea god, Neptune.

One of the highlights of this marvel of art and architecture is the **Great Hall** with its splendid marble arches and columns,

The Great Hall, with its splendid marble arches and columns

grand staircases, bronze statues, rich murals, and stained-glass skylights.

Equally impressive is the **Main Reading Room**, where eight huge marble columns, and 10-ft (3-m) high female figures, personifying aspects of human endeavor, dwarf the reading desks. The domed ceiling soars to a height of 160 ft (49 m). There are 10 other reading rooms in the Jefferson Building, notably the African and Asian Reading Rooms.

The staircase landing near the Visitors' Gallery, overlooking the Main Reading Room, is dominated by a beautiful marble mosaic figure of Minerva.

The Library's treasures include one of only three perfect vellum copies of the 15th-century Gutenberg Bible, the first book printed using movable metal type.

**★ The Rotunda**
Completed in 1824, the 180-ft (55-m) Rotunda is capped by *Apotheosis of Washington*, a fresco by Brumidi.

**★ Old Senate Chamber**
This sumptuous chamber was occupied by the Senate until 1859, and then by the Supreme Court for 75 years. It is now used mainly as museum space.

**US Capitol**
The Capitol also marks the center of Washington, DC. The city's four quadrants radiate out from the middle of the building.

---

# ③ US Supreme Court

**Map** F4. 1st St between E Capitol St & Maryland Ave NE. **Tel** (202) 479-3211.
Ⓜ Capitol S. **Open** 9am–4:30pm Mon–Fri. **Closed** federal hols. ♿
Lectures: 🌐 **supremecourtus.gov**

The judicial branch of the US government and the highest court in the land, the Supreme Court is the last stop in the disposition of the nation's legal disputes and issues of constitutionality. Groundbreaking cases settled here include *Brown v. Board of Education*, which abolished racial segregation in schools, and *Miranda v. Arizona*, which declared that crime suspects were entitled to a lawyer before they were interrogated.

As recently as 1929, the Supreme Court was still meeting in various sections of the US Capitol. Then, at Chief Justice William Howard Taft's urging, Congress authorized a separate building to be constructed. The result was a magnificent Corinthian edifice designed by Cass Gilbert that opened in 1935. Allegorical sculptures depicting the Contemplation of Justice and the Authority of the Law stand beside the steps.

The Great Hall that leads to the courtroom is an expanse of marble, lined with columns and the busts of former chief justices. The elegant court chamber itself has a coffered plaster ceiling decorated with gold leaf, and a frieze running around the walls that depicts both real and allegorical legal figures. The exhibit hall has displays on legal systems from around the world and an array of judges' robes.

Visitors may watch the court in session from October through April – check the calendar on the website. Admission is on a first-come, first-served basis. When the court is not in session, public lectures on the Supreme Court are held every hour on the half hour in the Courtroom.

The impressive Neo-Classical façade of the US Supreme Court

# The Mall

This boulevard, between the Capitol and the Washington Monument, stretches for 1 mile (1.6 km) and is the city's cultural heart; the many great museums of the Smithsonian Institution can be found along this green strip. At the northeast corner of the Mall is the National Gallery of Art. Directly opposite is one of the most popular museums in the world – the National Air & Space Museum – a soaring construction of glass and steel. Both the National Museum of American History and the National Museum of Natural History, on the north side of the Mall, draw huge numbers of visitors.

⑥ ★ **National Museum of Natural History**
The central Rotunda was designed in the Neo-Classical style and opened to the public in 1910.

⑧ ★ **National Museum of American History**
From George Washington's uniform to this flag that was raised after a victory in the War of 1812, US history is documented here.

Sculpture Garden

9TH STREET NW

12TH STREET NW

MADISON DRIVE NW

**Smithsonian Castle**, with its elegant Victorian façade, is the main information center for all Smithsonian activities.

JEFFERSON DRIVE SW

Washington Monument

0 meters       100
0 yards         100

⑦ **National Museum of African Art**
Founded in 1965 and located underground, this museum houses a comprehensive collection of ancient and modern African art.

**Freer Gallery of Art**
displays masterpieces of American and Asian art.

**Arthur M. Sackler Gallery**
holds an extensive collection of Asian art, which was donated to the nation by New Yorker Arthur Sackler.

National Museum of African Art

**The Arts & Industries Building**
a masterpiece of Victorian architecture, was built in 1881. It is closed for major renovation until further notice.

⑤ ★ **National Gallery of Art**
This gallery's fine collection of art treasures, such as *The Alba Madonna* (c.1510) by Raphael, chronicles the history of art from the Middle Ages to the 20th century.

THE MALL

**Locator Map**

**Key**

— Suggested route

## ④ **National Air & Space Museum**

**Map** D5. 601 Independence Ave, SW. **Tel** (202) 633-1000. **M** Smithsonian. 32, 34, 36, 52. **Open** 10am–5:30pm daily. **Closed** Dec 25. 10:15am, 1pm. **nasm.si.edu**

Opened on America's Bicentennial on July 1, 1976, the Air & Space Museum is today the most visited site in Washington. The museum's entrance leads into the lofty **Milestones of Flight** gallery, which displays many of the firsts in air and space travel. These include the 1903 Wright *Flyer*, the first powered, heavier-than-air machine to achieve controlled, sustained flight, built by the Wright Brothers; the *Spirit of St. Louis*, in which Charles Lindbergh made the first transatlantic solo flight in 1927; and the *Apollo 11* Command Module, which carried astronauts Buzz Aldrin, Neil Armstrong, and Michael Collins on their historic mission to the moon in 1969. Another gallery that attracts crowds is the **Space Race**, where exhibits include space suits, a working model of the *Columbia* Space Shuttle, and the Skylab, an orbiting workshop for three-person crews.

An eye-catching exhibit in the **Pioneers of Flight** gallery is the red Lockheed Vega in which Amelia Earhart became the first woman to make a solo transatlantic flight in 1932. The very popular **World War II Aviation** gallery displays fighter aircrafts from the American, British, German, and Japanese air forces.

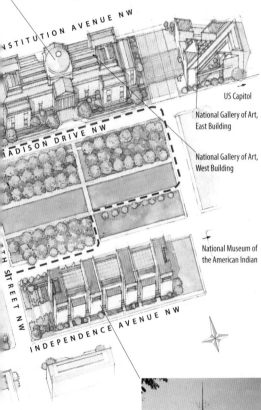

US Capitol

National Gallery of Art, East Building

National Gallery of Art, West Building

National Museum of the American Indian

**Hirshhorn Museum**, an unusual cylindrical-shaped addition to the Mall, houses contemporary art. Only a small selection of the 18,000 works it holds is on display at any one time.

④ ★ **National Air & Space Museum**
The clean, modern design of the National Air & Space Museum echoes the technological marvels on display inside.

Milestones of Flight gallery in the National Air & Space Museum

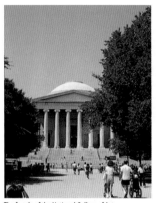

The façade of the National Gallery of Art

## ⑤ National Gallery of Art

**Map** E4. West Building: Constitution Ave between 4th & 7th Sts, NW. East Building: 4th St between Madison Drive & Constitution Ave, NW. **Tel** (202) 737-4215. Ⓜ Archives/Navy Memorial, Judiciary Square, Penn Quarter, Smithsonian. 🚌 32, 34, 36, 70. **Open** 10am–5pm Mon–Sat, 11am–6pm Sun. **Closed** Jan 1, Dec 25. 🎦 call (202) 842-6690. 🛈 call (202) 842-6176. ♿ 📷 🖼 🌐 **nga.gov**

One of Washington, DC's top attractions, this superb museum was established when American financier Andrew Mellon bequeathed his collection of European art to form the basis of a National Gallery of Art. Spurred on by his example, other collectors left their art to the proposed museum.

Of the two main buildings, the stately Neo-Classical-style West Building, opened in 1941, features European art from the 13th to the 19th centuries. The galleries of the modern East Building are closed until late 2016, although the atrium remains open. An underground concourse, with a cafeteria and shops, joins the two buildings.

Matching wings flank a central rotunda in the **West Building**. West of the rotunda are the galleries displaying Italian, Dutch, Flemish, and Spanish art. The Italian paintings include works by Giotto, Botticelli, Raphael and Leonardo da Vinci; and other masterpieces on display include works by Rembrandt, Van Dyck, Rubens, Goya, El Greco, and Velasquez. The sculpture galleries here display decorative arts from the Middle Ages to the 20th century. Galleries east of the rotunda house an outstanding collection of French Impressionist and Post-Impressionist art. Among its highlights are Monet's *Woman with a Parasol,* Degas' *Four Dancers,* and Toulouse-Lautrec's *Quadrille at the Moulin Rouge.* Portraits by John Singer Sargent and James McNeill Whistler are among the gallery's important collection of American paintings. Adjacent to the West Building is a Sculpture Garden, which is transformed into an ice-skating rink in winter.

The huge **East Building** is designed to accommodate large pieces of modern art. Centered in its courtyard is a giant red, blue, and black mobile by Alexander Calder, completed in 1976. Near the entrance is a sculpture by Henry Moore; the atrium displays a 1977 tapestry by Joan Miró.

## ⑥ National Museum of Natural History

**Map** D4. Constitution Ave & 10th St, NW. **Tel** (202) 633-1000 (recorded message after museum hours). Ⓜ Smithsonian. 🚌 32, 34, 36. **Open** 10am–5:30pm daily (later on some dates in spring and summer; check calendar). **Closed** Dec 25. 🎦 10:30am & 1:30pm Mon–Fri. 🛈 ♿ 📷 📧 🖼 🌐 **nmnh.si.edu**

Established in 1910, this vast museum's collection of 120 million artifacts includes samples from the world's diverse cultures, as well as fossils and living creatures from land and sea. The museum's entrance leads into the lofty Rotunda, where visitors are greeted by the impressive sight of a massive African Bush elephant. To the right of the Rotunda is one of the most popular areas of the museum, the **Dinosaur Hall**, although it is closed until 2019 while a major renovation project is carried out. Also on the ground floor is **Ocean Hall**, where exhibits explore the magnificence of the ocean, as well as man's relationship to it. To the left of the Rotunda is an IMAX® Theater and the Hall of Mammals with its huge 25,000 sq ft of stunning displays.

On the second floor is the **Gems and Minerals** collection, whose highlight is the 45.52-carat Hope Diamond. The largest deep blue diamond in the world and famed for its stunning color and clarity, it once belonged to Louis XVI of France. Also on the second floor is the highly popular **Insect Zoo**, with its giant hissing cockroaches and large leaf-cutter ant colony.

Elephant exhibit in the Rotunda at the National Museum of Natural History

## ⑦ National Museum of African Art

**Map** D5. 950 Independence Ave, SW. **Tel** (202) 633-1000. Ⓜ Smithsonian. **Open** 10am–5:30pm daily. **Closed** Dec 25. 🎦 ♿ 🖼 📷 🌐 **si.edu/nmafa**

This quiet museum is missed by many visitors, perhaps because much of its exhibition space is underground. The small entrance pavilion at the ground level leads to three subterranean floors where the exhibits are displayed. The 7,000-piece permanent collection includes both modern and ancient art from Africa, although the majority of pieces date from the 19th and 20th centuries. Traditional African bronzes, ceramics, and pottery are on display, as are stunning ivory and gold objects, brightly colored *kente* textiles from Ghana, and photographs.

## ⑧ National Museum of American History

**Map** D4. 14th St & Constitution Ave. **Tel** (202) 633-1000 (recorded message outside opening hours). Ⓜ Smithsonian–Federal Triangle. 🚌 32, 34, 36. **Open** 10am–5:30pm daily. **Closed** Dec 25. ⬛ Ⓖ 🏠 ✍ ⬛ 🔎 Ⓦ **americanhistory.si.edu**

This museum showcases America's past. A dramatic, central five-story atrium is surrounded by displays of artifacts representing the breadth of the museum's collection. Fascinating and diverse exhibits cover the USA's cultural, social, technological, and political history.

The first floor's east wing is devoted to America's history of transportation and technology. Displays range from steam locomotives to ancient gold coins. Another popular exhibit is a *Model T* Ford. This vehicle was an engineering landmark that heralded the beginning of the motor age.

Popular exhibits elsewhere include the actual kitchen of famous American cook, Julia Child (1912–2004) that she used in her house in Cambridge, Massachusetts. A beloved figure, she taught American households how to cook and enjoy French cuisine.

First ladies' gowns worn to the presidents' inaugural balls are also a memorable exhibit. Jackie Kennedy's and Nancy Reagan's haute couture gowns are all kept at the museum – as well as Rosalynn Carter's "off the rack" one.

Of great historical and cultural significance is the Star-Spangled Banner that flew over Fort McHenry in 1814, and which inspired the Francis Scott Key poem that later became the US national anthem. The fragile flag is dramatically displayed in an environmentally controlled exhibit on the second floor.

Ford's Model T, in the National Museum of American History

The extent of the museum's collection is huge, from science to objects that represent the lives and offices of the presidency, to American popular culture exhibits, such as the ruby slippers worn by Judy Garland in *The Wizard of Oz*.

## ⑨ Smithsonian American Art Museum & National Portrait Gallery

**Map** D4. Smithsonian American Art Museum: 8th & G Sts NW. **Tel** (202) 633-1000. **Open** 11:30am–7pm daily. **Closed** Dec 25. Ⓦ **americanart.si.edu** National Portrait Gallery: 8th & F Sts NW. **Tel** (202) 633-1000. **Open** 11:30am–7pm daily. **Closed** Dec 25. Ⓜ Gallery Place–Chinatown. ⬛ Ⓖ 🏠 ✍ ⬛ 🔎 Ⓦ **npg.si.edu**

Nowhere in Washington is the city's penchant for copying Greek and Roman architecture more obvious than in the former US Patent Office building, now the home of the Smithsonian American Art Museum and the National Portrait Gallery. The Patent Office was converted into the twin museums in 1968. The art museum contains a wealth of works by American artists, reflecting the history and culture of the country. The highlight of the American folk art collection is an amazing

piece of visionary art called *Throne of the Third Heaven of the Nations' Millennium* (c.1950–64), created out of light bulbs, silver and gold foil, and old furniture by a Washington janitor by the name of James Hampton. Among the 19th- and early 20th-century works, the Western landscapes by Albert Bierstadt stand out. Especially dramatic is his painting *Among the Sierra Nevada, California*, which captures the vastness of the American West. Another outstanding work from this period is *Achelous and Hercules* by Thomas Hart Benton (1889–1975). In this mythical analogy of early American life, Hercules symbolizes man taming the wild and then enjoying the fruits of his labor. Works by Modernists Jasper Johns, Andy Warhol, and Robert Rauschenberg are among the other treasures of this museum.

The National Portrait Gallery is America's family album, featuring paintings, sculptures, etchings, and photographs of thousands of famous Americans. Assembled here are such diverse works as Gilbert Stuart's famous portrait of George Washington (which features on the one-dollar bill), busts of Dr. Martin Luther King Jr. and the poet T.S. Eliot, and some photographs of actress Marilyn Monroe.

*George Washington* by Gilbert Stuart

Washington Monument, which dominates the city skyline

## ⑩ Washington Monument

**Map** C4. Independence Ave at 17th St, SW. **Tel** (202) 426-6841.
Ⓜ Smithsonian. 🚌 13, 52.
**Open** 9am–4:45pm daily.
**Closed** Jul 4, Dec 25. 🚻 📷
Interpretive talks. 🆆 nps.gov/wamo

Constructed from 36,000 pieces of marble and granite, the 555-ft (170-m) tall Washington Monument is one of the capital's most recognizable landmarks, clearly visible from almost all over the city. Conceived of as a tribute to the first president of the US, its construction began in 1848, but stopped in 1858 when funds ran out. The building work resumed in 1876 – a slight change in the color of the stone indicates the point at which construction stopped and then began again. The original design included a colonnade around the monument, but lack of funds prevented its construction.

Cleaned to a gleaming white, the monument has a capstone weighing 3,300 lbs (2,000 kg). It is topped by an aluminum pyramid, and surrounded by 50 flagpoles. The monument reopened in 2014 following repairs to damage caused by an earthquake in 2011. Exhibits now cover George Washington, the monument's engineering, and what happens if lightning strikes. There are stunning views across the city from the top (admission is free, but timed tickets are required for the elevator; the stairs are no longer accessible).

## ⑪ National World War II Memorial

**Map** C4. 17th St, NW, between Constitution Ave & Independence Ave. **Tel** (202) 426-6841.
Ⓜ Smithsonian or Federal Triangle.
**Open** 24 hours daily. 📷 on request.
🚻 🆆 nps.gov/nwwm

This 7.5-acre (3-ha) memorial was built to honor US veteran soldiers and civilians of World War II. It includes two 43-ft (13-m) pavilions, symbolic bas-relief panels, and fifty-six granite pillars, one for each of the country's states and territories. These are adorned with bronze wreaths of oak and wheat, which symbolize the nation's agricultural and industrial strength. The memorial was officially opened to the public in 2004.

## ⑫ United States Holocaust Memorial Museum

**Map** C5. 100 Raoul Wallenberg Place, SW. **Tel** (202) 488-0400.
Ⓜ Smithsonian. 🚌 13 (Pentagon shuttle). **Open** 10am–5:30pm daily (extended hours from Mar–Jun: 10am–6:30pm Mon–Fri). **Closed** Dec 25 & Yom Kippur. Time pass required for permanent exhibit. Advance passes available via the museum's website. 🚻 🆆 ushmm.org

Opened in 1993, the US Holocaust Memorial Museum bears witness to the systematic persecution and annihilation in Europe of six million Jews and others deemed undesirable by the Third Reich. The museum is meant to be experienced, not just seen. Within the exhibition space, which ranges from the intentionally claustrophobic to the soaringly majestic, are thousands of photographs and artifacts, 53 video monitors, and 30 interactive stations that contain graphic and emotionally disturbing images of violence, forcing visitors to confront the horror of the Holocaust. Starting from the top, the fourth floor documents the early years

Majestic statue of Jefferson

of the Nazi regime, with exhibits exposing their ruthless persecution of Jews. The third floor exhibits are devoted to the "Final Solution," the killing of six million "undesirable" people. Artifacts include a box car that carried prisoners to concentration camps.

On the second floor is the **Hall of Remembrance**, which houses an eternal flame that pays homage to the victims of the Holocaust, and the **Hall of Witness** on the first floor features temporary exhibits.

At the Concourse Level is the **Children's Tile Wall**. Over 3,000 tiles, painted by children, constitute this moving memorial to the one-and-a-half million children murdered in the Holocaust.

## ⑬ Jefferson Memorial

**Map** C5. S bank of the Tidal Basin.
**Tel** (202) 426-6841. Ⓜ Smithsonian.
**Open** 9:30am–11:30pm.
**Closed** Dec 25. Interpretive talks: 🚻
📷 🆆 nps.gov/thje

When this Neo-Classical-style memorial to the third US president, Thomas Jefferson (1743–1826), was completed in 1943, critics gave it the derisive nickname "Jefferson's Muffin." It was dismissed as far too "feminine" for so bold and influential a man who had played a significant part in drafting the Declaration of Independence in 1776. The dome of this round, colonnaded building covers a majestic 19-ft (6-m) statue of Jefferson, and a museum is housed in the basement of the building.

Jefferson Memorial stands on the banks of the scenic Tidal Basin. In the 1920s, hundreds of Japanese cherry trees were planted along its shores, and the sight of the trees in bloom is one of the most photographed in the city. Peak blooming time is between mid-March and mid-April. Rental paddle-boats are available at the Tidal Basin.

The colonnaded domed Jefferson Memorial, housing the bronze statue

## ⑭ Franklin D. Roosevelt Memorial

**Map** C5. W Basin Dr, SW. **Tel** (202) 426-6841. Ⓜ Smithsonian. 🚌 13.
**Open** 8am–midnight daily.
**Closed** Dec 25. ♿ 📷 Interpretive programs & talks: 🆆 **nps.gov/fdrm**

The memorial to President Franklin D. Roosevelt is a mammoth park of four granite open-air rooms, one for each of Roosevelt's terms *(see p59)*. The first room has the visitor center, and a bas-relief of Roosevelt's first inaugural parade. In the second room is a sculpture titled *Hunger*, recalling the hard times of the Great Depression. A controversial statue of Roosevelt in the third room shows the disabled president sitting in a wheelchair hidden by his Navy cape.

Dramatic waterfalls cascade into a series of pools in the fourth room, which also has a statue of Roosevelt's wife, Eleanor, and a relief of his funeral cortege carved into the granite wall. The water symbolizes the peace that Roosevelt was so eager to achieve before his death.

## ⑮ Martin Luther King, Jr. Memorial

**Map** B5. 1964 Independence Ave SW. **Tel** (888) 484-3373. Ⓜ Smithsonian. 🚌 13. **Open** 24 hours. Rangers are on hand to answer queries from 9:30am–11:30pm daily. ♿
🆆 **mlkmemorial.org**

The Martin Luther King, Jr. Memorial is located at the northwest corner of the Tidal Basin, a stone's throw from where his famous "I Have a Dream" speech was delivered, and is aligned along the axis of the Jefferson Memorial and Lincoln Memorial.

The centerpiece, a 30-ft (91-m) high relief of Martin Luther King, Jr., stands between two pieces of granite, and is based on a line from his "I Have a Dream" speech: "Out of a mountain of despair, a stone of hope". The memorial is set in a quiet and reflective space surrounded by Yoshino cherry blossom trees.

A 450-ft (140-m) inscription wall contains quotes from Dr. King's many sermons and speeches, commemorating those who lost their lives during the Civil Rights movement, and inspiring the modern world.

## ⑯ Lincoln Memorial

**Map** B4. 900 Ohio Drive SW. **Tel** (202) 426-6841. Ⓜ Smithsonian, Foggy Bottom. **Open** 24 hours. 📷 on request. ♿ 📷 🆆 **nps.gov/linc**

The Lincoln Memorial is one of Washington's most awe-inspiring sights, with the seated figure of President Abraham Lincoln in his Neo-Classical "temple," looming over a reflecting pool. The site chosen for the monument was a swamp, and before building began in 1914 it had to be drained. Concrete piers were poured for the foundation so that the building could be anchored in bedrock. As the memorial neared completion, architect Henry Bacon realized that the statue of Lincoln would be dwarfed inside the huge edifice. The original 10-ft (3-m) statue by Daniel Chester French was doubled in size and carved from 28 blocks of white marble. Engraved on the wall are the words of Lincoln's famous Gettysburg Address *(see p116)*.

## ⑰ Vietnam Veterans Memorial

**Map** B4. 21st St & Constitution Ave, NW. **Tel** (202) 426-6841. Ⓜ Foggy Bottom. **Open** 24 hours; rangers are on hand to answer queries from 9:30am–11:30pm daily. 📷 on request. ♿ 🆆 **nps.gov/vive**

Powerful in its symbolism and dramatic in its simplicity, this memorial consists of two triangular black walls, set into the earth at an angle of 125 degrees, one end pointing to the Lincoln Memorial and the other to the Washington Monument. The walls are inscribed with the names of the Americans who died in the Vietnam War, in chronological order from 1959 to 1975. The site is covered by tokens of remembrance placed by veterans and their families – poems, pictures, toys, and flowers – making this one of the most moving memorials on the Mall. A more conventional memorial was added in 1984 – a statue of three soldiers.

The Lincoln Memorial, one of Washington's most visited monuments

# ⑱ The White House

The official residence of the president, the White House was designed by Irish-born architect James Hoban. Known as the Executive Mansion, it was first occupied in 1800 by President John Adams. Burned by the British in 1814, the partially rebuilt edifice was reoccupied in 1817. In 1901, President Theodore Roosevelt renamed the building the White House and ordered the West Wing to be built. The East Wing was added in 1942, completing the building as it is today. Beautifully decorated with period furniture, valuable antiques, and paintings, the White House attracts more than a million and a half visitors every year.

**The White House**
The official residence of the US president for 200 years, the White House façade is familiar to millions of people around the world.

★ **State Dining Room**
Able to seat as many as 140 people, the State Dining Room was enlarged in 1902. A portrait of President Abraham Lincoln, by George P.A. Healy, hangs above the mantel.

## KEY

① **The stonework** has been painted over and over to maintain the building's white façade.

② **The West Terrace** leads to the West Wing and the Oval Office, the president's official office.

③ **The East Terrace** leads to the East Wing.

④ **The East Room** is used for large gatherings, such as dances and concerts.

⑤ **Treaty Room**

⑥ **The Green Room** was first used as a guest room before Thomas Jefferson turned it into a dining room.

⑦ **Blue Room**

★ **Red Room**
One of four reception rooms, the Red Room is furnished in red in the Empire Style (1810–30). The fabrics were woven in the US from French designs.

**Lincoln Bedroom**
President Lincoln used this room as his Cabinet Room, then turned it into a bedroom, furnishing it with Lincoln-era decor. Today it is used as a guest room.

③

⑤ ④

⑥

⑦

**★ Vermeil Room**
This ivory room houses seven paintings of First Ladies, including this portrait of Eleanor Roosevelt by Douglas Chandor.

**Diplomatic Reception**
This room is used to welcome friends and ambassadors. It is elegantly furnished in the Federal Period style (1790–1820).

## The White House Visitor Center

The Visitor Center has interesting exhibits about the history of the White House as well as royal gifts on display. There are also seasonal lectures by famous speakers on aspects of history in and out of the White House. The center has a monthly Living History program with actors portraying historic figures. The gift shop carries an extensive range, including the annual White House Christmas ornament. Tours of the president's official residence in the White House are extremely limited at this time. Guided tours can be booked only by special arrangement through a member of Congress or an embassy.

Façade of the
Visitor Center

The magnificent Renwick Gallery, a fine example of French Empire style

## ⑲ Renwick Gallery

**Map** C3. Pennsylvania Ave at 17th St, NW. **Tel** (202) 633-1000. **M** Farragut W. **Open** closed until 2016 for renovations. **W** americanart.si.edu

This magnificent red-brick building was designed by James Renwick in 1859. It originally housed the art collection of William Wilson Corcoran until it was moved to the current Corcoran Gallery of Art in 1897.

After efforts by First Lady Jacqueline Kennedy saved the building from destruction, it was bought by the Smithsonian. Refurbished and renamed, the Renwick Gallery opened in 1972. It is dedicated primarily to 20th-century American crafts and houses some impressive exhibits in every material including clay, glass, and metal.

Although the gallery is closed for renovation work until 2016, its French Empire-style exterior is worth seeing.

## ⑳ Corcoran Gallery of Art

**Map** C4. 500 17th St, NW. **Tel** (202) 639-1700. **M** Farragut W, Farragut N. **Open** check website for latest information on opening hours. **Closed** Dec 25. **W** corcoran.edu

A treasure trove of fine art, this privately funded collection was founded by William Wilson Corcoran, a banker. His collection soon outgrew its original home in the Renwick Gallery and moved to this massive edifice in 1897. Many of the European works were added in 1925 by art collector and US Senator William A. Clark. The gallery's masterpieces now include 16th-century paintings, including 17th-century works by Rembrandt, and 19th-century Impressionist paintings by Monet and Renoir. It also has the largest collection of paintings by Jean-Baptist Camille Corot outside France, and fine examples of African-American art. Paintings from the 20th century include works by Picasso, John Singer Sargent, and de Kooning. Chamber music concerts take place some Sundays at 4pm. Call for the schedule.

Lion Statue, guarding the Corcoran Gallery

## ㉑ The Kennedy Center

**Map** B4. New Hampshire Ave & Rock Creek Pkwy, NW. **Tel** (202) 467-4600. **M** Foggy Bottom. 🚌 80. **Open** 10am– 9pm daily; 10am–9pm Mon–Sat, noon–9pm Sun & hols (box office). 🎫 10am–5pm Mon–Fri, 10am–1pm Sat & Sun (call 416-8340). **W** kennedy-center.org

In 1958, President Eisenhower signed an act to begin fundraising for a national cultural center that would attract the world's best opera, music, and dance companies to the US capital. His successor, John F. Kennedy, was also an ardent supporter and fundraiser for this project but he was assassinated before the completion of the center, which was named in his honor.

Designed by Edward Durrell Stone, the center opened in 1971. The **Grand Foyer**, adorned with a remarkable bronze bust of Kennedy by sculptor Robert Berks, stretches 630 ft (192 m) and provides an impressive entrance to the three main theaters of this vast arts complex. In front of the foyer is the **JFK Terrace**, which runs the length of the center and offers glorious views of the Potomac River.

Of the three huge theaters, the **Eisenhower Theater**, with a bronze bust of Eisenhower, is at one end of the foyer. At the other end is the **Concert Hall**, which seats over 2,400 people and is the home of the National Symphony Orchestra. Between them is the sumptuous **Opera House**, hung with an enormous crystal chandelier, and with seating for more than 2,300 people. The Opera House is flanked by the **Hall of States**, with the flags of each of the 50 American states, and the **Hall of Nations**, with the flags of every country with which the US has diplomatic relations.

The impressive Grand Foyer of the Kennedy Center

## ㉒ Watergate Complex

**Map** B3. Virginia Ave between Rock Creek Pkwy & New Hampshire Ave, NW. Ⓜ Foggy Bottom-GWU. ♿

Located next to the Kennedy Center on the banks of the Potomac, the four rounded buildings that make up the Watergate Complex were completed in 1971 and designed to contain apartments, offices, and shops (today there are no longer any shops). The Watergate soon became one of Washington's most desirable addresses. In 1972, however, the complex found itself at the center of international news. Burglars, linked to President Nixon, broke into the offices of the Democratic Party headquarters in the complex to bug the telephones there, sparking off a major political scandal. Investigations by *Washington Post* reporters Bob Woodward and Carl Bernstein uncovered the extent of the president's involvement through incriminating tapes and proven bribery. This led to an impeachment hearing, but before Mr. Nixon could be impeached, he resigned. Vice-President Gerald Ford succeeded him.

## ㉓ Georgetown

**Map** A3. Old Stone House: 3051 M St, NW. **Tel** (202) 895-6070. **Open** phone ahead. 🚌 30, 32, 34, 36, 38. ♿ Ⓦ nps.gov/olst
Georgetown University: 37th & O Sts, NW. **Tel** (202) 687-0100. **Open** varies. 📷 call 687-3600 for details. ♿ Ⓦ georgetown.edu Dumbarton Oaks: 1703 32nd St, NW. **Tel** (202) 339-6401. **Open** 2–5pm Tue–Sun. **Closed** Federal hols, Dec 24. 📷 📷 ♿ house only. Ⓦ doaks.org

Georgetown developed well before Washington, DC. Native Americans had a settlement here, and by the mid-18th century Georgetown had a substantial population of immigrants from Scotland. With the construction of Washington Harbor and the Chesapeake and Ohio Canal in 1828, it soon grew into a wealthy port. Today one

The picturesque Old Stone House in Georgetown, built in 1765

of Washington, DC's most attractive neighborhoods, Georgetown is lined with elegant townhouses, many of them converted into upscale bars, restaurants, and boutiques. The two main business streets of the area are Wisconsin Avenue and M Street. On the latter is the historic **Old Stone House** (built in 1765), which may be the only building in Washington that predates the American Revolution. N Street, lined with historic buildings, has an array of 18th-century Federal-style mansions, as well as some fine Victorian townhouses. The 1794 Thomas **Beall House** (number 3017), is where Jackie Kennedy lived for a year after JFK's death.

More Federal houses can be seen lining the banks of the **Chesapeake and Ohio Canal**, which was built in 1828 and runs for 184 miles (296 km) from Georgetown to Cumberland, Maryland. The canal, with its ingenious transportation system of locks, aqueducts, and tunnels, fell out of use with the arrival of

The Riggs National Bank, on Wisconsin Avenue in Georgetown

the railroad in the 19th century. It is now a protected national park, offering many recreational facilities. Park rangers in period costume guide tours of the canal in mule-drawn barges, and boating is also popular, especially between Georgetown and Violette's Lock – the first 22 miles (35 km) of the canal. The towpath along the canal is ideal for walks and bike rides.

A major center of activity in this district is **Georgetown University**, founded in 1789. Among the historic buildings on its campus is the Gothic-inspired Healy Building, topped by a fanciful spiral.

Sprawling over 22 acres (9 ha) of land in Georgetown is the historic **Dumbarton Oaks** estate. Its superbly landscaped gardens surround a grand Federal-style brick mansion, which houses a priceless art collection assembled by pharmaceutical heirs Robert and Mildred Bliss.

The historic Dumbarton Oaks Conference, attended by President Franklin Roosevelt and British Prime Minister Winston Churchill, was held in the music room of this house in 1944, laying the groundwork for the establishment of the United Nations.

The Blisses donated the house to Harvard University, and it now houses a library, research institution, and museum, the highlight of which is its superb collection of Byzantine art. A new wing of the house, designed by Philip Johnson, houses pre-Columbian masks, gold jewelry from Central America, frescoes, and Aztec carvings.

Auguste Renoir's masterpiece, *The Luncheon of the Boating Party* (1881)

### ㉔ Phillips Collection

1600 21st St at Q St, NW. **Tel** (202) 387-2151. Ⓜ Dupont Circle. **Open** 10am–5pm Tue–Wed & Fri–Sat, 10am–8:30pm Thu, 11am–6pm Sun. **Closed** Mon, Jan 1, Jul 4, Thanksg., Dec 25. 🎨 📷 11am Fri & Sat. ♿ Ⓦ phillipscollection.org

This is one of the finest collections of Impressionist art in the world, and the first museum in the US devoted to modern art of the 19th and 20th centuries. Housed in the beautiful 1897 Georgian Revival mansion of the collection's founders, Marjorie and Duncan Phillips, this museum has a more intimate and personal ambience than the larger Smithsonian art museums.

Among the wonderful selection of Impressionist and Post-Impressionist works on display are *Dancers at the Barre* by Degas, *Self-Portrait* by Cezanne, *Entrance to the Public Gardens at Arles* by Van Gogh, and Renoir's masterpiece, *The Luncheon of the Boating Party* (1881).

Other great paintings in the collection include El Greco's *The Repentant Saint Peter* (1600), *The Blue Room* (1901) by Picasso, Piet Mondrian's *Composition No III* (1921–25), and *Ochre on Red* (1954) by Mark Rothko.

The museum hosts a number of special events, such as gallery talks, film retrospectives, and live jazz concerts. Especially popular are its Sunday afternoon concerts, staged in the Music Room, with performances by classical artists of world renown. These popular concerts are free to anyone who has purchased a ticket for the gallery on that day.

### ㉕ National Zoological Park

3001 Connecticut Ave, NW. **Tel** (202) 673-4800. Ⓜ Cleveland Park, Woodley Park-Zoo. **Open** Apr–Oct: 10am–6pm daily (buildings), 6am–8pm daily (grounds); Oct–Apr: 10am–4:30pm daily (buildings), 6am–6pm daily (grounds). **Closed** Dec 25. 🎨 call (202) 673-4671. ♿ 📷 🖥 Ⓦ natzoo.si.edu/

Located in a sprawling 163-acre (66-ha) park designed by Frederick Law Olmsted (the landscape designer of New York's Central Park), the National Zoo was established in 1887. Since 1964 it has been part of the Smithsonian Institution, which has developed it as a dynamic "biopark" where animals are studied in environments that replicate their natural habitats.

The Komodo dragon, a huge species of lizard, in the National Zoological Park

The zoo's most famous residents are the giant pandas, Mei Xiang, Tian Tian, and baby Bao Bao who can be seen roaming around the large trees, pools, and air-conditioned outdoor grottos in the **Giant Panda Exhibit**.

Equally popular with visitors is the **Great Ape House**, which houses lowland gorillas, each weighing around 400 lbs (180 kg), and arboreal orangutans.

The **Reptile Discovery Center** features the rare Komodo dragons, lizards that can grow up to a length of 10 ft (3 m) and weigh up to 200 lbs (90 kg).

In **Amazonia**, which re-creates the lush green Amazonian habitat, visitors can see poison arrow frogs and giant catfish, while the **Asia Trail** features red pandas and sloth bears.

Other rare creatures include the endangered Golden Lion Tamarins and red wolves.

### ㉖ Washington National Cathedral

Massachusetts & Wisconsin Aves, NW. **Tel** (202) 537-6200. 🚌 32, 34, 36. **Open** 10am–3:30pm Mon–Sat, 12:45–4pm Sun. 🌳 (free entry to garden). 🎨 group reservations call 537-6207. 📷 ♿ 🖥 📷 🔔 noon Mon–Sat, hourly 8am–11am & 4pm & 6:30pm Sun, 5:30pm Mon–Fri, 4pm Sat & Sun. Ⓦ nationalcathedral.org

The building of the Church of St. Peter and St. Paul (its official name) was financed entirely by donations. It is the world's sixth largest cathedral, measuring 518 ft (158 m) in length and 301 ft (95 m) from the ground to the top of the central tower. It uses building techniques of the Gothic style of architecture, evident in the pointed arches, rib vaulting, and exterior flying buttresses. Inside, sculpture, needlework, wrought iron, and wood carving depict the nation's history and biblical scenes.

Above the west entrance is a splendid relief of *The Creation* by Frederick Hart, which depicts mankind being formed from chaos. The pinnacles on the

Gothic-style architecture of the Washington National Cathedral

Cathedral towers are decorated with leaf-shaped ornaments. Above the south entrance is an exquisite stained-glass **Rose Window**, while in the nave another stained-glass window commemorates the *Apollo 11* space flight and contains a sliver of moon rock. The **High Altar** has carvings of 110 figures surrounding the central statue of Christ. The floor in front of the altar has stone from Mount Sinai. By the **Children's Chapel**, built to the scale of a six-year-old, is a statue of Jesus as a boy.

*The Creation*, National Cathedral

## ㉗ Arlington National Cemetery

Arlington, VA. **Tel** (877) 907-8585.
Ⓜ Arlington National Cemetery.
**Open** Apr–Sep: 8am–7pm daily;
Oct–Mar: 8am–5pm daily.
**Closed** Dec 25. 🎥 ♿

A sea of simple headstones covers Arlington National Cemetery, marking the graves of around 300,000 American servicemen killed in the nation's major conflicts – from the Revolution to the present. The focus of the cemetery, which sprawls over 624 acres (252 ha) of a hillside, is the **Tomb of the Unknowns**, honoring the thousands whose

bodies were never found or identified. Its four vaults are for soldiers from World Wars I and II, Korea, and Vietnam. Each vault held one unidentified soldier until 1998, when the Vietnam soldier was identified by DNA analysis and reburied in his hometown. Near it is the **Memorial Amphitheater**, which has hosted many state funerals, and where annual services are held on Memorial Day.

North of the Tomb of the Unknowns, an eternal flame burns at the **Grave of John F. Kennedy**, lit by his wife Jacqueline on the day of his funeral in December 1963. She and their infant son Patrick and an unnamed stillborn daughter are buried next to the late president. His brother Robert F. Kennedy is nearby. Close to Arlington House is the imposing **Tomb of Pierre L'Enfant**, the French architect responsible for planning the city of Washington. The cemetery also houses poignant memorials to the victims of the Lockerbie air crash and the *Challenger* Space Shuttle, which exploded seconds after take-off in January 1986.

The grand Georgian-Revival mansion at the top of the hill, above the Kennedy graves, is **Arlington House**, which was the home of the Confederate general Robert E. Lee (1807–70). When Lee left his home in 1861 to lead Virginia's armed forces during the Civil War, the Union confiscated the estate for a

military cemetery. The house, now a memorial to the general, is open to visitors.

## ㉘ The Pentagon

1000 Defense Pentagon, Hwy 1-395, Arlington, VA. **Tel** (703) 697-1776.
Ⓜ Pentagon. **Open** tours by appointment only; book online at **pentagontours.osd.mil**
Ⓦ **pentagon.afis.osd.mil**

The world's largest office building, the Pentagon is almost a city in itself. This enormous edifice houses 23,000 people who work for the US Department of Defense, which includes the Army, Navy, and Airforce, and 14 other defense agencies. Despite its enormous size – it has 17.5 miles (28 km) of corridors, and the entire US Capitol could fit into one of its five wedge-shaped sections – the building's efficient design ensures that it takes no more than seven minutes to walk between any two points in the Pentagon. Designed by army engineers, it is built from sand and gravel dredged from the Potomac and molded into concrete. The building was started in September 1941, and completed in January 1943 at a cost of $83 million.

The headquarters of the US military establishment and the ultimate symbol of America's military might, the Pentagon was one of the targets of terrorists who flew a hijacked American Airlines plane into one side of the building on September 11, 2001, killing 189 people. It has now been completely restored.

Uniform rows of headstones in Arlington National Cemetery

# Virginia

There is enough history and natural beauty in Virginia to satisfy the most avid sightseer. Mount Vernon, the perfectly preserved home of President George Washington, is close to Washington, DC. In eastern Virginia is the old capital, Williamsburg, a living museum of the Colonial era. To its west, the Skyline Drive reveals the spectacular beauty of the Shenandoah National Park and the Blue Ridge Mountains. The state capital, Richmond, retains a charming Old South aura.

## ❷ Alexandria

🏙 128,000. 🚉 Union Station, 110 Callahan St. Ⓜ King Street.
ℹ Ramsay House Visitor Center, 221 King St (703) 746-3301.
🌐 visitalexandriava.com

Old Town Alexandria has kept a special historical flavor, dating back to its incorporation in 1749. Accessible by Metro from Washington, Alexandria is still a busy port, with its lively Market Square. Its tree-lined streets are filled with elegant, historic buildings, among them the 1753 **Carlyle House**, a Georgian Palladian mansion on Fairfax

Façade of the elegant Carlyle House, built in 1752, Alexandria

Street. A guided tour of the house, now beautifully restored, provides fascinating details about 18th-century everday life.

On the same street is the **Stabler Leadbeater Apothecary Shop**, established in 1792. When it closed in 1933, the doors were locked with all its contents intact. Now reopened as a museum, the shop's 8,000 original objects include huge mortars and pestles, and jars of herbal remedies.

The **Boyhood Home of Robert E. Lee**, a Federal townhouse where General Lee (*see p197*) lived from the age of 11 until he went to the West Point Military Academy, is currently a private residence and not open to the public. The **Lee-Fendall House Museum** nearby is rich with artifacts from the Revolution to the 1930s Labor Movement. To its south is the 1773 **Christ Church**, a Georgian edifice where George Washington's pew is still preserved with his nameplate, as is that of Robert E. Lee.

On Union Street is the **Torpedo Factory Art Center**, displaying the work of local

## ❸ Mount Vernon

This country estate on the Potomac River was George Washington's home for 45 years. The house is furnished as it would have been during Washington's presidency (1789–97), and the 500-acre (202-ha) grounds still retain aspects of the original farm, such as the flower and vegetable gardens, the sheep paddock, and quarters for the slaves who worked the plantation.

**The Kitchen**, set slightly apart from the main house, has been completely restored.

**The Mansion Tour** shows visitors the study and dining room, Washington's bedroom, and the bed in which he died.

Overseer's House

**The Upper Garden**
The plants in this colorful garden replicate those grown in Washington's time.

**The Slave Quarters** housed the estate's slaves. Washington freed all his slaves in his will.

*For hotels and restaurants see pp234–9*

artists and craftsmen. From the nearby waterfront, there are boat tours on the Potomac River.

The **Farmers Market** in the center of town dates back to 1753, and George Washington regularly sent produce from his farm at Mount Vernon to be sold here. Today, shoppers can find fresh vegetables and fruit, flowers, baked goods, preserves, and local crafts.

### Carlyle House
121 N Fairfax St. **Tel** (703) 549-2997. **Open** 10am–4pm Tue–Sat, noon–5pm Sun; Nov–Mar: last tour 4pm. **Closed** Mon, Jan 1, Thanksgiving, Dec 25.

### Lee-Fendall House Museum
614 Oronoco St. **Tel** (703) 548-1789. **Open** 10am–3pm Tue, Wed–Sun. **Closed** Dec 25–Jan 31 (except 3rd Sun, Lee's birthday celebration). leefendallhouse.org

### Torpedo Factory Art Center
105 N Union St. **Tel** (703) 838-4565. **Open** 10am–6pm daily (to 9pm Thu). **Closed** Jan 1, Easter, Jul 4, Thanksgiving, Dec 25. torpedofactory.org

The elegant dining room at Kenmore House, Fredericksburg

## ❹ Fredericksburg

22,600. 706 Caroline St, (800) 678-4748. **Open** 9am–5pm daily (Memorial Day & Labor Day until 7pm). **Closed** Dec 25. visitfred.com

Fredericksburg's attractions are its historic downtown district and four Civil War battlefields, including those at Chancellorsville and The Wilderness. The Rising Sun Tavern and Hugh Mercer Apothecary Shop in the old downtown offer living history accounts of life in a town that began as a 50-acre (20-ha) port on the Rappahannock River.

**Kenmore Plantation and Gardens**, also in the heart of town, has beautiful rooms and gardens. The town's visitor center offers horse-and-carriage or trolley tours. The battlefields evoke the Union's long push toward Richmond during the Civil War (see p56).

### Kenmore Plantation & Gardens
1201 Washington Ave. **Tel** (540) 373-3381. **Open** Mar–Oct: 11am–5pm Mon–Sat, noon–5pm Sun; Nov–Dec: 10am–5pm Mon–Sat, noon–5pm Sun. **Closed** Jan–Feb, Thanksgiving, Dec 24–25, 31. kenmore.org

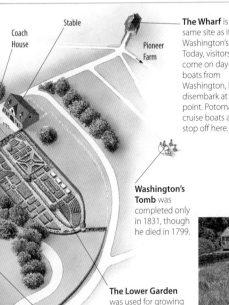

Coach House

Stable

Pioneer Farm

**The Wharf** is on the same site as it was in Washington's time. Today, visitors who come on day-trip boats from Washington, DC, disembark at this point. Potomac cruise boats also stop off here.

**Washington's Tomb** was completed only in 1831, though he died in 1799.

**The Lower Garden** was used for growing vegetables and berries.

**The Bowling Green** was added to the estate by Washington.

### VISITORS' CHECKLIST

**Practical Information**
S end of George Washington Memorial Pkwy, Fairfax County, VA. **Tel** (703) 780-2000. **Open** Mar & Sep–Oct: 9am–5pm daily; Apr–Aug: 8am–5pm daily; Nov–Feb: 9am–4pm daily. first floor. mountvernon.org

**Transport**
Yellow line to Huntington Station. Fairfax Connector bus 101 to Mount Vernon: call (703) 339-7200. Tour bus services & boat cruises available:

**The Pioneer Farm**
This exhibit demonstrates farming techniques pioneered by Washington. There is also a replica of his unique 16-sided treading barn, created using authentic tools.

# ❺ Colonial Williamsburg

As Virginia's capital from 1699 to 1780, Williamsburg was the hub of the loyal British colony. After 1780 the town went into decline. Then in 1926, John D. Rockefeller embarked on a massive restoration project. Today, in the midst of the modern-day city, the 18th-century city has been re-created. People in colonial dress portray the lifestyle of the original townspeople; blacksmiths, silversmiths, cabinetmakers, and bakers show off their skills; and horse-drawn carriages pass through the streets, providing visitors with a fascinating insight into America's past.

**Courthouse**
Built in 1770–71 this was the home of the county court for more than 150 years.

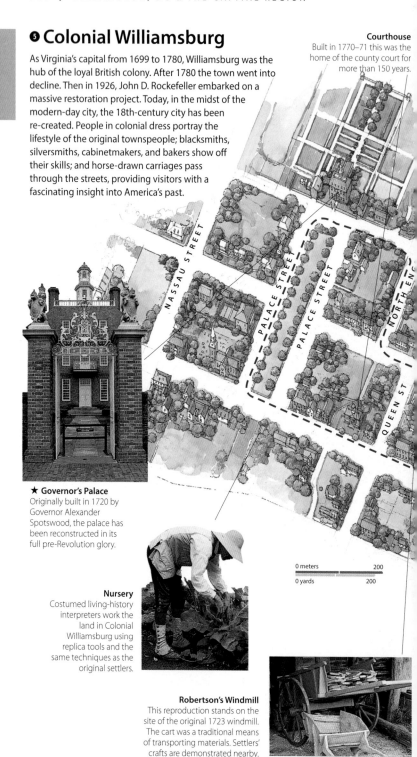

**★ Governor's Palace**
Originally built in 1720 by Governor Alexander Spotswood, the palace has been reconstructed in its full pre-Revolution glory.

**Nursery**
Costumed living-history interpreters work the land in Colonial Williamsburg using replica tools and the same techniques as the original settlers.

0 meters  200
0 yards  200

**Robertson's Windmill**
This reproduction stands on the site of the original 1723 windmill. The cart was a traditional means of transporting materials. Settlers' crafts are demonstrated nearby.

★ **Print Office**
This store stocks authentic 18th-century foods, including wine, Virginia ham, and peanuts.

**VISITORS' CHECKLIST**

**Practical Information**
🛈 1800-HISTORY. 📱 📷
Ⓦ colonialwilliamsburg.com

**Transport**
🚊 🚌 421 N Boundary St.

**Milliner**
Owned by Margaret Hunter, the milliner shop stocked a wide range of items. Imported clothes for women and children, jewelry, and toys could all be bought here.

**Raleigh Tavern**
The Raleigh was once an important center for social, political, and commercial gatherings. The building burned in 1859, but this reproduction evokes the original spirit.

★ **Capitol**
This is a 1945 reconstruction of the original 1705 building. The government resided in the West Wing, while the General Court was in the East Wing.

**Key**
— Suggested route

Jamestown Settlement, a re-creation of Colonial James Fort

## ❻ Jamestown & Yorktown

**ℹ** Jamestown Settlement & Yorktown Victory Center, (757) 887-1776. **W** historyisfun.org

Jamestown, established in 1607 on the banks of the James River, was the first permanent English settlement in the US. One of the early settlers was John Rolfe, who married Pocahontas, daughter of the Indian chief, Powhatan. But the colony didn't last long – disease, famine, and attacks by Algonquin Indians caused heavy loss of life and in 1699, the colony was abandoned.

Present-day Jamestown Island contains 1,500 acres (607 ha) of marshland and forest. The **Jamestown Settlement** is a re-creation of the original colony, complete with costumed interpreters and replicas of James Fort, an Indian village, and the ships that brought the first successful colonists to Virginia.

On the opposite side of the peninsula, 15 miles (24 km) away, Yorktown was the site of the decisive battle of the American Revolution in 1781. Battlefield tours at **Colonial National Historical Park** explain the siege at Yorktown, which ended with the surrender of the British forces.

**🏛 Jamestown Settlement**
**Tel** (757) 856-1200, (888) 593-4682. **Open** 9am–5pm daily (to 6pm Jun 15–Aug 15). **Closed** Jan 1, Dec 25. 🅿 ♿ 📷 **W** historicjamestowne.org

**🌿 Colonial National Historical Park**
**Tel** (757) 898-3400. **Open** 9am–5pm daily. **Closed** Jan 1, Thanksgiving, Dec 25. **W** nps.gov/colo

## ❼ Norfolk

**🏔** 262,000. **✈ 🚉 🚌 ℹ** 232 E Main St, (800) 368-3097, (757) 664-6620. **W** visitnorfolktoday.com

A historic Colonial port, located at the point where Chesapeake Bay meets the Atlantic Ocean, Norfolk is a busy maritime center with the world's largest naval base. The city's logo, a mermaid, is the theme of sculptures and emblems all over Norfolk. The downtown waterfront centers on the massive battleship USS *Wisconsin*, a part of the **Nauticus, The National Maritime Center**. The center offers multimedia presentations about naval battles, ships, and deep-sea creatures.

Another top attraction is the **Chrysler Museum of Art**, which displays the eclectic personal collection of automobile tycoon Walter Chrysler Jr. The works of art include paintings by Velasquez, Rubens, Degas, Renoir, and modern masters such as Roy Lichtenstein.

Neighboring Virginia Beach is the site of the 18th-century lighthouse at Cape Henry, where the English first landed in 1607. The waterfront is also home to the Virginia Aquarium and Marine Science Museum.

**🏛 Nauticus, The National Maritime Center**
1 Waterside Dr. **Tel** (757) 664-1000. **Open** 10am–5pm Tue–Sat, noon–5pm Sun; Jun 1–Sep 1:10am–5pm daily. **Closed** Mon, Thanksgiving, Jan 1, Dec 24 & 25. 🅿 ♿ 📷 **W** nauticus.org

## ❽ Richmond

**🏔** 198,300. **🚉 🚌 ℹ** 401 N Third St, (804) 783-7450. **W** visitrichmondva.com

The old capital of the Confederacy (see p57), Richmond still retains an aura of Old South gentility. Bronze statues of Civil War generals and other heroes line Monument Avenue, while Victorian mansions and brownstones testify to this area's postwar prosperity.

Civil War artifacts, including General Robert E. Lee's coat and sword, are among the exhibits at the **Museum of the Confederacy**. Next door, the White House of the Confederacy is a treasure of the Victorian age.

The graceful Neo-Classical **State Capitol** dominating downtown houses a life-size sculpture of George Washington by Jean Antoine Houdon. To its west is the serene **Hollywood Cemetery**, the resting place of presidents John Tyler and James Monroe, as well as of 18,000 Confederate soldiers who are buried under a communal pyramid. Palmer Chapel offers superb views of James River and Belle Isle. Farther uptown are two fine museums, the fascinating **Science Museum of Virginia** and the **Virginia Museum of Fine Arts**, which has collections ranging from ancient Egyptian, Indian, and Himalayan art to French Impressionist and modern American masterpieces. The museum's highlight, however, is the priceless Pratt Collection of Imperial Russian Art, which includes five fabulous jeweled Easter eggs made for the Tsar by the jeweler Peter Carl Fabergé.

Statue of Robert E. Lee in Richmond

**🏛 Virginia Museum of Fine Arts**
200 North Blvd. **Tel** (804) 340- 1400. **Open** 10am–5pm Wed–Sun. **Closed** Mon–Tue, Jan 1, Jul 4, Thanksg., Dec 25. 🅿 only exhibitions. ♿ 🖥 📷 **W** vmfa.museum

## ❾ Chincoteague

🏔 4,300. ℹ 6150 Community Drive, (757) 336-6161. 🆆 chincoteague-va.gov

The main tourist attraction on Virginia's sparsely developed Eastern Shore, Chincoteague draws fishermen, bird-watchers, and beachcombers. The town itself is primarily a service center, with hotels, motels, and restaurants catering to visitors bound for the **Chincoteague National Wildlife Refuge**, which protects several offshore islands, as well as coastal marshlands and a 10-mile (16-km) stretch of Atlantic Ocean beachfront.

A driving tour loops for over 3 miles (4.8 km) through the wildlife preserve, but the best way to see some of the numerous egrets, snow geese, herons, falcons, and other birds found here is by walking or paddling in a canoe.

**🦅 Chincoteague National Wildlife Refuge**
Tel (757) 336-6122. **Open** 6am–6pm daily. 🐾 ♿ limited.

## ❿ Charlottesville

🏔 45,000. 🚉 🚌 ℹ 610 E Main St, (434) 293-6789, (877) 386-1103.
🆆 visitcharlottesville.org

Charlottesville was Thomas Jefferson's hometown. It is dominated by the University of Virginia, which he founded and designed, and also by his home, **Monticello**.

It took Jefferson 40 years to complete Monticello, which he began building in 1769. It is now one of the most celebrated houses in the country. The entrance hall doubled as a private museum, and the library held a collection of around 6,700 books.

The 5,000-acre (2,023-ha) grounds include a large terraced vegetable garden where Jefferson grew and experimented with varieties. The remains of the slaves' quarters still stand; nearly 200 slaves worked the estate's plantations, and recent evidence suggests that one of them, Sally Hemmings, bore Jefferson's child.

The obelisk over Jefferson's grave in the family cemetery lauds him as "Father of the University of Virginia." The university's Neo-Classical buildings and grounds are open to visitors. Vineyards and wineries surround Charlottesville.

Michie Tavern *(see p238)*, joined to the Virginia Wine Museum, has been restored to its 18th-century appearance and serves typical Southern cuisine. Montpelier, on a 2,500-acre (1,012-ha) site, 25 miles (40 km) to the north, was the home of the fourth president, James Madison.

*The obelisk over Jefferson's grave*

**🚂 Monticello**
Route 53, 3 miles (4.8 km) SE of Charlottesville. **Tel** (434) 984-9822. **Open** Mar–Oct: 8am–5pm; Nov–Feb: 9am–4:30pm. **Closed** Dec 25. 🚫 📷 ♿ 📷 🆆 monticello.org

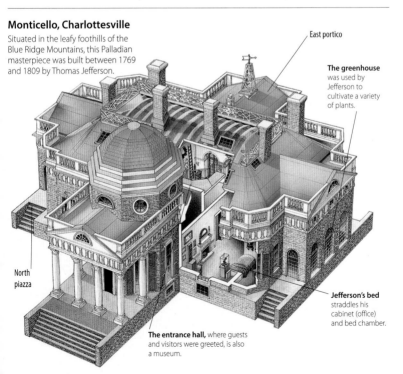

## Monticello, Charlottesville

Situated in the leafy foothills of the Blue Ridge Mountains, this Palladian masterpiece was built between 1769 and 1809 by Thomas Jefferson.

East portico

**The greenhouse** was used by Jefferson to cultivate a variety of plants.

North piazza

**Jefferson's bed** straddles his cabinet (office) and bed chamber.

**The entrance hall,** where guests and visitors were greeted, is also a museum.

A reconstructed building, Appomattox Court House National Historical Park

## ⓫ Appomattox Court House National Historical Park

ℹ️ (877) AT BLUE GREY, (434) 352-8987. **Open** 8:30am–5pm daily. **Closed** Jan 1, Martin Luther King Day, Presidents Day, Thanksgiving, Dec 25. 🅿️ ♿ 🆆 nps.gov/apco

This National Historic Park, located 3 miles (4.8 km) northeast of the town of Appomattox, re-creates the spot where Confederate General Robert E. Lee surrendered to US General Ulysses S. Grant to signal the end of the Civil War *(see p197)*. Today, markers trace the sites of the last skirmishes of the war, and 27 reconstructed and restored buildings replicate the scene where, on April 9, 1865, the two leaders and their armies put an end to that long, destructive war. In the last months of fighting, General Grant had captured the Confederate stronghold at Petersburg, while General Sherman's "March to the Sea" across Georgia surrounded Confederate forces from the South. With the fall of the Confederate capital at Richmond

on April 2, General Lee realized that victory was impossible. The terms of surrender were generous, since Union leaders hoped to promote reconciliation. When the Confederates laid down their arms, the Northern soldiers saluted their opponents.

Much of the original setting was destroyed in battle or later dismantled by souvenir hunters. Most of what stands here today was reconstructed by the National Park Service in the 1940s.

## ⓬ Blue Ridge Parkway

**Tel** (828) 271-4779.
🆆 nps.gov/blri

Stretching for 469 miles (755 km) along the crest of the Appalachian Mountains, the Blue Ridge Parkway *(see p51)* extends from the southern border of Shenandoah National Park all the way to North Carolina, ending finally at Great Smoky Mountains National Park *(see p264)*. Created as a public works project during the "New Deal" era in the depths of the 1930s Great Depression, the scenic route was begun in 1935 but was not completed until 1987. Mileposts along the way, measured from north to south, help travelers discover the points of interest along the route. Some of the highlights along the 216-mile (348-km) portion of the Blue Ridge Parkway in Virginia include a crossing of the James River at milepost 63 and the lakefront lodge in the Peaks of Otter section near milepost 86. The historic **Mabry Mill** at milepost 176 was in use as a backwoods sawmill and blacksmith shop until 1935.

This parkway passes through Asheville, North Carolina, and Roanoke, Virginia, and is primarily rural and scenic, with no advertising or commercial traffic allowed. Open all year, the peak travel season is fall.

The picturesque Mabry Mill at milepost 176 of the Blue Ridge Parkway

For hotels and restaurants see pp234–9

# ❽ Skyline Drive

Skyline Drive runs along the backbone of the Shenandoah National Park's Blue Ridge Mountains. Originally farmland, the government designated the area a national park in 1926. Deer, wild turkey, bears, and bobcats inhabit the park, and wildflowers, azaleas, and mountain laurel are abundant. The park's many hiking trails and its 75 viewpoints offer stunning natural scenery.

North entrance station

**② Whiteoak Canyon**
The Whiteoak Canyon Trail passes six waterfalls on its route.

**① Pinnacles Overlook**
The view of Old Rag Mountain with its outcroppings of granite is spectacular.

**⑤ Bearfence Mountain**
Although this is a bit of a climb, partly on rock scramble, it is not too difficult, and the reward is a breathtaking 360-degree view of the surrounding landscape.

**③ Big Meadows**
Close to the visitor center, this meadow retains its centuries-old state. It was probably kept clear by fires or lightning strikes. Herds of deer can be seen.

**④ Rapidan Camp**
At the end of Mill Prong Trail, this 164-acre (66-ha) resort was President Hoover's weekend retreat until 1932, when he donated it to the park.

**⑥ Lewis Mountain**
Quaint cabins, a campground, picnic area, camp store, laundry, and showers provide for campers and hikers here.

## Key

- – Hiking route
▬▬▬ Road

0 km      10
0 miles      10

## Tips for Walkers

**Starting point:** North at Front Royal, central at Thornton Gap or Swift Run Gap, south at Rockfish Gap.
**Length:** 105 miles (168 km), duration of 4–8 hrs depending on the number of stops.
**When to go:** Mid-October for fall leaf colors; spring and summer for wildflowers.
**What it costs:** No fee to travel the Blue Ridge Parkway.

Fall in Shenandoah National Park

# West Virginia

Set entirely within the Appalachian Mountains, this "Mountain State" remains largely forested, despite centuries of aggressive lumbering and mining. The state was part of Virginia until the Civil War, and its early European pioneers were less wealthy and generally very different from the genteel planters of eastern Virginia. As talk of secession grew, western Virginia aligned with the Union. Four years after abolitionist John Brown raided a federal arsenal in Harpers Ferry in a failed attempt to inspire a slave rebellion in 1859, West Virginia was declared a separate state. Today it is known for its woodworking, quilting, and basketry crafts, and traditional Appalachian music and dancing.

Blackwater Falls State Park, in Monongahela National Forest

## ⑭ Monongahela National Forest

200 Sycamore St, Elkins. **Tel** (304) 636-1800. **Open** 8am–4:45pm Mon–Fri.
**W** fs.udsa.gov/mnf

The eastern half of the state lies deep within the Allegheny Mountains, a part of the longer Appalachian Range. Much of this rugged terrain is protected as the vast Monongahela National Forest, which encompasses five federally designated wilderness areas and serves as the headwaters for six major river systems. Its landscapes of rhododendron, black cherry, highland bogs, blueberry thickets, and exposed rocks are the habitat for black bear, white-tailed deer, bobcat, otter, mink, and many other species. The forest's trails attract hikers, horseback riders, and mountain bikers, while in winter, the area is popular for downhill and cross-country skiing.

The small town of **Elkins**, the headquarters of the national forest, makes a convenient base to explore the area. The town's Augusta Heritage Center hosts residential summer programs on traditional folklife and folk arts, as well as bluegrass and old-time mountain music dances and concerts.

Northeast of Elkins, an 8-mile (13-km) stretch of the 124-mile (200-km) Allegheny Trail links two state parks – **Canaan Valley Resort State Park**, a downhill ski resort, and **Blackwater Falls State Park**, a good place for backcountry ski touring. Both parks have restaurants and provide facilities for lodging and camping. Farther south, Snowshoe Mountain Resort is the state's largest downhill resort in winter and a mountain biking center from spring to fall (rentals and guided trips are available). The nearby **Cass Scenic Railroad State Park** organizes vintage steam train rides across the mountaintops for panoramic views. Fall foliage rides are the most popular. Southeast of Elkins, the **Spruce**

Knob-Seneca Rocks National Recreation Area draws rockclimbers up the sandstone strata of Seneca Rocks, an hour's drive away. The 75-mile (121-km) Greenbrier River Trail, running parallel to the Virginia border, from White Sulphur Springs in the south all the way to the Cass Scenic Railroad State Park in the north, is a converted "rails-to-trails" rail-bed route, which is quite popular for bicycle tours.

🏕 **Spruce Knob-Seneca Rocks National Rec. Area**
ℹ️ (304) 567-2827. **Open** May–Sep: 9am–4:30pm Wed–Sun; Nov–Apr: 9am–4:30 pm Sat–Sun. ♿

🏕 **Cass Scenic Railroad**
Route 66/Main St, Cass. **Tel** (304) 456-4300. ♿ **Open** late May–Oct.
**W** cassrailroad.com

## ⑮ New River Gorge National River

Canyon Rim Visitor Center: US Hwy 19, Lansing. **Tel** (304) 465-0508. **Open** 8am–4:30pm daily. **Closed** Jan 1, Thanksgiving, Dec 25. ♿ **W** nps.gov/neri

The New River courses through a deep gorge in the southeastern corner of the state, drawing rafters for some of the most exciting white-water adventures in the eastern US. The National Park Service, located between Fayetteville and Hinton, oversees a stretch that falls 750 ft (225 m) within 50 miles (80 km), with a compact set of Class V rapids.

Rock climber above New River Gorge National River

Overlook at Hawk's Nest State Park, New River Gorge National River

The modern Canyon Rim Visitor Center and gorge bridge provide easy access to panoramic overlooks and rim hiking trails. The visitor center also distributes comprehensive lists of local rafting outfitters, while the nearby **Hawk's Nest State Park** offers modest lodge rooms and operates an aerial tram down to the river for boat rides during summer. The former mining town of Fayetteville is also a popular base for rafters and outfitters, while the old industrial town of Hinton holds a grittier appeal and is easily accessible to visitors via Amtrak.

🏞 **Hawk's Nest State Park**
Hwy 60, Ansted. **Tel** (304) 658-5212.
🚡 **Tram Rides, Boat Rides:** Call for seasonal operating days and hours.
W hawksnestsp.com

## ⓰ Harpers Ferry

🏕 300. 🚉 🚌 ℹ NPS Visitor Center, (304) 535-6029. W nps.gov/hafe

Nestled at the confluence of the Potomac and Shenandoah Rivers, where West Virginia meets Virginia and Maryland, is the tiny town of Harpers Ferry. Named after Robert Harper, the Philadelphia builder who constructed a ferry here in 1761, most of the historic downtown area is today the **Harpers Ferry National Historic Park**. It was here in 1859, that Maryland abolitionist John Brown led an ill-fated raid on the federal arsenal. Although his attempt failed, this event ignited the Civil War two years later.

The town looks just as it did in the 19th century, with small clapboard storefronts clinging to steep hillsides that slope down to the rushing rivers. Several historic buildings, including John Brown's Fort and the arsenal, are open to visitors.

The famous Appalachian Trail (see p182–3), which runs through town, has its headquarters at the **Appalachian Trail Conservancy**. The Trail is a 2,000-mile (3,220-km) footpath that stretches along the spine of the Appalachian Mountains from Georgia to Maine. With an Amtrak train station, Harpers Ferry is just an hour's ride from Washington, DC, making this remote region accessible for visitors without a car.

🚉 **Appalachian Trail Conservancy**
799 Washington St. **Tel** (304) 535-6331. **Open** 9am–5pm daily.
W appalachiantrail.org

Aerial view of Harpers Ferry, located at the confluence of the Potomac and Shenandoah Rivers

# Maryland

Maryland has an abundance of both natural attractions and historical sites. The rolling farmlands around Antietam in western Maryland are rich in Civil War heritage. Water-related tourism is a mainstay of southern Maryland's Chesapeake Bay, the longest inland shoreline in the US, which attracts sailors, fishermen, and seafood lovers who can indulge in the delicious local specialty – soft-shell blue crabs. The Eastern Shore on the Delmarva Peninsula, dotted with picturesque villages, is also graced by the wild beauty of Assateague and Chincoteague Islands.

## ❶ Antietam National Battlefield

Rte 65, 10 miles (16 km) S of Hagerstown. **Tel** (301) 432-5124. **Open** Jun–Sep: 8am–6pm daily; Oct–May: 8:30am–5pm. **Closed** Jan 1, Thanksgiving, Dec 25. 🅿 🏛 ♿
W **nps.gov/anti**

One of the worst battles of the Civil War was waged here on September 17, 1862, culminating in 23,000 casualties among the Confederate as well as the Union armies.

An observation tower offers a panoramic view of this historic battlefield. Antietam Creek runs peacefully under the Burnside Bridge, where the fighting was severe and much blood was spilled. The whole site has a haunted atmosphere even today. Although the battle did not end in a decisive victory, the horrendous bloodshed at Antietam inspired President Lincoln to issue the Emancipation Proclamation. The visitor center movie recreating the battle should not be missed.

## ❷ Frederick

🏠 50,000. 🚹 19 E Church St, (800) 999-3613, (301) 600-4046. **Open** 9am– 5pm daily.
W **visitfrederick.org**

Frederick's historic center, dating back to the mid-18th century, was renovated in the 1970s and is now a popular tourist attraction.

This charming town is a major antique center and home to hundreds of antique dealers. Its shops, galleries, and eateries are all in 18th- and 19th-century settings, and several historic houses in the town, beautifully restored and furnished with period artifacts, are open to visitors. Francis Scott Key, author of "The Star-Spangled Banner," is buried in Mt. Olivet Cemetery. Tourist information is available at the visitor center, which also conducts popular walking tours during the weekends.

## ❸ Baltimore

🏠 675,500. 🚹 401 Light St, (410) 837-4636, 877-BALTI MORE. 🚉 🚌
W **baltimore.org**

There is much to do and see in this pleasant port city of restaurants, antiques, arts, boats, and monuments. A good place to start is the Inner Harbor, the city's redeveloped waterfront, with its harborside shops and restaurants. The centerpiece, and one of Baltimore's most popular attractions, is the stunning **National Aquarium**, whose collection includes many exhibits, a seal pool, and a dolphin show.

The Harbor is also home to the **Maryland Science Center**, where "do touch" is the rule. It features a number of interactive exhibits, and the Planetarium and IMAX® Theater thrill visitors with images of earth and space.

The **American Visionary Art Museum**, also on the Inner Harbor, houses a collection of extraordinary works by self-taught artists whose materials range from matchsticks to faux pearls.

Uptown is the **Baltimore Museum of Art**, with its famous collection of modern art, including works by Matisse, Picasso, Degas, and Van Gogh. It also has a large collection of pieces by Andy Warhol and two sculpture gardens featuring works by Rodin and Calder. Also impressive is the **Walters**

The eye-catching architecture of the National Aquarium, Baltimore

**Art Gallery** on the elegant Mount Vernon Square, lined with Colonial brick townhouses. The gallery's collection includes Greek and Roman classical art, Southeast Asian and Chinese artifacts, Byzantine silver, pre-Columbian carvings, and jeweled objects by Fabergé. There are also paintings by Rubens, Monet, Manet, and the Victorian artist Alma-Tadema, whose beautiful *Sappho and Alcaeus* (1881) should not be missed.

The lively neighborhood of Little Italy is also worth a visit for its knockout Italian restaurants and the games of bocce (Italian lawn bowling), played around Pratt or Stiles Street on warm evenings.

The beautiful formal gardens of the William Paca House, in Annapolis

### 🐟 National Aquarium
501 E Pratt St, Pier 3. **Tel** (410) 576-3800. **Open** Mar–Jun & Sep–Oct: 9am–5pm daily (to 8pm Fri); Jul–Aug: 9am–7:30pm Sun–Thu, 9am–9:30pm Fri–Sat; Nov–Feb: 10am–4pm Mon–Thu, 10am–8pm Fri, 10am–5pm Sat & Sun. **Closed** Mon, Thanksgiving, Dec 24, 25. 🅿 ♿ 📷 **W** aqua.org

### 🏛 Maryland Science Center
601 Light St. **Tel** (410) 685-5225. **Open** 10am–5pm Tue–Thu, 10am–8pm Fri, 10am–6pm Sat, 11am–5pm Sun. **Closed** Mon, Thanksgiving, Dec 25. 🅿 ♿ 📷 **W** mdsci.org

### 🏛 Baltimore Museum of Art
N Charles St & 31st St. **Tel** (443) 573-1700. **Open** 11am–5pm Wed–Fri, 11am–6pm Sat & Sun. **Closed** Mon, Tue, Jan 1, Jul 4, Thanksgiving, Dec 25. 🎟 ♿ ✏ 📷 **W** artbma.org

### 🏛 Walters Art Museum
600 N Charles St. **Tel** (410) 547-9000. **Open** 10am–5pm Wed–Sun. **Closed** Dec 24, 25, Jan 1, Jul 4, Thanksg. 🅿 Sat & Sun. ♿ 📷 **W** thewalters.org

## ⓴ Annapolis
🏞 35,800. 🛈 Annapolis & Anne Arundel County Visitors Bureau, 26 West St, (410) 280-0445. **Open** 9am–5pm daily. **W** visitannapolis.org

The capital of Maryland, Annapolis, is regarded as the jewel of Chesapeake Bay. It is defined by the nautical character that comes with the 17 miles (27 km) of shoreline and the longtime presence of the **United States Naval Academy**. A walk down Main Street leads past the 200-year-old Maryland Inn, shops, and wonderful seafood restaurants that serve local fish, to the City Dock lined with boats. It is then a short walk to the 150-year-old US Naval Academy. Inside the visitor center is the *Freedom 7* Space Capsule that carried the first American, Alan Shepard, into space. The US Naval Academy Museum in Preble Hall is also worth visiting, especially to see the gallery of detailed ship models.

The **Maryland State House**, completed in 1779, is the oldest state capitol in continuous use. Its Old Senate Chamber is where the Continental Congress (delegates from each of the American colonies) met when Annapolis was briefly the capital of the United States in 1783–84. It was also here that the Treaty of Paris was ratified in 1784, formally ending the Revolutionary War.

Annapolis teems with Colonial-era buildings, most of them still in use. The 1765 **William Paca House**, home of Governor Paca who signed the Declaration of Independence, is a fine Georgian house with an enchanting garden, both of which have been lovingly restored. Another restored mansion worth visiting is the magnificent red-brick **Hammond Harwood House**, which boasts exceptionally fine woodcarving. Built in 1774, this masterpiece of Georgian design, a short walk west of the State House on Maryland Avenue, was named after the Hammond and Harwood families. Worth exploring are Cornhill and Duke of Gloucester streets, examples of the city's historic residential streets. Many tours are offered in Annapolis, including bus, boat, and walking tours. It is particularly enjoyable for tourists to view the city from the water by sightseeing boat, schooner, or kayak.

Tiffany window in the Naval Academy, Annapolis

### 🏛 US Naval Academy
Corner of King George, E of Randall St. **Tel** (410) 293-8687. **Open** 9am–5pm daily (photo ID required). **Closed** Jan 1, Thanksgiving, Dec 25. ♿

### 🏛 Maryland State House
State Circle. **Tel** (410) 974-3400. **Open** 9am–5pm Mon–Fri, 10am–4pm Sat & Sun (call ahead; bring photo ID). **Closed** Dec 25. 🎟 11am & 3pm. ♿

### 🏛 William Paca House
186 Prince George St. **Tel** (410) 267-7619. **Open** Mar–Dec: 10am–5pm daily (noon–5pm Sun). **Closed** Thanksgiving, Dec 24, 25. 🅿 📷

## ㉑ North Bay

🚌 ℹ 121 N Union St, Ste. B,
Havre de Grace, (410) 939-2100.

At the northern end of
Chesapeake Bay, the lovely
town of Havre de Grace is
home to the Concord Point
Lighthouse. Popular with artists
and photographers, the lighthouse has been in continuous
operation since the mid-1800s.
The **Havre de Grace Decoy
Museum** exhibits a fine
collection of working decoys
and chronicles how the
craft evolved from a purely
practical wildfowl lure into a
highly sophisticated form of
American folk art.

Across the bay to the east,
the lush forests of **Elk Neck
State Park** cover the tip of a
peninsula crowned by Turkey
Point Lighthouse, one of the
bay's oldest. The park offers a
sandy beach for swimming,
boat rentals, miniature golf,
and hiking trails.

Northeast of the park across
the Elk River is Chesapeake
City, where rooftops appear
much as they did 100 years ago
when the village grew to
service the Chesapeake and
Delaware Canal. Today, the
village is a "boutique town," with
fine shops and restaurants.
The **C & D Canal Museum** is
housed in the canal's original
pumphouse. Working models
of canal locks, the original
steam power plant, and a giant
waterwheel are on display.

🏛 **Havre de Grace Decoy Museum**
215 Giles St. **Tel** (410) 939-3739.
**Open** 10:30am–4:30pm Mon–Sat,
noon–4pm Sun. **Closed** public hols. ♿
🌐 **decoymuseum.com**

🏞 **Elk Neck State Park**
End of Route 272. **Tel** (410) 287-5333.

🏛 **C & D Canal Museum**
End of 2nd St. **Tel** (410) 885-5622.
**Open** 8am–4pm Mon–Fri. **Closed** Hols.

## ㉒ St. Michaels

🗺 1,900. 🚌 ℹ (800) 808-7622.
🌐 **stmichaelsmd.org**

St. Michaels, founded in 1677,
was once a haven for ship
builders, privateers, and
blockade-runners. Today, the
town is a destination for pleasure
boaters and yachts flying
international colors. B&Bs, shops,
and good restaurants abound.

**Chesapeake Bay Maritime
Museum** is one of Maryland's top
cultural attractions. The museum
features interactive exhibits on
boat building, historic boats,
decoys, and various other aspects
of Chesapeake Bay life. Several
vessels unique to the area are
anchored on the property, and
the **Hooper Strait Lighthouse**,
a fully restored 1879 screwpile
wooden structure, is open
for exploration.

🏛 **Chesapeake Bay Maritime
Museum**
213 North Talbot St. **Tel** (410) 745-
2916. **Open** 10am–5pm (until 6pm in
summer, 4pm in winter). ♿ 🅿
🌐 **cbmm.org**

The bay in Blackwater National Wildlife
Refuge, Easton

## ㉓ Easton

🗺 11,700. 🚌 ℹ 11 S Harrison St.
(410) 770-8000. 🌐 **eastonmd.org**

A handsome little town,
Easton is an interesting
combination of unique shops
and historic homes. A restored
1820s schoolhouse serves as
the premises of the **Academy
of the Arts**. Although the
emphasis is on Eastern Shore
artists, the gallery's permanent
collection includes works by
famous artists such as James
Whistler and Grant Wood.

Once a farm used by
muskrat trappers for the fur
trade, **Blackwater National
Wildlife Refuge** was
established in 1933 to provide
sanctuary for migrating
waterfowl. Geese number
35,000 and ducks exceed
15,000 at the peak of the fall
migration. The best time to
observe migratory birds is from
October through March;

Hooper Strait Lighthouse at Chesapeake Bay silhouetted by a pink and violet sunset

*For hotels and restaurants see pp234–9*

however, many songbirds and other animals can be seen all year round.

### 🎭 Academy Museum of the Arts
106 South St. **Tel** (410) 822-2787. **Open** 10am–8pm Tue–Thu, 10am–4pm Mon, Fri, Sat. **Closed** Sun. 🎨 W **academyartmuseum.org**

### 🦅 Blackwater National Wildlife Refuge
ℹ️ 2145 Key Wallace Dr, Cambridge. **Tel** (410) 228-2677. **Open** 8am–4pm Mon–Fri, 9am–5pm Sat & Sun. **Closed** Thanksgiving, Dec 25. 🎨

## ㉔ Crisfield
🏙️ 2,900. 🚌 ℹ️ 906 W Main St, Crisfield, (800) 782-3913. W **cityofcrisfield-md.gov**

Although the main industry here is tourism, this commercial seafood port supports a sport-fishing industry. From mid-May through October, the fish are running. The **J. Millard Tawes Museum** is named after a resident who became Maryland's 54th governor. The museum has displays on local history and marine life. It also offers walking tours through a boatyard and a seafood processing plant as well as trolley tours through historic Crisfield to the Ward Brothers waterfowl carving workshop and the crab-processing shanties of Jenkins Creek.

**Captain John Smith (1580–1631)**

### 🏛️ J. Millard Tawes Museum
3 North 9th St, Somers Cove Marina. **Tel** (410) 968-2501. **Open** 9am–5pm Mon–Sat; winter: 10am–4pm Mon–Fri. **Closed** Sun, week of Christmas, week after Christmas. 🎨 🎫 📷 ♿

### Environs
Accessible only by boat, **Smith Island**, 10 miles (16 km) to the west, was chartered in 1608 by Captain John Smith, founder of the Jamestown settlement (*see p195*). Ewell, at the island's north end, is where most of the population lives. Some claim that the local speech is reminiscent of the Elizabethan/Cornwall dialect brought here in the 1770s.

Ferris wheel at Trimper's Rides, Ocean City

## ㉕ Salisbury
🏙️ 29,000. 🚌 ℹ️ 8480 Ocean Hwy, (800) 332-8687.

The largest city on the Eastern Shore, Salisbury is known for its fine antique shops. It developed as a mill community in 1732 and soon became the principal crossroads of the southern Delmarva Peninsula. Salisbury's **Ward Museum of Wildfowl Art** contains the world's premier collection of wildfowl art. Here, wood is carved and painted to resemble wild birds in natural settings. The museum looks at the history of the art, from antique working decoys to contemporary carvings. **Pemberton Historical Park** is the site of Pemberton Hall, built in 1741 for Isaac Handy, a British Army colonel. The grounds are threaded by self-guided nature trails, and the manor house contains a small museum maintained by the local historical society.

### 🏛️ Ward Museum of Wildfowl Art
909 S Schumaker Dr. **Tel** (410) 742-4988. **Open** 10am–5pm Mon–Sat, noon–5pm Sun. 🎨 ♿ W **wardmuseum.org**

A specialist duck decoy maker at work in Crisfield

## ㉖ Ocean City
🏙️ 7,100. ℹ️ 4001 Coastal Hwy, 1-800-OC-OCEAN. W **ococean.com**

Soft beige sand extends endlessly along the Ocean City peninsula, fronted by miles of hotels. In summer, brightly colored umbrellas provide shade, while at night, the beach boardwalk that stretches from the inlet north past 27th Street is lively with strolling couples, singles, and families.

At the inlet, on the southern border of Ocean City, the **Ocean City Life-Saving Museum**, housed in a decommissioned 1891 Life-saving Station, relates the history of Ocean City and the US Life-saving Service.

North on the Boardwalk, **Trimper's Rides** began operating in 1902 with a steam-powered 45-animal carousel. Today, Trimper's includes a 1905 Herschell-Spellman merry-go-round glittering with jewels and fantasy animals, Ferris wheels, bumper rides, mechanized fortune-tellers, and a host of other entertainments.

Ocean City also has many miniature golf courses: visitors can play beneath plaster polar bears, bask in the tropics, or putt around rubber sharks.

### 🏛️ Ocean City Life-Saving Station Museum
813 South Atlantic Ave. **Tel** (410) 289-4991. **Open** May & Oct: 10am–4pm daily; Jun–Sep: 10am–10pm daily; Nov–Apr: call for hours. 🎨 W **ocmuseum.org**

### 🎡 Trimper's Rides
Baltimore & S 1st St on the boardwalk. **Tel** (410) 289-8617. **Open** mid-May–mid-Sep: 1pm–midnight Mon–Fri, noon–midnight Sat & Sun; mid-Sep–mid-May: limited hours. 🎨

# Delaware

Although Delaware is the country's second-smallest state, larger only than tiny Rhode Island, its importance in industry, banking, and technology far exceeds its size. This is mainly due to the laissez-faire tax and corporation laws that have attracted several large companies, who now base their headquarters here. Along with a significant history, stately country homes, and some of the nation's best museums, Delaware's 2,000 square miles (500,000 ha) also boasts more than 20 miles (32 km) of sandy beaches along the Atlantic Ocean.

Detail from *Washington Crossing the Delaware*, Delaware Art Museum

## ㉗ Wilmington

71,500. 100 W 10th St, (800) 489-6664.
visitwilmingtonde.com

This former Swedish colony is home to one of the country's finest art museums, the **Delaware Art Museum**. Its outstanding collections contain works by American illustrators such as Howard Pyle, and his students N.C. Wyeth and Maxfield Parrish. There are also paintings and sculpture by other 19th- and 20th-century American artists such as Winslow Homer. The galleries feature paintings and decorative arts from the English pre-Raphaelite movement, led by Dante Gabriel Rossetti. The romantic works, second only to those of London's Victoria and Albert Museum in the UK, were bequeathed to the museum in 1935 by the wealthy Wilmington industrialist Samuel Bancroft Jr.

Ⅲ **Delaware Art Museum**
2301 Kentmere Parkway. **Tel** (302) 571-9590. **Open** 10am– 4pm Wed–Sat, noon–4pm Sun.
delart.org

## ㉘ Winterthur

SR 52. **Tel** (800) 448-3883.
**Open** 10am–5pm Tue–Sun.
**Closed** Thanksgiving, Dec 25.
winterthur.org

Originally the home of Evelina du Pont and James Biderman, Winterthur was named after the Biderman ancestral home in Switzerland. Henry Francis du Pont inherited the house in 1927. Du Pont was one of the many post-World War I collectors, whose nationalistic sentiments caused them to take a fresh look at American decorative objects. His collection of American furniture is one of the most important assemblages of early American decorative arts in the world.

Winterthur showcases the du Pont family's fascination with American decorative arts and horticulture. The surrounding 982-acre (397-ha) grounds are landscaped beautifully, with miles of surfaced paths and scenic woodland trails. The part of the museum open to the public consists of two buildings, 175 period rooms, and two floors of exhibition galleries.

## ㉙ Hagley Museum/ Eleutherian Mills

Rte 141. **Tel** (302) 658-2400.
**Open** 9:30am–4:30pm daily; Jan–mid-Mar: 1:30pm (for one tour only) Mon–Fri; 9:30am–4:30pm Sat & Sun.
**Closed** Thanksgiving, Dec 25.
hagley.org

Picturesquely located on the banks of the Brandywine River, Hagley Yard is the origin of the du Pont fortune in America. Its serene setting is visible in spring when the river banks are ablaze with purple and pink rhododendrons and azaleas.

Eleuthere du Pont acquired the property and established a black powder (explosives) factory here in 1884. Factory buildings, storehouses, drying tables, and the workers' village are open to the public. Facing the river are the Eagle Roll Mill's "mixing rooms," with their 5-ft (1.5-m) thick walls, where powder explosions – there have been 299 blowouts in 20 years – did the least damage. Hagley Museum, at the entryway to the property, explores the history of the sites with exhibits and dioramas.

The modest du Pont family home, **Eleutherian Mills**, dates from 1803. It overlooks the powder works at the far end of the property and contains many original furnishings. The garden is verdant with a variety of native plants, shrubs, and trees.

Boxcar exhibit at Hagley, on the banks of the Brandywine River

The elegant French-style Nemours Mansion, built by Alfred I. du Pont

## ⑩ Nemours Mansion and Gardens

850 Alapocas Dr. **Tel** (302) 651-6912.
🚌 **Open** May–Dec: Tue–Sat.
🕙 🎟 9am, 11am, 1pm, 3pm;
call to make reservations.
Ⓦ **nemoursmansion.org**

Built by Alfred I. du Pont in
1909–1910, this Louis XVI-style
château is named after the
north-central French town that
Pierre Samuel du Pont de
Nemours, his great-great-
grandfather, represented as a
member of the French Estates
General in 1789. The mansion's
102 rooms are opulently
decorated with Oriental rugs,
tapestries, and paintings dating
from the 15th century.
The 300-acre (12-ha) gardens
are landscaped in the classic
French style.

## ⑪ New Castle

🚹 4,800. 🚌 ℹ 220 Delaware St,
(302) 322-9801.
Ⓦ **newcastlecity.delaware.gov**

Delaware's former capital is
today a well-preserved historic
site, with restaurants, shops,
and residential areas. The **New
Castle Courthouse** displays
artifacts that illuminate the
town's multinational origins;
Sweden, Holland, and Britain all
have claimed New Castle as
their own. Several historic
homes lie a short stroll from
each other. One, the **Amstel
House**, was the home of
Governor Van Dyke. The town's
most elegant dwelling place in
1738, its most famous guest was
George Washington.

### 🏛 New Castle Courthouse
211 Delaware St. **Tel** (302) 323-4453.
**Open** 10am–3:30pm Tue–Sat, 1:30–
4:30pm Sun. **Closed** Mon, public hols.

## ⑫ Lewes

🚹 3,000. 🚌 ℹ 114 E Third Street,
(302) 645-7777. Ⓦ **lewes.com**

The site of Zwaanendael
("Valley of the Swans"),
Delaware's original Dutch
settlement in 1631, Lewes is a
quiet town with a small beach,
sophisticated restaurants,
residences, and shops. The
**Zwaanendael Museum**, built in
1931, is a striking replica of the
Town Hall of Hoorn, home of
most of the settlers. Its exhibits
elaborate on the first
encampment as well as the
area's other historical aspects.
In 1682, the British Crown
granted the colony of Delaware
to Englishman William Penn
(see p108) who established one
of the nation's first public lands
by setting aside Cape Henlopen
for the citizens of Lewes.
Besides a bay and ocean
beaches, **Cape Henlopen
State Park** contains Gordon's
Pond Wildlife Area and the
Great Dune, which rises 80 ft
(24 m) above sea level.
The park's varied habitats are
home to many birds, reptiles,
and mammals, including
threatened shorebirds.
Attractions include hiking trails,
interpretive displays, a pier,
camping, and swimming.

### 🏛 Zwaanendael Museum
Kings Hwy & Savannah Rd. **Tel** (302)
645-1148. **Open** 10am–4:30pm
Tue–Sat, 1:30–4:30pm Sun.
**Closed** Mon, some public hols.

### 🏕 Cape Henlopen State Park
42 Cape Henlopen Dr. **Tel** (302) 645-
8983. 🏕

## ㉝ Rehoboth Beach

🚹 1,200. 🚌 ℹ 229 Rehoboth Ave,
(302) 227-6181.
Ⓦ **cityofrehoboth.com**

Rehoboth beach was originally
a Methodist summer camp.
A commercial strip of
restaurants and shops stretches
along Rehoboth Avenue,
meeting sand beaches at
Funland on the boardwalk.
The Outlets, between Lewes
and Rehoboth Beach, feature
every major outlet store, taking
advantage of the fact that there
is no sales tax in Delaware.
Three miles (5 km) south of
the beach, the 2,700-acre
(1093-ha) **Delaware Seashore
State Park** covers the strip of
land between the Atlantic
Ocean and Rehoboth Bay.
**Millsboro**, west of Reheboth
Bay, is home to the Nanticoke
tribe. In mid-September, the
tribe holds a public pow-wow
to preserve their heritage and
explain their beliefs.
South of the park, the 89-ft
(27-m) Fenwick Island
Lighthouse marks the Delaware-
Maryland border. Built in 1852,
it was decommissioned during
World War II.

### 🏕 Delaware Seashore State Park
Inlet 850. **Tel** (302) 227-2800.
🏕 Mar 1–Nov 30.

A Nanticoke Indian at the annual pow-wow,
Rehoboth Beach

# Practical Information

Washington, DC and the Capital Region is very rich in museums, cultural events, and entertainment, as well as in scenic sites and outdoor activities around its seashores, rivers, and mountains. This region offers excellent amenities for the large numbers of tourists that it attracts. Spring and fall are the best times to visit, as the summers are hot and humid in much of the region, and the winters cold and damp. However, spring, summer, and fall see the largest number of visitors, so it is best to make reservations.

## Tourist Information

The Capital Region is well-equipped to cater to visitors' needs. Visitor information desks at airports and within cities will provide guides and maps, information on guided tours, events, and festivals. Major hotels also have guest services desks. The **Smithsonian Information** line and website are useful resources for finding out about special events in the museums. State tourism bureaus are other reliable sources of comprehensive information.

## Personal Security

In recent years, Washington has made great efforts to clean up its streets and bring down crime. If you stick to the tourist areas and avoid outlying neighborhoods, you should not run into any trouble. When visiting sights off the beaten track, stay alert and study your map properly before you set off.

If you plan to hike alone, always carry a cell phone, and inform someone in advance about your itinerary.

## Getting Around

Travel within DC and the Capital Region is easy. Washington has a comprehensive public transportation system, and all major attractions in the capital are accessible on foot, or by **Metrorail, Metrobus** Circulator bus, or taxi. If you decide to drive in DC, be prepared for traffic jams and unexpected route changes. Avoid driving at night if you are unfamiliar with the area.

Several DC-based tour companies offer tours that include Mount Vernon, Williamsburg, and Monticello in Virginia. Baltimore and Annapolis, Maryland's major cities, are connected to DC by rail and bus. Car rental is widely available, but often expensive.

Both **Amtrak** trains and **Greyhound** buses are cheaper alternatives, but your choice of destination may be more limited. To explore many of the scenic parts of the Capital Region, it is best to travel by car. Visitors should avoid shortcuts and stay on well-traveled roads.

## Etiquette

Smoking is prohibited in all public buildings, restaurants, bars, and stores in the region. Cigarettes can only be purchased by those over 18 years old; proof of age may be required. The legal age for drinking alcohol in Washington is 21, and you may need a photo identification (ID) as proof of your age in order to purchase alcohol and be allowed into bars. It is illegal to drink alcohol in public parks or to carry an open container of alcohol in your car while driving. Penalties for driving under the influence of alcohol are quite severe, and may even include a jail sentence.

## Outdoor Activities

Maryland's Chesapeake Bay and Eastern Shore offer wonderful opportunities for boating, sailing, and fishing. For outdoor enthusiasts, other highlights of the Capital Region include hiking the **Appalachian Trail** in Virginia and West Virginia, white-water rafting in West Virginia, and cycling along the picturesque Chesapeake and Ohio Canal Towpath, which runs all the way from Washington to Maryland. There is also a 16-mile (26-km) biking trail from Washington to Mount Vernon. Delaware's Rehoboth Beach and Seashore State Park are a magnet for those in search of sea and sand.

Among spectator sports, the **Washington Redskins** (football), **Washington Nationals** (baseball) and the **Baltimore Orioles** (baseball) are hot tickets. If tickets have sold out, it is fun to watch the game along with other enthusiasts at a sports bar.

---

### The Climate of DC & the Capital Region

The Capital Region's climate varies greatly. In winter, temperatures can plummet below freezing. During this time, Virginia's Appalachian Mountains are covered with snow, attracting skiers and snowboarders. Summers can be very hot and humid, with almost continuous sunshine. Summer is also the season for the heaviest rainfall, especially between May and August, when the rain comes as a welcome break from the humidity. The rains taper off in September and October, when the weather is pleasantly mild. The region is at its best in spring and fall.

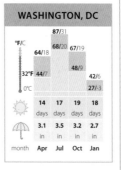

| WASHINGTON, DC | | | |
|---|---|---|---|
| | 87/31 | | |
| °F/C | 68/20 | 67/19 | |
| 64/18 | | | |
| | | 48/9 | |
| 32°F 44/7 | | | 42/6 |
| 0°C | | | 27/-3 |
| 14 days | 17 days | 19 days | 18 days |
| 3.1 in | 3.5 in | 3.2 in | 2.7 in |
| month Apr | Jul | Oct | Jan |

## Entertainment

Visitors to this region will never be at a loss for entertainment or cultural events. There are more free activities in DC than in any other American city. The weekend section of Friday's edition of the *Washington Post* provides listings of free concerts, gallery talks, films, book signings, poetry readings, plays, and concerts.

The **Kennedy Center** in Washington is home to the **Washington Opera Company** and the **National Symphony Orchestra**, two of the capital's crown jewels. It offers a magnificent dance and ballet season as well, featuring the world's finest companies, including the Bolshoi, the American Ballet Theater, and the Dance Theater of Harlem. The center also hosts touring theater companies and many top jazz performers. Other good jazz and blues venues are **Blues Alley** in Georgetown, the **Merriweather Post Pavilion** in Columbia, Maryland, and the **Nissan Pavilion** in Manassas, Virginia.

Film classics and film premieres are shown at the American Film Institute in Silver Spring, MD, and documentaries at the Library of Congress. Many of the capital's museums have regular series of film shows, lectures, and concerts.

Washington holds many seasonal cultural events. In June, there are nightly performances by the **Shakespeare Theatre Free for All** at Harmon Hall. Independence Day celebrations are spectacular along the Mall, with fireworks from the base of the Washington Memorial. Labor Day Weekend in September is marked by a free concert by the National Symphony Orchestra on the lawns of Capitol Hill. Tours of the White House are limited at present. Check at the White House Visitor Center or on its website *(see p211)* for the latest information.

## Shopping

Washington, DC as well as Maryland and Virginia are famous for their antique stores. Frederick, Maryland, has the **Emporium at Creekside Antiques**, which houses over 100 antique shops. A great place to shop are the museum shops in DC, which stock an incredibly wide range of products, from African textiles and artwork reproductions to contemporary American crafts. Popular department stores are **Macy's** in DC and Nordstrom in Arlington, Virginia. There are large malls in the Virginia and Maryland suburbs, and at Fashion Center in Pentagon City. Discount hunters should head for the 230 outlets at Potomac Mills, situated 30 miles (48 km) south of DC on I-95, or to Rehoboth Beach in Delaware, with its huge concentration of outlet stores.

Many shops in the Washington, DC area are closed on major holidays.

# DIRECTORY

## Tourist Information

**Delaware**
99 King's Hwy, Dover, DE 19901. **Tel** (866) 284-7483.
W **visitdelaware.com**

**Maryland**
401 E Pratt St, Baltimore, MD 21202.
**Tel** (866) 639-3526.
W **visitmaryland.org**

**Smithsonian Information**
1000 Jefferson Dr, SW Washington, DC.
**Tel** (202) 633-1000.
W **si.edu**

**Virginia**
901 E Byrd St, Richmond, VA 23219.
**Tel** 800-VISITVA.
W **virginia.org**

**Washington, DC**
901 Seventh St NW, Suite 400, Washington, DC 20001. **Tel** (202) 789-7000.
W **washington.org**

**West Virginia**
**Tel** (800)-225-5982.
W **wvtourism.com**

## Travel

**Amtrak**
**Tel** 800-USA-RAIL.
W **amtrak.com**

**Greyhound**
**Tel** (800) 231-2222.
W **greyhound.com**

**Metrorail & Metrobus**
600 Fifth St, NW, Washington, DC 20001.
**Tel** (202) 637-7000, (202) 638-3780 (TTY for hearing-impaired callers).
W **wmata.com**

## Sports & Outdoor Activities

**Baltimore Orioles**
Oriole Park at Camden Yards, 333 W Camden St, Baltimore, MD 21201.
**Tel** (888) 848-2473.
W **baltimore-orioles. mlb.com**

**Washington Nationals**
Nationals Stadium, 1500 S Capitol St, SE.
**Tel** (202) 675-6287.
W **nationals.com**

**Washington Redskins**
FedExField 1600, FedEx Way, Landover, MD 20785.
**Tel** (301) 276-6050 (ticket office), (301) 276-6000.
W **redskins.com**

## Entertainment

**Blues Alley**
1073 Wisconsin Ave, NW.
**Tel** (202) 337-4141.
W **bluesalley.com**

**Kennedy Center**
New Hampshire Ave & Rock Creek Pkwy, NW.
**Tel** (202) 467-4600.
W **kennedy-center.org**

**Merriweather Post Pavilion**
Columbia, MD.
**Tel** (410) 715-5550.
W **merriweather music.com**

**National Symphony Orchestra**
**Tel** (202) 467-4600.
W **kennedy-center.org**

**Jiffy Lube Pavilion**
7800 Cellar Door Dr, Haymarket, VA.
**Tel** (703 )754-6400.
W **livenation.com**

**Shakespeare Theatre Free for All**
Harmon Hall, 610 F St NW.
**Tel** (202) 334-4790.
W **shakespeare theatre.org**

## Shopping

**Emporium at Creekside Antiques**
112 E Patrick St, Frederick, MD. **Tel** (301) 662-7099.
W **emporiumantiques. com**

**Macy's Department Store**
12th & G St, NW.
**Tel** (202) 628-6661.
W **macys.com**

# Where to Stay

## Washington, DC

**ADAMS MORGAN: Adam's Inn** $
B&B
*1746 Lanier Place NW, 20009*
**Tel** *(202) 745-3600*
**w** adamsinn.com
A good choice for budget travelers, and located close to the zoo; some rooms here have shared baths.

**CAPITOL HILL: Courtyard
Washington Capitol Hill/
Navy Yard** $$
Family-friendly
*140 L St SE, 20002*
**Tel** *(202) 479-0027*
**w** marriott.com
A vibrant hotel offering well-appointed, comfortable rooms. Ask about their special promotions.

**CAPITOL HILL: Phoenix
Park Hotel** $$
Boutique **Map** 4E
*520 North Capitol St NW, 20001*
**Tel** *(800) 824-5419*
**w** phoenixparkhotel.com
This historic property, refurbished with an Irish theme, features the popular Dubliner restaurant.

### DK Choice

**CAPITOL HILL:
Hotel George** $$$
Boutique **Map** 4E
*15 E St NW, 20001*
**Tel** *(202) 347-4200*
**w** hotelgeorge.com
This chic Kimpton property has a hip political theme, state-of-the-art rooms, an exemplary spa, the excellent Bistro Bis restaurant, and one of the city's best bars. It is both eco-friendly and pet-friendly. There is a complimentary wine hour daily.

**DUPONT CIRCLE: The Swann
House** $$
B&B
*1808 New Hampshire Ave NW, 20009*
**Tel** *(202) 265-4414*
**w** swannhouse.com
A stunning historic mansion where amenities include Wi-Fi, a pool, and Jacuzzis in some rooms.

**DUPONT CIRCLE: Mansion
on O Street** $$$
Luxury **Map** 3B
*2020 O St NW, 20036*
**Tel** *(202) 496-2020*
**w** omansion.com
This 19th-century mansion has a quirky decor and many hidden rooms and passages for exploring.

**EMBASSY ROW: The Fairfax at
Embassy Row** $$$
Luxury
*2100 Massachusetts Ave NW, 20008*
**Tel** *(202) 293-2100*
**w** fairfaxhoteldc.com
A favorite of Washington's political elite, this Georgian-style hotel has glorious rooms with a historic feel.

**GEORGETOWN: Holiday Inn
Washington-Georgetown** $$
Family-friendly
*2101 Wisconsin Ave NW, 20007*
**Tel** *(202) 338-4600*
**w** holidayinn.com
A standard hotel with a fitness center and a pool in a great spot. Shuttle service to the Metro.

**GEORGETOWN:
Four Seasons** $$$
Business **Map** 3A
*2800 Pennsylvania Ave NW, 20007*
**Tel** *(202) 342-0444*
**w** fourseasons.com
This highly rated hotel on the edge of Georgetown offers large rooms, a great bar, and top service.

**LOGANS CIRCLE: Helix Hotel** $$
Boutique
*1430 Rhode Island Ave NW, 20005*
**Tel** *(202) 462-9001*
**w** hotelhelix.com
A colorful, chic hotel in a trendy neighborhood, with excellent service and a daily wine hour.

**THE MALL: Holiday Inn
Washington-Capitol** $$
Family-friendly **Map** 5D
*550 C St SW, 20024*
**Tel** *(877) 859-5095*
**w** holidayinn.com
This refurbished standard hotel offers the basics in a good location for the sites.

### Price Guide

Prices are based on one night's stay in high season for a standard double room, inclusive of service charges and taxes.

| | |
|---|---|
| $ | up to $150 |
| $$ | $150 to 300 |
| $$$ | over $300 |

**THE MALL: Mandarin
Oriental** $$$
Business **Map** 5D
*1330 Maryland Ave SW, 20024*
**Tel** *(202) 554-8588*
**w** mandarinoriental.com
Luxurious, elegant hotel with top amenities and one of the best restaurants in the city.

**PENN QUARTER: Hosteling
International** $
Hostel **Map** 3D
*1009 11th St NW, 20001*
**Tel** *(202) 737-2333*
**w** hiwashingtondc.org
Over 200 dorm-style rooms with shared baths, located close to the Smithsonian museums.

**PENN QUARTER:
Hotel Monaco** $$$
Boutique **Map** 4D
*700 F St NW, 20004*
**Tel** *(202) 628-7277*
**w** monaco-dc.com
A National Historic Landmark retro-fitted into a modern, colorful hotel with a chic bar and a popular restaurant.

**PENN QUARTER: The Willard** $$$
Luxury **Map** 4C
*1401 Pennsylvania Ave NW, 20004*
**Tel** *(202) 628-9100*
**w** washington.intercontinental.com
This stately, historic hotel has hosted countless presidents, as well as Martin Luther King Jr. and Charles Dickens.

Lobby of Sleep Inn & Suites, Ocean City, Maryland

**THE WHITE HOUSE AND FOGGY BOTTOM: The Hay-Adams** $$$
Luxury        Map 3C
*800 16th St NW, 20006*
**Tel** *(202) 638-6600*
🆆 hayadams.com
This historic, well-appointed property offers peaceful, elegant rooms close to the White House.

**THE WHITE HOUSE AND FOGGY BOTTOM: The Mayflower Renaissance Washington, DC Hotel** $$$
Business
*1127 Connecticut Ave NW, 20036*
**Tel** *(202) 347-3000*
🆆 marriotthotels.com
A grand hotel with historic charm and a stunning lobby. The formal afternoon tea is recommended.

# Maryland

**ANNAPOLIS: Maryland Inn** $$
Historic
*16 Church Circle, 21401*
**Tel** *(410) 263-2641*
🆆 historicinnsofannapolis.com
This lovely inn built in the 1760s offers comfortable, Victorian-style rooms and an inviting restaurant.

**ANNAPOLIS: Annapolis Marriott Waterfront** $$$
Luxury
*80 Compromise St, 21401*
**Tel** *(410) 268-7555*
🆆 annapolismarriott.com
A waterfront hotel with stunning views of Chesapeake Bay and the harbor. Spacious guest rooms.

**BALTIMORE: Wyndham Peabody Court** $
Value
*612 Cathedral St, 21201*
**Tel** *(410) 727-7101*
🆆 peabodycourthotel.com
This boutique-style property with a Renaissance façade is close to the Walters Art Gallery.

**BALTIMORE: Homewood Suites by Hilton** $$
Business
*625 S President St, 21202*
**Tel** *(410) 234-0999*
🆆 homewoodsuites3.hilton.com
All-suite options with kitchenettes and a daily breakfast buffet.

**BALTIMORE: Inn at the Black Olive** $$
B&B
*803 S Caroline St, 21231*
**Tel** *(443) 681-6316*
🆆 theblackolive.com
This eco-friendly inn with an organic restaurant offers all-suite rooms with spa bathrooms.

Room at the eco-friendly Inn at the Black Olive, Baltimore, Maryland

## DK Choice

**BALTIMORE: Four Seasons** $$$
Luxury
*200 International Dr, 21202*
**Tel** *(410) 576-5800*
🆆 fourseasons.com
A stunning waterfront urban retreat, Four Seasons is housed in a soaring glass tower and offers world-class service and spectacular views of the historic Inner Harbor. Amenities include a state-of-the-art fitness center, heated infinity-edge pool, and luxury spa treatments, as well as multiple dining options on site.

**OCEAN CITY: Sleep Inn & Suites** $
Value
*11 N Baltimore Ave, 21842*
**Tel** *(443) 664-4020*
🆆 sleepinn.com
Pleasant hotel close to the beach and the lively boardwalk with shopping, dining, and entertainment options nearby.

**OCEAN CITY: Princess Royale Oceanfront Hotel** $$
Luxury
*9100 Coastal Hwy, 21842*
**Tel** *(410) 524-7777*
🆆 princessroyale.com
Condos and family-friendly suites with fully equipped kitchenettes are situated on sandy beaches. There is an indoor heated pool.

# Virginia

**ALEXANDRIA: Hotel Monaco** $$
Business
*480 King St, 22314*
**Tel** *(703) 549-6080*
🆆 monaco-alexandria.com
Located in the historic Old Town, Hotel Monaco offers stylish rooms and suites. Free airport shuttle.

**CHARLOTTESVILLE: Omni Hotel** $$
Luxury
*212 Ridge McIntire Rd, 22903*
**Tel** *(434) 971-5500*
🆆 omnihotels.com
This luxurious hotel features a stunning seven-story glassed-in atrium and a beautiful lobby lush with greenery.

**CHINCOTEAGUE: Refuge Inn** $$
B&B
*7058 Maddox Blvd, 23336*
**Tel** *(757) 336-5511*
🆆 refugeinn.com
Family-friendly inn near the National Wildlife Refuge. Complimentary breakfasts.

**FREDERICKSBURG: Dunning Mills Inn All-Suite Hotel** $
Value
*2305-C Jefferson Davis Hwy, 22401*
**Tel** *(540) 373-1256*
🆆 dunningmills.com
Set in the woods near major Civil War battlefields and cemeteries, each suite here includes a kitchen and a dining area.

**NORFOLK: Courtyard Norfolk Downtown** $
Business
*520 Plume St, 23510*
**Tel** *(757) 963-6000*
🆆 marriott.com
This hotel is close to downtown attractions, as well as many entertainment, dining, and shopping options. It has an indoor pool and a whirlpool.

**RICHMOND: The Berkeley Hotel** $$
Business
*1200 E Cary St, 23219*
**Tel** *(804) 780-1300*
🆆 berkeleyhotel.com
A charming downtown hotel with lavish, traditional furnishings. Ask for a room with a balcony.

**For more information on types of hotels** *see pages 26–7*

**RICHMOND: Maury Place at Monument** $$
B&B
*3101 West Franklin St, 23221*
**Tel** *(804) 353-2717*
🅦 mauryplace.com
A cozy, elegantly decorated inn housed in a historic building. Complimentary gourmet breakfasts, wine, beverages, and snacks.

## DK Choice

**RICHMOND:
Jefferson Hotel** $$$
Historic
*101 West Franklin St, 23219*
**Tel** *(800) 424-8014*
🅦 jeffersonhotel.com
Located in the heart of downtown, this historic, upscale hotel has been an area staple since 1895. Jefferson has an elegant decor that features Southern antiques as well as a stained-glass domed skylight. Friendly staff cater to every whim. Complimentary transport service provided.

**VIRGINIA BEACH: Residence Inn Virginia Beach Oceanfront** $$
Value
*3217 Atlantic Ave, 23451*
**Tel** *(757) 425-1141*
🅦 marriott.com
This comfortable hotel offers stunning views, spacious suites with kitchens, and beach access.

**WILLIAMSBURG: Holiday Inn Hotel & Suites Williamsburg-Historic Gateway** $
Value
*515 Bypass Rd, 23185*
**Tel** *(757) 229-9990*
🅦 ihg.com
Kids eat for free in the welcoming bistro at this family-friendly hotel.

**WILLIAMSBURG:
Williamsburg Inn** $$$
Luxury
*136 E Francis St, 23185*
**Tel** *(877) 741-6852*
🅦 colonialwilliamsburg.com
A country estate-style inn with opulent decor, Regency-style furnishings, and marble bathrooms.

## West Virginia

**CHARLESTON: Marriott Charleston Town Center** $
Business
*200 Lee St E, 25301*
**Tel** *(304) 345-6500*
🅦 marriott.com
Convenient hotel near acclaimed white-water rafting destinations.

Palm court lounge in the opulent Jefferson Hotel, Richmond, Virginia

**HARPERS FERRY: The Jackson Rose Bed & Breakfast** $$
B&B
*1167 W Washington St, 25425*
**Tel** *(304) 535-1528*
🅦 thejacksonrose.com
Comfortable rooms feature original pine floors and high ceilings at this cozy B&B in a peaceful Federal-style mansion.

**MORGANTOWN: Waterfront Place Hotel** $
Business
*2 Waterfront Pl, 26501*
**Tel** *(304) 296-1700*
🅦 waterfrontplacehotel.com
This large waterfront hotel is popular with visitors to the university. It offers modern amenities including HD TVs.

**WHEELING: Oglebay Family Resort** $$
Value
*465 Lodge Dr, Oglebay Park, 26003*
**Tel** *(304) 243-4000*
🅦 oglebay-resort.com
A historic resort catering mostly to families, with golf, tennis, swimming, and kids' activities.

## DK Choice

**WHITE SULPHUR SPRINGS:
The Greenbrier** $$
Luxury
*300 W Main St, 24986*
**Tel** *(855) 453-4858*
🅦 greenbrier.com
A National Historic Landmark dating back to 1778, this world-famous resort is spread across 10,000 acres (4,047 ha) in the beautiful Allegheny Mountains. It offers many lodging options, from single rooms to four-bedroom estate houses, all with exquisite interior design. Golf, fine dining, and a mineral spa complete the experience.

## Delaware

**DOVER: Dover Downs Hotel & Casino** $
Value
*1131 N DuPont Hwy, 19901*
**Tel** *(302) 711-5882*
🅦 doverdowns.com
This sprawling casino complex offers full-service accommodations with access to top-notch entertainment and a luxurious spa.

**NEW CASTLE: Sheraton Wilmington South** $$
Business
*365 Airport Dr, 19720*
**Tel** *(302) 328-6200*
🅦 sheraton.com
An all-suite option offering rooms with separate living- and bedrooms, and all modern amenities.

**REHOBOTH BEACH: Boardwalk Plaza Hotel** $$
Luxury
*2 Olive St, 19971*
**Tel** *(302) 227-7169*
🅦 boardwalkplaza.com
Deluxe suites have whirlpools at this Victorian-style hotel with ocean views. Heated spa pool.

## DK Choice

**WILMINGTON:
Hotel Du Pont** $$
Luxury
*11th St and Market, 19801*
**Tel** *(302) 594-3100*
🅦 dupont.com/hotel
Hotel Du Pont has provided elegant accommodations to the likes of John F. Kennedy and Katharine Hepburn since 1913. The luxurious rooms feature imported linens and mahogany furnishings. The in-house restaurant, Green Room, serves exquisite French cuisine.

# Where to Eat and Drink

## Washington, DC

**CAPITOL HILL: Dubliner** $$
Irish       **Map** 4E
*4 F St NW, 20001*
**Tel** *(202) 737-3773*
A favorite of DC's Irish community for its pub food, such as fish and chips, Irish stew, and sandwiches.

**CAPITOL HILL: Tunnicliffs** $$
American
*222 7th St SE, 20003*
**Tel** *(202) 544-5680*
A local favorite since the 1980s, serving hearty pub fare, including burgers, quesadillas, and pizzas.

**GEORGETOWN: Das Ethiopian Cuisine** $$
Ethiopian
*1201 28th St NW, 20007*
**Tel** *(202)-333-4710*
Das has garnered good reviews for its delicious Ethiopian food and friendly service. It offers samplers for the uninitiated.

**GEORGETOWN: Pizzeria Paradiso** $$
Italian
*3282 M St NW, 20007*
**Tel** *(202) 337-1245*
This crowded pizzeria is known for thin-crust pizzas with a range of toppings. Large beer menu.

**GEORGETOWN: 1789** $$$
American
*1226 36th St NW, 20007*
**Tel** *(202) 965-1789*
Traditional cuisine and impeccable service define this upscale restaurant with an extensive wine list and delectable desserts.

### DK Choice

**THE MALL: Mitsitam Café** $$
Native American    **Map** 5F
*4th & Independence SW, 20565*
**Tel** *(866) 868-7774*
Probably the most unusual, and one of the best restaurants in DC. Located in the National Museum of the American Indian, this café serves Native American cuisine from many tribes. The menu changes seasonally, but always includes bison and salmon.

**THE MALL: CityZen** $$$
American      **Map** 5D
*1330 Maryland Ave SW, 20024*
**Tel** *(202) 787-6006* **Closed** *Sun & Mon*
An elegant place with a six-course tasting menu including fish and lamb, as well as vegetarian dishes.

**PENN QUARTER: Full Kee** $
Chinese      **Map** 3D
*509 H St NW, 20001*
**Tel** *(202) 371-2233*
One of the few Chinese eateries in Penn Quarter, Full Kee serves authentic Hong Kong-style food.

**PENN QUARTER: Jaleo** $$
Spanish      **Map** 4D
*480 7th St NW, 20004*
**Tel** *(202) 628-7949*
Tapas, paella, and sangrias make Jaleo a great place to enjoy a meal with friends.

**PENN QUARTER: Zaytinya** $$
Mediterranean      **Map** 3D
*701 9th St NW, 20001*
**Tel** *(202) 638-0800*
Run by chef José Andrés, this restaurant offers Turkish, Greek, and Lebanese cuisine.

**PENN QUARTER: Acadiana** $$$
Southern      **Map** 3D
*901 New York Ave NW, 20004*
**Tel** *(202) 408-8848*
A classy take on New Orleans food, with amazing gumbo, turtle soup, and oysters. Superb brunch.

**PENN QUARTER: Old Ebbitt Grill** $$$
American      **Map** 4C
*675 15th St NW, 20005*
**Tel** *(202) 347-4800*
DC's oldest saloon has been open since 1856. It is famous for its classic American fare and excellent seafood. Try the crab cakes.

**THE WHITE HOUSE AND FOGGY BOTTOM: Blue Duck Tavern** $$$
American      **Map** 3B
*1201 24th St NW, 20037*
**Tel** *(202) 419-6755*
Consistently rated one of the best restaurants in the city, the focus here is on food cooked in wood-burning ovens. Duck is a specialty.

**Price Guide**
Prices are based on a three-course meal per person, with a half-bottle of house wine, including tax and service.

| $ | up to $35 |
|---|---|
| $$ | $35 to 70 |
| $$$ | over $70 |

**THE WHITE HOUSE AND FOGGY BOTTOM: Founding Farmers** $$$
American      **Map** 3B
*1924 Pennsylvania Ave NW, 20006*
**Tel** *(202) 822-8783*
Everything at this restaurant is organic and made from scratch. The menu includes Yankee pot roast, shrimp and grits, and chicken pot pie. Vegetarians are also well catered to.

**FARTHER AFIELD: Ben's Chili Bowl** $
American
*1213 U St NW, 20009*
**Tel** *(202) 667-0909*
Everyone loves to eat at Ben's, including Bill Cosby and Barack Obama. It is highly acclaimed for its chili dog, gourmet burgers, subs, and the half-smoke.

**FARTHER AFIELD: Cactus Cantina** $
Mexican
*3300 Wisconsin Ave NW, 20016*
**Tel** *(202) 686-7222*
This cantina serves huge plates of Tex-Mex food. The large dining room is great for families and the patio is popular on sunny days.

**FARTHER AFIELD: 2Amys** $$
Italian
*3715 Macomb St NW, 20016*
**Tel** *(202) 885-5700*
Stop here for genuine Italian pizza or unmatched small plates, including devilled eggs, *burrata* (Italian cheese), eggplant confit, and olives.

The colorful, hispanic-themed interior of Jaleo, Washington, DC

**For more information on types of restaurants** *see pages 28–9*

# Maryland

### ANNAPOLIS: Dock Street Bar & Grill   $$
American
*136 Dock S, 21401*
**Tel** *(410) 268-7278*
Popular dining and nightlife spot, with water views and entertainment including DJs and local bands. Try the Maryland crab cakes.

## DK Choice

### ANNAPOLIS: Middleton Tavern Oyster Bar & Restaurant   $$$
Seafood
*2 Market Space, 21401*
**Tel** *(410) 263-3323*
This historic tavern, dating back to 1750, is situated across the street from the harbor. George Washington, Thomas Jefferson, and Benjamin Franklin were once guests. House specialties include fresh local oysters on the half shell, lump crab cakes, and filling pasta dishes.

### BALTIMORE: Isabella's Brick Oven Pizza & Panini   $
Pizzeria
*221 S High St, 21202*
**Tel** *(410) 962-8888*
Foodies flock to this family-run eatery in Little Italy for brick-oven pizzas, sandwiches made with fresh bread, and creative salads.

### BALTIMORE: Slainte Irish Pub and Restaurant   $
Irish/American
*1700 Thames St, 21231*
**Tel** *(410) 563-6600*
Authentic Irish pub popular with sports fans and young crowds for its draft beers, curry chips, and farmhouse burgers.

### BALTIMORE: LP Steamers   $$
Seafood
*1100 E Fort Ave, 21230*
**Tel** *(410) 576-9294*
This crab house provides an authentic Maryland experience in casual environs. Friendly waitresses and wooden mallets are on hand to help with the crab-picking process.

### BALTIMORE: Mama's On the Half Shell   $$
Seafood/American
*2901 O'Donnell St, 21224*
**Tel** *(410) 276-3160*
Cozy eatery with a menu focusing on seafood, particularly traditional Chesapeake recipes. Oyster stew and crab cakes are signatures.

Middleton Tavern Oyster Bar & Restaurant, Annapolis, Maryland

### BETHESDA: Mon Ami Gabi   $$
French
*7239 Woodmont Ave, 20814*
**Tel** *(301) 654-1234*
Authentic *steak-frites, bouillabaisse, crêpes,* and quiches are exquisitely flavorful at this popular restaurant with a casual yet romantic ambience. There is often live jazz music.

### BETHESDA: Jaleo   $$$
Spanish
*7271 Woodmont Ave, 20814*
**Tel** *(301) 913-0003*
The Bethesda outpost of José Andrés' popular tapas bar offers an impressive array of dishes. Enjoy them with sangria and be sure to leave room for the flan.

### HAGERSTOWN: Schmankerl Stube Bavarian Restaurant   $$
German
*58 S Potomac St, 21740*
**Tel** *(301) 797-3354*   **Closed** *Mon*
In a cozy atmosphere, waitstaff dressed in Bavarian garments serve imported beers and large portions of authentic German food, such as roasts, dumplings, and home-made desserts.

### OCEAN CITY: The Shark on the Harbor   $$
Seafood
*12924 Sunset Ave, 21842*
**Tel** *(410) 213-0924*
Seafood from the docks and fresh organic produce feature in dishes with local and Southern influences at this restaurant on the commercial fishing harbor.

# Virginia

### ALEXANDRIA: Gadsby's Tavern   $$
American
*138 N Royal St, 22314*
**Tel** *(703) 548-1288*
Historic tavern dating back to 1770, once frequented by former

presidents Washington and Jefferson. An on-site museum details the impressive history. Waiters in costume serve old-time fare such as prime ribs and pies.

### ALEXANDRIA: Le Refuge   $$
French
*127 N Washington St, 22314*
**Tel** *(703) 548-4661*   **Closed** *Sun*
Charming eatery across the street from the historic Christ Church serving "Country French" cuisine. *Bouillabaisse* and soft-shelled crabs are house specialties.

### CHARLOTTESVILLE: Citizen Burger Bar   $$
Hamburgers/American
*212 E Main St, 22902*
**Tel** *(434) 979-9944*
This welcoming eatery in an exposed-brick interior is popular for its gourmet burgers made with fresh meat from grass-fed cows and free-range chickens. The lengthy bar menu includes local craft beers and inventive cocktails. Friendly service.

### CHARLOTTESVILLE: Michie Tavern   $
American
*683 Thomas Jefferson Pkwy, 22902*
**Tel** *(434) 977-1234*
At this casual, buffet-style lunch spot with a Colonial touch, staff wear period clothing while the kitchen churns out hearty Southern food based on 18th-century recipes.

### RICHMOND: HogsHead Café   $
Barbecue
*9503 West Broad St, 23220*
**Tel** *(804) 308-0281*   **Closed** *Sun*
This small family-run café lures meat-lovers with its authentic smoky barbecue. The casual atmosphere bustles with friendly servers who dish out house favorites like hand-pulled pork sandwiches, tender ribs, and bacon-wrapped hot dogs.

**For key to prices** *see page 237*

**RICHMOND: Stella's** $$
Greek/Mediterranean
*1012 Lafayette St, 23221*
**Tel** *(804) 358-2011*
Inviting restaurant serving delicious food made from the freshest ingredients. The helpful waitstaff explain the menu's various dishes, most of which are for sharing.

**RICHMOND: Tarrant's Café** $$
American
*1 W Broad St, 23220*
**Tel** *(804) 225-0035*
Modeled after a 19th-century pharmacy, this affordable neighborhood eatery serves up fried oysters, baby back ribs, and shrimp and grits.

**VIRGINIA BEACH:**
**Route 58 Delicatessen** $
Delicatessen
*4000 Virginia Beach Blvd, 23462*
**Tel** *(757) 227-5868*
An authentic deli serving over-stuffed pastrami and corned beef sandwiches. Many items, such as smoked fish and *knishes*, are imported from New York.

## DK Choice

**WILLIAMSBURG: Christiana**
**Campbell's Tavern** $$
American
*Waller St, 23187*
**Tel** *(757) 229-2141*
This historic tavern, now run by Colonial Williamsburg, was once one of George Washington's favorites. Today, visitors can enjoy old-time seafood specialties such as sherried crab stew, shrimp and scallop brochette, and crab cakes, all served with spoon-bread or sweet potato muffins and to the sound of sea shanties.

**WILLIAMSBURG: The Trellis** $$
New American
*403 Duke of Gloucester St, 23187*
**Tel** *(757) 229-8610*
The Trellis's menu offers seasonal dishes such as home-made pâtés and terrines, as well as sweet red pepper soup with lump crab meat. The wine list features numerous labels from Virginia.

# West Virginia

**CHARLESTON:**
**The Chop House** $$$
Steak House
*1003 Charleston Town Ctr, 25389*
**Tel** *(888) 456-3463*
Popular with businesspeople and couples, the Chop House is

known for its hearty, gourmet cuts of USDA prime beef, premium seafood, and tasty side orders. Attentive service, fine cigars, and a lengthy wine list round out the experience.

## DK Choice

**HARPERS FERRY:**
**Canal House** $$
New American
*1226 W Washington St, 25425*
**Tel** *(304) 535-2880* **Closed** *Mon–Wed*
At the Canal House award-winning cuisine is served in a charming 1820s stone house that has, in the past, served as a hospital, military barracks, stained-glass studio, and a Montessori school. The kitchen utilizes local ingredients in creative dishes such as sweet potato-pumpkin soup and Asian vegetables with cellophane noodles.

**HUNTINGTON: Jim's Steak**
**and Spaghetti House** $$
American
*920 5th Ave, 25701*
**Tel** *(304) 696-9788* **Closed** *Sun*
Old-school and family-friendly, Jim's has traditionally served as a downtown meeting place for locals. Menu staples such as spaghetti, fish sandwiches, and home-made pies haven't changed much over the years.

**WHEELING: Later Alligator** $$
International
*2145 Market St, 26003*
**Tel** *(304) 233-1606* **Closed** *Sun*
This colorful café housed in an old saloon is frequented by regulars in the morning for its gourmet coffee. Popular items on the menu include freshly made *crêpes*, creative sandwiches, and home-made soups.

# Delaware

**DOVER: Doc Magrogan's**
**Oyster House** $$
Seafood
*1131 N Dupont Hwy, 19901*
**Tel** *(302) 857-3223*
Doc Magrogan's lures visitors from nearby casinos with its exceptionally fresh seafood and a wide variety of hand-crafted beers. Popular raw bar offerings include clams, mussels, crab, and oysters flown in fresh every day. The casual environs are reminiscent of a turn-of-the-century watering hole.

## DK Choice

**NEW CASTLE:**
**Jessop's Tavern** $$
American
*114 Delaware St, 19720*
**Tel** *(302) 322-6111* **Closed** *Sun*
Patrons fill wooden tables surrounded by Colonial-style decor to enjoy flavorful home-cooked food. The menu consists of authentic Early American dishes that incorporate English, Dutch, and Swedish recipes that were once common to the region. House favorites include oven-baked pot pies and fresh mussels steamed in Belgian beer, garlic, or West Indian spices. Warm service.

**REHOBOTH BEACH: The Back**
**Porch Café** $$$
New American
*59 Rehoboth Ave, 19971*
**Tel** *(302) 227-3674* **Closed** *Nov–Apr*
This welcoming eatery housed in an old beach house has been drawing crowds since 1974. The extensive wine list, enticing sea-food menu, and live music all contribute to the lively atmos-phere. Popular Sunday brunch.

**WILMINGTON: Harry's**
**Seafood Grill** $$$
Seafood/New American
*101 S Market St, 19801*
**Tel** *(302) 777-1500*
Harry's boasts innovative cuisine made with fresh ingredients, and served in an attractive space. The fresh raw bar offerings and award-winning crab cakes are always in demand. There is also a lively bar area and a breezy patio deck.

The Colonial-style Jessop's Tavern in New Castle, Delaware

For more information on types of restaurants *see pages 28–9*

# THE SOUTHEAST

# The Southeast at a Glance

Although the five Southeast states – North and South Carolina, Kentucky, Tennessee, and Georgia – share a common history and culture, they are quite distinct from one another. The region covers three different topographical areas. To the east, the low-lying coastal plains along the Atlantic include the historic cities of Savannah, Georgia, and Charleston, South Carolina, bordered by pristine beaches. The central Blue Ridge and Appalachian Mountains hold acres and acres of stunningly scenic wilderness, while in the inland foothills, linked to the Gulf of Mexico by the Mississippi and other broad rivers, are cities such as Louisville, Kentucky, and Tennessee's twin music capitals, Nashville and Memphis. Atlanta is the main commercial center.

**Lexington** *(see p272)* is Kentucky's main horse-breeding center. Visitors are allowed access to most of the stud farms surrounding the city.

**Nashville** *(see pp266–7)* is Tennessee's state capital as well as the nation's country music capital. The town's revitalized downtown, with its lively restaurants, cafés, and nightclubs, is the center of action, day and night.

**Atlanta** *(see pp262–3)*, Georgia's capital, is the place where Coca-Cola was born in the 1880s. Since then, the drink has become an international favorite. The hard-hitting TV news channel, CNN, is also based in Atlanta.

◄ Colorful azaleas blooming among the trees in one of Charleston's plantation gardens

**Locator Map**

0 kilometers 100

0 miles 100

**The Outer Banks** *(see p252)* are a long chain of narrow barrier islands that run along North Carolina's Atlantic Coast. Beside pristine beaches, the other attractions here include historic lighthouses and the site where the Wright Brothers launched their first successful flight.

Pikeville

Kingsport

Winston-Salem    Greensboro    Rocky Mount

Durham

**NORTH CAROLINA**    Raleigh    Beaufort
*(See pp250–53)*

Asheville

Charlotte    New Bern

Fayetteville

Greenville    Laurinburg    Jacksonville

**SOUTH CAROLINA**    Wilmington
*(See pp254–57)*

Greenwood    Florence

Athens    Columbia

**GEORGIA**    Orangeburg    Myrtle Beach
*ee pp258–63)*

Augusta

Macon

Dublin    Statesboro    Charleston

rdele    Savannah

Jesup

Brunswick    **Myrtle Beach** *(see p256),*
Waycross    South Carolina's premier
resort, is the capital of the
Valdosta    Grand Strand, a long sweep
of Atlantic coastline. The
beach and its environs
offer a wide variety of
seaside amusements.

*For hotels and restaurants see pp276–8 and pp279–81*

# THE SOUTHEAST

One of the country's most fascinating regions, the Southeast is home to two of America's most beautiful cities – Charleston and Savannah – as well as some of its most pristine beaches and expanses of primeval forests. Culturally, the region is famous for its vibrant musical traditons, as both country-and-western and the blues originated in Nashville and Memphis.

The Southeast's cities reflect the region's proud cultural heritage. Celebrated for their beauty and sophistication, Charleston and Savannah are urban gems, with lushly landscaped parks and gracious homes. Both actively preserve their stately architecture as well as support a fine range of hotels, restaurants, and cultural institutions. Other cities vary greatly. The quiet college town of Durham, North Carolina, rated the "most educated city in America," stands in direct contrast to burgeoning commercial centers such as Atlanta, Georgia, the economic capital of the "New South." Equally engaging are Nashville, the capital of country-and-western music, and Memphis, the birthplace of the blues.

The region's natural landscape is as memorable. Nearly a thousand miles of Atlantic coastline are formed by a long series of offshore barrier islands, ranging from Cape Hatteras to Cumberland Island on the Florida border. Just inland, and linked to the ocean by several broad rivers, is the heartland of the Colonial-era plantation country. Farther inland are the farmlands of North Carolina, the primary US producer of tobacco products, and the rolling bluegrass fields of Kentucky's verdant Horse Country. At the center lies unforgettable mountain scenery.

## History

Long before the arrival of the first Europeans, the region was home to a highly developed Native American culture, known as the Moundbuilders. Evidence of their large cities can be seen at Georgia's Ocmulgee National Monument. Later Indians, especially the Cherokee who lived in western North Carolina and northern Georgia, were among North America's most civilized tribes. Other tribes included the Creek, Tuscarora, Yamasee, and Catawba, but by the early 1800s, most of

Kentucky Derby, the annual horse-racing event held in Louisville's Churchill Downs

◀ Entrance to an elegant Southern home

Exhibits in the Civil War Museum, Bardstown, Kentucky

the Indians had been decimated by war and disease, or driven westward. Apart from a prominent Cherokee community in the far western corner of North Carolina, very few Indians survive in the region today.

In the early 1500s, explorers from Florida's Spanish colonies ventured here, lured by Indians' tales of great wealth. The Spanish were followed by the French and then the English. But it was only in 1670, under Charles II, that the first successful colony, called Carolina, was established near what is today Charleston. Carolina's first settlers came

### KEY DATES IN HISTORY

**1587** Sir Walter Raleigh sponsors the establishment of an ill-fated colony at Roanoke in present-day North Carolina

**1670** The first permanent English settlement in the Carolina colony is established at Charleston

**1729** Carolina divided into North and South

**1763** The Anglo-Spanish treaty fixes the Mississippi River as the western extent of the Southeast colonies

**1792** Kentucky becomes the 15th US state

**1795** The University of North Carolina, the country's first state-sponsored university, opens at Chapel Hill

**1838** The government forcibly expels the Cherokees westward on the "Trail of Tears"

**1861** Confederates attack on Fort Sumter

**1864** General Sherman spares Savannah at the end of his notorious "March to the Sea"

**1903** The Ohio-based Wright Brothers make the first successful powered airplane flight at Kitty Hawk, North Carolina

**1976** Georgia Governor Jimmy Carter elected 39th president of the United States

**1996** Atlanta hosts the centennial Olympics

**2002** Jimmy Carter wins the Nobel Peace Prize

from the congested English colony on Barbados, and it was their agricultural expertise that made the land-owning "planters" the wealthiest in the American colonies. Their wealth, however, was based on slave labor, and thousands of Africans were imported to clear the swamps, dig canals, and harvest the crops. Along the coast where the main crops, rice and indigo, were grown, the white colonists were a small minority, outnumbered four to one by the workers whose labor they exploited.

The great fortunes made in Carolina inspired the creation in 1732 of another colony, Georgia, located to the south. In many ways Georgia was a novel colony, funded by the government rather than private interests and founded with social, rather than commercial, intentions. For the first time in the Americas, slavery was banned, as was drinking alcohol and the presence of lawyers. The new colony, however, faltered and came under the control of Carolina, which introduced the slave-holding practices.

In December 1860, the state of South Carolina declared itself independent from the rest of the country. Though Georgia followed soon after, the other Southeast states remained with the Union. It was only after South Carolina forces attacked the fortress at Fort Sumter near Charleston, on April 12, 1861, that Tennessee and North Carolina joined the rebel cause. Ironically, only Kentucky, the birthplace of President Abraham Lincoln and Confederate President Jefferson Davis, remained divided – a true border state.

The impact of the four-year Civil War lasted for another 100 years, as the struggle against the iniquities of slavery gained momentum in the form of the Civil Rights Movement. While primarily a grassroots campaign, many of the battles were led by Atlanta-born Baptist minister Martin Luther King, Jr., who practiced the use of nonviolent direct action to win equality for black people. Though Dr. King

Grave of Dr. Martin Luther King, Jr. in Atlanta, a pilgrimage site for people from all over the world

was assassinated while participating in a strike by black sanitation workers in Memphis in 1968, the movement for Civil Rights eventually saw his colleague Andrew Young elected to Congress from Georgia. Young was later elected mayor of Atlanta in 1981.

## Society, Culture, & the Arts

The Southeast has been, and continues to be, a major contributor to American culture. Atlanta gave the world Coca-Cola and CNN, while Kentucky, particularly Colonel Sanders and his Kentucky Fried Chicken, spread the craze for fast food. Kentucky is also well known all over the world for its production of high-quality bourbon whiskey and high-speed horses.

Important though the region's cities are, they are also the conduit through which the outside world reaches into their hinterlands. Nashville's country music, for example, is deeply rooted in Appalachian folkways, while the blues and rock 'n' roll of Memphis emerge from the different ethnic and historical cultures of the broad Mississippi Delta. A roll call of the artists born and bred here spans all musical genres – the Everly Brothers, Bill Monroe, and Loretta Lynn are from Kentucky; John Coltrane, Doc Watson, Thelonius Monk, and Nina Simone hail from North Carolina; the Allman Brothers, James Brown, Otis Redding, and Gladys Knight came from Georgia; while Tennessee can take credit for Chet Atkins, Tina Turner, and Carl Perkins, and its favorite adopted son, Elvis Presley (1935–77).

This is also true of literature, which witnessed the creativity of such diverse writers as Alice Walker, Thomas Wolfe, Carson McCullers, and James Agee, and characters and settings such as "God's Little Acre" and "Catfish Row" from George Gershwin's opera Porgy & Bess. Music, literature, and the arts still dominate Southeastern culture, and numerous events and festivals are celebrated all over the region.

## Tourism

The Appalachain Mountains and their local constituents, the Blue Ridge and Great Smoky Mountains, offer miles of spectacular scenery in near-pristine condition. Much of the mountain landscape is now preserved in a series of local, state, and national parks and forests. The Great Smoky Mountains National Park, in particular, is one of the country's most popular, drawing millions of visitors each year. Other attractions include the beach resorts that proliferate along the Outer Banks in North Carolina, and Louisville's Kentucky Derby, reputed to be the biggest racing event in the country.

Local band performing in one of the many clubs in downtown Nashville, Tennessee

# Exploring the Southeast

Despite the Southeast's diverse landscape and topography, the region is compact enough to tour in about a week. The coastal cities of Charleston and Savannah, as well as the inland metropolises of Atlanta, Nashville, and Memphis, are well linked by road and short-haul airline flights. The broad crest of mountains that rise up at the center include such prime attractions as the scenic Blue Ridge Parkway and the Great Smoky Mountains National Park. Among the region's other highlights are Georgia's beautiful Golden Isles and Kentucky's spectacular mountain landscapes and bluegrass pasturelands, famous for their thoroughbred horse farms.

## Sights at a Glance

### North Carolina
1. Research Triangle Region
2. Winston-Salem
3. Blue Ridge Parkway
4. Asheville
5. Outer Banks
6. Roanoke Island
7. Beaufort

### South Carolina
8. *Charleston pp254–5*
9. Columbia
10. Myrtle Beach
11. Georgetown
12. Coastal Islands

### Georgia
13. Savannah
14. Golden Isles
15. Okefenokee Swamp National Wildlife Refuge
16. Americus
17. Macon

18. Athens
19. Dahlonega
20. Stone Mountain Park
21. *Atlanta pp262–3*

### Tennessee
22. Great Smoky Mountains National Park
23. Chattanooga
24. *Nashville pp266–7*
25. *Memphis pp268–9*

### Kentucky
26. Cumberland Gap National Historic Park
27. Mammoth Cave National Park
28. Berea
29. Daniel Boone National Forest
30. Lexington
31. Harrodsburg
32. Hodgenville
33. Bardstown
34. Louisville

**For keys to symbols** *see back flap*

## Key

— Highway
— Major road
— Railroad
--- State border

## Mileage Chart

**Atlanta, GA**

| 248<br>399 | Savannah, GA | | | | | | **10** = Distance in miles<br>10 = Distance in kilometers |
| 207<br>333 | 310<br>499 | Asheville, NC | | | | | |
| 324<br>522 | 115<br>185 | 268<br>432 | Charleston, SC | | | | |
| 250<br>402 | 497<br>800 | 294<br>473 | 551<br>887 | Nashville,TN | | | |
| 460<br>740 | 711<br>1143 | 506<br>814 | 787<br>1266 | 213<br>343 | Memphis,TN | | |
| 379<br>609 | 583<br>938 | 283<br>455 | 540<br>869 | 213<br>343 | 423<br>681 | Lexington, KY | |
| 422<br>678 | 658<br>1058 | 358<br>576 | 616<br>991 | 175<br>281 | 385<br>619 | 79<br>127 | Louisville, KY |

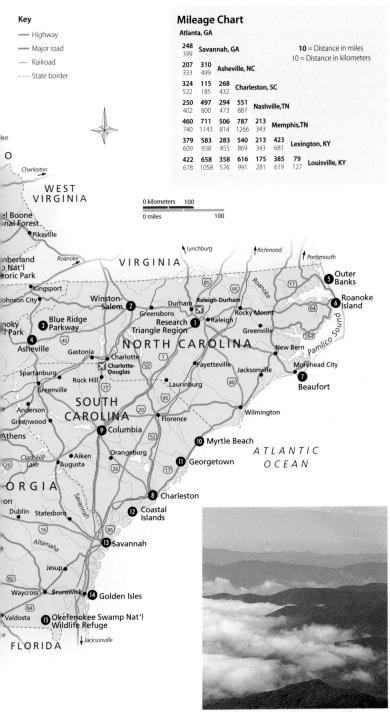

View of smoky mist from Clingman's Dome, Great Smoky Mountains National Park

*For hotels and restaurants see pp276–81*

# North Carolina

The site of the first English outpost in America in 1585, North Carolina became the 12th of the original 13 states in 1789 – it was also one of the country's 13 original colonies. While the population is increasingly based in cities, much of the state remains covered with fields of tobacco, a crop whose politics are the source of local and national debate. Still, the sight of green fields dotted with plank-wood, tin-roofed drying sheds continues to conjure up a classic image of North Carolina. Though tobacco-growing dominates the state's center, the east is lined by miles of pristine Atlantic Ocean beachfront, and the western mountains are among the most majestic found east of the Rockies.

🏛 **North Carolina Museum of History**
5 E Edenton St, Raleigh. **Tel** (919) 807-7900. **Open** 9am–5pm Mon–Sat, noon–5pm Sun. ♿ 🆆 ncdcr.gov/ncmoh

🏛 **North Carolina Museum of Art**
2110 Blue Ridge Rd, Raleigh. **Tel** (919) 839-6262. **Open** 10am–5pm Tue–Fri (to 9pm Fri), 10am–5pm Sat & Sun. ♿ 🆆 ncartmuseum.org

🗺 **UNC Visitor Center**
250 E Franklin St, Chapel Hill. **Tel** (919) 962-1630. **Open** 9am–5pm Mon–Fri. **Closed** Sat, Sun & public hols. 🆆 unc.edu

Façade of North Carolina Museum of History, Raleigh

## ❶ Research Triangle Region

🏙 2,000,000. ✈ 🚃 🚌 ℹ Durham Convention and Visitors' Bureau, 101 E Morgan St, Durham, (919) 687-0288, (800) 446-8604.

The state capital of Raleigh forms a regional triangle with the two major university towns of Durham and Chapel Hill. This region is the state's intellectual center, and has spawned the high-technology Research Triangle Park, a corporate campus located between the three cities.

Primarily a business region and gateway, the Triangle provides various urban conveniences and offers some interesting sights. Raleigh is known as the "City of Oaks" for the many oak trees lining the city's streets. Quiet downtown Raleigh includes a handful of modern state museums located across from the 1840 Greek

Revival State Capitol, including the Sports Hall of Fame, the Museum of Natural Sciences, and the **North Carolina Museum of History**. The latter is well known for a Civil War exhibit describing the state's divided loyalties. Other exhibits feature pirates, Native Americans, and vehicles. A few miles north toward the airport, the **North Carolina Museum of Art** holds three floors of statuary and paintings. Among these is the 16th-century *Madonna and Child in a Landscape* by the artist Lucas Cranach the Elder, which had been stolen by the Nazis. When this was discovered, the museum returned the painting to its original owner, who in turn, has now loaned it back to the museum.

Of the two university towns, the smaller Chapel Hill, with its wooded **University of North Carolina (UNC)** campus, Morehead Planetarium, art museum, and genteel Carolina Inn with its aristocratic clientele, is by far the quainter of the two. Downtown Durham, wedged between the three-part **Duke University** campus, is home to the Durham Bulls minor-league baseball team. It also hosts the annual September Blues Festival. A major landmark on the West Campus is the superb Neo-Gothic Duke Chapel, an imposing structure with a vast interior space. Alumni and students of the two universities enjoy the lively rivalry between their respective sports teams – the Duke's Blue Devils and UNC's Tar Heels.

## ❷ Winston-Salem

🏙 234,000. ✈ 🚌 ℹ 200 Brookstown Ave 27101, (336) 728-4200. 🆆 visitwinstonsalem.com

North Carolina's close ties with the tobacco industry are evident in the fact that two major US cigarette brands have been named after this twin city. Moravian immigrants first settled here in 1766. Their descendants celebrate their roots at **Old Salem**, an interesting restoration of a Colonial village, where guides dressed in period costume demonstrate traditional crafts. They also relate the story of this Protestant sect's journey from Moravia to this region. Gift shops throughout the village offer such Moravian wares as handmade lace and pewter ornaments. The complex is set invitingly on a hill and is compact enough to be covered in an hour or two.

Adjacent to the village is the **Museum of Early Southern Decorative Arts**. Guides take

Actors dressed in period costume, Old Salem Colonial village

*For hotels and restaurants see pp276–81*

A panoramic view of lush vegetation and mountains from the Blue Ridge Parkway

visitors through 24 rooms exhibiting antebellum furnishings and artifacts from across the region. A children's museum is downstairs.

🏛 **Old Salem**
900 Old Salem Rd. **Tel** (336) 721-7300. **Open** 9:30am–4:30pm Tue–Sat, 1–4:30pm Sun. **Closed** Easter, Thanksgiving, Dec 24 & 25. 🅿 🔗 museum. **W** oldsalem.org

## ❸ Blue Ridge Parkway

ℹ (828) 298-0398. **W** nps.gov/blri

A scenic two-lane highway, the Blue Ridge Parkway *(see pp50–51)* runs 469 miles (755 km) south from Virginia along the Blue Ridge Mountain ridge-line. Its most scenic stretches lie in North Carolina, where the road meanders for 250 miles (402 km) past peaks, waterfalls, and the towering, 6,684-ft (2,037-m) Mount Mitchell.

The National Park Service's most popular destination with over 23 million visitors every year, the route has a maximum speed limit of 45 mph (72 km/h), which is strictly enforced. It is most scenic during spring and fall. Some sections close in winter. There are ample opportunities to detour to nearby trails and mountain towns such as Boone and Blowing Rock.

The parkway ends at the entrance to **Great Smoky Mountains National Park**, north

of Cherokee *(see p264)*. Here, at the reservation of the Eastern Band of Cherokee Indians, a museum relates the history of the Cherokee people, focusing on the forcible removal of the tribe in 1838 to Oklahoma on the "Trail of Tears." The town of Cherokee itself has a large Indian-run gambling casino.

## ❹ Asheville

🏔 85,700. 🚌 ℹ 36 Montford Ave, (828) 258-6129.
**W** exploreasheville.com

Surrounded by mountains, this town's commercial district retains many Art Deco buildings from its boom years as an early 20th-century resort. Downtown Asheville evokes the period of local author, Thomas Wolfe (1900–38), who wrote about his hometown in *Look Homeward Angel*. Today the modest "Dixieland" boardinghouse

Biltmore Estate in Asheville, one of the most visited house tours in America

described in the novel is preserved as the **Thomas Wolfe State Historic Site**. Asheville is said to be among the healthiest towns in the country, with many health-food stores, cafés, bookstores, organic restaurants, and a vibrant arts and music scene, patronized by a non-conformist and sophisticated populace. It is probably better known for its 250-room, art-studded, **Biltmore Estate** to the south of town. This French Renaissance-style mansion holds a collection of 18th- and 19th-century art and sculpture, and also has the distinction of being the largest residence in America. Beside the main Neo-Classical house, the splendid estate also has a winery, a deluxe inn *(see p276)*, and gardens designed by Frederick Law Olmsted, who also designed New York's Central Park. Visitors should expect long lines, as the estate attracts huge crowds, making it among the country's most visited house tours, along with the White House and Elvis Presley's "Graceland" *(see p269)*. Asheville also makes a great base for exploring the surrounding mountain region.

🏛 **Thomas Wolfe State Historic Site**
52 N Market St. **Tel** (828) 253-8304. **Open** 9am–5pm Tue–Sat. 🅿 🔗 **W** wolfememorial.com

🏛 **Biltmore Estate**
1 Lodge St. **Tel** (828) 225-1333. **Open** 8:30am–6:30pm daily. 🅿 **W** biltmore.com

Cape Hatteras National Seashore, protecting the Outer Banks' northern coast

## ⑤ Outer Banks

🏠 57,800. 🚹 1 Visitors Center Rd, Manteo, (877) 629-4386.
🌐 **outerbanks.org**

North Carolina's Atlantic coastline is made up of a long chain of narrow barrier islands known as the Outer Banks. Most of the northern coast is protected as part of the **Cape Hatteras National Seashore**, where long stretches of pristine beach, dune, and marsh shelter wild ponies, sea turtles, and many varieties of waterbirds. Offshore, two jet streams that meet in a fury stir up the wild currents, storms, and hurricanes that have earned North Carolina's coast its reputation as the "Graveyard of the Atlantic." The coastline's many historic lighthouses, life-saving stations, and pirate lore are as important a part of the Outer Banks' maritime heritage as is its seafood industry.

Wright Brothers commemorative marker

In the early 20th century, bridges built from the mainland brought in the tourist trade, and now hotels and resort-home developments line the northernmost coast from Corolla all the way to Nags Head. In addition to the sun, surf, and sand, this tourist region offers many historic attractions and family amusements, in the town of **Kill Devil Hills**. The "First in Flight" slogan found on coins and the state's license plates commemorates the Wright Brothers' first historic flight, which took place here.

The **Wright Brothers National Memorial** stands at the very site where Orville and Wilbur Wright launched *Flyer*, the first successful experiment in powered flight in 1903.

A few minutes drive south at **Jockey's Ridge State Park**, hang-gliders participate in a modern version of the Wright Brothers' adventures, while "sandboarders" ride the largest sand dune on the East Coast. "Sandboarding," or running headfirst down the sheer 110-ft- (34-m-) high sand wall, is a revered local tradition. The dune is also a great spot to watch the sunset. Fewer people venture to the inland side of the island, where a slow kayak ride through the tidal marsh, or a walk through the scenic maritime forest at **Nags Head Woods Preserve**, hold a quieter appeal. Peculiar to barrier islands, these maritime forests, on the rough Atlantic Coast, are lined with banks of sturdy live oaks that protect the lush vegetation from the onslaughts of the water and wind. Follow the signs to the preserve west off Hwy 158 close to the Wright Brothers Memorial.

The drive along the National Seashore is one of the country's most scenic routes, with many opportunities to visit lighthouses and walk along dune and marsh boardwalks. Among the dozens of lighthouses, the 1847 Bodie Island Lighthouse is the only one still in operation. A free ferry ride transports cars and passengers between **Hatteras Island** and **Ocracoke Island**. Hatteras's distinctive black-and-white spiral **Cape Hatteras Lighthouse**, built in 1870, is the tallest brick lighthouse in the world at 193 ft (59 m). The scenic village of Ocracoke has a good selection of inns, restaurants, and shops, which makes this remote port an inviting destination for an overnight stay. Visitors can connect with toll mainland ferries (reservations recommended) from here.

🏛 **Wright Brothers National Memorial**
US Hwy 158, milepost 8, Kill Devil Hills. **Tel** (252) 441-7430. **Open** 9am–5pm daily. **Closed** Dec 24, 25. 🅿 ♿
🌐 **nps.gov/wrbr**

🌿 **Nags Head Woods Preserve**
701 W Ocean Acres Dr, Kill Devil Hills. **Tel** (252) 441-2525. **Open** dawn–dusk daily. 🅿

🏛 **Cape Hatteras Lighthouse**
Hatteras Is, off Hwy 12, 1 mile (1.6 km) SE of Buxton. **Tel** (252) 995-4474. **Open** mid-Apr–mid-Oct: 9am– 4:30pm daily (to 5:30pm Jul–Aug). 🅿

⛴ **Ocracoke Island**
Ocracoke Car Ferry to Cedar Island or Swan Quarter. **Tel** (800) 293-3779 for fares & schedules (subject to change).

Cape Hatteras Lighthouse, the world's tallest brick lighthouse

The landscaped Elizabethan Gardens on Roanoke Island

## ➌ Roanoke Island

ℹ️ 1 Visitors Center Rd, Manteo, (877) 629-4386. 🅦 outerbanks.org

A marsh island lying between the Outer Banks and the mainland, Roanoke Island was the site of the first English settlement in North America. The first expedition to these shores, sponsored by Sir Walter Raleigh, was in 1584. In 1587, another ship carrying more than 100 colonists disembarked at the island to create a permanent settlement. But when the next group arrived three years later, all the earlier colonists, including the first English women and children to land in the present-day US, had vanished without a trace. Today, the **Fort Raleigh National Historic Site**, the adjacent **Elizabethan Gardens**, an outdoor drama, and the nearby theme park with a replica of a 16th-century sailing ship as its centerpiece, all relate the mysterious story of this legendary "Lost Colony."

At the northern tip of the island, Fort Raleigh preserves the ruins of the colony's original disembarkation point, and ranger-led tours reveal what little is known about it. The Elizabethan Gardens are ideal for a walk through landscaped paths and lawns. A short drive south, at the port of Manteo, the **Roanoke Island Festival Park** tells the story of the first ship of explorers through tours of a recreation of the *Elizabeth II*.

There is also a museum that relates both the Native and European history of the region, as the island was the site of ancient indigenous settlements.

### 🏛 Fort Raleigh National Historic Site
US Hwy 64/264, Manteo. **Tel** (252) 473-5772. **Open** 9am–5pm daily. **Closed** Dec 25. 🔲 Elizabethan Gardens only. 🅦 **nps.gov/fora**

### 🏛 Roanoke Island Festival Park
Port of Manteo. **Tel** (252) 475-1500. **Open** 9am–4pm or 6pm daily (seasonal, call & check). **Closed** Jan 1, Thanksgiving, Dec 24 & 25. 🔲 ♿ 🅦 **roanokeisland.com**

## ➐ Beaufort

🏙 12,800. ℹ️ (252) 726-8148 (Morehead City).

Beaufort's considerable charms lie in its historic B&B inns, seafood markets, and restaurants. The highlight of this coastal resort's small attractive waterfront is the **North Carolina Maritime Museum**, which interprets the boating, fishing, and pirate history of this coastline. A swashbuckling robot of Edward "Blackbeard" Teach, a notorious pirate who was captured and killed off the Outer Banks in November of 1718, welcomes visitors in the shell room. A popular event is the family-oriented, educational Pirate Day, which is dedicated to pirate lore and has costumes, flag flying, and treasure hunts. Other activities include boat-building and net-making classes, and kayaking excursions. At the docks, private ferries take passengers out to the deserted sands of Lookout Island, preserved from development as the **Cape Lookout National Seashore**. The ecology of Lookout Island is similar to Cape Hatteras, with virgin beaches, marshland, and dunes, all rich in birdlife, but the limited access makes it more remote and less visited. The town at the island's northern tip was abandoned in the 1970s.

### 🏛 North Carolina Maritime Museum
315 Front St. **Tel** (252) 728-7317. **Open** 9am–5pm Mon–Fri, 10am–5pm Sat, 1–5pm Sun. **Closed** Jan 1, Thanksgiving, Dec 25. ♿ 🅦 **ncmaritimemuseums.com**

### 🏖 Cape Lookout National Seashore
3601 Bridge St, Morehead City. **Tel** (252) 728-2250. **Open** 9am–5pm daily. **Closed** Jan 1, Dec 25. 🅦 **nps.gov/calo**

The waterfront at Salt Marsh and Newport River, Beaufort

# South Carolina

After separating from its sibling North Carolina in 1729, the South Carolina colony spread Upcountry, where Welsh, Irish, and Scottish immigrants established small owner-operated farms, in sharp contrast to the Lowcountry gentry. By the 1860s, however, the differences between the two had subsided and a unified South Carolina became the first Southern state to declare independence from the Union. Soon after, the first shot of the American Civil War was fired at Fort Sumter. Today, the state's "glory days" of resistance and revolution are re-created at plantations, museums, and monuments. Many visitors, however, head straight for the miles of beaches.

## ❽ Charleston

🗠 125,500. ✈ 🚗 🚌
ℹ 375 Meeting St, (843) 853-8000.
🎭 Spoleto Festival (late May–early Jun). 🖥 **charlestoncvb.com**

One of the south's most beautiful cities and South Carolina's first capital, Charleston is situated on the tip of a peninsula between the Ashley and Cooper Rivers. Named after King Charles II of England, the city was founded in 1670 and soon became a wealthy colony of tobacco, rice, and indigo plantations. The first shot of the Civil War was fired just off the city's harbor, where people gathered to watch the Confederate siege of Fort Sumter. Today, Charleston retains much of its original period architecture and is a popular destination for antebellum house-and-garden tours, horse-and-carriage rides, fine Southern cuisine, and plantation retreats.

The historic district's beautifully preserved architecture evokes the city's Colonial and early American past. The civic and religious buildings here range from styles as varied as Colonial and Georgian, Greek and Gothic Revival, to Italianate and Victorian. Among the highlights are distinctive Charlestonian residences, set perpendicular to the street with grand piazzas running along their lengths. The only high structures are the towering church steeples. Horse-and-carriage rides through tree-lined streets provide a graceful overview.

The charming 1772 Heyward-Washington House

A trip south from **Old City Market** to the Battery takes in many highlights along Church Street, including the old magazine, the Gothic French Huguenot Church, and the **Heyward-Washington House**. This 1772 house was built by rice planter Daniel Heyward and has a splendid collection of Charleston-made furniture. A half-block detour to the east on Chalmers leads to the Old Slave Mart, once one of the busiest in the American colonies. At the Battery, the **Edmondston-Alston House** features two floors of an opulent 1825 mansion overlooking the harbor. White Point Gardens Park lies to the

south, while in the north, **Waterfront Park**, with its walk-through fountain, stands across from the popular restaurant row. Visitors can explore the cobblestone alleyways in search of hidden gardens, gargoyles, and harbor views. To the west of Waterfront Park, the **Gibbes Museum of Art** reveals local history through landscape paintings and portraits of famous South Carolinians.

🏛 **Heyward-Washington House**
87 Church St. **Tel** (843) 722-2996.
**Open** 10am–5pm Mon–Sat, 1–5pm Sun. 🎫 **Closed** major public hols.
🏛 Edmondston-Alston House: 21 E Battery. **Tel** (843) 722-7171.
**Open** 10am–4:30pm Tue–Sat, 1–4:30pm Sun–Mon. **Closed** major public hols. 🎫 🏛 Gibbes Museum of Art: 135 Meeting St. **Tel** (843) 722-2706. **Open** 10am–5pm Tue–Sat, 1pm–5pm Sun. **Closed** major public hols. 🎫 ♿

## 🐟 South Carolina Aquarium

100 Aquarium Wharf. **Tel** (843) 720-1990. **Open** Mar–Aug: 9am–5pm daily; Sep–Feb: 9am–4pm daily. **Closed** public hols. 🎫 ♿
🖥 **scaquarium.org**

Picturesquely set overlooking the harbor, Charleston's aquarium provides an excellent introduction to the indigenous creatures found within the state's aquatic habitats. These range from Appalachian rivers and blackwater swamps, to salt marshes and coral reefs. An IMAX® Theater lies adjacent.

## 🏛 Fort Sumter Visitor Center

340 Concord St. **Tel** (843) 720-1990. **Open** 8:30am–5pm daily. **Closed** Jan 1, Dec 25. 🚢 boat tours. ♿ 🖥 **nps. gov/fosu**

An embarkation point for boat tours to Fort Sumter, the visitor center relates the story of the

Civil War cannon lying preserved at Fort Sumter

*For hotels and restaurants see pp276–81*

American Civil War's first battle. The fort, which stands on an island at the entrance to Charleston harbor, was controlled by Union troops. In April 1861, the Confederate army besieged the fort. When Union troops tried to bring in supplies, the Confederates, who had occupied nearby Fort Johnson, unleashed a 34-hour bombardment. Union forces finally surrendered on April 14, 1861, and the fort remained under Confederate control until 1865. Ironically, General Beauregard, the Confederate leader, was a student of the defending Union commander, Major Robert Anderson, at the US Military Academy at West Point, New York (see p101). Fort Sumter has been preserved unchanged since the end of the war. It is a National Monument.

### 🏛 Charleston Museum
360 Meeting St. **Tel** (843) 722-2996. **Open** 9am–5pm Mon–Sat, 1–5pm Sun. **Closed** public hols. 🎫 ♿ 🖥 charlestonmuseum.org

This museum presents a comprehensive overview of the city's history from pre-Colonial days. Its most distinctive exhibits are in the Native

Flowers in bloom at Audubon Swamp Gardens, Magnolia Plantation

American and Natural History galleries; the former has dugout canoes and costumed mannequins, and the latter has a number of mounted skeletons of prehistoric animals such as the Cretaceous dinosaur *Thescelosaurus neglectus*.

### 🏛 Ashley River Plantations
Middleton Place: 3550 Ashley River Rd. **Tel** (843) 556-6020. **Open** 9am–5pm daily. **Closed** Dec 25. 🎫 Drayton Hall: 3380 Ashley River Rd. **Tel** (843) 769-2600. **Open** 9:30am–3pm or 4pm (seasonal). **Closed** Jan 1, 1st week Feb, Thanksgiving, Dec 24, 25 & 31. 🎫 Magnolia Plantation: Rte 4/Hwy 61. **Tel** (843) 571-1266. **Open** 9am–4:30pm daily. 🎫

Within a short drive upriver, three house tours provide a glimpse of Charleston-style country living. Of them, the grandest is

**Middleton Place**, with its 1755 mansion located on a bluff overlooking the US's oldest landscaped gardens. Close by, **Drayton Hall** is one of the country's finest examples of Colonial architecture. Built in 1738, the Georgian Palladian mansion has been preserved in its original condition without electricity or plumbing. A daily program on African-American heritage is held here.

**Magnolia Plantation** has a more modest house, with a petting zoo and a motorized train ride. Prized attractions are the acres of riverfront informal gardens with charming pathways that lead through a profusion of flowers, and **Audubon Swamp Gardens**, a lush tupelo-and-cypress sanctuary.

## Downtown Charleston

① Charleston Historic District
② South Carolina Aquarium
③ Fort Sumter Visitor Center
④ Charleston Museum

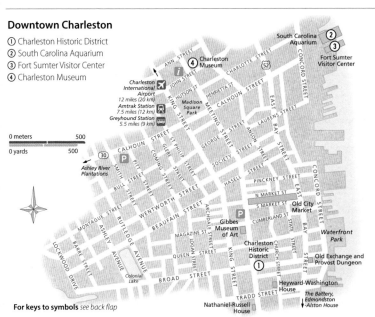

For keys to symbols *see back flap*

## ⊙ Columbia

🗺 131,600. 🚌 🚆 ℹ 900 Assembly St, (803) 545-0000.
Ⓦ **columbiacvb.com**

Situated at the fall line of the Congaree River – the area that marked the limit of inland navigation – this city was declared the state capital over Charleston in 1786. Although General William T. Sherman destroyed most of Columbia during the Civil War, the **State House** managed to survive intact. Today, six bronze stars mark the spots where Union cannonballs hit the 1855 copper-domed building, located in the center of the quiet downtown on Gervais Street.

On the banks of the river, the **South Carolina State Museum** is housed in an artfully recycled textile mill built in 1894. Informative exhibits on the state's natural, cultural, and industrial history are displayed. The adjacent **South Carolina Confederate Relic Room and Museum** maintains a huge collection of artifacts that trace the military history of South Carolina's participation in US wars from the Civil War onward, as well as an exhibit on the history and sometimes controversial meanings of the Confederate flag. While Southern traditionalists proclaim the flag a symbol of regional pride, many others see it as a symbol of white supremacy that should be abolished. A 20-minute drive south of town, the **Congaree Swamp National Park** offers visitors a close-up look at the

A view of the Grand Strand at Myrtle Beach

biodiversity found within a cypress swamp ecosystem. The swamp is at its best from late fall to early spring.

🏛 **South Carolina State Museum**
301 Gervais St. **Tel** (803) 898-4921.
**Open** 10am–5pm Tue–Sat, 1–5pm Sun. **Closed** Mon, Easter, Thanksgiving, Dec 25. 🅿 ♿
Ⓦ **museum.state.sc.us**

🏛 **South Carolina Confederate Relic Room & Museum**
301 Gervais St. **Tel** (803) 737-8095.
**Open** 10am–5pm Tue–Sat; 1–5pm first Sun of month. **Closed** public hols.
♿ Ⓦ **crr.sc.gov**

## ⊙ Myrtle Beach

🗺 23,000. 🚆 🚌 ℹ 1200 N Oak St, (843) 626-7444. Ⓦ **visitmyrtle beach.com**

This popular beach is the center of the "Grand Strand," a long sweep of the Atlantic coastline south of the North Carolina border, which is dominated by hotels, golf courses, amusement parks, and arcades. Its heyday was in the 1950s, when as a Spring Break destination, college students descended on this beach town for a week-long

party. "The Shag," South Carolina's official state dance, was invented here and caused a craze all over the country. The elite crowd vacations at exclusive resort communities, but everyone ventures to the nearby fishing village of **Murrell's Inlet** for seafood.

South of Myrtle Beach two attractions make a worthwhile detour. On the inland side of the coastal Hwy 17, 16 miles (26 km) south of the beach, is **Brookgreen Gardens**, landscaped around 550 works of statuary by 250 artists. Oceanside, **Huntington Beach State Park** offers access to an undeveloped beach and salt-marsh boardwalk, as well as an art studio that once belonged to Anna Huntington, the sculptor who created Brookgreen Gardens in the 1930s.

🗿 **Brookgreen Gardens**
US Hwy 17. **Tel** (843) 235-6000.
**Open** 9:30am–5pm daily. **Closed** Dec 25. 🅿 ♿ Ⓦ **brookgreen.org**

## ⊙ Georgetown

🗺 10,000. 🚌 ℹ 1001 Front St, (843) 546-8436. Ⓦ **visitgeorge.com**

Set along the banks of the Sampit River, Georgetown was the center of the state's lucrative rice trade, producing almost half the rice grown in the US in the 1840s. Downtown's **Rice Museum**, housed in the 1842 Old Market building, explains how the rice industry influenced almost every facet of life here. The museum's maritime gallery features examples of historic local watercraft. The museum leads out to a waterfront park

Civil War arms on display at the South Carolina State Museum, Columbia

*For hotels and restaurants see pp276–81*

where a wooden boardwalk makes an attractive marsh-side promenade.

The commercial district is reminiscent of a Southern small town in the early-to-mid-1900s, a quiet contrast to the Grand Strand or the bustle of Charleston. About 15 miles (24 km) south of Georgetown, **Hampton Plantation State Park** is an unfurnished 1750 Georgian house. Visitors are able to explore the mansion, which overlooks the remains of the old rice fields. The well maintained grounds include enormous live oak trees and beautiful camellia gardens.

Hampton Plantation State Park, Georgetown

### 🏛 Rice Museum
Front & Screven Sts. **Tel** (843) 546-7423. **Open** 10am–4:30pm Mon–Sat, 11:30am–3:30pm Sun. **Closed** public hols. 🅿 ♿ 🆆 **ricemuseum.org**

### 🏞 Hampton Plantation State Park
US Hwy 17. **Tel** (843) 546-9361. **Open** 9am–5pm daily (grounds), 9am–5pm Sat–Tue (house). **Closed** Thanksgiving, Dec 25. 🏞 house (grounds free).
🆆 **southcarolinaparks.com**

## ⑫ Coastal Islands
ℹ Lowcountry Visitors Center & Museum, I95 exit 33 & US17, (843) 717-3090. 🆆 **southcarolinalowcountry.com**

Extending from Georgetown south to beyond Savannah in Georgia, the remote islands of the Lowcountry are a semi-tropical region with a rich natural and cultural history. Shifting sand dunes, dense maritime forests

of live oak draped with Spanish moss and muscadine vines, and numerous lagoons and marshes harbor a mix of wildlife such as sea turtles, seabirds, alligators, ospreys, and dolphins.

The area's unique African-American history evolved around the common heritage of slaves, brought here from the rice-growing regions of West Africa, to cultivate this crop along the tidal creeks. Isolated on these islands, the Lowcountry Africans were able to perpetuate their cultural traditions over the generations. Today, their "Gullah" heritage remains distinct in the local language, music, cuisine, and folkways. To the east of Beaufort, two islands preserve the natural and cultural history. Both are accessible by car via Hwy 21, which offers a panoramic view of the Port Royal Sound marsh landscape.

On St. Helena Island, the renowned **Penn Center** is a touchstone of Gullah culture. A former school established in 1862 by Pennsylvanian abolitionists during the Civil War, the center has a distinguished history from the Civil Rights era. National leaders such as Martin Luther King Jr. and groups such as the Southern Christian Leadership Conference met here to advance the Civil Rights Movement. A modest museum located in the old schoolhouse relates numerous events from the center's past through photographs and other displays. The center also

Canoeing at the Hilton Head Island Resort, Coastal Islands

sponsors storytelling programs and an annual festival that celebrates Gullah culture.

Beyond St. Helena, **Hunting Island State Park** on Hunting Island preserves a natural barrier island environment. Its highlights include a pleasant, uncrowded beach, a coastside campground, and a 19th-century lighthouse.

**Hilton Head Island**, named after the English sea captain William Hilton who explored the island in 1664, is South Carolina's premier beach resort. It is dominated by several deluxe resort complexes, including the Westin Resort, Hyatt Regency, Crowne Plaza, Disney, and, of course, the Hilton, providing golf, tennis, and spa facilities. Among the other recreational opportunities are horseback riding, fishing, boating, sailing, and a variety of other water sports.

### 🏛 Penn Center
16 Penn Center Circle W, St. Helena. **Tel** (843) 838-2432. **Open** 11am–4pm Mon–Sat. **Closed** public hols. 🅿 ♿
🆆 **penncenter.com**

### 🏞 Hunting Island State Park
Hwy 21. **Tel** (843) 838-2011. **Open** Apr–Oct: 6am–9pm daily; Nov–Mar: 6am–6pm daily. 🏞

Port Royal Sound marshland at dusk, Coastal Islands

# Georgia

The last of the 13 original colonies, Georgia was founded by a British general, James Oglethorpe, to stop Spanish expansion up from Florida. While the state initially banned slavery, economic pressures from competing slave-holding colonies led to its introduction. As a result, it grew wealthy from slave labor on rice, indigo, and cotton plantations. Georgia was devastated during the Civil War, when General Sherman's "March to the Sea" set ablaze a swath of land across the state. Led by pragmatic Atlanta *(see pp262–3)*, Georgia was able to overcome the many hardships of its troubled past, and was well positioned to benefit from the economic boom in the late 20th century.

A colorful Halloween display on River Street, Savannah

## ⓭ Savannah

🏙 142,000. ✈ 🚆 🚌 ℹ 301 Martin Luther King Jr. Blvd, (912) 944-0455. 🔲 visitsavannah.com

Labeled the "most beautiful city in America" by the Paris newspaper *Le Monde*, the lushly landscaped parks and gracious homes of Savannah have earned it a reputation for scenic beauty and sophistication. It was established in 1733 on the banks of the Savannah River, 16 miles (26 km) from the Atlantic Ocean. Its founder, James Oglethorpe, laid out a town grid dotted with small squares designed to deter invaders. Today, even after the turmoil of the Revolution and Civil War, his design remains intact, with the squares now serving as scenic parks filled with statues and fountains. The city has one of the largest, and perhaps most beautiful, urban historic districts in the US, which now thrives as the city's downtown commercial center.

Horse-and-carriage tours provide an introduction to historic Savannah, though walking around is the best way to explore the area.

**River Street** is one of the city's central entertainment districts, lined with seafood restaurants, raucous taverns, and souvenir shops housed in old warehouses constructed of ballast-stones. Water taxis shuttle passengers to the modern Convention Center across the river on Hutchinson Island. Uphill, **Factors Walk** is a stately promenade on top of the bluff. A few blocks in from the river, **City Market** is another lively arts and entertainment district, housed in historic buildings.

Historic house museums throughout Savannah shed light on the city's history, architecture, and culture. Many homes and religious centers are open to tours year-round. Of these, the **Davenport House** on Columbia Square is considered one of the country's finest examples of Federal-style architecture, while nearby,

the **Owens-Thomas House** on Oglethorpe Square is among the finest Regency buildings, built by English architect William Jay in 1816. Other houses can be seen on the popular **Tour of Homes and Gardens**, held in spring.

A handful of museums also highlight different aspects of the city's history. The **Telfair Academy of Arts**, at the center of the historic district, displays a fine collection of Impressionist paintings and decorative arts within an 1818 Regency-style mansion. At the western edge of the district, the **Ships of the Sea Maritime Museum** holds ship models of all shapes and sizes within the palatial 1819 Scarborough House. Located just beyond the historic district, the **Ralph Mark Gilbert Civil Rights Museum** has exhibits relating to the city's history. In-depth African-American heritage tours also start at the museum.

Many more attractions await in the surrounding Lowcountry – the marsh-laden coastal region of Georgia and South Carolina *(see p257)*. A drive out on Hwy 80, east of the **Tybee Island** beach resort (18 miles/29 km east of downtown), passes the **Bonaventure Cemetery**, where singer Johnny Mercer and writer Conrad Aitken are buried. Also located en route is the behemoth brick **Fort Pulaski National Monument**, which rises like a medieval fortress at the mouth of the Savannah River.

🏛 **Davenport House**
324 E State St. **Tel** (912) 236-8097.
**Open** 10am–4pm Mon–Sat, 1–4pm Sun. **Closed** Jan 1, Mar 17, Easter, Jul 4, Thanksgiving, Dec 25. 🈂
🔲 davenporthousemuseum.org

Fort Pulaski National Monument, Savannah

Jekyll Island Club Hotel, one of many historic buildings on the Golden Isles

# ⑭ Golden Isles

 68,000 (Glynn County).
ℹ️ 4 Glynn Ave, (912) 265-0620.
**W** bgicvb.com

The Spanish called the barrier islands off Georgia's southern coast "the Golden Isles" – possibly after lost treasure or the golden hue of the marshlands in fall – a term that tourism promoters were happy to revive. While they are primarily beach resorts, the islands retain a number of historic sights. **Fort Frederica National Monument**, located on St. Simons, along a scenic stretch of the Frederica River that lies adjacent to Christ Church, holds the ruins of a fortified village built by James Oglethorpe in 1736. Another significant site is the quiet expanse of marsh off Demere Road, south of Fort Frederica, where the Battle of Bloody Marsh was fought in 1742. This decisive battle between English and Spanish forces determined which Colonial power would control this part of the American continent. Near the island's southern tip, Neptune Park in downtown St. Simons has the historic 1872 **St. Simons Lighthouse**, where visitors can climb to the top. Lying across Bloody Marsh from St. Simons, Sea Island is home to the luxurious Cloister Hotel. At the turn of the 20th century, **Jekyll Island** was the exclusive preserve of the nation's premier industrialists, such as the Vanderbilts, Goodyears, and Rockefellers. With the advent of World War II, however, this

St. Simons Lighthouse

vulnerable coastal island was deemed unsafe and the families moved elsewhere. Today, the island's historic district comprises the "cottages," as the millionaires' mansions were known, and the elegant Jekyll Island Club. The cottages have been restored and are now open as museums or inns. Among these are the 1892 Indian Mound Cottage, which passed into the hands of William Rockefeller in 1904, and Crane Cottage, which is now part of the Jekyll Island Club Hotel and features a fine restaurant. Other highlights are a former stable, now a small museum, and Faith Chapel, with its Tiffany windows. The historic Jekyll River Wharf, next to the Jekyll Island Club Hotel, has a popular seafood restaurant serving raw seafood, mainly fresh oysters. On the ocean side, a selection of franchise motels and restaurants offer family lodging and dining. There is also a campground located at the island's northern tip near "Boneyard Beach," where sun-bleached driftwood gives the beach its name.

🏛️ **Fort Frederica National Monument**
Frederica Rd, St. Simons Island.
**Tel** (912) 638-3639. **Open** 9am–5pm.
🅿️ ♿ **W** nps.gov/fofr

# ⑮ Okefenokee Swamp National Wildlife Refuge

Hwy 121, Folkston. 🚌 ℹ️ (912) 496-7836. **Open** sunrise–5:30pm (7:30pm in summer). **Closed** Dec 25.
🅿️ ♿ exhibits.

In the remote southeastern corner of the state, the Okefenokee Swamp is an exotic, primeval landscape of blackwater and cypress that harbors alligators, softshell turtles, otters, and all kinds of birdlife. The Seminole Indian name "Okefenokee," loosely translated as "trembling earth," characterizes the peat moss hammocks that bubble up from the water as a natural part of swamp ecology. Boat tours provide a close-up view at three sections of the swamp, including the **Okefenokee Swamp Park** near Waycross, and the wildlife refuge headquarters at **Folkston**, which provides details about overnight paddling trips into the swamp. Fargo, near the swamp's western entrance, is the nearest town to the **Stephen C. Foster State Park**, 18 miles (29 km) to the northeast. This section is perched on a peninsula in the deep recesses of the swamp. Camping facilities and cabins are available here.

🏕️ **Okefenokee Swamp Park**
Hwy 177, Waycross. **Tel** (912) 283-0583. **Open** 9am–5:30pm daily.
**Closed** Thanksgiving, Dec 25. 🅿️ ♿ exhibits only. **W** okeswamp.com

Suwanee Canal Recreation Area, Okefenokee Swamp Refuge

## 🔟 Americus

🏙 16,400. 🚌 ℹ️ 123 W Lamar St, (229) 928-6059.

Off the beaten track in south Georgia, the tidy county seat of Americus lies in a region of diverse attractions. The **Habitat for Humanity**, a worldwide organization offering "self-build" housing for the poor, has its headquarters downtown. Its Global Village and Discovery Center includes an international marketplace and up to 40 examples of habitat homes built around the world, including Papua New Guinea, Botswana, Ghana, and others.

Located 10 miles (16 km) north of town, Andersonville is the **National Prisoner of War (POW) Museum**. This marks a spot that was a notorious prisoner-of-war camp during the Civil War, which later became a veterans' cemetery. Almost 13,000 of the camp's inmates died from the terrible living conditions. Housed in a structure built to resemble a concentration camp, the museum's disturbing exhibits commemorate American POWs in conflicts from the Civil War through Vietnam to the Gulf and Iraqi wars.

The local high school in Plains, 10 miles (16 km) west of Americus, is part of the **Jimmy Carter National Historic Site**. It was here that a teacher predicted that her student would become president. Carter proved her right, and the school is now dedicated to the life of the Plains-area peanut farmer's son who became the 39th

Headstones at the Andersonville cemetery near Americus

president in 1976, in the wake of Nixon's resignation (see p213). The former president, recipient of the Nobel Peace Prize in 2002, lives here and teaches Sunday school at the Maranatha Baptist Church when he is in town. An excursion train runs from Cordele in the east through Plains up to Carter's boyhood farm in Archery.

### 🏛 Habitat for Humanity
121 Habitat St at W Lamar St. **Tel** (229) 924-6935. **Open** 9am–5pm Mon–Fri. **Closed** Sat & Sun. ♿ 🅿️

## 🔼 Macon

🏙 91,200. 🚌 ℹ️ 450 Martin Luther King Jr. Blvd, (478) 743-3401. 🌐 maconga.org

Founded on the south bank of the Ocmulgee River in 1823, Macon was laid out in a grid of avenues, which still exist in its historic district downtown. Uphill from here is one of the city's highlights, the Intown Historic District. This area has some of the city's most beautiful homes, a few of which are open to the public. The 1855 **Hay House Museum**, built in the Italian Renaissance style, features period characteristics such as trompe l'oeil marble, a ballroom, and hidden passages. The 1842 House Inn is also located here. Guided architectural tours begin at the visitor center. The city also has a vibrant musical history and was home to such greats as Little Richard and Otis Redding. The **Big House Museum**, located on Vineville Avenue, houses the **Allman Brothers Band Museum**, honoring the early years of the ultimate Southern rock band. The **Georgia Sports Hall of Fame** celebrates Georgia's athletes, such as Hank Aaron and Ty Cobb. Across the river from downtown, the **Ocmulgee National Monument** marks a historic mound complex built around 1100 as the capital of the Creek Confederacy.

Exterior of the Italianate Hay House Museum, Macon

### 🏛 Hay House Museum
934 Georgia Ave. **Tel** (478) 742-8155. **Open** 10am–4pm Tue–Sat, 1–4pm Sun. **Closed** Mon (all year), Sun (Jan, Feb, Jul, Aug), public hols. ♿

## 🔽 Athens

🏙 118,000. 🚌 ℹ️ 280 E Dougherty St, (706) 353-1820.

Home to the **University of Georgia** (UGA), Athens is well known as the state's intellectual and literary center. It has also gained repute as the originator of alternative music. Local bands such as REM, the B-52s, and Widespread Panic have made it big, and the 40-Watt Club on West Washington Street and the annual Athfest in June continue the tradition. The city is largely deserted in summer, while in fall it overflows with Georgia Bulldog fans for the home football games. The visitor center provides details about house and garden tours, such as the 1856 structure that now houses the Lyndon House Arts Center and the Founders Memorial Garden in North Campus. The university visitor center directs guests to the art museum, with its 19th- and 20th-century paintings and sculpture, and gives details on sports events and performances on campus.

UGA bulldog mascot

View from the Amicalola Falls, Amicalola State Park

# ⓳ Dahlonega

ℹ 13 S Park St, (706) 864-3711.
W **dahlonega.org**

The legendary Blue Ridge Mountain range extends across the state's northeastern corner. With abundant waterfalls and flowering forests, the region is well known for its cultural heritage of outstanding folk arts such as quilt-making, woodworking, and bluegrass music. The discovery of gold in the main town of Dahlonega in 1828 precipitated the nation's first gold rush, two decades before California's famous "Forty-Niners." The state's **Gold Museum**, housed in the 1836 courthouse in the center of Dahlonega's attractive town square, displays mining equipment, nuggets, and mining lore. The town also offers gold-panning and gold-mine tours as well as a complete set of coins minted in the US Mint that operated here from 1838 to 1861.

### 🏛 Gold Museum

1 Public Square. **Tel** (706) 864-2257.
**Open** 9am–5pm Mon–Sat, 10am–5pm Sun. **Closed** Jan 1, Thanksgiving, Dec 25. 🅿 ♿
W **gastateparks.org**

### Environs

About 18 miles (29 km) from Dahlonega, the **Amicalola Falls State Park** is the gateway to the southern terminus of the 2,144-mile (3,450-km) Appalachian Trail, a hiking route that leads from the top of Springer Mountain in Georgia north to Mount Katahdin, deep in Maine. Less ambitious hikers can head to the park's Len Foote Hike Inn, which offers ecologically sensitive, comfortably rustic overnight accommodations. The park also features a mountaintop lodge, restaurant, campground, and the Amicalola Falls. East of Dahlonega, along Hwy 441 at the Georgia–South Carolina border, the federally designated "Wild and Scenic" Chatooga River is considered one of the most daring rivers to navigate in eastern US. The book and the film *Deliverance* were based on this area (but locals don't appreciate being reminded of this). Visible from high above the river, Tallulah Gorge features a suspension bridge.

### 🏕 Amicalola Falls State Park & Lodge

Hwy 52. **Tel** (706) 265-4703.
**Open** 7am–10pm daily.
**Closed** Jan 1, Thanksgiving, Dec 25. 🅿 ♿ W **gastateparks.org**

# ⓴ Stone Mountain Park

US Hwy 78. ℹ (770) 498-5690. **Open** 6am–midnight (hours vary so call ahead). **Closed** Dec 24 & 25. 🅿 ♿ partial. W **stonemountainpark.com**

The centerpiece of this popular park, located about a 30-minute drive east of downtown Atlanta, is a bas-relief carved into the side of a massive granite mountain. The sculpture depicts three Confederate heroes – Jefferson Davis, president of the Confederacy, and generals Robert E. Lee and Stonewall Jackson. Its creator, Gutzon Borglum, began work here in 1924 and later sculpted the faces of four American presidents at Mount Rushmore *(see p443)*.

A sky-lift takes visitors up to the summit, and the walk down affords a close-up view of the unusual "monadnock" habitat – it harbors many species of plants that are more commonly associated with the desert than the humid Southeast. The huge lawn, lying between the granite wall and Stone Mountain Park Inn, is the location of various events such as the annual Fourth of July fireworks. Other attractions include the Geyser Towers, which lead visitors around and through a gushing geyser on rope bridges and net tunnels, an antebellum village, an ice rink, and paddle-wheel riverboat rides around the lake. A number of lodging and dining options are also available here.

The centerpiece bas-relief sculpture at Stone Mountain Park

# ㉑ Atlanta

🏘 444,000. ✈ 🚆 🚌 ℹ
Underground Atlanta, (404) 523-2311.
🌐 atlanta.net

Founded as a terminus for two railroad routes in 1837, Atlanta's importance as a transportation hub made it a Union target during the Civil War. After a 75-day siege, General William T. Sherman broke the Confederate defenses and set most of the town ablaze, a history recounted romantically in Margaret Mitchell's *Gone With the Wind*. Today, the city claims to be the "Capital of the New South" and has since been considered more brash and faster paced than its Southern neighbors.

## Exploring Atlanta

This cosmopolitan city is home to many industrial giants including Coca-Cola. Its entrepreneurial spirit led to an economic boom that lasted two decades, capped by a successful bid to host the Olympics in 1996. One of the city's landmarks, the **Centennial Olympic Park** downtown, commemorates this event. Yet another is **Turner Field**, where the former boxer Muhammad Ali famously lit the Olympic torch in the stadium. Downtown's attractions, **Georgia Aquarium**, **World of Coca-Cola**, and the **Martin Luther King Jr. National Historic Site**, are all within a mile of these Olympic landmarks. A short Metro ride north leads to the city's exceptional **High Museum** in midtown. East of midtown lie the residential neighborhoods of Virginia Highlands and Little Five Points, with their superb specialty restaurants.

## 🏛 World of Coca-Cola

121 Baker St. **Tel** (404) 676-5151.
**Open** 9am–5:30pm daily (last adm: 4pm). Hours may vary so call or check website. **Closed** Thanksgiving, Dec 25.
🎦 ♿ 🖥 🌐 worldofcoca-cola.com

World of Coca-Cola displays the world's largest collection of Coke memorabilia. Visitors can watch a 4D presentation,

The Centennial Olympic Park in downtown Atlanta

see a production line in operation, and sample from a range of 60 products.

## 🐟 Georgia Aquarium

225 Baker St. **Tel** (404) 581-4000.
**Open** 10am–5pm Sun–Fri, 9am–6pm Sat. 🎦 ♿ 🖥
🌐 georgiaaquarium.org

One of the world's largest aquariums housing 500 marine species in five habitats. The Ocean Voyageur features manta rays, whale sharks, and thousands of other fish in the six-million-gallon exhibit – the largest aquarium habitat in the world. Other tanks feature a brilliant rainbow of colored tropical fish.

## 🎬 CNN Studio

Marietta St at Techwood Dr. **Tel** (404) 827-2300.
**Open** 9am–5pm daily. 🎦 **Closed** Easter, Thanksgiving, Dec 25. ♿ with advance notice.

A 55-minute guided tour of CNN Studio takes visitors through the inner workings of the world's first 24-hour news station, located in a 14-story atrium global headquarters. Book in advance for the tour. The lobby gift shop sells merchandise ranging from Atlanta Braves paraphernalia to videos of Desert Storm coverage.

## 🏛 Martin Luther King Jr. National Historic Site

450 Auburn Ave. **Tel** (404) 331-5190.
**Open** 9am–5pm or 6pm. **Closed** Dec 25. ♿ 🌐 nps.gov/malu

Situated in a long reflecting pool beside an eternal flame, the crypt of the Nobel Peace Prize-winner Dr. Martin Luther King Jr. is a pilgrimage site for people from all over the world. The pool lies within the complex of the Center for Nonviolent Social Change, which has a gallery displaying portraits and memorabilia. Also located nearby is the original **Ebenezer Baptist Church**, where Martin Luther King Jr., his father, and grandfather presided. **The Martin Luther King Birthplace** is down the street to the east, while the **National Park Service Visitor Center**, housing portraits and exhibits that relate the area's role in the Civil Rights Movement, is right across the street.

This district preserves the heart of the **Sweet Auburn** neighborhood, which was the center of African-American life in the early 1900s.

Margaret Mitchell

## 🏛 Margaret Mitchell House and Museum

990 Peachtree St. **Tel** (404) 249-7015. **Open** 10am–5:30pm Mon–Sat, noon–5:30pm Sun. **Closed** Jan 1, Thanksgiving, Dec 24 & 25. 🎦 ♿ 🌐 atlantahistorycenter.com/mmh

Margaret Mitchell (1900–1949) wrote her magnum opus, *Gone With the Wind*, here in a basement apartment she affectionately called "the Dump." The three-story Tudor Revival house has had a dramatic history. It was abandoned, threatened by urban renewal, and then

The pool, eternal flame, and crypt at Dr. Martin Luther King Jr. National Historic Site

*For hotels and restaurants see pp276–81*

High Museum of Art, Atlanta

torched several times by arsonists, once on the eve of the Olympics opening. Various exhibits tell the story of the Georgia-born writer and reveal the extent of the house's restoration. Mementos from the famous film, such as Scarlett O'Hara's bonnet, are also on display.

### 🏛 High Museum of Art

1280 Peachtree St NE. **Tel** (404) 733-4444. **Open** 10am–5pm Mon–Sat, noon–5pm Sun. **Closed** public hols.
🅿 ♿ 🆆 high.org

One of the country's best museums, the High Museum of Art lies in the city's premier arts district and is housed behind a colorful Alexander Calder sculpture in a strikingly modern Richard Meier structure. The museum doubled in size with the addition of Renzo Piano's

sculpturally styled buildings and open plaza. Its extensive permanent collection careens from regional folk art and 19th-century American art to 18th-century Asian ceramics and sub-Saharan artifacts. Among the museum's packed calendar of events are blockbuster traveling exhibits, art films, make-art events, and lectures.

### 🏛 Atlanta History Center

130 W Paces Ferry Rd. **Tel** (404) 814-4000. **Open** 10am–5:30pm Mon–Sat, noon–5:30pm Sun. 🅿 ♿
🆆 atlantahistorycenter.com

The center contains a museum and two historic houses. Exhibits such as **Shaping Traditions: Folk Arts in a Changing South** trace the evolving character of Southern Folk Art.

Contrasting examples of rural and urban life are presented in the two houses. The Tullie Smith Farm, with its livestock and traditional crafts demonstrations, is a typical mid-1800s farmhouse, while the elegant 1928 Swan House has a grand interior staircase and swan motifs throughout.

### 🏛 Fernbank Natural History Museum

767 Clifton Rd NE. **Tel** (404) 929-6300. **Open** 10am–5pm Mon–Sat, noon–5pm Sun. **Closed** Thanksg., Dec 25.
🅿 ♿ 🆆 fernbankmuseum.org

This museum is housed in a striking modern building centered around a skylit four-story atrium. It has natural history exhibits ranging from plate tectonics to bubble science. Of local interest is its coverage of Georgia's diverse ecosystems, including the Appalachian forest, the coastal plain, and a particular favorite, the exotic Okefenokee Swamp habitat (see p259). The museum's IMAX® Theater features frequent "IMAX® and Martinis" nights, and there is also an on-site café. A number of in-town nature trails weave through the forest outside.

### 🏛 Jimmy Carter Library & Museum

441 Freedom Pkwy. **Tel** (404) 865-7100. **Open** 9am–4:45pm Mon–Sat, noon–4:45pm Sun. **Closed** Jan 1, Thanksgiving, Dec 25. 🅿 ♿
🆆 jimmycarterlibrary.gov

Located on a hilltop site 2 miles (3 km) from downtown Atlanta, the library highlights the humanitarian successes of President Carter's administration (see p260). These include the Camp David accords, Panama Canal treaties, and human-rights and energy policies. A popular attraction is an exact replica of the Oval Office at the White House as used by President Carter from 1977 to 1981.

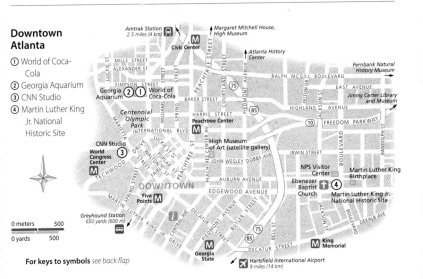

## Downtown Atlanta

① World of Coca-Cola
② Georgia Aquarium
③ CNN Studio
④ Martin Luther King Jr. National Historic Site

For keys to symbols *see back flap*

# Tennessee

Tennessee is made up of three distinct regions. Memphis anchors the western lowlands along the Mississippi River; Nashville, the state capital, heads the central plateau; and the east is dominated by the Appalachian Mountains, with Knoxville as its urban base. With the Cumberland and Tennessee Rivers feeding into the Ohio, then into the Mississippi, the state was well positioned to prosper from the steamboat trade, and later, the railroads. During the Civil War, Chattanooga was the scene of battles, while Memphis and Nashville were occupied by Union forces. Today, Tennessee is known for its tremendous contribution to American roots music, from bluegrass, country, gospel, and blues, to rockabilly, rock 'n' roll, and soul.

Visitors at a preserved log cabin, Cades Cove

## 🟢 Great Smoky Mountains National Park

ℹ️ US Hwy 441, Gatlinburg, (865) 436-1200. **Open** daily. ♿
🌐 nps.gov/grsm

The "Smokies," which earn their name from the smoke-like haze that clings to the ridge, hold some of the highest peaks in eastern US and support a diversity of plant life. With more than 10 million visitors each year, this is one of the country's most visited parks. Established as a national park in 1934, half of it is in Tennessee and the other half in North Carolina. The Tennessee entrance is through Gatlinburg and Hwy 441, which bisects this sprawling park along the Newfound Gap Road and meets up with the Blue Ridge Parkway (see p251) on the North Carolina side. Of the 800 miles (1,287 km) of trails, the most popular is the **Appalachian Trail**, which

straddles the state border through the park. Trails to the park's many scenic waterfalls are also popular. The hike to **Mount LeConte** offers panoramic views, and there is even a hike-in lodge that provides rustic overnight accommodations, for which reservations are required. The 6,643-ft- (2,025-m-) tall **Clingman's Dome**, Tennessee's highest peak, has an observation tower that offers fine views of the surrounding

landscape. At the western end of the Great Smoky Mountains National Park, **Cades Cove** still preserves the historic farm buildings that were erected back in the 1820s. These include structures such as log cabins, barns, and a still operating gristmill. Bicycling, horseback riding, fishing, and white-water rafting are some of the popular activities available to adventurous tourists in this beautiful park and its surrounding region.

Spectacular view from Clingman's Dome

### Flora of the Great Smoky Mountains

Sugar Maple

Magnolia

Mountain Laurel

Rhododendron

Famed for its incredible biodiversity, the Great Smoky Mountains shelter more than 1,500 species of flowering plants, including some 143 species of trees. The mountains' hardwood forests are made up of sugar maples, yellow birches, and poplars, while its spruce-fir forests are dominated by coniferous red spruce and Frasier fir. The understory consists of dense rhododendron and mountain laurel. Closely interwoven with Appalachian culture, the forest produces honeysuckle vines for basketry and various hardwoods for whittling and musical instruments, in addition to offering wild berries and fruits, medicinal plants (including ginseng), and harboring wild game.

# ㉓ Chattanooga

🏛 171,000. ✈ 🚌 ℹ 215 Broad St, (800) 322-3344.

🌐 chattanoogafun.com

Located on the banks of the Tennessee River along the Georgia border, Chattanooga is surrounded by several high landmasses – the plateaus of Lookout Mountain, Signal Mountain, and Missionary Ridge. Founded as a ferry landing by the Cherokee Indian Chief John Ross in 1815, Chattanooga was later occupied by white settlers after the Cherokees were forced out from here along the tragic "Trail of Tears" to Oklahoma in 1838 *(see p56)*. The railroad leading to Atlanta provided a natural target for the Union Army during the Civil War, and several battles were fought on this dramatic terrain.

Downtown Chattanooga is today a revitalized center surrounding the original site of the ferry landing known as Ross's Landing. Within this compact area are many of the city's most popular attractions such as the Chattanooga Regional History Museum, which covers the area's local history – Native American, Civil War, and cultural; the **Tennessee Aquarium**; the attractive Riverwalk promenade; and the pedestrian-only Walnut Street Bridge that spans the river to

Former Chickamauga battlefield, with cannons, statuary, and memorials

The Tennessee Aquarium, Chattanooga

Coolidge Park and Carousel. At the Tennessee Aquarium, visitors can trace the journey of a single drop of water from its origins in the Smoky Mountains through rivers, reservoirs, and deltas, then out into the Gulf of Mexico. Over 9,000 species of fish, amphibians, reptiles, mammals, and birds illustrate the state's varied habitats and ecosystems. An IMAX® Theater lies adjacent.

A short drive south of downtown on East Brow Road, the homespun **Battles for Chattanooga Electric Map** was originally known as "Confederama." It tells the story of local Civil War battles with 5,000 miniature soldiers and a series of tiny lights on large boards which are used to represent the advancing Confederate and Union troops. At the foot of Lookout Mountain, the station at St. Elmo Avenue is the start point for the mile-long **Lookout Mountain Incline Railway**. The train climbs a gradient of 72.7 percent up the side of Lookout Mountain for panoramic views. It was built in the 1890s to bring tourists up to the hotels that were once located on top. The **Chickamauga and Chattanooga National Military Park** of Point Park is a three-block walk away.

Lookout Mountain Incline Railway

The other section of the military park is the Chickamauga battlefield near Fort Oglethorpe across the border in northwest Georgia. The site at Point Park commemorates all the brave Confederate and Union soldiers who fought on the precipitous slopes of this steep plateau in the Battle Above the Clouds in 1863. This battle took place after Union forces were able to reverse an earlier Confederate victory and planted the US flag on the top of Lookout Mountain. At **Ruby Falls**, 3 miles (5 km) away, visitors descend by elevator to the floor of a cave, then walk past stalactites and stalagmites to the 145-ft (44-m) waterfall. A light show transforms the lovely natural surroundings of the falls into a somewhat gaudy display.

On the Georgia side of Lookout Mountain, **Rock City Gardens** has natural limestone rock formations beautified by the Enchanted Trail, a Lover's Leap, and little gnomes peering out from the crevices.

🐠 **Tennessee Aquarium**
1 Broad St. **Tel** (423) 265-0695. **Open** 10am–6pm daily. **Closed** Thanksgiving, Dec 25. 🅿 ♿ 🌐 tnaqua.org

🏛 **Chickamauga & Chattanooga National Military Park**
110 Point Park Rd. **Tel** (423) 821-7786. **Open** 8:30am–5pm daily. **Closed** Dec 25. ♿ 🌐 nps.gov/chch

🧗 **Ruby Falls**
**Tel** (423) 821-2544. **Open** 8am–8pm daily. **Closed** Dec 25. 🅿
🌐 rubyfalls.com

## ㉔ Nashville

🏙 609,600. ✈ 🚌 ℹ Broadway at Fifth St, (615) 259-4747.
🌐 **visitmusiccity.com**

Best known today as the capital of country music, Nashville is a friendly and fun place to visit. Its musical history dates to 1927, when a radio broadcaster, changing from music from the Grand Opera to the more popular Barn Dance show, introduced the upcoming selection as the "Grand Ole Opry." A musical legend was thus born and has flourished ever since. The city, however, has more to it than just music. It was founded as Fort Nashborough on the banks of the Cumberland River in 1779 and was named the state capital of Tennessee in 1843. It is also the financial center of the region and home to Vanderbilt University, one of the country's most prestigious institutions.

### Exploring Nashville

Nashville's vibrant downtown area is anchored by the Country Music Hall of Fame. Most of the city's major attractions are within comfortable walking distance, such as the imposing **State Capitol** at the top of the hill, the historic Ryman Auditorium on Fifth Avenue, and the scenic riverfront with its reconstructed fort – a replica of the original outpost. Plenty of restaurants, cafés, and nightclubs lie in the surrounding area, locally known as "the District." Devoted

Nashville's scenic riverfront

country music fans might want to venture 10 miles (16 km) east to see the Grand Ole Opry House. A similar trip 1.5 miles (2.4 km) west of downtown to Music Row, the heart of Nashville's recording industry, might also interest ardent fans or aspiring songwriters.

### 🏛 Country Music Hall of Fame & Museum

222 Fifth Ave S. **Tel** (615) 416-2001. **Open** 9am–5pm daily. **Closed** Tue (Jan–Feb), Jan 1, Thanksgiving, Dec 25. 🅿 ♿
🌐 **countrymusichalloffame.org**

Legendary Hank Williams

"Spreading the gospel of country music," the Country Music Hall of Fame honors scores of such outstanding musicians as Patsy Cline, Merle Haggard, and Hank Williams in a huge rotunda at a grand downtown location. In keeping with its exhibits, the building itself has been specially designed to resemble the black and white keys of a giant piano. Inside there is a beloved collection of vintage guitars, costumes, string ties, cowboy boots, well-known lyrics composed on bar napkins, and the celebrated golden Elvis Cadillac. A country music primer explains the academic distinctions between the subgenres of bluegrass, Cajun, honky-tonk, and rockabilly.

### 🎭 Ryman Auditorium

116 Fifth Ave N. **Tel** (615) 889-3060. **Open** 9am–4pm.
**Closed** Thanksgiving, Dec 25. 🅿 ♿
🌐 **ryman.com**

This landmark auditorium is still an evocative setting for live performances. The Grand Ole Opry was broadcast from here for 31 years, from 1943 to 1974, when it moved to the new Opry House. Daytime tours of the Mother Church of Country Music are available, but the best way to see the 2,000-seat theater is by taking in a show; performers from B.B. King to the Dixie Chicks and Sheryl Crow are typical of the

Façade of the Ryman Auditorium, a Nashville landmark

diverse all-star lineup. Within a few blocks of Ryman Auditorium, the modern **Nashville Convention Center**, **Bridgestone Arena**, and nightclubs also feature all kinds of music – country, bluegrass, and blues.

### 🏛 Musicians Hall of Fame at Nashville Municipal Auditorium

417 Fourth Ave N. **Tel** (615) 244-3263. **Open** 10am–5pm Mon–Sat. **Closed** Jan 1, Easter, Jul 4, Thanksgiving, Dec 25. 🅿 ♿ 🌐 **musicians halloffame.com**

Learn all about the musicians who created the greatest recordings of all time at the Musicians Hall of Fame. Visitors can see guitars, drums, and other instruments played by musicians such as Jimi Hendrix, as well as those played by such lesser-known session musicians as drummer Hal Blaine.

### 🏛 Tennessee State Museum

505 Deaderick St. **Tel** (615) 741-2692. **Open** 10am–5pm Tue–Sat, 1–5pm Sun. **Closed** public hols. ♿
🌐 **tnmuseum.org**

Although the main focus of this museum is the Civil War, it also covers other aspects of the state's past. Starting with a dugout canoe, exhibits showcase local Native American history, early pioneer life, slavery, the Civil Rights Movement, the river trade, and the Natchez Trace route. There is also a large collection of 19th-century decorative arts, such as European and American antique furnishings.

Exterior of the Grand Ole Opry House in Nashville

### 🏛 Grand Ole Opry House

2804 Opryland Dr. **Tel** (615) 871-6779.
**Open** some evenings, call in advance
for tickets and show information. 🅿
♿ **W** opry.com

Located 10 miles (16 km)
east of downtown in a gulch
of Opry-themed development
called Music Valley, the
4,400-seat modern Opry House
continues the "world's longest
running radio show" beyond its
75th year. The Who's Who of
country music grace the stage
of this legendary institution (live
broadcast on 650 WSM-AM).
The nearby Grand Ole Opry
Museum tells the Opry story
with wax figurines. The
complex contains the fabulous
Opryland Hotel with its
spectacular indoor gardens.

### 🏛 Belle Meade Plantation

110 Leake Ave. **Tel** (615) 356-0501.
**Open** 9am–5pm Mon–Sat,
11am–5pm Sun. **Closed** Jan 1,
Thanksgiving, Dec 25. 🅿 ♿ partial.
**W** bellemeadeplantation.com

A 20-minute drive southwest of
downtown, Belle Meade is
among the state's best-
preserved antebellum estates.
The 1853 Greek Revival mansion
was once the centerpiece of a
5,300 acre (2144.8 ha)
plantation and has been
restored to its former splendor.
Guides in period costume
offer tours of the mansion
and outbuildings, including an
1832 slave cabin. A Sunday
summer concert series features
live performances on the
spacious grounds.

### 🏛 The Hermitage

4580 Rachel's Lane. **Tel** (615) 889-2941.
**Open** Apr–mid-Oct: 8:30am–5pm;
mid-Oct–Mar: 9am–4:30pm. **Closed**
3rd week in Jan, Thanksg., Dec 25. 🅿
**W** thehermitage.com

The home of Tennessee's foremost political and military hero,
Andrew Jackson, this estate is a
20-minute drive east of downtown. After distinguishing himself
as a military leader in the War of
1812, Jackson became the state's
single Congressional representative before Tennessee gained
statehood. He was elected the
seventh president of the United
States in 1828 and re-elected in
1832, serving two terms. Most
of the contents of the house
remain intact from Jackson's
time. He is buried in the garden.

### 🏛 Natchez Trace Parkway

Originally a series of Indian trails,
the Natchez Trace Parkway,
which links Nashville with
Natchez in Mississippi, is today
a national historic parkway
*(see p362)*. Its northern terminus
lies 15 miles (24 km) southwest
of town. Here, the contour of
the Trace is more rolling and
deeply forested than farther
down in Mississippi.

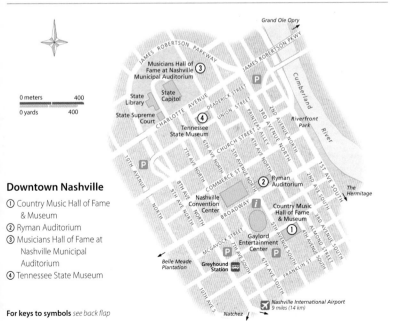

## Downtown Nashville

① Country Music Hall of Fame
   & Museum
② Ryman Auditorium
③ Musicians Hall of Fame at
   Nashville Municipal
   Auditorium
④ Tennessee State Museum

**For keys to symbols** *see back flap*

A neon B.B. King's Blues Club sign on Beale Street

# ㉕ Memphis

🏙 655,000. 🚉 🚌 🚗 ℹ 119 N Riverside Dr, (901) 543-5333.
🅆 **memphistravel.com**

Memphis sits on the banks of the Mississippi River at Tennessee's southwestern corner, where it meets the states of Arkansas and Mississippi. The city is most closely associated with two very different American icons – Civil Rights leader Dr. Martin Luther King Jr., and the singer Elvis Presley.

Since the early 20th century, Memphis has been synonymous with music. As the birthplace of rock 'n' roll, which originated from blues (see p361), the city celebrates this legacy in its many nightclubs and saloons, and out on the streets. Even its festivals revolve around music. Highlights include Elvis's birthday on January 8; "Memphis in May," a month-long series of concerts and cookouts (Memphis is also famous for its barbecue); the W.C. Handy Awards, the blues answer to the Grammys, also in May; Elvis Week or "Tribute Week" around August 16; and the Music and Heritage Festival on Labor Day weekend.

B.B. King, Rock-N-Soul Museum

## 🏛 Beale Street
A thriving commercial center for the city's African-American community, Beale Street's heyday was in the first half of the 20th century. After a period of decline, this historic street has now been resurrected as the heart of a vibrant entertainment district, rivaling New Orleans' Bourbon Street (see p348) in popularity. Restaurants, nightclubs, saloons, and shops line a four-block stretch. Many statues also punctuate the strip on either side. There is one of Elvis Presley opposite the Orpheum Theatre, and one of W.C. Handy stands at the entrance to a plaza where many outdoor festivals take place. A block away, **W.C. Handy's Home**, a tiny white shotgun shack, is now a museum to the man who has often been called the "Father of the Blues."

At the center of the strip stands the **A. Schwab's Dry Goods Store** at 163 Beale. This shop has been open here since 1876. Many nights Beale Street is closed to traffic, and people come to listen to live music emanating from every door. A short walk from Beale Street, **AutoZone Park** is the red and green stadium of the Memphis Redbirds baseball franchise. It lies across from the landmark **Peabody Hotel** at 149 Union Avenue, where the famous ducks march twice a day to and from the lobby to the fountain where they can be seen frolicking all day (see p278).

## 🏛 National Civil Rights Museum
450 Mulberry St. **Tel** (901) 521-9699.
**Open** 9am–5pm Mon–Sat, 1–5pm Sun. **Closed** Tue. 🅿 🚻
🅆 **civilrightsmuseum.org**

The museum was once the Lorraine Motel, where Dr. Martin Luther King Jr. was tragically assassinated on April 4, 1968. Room 306 is preserved as it was on the day of his killing and a memorial wreath rests outside the window. Across the street, the assassination scene is re-created in the bathroom from which James Earl Ray apparently fired his fatal shot.

## 🏛 Memphis Rock-N-Soul Museum
Fedex Forum, 191 Beale St. **Tel** (901) 205-2533. **Open** 10am–7pm daily. **Closed** Jan 1, Thanksg., Dec 25. 🅿 🚻 🅆 **memphisrocknsoul.org**

The intersection between history and race, and its expression in song, is explained with outstanding musical accompaniment at this museum. It is located opposite the Gibson Guitar factory, which offers a fascinating tour. The exhibit is sponsored by the Smithsonian Institute and examines the blues and country roots of rock 'n' roll with a fascinating movie, and displays of old instruments as well as vintage jukeboxes, stage costumes, and profiles of artists. A digital audio tour features more than six hours of fabulous music. Music fans may want to travel 10 minutes south to the Stax Museum of American Soul Music, in the old Stax Records recording studio.

## 🏛 Mud Island
Via Front & Main Sts. **Tel** (901) 576-7241. **Open** early Apr–Oct: 10am–5pm Tue–Sun. 🅿 🚻 🅆 **mudisland.com**
Reached via monorail, Mud Island holds the **Mississippi River Museum**, which tells the story of the river with artifacts such as an 1870 steamboat replica. The museum also has many Native American exhibits and galleries on the origins of the blues as an influential musical form. The most engaging exhibit, however, is located outside where water courses through a replica of the Mississippi for a five-block-long stretch, ending at a swimming pool shaped like the Gulf of Mexico.

Elvis Presley's grave in his lavish Graceland estate

### Center for Southern Folklore

119 S Main St. **Tel** (901) 525-3655. **Open** 11am–5pm Mon–Fri, 11am–6pm Sat. **Closed** Thanksgiving, Dec 25. ☑ hourly. ☑ shows. ♿
**W** southernfolklore.com

A touchstone for all that is authentically Southern, the center offers a great café, folk art gallery, gift shop, and a stage for shows ranging from jug bands to puppetry, with plenty of blues, soul, folk, rock, and gospel in between. It also sponsors the acclaimed Music and Heritage Festival.

### Sun Studio

706 Union Ave. **Tel** (901) 521-0664. **Open** 10am–6pm daily. **Closed** Thanksgiving, Dec 25. ☑ ♿
**W** sunstudio.com

Famous musicians from all over the world come to record in the legendary studio that launched the careers of Elvis, B.B. King, Johnny Cash, Jerry Lee Lewis, Roy Orbison, and others. Founded in 1954 by Sam Philips, the studio's exhibits include Elvis's original drum set and microphone. Souvenir items with the familiar yellow rooster logo are on sale, and visitors can also make their own souvenir recordings.

### Graceland

3734 Elvis Presley Blvd. **Tel** (901) 332-3322. **Open** 9am–5pm Mon–Sat, 10am–4pm Sun (but times can vary). **Closed** Tue (Dec–Feb), Jan 1, Thanksgiving, Dec 25. ☑ ♿
**W** elvis.com

A 10-minute drive from downtown, Graceland attracts more than 700,000 visitors each year to the estate that Elvis Presley bought as a 22-year-old superstar and called his home until his death in 1977.

Starting at the grand visitor complex, guests are taken by van through the metal gates up the drive to the house to view the front rooms, famous Jungle Room den, gallery, racquetball court, and Memorial Gardens, where Elvis is buried. The tour is self-guided. Across the street, additional admission charges are needed to see Elvis's car collection, his two airplanes, and a **Sincerely Elvis** exhibit with home movies and personal effects. Unofficial souvenir shops along **Elvis Presley Boulevard** offer some bizarre but entertaining items, such as Elvis-emblazoned nail clippers and beach towels.

### Full Gospel Tabernacle Church

787 Hale Rd. **Tel** (901) 396-9192. ✝ 11am Sun. ☑ donation.
The Reverend Al Green left a successful recording career in the 1970s (his hits included songs such as "Tired of Being Alone") to pursue his calling. He often presides over Sunday services at his church in South-side Memphis, not far from Graceland. Visitors to the electric gospel service should show respect by wearing decent attire, donating a little, and staying for the entire service.

## Downtown Memphis

① Beale Street
② National Civil Rights Museum
③ Memphis Rock-N-Soul Museum
④ Mud Island
⑤ Center for Southern Folklore

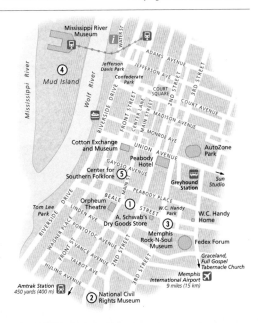

0 meters ———— 500
0 yards ———— 500

**For keys to symbols** see back flap

# Kentucky

With its Appalachian Mountain landscapes and rolling rural pasturelands, where horses run on acres and acres of bluegrass, Kentucky is easily one of the most picturesque states in the country. The lands west of the mountains were once inhabited by Indian tribes who strenuously opposed the encroachment of white settlers. Today, Kentucky is widely known for its horses, and many thoroughbred stud farms are centered around Lexington. One of the most prestigious horse races, the Kentucky Derby, takes place in Louisville. This state is also famous for its downhome style of country music, and Hwy 23 along its eastern border has been designated the Country Music Highway.

A cannon at Fort McCook, Cumberland Gap National Historic Park

## ❽ Cumberland Gap National Historic Park

US Hwy 25 E, Middlesboro. ℹ️ (606) 248-2817. **Open** 8am–5pm daily. **Closed** Dec 25. ♿ 🅦 nps.gov/cuga

Situated in the southeastern corner where Kentucky meets the states of Virginia and Tennessee, the Cumberland Gap is a natural pass through the Cumberland Mountains, once used by migrating deer and bison. It was first explored by Dr. Thomas Walker in 1750 on behalf of a land company. Some five years later, the legendary fur trapper and explorer Daniel Boone ran his Wilderness Road through the Gap, thus opening the way for some 200,000 pioneers to establish homesteads in the interior wilderness.

This rugged area is thickly forested, and many sights, such as the Sand Cave sandstone overhang and White Rocks sandstone outcrop, are accessible only by hiking trails. The hardwood and softwood forests shelter wild turkeys, white-tailed deer, and many varieties of songbirds.

The Gap was also a strategic point in the Civil War. It was held alternately by Confederate and Union forces, and the fortifications can still be seen throughout the park. Today, a four-lane Interstate Highway and a railroad tunnel run through the Gap. A drive up to **Pinnacle Overlook** leads to a short trail for a view of three states, most dramatic during fall.

## ㉗ Mammoth Cave National Park

I-65 exit 53. ℹ️ (270) 758-2180. **Open** Mar–Oct: 8am–6pm daily, Nov–Feb: 8:45am–5pm. **Closed** Dec 25. 🎟️ fee.

Halfway between Louisville (see p273) and Nashville (see p266), this park offers guided tours of one of the largest cave systems known, formed by underground rivers that left a dramatic landscape of stalactites and stalagmites. Guests are free to choose from tours with names such as "Historic" or "Wild Cave Tour" (helmets provided). Evidence suggests that the cave had been inhabited as far back as 4,000 years ago. The Green River runs its course above Mammoth Cave, an area that is crisscrossed by several hiking trails.

## ㉘ Berea

🏨 14,200. ℹ️ (800) 598-5263. 🎪 Berea Crafts Festival (Jul). 🅦 berea.com

Home to Berea College, dedicated to educating disadvantaged Appalachian youth, Berea is known as a highlands crafts center. Typical crafts include woodworking, pottery, and textiles. The town hosts the Kentucky Guild of Artists Fair, the Craftmen's Fair, as well as the Berea Crafts Festival. Year-round, there are public tours of artisans' studios, such as **Weaver's Bottom**, founded in 1983.

### 🏛️ Weaver's Bottom

140 N Broadway. **Tel** (859) 986-8661. **Open** 9am–5pm Mon–Sat. **Closed** Dec 25. 🔗

The path leading into the interior of Mammoth Cave

View of dense forest foliage from the Zilpo Road National Scenic Byway, Daniel Boone National Forest

## ㉙ Daniel Boone National Forest

1700 Bypass Rd, Winchester. **i** (859) 745-3100. **Open** 8am–4:30pm daily. **Closed** Jan 1, Thanksg., Dec 25. **W** fs.usda.gov/dbnf

Named after the legendary pioneer and fur trapper Daniel Boone, who lived in Kentucky, this National Forest protects some of the most dramatic scenery in the state. The dense forest provides shelter to over 35 endangered species, including red-cockaded woodpeckers, big-eared bats, and bald eagles. The **Sheltowee Trace National Recreation Trail** runs the entire 260-mile (418-km) length of the forest, from Morehead near the Ohio border in the north to Pickett State Rustic Park in Tenessee. Also near Morehead, **Cave Run Lake** is popular for boating, and

the **Zilpo Road National Scenic Byway** offers a good chance to see the forest's rich variety of wildlife on a short drive. The central area east of Stanton features the **Natural Bridge State Resort Park**, a naturally occuring archway surrounded by rugged terrain, and the picturesque **Red River Gorge**, both of which offer great hiking, canoeing, and white-water rafting opportunities. At the southern end, **Cumberland Falls State Resort Park** offers lodging, camping, and swimming.

### 🏕 Cumberland Falls State Resort Park

7351 Hwy 90, Corbin. **Tel** (606) 528-4121. **Open** daily. **&** **W** parks.ky.gov

### Environs

Visitors to the southern portion of the park might want to detour to **Corbin**, off I-75, 50 miles (80 km) north of the state's southern border with Tennessee. Corbin is notable as the original home of Kentucky Fried Chicken, where Colonel Harland Sanders first served the special recipe that went on to become a global franchise. The kitchen where the famous herbs and spices were first put together is on display, along with KFC artifacts.

Chairlifts carrying visitors up to the Natural Bridge

## Country & Bluegrass Music

Country singer Billy Ray Cyrus in concert

As the Mississippi Delta is to blues music, so the stretch of eastern Kentucky (along with West Virginia) is home to the greatest proportion of country music artists in America. British, Irish, and Scottish immigrants brought Elizabethan ballads, rhythms, and instruments to the area, which they then forged into a distinctly American style known as "country." It was characterized by fast fiddling, occasional yodeling, and laments on the hardscrabble life of the American Southeast. Hwy 23, which runs from Ashland to Pikeville along the state's eastern border, has been dubbed the "Country Music Highway" to commemorate the vast number of artists who come from here. Along its length, the route passes by the hometowns of Billy Ray Cyrus, the Judds, Loretta Lynn, Patty Loveless, and Dwight Yoakum.

Kentucky's vast bluegrass pasturelands defined a particular style of country music known as "bluegrass." This evolved from the musical style played in the late 1940s by Bill Monroe and his Bluegrass Boys. The name "bluegrass" stuck, and this acoustic folk style remains popular in the region today. Traditional bluegrass acoustic stringed instrucments include the fiddle, guitar, mandolin, five-string banjo, and bass and dobro guitars. Song lyrics are usually about the everyday lives of the people from whom the music originated.

Thoroughbred racehorses grazing in pastures near Lexington

## ⑳ Lexington

🏛 305,500. ✈ 🚌 ℹ 301 E Vine St, (859) 233-1221. 🌐 visitlex.com

Kentucky's second largest city, Lexington is also the capital of the state's horse country. The surrounding bluegrass-covered countryside is lined with hundreds of thoroughbred stud farms, where many Kentucky Derby winners are bred, reared, and trained. Most farms are open to visitors, who are welcome either on their own with advance reservations or as part of an organized tour. The visitor center supplies lists of farms and tour operators.

About 6 miles (9.6 km) north of town lies the **Kentucky Horse Park**, a state-operated working farm that serves as an equestrian theme park. Here, visitors can watch live shows, ride ponies, sign up for escorted trail rides, take carriage tours, and go swimming and camping. The park's **International Museum of the Horse** is a monument to the role of the

horse in the development of human history. The adjacent **American Saddlebred Museum** is named for, and focuses on, America's first registered horse breed. Outside, the Man o' War Memorial marks the grave of the beloved thoroughbred who won several acclaimed races. In town, the 1803 **Mary Todd Lincoln House** preserves the girlhood home of Abraham Lincoln's wife.

🏛 **Kentucky Horse Park**
4089 Iron Works Pkwy. **Tel** (859) 233-4303. **Open** mid-Mar–Oct: 9am–5pm daily. **Closed** Nov–mid-Mar: Mon & Tue, major public hols. 🎫 ♿
🌐 kyhorsepark.com

## ㉛ Harrodsburg

🏛 8,300. ✈ 🚌 ℹ 124 S Main St, (859) 734-2364.
🌐 harrodsburgky.com

A large number of Shaker families from New England relocated in and around Harrodsburg in 1805 and

established a farming community renowned for its handicrafts. It grew to a sizeable population of around 500 in 1830 and then, in part due to the Shaker belief in celibacy, it grew less cohesive and became scattered by 1910. The area's premier attraction is the **Shaker Village of Pleasant Hill**, America's finest, largest, and most completely restored Shaker community and living-history museum. The architecture and furnishings at the village reflect the spare, utilitarian style that typifies the Shaker values. Artisans demonstrate crafts such as woodworking and weaving.

🏛 **Shaker Village of Pleasant Hill**
3501 Lexington Rd. **Tel** (859) 734-5611. **Open** 10am–5pm daily (to 4:30pm Nov–Mar). **Closed** Dec 24 & 25. 🎫 ♿ partial.
🌐 shakervillageky.org

## ㉜ Hodgenville

🏛 3,200. ℹ 72 Lincoln Square, (270) 358-3411.

Hodgenville is the base for the **Abraham Lincoln Birthplace National Historic Site**, located 3 miles (5 km) to its south. The site commemorates the 16th US president's Kentucky roots by preserving his childhood home. Here, 56 steps representing the years of Lincoln's life lead up to a granite-and-marble Memorial Building built around a 19th-century log cabin, where the president was born. The site

Barrel making in the Shaker Village of Pleasant Hill, Harrodsburg

*For hotels and restaurants see pp276–81*

also encompasses a large portion of the original Lincoln family farmland.

### 🏛 Abraham Lincoln Birthplace National Historic Site

7120 Bardstown Rd (Hwy 31 E). **Tel** (270) 358-3137. **Open** 8am–4:45pm or 6:45pm (seasonal). **Closed** Jan 1, Thanksg., Dec 25. ♿ Ⓦ **nps.gov/abli**

The Hodgenville log cabin in which Abraham Lincoln was born

## ㉝ Bardstown

🏠 12,800. 🛈 107 E Stephen Foster Ave, (502) 348-4877.
Ⓦ **visitbardstown.com**

The self-proclaimed "Bourbon Capital of the World," Bardstown is surrounded by the state's largest whiskey distilleries, which have earned Kentucky its legendary reputation as the whiskey-making center of the US. (Bourbon is made from corn, malt, and rye, and is aged in charred white oak barrels.) The most popular distillery, James Beam, known in countless country songs as "Jim Beam," lies 14 miles (22.5 km) west of Bardstown, while a 20-mile (32-km) drive south leads to the famed Maker's Mark distillery, Kentucky's oldest distillery operating in the same site.

Stephen Foster statue, My Old Kentucky Home State Park, Bardstown

However, Bardtown's most popular attraction is **My Old Kentucky Home State Park.** Here, guides lead visitors through the historic mansion that, according to legend, inspired composer Stephen Foster to write "My Old Kentucky Home," the state's beloved anthem. The park also hosts outdoor musicals.

### 🏛 My Old Kentucky Home State Park

US Hwy 150. **Tel** (502) 348-3502. **Open** 9am–5pm daily. **Closed** Thanksgiving, late Dec–early Jan. ♿ ♿

## ㉞ Louisville

🏠 253,000. ✈ 🚌 🛈 30 Market St, (502) 584-2121.

Founded at the falls of the Ohio River in 1788, Louisville (pronounced "Looavul") is home to one of the world's most famous horse races, the Kentucky Derby. What Mardi Gras is to New Orleans, or the Masters Tournament is to Augusta, the Derby is to Louisville – it is the event around which all local calendars revolve. Since it first began in 1875, three-year-old horses have run the track at Churchill Downs on the first Saturday in May. Kentucky's high society turns out in spring finery for this social event of the year, with hats and seersucker suits constituting battle uniform. Mint juleps, the Southern concoction of bourbon, ice, sugar, and fresh mint are the unofficial beverage of choice. "My Old Kentucky Home" plays while the horses are led onto the track for an event that lasts less than two minutes. Winners take home the coveted trophy, decorated with lucky silver horseshoes in a "U" shape "so that the luck doesn't spill out." The adjacent **Kentucky Derby Museum** showcases horse-racing history and offers "backside track tours" through the Churchill Downs track. A couple of blocks from

Gigantic baseball bat outside the Louisville Slugger Museum

the historic district on the waterfront, the **Louisville Slugger Museum** produces the worldclass baseball bat in a factory marked by a landmark 120-ft- (36-m-) high bat.

The **Speed Art Museum** (located on East Market St until 2016 due to renovations) has a large collection of Renaissance paintings and sculpture. At the Riverfront Plaza on the banks of the Ohio River at Main and Fourth Streets, several paddle-wheelers tour the area, and a fountain periodically shoots water 375 ft (114.3 m) into the air. The surrounding historic district's old warehouses have been recast as cafés, galleries, and shops.

Located 2 miles (3.2 km) northeast of downtown, Cave Hill Cemetery is one of the largest and most beautiful in the US. Many Louisvillians go visit the grounds just to feed the ducks, or take in the landscaped lawns. Thirty miles (48.2 km) southwest of Louisville, the exterior of the federal gold bullion repository at **Fort Knox** can be seen.

### 🏛 Kentucky Derby Museum

704 Central Ave. **Tel** (502) 637-1111. **Open** 9am–5pm Mon–Sat (from 8am Mar 15–Nov 30), 11am–5pm Sun. **Closed** Breeder's cupdays, first Fri & Sat in May, Thanksgiving, Dec 25. ♿ ♿ Ⓦ **derbymuseum.org**

### 🏛 Louisville Slugger Museum

800 W Main St. **Tel** (877) 775-8443. **Open** 9am–5pm Mon–Sat, noon–5pm Sun (extended hours in summer). ♿ ♿ Ⓦ **sluggermuseum.com**

# Practical Information

Successful traveling around the Southeast requires a great deal of advance planning, as there is so much to see and do in the vast area. With miles of sandy beaches, picturesque historic cities such as Charleston, the stunning rugged wilderness of the Blue Ridge and Appalachian Mountains, and rolling hills and valleys of the foothills, the Southeast truly has it all. In addition to myriad natural wonders, the region also offers burgeoning commercial centers such as Atlanta, and engaging cultural towns including Memphis, the birthplace of the blues, and Nashville, the commercial and cultural capital of "country-western" music, arts, and entertainment.

## Tourist Information

Each of the five Southeast states, North Carolina, South Carolina, Kentucky, Tennessee, and Georgia, publishes travel information that can be ordered by phone or via websites. State "Welcome Centers" located along most major highways greet visitors as soon as they enter each of the Southeast states. Open between 8am and 5pm daily, these centers offer free road maps and a full range of tourist information, covering climate, transportation, attractions, and accommo-dations. More information is available from a multitude of tourism bureaus across the five states.

## Natural Hazards

The end of summer in the Southeast can be very pleasant, but this is also the main hurricane season, and potentially one of the most troubling times for visitors. Hurricane season stretches from August to the end of the year, but since storms form in the Atlantic Ocean near the Equator, emergency alert systems usually give at least a day or two warning before strong winds and heavy rains arrive.

Watch out for tornadoes and thunderstorms in late spring and summer, especially in the south, where they strike suddenly and create flash floods. If a tornado watch or warning is issued, take cover straight away.

## Getting Around

Like much of the US, the Southeast is a region where it can be hard to get around without a car. **Greyhound** buses do serve some larger towns and cities, and visitors can also take **Amtrak** trains to travel around the Southeast. Nevertheless, driving is the best way to get around the region, as public transportation can be limited. Seat belts are required for drivers and front-seat passengers in all of the five states. Most states also require seat belts for back-seat passengers, and child seats are required for all automobile occupants aged 4 and under. Speed limits vary, but are usually 70 to 75 mph (112 to 120 km/h) on Interstate Highways outside of densely populated urban areas, weather permitting.

## Etiquette

Compared to the rest of the country, Southerners are largely teetotal. Many of them are Baptists, a religion that frowns on the consumption of alcohol. "Dry" counties can still be found in some rural areas, particularly in the mountains where alcohol cannot be legally served or sold to the public. But exceptions to this tradition are legendary. Makers of "moonshine" a 100-proof home-made whiskey typically distilled from corn, gained an outlaw reputation in the days of the Prohibition for evading federal agents by hiding stills deep in the woods and working them by cover of darkness – hence the name "moonshine".

Drinking mint juleps on the day of the Kentucky Derby in Louisville is such a revered local custom that girls start collecting the traditional sterling silver "julep cups" as young as 12 years of age.

## Festivals

The southeast states stage a diverse range of annual community, regional, and national festivals. In February, cultural sites all over the Southeast, especially the Martin Luther King Jr. Center for Non-Violent Social Change in Atlanta, celebrate the **Black History Month** with various special programs. In March, Savannah, Georgia, hosts a lively

## The Climate of the Southeast

The region's states have a mild climate with temperatures rarely dipping below freezing in winter, though summer in the low-lying areas can be very hot. Spring sees azaleas and other blossom in the region's famous gardens. Summer, with its sunny days and warm water along sandy beaches, is the most popular time for travel. The end of summer is the primary hurricane season. In inland areas, leaves change color on mountain hardwood trees in October. In winter, snow can fall across many areas.

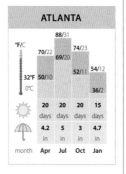

| ATLANTA | | | |
|---|---|---|---|
| | 88/31 | | |
| 70/22 | 74/23 | | |
| °F/C | 69/20 | | |
| | | 52/11 | 54/12 |
| 32°F 50/10 | | | 36/2 |
| 0°C | | | |
| 20 days | 20 days | 20 days | 15 days |
| 4.2 in | 5 in | 3 in | 4.7 in |
| month Apr | Jul | Oct | Jan |

St. Patrick's Day celebration, when thousands come together to drink beer, dance, sing, and celebrate real or imagined Irishness. March and April are also ideal months for enjoying house-and-garden tours and the blossoms of the Southeast's many fruit trees, celebrated in events like the Cherry Blossom Festival of Macon, Georgia, where visitors can see more than 200,000 trees that line the city streets.

Throughout May, one of the country's largest music and arts festivals takes place in historic Charleston, South Carolina, as part of the Spoleto Festival USA.

Summer brings a deluge of outdoor events. Bands, fireworks, and street festivals are the norm for community celebrations of the July 4 Independence Day holiday. One of the largest fireworks displays in the US is staged at Stone Mountain, outside Atlanta. Numerous county and state fairs crop up around this time, as do music festivals such as Old Time Fiddlers' Jamboree in Smithville, Tennessee. The end of summer brings Elvis Week in Memphis, Tennessee, celebrating the life and times of Elvis Presley with a week-long festival around the anniversary of his death on August 16.

A highlight of autumn is the Tennessee Fall Homecoming, an Appalachian-themed crafts and culture festival that takes place annually at the Museum of Appalachia. At the end of the year, an old-fashioned Christmas is re-created at the living-history village of Old Salem, outside Winston-Salem in North Carolina.

## Sports & Outdoor Activities

The cities of the Southeast host a wide array of professional and amateur sports teams, and there are many minor league teams in smaller cities. Especially in basketball and football, hundreds of high-quality and passionately supported sports teams are fielded by public and private colleges and universities. Atlanta has major league teams in all four main American spectator sports (baseball, football, hockey, and basketball), but professional NFL football is also played in Charlotte, North Carolina, and Nashville, Tennessee. At the minor league level, Memphis has an enormous downtown stadium for their Class AAA baseball team, the Redbirds; Nashville, Charlotte, and Louisville also have high-quality Class AAA baseball teams. Baseball season

runs from April to September, football from September through January, and basketball from winter through mid-spring.

In other sports, the Kentucky Derby in early May draws hundreds of thousands of horse-racing fans from all over the world. Golf fans flock to Augusta, Georgia to watch the Masters tournament in April. NASCAR stock car races are the region's most popular attractions, drawing more than 200,000 people to races at Atlanta, Bristol, Concord, Rockingham, and Darlington.

Numerous state parks provide opportunities for camping, boating, fishing, and hiking. The coastal states of the Southeast are known to excel in beach activities.

## Entertainment

The birthplace of the blues, rock 'n' roll, and country-and-western music, the Southeast is a great place to enjoy live music. Hundreds of events take place all over the region almost every night. Besides the various nightclubs hosting talented musicians, the major entertainment venues of the region include the legendary Grand Old Opry in Nashville and B.B. King's Blues Club in Memphis.

# DIRECTORY

## Tourist Information

### Georgia
Tel (800) 847-4842.
W exploregeorgia.org

### Kentucky
Tel (800) 225-8747.
W kentuckytourism.com

### North Carolina
Tel (800) 847-4862.
W visitnc.com

### South Carolina
Tel (800) 872-3505.
W discoversouthcarolina.com

### Tennessee
Tel (800) 462-8366.
W tnvacation.com

## Travel

### Amtrak
Tel (800) 872-7245.
W amtrak.com

### Greyhound
Tel (800) 231-2222.

## Parks & Outdoor Information

### Georgia
205 SE Butler St, Atlanta.
Tel (800) 864-7275.
W gastateparks.org

### Kentucky
2200 Capital Plaza Tower, Frankfort.
Tel (800) 255-7275.
W parks.ky.gov

### North Carolina
1615 Mail Service Center, Raleigh.
Tel (919) 733-4181.
W ncsparks.com

### South Carolina
1205 Pendleton St, Columbia.
Tel (803) 734-0156.
W southcarolinaparks.com

### Tennessee
401 Church St, Nashville.
Tel (615) 532-0001, (800) 421-6683.
W tnstateparks.com

### Kentucky Derby
Tel (800) 928-3378.
W kdf.org

## NASCAR
W nascar.com

### Atlanta Falcons
Tel (404) 223-8000.
W atlantafalcons.com

### Carolina Panthers
Tel (704) 358-7000.
W panthers.com

### Tennessee Titans
Tel (615) 565-4000.
W titansonline.com

## Entertainment

### B.B. King's Blues Club
143 Beale St, Memphis, Tennessee.
Tel (901) 524-5464.

### Grand Old Opry
Nashville, Tennessee.
Tel (615) 889-3060.

# Where to Stay

## North Carolina

### ASHEVILLE: Cedar Crest Victorian Inn $$
B&B
*674 Biltmore Ave, 28803*
**Tel** *(828) 252-1389*
W cedarcrestinn.com
A romantic Queen Anne-style mansion with spacious rooms and period furnishings. Hot breakfasts are included.

### DK Choice

### ASHEVILLE: Inn on Biltmore Estate $$$
Luxury
*1 Lodge St, 28803*
**Tel** *(828) 225-1333*
W biltmore.com
This elegant hotel on the grounds of the famed Biltmore Estate offers luxurious lodgings and gracious hospitality. The rooms boast exquisite furnishings and lovely views of the woodlands. Leisure activities such as hiking, cycling, and cooking classes are available. Enjoy mountain views, relaxing on the veranda, or afternoon tea in the library. The fine-dining restaurant serves food and wine sourced from the estate.

### CHAPEL HILL: Carolina Inn $$
Historic
*211 Pittsboro St, 27516*
**Tel** *(919) 933-2001*
W carolinainn.com
Spacious rooms feature antique furnishings and modern amenities at this hotel next to the University of North Carolina There's a fine-dining restaurant on site.

### CHARLOTTE: Charlotte Marriott City Center $$
Boutique
*100 W Trade St, 28202*
**Tel** *(704) 333-9000*
W marriott.com
This Marriott, located close to shops, restaurants, and museums, offers richly appointed rooms and excellent service.

### CHARLOTTE: Ritz-Carlton $$$
Luxury
*201 E Trade St, 28202*
**Tel** *(704) 547-2244*
W ritzcarlton.com/charlotte
Offering a quiet retreat, this eco-friendly hotel has well-appointed rooms, a luxurious spa, and a rooftop garden with beehives. Excellent service.

### DURHAM: Homewood Suites by Hilton $
Value
*3600 Mt Moriah Rd, 27707*
**Tel** *(919) 401-0610*
W homewoodsuites3.hilton.com
At this small but tastefully decorated hotel, comfortable suites feature homey furnishings, full kitchens, and workspaces. Complimentary breakfasts.

### KILL DEVIL HILLS: Sea Ranch Resort $
Value
*1731 N Virginia Dare Trail, 27948*
**Tel** *(800) 334-4737*
W searanchresort.com
Suites at this coastal-style oceanfront resort come with full kitchens. There's a pool, fitness center, and game room on site.

### NAGS HEAD: Surf Side Hotel $$
B&B
*6701 Virginia Dare Trail, 27959*
**Tel** *(252) 441-2105*
W surfsideobx.com
This oceanfront hotel offers great sea views and a range of rooms in varying sizes; all are cozy and well-appointed. Relaxing ambience and friendly service.

### RALEIGH: Holiday Inn Raleigh – North $
Value
*2805 Highwoods Blvd, 27604*
**Tel** *(919) 872-3500*
W ihg.com/holidayinn
Guest rooms are spacious, comfortable, and well-equipped at this modern hotel, conveniently located near the main highway, . There is an outdoor seasonal swimming pool as well.

The historic Carolina Inn, full of Southern charm, in Chapel Hill, North Carolina

### Price Guide

Prices are based on one night's stay in high season for a standard double room, inclusive of service charges and taxes.

| $ | up to $150 |
| $$ | $150 to $300 |
| $$$ | over $300 |

## South Carolina

### CHARLESTON: John Rutledge House Inn $$
B&B
*116 Broad St, 29401*
**Tel** *(843) 723-7999*
W johnrutledgehouseinn.com
This historic property, close to the Battery and other key attractions, was built in 1763 as the residence for John Rutledge, one of the signatories of the US Constitution. It offers handsome rooms with Southern charm.

### CHARLESTON: Kings Courtyard Inn $$
B&B
*198 King St, 29401*
**Tel** *(843) 723-7000*
W kingscourtyardinn.com
This inviting B&B dating back to 1853 is surrounded by numerous shopping and dining options. The attractive rooms are filled with historic artifacts.

### DK Choice

### CHARLESTON: The Restoration on King $$$
Boutique
*75 Wentworth St, 29401*
**Tel** *(843) 518-5100*
W restorationonking.com
This beautifully restored property combines the service of a high-end hotel with the amenities of a fully furnished apartment. Spacious suites feature exposed brick and other original elements. Contemporary furnishings and modern facilities are comfortable as well as luxurious. Some suites have patios. Southern hospitality includes wine and cheese on the rooftop terrace.

### COLUMBIA: Hampton Inn Columbia $
Value
*822 Gervais St, 29201*
**Tel** *(803) 231-2000*
W hamptoninncolumbia.com
Located in the historic downtown, this inn offers comfortable rooms with modern amenities and complimentary breakfasts.

**HILTON HEAD: Omni Hilton Head** $$
Boutique
*23 Ocean Ln, 29928*
**Tel** *(843) 842-8000*
w omnihotels.com
This oceanfront resort with tropical landscaping offers all-suite options with mini-kitchens. On-site amenities include golf, biking, a spa, and pools for kids and adults.

**MYRTLE BEACH:**
**The Breakers Resort** $$
Value
*2100 N Ocean Blvd, 29578*
**Tel** *(855) 861-9550*
w breakers.com
A family-friendly favorite on the beach, The Breakers boasts a variety of comfortable rooms, kids' play areas, and multiple pools. Great views.

# Georgia

**ATLANTA: Four Seasons Hotel** $$
Boutique
*75 14th St, 30309*
**Tel** *(404) 881-9898*
w fourseasons.com
A stunning midtown spot known for its exemplary service. Rooms are large and comfortable, and the impressive lobby features a red marble staircase.

**ATLANTA: Omni Hotel at CNN Center** $$
Value
*100 CNN Center, 30303*
**Tel** *(404) 659-0000*
w omnihotels.com
Large guest rooms featuring marble baths and city views are on offer at this hotel close to Centennial Olympic Park and other attractions.

**ATLANTA: Stonehurst Place** $$
B&B
*923 Piedmont Ave NE, 30309*
**Tel** *(404) 881-0722*
w stonehurstplace.com
This elegant award-winning hotel boasts individually designed rooms with original artwork, luxury amenities, and superior service. Great location.

**ATLANTA: Westin Buckhead** $$
Value
*3391 Peachtree Rd NE, 30326*
**Tel** *(404) 365-0065*
w westinbuckheadatlanta.com
The spacious rooms and marble bathrooms are ultra-comfortable at this sleek, modern hotel with minimalist decor and contemporary art on the walls.

Elegant room at Stonehurst Place, Atlanta, Georgia

## DK Choice

**ATLANTA: The St. Regis** $$$
Luxury
*88 W Paces Ferry Rd, 30305*
**Tel** *(404) 563-7900*
w stregisatlanta.com
A renowned choice in the exquisite Buckhead neighborhood, this boutique resort is one of the best in the city. Rooms are spacious, with luxurious amenities, custom furnishings, and original artwork, and impeccable service. Some suites offer the unique St. Regis Butler Service. The on-site pool and spa are outstanding.

**AUGUSTA: Hilton Garden Inn** $
Value
*1065 Stevens Creek Rd, 30907*
**Tel** *(706) 739-9990*
w hiltongardeninn3.hilton.com
Head here for comfortable accommodations near local attractions. Modern guest rooms have workstations plus access to a restaurant and convenience store.

**JEKYLL ISLAND:**
**The Beachview Club** $$
Value
*721 N Beachview Dr, 31527*
**Tel** *(912) 635-2256*
w beachviewclub.com
In a prime location and set in lovely grounds with old oak trees, the elegant rooms here have kitchenettes; some benefit from ocean views.

**SAVANNAH: East Bay Inn** $$
Boutique
*225 E Bay St, 31401*
**Tel** *(912) 238-1225*
w eastbayinn.com
These beautiful accommodations near bustling River Street offer classic style with modern comforts and friendly service. The evening reception includes complimentary beverages and appetizers.

**SAVANNAH: The Gastonian** $$$
Historic
*220 E Gaston St, 31401*
**Tel** *(912) 232-2869*
w gastonian.com
Luxurious rooms have antiques and working fireplaces in this elegant house with gardens.

**SAVANNAH: Kehoe House** $$$
B&B
*123 Habersham St, 31401*
**Tel** *(912) 232-1020*
w kehoehouse.com
This restored 1892 mansion overlooks Columbia Square. Rooms have antique furnishings. There is an evening wine and hors d'oeuvres reception.

**ST. SIMONS: Ocean Lodge** $$$
Luxury
*935 Beachview Dr, 31522*
**Tel** *(912) 291-4300*
w oceanlodgessi.com
The Ocean Lodge boasts stunning old-world architecture and villa-style rooms with deluxe amenities. Rooftop restaurant.

**TYBEE ISLAND: Surf Song Bed & Breakfast** $$
Historic
*21 Officers Row, 31328*
**Tel** *(912) 472-1040*
w tybeesurfsong.com
Beach-style furnishings and a wraparound porch add fun and character to this renovated Victorian home near the ocean, .

# Tennessee

**CHATTANOOGA: Chattanooga Choo Choo Hotel** $
Historic
*1400 Market St, 37402*
**Tel** *(423) 266-5000*
w choochoo.com
Popular with train enthusiasts, guests at this family-friendly hotel sleep in standard rooms or in a Victorian train car.

**For more information on types of hotels** *see pages 26–7*

**GATLINBURG: Zoder's Inn & Suites** $
B&B
*402 Pkwy, 37738*
**Tel** *(865) 436-5681*
W zoders.com
This tranquil property located in a secluded area beside a beautiful mountain stream offers comfortable rooms in a variety of sizes. Complimentary Continental breakfasts are served, and there's cheese and wine in the evening.

**MEMPHIS: Elvis Presley's Heartbreak Hotel** $
Value
*3677 Elvis Presley Blvd, 38116*
**Tel** *(901) 332-1000*
W elvis.com
A kitschy hotel with 1950s decor, located across the street from Elvis Presley's home, Graceland. Rooms are spacious and have kitchenettes. Elvis videos play on the in-house TV channel.

## DK Choice

**MEMPHIS: Peabody Hotel** $$
Historic
*149 Union Ave, 38103*
**Tel** *(901) 529-4000*
W peabodymemphis.com
This famous downtown hotel is a tourist destination in its own right. The popular, twice-daily "march of the ducks" draws spectators to the lobby as the house mallards walk down the red carpet to the fountain. Known as the South's Grand Hotel, it features large rooms with fine furnishings and luxurious amenities, and boasts a prime location near Beale Street and other attractions.

**NASHVILLE: Hotel Preston** $$
Boutique
*733 Briley Pkwy 37217*
**Tel** *(615) 361-5900*
W hotelpreston.com
This creative hotel features eclectic art, eye-catching colorful decor, and offbeat touches. The distinctive rooms are ultra-comfortable, and the service is friendly and personalized.

**NASHVILLE: The Hermitage Hotel** $$$
Luxury
*231 6th Ave N, 37219*
**Tel** *(615) 244-3121*
W thehermitagehotel.com
A charming historic property known for its Southern hospitality. Accommodations are luxurious, warm, and inviting, with views of downtown.

Swimming pool at Hotel Preston, Nashville, Tennessee

**NASHVILLE: Union Station Hotel** $$$
Boutique
*1001 Broadway, 37203*
**Tel** *(615) 726-1001*
W unionstationhotelnashville.com
In a former train station, this hotel has a dramatic barrel-vaulted lobby and offers elegant, uniquely designed rooms with contemporary decor.

# Kentucky

**LEXINGTON: Gratz Park Inn** $$
B&B
*120 W 2nd St, 40507*
**Tel** *(859) 231-1777*
W gratzparkinn.com
Rooms offer modern comforts and luxury bedding at this intimate historic inn with antique reproduction mahogany furnishings, hardwood floors, and regional artworks .

**LEXINGTON: Hilton Lexington Downtown** $$
Boutique
*369 W Vine St, 40507*
**Tel** *(859) 231-9000*
W hilton.com/lexington
This centrally located chain property offers comfortable rooms with quality amenities. It is close to local attractions and attached by skywalk to shopping and dining destinations.

**LOUISVILLE: Econo Lodge Downtown** $
Value
*401 S 2nd St, 40202*
**Tel** *(502) 583-2841*
W econolodge.com
Convenient for both business and leisure travelers, the well-appointed rooms here have refrigerators and microwaves. There's a free Continental breakfast and an exercise room.

**LOUISVILLE: Galt House Hotel** $
Value
*140 N Fourth St, 40202*
**Tel** *(502) 589-5200*
W galthouse.com
A large waterfront hotel with several on-site restaurants and a lovely rooftop garden. It offers an array of room types with luxurious amenities and warm service.

**LOUISVILLE: The Brown Hotel** $$
Luxury
*335 W Broadway, 40202*
**Tel** *(502) 583-1234*
W brownhotel.com
One of the city's most treasured landmarks, this hotel features Georgian Revival-style architecture, a grand lobby, and comfortable, elegant rooms.

## DK Choice

**LOUISVILLE: Seelbach Hilton** $$
Historic
*500 S 4th St, 40202*
**Tel** *(502) 585-3200*
W seelbachhilton.com
This elegant hotel, built in 1905, has hosted many famous figures and was notably referenced in *The Great Gatsby* by F. Scott Fitzgerald. It boasts an old-world charm, countered by the luxurious rooms with modern comforts and amenities. The opulent decor features marble, fine woodwork, and art from around the world.

**LOUISVILLE: 21c Museum Hotel** $$$
Boutique
*700 W Main St, 40202*
**Tel** *(502) 217-6300*
W 21cmuseumhotels.com
This unique hotel is also partly a contemporary art museum. The cozy rooms are distinctive and stylish. Superb hospitality.

# Where to Eat and Drink

## North Carolina

**ASHEVILLE: Laughing Seed Café** $
Vegetarian
*40 Wall St, 28801*
**Tel** *(828) 252-3445*
Serving seasonal, farm-to-table dishes with an international flair, as well as local beers and fresh fruit elixirs, this café sources organic ingredients from local farms. Covered patio, colorful bar.

**ASHEVILLE: Tupelo Honey** $
Southern
*12 College St, 28801*
**Tel** *(828) 255-4863*
An upscale yet casual spot with homey decor. The creative menu features old Southern favorites, with healthier versions of classic comfort foods prepared with fresh, local, and organic ingredients.

**BEAUFORT: Clawson's 1905 Restaurant & Pub** $
New American
*425 Front St, 28516*
**Tel** *(252) 728-2133* **Closed** *Sun*
This popular restaurant and pub on the historic waterfront is housed in an early-1900s grocery store. It offers large combination platters of seafood and meats, with local microbrews.

**CHAPEL HILL: Mama Dip's** $
Southern
*408 W Rosemary St, 27514*
**Tel** *(919) 942-5837*
This spacious venue has been serving down-home cooking since 1976. There are extensive breakfast, lunch, and dinner menus, with everything available to go. Traditional favorites include catfish gumbo, Brunswick stew, and fruit cobbler.

### DK Choice

**CHARLOTTE: Mert's Heart & Soul** $
Soul Food
*214 N College St, 28202*
**Tel** *(704) 342-4222*
Numerous locals and tourists label this Uptown favorite as "the heart and soul of Charlotte." Mert's is known for its regional Southern, Lowcountry-country, and Gullah-inspired home-made dishes. House favorites include mac 'n' cheese, buttery cornbread, Charleston red rice, and shrimp and grits. Friendly and personable staff.

**CHARLOTTE: Upstream** $$
Seafood
*6902 Phillips Pl Ct, 28210*
**Tel** *(704) 556-7730*
The day's freshest catch is turned into innovative, Asian-tinged dishes and gourmet sushi here. There is an award-winning wine list and a popular Sunday brunch.

**DURHAM: Dame's Chicken & Waffles** $
New American
*317 W Main St, 27701*
**Tel** *(919) 682-9235*
This eclectic restaurant serves its namesake Southern classic dish with a modern spin. Fluffy waffles are topped with sweet crème butters and crispy, perfectly fried chicken.

**NAGS HEAD: Sam & Omie's** $
American
*7228 S Virginia Dare Trail, 27959*
**Tel** *(252) 441-7366* **Closed** *Dec–Feb*
This casual and funky favorite started in 1937 as a breakfast spot for fishermen. Standard fare includes seafood and burgers. Friendly bar.

**RALEIGH: The Pit** $
Barbeque
*328 W Davie St, 27601*
**Tel** *(919) 890-4500*
Authentic pit-cooked barbecue dishes are served in a restored 1930s warehouse. The award-winning cuisine uses free-range meats and local produce. Superb wine and spirit lists.

**RALEIGH: The Raleigh Times** $$$
American
*14 E Hargett St, 27601*
**Tel** *(919) 833-0999*
The city's past is on display in this beautifully restored 1906 building. The menu includes creative bar fare, inventive drinks, and an extensive beer selection.

### Price Guide

Prices are based on a three-course meal per person, with a glass of house wine, including tax and service.

| | |
|---|---|
| $ | up to $30 |
| $$ | $30 to $50 |
| $$$ | over $50 |

## South Carolina

**CHARLESTON: Hominy Grill** $
Southern
*207 Rutledge Ave, 29403*
**Tel** *(843) 937-0930*
Housed in a charming old building, Hominy Grill is popular with locals for its traditional cuisine prepared with fresh local ingredients. House favorites include fried chicken, shrimp creole, and buttermilk pie.

### DK Choice

**CHARLESTON: Husk** $$$
Southern
*74–76 Queen St, 29401*
**Tel** *(843) 577-2500*
Food-lovers head to Husk in the historic downtown to try Chef Sean Brock's acclaimed modern interpretations of traditional Southern food. The ingredient-driven menu changes daily while focusing on artisanal products, in-house pickling and charcuterie. Knowledgeable servers.

**CHARLESTON: Magnolia's** $$$
Southern
*185 E Bay St, 29401*
**Tel** *(843) 577-7771*
Housed in an old building, Magnolia offers excellent service and attention to detail. The menu features classic Southern dishes such as fried green tomatoes and pecan-crusted flounder.

Husk, in a late 19th-century historic building in downtown Charleston, South Carolina

**For more information on types of restaurants** *see pages 28–9*

Entrance to the Wilkes House inn, housing Mrs. Wilkes' Dining Room, Savannah, Georgia

### COLUMBIA: Al's Upstairs Italian Restaurant $$
Italian
*300 Meeting St, W Columbia, 29169*
**Tel** *(803) 794-7404*　**Closed** *Sun*
Housed in a 1900s building with stunning city views. Entrées here feature fresh Atlantic seafood, hand-cut steaks, Italian specialties, and innovative pasta dishes.

### COLUMBIA: Blue Marlin $$
Seafood
*1200 Lincoln St, 29201*
**Tel** *(803) 799-3838*
Set in a converted train station, Blue Marlin serves Lowcountry cuisine, with an emphasis on seafood and hand-cut steaks. The house favorites include oysters Bienville and Firecracker flounder.

### HILTON HEAD: A Lowcountry Backyard $$
Southern
*32 Palmetto Bay Rd, 29928*
**Tel** *(843) 785-9273*
This popular eatery is known for its creative take on Lowcountry-country cuisine made using local and seasonal ingredients. Lively outdoor patio. Friendly servers.

### MYRTLE BEACH: Mr. Fish $
Seafood
*6401 N Kings Hwy, 29572*
**Tel** *(843) 839-3474*
This landmark restaurant and seafood market serves the freshest fish in town. The classic fried dishes, hearty gumbo, and sushi are impressive. Gluten-free pizzas and healthy fare are also available.

### MYRTLE BEACH: The Library Restaurant $$$
French/European
*1212 N Kings Hwy, 29577*
**Tel** *(843) 448-4527*
Established in 1974, this is the top choice for special-occasion dining. Tuxedoed staff serve classic Continental dishes such as Steak Diane and flambéed desserts.

# Georgia

### ATHENS: Cali N Tito's $
Latin American
*1427 S Lumpkin St, 30608*
**Tel** *(706) 227-9979*
Authentic Latin American flavors and tasty fish tacos are the main draw here. The colorful dining area and outdoor patio are lively. Payment by cash only.

### ATHENS: Last Resort Grill $$
Southern
*174–184 W Clayton St, 30601*
**Tel** *(706) 549-0810*
Housed in a historic building, with seating in booths or in the courtyard, this eatery attracts crowds for its modern Southern and Southwestern-influenced cuisine.

### ATLANTA: Colonnade Restaurant $$
American
*1879 Cheshire Bridge Rd NE, 30324*
**Tel** *(404) 874-5642*
A superb restaurant that has been defining local culinary traditions since 1927, serving dishes such as fried chicken, sirloin steak, and country vegetables. Friendly staff.

### ATLANTA: The Varsity $
American Diner
*61 N Ave NW, 30308*
**Tel** *(404) 881-1706*
This is the world's largest drive-in fast-food restaurant, dating back to 1928. Both locals and visitors line up for burgers, chili dogs, and other fast-food favorites.

### ATLANTA: La Grotta Ristorante Italiano $$
Italian
*2637 Peachtree Rd NE, 30305*
**Tel** *(404) 231-1368*　**Closed** *Sun*
This sophisticated restaurant serves fine Northern Italian fare, including seafood, beef, veal and chicken entrées, pastas, and decadent desserts. Lengthy wine list.

### ATLANTA: Bone's $$$
Steak House
*3130 Piedmont Rd NE, 30305*
**Tel** *(404) 237-2663*
This big-ticket steak house is a favorite with the business crowd and those looking to celebrate a special occasion. Prime, aged, and corn-fed beef, fresh seafood, and Maine lobster are the mainstays. Impressive wine list.

### ATLANTA: Holman & Finch Public House $$$
New American
*2277 Peachtree Rd NE, 30309*
**Tel** *(404) 948-1175*
Food-lovers are wowed by the ever-changing menu, full of obscure ingredients and nose-to-tail fare, at this modern restaurant. What some consider the city's best burger is sold in limited quantities nightly and also features in the Sunday brunch menu.

### JEKYLL ISLAND: Grand Dining Room $$$
Seafood
*371 Riverview Dr, 31527*
**Tel** *(912) 635-5155*
The elegant Grand Dining Room is decorated in Victorian style with high-backed chairs, fireplaces, and sparkling crystal. The Continental menu features buffalo bison burger, wild mushroom bisque, veal cheeks, and award-winning shrimp and grits.

## DK Choice

### SAVANNAH: Mrs. Wilkes' Dining Room $
Southern
*107 W Jones St, 31401*
**Tel** *(912) 232-5997*　**Closed** *Sat & Sun*
Guests gather each weekday morning to partake in a true Southern-style experience of sitting at communal tables and eating platters of traditional home-cooked favorites. Sample from the huge servings of fried chicken, cornbread dressing, sweet potato soufflé, black-eyed peas, mac 'n' cheese, BBQ pork, and okra gumbo. The lunch-only offerings change daily.

### SAVANNAH: Alligator Soul $$
Cajun/Creole
*114 Barnard St, 31401*
**Tel** *(912) 232-7899*
A welcoming downtown restaurant famed for its commitment to organic, local, and regional ingredients, with an emphasis on humanely treated animals. Organic cocktails and home-made desserts are popular.

**ST. SIMONS: Crabdaddy's** $$
Seafood
*1219 Ocean Blvd, 31522*
**Tel** *(912) 634-1120*
An extensive menu of tasty locally caught fish, served grilled, blackened, or steamed, is served at this popular restuarnat.

**SAVANNAH: The Olde Pink House** $$
New American
*23 Abercorn St, 31401*
**Tel** *(912) 232-4286*
This renowned restaurant in an 18th-century mansion serves New-Southern fare in an upscale setting. Live entertainment nightly.

**TYBEE ISLAND: Crab Shack** $
Seafood
*40 Estill Hammock Rd, 31328*
**Tel** *(912) 786-9857*
The menu at this family-friendly eatery includes regional favorites such as Lowcountry boiled and steamed oysters. Sit in the casual dining room or outdoors.

## Tennessee

**CHATTANOOGA: 212 Market Restaurant** $$
New American
*212 Market St, 37402*
**Tel** *(423) 265-1212*
The ever-changing menu of creative takes on contemporary American cuisine at this restaurant features local ingredients. The dining room has balcony seating and rustic decor.

**KNOXVILLE: The Tomato Head** $
Pizzeria
*12 Market Sq, 37902*
**Tel** *(865) 637-4067*
Gourmet pizzas are made here using the freshest ingredients. Breads, dressings, cookies, and

Modern interior of the Catbird Seat with an open-plan kitchen, Nashville, Tennessee

desserts are prepared daily. Musicians, poets, and other performers entertain diners.

### DK Choice

**MEMPHIS: Corky's BBQ** $
Barbecue
*5259 Poplar Ave, 38119*
**Tel** *(901) 685-9744*
A local favorite, this traditional barbecue joint serves hand-pulled pork shoulder, dry rub ribs, and tangy sauced ribs, all slow-cooked over hickory wood and charcoal. The walls are covered with pictures of famous customers, and there's a lively, family-friendly atmosphere.

**MEMPHIS: Gus' World Famous Fried Chicken** $
Southern
*310 S Front St, 38103*
**Tel** *(901) 527-4877*
This casual, no-frills restaurant is one of the world's best spots for authentic Southern fried chicken with all the down-home fixings.

**NASHVILLE: Arnold's Country Kitchen** $
Southern
*605 8th Ave S, 37203*
**Tel** *(615) 256-4455* **Closed** *Sat & Sun*
A lunchtime favorite serving meat-and-three dishes comprising a main entrée such as barbecue pork or roast beef, and tasty sides.

**NASHVILLE: Capitol Grille** $$$
Southern New American
*231 6th Ave N, 37219*
**Tel** *(615) 345-7116*
In an elegant setting dating back to 1910, black Angus beef, seafood, and the best local produce are turned into creative Southern fare.

**NASHVILLE: The Catbird Seat** $$$
New American
*1711 Division St, 37203*
**Tel** *(615) 810-8200* **Closed** *Sun-Tue*
At this buzzing venue, patrons sit around a U-shaped kitchen to watch their prix-fixe tasting feast being prepared.

## Kentucky

**BEREA: Boone Tavern Restaurant** $$
Southern
*100 Main St, 40404*
**Tel** *(859) 985-3700*
The menu at the homey Boone Tavern Restaurant includes signature dishes such as "chicken flakes in a bird's nest" and its famous spoonbread.

**LEXINGTON: Stella's Kentucky Deli** $
Deli
*143 Jefferson St, 40508*
**Tel** *(859) 255-3354*
This welcoming deli showcases local growers and producers and supports local food economies. Sandwiches, salads, soups, and desserts are all home-made.

**LEXINGTON: Jonathan at Gratz Park** $$$
New American
*120 W Second St, 40507*
**Tel** *(859) 252-4949*
Guests enjoy some of the city's finest food in this elegant dining room. Regional dishes are prepared with a modern twist, such as mushroom-dusted beef tenderloin. Excellent service.

**LOUISVILLE: Hammerheads** $
American
*921 Swan St, 40204*
**Tel** *(502) 365-1112* **Closed** *Sun*
Head here to sample an array of American pub food. A fine list of local craft beers and lively music contribute to the youthful vibe.

**LOUISVILLE: Havana Rumba** $$
Cuban
*4115 Oechsli Ave, 40207*
**Tel** *(502) 897-1959*
The Cuban owner of this place has carved out a niche in the local dining scene by providing an authentic experience. Guests enjoy flavorful recipes prepared with the freshest ingredients.

### DK Choice

**LOUISVILLE: Lilly's** $$
New American
*1147 Bardstown Rd, 40204*
**Tel** *(502) 451-0447* **Closed** *Sun & Mon*
Innovative food and an inviting atmosphere make this charming bistro popular with locals and visitors alike. The kitchen utilizes garden-fresh produce to create an ever-changing menu of original dishes such as chili-braised lamb shoulder, house-made pumpkin ravioli, and local heritage pork served in seven ways. Friendly, well-informed servers explain the menu.

**LOUISVILLE: Jack Fry's** $$$
New American
*1007 Bardstown Rd, 40204*
**Tel** *(502) 452-9244*
This speakeasy, established in 1933, has a colorful history. Today, it is popular for its live jazz, expertly made cocktails, and a varied menu of delicious regional fare.

1930s hotels lining Ocean Drive, Miami Beach, Florida ▶

# FLORIDA

# FLORIDA

For the majority of Florida's 96 million-plus annual visitors, the typical travel poster images of Florida – sun, sea, sand, and Mickey Mouse – are reason enough to jump on the next plane. The Sunshine State deserves its reputation as the perfect family vacation spot, but Florida is much richer in its culture, landscape, and character than its stereotypical image suggests.

Both climatically and culturally, Florida is a state divided – a bridge between temperate North America and tropical Latin America and the Caribbean. In the north, roads are lined with stately live oak trees and people speak with a southern drawl, while, in the south, shade from the subtropical sun is cast by palm trees, and the inhabitants of Miami are as likely to speak Spanish as English.

For most visitors, Florida's prime attractions lie along the coasts, where the beaches are varied and abundant enough to satisfy every visitor. However, great rewards await those who want to explore farther. The lush forests and rolling hills of the north provide some of the loveliest countryside in the state. Equally exciting are the so-called "wild areas," such as the Everglades, which harbor an extraordinary diversity of plant and animal life, and where alligators and snakes are living reminders of the inhospitable place that Florida was not much more than 100 years ago.

## History

At first glance, Florida appears to be a state without history. Yet behind its modern veneer lies a long and rich past, molded by different nationalities and cultures. Until the 16th century, Florida supported a large indigenous population, whose complex political and religious systems demonstrated a high degree of social organization. However, colonization soon decimated the Indians through warfare and disease. In 1513, the Spanish explorer Juan Ponce de León discovered Florida and named it after Pascua Florida, the Feast of the Flowers (Easter). For almost 200 years several Spanish conquistadors attempted unsuccessfully to search for

Deerfield Beach, a quiet coastal resort within easy reach of Boca Raton

◀ Aerial vista of Miami's South Beach, Florida

gold and colonize the region. Their primary concern was Florida's strategic position. The Gulf Stream carried Spanish galleons laden with gold and treasure from the New World colonies past Florida's coast on their journey back across the Atlantic, and it was thus vital that "La Florida" not fall into enemy hands.

Initially it was the French who troubled the Spanish, but the real threat to their control came in 1742 when English colonists from Georgia defeated them and finally acquired Florida about 20 years later. Though Florida was returned to Spain in 1783, numerous boundary disputes followed. It was only after Andrew Jackson, the ambitious US general, captured Pensacola that the official US occupation took place in 1821. During this period, the plantation system was firmly established in north Florida. The principal cash crop was cotton, for which intensive slave labor was required to work in the fields.

**Henry Flagler,**
**1830–1913**

American attempts to subdue the Seminole Indians and take over their land led to over 65 years of conflict. When the Third Seminole War ended in 1858, the Indians retreated to the Everglades, where they still live. Soon after came the Civil War, by the end of which, in 1865, Florida was in ruins. But the state recovered rapidly. Railroad barons, such as Henry Flagler and Henry Plant, built a network of railroads and opulent hotels, which attracted wealthy visitors from the north. Tourism flourished in the early 20th century, and by 1950 it had become Florida's top industry. The launch of the NASA space program at Cape Canaveral in the 1950s also helped boost the state's prosperity.

## Society & Culture

The state "where everyone is from somewhere else," Florida has always been a cultural hodgepodge. The earliest inhabitants were indigenous people, who were members of many tribes. Spanish, French, and British rule brought a diversity to the state that continues to this day.

Americans have poured into this land of opportunity since World War II; the twentieth most populous state in the US in 1950, Florida is now ranked third. The largest single group to move south has been the retirees, for whom Florida's climate, lifestyle of leisure, and low tax rates hold great appeal after a life of hard work. While super-rich communities like Palm Beach fit the conservative and staid image that some people still have of

### KEY DATES IN HISTORY

**1513** Ponce de León discovers "La Florida"

**1565** Pedro Menéndez de Avilés founds St. Augustine after defeating the French

**1763** Britain acquires Florida

**1783** Britain returns Florida to the Spanish

**1785–1821** Spanish-American border disputes

**1821** Florida becomes part of the US; Andrew Jackson becomes the first American governor

**1845** Florida becomes the 27th state

**1852** Harriet Beecher Stowe publishes the anti-slavery epic, *Uncle Tom's Cabin*

**1886** Henry Flagler starts construction of the Florida East Coast Railway

**1958** *Explorer I* is launched after NASA chooses Cape Canaveral as the site of its space program

**1959** Over 300,000 Cubans flee to Florida

**1971** Walt Disney World® opens

**1992** Hurricane Andrew devastates south Florida

**2000** George W. Bush appointed president after the Florida election debacle

**2003** Space Shuttle *Columbia* explodes on reentry and *Spirit*, a rover, heads for Mars

**2004** Four hurricanes hit Florida in a six-week period

**2011** *Atlantis'* last launch ends manned shuttle program

Space shuttle *Discovery* lifts off from the Kennedy Space Center, Cape Canaveral

Mural inside the US Federal Courthouse, Miami

such as car racing, and the Daytona International Speedway attracts thousands of visitors every year. Spring baseball training also draws teams and lots of fans south, while the fashion trade brings models by the dozen and plenty of glamour to Miami.

It is tourism, however, that fills the state's coffers. The Walt Disney World® Resort may appear to dominate the industry, but Florida makes the most of all its assets. Its superb beaches and the promise of winter sunshine have lured millions of vacationers through the years. Beside beaches and theme parks, there are natural habitats, state-of-the-art museums, and towns, such as St. Augustine and Pensacola, that still retain their Spanish Colonial ambience.

Florida, the reality is very different. An increasing number of the new arrivals are young people for whom Florida is a land of opportunity, and a place to enjoy the good life. Today, the younger generation has helped turn Miami's South Beach into one of the country's trendiest resorts.

From 1959 on, there has also been massive immigration from Latin America; Miami-Dade County in particular has a huge Hispanic community, with a distinct Cuban flair. Central Florida has become home to many Hispanic people, from Puerto Rico, Mexico, and Central and South America, along with immigrants from around the Caribbean. This ethnic diversity is celebrated in an endless cycle of exuberant festivals, music, and local food.

Beach buggie, Daytona Beach

Conservation is a major issue in Florida today. After decades of intense urban development, Floridians have finally learned the importance of preserving their rich and varied natural heritage. Great swathes of the natural landscape have already disappeared beneath factories, condos, and cabbage fields, but those involved in industry and agriculture are acting more responsibly, and water use is now strictly monitored. Florida's natural treasures, from its freshwater swamps and hardwood forests to its last remaining panthers, are now protected for posterity.

## Economics & Tourism

For most of Florida's history, its main source of revenue has been agriculture – citrus fruits, vegetables, sugar, and cattle, which was originally introduced by the Spanish colonists. In fact, Florida produces over 70 percent of the citrus fruits consumed in the United States today, while Kissimmee is known as the "cow capital" of the state. High-tech industry is significant as well, and the proximity of Miami to Latin America and the Caribbean has made it the natural route for trade with the region. This proximity has also contributed to the state's flourishing cruise industry. Florida's warm climate has also generated high-profile moneyspinners,

A vibrant mural in Key West's Bahama Village

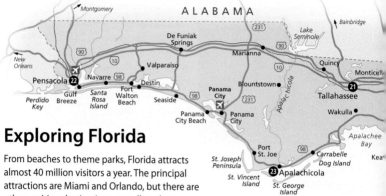

# Exploring Florida

From beaches to theme parks, Florida attracts almost 40 million visitors a year. The principal attractions are Miami and Orlando, but there are other exciting destinations as well, such as St. Augustine and Pensacola, established by Spanish colonialists in the 16th century. For nature lovers, the Everglades is a thrilling experience, while the Keys offer a choice of activities, such as fishing, diving, and snorkeling. An extensive road network links the main towns, so traveling by car in Florida is both quick and enjoyable.

Art Deco motif, commonly seen in Miami

## Sights at a Glance

## Key

— Highway

— Major road

---- Railroad

## Mileage Chart

**Miami**

| | | | | | | | | | |
|---|---|---|---|---|---|---|---|---|---|
| **70** / 113 | **Palm Beach** | | | | | | 10 = Distance in miles | | |
| **237** / 381 | **171** / 275 | **Orlando** | | | | | 10 = Distance in kilometers | | |
| **314** / 505 | **247** / 398 | **107** / 172 | **St. Augustine** | | | | | | |
| **504** / 811 | **438** / 705 | **257** / 414 | **205** / 330 | **Tallahassee** | | | | | |
| **707** / 1138 | **642** / 1033 | **450** / 724 | **399** / 642 | **197** / 317 | **Pensacola** | | | | |
| **279** / 449 | **200** / 322 | **84** / 135 | **190** / 306 | **274** / 441 | **468** / 753 | **Tampa** | | | |
| **262** / 422 | **228** / 367 | **106** / 171 | **212** / 341 | **299** / 481 | **490** / 789 | **24** / 39 | **St. Petersburg** | | |
| **230** / 370 | **195** / 314 | **131** / 211 | **236** / 380 | **333** / 536 | **520** / 837 | **60** / 97 | **35** / 56 | **Sarasota** | |
| **161** / 259 | **233** / 375 | **394** / 634 | **478** / 769 | **641** / 1032 | **873** / 1405 | **426** / 686 | **410** / 660 | **376** / 605 | **Key West** |

A lifeguard keeping watch on a Panhandle beach

GEORGIA

FLORIDA

**19** Fernandina Beach
*Amelia Island*

Jacksonville

Jacksonville

Jacksonville Beach

Lake City

Mandarin

**18** St. Augustine

Gainesville

Gainesville

Ocala
National
Forest
**20**

Palatka

Marineland

Flagler Beach

Cross Creek

Ocala

Silver
Springs

*Lake George*

**Daytona Beach**
**17** Daytona Beach

Crystal River

Homosassa Springs

*Ponce Inlet*
New Smyrna Beach

Mount Dora

Sanford
**Sanford**

**8** Canaveral National
Seashore & Merritt Island

Weeki Wachee

Orlando

**13** Winter Park

Universal
Orlando® Resort
**10**

Orlando
**12** International
Drive
**14**

**7** Kennedy Space Center

Cape Canaveral

Dade City

Walt Disney
World® Resort
**9**

SeaWorld®
**11** Orlando
& Discovery Cove®

**6** Cocoa Beach

*Indian River*

LEGOLAND®

Lakeland
**15**

Winter
Haven
**16**

Disney
Wilderness
Preserve

Melbourne

*Sebastian Inlet*

Tampa
**24**

St.Petersburg
Clearwater

Gibsonton

Bartow

Lake
Wales

*FLORIDA'S TURNPIKE*

Clearwater

tersburg
**25**

*Tampa Bay*

Yeehaw
Junction

Vero Beach

ATLANTIC
OCEAN

Anna Maria

Bradenton

Sarasota
**26**

Arcadia

Okeechobee

Fort Pierce

*Hutchinson Island*

Venice

Port Charlotte

*Lake
Okeechobee*

*St. Lucie Canal*

Stuart

Boca Grande
*Cayo Costa*
Lee Island Coast
**27**
*Captiva Island*

Fort Myers

*Caloosahatchee*

Clewiston

Pahokee

Belle
Glade

**5** Palm Beach

Palm
Beach

Lake Worth

Fort Myers

Immokalee

Loxahatchee
National Wildlife
Refuge
**4**

Delray Beach

**3** Boca Raton

*Sanibel Island*

Bonita
Springs

Naples

**28**

Big Cypress
Swamp

Fort Lauderdale
Hollywood

**2** Fort Lauderdale

Hollywood

*Marco Island*

Ochopee

Everglades
City

Miami

**1** Miami

*Ten Thousand Islands*

**29**

Everglades
National Park

Florida
City

*Biscayne
Bay*

**30** Biscayne
National Park

Flamingo

*John Pennekamp
State Park*

*Florida Bay*

Key Largo

Tavernier

Islamorada

*Indian &
Lignumvitae Keys*

The Keys **31**

*Lower Keys*
**Key West**

Marathon

Pigeon Key

*Dry
Tortugas*

**32** Key West

Florida Keys

0 kilometers    50

0 miles    50

# ❶ Miami

A small trading post a century ago, Miami, or Greater Miami, now covers 2,000 sq miles (5,180 sq km) and has a population of five million. The metropolis incorporates many districts and cities and comprises Miami-Dade County. Miami's top sights are its beaches, especially fun-filled South Beach. Other sights include Little Havana, the heart of the city's Cuban population, and the leafy suburbs of Coral Gables and Coconut Grove.

Miami Beach, a city in its own right, linked by causeways to the mainland

## Key

- Sight/Place of interest
- Beach area
- Expressway

## Getting Around

Public transportation in Miami is run by the Miami-Dade Transit Agency, which operates the buses, the Metrorail commuter rail network, and downtown's elevated Metromover. However, the best way to get around is by car, while taxis are recommended at night.

## Sights at a Glance

① South Beach
② Holocaust Memorial
③ Bass Museum of Art
④ Biscayne Bay Boat Trips
⑤ Museum Park
⑥ Miami-Dade Cultural Center
⑦ Downtown
⑧ Little Havana
⑨ Coral Gables
⑩ Biltmore Hotel
⑪ Venetian Pool
⑫ Coconut Grove Village
⑬ *Vizcaya p297*

### Greater Miami
**(see inset map)**

⑭ North Beaches
⑮ *Ancient Spanish Monastery p298*
⑯ Key Biscayne
⑰ Fairchild Tropical Botanic Garden
⑱ Zoo Miami
⑲ Wings Over Miami

### Key

- Area of main map
- Highway
- Major road
- Other road

**Greater Miami**

Lifeguard hut in South Beach to match buildings on Ocean Drive

# ① South Beach

**Map** F2. 🚌 M, S, C, H, G, L, F, M, Night Owl, Airport Owl. 🛈 1001, Ocean Drive, (305) 763-8026. 🌐 **mdpl.org**

This trendy district, also known as SoBe, extends from 6th to 23rd Streets between Lenox Avenue and Ocean Drive. A hedonistic playground, enlivened by an endless parade of fashion models, body builders, and drag queens, SoBe is also home to the world's largest concentration of well-preserved Art Deco buildings.

The 800-odd buildings along Ocean Drive were, in fact, modest hotels built in the 1930s by architects, the most famous of whom was Henry Hohauser, who used inexpensive materials to create an impression of stylishness. The present use of bright colors, known as Deco Dazzle, was introduced in the 1980s by designer Leonard Horowitz.

**Collins and Washington Avenues**, too, have their share of Art Deco buildings, such as the classic Marlin Hotel at 1200 Collins Avenue, one of the finest representations of Streamline Moderne. Farther north is the luxury Delano Hotel *(see p326)*, with its striking non-Deco interior of billowing white drapes and original Gaudi and Dali furniture. Other buildings of interest are the 1920s Mediterranean Revival Old City Hall and the austere Miami Beach Post Office on Washington Avenue. Inside the Post Office is a mural showing the arrival of Juan Ponce de León, the Spanish conquistador who discovered Florida in 1513. Also on Washington Avenue is the Wolfsonian Museum–FIU, built in the 1920s, which has an excellent collection of fine and decorative arts.

Between Washington and Drexel Avenues is **Española Way**, a small, pretty enclave of Mediterranean Revival buildings, where ornate arches, capitals, and balconies adorn salmon-colored, stuccoed frontages. Built from 1922–25, this street is said to be the inspiration for Addison Mizner's Worth Avenue in Palm Beach *(see p301)*. Offbeat art galleries and boutiques line this leafy street, and on weekends craft booths are set up here.

The pedestrian **Lincoln Road Mall** is Miami's up-and-coming cultural corner, dominated by the ArtCenter South Florida. Established in 1984, the ArtCenter has three exhibition areas and a dozen studios that double as work-in-progress and selling space, as well as independent galleries. The galleries are usually open in the evenings when the mall comes alive as theatergoers frequent the restored Art Deco Colony Theatre. After a heavy dose of modern art, the stylish restaurants and cafés, such as Van Dyke at 846, along Lincoln Road, offer respite.

**The Beach**, extending for 10 miles (16 km) up the coast, evolved into a spectacular winter playground after the

---

## Ocean Drive: Deco style

The splendid array of buildings on Ocean Drive illustrates Miami's unique interpretation of the Art Deco style, popular all over the world in the 1920s and '30s. Florida's version, often called Tropical Deco, uses motifs such as flamingoes, sunbursts, and jaunty nautical features, appropriate to South Beach's seaside location. Three main styles exist: traditional Art Deco, futuristic Streamline Moderne, and Mediterranean Revival, inspired by French, Italian, and Spanish architecture. A spirited preservation campaign, led by Barbara Capitman in the 1970s, made this area the first 20th-century district in the country's National Register of Historic Places.

**A flamingo** is etched into glass doors in the Beacon's lobby.

**Beacon** *(1936)*
A contemporary color scheme, an example of Horowitz's Deco Dazzle, brightens the abstract decoration above the first-floor windows.

bridge connecting the island with the mainland was built in 1913. Much of the sand flanking the beach was imported several decades ago, and it continues to be replenished to counter coastal erosion. The vast stretches of sand are still impressive and draw large crowds of people.

The beach constantly changes atmosphere. Surfers predominate up to 5th Street. The vast beach beyond is an extension of SoBe's lively persona, with colorful lifeguard huts and posing bathers. Alongside runs Lummus Park, where Yiddish is spoken by the mainly Jewish population. Around 21st Street, the clientele is predominantly gay.

The stretch north of 23rd Street is sometimes known as **Central Miami Beach**. The most eye-catching sight here is the impressive Fontainebleau Hotel (pronounced "Fountainblue" locally). Completed in 1954, this curvaceous structure was architect Morris Lapidus' (1903–2001) interpretation of a modern French château. With its grandeur, pool, and waterfall, the hotel was the ideal setting for the 1960s James Bond film classic, *Goldfinger*.

## ② Holocaust Memorial

**Map** F2. 1933–45 Meridian Ave. **Tel** (305) 538-1663. A, FM, G, L, W. **Open** 9:30am–sunset daily. holocaustmemorialmiamibeach.org

Miami Beach has one of the largest populations of Holocaust survivors in the world, hence the great appropriateness of Kenneth Treister's gut-wrenching memorial, finished in 1990. The centerpiece is an enormous bronze arm and hand stretching skyward, representing the final grasp of a dying person. It is stamped with a number from Auschwitz and covered with more than 100 life-size bronze statues of men, women, and children in the throes of the most unbearable grief. Titled *The Sculpture of Love and Anguish*, this is one of the most powerful contemporary sculptures in Florida today. Around the central plaza is a tunnel lined with the names of Europe's concentration camps, a graphic pictorial history of the Holocaust, and a granite wall Inscribed with the names of thousands of victims who perished.

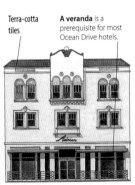
The Holocaust Memorial

*Coronation of the Virgin* (c.1492) by Domenico Ghirlandaio

## ③ Bass Museum of Art

**Map** F2. 2100 Collins Ave. **Tel** (305) 673-7530. M, S, C, H, G, L. **Open** noon–5pm Wed–Sun. **Closed** Mon, Tue, public hols. bassmuseum.org

This Mayan-influenced, 1930s Deco building has a good collection of European paintings, sculpture, and textiles donated in 1964 by the philanthropists John and Johanna Bass. The collection, dating from the 15th to 17th centuries, includes Renaissance works, paintings from the northern European schools, featuring paintings by Rubens, and huge 16th-century Flemish tapestries. The permanent galleries have more than 2,800 pieces on display.

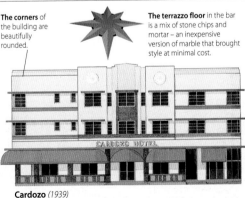

Terra-cotta tiles

**A veranda** is a prerequisite for most Ocean Drive hotels.

**The corners** of the building are beautifully rounded.

**The terrazzo floor** in the bar is a mix of stone chips and mortar – an inexpensive version of marble that brought style at minimal cost.

**Adrian** *(1934)*
Its Mediterranean inspiration and subdued colors make the Adrian stand out from other buildings.

**Cardozo** *(1939)*
A late Henry Hohauser work and Barbara Capitman's favorite, this Streamline gem replaces traditional Art Deco details with curved sides and aerodynamic racing stripes.

## ④ Biscayne Bay Boat Trips

**Map** D3. Bayside Marketplace.
Ⓜ College/Bayside. 🚌 16, 3, C, 95, BM, S, FM, Night Owl. Island Queen Cruises: (305) 379-5119. Duck Tours: (305) 673-2217. All other tour boats: (305) 577-3344.

A leisurely way to view the sprinkling of exclusive private island communities around Biscayne Bay is to take one of the many cruises from **Bayside Marketplace**. Tours, such as "Estates of the Rich and Famous" run by Island Queen Cruises, leave regularly and last about 90 minutes.

Tours begin by sailing past Dodge and Lummus islands, where the world's busiest cruise port is situated. This port, which contributes an annual income of more than $5 billion to the local economy, handles more than three million cruise passengers a year.

Near the eastern end of MacArthur Causeway is the US Coastguard's fleet of high-speed craft. Opposite lies the unbridged Fisher Island, separated from South Beach by Government Cut, a water channel dredged in 1905. A restricted beach for African-Americans in the 1920s, this is now, ironically, a highly exclusive residential enclave, with homes rarely costing less than $500,000. The tour continues north around the man-made Star, Palm, and Hibiscus islands, where real estate lots were sometimes sold "by the gallon." Among the lavish mansions are the former homes of Frank Sinatra and Al Capone, as well as the present

abodes of stars such as Gloria Estefan and Julio Iglesias.

Other boat trips include nighttime cruises, deep-sea fishing excursions, and a tall-ship cruise. Duck Tours take place on an amphibious vehicle that departs several times a day from South Beach, just off Lincoln Road. The tour takes in points of interest in South Beach and heads into Miami before "splashing" into Biscayne Bay for a closer look at the homes of the rich and famous on Star Island. Bayside Marketplace is a fun complex with several shops, bars, and restaurants, including the Hard Rock Café, complete with a guitar erupting from its roof. **Bayfront Park** is nearby. At its center is the Torch of Friendship, commemorating John F. Kennedy, surrounded by the coats of arms of Central and South American countries; a plaque from the city's exiled Cuban community thanks the US for allowing them to settle here.

## ⑤ Museum Park

**Map** D3. Biscayne Boulevard
Ⓜ 11th St, Park West. 🚌 2, 3, 11, 35, 103, 119, 137, 207, Night Owl. Pérez Art Museum Miami: 1103 Biscayne Boulevard. **Tel** (305) 375-3000. **Open** 10am–6pm Tue–Sun (to 9pm Thu). 🅦 **pamm.org**

This large park houses the **Pérez Art Museum Miami**, which replaced the Miami Art Museum in 2013. The museum's collection consists of 20th-century and contemporary international art, with an emphasis on art of the Americas. The Frost Museum of Science is expected to open in the park during 2015.

Miami-Dade Cultural Center, in downtown Miami

## ⑥ Miami-Dade Cultural Center

**Map** D3. 101 West Flagler St.
Ⓜ Government Center. 🚌 all buses to Miami Ave. HistoryMiami: **Tel** (305) 375-1492. **Open** 10am–5pm Mon–Sat, noon–5pm Sun. 🎨 ♿ Main Public Library: **Open** Mon–Sat.

Designed by the celebrated American architect Philip Johnson in 1982, the Miami-Dade Cultural Center is a large complex, with a Mediterranean-style central courtyard and fountains. It includes a museum and library. The Museum of HistoryMiami concentrates on pre-1945 Miami. Besides displays on the Spanish colonization and Seminole culture, there is a fascinating collection of old photographs. These bring to life Miami's early history, from the hardships endured by the early pioneers to the fun-filled Roaring Twenties.

## ⑦ Downtown

**Map** D3. Ⓜ various stations. US Federal Courthouse: 301 N Miami Ave. **Tel** (305) 523-5100. Ⓜ Arena/State Plaza. **Open** 8am–5pm Mon–Fri. **Closed** public hols. ♿

When the development of Miami took off with the arrival of the Florida East Coast Railway in 1896, the early city focused on one square mile (2.5 km) on the banks of the Miami River. Today, this is the site of present downtown and the hub of the city's financial district. Its futuristic skyscrapers are a monument to the banking boom of the 1980s, when the city emerged as a major financial and trade center. The raised track of the Metromover, a driverless shuttle launched in

One of the lavish mansions seen during a Biscayne Bay boat tour

View of downtown Miami's skyline from the MacArthur Causeway

1986, provides a swift but good overview of the area.

Among the most striking high-rises here are the Southeast Financial Center and the Miami Tower, built in 1983, and famous for its changing nighttime illuminations. Older structures include the Alfred I. DuPont Building (1938) and the Ingraham Building (1927), a Neo-Classical/Renaissance Revival work.

The **US Federal Courthouse**, completed in 1931, is an imposing Neo-Classical building, with a pleasant, Mediterranean courtyard. It has hosted a number of high-profile trials, including that of Manuel Noriega, the former Panamanian president, in 1990. Its main attraction is the mural on the second floor. Designed by Denman Fink *(see p296)*, it depicts Miami's transformation from a wilderness into a modern city. Entry is often restricted, especially during high-profile cases.

Freedom Tower (1925)

Miami's oldest Catholic parish, **Gesu Church** built in 1925, is on Northeast 2nd Street. It is noted for its fine stained-glass windows, made in Munich, Germany. The **Freedom Tower**, on Biscayne Boulevard, is loosely modeled on the Giralda in Seville. As first home to the now-defunct *Miami News*, it was the reception center for Cuban exiles in the 1960s and is now a cultural center. Macy's (formerly Burdines, founded in 1898) is on Flagler Street.

## ⑧ Little Havana

**Map** C3. 🚌 8 from Downtown, 17, 12, 6. El Titan de Bronze: 1071 SW 8th St. **Tel** (305) 860-1412. **Open** 9am–5pm Mon–Sat.

As its name suggests, the 3.5-sq-mile (9-sq-km) area comprising Little Havana has been the surrogate homeland of Cuban immigrants since the 1960s. The atmosphere here, especially on the streets, is vibrant and reflects the Cuban way of life. Spanish is spoken everywhere, while a salsa beat emanates from every other shop, and *bodegas* (canteens) sell Cuban specialties. The main commercial thoroughfare and sentimental heart is **Calle Ocho** (Southwest 8th Street), with its liveliest stretch between 11th and 17th Avenues. The small but authentic **El Titan de Bronze**, near Calle Ocho and 11th Avenue, is a cigar shop with cigars handcrafted in the traditional Cuban style by rollers who have worked in the finest factories in the world. The leaves are grown in the Dominican Republic, reputedly from Cuban tobacco seeds, the world's best.

The district's nationalistic focal point, **Cuban Memorial Boulevard**, as Southwest 13th Avenue is known, is dotted with memorials in honor of Cuban heroes. The most prominent is the Brigade 2506 Memorial's eternal flame commemorating the disastrous Bay of Pigs invasion in 1961. On April 17, people gather here to remember the Cubans who died in the attempt to overthrow Fidel Castro's regime. Beyond are other memorials to heroes who fought against Cuba's Spanish colonialists in the 1880s. At intervals, too, along Calle Ocho between 12th and 17th Avenues, are stars on the pavement honoring modern-day Latin celebrities such as Julio Iglesias and Gloria Estefan in Little Havana's version of Hollywood's Walk of Fame.

Salsa music album covers

North of Calle Ocho, at West Flagler Street and Southwest 17th Avenue, the Plaza de la Cubanidad has a map of Cuba sculpted in bronze. There's a flourish of banners advertising the headquarters of Alpha 66, Miami's most hard-line anti-Castro group.

Also in this district are the tiny Máximo Gómez Park, or Domino Park, and Woodlawn Cemetery. The Versailles restaurant, nearby, is the Cuban community's cultural and culinary bastion.

A Cuban mural in Little Havana, symbolizing nostalgia for the homeland

## ⑨ Coral Gables

**Map** A4. Lowe Art Museum: **Tel** (305) 284-3535. 🚇 Metrorail (University). 🚌 52, 56, 72. **Open** 10am–4pm Tue–Sat, noon–4pm Sun. **Closed** major public hols. 🐾 ♿ Miracle Mile: 🚇 Metrorail (Douglas Rd), then bus J or 40, 42, 24 from downtown.

Aptly named the City Beautiful, Coral Gables is a separate city within Greater Miami. In the 1920s, George Merrick planned this aesthetic wonderland with Denman Fink as artistic advisor, Frank Button as landscaper, and Phineas Paist as architectural director. Regulations guarantee that new buildings follow the same part-Italian, part-Spanish style advocated by Merrick. Major landmarks here include the Spanish Baroque **Coral Gables Congregational Church**, the district's first church, the Spanish Renaissance Coral Gables City Hall, and the **Lowe Art Museum**, the first art museum in South Florida, located in the University of Miami's campus.

Its main shopping street was named **Miracle Mile** (the walk along one side and down the other being the mile in question) by a developer in 1940. The Colonnade Hotel was built in 1926 by Merrick as the headquarters for his real estate business. Nearby, at Salzedo Street and Aragon Avenue, is the Old Police Station Building, built in 1939.

Coral Gables Congregational Church

South view of the Biltmore Hotel, Coral Gables' most famous landmark

## ⑩ Biltmore Hotel

**Map** A4. 1200 Anastasia Ave. **Tel** (855) 311-6903. 🚇 Metrorail (S Miami) then bus 72. ♿ 🍴 Sun free. 🌐 **biltmorehotel.com**

During its heyday in the 1920s, this hotel hosted figures such as Al Capone, Judy Garland, and the Duke and Duchess of Windsor. During World War II, it served as a military hospital and remained a veterans' hospital until 1968. After a $55-million restoration in 1986, it went bankrupt in 1990 but reopened two years later. The Biltmore's most striking feature is a 315-ft (96-m) near replica of Seville Cathedral's La Giralda, also the model for Miami's Freedom Tower *(see p295)*. Inside is a grand lobby, lined with Herculean pillars. The Biltmore has one of the largest hotel swimming pools in the US, where its famous instructor, Johnny Weissmuller – known for his role as Tarzan – set a world record in the 1930s.

## ⑪ Venetian Pool

**Map** A4. 2701 De Soto Blvd. **Tel** (305) 460-5306. 🚇 Metrorail (S Miami) then bus 72. **Open** Apr–May & Sep–Oct: 11am–5:30pm; mid-Jun– mid-Aug: 11am–7:30pm Mon–Fri; Nov–Mar: 10am–4:30pm; all year: 10am–4:30pm Sat & Sun. **Closed** Mon in Sep–May, Jan 1, Thanksgiving, Dec 24 & 25. 🐾 ♿ 🌐 **coralgablesvenetian pool.com**

Perhaps the most beautiful swimming pool in the world, the Venetian Pool was ingeniously fashioned from a coral rock quarry in 1923 by Denman Fink and Phineas Paist. Pink stucco towers and vine-covered loggias, candy-cane Venetian poles, a cobblestone bridge, fountains, waterfalls, and numerous caves surround crystal-clear, spring-fed waters, which are great for swimming. The pool was once one of the most fashionable social spots in Coral Gables – in the lobby are a series of photographs of beauty pageants staged here during the 1920s. This beautiful public swimming pool is definitely worth a visit, for a swim or just a look.

Venetian Pool, ingeniously created in the 1920s out of an old coral rock quarry

*For hotels and restaurants see pp326–31*

# ⑫ Coconut Grove Village

**Map** B4. 🚇 Metrorail (Coconut Grove). 🚌 42 from Coral Gables, 48 from downtown, 6, 27, 22.

Miami's oldest community, Coconut Grove was a fabled hippie hangout in the 1960s. Today, "the village," as it is simply known, is famous for its cafés and restaurants, especially at night or on weekends. This is also the city's most relaxed shopping area with many boutiques and two malls – the outdoor CocoWalk, and the stylish Streets of Mayfair. In contrast are the food stalls of the colorful farmers' market, held every Saturday at McDonald Street and Grand Avenue.

On Grand Avenue, too, are the simple homes of the local Bahamian community, descendants of the Wreckers *(see p323)*, who lived here from the mid-1800s. The exuberant Goombay Festival, a party with a parade, great food, and Caribbean music, is held here every June.

In a shady, affluent neighborhood south along Main Highway, is the **Barnacle**,

Coconut Grove Village, a lively area of shops, cafés, and bars

home of Ralph Monroe, a Renaissance man who made his living from ship building and wrecking. At 3400 Devon Road is the picturesque **Plymouth Congregational Church**, built in 1916.

# ⑬ Vizcaya

**Map** C4. 3251 S Miami Ave. **Tel** (305) 250-9133. 🚇 Metrorail (Vizcaya). 🚌 48. **Open** 9:30am–4:30pm Mon, Wed–Sun. **Closed** Thanksgiving, Dec 25. 🚫 📷 ♿ limited. 🚻 🖥 📷
🌐 vizcayamuseum.org

Florida's grandest residence was completed in 1916 as the winter retreat for millionaire industrialist James Deering. His vision was to replicate a 16th-century Italian estate, but one that had been altered by succeeding generations. As a result, Vizcaya and its opulent rooms come in a blend of styles from Renaissance to Neo-Classical, furnished with the fruits of Deering's shopping sprees around Europe. The formal gardens, a rarity in Florida, beautifully combine Italian and French garden features with tropical foliage. They are dotted with sculptures

**Statue of Pulcinella**

and quaint buildings, including a Japanese tea house. Deering would always ask of his architect: "Must we be so grand?" fearing that Vizcaya would be too costly to support. After Deering's death in 1925, it proved to be so until it was bought by Miami-Dade County in 1952. The house and gardens were opened to the public thereafter.

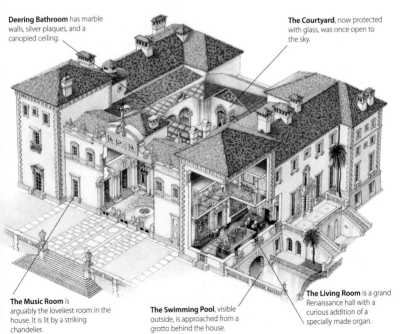

**Deering Bathroom** has marble walls, silver plaques, and a canopied ceiling.

**The Courtyard**, now protected with glass, was once open to the sky.

**The Music Room** is arguably the loveliest room in the house. It is lit by a striking chandelier.

**The Swimming Pool**, visible outside, is approached from a grotto behind the house.

**The Living Room** is a grand Renaissance hall with a curious addition of a specially made organ.

# Greater Miami

The areas north of Miami Beach and downtown and south of Coral Gables are seldom very scenic, but they are still well worth exploring for the great beaches and family amusements. To the south of the city, past citrus groves, coastal mangrove swamps, and the edges of the Everglades, visitors can find the city's zoo, along with several stunning gardens. The area was hit hard by Hurricane Andrew in 1992 but all affected areas have since completely recovered.

Beach at Haulover Park, under the protective eye of a lifeguard

## ⑭ North Beaches

**Map** F4. Collins Ave. 🚌 K, S, or T from South Beach or downtown.

The Barrier Islands to the north along Collins Avenue are occupied mainly by posh residential areas and inexpensive resorts, popular with package tours. A quiet strip of sand between 79th and 87th Streets separates Miami Beach from **Surfside**, a simple community popular with French Canadians. At 96th Street Surfside merges with **Bal Harbour**, a stylish enclave known for its flashy hotels and one of Miami's swankiest malls, Bal Harbour Shops. To the north is the pleasant **Haulover Park**, with a marina on the creek side and dune-backed sands facing the ocean.

## ⑮ Ancient Spanish Monastery

**Map** F4. 16711 W Dixie Hwy, N Miami Beach. **Tel** (407) 945-1461. 🚌 H from South Beach, 3 from downtown. **Open** 10am–4:30pm Mon–Sat, 11am–4:30pm Sun. **Closed** public hols, may close Sat or Sun for special events. 🅿 ♿
🆆 spanishmonastery.com

These monastery cloisters have an unusual history. Built in Spain between 1133 and 1141, they were bought in 1925 by newspaper tycoon William Randolph Hearst *(see p676)*, who had their 35,000 stones packed into

crates. An outbreak of foot-and-mouth disease led to the crates being opened (to check the packing straw), and the stones were repacked incorrectly. Once in New York, they remained there until 1952,

when it was decided to piece together "the world's largest and most expensive jigsaw puzzle." The cloisters resemble the original, but there is still a pile of unidentified stones in a corner of the gardens.

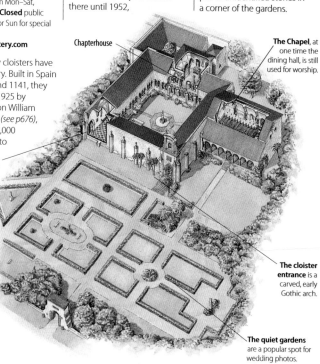

Chapterhouse

**The Chapel**, at one time the dining hall, is still used for worship.

Statue of Alphonso VII, patron of the monastery

**The cloister entrance** is a carved, early Gothic arch.

**The quiet gardens** are a popular spot for wedding photos.

The bell outside the chapel door

The tranquil, palm-fringed lakes of the Fairchild Tropical Botanic Garden

## ⑯ Key Biscayne

**Map** F5. 7 miles (11 km) SE of downtown. B. Bill Baggs Cape Florida State Park: **Tel** (305) 361-5811. **Open** daily. **W** **floridastateparks.org**

The view of downtown from Rickenbacker Causeway, connecting the mainland to Virginia Key and Key Biscayne, is one of Miami's best. Views aside, this has some of the city's top beaches. The most impressive is at Crandon Park in the upper half of the Key, which is 3 miles (5 km) long and enormously wide, with palm trees and picnic areas. At the southern end, the **Bill Baggs Cape Florida State Park** has a shorter beach joined to more picnic areas by boardwalks across the dunes.

## ⑰ Fairchild Tropical Botanic Garden

**Map** F5. 10901 Old Cutler Rd. **Tel** (305) 667-1651. 65 from Coconut Grove. **Open** Office: 8am–5pm daily. Gardens: sunrise–sunset daily. **Closed** Dec 25. **W** **fairchildgarden.org** Mattheson Hammock Park: **Tel** (305) 665-5475. **Open** 6am–sunset daily.

Established in 1938, this beautiful tropical garden is also a major botanical research institution. One of the world's largest collections of palm trees (550 of the 2,500 known species) stands around a series of man-made lakes. The garden also has an impressive array of cycads – relatives of palms and ferns that bear unusual giant red cones – as well as countless other trees and plants, including a comical-looking sausage tree.

Guides on the 40-minute tram tours describe how plants are used in the manufacture of medicines and perfumes (the flowers of the ylang-ylang tree, for example, are used in Chanel No. 5). The waterfront **Mattheson Hammock Park** is next door to the Fairchild Tropical Garden. Its highlight is the Atoll Pool, an artificial salt-water swimming pool circled by sand and palm trees alongside Biscayne Bay.

Palms in Fairchild Tropical Garden

## ⑱ Zoo Miami

**Map** E5. 12400 SW 152nd St, Miami. **Tel** (305) 251-0400. Metrorail (Dadeland North) then Zoo Bus. **Open** 9:30am–5:30pm daily. **W** **miamimetrozoo.com**

This enormous zoo is considered one of the country's best. Animals are kept in spacious landscaped habitats, separated from humans by moats. Highlights include lowland gorillas, Malayan sun bears, and white tigers. The Petting Zoo is a favorite with kids, and the Wildlife Show demonstrates the agility of the big cats. Take the 20-minute ride on the monorail for an overview of the zoo, and then visit what you like; or take the monorail to Station 4 and then walk back.

## ⑲ Wings Over Miami

**Map** F5. 14710 SW 128th St, adjacent to Tamiami Airport. **i** (305) 233-5197. **Open** 10am–5pm Wed–Sun. **Closed** public hols. **W** **wingsovermiami.com**

This museum is dedicated to the preservation of old aircraft. Its hangars contain a superb collection of finely preserved examples of aircraft that are still in operation, including a 1943 AT6D Texan "Old Timer," a Douglas B-23 Dragon, and a British Provost Jet, as well as a wide range of other fascinating exhibits such as a machine-gun turret.

All these planes take to the sky during the Memorial Day weekend celebration, while in February, they are joined by B-17 and B-24 bombers in the Wings of Freedom event.

White tiger in front of a mock Khmer temple at Zoo Miami

## ❷ Fort Lauderdale

🏙 170,000. ✈ 🚋 🚌 🚢 **i** 100 East Broward Blvd, Ste 303, (954) 765-4466.

Proclaimed the "Yachting Capital of the World," Fort Lauderdale's character is defined by its waterways, which branch from the New River. The area around the mouth of the river is known as the **Isles**. This is the city's prime area, with mansions behind lush foliage and luxurious yachts moored in the waterways.

Millions of visitors head for the barrier islands lying along the coast between the beaches and the Intracoastal Waterway. The waterway crosses **Port Everglades**, the world's second largest cruise port after Miami. Riverboat cruises and water taxis are also available.

**Las Olas Boulevard**, the city's busiest street, is lined with eateries and boutiques. The fine **Museum of Art**, also located here, is best known for its works by the CoBrA artists, a group of 20th-century Expressionist painters from Copenhagen, Brussels, and Amsterdam.

Water taxi on the New River, Fort Lauderdale

Downtown is the city's business and cultural center. **Riverwalk**, a 1.5-mile (2.4-km) stretch along the New River's north bank, links most of the city's historical and cultural landmarks; it starts at **Stranaham House** (1901), which originally served as a trading post, post office, and

Peach-pink Mizner Park, one of Boca Raton's shopping malls

bank. **Old Fort Lauderdale** runs along Southwest 2nd Avenue and has a few early 1900s buildings, such as the Fort Lauderdale History Center. The city has the liveliest beaches on the Gold Coast, especially toward the end of Las Olas Boulevard, where skaters cruise past bars and shops. To the west is Sawgrass Mills, Florida's largest mall, with its own indoor theme park, Wannado City.

## ❸ Boca Raton

🏙 87,800. 🚋 **i** 1555 Palm Beach Lakes Blvd, (561) 233-3000.

Affluent Boca Raton was originally a sleepy pineapple-growing settlement that architect Addison Mizner (1872–1933) envisaged as the "greatest resort in the world." The nucleus of his vision was the ultra-luxurious Cloister Inn, finished in 1926, with his trademark Spanish details. The hotel is now part of the exclusive **Boca Raton Resort and Club**. Weekly tours for nonresidents are arranged by the Boca Raton Historical Society, based at the Mizner-designed Town Hall.

Just opposite is the open-air **Mizner Park**, perhaps the most impressive of Boca Raton's dazzling malls. Located in a spectacular setting within Mizner Park is the **Boca Raton Museum of Art**. This museum contains 44,000 sq ft (4,088 sq m) of space for world-class exhibitions and an impressive display of contemporary art.

The verdant and historic **Old Floresta** district, a mile (1.6 km) west of the Town Hall, has 29 Mediterranean-style houses built by Mizner.

Boca Raton's long, undeveloped beach is reached via beachside parks, such as **Red Reef Park**, which also has the informative **Gumbo Limbo Nature Center**. The most northerly of the parks, **Spanish River Park** is also the most attractive, with pleasant picnic areas shaded by pines and palm trees. It also has a lovely lagoon on the Intracoastal Waterway, next to an observation tower.

🏛 **Boca Raton Museum of Art**
501 Plaza Real, Mizner Park.
**Tel** (561) 392-2500. **Open** 10am–5pm Tue–Fri (to 9pm Wed), noon–5pm Sat & Sun. **Closed** public hols. ♿ ♿
🌐 bocamuseum.org

## ❹ Loxahatchee National Wildlife Refuge

10216 Lee Rd. **Tel** (561) 732-3684.
🚋 Boynton Beach. 🚌 Refuge: **Open** daily. **Closed** Dec 25. ♿ ♿ 📷
Visitor Center: **Open** May–Oct: Wed–Sun; Nov–Apr: daily. **Closed** Dec 25.

The northernmost part of the Everglades *(see p321)*, this 221-sq-mile (572-sq-km) refuge is known for its superb wildlife. The best time to visit is in winter, when migrating birds arrive here from the north.

Cyclists and skaters enjoying the beachfront in Fort Lauderdale

*For hotels and restaurants see pp326–31*

An alleyway along Worth Avenue, Palm Beach's most exclusive street

The visitor center, off Route 441, has a display that explains the Everglades' ecology, and there are also two trails. The Cypress Swamp Boardwalk is lined with wax myrtle trees, and the longer Marsh Trail is a bird-watcher's paradise, with ibis, herons, and anhingas. Visitors can also spot turtles and alligators. Those with canoes can explore the 5.5-mile (9-km) canoe trail, and there are also numerous nature walks.

## ❺ Palm Beach

🔼 8,500. ✈ 🚗 🚌
ℹ️ 45 Cocoanut Row, (561) 655-3282.

Essentially a winter resort for the rich and famous, Palm Beach was created at the end of the 19th century by the railroad baron Henry Flagler. In the 1920s Addison Mizner built luxurious Spanish-style mansions for its residents, a trend that established its unique look and influenced future architectural styles. Palm Beach's major sights can be viewed in the area between Cocoanut Row and South County Road. Of these, the **Flagler Museum** (formerly Whitehall), Flagler's 55-room winter residence, has a grand marble entrance hall, an Italian Renaissance library, and a Louis XV ballroom. Flagler's private railroad car is on display on the South Lawn.

To the south, the **Society of the Four Arts**, founded in 1936, has two libraries, an exhibition space, and an auditorium for concerts and films. Other interesting buildings include the Town Hall, built in 1926, the Mizner Memorial Park, and **The Breakers**, a mammoth Italian Renaissance structure and Palm Beach's grandest hotel (see p326).

The epitome of Palm Beach's opulent lifestyle, however, is **Worth Avenue**. Stretching across four blocks from Lake Worth to the Atlantic Ocean, this is the town's best known thoroughfare. It first became fashionable with the construction of the Everglades Club in 1918, a collaborative effort between Mizner and his patron, Paris Singer, heir to the sewing machine fortune. Today, Worth Avenue boasts a spectacular mix of glitzy fashion boutiques, art galleries, and shops.

Picturesque alleyways, reminiscent of the backstreets of Spanish villages, connect with Worth Avenue. These interlinking pedestrian alleys, created by Mizner, are a riot of arches, twisting flights of stairs, cascading bougainvillea, and courtyards. The Esplanade, an open-air mall, is at the eastern end.

The multimillion-dollar mansions of Palm Beach are located in the suburbs. Some were built by Mizner and his imitators in the 1920s, but since then hundreds of other houses have proliferated in styles from Neo-Classical to Art Deco. The most easily visible are on a ridge along South Ocean Boulevard, nicknamed "Mansion Row." The most elaborate residence, Mar-a-Lago (# 1100), is now a top-end private club owned by millionaire Donald Trump.

### 🏛 Flagler Museum
1 Whitehall Way. **Tel** (561) 655-2833. **Open** 10am–5pm Tue–Sat, noon–5pm Sun. **Closed** Jan 1, Thanksgiving, Dec 25. 🔲 🔲 limited. 🔲 🔲 🔲
**W** flaglermuseum.us

Flagler Museum at Palm Beach, formerly Henry Flagler's winter home

## ❻ Cocoa Beach

🏔 11,200. 🚌 Merritt Island. 🛈 400 Fortenberry Rd, (321) 459-2200.

This large, no-frills resort calls itself the East Coast's surfing capital. Surfing festivals set the tone, along with win-your-weight-in-beer competitions. Motels, restaurants, and gift and souvenir shops characterize the main street. The dazzling **Ron Jon Surf Shop** has surf boards galore (for sale and rent) and a huge T-shirt collection. In front of its flashing towers are sculptures of sports figures.

## ❼ Kennedy Space Center

Off Rte 405, 6 miles (9.6 km) E of Titusville. **Tel** (321) 449-4444. 🚌 Titusville. **Open** 9am–7pm daily (closing time varies Sep–Dec; check website). **Closed** Dec 25. The center occasionally closes for operational requirements; always call ahead. 🅿 ♿ wheelchairs available at Information Central. 🅿 📷 **Tel** (321) 867-4636. 🆆 **kennedyspacecenter.com**

When Cape Canaveral was chosen as the site for NASA's (National Aeronautics and Space Administration) space program in the 1960s, the area came to be known as the Space Coast. The Kennedy Space Center on Merritt Island was the launching place for shuttle flights to the International Space Center until 2011. The historic space shuttles no longer fly, but future vehicles will launch from the area. The center was also the site of the historic launch of *Apollo 11* in July 1969, when President John F.

Rockets on display at the Cape Canaveral Air Force Station

Kennedy's dream of landing a man on the moon was realized. The **Visitor Complex**, built in 1967 for astronauts and their families to view space center operations, is a 131-sq-mile (340-sq-km) facility that includes many attractions. Its highlight is the two **IMAX® Theaters**, which show films on space exploration on screens that are five floors high. Footage from the shuttle missions offer breathtaking views of Earth from space. West of the entrance, the **Rocket Garden** is where visitors can walk through a group of rockets, each representing different stages in space history. **Robot Scouts**, located to the east of Rocket Garden, reveals the latest planetary explorer robots, while

**Exploration in the New Millennium** shows visitors what the future holds for space exploration; guests can even touch a piece of a Mars meteorite. The **Astronaut Encounter** in the same building is where visitors can meet real astronauts.

Guests can also climb aboard **Explorer** – a life-size replica of the Space Shuttle, at Shuttle Plaza in the northeastern corner of the Complex. Alongside Explorer are an external fuel tank, rocket boosters, and the Mission Status Center. Shuttles were the ingenious alternative to the very expensive, single-use crafts, used in the Apollo missions. Designed in the late 1970s, these re-usable spacecraft became the backbone of the space program. Close by, the **Astronaut Memorial** honors the astronauts, from the *Apollo 1* to the Space Shuttle *Columbia* missions, who died in the service of space missions.

Close to the entrance of the Complex, an all-glass rotunda leads to **Early Space Exploration**, which showcases key figures from the early days of rocketry. In the **Mercury Mission Control Room**, visitors view

A life-size replica of the space shuttle *Explorer*, Kennedy Space Center

## Timeline of American Space Exploration

| 1950 | 1960 | 1970 | 1980 | 1990 | 2000 | 2010 | 2020 |
|------|------|------|------|------|------|------|------|

Above the line:
- **1958** First American satellite, the *Explorer 1*, is launched (Jan 31)
- **1962** John Glenn orbits the earth in *Mercury* spacecraft
- **1975** American *Apollo* and Russian *Soyuz* vehicles dock in orbit (Jul 17)
- **1981** *Columbia* is the first shuttle in space (Apr 12)
- **1996** *Mars Pathfinder* sent to gather data from the surface of Mars
- **2003** Space Shuttle *Columbia* breaks up upon re-entry into the atmosphere (Feb 1)

Below the line:
- **1961** Alan Shephard becomes the first American in space
- **1969** Neil Armstrong and Buzz Aldrin (*Apollo 11*) walk on the moon (Jul 24)
- **1986** The *Challenger* explodes, killing its crew (Jan 28)
- **1990** The Hubble telescope is launched (Apr 24)
- **2011** Final flight of shuttle *Atlantis* and the end of the 30-year Space Shuttle Program

*For hotels and restaurants see pp326–31*

Launch pads seen on Kennedy Space Center Tours

the actual consoles from which the first eight manned missions were monitored. Footage and interviews with some of the personnel are the highlights. Next are displays of some of the authentic Mercury and Gemini spacecraft.

The Center offers a number of interesting tours. The **Kennedy Space Center (KSC) Bus Tour** leaves from the Visitor Complex and offers an overall tour. Visitors enter secured areas, where guides explain the inner workings of each facility. Each tour can take between two and six hours.

The **Apollo/Saturn V Center** features an actual 363-ft (110-m) Saturn V moon rocket, used by the Apollo missions. Visitors can watch the launch of *Apollo 8*, the first manned mission to the moon, in the Firing Room Theater, followed by a film at the Lunar Theater, which shows footage of the moon landing. This is also the only place in the world where guests can dine next to a genuine moon rock, at the Moon Rock Café.

The multimedia exhibit surrounding the Space Shuttle *Atlantis* showcases the spacecraft that orbited Earth on 33 missions from 1985 to 2011. The shuttle is displayed as only astronauts have previously seen it, with its payload bay doors open. Simulators and exhibits portray the day-to-day mission jobs and the history of the shuttle program.

Kids will enjoy the **Angry Birds Space Encounter**, an

attraction that teaches physics and engineering through video games. There are two special-interest tours – **Discover KSC: Today and Tomorrow**, an insider's view of the entire space shuttle program, and the **Cape Canaveral: Then & Now Tour**, an expedition to the Mercury, Gemini, and Apollo launch pads. It takes visitors to the Air Force Space & Missile Museum, where America's first satellite was launched, then to the launch complex where Alan Shepard lifted-off on America's first human space flight. The tour concludes at the Apollo/Saturn V Center. Visitors should remember that the Kennedy Space Center and Cape Canaveral are working space launch facilities, and tours may be altered or closed due to operational requirements. Outside the Center, prime viewing sites for rocket launches are in Titusville and Cocoa Beach.

### Environs
The **US Astronaut Hall of Fame** at Titusville, 9 miles (14 km) west of KSC, offers exciting opportunities to experience weightlessness and ride flight simulators with G-forces.

## ❽ Canaveral National Seashore & Merritt Island

🚌 Titusville. 🌐 nps.gov/cana

These adjacent preserves on the Space Coast share an astounding variety of fauna and a range of habitats including estuaries and hardwood hammocks. Visitors can often

see alligators and the endangered manatee, but the highlight is the rich birdlife.

The **Canaveral National Seashore** has a pristine 24-mile (39-km) stretch of beach. Apollo Beach at the northern end, and Playalinda Beach to the south are fine for sunbathing, but swimming can be hazardous, and there are no lifeguards. The top of Turtle Mound offers splendid views of Mosquito Lagoon (aptly named, so be sure to bring repellent in spring and summer).

Route 402 to Playalinda Beach has views of the Kennedy Space Center's launch pads. It also crosses **Merritt Island National Wildlife Refuge**, which covers an area of 220 sq miles (570 sq km). Much of the refuge lies within the Space Center and is out of bounds. Winter is the best season to visit. To view the local wildlife, follow the Black Point Wildlife Drive, which has the 5-mile (8-km) Cruickshank Trail. Be sure to pick up the informative leaflet at the drive's entrance. The Visitors' Information Center has displays on the habitats and wildlife in the refuge. One mile (1.6 km) farther east, the Oak Hammock and Palm Hammock trails have short boardwalks across the marshland for bird-watchers.

🌐 **Canaveral National Seashore**
Rte A1A, 20 miles (32 km) N of Titusville or Rte 402, 10 miles (16 km) E of Titusville. **Tel** (321) 267-1110. **Open** daily. 🦅

🌐 **Merritt Island National Wildlife Refuge**
Rte 406, 4 miles (6.5 km) E of Titusville. **Tel** (321) 861-0667. **Open** daily.

---

### Space Coast Birdlife

The Space Coast is a bird-watcher's paradise. Its magnificent and abundant birdlife is best viewed early in the morning or shortly before dusk. Between November and March, in particular, the marshes and lagoons teem with migratory ducks and waders, as up to 100,000 birds arrive from colder northern climates. Royal terns, white ibis, black skimmers, brown pelicans, and sandhill cranes are some of the birds that are frequently seen.

Brown pelican

# ❾ Walt Disney World® Resort

Walt Disney World® Resort, covering 43 sq miles (69 sq km), is the largest entertainment complex on earth. The main draw is its theme parks: Magic Kingdom®, Epcot®, Disney's Hollywood Studios®, and Animal Kingdom®. A self-sufficient vacation spot, the Resort offers more than 30 lodgings right on site, along with golf courses, water parks, a sports complex, hiking and riding trails, and lakes for boating. Peerless in its imagination and attention to detail, the Resort is also a hermetic bubble cocooned from the real world. Everything runs like clockwork, and nothing shatters its illusions of fantasy. Unless you're a confirmed cynic, Walt Disney World® Resort will amaze you.

## Useful Numbers

**General Information**
Tel (407) 939-6244.

**Accommodation Information/Reservations**
Tel (407) 939-6244.

**Dining Reservations**
Tel (407) 939-3463.
Ⓦ disney.go.com

## When to Visit

The busiest times of the year are Christmas and Easter, June to August, and the last week in February. At these times, the parks approach capacity – some 90,000 people in the Magic Kingdom® alone. Even so, all the rides operate and the parks remain open for much longer. During the off-season, 10,000 visitors a day might visit the Magic Kingdom®, and certain attractions may be closed for maintenance. The weather is also a factor – in July and August, hot and humid afternoons are regularly punctuated by thunderstorms. Between October and March, the temperatures and humidity are much more comfortable and permit a more energetic schedule.

## Length of Visit

Walt Disney World® offers at least a week of entertainment. To enjoy it to the full, give Magic Kingdom® and Epcot® two days each, and a day each for Disney's Hollywood Studios® and Animal Kingdom®. Keep three nights to see the splendid fireworks displays of Fantasmic!, Fantasy in the Sky, and IllumiNations.

## Getting Around

An extensive transportation system handles an average of 200,000 guests each day. Even if you stay outside Walt Disney World® Resort, many nearby hotels offer free shuttle services to and from the theme parks. Check when you make your reservation. The transport hub of Walt Disney World® is the **Ticket and Transportation Center** (TTC). Connecting it to the Magic Kingdom® are two monorail services. A third monorail links the TTC to Epcot®. Ferries run from the TTC to the Magic Kingdom®. They also connect the Magic Kingdom® and Epcot® with resorts in their areas. Buses link everything in Walt Disney World®, including direct links to Magic Kingdom®. Residents and pass holders can use the entire transportation system for free, while one-day tickets allow holders to use the ferries and monorails between the TTC and Magic Kingdom®.

## Disabled Travelers

Wheelchairs can be borrowed at the park entrance, and special bypass entrances allow disabled guests to board rides without waiting in line. Staff, however, are not allowed to assist with lifting for safety reasons.

## Very Young Children

Parents with pre-school age kids can make use of the unique system known as "switching off," where they can enjoy various rides and attractions one at a time while the other parent stays with the child, without having to line up twice.

The Resort can be exhausting, so it is a good idea to rent a stroller from any park entrance. Take frequent breaks from the excitement and the heat by building in time for snacks or naps.

If you've come with young kids you should focus mainly on the Magic Kingdom®.

**Walt Disney Resort**

**Key**
- ▨ Magic Kingdom® Resort Area
- ▨ Disney Village Resort Area
- ▨ Epcot® Resort Area
- ▨ Studio Resort Area

MAGIC KINGDOM®
Ticket and Transportation Center
Disney's animal kingdom®
Epcot®
Disney's Hollywood Studios®
Downtown Disney®
Exit 27
Exit 26B
Typhoon Lagoon
Exit 25B

0 meters 800
0 yards 800

## Safety

The resort's first-rate security force means problems are dealt with promptly. Cast members are trained to watch out for unaccompanied children and escort them to lost children centers.

## Parking

Visitors to the Magic Kingdom® must park at the TTC and use public transportation; Epcot® and Disney's Hollywood Studios® have their own parking lots. Parking is free for Disney Resort residents; others must pay, but only once a day regardless of how many times they move their vehicle.

## Advantages of Staying in the Resort

Lodgings in the resorts and in Walt Disney World Swan and Dolphin (operated independently but Disneyesque in every other respect) are of a very high standard. However, even the lowest-priced places are more expensive than many hotels outside Walt Disney World®.

Nevertheless, a few practical reasons to stay there are:
• Proximity to parks and free use of Disney's transportation.
• Early entry privileges into the parks (up to 90 minutes). Check in advance with each park for details.
• Guaranteed admission to the theme parks even when the parks are otherwise full.
• The possibility of dining with your favorite Disney character in your hotel.
• The delivery of shopping purchases made anywhere within the Resort.
• Note that the hotels close to the Marketplace (which are not run by Disney) offer few of the above mentioned privileges. For information on hotel listings see page 327.

## Resort Dining

Visitors should make reservations in advance for any full-service restaurant in Walt Disney World® Resort, especially in the theme parks and above all in Epcot®. Whether or not you are staying at one of the resorts, reservations for dining can be made 60 days in advance. Some tables are held for same-day reservations, so make your reservation as early in the morning as possible. For restaurant details, see page 330.

## Meeting Mickey

For many youngsters, meeting the Disney characters is the high point of their visit. Apart from seeing them in the parks, you can also meet them in numerous restaurants (usually at breakfast!). Each park and many resorts also offer "character dining," but you must book ahead.

# DIRECTORY

## Information

### Tickets & Types of Passes
You can buy one-day, or two- to 10-day, one-park tickets, but if you're planning to visit more than one park, consider adding the following options:
**Park Hopper Add-On:** entitles entry to all four parks.
**Water Park Add-On** or **Park Hopper and Water Park Add-On:** gives access to any combination of parks.
**Seasonal, Annual and Premium Annual Passes:** cost little more than a 7-day park hopper for an entire year of visits. Child pricing applies to ages 3–9. Prices depend on length of stay.
**FastPass+** allows guests to reserve fast admission to rides and attractions such as shows, parades, and fireworks in advance. Guests staying at a Disney Resort Hotel can make FastPass+ reservations up to 60 days in advance of their visit.

## Busiest Days
Each of the theme parks is busiest on certain days:
**Magic Kingdom®:** Monday, Thursday, and Saturday.
**Epcot®:** Tuesday, Friday, and Saturday.
**Disney's Hollywood Studios®:** Wednesday and Sunday.

### Opening Hours
When the theme parks are busiest, opening hours are the longest: 9am to 10/11pm or midnight. In less busy periods, hours are 9am to 6/7/8pm. The parks open early for pass holders and guests at any of the Resort hotels. Call to check details.

### The Ideal Schedule
To avoid the worst of the crowds and heat, arrive early and visit the popular attractions first. Take a break in the afternoon, when it is hot and parks are busy, and return in the evening to see parades and fireworks.

## Top Tips
• Lines are shortest at the start and end of the day, and during parade and meal times. The wait for a show is rarely longer than the show itself.
• Parks fill rapidly after the first hour of opening. Until then, you can often just walk onto rides for which there will be a line later.
• After a thunderstorm, the water parks are often almost empty, even at the busiest times of the year.
• Information regarding timings of shows, parades, and rides, and tips such as the waiting times at various attractions, are usually available at each park. Check at bulletin boards, Information Centers, and Guest Services.
• Ask for a Park Map.
• During parades, other attractions are quiet.
• Wear a comfortable pair of shoes, as the parks entail a lot of walking.
• There is very little shade, so be sure to wear a hat.

## Magic Kingdom®

Magic Kingdom® is the essential Disney theme park. Disney characters fill its cheerful acres, and seven lands evoke different themes.

It is best to head straight for **Space Mountain®**, a superb coaster in Tomorrowland®. It shoots around in stygian blackness against projections of asteroids and galaxies. Another popular attraction is **Monsters, Inc. Laugh Floor.** Guests find the power of laughter in an interactive adventure inspired by the movie. **Buzz Lightyear's Space Ranger Spin** is a fabulous journey in a two-seater car. It is fitted with laser cannons and a control, so you can shoot at targets with a laser beam.

**Fantasyland®**, dominated by Cinderella's Castle, forms the core of the Magic Kingdom®. Additions resulting from a major expansion include the very popular **Be Our Guest Restaurant** inside the **Beast's Castle**, **Seven Dwarfs Mine Train** ride, and a choice of Disney character rides inside the **Storybook Circus**, with its colorful circus tents. **The Many Adventures of Winnie the Pooh** uses the latest technology, lighting, and sound effects to create an enchanting experience, while

**Peter Pan's Flight** combines the feeling of flying with the delight of perfectly matched music and movement. **"it's a small world"** is a musical indoor voyage and one of the most popular rides at Disney.

**The Haunted Mansion®** in Liberty Square leads visitors through a spook-ridden mansion and graveyard.

Set in the Wild West, Frontierland® offers a journey on a runaway train known as **Big Thunder Mountain Railroad**. The fun **Country Bear Jamboree** is an Audio-Animatronics® animal show, and **Splash Mountain®** is an exciting flume ride.

**Adventureland®** is a fusion of Africa and the Caribbean. **The Jungle Cruise** goes past an animatronically animated setting of Africa. Another voyage, **Pirates of the Caribbean®**, leads you into underground prisons and past 16th-century galleons.

Main Street USA is famous for the **Festival of Fantasy**, a fantasy of music, live action, and illuminated floats. In peak season, it takes place at 7pm and again at 9pm. The afternoon parade is best viewed from Frontierland®. The evening parade also features **Wishes℠ Nighttime Spectacular** – an extravaganza of fireworks and music.

## Epcot®

Epcot®, an acronym for the Experimental Prototype Community of Tomorrow, was Disney's dream of a techno-logically advanced community that represented a utopian vision of the future.

The enormous 250-acre (101 ha) park is divided into two halves: **Future World**, with an emphasis on entertainment and education; and **World Showcase**, which represents the art, culture, and culinary skills of different countries around the globe. Boats cross the World Showcase Lagoon frequently and are a con-venient method of getting here.

The unmistakable seven-and-a-half-thousand-ton globe of **Spaceship Earth** is the focal point of Future World. It takes visitors past superbly crafted tableaux and Animatronics® scenes portraying future possibilities in technology. Since most people visit here first, there are long lines in the mornings, so it is best seen in the afternoon.

**Test Track**, one of Epcot's® top rides, places visitors in a simulator that moves on tracks at high speeds. You test a prototype sports car at over 66 mph (106 km/h) on a raised roadway. Try to visit this ride first in the morning. The popular **Mission: SPACE** uses state-of-the-art technology to simulate a ride to Mars in a rocket. This may cause motion sickness.

**The Imagination Pavilion** features **Journey into Imagination with Figment**, an upbeat ride, which explores ideas relating to the arts and sciences.

At **The Seas with Nemo & Friends Pavilion** visitors can watch sea life through transparent walls, climb aboard a "Clamobile" to search for Nemo, or enjoy the interactive show, "Turtle Talk with Crush."

**The Land Pavilion** has a tremendously popular attraction called Soarin'. Visitors are lifted high off the ground in a simu-lated hang-glider trip. The wind whips through your hair and your feet dangle above treetops as you "fly" over California. World Showcase has architectural

### Eating & Drinking

The typical fare at **Magic Kingdom®** is fast food. However, try the Liberty Tree Tavern or Crystal Palace for quieter dining. Cinderella's Royal Table in the castle has a regal ambience, and the Be Our Guest Restaurant offers upscale French cuisine.

The dining at **Epcot®** is superb, particularly **World Showcase**, where reservations are required. Recommended are: **Mexico:** the San Angel Inn serves interesting but pricey Mexican cuisine. **Italy:** Tutto Italia Ristorante serves pasta and fine Italian specialties. **Japan:** you can eat communally, either in the Mitsukoshi Teppan Edo or at the bar of Mitsukoshi Tokyo Dining for sushi and tempura. **France:** the upscale Monsieur Paul (dinner only); Les Chefs de France, an exclusive restaurant with haute cuisine; and **Canada:** Le Cellier Steakhouse for steaks and crêpes.

At **Disney's Hollywood Studios®**, you can soak up the atmos-phere at three of the full-service restaurants. The costly Hollywood Brown Derby replicates Hollywood's Original Brown Derby, where the stars met in the 1930s. Children prefer the Sci-Fi Dine-In Theater Restaurant, where you sit in mini-Cadillacs and watch old sci-fi films. For dining without a reservation, try Hollywood & Vine, which serves pasta, salads, seafood, ribs, and steaks.

*For hotels and restaurants see pp326–31*

showpieces of 11 different countries, with replicas of famous buildings. Each pavilion is staffed by people from the country it represents, selling ethnic products and food. The best live shows are the acrobats at China and the Off Kilter music show at Canada. Highlights include **Reflections of China** – a Circle-Vision film on China's ancient sites; **Maelstrom** in Norway – an exciting trip through fjords; and **Impressions de France** – a film offering a whirlwind tour of France. Do not miss **IllumiNations**, a *son-et-lumière* show with lasers, fire- and waterworks. It is staged near closing time around World Showcase Lagoon.

## Disney's Hollywood Studios®

Disney's Hollywood Studios®, formerly known as Disney-MGM Studios, opened in 1989, both as a theme park and as a working film and TV studio. Although most of the working film section has been shut down, it combines top-notch shows and rides, based on Disney and Hollywood films (to which Disney bought the rights), with entertaining tours.

At Hollywood Boulevard, Art Deco styled buildings vie with a replica of Mann's Chinese Theater. The best shops are located here: Celebrity 5 & 10 has a range of affordable movie souvenirs, such as clapper boards and Oscars®, and the pricey Sid Cahuenga's One-Of-A-Kind stocks rare film memorabilia such as autographed photos and famous actors' clothes. **The Great Movie Ride** carries visitors past enormous movie sets, where scenes from films are re-created using live action.

Sunset Boulevard is an evocation of the famous Hollywood street in the 1940s. Re-created theaters and storefronts are dominated by the Hollywood Tower Hotel. This lightning-ravaged hotel is the spot for Orlando's scariest ride – **The Twilight Zone Tower of Terror™** – in which you are strapped into an elevator for a voyage inspired by the 1950s TV show *The Twilight Zone*™. Its high point is the ghastly 13-story plunge, repeated no fewer than seven times. The **Rock 'n' Roller Coaster® Starring Aerosmith** accelerates to 60mph (96 km/h) in 2.8 seconds in the dark, and pulls 5G in the first corkscrew.

Animation Courtyard gives visitors a glimpse behind the scenes during the creation of Disney's Audio-Animatronics®. The **Magic of Disney-Animation** is a guided visit with a Disney artist, while **Disney Junior – Live on Stage!** is an interactive show featuring Disney Pals from Mickey Mouse Clubhouse and Little Einsteins™.

At Mickey Avenue, **The Legend of Jack Sparrow** allows kids to meet their favorite pirate. Pixar Place's **Toy Story Midway Mania!** is a 4-D midway-style game-playing adventure.

**Disney's Hollywood Studios® Backlot Tour** has a tram ride that takes visitors for a peek at the camera, wardrobe, and lighting departments. It ends in Catastrophe Canyon, in the midst of a flood and explosions. The walking tour demonstrates special effects.

Streets of America is a clever re-creation of the Big Apple, San Francisco, Chicago, and other cities. Its highlight is the spectacular **Muppet™ Vision 3-D**, a slapstick 3-D movie starring the Muppets. Trombones, cars, and rocks launch themselves at you out of the screen – so realistic that children often grasp the air expecting to touch something.

Echo Lake offers the sensational **Star Tours** ride, based on the *Star Wars* films and includes an intergalactic battle. The **Indiana Jones™ Epic Spectacular** is a 30-minute live show featuring edge-of-your-seat stunts and adventures.

At 5pm, the park holds a parade based on one of Disney's animated films. The evening show, **Fantasmic!** is the finest of its kind in Florida. It combines music, lasers, animation, and over a hundred actors and dancers. Although it seats 10,000 people, you still need to arrive 2 hours early to get a good seat.

## Disney's Animal Kingdom®

This park has both real and mythical beasts, spread over seven different "lands."

At Discovery Island®, the **It's Tough to be a Bug®** show is a superb 3-D presentation. The now-closed Camp Minnie-Mickey is due to re-open as an alien land based on the Avatar movies in 2017. The **Festival of the Lion King** show here is excellent.

Africa offers the fabulous **Kilimanjaro Safaris®**, where you see animals roaming freely.

Asia features gibbons, birds, and tigers in a re-creation of Indian ruins. Tapirs and Komodo dragons are found on the **Maharaja Jungle Trek®**, the climax of which are the Bengal tigers that roam the ruins. **Expedition Everest™ – Legend of the Forbidden Mountain** is a huge attraction where visitors ride a train through the misty unknown. DinoLand U.S.A. has the wild **DINOSAUR** ride, where a motion simulator bucks and weaves, trying to ensnare and avoid dinosaurs. **Primeval Whirl®** and **TriceraTop Spin** attempt to spin visitors dizzy.

## The Rest of Walt Disney World® Resort

Walt Disney World® Resort has over 30 resorts *(see p327)*, two water parks, a campground, nearly 300 restaurants, nightclubs, a shopping village, and half a dozen golf courses.

Of the water parks, **Blizzard Beach**, a reconstructed Alpine ski resort, claims to have the tallest freefall slide in the world. At **Fort Wilderness Resort and Campground**, activities include horseback riding, fishing, and biking. Jet skiing, rental boats, and fishing gear are also available at the **Marketplace** and at all lakeside resorts. The Marketplace is an outdoor mall with lots of shops – The World of Disney® sells mountains of merchandise; and **Disney's West Side** has blues clubs and the famous Cirque du Soleil®, an avant-garde circus spectacle with more than 70 performers.

# ⑩ Universal Orlando® Resort

Once a single movie park, Universal Orlando® Resort now boasts two theme parks, an entertainment complex, and three resorts. Together, Universal Studios Florida®, Islands of Adventure®, and Universal CityWalk® present a formidable reason to spend time away from Walt Disney World® Resort. The parking lot feeds into Universal CityWalk® where there is a series of moving walkways to a fork leading to the two separate parks.

Universal's globe, the logo for the combined complex of parks

## Tackling the Parks

The busiest seasons are during Christmas and Easter. During the off-season, check with Guest Services for special deals on tickets. Arrive early to combat the long lines for rides (the gates open an hour before opening time). Arrive 15 minutes early for shows to ensure a seat. Children may find most rides too intense but there are some child-friendly attractions: ET Adventure®, the Woody Woodpecker's Nuthouse®, A Day in the Park with Barney™, Animal Actors on Location!℠, Jurassic Park River Adventure®, and the Seuss Landing™.

### Eating & Shopping

There are plenty of options for dining. The Hard Rock Café® is the largest in the world. Lombard's Seafood Grill specializes in fish dishes, while Universal Studios Classic Monsters Café serves Californian and Italian cuisine, and has a great buffet. Most rides and attractions have their own stores. Dinostore, near Jurassic Park River Adventure®, sells all things dinosaur-related, while Universal Studios Store has everything from fake Oscars to oven mitts with the Universal logo.

## Universal Studios Florida®

The entrance is known as Front Lot, as it is built to look like the front lot of a 1940s Hollywood film studio. Actors in costumes wander the streets playing characters including Woody Woodpecker, Scooby Doo, and legends such as Marilyn Monroe and the Marx Brothers.

The next area is Production Central, home of **Shrek 4-D**, **Transformers: The Ride** and **Despicable Me Minion Mayhem** 3-D rides, and the high-speed **Hollywood Rip Ride Rockit** coaster.

**The Wizarding World of Harry Potter™ – Diagon Alley** is a separately ticketed area featuring an Escape from Gringotts™ thrill ride, restaurants, and shops, and connected by a Hogwarts Express steam train to the **Wizarding World of Harry Potter – Hogsmeade™**.

The New York area has more than 60 façades, some of which replicate real buildings, others reproduce famous movie settings. There are cut-outs of the Guggenheim Museum, Macy's department store, and Louie's Italian Restaurant, scene of a shootout in the original *Godfather* movie. **Revenge of the Mummy®** is a high-speed roller coaster that propels you though Egyptian passageways and includes frighteningly lifelike robotics. The other ride here is **Twister…Ride It Out®**, which pits visitors against a simulated tornado, and lets them experience the terrifying power of the elements standing inside 20 ft (6 m) of the five-floor-high funnel of winds.

In the section known as Hollywood, sets of Hollywood Boulevard and Rodeo Drive pay tribute to Hollywood's golden age, from the 1920s to the '50s – with the famous Mocambo nightclub, the Beverly Wilshire Hotel and top beauty salon, Max Factor. There is even a replica of the Hollywood Walk of Fame.

Hollywood's most popular attraction is **Terminator 2®: 3-D**, a ride that uses superb robotics and 3-D technology to catapult the audience into the action alongside the star of the *Terminator* films, Arnold Schwarzenegger.

The **Universal Orlando's Horror Make-Up Show** offers a behind-the-scenes look at scary make-up effects. This show closes during winter.

The **Simpsons Ride™** allows visitors to swoop, soar, and smash their way through Krustyland, before visiting Springfield USA for treats from Krusty Burger and Moe's Tavern. In the incredibly addictive **Men In Black™ – Alien Attack™**, visitors join Will Smith in a simulator, battling aliens with

Thrill-seekers enjoying a ride on the Incredible Hulk Coaster®

The entrance to Universal Studios Florida® theme park

lasers and cannons. In Woody Woodpecker's Kid Zone, the enchanting **ET Adventure**® is based on Steven Spielberg's 1982 film. Guests soar off to ET's home planet on a flying bicycle, gliding over a twinkling cityscape, before arriving at a world inhabited by ET lookalikes.

The San Francisco section's big draw is **Disaster!**℠ Take a trip into the world of disaster movies, experience special effects, and board a moving subway train set in the final scene of a disaster movie. At the end, watch the trailer starring you, in your very own "major movie motion picture."

At **Beetlejuice's Graveyard Revue™** join the classic Universal Monsters as they unleash their hot sound in a spooktacular rock 'n' roll revue that is loud enough to wake the dead. A popular attraction is **Fear Factor Live**, the first ever theme park experience based on a reality TV show. Casting takes place 75 minutes before the show, which tests the courage and strength of participants.

## Universal's Islands of Adventure®

One of the world's most technologically advanced theme parks, Islands of Adventure® demands a day's visit of its own. The first island visitors encounter is the Marvel Super Hero Island® where the theme draws from the Marvel Comics' Super Hero stable of characters. The **Incredible Hulk Coaster**®, probably Florida's best, is a green leviathan that

accelerates you to over 40 mph (64 km/h) in two seconds before turning upside down at 110 ft (33.5 m) above the ground. The **Amazing Adventures of Spiderman** shows a stunning integration of 3-D technology with motion simulation. Toon Lagoon, where cartoons transmute into reality, hosts a wet ride – **Popeye & Bluto's Bilge-Rate Barges**®, a twisting, churning, and splashing raft ride. Jurassic Park boasts the **Jurassic Park River Adventure**®, a cruise where visitors see friendly dinosaurs before being diverted due to a raptor breakout. The **Pteranodon Flyers**® ride flies pairs of riders over the island on an 80-second trip, while the **Discovery Center**® is an interactive natural history exhibit where guests can view the results of mixing DNA from various species, including themselves.

**The Wizarding World of Harry Potter – Hogsmeade™** takes visitors to Hogwart's Castle, Diagon Alley, and features the parks' most popular rides: The Dragon Challenge™ coasters, and Harry Potter and the Forbidden Journey™, a tour de force mix of roller coaster and film that leaves riders gasping. The faint of heart have the option of touring the castle and skipping the ride. Stage shows include the Eighth Voyage of Sinbad® Stunt Show, and Poseidon's Fury®, with myriad special effects. Seuss Landing™, based on the popular Dr. Seuss children's books, the creation of

### VISITORS' CHECKLIST

**Practical Information**
1000 Universal Studios Plaza, exits 29 or 30B on I-4.
**Tel** (407) 363-8000.
W universalorlando.com
**Open** 9am–6pm daily; extended evening hours in summer & on public hols. 🦽 ♿ 📷 ⚡

**Transport**
🚌 7, 11, 18, 21 from Orlando.

Theodor Seuss Geisel, caters to children. The **Cat in the Hat™** ride serves as an introduction to the characters. There are also a host of innovative rides that captivate younger children.

## Universal CityWalk®

Inspired by many of popular culture's innovators, such as Bob Marley, Universal CityWalk® is a 30-acre (12-ha) entertainment complex of restaurants, nightclubs, and cinemas. Open between 11am and 2am, its dazzling array of restaurants range from Emeril's (a top TV chef) to the nostalgic Bubba Gump Shrimp Co.™, and the famous Hard Rock Café®. A restaurant known as "Bob Marley – A Tribute to Freedom℠," is an exact replica of this famous musician's home. Among the many nightclubs are Hard Rock® Live! and the groove dance club where visitors can watch live musical performances. The complex also has stores and movies, and its stages host concerts, art festivals, and celebrity appearances. A lagoon provides a picturesque setting to sip a cool drink or take a moonlight stroll.

Flight of the Hippogriff™ ride, part of the Wizarding World of Harry Potter – Hogsmeade™

# ⓫ SeaWorld® Orlando & Discovery Cove®

In scale and sophistication, SeaWorld® is one of the world's most impressive marine-life adventure parks. Established in 1973 to promote its educational, research, and conservation programs, the park abounds in fun as well as entertainment. The One Ocean℠ and Blue Horizons shows, featuring killer whales, top the bill. Next to SeaWorld® is Discovery Cove®, an all-inclusive park, where guests can swim with rays and dolphins. Aquatica is SeaWorld®'s third park, with animals, coasters, and water rides, including the spectacular Dolphin Plunge.

Dolphin Cove®, where everyone can touch and feed the dolphins

## Exploring SeaWorld®

SeaWorld® is less crowded than Orlando's other theme parks. Most of the presentations are either walk-through exhibits or stadium shows. Arriving 15 minutes early guarantees a good seat. Show timings overlap, so guests cannot leave a show just in time for another. However, it is possible to get a seat in the Clyde and Seamore (Sea Lion and Otter) show by leaving the Shamu Stadium while the performers are taking their bows. The best time to see

shows such as Wild Arctic and Shark Encounter is while visitors are busy watching the stadium events. Young children enjoy meeting the actors in furry suits who play the parts of Shamu and Crew – guests can normally find them near SeaWorld®'s exit around closing time. The 400-ft (122-m) Sky Tower ride offers a superb overview of the park. For more information, go to Guest Services near the exit gate.

## Exhibits & Rides

Three meticulously landscaped habitats are incorporated in **Key West at SeaWorld®**. Dolphin Cove, a wave pool in the style of a Caribbean beach, offers underwater viewing of bottlenose dolphins and the chance to pet and feed them. Visitors can also touch one of the 200 rays at Stingray Lagoon, while Turtle Trek offers a 360-degree 3-D showcase, and the chance to experience life as a turtle.

Shamu, the park's official mascot

**Pacific Point Preserve** recreates the rugged north Pacific Coast in the form of a large, rocky pool. Watch harbor seals, South American fur seals, and noisy California sea lions basking on the rocks or gliding effortlessly through the water.

Most of the other wildlife at SeaWorld® is viewed through glass. **Manatee Rescue** offers a splendid underwater view of these irresistibly appealing herbivores *(see p319)*.

In the fabulous **Antarctica: Empire of the Penguin**, visitors are transported above and below the waterline in the icy world of the South Pole, with a mix of live penguins and motion-based simulator rides.

Billed as the world's largest collection of dangerous sea creatures, **Shark Encounter** is very popular. Moray eels, barracuda, and pufferfish are the tantalizing appetizers before a main course of sharks, whose toothy grins are a short distance away, as visitors walk through a glass tunnel inside their aquarium. **Wild Arctic** is a thrilling, hi-tech ride that simulates a helicopter flight through blizzards and avalanches. Visitors arrive at Base Station Wild Arctic, created around an old expedition ship, and encounter polar bears, harbor seals, walruses, and beluga whales.

SeaWorld®'s **Journey to Atlantis**, a water coaster with a mythological twist, and **Kraken**, a winner of the annual Orlando roller-coaster competition, are hot tickets. **Manta** is a roller coaster that simulates the water and airborne journey of a giant manta ray. **Aquatica** is a water park that offers thrilling rides, including **Ihu's Breakaway Falls**. This 80-ft- (24-m-) high attraction is Orlando's tallest, steepest, and only multi-drop tower ride. Riders drop into one of four slides through a trap door.

## TOP TIPS

• SeaWorld® allows guests to feed many of the animals, but it restricts both the type and the amount of food, which must be purchased from them. If this is something you would like to do, check with Guest Services as soon as you enter the park for feeding times and food availability.

• Build your schedule around the four main types of presentations: One Ocean℠, A'Lure, Sea Lion and Otter, and Blue Horizons shows.

• Bring a waterproof plastic bag for your camera as, especially during One Ocean℠ and Blue Horizons shows, people sitting in the first 12 rows often get splashed by salt water.

• Journey to Atlantis is guaranteed to get you wet, so reserve this for the hottest part of the day.

• The gentle pace of SeaWorld® means that visiting after 3pm is a less crowded experience.

## Shows & Tours

The park's number one show, **One Ocean<sup>SM</sup>** is a revolutionary show that features SeaWorld®'s entire family of killer whales performing awe-inspiring choreography to an original score. The multisensory show features dancing fountains and an impressive sound system, which combine to deliver an educational message to old and young alike.

**Blue Horizons** is another stunning theatrical spectacular that showcases graceful dolphins and false killer whales, a rainbow of exotic birds, and an entire cast of world-class divers and aerialists in elaborate costumes. The vivid imagination of a young girl sets the stage for an emotional adventure involving the power of the sea and the elegance of flight.

The **Clyde and Seamore Take Pirate Island** show, held in the Sea Lion and Otter Stadium, features two sea lions (Clyde and Seamore), otters, and a walrus in a swashbuckling adventure of lost loot, pirate ships, and hilarity on the high seas.

The Nautilus Theater hosts **A'Lure, the Call of the Ocean**, the spectacular tale of the Sea Sirens whose hypnotic calls have lured fishermen into their underwater lairs for centuries. It is a mariner's story that comes to life with athletic flying performers, gravity-defying aerial tumblers, and amazing silk yo-yo artists.

Another show, **Pets Ahoy**, features talented cats, birds, dogs, and pigs, all of whom have been rescued from animal shelters. Other exhibits include **Shamu's Happy Harbor**, a play area for smaller children, and **Dolphin Nursery** for new dolphin moms and their calves.

The **Hubbs–SeaWorld Research Institute** runs a number of nonprofit "Research, Rescue and Rehabilitation" projects. It has helped thousands of manatees, dolphins, and whales in difficulty – nursing and operating on them. Those that recover fully are released into the wild. Several tours such as The Sharks! tour, offer a glimpse of this work. If interested, inquire at Guest Services. Various **Exclusive Park Experiences** are on offer, including the Behind the Scenes Tour; Marine Mall Keeper Experience; and a Family Fun Tour, which combines animal feedings, show tickets, and a meal.

Cuddly versions of SeaWorld® stars

## Discovery Cove®

Just across the road from SeaWorld®, Discovery Cove® is a quiet revolution in Florida's theme parks. With a capacity of only 1,000 guests a day (the car park is limited to only 500 cars), it offers some unforgettable experiences, the most vaunted of which is an opportunity to swim with Atlantic bottlenose dolphins.

Discovery Cove® has been conceived as a private island. Its five main areas are set within beautifully landscaped grounds with waterfalls, pools, and niches connected by beaches. **Grand Reef** abounds with grottoes and a shipwreck, and offers the opportunity to swim alongside threateningly large sharks,

separated from visitors by a transparent plexi-glass wall. At the **Free Flight Aviary**, guests can feed birds, while **Ray Lagoon** offers the chance to snorkel above rays, some of which grow up to a length of 5 ft (1.5 m). The warm waters of **Rainforest River** are inviting to swimmers and snorkelers who can float lazily past lagoons, a waterfall, and thick rainforest. There is also an underwater cave. The **Dolphin Lagoon** has a 15-minute orientation session, followed by 30 minutes of wading and swimming with these highly intelligent mammals; you will usually be with eight other people. The "Trainer for a Day" session includes more in-depth interaction and a behind-the-scenes tour.

It's a good idea to split your party into two for the dolphin experience, to be able to take each other's photographs. Do not bring any sunscreen, as the park has its own "fish friendly" one, the only brand permitted. The package price (no child reductions) includes the dolphin experience (children under six cannot participate), all equipment, a free snorkel, a meal, and 14 days' admission to SeaWorld® or Busch Gardens, Tampa Bay. For an additional charge, visit Sea Venture, an underwater walking tour of the Grand Reef. Despite the price, the park is very popular, so book well ahead.

A performing killer whale, one of the star attractions at SeaWorld® Orlando

Downtown Orlando, dominated by the SunTrust Center

# ⑫ Orlando

🏠 249,000. ✈ 🚆 🚌 ℹ 8723 International Dr, (407) 425-1234.
W **visitorlando.com**

Orlando was just a sleepy provincial town until the 1950s. However, its proximity to Cape Canaveral and the theme parks soon transformed it into a burgeoning business center. Downtown, with its glass-sided high-rises, comes to life only at night, when both visitors and locals flock to the many bars and restaurants around Orange Avenue, the town's main street.

During the day, the area around **Lake Eola**, east of Orange Avenue, offers a peaceful midtown oasis for visitors and families. The residential districts north of downtown have many parks and museums, including the serenely beautiful Harry P. Leu Gardens and **Loch Haven Park**, which houses a trio of museums. The most highly regarded of these is the **Orlando Museum of Art**. Its collections include pre-Columbian artifacts with figurines from Peru, African art, and American paintings from the 19th and 20th centuries. The park is also home to the John and Rita Lowndes Shakespeare Center, which includes the 350-seat Margeson Theater and two other theaters. The Center holds the Orlando-UCF Shakespeare Festival and the annual Orlando Fringe Theatre Festival.

The **Maitland Art Center**, on Packwood Avenue in the leafy neighboring town of Maitland, occupies studios designed in the 1930s by artist André Smith as a winter retreat for fellow artists. Set around courtyards and gardens, the buildings show a profusion of Mayan and Aztec motifs. The studios are still used, and exhibitions of contemporary American crafts are held often here.

At Loch Haven Park is the **Orlando Science Center**. Covering 207,000 sq ft (19,200 sq m) of floor space, the center's aim is to offer a stimulating environment for experimental science learning. It thus provides a huge range of exciting state-of-the-art interactive exhibits. Among its attractions are the Dr. Philips CineDome, which also functions as a planetarium, its dinosaur fossils collection, and the ShowBiz Science exhibit, which reveals some of the tricks and special effects used in movies.

🏛 **Loch Haven Park**
N Mills Ave at Rollins St. Orlando Museum of Art: **Tel** (407) 896-4231. **Open** Tue–Sun. **Closed** public hols.
🅿 ♿ W omart.org

🏛 **Orlando Science Center**
777 East Princeton St. **Tel** (407) 514-2000. **Open** 10am–5pm Thu–Tue. **Closed** some major public hols. 🅿
📷 🎥 ♿ W osc.org

# ⑬ Winter Park

🏠 28,000. 🚆 🚌 ℹ 507 N New York Ave, (407) 644-8281. Scenic Boat Tour: **Tel** (407) 644-4056. 🚤
W **scenicboattours.com**

Orlando's most refined area took off in the 1880s, when wealthy northerners came south and began to build winter retreats here. The **Charles Hosmer Morse Museum of American Art** probably has the finest collection of works by Art Nouveau craftsman, Louis Comfort Tiffany. There are superb examples of his jewelry, lamps, and many of his windows, including the *The Four Seasons* (1899). To the south of Winter Park is **Rollins College**, dotted with 1930s Spanish-style buildings. The finest is the **Knowles Memorial Chapel**, whose main entrance has a relief of a meeting between the Seminole Indians and the Spanish conquistadors. The college's **Cornell Fine Arts Museum**'s impressive collection of Italian Renaissance paintings is the oldest in Florida. The **Scenic Boat Tour** explores the nearby lakes and canals.

Tiffany's *Four Seasons* window, Winter Park

🏛 **Charles Hosmer Morse Museum of American Art**
445 Park Ave N. **Tel** (407) 645-5311. **Open** Tue–Sun. **Closed** public hols.
📷 ♿ W morsemuseum.org

Main entrance of Knowles Memorial Chapel, Winter Park

The sinking home of Ripley's Believe It or Not!, International Drive

## ⓮ International Drive

🚊 Orlando. 🚌 Orlando. ℹ️ Visitor Center, 8723 International Drive, (407) 363-5872.

A stone's throw from Walt Disney World®, "I Drive" is a 3-mile (5-km) ribbon of hotels, shops, and theaters. Its most popular attraction is **Wet 'n' Wild**, known for its big-thrill rides. The Storm and Mach 5 feature terrifying descents down near-vertical slides, and there is also the watery Kid's Playground.

Filled with fantastic objects, illusions, and film footage of strange feats, **Ripley's Believe It or Not!** was created by the American cartoonist, Robert Ripley. It is housed in a building that appears to be falling into one of Florida's sinkholes, which occur due to the erosion of the limestone bedrock. **Titanic The Experience** displays artifacts, movie memorabilia, and re-creations of the ship's interior. Two blocks from the mall is Orlando's **Official Visitor Information Center**, which has coupons for many attractions, such as discounts on admission and bargain meals.

## ⓯ LEGOLAND®

One Legoland Way, Winter Haven. **Tel** (877) 350-5346. 🚊 Winter Haven. **Open** 10am–5pm daily. **Closed** Tue & Wed in slow periods. 🅿️ ♿

🌐 florida.legoland.com

Enjoy an action-packed day of adventure and education in a beautiful setting on the shores of Lake Eloise. LEGOLAND® Florida, the fifth of its kind – and the largest – is

another of Florida's impressive family-friendly theme parks. It is located just 45 minutes from both Walt Disney World® Resort and Tampa, in the city of Winter Haven. Built on the site of the former Cypress Gardens, the native plants and exotic species, including the original Banyan tree planted when the gardens opened in 1939, have been carefully preserved.

The park contains ten different zones, ensuring an exciting experience for every family member. **The Beginning** features a 100-ft- (30-m-) high rotating platform offering a 360-degree view of the whole park, while **Fun Town** has a two-story carousel, and 4-D movie theater. **Castle Hill** brings the medieval era to life, and **Miniland USA** presents eight miniature replicas of American landmarks. With its life-sized LEGO® dinosaur and roller coasters, **Land of Adventure** will delight thrill-seekers, while **XTreme** caters for more

courageous visitors with its LEGO Technic® Test Track Coaster, and Aquazone® Wave Racers. **LEGO® City** and **Imagination Zone** offer an entire scaled-down town and hands-on display. Younger visitors will enjoy **Duplo Valley** and **Pirate's Cove**. The **Water Park** features a raft river, a wave pool, and high-speed slides.

## ⓰ Disney Wilderness Preserve

2700 Scrub Jay Trail, 12 miles (18 km) SW of Kissimmee. **Tel** (407) 935-0002. 🚊 Kissimmee. 🚌 Kissimmee. **Open** 9am–5pm daily. **Closed** Sat & Sun in Jun–Sep. 🅿️ 🎫 Sun 1:30pm Oct–May.

Orlando's best wilderness preserve is a haven for native plants and animals, and also for people wanting to get away from the crowds. Unlike other Disney attractions, there are no thrill rides on these 12,000 acres (18.75 sq miles), but there is still plenty to do. There is an off-road buggy tour on Sundays, and three hiking trails that lead to Lake Russell. The interpretive trail is 0.8-mile (1.2-km) long and visitors can learn about nature along the way. The longer trails are mostly unshaded, so bring sunscreen, a hat, plenty of water, and insect repellent.

Lake Russell, one of many lakes at the Disney Wilderness Preserve

# ⓱ Daytona Beach

🏙 62,000. ✈ 🚌 ℹ 126 E Orange Ave, (386) 255-0415.
🌐 daytonabeach.com

This resort is famous for its 23-mile (37-km) beach, lined with a wall of hotels. The old-fashioned boardwalk offers concerts in the bandstand, arcades, and go-karts. During the April Spring Break, nearly 200,000 college students descend on the beach for this ritual party.

This is also one of the few beaches in Florida where cars are allowed on the sands, a hangover from the days when motor enthusiasts, such as Louis Chevrolet and Henry Ford, raced on the beaches. The **Daytona International Speedway** nearby draws huge crowds, especially during the Speedweek in February and the Motorcycle Weeks in March and October (see p38).

Across the Halifax River downtown, the **Halifax Historical Society Museum** occupies a 1910 bank building and displays local history. To the west, the **Museum of Arts and Sciences** has exhibits from 1640 to 1920 and a planetarium. **Gamble Place**, run by the museum, is a hunting lodge built in 1907 for James N. Gamble, of Procter & Gamble fame. Museum tours include the Snow White House, built for Gamble's grandchildren.

🏛 **Museum of Arts & Sciences**
1040 Museum Blvd. **Tel** (386) 255-0285. **Open** Tue–Sun. **Closed** public hols. 🅿 ♿ 🌐 moas.org

# ⓲ St. Augustine

🏙 14,000. 🚌 1711A Dobbs Rd, (904) 827-9273. ℹ 10 Castillo Dr, (904) 825-1000. 🎨 Arts & Crafts Spring Festival (Apr). 🌐 floridashistoriccoast.com

America's oldest continuously occupied European settlement was founded by the Spanish colonist Pedro Menéndez de Avilés on the feast day of St. Augustine in 1565. Today, this town has many attractions for the modern tourist, not least its 43 miles (69 km) of beaches and the fact that it is within easy reach of several golf courses and marinas. St. Augustine burned down in 1702 but was soon rebuilt in the lee of the **Castillo de San Marcos**. This mighty fortress is the largest and most complete Spanish fort in the US. Constructed of coquina, a sedimentary limestone formed by seashells and corals that could withstand the impact of cannonballs, this is a superb example of 17th-century military architecture.

The historic heart of St. Augustine is compact and easy to explore on foot. Horse-drawn carriage tours are popular and depart from Avenida Menendez, north of the Bridge of Lions, which was opened across Matanzas Bay in 1927. The 18th-century City Gate is the entrance to the **Old Town**. Its focus is the pedestrianized St. George Street, lined with attractive stone buildings. Some

*Cleopatra (c.1890) by Romanelli, Lightner Museum*

of the main attractions here are the **Spanish Quarter Village**, a museum that re-creates an 18th-century garrison town, and **Peña-Peck House**, a fine First Spanish Period home dating to the 1740s. The **Oldest Wooden Schoolhouse**, built from cypress and red cedar wood in the mid-1700s, is also located on this street. The heart of the Spanish settlement is **Plaza de la Constitution**, a leafy square flanked by Government House Museum and the grand Basilica Cathedral. The splendid **Flagler College** started out as the Ponce de Leon Hotel, built by Henry Flagler (see p286) in 1883, a year after he honeymooned in St. Augustine. Its gilded and stuccoed cupola has symbolic motifs representing Spain and Florida, notably the golden mask of the Timucuan Indian sun god and the lamb – a symbol of Spanish knighthood. Ask about the face hidden in the mosaic floor. The other resorts Flagler built here are the Cordoba and Alcazar Hotels. The latter, a three-floor Hispano-Moorish structure, is now the **Lightner Museum**, devoted to the country's Gilded Age. Its exhibits include glass works by Louis Tiffany, and its Grand Ballroom houses an eclectic exhibit of "American Castle" furniture. The lovely **Ximenez-Fatio House** is now a museum run by the National Society of Colonial Dames. It seeks to re-create the genteel boardinghouse that it was in the 1830s, when invalids and adventurers first visited Florida in order to escape from the harsh northern winters.

🏛 **Castillo de San Marcos**
1 S Castillo Dr. **Tel** (904) 829-6506. **Open** 8:45am–5:15pm daily. **Closed** Dec 25. 🅿 ♿ limited. 🎥 call for details. 🌐 nps.gov/casa

🏛 **Lightner Museum**
75 King St. **Tel** (904) 824-2874. **Open** daily. **Closed** Dec 25. 🅿 ♿ 🌐 lightnermuseum.org

Cars cruising the hard-packed sands of Daytona Beach

*For hotels and restaurants see pp326–31*

Fernandina's Beech Street Grill with Chinese Chippendale motifs

## ⑲ Fernandina Beach

🚹 12,000. 🚉 Jacksonville. 🚌 Jacksonville. 🛈 961687 Gateway Blvd Ste 101 G, (904) 261-3248.

The town of Fernandina Beach on Amelia Island, just across the St. Mary's River from Georgia, was famous as a pirates' den until the early 1800s. Its harbor attracted a motley crew of foreign adventurers, whose various allegiances earned the island its soubriquet, the "Isle of Eight Flags." Today, Fernandina is better known as a charming Victorian resort and Florida's primary source of sweet Atlantic white shrimp: more than 2 million pounds (900,000 kilos) are harvested by shrimping fleets each year.

Occupying a large section of the town's **Historic District**, the Silk Stocking District was named after the affluence of its original residents. Sea captains and timber barons built homes here in a variety of styles. Queen Anne houses with turrets jostle with graceful Italianate residences and fine Chinese Chippendale structures, such as the **Beech Street Grill**. The weathered buildings on Centre Street once housed chandleries and naval stores. Antique shops and gift shops have now replaced them; the 1878 Palace Saloon, however, still serves a wicked Pirate's Punch at the mahogany bar adorned with hand-carved caryatids. Farther south, the

**Amelia Island Museum of History** occupies the former jail and offers twice daily, 90-minute guided history tours recounting the island's turbulent past – from the time of its first Indian inhabitants to the early 1900s.

**Fort Clinch State Park**, at the island's northern tip, has trails, beaches, and campsites, as well as a fort that dates from 1847. Park rangers dress in Civil War uniforms and perform 19th-century war re-enactments one weekend a month.

🏛 **Amelia Island Museum of History**
233 S 3rd St. **Tel** (904) 261-7378. **Open** daily. **Closed** public hols. 🅿 🚹 limited. 🎥 compulsory, two tours daily.
🌐 ameliamuseum.org

## ⑳ Ocala National Forest

**Open** daily. 🏕 campgrounds & swimming areas. 🚹 🏕 Visitor Center: 3199 NE Co Rd. **Tel** (352) 236-0288. Juniper Springs Canoe Rental: **Tel** (352) 625-2808.

Between Ocala and the St. John's River, the world's largest sand pine forest covers 366,000 acres (148,000 ha) and is crisscrossed by rivers and hiking trails. One of the last refuges of the endangered Florida black bear, it is also home to animals such as deer and otter, and a variety of birds such as bald eagles, barred owls, wild turkey, and several wading birds.

Hiking trails vary from boardwalks and short loop trails to the 66-mile (106-km) stretch of the National Scenic Trail. Bass-fishing is popular, and there are swimming holes and campgrounds at the recreation areas of Salt Springs and Alexander Springs.

Canoe rental is widely available; the 7-mile (11-km) canoe run down Juniper Creek from the **Juniper Springs Recreation Area** is one of the finest in Florida. The Salt Springs trail is especially good for bird-watching. There are guides at the main visitor center on the forest's western fringe or at the centers at Salt Springs and Lake Dorr, on Route 19.

### Environs

**Silver Springs**, on the western border of Ocala National Forest, 29 miles (46 km) west of the Juniper Springs Recreation Area, is the world's largest artesian spring and Florida's oldest tourist attraction. Its famous glass-bottomed boat tours have been running since 1878. Jeep safaris and "Jungle Cruises" also travel through the Florida outback, where the early Tarzan movies starring Johnny Weissmuller were filmed. Wild Waters, next to the springs, is a lively water park. The quieter **Silver River State Park**, 2 miles (3 km) southeast, has a lovely walking trail through a hardwood hammock and cypress swamp, leading to a swimming hole in a bend of the crystal-clear river.

🌲 **Silver River State Park**
1425 NE 58th Ave, Ocala. **Tel** (352) 236-7148. **Open** daily. 🅿 🚹

Juniper Springs, Ocala National Forest

## ❷ Tallahassee

🏠 186,000. ✈️ 🚉 918 Railroad Ave, (800) 872-7245. 🚌 ℹ️ 106 E Jefferson, (850) 606-2305. 🎭 Springtime Tallahassee (Mar–Apr).

Encircled by rolling hills, Florida's dignified state capital is gracious and uncompromisingly Southern. Tallahassee grew dramatically during the plantation era, and the elegant townhouses built in the 1800s can still be seen around Park Avenue and Calhoun Street. The Chamber of Commerce, on Duval Street, is housed in the city's oldest building, an 1830 Classical-Revival mansion, known as "The Columns."

A major landmark, the Neo-Classical **Old Capitol Building** in downtown Tallahasse has been beautifully restored to its 1902 state, with striped awnings. Once inside, guests can visit the Supreme Court chamber and the Senate. The high-rise **New Capitol Building** behind it offers a fabulous view of the city. The **Museum of Florida History** situated on Bronough Street, covers about 12,000 years of the region's history.

The Old and the New Capitol Buildings, Tallahassee

### Environs

During the 1820s and 1930s, the area around Tallahassee was Florida's most important cotton-growing region. A tour along the canopied roads of the old **Cotton Trail** takes visitors past former cotton plantations and cattle pastures. The **Goodwood Museum and Gardens** retains its lovely 1830s mansion; Bradley's Country Store, set up in 1927, still serves their famous home-made sausages. Located

15 miles (24 km) south of Tallahassee, **Wakulla Springs State Park** has one of the world's largest freshwater springs, which pumps 700,000 gal (2.6 million liters) of water a minute into a large pool. Here, visitors can swim or snorkel in its clear waters or ride in a glass-bottomed boat. Boat trips on the Wakulla River are the best way to see alligators and wading birds. The elegant Wakulla Springs Lodge was built in the 1930s.

🦆 **Wakulla Springs State Park** 550 Wakulla Park Dr, Wakulla Springs. **Tel** (850) 926-0700. **Open** daily. 🎫 ♿ 🖥️ floridastateparks.org

## ❷ Pensacola

🏠 53,000. ✈️ 🚉 980 E Heinburg St, (850) 433-4966. 🚌 (850) 476-4800. ℹ️ 1401 E Gregory St, (850) 434-1234. 🎭 Fiesta of Five Flags (Jun). 🖥️ visitpensacola.com

One of Florida's earliest Spanish settlements, Pensacola was established by Don Tristan de Luna, who sailed into Pensacola Bay in 1559. The city features diverse architectural styles, from

# The Beaches of the Panhandle

Lying between Perdido Key and Panama City Beach are some of Florida's most beautiful beaches. The brilliant sand, consisting mainly of quartz, is washed down from the Appalachian Mountains. One can choose between quiet, pristine beaches and more lively resorts, with ample opportunities for water sports. The main season is April–July.

① **Perdido Key** is the location of Florida's most westerly shores, which are inaccessible by car and quieter than most.

② **Quietwater Beach**, on Santa Rosa Island, is not the Panhandle's finest but is an easy hop from Pensacola.

③ **Pensacola Beach** has miles of pristine sand and a string of shops, hotels, and bars. Large crowds gather here on weekends to sunbathe and swim.

④ **Navarre Beach** is quieter than Pensacola but nevertheless has good facilities, water sports, and a pier for fishing.

| 0 km | | 15 |
| --- | --- | --- |
| 0 miles | | 10 |

Colonial cottages to elegant Classical-Revival homes. Pensacola was wiped out by a hurricane two years after it was established, but it was soon rebuilt, and over the next 300 years the city was occupied by the Spanish, French, English, and the Americans. The 1800s were a period of prosperity ushered in by the timber boom, and much of today's downtown dates from this time.

Pensacola's oldest quarter, the **Historic Pensacola Village**, has a number of museums and houses, built by wealthy pioneers and traders. There are daily tours from Tivoli House on Zaragoza Street. Forming a backdrop to the Museum of Commerce is a cleverly constructed Victorian streetscape, complete with a printer's workshop, a saddlery, and an old-time music store. Florida's earliest church, the Old Christ Church (1832), stands in the leafy Seville Square shaded by oaks and magnolia trees.

The **TT Wentworth, Jr., Florida State Museum**, set in a Spanish Renaissance Revival building, has an eclectic collection that includes oddities such as a shrunken head from pre-Columbian times and old Coca-Cola bottles.

Farther north, the **North Hill Preservation District** has 19th- and 20th-century houses, built on the sites of British and Spanish forts. Even today, cannonballs are found in local gardens. A very striking home is the McCreary House on North Baylen Street. A Queen Anne home built in 1900, it has a gabled roof and tower. Lying between the two districts, **Palafox Street** is the city's commercial hub.

**🏛 TT Wentworth, Jr., Florida State Museum**
330 S Jefferson St. **Tel** (850) 595-5985 **Open** Tue–Sat. **Closed** public hols. 🎫
**♿ 🌐 historicpensacola.org**

Guides in 19th-century costume in the Historic Pensacola Village

# ㉓ Apalachicola

🏔 2,300. 🚌 Tallahassee. ℹ 122 Commerce St, (850) 653-9419.
🌐 **apalachicolabay.org**

A riverside customs station established in 1823, Apalachicola's first 100 years were its finest. It flourished first with the cotton trade, and later with the lumber boom. Today, pines and hardwoods still stand in the **Apalachicola National Forest**. The area offers hiking trails, canoeing opportunities, and campsites. Oystering in the Apalachicola River began in the 1920s. Oyster boats still pull up at the dockside, and Water Street has many places where fresh oysters are available.

A walking map of the old town, available at the Chamber of Commerce, takes in buildings from the cotton era, such as the 1838 Greek Revival Raney House. The **John Gorrie State Museum** houses a model of Gorrie's patent ice-making machine. Designed to cool yellow fever patients, the doctor's 1851 invention was the vanguard of modern refrigeration and air conditioning.

**⑤ Fort Walton Beach** is a relaxed resort, ideal for family holidays. It is also one of the best beaches for water sports.

**⑨ Panama City Beach** is a buzzing place, lined with condos and amusement parks; it's the Panhandle's biggest resort. Water sports facilities are excellent here.

**⑦ Santa Rosa Beach**, an undeveloped beach, is backed by dunes and marshlands teeming with birds and other wildlife.

**⑥ Destin** attracts bathers, water sports fans, and deep-sea fishing enthusiasts to its splendid beach.

**⑧ Grayton** has boardwalks across the dunes, which lead to one of the finest beaches in the country.

**⑩ St. Andrews** has a superb beach that, unlike Panama City Beach, is well protected against developers.

Valparaiso
Choctawhatchee Bay
Seaside
Panama City

The high-rise skyline of downtown Tampa on the Gulf Coast

## ❷❹ Tampa

🚹 347,000. ✈ 🚉 601 Nebraska Ave, (800) 872-7245. 🚌 610 Polk St, (800) 231-2222. 🚢 Channelside Dr, (800) 741-2297. 🛈 401 E Jackson St, (813) 223-1111. 🎭 Gasparilla Festival (Feb). 🅦 visittampabay.com

Situated at the mouth of the Hillsborough River, Tampa is one of Florida's fastest-growing cities. A perfect harbor, Tampa Bay was a magnet to the Spanish, who arrived here in 1539. However, the city's greatest period of prosperity was in the 1800s, when railroad baron Henry Plant extended his railroad here and made it an important center for trade.

Tampa's downtown area is centered around the partly pedestrian Franklin Street, which has the historic Tampa Theater. To its southeast, on North Ashley Drive, is the **Tampa Museum of Art**. This museum's exhibits range from Greek, Roman, and Etruscan antiquities to 20th-century American art.

The former Tampa Bay Hotel, which houses the **Henry B. Plant Museum**, is the city's premier landmark, its Moorish minarets visible from all over the city. Plant commissioned the building in 1891, and its construction alone cost $3 million. Currently a part of the University of Tampa, the south wing has been preserved as a museum. Its splendidly furnished interior retains the original 18th-century French furniture.

The **Florida Aquarium** is on Channelside Drive. It displays a variety of sea creatures such as seabirds, otters, and baby alligators living in tanks that replicate their natural habitats.

Located 3 miles (5 km) east of downtown, **Ybor City** was created by Spaniard Don Vicente Martinez Ybor, when he moved his cigar business from Key West to Tampa in the late 1800s. About 20,000 migrant workers settled here, and the legacy of the cigar boom is still visible on 7th Avenue, with its Spanish tiles and wrought-iron balconies. Today, the area is known for its lively shops, clubs, and restaurants, including the Columbia Restaurant, Florida's oldest establishment.

Northeast of downtown, the **Museum of Science and Industry** features various exhibits including an IMAX® Cinema. The GTE Challenger Learning Center, a living memorial to the Space Shuttle *Challenger*, has simulators and a mission control room. Nearby is Tampa's biggest attraction – **Busch Gardens**. This theme park incorporates an unusual zoo that re-creates colonial-era Africa. The zoo supports over 2,600 animals, with giraffes and zebras roaming freely over the "Serengeti Plain." Lions and other African animals can be seen on a unique Edge of Africa safari ride. Thrill-seekers can ride the 300-ft-(91-m-) high Falcon's Fury coaster.

Greek vase, Tampa Museum of Art

### 🚌 Busch Gardens
Busch Blvd, Tampa. **Tel** (888) 800-5447. **Open** 10am–6pm daily, extended hours for summer & hols. 🅿 ♿ 📷 🅦 buschgardens.com

## ❷❺ St. Petersburg

🚹 246,000. ✈ 🚉 180 9th St North, (727) 898-1496. 🛈 100 2nd Ave N, (727) 821-4715. 🎭 Festival of the States. 🅦 stpete.com

Established in 1875, "St. Pete," as it is often called, was originally a retired person's mecca. Times have changed however, and extensive renovations have rejuvenated the downtown waterfront area.

The city's claim to fame is the prestigious **Salvador Dalí Museum**, which has the largest private collection of the Spanish artist's work in the world, worth more than $350 million. It was opened in 1982, 40 years after the Ohio businessman Reynolds Morse first met Dalí and began collecting his works. There are 95 oil paintings, 100 watercolors and drawings, 1,300 graphics, sculptures, and other objects. Spanning the years 1914–70, they range from Dalí's early figurative paintings to his first experiments in Surrealism, as well as those mature, large-scale paintings described as his "masterworks."

The city's best-known landmark is **The Pier**, which has a string of shops and restaurants. Close by, the **St. Petersburg Museum of History** focuses on the city's history and has exhibits ranging from mastodon bones and native pottery to a replica of the sea plane that made the world's first flight with a paying passenger in 1914.

The modern Palladian-style **Museum of Fine Arts**, near the bay, is famous for its wide-ranging collection of European, American, and Asian works. Supreme among the French Impressionist paintings are *A Corner of the Woods* (1877) by Cézanne and Monet's classic *Parliament, Effect of Fog, London* (1904).

### 🏛 Salvador Dalí Museum
1 Dalí Blvd. **Tel** (727) 823-3767. 🚌 4, 32, trolley from The Pier. **Open** 10am–5:30pm Mon–Sat (10am–8pm Thu), noon–5:30pm Sun. **Closed** Thanksgiving, Dec 25. 🅿 📷 ♿ 📷 🎦 🅦 thedali.org

South Lido Park Beach on Lido Key, one of Sarasota's off-shore islands

## Environs

The Gulf Coast's much-advertised "361 days of sunshine a year," lures tourists from all over the world to the beaches between St. Petersburg and Clearwater. Known as the Holiday Isles or the Suncoast, the strip encompasses 28 miles (45 km) of barrier island beaches. St. Pete Beach is the busiest, with excellent water sports facilities; the **Fort de Soto Park** beaches have been ranked among the top 10 in the US. Florida's famous sea cows, or manatees, found all along in the coastal waters, are gentle herbivorous giants that grow to a length of 10 ft (3 m). Once plentiful, today only about 2,500 survive.

## ㉖ Sarasota

🏙 53,000. ✈ 🚌 575 N Washington Blvd, (941) 955-5735; Amtrak bus, (800) 872-7245. 🛈 655 N Tamiami Trail, (941) 957-1877. 🎪 Circus Festival (Jan). 🌐 visitsarasota.org

Known as Florida's cultural center, Sarasota's affluence is often credited to the millionaire circus owner, John Ringling, who invested much of his fortune, estimated at $200 million, in the area. His legacy is best seen at his house and in his splendid collection of European art, Sarasota's biggest attraction. The **Ringling Museum Complex** comprises the Museum of Art, a colorful Circus Museum, and the

Ca'd'Zan – Ringling's winter residence overlooking Sarasota Bay. Ringling had a particular love for Italy, and his fine collection of Italian Baroque paintings are the cornerstone of his collection. The highlight of the Museum of Art is the Rubens Gallery. Also noteworthy are the Astor Rooms, displaying the lavish 19th-century interiors of a New York mansion.

Sarasota has an attractive waterfront setting, and numerous artists and writers have settled here. The restored storefronts in the downtown area around Palm Avenue and Main Street house antique shops, bars, and restaurants.

The nearby barrier islands – Longboat Key, Lido Key, and Siesta Key – have great beaches and excellent tourist accommodations. **South Lido Park Beach** on Lido Key has a lovely woodland trail. The broad **Siesta Key Beach** is always lively, while Turtle Beach is quieter and has the only campsite on these Keys. Longboat Key is well known for its golf courses. Most of the beaches offer excellent water sports facilities.

## Ringling Museum Complex: Ca'd'Zan

The Ca'd'Zan (House of John), modeled after a Venetian palace with Renaissance and Baroque features, is set off by a 200-ft (60-m) marble terrace. Its opulence epitomizes the life of the American super-rich of the early 20th century.

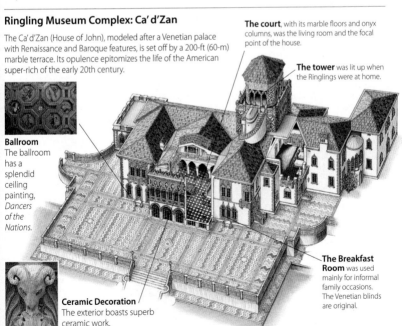

**The court**, with its marble floors and onyx columns, was the living room and the focal point of the house.

**The tower** was lit up when the Ringlings were at home.

**Ballroom**
The ballroom has a splendid ceiling painting, *Dancers of the Nations.*

**The Breakfast Room** was used mainly for informal family occasions. The Venetian blinds are original.

**Ceramic Decoration**
The exterior boasts superb ceramic work.

Beachfront cottages on Sanibel Island, Lee Island Coast

# ⑳ Lee Island Coast

✈ 📧 2275 Cleveland Ave, Fort Myers, (800) 231-2222. 🚹 1159 Causeway Rd, Sanibel, (239) 472-1080. Boat Services: Tropic Star (239) 283-0015; Captiva Cruises (239) 472-5300; North Captiva Island Club Resort (239) 395-1001.

This coastline offers an irresistible combination of sandy beaches, beautiful sunsets, and exotic wildlife. Of the two most popular islands, **Sanibel** has manicured gardens and rows of shops and restaurants along Periwinkle Way, the town's hub. Most of the beaches with public access are along Gulf Drive, the best being Turner and Bowman's beaches.

The **Sanibel Captiva Conservation Foundation** on Sanibel-Captiva Road, protects a chunk of the island's wetland. It has 4 miles (6 km) of boardwalk trails and an observation tower, which is a vantage point for viewing birds. The **JN "Ding" Darling National Wildlife Refuge** occupies two-thirds of Sanibel. Its wildlife includes raccoons, alligators, and birds such as roseate spoonbills, bald eagles, and ospreys. The popular scenic "Wildlife Drive" can be covered by bike or car. Paths and canoe trails are lined with red mangrove and sea grape. Canoes and fishing boats are available for rent.

**Captiva Island**, the other popular island, is less developed. However, visitors can enjoy the ambience of the old-fashioned South Seas Plantation Resort with its busy marina, which is the starting point for boat trips to

Cayo Costa Island – a beautiful, untouched barrier island.

Both islands are best known for their shells, and visitors soon get drawn into the shell-collecting culture. Other less developed islands lie close by and can be explored by boat.

🦅 **JN "Ding" Darling National Wildlife Refuge**
Mile Marker 2, Sanibel Captiva Rd. **Tel** (239) 472-1100. **Open** Sat–Thu. **Closed** public hols. 🅿 📷

## Environs
**Fort Myers**, about 25 miles (40 km) east of the Lee Island Coast, is an old-fashioned city that was put on the map in the 1880s by one of America's most famous inventors, Thomas Alva Edison (1847–1931). The Edison Winter Home is Fort Myers' most enduring attraction. Edison built his estate in 1886, and the house, laboratory, and botanical gardens are much as he left them. The laboratory contains his original equipment and is still lit by carbon filament light bulbs, which have been in

Original equipment in Thomas Edison's laboratory, Fort Myers

constant use since Edison invented them. The museum displays personal items, phonographs, and a 1916 Model T car that was given to Edison by Henry Ford, his great friend. Next door, the Ford Winter Home has a few early Ford cars on display.

The Fort Myers Historical Museum, on Peck Street, is housed in the former railroad station. Interesting exhibits include a model of Fort Myers in the 1900s, and a P-39 bomber that crashed in the 1940s. To the south of the city are a handful of lively beaches.

# ⑳ Big Cypress Swamp

Big Cypress National Preserve: **Tel** (239) 695-1201. **Open** daily. **Closed** Dec 25. ♿ Fakahatchee Strand Preserve State Park: **Tel** (239) 695-4593. **Open** daily. ♿ Audubon of Florida's Corkscrew Swamp Sanctuary: **Tel** (239) 348-9151. **Open** daily. 🅿 ♿

Home to several hundred plants and animals including the endangered Florida panther, this vast, wetland basin features islands of slash pine, prairies, and hardwood hammocks. A third of the swamp is covered by cypress trees growing in long, narrow forests or "strands." The Tamiami Trail (US 41) stretches from Tampa to Miami and cuts directly through the swamp.

**Big Cypress National Preserve** is the swamp's largest protected area. Visitors can stop at the Oasis Visitor Center for information and enjoy the views from US 41. The **Fakahatchee Strand Preserve State Park** lies to the west. The few remaining specimens of old growth cypresses, some of which are 600 years old, are found at Big Cypress Bend. The country's largest cluster of royal palms are also found here. Route 846 leads to **Audubon of Florida's Corkscrew Swamp Sanctuary**, with its old-growth cypresses. It is famous for its birds and is a winter nesting area for endangered wood storks.

# 29 Everglades National Park

**Open** daily. *i* all centers open Dec–Apr: daily; check for rest of year. Ernest F. Coe Visitor Center: **Tel** (305) 242-7700. **Open** 8am–5pm all year. Gulf Coast Visitor Center: (Everglades City) **Tel** (239) 695-3311; boat tours & canoe rental (239) 695-2591. Shark Valley Information Center: **Tel** (305) 221-8776; tram tours & cycle rental (305) 221-8455. Royal Palm Visitor Center: **Tel** (305) 242-7700. Flamingo Visitor Center: **Tel** (239) 695-2945. For canoe, bicycle rental & boat tours, call (239) 695-3101. *most boardwalks are accessible. ⚠ (800) 365-2267 to book. **w** nps.gov/ever

Covering 1.4 million acres (566,580 ha), the Everglades National Park makes up only a fifth of the world-famous Everglades – low-lying wetlands formed from the overspill of Lake Okeechobee. The unique landscape consists of a vast expanse of sawgrass prairie, broken by tree islands, hammocks, and meandering channels. A paradise for wildlife, the park has a wide range of fauna, including 400 species of birds.

The main entrance lies 10 miles (16 km) west of Florida City. Inside are walking trails, most of them elevated boardwalks; some are suitable for bicycles. Boats and canoes can be rented. The best time to visit is during winter. South of the main entrance lies the informative Royal Palm Visitor Center and two boardwalk trails. The popular **Anhinga Trail** attracts wildlife in the dry winter months, and its open site is excellent for photographs. Alligators congregate at the "gator hole" (a pond that is hollowed out by alligators in the dry season to reach the water below) at the head of the trail, and a wide range of fauna, including deer, raccoons, and the splendid anhinga bird, can be spotted. Close by, the **Gumbo Limbo Trail** offers the best chance to explore a tropical hardwood hammock but is ridden with mosquitoes. Watch for the pretty bromeliads, non-parasitic members of the pineapple family that grow on other plants, and the trail's namesake, the gumbo-limbo tree with its red bark.

A short distance to the west, **Long Pine Key's** campsite is beautifully situated and is one of the main reasons that people stop here. Several shady trails lead off from it: do not stray from the paths as the limestone bed-rock has "solution holes" created by rain, which are deep and difficult to spot.

**Shark Valley** lies north of Long Pine Key, near the park boundary. The area is best visited by taking a tram tour or a bicycle along the 15-mile (25-km) loop road. A 60-ft (18-m) tower at its end offers great views. The valley is home to the Seminole Indians, who settled here in the 19th-century after being driven into the Everglades by land-hungry Europeans *(see p286)*.

The elevated **Pa-hay-okee Overlook** lies northwest of Long Key Pine. The expanse of sawgrass prairie seen from here is typical of the Everglades landscape. The view from the observation tower is worth the climb: tree islands break the horizon, and a multitude of birds, such as hawks, roseate spoon-bills, great blue herons, and snail kites, can be easily spotted.

The **Mahogany Hammock Trail** leads through one of the park's largest hammocks, and it has a variety of fauna and flora. Trails such as West Lake Trail and Snake Bight Trail lie between Mahogany Hammock and **Flamingo** on Florida Bay and are especially rich in birdlife. Flamingo has the park's only hotel and also offers a wide choice of activities such as hiking, fishing, boating, and wildlife viewing. An overnight stay at the campsite is a must, especially for bird-watching. The bays around Flamingo have manatees *(see p319)*, as well as the rare, endangered American crocodile. The Flamingo Visitor Center has information about ranger-led activities: talks, slideshows, and walks through the swamp. Canoeing is the best way to explore the watery trails around Flamingo. These range from short trips to a week-long adventure of the remote Wilderness Waterway, leading past Whitewater Bay along the park's western coast. Northwest of Flamingo, the park's western entrance is marked by the island of Chokoloskee.

Today, the Everglades are under threat. Irrigation canals have disrupted the flow of water from Lake Okeechobee, which could prove disastrous for this delicate ecosystem.

Visitors should follow a few, simple safety tips. Bring insect repellent and protection against the sun. Follow park rules and respect all wildlife. Note that some shrubs and trees are poisonous, as are some caterpillars, spiders, and snakes. Do not wander off the pathways, and drive slowly because animals often venture onto the road.

Park ranger

Boardwalk through swamps in the tropical wilderness of the Everglades National Park

## ㉚ Biscayne National Park

9700 SW 328th St, Convoy Point.
📷 Miami. 📞 **Tel** (305) 230-7275.
**Open** daily. **Closed** Dec 25. ♿ limited.
⚠️ Boat Tours: **Tel** (305) 230-1100.
🌐 **nps.gov/bisc**

Dense mangrove swamp protects the shoreline of Biscayne National Park, which incorporates the northernmost islands of the Florida Keys. Its waters hold the park's greatest draw – a living coral reef with myriad forms and over 200 types of tropical fish. The barrier islands are unoccupied, so the coral here is healthier and the water even clearer than in the more popular parks farther south. Activities include glass-bottomed boat tours, snorkeling, and diving – all arranged by the visitor center.

## ㉛ The Keys

📷 Miami.

Running southwest off the tip of the Florida peninsula are the Keys, a chain of fossilized coral islands protected by North America's only coral reef. Visitors flock to the resorts here to enjoy several activities ranging from fishing to snorkeling.

From the 1500s, the Keys lured a succession of settlers, pirates, and "wreckers." Its development, however, took off in the early 1900s, when rail baron Henry Flagler (*see p286*) constructed the Overseas Railroad across the Keys. It has since been replaced by the magnificent Overseas Highway, which ends at Key West.

Bahia Honda's beautiful beach, the finest in the Florida Keys

The largest island in the Upper Keys is **Key Largo**, named "long island" by Spanish explorers. One of its highlights is the *African Queen*, the boat used in the eponymous 1951 film, which makes short pleasure trips. The island's greatest draws, however, are the diving and snorkeling opportunities just offshore in the **John Pennekamp Coral Reef State Park**. The park has a visitor center, swimming areas, and woodland trails, but it is best known for its fabulous underwater reaches, which provide a glimpse of the extraordinary forms of coral reef life.

Gold ornament from a treasure ship

**Islamorada**, south of Key Largo, declares itself as the "Sport Fishing Capital of the World." Encompassing seven islands, it is known for its outstanding big game fishing. The Whale Harbor Marina on Upper Matecumbe Key bristles with impressive deep-sea charter craft, used to catch

blue-water fish. Fishing boats, based here, offer half-day trips, even if visitors are not expert anglers.

Long Key Bridge marks the beginning of the Middle Keys. The **Dolphin Research Center**, a nonprofit concern on Grassy Key, conducts the delightful "Dolphin Encounter," where one can swim with these endearing marine mammals. It is also a rest home for sick and injured dolphins. The heavily developed **Marathon Key** is the main center of the Middle Keys. Its primary appeal lies in fertile fishing grounds, and enthusiasts can choose from a range of angling techniques, including spear-fishing and line-fishing. Crane Point Hammock has 64 acres (26 ha) of tropical forest and mangroves, and several trails, while the **Museum of Natural History of the Florida Keys** explains the islands' history, geology, and ecology.

The Lower Keys are more rugged and less developed than the Upper and Middle Keys. The vegetation is more wooded and supports a different flora and fauna. The most striking change, however, is in the slow and languid pace of life.

After crossing the Seven Mile Bridge, visitors can head for the **Bahia Honda State Park**, which has the finest beach in the Keys. Brilliant white sand is backed by tropical forest,

### Fishing in the Florida Keys

Deep-sea fishing from a sports boat

Islamorada, Marathon, and Key West are the area's major fishing centers, and small marinas throughout the region offer boats for rent. There are options to suit most budgets and abilities, and one can book places on fishing party boats or hire guides. Deep-sea fishing, an exhilarating option, appeals to the Hemingway spirit of the angler, while backcountry fishing calls for stealth and cunning. The numerous bait and tackle shops rent out gear and sell licenses.

with unusual species of trees, such as silver palm and yellow satinwood. Canoes, kayaks, and water sports gear are available to rent. The adjacent **Looe Key National Marine Sanctuary** is a spectacular dive location, with abundant marine life.

The second largest island, **Big Pine Key** is the Lower Keys' main residential community and the best place to see the diminutive Key deer. The turning near MM 30 leads to the **Blue Hole**, a flooded quarry whose viewing platform is ideal for watching the deer and other wildlife.

**Key Largo**
ℹ MM 106, (305) 451-1414, (800) 822-1088. 🌐 fla-keys.com

🏞 **John Pennekamp Coral Reef State Park**
MM 102.5. **Tel** (305) 451-1202. **Open** daily. ♿ 🚻 limited.

## 🟤 Key West

🏨 25,000. ✈ 🚌 ⛴ ℹ 402 Wall St, (305) 294-2587.

The southernmost settlement in the US, Key West is a magnet for people who want to leave the rest of America behind. In the 16th century, it became a haven for pirates and "wreckers." "Wrecking," or the salvage of shipwrecks on the Keys' coral reef, was the business that first made Key West rich.

It soon became Florida's wealthiest city, and its opportunistic lifestyle attracted a stream of settlers from the Americas, the Caribbean, and Europe; their legacy is visible in the island's unique architecture and cuisine. An influx of writers and a large gay community have further added to Key West's cultural cocktail.

Most of the sights are within a few blocks of **Duval Street**, the main axis of Old Key West. By-lanes, such as Fleming Street, have many fine 19th-century wooden buildings, which contrast with the simple homes erected to house Cuban cigar-workers.

The **Wreckers' Museum** on Duval Street was originally the home of the wreck captain Francis B. Watlington. Built in 1829, its design displays some eccentric maritime influences, such as a hatch used for ventilation in the roof. It is stuffed with nautical bric-a-brac. Farther down, the **San Carlos Institute**, founded in 1871, is a Cuban heritage center. The garden of **Heritage House Museum**, on Caroline Street, has the Robert Frost cottage, named after the famous American poet who frequently stayed here. At the northern edge of the Old Town is **Mallory Square**, which comes to life at sunset, when a variety of performing artists amuse the crowds.

The **Bahama Village** on the western fringe of the Old Town is named after Key West's

earliest settlers. It has a lively Caribbean flavor with a number of brightly painted clapboard buildings.

A prime attraction is the Spanish-Colonial style **Hemingway Home**, where novelist Ernest Hemingway lived from 1931 to 1940. The room where he penned several of his most famous works, such as *To Have and Have Not* (the only book set in Key West), is above the carriage house. His library, travel mementos, and memorabilia, such as the cigar-maker's chair on which he sat and wrote, are on display.

The **Mel Fisher Maritime Museum** on Green Street displays fabulous shipwreck treasures such as coins, jewels, and crucifixes. These were salvaged by the late Mel Fisher, who discovered the wrecks of the Spanish galleons *Nuestra Señora de Atocha* and *Santa Margarita*, about 40 miles (64 km) west of Key West in 1985. Inside were 47 tons of gold and silver bars, and 70 lbs (32 kg) of raw emeralds that sank with the galleons in 1622.

Diver's helmet, Mel Fisher Museum

The **Conch Train** and **the Old Town Trolley Tour** are convenient options for exploring the town.

🚃 **Hemingway Home**
907 Whitehead St. **Tel** (305) 294-1136. **Open** daily. ♿ 🚻 limited. 🌐 hemingwayhome.com

## Florida's Coral Reef

North America's only live coral reef extends 200 miles (320 km) along the length of the Keys, from Miami to the Dry Tortugas. A complex and delicate ecosystem, it protects these islands from oceanic storms. Coral reefs are created over thousands of years by tiny marine organisms known as polyps and are home to a multitude of plants and sea creatures, including 500 species of fish.

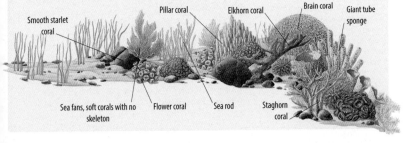

Smooth starlet coral · Pillar coral · Elkhorn coral · Brain coral · Giant tube sponge · Sea fans, soft corals with no skeleton · Flower coral · Sea rod · Staghorn coral

# Practical Information

With nearly 95 million visitors a year, Florida is very well geared for catering to tourists' needs. It is the ultimate family vacation destination. A strong emphasis is placed on entertaining children, and the superb facilities available make traveling with youngsters a real pleasure. Given its warm climate, Florida is a winter destination for many visitors. The peak season runs from December to April, when the beaches and other attractions are at their busiest. Anyone visiting Walt Disney World® or other theme parks should be prepared for long lines during the peak season.

## Tourist Information

Most large cities in Florida have a Convention and Visitor's Bureau (CVB), offering a huge array of brochures. Most hotels also have a brochure rack or free "WHERE" magazines that list museums, entertainment, shopping, and dining. To get information before you leave home, call or write for a vacation pack, issued by Visit Florida.

## Security & Health

Though crimes against tourists have fallen since the 1990s, it is best to take precautions in urban areas, especially in Miami. Avoid deserted neighborhoods at night. Carry as little money as possible, and leave valuables at home or check them at the hotel reception desk (it is best not to leave valuables in your hotel room). If attacked, hand over your wallet at once, and do not try to resist. In case of a serious illness or accident, hospitals provide good treatment. Minor ailments can be treated at the 24-hour walk-in clinics. Medical care is expensive, so be sure your insurance documents are up-to-date. In an emergency dial 911. For non-emergency assistance, contact **Miami-Dade Police Information**.

## Natural Hazards

Hurricanes are infrequent but devastating when they do occur. If a storm is imminent follow the announcements on local radio and television. The **National Hurricane Center** in Miami gives details on impending hurricanes. On beaches, keep an eye on children as riptides are a danger in some places.

The worst climatic hazard is the sun. Use sunscreen, wear hats, and drink plenty of fluids to avoid dehydration. Alligators are a thrilling sight in the Everglades but they can and do kill, so treat them with respect. Look out for spiders, scorpions, and venomous snakes native to Florida. It is best not to touch unfamiliar vegetation. Wear insect repellent when visiting parks and nature preserves.

## Driving in Florida

Driving in Florida is a delight because of its excellent road network, inexpensive gasoline, and affordable car rentals. The fastest routes are the Interstate Highways, referred to as I-10, I-75, and so on. Be warned that local drivers change lanes frequently on expressways, so stick to the right and be alert near exits. Speed limits can vary within a few miles, from 55–70 mph (90–105 km/h) on highways, to 20–30 mph (32–48 km/h) in residential areas, and 15 mph (24 km/h) near schools. Speed limits are rigorously enforced, and speeding fines can be as much as $500.

In the event of a serious breakdown, call the emergency number on the rental agreement and the agency will provide a new vehicle. The **American Automobile Association (AAA)** also has its own breakdown service and will assist its members.

Miami has had a bad reputation for crimes against motorists, but be careful in other areas as well. Avoid driving in unfamiliar territory after dark. If you have to refer to a map, stop only when you are in a well-lit area. Ignore any attempt by anyone to stop you from driving.

## Etiquette

Dress in Florida is mostly casual, but it is illegal for women to go topless on beaches, except in a few places, such as Miami's South Beach. Drinking alcohol on beaches and in other public places is illegal, as is smoking in buses, trains, taxis, and in most public buildings. All restaurants and cafés are non-smoking in Florida.

## The Climate of Florida

With its warm climate, Florida is a year-round destination. Its climatic divide between the temperate north and the subtropical south means that the state has two distinct tourist seaons. In south Florida (including Orlando), the busiest time is when tourists come to enjoy the mild winters. Here the summers can be uncomfortably hot. In the north, the Panhandle attracts most visitors in the summer. Despite this difference, the Sunshine State by and large lives up to its reputation of clear, blue skies and a pleasant climate.

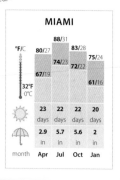

| MIAMI | | | | |
| --- | --- | --- | --- | --- |
| °F/C | 80/27 | 88/31 74/23 | 83/28 72/22 | 75/24 61/16 |
| | 67/19 | | | |
| 32°F 0°C | | | | |
| ☀ | 23 days | 22 days | 22 days | 20 days |
| ☂ | 2.9 in | 5.7 in | 5.6 in | 2 in |
| month | Apr | Jul | Oct | Jan |

## Sports & Outdoor Activities

Florida's climate makes the state a top destination for all sports enthusiasts, from golfers and tennis players to canoeists and deep-sea divers. The best sources of information on outdoor activities are the **Florida Sports Foundation** and the **Department of Environmental Protection (DEP)**.

Water sports of all kinds are well represented, with wonderful beaches on both the Atlantic and Gulf coasts. Most resorts offer the full range from windsurfing to jet-skiing. Water-skiing can also be enjoyed on lakes and inland waterways. The state provides ample opportunities for canoeing as well, with the Wilderness Waterway in the Everglades National Park being a favorite run.

Florida has superb diving and snorkeling sports. The country's only living coral reef skirts the state's southeast coast, stretching the length of the Keys. Excellent guided snorkeling trips are available to view the coast's coral and fish. For information on diving, contact the **Keys Association of Dive Operators**.

Fishing off the pier is popular at coastal spots, but the state is best known for its sport fishing.

Deep-sea fishing boats can be chartered at seaside resorts; the biggest fleets are in the Panhandle and the Keys. Many rivers and parks offer freshwater fishing. The **Florida Game and Fresh Water Fish Commission** provides details on locations and licensing costs.

Outdoor adventure tours to wilder areas, such as the Everglades, are organized by some companies, including **Build a Field Trip.**

## Entertainment

Whether your preference is for a Broadway drama, a lavish Las Vegas-style floor show, or a small cruise, Florida has something for everyone. **Walt Disney World® Resort**, **Universal Orlando® Resort**, and other attractions offer the best in family entertainment, with theme parks galore to thrill children during the day and dinner shows at night. Here, meals are served, generally themed to the show you are watching. Water parks, throughout Florida, are also big draws.

Lavish road shows are the highest-quality productions in Florida. The state has its own theater groups, orchestras, and opera companies, such as the the **Symphony of the Americas**

and the **Florida Grand Opera**. Some of the best places to dance are clubs offering live and varied music. Nightclubs require an ID to prove that you are over 18.

Florida is the world's leading departure point for cruises to the Caribbean. You can also go on mini-cruises, for a day or just an evening, for around $40. Evening cruises usually entail dinner and dancing; casino cruises, operating out of Miami and Port Everglades, are the rage. Fort Lauderdale and St. Petersburg also have popular tour boats.

## Shopping

Shopping is also a very popular pastime in Florida, attracting many overseas shoppers. Although the state has some very upscale stores, often clustered in shopping districts such as the exclusive Worth Avenue in Palm Beach, it is best known for its discount stores. If searching for gifts or souvenirs, the theme parks and seaside tourist centers offer a vast choice. Florida is also famed for its citrus fruit, which you can buy fresh or preserved as colorful candies and jellies. Other buys include seashells, Seminole crafts, Latin music, and hand-rolled cigars.

# DIRECTORY

## Tourist Information

**Tel** (866) 972-5280.
w visitflorida.com

## Emergency Numbers

**All Emergencies**
**Tel** 911 to alert police, fire, or medical services.

**Miami-Dade Police Information**
**Tel** (305) 476-5423.

**National Hurricane Center**
**Tel** (305) 229-4470, recorded message with hurricane details.

**American Automobile Assn. (AAA)**
**Tel** (800) 222-1134.

**AAA General Breakdown Assistance**
**Tel** (800) 222-4357. NOTE: Rentals also provide 24-hour assistance.

## Sports

**Department of Environmental Protection (DEP)**
3900 Commonwealth Blvd, Tallahassee, FL 32399. **Tel** (850) 245-2052.

**Florida Sports Foundation**
Tallahassee, FL 32308. **Tel** (850) 488-8347.
w flasports.com

## Backcountry Pursuits

**Build a Field Trip**
Fort Lauderdale, FL 33308. **Tel** (954) 772-7800.

## Fishing

**Florida Fish and Wildlife Conservation**
**Tel** (850) 488-4676.
**Tel** (888) 347-4356 (fishing licenses).
w myfwc.com

## Diving & Snorkeling

**Keys Association of Dive Operators (KADO)**
w divekeys.com

## Entertainment

**Florida Grand Opera**
1200 Coral Way, Miami.
**Tel** (305) 854-7890.

**Symphony of the Americas**
2425 E Commercial Blvd, Fort Lauderdale.
**Tel** (954) 335-7002.

**Universal Orlando® Resort**
**Tel** (407) 363-8000.
w universalorlando.com

**Walt Disney World® Resort**
**Tel** (407) 934-7639 (for reservations).
w disneyworld.com

# Where to Stay

## Miami

### CORAL GABLES: Courtyard by Marriott $$
Modern     **Map** B4
*2051 Le Jeune Rd, 33134*
**Tel** *(305) 443-2301*
**W** marriott.com
A comfortable, six-story hotel with motel-style decor and a rooftop pool. Airport shuttle.

### DK Choice
### CORAL GABLES: Biltmore Hotel $$$
Resort     **Map** A4
*1200 Anastasia Ave, 33134*
**Tel** *(855) 311-6903*
**W** biltmorehotel.com
Large rooms and legendary suites match the élan of this luxurious Spanish-style 1920s landmark, complete with a Giralda-inspired bell tower. Facilities include a Donald Ross golf course, 10 tennis courts, and a gigantic pool, along with four excellent restaurants.

### DOWNTOWN: Mandarin Oriental $$$
Luxury     **Map** D3
*500 Brickell Key Dr, 33131*
**Tel** *(305) 913-8288*
**W** mandarinoriental.com
Frequented by celebrities, this Asian luxury hotel boasts a lavish spa and five-star dining.

### MIAMI BEACH: Aqua $$
Modern     **Map** F2
*1530 Collins Ave, 33139*
**Tel** *(305) 538-4361*
**W** aquamiami.com
Modern rooms, a sundeck, and a garden feature here. Continental breakfast is included.

### MIAMI BEACH: Clay Hotel $$
Historic     **Map** F3
*1438 Washington Ave, 33139*
**Tel** *(305) 534-2988*
**W** clayhotel.com
In an atmospheric 1930s building full of South Beach history, this hotel has a lovely patio and well-lit rooms. Book early.

### DK Choice
### MIAMI BEACH: The Angler's $$$
Luxury     **Map** F3
*660 Washington Ave, 33139*
**Tel** *(305) 534-9600*
**W** theanglersresort.com
Choose from spacious suites, studios, or villas in the four majestic buildings of this Mediterranean Revival complex. Some units come with private gardens, Jacuzzis, and rooftop terraces. Luxurious poolside or in-room spa treatments are offered.

### MIAMI BEACH: The Delano $$$
Luxury     **Map** F2
*1685 Collins Ave, 33139*
**Tel** *(305) 672-2000*
**W** delano-hotel.com
This Philippe Starck-inspired hotel is famous for its decor and celebrity clientele. The rooms have stark all-white decor, and there is a great pool and bar.

### MIAMI BEACH: Fountainebleu Hotel $$$
Resort     **Map** F2
*4441 Collins Ave, 33140*
**Tel** *(305) 538-2000*
**W** fontainebleau.com
Fabulously retro, this lavishly renovated hotel features Las Vegas-style glitzy decor, plus a spectacular pool and spa.

> **Price Guide**
> Prices are based on one night's stay in high season for a standard double room, inclusive of service charges and taxes.
>
> $        up to $150
> $$       $150 to $300
> $$$      over $300

### MIAMI BEACH: W South Beach $$$
Luxury     **Map** F2
*2201 Collins Ave, 33139*
**Tel** *(305) 938-3000*
**W** wsouthbeach.com
This stunning W Hotels flagship has spacious rooms with glass balconies, kitchenettes, and ocean vistas.

## The Gold & Treasure Coasts

### FORT LAUDERDALE: The Hotel Deauville $
Hostel
*2916 N Ocean Blvd, 33308*
**Tel** *(954) 568-5000*
**W** thedeauvillehotel.com
Close to the beach, this hotel has clean dorms and rooms with a communal kitchen and a pool.

### DK Choice
### FORT LAUDERDALE: Lago Mar Resort $$$
Resort
*1700 S Ocean Ln, 33316*
**Tel** *(954) 678-3915*
**W** lagomar.com
There may be more lavish resorts but few as gracious or unpretentious as this familly-run charmer. It offers a huge private beach, lagoon pool, tennis courts, golf putting course, and even a giant outdoor chessboard. Great for families and couples.

### HOLLYWOOD: Seminole Hard Rock Hotel and Casino $$$
Luxury
*1 Seminole Way, 33314*
**Tel** *(954) 327-7625*
**W** seminolehardrockhollywood.com
Rooms are spacious and there is a lavish pool, but the entertainment and casino are the big draws here.

### PALM BEACH: The Breakers $$$
Resort
*1 S County Rd, 33480*
**Tel** *(561) 655-6611*
**W** thebreakers.com
Classy and expansive oceanfront resort, offering spa, golf, tennis with instructors, family programs, and luxurious rooms.

The luxurious Biltmore Hotel, a landmark in Coral Gables

Works of art adorning the walls in the Grand Bohemian, downtown Orlando

### WEST PALM BEACH:
**Palm Beach Hibiscus** $$
B&B
*213 South Rosemary Ave, 33407*
**Tel** *(561) 833-8171*
[W] palmbeachhibiscus.com
B&B fans will love this beautifully restored 1920s home furnished with old-world elegance. Rooms come with a private balcony or a terrace, and there's a small pool.

## Orlando & the Space Coast

### COCOA BEACH:
**The Inn at Cocoa Beach** $$
B&B
*4300 Ocean Blvd, 32931*
**Tel** *(321) 799-3460*
[W] theinnatcocoabeach.com
Located directly on the beach, this inn has individually decorated rooms. There is an evening wine and cheese reception.

### KISSIMMEE: Gaylord
**Palms Resort** $$$
Resort
*6000 W Osceola Pkwy, 34747*
**Tel** *(407) 586-0000*
[W] gaylordpalms.com
This big, lavish convention center and resort has three Florida-themed areas and a water park.

### ORLANDO: Grand Bohemian $$$
Luxury
*325 S Orange Ave, 32801*
**Tel** *(407) 313-9000*
[W] grandbohemianhotel.com
Great rooms, fine art, a pool, and a jazz-themed bar make this a top choice in downtown Orlando.

### ORLANDO: Villas of
**Grand Cypress** $$$
Resort
*1 N Jacaranda, 32836*
**Tel** *(407) 239-4700*
[W] grandcypress.com
This landscaped private complex has extravagant villas with

kitchens, patios, and bathrooms with Roman tubs. There's a free shuttle to the theme parks.

### UNIVERSAL ORLANDO®:
**Hard Rock Hotel** $$$
Luxury
*5800 Universal Blvd, 32819*
**Tel** *(407) 503-2000*
[W] hardrockhotelorlando.com
With a fun "rock 'n' roll" theme, this Hard Rock flagship has spacious rooms, a spa, and walking paths.

### DK Choice

**UNIVERSAL ORLANDO®:**
**Loews Portofino**
**Bay Hotel** $$$
Luxury
*5601 Universal Blvd, 32819*
**Tel** *(407) 503-1000*
[W] loewshotels.com
A beautifully re-created Italian village, complete with canals and festive piazza, complements the pools and Mandara Spa at this luxury hotel. Perks include skipping lines at the Universal theme parks, free rides on Express Unlimited, and on-site water taxis and shuttle buses.

### WALT DISNEY WORLD®:
**Disney's All Star Resorts** $$
Resort
*World Dr & Osceola Pkwy, Lake Buena Vista, 32830*
**Tel** *(407) 934-7639*
[W] disneyworld.com
Disney's least expensive lodgings offer small rooms within themed towers and lots of fun activities.

### WALT DISNEY WORLD®:
**Animal Kingdom Lodge** $$$
Luxury
*2901 Osceola Pkwy, Lake Buena Vista, 32830*
**Tel** *(407) 938-3000*
[W] disneyworld.com
Luxury safari lodge, with views of more than 200 animals roaming the savannah. Shuttle ride to park.

### WALT DISNEY WORLD®:
**Disney's Coronado**
**Springs Resort** $$$
Resort
*1000 W Buena Vista Dr, 32830*
**Tel** *(407) 939-1000*
[W] disneyworld.com
A luxury haven featuring a Mayan pyramid pool and evening campfires. There's also mini-golf and a fitness center.

### WALT DISNEY WORLD®:
**Disney's Port Orleans Resort** $$$
Resort
*1251 Riverside Dr, Lake Buena Vista, 32830*
**Tel** *(407) 934-5000*
[W] disneyworld.com
With wrought-iron balconies, horse-drawn carriages, and a lagoon lake, this resort has a fantastic New Orleans ambience.

## The Northeast

### AMELIA ISLAND: Omni Amelia
**Island Plantation** $$$
Resort
*39 Beach Lagoon, 32034*
**Tel** *(904) 261-6161*
[W] omnihotels.com
This sprawling Omni playground has everything for an active vacation: a beach, indoor and outdoor pools, kids' pool, golf, tennis center, and nature trails.

### FERNANDINA BEACH: Elizabeth
**Pointe Lodge** $$$
B&B
*98 S Fletcher Ave, 32034*
**Tel** *(904) 277-4851*
[W] elizabethpintelodge.com
An award-winning Nantucket-style shingled beach house with ocean views, elegant rooms, delicious breakfasts, and evening wine and *hors d'oeuvres*.

### JACKSONVILLE: Hyatt
**Regency Riverfront** $$
Modern
*225 E Coastline Dr, 32202*
**Tel** *(904) 588-1234*
[W] jacksonville.hyatt.com
Modern high-rise on the river-walk with comfortable rooms, full services, a rooftop pool, and a spa.

### PONTE VEDRA BEACH: Ponte
**Vedra Inn** $$$
Resort
*200 Ponte Vedra Blvd, 32082*
**Tel** *(904) 285-1111*
[W] pontevedra.com
A landmark since 1928, this Spanish-style five-star resort offers well-furnished rooms and suites, a beach, pools, golf courses, and a spa.

**For more information on types of hotels** *see pages 26–7*

Lobby of the opulent Casa Monica Hotel, St. Augustine

## DK Choice

**ST. AUGUSTINE:**
**Casa Monica Hotel** $$$
Historic
*95 Cordova St, 32084*
**Tel** *(904) 827-1888*
Ⓦ casamonica.com
Old Spanish charm pervades this fully restored 1888 beauty, from the frescoed lobby to the atmospheric guest rooms and the guitar music in the Cobalt lounge. Rooms have all modern conveniences and the pool deck is a welcome private haven.

## The Panhandle

**FORT WALTON BEACH:**
**Ramada Plaza Beach Resort** $$
Modern
*1500 E Miracle Strip Pkwy, 32548*
**Tel** *(850) 243-9161*
Ⓦ ramadafwb.com
Comfortable well-equipped rooms, plus a beach, waterfall, grotto pool, and a playground.

**PANAMA CITY BEACH:**
**Wyndham Bay Point Resort** $$
Resort
*4114 Jan Cooley Dr, 32408*
**Tel** *(850) 236-6000*
Ⓦ wyndham.com
This luxury resort features two golf courses, a spa, five pools, and a shuttle to the beach.

**PENSACOLA: Lee House** $$$
B&B
*400 Bayfront Pkwy, 32502*
**Tel** *(850) 912-8770*
Ⓦ leehousepensacola.com
This spacious B&B has nine individually styled guest rooms. Its wide porches overlook Seville Square and Fountain Park.

**PENSACOLA BEACH:**
**Portofino Island Resort** $$$
Resort
*10 Portofino Dr, 32561*
**Tel** *(850) 916-5000*
Ⓦ portofinoisland.com
Five Mediterranean-style condos house apartments with kitchens at this resort with a spa, pools, golf, and kids' activities.

## DK Choice

**SANTA ROSA BEACH:**
**Watercolor Inn** $$$
B&B
*34 Goldenrod Circle, 32459*
**Tel** *(850) 534-5000*
Ⓦ watercolorresort.com
Right next to the beach., Watercolor Inn is a luxurious but relaxed beach house with huge rooms, king-sized beds, walk-in showers, and balconies for sunset-watching. Complimentary bikes, canoes, and kayaks are on offer.

**TALLAHASSEE:**
**Governors Inn** $$$
Historic
*209 S Adams St, 32301*
**Tel** *(850) 681-6855*
Ⓦ thegovinn.com
A convenient downtown choice with old-fashioned warmth and rooms named after past governors. Free Continental breakfast and a happy hour.

## The Gulf Coast

## DK Choice

**FORT MYERS BEACH:**
**Edison Beach House** $$$
B&B
*830 Estero Blvd, 33931*
**Tel** *(239) 463-1530*
Ⓦ edisonbeachhouse.com
This five-story beachside inn cannot be beaten for its space and amenities. The airy suites are fitted with beach-style wicker furniture and ceiling fans, and have full kitchens, washer-dryers, and balconies. There is a heated pool and children's playhouse as well.

**SANIBEL ISLAND:**
**Sanibel Inn** $$$
B&B
*937 E Gulf Dr, 33957*
**Tel** *(239) 472-3181*
Ⓦ sanibelinn.com
Spacious and well-equipped rooms and condos. Great beach, plus tennis and biking facilties.

**SARASOTA:**
**Turtle Beach Resort** $$$
Resort
*9049 Midnight Pass Rd, Siesta Key, 34242*
**Tel** *(941) 349-4554*
Ⓦ turtlebeachresort.com
This private bayside cottage complex offers themed studios and suites with private patios and hot tubs.

**ST. PETERSBURG: Renaissance**
**Vinoy Resort** $$$
Historic
*501 5th Ave NE, 33701*
**Tel** *(727) 894-1000*
Ⓦ marriott.com
This beautifully restored classic hotel has retained the grandeur of the past, while adding top amenities including a lavish pool.

**TAMPA: Hilton Garden Inn** $$
B&B
*1700 E 9th Ave, 33605*
**Tel** *(813) 769-9267*
Ⓦ hiltongardeninn.com
A comfortable full-service hotel with well-equipped rooms in a great location near Ybor City.

## The Everglades & the Keys

**ISLAMORADA:**
**The Moorings Village** $$$
Luxury
*123 Beach Rd, 33036*
**Tel** *(305) 664-4708*
Ⓦ themooringsvillage.com
Eighteen beautifully furnished cottages have porches and balconies, plus an excellent spa.

## DK Choice

**KEY LARGO: Kona Kai**
**Resort & Gallery** $$$
Resort
*97802 Overseas Hwy, 33037*
**Tel** *(305) 852-7200*
Ⓦ konakairesort.com
Kona Kai is a unique resort for adults only. It offers tropical-themed cottage suites set in a botanical garden with over 250 rare plants. Amenities include garden tours, beach games, kayaks, paddleboats, a freshwater pool, and a Jacuzzi.

**KEY WEST: Marquesa Hotel** $$$
Historic
*600 Fleming St, 33040*
**Tel** *(305) 292-1919*
Ⓦ marquesa.com
Light, airy rooms come with ceiling fans in three beautifully restored 1880s homes and one newer unit.

# Where to Eat and Drink

## Miami

**COCONUT GROVE: Jaguar** $$
Latin American     Map B4
*3067 Grand Ave, 33133*
**Tel** *(305) 444-0216*
Artfully seasoned Latin dishes
and many grilled items feature in
Jaguar's colorful tropical menu.
Ceviche bar with taster platters.

**CORAL GABLES: Seasons 52** $$
American     Map B4
*321 Miracle Mile, 33134*
**Tel** *(305) 442-8552*
Head here for a variety of fresh,
healthy food, with no entrée over
475 calories, and dishes such as
cedar-plank roasted salmon and
grilled T-bone lamb chops.

**DOWNTOWN: Michael's
Genuine Food & Drink** $$$
American     Map D3
*130 NE 40th St, 33137*
**Tel** *(305) 573-5550*
Ingredients are sourced fresh from
the farm or the sea at this trendy
restaurant serving dishes ranging
from small to extra-large servings.

**DOWNTOWN: Tuyo** $$$
Latin American     Map D3
*415 NE 2nd Ave, 33132*
**Tel** *(305) 337-3200*    **Closed** *Sun &
Mon*
The daily-changing menu at this
romantic restaurant with
fantastic city-bay views features
delicious "Floribbean" cuisine
created by blending fresh local
ingredients with Latin spices.

**LITTLE HAVANA: Versaille** $
Cuban     Map C3
*3335 8th St, 33135*
**Tel** *(305) 444-0240*
Choose from two sampler plates
for a delicious introduction to
Cuban cuisine at Little Havana's
best-known restaurant.

**MIAMI BEACH: Shake Shack** $
American     Map F2
*1111 Lincoln Rd, 33139*
**Tel** *(305) 434-7787*
Come to Shake Shack for quality
burgers at bargain prices, plus
great fries and shakes worth
standing in line for.

**MIAMI BEACH: Tap Tap Haitian** $
Haitian     Map F3
*819 5th St, 33139*
**Tel** *(305) 672-2898*
This is a restaurant, art gallery,
and cultural center all in one.
Authentic Haitian dishes include
steamed whole fish in lime sauce,
shrimp in Creole sauce, goat
stew, and banana fritters.

**MIAMI BEACH: News Café** $$
American     Map F2
*800 Ocean Dr, 33139*
**Tel** *(305) 538-6397*
Large crowds flock to this round-
the-clock café serving crab cakes,
grilled salmon, pizza, and pasta.

### DK Choice

**MIAMI BEACH:
15 Steps** $$$
American     Map F2
*4525 Collins Ave, 33140*
**Tel** *(305) 674-5594*
The creative menu at this farm-
to-table restaurant inside the
Eden Roc Hotel changes daily
to include the best of each
season's bounty, relying heavily
on local produce. The excellent
*prix-fixe* three-course dinner is a
treat. South Beach location.

**FARTHER AFIELD:
Rusty Pelican** $$$
American
*3201 Rickenbacker Causeway, 33149*
**Tel** *(305) 361-3818*
With a creative chef at the helm
and stunning bay and city views,

---

**Price Guide**
Prices are based on a three-course meal
per person, with a glass of house wine,
including tax and service.

| | |
|---|---|
| $ | up to $35 |
| $$ | $35 to $70 |
| $$$ | over $70 |

---

this restaurant offers sushi, land,
or sea entrées, a bargain *prix-fixe*
menu, and plates to share.

## The Gold &
Treasure Coasts

### DK Choice

**BOCA RATON: Sapori** $$$
Italian
*301 via de Palmas, 33432*
**Tel** *(561) 367-9779*
Translating to "flavors," Sapori is a
small, unpretentious restaurant
rightly known for its flavorful fish
dishes and some of the city's
best pasta. Expect surprises such
as short rib ravioli or sweet-and-
sour salmon filet. There are
often special events when chef
Marco Pindo explains ingredients
and shows how dishes are made.

**FORT LAUDERDALE:
The Floridian** $
Diner
*1410 E Las Olas Blvd, 33301*
**Tel** *(954) 463-4041*
Open around the clock, this old-
time diner serves big portions of
hearty fare at great prices.

**FORT LAUDERDALE: Greek
Islands Taverna** $$$
Greek
*3300 N Ocean Blvd, 33308*
**Tel** *(954) 568-0008*
At this excellent Greek restaurant
loyal patrons line up to sample
the *meze*, fresh fish, and lamb.
Greek and international wines.

### DK Choice

**PALM BEACH: Buccan** $$$
American
*350 S County Rd, 33480*
**Tel** *(561) 833-3450*
With a star chef from Miami, an
energetic vibe, and a creative
menu of many small plates to
share, Buccan stands out from
the crowd. Along with steak
and swordfish, it serves delicious
short-rib empanadas, hot dog
paninis, and conch ceviches.

Homey interior of The Floridian, Fort Lauderdale

**For more information on types of restaurants** *see pages 28–9*

**POMPANO BEACH:**
**Café Maxx**          $$$
American
*2601 E Atlantic Blvd, 33062*
**Tel** *(954) 782-0606*
Café Maxx has been serving
innovative offerings since 1984.
Try the jerk-spiced sea scallops,
and pine-nut-crusted rack of lamb.

# Orlando & the Space Coast

**COCOA: Café Margaux**          $$$
French
*220 Brevard Ave, 32922*
**Tel** *(321) 639-8343*      **Closed** *Sun*
A fine-dining venue, with creative
dishes such as filo-encased
Norwegian salmon, and pork loin
stuffed with pear, brie, and walnut.

**LAKE BUENA VISTA:**
**Hemingway's**          $$$
Seafood
*Hyatt Regency Resort, 1 Grand
Cypress Blvd, 32836*
**Tel** *(407) 239-1234*
Inspired by Ernest Hemingway's
fishing exploits, this restaurant
offers great seafood such as local
swordfish and Florida rock shrimp.
Try the signature drink, Papa's
Doble, concocted by Hemingway.

**ORLANDO: Little Saigon**          $
Vietnamese
*1106 Colonial Dr, 32803*
**Tel** *(407) 423-8539*
A neighborhood favorite, Little
Saigon offers authentic and
delicious appetizers, and
noodle and rice dishes.

## DK Choice

**ORLANDO: Christini's
Ristorante**          $$$
Italian
*7600 Dr. Phillips Blvd, 32819*
**Tel** *(407) 583-4472*
Having received several awards
for both its food and wine, this
has been a bastion of fine dining
since 1984. Beautiful wood
paneling, paintings, and
celebrity photographs add to
the warm ambience. Delicious
meat dishes, as well as less
expensive chicken and pasta
dishes are on the menu.

**UNIVERSAL ORLANDO®:**
**Emeril's Orlando**          $$$
Creole
*6000 Universal Blvd, 32819*
**Tel** *(407) 224-2424*
New Orleans' favorites are re-
created in a lofty, modern setting
with an open kitchen. Kids' menu.

Hemingways, a restaurant specializing in seafood, Lake Buena Vista

## DK Choice

**WALT DISNEY WORLD®:**
**Boma – Flavors of Africa**          $$
African
*Animal Kingdom Lodge, 2901
Osceola Pkwy, 32830*
**Tel** *(407) 938-4722*
Boma features all the colors
and flavors of an African
market – with a thatched roof,
tree-trunk tabletops, and an
amazing array of serving
stations offering delicately
spiced meats and fish, along
with curries, plus mac 'n' cheese.

**WALT DISNEY WORLD®:**
**Ohana**          $$
Polynesian
*Polynesian Resort, 1600 Seven
Seas Dr, 32836*
**Tel** *(407) 824-1334*
Amid storytellers, coconut races,
and other festive fun, Ohana
offers excellent Polynesian food
cooked in an open pit and served
on skewers.

**WALT DISNEY WORLD®:**
**Cinderella's Royal Table**          $$$
American
*Fantasyland, Magic Kingdom Dr,
32830*
**Tel** *(407) 939-3463*
Experience fairy-tale dining in a
grand hall with Cinderella and
her prince. A souvenir photo is
included in the tab.

**WALT DISNEY WORLD®:**
**Les Chefs de France**          $$$
French
*Epcot World Showcase, 32830*
**Tel** *(407) 827-8709*
The brasserie menu here is
created by famous French chefs,
with dishes such as *Coquille
St. Jacques* and duckling with
cherries for the adults. Kids get
their own menu and visits from
*Ratatouille's* Chef Remy.

**WINTER PARK:**
**Ravenous Pig**          $$$
Gastropub
*1234 N Orange Ave, 32789*
**Tel** *(407) 628-2333*      **Closed** *Sun &
Mon*
From pub fare such as tacos
and burgers, to more creative
items like pork porterhouse and
tea-smoked salmon, Ravenous
Pig has something for everyone.

# The Northeast

**DAYTONA BEACH: Aunt
Catfish's On the River**          $$$
Southern seafood
*4009 Halifax Dr, Port Orange, 32127*
**Tel** *(386) 767-4768*
A laid-back Old South outpost on
the river, well known for its buffet
bar. Feast on grilled or fried catfish,
fried alligator and coconut shrimp.

**JACKSONVILLE: Bistro Aix**          $$$
American
*1440 San Marco Blvd, 32207*
**Tel** *(904) 398-1949*
This hip bistro in Jacksonville's
historic area offers small plates,
pizzas, and French standbys such
as mussels and *steak-frites*.

## DK Choice

**JACKSONVILLE:
Matthew's Restaurant**          $$$
American
*2107 Hendricks Ave, 32207*
**Tel** *(904) 396-9922*      **Closed** *Sun*
With sleek and elegant decor
and a 2,000-bottle wine cellar,
this is a great fine-dining venue.
Matthew Meure's beautifully
presented fare is well-priced,
given the high quality. Excellent
entrées include pistachio-
crusted Arctic char, and steak
with portobello mushrooms
and Gorgonzola cheese.

**ST. AUGUSTINE: The Floridian** **$$**
Southern
*39 Cordova St, 32084*
**Tel** *(904) 829-0655* **Closed** *Tue: lunch*
Head to the Floridian for Southern comfort – pickled pepper shrimps, chicken, and waffles – along with sandwiches, salad bowls, and vegetarian choices.

**ST. AUGUSTINE:**
**95 Cordoba** **$$$**
International
*95 Cordoba St, 32084*
**Tel** *(904) 824-0402*
Get a taste of Old Spain in St. Augustine with appetizers such as *escargot* and fried green tomatoes, and entrées that include *osso buco*, lobster, and bass with black-eyed pea mash.

## The Panhandle

**DESTIN: Marina Café** **$$$**
American seafood
*404 Harbor Blvd, 32541*
**Tel** *(850) 837-7960*
In an elegant nautical dining room with outdoor deck seating and great harbor views, formal cuisine such as steaks and seafood is paired with delicious wines.

**FORT WALTON BEACH:**
**Pandora's Steakhouse** **$$$**
Steak House
*1120B Santa Rosa Blvd, 32548*
**Tel** *(850) 244-8669* **Closed** *Mon*
This family-owned steak house is famous for its steak grilled over a wood-burning open pit. Seafood options and a children's menu are also available.

### DK Choice

**PANAMA CITY BEACH:**
**Firefly** **$$$**
American
*535 Richard Jackson Blvd, 32407*
**Tel** *(850) 249-3359*
Firefly provides a unique dining experience beneath a giant oak tree with twinkling lights, and is a great choice for a romantic meal. The menu features she-crab soups, rack of lamb, double-cut pork chops, and lobster tail. Martinis in the Library Lounge, a sushi happy hour, and a kids' menu are on offer.

**PENSACOLA: Five Sisters**
**Blues Café** **$$**
Southern
*421 W Belmont St, 32501*
**Tel** *(850) 912-4856*
Enjoy live music and relish traditional specials including

gumbo, fried chicken, crab cakes, pulled pork, and pot roast. There's also an excellent Sunday brunch.

**TALLAHASSEE:**
**Cypress Restaurant** **$$$**
Southern
*320 E Tennessee St, 32301*
**Tel** *(850) 513-1100* **Closed** *Sun dinner & Mon*
This chef-owned restaurant boasts of a sophisticated menu featuring kumquat-glazed duck breast, pecan-crusted grouper, and some of the best shrimp and grits in town.

## The Gulf Coast

### DK Choice

**ANNA MARIA ISLAND:**
**Beach Bistro** **$$$**
American
*6600 Gulf Dr, Holmes Beach, 34217*
**Tel** *(941) 778-6444*
One of Florida's top-rated restaurants, Beach Bistro is a great spot for a romantic meal, with beautiful sunset views over the sea. Delicacies on offer include Floridian grouper with cashew-toasted coconut crust, bouillabaisse filled with lobster tail, and sliders of sirloin, foie gras, and Béarnaise on a sweet roll.

**CLEARWATER BEACH:**
**Frenchy's South Beach Café** **$$**
American
*351 S Gulfview Dr, 33767*
**Tel** *(727) 441-9991*
This casual beach café is known for its tasty specialty grouper sandwiches. It also serves she-crab soup, salads, and seafood platters.

Seafood dish at the highly acclaimed Beach Bistro on Anna Maria Island

**SARASOTA: Yoders** **$**
American
*3434 Bahia Vista St, 34239*
**Tel** *(941) 955-7771* **Closed** *Sun*
Yoders has been serving Amish treats since 1975, including big breakfasts, delicious fried chicken, and pies. No alcohol.

**ST. PETERSBURG: The Moon**
**Under Water** **$$**
Pub/British
*332 Beach Dr NE, 33701*
**Tel** *(727) 896-6160*
This trendy pub with 17 traditional and craft beers on tap serves excellent fish 'n' chips, along with burgers and pot pies.

### DK Choice

**TAMPA:**
**Columbia Restaurant** **$$$**
Spanish
*2117 E 7th Ave, Ybor City, 33605*
**Tel** *(813) 248-4961*
Florida's oldest restaurant has grown to fill a city block, but has maintained the quality of its Spanish-Cuban menu and signature dishes such as paella and snapper Alicante. Flamenco dancers add to the charm.

## The Everglades
## & the Keys

**KEY LARGO:**
**Mrs. Mac's Kitchen** **$$**
Seafood
*99336 Overseas Hwy, MM 99.4, 33037*
**Tel** *(305) 451-3722* **Closed** *Sun*
The menu here features good-old down-South cooking, such as chili, conch chowder, crab cakes, fresh fish, and home-made pies.

**KEY WEST: Seven Fish** **$$**
American
*632 Olivia St, 33040*
**Tel** *(305) 296-2777* **Closed** *Tue*
A corner bistro where *mahi mahi* and meatloaf share the menu with banana chicken, and crab and shitake mushroom pasta.

### DK Choice

**KEY WEST: Café Sole** **$$$**
French/Floridian
*1029 Southard St, 33040*
**Tel** *(305) 294-0230*
This small café has at its helm a talented chef whose unique menus combine the best of Provence and Florida, such as lobster bisque and French onion soup, conch carpaccio, and duckling a l'orange.

**For more information on types of restaurants** *see pages 28–9*

# THE DEEP SOUTH

# The Deep South at a Glance

Comprising the four states of Louisiana, Arkansas, Mississippi, and Alabama, the Deep South is one of the most distinctive parts of the United States. From the broad plains of the mighty Mississippi River and the bayous of Louisiana's Cajun Country to the hardscrabble forests of Arkansas' Ozark Mountains, the region is both geographically and culturally diverse. While opulent mansions, antebellum homes, and Civil Rights Movement sights are aspects of its past, the Deep South's special charms rest with the people and their natural appreciation of the good things in life. America's two most beloved musical creations – jazz and the blues – were born here, a legacy that is celebrated throughout the region, particularly in New Orleans. This city's universal reputation for nonstop fun is best experienced during Mardi Gras.

0 kilometers 100
0 miles 100

**Hot Springs** *(see p358)*, Arkansas, is home to the historic Bathhouse Row, where the Buckstaff Bathhouse still offers spa facilities. Former president Bill Clinton spent his youth in this city.

Mountain Home

Fayetteville

Jone

Fort Smith

ARKANSAS
*(See pp358–59)*

Conway

Hot Springs • Little Rock

Pine Bluff

Texarkana

Greenville

El Dorado

Shreveport

Ruston

Tallulah

LOUISIANA
*(See pp342–57)*

Natchez

Alexandria

M

De Ridder

Ba
Rc

Lake Charles    Lafayette

Morgan City

**Lafayette** *(see p356)* is the heart of Louisiana's Cajun Country, where the descendants of French Canadian immigrants still preserve their language and culture. Much of this local culture can be found in restaurants and nightclubs, at the city's museums and historic parks, as well as out in the surrounding swamps.

◄ View of Ozark Mountains forests, Arkansas

**Locator Map**

**Selma** *(see p364)* is one of the many towns in Alabama that played a significant role during the Civil Rights Movement in the 1950s and '60s. An important sight here is the the National Voting Rights Museum, which tells the story of the successful Selma-to-Montgomery March led by Dr. Martin Luther King Jr. in 1965.

**The Gulf Coast** *(see p363)* has traditionally been dominated by the seafood industry, but over the last decade, lavish Las Vegas-style casinos have proliferated along the coast. The area hit by Hurricane Katrina and oil spills in the past few years has recovered admirably, and welcomes all visitors.

**New Orleans** *(see pp342–51)*, the region's cultural capital, is characterized by wrought-iron balcony railings, distinctive food, lively bars, and the annual Mardi Gras festivities.

*For hotels and restaurants see pp368–73*

# THE DEEP SOUTH

With its warm, semitropical climate and easygoing temperament, the Deep South is perhaps the most culturally diverse region of the United States. Multiethnic and all-embracing in a friendly, hospitable way, the region offers visitors an unforgettable introduction to Southern charm, as embodied by the pleasure-seeking lifestyle of New Orleans.

Some 14 million people live in the Deep South, in a region covering about 200,000 sq miles (517,998 sq km), which is similar in size and population density to neighboring Texas. While the four states share a natural appreciation for the good things in life, they are otherwise quite different. Louisiana epitomizes French Catholic culture, whereas Mississippi and Alabama were the heart of the Confederacy during the Civil War. Arkansas differs in its rugged landscape matched by its people's pride in the state's mountain heritage. Most residents of the primarily rural Deep South have family roots reaching deep into history, and a rare continuity exists between past and present.

The rich bottomlands that line the meandering path of the Mississippi River across parts of Mississippi, Arkansas, and Louisiana once yielded the world's largest crops of cotton, and it was here that some of the greatest early American fortunes were made. However, the industry's labor-intensive demands were based on the inequities of slavery, which have haunted the economy and culture of the Deep South for two centuries.

## History

Some of the region's earliest known inhabitants were the agricultural communities of the Mississippian culture, whose members cultivated extensive fields of corn, beans, and squash, and constructed elaborate mounds for their religious and political rituals. The 3,700-year-old effigy mounds at Poverty Point in northeastern Louisiana, one of North America's oldest, largest, and most significant archaeological remains, dates from this period.

When Spanish conquistador Hernando de Soto and his troops first encountered the Mississippian cities, they soon

The steamboat *Natchez* leaving Mississippi River port

◀ Colorfully painted ironwork gracing a building in New Orleans, Louisiana

Dennis Malone Carter's painting, *The Battle of New Orleans*

decimated the people and their culture. Thereafter, other more dispersed Indian groups rose to power, most notably the Chickasaw, Choctaw, Quapaw, Creek, and Cherokee tribes. The Creek Indians of central and northern Alabama were perhaps the most successful, numbering some 15,000 at their peak. In the early 1700s, European colonists supported the Creeks, and supplied them with guns and ammunition in exchange for their help in

vanquishing the other tribes. A century later, the Creeks themselves were under assault, and by 1816 they had been forced to give up their vast and fertile territory to the incoming Americans. The story of most other Deep South Indians is similar, ending tragically in the 1830s, when they were moved to distant Oklahoma. A few, including the Choctaw tribe in central Mississippi, still live on their ancestral lands.

While English-speaking Americans dominate the past and present, the French and Spanish carried out much of the early exploration and settlement. Louisiana and Arkansas were under nominal French control until 1803, while Alabama and Mississippi were part of the Spanish colony of West Florida until 1814. Boundaries and allegiances varied until the US took control, through the Louisiana Purchase of 1803, and by the multiple battles with England, Spain, and their Indian allies.

With the defeat of the British at the Battle of New Orleans in January 1815, the Deep South entered an era of unprecedented growth and prosperity. New Orleans became the fourth-largest US city and the nation's second-busiest port. Steamboats plied the Mississippi River, as chronicled by writer Mark Twain (1835–1910), himself a former steamboat captain.

By the mid-1800s, wealthy individuals from the Carolinas, in particular, introduced the slave-owning, cotton-growing plantation culture that would reap huge fortunes and lead inexorably toward the Civil War. Mississippi, the second state to secede from the US, provided the rebel Confederacy with its president, Jefferson Davis, while Montgomery, Alabama, served as its first capital. The fall of Vicksburg in 1863 effectively ended Confederate control of the Mississippi, and after the war much of the region lay in ruins.

The post-Civil War economic and social wasteland gave rise to a doctrine of white supremacy and racist violence that

## KEY DATES IN HISTORY

**1539** Hernando de Soto leads the first European expedition to the Deep South

**1699** Fort de Maurepas, near present-day Biloxi, Mississippi, becomes capital of France's Louisiana colony

**1723** Louisiana's capital moved to New Orleans

**1803** Louisiana Territory purchased from Napoleonic France (the Louisiana Purchase)

**1814** Creek and Chickasaw Indians are forced to relinquish their territorial claims

**1812** Louisiana becomes a state

**1817** Mississippi becomes a state

**1819** Alabama becomes a state

**1836** Arkansas becomes a state

**1935** Populist Louisiana governor Huey "Kingfish" Long assassinated in Baton Rogue

**1955** Montgomery Bus Boycott

**1962** African-American student James Meredith becomes the first nonwhite person to attend classes at the University of Mississippi

**1992** Former Arkansas governor Bill Clinton is elected 42nd president of the United States

**2005** Hurricane Katrina hits the southern US, destroying towns and cities and killing thousands of people in New Orleans and the Gulf Coast

**2010** Oil spill off Louisiana is the largest in US history; it causes environmental and economic destruction

plagued the region the following century. It wasn't until the 1950s and '60s, when the dramatic confrontations of the Civil Rights Movement, such as those at Selma, Alabama, in 1965, began to change things for the better.

## People & the Economy

The Deep South is remembered for its often troubled history as well as its people's resolute and indomitable spirit to cope with the problems of the past. Despite a large exodus of African-Americans to northern US cities after the Civil War, descendants of slaves still form a large percentage of the population, and the slow but steady process of overcoming racial segregation has transformed the region. Today, while racial discrimination is illegal, in reality there remains a distinct gap in opportunities between whites and nonwhites.

Another distinctive group of people, Louisiana's Cajuns, live in the watery region north and west of New Orleans. A third very different culture is found in the densely forested mountains of Arkansas and northern Alabama. Long denigrated as "hill-billies" like their figurative cousins in Tennessee, Kentucky, and West Virginia, these mountain people have a fiercely protected independence and self-reliance. Hunting and fishing, both for recreation and sustenance, are still popular, as are traditional crafts and the so-called "bluegrass" music derived from the folk music of the Scottish and Irish forebears of this group.

As the cotton-based economy of plantation and Reconstruction days disappeared, little emerged to take its place. Thanks to inexpensive imports, the region's once-thriving textile industry has all but disappeared. Except for the steel mills of Birmingham, Alabama, the corridor of petrochemical factories along the Mississippi in Louisiana, or the gambling centers in the Mississippi Delta and along the Gulf of Mexico, the Deep South still suffers from a major lack of industry and employment opportunities. Success stories include the world-dominating retail might of Walmart, which started in Arkansas, and still has its corporate headquarters there. In contrast, one of the region's economic darlings of the 1990s, the Mississippi-based telecommunications company, WorldCom, crashed into bankruptcy in 2002.

## Culture & the Arts

If culture and the arts were the most valuable market commodities, the Deep South would probably be the wealthiest region in the country. The region has been instrumental in creating some of the world's most popular forms of musical, literary, and culinary expression. Jazz, for example, grew from the bubbling melting pot of Creole culture that was New Orleans after the Civil War, while the blues and its offspring, rock 'n' roll, emerged from the slave songs of the Mississippi Delta. Writers such as Tennessee Williams and William Faulkner, and novels like Harper Lee's classic *To Kill a Mockingbird*, helped earn the Deep South a place in world literature, while the mélange of Cajun, Creole, "Soul Food," and barbecue make it a delicious place to travel for culinary delight.

Statue of William Faulkner in the courthouse square in downtown Oxford, Mississippi

# Exploring the Deep South

Stretching from the Gulf Coast to the Appalachians in the north and the Great Plains in the west, the Deep South region sprawls across some 200,000 sq miles (517,998 sq km). Although large in area, the population is sparse and the transportation facilities limited. As elsewhere in the US, a car is the best way to get around. New Orleans has the region's major airport, while smaller airports serve other cities.

**Key**

— Highway

— Major road

— Railroad

– – State border

## Sights at a Glance

**Louisiana**

① New Orleans pp342–51
② Plantation Alley
③ Baton Rouge p355
④ Lafayette
⑤ Bayou Teche
⑥ Natchitoches
⑦ Shreveport

**Arkansas**

⑧ Little Rock
⑨ Hot Springs
⑩ Mountain View
⑪ Eureka Springs

**Mississippi**

⑫ Clarksdale
⑬ Oxford
⑭ Tupelo
⑮ Vicksburg National Military Park
⑯ Jackson
⑰ Natchez Trace Parkway
⑱ Natchez
⑲ Gulf Coast

**Alabama**

⑳ Mobile
㉑ Selma
㉒ Montgomery
㉓ Tuskegee
㉔ Birmingham
㉕ Huntsville

Statue of General Tilghman, Vicksburg
National Military Park

## Mileage Chart

**New Orleans, LA**

| | | | | | | | |
|---|---|---|---|---|---|---|---|
| **80** <br> 129 | **Baton Rouge, LA** | | | | | **10** = Distance in miles | |
| **529** <br> 851 | **480** <br> 772 | **Little Rock, AR** | | | | 10 = Distance in kilometers | |
| **345** <br> 555 | **333** <br> 536 | **221** <br> 356 | **Oxford, MS** | | | | |
| **185** <br> 298 | **173** <br> 278 | **344** <br> 553 | **174** <br> 280 | **Jackson, MS** | | | |
| **144** <br> 232 | **199** <br> 320 | **573** <br> 922 | **402** <br> 647 | **189** <br> 304 | **Mobile, AL** | | |
| **343** <br> 552 | **399** <br> 642 | **377** <br> 607 | **187** <br> 301 | **238** <br> 382 | **258** <br> 415 | **Birmingham, AL** | |

A jazz pub, one of many in New Orleans

# ❶ New Orleans

Located in southeast Louisiana, New Orleans lies between Lake Pontchartrain and a bend in the Mississippi. It covers an area of 199 sq miles (516 sq km) and prior to Hurricane Katrina (August 2005) it had a population of nearly 500,000. Since then the population has been reduced to 370,000. The city's historic areas were largely unaffected by the storm. The topmost tourist destination is the French Quarter, where the legendary Royal and Bourbon Streets are located. Beyond this lie the Central Business District centered along the waterfront, the verdant Garden District, and the area around City Park.

Diners at the popular
Acme Oyster House

## Sights at a Glance

① Old US Mint
② Old Ursuline Convent
③ French Market
④ Café du Monde
⑤ Jackson Square
⑥ St. Louis Cathedral, Cabildo, & Presbytère
⑦ Washington Artillery Park and Moonwalk
⑧ St. Louis Cemetery #1
⑨ Hermann-Grima Historic House
⑩ Bourbon Street
⑪ Royal Street
⑫ Steamboat Natchez
⑬ Custom House
⑭ Audubon Aquarium of the Americas
⑮ Mardi Gras World
⑯ Outlet Collection at Riverwalk

**Greater New Orleans**
*(see inset map)*
⑰ Garden District
⑱ City Park

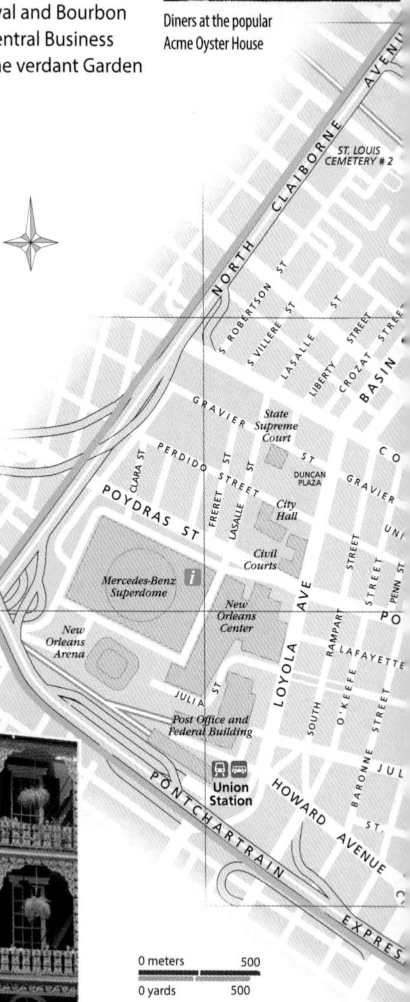

Royal Street and its well-known LaBranche buildings

For keys to symbols *see back flap*

## Getting Around

Although most of the city's popular tourist sights in and near the French Quarter are easily accessible on foot, New Orleans also has a useful public transportation system. Bus routes cover the city, and no visitor should miss the opportunity to take a trip on the city's streetcars. Riverboats also provide a relaxing and pleasant way to see the sights along the basin of the Mississippi River. Taxis are affordable and convenient, and are recommended for all trips planned for after dark.

**Key**

Sight/Place of interest

Highway

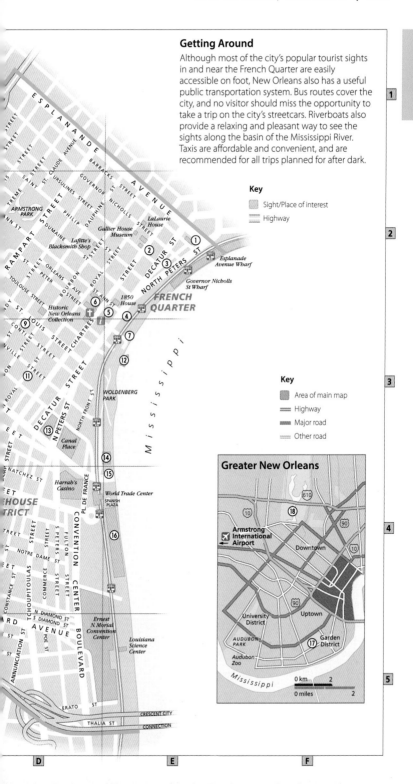

**Key**

Area of main map

Highway

Major road

Other road

**Greater New Orleans**

Neo-Classical façade of the Old US Mint

## ① Old US Mint

**Map** E2. 400 Esplanade Ave. **Tel** (504) 568-6968. 🚋 Riverfront. 🚌 3, 55. **Open** 10am–4:30pm Tue–Sun. **Closed** public hols. 🅿 ♿ 📷 📷 🅦 crt. state.la.us/museum/properties/usmint

This Greek Revival building, built in 1835 by William Strickland, functioned as a mint until 1909, turning out a variety of coinage, including Confederate and Mexican currency. It then became a federal prison and was later used by the Coast Guard. In the late 1970s, it was taken over by the state and converted into a museum to house the **New Orleans Jazz Collection**. The exhibit tells the story of jazz *(see p347)* through a collection of original musical instruments, vintage photographs, and historic documents. Among the instruments displayed are the ebony clarinet George Lewis used to record "Burgundy Street Blues," and the cornet Louis Armstrong learned to play on. At the entrance are a series of photographs of early bands and musicians, as well as a steamboat scale model.

The building also houses the **History of the Old US Mint Exhibition**, which displays gold and silver coins formerly minted here. On the third floor, the **New Orleans Mint Performing Arts Center** offers live musical and theatrical performances for a modest fee.

Vintage photograph, New Orleans Jazz Collection

## ② Old Ursuline Convent

**Map** E2. 1100 Chartres St. **Tel** (504) 529-3040. 🚋 Riverfront. 🚌 3, 55. **Open** 10am–4pm Mon–Sat. 📷 🅦 oldursulineconvent.org

The oldest building in the Mississippi Valley, the Old Ursuline Convent was built in 1752, some 25 years after the Ursuline Sisters first arrived in New Orleans. With its steep-pitched roof punctuated by a row of dormers and tall chimneys, it is a typical French Colonial structure and one of the few to remain from that period. In the 1820s, the nuns moved to new quarters, and the convent became the first official residence for the bishops and archbishops of New Orleans, and the home of the arch-diocesan archives. Later, it became part of a parish.

The current chapel, now known as Our Lady of Victory, was consecrated in 1845.

Old Ursuline Convent, dating from 1752

## ③ French Market

**Map** E2. N Peters St, from St. Ann to Barracks St. 🚋 Riverfront. 🚌 3, 5, 48. **Open** 9am–6pm daily. ♿ 📷 📷 👫 🅦 frenchmarket.org

A New Orleans institution since 1791, this area served as a trading place for Native Americans long before European settlement. Officially the French Market is five blocks between St. Ann and Barracks Streets, beginning roughly at Café du Monde and ending at the Old Mint museum. In daily use, the term "French Market" usually denotes the open-air markets from St. Philip to Barracks, which stock many New Orleans specialties. The Farmers Market (beginning at Ursulines Street) offers fresh Louisiana produce, seafood, and spices. Strawberries in the spring and the pecans in the fall are especially prized.

The majority of the space is now given over to the **Flea Market** – all kinds of items, ranging from jewelry and pottery to African arts and crafts, can be bought at the stalls and tables around the French Market buildings. It's a good place to get souvenirs, such as T-shirts and prints. The Flea Market stands on the site of the notorious neigh-borhood around Gallatin Street, which was once inhabited by criminals, prostitutes, and visiting sailors.

Inside, visitors can admire the splendid pine and cypress ceiling, two superb Bavarian stained-glass windows, and a window depicting the Battle of New Orleans, beneath an image of Our Lady of Prompt Succor. The nuns' old kitchen and laundry is now the rectory.

A formal French garden containing a handsome iron gazebo lies in front of the building. It is accessed via the porter's lodge.

## ④ Café du Monde

**Map** E2. 6800 Decatur. **Tel** (504) 525-4544. 🚋 Riverfront. 🚌 3, 5, 55. **Open** 24 hours daily. **Closed** Dec 25. ♿ 🖥
📷 W **cafedumonde.com**

Everyone who visits New Orleans stops here for a plate of sugar-dusted *beignets* (square French donuts) accompanied by plain *café au lait* or the famous chicory-flavored version. These are the only items offered at this coffee house dating from 1862, where visitors can relax at a table under the arcade and listen to the street musicians, or simply watch people as they go by.

During the mid-19th century there were 500 similar coffee houses in the French Quarter. Coffee was one of the city's most important commodities, and the coffee trade helped the economy recover after the Civil War, when New Orleans vied with New York City to control coffee imports. Chicory-flavored coffee was conceived during the Civil War, when the root was used to stretch the coffee supply.

Taking a break at Café du Monde with coffee and *beignets*

## ⑤ Jackson Square

**Map** E2. 🚋 Riverfront. 🚌 3, 5, 55.

Once little more than a muddy field called the Place d'Armes where troops were drilled, criminals were placed in the stocks, and executions were carried out, this square lies in the heart of the French Quarter. It was renamed in honor of General Andrew Jackson *(see p267)* who defeated the British at the Battle of New Orleans in 1815. The gardens and

Jazz band playing in Jackson Square

pathways, as they exist today, were laid out in 1848, when the beautification of the square took place under the patronage of Baroness Micaela Pontalba, then one of the city's most colorful personalities. Under her auspices, the Pelanne brothers designed the handsome wrought-iron fence that encloses the square. At the center stands a statue of General Jackson astride a rearing horse, sculpted by Clark Mills for $30,000. The inscription "The Union must and shall be preserved," on the plinth was added by Union General Benjamin "Beast" Butler, when he occupied the city during the Civil War.

Today, the square is a lively meeting place, where artists exhibit their works and musicians entertain visitors throughout the week.

A developer like her philanthropist father Don Andrés Almonester y Rojas *(see p346)*, the baroness also commissioned the **Pontalba Buildings**, flanking the uptown and downtown sides of Jackson Square. Built at a cost of over $300,000, they were considered the best and the largest apartments of their kind at that time. These elegant apartment buildings are based on plans the baroness brought back from Paris after she separated from her husband. The design of the initials A and P (for Almonester and Pontalba) in the cast-iron railings of the balconies and galleries is attributed to one of the baroness's sons, an artist.

The **National WWII Museum** is the world's most extensive museum commemorating World War II, with everything from tanks to personal diaries. It has been designated by Congress as the country's official World War II Museum. It is located in New Orleans because this is where Andrew Higgins designed and built the amphibious landing craft that Eisenhower considered essential for the Allies' victory.

🏛 **National WWII Museum**
945 Magazine St, Warehouse District. **Tel** (504) 528-1944. **Open** 9am–5pm daily. **Closed** public hols. ♿ 🅿
W **nationalww2museum.org**

### New Orleans Ironwork

The shadows cast by New Orleans ironwork add a romantic touch to the city. Wrought iron, which came first, was fashioned by hand into beautiful shapes by German, Irish, and African-American artisans. Cast iron, on the other hand, was poured into wooden molds and allowed to set. As a result, the latter has a somewhat solid, fixed appearance, unlike wrought iron, which is handmade and has a more fluid aspect. Both kinds of ironwork can be seen throughout the city, particularly in the French Quarter and the Garden District, where balconies, fences, window grilles, and gates are adorned with decorative motifs such as abstracts, cherubs, fruit, flowers, and animals.

Ironwork on the Pontalba Buildings

St. Louis Cathedral

## ⑥ St. Louis Cathedral, Cabildo, & Presbytère

**Map** D2. Jackson Square. **Tel** (504) 525-9585 (St. Louis Cathedral), (504) 568-6968 (Cabildo & Presbytère). 🚋 St. Charles Ave, Canal. 🚌 3, 5, 55, 81. **Open** 10am–4:30pm daily (St. Louis Cathedral); 9am–5pm Tue–Sun (Cabildo & Presbytère). 📷 Cabildo & Presbytère. ✝ St. Louis Cathedral, regular services throughout the day. 🚻 📷 📷 🔲 stlouiscathedral.org

This complex of buildings comprises the cathedral, Cabildo, and Presbytère. St. Louis Cathedral stands on the site of two earlier churches that were destroyed. The current building, begun in 1789, was dedicated as a cathedral in 1794. Inside are superb murals and a carved-wood Baroque main altar.

The Cabildo, designed by Guilberto Guillemard, was built and financed in 1795 by Don Andrés Almonester y Rojas. It served as a capitol for the legislative assembly of the Spanish Colonial government and subsequently as the City Hall. From 1853 to 1911 it housed the state Supreme Court. The Louisiana Purchase (*see p338*) was signed in the Sala Capitular in 1803.

The Casa Curial, or Presbytère, was built between 1794 and 1813, and used as a courthouse until 1911. It now houses the Mardi Gras Museum, featuring colorful objects and memorabilia.

## ⑦ Washington Artillery Park and Moonwalk

**Map** E3. Decatur St, between St. Ann & St. Peter sts. 🚌 3, 5, 55. 🚊 Riverfront.

Washington Artillery Park faces Jackson Square from Decatur Street. Inside the park is an austere concrete amphitheater with a central staircase leading to the Moonwalk. This community boardwalk was named after former New Orleans Mayor Maurice "Moon" Landrieu, who approved the construction of flood walls that made the riverfront area accessible to the public.

The park was built in 1976 and was once used as a military training ground, but today the amphitheater and Moonwalk are favored by street performers. Crowds often gather to enjoy performances by musicians, including guitarists, clarinettists, saxophonists, trombonists, and steel drummers, who play with an open case at their feet to collect donations.

The breeze along the waterfront can provide a welcome break from the humidity of the city, and it's also the perfect vantage point from which to see the river, Jackson Square, and the surrounding area. Stone steps lead down to where you can dangle your feet in the water, but don't attempt to stand in it, as the current is deceptively powerful.

## ⑧ St. Louis Cemetery #1

**Map** C2. Basin St between St. Louis & Conti. **Tel** (504) 596-3050. 🚌 46, 48, 52, 57. **Open** 9am–3pm Mon–Sat, 9am–noon Sun. 🚻 📷

The city's oldest surviving cemetery was established in 1789. This fascinating place, with its rows of mausoleums, is the resting place of many legendary local residents. The most famous of all is probably Marie Laveau. Crowds visit her tomb, marking it with an "X" (symbolically requesting that she grant a particular wish). By 1829, St. Louis Cemetery #1 was filled, mostly with victims of yellow fever, and the nearby **St. Louis Cemetery #2** was established as an extension. Many of the city's 19th-century Creole aristocracy are buried here in ornate mausoleums.

Statue of an angel, St. Louis Cemetery #1

However, the cemeteries should not be visited alone, as they are in secluded areas where muggers and pickpockets operate. It is advisable for visitors to join guided tours, given by the **Save Our Cemeteries** organization and by **Gray Line Tours**. Both companies provide plenty of excellent local information.

📷 **Gray Line Tours**
**Tel** (504) 569-1401.
🔲 graylineneworleans.com

📷 **Save Our Cemeteries**
**Tel** (504) 525-3377.

---

### Voodoo Worship

Voodoo arrived in New Orleans from Africa, via the Caribbean, where it originated as a form of ancestor worship among the West African tribes, who were brought to North America as slaves. During the slave uprising in Saint Dominique in 1793, many of the planters from Haiti fled to New Orleans, bringing their slaves (and voodoo) with them. Marie Laveau (c.1794–1881), the voodoo queen, used Catholic elements such as prayer, incense, and saints in her rituals, which she opened to the public for an admission fee. The voodoo calendar's high point was the celebration she held along Bayou St. John on St. John's Eve.

Portrait of Marie Laveau

# New Orleans Jazz

Jazz is America's original contribution to world culture. It evolved slowly and almost imperceptibly from a number of sources – the music played at balls, parades, dances, and funerals, and New Orleans' unique blend of cultures. Its musical inspirations included African work chants and spirituals, as well as European and American folk influences – the entire mélange of music that was played in 19th-century New Orleans.

**Trumpeter Oscar "Papa" Celestin**, the founder of the Tuxedo Brass Band in 1911, also composed "Down by the Riverside."

**Kid Ory's trombone**, which he played while performing with King Oliver and others, is displayed at the Old US Mint.

### Storyville Jazz Salon

*The 38-block area bounded by Iberville, Basin, Robertson, and St. Louis Streets, was the city's legal red-light district from 1897 to 1917. Known as Storyville, many early jazz artists, including Jelly Roll Morton, King Oliver, and Edward "Kid" Ory, entertained at the bordellos, playing behind screens.*

**Riverboat Jazz Bands** came into being after Storyville was closed down in 1917. New Orleans' best musicians either performed on boats or migrated to northern cities. Pianist Fate Marable's band included Louis Armstrong, who played the cornet.

**Congo Square**, now in Louis Armstrong Park, was where slaves gathered every Sunday to celebrate their one day off by playing music and dancing.

**Louis Armstrong**, the internationally famous jazz trumpeter, began singing on the streets of New Orleans. He played with Kid Ory before leaving the city in 1923 to join King Oliver's band in Chicago.

Master bedroom at the Hermann-Grima Historic House

## ⑨ Hermann-Grima Historic House

**Map** D3. 820 St. Louis St. **Tel** (504) 525-5661. 🚌 3. **Open** 10am–2pm Mon, Tue, Thu, Fri; noon–3pm Sat; Wed tours by appt. **Closed** public hols. 🚫 📷 🎥 ♿ 🅦 hgghh.org

This gabled brick house is one of the French Quarter's few examples of American Creole-style architecture. It was built in 1831 by William Brand for Samuel Hermann, a German-Jewish merchant who lost his fortune in 1837 and sold the house to Judge Felix Grima. It features a central doorway with a fanlight and marble steps; another window with a fanlight graces the second floor. Inside, the floors and doors are made of cypress. The three-story service quarters are in a building off the parterre garden behind the house. They contain a kitchen with a rare four-burner wood-fired stove with a beehive oven.

## ⑩ Bourbon Street

**Map** D3. 🚌 3, 55, 89.

Today Bourbon Street, rather than Basin Street, is synonymous with sin. This legendary street, named after the French royal family of Bourbon, is lined with bars that offer vats of such lethal concoctions as Brain Freeze, Nuclear Kamikaze, and Sex on the Bayou, most often to the accompaniment of blasting rock or blues. Other places offer everything from peep shows, topless dancers, and strip joints, to drag shows and gay action. During Mardi Gras, the sidewalks and overhanging balconies are jammed with crowds and drinking revelers.

Some of the most famous establishments near this lively street include **Pat O'Brien's** (St. Peter Street), which is well-known for its rum-based "Hurricane" cocktail, **Preservation Hall** (St. Peter Street), a top-quality jazz venue, and **Arnaud's** (Bienville Street), a restaurant that is a true New

Fire fountain at Pat O'Brien's, near Bourbon Street

Orleans classic. **Galatoire's**, close to Arnaud's, is another premier New Orleans restaurant *(see p372).* **Lafitte's Blacksmith Shop**, at 941 Bourbon Street, is considered one of the finest bars in New Orleans. Constructed sometime before 1772, it is a good example of the brick-between-posts French-style building, in which soft local bricks are supported by cypress timbers and protected by plaster. Inside, several small fireplaces warm the place on cool evenings, and there is also a small patio containing a sculpture of Adam and Eve, created by an artist as payment for his bar bill.

Despite its name, there is no concrete evidence that the pirate brothers, Jean and Pierre Lafitte, operated a smithy here as a front for their smuggling activities. They were also prominent slave traffickers, selling "black ivory" to Louisiana's prominent slave-holding families. The brothers earned local gratitude by warning the Americans of the planned British attack on New Orleans in 1815, and they fought bravely in the ensuing battle.

Just up from Lafitte's is the oldest gay bar in the country, **Café Lafitte in Exile**. It is so called because, until the early 1950s, gays frequented the old Lafitte's; when the bar changed hands, its new owner refused to renew the lease, and its gay patrons established their new quarters here. It has remained a popular alternative ever since.

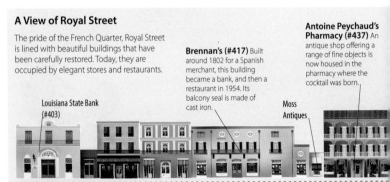

### A View of Royal Street

The pride of the French Quarter, Royal Street is lined with beautiful buildings that have been carefully restored. Today, they are occupied by elegant stores and restaurants.

**Brennan's (#417)** Built around 1802 for a Spanish merchant, this building became a bank, and then a restaurant in 1954. Its balcony seal is made of cast iron.

**Antoine Peychaud's Pharmacy (#437)** An antique shop offering a range of fine objects is now housed in the pharmacy where the cocktail was born.

Louisiana State Bank (#403)

Moss Antiques

Lafitte's Blacksmith Shop, Bourbon Street

## ⑪ Royal Street

**Map** D3. 🚋 St. Charles Ave. 🚌 3, 5, 55, 81, 82.

Antique shops filled with beautiful, often French, objects line Royal Street, undoubtedly the most fetching street in the French Quarter. In the early colony, this was the city's financial center and its main and most fashionable street. Today, many of the antique stores occupy handsome landmarks. Their merchandise includes crystal chandeliers, massive inlaid armoires, and ormolu furnishings – treasures associated with an opulent Southern lifestyle.

The **Historic New Orleans Collection**, born of one couple's interest in the Battle of New Orleans (1815), is housed in a complex of houses built for Jean François Merieult and his wife in 1792. The collectors were General and Mrs. L. Kemper Williams, who lived in the residence at the rear of the courtyard from the 1940s to the '60s.

The museum's ten galleries display historical artifacts, ranging from maps and paintings to furnishings and decorative objects. The Empire Gallery displays tables, chests, and sofas, alongside portraits of such native New Orleanians as Madame Auguste de Gas, mother of artist Edgar Degas. The museum's other galleries include the Plantation Gallery, the Louisiana Purchase Gallery, the Victorian Gallery, and the Spanish Colonial Gallery.

Farther away are **Gallier House Museum**, an attractive 19th-century residence that combines Creole and American architectural elements, and the lovely **Lalaurie House**, associated with ghosts. Also on Royal Street is **Rumors**, a gift shop that sells Mardi Gras souvenirs all year long – masks, beads, Krewe costumes (see p351), and posters are all available for sale here.

### 🏛 Historic New Orleans Collection
533 Royal St. **Tel** (504) 523-4662. **Open** 9:30am–4:30pm Tue–Sat.
W hnoc.org

Artifacts from the Historic New Orleans Collection on Royal Street

Steamboat *Natchez*, offering regular two-hour cruises

## ⑫ Steamboat Natchez

**Map** E3. Woldenberg Riverfront park wharf. **Tel** (504) 586-8777, (800) 233-2628. 🚋 Riverfront. 🚌 45, 87. **Open** Jazz Cruises: board 11am & 2pm daily; also 6pm some Thu–Sun. 🎫♿🚻 📷 W steamboatnatchez.com

A reminder of the old days of river travel, the Steamboat *Natchez* is typical of the steamboats that traveled the length of the Mississippi, taking three to five days to get from Louisville, Kentucky (see p273), to New Orleans. The boatmen, notorious brawlers in search of women and liquor at the end of a trip, established New Orleans' reputation as the "City of Sin." In their heyday, from 1830 to 1860, some 30 steamboats lined up at the levee. The era ended by the close of the 19th century as railroads and highways replaced them. Today, daily cruises offer visitors a glimpse into a forgotten lifestyle. Creole food and local drinks are available to enjoy on board.

---

**St. Anthony's Garden** This beautiful garden stands at the back of St. Louis Cathedral. Its serenity belies the fact that it was a staging ground for duels in the 18th century.

**The LaBranche Buildings (#700)** Embellished with fine oak-leaf ironwork, these buildings were constructed in 1835 for sugar planter Jean Baptiste LaBranche.

**Locator Map**

### ⑬ Custom House

**Map** D3. 423 Canal St. 🚋 3. 🚋 Canal.
**Open** daily. **Closed** some public hols.
🅿 📷 💻 🌐 **auduboninstitute.
org**

Perhaps the most important
Federal-style structure in the
South, this Quincy granite
building took 33 years to
complete (1848–81). The Marble
Hall is a dramatic space under a
ground-glass ceiling supported
by 14 marble columns.

### ⑭ Audubon Aquarium of the Americas

**Map** E3. Canal St at Mississippi River.
**Tel** (504) 581-4629. 🚋 Riverfront. 🚌
3, 5, 55, 57. **Open** 10am–5pm daily.
**Closed** Mardi Gras, Dec 25. 🅿 ♿ 🚻
♿ 📷 🌐 **auduboninstitute.org**

Focusing on the waters around
New Orleans, from the Mississippi
and the swamps to the Gulf of
Mexico and the Caribbean, this
complex features some 600
species of marine life. Highlights
include the 30-ft- (9-m-) long
Great Maya Reef exhibit of a
submerged city of the Yucatan
Peninsula, with ruins, lion fish,
sponges, moray eels, spiny
lobsters, and many other exotic
sea creatures that inhabit a coral
reef. The penguin exhibit
showcases an active colony of
warm weather penguins from
South America and Africa. On
the second floor, there are
cownose stingrays that can be
touched. Other tanks contain
species that illustrate everything
there is to know about life

King Copán statue in the Great Maya Reef
exhibit, Audobon Aquarium of the Americas

Entrance to the upscale Outlet Collection at Riverwalk in downtown New Orleans

beneath the ocean, including
how fish communicate. The
complex also includes New
Orleans Zoo, the Insectarium,
and the Entergy IMAX® Theater.
Daily riverboat cruises can also
be taken from here.

### ⑮ Mardi Gras World

**Map** E4. 1380 Port of New Orleans
Place. **Tel** (504) 361-7821.
**Open** 9:30am–4:30pm daily. 🅿 🚻
💻 📷 🌐 **mardigrasworld.com**

Visitors to this surreal and
colorful attraction used to have
to cross the river on a ferry to
Algiers, until owner Blaine Kern
moved to a larger warehouse
near the French Quarter in
2009. A free shuttle is available
from Canal Street. Blaine Kern is
often called "Mr. Mardi Gras"
because many of the massive
carnival floats, sculptures, and
props are constructed here in
his warehouse.

The tour begins with coffee
and the traditional King Cake.
A short film shows the floats
and the stages of their
production, from the original
drawings and molds to the end
result. Visitors can try on some
of the flamboyant costumes
worn by Krewe members in
past parades. Visitors can also
wander through the
warehouses and view huge
decorative figures made of
fiberglass or Styrofoam overlaid
with papier-mâché. The cost of
making the floats is usually
borne by each Krewe and can
range from anywhere between
$300 and $3,000.

### ⑯ Outlet Collection at Riverwalk

**Map** E4. 1 Poydras St.
**Tel** (504) 522-1555. 🚋 Riverfront.
🚌 3, 55, 57, 65. 🚻 📷 💻
🌐 **riverwalkneworleans.com**

Modern and expansive, this
indoor shopping mall on the
riverfront opened in 2014,
replacing the Riverside
Marketplace. More than 70
national outlet stores occupy
this vast mall. Last Call Studio by
Neiman Marcus and Forever 21
are the anchor stores, along
with other popular outlets,
including Coach and Coach,
Gap, Kenneth Cole, Ann Taylor
Loft, New Balance, Guess,
American Eagle Outfitters, and
Tommy Bahama. In addition to
plentiful shopping opportunities, the mall has an outdoor
walkway that runs along the
Mississippi River, giving visitors
one of the best views of the
river and its traffic in the city.
International and other cruise
ships dock alongside the mall,
the most notable being those
operated by the Delta Queen
Steamboat Company, which
was established in 1890. Several
information plaques attached to
railings along the walkway
describe everything from the
types of boats plying the river to
the seagulls that drift up from
the Gulf of Mexico.

The **Spanish Plaza**, near the
entrance, has a fountain in the
center. Surrounding it is a
circular mosaic bench, depicting
the coats of arms of the city's
Spanish immigrants.

*For hotels and restaurants see pp368–73*

St. Charles Avenue Streetcar, a New Orleans landmark

# ⑰ Garden District

Between Jackson & Louisiana Aves, & St. Charles Ave & Magazine St. 🚋 St. Charles. 🚌 11, 14, 27.

When the Americans arrived in New Orleans after the Louisiana Purchase in 1803, they settled upriver from the French Quarter. This area is referred to as the Garden District because of the lush gardens planted with magnolia, camellia, azalea, and jasmine. A residential neighborhood, it is filled with large mansions built by wealthy city planters and merchants. Some of the grand residences here are the Robinson House and Colonel Short's Villa, which has a handsome cast-iron cornstalk fence.

A romantic New Orleans experience is to take a ride on the slow-moving **St. Charles Avenue Streetcar** to uptown New Orleans. The last of the sort that featured in Tennessee Williams' *A Streetcar Named Desire*, it travels 6.5 miles (10.5 km) from Canal Street to Carrollton Avenue. Along the way it passes many famous landmarks. The most prominent are Lee Circle with its memorial to Confederate general Robert E. Lee, the Gothic Revival Christ Church, Touro Synagogue, the Latter Public Library, and Loyola and Tulane Universities.

Just off St. Charles Avenue is one of the loveliest urban parks in the country. The 340-acre (137-ha) Audubon Park was originally the sugar plantation of Jean Etienne Boré, who developed the commercially successful sugar granulation process. It was also the location of the 1884 World Exposition. The **Audubon Zoo** occupies 58 acres (23 ha) of the park's grounds. Beautifully landscaped, the zoo opened in 1938 but was completely redesigned in the 1980s. Today, the animals live in open paddocks that replicate their natural habitats. The Louisana Swamp, where white alligators bask along the banks or float in the muddy lagoon, is one of the most engaging exhibits.

Evocative statue in the City Park's New Orleans Botanical Gardens

# ⑱ City Park

🚌 45, 46, 48, 87, 90. New Orleans Museum of Art: **Tel** (504) 658-4100. **Open** 10am–6pm Tue–Thu, 10am–9pm Fri, 11am–5pm Sat & Sun. **Closed** public hols. 🚻 🚺 🅦 noma.org

The fifth largest urban park in the US, the 1,500-acre (607-ha) City Park is a New Orleans institution, where visitors can relax and enjoy the semitropical Louisiana weather. The **New Orleans Botanical Gardens** and the prestigious **New Orleans Museum of Art** share this space with moss-draped live oaks, lagoons for boating and fishing, and the championship Bayou Oaks Golf Course.

Housed in an impressive Beaux Arts building, the museum has an astonishingly varied collection. Originally the Delgado Museum of Art, it was founded in 1910 when Isaac Delgado, a millionaire bachelor, donated the original $150,000 to construct an art museum in City Park. In 1971 it was renamed the New Orleans Museum of Art in deference to some of its later benefactors. The New Orleans Botanical Garden was created in the 1930s. Then, it was primarily a rose garden, but today there are more than 2,000 varieties of plants from around the world organized as themed gardens. Highlights include the Historic Train Garden with miniature trains and streetcars moving through a New Orleans made of plant materials, the Conservancy of Two Sisters, the Butterfly Walk, and the Lord and Taylor Rose Garden.

## Mardi Gras

Culminating on the day before Ash Wednesday – Mardi Gras – Carnival festivities in New Orleans are celebrated with lavish masked balls, presented by groups of citizens known as "Krewes." Although most balls are private, many Krewes also put on parades, with ornate costumes and colorful floats. Many Carnival traditions began with the Krewe of Rex. The symbolic purple, green, and gold colors used for masks, banners, and other decorations are derived from the original costume worn by Rex, the King of Mardi Gras, in the 1872 parade. The tradition of throwing souvenir doubloons (coins), beads, and dolls from the floats to the crowds began in 1881.

Colorful costume for one of the many Mardi Gras parades

# Louisiana

Renowned for its exotic landscape of bayous and swamps, antebellum plantation homes, jazz, and fine food, Louisiana is a state richly steeped in history and tradition. Its predominant French heritage is the legacy of the French settlers who named the colony for Louis XIV. Both France and Spain colonized Louisiana before the United States finally acquired the territory through the Louisiana Purchase of 1803. Louisiana became a state in 1812 and in the following decades played a strategic role in the Civil War and the painful struggle for Civil Rights. Today, the state preserves both its Colonial history as well as its distinct Creole and Cajun heritage. Highlights include the beautiful plantations along the Mississippi and the cultural delights of Cajun Country.

## ❷ Plantation Alley

Hwy 18 from New Orleans, which joins Hwy 1. ℹ️ New Orleans Convention & Visitors' Bureau, (504) 566-5011; the bureau maintains a list of tour operators.

Before the Civil War, the Mississippi River was lined with plantations producing first indigo, then cotton, rice, and sugar. At the time, this was one of the nation's wealthiest regions and home to two-thirds of America's millionaires. Of the 350 opulent estates that once flourished here, around 40 remain. Of these about a dozen are open to the public on a stretch of the Great River Road (see pp50–51) between New Orleans and Baton Rouge, known as "Plantation Alley."

Today, large neighboring petrochemical plants have replaced sugar cane and cotton as the mainstay of the riverside economy. High levees, reinforced by the Army Corps of Engineers after the flood of 1927, block the river from the road. The tradition since the 1880s has been to light bonfires atop them each Christmas Eve, to illuminate the way for Santa Claus.

**Oak Alley Plantation** in Vacherie, is 40 miles (64 km) west from New Orleans airport. A quarter mile of arching live oaks, planted some 300 years ago, leads to this striking 1839 house. The picture of the Greek Revival mansion down the long arcade seems the archetypal Deep South image. Both the house and garden have been used as a location for several movies, including *Interview with the Vampire* (1994). The mansion offers five B&B cottages for overnight stay. To its east, **Laura Plantation** has an 1805 Creole house constructed of cypress, designed by Senegalese builders. The plantation slaves are thought to be the source of various Senegalese folk tales, including the famous *Br'er Rabbit* stories translated into English by Joel Chandler Harris.

A 15-minute drive from New Orleans, **Destrehan Plantation**, built in 1787, is the oldest documented plantation home in the Lower Mississippi Valley. The French Colonial-style home features demonstrations of indigo dyeing and other crafts like bousillage construction, a method using a mixture of clay and Spanish moss. San Francisco Plantation, near Garyville, is a 40-minute drive away from New Orleans. Built in 1856, under centuries-old spreading live oak trees, this galleried home in the Creole open-suite style is listed as a National Historic Landmark. It has now fully reopened after being restored following a fire in 2005.

Closest to Baton Rouge and the area's largest plantation home, the palatial 1860 **Nottoway Plantation** occupies an area of 53,000 sq ft (4,924 sq m), and comprises 65 rooms, 165 doors, and 200 windows. Completed in 1859, its largest room is the Grand White Ballroom, where the owner, John Hampden Randolph, celebrated his daughters' weddings.

In addition to guided house tours, several plantations now operate restaurants and comfortable B&B inns.

🏛️ **Oak Alley Plantation**
3645 Hwy 18 Vacherie. **Tel** (225) 265-2151. **Open** 9am–5pm daily. **Closed** Jan 1, Mardi Gras, Thanksgiving, Dec 25. 🅿️ ♿ 🆆 **oakalley plantation.com**

🏛️ **Laura Plantation**
2247 Hwy 18. **Tel** (225) 265-7690. **Open** 9am–5pm daily. **Closed** Jan 1, Mardi Gras, Easter, Thanksg., Dec 25. 🅿️ ♿ 🆆 **lauraplantation.com**

🏛️ **Destrehan Plantation**
13034 River Road, Destrehan. **Tel** (985) 764-9315. **Open** 9am–4pm daily. **Closed** public hols. 🅿️ 🆆 **destrehanplantation.org**

🏛️ **Nottoway Plantation**
White Castle. **Tel** (225) 545-2730. **Open** 9am–4pm daily. **Closed** Dec 25. 🅿️ ♿ 🆆 **nottoway.com**

The Grand White Ballroom, Nottoway Mansion, in Plantation Alley

*For hotels and restaurants see pp368–73*

Louisiana Old State Capitol, Baton Rouge

# ❸ Baton Rouge

🏙 230,000. ✈ 🚌 1253 Florida Blvd, (225) 383-3811. 🛈 359 Third St, (225) 382-3582. 🎭 Bayou Country Superfest (late May).
🌐 **visitbatonrouge.com**

Established by the French in 1699 to control access to the Mississippi, Baton Rouge ("Red Stick") was named for the spikes hung with bloody fish heads that marked the boundary between two Native American territories. The capital of Louisiana since 1849, this city is a favored tourist destination. Baton Rouge's population grew dramatically after Hurricane Katrina as people from New Orleans, made homeless, relocated here. North of downtown, the **State Capitol**

was built in 1932 under the tireless direction of ex-governor and US senator Huey Long (1893–1935), who persuaded legislators to approve the $5 million construction budget. Ironically, Long was assassinated in the building in 1935. This 34-story structure, the country's tallest capitol, offers superb city views from its 27th-floor observation deck. To the south, the autocratic senator's penchant for lavish buildings is further reflected in the **Old Governor's Mansion**, built in 1930 and modeled on the White House. Today, this restored Greek Revival structure displays such memorabilia of past governors as Jimmie Davis's guitar and Huey Long's pajamas. The ornate 1849 Gothic Revival **Louisiana Old State Capitol**, to the southwest, holds interactive exhibits on the state's tumultuous political history. Outside, an observation plaza

overlooks the river, where the massive World War II-era destroyer, **USS Kidd**, offers public tours. Farther south, visitors can get a feel of the antebellum era first hand at the 1791 **Magnolia Mound Plantation**, a 16-acre (6-ha) French-Creole style home and working plantation.

A short, 10-minute drive southwest from downtown leads to the attractive, tree-shaded **Louisiana State University** campus and the **LSU Rural Life Museum**, maintained by the university. Unlike the grand plantation restorations, this museum, with its simple artifacts, reveals how the common owner-operated farming families lived in the 19th century.

Statue in the new State Capitol

🏛 **Louisiana Old State Capitol**
100 N Blvd. **Tel** (225) 342-0500.
**Open** 9am–4pm Tue–Sat.
**Closed** Sun, Mon & public hols. ♿
🌐 **louisianaoldstatecapitol.org**

🏛 **LSU Rural Life Museum**
I-10 exit 160, at 4650 Essen Ln. **Tel** (225) 765-2437. **Open** 8am–5pm daily. **Closed** Jan 1, Easter, Thanksg., Dec 24, Dec 25. 📷 ♿ 🌐 **rurallife.lsu.edu**

## Downtown Baton Rouge
① State Capitol
② Old Governor's Mansion
③ Louisiana Old State Capitol
④ USS Kidd

For keys to symbols see back flap

Cathedral of St. John the Baptist, Lafayette

# ❹ Lafayette

🚹 120,600. ✈ 🚉 🛈 1400 NW Evangeline Thruway, (337) 232-3808.
🌐 lafayettetravel.com

The unofficial "Capital of French Louisiana" is an entertaining introduction to the world of bayous, alligators, superb cuisine, and lilting Cajun accents. When the first Acadians arrived here in 1765, they settled along the bayous and prairies west of New Orleans, working as farmers to make a living from the swamps and marshes.

Lafayette evolved from a small settlement, set up in 1821 around a church, now the towering **Cathedral of St. John the Baptist**, near the Vermilion River. Today, the town is the heart of Cajun Country, distinguished by its unique cultural heritage.

Lafayette's living history museum, **Vermilionville** (the original name of the town), evokes 19th-century Acadiana with its characteristic French-influenced architecture. The buildings here are constructed of bousillage (see p354), and have high-pitched roofs. Both Vermilionville and nearby **Jean Lafitte National Historical Park Acadian Cultural Center** feature exhibits as well as demonstrations on the skills needed to survive in 18th- and 19th-century Louisiana.

These include the netmaking that was vital for a life that depended on harvesting food from the bayou, and the woodcraft that built plows and the shallow-draft wooden pirogue. The National Park Service, which operates the Jean Lafitte National Historic Park, also maintains other Acadian cultural centers in the wetlands region in Thibodaux (100 miles/160 km to the southeast), and in the prairie region in Eunice that lies about 30 miles (48 km) to the northwest.

🏛 **Vermilionville**
300 Fisher Rd. **Tel** (337) 233-4077. **Open** 10am–4pm Tue–Sun. **Closed** Mon, Jan 1, Martin Luther King Jr. Day, Thanksgiving, Dec 24, 25, & 31. ♿♿
🌐 vermillionville.org

🏛 **Jean Lafitte National Historical Park Acadian Cultural Center**
501 Fisher Rd. **Tel** (337) 232-0789. **Open** 8am–5pm daily. **Closed** Mardi Gras, Dec 25. ♿ 🌐 nps.gov/jela

# ❺ Bayou Teche

Hwy 31 runs from Breaux Bridge to New Iberia. 🛈 2513 Hwy 14, (337) 365-1540. 🌐 iberiatravel.com

Bayou Teche (pronounced "Tesh") meanders north-to-south alongside a scenic route between Lafayette and the Atchafalaya Swamp. Stretching

between Breaux Bridge and New Iberia, the 25-mile (40-km) length of Hwy 31, with its lush vegetation and beautiful moss-draped oaks, offers a true flavor of the region.

In downtown **Breaux Bridge**, a tiny drawbridge over Bayou Teche proclaims the town "the Crawfish Capital of the World." The town also hosts the annual Crawfish Festival in May.

At **Lake Martin**, the Nature Conservancy's Cypress Island Preserve offers an opportunity to see swamp wildlife from a hiking trail and boat tours. The preserve has a world-class wading bird rookery.

Farther south, in **St. Martinville**, the famous Evangeline Oak marks the spot where Evangeline and her lover Gabriel were supposed to be reunited. Both their tragic tale and the Acadian saga are narrated in *Evangeline*, Henry Wadsworth Longfellow's 1847 poem. Nearby, St. Martin de Tours Church dates back to the town's founding in 1765. An adjacent museum displays carnival costumes.

Just outside town, the evocative **Longfellow-Evangeline State Historic Site** offers tours of an 18th-century sugar plantation house. Bayou Teche flows through the town of **New Iberia**, famous for its grand plantation home – the 1834 Shadows-on-the-Teche, which is now a museum.

A detour to Avery Island leads to the **McIlhenny Tabasco Company**, a popular stop for gourmands where a guide presents information about

Shadows-on-the-Teche plantation house in New Iberia, Bayou Teche

The Fort St. Jean Baptiste reconstruction in Natchitoches

the company's history and manufacturing. The adjacent **Jungle Gardens** is a natural swamp, which also offers tours.

### 🏠 Longfellow-Evangeline State Historic Site
1200 N Main St, St. Martinville. **Tel** (337) 394-3754. **Open** 9am–5pm Tue–Sat. **Closed** Jan 1, Thanksgiving, Dec 25. 🅿 📵 crt.state.la.us/parks

### 🏛 McIlhenny Tabasco Company
Avery Island. **Tel** (337) 365-8173. **Open** 9am–4pm daily. **Closed** pub. hols. ♿ 📵 tabasco.com/avery-island

## ❻ Natchitoches
🔢 39,500. 🚌 ℹ 781 Front St, (318) 352-8072, (800) 259-1714.
📵 natchitoches.net

The oldest permanent settlement in Louisiana, Natchitoches ("Nack-a-tish") was founded on the banks of the Cane River by the French in 1714. The town's compact 33-block riverfront district retains much of its 18th-century Creole architecture, with elaborate ironwork and spiral staircases. South of downtown, **Fort St. Jean Baptiste** re-creates the 1732 frontier outpost designed to deter Spanish expansion eastward from Texas.

The surrounding Cane River Country has several plantation house tours. Of these, **Melrose Plantation** was visited by such writers as John Steinbeck and William Faulkner. The family-friendly **Louisiana Sports Hall of Fame & Northwest Louisiana History Museum** showcases Louisiana athletes and sports figures, features sports-themed exhibits, and explores the area's cultural traditions.

### 🏛 Melrose Plantation
LA 119. **Tel** (318) 379-0055. **Open** 10am–5pm Tue–Sun. **Closed** public hols. 🅿 📵 melroseplantation.org

### 🏛 Louisiana Sports Hall of Fame & Northwest Louisiana History Museum
800 Front St. **Tel** (318) 35/-2492. **Open** 10am–4pm Tue–Sat, 1–5pm Sun. 🅿

## ❼ Shreveport
🔢 199,300. 🚌 ℹ 629 Spring St, (318) 222-9391. 📵 shreveport-bossier.org

Situated near the Texas border, Shreveport was founded on the Red River in 1839. Agriculture and river transport trade were mainstays of the local economy until the turn of the 20th century, when the discovery of oil made the city a boom town. Shreveport declined after the oil industry moved offshore. However, today, along the riverfront there are six floating casinos, several museums, and a river cruise. The welcoming town hosts a number of cultural activities, while the annual Louisiana State Fair, held here in late October or early November, attracts more than 300,000 visitors.

### Environs
About 165 miles (265 km) from Shreveport in the far northeastern corner of Louisiana state is one of the most significant archaeological sites located in the eastern part of the country. **Poverty Point National Monument** *(see p337)* outside Epps retains the religious mounds built by the early civilization that flourished in the Lower Mississippi basin around 600 BC. Visitors can get here by Highway 577.

### 🏠 Poverty Point National Monument
Hwy 577. **Tel** (888) 926-5492. **Open** 9am–5pm daily. **Closed** Jan 1, Thanksgiving, Dec 25. 🅿 📵 nps.gov/popo

Exhibition at Poverty Point National Monument, outside Epps

### The Acadians – Cajun Country

The Acadians, or "Cajuns," were originally French immigrants who had founded a colony in Nova Scotia, Canada, in 1604, naming it l'Acadie after the legendary Greek paradise, Arcadia. Exiled by the British in 1755, they finally settled along the isolated bayous of Louisiana, where they developed a rich French-influenced culture, deeply rooted in its music and cuisine. Acadian culture is best seen in the region's many festivals. Of these the Courir de Mardi Gras, literally "Fat Tuesday Run," is a distinctly Cajun version of the Mardi Gras *(see p351)*. Colorfully dressed and masked horseback riders ride from house to house, ostensibly collecting ingredients for a community gumbo. They then triumphantly parade through the town, before gathering together for food, drink, music, and frivolity. "Acadiana" is a 22-parish region comprising the wetlands area near New Orleans, the prairies north of Lafayette, and the remote southwestern coast.

Acadian dress

# Arkansas

Aptly known as the "Natural State," Arkansas abounds in mountains, valleys, dense woodlands, and fertile plains. Its two mountain ranges, the Ozark and the Ouachita, are separated by the Arkansas River, which flows through the state capital, Little Rock. The birthplace of former president Bill Clinton, the state actively promotes sights associated with him, including his birthplace, Hope, his boyhood home in Hot Springs, and Little Rock, where he served as governor and waged his campaign for presidency. This former frontier state remains largely wild even today, with vast areas of natural beauty, famous for adventure sports.

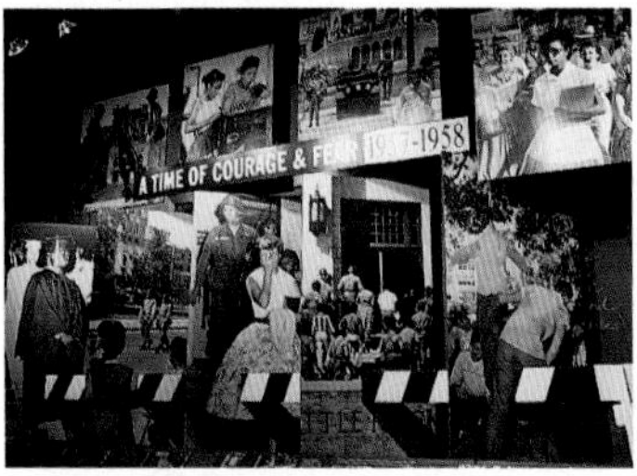


Display in the Central High Visitor Center, Little Rock

## ❽ Little Rock

194,000. 615 E Capitol Ave, (501) 371-0076. **littlerock.com**

Founded on the Arkansas River, near a boulder for which it is named, Little Rock was another modest-sized Southern state capital until native son Bill Clinton was elected 42nd US president in 1993. As a result, executive attention has helped revitalize the city. A center for much activity is Little Rock River Market District, lined with lively clubs, restaurants, cafés, and shops. Adjacent to the district is the **William J. Clinton Presidential Center**, which houses a library and museum where exhibits tell the inside story of the presidency. The **Old State House State History Museum**, west of Main Street, is where Clinton celebrated his 1992 and 1996 presidential victories.

In 1957, the contentious desegregation of Little Rock Central High School catapulted the city to the forefront of the national struggle for Civil Rights. Despite the Supreme Court ban, the governor refused to integrate the school, forcing President Eisenhower to send in the 101st Airborne Division to protect the "Little Rock Nine" (the first nine black students). Today, the **Little Rock Central High School National Historic Site Visitor Center** documents this story; it is located across the intersection from the school.

**Little Rock Central High School National Historic Site Visitor Center**
2120 Daisy L. Gatson Bates Dr. **Tel** (501) 396-3000. **Open** daily. **Closed** some pub. hols. **nps.gov/chsc**

**Old State House State History Museum**
300 W Markham St. **Tel** (501) 324-9685. **Open** daily. **Closed** some public hols. **oldstatehouse.com**

**William J. Clinton Presidential Center**
1200 Pres. Clinton Ave. **Tel** (501) 374-4242. **Open** daily.

## ❾ Hot Springs

40,000. 629 Central Ave, (501) 321-2277. **hotsprings.org**

In its heyday in the early 20th century, this was a popular resort for people seeking restorative cures from the thermal springs flowing from the southwestern slope of Hot Springs Mountain. The area became the first US federal reserve park in 1832 and a national park in 1921. The original "Bathhouse Row" is now a National Historic Landmark District within **Hot Springs National Park**. The visitor center is housed in

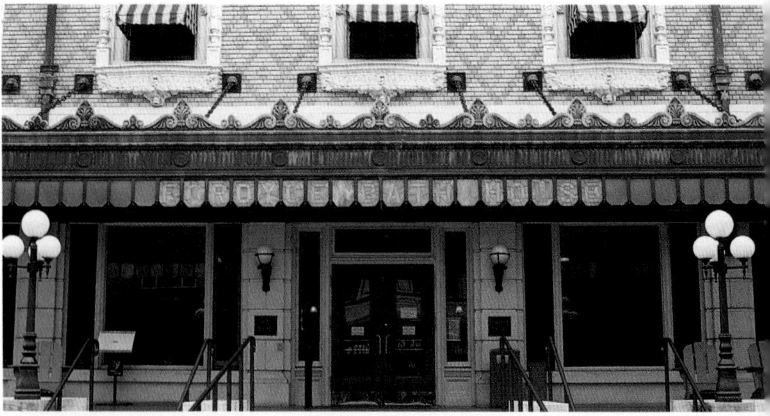


Exterior of the Spanish-style Fordyce Bathhouse, the visitor center for Hot Springs National Park

the opulent Spanish Renaissance-style 1915 Fordyce Bathhouse. Only the **Buckstaff Bathhouse** today remains in operation, offering spa facilities. Some hotels in the area also offer full bathing facilities.

At the Row's south end, the city visitor center distributes maps to sights associated with President Clinton, who spent his childhood in the city. Hot Springs High School, where Clinton graduated in 1964, is now an apartment building with a "cultural campus" that has exhibits from Clinton's teenage years. Visitors can also tour sights such as Clinton's church and his favorite burger joint. A scenic drive to the summit of Hot Springs Mountain leads to an observation tower offering panoramic views of the Ouachita Mountains, the city, and the forests and lakes that surround it.

### 🏛 Hot Springs National Park
369 Central Ave. **Tel** (501) 620-6715. **Open** 9am–5pm daily. **Closed** Jan 1, Thanksgiving, Dec 25. 🚻
**W** nps.gov/hosp

### 🏛 Buckstaff Bathhouse
509 Central Ave, Bathhouse Row. **Tel** (501) 623-2308. **Open** varies seasonally so check website. **Closed** Jan 1, Jul 4, Thanksgiving, Dec 25. 🚻 🚻 **W** buckstaffbaths.com

## ❿ Mountain View

🏔 2,700. 🛈 107 N Peabody, (888) 679-2859.

Nestling deep in the hills and valleys of the remote Ozark Mountains, the secluded hamlet of Mountain View is a haven for outdoor enthusiasts. A short drive to the north is the **Ozark Folk Center State Park**. The park celebrates the Ozark Mountain region's cultural heritage with living history exhibits, crafts demonstrations, festivals, and traditional music performances held at the state park theater. It also offers hiking trails, a lodge open year round, a lively restaurant, and a swimming pool. The nearby "Wild and Scenic" **Buffalo National River** is highly popular for float

fishing and canoeing; many local outfitters organize guided canoe trips of the river. The National Forest Service maintains several campgrounds in the area.

### 🎭 Ozark Folk Center State Park
1032 Park Ave. **Tel** (870) 269-3851. **Open** Apr–late Nov: 10am–5pm Tue–Sat, 10am–4pm Sun, Mon. 🚻 🚻
**W** ozarkfolkcenter.com

### Environs
About 15 miles (24 km) northwest of Mountain View, via Hwy 14, lie **Blanchard Springs Caverns**, which feature an extensive collection of limestone cave formations and an underground stream open for public tours. The ever-changing crystalline formations in these "living" caves are the result of minerals deposited by dripping water. Exploring the magnificent caves can be difficult because of the damp air and cramped conditions. However, both the two main routes, the half-mile (1-km) Dripstone Trail as well as the 1.2-mile (2-km) Discovery Trail, offer an unforgettable experience of life underground. A visitor center features exhibits and videos that describe the caves and their long process of creation.

### 🎭 Blanchard Springs Caverns
off Hwy 14. **Tel** (870) 757-2211. **Open** mid-Apr–Oct: 9am–5pm daily; Oct–Apr: 9:30am–4pm Wed–Sun. **Closed** Jan 1, Thanksgiving, Dec 25. 🚻

Inclined streets of the Victorian commercial area, Eureka Springs

## ⓫ Eureka Springs

🏔 2,400. 🛈 516 Village Circle, (479) 253-8737. **W** eurekasprings.org

The seven-story high statue of Jesus, "**Christ of the Ozarks**," towers above the former resort town of Eureka Springs. After nearly a century of decline, the town has benefited by its development as an artists' community, as a romantic getaway, and by the establishment of country music performances in the style of Nashville's Grand Ole Opry (see p267) held at the Hoe-Down and Pine Mountain Jamboree. For almost 30 years running, the Great Passion Play has been performed at the **Sacred Arts Center**. This outdoor drama depicts the days leading up to the death of Jesus Christ.

Christ of the Ozarks, Eureka Springs

The religious tone of the town is perpetuated in the **Bible Museum** with its collection of more than 6,000 Bible editions in 625 languages, including several rare first editions. Eureka Springs Historic Gardens and a scenic railroad are the town's other attractions. Many visitors also tour the well-preserved Victorian buildings and savor the magic of the town's forested mountain setting.

### 🏛 Sacred Arts Center
935 Passion Play Rd. **Tel** (800) 882-7529. **Open** Apr–Oct: call for times. 🚻

# Mississippi

The birthplace of Tennessee Williams, Elvis Presley, B.B. King, and Oprah Winfrey, Mississippi is a complex state best known for blues music, antebellum plantation homes, and a lamentable Civil Rights history. The endless horizon of cotton fields can be found in the northwest Delta region, while in the northeastern corner is the hardscrabble hill area around Tupelo. The state capital, Jackson, sits in the central plain and is the urban center of this largely rural state. Today, Mississippi offers such contrasting diversions as glittering Las Vegas-style casinos on the Gulf Coast and the Mississippi River, excellent Vietnamese seafood restaurants, and ferry rides to deserted beaches.

Ventress Hall, University of Mississippi campus, Oxford

## ⑫ Clarksdale

🏠 23,000 (Clarksdale). 🚉 🚌 Greenwood. ℹ️ 1540 DeSoto Ave, Hwy 49, Clarksdale, (662) 627-7337.

The Mississippi Delta, a vast, alluvial basin, cleared of its once-thick forests, and blanketed with cotton fields, is the birthplace of blues music. The **Delta Blues Museum** in downtown Clarksdale is the touchstone for music lovers from around the world. Located in a renovated 1920s freight depot, this museum is a repository of blues music, with personal belongings, photographs, instruments, and videos of such resident legends as Robert Johnson, Howlin' Wolf, and Muddy Waters. Exhibits include the wooden "Muddywood" guitar created by Z.Z. Top with planks from the original House of Blues, the birthplace of Muddy Waters. The Sunflower River Blues and Gospel Festival is held outside the museum each August. The Delta's creative legacy extends beyond music. The annual Tennessee Williams festival celebrates the work of the famous playwright who spent his childhood in Clarksdale.

About 55 miles (88 km) south of Clarksdale, the **Cottonlandia Museum** in Greenwood documents the history of the Delta with a special emphasis on cotton, the industry that fueled the culture and economy of the region. A 24-mile (38-km) drive south

Catfish farm sign

brings visitors to Greenville, the largest town in the Delta. The visitor center of this major riverport occupies a riverboat docked at the foot of the bridge. The Mississippi Delta Blues Festival is held in town every September. Other sights include the tiny museum in Leland honoring Jim Henson, the creator of the Muppets; Belzoni, said to be the "Catfish capital of the World," located in the county that has the most farm-raised catfish; and Indianola, the hometown of B.B. King.

🏛 **Delta Blues Museum**
1 Blues Alley, Clarksdale. **Tel** (662) 627-6820. **Open** Mar–Oct: 9am–5pm Mon–Sat; Nov–Feb: 10am–5pm Mon–Sat. **Closed** Jan 1, Jul 4, Thanksgiving, Dec 25. ♿ ♿
🌐 deltabluesmuseum.org

🏛 **Cottonlandia Museum**
1608 Hwy 82 W. **Tel** (662) 453-0925. **Open** 9am–5pm Mon–Fri, 10am–4pm Sat. **Closed** major public hols. ♿ ♿
🌐 cottonlandia.org

## ⑬ Oxford

🏠 14,000. 🚌 ℹ️ (662) 232-2367.
🌐 oxfordcvb.com

Home to the stately 1848 University of Mississippi, fondly known as "Ole Miss," the appealing college town of Oxford is the state's intellectual and cultural center. The local literary landmark is the secluded 1844 **Rowan Oak**, home of William Faulkner, one of the most influential writers of the time and pioneer of the Southern Gothic literature movement. The plot outline of *A Fable*, the book the Nobel Prize-winning author was working on at his death, can be seen inscribed on the walls. A Faulkner statue stands in downtown's classic courthouse square, surrounded by sophisticated galleries, restaurants, cafés, and live music venues.

The University of Mississippi campus houses the **University Museums**. In addition to classical Greek and Roman antiquities, the adjacent

One of the many riverboat casinos in the Mississippi Delta

*For hotels and restaurants see pp368–73*

museums hold a small but dynamic collection of Southern folk art.

### 🏠 Rowan Oak
916 Old Taylor Rd. **Tel** (662) 234-3284. **Open** 10am–4pm Tue–Sat, 1–4pm Sun. **Closed** some public & university hols. &

### 🏛 University Museums
University Ave at Fifth St. **Tel** (662) 915-7073. **Open** 10am–6pm Tue–Sat, 1–4 pm Sun. **Closed** some public & university hols. & W olemiss.edu

## ⑭ Tupelo
🏙 37,000. 🛈 399 E Main St, (662) 841-6521. W **tupelo.net**

An hour's drive west from Oxford, Tupelo is the birthplace of Elvis Presley, one of the world's most enduring cultural icons. Here, in a modest, two-room shotgun shack on the eastern fringe of town, the King of Rock 'n' Roll was born in 1935, along with his stillborn twin Jesse. Elvis lived in Tupelo until age 13, when the family was forced by financial constraints to move to Memphis *(see p268)*. Today the **Elvis Presley Birthplace**, refurbished to look as it did in 1935, is a pilgrimage site for Elvis fans the world over. An adjacent museum holds a unique private collection of Elvis memorabilia. A chapel, which overlooks the birthplace, features Elvis's own bible.

The Tupelo Automobile Museum, the first of its kind in the state, displays

Grave markers in Vicksburg National Military Park

more than 150 restored cars and includes a replica of a vintage garage.

Tupelo offers all the basic necessities for lodging and dining, and serves as a pit stop for the famous Natchez Trace Parkway *(see p362)*.

### 🏠 Elvis Presley Birthplace
306 Elvis Presley Dr. **Tel** (662) 841-1245. **Open** 9am–5pm Mon–Sat, 1–5pm Sun. **Closed** Thanksgiving, Dec 25. 🅿 &
W **elvispresleybirthplace.com**

## ⑮ Vicksburg National Military Park
3201 Clay St. 🛈 (601) 636-0583. **Open** 8am–5pm daily. **Closed** Dec 25. 🅿 & W **nps.gov/vick**

The Vicksburg National Military Park, established in 1899, commemorates one of the most tragic sieges in Civil War history *(see p57)*. Its strategic location, high on the bluffs overlooking the Mississippi River, made Vicksburg the target of Union forces, which wanted to gain control of the vital river corridor and cut the Confederacy in half. On March 29, 1863, the Union Army surrounded the city. After a 47-day siege, the Confederates surrendered on July 4, 1863, giving the North undisputed control of the river and sounding the death knell of the Confederacy. The impact of defeat was so severe that Vicksburg's citizens refused to recognize the Fourth of July holiday until the mid-20th century. The campaign's story is retold in statuary headstones, earthworks, and artifacts at the park. Guided tours bring the landscape to life, where re-enactments of the Civil War are held from June through August.

Statue of young Elvis at Tupelo, his birthplace

### Blues Music
The sound at the root of all contemporary popular music heard around the world springs from the large, flat, alluvial basin called the Mississippi Delta. Here African rhythms, work chants, and spirituals evolved into a distinctive style of music known as the blues. When Alabama musician W.C. Handy came through the Delta in 1903, he declared it "the weirdest music I ever heard," and carried the sound up to Memphis, where he recorded the Memphis Blues. Along with the Great Migration of African-Americans from the rural South to the industrial North in the early 1900s, the blues reached Chicago, where such famous artists as Muddy Waters electrified the sound. Rock 'n' roll is said to be born from this sound.

Muddy Waters figure in Delta Blues Museum

Old gas station at the Mississippi Agriculture and Forestry Museum

## ⑯ Jackson

🏙 174,000. ✈ 🚆 🚌 ℹ 921 S President St, (601) 960-1891.

Founded on a bluff above the Pearl River, Mississippi's capital city was named after popular national hero General Andrew Jackson (see p267). During the Civil War, the city was torched on three separate occasions by Union General William Tecumseh Sherman, earning it the nickname "Chimneyville." The few buildings that survive are treasured landmarks today. Of these, the old 1839 Capitol, now the **Old Capitol Museum of Mississippi History**, presents an overview of the state's Civil Rights history, juxtaposing stark black-and-white video footage of violent clashes between the police and protesters, with plainspoken commentary. Upstairs, the museum features revolving exhibits on such topics as author Eudora Welty, a Jackson resident, or "Pride of the Fleet" about the battleship USS *Mississippi*. A small, 20th-century room elaborates on the impact of the cotton and lumber industries on the state's economy, ecology, and society. Yet the city itself is the best historical exhibit. From the Old Capitol building, it is a short walk along Capitol Street to the Governor's Mansion and the Lamar Life Building, with its clock tower and gargoyles. The **Mississippi State Capitol**, built in 1903, resembles the US Capitol in Washington, DC, and houses the legislative, judicial, and executive branches of the

state government. Jackson is also home to the **Mississippi Agriculture and Forestry Museum**, a very appealing family attraction that celebrates the state's rural heritage. Among its exhibits are an 1850s homestead, complete with livestock and gardens, and a 1930s small-town Main Street with a general store. The Chimneyville Crafts Gallery, a handicraft store on the grounds, displays and sells folk arts, including Choctaw crafts. The expansive site also has a lively cafeteria. The adjacent Sports Hall of Fame honors the state's beloved athletes and college teams with enjoyable interactive exhibits.

Other sights in Jackson include the local zoo, Mynelle Gardens, the Mississippi Museum of Natural Science, and the Mississippi Museum of Art. All these attractions, plus the city's growing reputation as a blues venue, make Jackson a pleasant stop for visitors coming through the Natchez Trace Parkway.

🏛 **Old Capitol Museum of Mississippi History**
Old Capitol, 100 S State St. **Tel** (601) 576-6920. **Open** daily. **Closed** public hols. 🌐 mdah.state.ms.us/oldcap

🏛 **Mississippi Agriculture & Forestry Museum**
1150 Lakeland Dr. **Tel** (601) 432-4500. **Open** 9am–5pm Mon–Sat. **Closed** Sun, Jan 1, Thanksgiving, Dec 25. 📷 ♿ 🌐 mdac.state.ms.us/departments/museum

## ⑰ Natchez Trace Parkway

Visitor Center: Mount Locust. **Tel** (662) 680-4027. **Open** 8am–5pm daily. 🌐 nps.gov/natr

Established as a National Historic Parkway in 1938, this 450-mile (724-km) highway linking Natchez with Nashville, Tennessee (see pp266–7), was originally an animal trail. Later, it evolved into a footpath and played a vital role in the development of the country's midsection by linking the Ohio River Valley and the Gulf of Mexico. Pioneers used the route to transport their crops and produce downriver by barge to Natchez, where they sold both their goods and barges for scrap lumber, and then returned north on foot.

Today, the Natchez Trace Parkway (see pp50–51) is a scenic, year-round destination. No commercial traffic is permitted in this haven for hikers, motorists, and cyclists, and the speed limit is a leisurely 50 mph (80 km/h).

Natchez Parkway sign

The parkway preserves several historical sites, such as **Emerald Mound**. Situated near Natchez, it dates from AD 1400 and is the second largest Native American ceremonial mound in the country. A detour west, along Hwy 552, leads to the "**Ruins of**

Natchez Trace Parkway, a historic wooded trail

Windsor," where a ghostly set of 23 towering Corinthian columns serves as a poignant reminder of a mansion that burned down in 1890. The **Mount Locust** visitor center is located 15 miles (24 km) northeast of Natchez in a restored 1783 inn.

## ⓲ Natchez

🏙 20,000. 🚌 🚐 ℹ 640 S Canal St, (601) 446-6345.

Best known for its fine antebellum architecture, Natchez is an attractive town on the bluffs above the Mississippi River. The first capital of the state of Mississippi, it is the oldest settlement on the entire river, and is surrounded by a wealth of natural resources, with a growing industrial sector. Many of its historic buildings lie within easy walking distance of the compact downtown district. Some of these gems include the oldest house in town, the 1798 **House on Ellicott's Hill**; the stately and palatial **Stanton Hall** (1857); the unfinished **Longwood** (1860), whose construction was interrupted by the Civil War; and **Rosalie**, an 1829 brick mansion atop the bluff that served as Union headquarters during the Civil War.

Many house museums are open all year, but many more can be seen during the **Natchez Pilgrimage** held in the spring and fall (see p40). A short drive east of downtown is **Melrose**

Plantation, the US's most intact antebellum estate. It displays African-American history in slave quarters alongside the 1845 Greek Revival mansion. At the south end of town, a mile (1.6 km) off Hwy 61, is the Grand Village of the Natchez Indians, a historic village with Indian mounds, replicas of huts, nature trails, and a small museum.

🏛 **House on Ellicott's Hill**
Jefferson & Canal Sts. **Tel** (601) 442-2011. **Open** 10am–3pm Fri, Sat. **Closed** Dec 25. 🅿 ♿
W **natchezgardenclub.com**

🏛 **Natchez Pilgrimage Tour**
**Tel** (601) 446-6631, (800) 647-6742.
W **natchezpilgrimage.com**

## ⓳ Gulf Coast

🏙 156,000 (Biloxi & Gulfport). 🚐 🚌 ℹ 942 Beach Dr, Gulfport, (228) 896-6699. W **gulfcoast.org**

Lingering French influences and a maritime heritage combine to make the scenic Gulf of Mexico coastline unlike the rest of Mississippi. In 1699, two Québcois brothers, Pierre le Moyne, Sieur d'Iberville, and Jean Baptiste le Moyne, Sieur de Bienville, reached what is now Ocean Springs, to set up France's first permanent settlement in the South. In 1704, the French government sponsored the transport of 20 young women as prospective brides for the male colonists. Armed with

Fishing schooners lining the waterfront on the Gulf Coast

their trousseaux in state-issued suitcases or "cassettes," the "cassette girls" were housed on Ship Island. After the Americans gained control of the coast, they built **Fort Massachusetts** in the mid-1800s on Ship Island. During the Civil War, the Union used the fort to house POWs, including a troop of African-American Confederates from Louisiana.

In August 1965, Hurricane Camille, one of the worst storms to hit mainland US, split Ship Island into two – West Ship and East Ship (although it is still referred to locally in the singular). Today, both are part of the **Gulf Islands National Seashore**. A ferry transports passengers to the beach and for tours of the historic fort. Boating is a popular recreation – visitors can take boat and kayak trips to deserted islands, or fishing charters on traditional shrimp boats. The **Walter Anderson Museum of Art** exhibits works by the late painter, potter, naturalist, and writer Walter Anderson, reflecting his love for the Mississippi coast.

🏖 **Gulf Islands National Seashore**
3500 Park Rd, Ocean Springs. **Tel** (228) 875-9057. W **nps.gov/guis**

🏛 **Walter Anderson Museum of Art**
510 Washington Ave, Ocean Springs. ℹ (228) 872-3164. **Open** 9:30am–4:30pm Mon–Sat, 12:30-4:30pm Sun. W **walterandersonmuseum.org**

Longwood, the octagonal, domed house, in Natchez

# Alabama

Alabama slopes from the Cumberland Plateau in the northeast, across forested ridges and fertile plains to the Gulf of Mexico at Mobile Bay. The first European presence was established by the French along the coast in the early 1700s. During the next 100 years, settlement increased as overland immigrants from Tennessee and Georgia moved here, ousting the Choctaw, Cherokee, and Creek Indians from their ancestral lands. With progress, cotton fed the port of Mobile, and the steel industry drove Birmingham's economy. Today, the state is known for its diverse landscape, its antebellum architecture, and, most importantly, its Civil Rights history.

Reconstructed Fort Conde, Mobile

## ⑳ Mobile

🚹 203,000. ✈ 🚊 🚌 **ℹ** 1 S Water St, (251) 208-2000.

This beautiful port city was founded as a French colony in 1702. Later it served as a strategic Confederate port until the final days of the Civil War. Today, the city retains both its French and Southern flavor and is best known for its **Mobile Carnival Museum**, which includes memorabilia dating from the early 1800s.

At the head of Mobile Bay is **Fort Conde**, a partially reconstructed fort built by the French. Moored nearby is the World War II battleship, USS *Alabama*. A scenic loop drive around the bay leads to two other historic forts, Fort Morgan to the east, and Fort Gaines on Dauphin Island. Both are havens for birdlife.

**🏛 Fort Conde**
150 Royal St. **Tel** (251) 208-7304.
**Open** 8am–5pm daily.
**Closed** public hols, Mardi Gras.

## ㉑ Selma

🚹 21,000. **ℹ** 912 Selma Ave, (334) 875-7241. **W** **selmaalabama.com**

Situated on a bluff high above the Alabama River, this city was the site of one the most notorious scenes in Civil Rights history. On March 7, 1965, a day that became known as "Bloody Sunday," 600 Civil Rights protesters heading toward Montgomery, the capital, violently clashed with the police at Edmund Pettus Bridge.

Display inside the Voting Rights Museum in Selma

A few weeks later, however, Dr. Martin Luther King Jr. led a successful march to the State Capitol steps. The **National Voting Rights Museum** encapsulates the story, and an annual re-enactment pays tribute to the event.

Before the Civil Rights era, Selma's place in history was assured as the "Arsenal of the Confederacy." It produced weapons, cannons, and ironclad ships. Much of the city was destroyed during the war, but the townscape along the river remained intact. The city's 1891 cherry-red train depot has exhibits on local history.

**🏛 National Voting Rights Museum**
6 US Hwy 80 E. **Tel** (334) 418-0800.
**Open** 10am–4pm Mon–Thu, by appt Fri–Sun. 🅿 🚻 **W** nvrmi.com

## ㉒ Montgomery

🚹 224,000. 🚌 **ℹ** 300 Water St, (334) 262-0013. **W** **visiting montgomery.com**

Alabama's capital city since 1846, Montgomery was also the Confederacy's first capital during the Civil War. In 1861, Jefferson Davis was sworn in as the Confederate president on the steps of the Greek Revival State Capitol. Across the street, the **First White House of the Confederacy** is now a museum related to those times.

The city also played a pivotal role during the Civil Rights Movement. The segregation of the city's transportation system led to an act of defiance by Rosa Parks, when she refused to surrender her bus seat to a white man. In 1956, the young Dr. Martin Luther King Jr. supported the year-long Montgomery Bus Boycott, which ultimately brought about the desegregation of the city's public transportation system. Its success was significant as it not only strengthened the movement, but also saw the rise of King as the campaign's leader. The city's landmark **Civil Rights Memorial**, designed by Vietnam Veterans Memorial

Montgomery's Civil Rights Memorial Fountain

artist Maya Lin *(see p209)*, honors 40 martyrs who sacrificed their lives in the fight for racial equality.

Montgomery is also associated with two major figures of 20th-century arts. Local girl Zelda Fitzgerald and her husband, writer F. Scott Fitzgerald, lived here in 1931, while he was writing *Tender is the Night*. Their house is now a museum. In 1958, country singer Hank Williams played his final concert in the city three days before his death. Williams is buried in Oakwood Cemetery, and a statue of the singer stands downtown.

**First White House of the Confederacy**
644 Washington Ave. **Tel** (334) 242-1861. **Open** 9am–4pm Mon–Sat **Closed** Sun & state hols.

## ❷❸ Tuskegee

13,000. 121 Main St, (334) 727-6619.

Former slave Booker T. Washington founded the Tuskegee Normal and Industrial Institute here in 1881 to improve educational opportunities for African-Americans. The school evolved into **Tuskegee University**, best known for

agriculturist George Washington Carver's innovations that revolutionized agricultural growth in the region. The "Tuskegee Airmen," the group of African-American pilots who distinguished themselves in World War II, also graduated from the institute, now part of the Tuskegee Institute National Historic Site.

## ❷❹ Birmingham

212,000. 2200 9th Ave N, (205) 458-8000.

The largest city in Alabama, Birmingham was once the region's foremost producer of steel. Celebrating the city's industrial past is **Sloss Furnaces National Historic Landmark**, a museum housed in an old steel mill, and a 55-ft- (17-m-) high iron statue of Vulcan, the Roman god of fire, on the summit of Red Mountain, the source of the iron ore. Today, the city's attractions are typical of a modern Southern city – antebellum houses, botanical gardens, and the acclaimed **Birmingham Museum of Art**, with its fine collection of Wedgwood. Yet the most moving landmarks are those that relate to the city's African-American

history. These can be seen within walking distance of the central downtown district's visitor center, where maps as well as tours are available.

The **Birmingham Civil Rights Institute** uses vintage film footage to explain the city's Civil Rights Movement. Among the exhibits is the door of the cell in which Dr. Martin Luther King Jr. wrote his famous "Letter from a Birmingham Jail," arguing that individuals have the right to disobey unjust laws. Down the street, the restored Sixteenth Street Baptist Church stands as a memorial to four black girls killed by a Ku Klux Klan bomb in 1963. To its southeast, in the historic **Carver Theatre**, the Alabama Jazz Hall of Fame hosts live music performances and celebrates the achievements of such artists as Dinah Washington, Nat King Cole, W.C. Handy, and Duke Ellington. At the north end of town, the **Alabama Sports Hall of Fame** honors beloved native African-American athletes such as Joe Louis and Jesse Owens.

Dr. Martin Luther King Jr.

**Birmingham Civil Rights Institute**
520 16th St N. **Tel** (205) 328-9696. **Open** 10am–5pm Tue–Sat, 1–5pm Sun. **Closed** public hols. (Sun free). bcri.org

## ❷❺ Huntsville

163,000. 500 Church St, (256) 533-5723. huntsville.org

Set in a curving valley in northern Alabama, the cotton market town of Huntsville developed into a space and military research and development and manufacturing center after World War II. Home to the NASA-Marshall Space Flight Center, the city's main attractions are the US Space and Rocket Center and its bus tours. Exhibits include Apollo capsules and a life-size space shuttle. A camp here also teaches children about space exploration.

George Washington Carver Museum, Tuskegee University

# Practical Information

Advance planning is necessary for a successful tour around the Deep South, simply because there is so much to see and do. New Orleans, the region's most exotic city, is packed with entertainment and music venues, clubs, hotels, and restaurants, while many small towns and the expansive and diverse areas between them often double as low-key resort areas, catering to city-dwellers in need of a change of pace. Depending upon the time, visitors can explore significant historical sights, appreciate stunning scenery, gaze at the well-manicured gardens of former plantation homes, take in a local celebration, or simply relax alongside a lazy river.

## Tourist Information

Each of the Deep South states publishes a wide variety of informative travel guides, which may be ordered by telephone or accessed via websites. As soon as visitors enter Louisiana, Mississippi, Alabama, or Arkansas, they may check in one of a dozen official "Welcome Centers" along major highways. Staffed by helpful volunteers and open from 8am to 5pm daily, these centers offer free road maps and a full range of tourist information. Such information is also available from the multitude of local and regional tourism bureaus across all four states.

## Natural Hazards

The Deep South is prone to hurricanes and occasional tornadoes from early June to November each year. In August 2005, Hurricane Katrina hit the Gulf Coast, destroying much of New Orleans and coastal towns and killing thousands. If planning a visit, visitors should follow the storm forecasts for the Gulf and Caribbean. The **National Hurricane Center** in Miami provides information on impending hurricanes. When a Hurricane Warning is posted in the area you are visiting, either cancel your trip or evacuate the area. Follow the broadcasts about emergency procedures on radio and television.

The biggest hazard is the sun. Use high-factor sunscreen and wear a hat. Also, drink plenty of fluids to avoid getting dehydrated. Biting and stinging insects, especially mosquitoes, are a nuisance between April and November, so remember to carry insect repellent.

## Getting Around

Like much of the US, the Deep South is a region where it can be difficult to get around without a car. Seat belts are mandatory for drivers and front-seat passengers in all Deep South states. Most states also require seat belts for back-seat passengers. All automobile occupants under the age of four require child safety seats.

Public transportation options are limited. **Greyhound** buses only serve some larger towns and cities, while **Amtrak** runs two train routes – north–south across the Mississippi Delta between Memphis and New Orleans, and east–west, connecting New Orleans with western cities. Mississippi river cruises fell into decline following Hurricane Katrina in 2005, but **American Cruise Lines** and **Blount Small Ship Adventures**, although expensive, offer itineraries of varying lengths.

## Etiquette

The old-world traditions of the Deep South, hospitality and courtesy, especially toward women, are legendary. Addressing people politely, with a "sir" or "ma'am" will be much appreciated, and will help social interaction.

Check for non-smoking signs as smoking is prohibited in most public buildings, including stores and restaurants. Although the laws for drinking alcohol vary from state to state, the legal age is 21. Only in New Orleans is it permissible to drink on the streets, though only in plastic containers called "go cups."

## Festivals

The Deep South states stage a diverse range of annual community, regional, and national festivals. The nation's biggest party, and one of the world's most colorful and lively annual events, is the 10-day-long series of celebrations leading up to **Mardi Gras**, French for "Fat Tuesday." The carnival parades, music, drinking, and dancing are at their liveliest in New Orleans, though smaller but no less energetic celebrations are

## The Climate of the Deep South

The climate across this region does not vary much from state to state, although seasonal differences are distinct. Winter is rather wet, while the summer heat and humidity can be sweltering. By September the weather is fine again, though late summer storms or hurricanes can put a damper on travel. Spring and autumn are the ideal times to plan an extended trip. Spring flowers, such as magnolia blossoms, set the tone for the early months of the year.

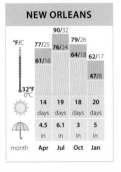

**NEW ORLEANS**

| °F/C | 90/32 | | |
|---|---|---|---|
| | 77/25 76/24 | 79/26 | |
| | 61/16 | 64/18 | 62/17 |
| | | | 47/8 |
| 32°F 0°C | | | |

| | 14 days | 19 days | 18 days | 20 days |
|---|---|---|---|---|
| ☔ | 4.5 in | 6.1 in | 3 in | 5 in |
| month | Apr | Jul | Oct | Jan |

also held in several other Deep South towns, including Mobile, Alabama.

Spring is a fine time to be in Mississippi, especially if you can time your trip to enjoy the *"Gone With the Wind"*-like re-creations of the **Natchez Pilgrimage**, a month-long celebration of the antebellum "Old South." Many of the city's historic homes are open to the public, and several pageants and performances take place.

Summer brings a profusion of outdoor events, and fireworks, bands, and street festivals are the norm for community celebrations of the July 4 Independence Day holiday. Numerous county and state fairs take place in the country-side in July and August, as do a number of music festivals such as the **B.B. King Homecoming Festival** in Indianola, Mississippi, the first of many blues-themed festivals that take place in and around the Mississippi Delta. Later in the summer comes the grand **Mississippi Delta Blues and Heritage Festival**, held in September in Greenville, Mississippi. In October, the historic homes of Natchez and Vicksburg are again opened to the public during the **Fall Pilgrimage**. Lucky visitors may sample freshly made, sugary pralines, sold by vendors.

## Sports & Outdoor Activities

The towns and cities of the Deep South are not large enough to support top-tier professional sports teams, but they field dozens of minor league teams and hundreds of high-quality sports teams of various public and private colleges and universities. New Orleans has the New Orleans Pelicans basketball team and the New Orleans Saints football team, which plays in the **Superdome**, one of the world's largest indoor sports arenas. The main events of the college sporting seasons are football and basketball games between regional rivals, including Louisiana State University Tigers, the University of Alabama's Crimson Tide, and the Rebels of the University of Mississippi. Baseball season runs from April to September, football from September through January, and basketball from winter through mid-spring.

Although both fishing and boating are also prominent, fishing is by far the more popular of the two sports. Lake fishing for bass or crappie is available in many state parks, while Arkansas streams offer trout fishing. Deep-sea fishing for grouper, tarpon, or snapper, or by net for the shrimp, can be arranged from Gulf of Mexico ports such as Biloxi, Mississippi, Mobile, Alabama, or Grand Isle, Louisiana. Visitors should check with the various state fish and game departments to see which permits are required.

## Entertainment

The birthplace of jazz and a melting pot of American music, New Orleans is a showcase for all types of performance. Local newspapers such as the *Times-Picayune* or the weekly *New Orleans Magazine* carry detailed listings of the events and activities. A major venue for music in New Orleans is the historic **Preservation Hall**, where traditonal "Dixieland" jazz may be heard most nights. A huge range of nightclubs in the tourist-dominated French Quarter as well as in the uptown area offer live musical entertainment. For traditional Cajun music, head to Lafayette and the roadhouse restaurant, **Prejean's**, the most reliable of the music venues in the region.

Many other cities also host popular musical events. Blues festivals take place all over Mississippi and Arkansas during summer. A wonderful place to listen to the blues is **Ground Zero Blues Club**, in Clarksdale, Mississippi.

# DIRECTORY

## Tourist Offices

**Alabama**
Tel (334) 242-4169.
W alabama.travel

**Arkansas**
Tel (800) 628-8725.
W arkansas.com

**Louisiana**
Tel (800) 994-8626.
W louisianatravel.com

**Mississippi**
Tel (601) 359-3297.
W visitmississippi.org

## Natural Hazards

**National Hurricane Center, Miami**
Tel (305) 229-4470.
W nhc.noaa.gov

## Travel

**Amtrak**
Tel (800) 872-7245.
W amtrak.com

**Greyhound**
Tel (800) 231-2222.
W greyhound.com

## River Cruises

**American Cruise Lines/ Blount Small Ship Adventures**
Tel (800) 510-4002.
W mississippi rivercruises.com

## Festivals

**B.B. King Homecoming Festival**
Tel (662) 887-4454.

**Mardi Gras, New Orleans**
Tel (800) 672-6124.
W neworleans online.com

## Sports

**Superdome**
Tel (504) 587-3663.
W superdome.com

## Departments of Fish & Game

W fws.gov

**Alabama**
Tel (334) 242-3465.

**Arkansas**
Tel (501) 223-6300.

**Louisiana**
Tel (225) 765-2800.

**Mississippi**
Tel (601) 432-2400.

## Entertainment

**Ground Zero Blues Club**
Tel (662) 621-9009.

**Prejean's**
Tel (337) 896-3247.
W prejeans.com

**Preservation Hall**
Tel (504) 522-2841.
W preservation hall.com

# Where to Stay

## Louisiana

### BATON ROUGE: Hilton Baton Rouge Capitol Center $$
Business
*201 Lafayette St, 70801*
**Tel** *(225) 344-5866*
**w** hilton.com
Historical grandeur is mixed with modern amenities and excellent service here. The garden deck overlooks the Mississippi River.

### DK Choice

**BATON ROUGE:
The Stockade** $$
Inn/B&B
*8860 Highland Rd, 70808*
**Tel** *(225) 769-7358*
**w** thestockade.com
Situated near Louisiana State University and downtown, this Spanish-style hacienda is named after the Union stockade that occupied the site during the Civil War. Each of the elegant guest rooms features regional art and lovely antiques. Spread over 30 acres (12 ha) of wooded grounds, The Stockade provides ample nature-spotting opportunities for wildlife lovers and bird-watchers.

### BREAUX BRIDGE: Cajun Country Cottages B&B $$
B&B
*1138A Lawless Tauzin Rd, 70517*
**Tel** *(337) 332-3093*
**w** cajuncottages.com
These secluded cottages on a former plantation site overlook a huge lake. Relax on porch swings, or go canoeing and fishing.

Lobby of the charming Hotel Mazarin, New Orleans

### LAFAYETTE: Blue Moon Saloon and Guesthouse $
Value
*215 E Convent St, 70501*
**Tel** *(337) 234-2422*
**w** bluemoonpresents.com
Private and shared rooms have a range of amenities. The saloon features live music on most nights.

### LAFAYETTE: Courtyard by Marriott $$
Business
*214 E Kaliste Saloom Rd, 70508*
**Tel** *(337) 232-5005*
**w** marriott.com
This modern hotel near the airport offers comfortable rooms with many amenities.

### NATCHITOCHES: Queen Anne B&B $$
B&B
*125 Pine St, 71457*
**Tel** *(800) 441-8343*
**w** queenannebandb.com
This warm and welcoming inn has a range of amenities and activities.

### NEW IBERIA: Rip Van Winkle Gardens $$
B&B
*5505 Rip Van Winkle Rd, 70560*
**Tel** *(337) 359-8525*
**w** ripvanwinklegardens.com
Located in semi-tropical gardens, these romantic Cajun Country cottages come with luxury beds and amenities.

### NEW ORLEANS: Auld Sweet Olive B&B $
B&B
*2460 N Rampart St, 70117*
**Tel** *(504) 947-4332*
**w** sweetolive.com
This arty B&B just outside the French Quarter has serene rooms and a lush tropical courtyard. Complimentary breakfasts.

### NEW ORLEANS: Ashton's Bed & Breakfast $$
B&B
*2023 Esplanade Ave, 70116*
**Tel** *(504) 942-7048*
**w** ashtonsbb.com
A family-run B&B in a Greek-Revival mansion shaded by old oaks, with complimentary extras.

### NEW ORLEANS: Hotel Mazarin $$
Boutique **Map** 3D
*730 Bienville St, 70130*
**Tel** *(504) 581-7300*
**w** hotelmazarin.com
Modern, well-appointed rooms with New Orleans charm are centered around a courtyard.

### NEW ORLEANS: Hotel Modern $$
Boutique **Map** 4C
*936 St Charles Ave, 70130*
**Tel** *(504) 962-0900*
**w** thehotelmodern.com
This stylish, contemporary hotel oozes Old World charm. The cozy rooms boast luxury bedding and designer amenities.

### DK Choice

**NEW ORLEANS: Hotel Monteleone** $$
Historic **Map** 3D
*214 Rue Royale, 70130*
**Tel** *(504) 523-3341*
**w** hotelmonteleone.com
Legendary hospitality and a prime location are the hallmarks of this excellent family-run hotel. In a historic building, it features an elegant, expansive lobby as well as luxurious rooms and suites. The rooftop swimming pool is a delight, and the famous revolving Carousel Bar is a favorite gathering spot for visitors and locals alike.

### NEW ORLEANS: International House Hotel $$
Boutique **Map** 3D
*221 Camp St, 70130*
**Tel** *(504) 553-9550*
**w** ihhotel.com
The penthouse rooms afford great views at this fashionable, stylish hotel with a lobby bar. .

### NEW ORLEANS: Le Pavillon $$
Historic **Map** 4C
*833 Poydras St, 70112*
**Tel** *(504) 581-3111*
**w** lepavillon.com
This upscale hotel comes with a dazzling lobby, a rooftop pool, lavishly appointed rooms, and first-class service.

### NEW ORLEANS: Roosevelt Hotel $$
Historic **Map** 3C
*123 Baronne St, 70112*
**Tel** *(504) 648-1200*
**w** therooseveltneworleans.com
A majestic lobby and the swanky Sazerac Bar set this elegant hotel apart. It offers luxuriously decorated rooms and a decadent spa.

**NEW ORLEANS: Royal
Sonesta** $$
Boutique **Map** 3D
*300 Bourbon St, 70130*
**Tel** *(504) 586-0300*
W sonesta.com/RoyalNewOrleans
Head here for French flair with
wrought-iron balconies and
French doors. There's a pretty
tropical courtyard.

**NEW ORLEANS: Ritz-Carlton
New Orleans** $$$
Business **Map** 3D
*921 Canal St, 70112*
**Tel** *(504) 524-1331*
W ritzcarlton.com
Decorated in the grand Garden
District Mansion style, this hotel
offers high-end luxury and
excellent hospitality. Rooms have
high ceilings and marble baths.

**NEW ORLEANS: Windsor
Court Hotel** $$$
Historic **Map** 4D
*300 Gravier St, 70130*
**Tel** *(504) 523-6000*
W windsorcourthotel.com
Boasting English decor and great
service, rooms here are
exceptionally large and
comfortable. Do not miss the
classy high-tea service (Thu–Sun).

**ST. FRANCISVILLE: Barrow
House Inn** $
B&B
*9779 Royal St, 70775*
**Tel** *(225) 635-4791*
W topteninn.com
This romantic B&B features
elegant suites furnished with
American antiques from the
mid-19th century and offers
excellent attentive service.

**ST. MARTINVILLE: Bienvenue
House** $
B&B
*421 N Main St, 70582*
**Tel** *(337) 394-9100*
W bienvenuehouse.com
Offering true Southern
hospitality, this B&B has elegant
guest rooms with individual
themes and arty decor.
The porch swings are great for
relaxing on. Gourmet breakfasts.

**VACHERIE: Oak Alley
Plantation** $$
Historic
*3645 Hwy 18, 70090*
**Tel** *(225) 265-2151*
W oakalleyplantation.com
This historic Greek Revival-style
plantation house has featured
in many movies, including
the blockbuster *Interview With
the Vampire*. It offers private
cottages in a spectacular
setting. Full breakfast is included.

Balcony of a suite at the luxurious Ritz-Carlton, New Orleans

# Arkansas

## DK Choice
**BENTONVILLE:
21c Museum Hotel** $$
Boutique
*200 NE A St, 72712*
**Tel** *(479) 286-6500*
W 21cmuseumhotels.com
A boutique hotel and
contemporary art museum,
21c Museum Hotel features
exhibitions and installations, as
well as live events. The intimate
rooms make use of natural light,
bold colors, and original art, and
boast luxurious amenities. The
on-site restaurant serves
inventive local fare.

**EUREKA SPRINGS: 1886
Crescent Hotel & Spa** $$
Historic
*75 Prospect Ave, 72632*
**Tel** *(855) 725-5720*
W crescent-hotel.com
This hotel in a Victorian building
famous for being haunted
features a spa, beautiful gardens,
and a porch with rocking chairs.

**FAYETTEVILLE:
The Chancellor Hotel** $
Boutique
*70 NE Ave, 72701*
**Tel** *(855) 285-6162*
W hotelchancellor.com
A modern, sophisticated hotel
with a casual ambience, luxury
amenities, and first-class service.

**HOT SPRINGS: The B Inn** $
Value
*316 Park Ave, 71901*
**Tel** *(501) 547-7172*
W bhotsprings.com
Steps away from the Hot
Springs National Park and
downtown, this inn offers
comfortable rooms with
book-related themes.

**LITTLE ROCK: Legacy
Hotel and Suites** $
Value
*625 W Capitol Ave, 72201*
**Tel** *(501) 374-0100*
W legacyhotel.com
An elegant hotel with well-
appointed rooms, an intimate
courtyard, and a business center.

**LITTLE ROCK: Wyndham
Riverfront** $
Business
*2 Riverfront Dr, 72114*
**Tel** *(501) 371-9000*
W wyndham.com
Comfortable rooms, a full business
center on site, and shuttle service.

**LITTLE ROCK:
The Capital Hotel** $$
Historic
*111 W Markham, 72201*
**Tel** *(501) 374-7474*
W capitalhotel.com
Large, tastefully appointed rooms
sit in an historic architectural gem
with a marble lobby and sweeping
staircase. Elegant style and service.

**MOUNTAIN VIEW: Ozark Folk
Center Dry Creek Cabins** $
Value
*1032 Park Ave, 72560*
**Tel** *(870) 269-3871*
W ozarkfolkcenter.com
Cabins in a wooded setting come
with porches and homey decor.
There's an excellent folk center.

# Mississippi

**BILOXI: Beau Rivage
Resort & Casino** $$
Boutique
*875 Beach Blvd, 39530*
**Tel** *(228) 386-7444*
W beaurivage.com
This beachfront casino complex
offers many dining, shopping,
and entertainment options,
as well as luxurious rooms.

Shack Up Inn, housed in authentic sharecropper shacks, Clarksdale

**CLARKSDALE: Shack Up Inn** $
Value
*1 Commissary Circle, 38614*
**Tel** *(662) 624-8329*
W shackupinn.com
These sharecropper shacks with modern amenities have a minimum 2-night stay on weekends. Under 25s are not allowed.

**JACKSON: Old Capitol Inn** $
Boutique
*226 N State St, 39201*
**Tel** *(601) 359-9000*
W oldcapitolinn.com
Head here for the rooftop deck with hot tub and patio, Southern breakfast, and evening wine hour.

**DK Choice**

**NATCHEZ: Monmouth Historic Inn** $$
B&B
*36 Melrose Ave, 39120*
**Tel** *(601) 442-5852*
W monmouthhistoricinn.com
One of the most romantic inns in America, this award-winning B&B is housed in an 1818 plantation home surrounded by oaks. Rooms are appointed in grand antebellum style with antiques. It offers complimentary wine tastings and house tours, plus packages for special occasions, golfers, and foodies.

**OCEAN SPRINGS: Travelodge** $
Value
*500 Bienville Blvd, 39564*
**Tel** *(228) 215-1144*
W travelodge.com
Pleasant motel located near local attractions. On-site barbecue grills.

**OXFORD: Hampton Inn** $
Business
*110 Heritage Dr, 38655*
**Tel** *(662) 232-2442*
W hamptoninn.com
This modern hotel near the university offers clean rooms and a complimentary hot breakfast.

**OXFORD: The 5 Twelve** $$
Inn/B&B
*512 Van Buren Ave, 38655*
**Tel** *(662) 234-8043*
W the5twelve.com
Rooms feature English country-style decor and claw-foot tubs at this Greek Revival manor house exuding Southern charm. .

**VICKSBURG: Baer House Inn** $
Inn/B&B
*1117 Grove St, 39183*
**Tel** *(601) 883-1525*
W baerhouseinn.ms
A full breakfast service and evening social hour are included in your stay at this Victorian mansion with period antiques.

# Alabama

**BIRMINGHAM: Cobb Lane B&B** $
Inn/B&B
*1309 19th St S, 35205*
**Tel** *(205) 918-9090*
W cobblanebandb.com
This Victorian B&B with a genteel atmosphere offers true Southern hospitality, luxurious rooms, and elegant breakfasts.

**DK Choice**

**BIRMINGHAM: Hotel Highland at Five Points South** $$
Boutique
*1023 20th St S, 35205*
**Tel** *(205) 933-9555*
W thehotelhighland.com
Sporting sophisticated rooms with modern, handcrafted furnishings and the finest linens from Brazil, this is a hip, ultra-chic hotel. Unique design features, flat-screen TVs, and wet bars add style to each room. Head to the trendy Martini Bar for its award-winning cocktails. Attentive service and prime location make this the ideal choice.

**HUNTSVILLE: Marriott Huntsville** $
Business
*5 Tranquility Base, 35805*
**Tel** *(256) 830-2222*
W marriott.com
Located on the grounds of the US Space and Rocket Center, rooms here are generously furnished, comfortable, and quiet. Helpful staff.

**MOBILE: Kate Shepard House B&B** $$
B&B
*1552 Monterey Pl, 36604*
**Tel** *(251) 479-7048*
W kateshepardhouse.com
This Queen Anne-style B&B built in 1897 is close to downtown. It features original fireplace mantles and hardwood floors. Complimentary full breakfasts.

**MOBILE: The Battle House** $$
Historic
*26 N Royal St, 36602*
**Tel** *(251) 338-2000*
W rsabattlehouse.com
This richly historic downtown hotel boasts a stunning, opulent lobby, classic Southern charm, and luxurious rooms with modern amenities. The full service spa on site offers a range of services.

**MONTGOMERY: Doubletree Hotel** $$
Business
*120 Madison Ave, 36104*
**Tel** *(334) 245-2320*
W doubletree3.hilton.com
Rooms are modern and comfortable at this hotel in a convenient location near important historical sites as well as shopping and dining options. There is a stylish restaurant and bar on site.

**ORANGE BEACH: The Island House Hotel** $$
Boutique
*26650 Perdido Beach Blvd, 36561*
**Tel** *(251) 981-6100*
W islandhousehotel.com
This is a luxurious vacation hotel with attentive staff and deluxe amenities. All rooms at this hotel face the gulf, with balconies overlooking the private beach.

**SELMA: St. James Hotel** $
Historic
*1200 Water Ave, 36701*
**Tel** *(334) 872-0332*
W historicstjameshotel.com
Historic riverfront hotel with comfortable rooms. The wrap-around porches offer views of the famed Edmund Pettus Bridge.

# Where to Eat and Drink

## Louisiana

**BATON ROUGE: Boutin's Cajun Restaurant** $
Cajun/Creole
8322 Bluebonnet Blvd, 70810
Tel (225) 819-9862
Head here for authentic favorites like crawfish *étouffée* (a Cajun stew of shellfish or chicken) and shrimp and oysters *en brochette*. There is live Cajun music on most nights.

**BATON ROUGE: The Chimes** $
Cajun/Creole
3357 Highland Rd, 70802
Tel (225) 383-1754
The menu at Chimes features standard bar fare, Cajun and Creole classics, blackened seafood, and desserts. Extensive beer list.

**BREAUX BRIDGE: Café des Amis** $
Cajun/Creole
140 E Bridge St, 70517
Tel (337) 332-5273 **Closed** Mon
Don't miss the Saturday Zydeco breakfast at this cultural gem. *Étouffée*, *couche couche* (a Cajun breakfast of steamed cornmeal), and BBQ shrimp are specialties.

### DK Choice

**LAFAYETTE: Prejean's** $
Cajun
3480 US I-49 N, 70507
Tel (337) 896-3247
The bayou theme at Prejean's attracts both locals and tourists. The menu includes authentic gumbos, bisques, blackened catfish *étouffée*, eggplant Pirogue, and a savory cheesecake made with crawfish and alligator-stuffed sausage. There is live Cajun music nightly and during weekend brunch service.

**LAFAYETTE: Café Vermilionville** $$
Cajun/Creole
1304 W Pinhook Rd, 70503
Tel (337) 237-0100 **Closed** Sun
Housed in a 19th-century inn, this restaurant has two Cajun menus – one featuring traditional favorites, the other seasonal chef creations.

**NATCHITOCHES: The Landing** $
Cajun/Creole
530 Front St, 71457
Tel (318) 352-1579 **Closed** Mon
At this casual eatery with friendly service po'boys are a lunch favorite, while the dinner menu features Creole- and Cajun-style seafood, meat, and pasta entrées.

**NEW ORLEANS: Acme Oyster House** $
Seafood **Map** 3D
724 Iberville St, 70130
Tel (504) 522-5973
A classic eatery popular for super-fresh oysters served fried, chargrilled, or freshly shucked and raw. The menu also includes seafood platters and regional favorites like red beans and jambalaya.

**NEW ORLEANS: Café du Monde** $
French café **Map** 2E
800 Decatur St, 70116
Tel (504) 525-4544
A steadfast favorite with locals and tourists alike. The solitary menu item is tasty beignets, best enjoyed with exquisite *café au lait*. Open around the clock.

**NEW ORLEANS: Casamento's** $
Seafood
4330 Magazine St, 70115
Tel (504) 895-9761 **Closed** Jun–Aug; Sun & Mon
This tiny restaurant has been serving fresh oysters and seafood since 1919. The short menu includes oyster loaf, gumbo, and freshly shucked raw oysters.

**NEW ORLEANS: Cochon Butcher** $
Sandwiches
930 Tchoupitoulas St, 70130
Tel (504) 588-7675
This deli and butcher shop is the sister restaurant of Chef Donald Link's Cochon. Highlights include house-cured meats and sausages, duck pastrami sliders, buckboard bacon melt, pancetta mac 'n' cheese, and bacon pralines.

**NEW ORLEANS: Mother's** $
Cajun/Creole **Map** 4D
401 Poydras St, 70130
Tel (504) 523-9656
Casual and boisterous, this diner-style restaurant is favored for its breakfasts, heaped po'boys, and other Creole standards. The famed Ferdi po'boy includes roast beans, baked ham, and "debris."

**NEW ORLEANS: Napoleon House** $
Creole **Map** 3D
500 Chartres St, 70130
Tel (504) 524-9752 **Closed** Sun
This European-style bar and café is housed in a historic landmark building dating to 1797. The casual atmosphere, classical music, and back courtyard are perfect for a classic Pimm's cup or a *muffuletta* (a special local sandwich).

**Price Guide**
Prices are based on a three-course meal for one, with a glass of house wine, including tax and service.

$      up to $35
$$      $35 to $70
$$$      over $70

**NEW ORLEANS: Parkway Bakery and Tavern** $
Sandwiches
538 Hagan Ave, 70119
Tel (504) 482-3047 **Closed** Tue
A busy po'boy shop with a long history. Roast beef, fried shrimp, and "dressed" (topped with tomatoes, lettuce, pickles, and mayonnaise) po'boys are popular. There is plenty of outdoor seating.

**NEW ORLEANS: Port of Call** $
Burgers **Map** 2F
838 Esplanade Ave, 70116
Tel (504) 523-0120
The always packed Port of Call serves burgers topped with grated cheese or mushrooms, and giant baked potatoes. Steaks and sides are available too. Try the potent Monsoon cocktail at the bar.

**NEW ORLEANS: Emeril's** $$
Modern Creole **Map** 4D
800 Tchoupitoulas St, 70130
Tel (504) 528-9393
This is one of the finest eateries of its kind in the city, owned by famous chef Emeril Lagasse. The expansive menu promises Creole ingredients and flavors. Try the legendary banana cream pie.

**NEW ORLEANS: Irene's Cuisine** $$
Italian/Creole **Map** 2E
539 St Philip St, 70116
Tel (504) 529-8811
This cozy venue offers Creole-Italian specialties including seasoned rosemary chicken, seared chops, pan-sautéed fish fillets, and pasta. Decadent desserts.

The popular Emeril's in New Orleans, serving Creole cuisine

**For more information on types of restaurants** see pages 28–9

**NEW ORLEANS:**
**Jacques-Imo's** $$
Cajun/Creole
*8324 Oak St, 70118*
**Tel** *(504) 861-0886* **Closed** *Sun*
This restaurant combines an
eclectic menu with funky decor
and a raucous atmosphere.
Try the fried chicken, shrimp
Creole, and alligator cheesecake.

**NEW ORLEANS: K-Paul's**
**Louisiana Kitchen** $$
Cajun/Creole **Map** 3D
*416 Chartres St, 70130*
**Tel** *(504) 596-2530* **Closed** *Sun*
Originator of the "blackened" craze
in the 1980s, K-Paul's still attracts
crowds with its signature spicy-
hot seasonings and rich sauces.
Favorites include gumbo, soft-
shell crab, and jambalaya. Pleasant
alfresco seating on the balcony.

**DK Choice**

**NEW ORLEANS:**
**Antoine's** $$$
Creole **Map** 3D
*713 St. Louis St, 70130*
**Tel** *(504) 581-1422*
This legendary restaurant has
been operating since 1840,
making it the oldest fine-dining
restaurant in New Orleans.
Classic and elegant, it features
fourteen upscale dining rooms
and a quintessential French-
Creole menu. Signature dishes
include eggs Sardou and oysters
Rockefeller. Try the Sunday Jazz
brunch. A drink at the attached
Hermes Bar is an equally
refined experience.

**NEW ORLEANS: Commander's**
**Palace** $$$
Creole
*1403 Washington Ave, 70130*
**Tel** *(504) 899-8221*
At this celebrated landmark
housed in a Victorian-era
building, the menu features both
traditional and innovative dishes,
including classic turtle soup. It
boasts excellent service and an
impressive wine list. Ask for a
table in the lovely garden.

**NEW ORLEANS: Galatoire's** $$$
Creole **Map** 3D
*209 Bourbon St, 70130*
**Tel** *(504) 525-2021* **Closed** *Mon*
This upscale, refined establish-
ment with marble floors and
black-tie waiters exudes elegance
and charm, and has a history
dating back to 1905. The
impeccable cuisine and service
draw regulars. The *remoulade*,
Godchaux salad, and soufflé
potatoes are top choices.

Table setting in the Garden Room at Commanders Palace, New Orleans

# Arkansas

**BENTONVILLE: Tusk & Trotter** $$
New American
*110 SE A St, 72712*
**Tel** *(479) 268-4494*
This casual restaurant features a
sophisticated menu of regional
comfort food with an innovative
twist. Try the risotto balls, pig's-
ear salad, or chicken and waffles.

**EUREKA SPRINGS: The Balcony**
**Restaurant** $
American
*12 Spring St, 72632*
**Tel** *(479) 253-7837*
The balcony of a historic hotel
houses this casual restaurant,
which overlooks the town's main
street. The long menu includes
family favorites such as soups,
salads, burgers, and sandwiches.

**DK Choice**

**HOT SPRINGS:**
**McClard's BBQ** $
Barbecue
*505 Albert Pike, 71913*
**Tel** *(501) 623-9665* **Closed** *Sun &*
*Mon*
A favorite of then-Governor Bill
Clinton, McClard's has been in
business since 1928. It is widely
considered the best barbecue
joint in Arkansas. Ribs are cooked
and smoked in an old-fashioned
pit and smothered with a
legendary special sauce. The
hot tamales, slow-cooked beans,
and coleslaw are equally popular.

**HOT SPRINGS: Belle Arti**
**Ristorante** $$
Italian
*719 Central Ave, 71901*
**Tel** *(501) 624-7474*
A popular restaurant with an old-
world ambience, Belle Arti features
artistically presented cuisine,
including steak, seafood, chicken,
pasta, fine wines and desserts.

**LITTLE ROCK: Doe's Eat Place** $
Steak House
*1023 W Markham St, 72201*
**Tel** *(501) 376-1195* **Closed** *Sun*
T-bone, porterhouse, and sirloin
steaks are cooked to order and
served family-style in this eatery.
Sides include new potatoes,
French fries, and Texas toast.

**LITTLE ROCK: Whole Hog Café** $
Barbecue
*2516 Cantrell Rd, 72202*
**Tel** *(501) 664-5025*
Delicious pulled pork, smoked
chicken, and the famous BBQ ribs
come with a choice of seven
sauces and a range of sides at this
award-winning eatery.

**LITTLE ROCK: Cajun's Wharf** $$
Cajun/Creole
*2400 Cantrell Rd, 72202*
**Tel** *(501) 375-5351* **Closed** *Sun*
The menu at this lively
restaurant, bar, and dance
club includes a good selection
of fresh seafood and aged
Angus beef. Great wine list.

**MOUNTAIN VIEW: Skillet**
**Restaurant** $
Southern
*1032 Park Ave, 72560*
**Tel** *(870) 269-3139* **Closed** *Dec–Mar*
At this country-style restaurant in
the Ozark Folk Center, diners enjoy
an extensive menu and great
weekend buffets plus great views
of the garden and wildlife
feeding stations.

# Mississippi

**BILOXI: Mary Mahoney's Old**
**French House** $$
Seafood
*110 Rue Magnolia, 39530*
**Tel** *(228) 374-0163* **Closed** *Sun*
A charming eatery in a historical
1737 house with period decor. The
menu features fresh Gulf seafood,
meats, and a choice of desserts.

**CLARKSDALE: Ground Zero
Blues Club** $
Southern
*252 Delta Ave, 38614*
**Tel** *(662) 621-9009* **Closed** *Sun*
Actor Morgan Freeman's club and
restaurant is known for live blues
music, great barbecue, burgers,
and special plate lunches.

**HATTIESBURG: Leatha's BBQ** $
Barbecue
*6374 US Hwy 98, 39402*
**Tel** *(601) 271-6003*
This friendly, family-run restaurant
serves delicious barbecued dishes,
such as juicy ribs and pulled pork,
and equally tasty sides.

**JACKSON: Walker's Drive In** $$
Southern/New American
*3016 N State St, 39216*
**Tel** *(601) 982-2633* **Closed** *Sun*
A sophisticated diner serving
regional favorites with a
modern touch. Try the
barbecued oysters with brie,
redfish with charred tomato
butter, and braised pork shank.
There's an extensive wine list.

**NATCHEZ: Carriage House
Restaurant** $
Southern
*401 High St, 39120*
**Tel** *(601) 445-5151* **Closed** *Dinner;
Mon & Tue*
This charming carriage house on
the grounds of Stanton Hall
serves traditional and
contemporary Southern food,
such as fried chicken, tomato
aspic, and Longwood salad.

**DK Choice**

**OXFORD: Ajax Diner** $
Southern
*118 Courthouse Sq, 38655*
**Tel** *(662) 232-8880* **Closed** *Sun*
Ajax Diner offers down-home
food in a prime location with
an eclectic decor. A menu of
creative spins on local favorites
such as chicken and dumplings,
casseroles, hot tamale pie, and
meatloaf can be enjoyed by
diners at booth and bar seating.
For dessert, be sure to save
room for the warm pies and
cobblers à la mode.

**OXFORD: City Grocery** $$
Southern
*152 Courthouse Sq, 38655*
**Tel** *(662) 232-8080* **Closed** *Sun*
Eclectic regional cuisine is served
in a picturesque location with an
old Southern feel. Shrimp and
grits is the star dish, but there is
also a choice of innovative salads,
seafood, sandwiches, and meats.

**VICKSBURG: Café Anchuca** $
American
*1010 1st E St, 39183*
**Tel** *(601) 661-0111*
Located in an antebellum house,
Café Anchuca offers a small lunch
menu of soups and sandwiches
and a dinner menu of Southern
favorites and home-made
desserts. Popular Sunday brunch.

# Alabama

**BIRMINGHAM: Bob Sykes
Bar-B-Q** $
Barbecue
*1724 9th Ave N, 35020*
**Tel** *(205) 426-1400* **Closed** *Sun*
This family-run landmark has been
serving since 1957. Try the
succulent pork and chicken, slow-
roasted over hickory wood. Also
on the menu are ribs, sandwiches,
baked beans, and dessert pies.

**BIRMINGHAM: Café Dupont** $$
New American
*113 20th St N, 35203*
**Tel** *(205) 322-1282* **Closed** *Sun & Mon*
A classy restaurant serving dishes
made with local ingredients. The
menu has steaks, seafood such as
oysters and okra with cayenne
butter sauce, and beignets.

**DK Choice**

**BIRMINGHAM: Highlands
Bar & Grill** $$$
Southern
*2011 11th Ave S, 35205*
**Tel** *(205) 939-1400* **Closed** *Sun &
Mon*
This internationally acclaimed
eatery serves French-inspired
Southern fare. Upscale and
elegant, with refined service,
the main dining room is perfect
for special occasions, while the
more casual bar area is a friendly
spot to relax or enjoy a small
meal. The dishes are made with
seasonal ingredients.

**BIRMINGHAM: Hot and Hot
Fish Club** $$$
Seafood
*2180 11th Court S, 35205*
**Tel** *(205) 933-5474* **Closed** *Sun & Mon*
Helmed by a James Beard-
nominated chef, there's a daily-
changing and seasonal menu
here plus delicious cocktails. The
dining room is airy, while the
chef's counter offers a great view
of the open kitchen.

**HUNTSVILLE: Little Paul's
Gibson Barbecue** $
Barbecue
*815 Madison St SE, 35801*
**Tel** *(256) 536-7227* **Closed** *Sun*
Savor large portions of hickory-
smoked pork, ribs, chicken, and
beef as well as their famous fried
catfish and home-made pie at this
popular family-owned restaurant. .

**MOBILE: Wintzell's** $
Seafood
*605 Dauphin St, 36602*
**Tel** *(251) 432-4605*
A Gulf Coast destination since
1938, Wintzell's offers fried,
boiled, and grilled seafood, and
Southern favorites; try the fried
green tomatoes and gumbo.
Oysters are served cold and fresh.

**MONTGOMERY: Chris's Famous
Hot Dogs** $
Diner
*138 Dexter Ave, 36104*
**Tel** *(334) 265-6850* **Closed** *Sun*
This family-run diner has been in
business since 1917. Their famous
hot dogs come with mustard,
onions, sauerkraut, and a chili
sauce. Soups, burgers, chicken
fingers, and pie are also available.

**TUSCALOOSA: Dreamland** $
Barbecue
*5535 15th Ave E, 35405*
**Tel** *(205) 758-8135*
A small, well-worn, and friendly
family-owned joint serving slabs
of ribs with white bread to soak
up the sauce. The freshly made
banana pudding is unbeatable.

Wintzell's, a famous seafood bar in Mobile

**For more information on types of restaurants** *see pages 28–9*

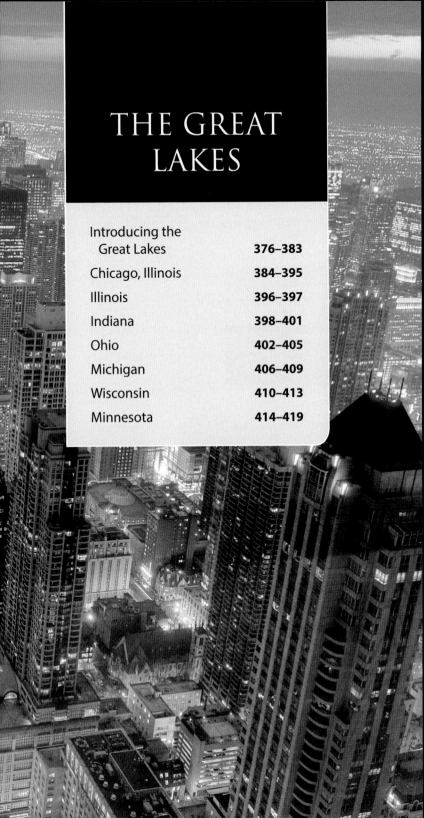

# THE GREAT LAKES

# The Great Lakes at a Glance

Spreading between the Colonial-era landscapes of the East Coast and the wide-open spaces of the Wild West, this region stakes a strong claim to being the most "American" part of the US. Home to more than one in five Americans, the Great Lakes is energetic and surprisingly varied. With its bustling big cities and sleepy small towns, idyllic rural scenes and sublime waterfront parks, industrial might and broad swaths of pristine natural beauty, the attractions here are as varied as the six states of Illinois, Ohio, Michigan, Indiana, Wisconsin, and Minnesota that form the center of America's heartland.

0 km    100
0 miles    100

**Voyageurs National Park** *(see p419)* in Minnesota covers endless stretches of watery wilderness near the Canadian border. The park, with its lakes and islands, is a prime outdoor destination.

Crookston

Grand Rapids

Duluth

**MINNESOTA**
*(See pp414–19)*

St. Cloud

Willmar

Minneapolis-
St. Paul

Eau Claire

Rochester

La Crosse

**WISCO**
*(See pp4*

Madiso

Rock

**Wisconsin's** natural wonders attract hikers, bikers, and campers' who explore the state's glacial moraines, lakes, and valleys through well-marked trails.

Daver

Peoria

**ILLIN**
*(See pp3*

Springfield

**Springfield** *(see p397)* is the capital of Illinois, a state characterized by vast expanses of rich, flat farmland. Abraham Lincoln, who lived here for 31 years (1830–61), delivered his famous "House Divided" speech in 1858 at the Old State Capitol.

M
Ve

◀ The Chicago skyline at night, viewed from the John Hancock Building

**Chicago** *(see pp384–95)*, the region's largest city, is located on the southwestern edge of Lake Michigan. One of the world's most celebrated centers of architectural innovation, the city has attracted many of North America's most influential architects. The most significant of these was Frank Lloyd Wright.

**Locator Map**

**Detroit** *(see pp406–407)*, still known as the Motor City, is also Michigan's main city and commercial center. Downtown's Hart Plaza, at the riverfront, is the site of the city's lively summer festivals.

**Ohio** is a curious combination of a rural and heavily industrial state. It also contains some of the earliest examples of Native American cultures, such as the symbolic earthen Serpent Mound.

**Indianapolis** *(see p400–401)* Monument Circle is the dominant feature of downtown. The city's many excellent museums add to its status as Indiana's state capital.

*For hotels and restaurants see pp422–7*

# THE GREAT LAKES

Surrounding the world's largest bodies of fresh water, the Great Lakes region is a land of epic proportions. From the towering skyscrapers of Chicago, Illinois, and the factories of Detroit, Michigan, to the seemingly endless plains of Indiana, the bountiful pastures of Wisconsin, and Minnesota's watery wilderness, this is one of the most exciting destinations in the country.

Spreading west from the original American colonies to beyond the Mississippi River, the Great Lakes region formed the first frontier of the early United States. The lakes themselves – Ontario, Erie, Huron, Michigan, and Superior – were a conduit for trade and exploration, and a key to the region's development. Plentiful harvests from the fertile soils, lumber from the forests, and ore from the region's mines all came together to support the growth of such cities as Chicago, Cleveland, Detroit, and Minneapolis. From the mid-19th century on, immigrants from all over the country and around the world came here to work on farms and in factories, thus establishing the diverse cultures and traditions that still flavor Great Lakes life. While industry and agriculture have given way to the service economy, the region's history and heritage have now become important tourist attractions, enhancing the natural beauty of its many lakes, rivers, and forests.

## History

Long before the United States was founded, the region surrounding the Great Lakes was home to some of the most developed and powerful Native American cultures. Evidence of one of the most significant archaeological remnants in North America can be found in southern Ohio and Illinois, where the enigmatic mound-builder culture constructed the largest cities north of Mexico. Of these, the most impressive is at Cahokia. Farther north, spanning the international border between the US and Canada – which runs right through the center of the Great

A 1920s photograph showing parked automobiles at Detroit's Cadillac Square

◄ A church on Mackinac Island at sunset with harbor lighthouses in the background

Lakes – Native Americans were grouped together into many distinct though related tribes. The Huron and Ojibwe in the north, and the Fox, Shawnee, and Menominee in the south and west had developed intricate trade and cultural relationships. However, after some 100 years of European contact, large Native populations had been decimated through disease and internecine warfare.

Replica of Christopher Columbus's ship *Santa Maria* in Columbus, Ohio

Initially, early European exploration of this part of the New World was dominated by the French. Traveling from their colony at Quebec, the first French explorers were rapidly followed by fur-trading "voyageurs" who bartered tools and weapons for beaver pelts. At the same time, French Jesuit missionaries began to establish commercial, military, and religious outposts at Sault Sainte Marie in 1668 and at Detroit in 1701. Until the mid-1700s, religion and the fur trade remained the main points of contact between Indians and Europeans.

The pace of settlement accelerated after the end of the Seven Years' War in Europe in 1763, and the Americans and British acquired territorial control of the region. Within a few decades Ohio, Indiana, and Illinois had changed from isolated frontier territories to states. Following the completion of the Erie Canal in 1825, and improved transportation on the lakes, settlers were able to reach the previously distant lands of Michigan and Wisconsin. In 1858, Minnesota became the last of the Great Lakes states to join the nation.

## Immigrants & Industry

The opening up of the Great Lakes region to settlement coincided with a major influx of immigrants. From the 1840s on, immigration increased tenfold as more than 200,000 people, mostly Irish and Germans fleeing the potato famine and political unrest respectively, came to America every year. Many settled in ethnic enclaves in rapidly growing cities such as Chicago, Detroit, Cincinnati, and

### KEY DATES IN HISTORY

**1620** Etienne Brule is the first European to explore present-day Michigan and Wisconsin

**1673** Jesuit missionary Jacques Marquette and explorer Louis Jolliet cross the northern Great Lakes and descend the Mississippi River

**1750** The population of Detroit, the only large Great Lakes settlement, numbers 600

**1763** France surrenders its Great Lakes territorial claims to Great Britain

**1783** The US acquires the region from Britain, and forms the Northwest Territory

**1803** Ohio is the first to become a state in the Great Lakes area

**1903** Henry Ford establishes the Ford Motor Company in Detroit

**1911** First Indy 500 auto race held in Indianapolis

**1968** Chicago police attack anti-Vietnam War protestors at the Democratic National Convention

**1998** Ohio native John Glenn, at age 77, becomes the oldest American to travel into space

**2000** Former WWF champion Jesse "The Body" Ventura is elected Governor of Minnesota

**2009** Chicago resident Barack Obama becomes the first African-American US president

Historical Museum, on the Mississippi, Winona, MN

Cleveland, where some three-quarters of residents were either foreign-born or first-generation Americans.

Large numbers of other immigrants set up wheat and dairy farms on recently cleared forests, or found work in other resource-based industries. Copper mining in Michigan's Upper Peninsula, for example, produced more than 75 percent of the nation's supplies between 1850 and 1900. With a total value of nearly $10 billion, this mining boom was ten times more lucrative than the legendary California Gold Rush of 1849. Another major industry was food processing. Meat-packing, which was concentrated on the huge stockyards of Chicago and Minneapolis, relied on the railroads to transport millions of cattle and pigs from across the Midwest. The Great Lakes also came to dominate grain processing, and some of the nation's largest companies, including the world-famous Kellogg's and General Mills, are still based here.

The early 20th century witnessed the largest and most enduring industrial boom, mainly because of the mutually dependent growth of the steel and automobile industries, both largely based in the Great Lakes region. Dearborn and Detroit, headquarters of Ford Motor Company as well as other smaller companies that evolved into the giant General Motors, emerged as the "Motor City." Despite competition from other countries, the Great Lakes automobile industry flourished and in turn supported a network of other industries, such as the iron mines in Minnesota, steel mills in Indiana, and rubber plants in Ohio.

## Politics & Culture

The success of the industries may have reaped huge fortunes for their owners, but the workers' conditions were often dire. This exploitation led to a number of violent battles, particularly around Chicago, such as the riots in Haymarket Square in 1886 and the bitter strike against the Pullman Palace Car company in 1894. The growth of unions gave workers some semblance of political power, which in turn supported a number of Left-leaning social movements. The Great Lakes in general, and Minnesota and Wisconsin in particular, were early strongholds of the Populist and Progressive movements, which in the early 1900s proposed such now-accepted innovations as the 8-hour workday and graduated rates of income tax. Unions continue to be very active in the region.

This social awareness also influenced art and literature. Diego Rivera's massive mural on the walls of the Detroit Institute of Art depicts workers struggling under the demands of industrialization. The region's great literary works include Hamlin Garland's depictions of life on the Wisconsin frontier, Sherwood Anderson's *Winesburg, Ohio*, the vivid exposés of Sinclair Lewis, and the stories of St. Paul native F. Scott Fitzgerald.

A view of Detroit's gleaming skyscrapers, including the Renaissance Center, from across the Detroit River

# Exploring the Great Lakes

Encompassing large cities as well as vast stretches of farmland and places of natural beauty, the Great Lakes covers a broad area that is best explored by car. While the major towns and cities are linked by both Interstate highways and Amtrak trains, public transportation is otherwise limited, but there is a seasonal ferry service across Lake Michigan. Chicago is the region's largest and most cosmopolitan city; other cities include Indianapolis, Detroit, Cleveland, Cincinnati, Milwaukee, and Minnesota's Twin Cities of Minneapolis & St. Paul.

Visitors near Old Mission Lighthouse, Lake Michigan Shore, Michigan

## Sights at a Glance

**For keys to symbols** see back flap

**Key**

- Highway
- Major road
- Railroad
- State border
- International border

**Mileage Chart**

10 = Distance in miles
10 = Distance in kilometres

| | | | | | | |
|---|---|---|---|---|---|---|
| **Chicago, IL** | | | | | | |
| **181** | | | | | | |
| 291 | **Indianapolis, IN** | | | | | |
| **297** | **113** | | | | | |
| 478 | 182 | **Cincinnati, OH** | | | | |
| **342** | **317** | **243** | | | | |
| 550 | 510 | 391 | **Cleveland, OH** | | | |
| **283** | **317** | **256** | **168** | | | |
| 455 | 510 | 412 | 270 | **Detroit, MI** | | |
| **93** | **278** | **395** | **435** | **375** | | |
| 150 | 447 | 636 | 700 | 604 | **Milwaukee, WI** | |
| **409** | **595** | **707** | **751** | **695** | **336** | |
| 658 | 958 | 1138 | 1207 | 1118 | 541 | **Minneapolis, MN** |

# ❶ Chicago

Chicago, a city of almost 3 million people, covers 237 sq miles (614 sq km) of the US's Midwest. Situated at the southwest edge of the vast Lake Michigan, the city claims 26 miles (42 km) of lakefront. Despite burning to the ground in 1871 and witnessing terrible social unrest, the city was soon rebuilt and emerged as the financial capital of the Midwest. Today, this third-largest city in the US is world-famous for its innovative architecture, its vibrant cultural and educational institutions, and for its colorful and turbulent political history. It is also home to US President Barack Obama.

## Sights at a Glance

① Chicago History Museum
② Newberry Library
③ Magnificent Mile
④ John Hancock Center
⑤ Navy Pier
⑥ Chicago Children's Museum
⑦ Millennium Park
⑧ Art Institute of Chicago
⑨ Willis Tower
⑩ *The Loop pp388–9*
⑪ South Loop
⑫ Museum Campus

### South Side
*(see inset map)*

⑬ Museum of Science & Industry
⑭ University of Chicago
⑮ DuSable Museum of African American History

### Greater Chicago
*(see inset map)*

⑯ Lincoln Park Zoo
⑰ *Oak Park pp394–5*

## Getting Around

Although Chicago is a sprawling Midwestern metropolis, many of the city's sights and main cultural centers are located downtown, making the city a walker's dream. The city's public transportation is inexpensive and efficient. The train system, known as the "L" for "elevated," is the easiest way to get around. Buses crisscross the city and bus drivers are helpful. Free trolleys go to popular sites during summer. Taxis are affordable, convenient, and readily available.

### Key

- Sight/Place of interest
- Railroad line
- Expressway

**Greater Chicago**
Area of main maps

O'Hare
International
Airport

DOWNTOWN

Lake
Michigan

Lombard

SOUTHSIDE

0 km      5

0 miles      5

**Key**

Area of main map

Highway

Major road

Other road

0 meters      800

0 yards      800

OLN
RK

LASALLE DRIVE

NORTH BLVD

NORTH STATE PARKWAY

sion

VISION ST

**GOLD COAST**

EAST ELM ST

EAST CEDAR ST

EAST BELLEVUE PL

EAST OAK ST

*Drake Hotel*

NORTH

ST

RUSH ST

EAST DELAWARE PL

ON ST

④

EAST PEARSON ST

M  E  **CHICAGO AVE**

**STREETERVILLE**

EAST HURON STREET

③  ERIE  STREET

FAIRBANKS

EAST ONTARIO STREET

M

EAST OHIO STREET

rand

EAST GRAND AVE

N MICHIGAN AVE

N DEWITT PL

N LAKE SHORE DRIVE

N MCCLURG COURT

MILTON
LEE OLIVER
PARK

STREETER DRIVE

⑥ ⑤

*Tribune
Tower*

*Wrigley
Building*

*Chicago*

EAST NORTH WATER ST

*River*

EAST  WACKER  DRIVE

DRIVE

M State

EAST RANDOLPH ST

ke

Randolph

**Millennium
Station**

M  Madison

M  S WABASH

DALEY
BICENTENNIAL
PLAZA

⑦

EAST MONROE DRIVE

⑩  M  Adams

⑧

*GRANT
PARK*

E JACKSON DR

*Chicago
Harbor*

E VAN BUREN ST

**Van Buren
Street Station**

*Lake
Michigan*

y

/AY

M  Harrison

EAST BALBO AVE

S COLUMBUS DRIVE

E BALBO DR

*GRANT*

SOUTH STATE ST

*Hilton
Chicago*

*PARK*

COLUMBUS DRIVE

M  Roosevelt

D

**Museum Campus/
11th Street Station**

⑫

*John G. Shedd
Aquarium*

*Adler
Planetarium*

*Field
Museum*

EAST SOLIDARITY DRIVE

OLD LAKE SHORE DRIVE

SOUTH LAKE SHORE DRIVE

MCFETRIDGE DRIVE

*NORTHERLY
ISLAND
PARK*

*Burnham
Park Harbor*

*Northerly
Island*

E WALDRON DR

The marquee and sign of the opulent
Chicago Theater

**For keys to symbols** *see back flap*

D          E          F

Original Neo-Georgian entrance to the Chicago History Museum

## ① Chicago History Museum

**Map** D1. 1601 N Clark St. **Tel** (312) 642-4600. Ⓜ Clark/Division, then bus 22, 36. 🚌 11, 151, 156. **Open** 9:30am–4:30pm Mon–Sat, noon–5pm Sun. **Closed** Jan 1, Thanksg., Dec 25. 📷 ♿ 🅿 (call for times). 🅿 Concerts, lectures, films. 🅦 chicagohistory.org

The city's oldest cultural institution, the 1856 Chicago Historical Society is a major museum and research center, with a library open for public research. It traces the history of Chicago and Illinois, from its first explorers through the development of the city to the major events in modern-day Chicago. Miniature dioramas depict great events such as the Great Fire of 1871, the Chicago River during the Civil War, and the bustling LaSalle Street in the mid-1860s.

The American Wing holds one of only 23 copies of the Declaration of Independence, and a 1789 copy of the American Constitution, first printed in a Philadelphia newspaper. The building has two faces – the original 1932 Neo-Georgian structure, and a 1988 addition with a three-story, glass-and-steel atrium entrance.

## ② Newberry Library

**Map** D2. 60 W Walton St. **Tel** (312) 943-9090. Ⓜ Chicago or Clark/Division stops (red line). **Open** hours for lobby, book rooms, & exhibits vary. Call ahead. **Closed** public hols. ♿ 📷 3pm Thu; 10:30am Sat. 🖼 Exhibits, lectures, concerts. 🅦 newberry.org

Founded in 1887 by banker Walter Newberry, this independent research library for the humanities was designed by Henry Ives Cobb, master architect of the Richardsonian Romanesque style.

The collection spans cartography, Native American history, Renaissance studies, the history of printing, genealogy, and such rarities as first editions of Milton's *Paradise Regained* and a 1481 edition of Dante's *Divine Comedy*.

## ③ Magnificent Mile

Michigan Ave, between E Walton Pl & E Kinzie St.

The Magnificent Mile, a stretch of Michigan Avenue north of the Chicago River, is the city's most fashionable street. Almost completely destroyed in the 1871 fire, the street grew into Chicago's premier shopping district after the opening of the Michigan Avenue Bridge in 1920. Exclusive shops line the wide boulevard, while modern retail outlets and skyscrapers rub shoulders with historic buildings.

To the north lies the Gothic Revival-style **Fourth Presbyterian Church**. Its exposed buttresses, stone spire, and recessed main window reflect the influences of medieval European churches.

To its right are two historic castellated structures, the **Water Tower** and the **Pumping Station**, among the few buildings that survived the 1871 fire. The tower, originally housing a standpipe, is now home to a photography gallery and a theater. The station still fulfills its original purpose of

Open-air skywalk topping the John Hancock Center

## Architecture in Chicago

Chicago is world famous as a center of architectural innovation, a city where architects have pushed the boundaries of creativity. This reputation had its beginnings in the tragic fire of 1871. Working on a blank slate, architects rose to the challenge of reshaping a devastated city. It was in Chicago that the world's first skyscraper was built, and here that Frank Lloyd Wright developed his Prairie School of architecture.

**Gothic Revival** style, represented by the Water Tower, drew from medieval European architecture.

**Italianate design** style was inspired by Renaissance palaces and villas of northern Italy. The elegant Drake Hotel exemplifies this style.

**Richardsonian Romanesque** style – typified by rough-cut stone, round arches, and recessed windows – can be seen in the Newberry Library.

umping water and houses a
sitor Information Center (163
Pearson St) and café. Across
the street, **Water Town Place**
contains eight floors of upscale
boutiques and restaurants.
Other "vertical shopping malls"
on the street include The Shops
at North Bridge.

Slightly south, the Gothic-
style **Tribune Tower**, office of
the *Chicago Tribune*, holds rock
fragments from world-famous
sites, such as St. Peter's Basilica
in Rome, the Forbidden City in
Beijing, and even a 3.3-billion-
year-old piece of moon rock
embedded in its exterior walls.

At the southernmost end of
the street is the beloved two-
part **Wrigley Building**. This
white terra-cotta structure
features a giant four-sided clock
and a quiet courtyard, which is
open to the public.

Chicago visitor centers
(www.explorechicago.org) offer
details about walking and bus
tours of the city.

## ④ John Hancock Center

**Map** D2. 875 N Michigan Ave.
360 Chicago: **Tel** (888) 875-8439.
Ⓜ Chicago (red line). 🚌 145, 146,
147, 151. **Open** 9am–11pm daily. 🏛
To observatory (children under 3 free).
♿ 🖊 🅿 Ⓦ jhochicago.com

Affectionately called "Big John"
by Chicagoans, the 100-story,
cross-braced steel John
Hancock Center stands out in
the Chicago skyline. The tapering
obelisk tower's major attraction

is 360 Chicago (formerly the
Hancock Observatory) on
the 94th floor. Here, 1,127 ft
(344 m) above the Magnificent
Mile, an open-air (screened)
skywalk offers spectacular views
of the city. The elevator ride to
the top at 20 mph (32 km/h) is
one of the fastest in the US.

Designed by architect Bruce
Graham of Skidmore Owings
and Merrill and engineer Fazlur
R. Khan, the center houses
offices, condominiums, and
shops in 2.8 million sq ft
(0.26 million sq m) of space.

## ⑤ Navy Pier

**Map** D2. 600 E Grand Ave. **Tel** (800)
595-7437. 🚌 29, 56, 65, 66, 120, 121,
124. **Open** 10am; closing times vary
by day & season. **Closed** Thanksgiving,
Dec 25. ♿ 🖊 🖥 🅿 ℹ Lake
cruises: Ⓦ navypier.com

Navy Pier is a bustling
recreational and cultural center.
Designed by Charles S. Frost, the
3,000-ft- (915-m-) long and
400-ft- (120-m-) wide pier was

**The giant Ferris wheel, Navy Pier Park**

the largest in the world
when built in 1916. Over
20,000 timber piles were used
in its construction.

Originally a municipal wharf,
the pier was used for naval
training during World War II.
After a four-year renovation,
Navy Pier opened in its
present incarnation in 1995.
Navy Pier Park has a 150-ft
(45-m) Ferris wheel, an old-
fashioned carousel, an outdoor
amphitheater, ice skating, and an
IMAX® 3D theater. The Smith
Museum features Victorian to
contemporary stained glass.

## ⑥ Chicago Children's Museum

**Map** E3. 700 E Grand Ave. **Tel** (312)
527-1000. 🚌 29, 56, 65, 66, 120, 121,
124. **Open** 10am–5pm daily (until
8pm Thu). **Closed** Thanksg., Dec 25.
🏛 (free first Mon of month). ♿ 📷
🅿 Special activities daily:
Ⓦ chicagochildrensmuseum.org

Chicago Children's Museum,
focusing on activating the
intellectual and creative
potential of children ages 1 to
12, is an activity center for the
whole family and has many
hands-on and interactive
exhibits. The Dinosaur
Expedition is where children
can dig for bones in an
excavation pit, or simply slide,
climb, and jump around.
Children can also climb
on a ship, hide in a
treehouse, and make
art to take home.

**Queen Anne** style, once
popular design for
Chicago residences, is
exemplified by row
houses in Crilly Court.

**Chicago School**,
developed here, led to an
engineering and aesthetic
revolution with
commercial skyscrapers
like the Reliance building.

**Neo-Classical** style
has classical Greco-
Roman elements, as
seen in the Chicago
Cultural Center.

**International Style**
stresses severe geometry
and large expanses of
glass. Willis Tower is a
fine example.

**Post-Modern** architecture, an
eclectic style without strict
rules, is seen in the Harold
Washington Library Center.

### ⑦ Millennium Park

**Map** D4. 55 N Michigan Ave. **Tel** (312) 742-1168. Ⓜ Madison. **Open** 6am–11pm daily. ☑ free tours at 11:30am & 1pm daily. 🐾 ✏ 🖥 Ⓦ millenniumpark.org

The award-winning center for art, music, architecture, and landscape design opened in 2004 on 24.5 acres (10 ha) of former railroad property. The park is bordered by Michigan Avenue, Columbus Drive, and Randolph and Monroe Streets. The nearby Welcome Center, at 201 East Randolph Street, is a good place to find out about what the park has to offer.

Unusual design elements within the park include Frank Gehry's spectacular Jay Pritzker Pavilion, with its roof of massive, curling, stainless-steel ribbons, that looms 120 ft (37 m) high. This outdoor concert venue hosts the Grant Park Music Festival series of concerts each summer, as well as other free concerts and events. Another Gehry-designed ribbon of the same material forms a 925-ft- (282-m-) long-, winding bridge that connects the park to Daley Bicentennial Plaza.

The Neo-Classical façade of the Art Institute of Chicago

Video images of the faces of 1,000 local residents rotate over the two 50-ft- (15-m-) tall towers of glass blocks which make up the interactive Crown Fountain designed by Spanish artist Jaume Plensa. Water pours out of the towers from spring to fall, landing in a shallow reflecting pool that is popular with local families.

Other unique features within the park are the contemporary 5-acre (2-ha) Lurie Garden with its dramatically lit hedges and perennial garden, and British artist Anish Kapoor's Cloud Gate sculpture, which resembles a giant drop of mercury and allows visitors to view themselves as a part of the Chicago skyline.

### ⑧ The Art Institute of Chicago

**Map** D4. 111 S Michigan Ave. **Tel** (31 443-3600. Ⓜ Adams. 🚌 1, 3, 6, 7, 126, 145, 147, 151. 🚇 Van Buren St. **Open** 10:30am–5pm daily (to 8pm Thu). **Closed** Jan 1, Thanksg., Dec 25 ☑ (under 14s free; separate adm to some exhibits). 🐾 ✏ ✎ 📷 Ⓟ Exhibits, lectures, films. Ⓦ artic.edu

The extensive collections at the Art Institute of Chicago represent nearly 5,000 years of creativity through paintings, sculptures, textiles, photograph cultural objects, and decorative artifacts. Founded by civic leaders and art patrons in 1879 as the Chicago Academy of Fine Arts, the museum became the Art Institute of

### ⑩ The Loop

The Loop gets its name from the elevated track system that circles the center of downtown. Screeching trains and a steady stream of people add to its bustle. In the canyon vistas, through the historic buildings and modern edifices, you can catch glimpses of the bridges spanning the Chicago River. The renovation of warehouses and historic theaters is helping to enliven the Loop at night.

**Marquette Building**, an early skyscraper (1895), was designed by William Holabird and Martin Roche, central Chicago School figures and architects of more than 80 buildings in the Loop.

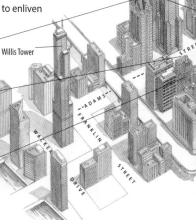

Willis Tower

**190 South LaSalle Street** (1987), designed by Philip Johnson, has a white-marble lobby with a gold-leafed, vaulted ceiling.

**The Rookery**, designed by Burnham and Root in 1888, typifies the Richardsonian Romanesque style.

**Chicago Board of Trade** occupies a 45-story Art Deco building, a statue of Ceres atop its roof. The frenetic action inside can be observed from a viewers' gallery.

*For hotels and restaurants see pp422–7*

## ⑨ Willis Tower

**Map** C4. 233 S Wacker Dr.
Observatory: **Tel** (312) 875-9696.
Ⓜ Quincy. 🚌 7, 126. **Open** Apr–Sep:
9am–10pm daily; Oct–Mar: 10am–
8pm daily; last adm 30 min before
closing. 🎟 (children under 3 free).
♿🖊🏛🅿🖥 **theskydeck.com**

At a height of 1,450 ft (442 m),
Willis Tower (formerly known as
the Sears Tower) is one of the
world's tallest buildings.
Boasting the highest occupied
floor and the highest height to
the rooftop, it was designed by
Bruce Graham, of Skidmore
Owings and Merrill, and
engineer Fazlur Khan. Over 110
concrete caissons, anchored in
bedrock, support the tower's
222,500 tons.

Today, the tower contains
3.5 million sq ft (0.3 million sq m)
of office space, more than 100
elevators, and almost enough
telephone cable to circle the
earth twice. The elevator to the
glass-enclosed 103rd-floor
Skydeck travels at 1,600 ft
(490 m) per minute, and offers
stunning views. Nearby, the
12-story **Rookery** building, the
world's tallest when it opened
in 1888, is one of the city's

View of the Willis Tower and Skydeck,
looking northeast

most-photographed edifices. Its
dark red-brick façade with terra-
cotta trim gives way to a two-
tiered court, remodeled in 1907
by Frank Lloyd Wright, who was
nearing the peak of his fame. He
covered the iron columns and
staircases with white marble,
inlaid with gold leaf.

### 🏛 The Rookery

209 S LaSalle St. 📷 for tours,
call Chicago Architectural
Foundation, (312) 922-3432.
**Closed** public hols. ♿

*[left column, partial]*

hicago in 1882. Outgrowing
wo homes as wealthy
atrons donated their art
ollections, it finally settled
 this Neo-Classical structure.
he addition of the Modern
ing has made this the
cond-largest museum in the
nited States.

The museum's holdings
an from 3rd-millennium-BC
gyptian and Chinese artifacts
 modern and contemporary
merican and European art.
hough best known for its
orld-famous Impressionist
nd Post-Impressionist
ollection, with such master-
eces as Paul Cézanne's *The
asket of Apples* (c.1895), Henri
e Toulouse-Lautrec's
 *the Moulin Rouge* (1895),
nd Claude Monet's six
ersions of a wheat field, the
useum represents almost
very major artistic movement
 the 19th and 20th centuries.
articularly strong are examples
f Cubism, Surrealism, and
erman Expressionism.

The 35,000-strong exquisite
sian collection is also
oteworthy for its Japanese
oodblock prints, and Indian
nd Chinese historic artifacts.

**The "Elevated"** train tracks that opened in 1892 total 224 miles (360 km) and extend as far as O'Hare and Midway airports.

**Locator Map**

**Auditorium Building**, an 1889 multipurpose skyscraper, features one of Adler and Sullivan's best interiors in its seventh-floor, birch-paneled recital hall.

**Fine Arts Building**, designed by Solon S. Beman in 1885, was originally a wagon carriage showroom. It once also housed Frank Lloyd Wright's studio.

**Monadnock Building's** north half is one of the tallest buildings constructed entirely of masonry.

**Santa Fe Center**, a classic Chicago School building, with an elegant two-story atrium, houses the Chicago Architecture Foundation.

**Federal Center** is a three-building office complex designed around a central plaza by Ludwig Mies van der Rohe.

**Key**

— Suggested route

Rowe Building, Printing House Row District

## ⑪ South Loop

**Map** D4. Ⓜ Harrison, Roosevelt.
🚌 via State St & Dearborn St buses
(near South Side: Michigan Ave bus 3).

Located a short walk south of the downtown core, the South Loop has changed dramatically, from a run-down industrial district to a residential and retail neighborhood. The South Loop developed as an industrial area in the late 1800s, but after World War II manufacturers left and the area declined. In the 1970s, with the conversion of the district's derelict warehouses to fashionable lofts, businesses sprang up as Chicagoans took advantage of the area's proximity to downtown.

This transformation is most evident in the two blocks of the **Printing House Row Historic District**, which in the 1890s had earned Chicago the title of the printing capital of the US. By the 1970s, with the closing of the nearby Dearborn Station, manufacturers withdrew and the area fell into decline. Many of the massive buildings erected for the printing trade remain today. Their conversion into stylish condominiums and office lofts has led to the revitalization of the neighborhood and an influx of commercial activity. The Second

Franklin Building has ornamental tilework illustrating the history of printing over its entranceway, while the Rowe Building houses Sandmeyer's bookstore, specializing in local authors and travel literature. The nearby Richardsonian Romanesque-style **Dearborn Station Galleria**, Chicago's oldest surviving passenger train station building, has also been converted into a shopping mall. Its square clock tower is a landmark. Dominating the South Loop, at State and Congress, is the world's largest public library building, the **Chicago Public Library, Harold Washington Library Center**, holding close to 9 million books and periodicals on its 70 miles (113 km) of shelving. This Post-Modern giant pays tribute to many of Chicago's historic buildings, through its varied architectural features. Artwork is displayed throughout the building, including work by Cheyenne artist Heap of Birds. The library also showcases exhibits relating to Chicago's history.

To the southeast, the **Museum of Contemporary Photography** focuses on American photography produced since 1936, with selections from its 9,000-strong collection and temporary exhibitions. On the same block, the **Spertus Museum** is Chicago's Jewish Museum. It is part of the Spertus Institute of Jewish Studies, which moved into a new facility in 2007. The museum invites visitors to learn about the Jewish experience through a series of thought-provoking exhibitions

and programs on Jewish history, religion, art, and culture over the centuries and today. Often these exhibitions draw from Spertus's own world-class collection of art and artifacts, including ritual objects, textiles and jewelry.

A computer lists the names of people lost in the Holocaust by Chicago families – it takes a full day to read the list – and an exhibition is geared to teaching young people about it.

The Asher Library, on the fifth floor, is one of the largest public Jewish libraries in North America, with over 110,000 books and 1,000 Jewish films on video and DVD. An interactive Children's Center promotes literacy and storytelling.

A short walk east leads to Grant Park's **Buckingham Fountain** and **South Michigan Avenue**, which is an excellent place to admire the varied architectural styles for which the city is famous. Farther along the street lies the opulent Hilton Chicago. Decorated in French Renaissance style, this 25-story hotel was the largest in the world when it opened in 1927. Buddy Guy's Legends presents big-name and local blues acts one block away, in an enlarged nightclub that also serves Cajun food. Owner and blues legend Buddy Guy is often there himself.

Judaic art showcased in the Spertus Museum

📷 **Chicago Public Library, Harold Washington Library Center**
400 S State St. **Tel** (312) 747-4300.
Ⓜ Library. **Open** 9am–9pm Mon–Thu, 9am–5pm Fri & Sat, 1–5pm Sun.
**Closed** public hols. 🚻 call (312) 747-4050. 🎫 📷 Exhibits, lectures, films. 🖥 **chipublib.org**

🏛 **Spertus Museum**
610 S Michigan Ave. **Tel** (312) 322-1700. Ⓜ Harrison. **Open** 10am–5pm Sun–Thu. **Closed** Sat, public & Jewish hols. 🚸 (children under 5 free; all get in free 10am–noon Wed, 2–6pm Thu). 🚻 🎫 📷 Concerts, lectures, films. 🖥 **spertus.edu**

# Museum Campus

p E5. S Lake Shore Dr. Ⓜ
osevelt, then free trolley. 🚌 12,
6. 🚆 Roosevelt, then free trolley.

e Museum Campus is a vast
.efront park connecting three
orld-famous natural science
useums. This 57-acre (23-ha)
tension of Burnham Park was
eated by the relocation of
ke Shore Drive in 1996.
Located in the southwest
rt of the lush green
mpus is the Daniel
rnham-designed
eo-Classical structure
ousing the **Field
useum**. This great
tural history museum
olds an encyclopedic
llection of zoological,
ological, and
hropological objects
om around the world.
ounded in 1894 (with
nding from Marshall
eld) to house objects from
e 1893 World's Columbian
xposition, the museum now
olds over 20 million objects.
Particular strengths of the
useum include such dinosaur
ssils as "Sue" – the most
omplete *Tyrannosaurus rex*
eleton ever found – Native
dian and Ancient Egyptian
tifacts, and extensive displays
n mammals and birds.
The permanent "Ancient
mericas" exhibit covers Ice Age
Aztec cultures. The Hall of
des displays more than
00 artifacts from Neolithic
mes to the Bronze Age and
hinese Dynasties. The
ghlight is a 300-lb (136-kg) jar
om the palace of Emperor
uanlong. The Underground
dventure is a subterranean
xhibit where visitors can walk,

*Xochpilli, Aztec God
of Flowers, Field
Museum*

through worm tunnels, meet
giant bugs, and feel reduced
to insect size.

A short walk northeast along
terraced gardens leads to the
**John G. Shedd Aquarium**,
housing more than 32,500
saltwater and freshwater
animals, representing 1,500
species of fish, birds, reptiles,
amphibians, invertebrates, and
mammals. Named for its
benefactor, a prominent
Chicago businessman, the
aquarium opened in
1930 in a Neo-Classical
building. The
remodeled Oceanarium
has a magnificent
curved wall of glass
facing Lake Michigan,
whose water flows into
its tank. This marine-
mammal pavilion
showcases beluga
whales and dolphins.
The aquarium's exhibits
can be viewed from many
viewpoints, some under water.

Farther east, the Museum
Campus houses the **Adler
Planetarium and Astronomy
Museum** featuring one of the
world's finest astronomical
collections, with artifacts dating
as far back as 12th-century
Persia. Antique astronomical
instruments include the world's
oldest known window sundial.
It also has the world's first
virtual-reality theater. Spectacular
sky shows complement displays
on navigation and space
exploration. State-of-the-art

Beluga whale at the Oceanarium in the
John G. Shedd Aquarium

technology enables visitors to
explore exhibits hands-on.
Funded by businessman Max
Adler, this 12-sided, Art Deco
structure was designed by
Ernest Grunsfeld in 1930 and is
now a historical landmark.

🏛 **Field Museum**
1400 S Lake Shore Dr. **Tel** (312) 922-
9410. **Open** 9am–5pm daily. **Closed**
Dec 25. 🅿 ♿ via east entrance. 📷
📷 🎥 🅿 Lectures, films, events:
🌐 fieldmuseum.org

🏛 **John G. Shedd Aquarium**
1200 S Lake Shore Dr. **Tel** (312) 939-
2438. **Open** Jul–Sep: 8:30am–6pm
daily; Oct–Jun: 9am–5pm Mon–Fri,
9am–6pm Sat & Sun. **Closed** Dec 25.
📷 ♿ 📷 🍴 📷 🎥 🅿 Lectures:
🌐 shedd.org

🏛 **Adler Planetarium &
Astronomy Museum**
1300 S Lake Shore Dr. **Tel** (312) 922-
7827. **Open** 10am–4pm daily (to
4:30pm Sat & Sun). **Closed**
Thanksgiving, Dec 25. 📷 separate
adm to theaters. ♿ 🍴 📷 🎥
🅿 Lectures, films, light shows.
🌐 adlerplanetarium.org

---

## Old Money

Chicago has a beautiful sound because Chicago
means money – so the late actress Ruth Gordon
reputedly said. By the beginning of the
20th century the city was home to 200
millionaires. One of the most prominent was dry-
goods merchant and real-estate mogul Potter
Palmer who, with his socialite wife Bertha Honoré,
had an enormous impact on the city's cultural and
economic life. In 1882, Palmer built an opulent
home at North Lake Shore Drive. Perhaps no feature of the mansion
epitomized the family's wealth as much as the doors: there were
no outside handles, as the doors were always opened from inside,
by servants. Department-store owner Marshall Field was less
ostentatious. Although he rode in a carriage to work, he stopped
short of his store to walk the last few blocks so people would not see
his mode of transport. Likewise, he asked the architect of his
$2-million, 25-room mansion not to include any frills.

*Potter Palmer*

e monumental Neo-Classical entrance to
eld Museum

View of the Museum of Science and Industry from across Columbia Basin

## ⑬ Museum of Science & Industry

**Map** B5. 57th St & S Lake Shore Dr. **Tel** (773) 684-1414, (800) 468-6674. Ⓜ Garfield, then eastbound bus 55. 🚌 1, 6, 10. 🚆 55th-56th-57th St, 59th St. **Open** 9:30am–4pm Mon–Sat. **Closed** Dec 25. 🅿 Films. 🆆 **msichicago.org**

The Museum of Science and Industry celebrates scientific and technological accomplishments, with an emphasis on achievements of the 20th and 21st centuries. With its collection of over 800 exhibits and 35,000 artifacts, the museum makes the exploration of science and technology an accessible experience.

Though best known for its exhibits on space exploration, biology, and transportation, this largest science museum in the Western Hemisphere has more than enough to keep visitors of all ages engaged for a full day.

The **Henry Crown Space Center** features the Apollo 8 Command Module, the first manned spacecraft to circle the moon, in 1968, a replica of NASA's Apollo Lunar Module Trainer, and a 6.5-oz (185-gm) piece of moon rock. A 20-minute movie simulates the experience of blasting off in a space shuttle, complete with shaking seats, allowing viewers to feel like astronauts, if only briefly.

The transportation section features outstanding examples of transport from train and plane to automobile. In **All Aboard the Silver Streak**, visitors can climb aboard a record-breaking 1930s train that revolutionized industrial design. **Take Flight** explores the inner workings of a 727 jetliner, cantilevered to the museum's balcony, and simulates a 7-minute San Francisco-to-Chicago flight.

Visitors can walk through a 16-ft- (5-m-) tall replica of the human heart, seeing it from the perspective of a blood cell, and calculate the number of times their heart has beaten since birth, or look inside the human body in a detailed exhibit on anatomy. **Genetics: Decoding Life** explores the ethical, biological and social issues of this field of research.

A few exhibits fall outside the museum's defined focus but prove to be enduring crowd-pleasers, such as a toy factory staffed by robots, and the five-story, wraparound Omnimax theater. Colleen Moore's Fairy Castle is an exquisite dollhouse with at lea 2,000 miniature furnishings.

## ⑭ University of Chicago

**Map** A5. Bounded by 56th & 59th St Ellis & Woodlawn Aves. Ⓜ Garfield (green line), then bus 55. 🚆 59th.

The University of Chicago was founded in 1890 with the endowment of John D. Rockefeller, on land donated b Marshall Field *(see p391)*. Today, this outstanding private university has one of the greatest number of Nobel laureates among faculty, alumn and researchers of any US university. It is particularly lauded in the fields of economics, chemistry, and physics. Henry Ives Cobb designed 18 of the university's limestone buildings and developed its cloistered quadrangle plan (along the lines of Cambridge and Oxford

### From Plaster to Stone

Originally built as the Palace of Fine Arts for the 1893 World's Fair, this structure later became the first home of the Field Museum of Natural History. Based on Classical Revival style, this plaster-clad building was designed by Charles B. Atwood. After the Field Museum moved out, the building sat in a state of disrepair until the mid-1920s, when Julius Rosenwald, chairman of Sears Roebuck and Co., campaigned to save it,

The original building during the 1893 World's Columbian Exposition

launching a million-dollar reconstruction program. Exterior plaster was replaced with 28,000 tons of limestone and marble in an 11-year renovation. The Museum of Science and Industry opened in 1933, in time for the Century of Progress World's Exposition.

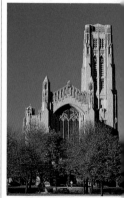
The Rockefeller Memorial Chapel, University of Chicago

Robie House, a masterpiece of the Prairie School of architecture

before the Boston firm Shepley Rutan and Coolidge took over as the main architects in 1901. Now the campus features designs from more than 70 architects.

The north entrance houses the ornamental Cobb Gate, a gargoyled ceremonial gateway donated by Henry Cobb in 1900. Across the street, the Regenstein Library holds rare book and manuscript collections, along with millions of other volumes.

Situated at the northern end of the campus is the light-filled, intimate **Smart Museum of Art**. Named after its benefactors, David and Alfred Smart, the museum holds more than 10,000 objects, including antiquities and Old Master prints, Asian paintings, calligraphy, and ceramics, spanning five centuries of Western and Eastern civilizations. The museum's café, with tall windows overlooking the tranquil sculpture garden, is a great spot for a quiet lunch. Outside the museum, sculptor Henry Moore's *Nuclear Energy* marks the spot where, in 1942, a team of scientists led by Enrico Fermi ushered in the atomic age with the first controlled nuclear reaction.

In the southeast of the vast campus lies the **Oriental Institute Museum**, the exhibition arm of the university's Oriental Institute, whose scholars have excavated in virtually every region of the Near East since 1919. Highlights of the museum's collections include a reconstruction of an Assyrian palace (c.721–705 BC) and a 17-ft (5-m) sculpture of King Tutankhamen, the tallest ancient Egyptian statue in the Western Hemisphere (c.1334–25 BC). Opposite the museum, the massive Gothic-style **Rockefeller Memorial Chapel**, topped with a 207-ft (63-m) carillon tower, is among the tallest buildings on campus. John D. Rockefeller had requested that this limestone-and-brick structure representing religion be the university's dominant feature. Two blocks north lies Frank Lloyd Wright's world-famous **Robie House** (1908–1910), currently being restored. Designed for Frederick Robie, a bicycle and motorbike manufacturer, the home is one of Wright's last Prairie School houses: Wright left both his family and his Oak Park practice during its three-year construction. The exterior design of the house perfectly captures the prairie landscape of flat, open fields. The roof's sweeping planes embody the house's aesthetic of bold rectilinear simplicity. Steel beams support the overhanging roof. Also bold but simple, the interior is

Statue of King Tutankhamen, Oriental Institute Museum

furnished with Wright-designed furniture. The house is an organic whole, underscored by the harmonious interplay between the exterior and interior.

🏛 **Smart Museum of Art**
5550 S Greenwood Ave. **Tel** (773) 702-0200. **Open** 10am–4pm Tue–Fri (until 8pm Thu), 11am–5pm Sat, Sun. **Closed** public hols. 🔲 🖥 🎦 Ⓦ smartmuseum.uchicago.edu

🏛 **Oriental Institute Museum**
1155 E 58th St. **Tel** (773) 702-9514. **Open** 10am–6pm Tue & Thu–Sat (until 8:30pm Wed), noon–6pm Sun. **Closed** public hols. 🔲 🎦 Special events. Ⓦ oi.uchicago.edu

🏠 **Robie House**
5757 S Woodlawn Ave. **Tel** (312) 994-4000. **Open** Thu–Mon. **Closed** Jan 1, Thanksgiving, Dec 25. 🎦 (children under 4 free). 🎦 11am–2pm (reservations advised). Ⓦ gowright.org; Ⓦ oi.uchicago.edu

## ⑮ DuSable Museum of African American History

**Map** A5. 740 E 56th Pl. **Tel** (773) 947-0600. Ⓜ Garfield (green line), then bus 55. 🚌 4, 10. **Open** 10am–5pm Tue–Sat, noon–5pm Sun. **Closed** public hols. 🎦 (children under 5 free; free on Sun). 🔲 🎦 book in advance. 🎦 Ⓟ Lectures, films. Ⓦ dusablemuseum.org

Founded in 1961 to preserve and interpret the diverse historical experiences and achievements of African Americans, the DuSable Museum highlights the accomplishments of the ordinary and extraordinary alike.

The 9-ft by 8-ft (2.7-m by 2.4-m) substantial wooden Freedom Now mural depicts the experiences of African-Americans throughout 400 years of US history. Other exhibits include memorabilia from the life and political career of Chicago's first black mayor, Harold Washington. The museum showcases local artwork, and traveling show topics have included black film history and African-Americans on postage stamps.

# Greater Chicago

Visitors eager to discover more of Chicago will not be disappointed by the rich mix of historical sights, recreational activities, and picturesque suburbs that the city's outlying areas have to offer. For lovers of architecture, Oak Park is a must-see for its Frank Lloyd Wright designs. Other Chicago neighborhoods, such as Wicker Park and Lakeview, are ideal day-trip destinations. The vast expanse of Lincoln Park offers a respite from the bustle of the city in its lush gardens, flowering plants, and a zoo, famed for its naturalistic animal habitats.

Frank Lloyd Wright's Home and Studio, Oak Park

A lowland gorilla at the zoo's Regenstein Center for African Apes

## ⑯ Lincoln Park Zoo

2200 N Cannon Dr. **Tel** (312) 742-2000. Ⓜ Fullerton, Armitage. ▣ 22, 36, 73, 151, 156. **Open** 9am–6pm daily (Nov–Mar: 9am–5pm). ⬛⬛⬛⬛ on N Cnnon Dr. Workshops, special events. Ⓦ lpzoo.org

Located in the heart of Lincoln Park, this zoo is easily accessible from downtown. Established in 1868 with the gift of two swans

from New York's Central Park, Lincoln Park Zoo is the country's oldest free zoo. Today, more than 1,000 mammals, reptiles, and birds from around the world live here in realistic habitats. A world leader in wildlife conservation, the zoo shelters such animals as the threatened Grévy's zebra from Africa and the endangered Bactrian camel from Mongolia, as well as a giraffe, black rhino, polar bear, and other species in its many outdoor habitats. A 1912 historic building houses rare cats, including Amur tigers. The zoo's large collection of lowland gorillas bears testimony to a successful breeding program. A working farm with cows, horses, pigs, and chickens is popular with kids for the daily milking demonstrations.

Lincoln Park, Chicago's largest, offers walking and biking paths that wind along ponds, lagoons, and sandy beaches.

## ⑰ Oak Park

Bounded by North Ave, Roosevelt Rd, Austin Blvd, & Harlem Ave. ⓘ (708) 848-1500. Ⓜ Oak Park (green line); Harlem/Lake (green line). ▣ Oak Park (Union Pacific/ West line). Visitor Center: 158 N Forest Ave. **Open** 10am–3:30pm Mon–Fri, 11am–3:30pm Sat–Sun. **Closed** Jan 1, Thanksg., Dec 25. ⬛⬛ Frank Lloyd Wright Preservation Trust: 931 Chicago Ave. **Tel** (312) 994-4000. ⬛ Ⓦ gowright.org Ⓦ visitoakpark.com

Frank Lloyd Wright moved to Oak Park in 1889, at the age of 22. During the next 20 years here, he created many groundbreaking buildings as his legendary Prairie School style evolved. This tranquil community is now home to 25 Wright buildings – the largest grouping of his work anywhere. The best place to feast on Wright's achievement is the superbly restored **Frank Lloyd**

Pink flamingos in the Waterfowl Lagoon at Lincoln Park Zoo

*For hotels and restaurants see pp422–7*

Unity Temple, Frank Lloyd Wright's "little jewel," Oak Park

**Wright Home and Studio**, designed by Wright in 1889. This was also where he developed his influential architectural style.

Nearby are two private homes that reveal Wright's versatility. The 1902 **Arthur Heurtley House** is typically Prairie style, with its row of windows spanning the low roofline, and a simple but elegant entrance arch. The 1895 **Moore-Dugal House**, across the street, is a hybrid of styles, rich with Tudor-Revival and Gothic elements.

At the southern end of Oak Park is the masterful **Pleasant Home**, a 30-room Prairie-style mansion designed in 1897 by George W. Maher. The house holds extraordinary

art glass – designed panels of leaded glass. It also includes intricate woodwork, and decorative motifs, and a display on the area's history.

Wright was especially proud of **Unity Temple**, his design for the Unitarian Universalist Congregation. He called this church one of his most important designs, his first expression of an "entirely new architecture." It was built between 1906 and 1908, using a then-unusual technique of poured reinforced concrete, in part because of a budget of only $45,000. Unity Temple is a masterpiece of powerful simplicity wedded with functional ornamentation.

Oak Park is also famous as the birthplace of the famed US writer Ernest Hemingway (1899–1960), who lived here until the age of 20. Although Hemingway *(see p323)* rejected the conservative mind-set of this Chicago suburb, saying it was full of "wide lawns and narrow minds," Oak Park continues to pride itself on its literary association. The **Ernest Hemingway Birthplace**, a grand Victorian home decorated with turn-of-the-20th-century furnishings, has displays on this Nobel Prize-winner's life. The **Ernest Hemingway Museum**, features several artifacts from Hemingway's early life.

The Victorian house in which Ernest Hemingway was born

## Oak Park

① Frank Lloyd Wright Home and Studio
② Arthur Heurtley House
③ Moore-Dugal House
④ Pleasant Home
⑤ Unity Temple
⑥ Ernest Hemingway Birthplace
⑦ Ernest Hemingway Museum

0 meters    400
0 yards     400

**For keys to symbols** *see back flap*

# Illinois

Except for the densely populated area around Chicago (*see pp384–95*), Illinois is a predominantly rural state. Large expanses of rich, flat farmland are dotted with scenic byways, quaint historic towns, and wine trails. Known as the "Land of Lincoln," most of the sites related to the president are concentrated in Springfield, the heart of the state. Some rather unusual and picturesque scenery can be found in the hilly "Driftless Region" along the Mississippi in the northwest, and in the rugged "Illinois Ozarks" in the southwest.

Rock River, overlooked by the statue of Sac hero Black Hawk, southwest of Rockford

## ❷ Rockford

🏙 150,000. ✈ 🚌 ℹ️ 102 N Main St, (800) 521-0849. 🌐 gorockford.com

Dubbed the Forest City in the late 1800s, Rockford today has beautiful public and private gardens and miles of parkland along the Rock River, which bisects the city. Of its three most-visited gardens, the **Klehm Arboretum and Botanic Garden** contains 150 acres (61 ha) of plants. **Anderson Japanese Gardens** has a teahouse and a 16th century-style guest house. **Sinnissippi Gardens** features an aviary, lagoon, and recreation path with views of downtown's historic buildings, including the Coronado Theater, a gilded 1927 Moorish movie palace.

On the town's east side, the **Midway Village and Museum Center** is both a living history center and local history museum. Exhibits tell the story of ethnic groups who flocked to the city's factories. The grounds have been turned into a 19th-century village, with restored buildings from the area.

The growth of Rockford followed the tragic 1830s Blackhawk War between the Sac Indians of northern Illinois and the US Army, determined to displace the tribes from their farmlands. After the Sacs lost, they were relocated to Iowa. A stone statue of the Sac warrior Chief Blackhawk is located 27 miles (43 km) southwest of Rockford.

🌼 **Klehm Arboretum & Botanic Garden**
2715 S Main St. **Tel** (815) 965-8146. **Open** 9am–4pm daily. 🅿️ ♿ 🌐 klehm.org

🌼 **Anderson Japanese Gardens**
318 Spring Creek Rd. **Tel** (815) 229-9390. **Open** May–Oct: 9am–6pm Mon–Fri, 9am–4pm Sat, 10am–4pm Sun. 🅿️ ♿ 🌐 andersongardens.org

🌼 **Sinnissippi Gardens**
1300 N 2nd St. **Tel** (815) 987-8858. Greenhouse: **Open** 9am–4pm daily. ♿ 🌐 rockfordparkdistrict.org

## ❸ Galena

🏙 3,600. ✈ 🚌 ℹ️ 101 Bouthillier, (877) 464-2536. 🌐 galena.org

Perched on a bluff overlooking the Galena River near its confluence with the Mississippi, this immaculately preserved town is a relaxing tourist destination with 19th-century homes, historical landmarks, and antique shops. Its status as the shipping center for the region's many lead mines

made Galena the busiest Mississippi River Valley port between St. Louis and St. Paul in the 1840s.

The town's population peaked at 15,000 during the Civil War, when the elite erected many magnificent homes in a wide variety of ornate styles.

Many of Galena's historic homes are now open to visitors. The **Belvedere Mansion**, built in 1857 by a local steamboat owner, is a 22-room Italianate structure with a varied collection of period furnishings and some quaint recent additions, including the draperies from the *Gone with the Wind* movie set. Civil War general and US president Ulysses S. Grant lived quietly in Galena, between the signature events of his military career and time in the White House. His small, Federal-style 1860 home contains many of Grant's original possessions and furnishings.

The **Galena/Jo Daviess County History Museum** chronicles Galena's lead mining and Civil War shipping days. Informative 1-hour walking tours of Main Street begin at 10am on Saturdays from May through to October.

🏛 **Belvedere Mansion**
1008 Park Ave. **Tel** (815) 777-0747. **Open** mid-May–mid-Nov: 11am–4pm. 🅿️

🏛 **Galena/Jo Daviess County History Museum**
211 S Bench St. **Tel** (815) 777-9129. **Open** 9am–4:30pm daily. **Closed** Jan 1, Easter, Thanksgiving, Dec 24, 25, 31. 🅿️ ♿ 🌐 galenahistorymuseum.org

A view of Galena with its historic landmarks

Cozy Dog Drive-in, a popular Route 66 café

# ❹ Springfield

🏨 111,000. ✈ 🚲 🚌 ℹ️ 109 N 7th St, (800) 545-7300. 🌐 **visit–springfieldillinois.com**

The state capital since 1837, Springfield gained fame as the adopted hometown of 16th US president, Abraham Lincoln, who lived here for 24 years before assuming the presidency in 1861. The **Abraham Lincoln Presidential Library and Museum** is full of artifacts, interactive displays, and special-effect theaters. The four-block **Lincoln Home National Historic Site** is a pedestrian-only historic district, with restored 19th-century homes, gaslights, and wooden sidewalks surrounding the neat frame house where Lincoln and his wife, Mary, lived for 16 years.

An on-site visitor center provides details about the city's other Lincoln-related attractions, including his law office, tomb, and the 1853 **Old State Capitol**. It was here that he delivered his famous 1858 "House Divided" speech, outlining the sectional differences that would soon plunge the nation into the Civil War. Lincoln's political career began in 1834, when he was elected to the Illinois General Assembly.

The town's other attraction is the elegant **Dana-Thomas House**, a 1904 Prairie-style home designed by Frank Lloyd Wright (see p394–5). It contains much of Wright's original white oak furniture, light fixtures, art-glass doors, windows, and light panels. Many Wright experts consider this to be the best-preserved of the houses designed by the famous architect.

Springfield is also rich in Route 66 lore (see pp50–51). The old road follows a clearly marked path through the city, leading to the southside **Cozy Dog Drive-in**, a legendary Route 66 eatery, which claims to have invented the corn dog. The café's Route 66 Museum and its trademark "cozy dogs," still available at rock-bottom prices, make it a popular tourist destination (closed on Sunday and some holidays).

🏛 **Lincoln Home National Historic Site**
413 S 8th St. **Tel** (217) 391-3226. **Open** 8:30 am–5pm daily. **Closed** Jan 1, Thanksgiving, Dec 25. ♿
🌐 **nps.gov/liho**

🏛 **Old State Capitol**
5th & Adams Sts, Springfield. **Tel** (217) 785-9363. **Open** May–Sep: 9am–5pm daily; Sep–Apr: 9am–5pm Tue–Sat. **Closed** public hols. ♿
🌐 **oldstatecapitol.org**

# ❺ Southern Illinois

🚌 ℹ️ (800) 248-4373.
🌐 **southernmostillinois.com**

In Southern Illinois, flat farm-lands give way to rolling hills and forests along the Mississippi and Ohio Rivers. This terrain provided strategic vantage points from which Native Americans and, later, French traders and missionaries could monitor river traffic.

Near the confluence of the Mississippi, Missouri, and Illinois Rivers (90 miles/145 km southwest of Springfield) are the remains of the largest prehistoric Native American city north of Mexico. The **Cahokia Mounds State Historic and World Heritage Site** contains more than 100 earthen mounds dating from 1050 to 1250, when 15,000 people of the Mississippian culture are estimated to have occupied the city. The flat-topped Monks Mound covers 14 acres (6 ha) and rises, in four terraces, to a height of 100 ft (30 m), providing sweeping views of the nearby river valleys and the Gateway Arch (see p450), about 12 miles (19 km) away in downtown St. Louis. The site's interpretive center recounts the fascinating story of these mounds, which were mysteriously abandoned by around 1500.

Further evidence of Native American habitation is abundant in the rugged, unglaciated "Illinois Ozarks," or "Little Egypt" region, where the Ohio River separates the state from Kentucky. The forested ridges and hollows of the sprawling **Shawnee National Forest** can be viewed most dramatically at the Garden of the Gods, an area of rocky sandstone outcroppings, and Shawnee Hills, home to a winery trail.

🏛 **Cahokia Mounds State Historic Site**
30 Ramey St, Collinsville. **Tel** (618) 346-5160. **Open** 8am–sunset daily. Visitor Center: **Open** 9am–5pm daily (closed Mon & Tue Nov–Apr). **Closed** public hols. ♿
🌐 **cahokiamounds.org**

Grass-covered mounds in the Cahokia Mounds State Historic Site

# Indiana

Unlike the other states of the Great Lakes region, Indiana has only a short, 45-mile (72-km) stretch of shoreline along Lake Michigan. As a result, the state's history has centered on its extensive river systems – the Maumee/Wabash in the north, and the Ohio in the south – and the development of the railroads and highways that linked Indiana to key Midwestern and Eastern markets. Indiana today is an engaging place to explore by car, especially along its hilly Ohio River backroads and Amish-country scenic lanes.

## ❻ New Harmony

🏠 900. 🛈 Atheneum/Visitor Center, 401 N Arthur St, (800) 231-2168.
**w** newharmony.org

America's two most successful utopian communities flourished in this neat village on the eastern banks of the Wabash River. The first, the Harmonie Society, was founded by a Pennsylvania-based German Lutheran separatist group in 1814. The sect followed a doctrine of perfectionism and celibacy in anticipation of the second coming of Christ, focusing on the development of profitable agricultural and manufacturing enterprises.

In 1825, the Harmonists returned to Pennsylvania, after selling the town and the surrounding lands to Scottish textile magnate Robert Owen. The latter, too, sought to create an ideal society based on free education and the abolition of social classes and personal property ownership. The colony failed after two years, but Owen's sons, David and Robert, pursued their father's ideas and later established the Smithsonian Institution in Washington, DC.

The tree-lined town is now a State Historic Site with 25 well-preserved Harmonist buildings, an inn, and many beautiful manicured gardens. These include the reconstructed Labyrinth, a mazelike set of hedges arranged in concentric circles around a stone temple that stands at the center.

🏛 **Historic New Harmony**
603 West St. **Tel** (800) 231-2168.
**Open** Mar–Dec daily. ⏰ 10am, 2pm daily. 🐾 ♿

Monroe County Courthouse, Bloomington, a Beaux Arts building

## ❼ Bloomington

🏠 70,000. ✈ 🚆 🛈 2855 N Walnut St, (800) 800-0037.
**w** visitbloomington.com

Surrounded by rugged limestone outcrops, this city is home to the leafy Indiana University campus. Quarrying of the limestone deposits fueled Bloomington's 19th-century growth, the results of which can still be seen in the city's magnificent public buildings. A prime example is the 1906 Beaux Arts **Monroe County Courthouse**, at the center of the Courthouse Square Historic District located downtown.

On the campus are a variety of historic buildings and outdoor spaces. The 1941 Auditorium displays 20 panels of Thomas Hart Benton's 1933 *Century of Progress*

murals, painted for the World's Fair. The **Tibetan Cultural Center** is the only one in the US and is a haven for meditation. The **Indiana University Art Museum** was designed by architect I.M. Pei. It includes works by Henri Matisse, Claude Monet, Auguste Rodin, and Andy Warhol, as well as Picasso's 1934 *L'Atelier (The Studio)*.

🏛 **Indiana University Art Museum**
1133 E 7th St. **Tel** (812) 855-5445.
**Open** 10am–5pm Tue–Sat, noon–5pm Sun. **Closed** public hols. ♿
**w** artmuseum.iu.edu

## ❽ Indiana Dunes National Lakeshore

🛈 Dorothy Buell Memorial Visitor Center, Hwy 20 & Hwy 49. **Tel** (219) 926-7561. **Open** 8:30am–4:30pm daily (to 6pm in summer). **Closed** Jan 1, Thanksgiving, Dec 25. 🐾 ♿
**w** nps.gov/indu

One of the nation's most diverse groups of ecosystems is contained within the 23-sq-mile (61-sq-km) Indiana Dunes National Lakeshore. Only a 30-minute drive from downtown Chicago, this stunning refuge is located along the 25-mile (40-km) stretch of the Lake Michigan shore. Its ecosystems include bogs, swamps, marshes, glacial moraines, prairies, forests, oak savannas, and dunes linked by scenic roads and a network of hiking and biking trails. The Beyond the Beach Discovery Trail leads to the area's natural treasures. The park is also known as a bird-watcher's paradise, as herons, cardinals, kingfishers, and towhees are frequently spotted here.

Deer at the Indiana Dunes National Lakeshore

# ❾ South Bend

🏛 107,789. ✈ 🚆 🚌 ℹ 401 E Colfax Ave, (800) 519-0577.
🌐 **exploresouthbend.org**

South Bend is widely known today as the home of the Roman Catholic **University of Notre Dame**. The 11,400-student institution was established in 1842 by Father Edward Sorin, a priest from the Congregation of the Holy Cross.

While religion is still important, the students and countless alumni are equally passionate about the Notre Dame "Fighting Irish" football team, one of the most successful in college football history. In fact, one of the most famous sculptures at the art-filled campus is a large mural of Christ known as *The Word of Life* that students call "Touchdown Jesus."

Guided tours are available at the **Morris Performing Arts Center**, which was built in 1921 and renovated in 2011. It cost $1 million to construct and was the most modern theater in the nation when it opened as a vaudeville house. Many celebrities, from Frank Sinatra to Jerry Seinfeld, have performed here.

South of downtown, the **Studebaker National Museum** contains the horse-drawn carriages and early automobiles manufactured by the town's now-defunct Studebaker corporation. The collection includes the carriage in which President Lincoln rode to Ford's Theater the night he was assassinated in Washington, DC, and a 1909 backward-forward automobile that shuttled US senators between their offices and the Capitol.

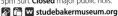
Amish horse-drawn carriage

🎭 **Morris Performing Arts Center** 211 N Michigan St. **Tel** (800)-537-6415. **Open** 10am–5pm (box office). 🌐 **morriscenter.org**

🏛 **Studebaker National Museum** 201 S Chapin St. **Tel** (888) 391-5600. **Open** 10am–5pm Mon–Sat, noon–5pm Sun. **Closed** major public hols. 🅿 🏛 🌐 **studebakermuseum.org**

"Touchdown Jesus" mural at Notre Dame, South Bend

# ❿ Shipshewana

🏛 525. 🚌 ℹ 780 S Van Buren St, (800) 254-8090. 🌐 **backroads.org**

This small village, nestled in the rolling farmlands of northeastern Indiana, has one of the world's largest Amish communities (*see p119*). The town's **Menno-Hof Mennonite Anabaptist Interpretive Center** provides a detailed background on the European Anabaptist movement, which gave rise to the Mennonite, Hutterite, and Amish sects. Religious persecution in the 19th century led to the large-scale immigration of Anabaptists to the US and Canada. Exhibits at the center re-create this dark period as well as examining the sects and their lifestyles as they are today.

Local Amish farmers, with their distinctive black hats, white shirts, and black suits, riding horse-drawn buggies, are frequent sights in Shipshewana and the surrounding villages of Bristol, Elkhart, Goshen, Middlebury, Nappanee, and Wakarusa. Tourists come to the villages in search of furniture, dairy, baked goods, and quilts.

🏛 **Menno-Hof Mennonite Anabaptist Interpretive Center** 510 S Van Buren St. **Tel** (260) 768-4117. **Open** Apr–Dec: 10am–5pm Mon–Sat (Jun–Aug: to 7pm Mon–Fri). **Closed** Jan 1, Thanksgiving, Dec 25. 🅿 🚻 🌐 **mennohof.org**

# ⓫ Fort Wayne

🏛 206,000. ✈ 🚌 ℹ 927 S Harrison St, (800) 767-7752.
🌐 **visitfortwayne.com**

Fort Wayne's location at the confluence of the St. Mary's, St. Joseph, and Maumee Rivers made it a strategic site for the Native Americans, French fur traders, British armies, and American settlers who sought to control the access to the Great Lakes. The city's prosperity during the railroad era is exemplified in the fascinating downtown Allen County Courthouse, constructed in 1902.

Visitors use the Sky Safari to glide over treetops and animal quarters at the **Fort Wayne Children's Zoo**, which is the city's biggest attraction. An extensive array of Australian animals has earned accolades nationally, while the African Journey brings visitors up close to a menagerie of lions, hyenas, mongooses, and other species found on the continent.

🦁 **Fort Wayne Children's Zoo** 3411 Sherman Blvd. **Tel** (260) 427-6800. **Open** Apr–Oct: 9am–5pm daily. 🅿 🚻 🌐 **kidszoo.org**

A view of the Allen County Courthouse in Fort Wayne

Architecture of modern downtown Indianapolis

# ⑫ Indianapolis

🏛 860, 500. ✈ 🚉 🚌
ℹ 200 S Capitol Ave, (800) 323-4639.
w **visitindy.com**

Known as "The Crossroads of America," Indianapolis is much more than a transportation hub where multiple railroads and Interstate highways intersect. The city's many parks and monuments, and vibrant in-town neighborhoods make it one of the region's most surprising and satisfying destinations.

Selected as the state capital in 1820, Indianapolis was laid out on the banks of the shallow White River, with a network of wide boulevards radiating outward from the central **Monument Circle**, which is dominated by the towering 1901 Beaux Arts obelisk, the Soldiers' and Sailors' Monument.

The city's first-rate museums and lively arts and theater scenes are complemented by an active interest in sports. Every Memorial Day, the world's largest, single-day sporting event – the Indiana-polis 500 auto race – fills the **Indianapolis Motor Speedway** with nearly 300,000 fans. Built in 1909 as a 2.5-mile (4-km) test track for the city's then-burgeoning automotive industry, the speedway played host to the first Indy 500 in 1911. The race was the brain-child of Indianapolis auto-parts manufacturer Carl Fisher, who later gained fame as the tireless promoter of the Lincoln Highway (now US 30), the nation's first transcontinental highway, from New York to San Francisco.

The track's Hall of Fame displays more than 75 racing cars and other Indy 500 memorabilia, in addition to examples of the Stutz, Cole, Marmon, National, and Duesenberg automobiles built in the city before the industry centralized in Detroit. Visitors can also take a guided bus tour around the famous track.

The five-story **Children's Museum of Indianapolis**, which opened in 1976, has been consistently rated as one of the country's best, and is the largest in the world. The museum's 11 galleries and 10 percent of its 120,000 artifacts are displayed in a manner that encourages hands-on, interactive exploration of the sciences, history, world cultures, and the arts. Among the many highlights here are an authentic Indy 500 race car, a restored carousel, a dinosaur discovery exhibit, and Anne Frank Peace Park, with sculptures of the world's Seven Wonders.

The **Indiana State Museum** is among the sites within the

Display in the Indianapolis Motor Speedway Hall of Fame

downtown **White River State Park**, a 250-acre (101-ha) urban oasis. The spacious museum is constructed of locally sourced materials, including Indiana limestone, sandstone, brick, steel, extruded aluminum, and glass. Focusing on Indiana's natural and cultural history, the museum displays extensive exhibits from prehistoric fossils to contemporary pop culture icons.

**Lockerbie Square District**, northeast of downtown, is the city's oldest surviving 19th-century immigrant neighborhood. Immortalized in the poetry of resident James Whitcomb Riley (1849–1916), the square preserves modest workers' cottages, restored cobblestone streets, and period street lights. Riley's 1872 brick Italianate home is now a museum and National Historic Landmark.

Situated on the grounds of the Oldfields estate of local pharmaceutical pioneer J.K. Lilly Jr., 5 miles (8 km) north of downtown, the **Indianapolis Museum of Art** houses a wide-ranging collection of American, European, Asian, and African art. Among the museum's more acclaimed holdings are Winslow Homer's *The Boat Builders*, Edward Hopper's *Hotel Lobby*, Georgia O'Keeffe's *Jimson Weed*, and many of Paul Gauguin's works from his 1886 visit to the French artists' colony of Pont-Aven.

The restored Oldfields-Lilly house and superb gardens, designed by Percival Gallagher of the famed Olmsted Brothers landscape architecture firm, have been carefully restored to their original 1920s grandeur. The house and extensive wooded grounds and gardens are open for tours.

The **Eiteljorg Museum of American Indians and Western Art**, also in the White River State Park, has one of the most impressive collections of Native American and Western American art in the US. Establi-shed in 1989 by Harrison Eiteljorg, a successful Indianapolis

George Carlson's *The Greeting* (1989) outside Eiteljorg Museum

businessman and art collector, the museum is housed in a Southwest-inspired adobe building, in deference to Eitel-jorg's large collection of works from the early 20th-century Taos Society of Artists *(see p538)*, who included Native American, Western American, and Hispanic themes into their work.

On view are paintings by such celebrated artists as Georgia O'Keeffe, Frederic Remington, and Charles M. Russell, whose *Indians Crossing the Plains* is a famous depiction of vanishing Native American culture on the late 19th-century Great Plains. Many Native American artifacts are also displayed.

**⊞ Indianapolis Motor Speedway**
Hall of Fame, 4790 W 16th St. **Tel** (317) 492-6784. **Open** 9am–5pm daily (extended hours in May). **Closed** Thanksgiving, Dec 25. 🚫 (children under 6 free). 🚻 **W** brickyard.com

**⊞ Indianapolis Museum of Art**
4000 Michigan Rd. **Tel** (317) 920-2660. **Open** 11am–5pm Tue–Sat (until 9pm Thu, Fri), noon–5pm Sun. **Closed** Jan 1, Thanksgiving, Dec 25. 🚫 for special exhibits. 🚻 **W** imamuseum.org

**⊞ Eiteljorg Museum of American Indians & Western Art**
500 W Washington St. **Tel** (317) 636-9378. **Open** 10am–5pm Mon–Sat, noon–5pm Sun. **Closed** Jan 1, Thanksgiving, Dec 25. 🚫 (children under 5 free). 🕐 1pm daily. 🚻 **W** eiteljorg.org

# ⑬ Columbus

🏠 39,000. 🚌 **i** 506 5th St, (800) 468-6564. **W** columbus.in.us

One of the world's most concentrated collections of modern architecture can be found in this small southern Indiana city. From 1942 on, after the completion of architect Eliel Saarinen's **First Christian Church**, Columbus garnered international attention for the more than 70 churches, schools, banks, and commercial and public buildings constructed here. Today, the city's commitment to high-quality design has resulted in Columbus being ranked sixth on the American Institute of Architects' list of cities marked by innovation in architecture and design.

A philanthropic foundation endowed by the city's largest employer, Cummins Engine, attracted some of the world's most distinguished architects. Among those who left their stamp on the city environment are Robert Trent Jones, Richard Meier, Robert Venturi, Alexander Girard, and I.M. Pei, whose 1969 Cleo Rodgers Memorial Library is at 536 5th Street. The **Columbus Architecture Tours** allow visitors to catch a glimpse of these architectural delights.

**🏛 Columbus Architecture Tours**
506 5th St. **Tel** (800) 468-6564. 🕐 daily; times and frequency depends on time of year. 🚫 🚻

# ⑭ Ohio River Valley

**i** 601 W First St, (800) 559-2956. **W** visitmadison.org

From Indiana's southeastern border with Kentucky, Route 56 and 156 follow the serpentine Ohio River for nearly 80 miles (129 km) as it winds lazily through the river towns of Rising Sun, Patriot, Florence, and Vevey. These two highways are the best way to explore both the river valley and the southern hill country.

The antebellum river port of **Madison**, 90 miles (145 km) southeast of Indianapolis, is one of the best-preserved towns on the river. Many of its residential and commercial buildings have benefited from a generous grant from the National Trust for Historic Preservation. The town's notable architectural charms include the Greek Revival **Lanier Mansion**, which was built in 1844 for railroad magnate James Lanier, and the Shrewsbury-Windle House, an 1849 riverboat entrepreneur's home featuring an elegant, free-standing circular staircase. Downtown is the restored 19th-century office of progressive frontier physician Dr. William D. Hutchings.

**⊞ Lanier Mansion State Historic Site**
601 W 1st St Madison. **Tel** (812) 265-3526. **Open** 9am–5pm daily. **Closed** public hols. 🕐 every hour until 4pm. 🚫 (children under 2 free).

Exterior of Eliel Saarinen's First Christian Church (1942), Columbus

# Ohio

Ohio is a study in contrasts. As one of the nation's largest agricultural producers, the state is dotted with picturesque farmland, small towns steeped in history, and more recently settled Amish areas where horse-drawn buggies and barns are a thing of the present. Ohio also contains several of the country's most urbanized industrial centers along the Ohio River – the state's southern and eastern border – and in port cities that lie along the shores of Lake Erie.

Art Deco façade of the Union Terminal, Cincinnati

## ⓯ Cincinnati

🏙 331,285. ✈ 🚆 🚌 ℹ 525 Vine St, (800) 344-3445. 🌐 cincyusa.com

Built on a series of steep hills overlooking the Ohio River, Cincinnati was once called "Porkopolis" for its slaughter-houses and belching factories. Later, its winding side streets and stunning views from the hilltop Mount Adams neighborhood inspired British prime minister Winston Churchill to call it "the most beautiful of America's inland cities." The city is today a vibrant corporate center with a revitalized riverfront entertainment and parks district.

Cincinnati's location at the intersection of the Ohio Canal and the Miami and Ohio Rivers, and its strategic perch on the border of the slaveholding South and the industrializing North, made it a heterogeneous cultural and commercial crossroads. Many prominent locals, including writer Harriet Beecher Stowe, whose home is now a state historic site, strongly supported the anti-slavery movement. The dynamic **National Underground Railroad Freedom Center** focuses on the city's one-time heroic past. Cincinnati's most celebrated landmark is the 1867 stone and steel suspension bridge, built by Brooklyn Bridge engineer John A. Roebling to link this city with Covington, Kentucky, across the Ohio River. Another landmark is the 1933 Art Deco **Cincinnati Museum Center** at **Union Terminal**, west of downtown. The refurbished terminal now houses attractions that specialize in city history, children's activities, and natural history/science. The enlarged **Contemporary Arts Center** adds creative energy downtown. The innovative sixth-floor UnMuseum encourages interaction, especially among children.

On the eastern part of town, the **Cincinnati Art Museum** overlooks Eden Park. The museum's extensive collections include Roman, Greek, Egyptian, Asian, and African artifacts. Among its exhibits of contemporary art is a specially commissioned portrait by Andy Warhol of the controversial Cincinnati Reds baseball great, Pete Rose.

### 🏛 The Cincinnati Art Museum
953 Eden Park Dr. **Tel** (877) 472-4226. **Open** 11am–5pm Tue–Sun. **Closed** public hols. 🚫 ♿ 🌐 cincinnatiartmuseum.org

## ⓰ Dayton

🏙 166,000. ✈ 🚌 ℹ 1 Chamber Plaza, Suite A, (800) 221-8235. 🌐 daytoncvb.com

This pleasant city on the Great Miami River is known as the "Birthplace of Aviation." It was here that aviation pioneers Wilbur and Orville Wright (see p252), carried out much of their research and experimentation, which led to their successful flight in 1903 in Kitty Hawk, North Carolina. Five miles northeast lies the **Dayton Aviation Heritage National Historical Park** at the spot where the brothers tested their second and third aircraft in 1904 and 1905. The **Carillon Historical Park** holds the Wright Flyer III aircraft – the first capable of executing a turn. Over 300 aircraft and missiles from the post-Wright aviation era are at the **National Museum of the US Air Force**. Also within the area is the **National Aviation Hall of Fame**.

Overlooking the Great Miami River, the Italian Renaissance-style **Dayton Art Institute** features a large collection of European and American paintings, such as Claude Monet's Waterlilies and Edward Hopper's High Noon.

### 🏛 Carillon Historical Park
1000 Carillon Blvd. **Tel** (937) 293-2841. **Open** 9:30am–5pm Tue–Sat, noon–5pm Sun & public hols. 🚫 (children under 3 free). ♿ 🌐 carillonpark.org

### 🏛 Dayton Art Institute
456 Belmonte Park N. **Tel** (937) 223-5277. **Open** 10am–5pm Wed–Sun (to 8pm Thu). 🚫 (children under 17 free). 🌐 daytonartinstitute.org

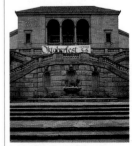

Italian Renaissance-style Dayton Art Institute, Dayton

*For hotels and restaurants see pp422–7*

The 1,348-ft (411-m) Serpent Mound

## ⓱ Serpent Mound

3850 Rte 73, Peebles. **Tel** (800) 752-2757. Museum and Grounds: **Open** Apr–Oct: 10am–5pm daily; Nov–mid-Dec, Mar: 10am–4pm Sat–Sun.

The largest serpent-shaped effigy mound in the US, the 1,348-ft- (411-m-) long Serpent Mound overlooks Brush Creek in the Ohio River Valley. Although its exact age is unknown, research suggests that the mound was constructed between 800 BC and AD 400 by the ancient Adena people, Ohio's earliest farming Native American community.

The 5-ft- (1.5-m-) high, 20-ft-(6-m-) wide mound appears to represent an uncoiling serpent, with a tightly coiled tail at one end and a mouthlike opening, swallowing an oval-shaped egg, at the other. An on-site museum describes the mound's history and its protection under an 1888 law, the first in the US to safeguard important archaeological sites.

## ⓲ Hopewell Culture National Historical Park

16062 Rte 104, Chillicothe. **Tel** (740) 774-1126. **Open** 8:30am–5pm daily (until 6pm Memorial Day to Labor Day). **Closed** Jan 1, Thanksgiving, Dec 25. **nps.gov/hocu**

Located in the Scioto River Valley, this 120-acre (48-ha) park preserves 23 Native American burial mounds built by the Hopewell people, who lived here from 200 BC to AD 500. The Hopewell culture, which emerged from the Adena culture, covers a broad network of beliefs and practices among different Native groups spread over the eastern US. As characteristic of the culture, the mounds are arranged in geometric shapes, ringed by an earthen wall. A visitor center provides an in-depth look at the social and economic life of the long-vanished Hopewell peoples, based on the archaeological work conducted here.

## ⓳ Columbus

711,000. ✈ 🚆 🚌

ℹ 277 W Nationwide Blvd, (614) 221-6623, (800) 354-2657.

**experiencecolumbus.org**

Ohio's capital since 1816, Columbus has grown from a sleepy, swampy lowland site on the east bank of the Scioto River to become a bustling cultural, political, and economic center. Downtown's central feature is the Greek-Revival style **Ohio Statehouse**. Built between 1839 and 1861, the structure is surmounted by a unique drum-shaped cupola marked by a 29-ft-(9-m-) wide skylight.

The **Ohio History Center** is the best place to begin the exploration of Columbus. Its interactive displays trace Ohio's evolution from an 18th-century frontier outpost to its current urban and industrial status. Nationally acclaimed attractions include the **COSI** (Center of Science and Industry) outdoor science park and 300 interactive indoor exhibits. The **Columbus Zoo**

Franklin Park Conservatory and Botanical Garden, Columbus

**and Aquarium** is home to more than 9,000 creatures and television celebrity Jack Hanna is Director Emeritus.

The **Franklin Park Conservatory and Botanical Garden**, built in 1895, has a bonsai and sculpture garden. It also has indoor simulations of exotic climates.

### 🏛 Ohio History Center
1982 Velma Ave. **Tel** (614) 297-2300. **Open** 10am–5pm Wed–Sat, noon–5pm Sun. **Closed** most public hols. (children under 6 free). 
**ohiohistory.org/places/ohc**

### 🌿 Franklin Park Conservatory & Botanical Garden
1777 E Broad St. **Tel** (614) 645-8733, (800) 214-7275. **Open** 10am–5pm daily (until 8pm Wed). **Closed** Thanksgiving, Dec 25. (children under 3 free). 
**fpconservatory.org**

## ⓴ Berlin

3,100. 🚌 ℹ 35 N Monroe St, Millersburg, (330) 674-3975, (877) 643-8824. **visitamishcountry.com**

Much of Ohio's large Amish population is concentrated in Holmes County in the north-central part of the state, about 90 miles (145 km) northeast of Columbus. Berlin is the oldest village in Holmes County. Most of its early settlers, originally from Germany or Switzerland, moved to Ohio after having first settled in Pennyslvania .

Lying just outside Berlin village, **Schrock's Amish Farm** provides a good overview of the reclusive Amish, who have maintained their simplified 19th-century way of life. The farm has a multimedia visitor center and offers a tour of a working farm, complete with freshly baked goods and buggy rides.

Visitors are requested to drive carefully along the rural backroads and busier thoroughfares, out of respect for the slow-moving, horse-drawn carriages.

**Schrock's Amish Farm**
4363 SR 39. **Tel** (330) 893-3232. **Open** Apr–Oct: 10am–5pm Mon–Fri, 10am–6pm Sat.

View of the Cleveland skyline from The Flats

# ❷ Cleveland

🗺 478,000. ✈ 🚊 🚌 ℹ 334 Euclid Ave, (800) 321-1001.
🌐 **positivelycleveland.com**

Cleveland is a hard-working, vibrant, and ever-changing place. Founded in 1796 by speculator Moses Cleaveland, the city evolved from a frontier town into a bustling commercial port in 1832, when the Ohio and Erie Canal linked Cleveland to the Ohio River.

Cleveland's steel industry was born after the Civil War, when railroads linked the city with Minnesota's Iron Range and the coalfields of western Pennsylvania. The industry thrived in the early 1900s, catering to the Detroit auto-mobile industry's demand for easily transported steel. After World War II, however, the city's fortunes faded as industries moved away, leaving behind vast polluted landscapes and scores of unemployed workers.

Cleveland's "Rust Belt" image is today a thing of the past. The city now encompasses 30 sq miles (77 sq km) of pristine parkland. **The East 4th Street District** and the historic **Warehouse District** are the entertainment hubs.

A signature feature since 1927, the 52-story Beaux Arts **Terminal Tower**, was designed as a "city within a city." It made maximum use of vertical space, squeezing an office building, railroad station, and hotel into its confines. The 42nd-floor observation deck offers grand views of the city and, on a clear day, one can see the Canadian shoreline.

The 1995 **Rock and Roll Hall of Fame and Museum** on the Lake Erie waterfront in downtown, put Cleveland at center stage of the nation's entertainment scene. The massive 150,000-sq-ft (13,935-sq-m) I.M. Pei-designed museum traces the development of the musical genre, beginning with its roots in the Mississippi Delta blues *(see pp360–61)* and Appalachian string bands. On display are memorabilia ranging from Chuck Berry's Gibson electric guitar to a Cub Scout shirt worn by Jim Morrison. To its west, the **Great Lakes Science Center** uses interactive exhibits to stimulate public interest in the complex ecosystem of the Great Lakes region.

The **Greater Cleveland Aquarium** has a dynamic underwater walk-through experience.

Cleveland's principal cultural attractions lie about 4 miles (6 km) east of downtown, around University Circle. Surrounding this expanse of parkland near the Case Western Reserve University campus are a series of early 20th-century buildings that now contain several fine museums. Among

them is the **Cleveland Museum of Art**, with its superb collection of ancient Egyptian relics and pre-Columbian artifacts. Its European painting collection includes such masterpieces as Renoir's *Mother and Child* and van Gogh's *Landscape with Wheelbarrow*. Facing this museum, the city's popular **Botanical Garden** features 10 acres (4 ha) of outdoor gardens, as well as a Japanese garden and a peace garden.

🏛 **Rock and Roll Hall of Fame and Museum**
1100 Rock and Roll Blvd. **Tel** (216) 781-7625. **Open** 10am–5:30pm daily (till 9pm Wed). **Closed** Thanksgiving, Dec 25. 🎫 (under 9s free). ♿
🌐 **rockhall.com**

🏛 **Greater Cleveland Aquarium**
2000 Sycamore St. **Tel** (216) 298-4918, (888) 262-4748. **Open** 10am–6pm daily. 🎫 ♿ 🌐 **greatercleveland aquarium.com**

🏛 **Cleveland Museum of Art**
11150 East Blvd. **Tel** (216) 421-7340, (888) 262-4748. **Open** 10am–5pm Tue–Sun (until 9pm Wed, Fri, Sat). **Closed** Mon, Jan 1, Jul 4, Thanksgiving, Dec 25. ♿
🌐 **clevelandart.org**

**Environs**
Located 25 miles (40 km) west of Cleveland, **Oberlin** is home to Oberlin College, one of the first to admit African-American and female students. The **Allen Memorial Art Museum** on campus displays American, Asian, and European art.

The steel manufacturing center, **Canton**, 60 miles (96 km) south of Cleveland, is famed for the **Pro Football Hall of Fame**, which has been visited by millions of fans.

The Rock and Roll Hall of Fame and Museum in downtown Cleveland

Perry's Victory Memorial at Put-in-Bay,
Lake Erie Islands

## ㉒ Lake Erie Islands

🏖 ℹ️ 770 SE Catawba Rd, Port
Clinton, (800) 441-1271.
W **shoresandislands.com**

Located just offshore from the
Marblehead Peninsula
separating Sandusky Bay from
Lake Erie, the Lake Erie Islands
are a prime summer tourist
destination. The islands include
the bucolic, peaceful Kelleys
Island and the rowdier South
Bass Island, with the village
of Put-in-Bay as its lively
nightlife center.

Home of the Erie, Ottawa,
and Huron Indian tribes until
the 19th century, the Lake Erie
Islands rose to national
prominence during the War of
1812. On September 10, 1813,
US Navy Commodore Oliver
Hazard Perry defeated the more
heavily fortified British fleet in
the pivotal Battle of Lake Erie,
fought off South Bass Island.
A visitor center and a 352-ft
(107-m) granite column at Put-
in-Bay, **Perry's Victory and
International Peace Memorial**,
commemorates his victory and
his famous message to US
General William Henry Harrison:
"We have met the enemy and
they are ours."

**Kelleys Island State Park** has
the fascinating Glacial Grooves, a
series of deep limestone grooves
caused by the movement of a
heavy glacial wall. These grooves
have been protected from
quarrying since 1923.

Short ferry rides from nearby
Sandusky and Marblehead are
available. The Marblehead
Lighthouse, built in 1821,
is a popular regional icon.

🏛 **Perry's Victory & International
Peace Memorial**
93 Delaware Ave, Put-in-Bay, S Bass
Island. **Tel** (419) 285-2184.
**Open** late Apr–Oct: 10am–5pm daily,
or by appointment. 🎟 (children
under 16 free). ♿ W **nps.gov/pevi**

🌲 **Kelleys Island State Park**
Kelleys Island. **Tel** (419) 746-2546.
**Open** 6am–10pm daily. ♿
W **ohiostateparks.org**

## ㉓ Sandusky

🏙 29,800. 🚍 🚌 🚐 ℹ️ 4424 Milan
Rd, Sandusky, (800) 255-3743.
W **shoreandislands.com**

Sandusky was once one of the
Great Lakes' largest coal-
shipping ports. Today, its ferry
terminal provides easy access to
many of the Lake Erie Islands.
The city is, however, best
known for the 364-acre (147-ha)
**Cedar Point Amusement Park**,
which claims to have the
world's largest collection of
roller coasters. They range from
rickety old wooden ones to the
high-speed Magnum,
Millennium Force, and Top
Thrill Dragster. Windseeker,
a 30-story tall swing ride, is
another exciting ride. Cedar
Point also includes a water
park, the children-centered
Camp Snoopy, and a sandy
Lake Erie beach.

🎢 **Cedar Point Amusement Park**
1 Cedar Point Dr. **Tel** (419) 627-2350.
**Open** mid-May–Labor Day:
10am–8pm or later daily; Labor Day–
end of Oct: days vary, call first. 🎟 ♿
W **cedarpoint.com**

## ㉔ Toledo

🏙 314,000. ✈ 🚍 🚌 ℹ️ 401
Jefferson Ave, (800) 243-4667.
W **dotoledo.org**

One of the world's leading glass
manufacturing centers and the
third-busiest Great Lakes port,
Toledo occupies a Maumee
River site steeped in history.
The 1794 Battle of Fallen
Timbers that took place nearby
opened northwestern Ohio and
Indiana to white settlement.
The area was also a strategic
one during the War of 1812.

Today, the city is famed for
the **Toledo Museum of Art**, a
Neo-Classical marble structure
in the historic Old West End
founded by local glass tycoon
Edward Drummond Libbey. The
museum features one of
the world's largest collections
of ornamental glass, housed in
the Post-Modern **Glass
Pavilion** that opened in 2008.
The nearby **Fort Meigs State
Memorial**, which is a
reconstructed fort dating from
the War of 1812, was rebuilt in
2003. It features a museum and
interactive displays, and various
outdoor re-enactments are
organized throughout the
summer by staff and volunteers
in period costume. Fort Meigs,
about 10 miles (16 km) south
of Toledo in Perrysburg,
commemorates the stockade
that withstood two British and
Native American sieges in 1813.

🏛 **Toledo Museum of Art**
2445 Monroe St. **Tel** (419) 255-8000.
**Open** 10am–4pm Tue–Sat (to 10pm
Fri, 6pm Sat), noon–6pm Sun. **Closed**
Jan 1, Jul 4, Thanksgiving, Dec 25. ♿
W **toledomuseum.org**

A roller-coaster ride at Cedar Point Amusement Park, Sandusky

# Michigan

This inland state has a rich maritime history. Michigan's principal landmass, the so-called Lower Peninsula, is a mitten-shaped area surrounded by three Great Lakes – Michigan, Huron, and Erie. This landmass contains the largest cities, including Detroit, and accounts for most of Michigan's industry and population. In the 19th century, the Lower Peninsula, with its wind-blown dunes and rolling cherry orchards, was a prime destination. The rugged Upper Peninsula to the northwest, whose northern border is Lake Superior, only became part of the state in 1834. It has also become a popular tourist getaway.

The annual jazz festival in Detroit's Hart Plaza

## ⑳ Detroit

🗺 951,270. ✈ 🚉 🚌
ℹ 211 W Fort St, (800) 338-7648.
🌐 visitdetroit.com

Known today as the "Motor City," Detroit (meaning "the Strait" in French) was founded in 1701 by the French fur trader Antoine de la Mothe Cadillac. The city has since evolved from a ship-building center into a leading manufacturer of railroad equipment, cars, and bicycles. Its massive industrial growth, however, took place after Henry Ford began manufacturing automobiles in Detroit in 1896. By the 1920s, most American automobile manufacturers – Ford, General Motors, Pontiac, and Chrysler – had moved their headquarters and production facilities to the city.

The automobile industry still dominates Detroit. A web of highways fans out from the city's revitalized downtown. The city's present focal point is the huge riverfront **Renaissance Center**, General Motors' current headquarters. Nearby, **Hart Plaza** hosts year-round

riverfront festivals, including the Detroit Jazz Festival during Labor Day weekend. Directly across, the 25-ft (8-m) Big Fist outdoor sculpture on Woodward Avenue, is a tribute to the local African-American boxer Joe Louis, known as "The Brown Bomber." East of downtown is the lively Greektown neighborhood and restaurant district centered on Monroe Avenue. Just north of downtown are **Comerica Park** and **Ford Field**, two famous sports venues.

### 🏛 Charles H. Wright Museum of African American History

315 E Warren Ave. **Tel** (313) 494-5800. **Open** 9am–5pm Tue–Sat, 1–5pm Sun. **Closed** Mon, public hols. 🎟 &
🌐 thewright.org

Built in 1997, this center commemorates the contributions made by Detroit's large African-American population to the city's commercial and cultural progress. It depicts the Middle Passage of enslaved Africans across the Atlantic, the Underground

Railroad, the Civil Rights Movement, and other milestones in African-American history. There is an exciting program of changing exhibits, as well as some that are long-term. One of these, aimed at very young children, is called "A is for Africa" and has 26 interactive stations and a three-dimensional "dictionary."

### 🏛 Detroit Institute of Arts

5200 Woodward Ave, Detroit Cultural Center. **Tel** (313) 833-7900. **Open** 10am–4pm Wed–Thu, 10am–10pm Fri, 10am–5pm Sat–Sun. **Closed** Mon, Tue, public hols. 🎟 (children under 6 free). 🌐 dia.org

The museum's centerpiece is a vast 27-panel mural by Mexico City artist Diego Rivera. His controversial *Detroit Industry* depicts the automobile manufacturing process in a stark way, reflecting the artist's Leftist views of the relationship between management and labor.

The museum's outstanding collections range from pre-Columbian, Native American, and African art to 17th-century Dutch and Flemish paintings. It has a large selection of 19th-century American paintings.

### 🏛 Detroit Historical Museum

Detroit Historical Museums & Society
5401 Woodward Ave. **Tel** (313) 833-1805. **Open** 9:30am–3pm Wed–Fri, 10am–5pm Sat, noon–5pm Sun. **Closed** public hols. 🎟 (children under 4 free). &
🌐 detroithistorical.org

The renovated "Streets of Old Detroit" display, as well as a permanent exhibit on Detroit's automotive heritage, are the main features of this museum in the Detroit Cultural Corridor near Wayne State University. The society's **Historic Fort Wayne and Tuskegee Airmen Museum**,

*Nymph and Eros*, on display at the Detroit Institute of Arts

*For hotels and restaurants see pp422–7*

along the Detroit River on the city's southwest side, incorporates many of the surviving buildings from Fort Wayne, the last military bastion to defend the city. The fort is open Saturday and Sunday, and the museum is open by appointment only. The society also operates the **Dossin Great Lakes Museum** in Belle Isle Park on the Detroit River.

### 🏛 Motown Historical Museum

2648 W Grand Blvd. **Tel** (313) 875-2264. **Open** 10am–6pm Tue–Sat (also Mon during summer). **Closed** Sun, public hols. 🛗
**w** motownmuseum.org

During the early 1960s, the Motown record label revolutionized American popular music with its trademark "Motown Sound" – a melodic blend of pop, soul, and rhythm and blues. The creative genius of label founder Berry Gordy Jr. and his stable of talented artists such as Marvin Gaye, Smokey Robinson, Stevie Wonder, the Temptations, and Diana Ross and the Supremes are honored in this museum, housed in the original brick building where hit

Vintage transportation on display at the Henry Ford Museum in Dearborn

records such as "Heard It Through the Grapevine" and "Baby Love" were produced. The renovated building, called Hitsville USA by Gordy, has a wide-ranging display of old photographs, instruments, and recording equipment, including the original "Studio A" where the classic sounds were first created. Displays narrate the story of Motown as the singlemost successful independent African-American-controlled record label in the history of the country. Today this label is owned by the PolyGram Corporation.

### Environs

The suburb of Dearborn, 8 miles (13 km) west of Detroit, is home

to the **Henry Ford**, an indoor and outdoor museum that has one of the nation's most impressive collections of Americana. Within the complex is the **Henry Ford Museum**, which displays vintage transportation and other artifacts; this is also the starting point for the high-tech Ford Rouge Factory Tour. The open-air Greenfield Village exhibits Ford's eclectic collection. These include diverse objects: a cot used by George Washington; the chair in which Abraham Lincoln was shot; inventor Thomas Edison's laboratory; John F. Kennedy's presidential limousine; the Rosa Parks bus; and the Dayton home and bicycle shop of Orville and Wilbur Wright.

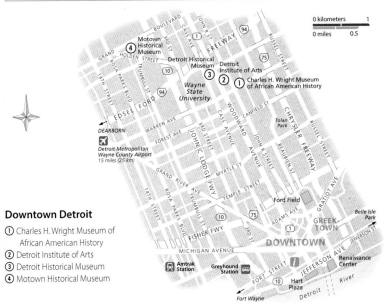

## Downtown Detroit

① Charles H. Wright Museum of African American History

② Detroit Institute of Arts

③ Detroit Historical Museum

④ Motown Historical Museum

**For keys to symbols** see back flap

University of Michigan campus,
Ann Arbor

# ❷ Ann Arbor

🏙 114, 000. ✈ 🚃 🚌 *i* 120 W
Huron St, (800) 888- 9487.
Ⓦ visitannarbor.org

A picturesque, mid-size city, with a vibrant pedestrian-friendly downtown, Ann Arbor is a bastion of laid-back liberalism and environmental activism on the western fringe of Detroit. The city's independent streak springs from the professors and students affiliated with the **University of Michigan**, the city's largest employer.

Music, film, and art festivals are a year-round tradition. One of the nation's largest outdoor art fairs is held in the city. This annual July event attracts more than 1,000 artists and 500,000 art fans and dealers.

**The Hands On Museum** introduces children to science, math, and technology in fun, interactive ways. Inside the nine galleries are at least 250 interactive exhibits; in one gallery preschoolers can dress up like firefighters and splash in water.

The 2,800-acre (1,133-ha) Gothic central campus of the University of Michigan straddles Washtenaw Avenue, southeast of downtown. The **Kelsey Museum of Archaeology**, on the main campus, houses a variety of Greek, Roman, Egyptian, and Near Eastern artifacts.

# ❷ Lansing

🏙 119,128. ✈ 🚃 🚌 *i* 500 E
Michigan Ave, (888) 252-6746.
Ⓦ lansing.org

A government and industrial center, this city benefits from its proximity to the Michigan State University in adjacent East Lansing. Selected as the state capital in 1847, the subsequent arrival of railroads in 1871 and the completion of the downtown statehouse in 1879 fueled the city's growth. The **Michigan Historical Museum** recounts the construction of the Second Renaissance Revival-style State Capitol and traces the state's history from the prehistoric era to the present through various interactive exhibits.

Lansing's status as a major automotive manufacturing center is linked to the business founded by Ransom E. Olds, who began building prototype vehicles here in 1885. He later produced the Curved Dash Olds, considered by many to have been the world's first mass-produced automobile. The **R.E. Olds Transportation Museum** has the distinction of showcasing an original 1901 Curved Dash Olds Runabout and a variety of classic Oldsmobiles from the 1930s and 1940s. Also in the collection is the last model, manufactured in 2004. Displays change quarterly.

🏛 **R.E. Olds Transportation Museum**
240 Museum Dr. **Tel** (517) 372-0529.
**Open** 10am–5pm Tue–Sat, noon–5pm Sun. **Closed** Nov–Mar: Sun. ♿

Exhibit from the Olds Museum

# ❷ Grand Rapids

🏙 197,800. ✈ 🚃 🚌 *i* 171
Monroe Ave, Suite 700, (800) 678-9859. Ⓦ experiencegr.com

Grand Rapids owes its reputation as a major furniture manufacturing center to the Grand River that flows through the heart of the city. The water-powered lumber mills that were set up along its banks in the 19th century formed the foundation for the growth of fine furniture makers such as Herman Miller and Steelcase.

East of downtown is the fashionable **Heritage Hill Neighborhood**, a historic district. **Grand Rapids Public Museum** explores the history of the town and has a planetarium. Affiliates include the stately 1895 **Voigt House Victorian Museum**, with its grand period furnishings, and the 1909 **Meyer May House**, one of Frank Lloyd Wright's last Prairie-style family homes. A scenic gathering spot is the spacious **Frederik Meijer Gardens and Sculpture Park**.

Also in town is the **Gerald R. Ford Museum**. It traces the career of the 38th president, who grew up in Grand Rapids, where his father ran a paint and varnish company. The museum includes a holographic tour of the White House and a replica of the Oval Office.

🏛 **Grand Rapids Public Museum**
272 Pearl St NW. **Tel** (616) 929-1700.
**Open** hours vary. 📷 ♿
Ⓦ grmuseum.org

Frank Lloyd Wright's 1909 Meyer May House in Grand Rapids

Hikers at Sleeping Bear Dunes National Lakeshore, Lake Michigan Shore

# 29 Lake Michigan Shore

🚆 🚌 **i** 741 Kenmoor Ave, Grand Rapids, (800) 442-2084. **W** wmta.org

A major tourist destination since wealthy Chicagoans first came here in the late 1800s, the Lake Michigan Shore is lined with sandy beaches, 19th-century resorts, working ports, and many scenic lighthouses. The resort town of Saugatuck makes an ideal base to explore the shore. A noteworthy attraction 20 miles (32 km) south is the excellent **Michigan Maritime Museum**, narrating the history of fishing, shipping, and shipbuilding on the Great Lakes.

Located 200 miles (322 km) to the north on US 31, **Sleeping Bear Dunes National Lakeshore** incorporates many ecosystems and its signature sand dunes, which tower some 460 ft (140 m) above the lakefront beaches and an inland lake. The park's ghost forest of sand-buried trees can be explored through hiking trails or a 7-mile (11-km) drive.

The busy community of **Traverse City**, 30 miles (48 km) north of Sleeping Bear Dunes, is a convenient base to visit the picturesque Old Mission Peninsula. A short trip toward the north along Route 37 provides beautiful views of green rolling hills, cherry orchards, and the lake. At its tip stands the Old Mission Point

Lighthouse, built in 1870. The white wooden structure sits exactly on the 45th parallel.

🏛 **Michigan Maritime Museum**
260 Dyckman Rd, South Haven.
**Tel** (800) 747-3810. **Open** May–late Sep:10am–5pm daily; off-season hours vary, call ahead. 🅿 ♿
**W** michiganmaritimemuseum.org

❌ **Sleeping Bear Dunes National Lakeshore**
9922 Front St, Empire. **Tel** (231) 326-5134. **Open** Park: year-round. Visitor Center: Memorial Day–Labor Day: 8am–6pm daily; Labor Day–Memorial Day: 8:15am–4pm daily. **Closed** Jan 1, Thanksgiving, Dec 25. 🅿 ♿
**W** nps.gov/slbe

# 30 Mackinac Island

🗺 500. 🚆 🚌 **i** Main St, (800) 454-5227. **W** mackinacisland.org

The limestone outcrop of Mackinac Island, covering 4 sq miles (10 sq km), sits in the middle of the Straits of Mackinac, separating the Lower and Upper Peninsulas. Ferries that depart regularly from Mackinaw City and St. Ignace on the mainland are the only way to reach the island, where no cars are permitted. The principal landmark here is the 1887 **Grand Hotel** *(see p423)*, a classic Gilded Age summer resort that has the world's longest front porch, at 660 ft (201 m). Fort Mackinac, overlooking the harbor, is in the **Mackinac Island State Park**. This restored fort commemorates the island's 18th-century past as a French,

British, and American military outpost through a variety of demonstrations as well as multimedia shows.

# 31 Upper Peninsula

🚆 🚌 **i** Iron Mountain, (906) 774-5480, (800) 562-7134.
**W** uptravel.com
Soo Locks Boat Tours: Dock #1, 1157 E Portage Ave, Sault Ste. Marie. **Tel** (800) 432-6301. **Open** May 1–Oct 15; call for tour schedule. 🅿 (children under 5 free). ♿ **W** soolocks.com

The sparsely populated wilderness of the 384-mile- (618-km-) wide Upper Peninsula is dotted with old lumber, mining, and fishing towns, and some of Michigan's most striking natural attractions. Also called the "UP," this region was first explored by 17th-century French adventurers, one of whom, Etienne Brule, established Michigan's oldest community, **Sault Sainte Marie**, on its northeastern tip.

One of its most popular attractions, **Pictured Rocks National Lakeshore**, stretches along Lake Superior. Although accessible by car from Hwy 28, this 40-mile (64-km) stretch of beaches and bluffs can be viewed more dramatically on guided cruises, departing from Munising.

For more rugged scenery, head west to **Porcupine Mountains Wilderness State Park** along Lake Superior. It is known for its forests, lakes, rivers, and a 90-mile (145-km) network of hiking trails.

Cannon at the British Landing, Mackinac Island State Park

# Wisconsin

Most Americans associate Wisconsin either with cheese – because of its advertised nickname of "America's Dairyland" – or with beer, from Milwaukee's many historic breweries. While both images are accurate, this predominantly agricultural state is the Midwest's premier vacation destination. Wisconsin's recreational jewels range from the gorgeous Apostle Islands on its northern Lake Superior coast to dozens of carefully maintained state parks, forests, and trails that allow hikers and bikers to explore glacial moraines, rugged lakeside cliffs, broad rivers, dense forests, and lush green valleys. The Ice Age National Scenic Trail stretches 1,000 miles (1,600 km).

Façade of the 1892 Pabst Mansion in Milwaukee

## ❷ Milwaukee

🏙 597,000. ✈ 🚆 🚌 ℹ 400 W Wisconsin Ave, (800) 554-1448. 🎭 Summerfest. 🆆 **milwaukee.org**

Like Chicago, its more famous neighbor 90 miles (145 km) to the south, this manufacturing and brewing center grew up on a swampy Lake Michigan marshland. Treaties signed with local Indian tribes opened the area to white settlement in the 1830s. The city's strong German ambience dates to the arrival of "Forty-Eighters," the revolutionaries who fled Germany after an aborted attempt to overthrow the monarchy in 1848. By the 1870s, Milwaukee had as many as six daily German-language newspapers.

Pabst, Blatz, Schlitz, and Miller were the beers that "made Milwaukee famous." This tradition took such strong root in the city that even the local baseball team came to be called the Brewers. Milwaukee's

wealthy beer barons were active philanthropists, investing in the arts, architecture, and social causes. The city's spectacular Lake Michigan shoreline hosts a long schedule of festivals, the most popular being Summerfest, an 11-day culinary and musical extravaganza that takes place in late June and early July.

The **Harley-Davidson Museum**, which sits in a 20-acre (8-ha) campus, celebrates a century of motorcycle manufacturing in Milwaukee and is a global mecca for bikers. The building's industrial design includes 80-ft- (24-m-) high towers of exposed galvanized steel. Inside are about 140 Harley vehicles and 16,000 smaller artifacts. Interactive features engage the interest of both children and adults.

The **Milwaukee County Historical Society** is located in the heart of downtown. Housed in a restored stately Beaux Arts bank building, the institution provides an

excellent introduction to the city's economic, political, and social history.

To its southwest, the 150,000-sq-ft- (13,935-sq-m-) **Milwaukee Public Museum** is part science museum, part local and cultural history center. Its interactive, child-targeted science holdings include the world's largest dinosaur skull and a glass-enclosed tropical butterfly garden. The museum's pre-Columbian and Native American exhibits paint a vivid and honest portrait of the culture and fate of the continent's Native Americans, while the "Streets of Old Milwaukee" provides a fascinating glimpse of this metropolitan melting pot.

Captain Frederick Pabst, a successful Milwaukee brewer, amassed a fortune with his popular Pabst Blue Ribbon beer brand and real-estate investments. The cornerstone of his empire, the 1892 Flemish Renaissance-Revival-style **Pabst Mansion**, lies at the west end of the city's grand Wisconsin Avenue. At that time the 37-room palace was considered one of the world's most technologically sophisticated houses, as it was equipped with full electrical service, a heating system, and nine bathrooms.

Located in the city's Historic Third Ward warehouse district, south of downtown and a mecca for upscale shopping and entertainment, the **Eisner:**

Spectacular entrance of the Milwaukee Art Museum

**American Museum of Advertising and Design** critically assesses the impact of advertising on culture and society. It is one of the few museums in the country dedicated to this subject. Exhibits focus on topics as diverse as the marketing of US presidents and the use of sports heroes to market beer.

Eastward, the lakefront **Milwaukee Art Museum** was established in 1888 and holds a 20,000-piece collection, renovated galleries, and a vast reception hall, designed by Spanish architect Santiago Calatrava. This pavilion has a grand, winglike sunshade to complement the museum's windswept setting. Its signature collections are its Frank Lloyd Wright decorative arts holdings.

Pabst Brewing Company closed in 1996, but the 14 German Renaissance-Revival buildings on the historic campus are being renovated. The former headquarters, called **Best Place**, is open for guided tours.

The Miller Brewing Company, the only longtime brewer still in operation in the city, is at the town's western edge. This firm, which produces the top-selling Miller beers, opened in 1855, when immigrant brewer Frederick Miller purchased the floundering Plank Road Brewery. Today, it is the second-largest brewer in the US, after the St. Louis-based Anheuser-Busch *(see p451)*. The **MillerCoors Brewery Tour** takes visitors on an hour-long tour of its brewery and the nearby Caves Museum, where beer was naturally cooled deep inside Milwaukee's bluffs. The tour covers the company's rich history, as well as the modern technology used to brew the beer today. Complimentary MillerCoors beverages, including sodas for children, are offered at the end of the tour.

Milwaukee's other major sight is the **Annunciation Greek Orthodox Church**, one of Frank Lloyd Wright's last commissions. Designed in 1956, it was opened in 1961, two years after Wright's death.

**Ⅲ Harley-Davidson Museum**
400 Canal St. **Tel** (877) 436-8738. **Open** 10am–6pm daily (until 8pm Thu). 🎟 (children under 5 free). 🎞 ♿ 🖥 **harley-davidson.com**

**Ⅲ The Eisner: American Museum of Advertising & Design**
208 N Water St. **Tel** (414) 847-3290. **Open** 11am–5pm Wed–Fri, noon–5pm Sat, 1–5pm Sun. **Closed** public hols. 🎟 (children under 12 free). ♿ 🖥 **eisnermuseum.org**

**Ⅲ Milwaukee Art Museum**
700 N Art Museum Dr. **Tel** (414) 224-3200. **Open** 10am–5pm daily, (until 8pm Thu). **Closed** Thanksgiving, Dec 25. 🎟 (children under 13 free). ♿ 🖥 **mam.org**

**Ⅲ Best Place**
901 W Juneau Ave. **Tel** (414) 630-1609. **Open** Wed–Sun. 🎟 🎞 ♿ 🖥 **bestplacemilwaukee.com**

**⚑ MillerCoors Brewery Tour**
4251 W State St. **Tel** (800) 944-5483. **Open** Call (414) 931-2337 for free guided tours. ♿ **Closed** Sun, public hols. 🖥 **millerbrewing.com**

## ❸ Door County

🚗 🚌 🄘 1015 Green Bay Rd, Sturgeon Bay, (920) 743-4456, (800) 527-3529. 🖥 **doorcounty.com**

Stretching like the spout of a teapot, between Green Bay and Lake Michigan, the Door Peninsula is a rugged New England-like expanse of rolling hills, lakeside cliffs, and pretty port villages. The county comprises the northern two-thirds of the peninsula and derives its name from the French-Canadian voyageurs' sobriquet for the treacherous shipping channel off the peninsula's northern point – Porte des Morts, or "Death's Door." The area's fishing and shipping heritage is on display at the **Door County Maritime Museum**, in downtown Sturgeon Bay, the county's largest port and southernmost city. A few miles north, on Highway 57, is **The Farm**, a traditional Wisconsin dairy farm and petting zoo, replete with an array of animals – cows, goats, pigs, chickens, horses, and barn cats. The peninsula's 250-mile (402-km) shoreline is lined with more than a dozen county parks

The historic 1868 Eagle Bluff Lighthouse in Door County, restored to its former glory

and five magnificent state parks. The largest of these is the 6-sq-mile (15-sq-km) **Peninsula State Park**, between the picturesque communities of Fish Creek and Ephraim on the northwestern coast. After traversing the park's miles of hiking and biking trails and visiting the restored Eagle Bluff Lighthouse, visitors can take in a performance at Peninsula Players, the nation's oldest resident summer stock theater company.

**Washington Island**, 6 miles (10 km) across the Porte des Morts Straits to the northeast of Newport State Park, can be reached, year-round, via a short ferry ride. The island was home to the Potawatomi Indians until a hardy group of Icelandic immigrants arrived in the 19th century. The latter's descendants continue to farm the island's fertile soil and to welcome day-trippers who come in search of peace, quiet, and splendid lake views.

**Ⅲ Door County Maritime Museum**
120 N Madison Ave, Sturgeon Bay. **Tel** (920) 743-5958. **Open** 10am–5pm daily (Memorial Day–Labor Day: 9am–6pm daily). **Closed** some public hols. 🎟 ♿ 🖥 **dcmm.org**

**❂ Peninsula State Park**
9462 Shore Rd, Fish Creek. **Tel** (920) 868-3258. **Open** 6am–11pm daily. 🎟 ♿ 🖥 **dnr.state.wi.us**

Guided boat tour along the Wisconsin River

## ❸ Wisconsin Dells

🏙 2,400. ℹ 701 Superior St, (800)
223-3557. 🌐 wisdells.com

Wisconsin Dells has one of the
most spectacular locations along
the Wisconsin River as it winds
through an awe-inspiring,
15-mile (24-km) stretch of
deep sandstone canyons.
The area's natural beauty and
a variety of man-made
attractions make it a prime
summer vacation destination.
Among the highlights are the
guided **Dells Boat Tours**, which
offer excursions past the storied
cliffs through the Upper and
Lower Dells. The highest
concentration of water parks
in the world – 22 are indoors –
make the area popular with
families in winter, too.

The region owes much of
its popularity to photographer
H.H. Bennett, whose late
19th-century photographs of
the Wisconsin River's rugged
landscapes became famous
throughout America. The
Wisconsin Historical Society
operates the **H.H. Bennett
Studio and History Center**.

**Dells Boat Tours**
Upper & Lower Dells Docks.
**Tel** (608) 254-8555.
**Open** Apr–Oct: 10am–7pm daily (until
4pm spring, fall). 🅿 ♿
🌐 dellsboats.com

**H.H. Bennett Studio &
History Center**
215 Broadway, Wisconsin Dells.
**Tel** (608) 253-3523. **Open** May–Oct:
10am–4pm daily (Jun–Aug: open
some eves). 🅿 (children under 5
free). ♿ 🌐 wisconsinhistory.org/
hhbennett

## ❸ Baraboo

🏙 10,700. ℹ 600 W Chestnut St,
(800) 227-2266. 🌐 baraboo.com

This tiny town was the winter
base of the Ringling Brothers
Circus *(see p319)* from 1884 until
1918. Thereafter, the troupe
merged with its popular rival
Barnum and Bailey to create the
Ringling Brothers, Barnum and
Bailey Circus, the largest in
the United
States. The
**Circus World
Museum**,
located on the
original Ringling
wintering
grounds, has a
museum with one
of the world's
largest collections
of carved and
painted circus wagons.
Live performances by clowns,
trapeze artists, an elephant, and
horse riders take place under
the Big Top during the summer.

The **International Crane
Foundation** shelters all 15
species of the bird.

Circus World Museum,
Baraboo

**Circus World Museum**
550 Water St. **Tel** (866) 693-1500.
**Open** mid-Mar–mid-May & Sep–Oct:
10am–4pm daily; mid-May–mid-Jun:
9am–6pm daily; mid-Jun–Sep:
9:30am–6pm Mon–Fri. 🅿 (children
under 5 free). ♿ 🌐 circusworld
museum.com

## ❸ Madison

🏙 240,000. ✈ 🚉 🚌 ℹ 21 N Park
St, (800) 373-6376.
🌐 visitmadison.com

Nestled on a narrow isthmus of
land between Lake Mendota
and Lake Monona, Madison is
one of the country's most
attractively situated capital cities.
Established as the territorial
capital in 1836, it became the
state capital and home of the
lakeside University of Wisconsin
campus when Wisconsin
achieved statehood, in 1848.

The majestic, 200-ft (60-m)
dome of the **Wisconsin State
Capitol** rises above the city's
beautiful downtown. Among its
key interior features are a

rotunda encircled by marble
Corinthian columns and an
exquisite four-panel, glass
mosaic symbolizing the
themes of liberty and justice.

Madison is considered one of
the nation's best places to live
and work. The University of
Wisconsin and the city's liberal
political leanings have drawn
scores of artists, environ-
mentalists, and health-food
devotees to the area. As a
result, downtown features a
variety of bookshops,
galleries, and
restaurants that are
vegetarian-friendly.
A network of biking
and walking trails
provides access to the
shimmering lakes
around the city of
Madison.

The **Monona Terrace
Community and Convention
Center**, completed in 1997 from
plans proposed by Frank Lloyd
Wright *(see p394–5)*, has a
tranquil rooftop garden that
provides great views of
downtown and Lake Monona. It
includes a memorial to soul
singer Otis Redding, who died in
a plane crash on the lake in 1967.

**Wisconsin State Capitol**
2 E Main St. **Tel** (608) 266-0382. **Open**
8am–6pm Mon–Fri, 8am–4pm Sat–
Sun. 🅿 🅿 ♿ 🌐 wisconsin.gov

**Monona Terrace Community
& Convention Center**
2 blocks E of Capitol Square. **Tel** (608)
261-4000. **Open** 8am–5pm daily.
🅿 1pm daily. ♿
🌐 mononaterrace.com

Majestic dome of the Wisconsin State
Capitol, Madison

Taliesin, architect Frank Lloyd Wright's sprawling estate in Spring Green

## ❸ Spring Green

🏔 1,300. 🚌 ℹ 150 E Jefferson St, (800) 588-2042. 🌐 **springgreen.com**

This handsome farming community lies just north of the Wisconsin River. In 1911, architect Frank Lloyd Wright, who spent his childhood in nearby Richland Center, built **Taliesin** ("Shining Brow" in Welsh) on a bluff overlooking the river. The 600-acre (240-ha) estate was Wright's home until his death in 1959 and included a school where his disciples were instructed in his Prairie-style design philosophy. Today, the Taliesin Fellowship runs the school and an architectural firm on the grounds. Guided tours lead visitors through Wright's eclectic home and gardens. About 9 miles (14 km) north of Spring Green is the **House on the Rock**. This sprawling resort complex has a home built on top of a 60-ft (18-m) chimney rock. The house, built in the 1940s by eccentric architect Alex Jordan, is the focal point for a rambling museum exhibiting Jordan's vast collection of Americana.

🏠 **Taliesin**
5607 County Rd C, Spring Green.
**Tel** (608) 588-7900, (877) 588-7900.
**Open** May–Oct: 9am–6pm daily. 🚫
♿ 🌐 **taliesinpreservation.org**

🏠 **House on the Rock**
5754 Hwy 23. **Tel** (608) 935-3639.
**Open** Mar–Oct: 9am–5pm daily (to 6pm Jun–Aug). **Closed** most weekdays Nov–Mar; Thanksgiving, Dec 25. 🚫 ♿
🌐 **houseontherock.com**

## ❸ La Crosse

🏔 51,000. ✈ 🚇 🚌 ℹ 410 Veterans Memorial Dr, (800) 658-9424.
🌐 **explorelacrosse.com**

Founded as a trading post in 1842, La Crosse emerged as a key railroad junction after the Civil War. The city's well-preserved downtown district, and tree-lined neighborhoods around the University of Wisconsin-La Crosse campus add to its charm. It also makes a fine base for exploring the Mississippi River towns along the Great River Road Scenic Byway *(see p51)* as it passes through the state.

Sailor mannequins for sale at Bayfield

East of downtown, **Grandad Bluff**, 600 ft (180 m) above the city, offers superb views of La Crosse and the Mississippi River

Grandad Bluff, an observation point east of downtown La Crosse

Valley. Rides on restored paddlewheel steamboats offer a relaxed way to enjoy great views of the river. Another alternative may be **Perrot State Park**, 30 miles (48 km) north of La Crosse. In Trempeleau, south of the park entrance, stands the Trempeleau Hotel, the town's only building to have survived a fire that took place in 1888.

## ❸ Apostle Islands

🚌 Bayfield. ℹ (800) 447-4094.
🌐 **bayfield.org**

Off the state's northeastern Lake Superior coast lie a group of 22 islands, the remains of retreating glaciers from the last Ice Age. They were named the Apostle Islands by 17th-century French missionaries, who incorrectly assumed that the archipelago included only 12 islands. Today, 21 islands form part of the **Apostle Islands National Lakeshore**. The old-growth forests here provide the habitat for resident bald eagles and black bears, while vast stretches of sand beaches with sea caves, carved by the wind and lake into craggy, brownstone cliffs, make the Apostle Islands a popular destination for those interested in ecotourism.

A local cruise service from **Bayfield**, on the mainland, ferries visitors to the islands, one of which holds the 1881 Sand Island Light Station, with its octagonal tower built from locally quarried sandstone. The 22-chain archipelago offers the area's best sea kayaking. Various outfitters in Bayfield rent kayaks and provide guided charter tours.

🏕 **Apostle Islands National Lakeshore**
415 Washington Ave, Bayfield.
**Tel** (715) 779-3397. Visitor Center:
**Open** 8am–4:30pm Mon–Fri.
**Closed** mid-Oct–Apr: Sat & Sun;
federal holidays. 🚫 ♿
🌐 **nps.gov/apis**

# Minnesota

Minnesota has been seductively nicknamed "The Land of 10,000 Lakes." While beautiful lakes have added to the state's appeal as an affordable outdoors destination, it was the meandering rivers that actually shaped Minnesota's history as an important trading and agricultural hub. Many of these rivers, streams, and lakes have now been preserved and offer a rare solitude and natural splendor in vast stretches of its watery wilderness.

*Spoonbridge and Cherry* at the Minneapolis Sculpture Garden, Walker Art Center

## ❹ Minneapolis & St. Paul

Minneapolis: 🅰 368,400. ✈ 🚌 🚆
ℹ 250 Marquette Ave S, (888) 676-6757. 🆆 minneapolis.org
St. Paul: 🅰 287,150. ✈ 🚌 🚆 ℹ
175 W Kellogg Blvd, (800) 627-6101.
🆆 visitstpaul.com

The Twin Cities, separated by the Mississippi, are a study in contrasts. Flamboyant Minneapolis, with its modern skyscrapers, is an urbane, commercial center where most of the state's corporate headquarters, museums, and high-end retail stores are located. St. Paul, the state capital, is more sedate, but has a colorful history, well-preserved downtown, and architectural and cultural attractions.

**Exploring Minneapolis**
Downtown revolves around the pedestrian **Nicollet Mall**, which hosts various cultural events, and the Mississippi riverfront, which is home to the acclaimed Guthrie Theater, the unusual Mill City Museum, and historic Stone Arch Bridge. It also offers walking trails near the water. The **Uptown** neighborhood, on the southwest, revolves around the Chain of Lakes, with its lakeside biking and jogging trails. The country's largest enclosed shopping mall, the **Mall of America**, is in the southern suburb of Bloomington. A light rail system links Mall of America, the international airport, and downtown Minneapolis & St. Paul.

### 🏛 Walker Art Center
1750 Hennepin Ave. **Tel** (612) 375-7600. **Open** 11am–5pm Tue–Sun (until 9pm Thu). **Closed** public hols. 🎟 (free 5–9pm Thu; children under 18 free). 🎟 2pm Thu–Sun. ♿
🆆 walkerart.org

The performing, visual, and media arts are the focus of the exhibits at the Twin Cities' most complete contemporary art resource. Among the highlights are the minimalist work of sculptor Donald Judd, including the restored 1971 *Untitled*, a group of six, large-scale aluminum cubes, and realist painter Edward Hopper's *Office at Night* (1940).

### 🏛 Minneapolis Institute of Arts
2400 3rd Ave S. **Tel** (612) 870-3131, (888) 642-2787. **Open** 10am–5pm Tue–Sun (until 9pm Thu). **Closed** Jul 4, Thanksg., Dec 24, 25. ♿
🆆 artsmia.org

Established in 1915, this is one of the region's largest and most highly regarded museums. Its traditional collection includes a wide range of Greek and Roman statuary, Italian and Dutch Renaissance paintings, as well as American works by Georgia O'Keeffe and regionalist Grant Wood.

The **Ulrich Architecture and Design Gallery** houses an astonishing collection of Prairie School furniture, architectural fragments, art-glass windows, and silver.

## Downtown Minneapolis

① Walker Art Center
② Minneapolis Institute of Arts
③ American Swedish Institute

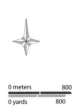

0 meters 800
0 yards 800

**For keys to symbols** *see back flap*

## American Swedish Institute

2600 Park Ave. **Tel** (612) 871-4907. **Open** noon–5pm Tue–Sun (until 8pm Wed, open 10am Sat). **Closed** public hols. 🅿️ ♿
🆆 americanswedishinst.org

Housed in a grand 1907 Romanesque mansion, this institute chronicles the contributions of Swedish-Americans to the state's history and culture. Guided tours of the house, built by Swedish newspaper publisher Swan Turnblad, allow visitors to view his collection of Swedish-American *kakelugnar* (porcelain tile stoves), wood carvings, textiles, and immigration artifacts.

## Exploring St. Paul

Founded in 1841 on the site of Pig's Eye, the notorious French-Canadian trading post, St. Paul flourished as the busiest river port on the Upper Mississippi. By the late 19th century, the new state capital had emerged as a railroad hub, powered by the completion of the railroad between St. Paul and Seattle in 1893. The stately Romanesque, Queen Anne, and Jacobean mansions along **Summit Avenue** date from those prosperous days. Downtown centers on the Art Deco City Hall and Courthouse on Kellogg Boulevard and St. Peter Street. The popular Minnesota Public Radio program *A Prairie Home Companion* is recorded live on many Saturdays at the **Fitzgerald Theater**, a beautifully restored 1910 vaudeville and movie palace at Exchange and Wabasha Streets. The city also hosts the annual Minnesota State Fair.

## Minnesota State Capitol

75 Rev. Dr. Martin Luther King Jr. Blvd. 📞 (651) 296-2881. **Open** 8:30am–5pm Mon–Fri, 10am–3pm Sat, 1–4pm Sun. **Closed** most public holidays. ♿

Designed by Cass Gilbert, architect of the US Supreme Court *(see p203)*, this monumental domed Beaux Arts structure features the sculpture *Progress of the State*, a group of gold-leafed copper and steel statues in the front.

*The sculpture Progress of the State, Minnesota State Capitol*

## City Hall & Courthouse

15 W Kellogg Blvd. **Tel** (651) 266-8500. **Open** 8am–4:30pm Mon–Fri. ♿

This Art Deco masterpiece, painstakingly restored from 1990 to 1993, is built of Indiana limestone and black Wisconsin granite. The structure appears to soar above the surrounding downtown. No detail was spared in the building's construction, with every light fixture, elevator door, railing, mailbox, door handle, and lock specially crafted in the ornate style of Art Deco.

## Minnesota History Center

345 Kellogg Blvd W. **Tel** (800) 657-3773. **Open** 10am–5pm Mon (public hols only), 10am–8pm Tue, 10am–5pm Wed–Sat, noon–5pm Sun. **Closed** most public hols (except when on Mon). 🅿️ ♿
🆆 mnhs.org/historycenter

A treasure trove of interactive exhibits that chronicles the state's 19th century history is housed in this interesting granite and limestone building. Exhibits such as a huge boxcar, giant grain elevator, lifelike meat-packing plant, and a replica of a 1930s dairy farm help visitors relive history from the point of view of a farmer or factory worker. The center's pop culture highlight, **Sounds Good to Me: Music in Minnesota**, showcases the music that originated here.

## Union Depot

214 4th St E. **Tel** (651) 202-2700. **Open** daily. 📷 ♿ 🆆 uniondepot.org

Built in 1881, the depot re-opened after a major renovation in 2014 as the Twin Cities' hub for public transit (Greyhound bus, Amtrak trains, and the regional light rail that connects Minneapolis and St. Paul). The architectural gem, on 33 acres (13 ha) near the Mississippi River, is open for guided tours.

---

## St. Paul

① Minnesota State Capitol
② City Hall & Courthouse
③ Minnesota History Center
④ Union Depot

0 meters 500
0 yards 500

MINNEAPOLIS 5 miles (9 km)

Minneapolis – St Paul International Airport 8 miles (14 km)

The Mississippi River, seen from the Great River Bluffs State Park, southeast of the river town Winona

# ❹ Mississippi River Towns

🏠 🚌 ℹ️ (763) 212-8556.
🌐 mnmississippiriver.com

The Mississippi River courses 572 miles (921 km) through Minnesota. It originates in the north-central part of the state and continues until its confluence with the St. Croix River near Hastings. South of the confluence, it widens and picks up speed, rushing through deep, fog-laden valleys along the Minnesota-Wisconsin border. The Great River Road Scenic Byway (see p51), or US 61, hugs the river's west bank, revealing breathtaking views of attractive towns and parks.

The 19th-century town of **Red Wing** was built on the site of a Dakota Sioux farming village. Today, the town is known as the headquarters of the Red Wing Shoe Company, the popular work boot manufacturer, established in 1905. A small downtown museum showcases its manufacturing process.

About 10 miles (16 km) southeast of Red Wing is **Frontenac State Park**, one of the premier bird-watching sites along the river, where over 260 species pause on their journeys north and south every year. Bald eagles and warblers flock to the diverse habitats of Lake Pepin,

the widest stretch of the river. The National Eagle Center in Wabasha houses injured raptors that cannot be returned to the wild. Picturesque **Winona**, 65 miles (105 km) southeast of Red Wing and located on an island in the river, is home to the Minnesota Marine Art Museum.

The beautiful **Great River Bluffs State Park**, about 20 miles (32 km) southeast of Winona, occupies one of the river's most scenic stretches.

# ❷ Rochester

🏙️ 90,000. ✈️ 🚌 ℹ️ 30 Civic Center Drive SE, (800) 634-8277.
🌐 visitrochestermn.com

The primary attraction in this southeastern Minnesota city is the **Mayo Clinic**, founded by the physician brothers Will and Charles Mayo in the early 1900s. They initiated the first collaborative medical practice, integrating the findings of a group of medical specialists to diagnose more effectively and treat serious illnesses. About 3,700 physicians and scientists, plus 49,000 health staff, work at three sites, treating more than a million people per year.

🏥 **Mayo Clinic**
200 1st St SW. **Tel** (507) 538-0440.
**Open** general tours at 10am Mon–Fri; art tours at 1:30pm Mon–Fri. 🎫 ♿
🌐 mayoclinic.org

# ❸ Pipestone National Monument

🏞️ 4,600. 🚌 ℹ️ 36 Reservation Ave, (507) 825-5464. Visitor Center:
**Open** 8am–5pm daily. **Closed** Jan 1, Thanksg., Dec 25. 🌐 nps.gov/pipe

Pipestone sits in the state's southwestern corner. The name derives from Dakota Sioux Indians, who lived here for generations, quarrying the region's soft red quartzite to craft elegant ceremonial pipes. The stone catlinite has been named in honor of artist George Catlin, who depicted this place in his 1838 masterpiece, *Pipestone Quarry*.

Indian craftsmen continue the tradition in the remains of the quarries. The pipes are then sold at the adjoining Cultural Center.

Visitors negotiating a trail through Pipestone's quarries

# ⓭ Brainerd Lakes Area

🏙 65,000. ✈ 🚌 ℹ 124 N 6th St, Brainerd, (800) 450-2838.
🌐 **explorebrainerdlakes.com**

Founded by the Northern Pacific Railroad in 1871, the Upper Mississippi River city of Brainerd was carved out of a dense forest, felled to meet the demands of the state's lumber boom. The area's heritage as a hard-working railroad and lumber town is personified in the flannel-shirted, bearded character of Paul Bunyan, the mythical Herculean Minnesota woodsman, and his massive pet, Babe, the Blue Ox. His name seems to appear at every turn; the Paul Bunyan Trail bike route and Paul Bunyan Scenic Byway backroads auto tour are two examples.

Brainerd International Raceway's drag strip is famous for being the fastest place to race in the world.

Brainerd is also the gateway to north-central Minnesota's lake region, where the state's trademark lodge-resorts were first developed on the shores of more than 500 freshwater lakes.

**Babe, the Blue Ox**

**Mille Lacs Lake**, 40 miles (64 km) southeast of Brainerd, is bordered by beautiful state parks and the Mille Lacs Band of Ojibwe tribal reservation. The Minnesota Historical Society collaborated with the tribe to develop the **Mille Lacs Indian Museum**, on the lake's southwest shore.

The restored railroad Depot, the centerpiece of downtown Duluth

# ⓮ Duluth

🏙 87,000. ✈ 🚌 ℹ 21 W Superior St, (800) 438-5884.
🌐 **visitduluth.com**

Minnesota's third-largest city, Duluth is one of the Midwest's most enjoyable destinations. Clinging to the sides of the 800-ft (240-m) high granite slopes that ring its lively downtown, this city successfully juxtaposes numerous nature preserves with operating industries, which fuel its bustling port. Its most striking feature is the **Aerial Lift Bridge**, a huge steel structure linking the mainland to the mouth of the Duluth harbor with a 385-ft (115-m) span. The bridge can raise at the rate of 138 ft (41 m) a minute to allow hulking freighters to pass into the harbor. One of these massive ships, the docked 610-ft (186-m) SS *William A. Irwin*, is now a museum.

The **Great Lakes Aquarium**, an "all-freshwater" aquarium, provides a close-up view of the bridge in action. The Amazing Amazon exhibit features creatures from the largest river in the world. In Canal Park, next to the bridge, the **Lake Superior Maritime Visitor Center** details the shipping history of the Upper Great Lakes. It also relates the US Army Corps of Engineers' feat of constructing the Aerial Lift Bridge in 1930.

The centerpiece of the redbrick-paved streets of Duluth's attractive downtown is the 1892 **Depot**, or **St. Louis County Heritage and Arts Center**. The restored brownstone railroad depot houses the **Duluth Art Institute**, **Lake Superior Railroad Museum**, and several performance art companies. Depot Square, a re-creation of early 20th-century Duluth, features the waiting room where US immigration officials processed many of the state's Scandinavian and German immigrants.

The **North Shore Scenic Railroad** offers sightseeing trips from the depot in period trains (from May to early October). The excursions head north along the shore of Lake Superior, with spectacular views of waterfalls and cliffs plunging down to the shoreline. Motorists can also experience this magical trip on the North Shore Scenic Drive, a section of old Hwy 61 along the lakeshore from Duluth all the way to the Canadian border.

🏛 **The Depot/St. Louis County Heritage & Arts Center**
506 W Michigan St. **Tel** (218) 727-8025.
**Open** Jun–Sep: 9:30am–6pm daily; Sep–May: 10am–5pm Mon–Sat, 1–5pm Sun. 🅿 ♿
🌐 **duluthdepot.org**

Mille Lacs Lake, Minnesota's second-largest lake, southeast of Brainerd

The Mesabi Range, one of the three ranges that comprise the Iron Range

## 🔴 Iron Range

📧 🛈 111 Station 44 Rd, Eveleth (800) 777-8497.

When iron ore was discovered in northeastern Minnesota in the 1880s, waves of immigrant workers came to boomtowns that grew up along three ranges – the Vermilion, Mesabi, and Cuyuna. These ranges collectively came to be known as the Iron Range district. By the 1960s, the mines' productivity diminished and many were shut down, decimating local communities and leaving behind empty mining pits. But in the past three decades, a growing tourist interest in the mining era has revitalized the Iron Range district.

About 225 miles (362 km) north of Minneapolis, the **Soudan Underground Mine** is Minnesota's oldest and deepest iron mine. It opened in 1884, closed in 1962, and is now part of a 5-sq-mile (13-sq-km) state park. Visitors can go a half-mile (1 km) underground into the heart of the mine that also holds an atomic physics lab.

The Iron Range city of Chisholm, 45 miles (72 km) southwest of Soudan, is home to the **Minnesota Discovery Center**. The center presents a theme-park version of the Iron Range story with living history interpreters and trolley rides. Its highlight is the Minnesota CCC History Museum, commemorating the achievements of the state's Civilian Conservation Corps,

a Depression-era program that put 84,000 young men to work on soil and forest conservation projects.

### 🏛 Soudan Underground Mine State Park
1379 Stuntz Bay Rd, Soudan. **Tel** (218) 753-2245. **Open** call for times. 🅿 ♿

### 🏛 Minnesota Discovery Center
1005 Discovery Dr, Chisholm. **Tel** (800) 372-6437. **Open** 10am–5pm Tue–Sat (to 9pm Thu). 🅿 (children under 3 free). ♿
🌐 **mndiscoverycenter.com**

## 🔴 Boundary Waters Canoe Area Wilderness

🛬 📧 🛈 1600 E Sheridan St, Ely, (800) 777-7281, (888) 922-5000.
🌐 **ely.org** 🌐 **grandmarais.com**

The largest, and also the most visited, wilderness preserve east of the Rocky Mountains, the Boundary Waters Canoe Area Wilderness stretches for almost 200 miles (322 km) along the Canadian border in the state's northeastern corner. One of the country's most unspoiled natural regions, this vast area attracts many adventurers seeking an escape from civilization. The region is also one of the world's largest canoeing and fishing destinations, with more than 1,200 miles (1,932 km) of canoe routes which snake through 1,000 streams and lakes in the dense Superior National Forest.

**Statue outside Ironworld**

To preserve the area's unique appeal, there is a limit on the number of campers as well as restrictions on the use of motorized watercraft. The area has no roads, and campers have to carry their equipment from lake to lake via portage methods perfected by the Ojibwe Indians.

Most camping parties begin their exploration at Ely, 240 miles (386 km) north of Minneapolis. One of the park's far-western entry points. The **Dorothy Molter Museum** is a memorial to the wilderness area's last human resident, who ran a resort here and died in 1986. The **International Wolf Center** in town promotes the survival of the region's once-threatened wolf population through interactive exhibits and close views of the resident gray and Arctic wolf. Also in Ely is the North American Bear Center, a research, education, and rehab facility.

Visitors can also take the 63-mile (101-km) Gunflint Trail, a scenic road into the north-eastern corner of the Boundary Waters area. Motorists are encouraged to fill up the tank and pack food and water. Moose may be seen while driving.

### 🏛 Dorothy Molter Museum
2002 E Sheridan St. **Tel** (218) 365-4451. **Open** Memorial Day–Labor Day: 10am–5:30pm Mon–Sat, noon–5:30pm Sun (children under 5 free). ♿ 🌐 **rootbeerlady.com**

### 🏛 International Wolf Center
1396 Hwy 169, Ely. **Tel** (218) 365-4695. **Open** 10am–5pm (Jun–Aug: to 7pm). **Closed** Oct–May: Mon–Thu; Nov–May: Sun. 🅿 (children under 3 free). ♿ 🌐 **wolf.org**

Kayakers on Moose Lake, near Ely, Boundary Waters Wilderness

*For hotels and restaurants see pp422–7*

# ㊽ Voyageurs National Park

ℹ 3131 Highway 53 S, International Falls, (218) 283-6600. 🚌 🚐
ⓦ nps.gov/voya

Pelicans on one of the numerous lakes of Voyageurs National Park

The watery Rainy Lake borderlands west of Superior National Forest contain the old Voyageur Highway, an old network of lakes, streams, and portage routes used by Native Americans and French-Canadian trappers to move furs from the Minnesota and Northern Ontario forests across the Great Lakes to Montreal. The route was taken over by the British after the French and Indian War, and extended as far west as the Canadian province of Alberta.

Lithograph of a fur trapper's cabin

Today, 218,000 acres (87,200 ha) of this Canadian Shield wilderness are preserved in the Voyageurs National Park, a water-based park with 30 large lakes, beaver ponds, and islands – the habitat of large packs of Eastern timber wolves.

Rainy Lake, the finest fishing lake in the park, abounds in walleye, pike, and bass. The Rainy Lake Visitor Center, near International Falls, 295 miles (475 km) north of Minneapolis

and 160 miles (258 km) west of Duluth, is one of three staffed access points to the park and the only one open year-round. The center features interactive exhibits concerning the fur trade and provides information about naturalist-guided tours.

Although most vistors traverse the park's vast area using boat (motorized watercrafts are permitted here) and canoe, hikers can take advantage of a network of hiking trails, including a self-guided trek to Locater Lake and the Cruiser Lake Trail. This trail is the only means of exploring the roadless Kabetogama Peninsula. Shorter guided tours are available at the park visitor centers.

For those people keen on boating, the border city of International Falls is the home base for stocking up on supplies or arranging a boat or

canoe rental. The town's Boise Paper Solutions houses what the company claims to be the "largest, fastest paper machine in the world." In winter, the Voyageurs National Park offers opportunities for such activities as snowmobiling, ice fishing, snowshoeing, and cross-country skiing.

## Wolves

Inside Voyageurs National Park is one of the largest wolf populations in the US. The animals that roam here are gray wolves, one of three species of wolves in the world. Wolves live in packs, dominated by two adult parents, their offspring of the past 2–3 years, and several unrelated members. Contrary to folklore, wolves tend to shy away from humans.

Gray wolf

Aerial view of the many islets in wild, spectacular Voyageurs National Park

# Practical Information

Traveling around the Great Lakes states requires a lot of planning, since there is so much to see and do in such a wide area. From the towering skyscrapers of bustling big cities such as Chicago to the idyllic pastures of Wisconsin, the attractions here are as varied as the six states that form the Great Lakes region. With its rolling hills, endless farmlands, and sublime waterfront wilderness, America's heartland abounds in pristine wonders that offer a wide choice of outdoor pursuits.

## Tourist Information

Each of the Great Lakes states houses at least one state Welcome Center that offers a full range of tourist information, as well as clean restrooms. Most airports have information desks stocked with free brochures and maps. All the larger cities and many smaller towns have Convention & Visitors' Bureaus or Chambers of Commerce, with free directories of attractions, accommodations, and events.

## Natural Hazards

Winters in the northern parts of Michigan, Minnesota, and Wisconsin can be very cold, with blizzards and snowstorms a common occurrence. Visitors should dress warmly and pack a small snow shovel, gloves, and a hat when traversing this region between November and April. Ice and snow can make driving extremely treacherous.

## Getting Around

Most major cities have limited public bus systems. Light rail, subway, and/or commuter train services only run in Chicago, Minneapolis, St. Paul, and Cleveland. The Woodward Avenue streetcar in Detroit is expected to expand the People Mover loop downtown in 2016.

However, driving is the best way to get around this region. Seat belts are a must for drivers, front-seat passengers, and back-seat passengers. Child seats are mandatory for occupants aged four and under (seven and under in Indiana, Illinois, Minnesota, and Michigan). Helmets are compulsory for motorcyclists under the age of 18 in all of the Great Lakes states, except Michigan, where motorcyclists aged 20 and under must wear helmets, and Illinois, which has no restrictions regarding helmet usage. Speed limits vary, but are usually 65–70 mph (105–113 km/h) on Interstate Highways outside urban areas.

## Etiquette

Residents of the Great Lakes are friendly and polite – especially in Minnesota, where the phrase "you bet" epitomizes their helpful attitude. Visitors to the Amish communities in Indiana and Ohio will be impressed by the shy, reserved manner of the Amish, whose simple, black outfits and horse-driven buggies are common sights. Many prefer not to be photographed, so ask their permission first.

## Festivals

The Great Lakes states stage a diverse range of annual, community, regional, state, and cultural festivals. As an expression of Chicago's strong Irish heritage, the city actually dyes the Chicago River green as part of its boisterous **St. Patrick's Day Parade**. The Mexican-American population residing in the region celebrates **Cinco de Mayo** (early May) festivals in many of the Great Lakes cities; it is celebrated in a big way especially in Chicago, Kansas City, and St. Paul. Summer brings a deluge of outdoor events, starting on Memorial Day weekend with the Indianapolis 500 auto race. Fireworks are the norm for various county and state fairs that crop up in July and August. The Minnesota State Fair (August), held in St. Paul, is one of the largest summer events, along with Milwaukee's immensely popular **Summerfest**. Milwaukee also hosts a series of ethnic summer festivals on its lakefront, such as Irish Fest, a huge celebration of Irish culture.

## Sports

The Great Lakes region harbors a wide array of professional and amateur sports teams, with major pro baseball, football, and basketball franchises operating in nearly all of the major cities. The onset of spring signals the beginning of the baseball season, with fans flocking to historic **Wrigley Field**, home of the Chicago Cubs. Ohio boasts some of the region's best minor

---

## The Climate of the Great Lakes

Weather in most of the Great Lakes states is fairly consistent. Temperatures tend to be cooler in the northern states of Michigan, Wisconsin, and Minnesota, where cold, snowy winters lure residents to ski. The southern regions of Ohio, Indiana, and Illinois witness a more temperate climate. Summer months are ideal for touring the lakeside areas in Ohio, Wisconsin, Michigan, and Minnesota. Cooler temperatures and fall colors make September to October ideal for an extended trip to Chicago and scenic drives through the rugged forests of Michigan's Upper Peninsula.

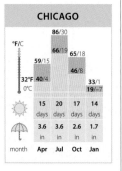

**CHICAGO**

| °F/C | Apr | Jul | Oct | Jan |
|---|---|---|---|---|
| | | 86/30 | | |
| | | 66/19 | 65/18 | |
| | 59/15 | | | |
| | | | 46/8 | |
| 32°F 0°C | 40/4 | | | 33/1 |
| | | | | 19/–7 |
| days | 15 days | 20 days | 17 days | 14 days |
| in | 3.6 in | 3.6 in | 2.6 in | 1.7 in |
| month | Apr | Jul | Oct | Jan |

league parks in Toledo, Akron, Columbus, Cleveland, Niles, and Dayton. This region also loves its football. The gregarious fans of the Chicago Bears and Cleveland Browns pro teams go head-to-head with the Wisconsin "Cheeseheads," who strip to the waist in the freezing cold to cheer on the Green Bay Packers. Several universities compete in the **Big Ten** conference that draws over 100,000 fans.

Winter brings basketball and hockey to the frozen region, with two NHL hockey teams, and many college teams.

Conseco Fieldhouse and Lucas Oil Stadium often host championship events in downtown Indianapolis.

## Outdoor Activities

Relatively short summers and long winters do not deter Great Lakes residents from enjoying the outdoors. On the contrary, the region's climate seems to encourage a more passionate pursuit of recreational activities, with mountain biking and cycling enthusiasts thronging paths and trails from April through early November. Northern Minnesota and Wisconsin are favorite canoe and kayak destinations, while sail- and motorboats are omnipresent on all of the Great Lakes throughout summer. Many fishing enthusiasts look forward to ice fishing in winter. Skiing and snowmobiling are also extremely popular.

Some of the region's best outdoors outfitters are located at Ely, entrance to the Boundary Waters Area Canoe Wilderness, and in Bayfield, gateway to the Apostle Islands National Lakeshore. For a list of outfitters in these locations, contact the **Ely Chamber of Commerce** or the **Bayfield Chamber**.

## Entertainment

Most of the region's most famous live music and theatrical venues are in Chicago. **Buddy Guy's Legends** and the **Kingston Mines** are the best places to hear authentic electric Chicago blues. **Blue Chicago** was the venue used to film *The Blues Brothers* movie. Comedy fans flock to Chicago's **Second City**, training ground for many *Saturday Night Live* cast members, and to St. Paul's **Fitzgerald Theater**, home base for Minnesota humorist Garrison Keillor's long-running *A Prairie Home Companion* radio program.

The summertime **Big Top Chautauqua**, situated near Wisconsin's Apostle Islands, holds similar, old-time comic and musical shows. Visitors can also check out rides at **Noah's Ark** in the world's waterpark capital, Wisconsin Dells.

## Shopping

The region's premier retail destination is Chicago's **Magnificent Mile**. This dense stretch of Michigan Avenue north of the Chicago River holds some the nation's premier specialty shops, augmenting the classic **Macy's** (formerly Marshall Field's) department store on State Street in the heart of the Loop. Another popular shopping destination is the pedestrian **Nicollet Mall** in Minneapolis. This pleasantly designed downtown district is far removed from the Twin Cities' **Mall of America**, the country's largest indoor mall. Tourists can also travel to the Amish communities in northern Indiana. **Shipshewana** has a busy flea market, where quilts, rugs, and baked goods can be bought at reasonable prices. **Fashion Outlets Chicago**, located near downtown Chicago, has a large selection of stores.

## DIRECTORY

### Tourist Offices

**Illinois**
Tel (800) 226-6632.
W enjoyillinois.com

**Indiana**
Tel (800) 677-9800.
W enjoyindiana.com

**Michigan**
Tel (888) 784-7328.
W michigan.org

**Minnesota**
Tel (888) 868-7476.
W exploreminnesota.com

**Ohio**
Tel (800) 282-5393.
W ohiotourism.com

**Wisconsin**
Tel (800) 432-8747.
W travelwisconsin.com

### Sports & Outdoor Activities

**Bayfield Chamber of Commerce**
Tel (800) 447-4094.

**Ely Chamber of Commerce**
Tel (800) 777-7281.

### Entertainment

**Big Top Chautauqua**
Ski Hill Rd.
Tel (888) 244-8368.
W bigtop.org

**Blue Chicago**
536 N Clark St.
Tel (312) 661-0100.

**Buddy Guy's Legends**
700 S Wabash Ave.
Tel (312) 427-1190.

**Fitzgerald Theater**
10 East Exchange St.
Tel (651) 290-1200.

**Kingston Mines**
2548 N Halsted St.
Tel (773) 477-4646.
W kingstonmines.com

**Noah's Ark**
1401 Wisconsin Dells Pkwy.
Tel (608) 254-6351.
W noahsarkwaterpark.com

**Second City**
1616 N Wells.
Tel (312) 337-3992.
W secondcity.com

### Shopping

**Fashion Outlets Chicago**
Tel (847) 928-7500.

**Macy's**
Tel (312) 781-1000.
W macys.com

**Magnificent Mile**
Tel (312) 642-3570.
W themagnificentmile.com

**Mall of America**
Tel (952) 883-8800.
W mallofamerica.com

**Nicollet Mall**
Tel (888) 676-6757.
W minneapolis.org

**Shipshewana Flea Market**
Tel (260) 768 4129.
W tradingplaceamerica.com

# Where to Stay

## Illinois

### ALTON: The Beall Mansion $$
B&B
*407 E 12th St, 62002*
**Tel** *(618) 474-9100*
W beallmansion.com
This historic inn with well-appointed rooms offers a complimentary, 24-hour, all-you-can-eat chocolate buffet.

### CHAMPAIGN-URBANA: I Hotel and Conference Center $
Value
*1900 S 1st St, 61820*
**Tel** *(217) 819-5000*
W stayatthei.com
Rooms feature commissioned art at this full-service hotel in the University of Illinois Research Park.

### CHICAGO: HI-Chicago $
Value                    **Map** 4D
*24 E Congress Pkwy, 60605*
**Tel** *(312) 360-0300*
W hichicago.org
This non-profit hostel near Lake Michigan offers clean dorm rooms, most with shared bathrooms.

### CHICAGO: Hotel Burnham $$
Business                 **Map** 4D
*1 W Washington St, 60602*
**Tel** *(312) 782-1111*
W burnhamhotel.com
The Reliance Building designed by Daniel Burnham is the setting for this classic hotel featuring stylish rooms, mosaic floors, and an evening wine hour.

### CHICAGO: Hotel Chicago $$
Business                 **Map** 3D
*333 Dearborn St, 60610*
**Tel** *(312) 245-0333*
W hotelsaxchicago.com
A trendy luxury hotel close to the best shops, restaurants, and bars. The service is excellent.

## DK Choice

### CHICAGO:
### The Drake Hotel $$
Business                 **Map** 2D
*140 E Walton Pl, 60611*
**Tel** *(312) 787-2200*
W thedrakehotel.com
The grande dame of hotels in Chicago, this historic Michigan Avenue destination boasts stunning city and water views. On-site restaurants include the Cape Cod Room seafood restaurant, where Marilyn Monroe carved her initials into the bar, and the Palm Court for high tea. Guests can enjoy the spacious fitness facility.

### CHICAGO: Ritz-Carlton Chicago $$$
Luxury                   **Map** 2D
*160 E Pearson St, 60611*
**Tel** *(312) 266-1000*
W fourseasons.com
This grand hotel perched above the Water Tower Place offers sleek elegance, antique cherrywood furnishings, and marble bathrooms.

### CHICAGO: Villa D' Citta $$$
B&B
*2230 N Halsted St, 60614*
**Tel** *(312) 771-0696*
W villadcitta.com
Set in the trendy Lincoln Park area, this inn boasts Italian architecture and romantic rooms with Jacuzzis.

### PEORIA: Mark Twain Hotel $$
Business
*225 NE Adams St, 61602*
**Tel** *(866) 325-6351*
W marktwainhotel.com
This boutique hotel offering rooms with a range of modern amenities suits both business and leisure travelers. Complimentary breakfasts.

**Price Guide**
Prices are based on one night's stay in high season for a standard double room, inclusive of service charges and taxes.

| | |
|---|---|
| $ | up to $150 |
| $$ | $150 to $250 |
| $$$ | over $250 |

### ROCKFORD: Cliffbreakers Riverside Resort $
Business
*700 W Riverside Dr, 61103*
**Tel** *(815) 282-3033*
W cliffbreakers.com
Individual decor and a hot breakfast are offered at these luxury accommodations.

### SPRINGFIELD: Carpenter Street Hotel $
Value
*525 N 6th St, 62702*
**Tel** *(217) 789-9100*
W carpenterstreethotel.com
A comfortable downtown option with complimentary breakfasts.

## Indiana

### FORT WAYNE: Don Hall's Guesthouse $
Value
*1313 W Washington Center Rd, 46825*
**Tel** *(260) 489-2524*
W donhalls.com
This family-friendly option offers a "water fun area" and a popular restaurant bustling with locals.

### INDIANAPOLIS: Residence Inn Indianapolis Downtown on the Canal $
Value
*350 W New York St, 46202*
**Tel** *(317) 822-0840*
W marriott.com
Set along a historic canal, where guests can feed ducks or rent paddle-boats, these apartment-style suites come with full kitchens.

## DK Choice

### INDIANAPOLIS: Conrad $$
Luxury
*50 W Washington St, 46204*
**Tel** *(317) 713-5000*
W conradhotels3.hilton.com
Guests enjoy rejuvenating wellness facilities, such as a state-of-the-art fitness room and heated indoor pool, at this luxury hotel in a prime downtown location. There are three excellent and popular fine-dining options on site, and two floors display world-class art.

Lobby of the European-style Bell Tower Hotel, Ann Arbor, Michigan

The historic Grand Hotel, Mackinack Island, Michigan

**INDIANAPOLIS:**
**JW Marriott** $$
Business
10 S West St, 46204
**Tel** (317) 860-5800
🌐 marriott.com
A sprawling downtown hotel
with more than 1,000 modern
rooms, a pool, and on-site dining.

**INDIANAPOLIS: Nestle Inn** $$
B&B
637 N East St, 46202
**Tel** (317) 610-5200
🌐 nestleindy.com
Within walking distance of key
sights, this downtown B&B offers
luxurious breakfasts, cooking
classes (for a fee), and top service.

**SOUTH BEND: Inn at**
**Saint Mary's** $$
B&B
53993 US 933, 46637
**Tel** (574) 232-4000
🌐 innatsaintmarys.com
An upscale inn on the campus of
St. Mary's College, adjacent to the
University of Notre Dame. A hot
breakfast buffet is included.

## Michigan

**ANN ARBOR: Bell Tower Hotel** $$
Business
300 S Thayer St, 48104
**Tel** (734) 769-3010
🌐 belltowerhotel.com
A European-style inn with old-
world elegance, located on the
University of Michigan campus.

**DETROIT: The Atheneum**
**Suite Hotel** $$
Business
1000 Brush St, 48226
**Tel** (313) 962-2323
🌐 atheneumsuites.com
An all-suite option in the middle
of the Greek district, close to
dining and nightlife options.

**DETROIT: Inn on Ferry Street** $$
Inn/B&B
84 E Ferry St, 48202
**Tel** (313) 871-6000
🌐 innonferrystreet.com
Four beautifully restored Victorian
mansions and two carriage houses
make up this welcoming inn.

**DETROIT: The Westin Book**
**Cadillac Detroit** $$
Luxury
1114 Washington Blvd, 48226
**Tel** (313) 442-1600
🌐 starwoodhotels.com
This Italian Renaissance-style
building dating back to 1924 is
listed in the National Register of
Historic Places.

### DK Choice

**MACKINAC ISLAND:**
**The Grand Hotel** $$$
Luxury
1 Grand Ave, 49757
**Tel** (906) 847-3331
🌐 grandhotel.com
This elegant hotel has been
hosting the Midwest's elite since
1887. It is perched high over the
Straits of Mackinac, with picturesque lake views and individually
appointed rooms filled with
antiques. The rates include
breakfast and dinner. Motorized
vehicles are not allowed on the
historic island; bikes and horse-
drawn carriages are the favored
modes of transportation.

**MACKINAW CITY: Best Western**
**– Dockside Waterfront Inn** $
Value
505 S Huron Ave, 49701
**Tel** (231) 436-5001
🌐 bestwestern.com
Some rooms have balconies at
this family-friendly inn. Guests can
enjoy the indoor water park and
a private sandy beach.

**TRAVERSE CITY:**
**Bayshore Resort** $$
Resort
833 E Front St, 49686
**Tel** (231) 935-4400
🌐 bayshore-resort.com
This beachside Victorian-style
property with breathtaking
views of the bay is accessible
only by boat or float plane.

## Minnesota

**DULUTH: Inn on**
**Lake Superior** $$
Resort
350 Canal Park Dr, 55802
**Tel** (218) 726-1111
🌐 theinnonlakesuperior.com
A lakefront property with year-
round pools and nightly campfires.
Complimentary hot breakfast bar.

**MINNEAPOLIS: Wales House** $
Inn/B&B
1115 SE 5th St, 55414
**Tel** (612) 331-3931
🌐 waleshouse.com
Close to the University of
Minnesota and popular with
visiting academics, this tastefully
appointed historic home has
spacious common areas.

**MINNEAPOLIS:**
**Commons Hotel** $$
Business
615 Washington Ave SE, 55455
**Tel** (612) 379-8888
🌐 commonshotel.com
Industrial chic decor and in-
room art galleries feature at
this boutique hotel on
the sprawling campus of the
University of Minnesota.

### DK Choice

**MINNEAPOLIS: Le Meridien**
**Chambers** $$
Luxury
901 Hennepin Ave, 55403
**Tel** (612) 767-6900
🌐 lemeridienchambers.com
Downtown Minneapolis's most
stylish hotel, Le Meridien
Chambers combines art, design,
and culinary skill across a pair
of landmark Revival buildings.
Special amenities include in-
room massage and beauty
services. The magnificent
Marin Restaurant and Bar serves
exquisite Northern California-
inspired cuisine. Over 200 pieces
of original artwork are displayed
at the hotel, and guests enjoy
free admission to the lauded
Walker Art Center by presenting
their artist-designed room key.

**For more information on types of hotels** see pages 26–7

Elegant lounge in the luxurious Ritz-Carlton, Cleveland

### ST. PAUL: Best Western Plus Kelly Inn $
Value
161 Saint Anthony Ave, 55103
**Tel** (651) 227-8711
W bestwestern.com
This inexpensive option near the main attractions offers clean, basic rooms and friendly staff.

### ST. PAUL: Saint Paul Hotel $$$
Luxury
350 Market St, 55102
**Tel** (651) 292-9292
W stpaulhotel.com
A historic hotel, in operation for over a century, offering classic decor and modern amenities.

## Ohio

### CINCINNATI: The Cincinnatian Hotel $$
Luxury
601 Vine St, 45202
**Tel** (513) 381-3000
W cincinnatianhotel.com
Dating back to 1882, this hotel offers rooms with fireplaces, balconies, and contemporary design.

### CINCINNATI: 21c Museum Hotel $$$
Business
609 Walnut St, 45202
**Tel** (513) 578-6600
W 21cmuseumhotels.com/cincinnati
This arty venue is a combination of a boutique hotel, contemporary art museum, and cultural center.

### CLEVELAND: Glidden House Inn $$
Inn/B&B
1901 Ford Dr, 44106
**Tel** (216) 231-8900
W gliddenhouse.com
Classy accommodations here are set in a 1910 mansion. A breakfast buffet is included.

### DK Choice

**CLEVELAND: The Ritz-Carlton, Cleveland** $$$
Luxury
1515 W 3rd St, 44113
**Tel** (216) 623-1300
W ritzcarlton.com
The high-end Ritz-Carlton offers well-appointed guest rooms and suites, all featuring luxurious marble baths as well as gorgeous panoramic views of Lake Erie. On-site features include fine dining and a state-of-the-art, 24-hour fitness center. The knowledgeable staff strive to cater to every need. Located within walking distance to key downtown attractions.

### COLUMBUS: The Blackwell $
Value
2110 Tuttle Park Pl, 43210
**Tel** (614) 247-4000
W theblackwell.com
This modern hotel and conference center is located on Ohio State University's campus. The stylish guestrooms feature state-of-the-art technology.

### COLUMBUS: The Lofts Hotel $$
Business
55 E Nationwide Blvd, 43215
**Tel** (614) 461-2663
W 55lofts.com
Trendy, loft-style rooms in an old converted warehouse come with plush furnishings and floor-to-ceiling windows, offering great downtown views.

### SANDUSKY: Kalahari Resort $$
Resort
7000 Kalahari Dr, 44870
**Tel** (419) 433-7200
W kalahariresorts.com/ohio
This family-friendly African-themed resort includes an indoor theme park, waterpark, go-karting, bowling, and miniature golf.

## Wisconsin

### MADISON: Edgewater Hotel $$
Business
666 Wisconsin Ave, 53703
**Tel** (608) 256-9071
W theedgewater.com
Deluxe rooms, a rooftop terrace, and a spa feature at this peaceful hotel overlooking Lake Mondota.

### MILWAUKEE: The Iron Horse Hotel $$
Business
500 W Florida St, 53204
**Tel** (414) 374-4766
W theironhorsehotel.com
A century-old warehouse has been converted into an upscale hotel that caters mostly to business travelers and motorcycle enthusiasts.

### DK Choice

**MILWAUKEE: The Pfister Hotel** $$
Luxury
424 E Wisconsin Ave, 53202
**Tel** (414) 273-8222
W thepfisterhotel.com
Guido Pfister, a successful Milwaukee merchant, built this grand downtown hotel in 1893 for $1million. It has since been restored to its grandiose former glory. It displays one of the largest hotel collections of Victorian art in the world. The martini and wine bar on the 23rd floor offers impressive city views.

### MILWAUKEE: Schuster Mansion Bed & Breakfast $$
B&B
3209 W Wells St, 53208
**Tel** (414) 342-3210
W schustermansion.com
An architectural gem in the historic Concordia neighborhood, minutes from downtown, offering spacious Victorian suites

### WISCONSIN DELLS: Black Hawk Motel $
Value
720 Race St, 53965
**Tel** (608) 254-7770
W blackhawkmotel.com
Rooms on offer here range from family-friendly cottages to romantic Jacuzzi suites.

### WISCONSIN DELLS: Cedar Lodge & Settlement $$
Resort
11232 Hillside Dr, 53965
**Tel** (608) 253-6080
W cedarlodgedells.com
Guests enjoy bonfires in the summer at this secluded property.

# Where to Eat and Drink

## Illinois

**CHICAGO: Carson's Prime Steaks** $$
American barbecue        Map 3C
*612 N Wells St, 60610*
**Tel** *(312) 280-9200*
A legendary spot serving up plates of sauce-slicked baby back ribs, barbecued pork chops, chicken, and shrimp since 1976.

### DK Choice

**CHICAGO: Girl & The Goat** $$
New American
*809 W Randolph St, 60607*
**Tel** *(312) 492-6262*
Nationally acclaimed chef Stephanie Izard wows guests with her inventive creations and rare delicacies, such as escargot ravioli and goat carpaccio with smoked trout roe. Enjoy local beers and cheeses at the lively bar. Rustic, inviting dining space.

**CHICAGO: Heaven on Seven** $$
American        Map 4D
*111 N Wabash Ave, 60602*
**Tel** *(312) 263-6443*    **Closed** *Sun*
Spicy Cajun and Creole fare is served on the seventh floor of a historic building. Jambalaya, crab cakes, and po'boys are house favorites. Breakfast and lunch only.

**CHICAGO: Russian Tea Time** $$
Russian        Map 4D
*77 E Adams St, 60603*
**Tel** *(312) 360-0000*
Dig into cold *borscht* and potato pancakes, meat-stuffed dumplings, and chicken kebabs at this eatery, which is reminiscent of a Moscow tearoom. Afternoon tea is served daily.

**CHICAGO: Trattoria No. 10** $$
Italian        Map 4D
*10 N Dearborn St, 60602*
**Tel** *(312) 984-1718*
This popular restaurant is known for modern takes on Italian classics such as grass-fed beef with mascarpone mashed potatoes, and farfalle pasta with duck confit and asparagus.

**CHICAGO: Everest** $$$
American/French        Map 4C
*440 S LaSalle St, 40th Floor, 60605*
**Tel** *(312) 663-8920*    **Closed** *Sun & Mon*
The renowned French chef offers delicious tasting menus in this exquisitely appointed dining room with crystal chandeliers and tuxedoed staff.

**CHICAGO: North Pond** $$$
New American
*2610 N Cannon Dr, 60614*
**Tel** *(773) 477-5845*    **Closed** *Mon*
This contemporary restaurant, nestled on a quiet pond in the middle of Lincoln Park, boasts one of the loveliest settings in the city. Serves exquisite foie gras.

**GALENA: Fried Green Tomatoes** $$
American
*213 N Main St, 61036*
**Tel** *(815) 777-3938*    **Closed** *Mon*
Set in a historic 1838 building, must-try dishes here include the namesake appetizer, and traditional pasta and meat dishes such as chicken *piccata* and veal marsala. Superb wine list.

**OAK PARK: Winberie's Restaurant and Bar** $$
American
*151 N Oak Park Ave, 60301*
**Tel** *(708) 386-2600*
An eclectic, creative menu and an extensive wine list are offered at this busy, bright restaurant and wine bar. Antiques and framed posters adorn the interior.

**PEORIA: One World Café** $$
International
*1245 W Main St, 61606*
**Tel** *(309) 672-1522*
A traditional eatery, One World Café serves breakfast and lunch all day and dinner entrées after 4pm. The coffee bar offers gourmet drinks, and the bar and lounge area is popular with locals.

**ROCKFORD: D'Arcy's Pint** $
Irish/American
*661 W Stanford Ave, 62702*
**Tel** *(217) 492-8800*
This family-friendly restaurant is known for its famous horseshoe sandwiches, a unique regional specialty where a choice of meat is served over Texas toast, topped with fries and cheese sauce.

## Indiana

**FORT WAYNE: Biaggi's Ristorante Italiano** $$
Italian
*4010 W Jefferson Blvd, 46804*
**Tel** *(260) 459-6700*
Part of a well-regarded chain, the popular Biaggi's entices diners with its delicious steak, seafood, and pasta dishes. Try the savory home-made ravioli.

### Price Guide

Prices are based on a three-course meal for one, with a glass of house wine, including tax and service.

| $ | up to $35 |
|---|---|
| $$ | $35 to $70 |
| $$$ | over $70 |

**INDIANAPOLIS: Bazbeaux Pizza** $
Pizza
*329 Massachusetts Ave, 46204*
**Tel** *(317) 636-7662*
This downtown outpost of a popular local pizza chain provides a quick, by-the-slice lunch option. It offers seating on a breezy sidewalk and in the casual dining room, and there's a welcoming bar with an eclectic menu of craft beers.

**INDIANAPOLIS: Yats** $
Cajun/Creole
*5363 N College Ave, 46220*
**Tel** *(317) 253-8817*
A local institution where the chalkboard behind the cashier displays the daily menu of delectable Cajun and Creole dishes. Savory jambalaya and flavorful chili cheese *étouffée* with crawfish prove popular.

**INDIANAPOLIS: Santorini Greek Kitchen** $$
Greek
*1417 Prospect St, 46203*
**Tel** *(317) 917-1117*    **Closed** *Sun*
This cheerful eatery, run by a brilliant chef-owner, serves what many label as the area's best Greek food. Friendly servers explain the menu's authentic touches. Friday and Saturday evenings feature live music and belly dancers.

North Pond dining room in Lincoln Park, Chicago

## DK Choice

**INDIANAPOLIS:**
**St. Elmo's Steak House** $$$
Steak House
*127 S Illinois, 46225*
**Tel** *(317) 635-0636*
A local landmark since 1902, St. Elmo's remains the city's restaurant of choice. The classic steak house menu rarely changes, and seemingly every table is topped with an order of the world-famous signature shrimp cocktail drenched in spicy sauce.

**SOUTH BEND: Sorin's at the Morris Inn** $$
New American
*N Notre Dame Ave, 46556*
**Tel** *(574) 631-2000* **Closed** *Mon*
Nestled in the University of Notre Dame's campus, this inviting eatery has been named after the institution's founder. The varied menu at Sorin's has something for everyone. Extensive wine list.

# Michigan

**ANN ARBOR: Zingerman's Delicatessen** $
American/Delicatessen
*422 Detroit St, 48104*
**Tel** *(734) 663-3354*
Once a traditional Jewish deli, Zingerman's is now renowned for its specialty foods. Try the made-to-order sandwiches with savory pastrami and chopped liver.

**DETROIT: Lafayette Coney Island** $
American
*118 W Lafayette Blvd, 48226*
**Tel** *(313) 964-8198*
Popular for the city's most iconic dish since 1914, the Coney Island – a hotdog served atop a steamed bun, dressed with chili, diced onions, and yellow mustard.

## DK Choice

**DETROIT: Slows Bar-B-Q** $
Barbecue
*2138 Michigan Ave, 48216*
**Tel** *(313) 962-9828*
Expect a lengthy wait for what is said to be the country's best barbecue and smoked meats served with sweet baked beans and gooey mac 'n' cheese. The bustling Corktown space features a sunny patio and lively bar area with over 50 craft beer taps.

**DETROIT: Cuisine** $$
French/New American
*670 Lothrop Rd, 48202*
**Tel** *(313) 872-5110* **Closed** *Mon*
One of the region's most creative restaurants, serving inventive food such as charcuterie plates, seared sea scallops, lobster ravioli, and duck confit in a welcoming space. Knowledgeable staff help guests choose from the excellent wine list.

**GRAND RAPIDS:**
**San Chez Bistro** $$
Spanish
*38 Fulton St W, 49503*
**Tel** *(616) 774-8272*
This award-winning bistro specializes in European and Mediterranean small plates. The fun, arty ambience is enlivened by patrons practicing painting or learning knife skills. The casual café area is popular for breakfasts.

**MACKINAC ISLAND: The Yankee Rebel Tavern** $$
American/International
*3 Astor St, 49757*
**Tel** *(906) 847-6249*
Large portions of American classics are served here in the heart of downtown, just a short walk from boat lines. The spacious seating, with large booths and tables, is perfect for gatherings of family and friends.

**MACKINAW CITY:**
**Dixie Saloon** $
American
*401 E Central St, 49701*
**Tel** *(231) 436-5449*
Dating back to 1890, this historic restaurant is located across from the Mackinac Island ferry, making it a great spot for a quick bite before a trip to the island. Window-side booths offer great views of the waterfront.

# Minnesota

**DULUTH: New Scenic Café** $$
New American
*5461 N Shore Dr, 55804*
**Tel** *(218) 525-6274*
Trek to Lake Superior's northern shore to sample this café's seasonal menu of local fare. Colorful gardens and local art add to the inviting, serene ambience.

**MINNEAPOLIS: Al's Breakfast** $
Diner
*413 14th Ave SE, 55414*
**Tel** *(612) 331-9991*
Al's is a tiny breakfast-only diner with just over a dozen seats. A varied mix of locals and tourists

Pulled pork dish at Brasa Premium, Minneapolis, Minnesota

wait in line for made-to-order classics such as buttermilk pancakes and filling omelets.

**MINNEAPOLIS: Brasa Premium** $
Creole/Latin American
*600 E Hennepin Ave, 55414*
**Tel** *(612) 379-3030*
Head to Brasa Premium for a Creole-tinged choice of slow-cooked meats and tasty sides, all made with local ingredients and sustainably raised meats. Options include savory rotisserie dishes, braises, and roasts.

## DK Choice

**MINNEAPOLIS: Nye's Polonaise Room** $$
Polish/American
*112 E Hennepin Ave, 55414*
**Tel** *(612) 379-2021*
In operation since 1949, this beloved supper club serves an assortment of filling Polish-American fare such as savory *pierogies* or fresh sausages with *sauerkraut*. It is popular for its retro ambience, complete with classic cocktails and live piano or polka music.

**ST. PAUL: Mickey's Diner** $
American
*36 W 7th St, 55116*
**Tel** *(651) 222-5633*
Operating since 1937, this dining car is open 24 hours a day, serving breakfasts, juicy burgers, and the house signature – savory stew.

**ST. PAUL: Forepaugh's Restaurant** $$$
International
*276 S Exchange St, 55102*
**Tel** *(651) 224-5606*
Award-winning cuisine is served in this elegant Victorian mansion. Well-informed servers help guests select from the lengthy wine list.

# Ohio

### CINCINNATI: Skyline Chili $
American
*1001 Vine St, 45202*
**Tel** *(513) 721-4715*
Diners enjoy the savory, meaty chili over hotdogs, baked potatoes, fries, or spaghetti at this popular regional chain with Greek roots dating back to 1949.

### CINCINNATI: The Celestial Restaurant $$$
Steak House
*1071 Celestial St, 45202*
**Tel** *(513) 241-4455*
Head to this romantic venue with panoramic views of the city skyline and Ohio River for standard steak house offerings, as well as fresh seafood dishes. There's an extensive wine list.

### CLEVELAND: Blue Point Grill $$
Seafood
*700 W St. Clair, 44113*
**Tel** *(216) 875-7827*
This comfortable restaurant offers an innovative menu of modern dishes, including fresh fish such as grouper, salmon, and sea bass. Varied wine list available.

## DK Choice

### CLEVELAND: Lola Bistro $$$
New American
*2058 E 4th St, 44115*
**Tel** *(216) 621-5652* **Closed** *Sun*
The famous chef-owner of Lola, Michael Symon, hosts a popular food show, but his home base is this upscale eatery. The inventive menu features the best local ingredients, including nose-to-tail items such as beef heart and pig's ear. The handsome environs and fine service is perfectly suited for romantic meals as well as business dinners.

### COLUMBUS: Schmidt's German Village Restaurant $
German
*240 E Kossuth St, 43206*
**Tel** *(614) 444-6808*
Staffers in traditional costumes serve up the generous lunch buffet, plus schnitzel, sausages, and other traditional dishes at one of the nation's most famous German restaurants.

### COLUMBUS: Thurman Café $
Hamburgers/American
*183 Thurman Ave, 43206*
**Tel** *(614) 443-1570*
A landmark since 1942, the small and cozy Thurman Café is known for its juicy burgers and authentic Coney Island hotdogs that are among the most popular in town. Friendly staff.

### LEBANON: The Golden Lamb Dining Room $$
American/Eclectic
*27 S Broadway, 45036*
**Tel** *(513) 932-5065*
This historic landmark was once a stagecoach tavern. Diners now enjoy Colonial dishes such as roast leg of lamb – the house specialty – in family-friendly environs in the state's oldest hotel.

# Wisconsin

### MADISON: Marigold Kitchen $
American
*118 S Pinckney St, 53703*
**Tel** *(608) 661-5559*
At this friendly breakfast and lunch spot near the State Capitol, the kitchen uses local organic ingredients to create inventive variations of familiar dishes, such as an omelet with artisanal cheese or hash with roasted duck.

### MADISON: The Old Fashioned $
American
*23 N Pinckney St, 53703*
**Tel** *(608) 310-4545*
This welcoming establishment highlights meats, cheeses, produce, and specialties from small Wisconsin producers in its menu. The Friday fish dinners and weekend roasts prove popular. There's a wide selection of local beers, wines, spirits, and specialty drinks.

### MILWAUKEE: Balisteri's Bluemound Inn $$
Italian
*6501 W Bluemound Rd, 53213*
**Tel** *(414) 258-9881*
Balisteri's is a popular venue offering particularly tasty pizzas, as well as an extensive menu of fresh seafood, fish, poultry, and steaks. There is a patio for outdoor eating and service is very friendly.

## DK Choice

### MILWAUKEE: Bartolotta's Lake Park Bistro $$$
French
*3133 E Newberry Blvd, 53211*
**Tel** *(414) 962-6300*
This lovely, upscale bistro is housed in a historic pavilion in the scenic Lake Park, perched on a bluff overlooking Lake Michigan. The award-winning kitchen produces exquisite French-accented cuisine such as foie gras mousse, *tartare de boeuf*, chicken liver mousse, and *steak-frites* as well as braised and rotisserie meats. There is an extensive wine list, and the elegant service and classy environs appeal to those celebrating special occasions.

### MILWAUKEE: Mader's $$$
German
*1041 N Old World 3rd St, 53203*
**Tel** *(414) 271-3377*
The fine service and gourmet German fare continue to lure local celebrities and families on special occasions at this historic restaurant and museum with artifacts dating back to when locals enjoyed a 20-cent dinner.

### WISCONSIN DELLS: High Rock Café $$
Eclectic/International
*232 Broadway, 53965*
**Tel** *(608) 254-5677*
A wide-ranging menu of creative dishes is on offer at this relaxed and popular eatery. There are soups, wraps, and sandwiches, as well as pastas, entrées, and homemade desserts. It is especially lively during big sporting events or the weekly Friday fish fry.

Dining room in Blue Point Grill in the heart of downtown Cleveland, Ohio

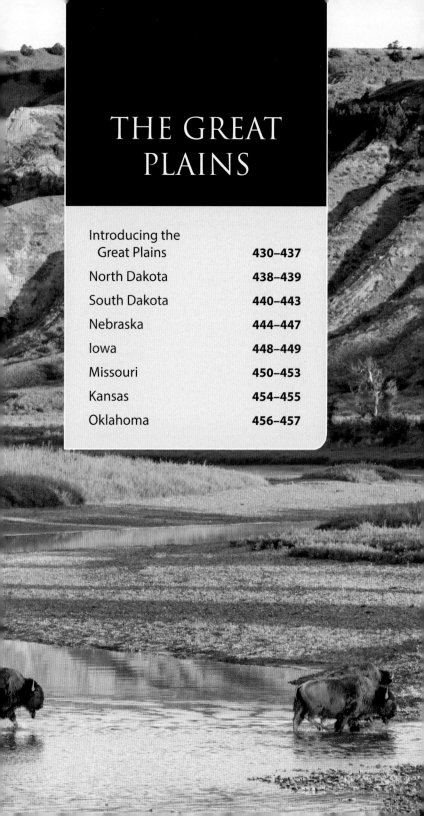

# THE GREAT PLAINS

# The Great Plains at a Glance

Centering on the midway longitude, the 100th meridian – which divides the United States roughly into East and West – this region is the essence of Middle America. Stretching from Canada to Texas, and sloping gradually from the foot of the Rocky Mountains to the floodplain of the Mississippi River, the Great Plains covers seven states, from North and South Dakota across Iowa, Nebraska, Missouri, Kansas, and Oklahoma. This largely rural and agricultural region is a place of small towns, wide-open spaces, and distant horizons. Museums, historic sights, and entertainment options can be found in cities such as Tulsa, St. Louis, Kansas City, Sioux Falls, and Oklahoma City.

**Theodore Roosevelt National Park** *(see p439)*, in North Dakota, was created in 1947 as a memorial in the president's honor. Today, herds of bison can frequently be seen roaming through the park's stark but beautiful badlands.

**Black Hills** *(see pp442–3)*, South Dakota's main attraction, is home to the Mount Rushmore National Memorial, with its giant, sculpted heads of four US presidents. Crazy Horse Memorial pays tribute to Native American heroes.

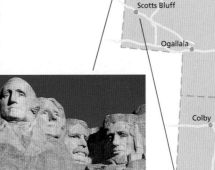

**Scotts Bluff** *(see p446)* is a major landmark on the Nebraska portion of the Oregon Trail. Vast, grassy expanses of open range still contain reminders of 19th-century overland routes, along which pioneer settlers traveled westward. The Oregon Trail from Independence, Missouri, followed the North Platte River as it headed northwest across the Rocky Mountains.

◄ Bison crossing the Little Missouri River in Theodore Roosevelt National Park, North Dakota

Williston

Minot

**NORTH DAKOT**
*(See pp438–39)*

Jamest

Bismarck

Bowman

Mobridge    Abe

**SOUTH DAKO**
*(See pp440–43)*

Pierre

Rapid City

Chadron    Valentine

Scotts Bluff

**NEBRASK**
*(See pp444–*

Ogallala    North Platte

Kearney

Colby

Ha

**KAN**
*(See pp4*

Dodge City    Hut

Clinton

Lav

**Des Moines** *(see p448)* is the state capital of Iowa, one of the country's largest agricultural producers, with a rich stock of hard-working farming communities. Iowa's green river valleys and lush cornfields encapsulate an idyllic image of a nearly vanished rural America.

**LOCATOR MAP**

**St. Louis** *(see pp450–51)* is one of Missouri's largest and most cosmopolitan cities. Its location on the route leading west made St. Louis an active commercial and cultural crossroads, a role symbolized by the Gateway Arch.

0 km 100
0 miles 100

okings

Spencer

Sioux City

Waterloo Dubuque

Cedar Rapids

Des Moines Iowa City Davenport

**IOWA**
*(See pp448-49)*

Omaha

Quincy

St.Joseph

Topeka Kansas City Columbia

**MISSOURI**
*(See pp450-53)* St. Louis

Lebanon

chita

Springfield

Poplar Bluff

Tulsa

homa Muskogee

AHOMA
*pp456-57)*

dmore

**Wichita** and **Dodge City** *(see p455)*, Kansas, were once cattle-drive destinations where cowboys conducted business and let off steam. The colorful past is replicated at Wichita's Old Cowtown Museum and Dodge City's Boot Hill and Front Street.

**Oklahoma** *(see pp456-7)* boasts more miles of the original Old Route 66 highway than any other state. This historic road, famous as the "mother road" in John Steinbeck's *The Grapes of Wrath,* has also been celebrated in blues and jazz. Old gas pumps, signboards, and other exhibits can be seen at some Route 66 museums, especially in Clinton.

# THE GREAT PLAINS

From an airplane, the Great Plains looks like a repeated pattern of rectangular fields and arrow-straight highways, prompting urban Americans to dub it "fly-over country." This predominantly rural and agricultural region, which stretches clear across the center of the country, embodies the all-American ideals of independence and hard-working self-sufficiency.

The Great Plains is deeply rooted, both literally and figuratively, at the center of the American psyche. Though city-dwellers on both the East and West coasts may deride the region's general lack of sophistication, its residents' obvious pride in traditional values and old-fashioned lifestyles explain why this area is still the ideal location for all that is essentially American.

In fiction and film, the region has spawned such all-American creations as Mark Twain's *Huckleberry Finn*, Dorothy in *The Wizard of Oz*, the pioneer family of *Little House on the Prairie*, and the homespun sentimentality of *Field of Dreams* and *The Bridges of Madison County*.

Its rural reaches, with their vast expanses of fertile farmlands, form the basis of the Great Plains identity. Larger cities, such as Tulsa, St. Louis, Kansas City, and Oklahoma City, hold the bulk of the population as well as the museums, historic sights, and a wide range of hotels and resturants.

Visitors can get a better sense of the region's culture by spending some time in bucolic, smaller towns.

**History**

Throughout the 17th and 18th centuries, French traders and fur trappers explored the region, coming into contact with the diverse Native American tribes who lived here. These tribes varied from the sedentary, agriculture-based cultures of the Caddo and Mandan people to the Pawnee, Osage, and Comanche Indians, whose livelihoods depended on hunting migratory herds of bison (or buffalo). As Europeans settled along the East Coast, other tribes relocated westward to the Great Plains. The most tragic mass migration to this region took place in 1838, when the Cherokee Nation was forced to relinquish all lands east of the Mississippi River. In exchange, they were granted land for "as long as the grass grows and the waters run," in what was

Prairie in Buffalo Gap National Grassland, Nebraska

◄ Dusk at Gateway Arch, Eero Saarinen's symbol of St. Louis, Missouri

Mural showing the Lewis and Clark expedition

then known as Indian Territory (present-day Oklahoma). More than 4,000 people died from hunger, disease, and exposure on the long journey, dubbed the "Trail of Tears," from North Carolina to Oklahoma. Native American influence on the region is hard to quantify, but its heritage survives in numerous place names, including those of each state – Iowa, Missouri, Oklahoma, Kansas, Nebraska, and the Dakotas.

Among the first Americans to explore the Great Plains were the legendary Lewis and Clark, whose expedition to the Pacific Ocean and back took almost three years, from 1803 to 1806. Remarkable as their journey was, the later expedition of the German Prince Maximilian made perhaps the most enduring contribution to the region's lore. Maximilian's journals, as well as artist Karl Bodmer's drawings and paintings of Indians, were published in Germany in 1838, and finally put the Great Plains on the international map.

Both expeditions embarked from St. Louis, the region's oldest city, founded as a distant French fur-trading frontier outpost. By the mid-19th century, Kansas City had joined St. Louis as an outpost for pioneers crossing the Great Plains on the legendary Santa Fe, California, and Oregon Trails.

After the Civil War, a series of transcontinental railroads followed many of the same routes, cutting down on travel time and transportation costs. The railroads, however, sliced across the migration routes for the bison herds, whose numbers dwindled from millions to near-extinction. As the railroads opened up the land, the Indians were forced onto reservations,

## KEY DATES IN HISTORY

**1738–43** French fur trader Pierre Gaultier du Varennes, Sieur de la Verendrye, explores the northern Great Plains

**1764** St. Louis established

**1803** The US buys much of the region from France as part of the Louisiana Purchase

**1833** German artist Karl Bodmer documents Native American lifestyles

**1882** "Buffalo Bill" stages the world's first rodeo in North Platte, Nebraska

**1890** Massacre of 300 Sioux Indians by the US Army at Wounded Knee on Pine Ridge Reservation, South Dakota

**1907** Hollywood actor John Wayne is born in Winterset, Iowa

**1930–37** Extended drought and sustained winds create the Dust Bowl

**1941** Mount Rushmore National Memorial completed

**1948** Work begins on Crazy Horse Memorial in the Black Hills of South Dakota

**1965** Gateway Arch completed in St. Louis on the site of the original 1764 settlement

**2000** Oklahoma City National Memorial dedicated on fifth anniversary of the Federal Building truck bombing

while homesteading settlers took their place. These family-run farms, growing wheat, corn, cattle, and pigs, are still emblematic of the region, though many farms are now operated on an industrial scale by absentee landlords. The high point of agriculture was the World War I era, when farm prices were high and mechanization had yet to replace horse-drawn plows and other labor-intensive methods. The economic low point came soon afterward, when a sudden postwar drop in prices and a decade of drought turned the region into the "Dust Bowl," forcing some 200,000 farmers and their families to move west to California, a saga movingly documented in John Steinbeck's *The Grapes of Wrath*.

## Geology & Climate

The land is what defines life in the Great Plains. Some 500 million years ago, a deep inland sea laid the foundation of layers of sedimentary rock, with their rich array of ancient fossils as well as the fossil fuels that industries rely on today. Above this solid rock, a series of Ice Age glaciers, scraping their way south from Canada, deposited the pulverized soil that makes the eastern half of the Great Plains – and Iowa in particular – some of the world's most fertile farmland. Exceptions to the typically horizontal landscape are found at its fringes. The rugged Ozark Mountains lie in southern Missouri and Oklahoma, while, in western South Dakota, the densely forested, gold-bearing granite peaks of the Black Hills rise high above the eroded sandstone of Badlands National Park.

While the underlying geology may make for uneventful scenery, the climate is any-thing but mild. The Great Plains experiences some of the nation's most extreme weather, particularly its fierce tornadoes. These powerful windstorms form with little warning in late spring and are most frequent along the "Tornado Alley," which runs through eastern Kansas, Missouri, and Oklahoma. The region also experiences

Prairie dog, Badlands

other weather extremes, such as flood-inducing rains, scorching summer heat and humidity, and frigid winter blizzards.

## People & Culture

The Great Plains is, by and large, conservative, with patriotism and religion the dominating cultural values. Yet it also is a region of varied cultural and political traditions. In the 19th century, Kansas was one of the prime anti-slavery battlegrounds, but at the turn of the 21st century the state insisted that biblical ideas of creationism be taught in school science classes.

Ethnically, however, the population is surprisingly diverse, and includes the Swedish settlement of Lindsborg. Many of the original immigrants were lured here from similar terrain in Europe, notably the steppes of Eastern Europe, by promises of land ownership. A significant number were adherents of nonconformist religions, such as the Mennonites, who came from German-speaking regions of Russia to settle in central Kansas and the Dakotas. Many German-style pastry shops operate in what may seem like quintessentially American small towns.

Native Americans also play an increasingly visible role in the region's identity, thanks both to burgeoning casinos operated by the various tribes and to a growing respect for their culture and heritage. Oklahoma, for example, has one of the country's largest Native American populations, numbering nearly 10 percent of the state's three million inhabitants.

Pine Ridge Indian Reservation in South Dakota

# Exploring the Great Plains

The Great Plains draws visitors in search of a taste of wholesome America. Its singular attraction is the countryside with its wide-open, seemingly endless spaces, where visitors can travel for miles without seeing more than a few railroad tracks, a set of power lines, or perhaps an occasional windmill or grain elevator. The Great Plains' highlights include the magnificent, sculpted Mount Rushmore National Monument, the eerie landscape of Badlands National Park, the tallgrass prairie covering the Flint Hills of Kansas, and historic frontier outposts such as St. Louis and Kansas City, two of the region's largest cities. A car is essential to make the most of a visit to the area.

## Sights at a Glance

**North Dakota**

1. Grand Forks
2. Devils Lake
3. Washburn
4. Theodore Roosevelt National Park
5. Bismarck & Mandan
6. Fargo

**South Dakota**

7. Mitchell
8. Pierre
9. Badlands National Park
10. Wall
11. Pine Ridge Indian Reservation
12. Black Hills pp442–3

**Nebraska**

13. Chadron
14. Ogallala
15. North Platte
16. Lincoln
17. Nebraska City
18. Omaha

**Iowa**

19. Sioux City
20. Des Moines
21. Amana Colonies
22. Cedar Rapids
23. Dubuque
24. Quad Cities (Davenport)
25. Iowa City

**Missouri**

26. St. Louis pp450–51
27. Jefferson City
28. Branson
29. Kansas City
30. St. Joseph

**Kansas**

31. Lawrence
32. Topeka
33. Flint Hills
34. Wichita
35. Dodge City

**Oklahoma**

36. Bartlesville
37. Tulsa
38. Tahlequah
39. Oklahoma City

### Key

— Highway
— Major road
— Railroad
- - State border

Winnipeg

### Mileage Chart

**Bismarck, ND**

**10** = Distance in miles
**10** = Distance in kilometers

| | | | | | | | |
|---|---|---|---|---|---|---|---|
| 350 | **Rapid City, SD** | | | | | | |
| 563 | | | | | | | |
| 607 | 524 | **Omaha, NE** | | | | | |
| 977 | 843 | | | | | | |
| 667 | 624 | 135 | **Des Moines, IA** | | | | |
| 1073 | 1004 | 217 | | | | | |
| 1039 | 953 | 434 | 434 | **St. Louis, MO** | | | |
| 1672 | 1534 | 698 | 698 | | | | |
| 786 | 702 | 183 | 194 | 247 | **Kansas City, MO** | | |
| 1265 | 1130 | 295 | 312 | 397 | | | |
| 1034 | 952 | 385 | 393 | 444 | 203 | **Wichita, KS** | |
| 1664 | 1532 | 620 | 632 | 715 | 327 | | |
| 1123 | 1040 | 519 | 546 | 500 | 349 | 161 | **Oklahoma City, OK** |
| 1807 | 1674 | 835 | 879 | 805 | 562 | 259 | |

Grand Forks

Fargo **6**

Watertown

MINNESOTA

Brookings

Minneapolis

Sioux Falls

IOWA

Mason City

Spencer

Sioux City **19**

Fort Dodge

Waterloo ⑳

Dubuque **23**

Chicago

Carroll

Ames

Amana Colonies **21**

Cedar Rapids **22**

Des Moines ⑳

Iowa City **25**

Davenport

Fremont

Omaha **18**

Creston ㉞

Quad Cities **24**

Burlington

Lincoln

Clarinda

Ottumwa

**16**

**17**

Nebraska City

Kirksville

Keokuk

ILLINOIS

Quincy

St. Joseph **30**

Kansas City

Moberly

Springfield

Topeka

Flint Hills **32**

**33**

**31** Kansas City **29**

Lawrence

Columbia

Lambert-St.Louis

**26** St. Louis

Indianapolis

Emporia

Sedalia ㉗

Jefferson City

Rolla

Lake of the Ozarks

Newton

Wichita

Fort Scott

MISSOURI

Farmington

Cape Girardeau

Arkansas City

Joplin

Springfield

West Plains

Sikeston

Fulton

Bartlesville **36**

Miami

Branson **28**

Bull Shoals Lake

Poplar Bluff

Tulsa **37**

**38**

Little Rock

Memphis

Muskogee

Tahlequah

ARKANSAS

OKLAHOMA

Little Rock

McAlester

Ardmore

Hugo

Durant

Dallas

Rolling wheat plains near Washburn, North Dakota

0 kilometers          200
0 miles          100

# North Dakota

A state of unexpected variety, North Dakota's vast blue skies, tiny farming communities, and endless wheat fields along its eastern half can lull visitors into a state of quiet contemplation. Toward the west, North Dakota's drier, more rugged Missouri Plateau contains the stark badlands of Theodore Roosevelt National Park and more than a dozen historic sites visited by Lewis and Clark *(see pp561–2)* on their 1803–1806 expedition up the Missouri River. The explorers spent 146 days in North Dakota on their outbound and return journeys. Vast tracts of undeveloped areas along the river north of the pleasant capital city of Bismarck still look much like they did in the early 19th century.

## ❶ Grand Forks

98,000. ✈ 🚌 🚂
ℹ 4251 Gateway Dr, (800) 866-4566.
W visitgrandforks.com

Located at the junction of the Red and Red Lake Rivers, the city attracted international attention in 1997, when the Red River flooded downtown, destroying many historic structures and inflicting huge damage. Massive cleanup, water control, and reconstruction efforts have helped Grand Forks overcome much of the flood's disastrous effects.

The **Empire Arts Center**, housed in the restored 1919 Empire Theatre, is now downtown's vibrant performing arts center. The University of North Dakota campus, 2 miles (3 km) west of downtown, is home to the **North Dakota Museum of Art**, with its good collection of contemporary art.

🏛 **Empire Arts Center**
415 Demers Ave. **Tel** (701) 746-5500.
**Open** call for times. ♿ 🅿
W empireartscenter.org

## ❷ Devils Lake

7,000. 🚌 🚂
ℹ 208 Hwy 2 W, (800) 233-8048.
W devilslakend.com

The primary recreational attraction in northeastern North Dakota is the 90-sq-mile (490-sq-km) glacial Devils Lake, 90 miles (150 km) west of Grand Forks. With miles of shoreline and no natural outlet, the lake is an excellent spot for fishing and boating.

**Fort Totten State Historic Site**, 14 miles (22 km) to the south, is one of the best-preserved United States Army bases from the post-Civil War era. Built in 1867, it remained in use as a military reservation until 1890, when it became a boarding school for Native American children. The restored buildings around the parade ground contain period furniture.

🏛 **Fort Totten State Historic Site**
Rte 57. **Tel** (701) 766-4441.
**Open** May–Sep: 8am–5pm. ♿ 🅿
W history.nd.gov/historicsites/
totten

## ❸ Washburn

1,700. ℹ (701) 462-8530.
W washburnnd.com

The key attraction in the area surrounding the sleepy Missouri River town of Washburn is the **Lewis and Clark Interpretive Center**. A stunning view of the Missouri River Valley greets visitors, who can also don buffalo robes, listen to Native American music, and view exhibits tracing the river's shifting course over the past 200 years.

The Center is an ideal starting point for a tour of the sites associated with Lewis and Clark's historic expedition. About 2 miles (3 km) west of the visitor center is the reconstructed **Fort Mandan**. It was here that Lewis and Clark's 44-man Corps of Discovery wintered between 1804 and 1805, en route to the Pacific Ocean.

The **Knife River Indian Village National Historic Site**, 20 miles (32 km) west of Washburn, contains the remains of the largest villages of the interrelated Mandan, Hidatsa, and Arikara tribes. Among these are a restored 50-ft x 12-ft (15-m x 4-m) earth lodge. The French trapper Charbonneau, and his Native American wife, Sacagawea, joined the Lewis and Clark expedition near this spot in 1804.

🏛 **Lewis & Clark Interpretive Center**
US 83 & Rte 200A. **Tel** (877) 462-8535.
**Open** 9am–5pm Mon–Sat, noon–5pm Sun. ♿ 🅿
W fortmandan.com

The reconstructed, high-stockaded façade of Fort Mandan, near Washburn

The Painted Canyon, Theodore Roosevelt National Park

## ❹ Theodore Roosevelt National Park

Medora. **Tel** (701) 623-4466.
**Open** 8am–4:30pm daily.
**Closed** Jan 1, Thanksgiving, Dec 25.
🐾 ♿ 🅦 nps.gov/thro

The tiny western North Dakota town of Medora is the gateway to the Theodore Roosevelt National Park and the remote, beautiful North Dakota badlands. The bill that created this park as a memorial to Roosevelt was signed on April 25, 1947, by President Truman. On November 10, 1978, the area was given national park status by virtue of another bill signed by President Carter.

The Theodore Roosevelt National Park is a sprawling one, covering over 110 sq miles (280 sq km) of land. It is divided into three areas – the North and South Units and Elkhorn Ranch. The butte-studded South Unit has the phantasmagoric **Painted Canyon** and can be explored on horseback or seen from an overlook from a 36-mile (58-km) self-guided auto tour. The North Unit features a dramatic, oxbow bend in the Little Missouri River. Its moonlike landscape is dotted with mushroom-shaped stone formations and windswept grasslands. Unlike the much-visited South Unit, this pocket lies in very isolated country. However, a 14-mile (22-km) auto route through this rugged landscape provides access to nature trails and numerous scenic overlooks.

## ❺ Bismarck & Mandan

🏙 120,000. ✈ 🚌 📧 ℹ 1600 Burnt Boat Dr, Bismarck, (800) 767-3555.
🅦 discoverbismarckmandan.com

Riverboat traffic, railroads, and the government were instrumental in the development of the state capital of Bismarck, founded in 1872 on the east bank of the Missouri River. The 19-story, Art Deco **North Dakota State Capitol** dominates the city's leafy, low-slung skyline. Known as the "Skyscraper of the Prairies," the 1933 structure is visible for miles in every direction, mainly because of its location on top of a small rise north of downtown. The **North Dakota Heritage Center**, abutting the Capitol, provides a fascinating introduction to the state's Native American heritage and territorial settlement. It also traces the story of the Capitol's design and construction.

Mandan, a gateway to the West, lies just across the Missouri. To the south of downtown is **Fort Abraham Lincoln State Park**, which contains On-a-Slant Indian Village, the excavated remains of a 17th-century Mandan Native American community, and several other reconstructed buildings. The fort was the last base for reckless George Armstrong Custer, who led the 7th Cavalry from here to their disastrous defeat at the Battle of Little Bighorn (see p573) in 1876.

🏛 **North Dakota Heritage Center**
Capitol Mall, Bismarck. **Tel** (701) 328-2666. **Open** 8am–5pm Mon–Fri, 10am–5pm Sat & Sun. ♿

🏛 **Fort Abraham Lincoln State Park**
4480 Fort Lincoln Rd. **Tel** (701) 667-6340. **Open** Apr 1–Memorial Day: 9am–5pm daily; Memorial Day–Labor Day: 9am–7pm; Labor Day–Sep 30: 9am–5pm. 🐾 ♿

## ❻ Fargo

🏙 216,000. ✈ 🚌 📧 ℹ 2001 44th St S, (800) 235-7654.
🅦 fargomoorhead.org

A grain-processing center, Fargo lies directly across the Red River from its sister city, Moorhead, Minnesota. Fargo's historic downtown includes the renovated 1926 **Fargo Theatre**, an Art Moderne structure that still presents art and period films as well as live performances. Southwest of the theater is the superb **Plains Art Museum**, housed in a restored 1904 International Harvester Company warehouse. This museum has the state's largest public art collection, with works by the region's Native American and folk artists. The **Roger Maris Baseball Museum**, in the West Acres Shopping Center, celebrates the achievements of Fargo's most famous native son, who hit 61 home runs in 1961, setting a record for most home runs in a season.

🎭 **Fargo Theatre**
314 Broadway. **Tel** (701) 239-8385.
**Open** call for schedule. 🐾 ♿

Exterior of the historic Fargo Theatre, Fargo

# South Dakota

Rivers, hills, buttes, rolling prairies, and badlands are South Dakota's defining geographical features. The Missouri River bisects the state from north to south, with the corn and soybean fields of the flatter eastern plains giving way to shortgrass prairie and rocky badlands as one heads west on the state's main east–west corridor, I-90. Culturally, the state is dominated by the heritage of the Dakota, Lakota, and Nakota Sioux tribes, who roamed and hunted the buffalo-rich area until they were moved onto reservations in the late 1800s. Over 60,000 Native Americans still reside here.

Exterior of the South Dakota State Capitol in Pierre

## ⑦ Mitchell

🏙 16,000. 🚌
ℹ 601 N Main St, (866) 273-2676.
🅦 cornpalace.com

Located in the fertile James River Valley, Mitchell is the state's corn, grain, and cattle center. The city's claim to fame is the world's only **Corn Palace**, a Moorish auditorium that was built in 1921 to house the city's Corn Belt Exposition. Colorful domes, minarets, and kiosks are the only permanent design features on the ever-changing façade of the palace. Every year, local artists use more than 3,000 bushels of corn and grasses to create new murals, which depict agricultural and myriad other scenes. This tradition dates back to 1892, when the Corn Real Estate Association constructed the first palace to showcase the area's crops, in an endeavor to lure settlers.

🏛 **Corn Palace**
**Open** Apr–May & Sep–Nov: 8am–5pm daily; Jun–Aug: 8am–9pm; Dec–Mar: 8am–5pm Mon–Sat. ♿

Mural at the Corn Palace, Mitchell

## ⑧ Pierre

🏙 14,000. ✈ 🚌
ℹ 800 W Dakota Ave, (800) 962-2034.
🅦 pierre.org

The second-smallest capital in the US, Pierre lies in the Missouri River Valley, and forms a leafy oasis in the shortgrass, largely treeless plains of central South Dakota. The 1910 **South Dakota State Capitol** has a grand marble staircase and overlooks a lake visited each spring and fall by thousands of migratory birds. A huge display of Christmas trees inside the Capitol begins at Thanksgiving.

The excellent **South Dakota Cultural Heritage Center** is built into the side of a Missouri River bluff, covered with shortgrass prairie. Its exhibits trace the history of South Dakota's Sioux tribes and also provide information on the diverse ethnic backgrounds of the state's homesteading white settlers. On display is a lead plate that was buried in a nearby river bluff in 1743 by the French-sponsored Verendrye expedition to mark the site as French territory. The **Verendrye Museum**, across the river in Fort Pierre, focuses on French trading and exploration activities.

🏛 **South Dakota State Capitol**
500 E Capitol Ave. **Tel** (605) 773-3011.
**Open** 8am–7pm Mon–Fri, 8am–5pm Sat, Sun.

🏛 **South Dakota Cultural Heritage Center**
900 Governors Dr. **Tel** (605) 773-3458.
**Open** 9am–6:30pm Mon–Sat, 1–4:30pm Sun. **Closed** Jan 1, Easter, Thanksgiving, Dec 25. ♿ ♿

## ⑨ Badlands National Park

ℹ Ben Reifel Visitor Center, Rte 240, S of I-90 exit 131. **Tel** (605) 433-5361.
**Open** Jun–Aug: 7am–7pm; Sep–Oct: 8am–5pm; Nov–May: 8am–4pm. ♿
♿ 🅦 nps.gov/badl

The eerie desolation of Badlands National Park is an awe-inspiring sight for travelers unprepared for such a stark, rugged landscape after miles of gentle, rolling South Dakota prairie. Formed over 14 million years ago from silt and sediment washing down from the Black Hills (*see pp442–3*), the Badlands were sculpted into their present craggy form by harsh sun and powerful winds.

Some of the region's most dramatically eroded buttes, pinnacles, and spires are contained in this 380-sq-mile (990-sq-km) park. The **Ben Reifel Visitor Center** is the gateway to several self-guided hiking tours and the 30-mile (48-km) Badlands Loop Road (Route 240). The scenic drive follows the northern rim of the 450-ft- (137-m-) high Badlands Wall escarpment and leads to several overlooks and trails that provide breathtaking vistas of

View of the eroded gullies from Changing Scenes Overlook in Badlands National Park

the eroded gullies below. The road loops back north to I-90 near **Sage Creek Wilderness Area**, where golden eagles, hawks, and various songbirds gather in a vast expanse of steep grasslands, festooned each summer with wild-flowers. The park-managed buffalo herd can be seen grazing on large stretches of prairie.

Wall Drug, a shopping and entertainment complex

## ⑩ Wall

🏘 800. 🚌 ℹ 501 Main St, (888) 852-9255. 🆆 wall-badlands.com

Wall has done a thriving tourist trade since 1936, when local pharmacist Ted Hustead put up signs along the highway offering free ice water. This primitive roadside advertising tactic soon grew into a statewide slew of billboards, which still line I-90 all the way across South Dakota. Hustead's small-town pharmacy, **Wall Drug**, is now a sprawling Wild West shopping and entertainment complex. Along with Western and Native American souvenirs are interactive exhibits of cowboys, homesteaders, gunfighters, and medicine-show hucksters.

The sprawling **Buffalo Gap National Grassland** lies south, west, and east of Wall. Its visitor center describes the ecological and cultural history of the grasslands. Exhibits outline the various habitats and illustrate the astonishing biodiversity of the shortgrass, mixed-grass, and tallgrass prairies, which once covered most of the region.

### 🏢 Wall Drug
510 Main St. **Tel** (605) 279-2175. **Open** 7am–5:30pm daily (extended summer hours). 🆆 walldrug.com

### 🌿 Buffalo Gap National Grassland Visitor Center
ℹ 708 Main St, (605) 279-2125. **Open** Memorial–Labor Day: 8am–5pm daily; Labor Day–Memorial Day: 8am–4pm Mon–Fri. ♿

## ⑪ Pine Ridge Indian Reservation

ℹ Oglala Sioux Tribe, Pine Ridge, (605) 867-6075.

Home to the Oglala Sioux tribe, the Pine Ridge Reservation is the nation's second-largest Native American reservation. The reservation lands abut the South Dakota–Nebraska border and extend west into the badlands region. The Oglala and their chief, Red Cloud, were relocated here in 1876. On December 29, 1890, the US Army's 7th Cavalry massacred about 300 Lakota men, women, and children at **Wounded Knee**.

This was the last in a series of misunderstandings concerning the ceremonial Ghost Dance, which the tribe believed would reunite them with their ancestors, bring the buffalo back, and help them regain their lost lands. A lone stone monument, about 10 miles (16 km) east of the village of Pine Ridge, marks the site.

The **Red Cloud Heritage Center**, on the Red Cloud Indian School campus near Pine Ridge, contains the gravesite of Chief Red Cloud. It also displays a range of Native American artifacts and contemporary art.

### 🏢 Red Cloud Heritage Center
4.5 miles (7 km) N of Pine Ridge Village on Hwy 18. **Tel** (605) 867-8257. **Open** 9am–7pm Mon–Fri, 11am–5pm Sat, Sun. **Closed** public hols. ♿ 🆆 redcloudschool.org

The Red Cloud Heritage Center at the Pine Ridge Indian Reservation

# ⑫ Black Hills

Known to the Lakota Sioux as Paha Sapa, these majestic hills were a mysterious, sacred place where Native Americans would retreat to seek guidance from the Great Spirit. In 1874, George Armstrong Custer's *(see p573)* expedition discovered evidence of gold deposits in the thickly forested, oddly shaped granite hills. A series of misleading treaties followed, forcing the Sioux to relinquish their land, as miners, speculators, and settlers rushed into these once-sacred hills to stake their claims. Today, the Black Hills harbor some of the state's most visited attractions, particularly Mount Rushmore National Memorial. The 125-mile by 65-mile (201-km by 105-km) area is linked by US 385 and US 16, which meanders from Rapid City, the main center in the area, to Wyoming.

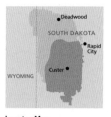

**Locator Map**
▨ Black Hills
▨ Area illustrated

**Crazy Horse Memorial**
When complete, the statue of the great Sioux warrior Crazy Horse will be the world's largest sculpture. So far, only the nine-story-high face is finished.

**Jewel Cave National Monument**
The underground attractions in the second-longest cave in the world are more varied than those at Wind Cave. Tough spelunking (cave exploring) tours allow participants into some of the more astounding areas. A simpler paved route offers a broad overview.

**Historic Deadwood**
The restored downtown re-creates Deadwood's past as a wild, lawless gold-mining town. Gunfighter Wild Bill Hickok was shot here in 1876, and Calamity Jane also left her mark here. Today, visitors try their luck in the historic gaming halls.

0 kilometers    10
0 miles    10

**Mount Rushmore National Memorial**
An American icon since its completion in 1941, the giant, sculpted heads of presidents George Washington, Thomas Jefferson, Theodore Roosevelt, and Abraham Lincoln took 14 years to create. Sculptor Gutzon Borglum's studio, tools, and models are preserved on site.

## VISITORS' CHECKLIST

**Practical Information**
ℹ️ Black Hills Visitor Information Center, Exit 61 off I-90, Rapid City, (605) 355-3600.
W **blackhillsbadlands.com**
Mount Rushmore National Memorial: **Tel** (605) 574-3165. **Open** call for timings. ♿
W **nps.gov/moru**
Crazy Horse Memorial: **Tel** (605) 673-4681. **Open** call for timings. 📷 ♿
W **crazyhorsememorial.org**
Custer State Park: **Tel** (605) 255-4515. **Open** call for timings. 📷 ♿ W **custerstatepark.com**
Wind Cave National Park: **Tel** (605) 745-4600. **Open** call for timings. 📷 ♿ W **nps.gov/wica** Jewel Cave National Monument: **Tel** (605) 673-8300. **Open** call for timings. **Closed** Jan 1, Thanksgiving, Dec 25. 📷 ♿ Visitor center only.
W **nps.gov/jeca**
The Mammoth Site: **Tel** (605) 745-6017. **Open** call for timings. 📷 ♿ W **mammothsite.com**
Deadwood: **Tel** (800) 999-1876. **Open** call for timings. ♿
W **deadwood.org**

**Transport**
✈️ Rapid City. 🚌 Rapid City.

### Key

— Custer State Park boundary
— Wind Cave NP boundary
⋯⋯ Major road

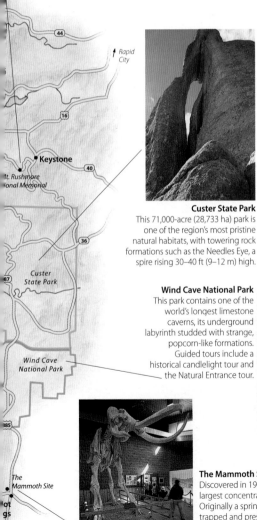

44

↑ Rapid City

16

● **Keystone**

40

Mt. Rushmore
...onal Memorial

36

**Custer
State Park**

87

**Wind Cave
National Park**

385

**The
Mammoth Site**

...ot
...gs

**Custer State Park**
This 71,000-acre (28,733 ha) park is one of the region's most pristine natural habitats, with towering rock formations such as the Needles Eye, a spire rising 30–40 ft (9–12 m) high.

**Wind Cave National Park**
This park contains one of the world's longest limestone caverns, its underground labyrinth studded with strange, popcorn-like formations. Guided tours include a historical candlelight tour and the Natural Entrance tour.

**The Mammoth Site**
Discovered in 1974, this site displays the world's largest concentration of Columbian mammoth fossils. Originally a spring-fed sinkhole where animals were trapped and preserved, only 30 percent of the 26,000-year-old site has been explored so far.

# Nebraska

Nebraska's vast, grassy expanses of open range, and ruts from old overland wagon routes, epitomize the geography and history of the Great Plains. The modern I-80 freeway stretches westward in the shadow of the wide Platte River Valley, the historic Oregon, Mormon, and Pony Express Trails, and the original Lincoln Highway (now US 30). Farther north, the sparsely settled central Nebraska Sandhills contain some of the nation's largest expanses of unbroken, mixed-grass prairie, while the Panhandle in the northwest is studded with rocky outcrops and jagged canyons. The state's two largest cities, Omaha and Lincoln, are in the southeast.

## ⑬ Chadron

🗺 5,600. ✈ ℹ 706 W 3rd St, (800) 603-2937. 🖥 chadron.com

Chadron is the ideal base to tour the Pine Ridge and Sandhills regions as well as explore aspects of the state's fascinating past. About 3 miles (5 km) east of town is the **Museum of the Fur Trade**. Built on the grounds of an 1833–49 American Fur Company post, the museum traces the history of the complex North American fur trade and its effect on Native American communities. One of its main features is a reconstructed trading post built into the sides of a low hill.

The area's key historical attraction is **Fort Robinson State Park**, just west of Crawford, which itself is 23 miles (37 km) west of Chadron. The park occupies the parade grounds, barracks, and officers' quarters of the US Army's Fort Robinson. The fort was built in 1874 to protect the nearby Red Cloud Indian Agency, where Sioux chief Red Cloud and his followers moved to before

being relocated at Pine Ridge (see p441). In 1877, the great Oglala Sioux chief, Crazy Horse (see p442), and 900 of his tribe surrendered and set up camp outside of the fort. In a series of tragic events, Crazy Horse was killed while federal troops attempted to imprison him. A restored blockhouse commemorates the site where he fell.

The excellent Fort Robinson Museum details the fort's other lives as an experimental cattle ranch and a training ground for the army's World War II canine corps. The fort's restored quarters provide accommodations for visitors, while horseback trails lead through the surrounding lonesome buttes and grassy plains. The park also harbors a large herd of longhorn cattle and more than 400 bison.

**Chadron State Park**, 8 miles (13 km) south of Chadron, is a quieter, more scenic alternative, with ample campgrounds and cabin facilities. Hiking and biking trails from the park crisscross the

spine of the 230-mile- (370-km-) long Pine Ridge escarpment. Hikers and mountain bikers seeking more challenging routes can follow the 25-mile (40-km) Pine Ridge Trail, a steep, meandering route leading through patches of meadows and thick stands of ponderosa pine. The trail is part of the Pine Ridge National Recreation Area, a craggy portion of the vast Nebraska National Forest, which runs along the brow of the escarpment, south of US 20, between Chadron and Crawford.

### 🏕 Fort Robinson State Park
US 20, 3 miles (5 km) W of Crawford. **Tel** (308) 665-2900. **Open** daily. ♿ 🖥 outdoornebraska.ne.gov

Martin Bay in Lake McConaughy State Recreation Area, near Ogallala

## ⑭ Ogallala

🗺 5,100. 🚌 ℹ 204 E A St, (800) 658-4390. 🖥 visitogallala.com

Located on the South Platte River near the junction of I-80, US 26, and Route 92, Ogallala is the gateway to the Panhandle part of the Oregon Trail tour (see p446). The city gained a rowdy reputation as the "Gomorrah of the Plains" soon after its founding in 1867, when the arrival of the railroad drew herds of cattle and hordes of Texas cowboys. Most modern visitors now come seeking camping, boating, hunting, and fishing supplies for their exploration of **Lake McConaughy State Recreation Area**, about 9 miles (14 km), to the north.

A refreshing oasis in the middle of the dry Panhandle plains, Lake McConaughy is the

Restored officers' quarters in Fort Robinson State Park, Chadron

state's largest reservoir. Known locally as "Big Mac," its cool waters are a prime breeding ground for rainbow trout, catfish, walleye, and white bass. The north shore is lined with fine sand beaches, while the marshes, woodlands, and grasslands on the lake's western end attract a wide variety of waterfowl. Loons, ducks, mergansers, and western grebes frequent Big Mac, making it one of the richest birding spots in the Great Plains region.

### 🦆 Lake McConaughy State Recreation Area
1475 Hwy 61 N. **Tel** (308) 284-8800. **Open** 8am–5pm daily; Memorial Day–Labor Day: 8am–5pm Sun–Thu, 8am–8pm Sat. 🌊

## ⓯ North Platte
🏠 27,000. ✈ 🚌 ℹ 219 S Dewey, (800) 955-4528. 🌐 visitnorthplatte.com

Now one of the country's major railroad centers, North Platte was the late 19th-century home of the famed William "Buffalo Bill" Cody *(see p574)*. The comfortable ranch house he built on the outskirts of town was the base of operations for his spectacular traveling Wild West show until 1902, when he founded Cody in Wyoming. Cody's home is now part of the **Buffalo Bill Ranch State Historical Park and State Recreation Area** that includes a horse barn and log cabin from one of his previous ranches. The nearby **Lincoln County Historical Museum** exhibits a replica of the famous North

Platte Canteen, which served countless pots of coffee and quantities of snacks to the troops who passed through the town during World War II.

### 🏛 Buffalo Bill Ranch State Historical Park and State Recreation Area
2921 Scouts Rest Ranch Rd. **Tel** (308) 535-8035. **Open** daily for camping; house and barn open May–Sep; check website for full info. **Closed** Oct–Apr. 🌊 ♿ 🌐 outdoornebraska.ne.gov

### 🏛 Lincoln County Historical Museum
2403 Buffalo Bill Ave. **Tel** (308) 534-5640. **Open** May–Sep: 9am–5pm Mon–Sat, 1–5pm Sun; winter: by appointment. 🌊 ♿

Cody's house in North Platte's Buffalo Bill Ranch State Historical Park

## ⓰ Lincoln
🏠 260,000. ✈ 🚃 🚌 ℹ 201 N 7th St, (402) 434-5348. 🌐 lincoln.org

State capital and Nebraska's second-largest city, Lincoln is also home to the University of Nebraska, whose Cornhuskers football team is so popular that it has sold out every home

Bronze statue surmounting the Nebraska State Capitol in Lincoln

game at the 77,000-seat Memorial Stadium since 1962. The city's principal landmark, however, is the 400-ft (120-m) Indiana limestone tower of the **Nebraska State Capitol**. Completed in 1932, the "Tower of the Plains" is surmounted by a bronze statue of a man sowing grain and visible for miles around. Intricate murals and ornate ceilings adorn the interior. The building houses the nation's only unicameral legislature, a vestige of cost-saving measures introduced by the state during the Great Depression of the 1930s.

The state's political history is related alongside its rich Native American heritage in the excellent **Nebraska History Museum**, located on 15th and P Streets. The **University of Nebraska State Museum**, in the downtown campus, has a wide-ranging collection of elephant fossils and Native American artifacts. In the nearby historic Haymarket District, several 19th-century warehouses have been converted into bars, restaurants, and shops.

### 🏛 Nebraska History Museum
15th & P Sts. **Tel** (800) 833-6747. **Open** 9am–4:30pm Mon–Fri, 1–4:30pm Sat & Sun. **Closed** public hols. ♿ 🌐 nebraskahistory.org

### 🏛 University of Nebraska State Museum
Morrill Hall, 14th & Vine Sts. **Tel** (402) 472-2642. **Open** 9:30am–4:30pm Mon–Sat (to 8pm Thu), 1:30–4:30pm Sun. **Closed** public hols. ♿ 🌐 museum.unl.edu

A colorful billboard in a parking lot welcoming visitors to North Platte

# The Oregon Trail

Founded by trader William Sublette in 1830, this formidable 2,000-mile (3,200-km) trail was the main wagon route between Independence, Missouri *(see p453)* in the east and Oregon to the west. The original route curved northwest after crossing the Missouri River near present-day Kansas City, passing through northeastern Kansas and southeastern Nebraska on the way to the Platte River. Between 1841 and 1866, a staggering 500,000 settlers bound for the fertile farmlands of Oregon and the goldfields of northern California passed through Nebraska, following the northern banks of the Platte, past a string of army forts to Ogallala. As the trail veered northwest, away from the flat landscape of the Platte River Valley and up into the craggy Panhandle plateau along the North Platte River, pioneers were awestruck by the massive rock formations that signaled the Rockies to the west.

**Locator Map**
*The Oregon Trail*

**Chimney Rock**, east of the town of Scottsbluff, rises 500 ft (152 m) above the mixed-grass plains. This was one of the more frequently noted sights found in travelers' diaries and sketchbooks.

### The Oregon Trail In Nebraska

*More than 428 miles (689 km) of the original Oregon Trail passed through the flat grasslands of Nebraska before it turned northwestward. Today, most of the old routes are easily accessible, with historic markers guiding travelers on I-80, along the Platte River, or Route 92 and US 26, which follows the trail's northwestern ascent of the North Platte. This undated illustration by William H. Jackson depicts the first covered wagon caravan, led by Smith-Jackson-Sublette, consisting of ten wagons drawn by five mules each, heading for Wind River Valley near present-day Lander in Wyoming.*

**Scotts Bluff National Monument** has a well-staffed visitor center, which runs various interpretive and living history programs. These include an excellent overview of the Oregon Trail history, as well as exhibits on the Mormon Trail. Visitors can hike to the summit of the 800-ft (244-m) sandstone outcropping and walk along still-visible Oregon Trail ruts.

Morton's mansion at Arbor Lodge State Historical Park, Nebraska City

# ⑰ Nebraska City

🏙 7,200. 🛈 806 1st Ave, (800) 514-9113. 🅦 nebraskacity.com

Sedate, tree-lined Nebraska City's origins were as a rowdy Missouri River way station, where families and adventurers bound for the Oregon Trail mingled with trappers, traders, and riverboat employees. Today, the city is best known as the birthplace of Arbor Day, established by Nebraska politician and newspaper editor Julius Sterling Morton (1832–1902). When he was Secretary of Agriculture under President Grover Cleveland, Morton introduced a resolution to make April 10 a state holiday to encourage farmers in Nebraska to plant trees as protection from high plains winds and soil erosion. Later, the date was changed to April 22, Morton's birthday. Arbor Day is still commemorated throughout the United States, although the date varies from state to state.

The city is also well known as the home of **Arbor Day Farm**, a 260-acre (105-ha) experimental farm, conference center, and forestry research center. Scenic hiking trails and guided tours offer casual explorations of the farm's apple orchards, windbreak arboretum, and a renewable energy plant.

The **Arbor Lodge State Historical Park** contains Morton's Georgian Revival mansion, greenhouse, and grounds. The park includes tours of the formal Italian garden and 52-room mansion, completed in 1902, and a carriage house with a stagecoach once driven by Wild West impresario Buffalo Bill (see p574).

### 🎇 Arbor Day Farm
2611 Arbor Ave. **Tel** (402) 873-8717. **Open** 9am–5pm Mon–Sat, 10am–5pm Sun (10am–5pm in winter; from 11am Sun). **Closed** Jan 1, Dec 25. 🅦 arbordayfarm.org

# ⑱ Omaha

🏙 421,600. ✈ 🚃 🚌 🛈 1001 Farnam St, Ste 200, (402) 444-4660. 🅦 visitomaha.com

Omaha evolved from a rough-and-tumble Missouri River town and outfitting post into a major railroad terminus with the construction of the trans-continental railroad in 1868 (see p562). The restored Old Market warehouse district just south of downtown preserves the city's historical roots. Its old commercial buildings and cobblestone streets are now home to some of the region's best restaurants, bookstores, and antique shops. A few blocks south, the city's landmark 1931 Art Deco Union Station has been refurbished and converted into the **Durham Western Heritage Museum**. This splendid local history museum features displays on Omaha's railroad and transportation heritage.

Just west of downtown is the pink marble **Joslyn Art Museum**, a Smithsonian affiliate and the crown jewel of Omaha's cultural attractions. The museum features 19th- and 20th-century European and American art. It also is a treasure trove of Western American art, with paintings, sculpture, and photographs by George Catlin, Frederic Remington, George Caleb Bingham, and Edward S. Curtis. The centerpiece of its Western collection are the watercolors and prints by Swiss artist Karl Bodmer (see p434), who documented life on the upper Plains when he traveled across North America with German naturalist Prince Maximilian of Wied in 1833.

North of downtown, the **Great Plains Black History Museum** relates the rarely told story of African-American migration and settlement on the Great Plains, beginning with the Exoduster group of freed slaves that left Reconstruction-ravaged Tennessee in the 1870s to homestead in Kansas. The **Mormon Trail Center**, about 5 miles (8 km) to the north, commemorates the 1846-48 migration of Mormons from the Midwest to Utah (see p511). Located on the pioneers' late 19th-century Winter Quarters campsite, a visitor center explains the religious persecution that led to the migration. It also displays a reconstructed Mormon Trail handcart and wagon.

### 🏛 Durham Western Heritage Museum
801 S 10th St. **Tel** (402) 444-5071. **Open** 10am–8pm Tue, 10am–5pm Wed–Sat, 1–5pm Sun. 🅦 durhammuseum.org

### 🎇 Joslyn Art Museum
2200 Dodge St. **Tel** (402) 342-3300. **Open** 10am–4pm Tue–Sat (to 8pm Thu), noon–4pm Sun. 

Art Deco façade of Omaha's Durham Western Heritage Museum

# Iowa

Stretching from the Mississippi on its eastern border to the Missouri River on the west, Iowa offers seemingly endless vistas of rolling hills, lush cornfields, old-fashioned barns, and clapboard country churches. It is one of the nation's largest agricultural producers, with a rich stock of tidy, hard-working farming communities. These are the images that make the state a perfect setting for Hollywood movies seeking to capture a nearly vanished rural America. Iowa also has a handful of lively cities, including the state capital Des Moines, with its excellent art and history museums.

## ⑲ Sioux City

🏙 83,000. ✈ 🚌
ℹ 801 4th St, (800) 593-2228.
🌐 visitsiouxcity.org

A busy railroad center and Missouri River port, Sioux City sits on the northern cusp of Iowa's green, shaggy Loess Hills. This unique ecosystem is comprehensively explained at the **Dorothy Pecaut Nature Center** in Stone State Park, about 3 miles (5 km) north of the city. The northern tip of the 200-mile (320-km) Loess Hills Scenic Byway, which traverses the hills, can be accessed from the park. The park also has one of the state's few surviving stands of tallgrass prairie and a network of bike and hiking trails.

Just south of downtown, the **Floyd Monument**, standing on a loess bluff, marks the 1804 burial of Sargent Charles Floyd, who was a member of Lewis and Clark's *(see p562)* Corps of Discovery. Floyd was the first and only member to die on the transcontinental journey of the three-year-long expedition. Exhibits from the voyage can be seen in the **Sergeant Floyd River Museum & Welcome Center** on the riverfront.

Floyd Monument

**🏛 Dorothy Pecaut Nature Center**
4500 Sioux River Rd. **Tel** (712) 258-0838. **Open** 9am–4pm Tue–Fri, 1–4pm Sat & Sun. **Closed** public hols. ♿

## ⑳ Des Moines

🏙 203,400. ✈ 🚌 ℹ 400 Locust St, Suite 265, (800) 451-2625.
🌐 catchdesmoines.com

The state capital draws its name from French voyageurs who explored the Raccoon and Des Moines River Valleys, calling the latter *La Rivière des Moines*, "River of the Monks." The city is now an important agricultural and entertainment center and home of the massive Iowa State Fair, which lures more than a million visitors every August.

Dominating the area east of downtown is the gold-leafed central dome of the **Iowa State Capitol**. Nearby is the **Iowa Historical Building**, with its displays on the state's Native American, geological, and cultural history. West of the Capitol, the Eliel Saarinen-designed **Des Moines Art Center** exhibits an impressive collection of paintings by Henri Matisse, Jasper Johns, Andy Warhol, and Georgia O'Keeffe. The Center's modern sculpture gallery was designed by I.M. Pei.

**🏛 Des Moines Art Center**
4700 Grand Ave. **Tel** (515) 277-4405. **Open** 11am–4pm Tue, Wed, Fri, 11am–9pm Thu, 10am–4pm Sat, noon–4pm Sun. ♿
🌐 desmoinesartcenter.org

**Environs**
Winterset, located about 35 miles (56 km) to the south, is the attractive seat of

Madison County and birthplace of Hollywood Western star John Wayne. The four-room house where the actor grew up is a much-visited museum today. The local Chamber of Commerce provides a map of the six covered bridges that inspired author Robert Waller's famous 1992 novel, *The Bridges of Madison County*.

A typical family home in the Amana Colonies

## ㉑ Amana Colonies

ℹ 622 46th Ave, Amana, (800) 579-2294. 🌐 amanacolonies.com

The seven Amana Colonies, along the Iowa River were settled in the 1850s by the Inspirationists, a mainly German religious sect. The colonists prospered, building a profitable woolen mill and a series of communal kitchens, shops, and factories. In 1932, residents voted to end their communal lifestyle, setting up a profit-sharing society instead.

One of the community businesses has since evolved into the Amana appliance manufacturer, while the 1857 Amana Woolen Mill is the state's only woolen mill still in operation. The **Amana Heritage Society & Museums** commemorate the success of the colonies' enterprises and their unique history in six separate museums and preserved historical sites.

**🏛 Amana Heritage Society & Museums**
705 44th Ave. **Tel** (319) 622-3567. **Open** Mar, Nov, Dec: Sat; Apr–Oct: 10am–5pm Mon–Sat, noon–4pm Sun.
♿ 🌐 amanaheritage.org

## 22 Cedar Rapids

126,600. ✈ 🚌 ℹ️ 87 16th Ave SW, Suite 200, (800) 735-5557.
W **cedar-rapids.com**

This town's downtown straddles the Cedar River. The Iowa artist Grant Wood lived in Cedar Rapids for much of his adult life and developed a Regionalist style that celebrated the people and landscapes of his home state. The **Cedar Rapids Museum of Art** has one of the country's largest collections of Wood's paintings, including the well-known *Young Corn*.

The Carl and Mary Koehler History Center details the area's early history, while the **National Czech and Slovak Museum & Library** celebrates the city's large Czech and Slovak immigrant population. Czech Village, a corridor along 16th Avenue Southwest, is still lined with shops selling Czech delicacies.

## 23 Dubuque

57,500. ✈ 🚌 ℹ️ 300 Main St, (800) 798-8844. W **traveldubuque.com**

Iowa's oldest city was established in 1788 by a French voyageur, Julian Dubuque. During the 19th century, the city's nouveau riche constructed luxurious homes atop the bluffs ringing the city. These citizens rode to and from downtown, 296 ft (90 m) below, via the **Fenelon Place Elevator**, an incline

View of Dubuque from the Fenelon Place Elevator

railway that is a major tourist attraction today.

The city's main attraction is the **National Mississippi River Museum and Aquarium**, a riverfront complex with exhibits on the mighty river's history and ecology. Aquariums replicate the habitat and ecosystem of the country's different rivers.

## 24 Quad Cities (Davenport)

480,000. ✈ 🚌 ℹ️ 1601 River Dr, Moline, IL (800) 747-7800.
W **visitquadcities.com**

Davenport is one of the four Mississippi River communities that comprise the sprawling 400,000-person "Quad Cities" area on both sides of the Iowa and Illinois border. It is the only city not blocked off from the river by flood-control walls. The excellent **Figge Art Museum**

west of downtown has one of the better collections of early 20th-century American Regionalist paintings. It displays works by Missouri's Thomas Hart Benton and Kansas-born John Steuart Curry, as well as the only painted self-portrait of Grant Wood. The **Putnam Museum of History and Natural Science** charts the early history of the Mississippi River Valley, and includes an aquarium and a giant-screen theater.

**Figge Art Museum**
225 W 2nd St. **Tel** (563) 326- 7804.
**Open** 10am–5pm Tue, Wed, Fri & Sat, 10am–9pm Thu, noon–5pm Sun.
**Closed** Mon, public hols. ♿
W **figgeartmuseum.org**

## 25 Iowa City

68,000. 🚌 ℹ️ 900 1st Ave, Coralville, (800) 283-6592.
W **iowacitycoralville.org**

Easygoing Iowa City is home to the 3-sq-mile (9-sq-km) University of Iowa campus and the school's noteworthy Iowa Writers' Workshop. The town served as the territorial and state capital until 1857, and the Old Capitol, now the **Old Capitol Museum**, is on campus.

About 10 miles (16 km) east of Iowa City is the **Herbert Hoover National Historic Site**. The president's boyhood home has been restored, along with a number of buildings constructed by the local Quaker community.

Boats sailing below a bridge that spans the mighty Mississippi River, Davenport

# Missouri

The Missouri River and the I-70 Interstate Highway bisect the state of Missouri, linking its two largest cities – St. Louis and Kansas City – and providing quick access to the centrally located state capital of Jefferson City. In southern Missouri, the rugged Ozark Mountain region is veined with beautiful streams and rivers, making the area a popular camping and canoeing destination.

Gateway Arch, symbol of the city of St. Louis

## ㉖ St. Louis

🏙 320,000. ✈ 🚆 🚌 🛈 308 Washington Ave, (314) 241-1764. 🌐 explorestlouis.com

Located just south of the point where the Missouri empties into the Mississippi River, St. Louis has been one of the country's most active crossroads. Founded by a French fur trader in 1764, this frontier city became a part of the US as a result of the Louisiana Purchase in 1803. It soon established itself as the "Gateway to the West," as steamboats chugged up the Missouri River into territories opened up by the Lewis and Clark expedition.

Scott trial plaque in the Old Courthouse

### 🏛 Gateway Arch-Jefferson National Expansion Memorial

Memorial Dr & Market St. **Tel** (314) 655-1700. **Open** 9am–6pm Labor Day–Memorial Day; 8am–10pm Memorial Day–Labor Day (summer). **Closed** Jan 1, Thanksgiving, Dec 25. 📷 ♿ Old Courthouse: 11 N 4th St. **Tel** (314) 655-1700. **Open** 8am–4:30pm daily. **Closed** Jan 1, Thanksgiving, Dec 25. ♿ 🌐 nps.gov/jeff Museum of Westward Expansion: **Tel** (314) 655-1600. **Open** Jun–Sep: 8am–10pm; Oct–May: 9am–6pm. ♿ 🌐 gatewayarch.com

*For hotels and restaurants see pp460–65*

Completed in 1965 on the site of fur trader Pierre Laclede's original 1764 settlement, Eero Saarinen's 630-ft- (192-m-) tall **Gateway Arch** symbolizes the city's role as a commercial and cultural gateway between the settled eastern US and the wide-open lands to the west. The excellent **Museum of Westward Expansion** at the base of the arch features several detailed exhibits on the 1803–1806 expedition by the explorers Lewis and Clark (*see p562*) and other 19th-century expeditions. The museum also includes two movie theaters. Elevator-like tram rides transport visitors to the top of the arch, where picturesque views of the surrounding city and Illinois farmlands make the cramped quarters well worth the 1-hour round trip.

The stately, domed **Old Courthouse** (1839–62) is one of the oldest buildings in the city of St. Louis. This Greek Revival structure was the site of two of the initial trials in the landmark Dred Scott case, which resulted in an 1857 decision by the US Supreme Court stating that African-Americans were not citizens of the country and had no rights under the laws of the US. The decision overturned an earlier suit by Scott, an African-American slave who had returned to St. Louis with his owners after nine years in free states, to win his freedom. It also deepened the sectional and racial differences that finally erupted in the American Civil War that lasted from 1861 to 1865.

A museum that stands within the Old Courthouse recounts the events of the famous Dred Scott trial for the benefit of visitors and depicts what life must have been like for ordinary people living in 18th-century St. Louis under the yoke of French and Spanish rule.

### 🏛 Laclede's Landing

Morgan St & Lucas St between I-70 & the Mississippi River. **Tel** (314) 241-5875. **Open** area open year-round; individual restaurant and club hours vary. ♿ 🌐 lacledeslanding.org

This vibrant restaurant and entertainment district consists of several blocks of restored 19th-century cotton, tobacco, and food warehouses that lie along the riverfront. The popular restaurants and blues clubs are known to attract large crowds, especially during the annual Big Muddy Blues Festival during the Labor Day weekend. The tall, six-story, cast-iron Raeder Place Building located on 719-727 N 1st Street, was built in 1873 and is one of the best-preserved warehouses in St. Louis. The 1874 Eads Bridge defines the Landing's southern boundary.

Raeder Building in Laclede's Landing area

## Forest Park

St. Louis Art Museum: 1 Fine Arts Dr.
Tel (314) 721-0072. **Open** 10am–5pm
Tue–Sun (until 9pm Fri). **Closed** Jan 1,
Thanksgiving, Dec 25.

w slam.org Missouri History
Museum: Jefferson Memorial Bldg.
Tel (314) 746-4599. **Open** 10am–5pm
Tue, 10am–8pm Wed–Mon.

w mohistory.org

Designed in 1876 by German-
trained landscape architect
Maximilian Kern, this 2-sq-mile
(5-sq-km) park is one of the
nation's largest urban green
spaces. The 1904 World's Fair,
known officially as the Louisiana
Purchase Exposition, was held
on the grounds, drawing nearly
20 million visitors. After the fair,
nearly all the grand Beaux Arts
structures designed by Cass
Gilbert were demolished. The
only exception, the Palace of
Fine Arts, is now home to the
**St. Louis Art Museum**. Its
sweeping collection of
American art includes paintings
by Missourians George Caleb
Bingham and Thomas Hart
Benton, and artists Georgia
O'Keeffe, Winslow Homer, and
Andy Warhol. The **Missouri
History Museum**, originally the
Jefferson Memorial Building, sits
on the site of the main entrance
to the 1904 fair. The Beaux Arts
building houses impressive

Brick exterior of Anheuser-Busch Brewery

exhibits depicting the
multicultural history of St. Louis.
Its holdings include an original
Louisiana Purchase transfer
document, a replica of aviator
Charles Lindbergh's 1927 *Spirit
of St. Louis* airplane, and extensive
displays on the World's Fair. An
interactive arts gallery explores
the city's rich musical history.

### Anheuser-Busch Brewery

1127 Pestalozzi St. **Tel** (314) 577-2626.
**Open** Jun–Aug: 9am–5pm Mon–Sat,
11:30am–5pm Sun; Sep–May:
10am–4pm Mon–Sat, 11:30am–4pm
Sun. budweisertours.com

The world's largest brewery,
Anheuser-Busch, was founded
in 1860 by entrepreneurial
German immigrants. Its famous
trademark Budweiser lager
brand is still very popular. The
complex contains many of

the company's 19th-century
brick structures. Tours include
a visit to the famous Clydesdale
horse stables.

### Missouri Botanical Garden

4344 Shaw Blvd. **Tel** (800) 642-8842,
(314) 577-5100. **Open** 9am–5pm daily.
Jun–Aug: to 8pm Wed (grounds only).
w mobot.org

This garden was created in 1859
by a wealthy St. Louis
businessman on the grounds of
his estate. The grounds contain
an English garden, a Japanese
garden, a Turkish-style Ottoman
garden, as well as a scented
garden for the visually impaired.
The geodesic-domed
Climatron® has exotic birds and
over 1,200 species of tropical
plants, including banana trees,
orchids, and epiphytes.

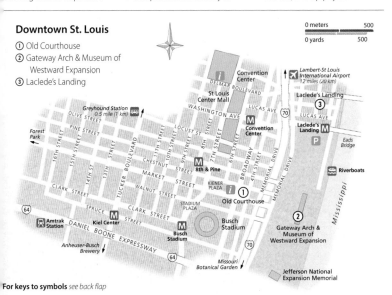

**Downtown St. Louis**

① Old Courthouse
② Gateway Arch & Museum of
   Westward Expansion
③ Laclede's Landing

The Classical Revival Missouri State Capitol, Jefferson City

## ㉗ Jefferson City

🏠 43,000. ✈ 🚉 🚌
ℹ 100 E High St, (800) 769-4183.
🌐 visitjeffersoncity.com

Soon after its founding as the state capital in 1821, Jefferson City grew into a busy Missouri River port. The **Jefferson Landing State Historic Site** preserves many structures from its original waterfront, including the 1839 Lohman Building. The Classical Revival **Missouri State Capitol**, completed in 1917, now houses the Missouri State Museum and a mural by Thomas Hart Benton. His bold 1935 *A Social History of the State of the Missouri* was criticized by Missouri's conservative power brokers for its stark depiction of the state's widespread poverty and seamier underclass.

🏛 **Jefferson Landing State Historic Site**
ℹ Jefferson St, (573) 751-2854.
**Open** 10am–4pm Tue–Sat.
**Closed** Jan 1, Thanksg., Dec 25. ♿

## ㉘ Branson

🏠 7,000. ℹ 269 State Hwy 248, (800) 214-3661. 🌐 explorebranson.com

This sleepy Ozark Mountain resort has radically transformed since the 1960s, thanks to the phenomenal success of several family-oriented tourist attractions. A musical pageant revolving around the Ozarks-based novel *The Shepherd of the Hills* was one of the area's first big hits. It is still staged in a picturesque, outdoor arena attached to a working, mountain farm.

*For hotels and restaurants see pp460–65*

The **Silver Dollar City** amusement park features high-tech roller coasters and water rides in a 19th-century Ozark pioneer setting, about 9 miles (14 km) west of town. The area's biggest draws are Branson's nightly music programs, presented at more than 30 alcohol-free performance venues crowded together on the "The Strip" (Route 76 W).

🏛 **Shepherd of the Hills Homestead**
5586 W Hwy 76, 2 miles W of Branson.
**Tel** (800) 653-6288. **Open** May–Oct: 9am–4pm. 🅿 ♿ 🌐 oldmatt.com

## ㉙ Kansas City

🏠 2,000,000. ✈ 🚉 🚌
ℹ 1100 Main St, (800) 767-7700.
🌐 visitkc.com

A delightful study in contrasts, Kansas City is rife with imagery associated with the Wild West. This vibrant city now contains beautifully landscaped parks and boulevards, sophisticated museums, fine public architecture, and high-end urban retail districts.

On the bluffs overlooking the Missouri River, just north of downtown, the **City Market** sits on the site of the town's original Westport Landing business district. The riverfront's 19th-century brick and cast-iron warehouses were converted into loft apartments and restaurants in the 1970s. Today, the 1930s City Market building houses an eclectic collection of shops, farmers' markets, retail outlets, and the Arabia Steamboat Museum, which displays artifacts salvaged from an 1856 wreck.

Northeast of the City Market, the **Kansas City Museum** is housed in a 50-room mansion in one of the city's most exclusive 19th-century neighborhoods. Its collections trace the city's evolution from a fur trading post into a powerful railroad and agricultural center. Walking tours are on offer at the visitor center, showing the limited exhibits that remain open during the museum's ongoing renovation. The Corinthian Hall and the Carriage House are currently closed.

"**Crossroads Arts District**" refers to the area stretching south of downtown to Penn Valley Park and Crown Center, roughly bounded on the east and west by Main Street and Broadway. The city's two most prominent architectural landmarks, **Union Station** and **Liberty Memorial**, are located here. The magnificent Beaux Arts Union Station, built in 1914, was one of the country's busiest and most glamorous railroad terminals. It rose to national prominence in 1933 when outlaw Pretty Boy Floyd gunned down an accomplice and several police officers in what became known as the Union Station Massacre. Renovated after years of neglect, the station is now a local history museum, children's science museum, and restaurant complex.

Kansas City skyline with Union Station in the foreground

Sprawling lawn of the Nelson-Atkins Museum of Art, Kansas City

The 217-ft (66-m) Liberty Memorial overlooks the old train depot on the grassy bluffs of Penn Valley Park. It houses the nation's only World War I museum. The "Torch of Liberty" observation tower offers a sweeping view of the city. To its south, the **Hallmark Visitors Center** presents the history of Hallmark, the well-known greeting card company.

Southeast of downtown, the **18th & Vine Historic Jazz District** commemorates the city's rich African-American heritage. In the 1930s, all-night jazz clubs showcased the innovative riffs of local musicians such as Count Basie, Lester Young, and Charlie Parker. This was Kansas City's heyday, when, under the free-wheeling "rule" of Tom Pendergast, a local concrete contractor, it was known as a "wide-open" town that stayed awake all night. Refurbished to form the backdrop for Robert Altman's 1996 film *Kansas City*, the district's premier attractions include the **American Jazz Museum**, which re-creates the city's swinging jazz era, and the **Negro Leagues Baseball Museum**, which honors talented African-American baseball players who toiled in low-paid obscurity for all-black teams in the US, Canada, and Latin America. In 1945, Kansas City Monarchs shortstop Jackie Robinson broke the color barrier by signing with the all-white Brooklyn Dodgers in the National League.

Once an outfitting post for travelers on the Santa Fe and Oregon Trails, the village of **Westport** became part of Kansas City in 1899. In the retail district along Westport Road, shops and restaurants occupy some of the city's oldest buildings, such as Kelly's Westport Inn, an 1837 tavern. Several blocks south of Westport, the **Country Club Plaza**, the nation's first planned suburban shopping district, was designed in 1922. To its east, the **Nelson-Atkins Museum of Art** has a stellar collection of paintings by Missouri's George Caleb Bingham and Thomas Hart Benton. The outdoor sculpture garden features 13 exclusive works by British artist Henry Moore.

Mural at the American Jazz Museum

🏛 **Kansas City Museum**
3218 Gladstone Blvd. **Tel** (816) 483-8300. **Open** 10am–4pm Wed–Sat, noon–4pm Sun. **Closed** Jan 1, Thanksgiving, Dec 25.
🈯 (free during renovation). ♿

🏛 **American Jazz Museum**
1616 E 18th St. **Tel** (816) 474-8463. **Open** 9am–6pm Tue–Sat, noon–6pm Sun. **Closed** public hols. 🈯 ♿
🌐 americanjazzmuseum.com

🏛 **Nelson-Atkins Museum of Art**
45th St & Oak St. **Tel** (816) 751-1278. **Open** 10am–4pm Wed, 10am–9pm Thu & Fri, 10am–5pm Sat, noon–5pm Sun. **Closed** public hols. ♿
🌐 nelson-atkins.org

## Environs

The suburb of **Independence**, 15 miles (24 km) east of downtown Kansas City, has one of the country's best westward expansion museums, the National Frontier Trails Center. It was also the home of Harry S. Truman, 33rd US president. His simple downtown home is now a national historic site.

# ㉚ St. Joseph

🏙 77,000. 🚌 ℹ️ 109 S 4th St, (800) 785-0360. 🌐 stjomo.com

Like many Missouri River communities, St. Joseph grew from a fur-trading post into a wagon-train outfitting center. Its position as the nation's western-most railroad terminal instigated local entrepreneurs to launch the Pony Express in the mid-1800s. This service sought to deliver mail from St. Joseph to Sacramento – a 1,966-mile (3,214-km) trip – in less than ten days. Informative displays in the **Pony Express Museum** relate the story of this short-lived enterprise, while the Patee House Museum preserves an 1858 hotel that served as the head-quarters of the Express. On its grounds is the house where the notorious Missouri outlaw Jesse James was killed by one of his former gang members in 1882.

🏛 **Pony Express Museum**
914 Penn St. **Tel** (800) 530-5930. **Open** 9am–5pm Mon–Sat, 1–5pm Sun. **Closed** Jan 1, Thanksgiving, Dec 24, 25 & 31. 🈯 ♿
🌐 ponyexpress.org

Bronze statue of a Pony Express rider, St. Joseph

# Kansas

For most Americans, Kansas conjures up images of rolling wheat fields, flatlands, sunflowers, and scenes from the 1939 film *The Wizard of Oz*. The real Kansas, however, is infinitely more interesting, both historically and geographically. Reminders of the state's turbulent 19th-century history as an Indian resettlement territory, anti-slavery battleground, and cattle-drive destination can be seen frequently as one traverses the principal Interstate Highways, I-335 and I-35, and the meandering backroads. Kansas is also home to the largest continuous area of natural tallgrass prairie left in North America, preserved in the undulating Flint Hills, and to the Museum at Prairiefire, a natural history museum, in Overland Park.

Entrance to the Kansas Natural History Museum, Lawrence

## ❶ Lawrence

🏙 88,000. 🚌 *i* 402 N 2nd St, (785) 865-4499. 🌐 **visitlawrence.com**

Founded by New England abolitionists in 1854, Lawrence's strong "free state" leanings made it a target for Missouri's pro-slavery "border ruffians," only 40 miles (64 km) to the east. The attractive, downtown retail district is lined with 19th-century stone and brick commercial buildings, reminders of the city's massive reconstruction drive after a destructive 1863 raid led by Confederate guerrilla William Quantrill.

A restored 1889 railroad depot houses the **Lawrence Visitor Information Center**, which relates key episodes in the city's history and provides information about the University of Kansas campus, just southwest of downtown. Situated astride a hill, known locally as Mount Oread, the campus includes the **Kansas**

Natural History Museum and the **Spencer Museum of Art**. Exhibits and events at Dole Institute of Politics promote civil discourse in a bi-partisan, balanced manner.

🏛 **Spencer Museum of Art**
1301 Mississippi St. **Tel** (785) 864-4710. **Open** 10am–4pm Tue–Sat (until 8pm Thu), noon–4pm Sun. **Closed** public hols. 🚻 🌐 **spencerart.ku.edu**

## ❷ Topeka

🏙 125,000. ✈ 🚌 *i* 1275 SW Topeka Blvd, (800) 235-1030. 🌐 **visittopeka.us**

A quiet government center, Topeka's most significant historical attraction is Kansas Regionalist painter John Steuart Curry's mural in the **Kansas State Capitol**, where a major renovation was completed in 2014. The mural, *The Settlement of Kansas*, depicts abolitionist John Brown in a dramatic confrontation with pro-slavery forces that threatened to make Kansas a slave state in the 1850s. More background on this tense period can be found at the superb **Kansas Museum of History**.

🏛 **Kansas Museum of History**
6425 SW 6th Ave. **Tel** (785) 272-8681. **Open** 9am–5pm Tue–Sat, 1–5pm Sun. **Closed** public hols. 🚻 🌐 **kshs.org**

## ❸ Flint Hills

🚗 🚌 *i* 501 Poyntz Ave, (800) 759-0134. 🌐 **manhattancvb.org**

The shaggy, rolling Flint Hills are among Kansas's most spectacular natural features. The best way to explore the area is to drive along the scenic 85-mile (137-km) stretch of Route 177, running south from the university town of **Manhattan**, across I-70, and down to Cassody at I-35. About 6 miles (10 km) southeast of Manhattan is **Konza Prairie**, the country's largest remaining parcel of virgin tallgrass prairie. The 13-sq-mile (35-sq-km) preserve contains a variety of spectacular hiking trails. The Flint Hills Discovery Center in Manhattan explores the biology, geology, and cultural history of the tallgrass prairie.

Route 177 intersects US 56 at **Council Grove** (40 miles/64 km south of Manhattan). The town takes its name from a huge oak tree, the Council Oak, which commemorates the spot where the Kansa and Osage tribes agreed to allow the old Santa Fe Trail to pass through their ancestral lands. The **Kaw Mission School**, now a state historic site, was set up by the Methodists from 1851 to 1854 in an attempt to "Westernize" male children from the Kaw (also known as Kansa or Kanza) tribe. This experiment did not succeed. The site now displays artifacts from the Mission School.

The red-roofed Chase County Courthouse, Cottonwood Falls, Flint Hills

Hikers at the Tallgrass Prairie National Preserve, Flint Hills

The **Tallgrass Prairie National Preserve**, 20 miles (32 km) south of Council Grove, protects what remains of a 17-sq-mile (45-sq-km), 19th-century cattle ranch. A hiking trail leads visitors from the ranch's Second Empire main house through large stands of native prairie. The ranching community of **Cottonwood Falls**, located about 3 miles (5 km) south on Route 177, contains another impressive Second Empire structure. Built in 1873, the red-roofed, limestone **Chase County Courthouse** is the oldest still in use in Kansas.

### 🏛 Konza Prairie
McDowell Creek Rd. **Tel** (785) 587-0441. **Open** sunrise-sunset daily.
**W** naturalkansas.org/konza

### 🦅 Tallgrass Prairie National Preserve
Hwy 177, 2 miles (3 km) N of Strong City. **Tel** (620) 273-8494. **Open** 9am–4:30pm daily. **W** nps.gov/tapr

## ❸❹ Wichita

🏛 660,000. ✈ 🚍 🚌
ℹ️ 515 S Main St, (800) 288-9424.
**W** visitwichita.com

Wichita developed in 1865 as a lawless railhead town, where cowboys driving cattle north from Texas on the Chisholm Trail *(see p475)* would stop to let off steam in the city's rowdy saloons and brothels. Those early cattle hands would not recognize today's Wichita, which has grown into a busy aircraft manufacturing and oil-refining

center. The town's colorful past is recreated at the **Old Cowtown Museum**. The original jail and period houses, as well as stores and saloons from surrounding rural communities are on display here. To its southeast is the **Mid-America All-Indian Center**, which depicts the 19th-century Great Plains lifestyles of the Kiowa, Cheyenne, and Lakota tribes. The main feature at the center is a reconstructed village. The "Gallery of Nations" features the flags of over 500 Indian nations.

Statue, Indian Center Museum, Wichita

### 🏛 Old Cowtown Museum
1865 Museum Blvd. **Tel** (316) 219-1871. **Open** Apr–Oct: 9:30am–4:30pm Mon–Sat, noon–4:30pm Sun; Nov–Apr: 10am–4pm Tue–Sat. 🅿 ♿
**W** oldcowtown.org

### 🏛 Mid-America All-Indian Center
650 N Seneca St. **Tel** (316) 350-3340. **Open** 10am–4pm Tue–Sat. **Closed** public hols. 🅿 ♿
**W** theindiancenter.org

## ❸❺ Dodge City

🏛 27,000. ✈ 🚌 ℹ️ 400 W Wyatt Earp Blvd, (800) 653-9378.
**W** visitdodgecity.org

The Wild West's two most colorful characters, lawmen Wyatt Earp and Bat Masterson, earned their tough reputations in Dodge City during its brief but boisterous heyday. Between 1872 and 1884, the town flourished as a High Plains buffalo-hunting, cattle-driving, and railroad center. The **Boot Hill Museum** re-creates the infamous Front Street strip of saloons and burlesque houses that earned Dodge City the sobriquet of "Hell on the Plains." The museum organizes various shows and stagecoach rides. On the museum grounds is Boot Hill cemetery.

Before hordes of cowboys and gun-toting buffalo hunters came to town, Dodge City was just another stop on the Santa Fe Trail. Ruts from the old wagon trail can still be seen 9 miles (14 km) west of Dodge City along US 50 and at the **Fort Larned National Historic Site**, 55 miles (88 km) east of Dodge City. The site contains several restored original sandstone structures from the US Army fort that protected travelers along the Santa Fe Trail from 1859 to 1878.

### 🚍 Boot Hill Museum
Front St & 5th Sts. **Tel** (620) 227-8188. **Open** Jun–Aug: 8am–8pm daily; Sep–May: 9am–5pm Mon–Sat, 1–5pm Sun. **Closed** Jan 1, Thanksgiving, Dec 25.
🅿 ♿ **W** boothill.org

Fort Larned National Historic Site, east of Dodge City

# Oklahoma

Bordered by six states, Oklahoma is a cultural, geographical, and historical crossroads, where jagged mountain ranges and High Plains mesas merge with forests, flatland wheat fields, and vast grassy ranges. The state has the nation's largest Native American population – more than 250,000 people representing 67 tribes – as a result of forced 19th-century migrations to the region, then known as the Indian Territory. Several "land runs" between 1889 and 1895 brought a huge influx of white and African-American settlers to this area, which joined the US in 1907 after oil was discovered.

*Praying Hands* at Oral Roberts University, Tulsa

## ➏ Bartlesville

🏙 36,000. ✈ 🚌 ℹ 201 SW Keeler, (800) 364-8708. 🅦 bartlesville.com

The state's first commercial oil well was drilled here in 1897, kicking off a large-scale oil boom. A replica of the original well, the Nellie Johnstone #1, now stands as a memorial in a downtown park. Today, the city's largest employer is still the Conoco-Phillips company, founded in 1917 as Phillips Petroleum, by two speculators from Iowa.

**Environs**
Frank Phillips's extensive 6-sq-mile (15-sq-km) rural estate, **Woolaroc Museum and Wildlife Preserve**, is located 12 miles (19 km) southwest of Bartlesville. The picturesque ranch includes a superb Western art collection, the Native American Heritage Center, and a wildlife preserve. About 45 miles (72 km) northwest of Bartlesville (via Pawhuska) is the Nature Conservancy's **Tallgrass Prairie Preserve**. In this vast expanse of rolling prairie, a herd of bison graze among stands of big bluestem grasses and blazing star wildflowers.

🏛 **Woolaroc Museum and Wildlife Preserve**
Rte 123, 12 miles (19 km) SW of Bartlesville. **Tel** (918) 336-0307. **Open** 10am–5pm Wed–Sun (and Tue from Memorial Day to Labor Day). **Closed** Mon, Thanksgiving, Dec 25. 🅿 👤 🅦 woolaroc.org

## ➐ Tulsa

🏙 394,000. ✈ 🚌 🚆 ℹ Williams Center Tower 2, 2 W 2nd St, (800) 558-3311. 🅦 visittulsa.com

Originally a railroad town, Tulsa prospered after the discovery of oil in 1901. Fortunes were made literally overnight, leading to the construction of Art Deco commercial buildings, roads, and bridges across the Arkansas River. Although Tulsa is still a major oil center, it also contains numerous man-made lakes, parks, and Arkansas River bike trails. Its top attraction is the **Thomas Gilcrease Institute**, a comprehensive art museum founded by a wealthy local oilman. Its collection includes a wide range of Native and Western American paintings by such well-known artists as George Catlin and Frederic Remington. The city's most popular roadside sight is the Prayer Tower Visitor Center and the 80-ft (24-m) bronze statue of a pair of hands folded in prayer at the entrance to Tulsa's **Oral Roberts University**.

🏛 **Thomas Gilcrease Institute**
1400 N Gilcrease Museum Rd, off US 64. **Tel** (918) 596-2700. **Open** 10am–5pm Tue–Sun. **Closed** Mon, Dec 25. 🅿 👤 🅦 gilcrease.org

## ➑ Tahlequah

🏙 17,000. 🚌 ℹ 123 E Delaware St, (800) 456-4860. 🅦 tourtahlequah.com

The capital of the Cherokee Nation, Tahlequah lies in the eastern Oklahoma Ozark Mountain foothills, the tribe's home since 1839. The city preserves several late 19th-century buildings, including the prison and the Cherokee National Capitol Building.

Of primary interest here is the **Cherokee Heritage Center**. Its attractions include a village dating from the 1875–90 Indian Territory era and a re-creation of a 17th-century settlement from the tribe's ancestral lands in the Appalachian Mountains. Exhibits at the Cherokee National Museum chronicle

Carriage on display at Woolaroc Museum and Wildlife Preserve, near Bartlesville

*For hotels and restaurants see pp460–65*

Earth lodges in the Cherokee Heritage Center, Tahlequah

the tribe's forced march along the "Trail of Tears" from North Carolina to Oklahoma in the 1830s *(see p434)*. This tragic event is also dramatized every year in June.

🏛 **Cherokee Heritage Center**
21192 S Keeler Dr, 3 miles (5 km) S of Tahlequah. **Tel** (888) 999-6007. **Open** 9am–5pm Mon–Sat. **Closed** pub. hols.
🅿 ⛽ 🅦 cherokeeheritage.org

## ㊴ Oklahoma City

🏛 599,000. ✈ 🚌 ℹ 123 Park Ave, (800) 225-5652. 🅦 visitokc.com

Oklahoma City was built and founded in a single day, April 22, 1889, as part of the first Oklahoma Territory land rush. Over 10,000 land claims were filed on that day, creating a city out of thin air. The city became the state capital in 1910 and saw its first oil strike in 1928. Today, there are more than 2,000 still-active oil wells, including one on the grounds of the Oklahoma State Capitol, within the city limits.

The **Oklahoma History Center** chronicles the state's intimate relationship with oil, as well as its pre-settlement history. The **National Cowboy Museum** contains one of the country's most comprehensive collections of Western-related art. Among its exhibits are works by such artists as Charles Russell and Albert Bierstadt. It also features a giant statue of the famed Wild West figure Buffalo Bill and a collection of Western actor John Wayne memorabilia. On a more somber note, the city has paid homage to the 168 people killed in the tragic 1995 Federal Building bombing incident *(see p434)* with the dignified **Oklahoma City National Memorial**. The 3.3-acre (1.3-ha) downtown memorial includes a museum, reflecting pool, and an American elm tree planted in the 1950s.

🏛 **Oklahama History Center**
2401 N Laird Ave. **Tel** (405) 521-2491. **Open** 10am–5pm Mon–Sat. **Closed** Jan 1, Thanksgiving, Dec 25.
⛽ 🅦 okhistorycenter.org

🏛 **National Cowboy Museum**
1700 NE 63rd St. **Tel** (405) 478-2250. **Open** 10am–5pm daily. **Closed** Jan 1, Thanksgiving, Dec 25. 🅿 ⛽
🅦 nationalcowboymuseum.com

The reflecting pool at the Oklahoma City National Memorial

---

## Old Route 66: The Historic "Mother Road"

Route 66 has been immortalized as the "mother road" traveled by the migrant Oklahoma family in author John Steinbeck's 1939 novel *The Grapes of Wrath* as they fled the drought-stricken Dust Bowl on the way to

Totem Pole Park

California. This historic highway, charted in 1926, was the first to link Chicago to Los Angeles. Old Route 66 heads southwest from the state's northeastern corner to its western border with Texas, meandering along the original two-lane alignment much of the way, frequently within sight of the modern interstates, I-44 and I-40, that parallel its original route. West of Oklahoma City, the route runs alongside I-40, with several sections of old road veering off the Interstate. The **Oklahoma Route 66 Museum** in Clinton sits across from a Best Western Motel where Elvis Presley slept on four separate occasions. The museum has one of the country's best Route 66 collections. The **National Route 66 Museum** in Elk City (30 miles/48 km west of Clinton) sports a smaller but equally engaging array of exhibits, including a pickup truck modeled after the one used in director John Ford's 1940 film adaptation of *The Grapes of Wrath*. Other sights along the route include the **Totem Pole Park** (about 4 miles/6 km east of Foyil) and the **Will Rogers Memorial Museum** at Claremore (27 miles/43 km east of Tulsa). Oklahoma's favorite son, humorist Will Rogers, was born in a log cabin in nearby Oologah. The museum relates the life story of this colorful actor and newspaper columnist, and screens several of his films.

# Practical Information

Up-to-date information is essential when planning an itinerary across the Great Plains, where cities and attractions are often separated by miles and miles of rolling prairie. A region of small towns, wide-open spaces, and distant horizons, the beautiful landscape of the Great Plains draws visitors searching for a taste of wholesome Americana. The best time to plan a trip is from mid-April through late October, but bear in mind that many of the historic sights are open only from Memorial Day (end May) to Labor Day (end August).

## Tourist Information

Travelers entering the Great Plains via a principal Interstate Highway are greeted with signs advertising a state "Welcome Center." These centers provide a full range of tourist information, as well as clean restrooms and coffee. Most of the region's major airports and train stations have information desks stocked with free brochures and maps. All of the larger cities and smaller towns operate Convention & Visitors Bureaus, which provide free directories of events, attractions, accommodations, and restaurants, both in print and online.

## Natural Hazards

Tornadoes usually occur during summer, particularly in the eastern portions of Kansas and Oklahoma, called "Tornado Alley." In the event of a tornado warning, travelers should first seek shelter in the basement of a solidly constructed building and then tune into a local radio station for additional information.

## Getting Around

Most of the major cities in the Great Plains have public bus systems that provide affordable but limited service. However, the convenient St. Louis Metrorail system is the only public rail transit system in the region.

## Driving in the Great Plains

Driving is the best way to explore the region, since most sights are usually situated far away from each other. Thus certain pre-cautions are necessary to ensure a safe journey. Seat belts are a must for drivers and front-seat passengers in all the states. Most states also require seat belts for back-seat passengers. Child seats are also mandatory, but age restrictions may vary from one state to another. Motorcyclists are required to wear helmets in in some states, especially if the rider is under 18 years of age.

Speed limits vary but are usually between 70 and 75 mph (112 and 120 km/h) on Interstate Highways, which are located outside crowded urban areas. Radar detectors are permitted in all the states.

## Etiquette

Great Plains residents tend to be friendly and polite. Drivers on the empty back roads usually acknowledge an oncoming car or truck by raising one or two fingers off of the steering wheel in a modified version of a wave. The polite response is to offer the same in return.

## Festivals

The Great Plains states stage a wide range of annual community, regional, and state festivals. The largest of the region's many fairs is the **Iowa State Fair**, held in August in Des Moines, while one of the country's friendliest Independence Day celebrations takes place in historic Independence, Missouri. All through summer, Native Americans in South Dakota hold several traditional "powwow" get-togethers. Other summer-time events are the historical productions staged by the Great Plains Chautauqua Society.

Musical festivals also abound in the region, with summer blues festivals in Kansas City, St. Louis, and Lincoln vying for top billing. The Walnut Valley bluegrass festival in Winfield, Kansas, and **Woody Guthrie Free Folk Festival** in his hometown Okemah, Oklahoma, are also very popular. Polka music, beer, and German food end the festival season at Missouri's **Oktoberfest**, in the Missouri River community of Hermann.

## Sports

Missouri has a monopoly on professional sports teams in the region, with Kansas City and St. Louis operating the region's

## The Climate of the Great Plains

This is a region of extremes, with hot summers and cold winters, especially in North and South Dakota. The southern states – Kansas, Missouri, and Oklahoma – have a more temperate climate, with milder winters. With its cooler nights and sunny days, June is perfect for touring the region's historic sites. Wildflowers are most colorful in May and September, while October's changing colors make it ideal for scenic drives through the wooded Ozark Mountains.

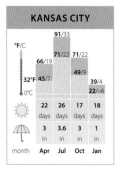

**KANSAS CITY**

| | Apr | Jul | Oct | Jan |
|---|---|---|---|---|
| °F/C | 66/19 | 91/33 71/22 | 71/22 49/9 | 39/4 |
| | 45/7 32°F | | | 22/-6 |
| | 0°C | | | |
| ☀ (days) | 22 days | 26 days | 17 days | 18 days |
| ☂ (in) | 3 in | 3.6 in | 3 in | 1 in |
| month | Apr | Jul | Oct | Jan |

only pro baseball (Kansas City Royals and St. Louis Cardinals) and football (Kansas City Chiefs and St. Louis Rams) franchises. Many of the states have minor league baseball teams as well, providing travelers with opportunities to watch up-and-coming players in cozier settings. Iowa is a mecca for minor league fans, with A-level teams in Burlington, Cedar Rapids, Clinton, and Davenport, and the AAA affiliate of the Chicago Cubs in Des Moines.

College football and basketball are also very popular, particularly in the southern Plains states. The annual **Kansas–Kansas State** football game is the seasonal climax to one of college football's most colorful intrastate rivalries.

## Outdoor Activities

In defiance of the stereotypical image of the Great Plains as flat and devoid of topography, hikers, cyclists, and mountain bikers flock to the region's hilly areas. Nebraska's Pine Ridge country, South Dakota's Badlands and Black Hills, and the Kansas Flint Hills are havens for campers and hikers. The 240-mile (386-km) **Katy Trail** bike path winds along the Missouri River for much of its route. Iowa's 7-day 500-mile (800-km) **RAGBRAI** cycling event is one of the world's largest, and North Dakota's Maah Daah Hey Trail in the Badlands is an International Mountain Bicycling Association Epic Ride. The August motorcycle rally and race in Sturgis, South Dakota, draws thousands of participants and spectators. Fishing and boating enthusiasts can choose from a range of mainly man-made lakes, such as Nebraska's Lake McConaughy. Streams and rivers in the Missouri Ozarks near Branson provide opportunities to fish and canoe.

## Entertainment

The busiest live music and theatrical venues in the Great Plains are in Branson, Kansas City, and St. Louis, with an array of clubs and theaters sprinkled in cities such as Tulsa, Lawrence, Lincoln, Omaha, Grand Forks, and Des Moines. The region's most spectacular outdoor performance venues include **The Muny** in Forest Park in St. Louis; Kansas City's **Starlight Theater**, in the city's bucolic Swope Park; and North Dakota's **Medora Musical**, featuring live Wild West musical programs on summer nights against the backdrop of the Theodore Roosevelt National Park badlands. A dizzying array of rides and activities awaits those who are more adventurous at the region's largest amusement parks, Kansas City's Worlds of Fun and Six Flags St. Louis.

## Shopping

The region's premier retail destination is Kansas City's elegantly designed Country Club Plaza. This 1920s urban shopping district has several higher-end specialty shops and department stores. A popular suburban shopping destination is the upscale Galleria mall in Clayton.

Iowa's Amana Colonies offer some of the best locally made products at the Amana Woolen Mill and Millstream Brewing Company. The best place to visit for Native American crafts and other merchandise is South Dakota. The Native American Educational and Cultural Center at the Crazy Horse Memorial in the Black Hills, and the Red Cloud Heritage Center on the Pine Ridge Reservation, offer a wide selection of handmade rugs, apparel, and other items. For Wild West souvenirs, travelers should visit Wall Drug, in Wall, located in South Dakota, for the widest selection.

# DIRECTORY

## Tourist Offices

**Iowa**
Tel (888) 472-6035.
w traveliowa.com

**Kansas**
Tel (800) 252-6727.
w travelks.com

**Missouri**
Tel (800) 411-5110.
w visitmo.com

**Nebraska**
Tel (800) 228-4307.
w visitnebraska.gov

**North Dakota**
Tel (800) 435-5663.
w ndtourism.com

**Oklahoma**
Tel (800) 652-6552.
w travelok.com

**South Dakota**
Tel (605) 773-3301,
(800) 732-5682.
w travelsd.com

## Road Conditions

**Iowa**
Tel (800) 288-1047.

**Kansas**
Tel (800) 585-7623.

**Missouri**
Tel (573) 751-2551.

**Nebraska**
Tel (800) 906-9069.

**North Dakota**
Tel (701) 328-2500.

**Oklahoma**
Tel (405) 425-2385.

**South Dakota**
Tel (866) 697-3511.

## Festivals

**Iowa State Fair**
PO Box 57130, Des
Moines, IA 50317.
Tel (515) 262-3111.
w iowastatefair.org

**Oktoberfest**
Hermann, MO.
Tel (800) 932-8687.
w visithermann.com

**Woody Guthrie Free
Folk Festival**
Okemah Industrial Park,
Okemah, OK.
Tel (918) 623-2440.
w woodyguthrie.com

## Entertainment

**Medora Musical**
Burning Hills
Amphitheater,
Medora, ND.
Tel (800) 633-6721.
w medora.com

**The Muny**
1 Theatre Dr, Forest Park,
St. Louis, MO.
Tel (314) 361-1900.
w muny.org

**Starlight Theater**
4600 Starlight Rd,
Kansas City, MO.
Tel (800) 776-1730.
w kcstarlight.com

# Where to Stay

## North Dakota

### BISMARCK: Wingate by Wyndham Bismarck $
Value
*1421 Skyline Blvd, 58503*
**Tel** *(701) 751-2373*
W wingatehotels.com
The ample rooms here come with sitting areas and refrigerators. Indoor pool. Breakfast is included.

### FARGO: Howard Johnson Inn Fargo $
Value
*301 3rd Ave, 58102*
**Tel** *(701) 232-8850*
W hojo.com
Comfortable rooms and a range of amenities, including a courtyard and a large indoor pool, make this a good family option.

### DK Choice

### FARGO: The Hotel Donaldson $$
Boutique
*101 Broadway, 58102*
**Tel** *(701) 478-1000*
W hoteldonaldson.com
This European-style boutique hotel is located in Fargo's revitalized downtown. The historic building features world-class accommodations and a restaurant serving renowned cuisine. Each of the artist-inspired rooms is unique. Enjoy exceptional hospitality, a nightly wine and cheese reception, and artisanal pastries served each morning. There is also a rooftop hot tub.

### FORT TOTTEN: Fort Totten Trail Historic Inn $
Value
*4 Historic Sq, 58335*
**Tel** *(701) 766-4874*
W tottentrailinn.com
Located at the Fort Totten Historic Site, rooms in former officers' quarters feature frontier decor. Complimentary Victorian tea and breakfast. Open May–September.

### GRAND FORKS: Staybridge Suites $
Value
*1175 42nd St S, 58201*
**Tel** *(701) 772-9000*
W ihg.com
Guests here enjoy comfortable rooms with full kitchens, a complimentary breakfast, and a reception with drinks and appetizers from Tuesday to Thursday.

## South Dakota

### DK Choice

### BADLANDS NATIONAL PARK: Cedar Pass Lodge $
Lodge
*20681 SD Hwy 240, 57750*
**Tel** *(605) 443-5460*
W cedarpasslodge.com
This beautiful lodge in the heart of Badlands National Park is a prime spot for exploring the area's eroded buttes and mixed-grass prairie. Built in 1928, the rustic, eco-friendly cabins are well-appointed, with modern amenities and hand-crafted pine furniture. Enjoy the surrounding nature while hiking one of the many trails. Open between April and October.

### CUSTER: Sylvan Lake Lodge & Resort $$
Lodge
*24572 Hwy 87, 57730*
**Tel** *(605) 574-2561*
W custerresorts.com
Options here include lakeside private cabins with kitchenettes and fireplaces or cozy main lodge rooms. This is a good place for hiking, bird-watching, and swimming.

### DEADWOOD: The Lodge at Deadwood $$$
Lodge
*100 Pine Crest Ln, 57732*
**Tel** *(605) 584-4800*
W deadwoodlodge.com
Comfortable rooms, many with private decks, enjoy panoramic views of the Black Hills. There is a huge range of outdoor activities.

Room at the family-friendly Howard Johnson Inn, Fargo, North Dakota

### PIERRE: Governor's Inn $
B&B
*700 W Sioux Ave, 57501*
**Tel** *(605) 224-4200*
W govinn.com
Spacious rooms at this inn come with microwaves and refrigerators, and a continental breakfast is included.

### RAPID CITY: Hotel Alex Johnson $$
Boutique
*523 6th St, 57701*
**Tel** *(605) 342-1210*
W alexjohnson.com
Native American decor and modern amenities feature at this comfortable landmark historic property close to Mt. Rushmore.

### SIOUX FALLS: Hilton Garden Inn $$
Boutique
*5300 South Grand Circle, 57108*
**Tel** *(605) 444-4500*
W hiltongardeninn3.hilton.com
The homey, well-appointed rooms here are comfortable. Complimentary airport shuttle.

## Nebraska

### LINCOLN: Cornhusker Hotel $
Value
*333 S 13th St, 68508*
**Tel** *(402) 474-7474*
W thecornhusker.com
Airy, elegant rooms mix old-world charm with modern convenience. Friendly service.

### LINCOLN: The Rogers House $$
B&B
*2145 B St, 68502*
**Tel** *(402) 476-6961*
W rogershouseinn.com
This renovated historic mansion offers unique rooms fitted with antique furnishings. Warm service.

### OMAHA: Cornerstone Mansion $
B&B
*140 North 39th St, 68131*
**Tel** *(402) 558-7600*
W cornerstonemansion.com
Rooms at this historic home built in 1894 boast period decor and have private baths.

The stunning setting of Chateau on the Lake, Branson, Missouri

**OMAHA: Element Omaha Midtown Crossing** $$
Boutique
*3253 Dodge St, 68131*
**Tel** *(402) 614-8080*
W elementomahamidtown
crossing.com
The eco-friendly studios and suites here have kitchens. Breakfast is included.

### DK Choice

**OMAHA: Magnolia Hotel** $$
Historic
*1615 Howard St, 68102*
**Tel** *(402) 341-2500*
W magnoliahotels.com
This historic property built in the style of a palace in Florence offers well-appointed, stylish rooms and suites and is known for its great service. Breakfast, an evening reception, and bedtime milk and cookies are included.

**SCOTTS BLUFF: Barn Anew Bed & Breakfast** $
B&B
*170549 County Rd L, 69351*
**Tel** *(308) 632-8647*
W barnanew.com
In a converted barn, Anew boasts views of Scotts Bluff Monument.

## Iowa

### DK Choice

**CEDAR FALLS: The Blackhawk Hotel** $
Historic
*115 Main St, 50613*
**Tel** *(319) 277-1161*
W blackhawk-hotel.com
Individually styled rooms feature original art at one of the oldest continuously operating hotels west of the Mississippi. The vintage Motor Lodge annex has mid-century modern rooms. There are bicycling trails nearby.

**CEDAR RAPIDS: The Hotel at Kirkwood Center** $
Boutique
*7725 Kirkwood Blvd SW, 52404*
**Tel** *(319) 848-8700*
W thehotelatkirkwood.com
This teaching hotel, where staff are assisted by competent hospitality students, offers stylish rooms, deluxe suites, and a comprehensive business center.

**DES MOINES: Hotel Fort Des Moines** $
Historic
*1000 Walnut St, 50309*
**Tel** *(515) 243-1161*
W hotelfortdesmoines.com
A renovated property with grand decor, spacious rooms, and elegant dining options.

**DUBUQUE: Hotel Julien Dubuque** $$
Boutique
*200 Main St, 52001*
**Tel** *(563) 556-4200*
W hoteljuliendubuque.com
High style, elegance, and sophisticated service complement richly appointed rooms with top amenities.

**MASON CITY: Historic Park Inn Hotel** $$
Historic
*7 W State St, 50402*
**Tel** *(641) 423-0689*
W wrightonthepark.org
The beautifully restored Frank Lloyd Wright hotel is a must for architecture fans.

## Missouri

**BRANSON: Chateau on the Lake** $$
Value
*415 N Hwy 265, 65616*
**Tel** *(417) 334-1161*
W chateauonthelake.com
Most rooms here have private balconies. The vast atrium features waterfalls and greenery.

**BRANSON: Hilton Promenade at Branson Landing** $$
Value
*3 Branson Landing Blvd, 65616*
**Tel** *(417) 336-5500*
W www3.hilton.com
Spacious, modern rooms at this hotel in the entertainment district come with stunning views.

### DK Choice

**KANSAS CITY: Hotel Savoy** $
B&B
*219 W 9th St, 64105*
**Tel** *(816) 842-3575*
W savoyhotel.net
This historic property has hosted many famous guests, including Teddy Roosevelt and John D. Rockefeller. The late 19th-century building features imported marble and original stained-glass windows. Elegant rooms have baths with antique claw-foot tubs and pedestal sinks. Enjoy complimentary breakfast at the famous Savoy Grill, the city's oldest restaurant.

**KANSAS CITY: Hotel Phillips** $$
Historic
*106 W 12th St, 64105*
**Tel** *(816) 221-7000*
W hotelphillips.com
Excellent service, elegantly designed rooms, and quality amenities feature at this boutique hotel.

**KANSAS CITY: The Raphael Hotel** $$
Boutique
*325 Ward Pkwy, 64112*
**Tel** *(816) 756-3800*
W marriott.com
Luxurious rooms, top service, and a romantic ambience are offered at this charming venue modeled after small European hotels.

**SPRINGFIELD: Holiday Inn Express** $
Value
*1117 E Saint Louis St, 65806*
**Tel** *(417) 862-0070*
W ihg.com
The large, tastefully decorated rooms at this centrally located hotel feature Mission-style furniture. Complimentary breakfast is served in the Great Room.

**ST. LOUIS: Moonrise Hotel** $$
Boutique
*6177 Delmar Blvd, 63112*
**Tel** *(314) 721-1111*
W moonrisehotel.com
This quirky hotel has well-appointed rooms, luxury amenities, and lunar-themed art.

For more information on types of hotels *see pages 26–7*

**ST. LOUIS: Napoleon's Retreat
Bed & Breakfast** $$
B&B
*1815 Lafayette Ave, 63104*
**Tel** *(314) 772-6979*
w napoleonsretreat.com
An elegant mansion with
spacious rooms in the heart of
Victorian St. Louis. Guests can
enjoy breakfast in the courtyard.

## Kansas

**COTTONWOOD FALLS:
Grand Central Hotel** $$
Historic
*215 Broadway, 66845*
**Tel** *(620) 273-6763*
w grandcentralhotel.com
Comfortable rooms come with
deluxe amenities at this small-
town property.

### DK Choice

**LAWRENCE: The Eldridge
Hotel** $
Historic
*701 Massachusetts St, 66044*
**Tel** *(785) 749-5011*
w eldridgehotel.com
Built in 1855, this was once a free
state hostelry for abolitionists. It
was attacked and destroyed
twice in the Civil War. Located
on "the most historic corner in
Kansas," the all-suite Eldridge
Hotel has comfortable, inviting
rooms with quality amenities
and complimentary Wi-Fi. There
is also a business center.

**TOPEKA: Hyatt Place** $
Value
*6021 SW 6th Ave, 66615*
**Tel** *(785) 273-0066*
w topeka.place.hyatt.com
These clean, plush rooms with
quality amenities are situated
close to shops. Top-notch service
is provided by excellent staff.

**TOPEKA: Senate Luxury Suites** $
Historic
*900 SW Tyler St, 66612*
**Tel** *(785) 233-5050*
w senatesuites.com
The spacious rooms have private
balconies with beautiful views at
this Victorian brick building with
inviting courtyards, .

**WICHITA: Hotel at Old Town** $
Historic
*830 E 1st St N, 67202*
**Tel** *(316) 267-4800*
w hotelatoldtown.com
Victorian elegance features at
this boutique hotel where rooms
include fully equipped kitchens.

The Skirvin Hilton in a historic building, Oklahoma City

**WICHITA: Courtyard Wichita at
Old Town** $$
Boutique
*820 E 2nd St N, 67202*
**Tel** *(316) 264-5300*
w marriott.com
Plush rooms here have a range of
amenities, and there's a lush
atrium and an airy courtyard.

## Oklahoma

**NORMAN: Montford Inn B&B** $$
Romantic
*322 W Tonhawa St, 73069*
**Tel** *(405) 321-2200*
w montfordinn.com
Heart-shaped jetted tubs for two,
private decks, and fireplaces in
cottage suites or rooms spell
romance in this quiet location.

**OKLAHOMA CITY: Marriott
Waterford** $
Value
*6300 Waterford Blvd, 73118*
**Tel** *(405) 848-4782*
w marriott.com
These inviting lodgings come
with volleyball and squash
facilities, an outdoor pool, and a
cocktail lounge. Excellent service.

### DK Choice

**OKLAHOMA CITY:
Colcord Hotel** $$
Historic
*15 N Robinson Ave, 73102*
**Tel** *(405) 601-4300*
w colcordhotel.com
A renovated historic landmark,
this majestic hotel's elegant
rooms have hip accents and
luxurious amenities. Plush
bedding and furniture are of
the highest quality. The
lobby's classic black-and-marble
decor exudes an Art Deco feel.
Exceptional service and
delicious complimentary
breakfasts top the experience.

**OKLAHOMA CITY: Rusty Gables
Guest Lodge** $$
B&B
*3800 NE 50th St, 73121*
**Tel** *(405) 424-1015*
w rustygables.com
The large suites boast fireplaces,
whirlpools, and Western decor at
this rustic lodge set atop a hill
outside the city. Horseback riding
and spa services are available.

**OKLAHOMA CITY: The Skirvin
Hilton** $$
Boutique
*1 Park Ave, 73102*
**Tel** *(405) 272-3040*
w www3.hilton.com
This architecturally restored
historic building with stylish
rooms and elegant suites is
located near the business
and entertainment districts.

**TULSA: Hilton Garden Inn
Tulsa South** $
Value
*8202 S 100th E Ave, 74133*
**Tel** *(918) 392-2000*
w hiltongardeninn.hilton.com
Comfortable rooms and all the
standard amenities are offered
at this reliable chain hotel. There
are also coin laundry and
babysitting services.

**TULSA: The Campbell Hotel** $$
Boutique
*2636 E 11th St, 74104*
**Tel** *(918) 744-5500*
w thecampbellhotel.com
This luxurious hotel with retro
glamor boasts Southern charm,
comfortable rooms, and a
great location.

**TULSA: Hotel Ambassador** $$
Boutique
*1324 S Main St, 74119*
**Tel** *(918) 587-8200*
w hotelambassador-tulsa.com
The spacious rooms at this
sophisticated, romantic hotel
come with marble baths and
plush bedding.

# Where to Eat and Drink

## North Dakota

**BISMARCK: Peacock Alley**   $
American
*422 E Main St, 58501*
**Tel** *(701) 255-7917*   **Closed** *Sun*
Housed in a historic 1915 hotel with antiques, photographs, and original wood furnishings, this restaurant offers a legendary food menu of flavorful classics and steaks, plus a bar menu of more than 20 beers on tap.

**FARGO: Café Aladdin**   $
Mediterranean
*530 6th Ave N, 58102*
**Tel** *(701) 298-0880*   **Closed** *Sun*
This casual eatery, popular with locals, offers quality service and a unique menu of Mediterranean dishes. The tasty gyros are piled high with meat and toppings and served in large portions.

**FARGO: Doolittles Woodfire Grill**   $$
New American
*2112 25th St S, 58103*
**Tel** *(701) 478-2200*
Doolittles boasts juicy meats with savory flavors cooked in a wood-fired rotisserie. The lively ambience is great for all occasions. An extensive wine list complements the menu.

**FARGO: HoDo Lounge**   $$
New American
*101 N Broadway, 58102*
**Tel** *(701) 478-6969*   **Closed** *Sun*
In the trendy Hotel Donaldson, HoDo Lounge's eclectic seasonal menu includes dishes made with local, organic ingredients. Bison, filet, and duck are highlights. Servers are knowledgeable.

### DK Choice

**GRAND FORKS: Sanders 1907 Dakota Cuisine**   $$$
American
*22 S 3rd St, 58201*
**Tel** *(701) 746-8970*   **Closed** *Sun & Mon*
This downtown establishment has been a local favorite for decades. The friendly proprietors strive to please with their tasty "Dakota cuisine," serving dishes such as grilled salmon, walleye, grilled rib-eye, lamb chops, and the signature prime ribs dish – Swiss Eiger beef. Exquisite food served by friendly staff in a cozy atmosphere makes this a must-visit restaurant.

## South Dakota

**CUSTER: State Game Lodge**   $$$
American
*13389 US Hwy 16A, 57730*
**Tel** *(605) 255-4541*   **Closed** *Nov–Apr*
Traditional fare supplemented with local trout, pheasant, and elk is served at this elegant eatery. The sandwiches and Custer State Park Buffalo Stew are favorites.

### DK Choice

**DEADWOOD: Jake's Fine Dining**   $$
New American
*677 Main St, 57732*
**Tel** *(605) 578-3656*
This fine-dining venue, owned by actor Kevin Costner, boasts an award-winning kitchen serving creative fare made with local ingredients. Choose from an extensive wine list to complement dishes such as salmon, duck, lamb, and buffalo. There is also a display featuring costumes worn by the actor in his films.

**PIERRE: La Minestra**   $$
Italian
*106 E Dakota Ave, 57501*
**Tel** *(605) 224-8090*
Try the pan-fried, pistachio-crusted walleye, one of La Minestra's signature dishes. Other tasty entrées include seafood and poultry. Reservations recommended.

**RAPID CITY: Firehouse Brewing Company**   $
Brewpub
*610 Main St, 57701*
**Tel** *(605) 348-1915*
Set in a 1915 historic firehouse. Head here for hand-crafted ales

Outdoor seating at the Firehouse Brewing Company, Rapid City, South Dakota

on tap plus hearty pub fare, such as pasta, buffalo wings, and gumbo, plus heavenly desserts.

**SIOUX FALLS: Parker's Bistro**   $$
American/Creole
*210 South Main Ave, 57105*
**Tel** *(605) 275-7676*   **Closed** *Sun*
This quaint restaurant offers exceptional cuisine made with local ingredients. The innovative menu changes seasonally. Fresh fish dishes and the weekly specials prove popular. Lengthy wine list.

**SIOUX FALLS: Foleys**   $$$
Steak House/Seafood
*2507 S Shirley Ave, 57106*
**Tel** *(605) 362-8125*
Foleys is a local favorite, popular for its expertly cooked steaks and seafood. Menu highlights include bone-in ribeye and Asiago trout. Excellent wine selection. The great atmosphere and service make for a memorable experience.

## Nebraska

### DK Choice

**LINCOLN: Billy's**   $
New American
*1301 H St, 68508*
**Tel** *(402) 474-0084*   **Closed** *Sun*
Located in a historic house, this elegant restaurant offers a glimpse into a grand era in American history. Each of the three lovely dining rooms is named for a famous Nebraskan. The menu includes steak, lamb, duck, veal, and seafood dishes as well as several vegetarian options. There is also a superb wine list. Exceptional service.

**LINCOLN: The Green Gateau**   $
French
*330 S 10th St, 68508*
**Tel** *(402) 477-0330*
The Green Gateau boasts an eclectic decor inspired by European country inns and serves contemporary French cuisine. The brunch is especially popular. Try the bisque, baked brie, and house-made desserts.

**For more information on types of restaurants** *see pages 28–9*

**OMAHA: The Grey Plume** $$
New American
220 S 31st Ave, 68131
**Tel** (402) 763-4447    **Closed** Sun
Seasonal cuisine made from local
produce and livestock features on
a daily-changing menu of pastas,
meats, and seafood.

**OMAHA: Flatiron Café** $$$
New American
1722 St. Marys Ave, 68102
**Tel** (402) 344-3040    **Closed** Sun
Head here for elegant dining near
the old market. The imaginative
menu includes portobello fries
and sake-marinated sea bass.

**YORK: Chances R** $
American
124 W 5th St, 68467
**Tel** (402) 362-7755
The multiple dining rooms at
Chances R feature turn-of-the-
century decor and antique
furnishings. The traditional home-
cooked food ranges from hearty
country breakfasts to pan-fried
chicken plus a prime-rib buffet.

## Iowa

**CEDAR RAPIDS:**
**The Class Act** $$
New American
7725 Kirkwood Blvd SW, 52404
**Tel** (319) 848-8777
This gourmet restaurant with
lovely decor is also a teaching
venue for culinary arts students.
The creative menu features
seasonal ingredients and an
innovative approach.

### DK Choice

**CORALVILLE: Iowa River**
**Power Restaurant** $
New American
501 1st Ave, 52241
**Tel** (319) 351-1904
This local favorite, housed in
an old power station with
fantastic views of the river,
offers a fine-dining menu in a
large space that includes a
lounge, quiet nooks, and a
patio. Seafood and steak are the
main draw. The Sunday brunch
is always popular.

**DES MOINES: Flying Mango** $
Caribbean
4345 Hickman Rd, 50310
**Tel** (515) 255-4111  **Closed** Sun & Mon
Innovative takes on barbecue,
smoked meats, and Cajun and
Creole cuisine, as well as
inventive cocktails, feature at
this casual eatery. Live music.

Attractive dining area of The Class Act,
Cedar Rapids, Iowa

**DES MOINES: Jethro's BBQ** $
Barbecue
3100 Forest Ave, 50311
**Tel** (515) 279-3300
Jethro's draws fans of smoked
meats, tasty sauces, juicy burgers,
and sides such as waffle fries and
jalapeño creamed corn.

**DES MOINES: Christopher's**
**Restaurant** $$
Italian
2816 Beaver Ave, 50310
**Tel** (515) 274-3694    **Closed** Sun
A local institution, Christopher's
boasts a menu of classic favorites
such as spaghetti and meatballs,
and creative dishes such as
tequila shrimp and olive chicken.

**DUBUQUE: Caroline's**
**Restaurant** $$
New American
200 Main St, 52001
**Tel** (563) 588-5595
An elegant restaurant within the
Hotel Julien, Caroline's serves
hearty breakfasts. Lunch includes
soups, salads, and sandwiches,
while the dinner menu has
delicious steaks and seafood.

## Missouri

**BRANSON: Billy Gail's Café** $
American
5291 Hwy 265, 65616
**Tel** (417) 338-8883
A great spot for breakfast or
brunch, the pancakes here are
bigger than the plate, the biscuits
with gravy are hot and fresh, and
the burgers are juicy.

**BRANSON: Vasken's Deli** $
Mediterranean/Deli
3200 Gretna Rd, 65616
**Tel** (417) 334-9182    **Closed** Sun
This charming deli serves
delicious platters and home-

made takeouts. Choose from tasty
gyros, salads, appetizers, and sand-
wiches. The baklava is a must-try.

### DK Choice

**KANSAS CITY: Arthur**
**Bryant's** $
Barbecue
1727 Brooklyn Ave, 64127
**Tel** (816) 231-1123
Founded in the 1920s, this
legendary barbecue joint with
minimal decor allows patrons
to focus on the flavors of tender,
slow-smoked meats. Enjoy ribs,
brisket, pulled pork, sausage,
and more, enhanced by regular
or spicy sauce. The sides and
"burnt ends" are equally popular.

**KANSAS CITY: Blue Bird Bistro** $
American
1700 Summit St, 64108
**Tel** (816) 221-7559
A colorful venue with some
original 1890s decor, this bistro
serves succulent organic meats
as well as savory vegetarian
dishes. Great for brunch.

**KANSAS CITY: EBT** $$$
Steak House/Seafood
1310 Carondelet Dr, 64114
**Tel** (816) 942-8870 **Closed** Sun & Mon
The decor here, salvaged from a
landmark department store,
evokes Victorian-era charm.
Menu highlights include crab-
stuffed halibut, Kobe strip steak,
and smoked duck breast.

**SPRINGFIELD: Springfield**
**Brewing Company** $
American/Brewpub
301 S Market Ave, 65806
**Tel** (417) 832-8277
A state-of-the-art brewery and
restaurant, this is the cornerstone
of downtown. It offers a wide
selection of craft beers plus pub
fare such as burgers and pastas.

**ST. LOUIS: Cunetto**
**House of Pasta** $
Italian
5453 Magnolia Ave, 63139
**Tel** (314) 781-1135    **Closed** Sun
Locals frequent this family-owned
institution for its dizzying range
of pastas and other entrées.
The toasted ravioli is popular.

**ST. LOUIS: Imo's Pizza** $
Pizzeria
904 S 4th St, 63102
**Tel** (314) 421-4667
St. Louis-style pizza, made with a
unique processed cheese, is the
main draw at Imo's. A salad bar,
sandwiches, and pastas are
available too. Open until late.

**ST. LOUIS: Remy's Kitchen & Wine Bar** $$
Mediterranean
*222 S Bemiston Ave, 63105*
**Tel** *(314) 726-5757* **Closed** *Sun*
Remy's offers a selection of small and large plates with an award-winning wine list. The bread pudding is a popular dessert.

## Kansas

**LAWRENCE: Free State Brewing Company** $
American
*636 Massachusetts St, 66044*
**Tel** *(785) 843-4555*
The headquarters of the beer producer as well as an eatery, Free State draws fans of craft beer. The menu features pub fare such as quesadillas, and fish 'n' chips.

### DK Choice

**LAWRENCE: Pachamama's** $$$
New American
*800 New Hampshire St, 66044*
**Tel** *(785) 841-0990* **Closed** *Sun & Mon*
The upscale Pachamama's is a local favorite for its appetizing array of eclectic dishes, with at least one vegetarian special every evening. The seasonal menu of flavorful "market cuisine" uses only the best ingredients. The Star Bar has its own embedded solar system.

**TOPEKA: Carlos O'Kelly's** $
Mexican
*3425 S Kansas Ave, 66611*
**Tel** *(785) 266-3457*
Traditional and Americanized Mexican dishes and margaritas are the specialties at this chain restaurant. Enjoy sizzling steak fajitas, burritos, chimichangas, and the traditional *buñuelos* for dessert.

**TOPEKA: Rowhouse Restaurant** $
New American
*515 SW Van Buren St, 66603*
**Tel** *(785) 817-6052* **Closed** *Sun–Tue*
The four-course menus at this quaint restaurant are based on seasonal ingredients and the chef's inspirations. They change weekly. Booking is recommended.

**WICHITA: Redrock Canyon Grill** $
Southwestern
*1844 N Rock Rd, 67206*
**Tel** *(316) 636-1844*
This casual, lively eatery offers sandwiches, rotisserie meats, and sides such as skillet cornbread and ranch calamari.

**WICHITA: Chester's Chophouse and Wine Bar** $$
Steak House
*1550 N Webb Rd, 67206*
**Tel** *(316) 201-1300*
Steaks are cooked over an oak-wood fire here and fresh fish is flown in daily. The extensive wine cellar stocks over 1,000 bottles. Indoor and outdoor seating offers sweeping water views.

## Oklahoma

### DK Choice

**CATOOSA: Molly's Landing** $$
Steak House/Seafood
*3700 N Old Hwy 66, 74015*
**Tel** *(918) 266-7853* **Closed** *Sun*
Set by the river near the woods, this log house has been a road-side attraction since 1979. The rustic interior is furnished with leather and treasures collected by the owners. Steak is the main draw, while grilled seafood and chicken dishes are also delicious.

**OKLAHOMA CITY: Flint** $
New American
*15 N Robinson Ave, 73102*
**Tel** *(405) 605-0657*
An upscale casual restaurant and lounge, Flint's menu includes delicious meats, seafood, and sandwiches as well as contemporary cuisine made with local ingredients. The outdoor lounge has a waterfall and a fireplace.

**OKLAHOMA CITY: Ted's Café Escondido** $
Tex-Mex
*2836 NW 68th St, 73116*
**Tel** *(405) 848-8337*
Standard dishes such as fajitas, burritos, and enchiladas are on offer at this regional Tex-Mex

chain. At lunch, enjoy complimentary tortillas and salsa, with *sopapillas* for dessert.

### DK Choice

**OKLAHOMA CITY: The Coach House** $$$
American
*6437 Avondale Dr, 73116*
**Tel** *(405) 842-1000* **Closed** *Sun*
The gracious Coach House, with its oak-paneled dining room, is considered one of the state's finest restaurants. The seasonal menu reflects the best local produce and regional specialties. The pecan cornbread crusted salmon is a crowd favorite. There is an extensive wine list.

**TULSA: White River Fish Market** $
Seafood
*1708 N Sheridan Rd, 74115*
**Tel** *(918) 835-1910* **Closed** *Sun*
This combo market and restaurant has the freshest fish around, with 12-ft (3.5-m) tanks displaying live seafood. The kitchen specializes in home-style recipes.

**TULSA: Villa Ravenna** $$
Italian
*6526 E 51st St, 74145*
**Tel** *(918) 270-2666* **Closed** *Mon*
Home-made pastas, meats, and seafood are the house specialties at this authentic family-owned eatery with a romantic, candlelit atmosphere. It offers a great range of fine wines. Live classical music features on weekends.

**TULSA: Warren Duck Club** $$$
American
*6110 S Yale Ave, 74136*
**Tel** *(918) 495-1000*
This fine-dining restaurant is known for its duck served with a selection of five sauces. There is a lengthy wine list and a delicious dessert buffet.

Caroline's Restaurant in the Hotel Julien, Dubuque, Iowa

**For more information on types of restaurants** *see pages 28–9*

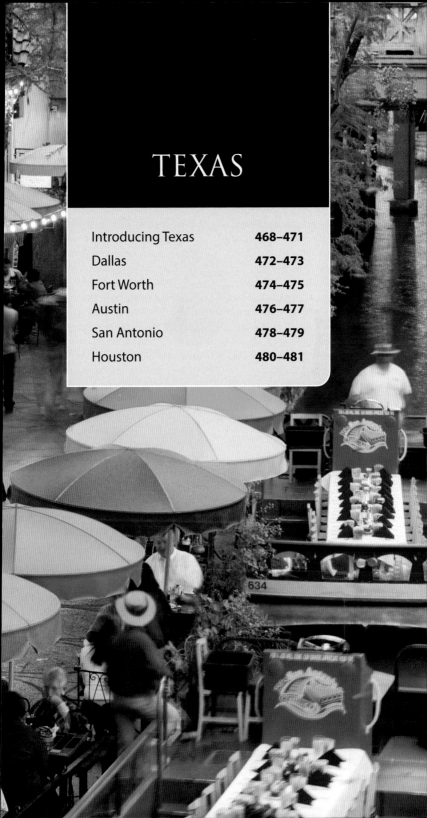

# TEXAS

634

# TEXAS

By almost any standard Texas is big. Stretching nearly 1,000 miles (1,600 km) across, and even longer north to south, it is by far the largest of the "Lower 48" states and also among the most populous, with 25 million residents. While its size has inspired a love of all things large, its past as an independent nation has given Texans a sense of pride and spirit of freedom, as is evident by the state flag that still carries the Lone Star, emblem of the Republic.

The huge scale of Texas seems to have encouraged a culture of exaggeration, and, according to residents, everything about the state is bigger, better, and brasher than anywhere else. The horns on the emblematic longhorn cattle, the great fortunes made from the state's supplies of oil, and even the onetime role of the Dallas Cowboys football team as "America's Team" – almost every aspect of life is imbued with a sense of superiority. Whether this is deserved or not is a matter of opinion, but contradiction is not what many Texans want to hear. As signs and songs all over the state say: "Don't Mess With Texas."

**Dome of Texas State Capitol, Austin**

### History

In Texas, history begins at the Alamo, a former Spanish mission and Mexican fort. "Remember the Alamo" was the battle cry of the Texas war of independence against Mexico. In December 1835, a band of rebellious American settlers commandeered the fort. Two months later, the vanquished Mexican army retaliated by attacking the fort for 13 days until all the 189 Americans inside were killed. Despite this setback, the freelance Americans under General Samuel Houston defeated the Mexicans in 1836 and declared the independent Republic of Texas. The Republic, which included parts of what are now New Mexico, Oklahoma, Colorado, and Wyoming, was annexed by the US in 1845. This move ignited the Mexican War, and after two years of sporadic fighting Mexico was forced to accept the loss of Texas, and the rest of the West, in 1848.

The second half of the 19th century was the heyday of the great cattle drives of the Wild West. Huge herds of Texas longhorn cattle, descendants of animals introduced by the Spanish colonists centuries before,

Plaque depicting a scene from the Texas War of Independence, the Alamo complex, San Antonio

◀ The colorful Riverwalk (Paseo del Rio), San Antonio

Sculpture of longhorn cattle outside the Dallas Convention Center

roamed the open range. Rounded up and driven by cowboys to towns such as Fort Worth and Dallas, these cattle were loaded onto trains and shipped to different markets located in the eastern US. After working on the range for weeks at a time, the cowboys' arrival into town was often heralded by a frenzy of gunplay and general debauchery.

## Economy & Culture

Though Texas has one of the nation's most diversified economies, historically it has been dependent upon two main

### KEY DATES IN HISTORY

**1519** Spanish explorer Alonso Alvarez de Pineda sets foot in what is now Texas

**1528** Cabeza de Vaca and a black African slave spend six years traveling across Texas

**1685** Rene-Robert Cavelier, Sieur de La Salle, establishes a short-lived French colony on the Gulf of Mexico at Matagorda Bay

**1716** Spain establishes Catholic missions in southern Texas

**1822** American immigrant Stephen F. Austin establishes a settlement along the Brazos River

**1836** Battle of the Alamo; Texas becomes a Republic

**1845** Texas becomes a state

**1870** Texas readmitted to the Union

**1900** Hurricane hits Galveston, killing 6,000

**1962** NASA's "Mission Control" in Houston

**1963** President John F. Kennedy assassinated in Dallas; Texas native Vice President Lyndon B. Johnson assumes leadership

**1986** Crude oil prices fall, damaging economy

**2001** Texas Governor George W. Bush is named as 43rd president, despite losing the popular vote

**2009** Bush's presidency ends and Barack Obama's begins

industries, oil and agriculture. Since the discovery of oil in the early 1900s, the state has remained the center of the US petroleum industry, producing almost 25 percent of the nation's output and controlling most of the vast quantities imported from overseas. In fact, it is hard to think of Texas without reference to the oil industry, thanks to images of gushers, "Texas Tea," and the machinations of the Ewing family on the 1980s TV show *Dallas*.

Agriculture, too, is very important. The livestock industry is still big business, so identified with its "cowboy culture" roots that boots, jeans, and a Stetson hat seem to be the official state costume. However, Texas also produces other crops such as cotton and citrus. The state's high-tech industry is led by Texas Instruments and Austin-based Dell Computer, while the huge military presence supports a major aeronautical engineering industry, particularly at NASA's "Mission Control" in Houston.

These frequently booming and often busting industries have created many fortunes. Texan wealth supports not only glitzy shops and fancy restaurants but has also endowed several excellent museums in Houston, Fort Worth, and other cities. However, the most authentic images of Texas are not of urban sophistication but of the down-home informality and vast open spaces of its rural reaches. Perhaps the best way to find its heart is to follow a dusty country road, stopping for coffee in a small-town café, with its parking lot full of pickup trucks, or watching the sun set over the ever-distant horizon.

Cowboys relaxing on a Texas ranch at sunset

# Exploring Texas

Texas is so large that it is a challenge to see all of it. Public transportation is negligible in this fossil-fueled state, where driving is an essential part of life. Many visitors fly between the main cities of Dallas, Austin, and Houston, and then rent a car to get around. About 90 percent of the state's 26 million residents live in the cities, which are equipped with restaurants, hotels, and visitor attractions. Out in the countryside, where the "real" Texas lives, facilities are few and far between. Even in the more popular areas, such as the Hill Country outside Austin, hotels and restaurants tend to be basic, and distances are so great that travel time can take up a large portion of the day.

## Sights at a Glance

1. Dallas pp472–3
2. Fort Worth pp474–5
3. Austin
4. Fredericksburg
5. Kerrville
6. New Braunfels
7. San Antonio pp478–9
8. Houston pp480–81
9. Big Thicket National Preserve
10. Galveston
11. Aransas National Wildlife Refuge
12. Corpus Christi
13. Padre Island National Seashore
14. Laredo
15. Rio Grande Valley
16. Big Bend National Park
17. Fort Davis
18. El Paso
19. Guadalupe Mountains National Park
20. Lubbock
21. Canyon
22. Amarillo
23. Abilene

Sparkling glass office towers, dominating the Dallas skyline

**For keys to symbols** see back flap

## Key

— Highway

— Major road

— Railroad

– – State border

⌁⌁ International border

## Mileage Chart

**Dallas**

| | | | | | | | | |
|---|---|---|---|---|---|---|---|---|
| **33** | **Fort Worth** | | | | 10 = Distance in miles | | | |
| 53 | | | | | 10 = Distance in kilometers | | | |
| **196** | **187** | **Austin** | | | | | | |
| 315 | 301 | | | | | | | |
| **260** | **232** | **78** | **Fredericksburg** | | | | | |
| 418 | 373 | 126 | | | | | | |
| **273** | **264** | **79** | **71** | **San Antonio** | | | | |
| 439 | 425 | 127 | 114 | | | | | |
| **239** | **269** | **164** | **240** | **197** | **Houston** | | | |
| 385 | 433 | 264 | 386 | 317 | | | | |
| **289** | **321** | **217** | **293** | **251** | **51** | **Galveston** | | |
| 465 | 517 | 349 | 472 | 404 | 82 | | | |
| **634** | **608** | **577** | **497** | **551** | **747** | **802** | **El Paso** | |
| 1020 | 978 | 929 | 800 | 887 | 1202 | 1291 | | |
| **360** | **340** | **506** | **444** | **512** | **599** | **649** | **432** | **Amarillo** |
| 579 | 547 | 814 | 715 | 824 | 964 | 1044 | 695 | |

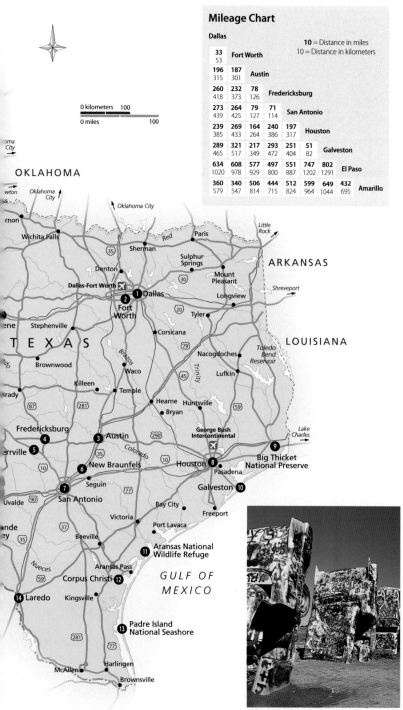

0 kilometers 100
0 miles 100

OKLAHOMA

Oklahoma City
Oklahoma City
Oklahoma City

Little Rock

Wichita Falls
Paris
Sherman
Red
Denton
Sulphur Springs
Mount Pleasant
35
Dallas-Fort Worth
1 Dallas
2 Fort Worth
Shreveport
30
Longview
20
Tyler

ARKANSAS

Stephenville
Corsicana
TEXAS
79
Nacogdoches
LOUISIANA
Brazos
Toledo Bend Reservoir
Brownwood
Waco
Trinity
Lufkin
Killeen
Temple
45
87
Hearne Huntsville
59
281
Bryan
Fredericksburg
4 3 Austin
290
George Bush Intercontinental
Lake Charles
rrville 5
35
Colorado
9
6 New Braunfels
10
10 Houston 8 Big Thicket National Preserve
7 Seguin
77
Pasadena
Uvalde 90
San Antonio
Galveston 10
Bay City
37
Victoria
Freeport
nde ey 35
Beeville
Port Lavaca
Nueces
11 Aransas National Wildlife Refuge
59
Aransas Pass
GULF OF MEXICO
14 Laredo
Corpus Christi 12
Kingsville
13 Padre Island National Seashore
281
77
Harlingen
McAllen
Brownsville

Amarillo's Cadillac Ranch, a pop-art display in northern Texas

The Dallas skyline, as seen from the Reunion Tower Observation area

# ❶ Dallas

🏙 1,888,000. ✈ 🚉 Union Station, 400 S Houston St. 🚌 Greyhound, 205 S Lamar St. ℹ 100 S Houston St, (214) 571-1300. 🎉 Cotton Bowl Parade (Jan 1); Dallas Blooms (mid- Mar–mid-Apr); Texas State Fair (Sep–Oct).
**W** visitdallas.com

When most people think of Texas, they think of Dallas, even though it is neither the state capital nor the biggest city. Located in the northeastern corner of the state, this is where the cotton fields and oil wells of East Texas meet the wide-open West Texas rangelands. With a forest of sparkling glass office towers dominating the downtown area, Dallas is the commercial and financial center of the "Lone Star" state, a role it has played since its days as the junction between the two main southwestern railroads. This fast-growing metropolis devoted to business has a huge concentration of technology firms, corporate headquarters, and wholesale markets. Infamous as the place where President Kennedy was assassinated, Dallas is nonetheless an energetic, enjoyable city, home to many prestigious museums, restaurants, and cultural venues.

Dallas is a sprawling city, merging into neighboring Fort Worth (see pp474–5). The nation's ninth-largest city features a lively downtown, where most of the visitor attractions are located. A square-mile grid of streets centering on Main Street holds the main commercial district that is also the home of some of Texas' best museums. The lively West End and hip Deep Ellum districts lie at the edges of downtown. Walking in Dallas is an option, but a car, a cab, or the DART trams can help make the most of a visitor's time.

## 🚋 Reunion Tower

300 Reunion Blvd E. **Tel** (214) 712-7180. **Open** call for hours. **Closed** may close for special events. 🅿 ♿
**W** reuniontower.com

Looking over Dallas from the western edge of downtown, this 50-story landmark is topped by a geodesic sphere containing a rotating restaurant run by celebrity chef Wolfgang Puck, a cocktail bar, and an observation area. Although not the city's tallest building, a title held by the 72-story Bank of America Tower located on Main Street, Reunion Tower does offer an unforgettable panoramic view of Dallas and its surrounding suburbs, and remains one of the city's most distinctive landmarks.

## 🏛 Sixth Floor Museum

411 Elm St. **Tel** (214) 747-6660. **Open** noon–6pm Mon, 10am–6pm Tue–Sun. **Closed** Thanksg., Dec 25. 🅿 ♿
**W** jfk.org

At the west end of downtown Dallas, this private museum meticulously re-creates the context while describing the controversial events of November 22, 1963, when President Kennedy was assassinated. Located in the former warehouse from which Lee Harvey Oswald shot and killed Kennedy, the exhibition concentrates on the life and times of Kennedy.

The corner window from which the shots were fired has been rebuilt to look like it did on the day of the assassination. A portion of the floor space documents the many conspiracy theories that question the official version of the president's murder.

## 🚋 West End Historic District

Bounded by highways and railroad tracks, this compact district of the century-old warehouses has been revitalized as the city's prime recreation center. There are sidewalk cafés, restaurants, and bars, along with shops and boutiques. Dallas World Aquarium features marine life, plants, and animals, and Old Red Museum showcases Dallas history.

## 🏛 Dallas Museum of Art

1717 N Harwood St. **Tel** (214) 922-1200. **Open** 11am–5pm Tue–Sun (until 9pm Thu). **Closed** Jan 1, Thanksgiving, Dec 25. 🅿 ♿
**W** dma.org

Modernist façade of the Dallas Museum of Art

Housed in an expansive modern building north of downtown, the wide-ranging collection of this museum gives a fine overview of art history. The main galleries are arranged by continent. Noteworthy among these is the Art of the Americas gallery, displaying treasures from ancient Maya and Inca civilizations through paintings by such American artists as Frederic Church and Thomas Hart Benton, with a special focus on Texas-made art of the Wild West. The European Sculpture and Painting gallery traces the evolution of art from Greek and Roman antiquities through the Renaissance, ending with a fine display of Modernist paintings. The world's most extensive collection of works by influential Dutch artist Piet Mondrian (1872–1944) is also on display.

### 🏛 Thanks-Giving Square

Pacific Ave. **Tel** (214) 969-1977.
🌐 thanksgiving.org

A peaceful and quiet oasis in bustling downtown, this pocket-sized park is packed with waterfalls, gardens, a bell tower, and an all-faiths chapel. A small museum traces the history of the American custom of Thanksgiving and expresses gratitude for life in all its myriad forms.

### 🏛 Fair Park

First Ave. **Tel** (214) 426-3400.
This 277-acre (111-ha) exhibition center is the site of the annual Texas State Fair. It hosts the famous annual Cotton Bowl football game as well as many concerts and theater festivals. Alongside an aquarium, a natural history museum, and an African-American history museum, a highlight here is the Hall of State, a huge Art Deco repository of exhibits tracing all things Texan.

### 🏛 Nasher Sculpture Center

2001 Flora St. **Tel** (214) 242-5100.
**Open** 11am–5pm Tue–Sun. 🅿 ♿
🌐 naschersculpture center.org

The Nasher Sculpture Center offers a peaceful oasis in the urban center of Dallas. The internationally important collection of more than 300 modern and contemporary sculptures was acquired by the late Raymond and Patsy Nasher. Works by such noted artists as Joan Miró, Jeff Koons, and Anish Kapoor are displayed in a handsome Italian travertine stone building with a glass roof. The outside space is used to display further sculptures in a garden-like setting, with fountains and many trees.

Mosaic mural in downtown's Thanks-giving Square

---

## Downtown Dallas

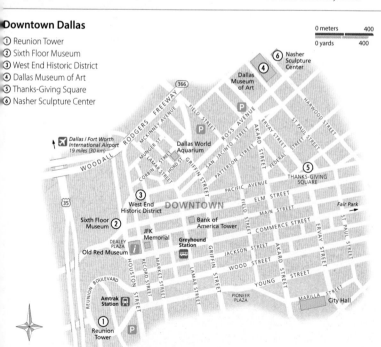

# ❷ Fort Worth

🏙 1,702,625. ✈ 🚌 Greyhound
Lines, 901 Commerce St. ℹ 415
Throckmorton St, (817) 336-8791.
🎪 Fort Worth Stock Show & Rodeo
(late Jan–early Feb); Main St Fort
Worth Arts Festival (Apr).
W fortworth.com

Unlike its flashy neighbor, Dallas, 25 miles (40 km) to the east, Fort Worth is smaller, much calmer, and more down-to-earth. In many ways it is also truer to its Texas roots. Founded in 1849 as a US Army outpost, Fort Worth boomed after the Civil War, when Chisholm Trail cattle drives made the city one of the country's largest livestock markets. Although cowboy culture lives on in the Stockyards District and the Amon Carter Museum, Fort Worth is also a capital of "high" culture, with some of the nation's finest performing arts spaces and organizations.

Fort Worth has three main areas of interest. Downtown Fort Worth revolves around Sundance Square, comprising more than a dozen blocks of historic buildings at the center of the city. To the north is the Stockyards District, where the Wild West culture is alive and well. About 2 miles (3 km) to the west, the Fort Worth Cultural District has some of the country's best museums. These are centered around the landmark Kimbell Art Museum, which along with the Amon Carter Museum traces the high points of European and American art. Other museums

The Water Gardens, designed by the architect Philip Johnson

include the excellent Modern Art Museum, and the Museum of Science and History, which also houses a planetarium.

While walking is enjoyable in and around downtown, a car is essential to get around the rest of city.

### 🎦 Sundance Square
**Tel** (817) 255-5700.
The heart of downtown Fort Worth, Sundance Square's name is a reminder of the city's Wild West past, when Chisholm Trail cattle drives used to come right through town, and cowboys and outlaws such as Butch Cassidy and the Sundance Kid frequented the city's many saloons. Filled with well-restored commercial buildings dating from the turn of the

Advertisement for Western wear in the Stockyards District

20th century, the brick-paved streets of Sundance Square are now lined with theaters, shops, and restaurants. The city's symphony, ballet, and opera companies are all housed here. An important museum in this area is the **Sid Richardson Collection of Western Art** on Main Street. Housed in a replica of an 1895 building, the museum exhibits 60 paintings of the famed artists Frederic Remington and Charles M. Russell. Also on Main Street is the trompe l'oeil mural of the Chisholm Trail by Richard Haas.

### 🏞 Water Gardens
Houston & Commerce Sts.
**Tel** (817) 392-7111.
Located on the site of Fort Worth's historic red-light district of Wild West saloons, this 5-acre (2-ha) park features a variety of waterfalls, cascades, streams, and fountains. Built in concrete and designed by architect Philip Johnson, the Water Gardens provide a welcome relief on hot summer days.

### 🎦 Fort Worth Stockyards National Historic District
**Tel** (817) 624-4741.
W fortworth
stockyards.org

With its cobblestoned streets, raised wooden sidewalks, and street lights like old-fashioned gas lights, this small but engaging ten-block neighborhood is located 2 miles (3 km) north of downtown. Known as the Stockyards District, it developed alongside the sprawling Fort Worth Stockyards, where each day more than 1 million head of cattle were sold and shipped to markets in the eastern United States. Though the stockyards ceased to be commercially viable many years ago, the complex preserves the old wooden pens and holds daily livestock auctions.

Today, the neighborhood offers a glimpse of what life in Texas was like a century ago.

One of the many cowboy-themed saloons of the Stockyards District

*For hotels and restaurants see p490–91*

Longhorn cattle being led through Stockyards National Historic District

A number of lively cowboy-themed saloons and honky-tonk nightclubs, many featuring live music, are also located here. The oldest and most atmospheric of these is the White Elephant Saloon. Also nearby are the Longhorn Saloon and **Billy Bob's Texas** (see p489). Said to be the largest nightclub in the world, Billy Bob's Texas is housed in a huge building and boasts 42 bar areas. Live bull-riding demonstrations also take place here on weekend nights. The district includes a small museum and a steam train. Other attractions include weekend rodeos and a daily parade of longhorn cattle down Exchange Avenue. Today, this is an up-and-coming area, where trendy bars and cafés spring up almost every day.

### 🏛 Kimbell Art Museum

3333 Camp Bowie Blvd. **Tel** (817) 332-8451. **Open** 10am–5pm Tue–Thu, noon–8pm Fri, 10am–5pm Sat, noon–5pm Sun. **Closed** Jan 1, Jul 4, Thanksg., Dec 25. 🖼 exhibitions only. 🚻 **www.kimbellart.org**

One of the most unforgettable museums and art collections in the United States, the Kimbell Museum is an architectural masterpiece, designed by Louis Kahn in 1971 as a series of vaulted roofs that seem to hover in mid-air. The gallery spaces are bathed in natural light, showing off the varied beauty of the diverse collections, which include pre-Columbian Mayan pottery, and jewelry, as well as rare ancient Asian bronzes. Paintings on display range from Renaissance and Baroque masterpieces by Rubens, Rembrandt, Tiepolo,

Sign for Billy Bob's Texas nightclub

and Tintoretto to a world-class collection of Post-Impressionist and early Modernist paintings by such celebrated masters as Cezanne, Picasso, and others.

### 🏛 Amon Carter Museum

3501 Camp Bowie Blvd. **Tel** (817) 738-1933. **Open** 10am–5pm Tue, Wed, Fri & Sat, 10am–8pm Thu, noon–5pm Sun. **Closed** Jan 1, Jul 4, Thanksg., Dec 25. 🚻 **www.cartermuseum.org**

Along with the Kimbell Art Museum across the street, the Amon Carter Museum anchors Fort Worth's much-vaunted Cultural District, which is located 2.5 miles (4 km) west of downtown. The Amon Carter Museum concentrates entirely on American art of the Wild West, housing seminal paintings, drawings, and sculptures by Thomas Moran, Frederic Remington, Charlie Russell, and Georgia O'Keeffe, among others. Said to be one of the foremost collections of cowboy art, the Amon Carter Museum also has the distinction of possessing the world's most extensive library. It has more than 100,000 photographs documenting the discovery, exploration, and settlement of the country's western frontier.

The Amon Carter Museum, which features cowboy art

## Cowboys

The romanticized image of the cowboy, as portrayed by Hollywood Westerns, was far removed from reality. During the 1880s, the demand for beef in the East and Midwest led to the Texas cattle trails, which linked the open ranges with railroads. Of these, the most famous was the Chisholm Trail to Abilene, Kansas. Cowboys traveled across the country on trail drives that were often fraught with danger. These poorly paid young men mostly rode the flanks of a herd to prevent cattle from wandering off. Those at the rear faced even more difficult conditions: Indian attacks, choking dust, long hours, and outlaw hustlers. From this tough life emerged the myth of the cowboy, celebrated in films, literature, music, and fashion. The first cowboy star was Buffalo Bill (see p574). Since then, the rugged roles played by John Wayne and Clint Eastwood fashioned popular perceptions of cowboys and life in the Wild West.

Magazine cover depicting a cowboy in action, 1913

Exterior of the Texas State Capitol in Austin

## ❸ Austin

🏙 735,000. ✈ 🚊 🚌 ℹ 209 E 6th St, (512) 478-0098, (866) 462-8784.
🌐 austintexas.org

The capital city of Texas, Austin is also home to a thriving high-tech industry as well as the state's main university. However, it is best known for hosting one of the liveliest popular music scenes in the country since the 1960s. Musicians as diverse as Janis Joplin and Willie Nelson achieved prominence in Austin. The exodus

Nightclub sign, Austin

of musicians from New Orleans following Hurricane Katrina has further enhanced the city's vibrant music scene.

Showcasing the Texan love of all things large, the **Texas State Capitol**, in the heart of downtown, is the largest such structure in the US. Built in 1888, it has 500 rooms covering some 8.5 acres (3.5 ha) of floor space. With its over 300-ft (92-m) high pink granite dome dominating the downtown skyline, the building is taller than the US Capitol in Washington (see pp202–203). In the rotunda beneath the dome, the floor contains the official seals of the six nations – Spain, France, Mexico, the Republic of Texas, the Confederacy, and the US – whose flags have all flown over Texas.

North of the Capitol complex, the expansive campus of the **University of Texas** spreads east from Guadalupe Street.

Centering on a landmark tower, the campus holds a number of museums and libraries. The new **Blanton Museum of Art** has over 17,000 works of art, from the Renaissance to Abstract Expressionism, many of which were donated by novelist James Michener. The **Lyndon Baines Johnson Presidential Library**, at the northeast edge of the campus, is a repository for all official documents of the Texas-born Johnson (1908–73), who served as US senator, vice-president, and US president following the assassination of John F. Kennedy (see p472). Videotapes trace the Civil Rights Movement, the Vietnam War, and other key events of his tumultuous career. A 7/8th scale reproduction of his Oval Office is displayed on the top floor of this monumental building.

🏛 **Texas State Capitol**
11th St & Congress Ave. **Tel** (512) 463-0063. **Open** 7am–10pm Mon–Fri, 9am–8pm Sat & Sun. **Closed** Jan 1, Easter, Thanksgiving, Dec 24–25. ♿

🏛 **Blanton Museum of Art**
200 E MLK at Congress. **Tel** (512) 471-7324. **Open** 10am–5pm Tue–Fri (to 9pm every third Thu), 11am–5pm Sat, 1–5pm Sun. **Closed** public hols. 🎟 (free Thu). ♿ 🏠 📷
🌐 blantonmuseum.org

## ❹ Fredericksburg

🏙 8,400. ℹ 302 E Austin St, (830) 997-6523.
🌐 visitfredericksburgtx.com

One of the loveliest small towns in Texas, and centerpiece of the rolling Hill Country that spreads over 25,000 sq miles (64,749 sq km) west of Austin, Fredericksburg was first settled by German immigrants in 1846. The town's strong Germanic heritage is kept alive by a number of biergarten (beer gardens) and Bavarian-style buildings such as the reconstructed Vereinskirche (community or union church) in the Marktplatz, off Main Street.

The town is also home to the **National Museum of the Pacific War**, which traces the history of US military activities in the South Pacific during World War II. The museum includes the steamboat-shaped Nimitz Hotel. The hotel was built in the 1850s by the family of US Admiral Chester Nimitz, the commander-in-chief of US forces, who was born in Fredericksburg. It operated as a hotel until the early 1960s and opened as a museum in 1967. The museum has been greatly expanded since, but the appearance of the old hotel has been preserved. The tranquil Japanese Peace Garden, gifted by the Japanese government, is at the back.

Located midway between Fredericksburg and Austin, the boyhood home of the Vietnam War-era, 36th US president has

Tank display in the National Museum of the Pacific War, Fredericksburg

been preserved as the **Lyndon B. Johnson National Historical Park**. Other features of the park, which includes sites over the surrounding area, are Johnson's one-room rural school, the ranch that served as his "Texas White House," and his grave.

German-style architecture in New Braunfels

### 🏛 National Museum of the Pacific War
340 E Main St. **Tel** (830) 997-8600. **Open** 9am–5pm daily. **Closed** Thanksgiving, Dec 25. 🖼 🛇 📷
**w** nimitz–museum.org

### 🏛 Lyndon B. Johnson National Historical Park
US 290 in Johnson City. **Tel** (830) 868-7128. **Open** 9am–5pm daily. **Closed** Jan 1, Thanksg., Dec 25. 🛇 📷
**w** nps.gov/lyjo

## ❺ Kerrville
🏔 21,000. 🚌 ℹ 2108 Sidney Baker St, (830) 896-1155.
**w** kerrvilletx.com

A picturesque resort and retirement community located in the rugged hills above the Guadalupe River, Kerrville is one of the largest towns in the Texas Hill Country. This friendly town is famous for the 18-day folk music festival it hosts annually at the Quiet Valley Ranch just south of town, starting Thursday before Memorial Day. While the festival now attracts singers and fans from all over the world, it still retains the homey, intimate atmosphere of the early years.

Another highlight in town is the **Museum of Western Art**, which showcases contemporary painting and sculpture depicting the working life of cowboys. Hundreds of musicians are attracted to the **Kerrville Folk Festival** held from late May to early June, which is outdoors and encourages camping and bonfires.

### 🏛 Museum of Western Art
1550 Bandera Hwy. **Tel** (830) 896-2553. **Open** 10am–4pm Tue–Sat. **Closed** Sun, Mon, some public hols. 🖼 🛇 **w** museumofwestern art.org

## ❻ New Braunfels
🏔 28,000. ℹ 390 S Seguin St, (800) 572-2626. **w** nbcham.org

A popular daytrip from San Antonio *(see pp478–9)*, New Braunfels was one of many towns settled by German immigrants in the tumultuous 1840s, when Texas was an independent republic offering land grants to Anglo-Saxon settlers. The German heritage still thrives in local architecture, cuisine, language, and festivals. Many historic and restored German-style buildings can be seen across the town. However, German influence is most evident in the numerous annual festivals celebrated here, such as the sausage and beer festivals and the Polka Festival, all of which help preserve the town's strong German roots.

Built on the site that the town's aristocratic founder Prince Carl of Solms-Braunfels, Germany, chose for his castle (it was never built), the **Sophienburg Museum and Archives** documents the town's history. Exhibits include several local artifacts and re-creations of pioneers' homes and shops, an early bakery, a doctor's office, and a pharmacy.

### 🏛 Sophienburg Museum and Archives
401 W Coll St. **Tel** (830) 629-1572. **Open** 10am–4pm Tue–Sat. **Closed** public hols. 🖼 📷
**w** sophienburg.com

Gallery inside Kerrville's Museum of Western Art, displaying paintings and sculptures exemplifying the life of cowboys

# ❼ San Antonio

The most historic city in Texas, San Antonio is also the most popular, both for its pivotal historic role and its natural beauty. Once home to the Comanche Indians, the riverside site drew the attention of Spanish missionaries, who founded Mission San Antonio de Valero in 1718. Later converted into a military outpost and renamed the Alamo, it was the site of the most heroic episode of the Texan revolution. Predominantly Hispanic and Mexican in character, San Antonio balances a thriving economy with a careful preservation of its past. Most of the historic sites lie within a block of the pedestrian-friendly Riverwalk in the downtown core.

The Arneson River Theater

★ **Riverwalk** (Paseo del Rio)
This tree-shaded path along the San Antonio River was built as a flood-control project during the Depression-era New Deal. Now a horseshoe-shaped, open-air promenade lined with shops, Riverwalk is a peaceful oasis in the middle of the city.

Arneson River Theater

★ **La Villita**
It was in this early 19th-century "little village" that the Mexicans officially surrendered to the Republic of Texas. The quaint village of stone and adobe buildings now houses craft workshops and boutique shops.

## Missions National Historical Park

This 819-acre (331-ha) historic park preserves four Spanish frontier missions, which, along with the Alamo, formed the northern edge of Spain's North American colonies in the 18th century. Still in use as Catholic parish churches, the former Missions San Jose, San Juan, Espada, and Concepcion spread south from downtown San Antonio along the 9-mile (14-km) "Mission Trail." The finest of the group, Mission San Jose, is known for the intricately carved stonework of the Rose Window adjacent to the sacristy.

Mission San Jose

**Key**

— Suggested route

**Buckhorn Saloon & Museum**
This intriguing museum is crowded with Wild West exhibits and stuffed animals from around the world.

LOSOYA STREET

S ALAMO STREET

E COMMERCE ST

EAST CROCKET ST

E MARKET STREET

Rivercenter Mall

Tower of the Americas

HemisFair Park

0 meters    200
0 yards     200

**VISITORS' CHECKLIST**

**Practical Information**
⚄ 1,592,000. 🛈 317 Alamo Plaza, **Tel** (210) 207-6700.
🎭 Riverwalk Mud Festival (Jan), Fiesta San Antonio (late Apr).
**W** visitsanantonio.com
**Open** Sep–May: 9am–5:30pm daily, Jun–Aug: 9am–5:30pm Sun–Thu, 9am–7pm Fri & Sat. **Closed** Dec 24, 25. 🎫 donation. ♿ 🎁 The Alamo: 300 Alamo Plaza, **Tel** (210) 225-1391. **W** thealamo.org

**Transport**
✈ 🚉 224 Hoefgren Ave.
🚌 Greyhound Lines, 500 N St. Mary's St. **Tel** (210) 223-3226.

**★ The Alamo**
"Remember the Alamo" was the battle cry that inspired Texans during their war for independence against Mexico (1835–1836). The secularized mission was the site of a long, bloody siege that took the lives of 189 Americans, shortly after which the Texas Republic was born.

**Institute of Texas Cultures**
On the grounds of HemisFair Park, this expansive museum chronicles the past and present of 27 distinct ethnic and cultural groups prominent in Texas.

# ❽ Houston

🏙 1,953,000. ✈ 🚌 902 Washington Ave. 🚍 Greyhound Lines, 2121 S Main St. ℹ 901 Bagby St, (713) 437-5200. 🎪 Houston Livestock Show (late Feb–early Mar); Art Car Parade (May); Thanksgiving Day Parade (Nov).
🌐 visithoustontexas.com

A city of constant change and great diversity, the story of Houston is a typical Texas success story. Founded in 1836 in what was then a swamp, the city was named in honor of Texas hero General Samuel Houston (see p468) and served as capital of the Texas Republic until 1839. A center for shipping cotton, Houston's fortunes faded after the Civil War, but it developed into a major port following the construction of a shipping channel to the Gulf of Mexico. The discovery of oil turned the city into a major petrochemical producer, and it has grown into the biggest city in Texas and the fourth-largest in the US. It has some of the world's finest art museums.

A huge, sprawling city that has grown to cover over 600 sq miles (1554 sq km), Houston is a thoroughly confusing place, lacking in an overall plan. The absence of any real visual order, the frequent changes in street names and directions, and the lack of public transportation and often heavy road traffic, can make matters worse.

In short, to see Houston visitors should be prepared to drive, and to get lost more than once. The main attractions for visitors lie southwest of downtown, on and around the **Rice University** campus.

Expansive gardens surrounding Ima Hogg's mansion, Bayou Bend

## 🏛 Menil Collection

1533 Sul Ross. **Tel** (713) 525-9400. **Open** 11am–7pm Wed–Sun. **Closed** Jan 1, Easter, Jul 4, Thanksgiving, Dec 25. ♿ 🌐 menil.org

One of the world's better assemblies of painting and sculpture, this collection was endowed by the family of Houston philanthropist Dominique de Menil, who died in 1997. It is housed in a striking modern building designed by Italian architect Renzo Piano. The most extensive display here is of Surrealist paintings, notably by René Magritte and Max Ernst. The museum also has a world-class collection of Cubist painting by Picasso and Braque in particular, as well as a full survey of 20th-century American paintings by Jackson Pollock, Jasper Johns, Robert Rauschenberg, and Cy Twombly. Separate galleries display ancient and medieval art of the Mediterranean. Also on view is a show of works by Native peoples of Africa, the South Pacific, and the Pacific North-west region of North America. Modern and contemporary works on paper is the fastest growing part of de Menil's

collection, with works by Paul Cézanne, Marlene Dumas, Jasper Johns, Piet Mondrian, Andy Warhol, and other noted artists. The Menil Drawing Institute, which will house this collection, is expected to open in 2017.

A short walk east from the main museum stands the ecumenical **Rothko Chapel**, a spare concrete space designed around a series of large, dark-colored abstract paintings by the artist Mark Rothko. Commissioned by the de Menil family and completed by architect Philip Johnson in 1971, the chapel is open from 10am to 6pm daily.

## 🏛 Museum of Fine Arts

1001 Bissonnet St. **Tel** (713) 639-7300. **Open** 10am–5pm Tue & Wed, 10am–9pm Thu, 10am–7pm Fri & Sat, 12:15pm–7pm Sun. **Closed** Jan 1, Thanksg., Dec 25. 📷 ♿ 🌐 mfah.org

The oldest art museum in Texas, and one of the largest in the US, the collections here range from Greek and Roman antiquities to Wild West sculptures by Frederic Remington. The striking Beck Building has European art of the late 19th and early 20th century, with a survey of works by Manet, Pissarro, Renoir, and other masters.

## 🌳 Bayou Bend

6003 Memorial Dr at Wescott St. **Tel** (713) 639-7750. **Open** 10am–5pm Tue–Sat, 1–5pm Sun. **Closed** Jan 1, Thanksgiving, Dec 25. 📷 ♿ 🌳

The largest public gardens in Houston surround the pink stucco mansion of oil heiress Ima Hogg (1882–1975), who survived her somewhat

Houston's Memorial Park, lying at the foot of the city

Neon signs light up the lively
Montrose District

unfortunate name to become
one of Houston's greatest
benefactors. The wealthy
philanthropist was not only
famous as a patron of the arts
but was also passionately
concerned with the well-being
of the city. Now run by the
Museum of Fine Arts, her home
displays a collection of decorative
arts, highlighted by a sugar
bowl crafted by Colonial hero
Paul Revere (see p148), and 5,000
pieces of furniture, ceramics,
and textiles. Also on display are
portraits by early American
artists John Singleton Copley
and Charles Willson Peale.

### Montrose District

"Montrose" is a catch name for
the lively collection of counter-
cultural-flavored galleries,
shops, nightclubs, cafés, and
restaurants that can be found
along Montrose Street and its
intersection with Westheimer
Road. Apart from the shopping
malls and downtown business
district, Montrose District is
one of the few walkable
neighborhoods in Houston and
is especially popular on
weekend nights.

### Space Center Houston

1601 Nasa Pkwy. Tel (281) 244-2100.
Open 10am–5pm Mon–Fri, 10am–
7pm Sat & Sun. Closed Dec 25.
spacecenter.org

Adjacent to the Johnson
Space Center, the mission
control for all manned US
explorations of space since
1965, this visitor-friendly
attraction traces the full
story of the Space Race.
Hands-on exhibits are
particularly appealing to
young people and let
visitors try on space
helmets, touch moon
rocks, or peer into actual
spaceships such as
those from the Mercury,
Gemini, and Apollo

programs. Computer
simulations let visitors fly
the space shuttle or land on
the moon. There are also
various changing exhibits. The
major attraction of the Space
Center is the tour of the
still-in-use mission control
facilities, where the historic
missions to the moon and back
were guided.

### San Jacinto Battleground

Hwy 134, 21 miles (34 km) SE of
downtown. Tel (281) 479-2431.
Open 9am–6pm daily.

The vast plains of Texas
can be seen for miles from
the foot of this 605-ft- (184-m-)
tall monument, claimed to be
one of the tallest in the
world. It marks the site of
the final battle for the
independence of the Texas
Republic in 1836. The slim
shaft is topped by a
massive "Lone Star." A
museum at the base traces
the history and culture of
the state, while an
adjacent theater hosts
a popular 42-projector,
multi-image
slide show.

San Jacinto tower

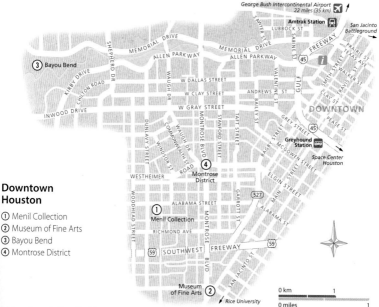

## Downtown Houston

① Menil Collection
② Museum of Fine Arts
③ Bayou Bend
④ Montrose District

For keys to symbols see back flap

Dense cypress swamp in the Big Thicket National Preserve

## ❾ Big Thicket National Preserve

Junction of US 69 & Hwy 420, 7 miles (11 km) N of Kountze. **Tel** (409) 951-6700. **Open** 9am–5pm daily. ♿
🅦 nps.gov/bith

Maintaining a unique mixture of mountains, plains, swamps, and forests, the Big Thicket National Preserve protects 15 distinct biologically diverse areas (9 land units and 6 water corridors) spread over 152 sq miles (393 sq km) along the Texas/Louisiana border.

Although much of the preserve is relatively inaccessible, the area once served as a hideout for runaway slaves and outlaws. Today, it is best known for housing a wide range of plants and animals. A series of short hiking trails offer close-up views of dense groves of resident oaks, cactus, carnivorous "pitcher plants," and millions of mosquitoes.

## ❿ Galveston

🏙 60,000. ✈ 🚌 🚆 ℹ 2328 Broadway, (888) 425-4753. 🅦 galveston.com

Though comparatively smaller than other Texas cities, Galveston rivals the rest of the state for historical significance and character. Originally a notorious hideout for slave-trading Gulf Coast pirate Jean Lafitte *(see p348)*, Galveston was burned to the ground by US forces in 1821. But by the 1890s the port had grown to be the largest and wealthiest city in Texas.

The economy soon declined following a devastating hurricane in 1900, which killed as many as 6,000 people. The subsequent rise of Houston also contributed to Galveston's fading fortunes.

Many of the city's grand Victorian mansions and 19th-century storefronts have been restored to their original glory. Many exuberantly designed buildings from that period survive in the Strand National Historic Landmark District, near the waterfront. **Ashton Villa** is one such building, and today it houses one of the Galveston Island Visitor Centers.

Often hailed as one of the state's best resorts on the Gulf of Mexico, the charming island city features more than 30 miles (48 km) of pristine, sandy beaches. Visitors can also indulge in the family-friendly fun of **Moody Gardens**, with its water-park pools, a ten-story Rainforest Pyramid offering an incredible tropical environment, and a series of massive aquariums showcasing life from the world's oceans.

### 🏛 Ashton Villa

2328 Broadway. **Tel** (409) 765-7834. **Open** call for information about tours and special events.

### 🌺 Moody Gardens

1 Hope Blvd. **Tel** (800) 582-4673. **Open** Apr–Oct: 10am–8pm daily; Nov–Mar: 10am–6pm daily. **Closed** Dec 25.
📷 ♿ 🅦 moodygardens.com

## ⓫ Aransas National Wildlife Refuge

Hwy 239. 65 miles (105 km) NE of Corpus Christi. **Tel** (361) 286-3559. **Open** dawn–dusk. **Closed** Thanksgiving, Dec 25. 📷 🅦 fws.gov/refuge/aransas

While sun worshipers flock to the Gulf Coast beaches in winter, birds and bird-watchers congregate slightly inland at the 109-sq-mile (283-sq-km) Aransas National Wildlife Refuge. Established in 1937 to protect the vanishing wildlife of coastal Texas, Aransas is today home to alligators, armadillo, boars, javelinas, coyotes, white-tailed deer, and many other species of wildlife. The most famous visitors here are the endangered whooping cranes, the tallest birds native to North

Bird-watching in Aransas

The ten-story Rainforest Pyramid in Moody Gardens, Galveston

*For hotels and restaurants see p490–91*

Padre Island National Seashore – a popular vacation destination

America. Standing 5 ft (1.5 m) tall, with white bodies, black-tipped wings, and red heads, the cranes migrate here from Canada between November and March, feeding in the saltwater marshes.

Ringed by tidal marshes and broken by long, narrow ponds, Aransas is an ever-changing land that is still being shaped by the turquoise-blue waters of San Antonio Bay and the storms of the Gulf of Mexico. Grasslands, live oaks, and red bay thickets that cover deep, sandy soils provide spectacular background scenery.

## ⑫ Corpus Christi

🏙 380,000. ✈ 🚌 ℹ 1823 N Chaparralb St, (800) 766-2322.
🌐 visitcorpuschristitx.org

The deepest commercial port in Texas and an extensive US military presence have made Corpus Christi one of the fastest-growing cities in the state. Its military importance is marked by the famous 910-ft-(277-m-) long aircraft carrier, the USS *Lexington*, moored along the 2-mile (3-km) downtown waterfront. To its south, the **Texas State Aquarium** explores the sea life of the Gulf of Mexico with whales, rays, and sharks, and re-creations of reefs similar to those that have grown around the Gulf's many offshore oil rigs. Texas river otters and the Kemp's Ridley sea turtle are also found here. "Corpus," as locals

call the city, looks out across the harbor to **Mustang Island State Park**, where over 5 miles (8 km) of sandy beach stretch along the Gulf of Mexico. At the park's north end, modern resorts detract from the natural scene, overshadowing the historic community of Port Aransas at the island's northern tip.

🗺 **Texas State Aquarium**
2710 N Shoreline Blvd. **Tel** (361) 881-1200. **Open** 9am–5pm daily (to 6pm Memorial Day–Labor Day).
**Closed** Thanksg., Dec 25. 🅿 ♿
🌐 texasstateaquarium.org

## ⑬ Padre Island National Seashore

ℹ Malaquite Visitor Center, (361) 949-8068. ⛰ 🌐 nps.gov/pais

Bordered by a pair of tourist resorts at its north and south ends, Padre Island is a slender sandbar that stretches for more than 110 miles (177 km) between Corpus Christi and the Mexican border. The central 65 miles (105 km) have been preserved as the Padre Island National Seashore, which, with few roads and no commercial development, is among the longest wild stretches of coastline in the country. The park is open throughout the year for camping, beach-combing, surfing, swimming, hiking, fishing, and various other activities. Coyotes and other native wild animals still roam the heart of the island.

This is one of the nation's most popular vacation spots. It receives an average of 800,000 visitors per year, especially during the Spring Break, when university students from colder climes in the northern Midwest flock here to unwind and party. South Padre Island marks the southern end of the Gulf Coast of Texas.

Sailing boats lining the waterfront of Corpus Christi

Façade of the Republic of the Rio Grande Museum, San Augustin Plaza, Laredo

## ⓮ Laredo

🏙 200,000. ✈ ℹ️ 501 San Augustin St, (800) 361-3360. 🌐 visitlaredo.com

Located on the north bank of the legendary Rio Grande (or Rio Bravo, as it is known in Mexico), Laredo is often referred to as the "Gateway to Mexico." It operates two international bridges to Mexico and is hence one of the principal US ports of entry into Mexico.

Located north of the Rio Grande, the original center of Laredo has been well preserved around the historic San Augustin Plaza. Here, the intriguing **Republic of the Rio Grande Museum** is housed in a building that once served as the Capitol of the short-lived independent republic that in 1840 included southern Texas and the three northernmost states of Mexico. The museum traces Laredo's role under six different national flags.

### 🏛 Republic of the Rio Grande Museum
1005 Zaragoza St. **Tel** (956) 727-3840. **Open** 9am–4pm Tue–Sat. **Closed** public hols. 🅿 ♿

## ⓯ Rio Grande Valley

ℹ️ FM 1015 Expressway 83, Welasco, (956) 968-2102.

Stretching along the Rio Grande for 200 miles (322 km) between Laredo and the Gulf of Mexico, the Rio Grande Valley is a bustling corridor of agricultural, commercial, and retirement communities all jumbled together in a complicated sprawl. Linked by east–west US 83, which becomes increasingly busy as it gets closer to the Gulf, the valley feels very different from the rest of Texas, thanks in part to the lush, temperate climate softened by moisture-laden breezes. Numerous roadside stands sell bags of grapefruits and bunches of red chili peppers, while convoys of trucks lumber past between warehouses and factories on both sides of the river.

The region's story from border banditry to bilateral trade is traced with permanent and changing exhibits at the **Harlingen Arts and Heritage Museum**, while numerous parks try to protect the region's varied natural heritage. The 525-acre (212-ha) **Sabal Palm Audubon Sanctuary** preserves the last stand of the stumpy native Sabal palm trees, which once lined the river for miles upstream.

### 🏛 Harlingen Arts and Heritage Museum
2425 Boxwood & Raintree Sts, Harlingen. **Tel** (956) 216-4901. **Open** 10am–4pm Tue–Sat, 1–4pm Sun. 🅿 ♿ 🎫 by appointment.

### 🦅 Sabal Palm Audubon Sanctuary
International Blvd, 6 miles (10 km) SE of Brownsville. **Tel** (956) 541-8034. **Open** 7am–5pm daily. **Closed** Jan 1, Thanksgiving, Dec 25. 🅿 ♿

## ⓰ Big Bend National Park

ℹ️ Panther Junction, (432) 477-2251. 🅿 🌐 nps.gov/bibe

One of the wildest and most isolated corners of the US, this diverse park covers 801,000 acres (324,154 ha) of southwest Texas. The name "Big Bend" comes from the 90-degree turn made by the Rio Grande as it carves its way toward the Gulf of Mexico through the volcanic rock of the San Vicente and Sierra del Carmen Mountains. Ranging from 1,500-ft- (457-m-) deep river canyons along the Rio Grande to the pine-forested Chisos Mountains, Big Bend offers a complete experience of the rivers, mountains, canyons, and deserts that define the American Southwest. These contrasts in topography have created a unique diversity

Fascinating rock formations at Big Bend National Park

*For hotels and restaurants see p490–91*

of plant and animal habitats. Coyotes, roadrunners, and javelinas roam among spring wildflowers and cacti.

## ⓱ Fort Davis

🏚 600. 🛈 Town Square, (432) 426-3015. 🌐 ftdavis.com

Situated in the scenic Davis Mountains at a height of 4,900 ft (1,494 m), Fort Davis is a popular destination for visitors seeking relief from a typical Texas summer. A key site during the Indian Wars of the 19th century, it was originally established in 1854 as a US Army fort along the main road between El Paso and San Antonio (see pp478–9). Today, it has been preserved as the **Fort Davis National Historic Site**. In summer, costumed interpreters help visitors on self-guided tours through some of the site's restored structures.

The area's high altitude and isolation from large cities has also made it a fine location for astronomical research. Located atop the 6,791-ft (2,070-m) Mount Locke, 17 miles (27 km) northwest of town, the **McDonald Observatory** gives visitors the opportunity to see stars and planets. The Hobby-Eberle spectroscope here has a 430-inch (1,092-cm) mirror, the world's largest.

### 🏛 Fort Davis National Historic Site
Hwy 17. **Tel** (432) 426-3224. **Open** 8am–5pm daily. **Closed** major public hols. 🅿 🚻 🌐 nps.gov/foda

### 🔭 McDonald Observatory
Hwy 118. **Tel** (432) 426-3640. **Open** 10am–5:30pm daily (call for evening schedule). **Closed** Jan 1, Thanksgiving, Dec 25. 🌐 mcdonaldobservatory.org

## ⓲ El Paso

🏚 722,000. ✈ 🚉 🚌 🛈 1 Civic Center Plaza, (915) 534-0600. 🌐 visitelpaso.com

Located on the northern bank of the Rio Grande, at one of the river's safest natural crossing

Catholic Ysleta Mission in El Paso

places, El Paso has long been part of the largest and liveliest international community along the US/Mexico border. In 1598, Spanish explorer Juan de Onate crossed the river from Mexico and named the place "El Paso del Rio del Norte." It took another 80 years before the city was established with a trio of Catholic missions at Ysleta, Socorro, and San Elizario. Still in operation, the missions are among the oldest communities in Texas. The story of the varying course of the Rio Grande (and so the international border), until a concrete channel was built in 1963, is detailed in a museum at the **Chamizal National Memorial**, a 55-acre (22-ha) park on the US side. Outside, a 1.8 mile (2.9 km) walking trail circles the park.

### 🏞 Chamizal National Memorial
800 S San Marcial St. **Tel** (915) 532-7273. Exhibits: **Open** 10am–5pm Tue–Sat. Grounds: **Open** 5am–10pm daily. **Closed** Jan 1, Thanksgiving, Dec 25. 🚻 🌐 nps.gov/cham

Guide dressed as an 1880s cavalry soldier in Fort Davis

---

## Visiting Mexico

A short, easy walk over the "International Bridge" from San Augustin Plaza, Laredo, leads visitors across the border into the typical Mexican border town of Nuevo Laredo. This trip gives visitors a deeper appreciation of the interdependence of these two very different yet increasingly similar countries. There is so much shared culture that, in the border areas at least, the differences between the US and Mexico are less striking than the similarities. Thanks mainly to the "Mexicanization" of the American side, where the population is more than 80 percent Latino, the food, music, and language is much the same. Nuevo Laredo, Juarez, and other Mexican cities are far larger and busier than their American counterparts, with a huge array of shops, restaurants, and bars offering a taste of Mexico. Elsewhere, along the more than 1,000-mile (1,609-km) border, dozens of small towns and villages are less frenetic, letting

"International Bridge" across the river to Nuevo Laredo, Mexico

visitors sample a taco while soaking up some south-of-the-border ambience. For US citizens, a trip across the border requires a passport. For non-citizens, however, it is vital to confirm their legal status and ensure that they can return to the US. For all travelers, it is far easier and usually quicker to cross the border on foot.

Towering El Capitan in Guadalupe Mountains

# ⑲ Guadalupe Mountains National Park

ℹ US 62/180, (915) 828-3251.
🌐 nps.gov/gumo

An almost road-free region on the Texas/New Mexico border, this national park covers 85,000 acres (34,398 ha) of rugged mountains that make up portions of the world's most extensive Permian limestone fossil reef, El Capitan, and the 8,749-ft (2,667-m) Guadalupe Peak, the highest point in Texas. Formed as part of the same prehistoric limestone that makes up the nearby (and more popular) Carlsbad Caverns National Park (see p552), the Guadalupe Mountains reward visitors with lofty peaks, spectacular views, unusual flora and fauna, and a colorful record of the past.

A short trail from the visitor center leads to the remains of a stone wall and foundations of a former frontier stagecoach station. This was built as part of the **Butterfield Trail**, which first established a link between St. Louis and California in 1858.

A few miles northeast of the visitor center, a forest of hardwood trees lines the trail of **McKittrick Canyon**. Here lies the site's most famous attraction, the spectacular red-and-orange foliage in October

and November. The hiking trails between the canyon walls that shelter a perennial stream are also very popular.

# ⑳ Lubbock

🏙 258,000. ✈ 🚌
ℹ 1500 Broadway, (806) 747-5232.
🌐 visitlubbock.org

Home to 30,000 sports-crazy students at Texas Tech University, Lubbock is a cattle-ranching and cotton-growing city that is perhaps best known for its musical progeny. Local musicians including Roy Orbison, Joe Ely, Waylon Jennings, and Tanya Tucker are all honored in Lubbock's guitar-shaped **Buddy Holly Center**, a musical Hall of Fame named for the city's favorite son, Charles Hardin Holley. A statue of Buddy Holly, one of rock and roll's most enduring icons, stands along 8th Street and Avenue Q.

Other aspects of Lubbock history are covered in the Texas Tech University's **Ranching Heritage Center**, an outdoor assembly of historic structures collected from all over Texas. On display are more than 30 original ranch buildings, from cowboy huts to stately overseers' mansions.

🏛 **Buddy Holly Center**
1801 Crickets Ave. **Tel** (806) 775-3560.
**Open** 10am–5pm Tue–Sat, 1–5pm Sun. **Closed** Jan 1, Easter, Jul 4, Thanksgiving, Dec 25. ♿ ♿
🌐 buddyhollycenter.org

🏛 **Ranching Heritage Center**
3121 4th St. **Tel** (806) 742-2498.
**Open** 10am–5pm Mon–Sat, 1–5pm Sun. **Closed** Jan 1, Thanksg., Dec 24–25. ♿ 🌐 nrhc.ttu.edu

# ㉑ Canyon

🏙 13,000. 🚌 ℹ 1518 5th Ave, (806) 655-7815.

Taking its name from the beautifully sculpted geology of nearby Palo Duro Canyon, this medium-sized Texas town is also home to the largest and best-known historical museum in the state. The **Panhandle-Plains Historical Museum**, housed in a stately 1930s complex on the campus of West Texas A&M University, holds over three million exhibits tracing the history of north-central Texas. Flint arrowheads from the Alibates quarry, north of Amarillo, highlight the culture of the region's prehistoric people, while geology and paleontology come together in exhibits exploring prehistoric dinosaurs and their relation to the region's petroleum industry. The story of another great Texas tradition, cattle ranching, is explored through the life of Wild West rancher Charles Goodnight, who owned a

---

## Buddy Holly (1936–59)

Singer, instrumentalist, and songwriter, Buddy Holly was one of the first major rock and roll music performers. Deeply influenced by local blues and country music, he began to sing in country groups while still in high school. By the mid-1950s, Holly was playing in small clubs throughout the Southwest. Drawn increasingly to rock music as exemplified by Elvis Presley, he recorded both alone and as lead performer with the Crickets. The group's energetic style, combining elements of country music and a strong background rhythm, together with Holly's unique hiccoughing vocals, quickly made them a success. Songs such as "Maybe Baby" and Holly's solo hit "Peggy Sue" became runaway hits. Holly's phenomenal career came to an abrupt end in 1959, when he died in a plane crash in Iowa.

Buddy Holly's statue, Lubbock

---

The rugged beauty of Palo Duro Canyon, the "Grand Canyon of Texas"

780-sq-mile (2,000-sq-km) ranch, and later led the fight to save native bison from extinction. Goodnight's home is now preserved in the enjoyable "Pioneer Town," located behind the museum.

About 12 miles (19 km) east of town, **Palo Duro Canyon State Park** protects the 60-mile- (97-km-) long, 1,100-ft (335-m) deep red and yellow sandstone gorge also known as the "Grand Canyon of Texas." A number of scenic drives and hiking routes run between the rim and the canyon floor, offering views of such geological oddities as the 300-ft- (91-m-) tall stone "Lighthouse." Palo Duro is also home to a wide variety of flora and fauna, including spring wildflowers, mule deer, and wild turkeys. In summer, one of the canyon's 600-ft (183-m) cliffs forms the backdrop for the

A sculpturally implanted Cadillac car at Cadillac Ranch, Amarillo

pageantry of *Texas*, a popular play on the history of the state.

🏛 **Panhandle-Plains Historical Museum**
2503 4th Ave. **Tel** (806) 651-2244. **Open** Jun–Aug: 9am–6pm Mon–Sat; Sep–May: 9am–5pm Tue–Sat. **Closed** Jan 1, Thanksgiving, Dec 24 & 25. 🅿 ♿ 🆆 panhandleplains.org

🌲 **Palo Duro Canyon State Park**
Hwy 217. **Tel** (806) 488-2227. **Open** 8am–6pm daily (Mar–Nov: later closing). 🅿 ♿ ⛺ 🆆 tpwd.state. tx.us/state-parks/palo-duro-canyon

## ㉒ Amarillo

🏙 185,000. 🛈 1000 S Polk St, (800) 692-1338. 🆆 visitamarillotx.com

The commercial heart of the sprawling Texas Panhandle region, and a key center for agriculture as well as oil, natural gas, and nuclear power industries, Amarillo was first settled in 1887 along the Santa Fe Railroad. The city later thrived thanks to its location along the legendary Route 66 (*see p50*). The route is now immortalized by **Cadillac Ranch**, a Pop Art work created from ten classic Cadillac cars planted nose-down in a pasture west of downtown. Another more typically Texas experience is the **Amarillo Livestock Auction**, where modern-day cowboys buy and sell their cattle.

🎡 **Cadillac Ranch**
S side of I-40 between Hope Rd & Arnot Rd exits. **Open** 24 hours. ♿

## ㉓ Abilene

🏙 116,000. 🚌 🛈 1101 N 1st St, (325) 676-2556. 🆆 abilenevisitors.com

Although named for the notorious Wild West town in Kansas, Abilene evolved from a frontier settlement to a solid, stable community. Also known as the "Buckle of the Bible Belt," thanks to its predominantly Christian colleges, where 8,000 students study, Abilene's past is kept alive at **Buffalo Gap Historical Village**, 14 miles (23 km) southwest of downtown. Founded in 1878, Buffalo Gap maintains over a dozen old buildings, such as a courthouse, a train station, and a school-house. Exhibits include Paleo-Indian artifacts and a frontier weapons collection.

🏠 **Buffalo Gap Historical Village**
133 William St. **Tel** (325) 572-3365. **Open** 10am–5pm Mon–Sat, noon–5pm Sun (to 6pm Jun–Aug). **Closed** Thanksgiving, Dec 25. 🅿 ♿ 🆆 buffalogap.com

Cowboy in Buffalo Gap Historical Village, Abilene

# Practical Information

In a state as vast as Texas, it helps greatly that information for travelers is readily accessible. Images of oil and cattle ranches immediately spring to mind and, while this is true for much of the state, Texas has much variety to offer. Stretching for nearly 800 miles (1,287 km) from east to west, the state offers everything from bayous and forests to prairies, bare windswept plains, and beautiful beaches. The dynamic, bustling big cities of Dallas and Houston are a contrast to the laid-back charm of the capital city of Austin, with its lush riverside parks, and historic San Antonio, with its predominantly Hispanic cultural ambience.

## Tourist Information

Along most major highways in Texas, there are "Welcome Centers," operated by the **Travel Division** of the Texas Department of Transportation. Open between 8am and 5pm daily, these centers offer a full range of tourist information, including details of weather and road conditions, attractions, and accommodations. Texas also publishes a magazine called *Texas Monthly* with travel stories and photographic essays on the wonders of the "Lone Star" state.

Most airports have information desks, and all major towns and cities have tourist-oriented Visitors' Bureaus or Chambers of Commerce.

## Natural Hazards

Texas has its fair share of natural hazards. Winter blizzards block roads and strand drivers under heavy snows, while, in spring, torrential rains that occur along with tornadoes and severe thunderstorms flood towns and cities located along streams a nd rivers. The most dangerous hazards are hurricanes, which can strike the Gulf Coast from June till December. Hurricane winds reach speeds of 75 to 150 mph (121 to 241 km/h) or more, but even more dangerous than the high winds is the storm surge, a dome of ocean water that can cause severe flooding along coastal rivers and bays. Fortunately, sophisticated warning systems are in place to give visitors plenty of time to get out of harm's way. Radio and TV stations broadcast storm watches and evacuation warnings.

## Getting Around

Public transportation is almost negligible in this state, although a few **Greyhound** routes cover some major cities. A single Amtrak route also shuttles along the southern part of the state. There is an excellent network of airports across the state, and many visitors fly between the major cities and then rent a car to get around the surrounding region.

Driving is essential in Texas and the comparatively low price of gas makes it a convenient option. Seat belts are required for drivers and passengers of all ages, whether in the front or back seats. Child seats are mandatory for all occupants under age 8, unless the child is more than 4 ft 9 inches (1.45 m) tall. Motor-cyclists under 21 years of age must wear helmets, while riders over 21 years must have proof of health insurance before they ride without a helmet. Radar detectors are permitted.

Speed limits for vehicles vary in Texas, with a state-wide maximum of 70 mph (113 km/h) allowed on Interstate Highways during daylight hours.

## Annual Events & Festivals

One of the best ways for visitors to get a feel for Texas is to take part in one of the state's huge range of annual events and festivals. Soon after the New Year sets in, the annual cleaning of the Riverwalk Canal in San Antonio launches the Mud Week, a ten-day festival of arts and entertainment. In March, Austin hosts the youthful South by Southwest festival of popular music.

The festival season really gets going in summer, starting at the end of May with the nationally acclaimed **Kerrville Folk Festival**. Many other local festivals, fairs, and events take place in towns all over the state, winding up with the massive **Texas State Fair**. This is one of the largest state fairs in the country, and is held in October in Dallas's extensive Fair Park. In addition to the national holidays, Texas also celebrates Confederate Heroes Day (January 19), Emancipation Day (June 19), and Lyndon Johnson's Birthday (August 27).

---

## The Climate of Texas

Despite its generally mild climate, weather across the vast state tends to vary greatly. Spring is ideal for travel, when the days are cool and wildflowers are in full bloom. Summer can be very hot and humid, with severe rains often causing floods along rivers and in low-lying areas. October is also good for travel, as temperatures are mild and the skies clear. In winter, snowstorms blow down from the Great Plains, and hurricanes hit the Gulf Coast.

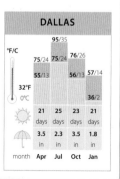

**DALLAS**

| °F/C | Apr | Jul | Oct | Jan |
|---|---|---|---|---|
| high | 75/24 | 95/35 | 76/26 | 57/14 |
| low | 55/13 | 75/24 | 56/13 | 36/2 |
| 32°F / 0°C | | | | |
| sun (days) | 21 days | 25 days | 23 days | 21 days |
| rain (in) | 3.5 in | 2.3 in | 3.5 in | 1.8 in |
| month | Apr | Jul | Oct | Jan |

## Sports

Springtime in Texas is synonymous with baseball, which is played at a variety of levels all over the state. Major league baseball is represented here by the **Houston Astros** and the **Texas Rangers**, both of whom play in state-of-the-art stadiums, though the Astros no longer play in the Astrodome – once the world's largest indoor space. Tickets for major league baseball games, however, can be expensive and hard to come by. In any case, a better sense of the game and its importance to Texas can be experienced by attending a Texas League baseball game, which may not be as slick, but is often more fun. Played in smaller arenas in front of a close-knit crowd of enthusiastic fans, the main Texas League teams is the **San Antonio Missions**.

As summer fades into fall, the American football season begins. A number of intense intrastate rivalries, such as that between the University of Texas and Texas A&M University, enliven the college football season. At the professional National Football League (NFL) level, the pride of Texas is the **Dallas Cowboys**, self-proclaimed "America's Team."

The New Year kicks off in Dallas with the Cotton Bowl, a championship football game played between two of the top universities in the country.

Winter is also basketball season, and games are played at all levels throughout the state. At the professional National Basketball Association level, Texas has the **Houston Rockets**, the **Dallas Mavericks**, and the **San Antonio Spurs**.

## Outdoor Activities

Visitors can participate in a vast range of outdoor activities all over Texas. From golf to fishing, river rafting to cycling, Texas has something for everyone at all levels and abilities. There are golf courses all over the state, most of them open to the public. Fishing, in a variety of freshwater lakes and in the Gulf of Mexico, is regulated by the **Texas Parks Department**. River rafting along the Rio Grande through **Big Bend National Park** draws people from all over the world, so advance reservations are essential. Biking is also a popular activity, and bicycles, helmets, and other accessories can easily be rented from shops in most Texas towns.

## Entertainment

Located in Fort Worth's lively Stockyard District, **Billy Bob's**, the world's largest honky-tonk, is just one of hundreds of nightclubs and performance venues all over this music-loving state. More upscale and refined music can also be enjoyed, thanks to the many orchestras in Texas. Fort Worth has one of the finest music venues, the **Bass Performance Hall**, home to the city's symphony, opera, and ballet.

## Shopping

Visitors wanting to bring home a souvenir of Texas should try cowboy boots. Western-wear shops all over the state may have the perfect pair, but some visitors may wish to take advantage of the discounts offered close by at El Paso-based **Tony Lama Boots**, one of the country's largest and most famous boot makers. For more upscale needs, nothing beats **Neiman-Marcus**, one of the nation's most exclusive department stores, which started in Dallas and is still in business downtown. The sales tax in Texas is 6.25 percent, and cities and counties may impose an additional tax of 2 percent.

# DIRECTORY

## Tourist Information

**Travel Division**
Texas Visitor Information:
W traveltex.com
Road Conditions Info:
**Tel** (800) 452-9292.
W drivetexas.org

## Natural Hazards

**National Hurricane Center**
W nhc.noaa.gov

## Getting Around

**Amtrak**
**Tel** (800) 872-7245.

**Greyhound**
**Tel** (800) 231-2222.

## Annual Events & Festivals

**Kerrville Folk Festival**
W kerrville-music.com

**Texas State Fair**
W bigtex.com

## Sports

**Dallas Cowboys**
**Tel** (972) 556-9900.

**Dallas Mavericks**
**Tel** (214) 747-6287.

**El Paso Chihuahuas**
**Tel** (915) 533-2273.

**Houston Astros**
**Tel** (713) 259-8000.

**Houston Rockets**
**Tel** (713) 627-3865.

**San Antonio Missions**
**Tel** (210) 675-7275.

**San Antonio Spurs**
**Tel** (210) 554-7787.

**Texas Rangers**
**Tel** (817) 273-5100.

## Outdoor Activities

**Big Bend National Park**
**Tel** (432) 477-2251.

**Texas Parks Deptartment**
**Tel** (512) 389-4800.

## Entertainment

**Bass Performance Hall**
525 Commerce St,
Fort Worth.
**Tel** (817) 212-4200.

**Billy Bob's**
Texas Rodeo Plaza,
Fort Worth.
**Tel** (817) 624-7117.

## Shopping

**Neiman-Marcus**
1618 Main St, Dallas.
**Tel** (214) 741-6911.
W neimanmarcus.com

**Tony Lama Boots**
7156 E Gateway, El Paso.
**Tel** (915) 772-4327.

# Where to Stay

**AUSTIN: Austin Motel** $
Value
*1220 S Congress Ave, 78704*
**Tel** *(512) 441-1157*
W austinmotel.com
This Austin motel has been family-owned and -operated since 1938. Its 1950s-style pool is popular with visiting artists and musicians in trendy South Congress.

### DK Choice

**AUSTIN: Driskill Hotel** $$$
Luxury
*604 Brazos St, 78701*
**Tel** *(512) 474-5911*
W driskillhotel.com
This historic hotel was built in 1886 as the showplace of a cattle baron. The finely appointed, comfortable guest rooms feature luxury bedding, terry robes, and high-end amenities. Marble floors, three-story columns, and a stained-glass dome ceiling add to the opulent atmosphere. Conveniently located in the heart of downtown, it is within walking distance of major attractions.

**AUSTIN: Hotel San Jose** $$$
Boutique
*1316 S Congress, 78704*
**Tel** *(512) 852-2350*
W sanjosehotel.com
Originally built in 1939 as an "ultramodern motor court," this property has been turned into a secluded, urban, bungalow-style hotel. It offers a variety of rooms with minimalist interiors, ranging from standards to grand suites.

**BIG BEND NATIONAL PARK:
Chisos Mountains Lodge** $
Value
*Basin Rural Station, 79834*
**Tel** *(432) 477-2292*
W chisosmountainslodge.com
The only lodging option in Big Bend National Park offers comfortable accommodations in the basin of the Chisos Mountains.

**DALLAS: Corinthian Bed &
Breakfast** $$
B&B
*4125 Junius St, 75246*
**Tel** *(214) 818-0400*
W corinthianbandb.com
This historic home in the Peak-Suburban Historic District offers a welcoming atmosphere among peaceful environs, not far from the heart of downtown.

Tremont House, a luxury hotel in a historic building, Galveston

**DALLAS: The Magnolia** $$
Historic
*1401 Commerce St, 75201*
**Tel** *(214) 915-6500*
W magnoliahoteldallas.com
A trendy hotel in the famous downtown Magnolia Petroleum Company building that dates back to 1922. The spacious rooms feature historic decor.

**DALLAS: Rosewood Mansion
on Turtle Creek** $$$
Luxury
*2821 Turtle Creek Blvd, 75219*
**Tel** *(214) 559-2100*
W rosewoodhotels.com
At this lovely hotel in the former palatial mansion of cotton magnate Sheppard King, the residential-style rooms have elegant marble bathrooms and private balconies.

**EL PASO: Camino Real Hotel** $
Historic
*101 S El Paso St, 79901*
**Tel** *(915) 534-3000*
W caminoreal.com
This 1912 landmark is full of historical grandeur, including a magnificent staircase, Italian-crafted marble, and a stunning Tiffany glass dome.

**FORT WORTH:
Stockyards Hotel** $$$
Historic
*109 E Exchange Ave, 76164*
**Tel** *(817) 625-6427*
W stockyardshotel.com
Set in the Stockyards National Historic District, this hotel offers rooms furnished with Western furniture, art, and antiques. All have modern conveniences.

**Price Guide**

Prices are based on one night's stay in high season for a standard double room, inclusive of service charges and taxes.

| | |
|---|---|
| $ | up to $150 |
| $$ | $150 to 250 |
| $$$ | over $250 |

**FREDERICKSBURG: Inn on
Barons Creek** $$
B&B
*308 South Washington St, 78624*
**Tel** *(830) 990-9202*
W innonbaronscreek.com
This welcoming inn in the heart of Texas Hill Country has well-appointed rooms and suites. It offers a complimentary breakfast, plus spa and fitness facilities.

**GALVESTON: Tremont House** $$$
Luxury
*2300 Ship's Mechanic Row, 77550*
**Tel** *(409) 763-0300*
W wyndham.com
In a lavish 1879 Victorian building with ornate architecture in the Strand Historic District, this hotel has period furnishings, birdcage elevators, and a rooftop terrace.

**HOUSTON: Hilton Americas** $$
Value
*1600 Lamar, 77010*
**Tel** *(713) 739-8000*
W hilton.com
Two sky-bridges connect this eco-friendly complex to the city's convention center. Downtown attractions are also nearby.

**HOUSTON: Hotel ZaZa** $$$
Boutique
*5701 Main St, 77005*
**Tel** *(713) 526-1991*
W hotelzaza.com
A short walk from the Museum of Fine Arts, this hotel in a historic building has hip, trendy rooms.

**SAN ANTONIO: Best Western
Plus Sunset Suites** $
Value
*1103 E Commerce St, 78205*
**Tel** *(210) 223-4400*
W bestwesternsunsetsuites.com
All-suite accommodations in a beautifully converted turn-of-the-century building. Located near the Alamo and Riverwalk.

**SAN ANTONIO: Menger Hotel** $$
Historic
*204 Alamo Plaza, 78205*
**Tel** *(210) 223-4361*
W mengerhotel.com
Built in 1859, right next to the Alamo, the rooms here are modern and comfortable. There is an impressive Victorian lobby.

**For more information on types of hotels** *see pages 26–7*

# Where to Eat and Drink

## AUSTIN: Chuy's $
Tex-Mex
*1728 Barton Springs Rd, 78704*
**Tel** *(512) 474-4452*
Originating in Austin, this chain restaurant serves low-cost Tex-Mex fare. Enjoy huge portions of enchiladas, nachos, and tacos. The signature items feature tasty Hatch green chilis. Elvis fans will appreciate the tributes.

## AUSTIN: Salt Lick BBQ $
Barbecue
*18300 FM 1826, Driftwood, 78619*
**Tel** *(512) 858-4959*
A legendary barbecue that serves brisket, ribs, sausage, turkey, and chicken smoked over a large open pit. Plenty of sides to choose from.

## AUSTIN: Threadgill's $
Southern
*6416 N Lamar Blvd, 78752*
**Tel** *(512) 451-5440*
This historic 1930s eatery is popular for American diner food with a Texan twist. Fried catfish, chicken-fried steak, and pecan pie are popular dishes. Check out their neon signs and memorabilia.

## AUSTIN: Uchi $$$
Japanese
*801 S Lamar Blvd, 78704*
**Tel** *(512) 916-4808*
Housed in a refurbished old home, Uchi serves award-winning contemporary Japanese cuisine. Local ingredients are combined with high-quality seafood from around the world.

## DALLAS: El Fenix $
Tex-Mex
*1601 McKinney Ave, 75202*
**Tel** *(214) 747-1121*
A casual, affordable haven operating since 1918. The fresh and generous portions of fajitas, burritos, and enchiladas are the house favorites. Warm ambience.

## DK Choice

### DALLAS: Sonny Bryan's Smokehouse $
Barbecue
*2202 Inwood Rd, 75235*
**Tel** *(214) 357-7120*
This chain has been serving legendary Texas barbecue since 1910. The rich and smoky meats, accompanied by savory sauces, are intensely flavorful. Traditional brisket, a favorite, often sells out. Pulled pork, ribs, and sausages are also popular.

## DALLAS: Mansion Restaurant $$$
New American/French
*2821 Turtle Creek Blvd, 75219*
**Tel** *(214) 443-4747*
Housed in the historic Sheppard King Mansion, this restaurant has a contemporary American menu with French influences. The Chef's Room specializes in formal dining.

## EL PASO: Café Central $$
New American
*109 N Oregon St, 79901*
**Tel** *(915) 545-2233*     **Closed** *Sun*
This elegant restaurant serves gourmet seasonal cuisine with a contemporary Southwest twist. Options include green chili soup, ahi tuna, and mango colada pie.

## FORT WORTH:
### Cattlemen's Steak House $$
Steak House
*2458 N Main St, 76164*
**Tel** *(817) 624-3945*
Juicy charcoal-grilled steaks are the star dishes at Cattlemen's. Try the thick sirloin, rib-eye, or T-bone steaks. Chicken, shrimp, and lobster are also available.

## HOUSTON: Torchy's Tacos $
Tex-Mex
*2411 S Shepherd Dr, 77019*
**Tel** *(713) 595-8226*
A favorite with locals for its tasty tacos. The creative menu features *queso*, and soft and crispy tacos, with Jamaican jerk chicken, fried avocado, and blackened salmon.

## HOUSTON: Américas $$$
Latin American
*2040 W Gray St, TX 77019*
**Tel** *(832) 200-1492*
This upscale establishment offers vibrant Latin cuisine, including *ceviche* and grilled meats in a modern space with rustic touches.

### Price Guide
Prices are based on a three-course meal for one, with a glass of house wine, including tax and service.

| | |
|---|---|
| $ | up to $35 |
| $$ | $35 to 70 |
| $$$ | over $70 |

## HOUSTON: Underbelly $$$
New American
*1100 Westheimer Rd, 77006*
**Tel** *(713) 528-9800*     **Closed** *Sun*
A trendy venue with an inventive take on Southern cuisine plus a popular wine bar. The weekly-changing menu offers creative seafood dishes and meats, such as goat and grass-fed beef prepared by the in-house butcher shop.

## SAN ANTONIO: Chris Madrid's $
American hamburgers
*1900 Blanco Rd, 78212*
**Tel** *(210) 735-3552*     **Closed** *Sun*
This popular cantina serves "Macho"-sized burgers, nachos, cold beers, and more. The revered *tostada* burger is topped with cheese, beans, chips, and salsa.

## SAN ANTONIO: Boudros $$
New American
*421 E Commerce St, 78205*
**Tel** *(210) 224-8484*
A trendy Riverwalk restaurant serving Texas beef, Gulf seafood, and Hill Country produce. Popular dishes include blackened prime rib and marinated Gulf tuna.

## SAN ANTONIO: Mi Tierra Café & Bakery $$
Mexican
*218 Produce Row, 78207*
**Tel** *(210) 225-1262*
A legendary spot, Mi Tierra is known for its festive decor, margaritas, and sizzling fajitas. The on-site bakery provides a huge choice of sweets.

Wine racks and dining area of the popular Underbelly, Houston

**For more information on types of restaurants** *see pages 28–9*

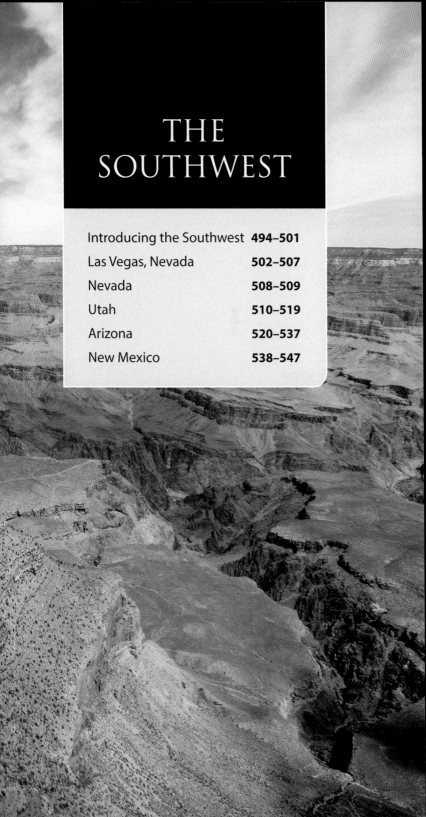

# THE
# SOUTHWEST

# The Southwest at a Glance

America's Southwest is made up of the states of Nevada, Utah, Arizona, and New Mexico. It also includes the Four Corners area, the only place in the US where four states – parts of Utah, Arizona, New Mexico, and Colorado – meet at a central point. The region boasts spectacular landscapes, dominated by desert, deep canyons, and high mesas. Equally fascinating is its multicultural heritage, influenced by Native American, Hispanic, and Anglo-American settlers. Today, this region offers visitors a range of sights, most of which are concentrated in the cities of Phoenix, Tucson, Albuquerque, Santa Fe, and Las Vegas.

Hopi-made coiled basket made of willow or yucca leaves

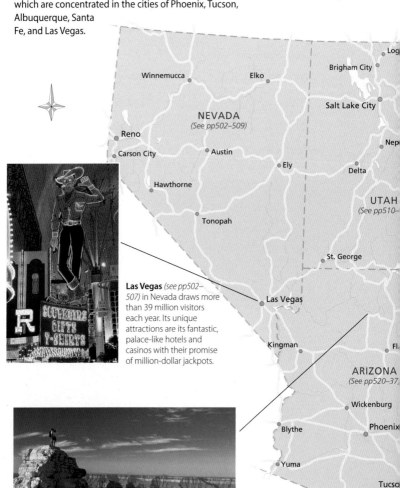

**Las Vegas** *(see pp502–507)* in Nevada draws more than 39 million visitors each year. Its unique attractions are its fantastic, palace-like hotels and casinos with their promise of million-dollar jackpots.

**The Grand Canyon** *(see pp530–33)* in Arizona is the second most-visited national park in the country. This is, however, just one of the many natural wonders in a state well-known for its stunning landscapes of pristine deserts, forested hills, and fertile meadows.

◄ The remarkable landscape of the Grand Canyon, Arizona

**Locator Map**

Cacti and dried chilies adorning a flower shop, Tucson

**Arches National Park** *(see pp512–13)* is just one of the many geological wonders in Utah, a state with the highest concentration of national parks in the United States. The dramatic and unpromising landscape of Utah also became the spiritual and worldly base of the Mormons. Salt Lake City, the state capital, is located northwest of the park.

Monticello

Farmington

Raton

Taos

Clayton

Santa Fe

Albuquerque

Grants

Tucumcari

**NEW MEXICO**
*(See pp538–47)*

Vaughn

Clovis

Socorro

Silver City

Tularosa

Roswell

Hobbs

Deming

Douglas

0 km        100

0 miles      100

**New Mexico** *(see pp538–47)* is one of the Southwest's most popular destinations. Its scenic beauty and rich cultural heritage have lured generations of artists, who have made Santa Fe and Taos vibrant creative centers. Albuquerque, the largest city, has many fine museums.

# THE SOUTHWEST

Distinguished by its dramatic landscape, the Southwest is a land of twisting canyons, cactus-studded deserts, and rugged mountains. For more than 15,000 years, the region was inhabited by Native Americans, but by the 20th century Anglo-American traditions had mingled with those of the Hispanic and Native peoples to create the region's multicultural heritage.

The states of Nevada, Utah, Arizona, and New Mexico make up America's Southwest. Perceptions of this region are influenced by the landscape – the red sandstone mesas of Monument Valley, the tall saguaro cacti of Arizona's Sonoran Desert, the staggering scale of the Grand Canyon, and New Mexico's adobe architecture. At its heart is its defining geological feature – the Colorado Plateau – a rock tableland rising more than 12,000 ft (3,660 m) above sea level and covering a vast area of around 130,000 sq miles (336,700 sq km). The plateau was created by the same geological upheavals that formed the Rocky Mountains. Subsequent erosion by wind, water, and sand molded both hard and soft rock to form the mesas, canyons, and mountains. Many of these natural wonders have been preserved as national parks.

The region's main city, Las Vegas, has been synonymous with glamor and entertainment ever since Nevada legalized gambling in 1931. Mobster Bugsy Siegel opened the first luxury hotel, the Flamingo, in 1946, and soon there was a proliferation of casinos. Some of the biggest names in show business, such as Frank Sinatra and Elvis Presley, as well as eccentric millionaire Howard Hughes, have all contributed to Vegas's image as the fun city of limos, showgirls, and glitzy lifestyles. This city of megaresorts and casinos is as popular for its wedding chapels, where more than 100,000 couples get married each year.

## History

The first Native American people were a society of hunters who inhabited the region between 10,000 and 8,000 BC. The introduction of new farming techniques and crops, especially corn from Mexico, saw the start of settled farming communities in around 800 BC. By AD 500 an agrarian society was well established, and large villages or pueblos began to develop. By 700 the three main cultures in the region were the Hohokam, the Mogollon, and the Ancestral Puebloan. Ancestral Puebloan people constructed elaborate dwellings that grew into large cities such as Chaco Canyon. However, in the 12th and 13th centuries,

The desert floor dotted with sagebrush, Monument Valley, Arizona

◀ Visitors taking a trip on a gondola around the Venetian Resort Hotel Casino, Las Vegas, Nevada

these settlements were mysteriously abandoned. It is thought that the people migrated to the Pueblo Indian settlements along the Rio Grande Valley and northwest New Mexico, where their descendants still live. The 15th century saw the arrival of the Navajo, who were hunters, and the fierce Apache warriors from Canada.

In the 1500s, the Spanish quest for wealth, particularly gold, led to the establishment of a permanent colony called New Mexico, which included all of the present-day states of New Mexico and Arizona, as well as parts of Colorado, Utah, Nevada, and California. Mexican independence from Spain was declared in 1821, paving the way for Anglo-American traders. The first Anglos (non-Spanish people of European descent) in the Southwest were "mountain men" or fur trappers, who helped open up the trade routes to the west. With the establishment of the Old Spanish and the Santa Fe Trails, this remote region became more accessible.

Ancient pottery bowl

The US government's vigorous expansion led to conflict with Mexico, and the region became a part of the United States in 1848. Soon, the settlers began to forcibly acquire Native land, and more than 8,000 Navajo were made to march "The Long Walk" to a reservation in New Mexico in 1864. Resentment against the Anglos instigated the Indian Wars, which finally ended with the surrender of Apache leader Geronimo in 1886.

At the same time, rich lodes of gold, silver, and copper were discovered in Arizona, and mining camps such as Bisbee and Tombstone became boomtowns. This was the Wild West of mining prospectors, ranch cowboys, and notorious outlaws, such as Billy the Kid, whose exploits form part of American folklore.

## Society & Culture

The Southwest is a crossroads of the three great cultures that shaped America – Native American, Hispanic, and Anglo-American. The Spanish language is prominent, not only in bilingual New Mexico but also in Arizona. A host of Native American languages are also spoken, reflecting the far longer history of the region's Native inhabitants. The Hopi and other Pueblo peoples trace their ancestry back to the Ancestral Puebloan peoples, while the Navajo occupy the country's largest reservation, stretching across the northern ends of both Arizona and New Mexico. The Apache and many other tribes have land here as well. Today, Native populations have a hand in governing their own lands, and many have diversified their business interests to regenerate their economy and are involved in tourism, running casinos, and the production of such crafts as pottery and rugs.

A variety of religions coexist in the Southwest. The most visible is Roman Catholicism, which was introduced in the 16th century by the Spanish colonists. It is today the main religion, although several

### KEY DATES IN HISTORY

**1800 BC** Corn brought from Mexico

**AD 800** Chaco Canyon under construction

**1400** Migrations of the Navajo and Apache

**1540–42** Francisco Vasquez de Coronado leads the search for gold in New Mexico

**1610** Santa Fe established as capital of New Mexico

**1680** The Pueblo revolt against the Spanish

**1821** Santa Fe Trail opened

**1848** Treaty of Guadalupe-Hidalgo cedes Mexican territory to the US

**1868** Navajo reservation founded in Four Corners region

**1869** The coming of the railroad

**1912** New Mexico and Arizona become 47th and 48th states of the United States

**1931–36** Hoover Dam constructed in Arizona

**1945** First atomic bomb tested in New Mexico

**1974** Central Arizona Project begins to extract water from the Colorado River

**1996** President Clinton signs Navajo-Hopi Land Dispute Settlement Act

**2009** A 4-mile (7-km) section of Las Vegas Boulevard is designated a National Scenic Byway

A typical Navajo rug

Protestant denominations exist as well. Utah's residents, however, are predominantly Mormon. Native American spiritual beliefs are complex, as each tribe has its own practices.

One of the region's most famous attributes is the quality of light found in the hills of northern New Mexico. Georgia O'Keeffe's landscape paintings in the 1940s helped to make the area around Santa Fe a mecca for artists. Today, the city has the country's second largest art trade after New York City. The smaller resort town of Taos is also famous for its resident painters and sculptors.

Santa Fe, as well as Phoenix, Tucson, and Albuquerque also offer opera, ballet, classical music, and major theatrical productions. The Phoenix Symphony and New Mexico Symphony Orchestra, based in Albuquerque, are best known for their concerts, while jazz and country music can be heard in almost every city and major town.

## Economics & Tourism

Today, New Mexico and Arizona are the country's fifth and sixth largest states. Despite the fact that the region's population is increasing, it remains one of the least populated in the United States. The cities of Phoenix, Tucson, Santa Fe, and Albuquerque account for around 60 percent of the region's population. Such intense urbanization has put tremendous pressure on the region's resources, particularly water, which has become one of the Southwest's most pressing issues.

The legacy of the two World Wars changed the Southwest's economic course. In the 1940s, New Mexico's sparsely populated and remote desert area of Los Alamos was chosen as the location for the top secret Manhattan Project, which developed the world's first atomic bomb. Since then, the region has been a major center for national defense research and development of nuclear weapon technology, as well as for research into space travel, with both state and federal governments as major employers. Today, other research projects, including bio-technology, especially the Genome Project (which maps all human genes) and computer technology, attract scientists to the Southwest.

Tourism is another of the region's principal employers. Vast wilderness areas and a warm climate make outdoor leisure popular in the Southwest. Its national parks, established in the early 1900s, draw ever-increasing numbers of tourists each year. There are also miles of hiking trails, rivers for white-water rafting, lakes for water sports, ski resorts, and some of the nation's finest golf courses. One of the best ways to experience the landscape is on a trail ride, and armchair cowboys can attend that great Southwestern event – the rodeo.

**FLAGSTAFF ROUTE 66**

Route 66 Flagstaff sign

The Southwest is as much a state of mind as it is a geographical region. The attractions of the landscape and a romantic sense of the past combine to conjure up the idealized legends of the "Wild West." For many, it is the chance to indulge the cowboy in their soul.

Horseback riding, a popular pastime in the Sonoran Desert near Tucson, Arizona

# Exploring the Southwest

The four states of the Southwest encompass many
natural wonders, such as the Grand Canyon and
Monument Valley in Arizona, and Zion National Park
in Utah. Beyond the scenic are the pueblo villages
along the Rio Grande in New Mexico and the glitter
of Las Vegas, Nevada's fastest growing city. Above all,
the region conjures up images of the Wild West,
as portrayed by Hollywood and preserved by
the myths around old mining towns, such as
Bisbee and Tombstone.

Chili wreath, Santa Fe

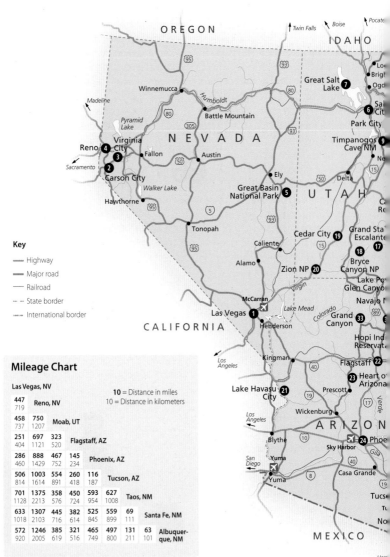

## Key

— Highway
— Major road
— Railroad
– – State border
··—·· International border

## Mileage Chart

| 10 = Distance in miles |
| 10 = Distance in kilometers |

| | | | | | | | | |
|---|---|---|---|---|---|---|---|---|
| **Las Vegas, NV** | | | | | | | | |
| 447 | **Reno, NV** | | | | | | | |
| 719 | | | | | | | | |
| 458 | 750 | **Moab, UT** | | | | | | |
| 737 | 1207 | | | | | | | |
| 251 | 697 | 323 | **Flagstaff, AZ** | | | | | |
| 404 | 1121 | 520 | | | | | | |
| 286 | 888 | 467 | 145 | **Phoenix, AZ** | | | | |
| 460 | 1429 | 752 | 234 | | | | | |
| 506 | 1003 | 554 | 260 | 116 | **Tucson, AZ** | | | |
| 814 | 1614 | 891 | 418 | 187 | | | | |
| 701 | 1375 | 358 | 450 | 593 | 627 | **Taos, NM** | | |
| 1128 | 2213 | 576 | 724 | 954 | 1008 | | | |
| 633 | 1307 | 445 | 382 | 525 | 559 | 69 | **Santa Fe, NM** | |
| 1018 | 2103 | 716 | 614 | 845 | 899 | 111 | | |
| 572 | 1246 | 385 | 321 | 465 | 497 | 131 | 63 | **Albuquer-que, NM** |
| 920 | 2005 | 619 | 516 | 749 | 800 | 211 | 101 | |

## Sights at a Glance

0 kilometers 100

0 miles 100

Mummy Cave Overlook in Canyon de Chelly, Arizona

# ● Las Vegas

The heart of Las Vegas, Nevada's most famous city, lies along Las Vegas Boulevard, a sparkling vista of neon known simply as "the Strip." The southern stretch of this 3.5-mile- (6-km-) long street that runs northeast through the city is home to a cluster of lavishly themed hotels, with their own shops, restaurants, and gaming casinos. They lure almost 37 million visitors every year, making Vegas the entertainment capital of the world. When the lights come on in the evening, these new megaresorts become a fantasyland with riotous design and architecture, such as that of the Luxor's striking pyramid with its sphinx. The exotically themed Aladdin Hotel is evidence of the city's ability to reinvent itself quickly – it took only two years to build.

A dazzling nighttime view of the Strip

**New York New York**
A replica of the Statue of Liberty forms part of the façade of this hotel, which is composed of a host of such Manhattan landmarks as the Empire State Building.

**Luxor**
The main portion of the hotel is a 365-ft- (111-m-) high, 30-story pyramid encased in 11 acres (4 ha) of bronze glass.

**The Monte Carlo** is filled with Corinthian colonnades and arches.

**Mandalay Bay's** interior, with its palm trees and bamboo, re-creates a 19th-century tropical paradise.

**Excalibur's** towers are a kitsch fantasy of medieval England.

TROPICANA AVE

LAS VEGAS BLVD

**Showcase Mall** is a striking building, with its giant neon Coca-Cola bottle. Attractions include M&M's World, World of Coca-Cola, and the Grand Canyon Experience.

**MGM Grand Hotel**
One of the largest hotels in the US with more than 5,000 rooms, the Grand displays a 45-ft- (15-m-) high statue of Leo, symbol of the Hollywood film studio, MGM.

**Tropicana**
The rooms, suites, and villas at the renovated Tropicana have a bright, South Beach-style decor, as seen at this poolside villa.

For hotels and restaurants see pp550–55

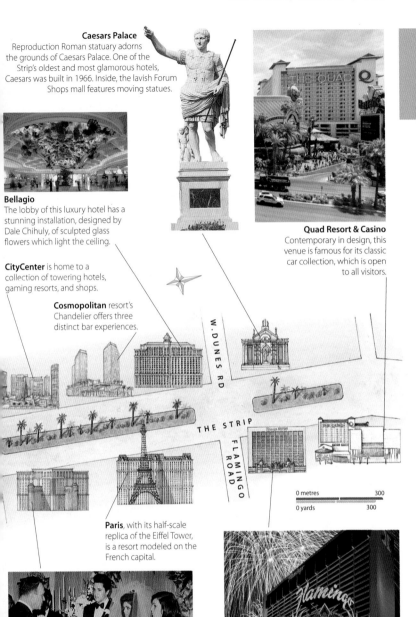

**Caesars Palace**
Reproduction Roman statuary adorns the grounds of Caesars Palace. One of the Strip's oldest and most glamorous hotels, Caesars was built in 1966. Inside, the lavish Forum Shops mall features moving statues.

**Bellagio**
The lobby of this luxury hotel has a stunning installation, designed by Dale Chihuly, of sculpted glass flowers which light the ceiling.

**CityCenter** is home to a collection of towering hotels, gaming resorts, and shops.

**Cosmopolitan** resort's Chandelier offers three distinct bar experiences.

**Quad Resort & Casino**
Contemporary in design, this venue is famous for its classic car collection, which is open to all visitors.

W. DUNES RD

THE STRIP

FLAMINGO ROAD

0 metres 300
0 yards 300

**Paris**, with its half-scale replica of the Eiffel Tower, is a resort modeled on the French capital.

**Planet Hollywood Resort & Casino**
The reputation of this hotel, which opened in 1963, as one of the glitziest on the Strip was sealed when Elvis married Priscilla here in 1967. Today the resort and casino have a sleek, modern Hollywood theme.

**Flamingo Las Vegas**
The flaming pink and orange neon feathers of the Flamingo hotel's façade is a famous Strip icon. New York City gangster Bugsy Siegel created the hotel and casino in 1946. He was killed just a year later by fellow gangsters.

# Las Vegas (The Strip Continued)

The legalization of gambling in Nevada paved the way for Las Vegas's casino-based growth. The first casino resort, the El Rancho Vegas Hotel-Casino, opened in 1941 and was located on the northern section of the Strip. A building boom followed in the 1950s, resulting in a plethora of resorts. The Sands, Desert Inn, Sahara, and Stardust hotels began the process that transformed the Strip into a high-rise adult theme park. Although many of these North Strip resorts remain, they are now unrecognizable, thanks to million-dollar rebuilding programs. The façades of the new casinos are designed now to encourage people to walk up and enter to enjoy the casinos, shops, shows, and restaurants inside.

The Venetian with replica of St. Mark's Campanile

**Treasure Island**
Sophisticated and hip, Treasure Island offers fine dining, entertainment, a casino, and a three-story shopping center.

**The Fashion Show Mall** is currently the largest shopping destination in Vegas, with more than 200 stores, an entertainment complex, and a food court serving both fast and fresh food.

**The Mirage** is both stylish and ornate – its beautiful, Strip-facing gardens feature an "erupting" volcano.

**Wynn Las Vegas & Encore**
This resort has it all: casinos, an exclusive golf course, oversized luxurious rooms, restaurants with award-winning chefs, nightclubs, and dozens of designer shops.

**Guardian Angel Cathedral**
Located on Cathedral Way, this chapel has elegant marble floors and imposing buttress support columns.

**⑯ The Venetian**
One of the world's most luxurious hotels with mock canals flowing through its shopping area.

SPRING MOUNTAIN RD

LAS VEGAS BLVD

SANDS AVE

*For hotels and restaurants see pp550–55*

**㉑ Circus Circus**
Lucky the clown beckons visitors to this resort, which offers circus acts and traditional carnival games on the mezzanine floor above the casino.

**㉒ Stratosphere Tower**
An observation deck at the top of this 1,149-ft (350-m) tower offers fine views of the city and the ring of mountains that rise from the desert.

**Riviera**
The colorful, neon-lit, and seemingly jewel-encrusted façade of Riviera highlights the hotel's hit shows, and is one of the most dazzling landmarks along North Strip.

W. SAHARA AVE

S. MAIN ST

THE STRIP

0 metres 300
0 yards 300

Neon lights at the Riviera Hotel

**Las Vegas Neon**

The twinkling, flashing neon sign remains the dominant icon of Las Vegas, even though several of the new themed megaresorts here have opted for a more understated look. Neon is a gas discovered by British chemist Sir William Ramsey in 1898. But it was a French inventor, Georges Claude, who, in 1910, discovered that an electric current passed through a glass tube of neon emitted a powerful, shimmering light. In the 1940s and '50s the craft of neon sign-making was elevated to the status of an art form in Las Vegas.

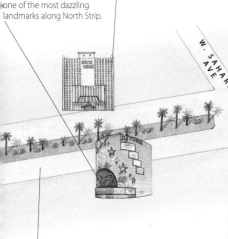

**Busy traffic on the Strip**
Although the Strip is very busy with traffic, it is increasingly pedestrian-friendly and makes for an enjoyable walk.

### Exploring Las Vegas

Rising like a mirage out of Nevada's beautiful southern desert, Las Vegas is a fascinating wonderland that promises fun to all its visitors. Beyond the allure of the Strip are the glittering malls and museums in the downtown area. For those who can tear themselves away from the city, the surrounding canyons, mountains, deserts, and parks offer a wealth of natural beauty and outdoor pleasures. Apart from tourism and gaming, Las Vegas is also famous for wedding chapels that offer a wide range of customized ceremonies.

### Siegfried & Roy's Secret Garden and Dolphin Habitat

Mirage Hotel, 3400 S Las Vegas Blvd S. **Tel** (702) 791-7111. **Open** 11am–6:30pm Mon–Fri; 10am–6:30pm Sat & Sun. 🅿 📷 Ⓦ **mirage.com**

The highlight here is the Dolphin Habitat, which has a 2.5-million-gallon (7,570,800-liter) saltwater aquarium for Atlantic bottlenose dolphins. Four connected pools, an artificial coral reef system, and a sandy bottom simulate the dolphins' natural environment. All of the dolphins were born here except for a few that were transferred from other facilities. Visitors can watch them swimming and playing with large balls through viewing windows.

The Secret Garden is a palm-shaded place with white tigers, lions, leopards, and black panthers. The animal enclosures are small, but the cats are rotated between the Secret Garden and larger quarters off-site.

### Fremont Street Experience

Light Shows: **Open** 6pm–midnight daily. ♿ Ⓦ **vegasexperience.com** Binion's: 128 E Fremont St. **Tel** (702) 382-1600. **Open** 24 hours. ♿ Ⓦ **binions.com** Four Queens: 202 E Fremont St. **Tel** (702) 385-4011. **Open** 24 hours. ♿ Ⓦ **fourqueens.com**

Known as "Glitter Gulch," Fremont Street was where the first casinos with neon signs and illuminated icons were located. However, during the 1980s and 1990s as the Strip became more glamorous, this street went into decline. To reverse the process, an ambitious $70-million project was initiated by the city in 1994 to revitalize the area. The street is now a colorful, bustling pedestrian mall, covered by a vast steel canopy, extending for five blocks, and from which the spectacular sound-and-light shows are projected every night. Gaze upward to experience high-resolution images presented by more than 12 million LED modules with concert-quality sound.

Established by Dallas bootlegger and gambler Benny Binion, the landmark **Binion's** retains an old-style Vegas atmosphere. Now managed by MTR Gaming, the legend continues with table games, slots, keno, and poker. Another historic casino along the Street is **Four Queens**. Named for the owner's four daughters, the casino has chandeliers and gilt mirrors, reminscent of 19th-century New Orleans. It also claims to have the largest slot machine in the world.

Façade of Binion's

### Discovery Children's Museum

360 Promenade Place. **Tel** (702) 382-5437. **Open** Jun–Labor Day: 10am–5pm Mon–Sat, noon–5pm Sun; Sep–May: 9am–4pm Tue–Fri, 10am–5pm Sat, noon–5pm Sun. **Closed** Mon (except school hols), Jan 1, Easter, Thanksgiving, Dec 24 & 25. ♿ ♿ Ⓦ **discoverykidslv.org**

Nine interactive galleries provide fun hands-on learning activities in science, arts, culture, and early childhood development. There is also a gallery for temporary exhibitions from leading museums.

### The Las Vegas Natural History Museum

900 Las Vegas Blvd. **Tel** (702) 384-3466. **Open** 9am–4pm daily. **Closed** Jan 1, Thanksgiving, Dec 25. ♿ ♿ Ⓦ **lvnhm.org**

A popular choice with families who need a break from the Strip resorts, this museum has an appealing range of exhibits. Dioramas re-create the African savanna, complete with leopards, cheetahs, and antelopes. The marine exhibit offers a chance to view live sharks and eels at close quarters. Animatronic dinosaurs and the hands-on discovery room, where visitors can dig fossils and operate a robotic baby dinosaur, are popular with children.

### Boulder City & Hoover Dam

🚷 12,500. 🛩 🚌 **Tel** (702) 494-2517. **Open:** summer: 9am–5:15pm; winter: 9am–4:15pm. 🅿 ♿

Named after Herbert Hoover, the 31st president, the historic Hoover Dam lies about 30 miles (48 km) east of Las Vegas. Before its construction, the Colorado River frequently flooded acres of farmland in Mexico and southern California. After much consideration, the dam was built between 1931 and 1935 across the Colorado River's Black Canyon. Hailed as an engineering marvel, it gave this desert region a reliable water supply and provided inexpensive electricity to Nevada, Arizona,

An animatronic *Tyrannosaurus rex* in roaring form at the Las Vegas Natural History Museum

he Hoover Dam as seen from above

nd California. This colossus of oncrete is today a huge tourist ttraction. Guided tours take isitors into the depths of the am; the top of the visitor center ffers superb views.

Just 8 miles (13 km) vest, Boulder City was uilt to house the dam's onstruction workers. It s one of Nevada's most ttractive well-ordered owns. Several 1930s uildings remain, such as he historic Boulder Dam Hotel, housing the Hoover Dam Museum.

### Lake Mead National Recreation Area
Las Vegas. **Tel** (702) 293-8906/990. Park: **Open** 24 hrs. Visitor Center: **Open** 9am–4:30pm Wed–Sun. **Closed** Jan 1, Thanksgiving, Dec 25. limited. nps.gov/lame

After the completion of Hoover Dam, the waters of the Colorado River filled the deep canyons, which once towered above the river, to create Lake Mead. This huge reservoir is the largest man-made body of water in the US. Its 700-mile (1,130-km) shoreline is home to forests, canyons, and flower-rich meadows. Dotted with beaches, marinas, and campgrounds, the reservoir area offers water sports such as sailing, water-skiing, swimming, and fishing. Striped bass and rainbow trout are popular catches.

### Valley of Fire State Park
29450 Valley of Fire Rd. Las Vegas. **Tel** (702) 397-2088. partial. parks.nv.gov/vf.htm
Lost City Museum of Archaeology: 721 S Moapa Valley Blvd, Overton. **Tel** (702) 397-2193. **Open** 8:30am–4:30pm daily. **Closed** Jan 1, Thanksg., Dec 25.

Hoover Dam sign

This spectacularly scenic state park is in a remote desert location some 60 miles (97 km) northeast of Las Vegas. It derives its name from the red sandstone formations that began as huge, shifting sand dunes about 150 million years ago. The extreme summer temperatures mean that spring or fall are the best times to explore the wilderness. Of the four well-maintained trails, the Petroglyph Canyon Trail is an easy half-mile (0.8 km) loop, which takes in several fine prehistoric Ancestral Puebloan rock carvings. One of the most famous depicts an *atlatl*, a notched stick used to add speed and distance to a thrown spear. Ancestral Puebloan people settled in the nearby town of Overton along Muddy River, around 300 BC. They left some 1,500 years later, perhaps because of a long drought. Archaeologists have discovered hundreds of prehistoric artifacts in the area, many of which are housed in Overton's **Lost City Museum of Archaeology**, just outside the town. Its large collection includes pottery, beads, woven baskets, and delicate turquoise jewelry, which was a local specialty.

### Red Rock Canyon
Las Vegas. **Tel** (702) 515-5350. **Open** 8am–4:30pm daily. **Closed** public hols. limited. nv.blm.gov/redrockcanyon/

From downtown Las Vegas it is a short, 10-mile (16-km) drive west to the low hills and steep gullies of the Red Rock Canyon National Conservation Area. Here, baked by the summer sun, a gnarled escarpment rises out of the desert, its gray limestone and red sandstone the geological residue of an ancient ocean and the huge sand dunes that succeeded it. The canyon is easily explored on a 13-mile- (21-km-) long scenic road that loops off Hwy 159 providing a good overview and great picnic spots, but the best way to explore these steep winding canyons is on foot. Watch for the bighorn sheep and desert tortoises when hiking.

Extraordinary rock formations in the Valley of Fire State Park

# Nevada

Nevada was known as the "Silver State" mainly because of the immense wealth that came out of the late 19th-century silver mines of the Comstock Lode, east of Reno. Today, it is synonymous with adult fun, thanks to the presence of the world's largest gambling and entertainment mecca of glittering Las Vegas *(see pp502–507)*. Away from its few cities, Nevada is mostly uninhabited desert, with ridge after ridge of rugged mountains dividing the endless sagebrush plains.

Façade of the impressive State Capitol in Carson City

## ❷ Carson City

🏙 55,000. ✈ ℹ 1900 S Carson St Suite 100, (775) 687-7410.
🌐 visitcarsoncity.com

The state capital and third largest city in Nevada, Carson City was named in honor of the Wild West explorer Kit Carson. Nestled at the base of the eastern escarpment of the Sierra Nevada, the city was founded in 1858, a year before the discovery of the Comstock Lode mines. It still retains a few old-fashioned casinos in its downtown core.

The excellent **Nevada State Museum**, down the street from the impressive State Capitol, is housed inside the 1870 US Mint building, where coins were made from Comstock silver. The museum holds a full-scale replica of a working mine, as well as displays on the natural history of Nevada and the Great Basin.

On the south side of Carson City, the **Nevada State Railroad Museum** preserves 60 steam engines and freight cars from the old Virginia & Truckee Railroad, which carried ore from

the Comstock Lode between 1869 and the 1930s. Later used in Hollywood films, the trains also offer excursions on summer weekends.

🏛 **Nevada State Museum**
600 N Carson St. **Tel** (775) 687-4810.
**Open** 8:30am–4:30pm Tue–Sun.
**Closed** Jan 1, Thanksg., Dec 25. ♿ ♿
🌐 museums.nevadaculture.org

🏛 **Nevada State Railroad Museum**
2180 S Carson St. **Tel** (775) 687-6953.
**Open** 9am–5pm Thu–Mon. **Closed** Jan 1, Thanksgiving, Dec 25. ♿ ♿
🌐 museums.nevadaculture.org

## ❸ Virginia City

🏙 1,000. ℹ 86 S C St, (800) 718-7587. 🌐 visitvirginiacitynv.com

Prospectors following the gold deposits up the slopes of Mount Davidson discovered one of the world's richest strikes, the Comstock Lode, in 1859. Almost overnight, the bustling camp of Virginia City grew into the largest settlement between Chicago and San Francisco. It had over 100 saloons and 25,000

Old-timers in a Wild West-themed saloon in Virginia City

residents, among whom was a journalist from Missouri who later became famous under the pseudonym Mark Twain.

Over the next 20 years, tons of gold and silver were mined here, but by the turn of the 20th century the town had begun to fade. However, the popular 1960s TV show *Bonanza* has given the city a new lease on life as one of Nevada's most enjoyable destinations. A National Historic Landmark, the city is located at an elevation of 6,220 ft (1,896 m). Its steep streets offer fine views of the surrounding mountains. The old main street, **C Street**, is packed with historic sites dotted alongside Wild West-themed saloons and souvenir shops. Up the hill along B Street, the elegant **Castle** is the state's best-preserved mansion. It was built in 1863–8 and in its heyday it was considered to be one of the finest mansions in the west. Although the interior is now closed to the public, you can still gain a glimpse of the amount of wealth that flowed through here in the 1860s.

The city's main historical museum fills the old **Fourth Ward School**, the Victorian Gothic landmark at the south end of C Street. It showcases the city's lively history with exhibits ranging from mining tools to Mark Twain, who began his career at the city's *Territorial Enterprise*. An intact classroom is preserved as it was in 1936, when the last class graduated.

🏫 **Fourth Ward School**
537 South C St. **Tel** (775) 847-0975.
**Open** May–Oct:10am–5pm daily.
**Closed** Nov–Apr. ♿ ♿
🌐 fourthwardschool.org

## ❹ Reno

🏙 190,000. ✈ 🚉 🚌 ℹ 4590 S Virginia St, (775) 687-7410.
🌐 visitrenotahoe.com

Self-proclaimed "The Biggest Little City in the World," Reno was Nevada's main gambling destination until it was surpassed by glitzy Las Vegas in the 1950s. The city also achieved national prominence

archway over Virginia Street in downtown Reno

the 1930s as a center for quick divorces. Although smaller than Las Vegas, Reno has a similar array of 24-hour-a-day casino-fueled fun. It also offers a huge variety of winter and outdoor activities, including 8 alpine ski resorts within the hour of Tahoe, dogsled tours, sleigh rides, sledding, snowshoeing, and cross-country skiing. The **Truckee River Whitewater Park** in downtown Reno is one of the premier white-water parks in the country, with 11 pools over a half-mile course. Kayaking, tubing, and rafting can be enjoyed by novice and experienced enthusiasts. All equipment is available for hire at the park.

The **National Automobile Museum**, on the south bank of the Truckee River, has one of the country's most extensive car collections. From early classics to 1960s hot rods, the museum – styled like a late-1940s Chrysler – showcases the cars in stage-set "streets" that provide evocative period backgrounds.

**🏄 Truckee River Whitewater Park**
Wingfield (off W 1st St).
**Tel** (775) 657-4634.

**🚗 National Automobile Museum**
10 S Lake St. **Tel** (775) 333-9300.
**Open** 9:30am–5:30pm Mon–Sat,
10am–4pm Sun. **Closed** Thanksgiving,
Dec 25. 🅿️ ♿ 🆆 automuseum.org

**Environs**
West of Reno, the startling beauty of **Lake Tahoe** (see p706) greets visitors at the Nevada/California border. Surrounded by summer resorts and winter ski areas, this is one of the most popular destinations in the western US.

## ❺ Great Basin National Park

ℹ️ 100 Great Basin Hwy, Baker, (775) 234-7331. **Open** 8am–4:30pm daily. **Closed** Jan 1, Thanksgiving, Dec 25. 🅿️ ♿ limited. 🆆 nps.gov/grba

Travelers driving along the "Loneliest Road in America" are beckoned by the towering silhouette of the 13,063-ft (3,982-m) Wheeler Peak which stands at the center of Great Basin National Park. Below the peak lies the park's centerpiece, the **Lehman Caves**, discovered when homesteader Absalom Lehman stumbled upon their small entrance in 1885. Their fantastic limestone formations, including thousands of stalactites and shields, can be seen on various guided tours that take place at intervals all through the day.

Tours start from the park visitor center, which offers hiking and camping details, along with exhibits on Great Basin's wildlife. The well-maintained **Wheeler Peak Scenic Drive** starts near the visitor center and passes through all the major Great Basin climate zones while climbing from 6,500 ft (1,982 m) to over 10,000 ft (3,048 m) in 12 steep miles (19 km). Great Basin National Park's remote location has made it one of the least-visited national parks in the country, so hikers and campers can find immense solitude among the limestone caves, alpine forests, ancient bristlecone pines, and glacial lakes.

Picturesque Wheeler Peak at Great Basin National Park

### The Loneliest Road in America

One of the country's most compelling drives, the Nevada portion of transcontinental US 50, stretching between Lake Tahoe in the west and Great Basin National Park on the Utah border, traverses over 400 miles (644 km) of corrugated country. Early explorers mapped this region, Pony Express riders raced across it, and the long-distance Lincoln Highway finally tamed it. But US 50 has long played second fiddle to busy I-80, the more popular route across the state. The Nevada Commission on Tourism now sponsors a tongue-in-cheek promotion where travelers on US 50 can get a certificate saying "I Survived the Loneliest Road in America."

Sign on US 50 highway

# Utah

Best known as world headquarters for the Mormon Church, Utah is also home to some of the most remarkable landscapes in the US. The inhospitably rugged sandstone canyons of the Colorado Plateau, which covers the southern half of the state, have been preserved within a series of unforgettably beautiful national parks, forests, and monuments. The towering snowcapped peaks of the Wasatch Mountains in the northern half of the state, a haven for skiers worldwide, played host to the 2000 Winter Olympics. West of the mountains sits the Mormon-dominated state capital Salt Lake City, Utah's only major city, bordered by its namesake lake.

Visitors looking out across the Great Salt Lake

## ❻ Salt Lake City

⛰ 181,700. ✈ 🚉 🚌 ℹ 90 South West Temple St, (801) 534-4900. Ⓦ visitsaltlake.com

Pleasant and friendly Salt Lake City makes a great stopover for weary travelers between Denver and San Francisco. Although its name derives from the undrinkable alkaline Great Salt Lake that spreads to the west, the city actually has abundant fresh water, thanks to the rain and snowmelt of the Wasatch Range, which rises to the east. Founded and controlled by the Mormons since 1847, the city spreads for miles and miles along the base of the snowcapped peaks.

Apart from its spectacular natural setting, Salt Lake City is known as the spiritual base of the Mormon church, which has its worldwide headquarters in Temple Square downtown. Here, the six spires of the main Mormon temple and the famous oblong auditorium of the **Mormon Tabernacle**, built in 1867, stand side by side. The

Mormon Tabernacle choir rehearsals are open to the public.

To the west of Temple Square, the amazing **Family History Library** holds records of Mormon family trees dating back to the mid-16th century. Eastward, the 1850 Beehive House has been preserved as it was when Mormon leader Brigham Young lived here. At its entrance stands the stately 76-ft (23-m) Eagle Gate, capped by a 4,000-pound (1,800 kg) eagle with an impressive wingspan of 20 ft (6 m). To the north, the domed **Utah State Capitol**, modeled after the US Capitol, features a series of exhibits on Utah's history.

**🏛 Mormon Tabernacle**
Temple Square. **Tel** (801) 240-1706. **Open** 9am–9pm daily. ♿
Ⓦ visittemplesquare.com

**🏛 Family History Library**
35 NW Temple St. **Tel** (866) 406-1830. **Open** 8am–5pm Mon, 8am–9pm Tue–Fri, 9am–5pm Sat. Always call in advance. **Closed** Sun, Jan 1, Jul 4, Thanksgiving, Dec 24, 25, 26. ♿
Ⓦ familysearch.org

## ❼ Great Salt Lake

Great Salt Lake State Park, I-80 exit 1C ℹ (801) 250-1898. **Open** Apr–Sep: sunrise–sunset daily; Oct–Mar: 9am–5pm daily. ♿ limited.

The largest salt lake in North America, the Great Salt Lake is a shallow remnant of the prehistoric Lake Bonneville. Depending on the weather, the lake covers an area ranging from 1,000 sq miles (2,590 sq km) to 2,500 sq miles (6,477 sq km). The salt flats stretching west from the lake to the Nevada border are so hard and expansive that they have long been used as a proving ground for automobile racers. Apart from some algae and microscopic brine shrimp, the lake itself supports almost no life. However, the **Antelope Island State Park**, located in the middle of the lake, is home to resident herds of bighorn sheep, mule deer, bison, and its namesake, the pronghorn antelope. Access to the island, lying about 40 miles (64 km) northwest of Salt Lake City, is by way of a 7-mile (11-km) long causeway. Visitors can camp or swim along the shore or take guided lake cruises.

West from Salt Lake City, toward the lake's south shore, the **Great Salt Lake State Park** offers a broad, sandy beach with a marina and observation deck.

**🦌 Antelope Island State Park**
I-15 exit 335. **Tel** (801) 773-2941. **Ope** Oct–Apr: 6am–6pm daily; May–Sep: 6am–10pm daily. 🅿 ♿ limited.

The impressive "Eagle Gate" looking toward the Utah State Capitol

*For hotels and restaurants see pp550–55*

# Park City

7,300. 🛈 1794 Olympic Parkway
528 Main Street, (435) 649-6100.
🖵 visitparkcity.com

hour's drive east from down-
wn Salt Lake City, through the
asatch Mountains, leads to this
pular resort. The city started
e in the 1860s as a silver mining
mp and still retains several
rn-of-20th-century buildings
ong its photogenic Main Street.
rk City has become world-
mous as the home of the
estigious **Sundance Film
stival**. Founded by actor and
rector Robert Redford in 1981,
e annual festival focuses on
dependent and documentary
ms and has become America's
remost venue for innovative
nema. The festival's popularity
linked to Park City's excellent
iing facilities, showcased in
e 2000 Winter Olympics.
sense of the town's history
an be obtained at **Park City
useum** in the old City Hall.

🏛 **Park City Museum**
528 Main St. **Tel** (435) 649-7457. **Open**
10am–7pm Mon–Sat, noon–6pm Sun
(May & Nov: 11am–5pm Mon–Sat,
noon–6pm Sun). **Closed** Jan 1, Thnksg.,
Dec 25. 🚻 ltd. 🖵 **parkcityhistory.org**

## 🔵 Timpanogos Cave National Monument

Hwy 92, American Fork. **Tel** (801) 756-
5238. **Open** mid-May–mid-Sep: times
vary; call ahead. **Closed** mid-Sep–
mid-May. 🅿 🖵 **nps.gov/tica**

One of the the most popular
destinations around Salt Lake
City, the Timpanogos Cave
National Monument lies deep
beneath the 11,750-ft (3,581-m)
summit of Mount Timpanogos.
The site preserves a trio of
massive limestone caverns
stretching nearly 1,800 ft (549
m) deep into the mountain.
Reached by way of a steep,
1.5 mile (2 km) uphill hike from
the visitor center, and linked
by man-made tunnels, the

Scenic view along Alpine Loop following
Highway 92

three caves are very cool
(43° F/ 6° C), very damp, and
full of spectacular limestone
formations. Electric lights
showcase the sundry stalactites,
stalagmites, crystalline helictites,
and other water-sculpted
formations, all of which are
still being formed. Only a
limited number of people
are allowed inside, so visitors
should come early in the day
or during the week, or call
ahead for reservations.

Timpanogos Cave is one
of the many highlights of the
drive along the 40-mile (64-km)
**Alpine Loop**, which follows
Highway 92 around the
landmark mountain. Many
campgrounds, picnic spots,
scenic views, and hiking trails
can be enjoyed by trekkers
along the way.

storic houses lining Main Street in Park City

## The Mormons

The Church of Jesus Christ of Latter Day Saints, a large Christian denomination,
was founded by Joseph Smith (1805–44), a farm worker from New York State.
In 1820 Smith claimed to have seen visions of the Angel Moroni, who led him
to a set of golden tablets, which he translated and later published as the
*Book of Mormon*, thus establishing the Mormon Church. Although this new
faith grew rapidly, it attracted hostility because of its political and economic
beliefs, and the practice of polygamy. Seeking refuge, the Mormons moved
to Illinois in 1839, where Smith was killed by an angry mob. Leadership passed
to Brigham Young, who led the members on an arduous journey west, in the
hope of escaping persecution and setting up a safe haven in the unpromising
landscape of Salt Lake Valley. The pioneers traveled across bleak prairies and
mountains in primitive wagons, braving the fierce weather. Young's followers
finally established successful farming communities across Utah's wilderness.
Today, Mormons form 60 percent of Utah's population.

Portrait of Brigham Young
(1801–77)

# ⑩ Arches National Park

Arches National Park has the the highest concentration of natural sandstone arches in the world. More than 80 of these natural wonders have formed over millions of years. The park "floats" on a salt bed, which once liquefied under the pressure exerted by the rock above it. About 300 million years ago, this salt layer bulged upward, cracking the sandstone above. Over time the cracks eroded, leaving long "fins" of rock. As these fins eroded, the hard overhead rock formed arches, which range today from the solid-looking Turret Arch to the graceful Delicate and Landscape Arches.

**Devil's Garden**
This area contains several of the park's most beautiful arches, including Landscape Arch, a slender curve of sandstone more than 300 ft (91 m) long, which is thought to be the longest natural arch in the world.

**Sunset Watch at Delicate Arch**
A natural amphitheater surrounds the arch, creating seating from which vistas of the La Sal Mountains are framed.

**The Windows Section**
*In the park's Windows Section, a one-mile loop trail leads to Turret Arch, then the North and South Windows Arches, located side by side. With excellent viewing spots available, many visitors photograph the North and South arches framed by the sandstone Turner Arch, as seen here.*

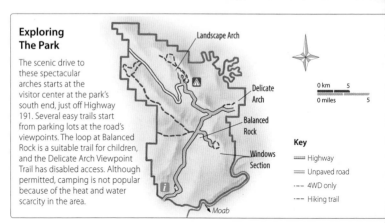

## Exploring The Park

The scenic drive to these spectacular arches starts at the visitor center at the park's south end, just off Highway 191. Several easy trails start from parking lots at the road's viewpoints. The loop at Balanced Rock is a suitable trail for children, and the Delicate Arch Viewpoint Trail has disabled access. Although permitted, camping is not popular because of the heat and water scarcity in the area.

Landscape Arch

Delicate Arch

Balanced Rock

Windows Section

Moab

0 km 5
0 miles 5

### Key

▬▬ Highway
═══ Unpaved road
--- 4WD only
--- Hiking trail

**For keys to symbols** *see back flap*

**Delicate Arch**
The most celebrated of all the
arches here, and a state symbol,
Delicate Arch appears on many
Utah license plates. It is reached
by a moderate 45-minute walk
over sandstone.

## VISITORS' CHECKLIST

**Practical Information**
*i* **Tel** (435) 719-2299.
Center: **Open** Apr–Oct:
8am–6pm daily; Nov–Mar:
8am–4:30pm daily. ♿ ♿
(campground, Park Avenue
Viewpoint, Delicate Arch
Viewpoint Trail & Balanced Rock
Trail.) 📷 📷 ⛺
w nps.gov/arch

**Arches are formed** through
a process that takes millions
of years; today's arches
continue to erode and
will eventually collapse.

**Balanced Rock**
This precariously balanced
boulder atop a sandstone spire is
one of the park's landmarks. Good
views are available from the trail
as well as the scenic road route.

Western-style, timber-clad gift store on
Main Street, Moab

## ⓫ Moab

🏠 6500. *i* Main & Center Sts, (435)
259-8825. **www**.discovermoab.com

A town of dramatic ups and
downs, Moab is currently riding
its second great boom since
the 1950s. Once a quiet
Mormon settlement, the
discovery in 1952 of several
major uranium deposits
outside town made Moab
one of America's wealthiest
communities. When the
uranium market declined in
the 1970s, the town was saved
by tourism and its proximity
to Arches and Canyonlands
National Parks. Many movies,
including some John Wayne
Westerns and the Indiana
Jones classics were shot here.

Today, Moab is a top
destination for lovers of the
outdoors. Mountain bikers
come here for the challenging
ride from Moab Rim, reached
by Moab Skyway, a scenic tram
ride offering panoramic views
of the area. Numerous hiking
trails and 4WD routes take in
some of this region's fabulous
landscapes. Moab is also a
major center for white-water
rafting on the Colorado River.
**Matheson Wetlands Preserve**
off Kane Creek Boulevard
has 2 miles (3 km) of hiking
trails along a riverside
wetland, home to birds and
indigenous wildlife.

🏞 **Matheson Wetlands Preserve**
Off Kane Creek Blvd. **Tel** (435) 259-
4629. **Open** dawn–dusk daily. ♿

**Park Avenue and the Courthouse Towers**
The large, rock monoliths known as Courthouse Towers bear an
uncanny resemblance to city skyscrapers. They can be seen from Park
Avenue, an easy, short trail.

*For hotels and restaurants see pp550–55*

# ⓬ Canyonlands National Park

Millions of years ago, the Colorado and Green Rivers cut winding paths deep into rock, creating a labyrinth of rocky canyons that form the heart of this stunning wilderness. At its center, the rivers' confluence divides the park's 527 sq miles (1,365 sq km) into three districts – the Needles, the Maze, and the grassy plateau of the Island in the Sky. Established as a national park in 1964, Canyonlands is growing in popularity. Most wilderness travel here requires a permit.

**VISITORS' CHECKLIST**

**Practical Information**
ℹ️ 2282 South West Resource Blvd, Moab, (435) 719-2313.
**Open** visitor center: 8am–5pm daily (longer late Mar–late Oct).
**Closed** Jan 1, Thanksgiving, Dec 25. 🅿️ ♿ 📷 🏕️ ⛰️
ⓦ nps.gov/cany

**Mesa Arch**
An easy and rewarding 500-yard (455-m) trail leads to Mesa Arch, a long, low curve of stone that perfectly frames the snowcapped La Sal Mountains in the distance.

**Key**
═══ Highway
▬▬▬ 4WD only
▪ ▪ ▪ Hiking route
——— National Park boundary

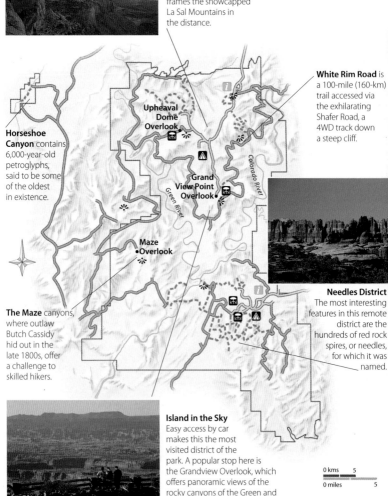

**White Rim Road** is a 100-mile (160-km) trail accessed via the exhilarating Shafer Road, a 4WD track down a steep cliff.

**Upheaval Dome Overlook**

**Horseshoe Canyon** contains 6,000-year-old petroglyphs, said to be some of the oldest in existence.

**Grand View Point Overlook**

Colorado River

Green River

**Maze Overlook**

**Needles District**
The most interesting features in this remote district are the hundreds of red rock spires, or needles, for which it was named.

**The Maze** canyons, where outlaw Butch Cassidy hid out in the late 1800s, offer a challenge to skilled hikers.

**Island in the Sky**
Easy access by car makes this the most visited district of the park. A popular stop here is the Grandview Overlook, which offers panoramic views of the rocky canyons of the Green and Colorado Rivers.

0 kms   5
0 miles   5

The deep crevices of the canyons in the wide valley around Green River

# ⑬ Green River

🏔 1,000. 🚹 885 E Main St, (435) 564-3427. **Open** Apr–Oct: 8am–8pm; Nov–Mar: 8am–5pm daily.

Located in a broad, bowl-shaped valley, the town grew around a ford of the wild Green River in the 19th and early 20th centuries. Today, it is a launching spot for white-water rafting on the Green and Colorado Rivers.

The **John Wesley Powell River History Museum** at Green River has 20,000 sq ft (1,860 sq m) of displays tracing the history of the area's exploration. Principally it examines the surveying and discoveries made by American geologist and ethnologist John Wesley Powell (1834–1902).

🏛 **John Wesley Powell River History Museum**
1765 E Main St. **Tel** (435) 564-3427. **Open** Apr–Oct: 8am–7pm daily; Nov–Mar: call for hours. **Closed** public hols.
📷 ☑ 🆆 jwprhm.com

# ⑭ Hovenweep National Monument

E of Hwy 191. **Tel** (970) 562-4282. **Open** 8am–5pm daily (to 6pm May–Sep). **Closed** Jan 1, Thanksgiving, Dec 25. 📷 ☑ ⚠ 🆆 nps.gov/hove

The six separate sets of ruins at this Ancestral Puebloan site were discovered by W.D. Huntington, leader of a Mormon expedition, in 1854. The culture at Hovenweep, a Ute word meaning "Deserted Valley," reached its peak between 1200 and 1275. Little is known

of the Utes beyond the clues found in the round, square, and D-shaped towers, and pottery and tools that they left behind.

Researchers have speculated that the towers might have been built as defensive fortifications, astronomical observatories, storage silos, or as religious structures for the entire community.

# ⑮ Lake Powell & Glen Canyon National Recreation Area

2 miles (3 km) N of Page on Hwy 98, off Hwy 160. 🚻 🚹 Carl Hayden Visitor Center, (928) 608-6404. **Open** Apr–Oct: 8am–5pm daily; Nov–Mar: 8am–4:30pm daily. ♿ visitor center only. 📷 🅿 🚽 🏕 ⚠ Page & Wahweap only. 🆆 nps.gov/glca, lakepowell.com

The Glen Canyon National Recreation Area (NRA), established in 1972, covers more than one million acres (400,000 ha)

of dramatic desert and canyon country around the 185-mile (298-km) long Lake Powell, named after John Wesley Powell. The lake was created by damming the Colorado River and its tributaries to supply electricity to the region's growing population.

The construction of the Glen Canyon Dam, completed in 1963, was controversial from the start. The spirited campaign, led by the environmentalist Sierra Club, continues to argue for the restoration of Glen Canyon, believing that ancient ecosystems are being ruined. Pro-dam advocates, however, firmly believe in its ability to store water, generate power, and provide recreation.

The "Y"-shaped recreation area follows the San Juan River east almost to the town of Mexican Hat, and heads northeast along the Colorado toward Canyonlands National Park. Within the area is the **Antelope Canyon**, a famously deep "slot" canyon. Other highlights include Lees Ferry, a 19th-century Mormon settlement that now offers tourist facilities, and the **Rainbow Bridge National Monument**. Rising 309 ft (94 m), this is the largest natural bridge in the world.

Today, the lake is busy with water-sports enthusiasts and houseboat parties, exploring the myriad sandstone side canyons. Glen Canyon is also one of the most popular hiking, biking, and 4WD destinations in the country.

Rose-colored sandstone of Antelope Canyon, in Glen Canyon NRA

## ⑯ Capitol Reef National Park

10 miles (16 km) E of Torrey, Hwy 24.
ℹ️ (435) 425-3791. **Open** Jun–Sep:
8am–6pm daily; Oct–May: 8am–
4:30pm daily. **Closed** public holidays.
🖼️ ♿ 📷 ⛰️ **W** nps.gov/care

Covering 378 sq miles
(980 sq km), this spectacular
park encloses a 100-mile
(160-km) long, colorful wall of
rock that was thrust up by the
earth 65 million years ago. The
strata that buckled upward
folded back on itself, trapping
water in the process. Around
100 years ago, prospectors
crossing the desert were forced
to stop at this wind-carved
Waterpocket Fold. They likened
the rock barrier to an ocean reef
and thought its round white
domes looked just like the US
Capitol building, hence the
park's name.

An adventurous drive along
the partly unpaved Notom-
Bullfrog Road provides a good
overview of the area. Cars can
negotiate the road in dry
weather, but extra gas and water
are essential. Capitol Gorge, to
the north, can be reached via a
scenic route, extending about
10 miles (16 km) into the heart
of the park. Guided walking tours
are available during summer, but
be aware that only experienced
hikers should attempt to
explore the backcountry here.

To the north lies the 1908
**Gifford Farmhouse**. Now a
cultural center, it is dedicated to
the 1880s Mormon settlement

that once flourished here.
Fremont Canyon, on its right,
features the famous Fremont
Petroglyphs, created by the
Ancestral Puebloans between
700 and 1250. Farther north is
the Cathedral Valley, named for
the rock monoliths that tower
over the desert.

## ⑰ Grand Staircase– Escalante National Monument

ℹ️ 755 W Main St, Escalante, (435)
826-5499. **Open** Mar–Oct: 8:30am–
4:30pm daily; Nov–Apr: 8:30am–
4:30pm Mon–Fri. **W** ut.blm.gov/
monument

Established by President Clinton
in 1996, this monument
encompasses 3,000 sq miles
(7,700 sq km) of pristine rock
canyons, mountains, and high
desert plateaus. It was named for
its four 12-million-year-old cliff
faces that rise in tiered steps
across the Colorado
Plateau. To preserve
its wild state, no
new roads, facilities,
or campgrounds
are being built here.
This vast untamed
area is best explored
on scenic drives
combined with day-long hikes.
About 9 miles (14 km) south of
Highway 12 stands **Kodachrome
Basin State Park**, a distinctive
landscape noted for its 67 free-
standing sand pipes or rock
chimneys, formed millions of
years ago as geyser vents.

**Vintage wagon outside Cedar City's museum**

🗺️ **Kodachrome Basin State Park**
**Tel** (435) 679-8562. **Open** dawn–dusk
daily. 🖼️ 📷 ⛺ ⛰️

## ⑱ Bryce Canyon National Park

*See pp518–19.*

## ⑲ Cedar City

🏔️ 20,500. ✈️ 🚌 ℹ️ 581 N Main St,
(435) 586-5124. **W** utah.com/
cedarcity

Founded by Mormons in 1851,
Cedar City developed as a
center for mining and smelting
iron. The Frontier Homestead
State Park Museum offers a
glimpse of this pioneering spirit
and features a large collection
of early vehicles. The town offers
a choice of hotels within an
hour's drive of Zion National
Park. Cedar City is popular for its
annual Shakespeare Festival,
staged in a replica of London's
Globe Theatre. East of town,
the spectacular
**Cedar Breaks
National
Monument**
features lime-
stone cliffs and a
lake topped by a
deep green forest.
In winter, the area is
a popular skiing resort.

🏕️ **Cedar Breaks National
Monument**
**Tel** (435) 586-9451. **Open** daily.
Visitor Center: **Open** late May–mid-
Oct: 9am–6pm daily. 📷
**W** nps.gov/cebr

Fishing in the lake at Cedar Breaks National Monument, near Cedar City

*For hotels and restaurants see pp550–55*

# ⑳ Zion National Park

At the heart of this beautiful national park lies Zion Canyon, perhaps the most popular of all of Utah's natural wonders. It was carved by the powerful waters of the Virgin River and then widened, sculpted, and reshaped by wind, rain, and ice. Its majestic walls rise up to 2,000 ft (600 m) and are shaped into jagged peaks and formations in shades of red and white. Wild meadows and luxuriant foliage along the river account for the area's abundant wildlife. The park shuttle is the only way into the canyon. A number of short walks, beginning at the shuttle stops, follow marked trails to the tough 16-mile (26-km) hike through the canyon and involves wading through the river.

### VISITORS' CHECKLIST

**Practical Information**
Hwy 9, near Springdale. **ℹ** Zion Canyon Visitor Center, (435) 772-3256. **Open** mid-Apr–mid-Oct: 8am–6pm daily (to 7:30pm in summer); mid-Oct–mid-Apr: 8am–5pm daily. 🅿 ♿ partial.
🗌 🗌 ⚠ **W** nps.gov/zion

The spectacular Zion–
Mt. Carmel Highway

### Zion Canyon

The Virgin River meanders quietly through banks of wildflowers, cotton-wood, oak, and willow trees, which grow beneath the sloping walls of the canyon. Be aware that sudden summer rainstorms may cause floods, so visitors are advised to check conditions first.

### Hiking

Numerous guided walking and hiking tours of Zion's geology and history leave daily from the visitor center. Emerald Pools Trail and Canyon Overlook Trail are particularly popular trails.

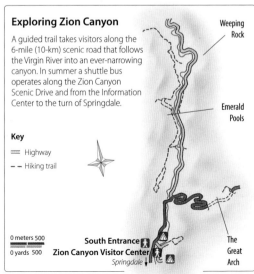

### Exploring Zion Canyon

A guided trail takes visitors along the 6-mile (10-km) scenic road that follows the Virgin River into an ever-narrowing canyon. In summer a shuttle bus operates along the Zion Canyon Scenic Drive and from the Information Center to the turn of Springdale.

**Key**

═══ Highway

– – Hiking trail

Weeping
Rock

Emerald
Pools

0 meters 500
0 yards 500

**South Entrance** 🧍
**Zion Canyon Visitor Center** 🧍
*Springdale* ↓

The
Great
Arch

**For keys to symbols** *see back flap*

# ⓲ Bryce Canyon National Park

A series of deep amphitheaters filled with flame-colored rock formations called hoodoos are the hallmark of Bryce Canyon National Park. Bryce is high in altitude, reaching elevations of 6,000–8,000 ft (1,829–2,438 m), with an 18-mile (30-km) scenic road running along the rim of Paunsaugunt Plateau. Highlights include views of vast fields of pink, orange, and red spires; the Paiute Indians, once hunters here, described them as "red rocks standing like men in a bowl-shaped recess." The canyon's maze of pillars and channels is best appreciated on foot.

**Sunrise Point**
From this lookout it is easy to see why early settler and Mormon farmer Ebenezer Bryce, after whom the park is named, called it "a helluva place to lose a cow."

PINK CLIFFS

Moss Cave

0 kilometers 2
0 miles 2

**Navajo Loop**
This 1.4-mile (2-km) round-trip trail zigzags sharply down the cliff face for 500 ft (150 m) to finish in a slow meander among slot canyons and rock stands. The climb back up the trail is particularly strenuous.

**KEY**

① **Sunset Point** is one of the major lookouts in Bryce Canyon. In spite of its name it faces east, so while sunrises can be spectacular here, sunsets can be a little anticlimactic.

② **Queen's Garden Trail**

③ **Fairyland Point**

**Thor's Hammer**
Carved into the pink cliffs of the highest "step" of the Grand Staircase *(see p516)*, this unusual landscape consists of eroded sandstone. Hoodoos such as Thor's Hammer are formed as rain and wind erode "fins" of harder rock that become columns, then further erode into strangely shaped hoodoos. The high altitude, ice, and wind continue the "carving" process today.

### Bryce Amphitheater
This panoramic vista of snow-covered rock spires is among the most popular views of the park. In both winter and summer the amphitheater is best seen from Inspiration Point.

### Natural Bridge
This graceful natural bridge is located a few yards from the park's scenic highway. It frames a picturesque view of the distant valley below. Officially, it is a natural arch and not a bridge, as it was formed not by a river but by the same natural forces (of wind, rain, and ice) that created the park's hoodoos.

### Agua Canyon
This overlook features some of the most delicate and beautiful of the park's formations, as well as a good view of the layered pink sandstone cliffs typical of the Paunsaugunt Plateau.

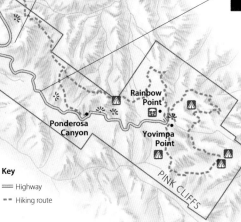

**Bryce Point**

**PINK CLIFFS**

**Swamp Canyon Butte**

**Noon Canyon Butte**

**Rainbow Point**

**Ponderosa Canyon**

**Yovimpa Point**

**PINK CLIFFS**

**Key**
— Highway
-- Hiking route

### Utah Prairie Dog
Now threatened, the Utah prairie dog lives only in southern Utah; those living in the park today constitute the largest remaining group.

*For hotels and restaurants see pp550–55*

# Arizona

Often referred to as the Grand Canyon State after its most famous sight, Arizona offers a range of stunning natural beauty. Its southwest corner features the hostile but eerily beautiful Sonoran Desert, bordered by the state's economic hub, Phoenix, and the city of Tucson. To the north, the landscape changes, rising through high desert plateaus, toward canyons and mountains, the romanticized "Wild West" of cowboy films. Here, the city of Flagstaff and the picturesque towns of Sedona and Jerome attract thousands of visitors. Over 25 percent of Arizona is Native American reservation land. The state also houses several Ancient Puebloan ruins.

London Bridge spanning a man-made waterway in Lake Havasu City

## ㉑ Lake Havasu City

🗺 45,000. ✈ 🚌 ℹ 314 London Bridge Rd, (928) 453-3444.
Ⓦ golakehavasu.com

California businessman Robert McCulloch founded Lake Havasu City in 1964. The resort city he built on the Colorado River was popular with the landlocked citizens of Arizona. His real brainwave, however, came four years later when he bought London Bridge and painstakingly transported it stone-by-stone from England to Lake Havasu. Some mocked McCulloch, suggesting that he had thought he was buying London's Gothic Tower Bridge, not this more ordinary one. There was more hilarity when it appeared that there was nothing in Havasu City for the bridge to span. Undaunted, McCulloch simply created the waterway he needed by digging a channel to divert water from Lake Havasu. Today, Lake Havasu City is one of the most visited outdoor recreation areas in Arizona, attracting families and sports enthusiasts alike.

## ㉒ Flagstaff

🗺 58,000. ✈ 🚉 Amtrak Flagstaff Station, 1 E Rte 66. 🚌 Flagstaff bus station, 399 S Malpais Lane.
ℹ Amtrak depot, 1 E Rte 66, (928) 774-9541. **Open** 8am–5pm Mon–Sat, 9am–4pm Sun. **Closed** public hols.
🎭 Flagstaff Festival of the Arts (early Jul–mid-Aug).
Ⓦ flagstaffarizona.org

Nestling among the pine forests of northern Arizona's San Francisco Peaks, Flagstaff is one of the region's most attractive towns. Its historic downtown, an attractive ensemble of red-brick buildings housing bars and restaurants, dates from the 1890s, when the town developed as a lumber center.

Flagstaff's lively café society owes much to the students of the **Northern Arizona University**, home to two campus art galleries. The Beasley Gallery holds temporary exhibitions and student work, while the Northern Arizona University Art Museum has the permanent Weiss collection, which includes works by the Mexican artist Diego Rivera.

Situated on Mars Hill is the 1894 **Lowell Observatory**, named for its benefactor, Percival Lowell, a member of one of Boston's wealthiest families. Lowell wanted to look for life on Mars and although he did not succeed, the observatory earned repute with its documented evidence of an expanding universe, along with the discovery of Pluto by astronomer Clyde Tombaugh.

A few miles northwest of downtown, set picturesquely in a pine forest, is the **Museum of Northern Arizona**. It holds one of the Southwest's most comprehensive collections of Southwestern archaeological artifacts, as well as fine art and natural science exhibits. The museum presents an excellent overview of Anasazi history and contemporary Navajo, Hopi, and Pai cultures.

The collections are arranged in a series of galleries around a central courtyard. The Archaeology Gallery provides a fine introduction to the region's historic cultures. The award-winning anthropology exhibition in the Ethnology Gallery documents 12,000 years of Hopi, Zuni, Navajo, and Pai tribal cultures on the Colorado Plateau. The museum shop sells Native American arts and crafts. A section has exhibits that focus on the variety of plants and animals found on the Colorado Plateau through the ages.

🏛 **Museum of Northern Arizona**
3101 N Fort Valley Rd. **Tel** (928) 774-5213. **Open** 9am–5pm daily.
**Closed** public hols. 🚭 ♿ 📷
Ⓦ musnaz.org

Native American exhibits, Museum of Northern Arizona in Flagstaff

# ㉓ Heart of Arizona Tour

The Verde River passes through the wooded hills and fertile meadows of central Arizona, before opening into a wide, green valley between Flagstaff and Phoenix. The heart of Arizona is full of charming towns such as Sedona, hidden away among stunning scenery, and the former mining town of Jerome. Over the hills lies Prescott, once the state capital and now a busy, likable little town with a center full of dignified Victorian buildings. The area's ancient history can be seen in its two beautiful pueblo ruins, Montezuma Castle and Tuzigoot.

## Tips for Drivers

**Recommended route:** From Sedona, take Hwy 89A to Tuzigoot, Jerome, & Prescott. Hwy 69 runs east from Prescott to Interstate Hwy 17, which connects to Camp Verde, Fort Verde, & Montezuma Castle.
**Tour length:** 85 miles (137 km).
**When to go:** Spring & fall are delightful; summer is very hot.

① **Sedona** Set among dramatic red rock hills, Sedona is a popular resort, known for its New Age stores and galleries as well as for its friendly ambience.

### Key

▬ Tour route
═ Other road

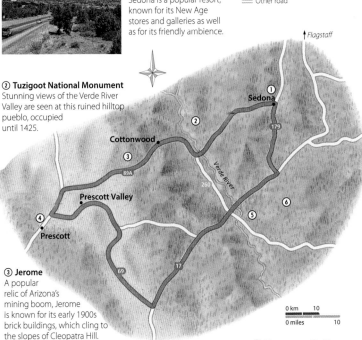

↑ Flagstaff

② **Tuzigoot National Monument** Stunning views of the Verde River Valley are seen at this ruined hilltop pueblo, occupied until 1425.

Cottonwood

Prescott Valley

④ Prescott

③ **Jerome** A popular relic of Arizona's mining boom, Jerome is known for its early 1900s brick buildings, which cling to the slopes of Cleopatra Hill.

↓ Phoenix

0 km 10
0 miles 10

⑥ **Montezuma Castle National Monument** The Ancestral Puebloan ruins here date from the 1100s and occupy one of the loveliest sites in the Southwest.

④ **Prescott** This cool hilltop town is set among the rugged peaks and lush woods of Prescott National Forest, making it a popular center for many outdoor activities.

⑤ **Camp Verde** A highlight of this little town is Fort Verde. Built by the US Army in 1865, this stone fort is manned by costumed guides.

## ㉔ Phoenix

🏔 1,300,000 (city only). ✈ 🚌
Greyhound Bus, 2115 E Buckeye Rd.
ℹ️ 50 North 2nd St, (602) 254-6500.
⛳ The PGA's Phoenix Golf Open (Jan).
🌐 visitphoenix.com

Stretching across the entire Salt River Valley, Arizona's capital, Phoenix, started out as a farming town in the 1860s and soon developed into the economic hub of the state. As it grew, it gradually absorbed the surrounding towns of Scottsdale, Mesa, and Tempe, and now has over a million people within the city and almost three million in Metropolitan Phoenix. Downtown Phoenix has many historic attractions while the metropolitan area, famed for the design studio Taliesin West, is also popular with tourists for its spas and resorts during the warm winter months.

### Exploring Downtown Phoenix

Downtown, where the city began in the 19th century, covers a few blocks east and west of Central Avenue and north and south of Washington Street. Washington Street houses the copper-domed **Arizona Capitol Museum**, originally the state legislature. The museum documents the state's political history.

More glimpses of the city's history can be seen in the attractive restored Victorian houses on the tree-lined **Heritage Square**, some of

Kachina doll, Heard Museum

which have been converted into tearooms and small museums. **Rosson House**, built in 1895 and decorated with period furnishings, is open to visitors. In the historic Stevens House, the small **Arizona Toy and Doll Museum** exhibits changing displays of historic dolls, furnished dollhouses, and toys.

Adjacent to these historic attractions stands the ultramodern **Arizona Science Center**, with over 300 interactive science exhibits offering virtual reality trips through the human body.

A short drive north of downtown leads to the highly acclaimed **Phoenix Art Museum**, renowned for its stimulating temporary exhibitions. The second floor houses works by 18th- and 19th-century American artists, particularly those connected with the Southwest. Among the exhibits are works by Georgia O'Keeffe and Gilbert Stuart, whose celebrated *Portrait of George Washington* (1796) is seen on every dollar bill.

The **Heard Museum**, farther north, was founded in 1929 by Dwight Heard, a wealthy rancher and newspaper tycoon, whose wife, Maie, amassed an extraordinary collection of Native Southwestern American art. The museum exhibits over 40,000 works, but its star attraction is the display of more than 500 *kachina* dolls. Apart from dolls, there's an award-winning display of Native American pottery, jewelry, and

textiles called Home: Native Peoples In The Southwest. The Sandra Day O'Connor Gallery displays temporary exhibitions.

### 🏛 Heard Museum
2301 North Central Ave. **Tel** (602) 252-8840. ℹ️ (602) 252-8848. **Open** 9:30am–5pm Mon–Sat, 11am–5pm Sun. **Closed** Dec 25. ♿ 🅿️ 📷 📚 🌐 heard.org

### Environs

About 7 miles (11 km) east of downtown is **Papago Park** with its distinctive red rock formations, outdoor activities, and museums. Immediately south of the park, the **Hall of Flame Fire Museum** houses a large collection of firefighting equipment dating from the early 1700s. In the center of Papago Park, the **Desert Botanical Garden** displays 4,000 arid plant species, including 139 that are rare, threatened, or endangered. A few miles north of Papago Park lies the former town of **Scottsdale**, founded in the late 19th century. Replete with air-conditioned malls, designer stores, hotels, cafés, and restaurants, it is also famous for its world-class golf courses. Scottsdale's quiet, tree-lined streets and desert setting attracted the visionary architect Frank Lloyd Wright *(see p394)* to establish his winter studio **Taliesin West** here in 1937. The 600-acre (240-ha) complex is now an architecture school and a working design studio. The muted tones of its low-lying buildings and use of local stone for irregular walls reflects Wright's enthusiasm for the desert setting.

The **Cosanti Foundation**, 4 miles (6 km) west of Taliesin West, was established by the Italian architect and student of Wright, Paolo Soleri (1919–2013), to

Arizona State Capitol Museum

The 1900 façade of the Arizona State Capitol Building, Phoenix

*For hotels and restaurants see pp550–55*

The unique Taliesin West, designed to blend with the desert landscape

further his study of what he termed "arcology": a combination of architecture and ecology to create new urban habitats. Today, the site consists of simple, low structures housing studios, a gallery, and craft workshops, where Soleri's workers make and sell their trademark windbells and cast bronzes.

South of the Cosanti Foundation is the **Camelback Mountain**, named for its humped shape. One of Phoenix's most distinctive landmarks, the mountain is a granite and sandstone outcrop formed by prehistoric volcanic forces. A steep climb, covering 1,200 ft (366 m) in the space of just over a mile, leads to the summit.

More glimpses of the area's Native American past can be found at the **Pueblo Grande Museum**. Located next to the ruins of a 1,500-year-old Hohokam settlement, it is dedicated to the study and understanding of the people who lived there from the 8th to the 14th centuries. Full-scale reproductions of original adobe Hohokam homes can be viewed along the museum trail, as well as some of the ancient artifacts such as cooking utensils and pottery. Many of these pieces come from the Archaeological Park, site of the settlement, originally excavated in 1887. The museum operates a varied program of educational workshops and activities, for both adults and children, to promote its mission of enhancing an understanding of the Hohokam culture.

## Sights at a Glance

① Arizona State Capitol Museum
② Heritage Square
③ Rosson House
④ Arizona Toy and Doll Museum
⑤ Arizona Science Center
⑥ Phoenix Art Museum
⑦ Heard Museum

Innovative design of the Cosanti Foundation gift shop, Scottsdale

**For keys to symbols** *see back flap*

# ㉙ Tucson

🏙 750,000. ✈ 🚉 Amtrak Station,
400 E Toole Ave. 🚌 Greyhound Lines,
2 S 4th Ave. ℹ 100 S Church Ave,
(520) 624-1817, (800) 638-8350.
🎭 La Fiesta de los Vaqueros (late
Feb); Tucson Folk Music Festival (May).
**W** visittucson.org

The second largest city in
Arizona, Tucson (pronounced
too-sahn) is located on the
northern boundary of the
Sonoran Desert, in a basin
surrounded by five mountain
ranges. The town's Colonial past
dates to the 1770s, when strong
resistance from the local Tohono
O'odham and Pima
Native tribes forced the
Spanish to move their
regional fortress, or
presidio, from nearby
Tubac to Tucson.

The city's main
sights are clustered
around the
University of Arizona
campus and the
historic downtown
area. The **Barrio** and
**El Presidio** historic
districts are located here. El
Presidio occupies the area
where the original Spanish
fortress was built. Today, many
of the historic buildings have
been converted into
restaurants, shops, and offices.
Five of El Presidio's oldest
dwellings, including the J. Knox
Corbett House, are located in
the Historic Block. They form a
part of the **Tucson Museum of**

**Stained-glass window in
St. Augustine Cathedral**

**Art**, with its excellent collection
of pre-Columbian artifacts, and
exhibitions of contemporary
American and European work.
Southeast of the museum, the
Pima County Courthouse, built
in 1927, is a fine example of
Spanish Colonial Revival style.

The **St. Augustine Cathedral**,
with its imposing sandstone
façade, is southwest of El
Presidio. Begun in 1896, the
cathedral is modeled after the
Spanish Colonial style of the
Cathedral of Querétaro in
central Mexico. The Barrio
Historic District, farther south,
was once a business district.
Today, its quiet streets
are lined with brightly
painted adobe
houses. On nearby
Main Street is the
"wishing shrine" of
El Tiradito, where a
young man was
killed as a
consequence of a
lovers' triangle. The
locals believe that if a
candle lit here burns
through a night,
their wishes will come true.

The University of Arizona
campus houses several
museums. The most notable is
the **Arizona State Museum**,
renowned for its collections of
artifacts covering 2,000 years of
Native history. Beyond downtown, Metropolitan Tucson
extends into the surrounding
mountain ranges. **Mount
Lemmon** (9,157 ft/2,790 m),

the highest peak, is to the north,
while to the west is one part of
the Saguaro National Park (the
other is to the east), where
vistas of the tall saguaro cacti
can be seen.

About 14 miles (22 km)
west of the university lies the
fascinating **Arizona-Sonora
Desert Museum**. Covering more
than 21 acres (8.5 ha), it includes
a botanical garden, zoo, and
natural history museum with
displays describing the history,
geology, and flora and fauna of
the Sonoran Desert.

Nearby is the **Old Tucson
Studios**, a Wild West theme park
originally built as a set for a
Western movie in 1939. Some
of Hollywood's most famous
Westerns, such as *Gunfight at
the OK Corral* (1957) and *Rio
Bravo* (1958) were filmed here.

The Southwest's oldest and
best preserved Mission church
lies south of Tucson. The **San
Xavier del Bac Mission**,
completed in 1797 by
Franciscan missionaries, is built
of adobe brick and is considered
the finest example of Spanish
Colonial architecture in the US.
Its highlights include an ornate
Baroque façade decorated with
carved figures of saints, a
glorious painted ceiling,
and a spectacular main altar.

🏛 **San Xavier del Bac Mission**
1950 W San Xavier Rd, 10 miles (16 km)
S of Tucson on I-19. **Tel** (520) 294-2624.
**Open** 7am–5pm daily. ♿ 🅿
**W** sanxaviermission.org

## Southwest Architecture

The Southwest has been witness to
a range of architecture styles from
Ancestral Puebloan adobe to Spanish
Colonial, and 19th- and early 20th-
century Mission and Pueblo Revival.
Colonizers brought their own forms that
mingled with the Native, creating a
unique plethora of multicultural styles.

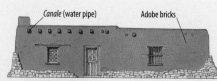

**This adobe home** in El Rancho de las Golondrinas
Museum in Santa Fe is made of adobe (sun-baked bricks
that are a mixture of mud, sand, and straw), cemented
with similar material, and replastered with mud.

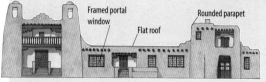

**The Santa Fe Museum of Fine
Arts** was the city's first building in
Pueblo Revival style, with adobe
walls, rounded parapets, framed
portal windows, and pueblo-style
multitiered stories.

Statue of Virgin Mary at the San Xavier del Bac Mission, Tucson

# ㉖ Nogales

🗺 20,800. 🚌 🚍 ℹ️ 123 W Kino Park, (520) 287-3685.
🌐 thenogaleschamber.com

The birthplace of jazz star Charles Mingus, Nogales is really two towns that straddle the US border with Mexico. It is a busy port of entry, handling huge amounts of freight, including much of the winter fruit and vegetables sold in North America. The town attracts large numbers of visitors in search of bargains at shopping districts on both sides of the border. There is a profound contrast between the quiet, ordered streets of the US side, and the ramshackle houses and bustling, large-scale street market across the border. Visas

Mexican pottery from Nogales

are usually required only for visitors traveling beyond town limits. US citizens should carry a passport or birth certificate for identification, while foreign nationals should carry their passport and make sure that their visa status enables them to re-enter the US.

# ㉗ Bisbee

🗺 6,500. 🚌 ℹ️ 478 Dart Road, (520) 432-3554. 🌐 discoverbisbee.com

The discovery of copper here in the 1880s sparked a mining rush, and by the turn of the century Bisbee was the largest city between St. Louis and San Francisco. Today, this is one of the Southwest's most atmospheric mining towns. Victorian buildings such as the landmark Copper Queen Hotel still dominate the historic town center, while attractive clusters of houses cling to the sides of the surrounding mountains. Visitors can tour the mines that once flourished here. The Bisbee Mining and Historical Museum illustrates the realities of mining and frontier life.

### Environs

Some 25 miles (40 km) north of Bisbee is **Tombstone**, one of the wildest towns in the West. Founded by a prospector in 1877, its name derives from the warning he received that "all you'll find out there is your tombstone." Instead, the silver he found led to a silver rush. Today, Tombstone is a living legend, famous as the site of the 1881 gunfight at OK Corral between the Earp brothers and the Clanton gang. The OK Corral is now a museum, where the infamous gunfight is re-enacted. The old seat of justice, Tombstone Courthouse, is a historic site.

# ㉘ Amerind Foundation

Dragoon Road, off I-10 exit 318.
**Tel** (520) 586-3666. **Open** 10am–4pm Tue–Sun. **Closed** Mon, public hols. 🦽
🌐 amerind.org

The Amerind Foundation is one of the country's most important private archaeological and ethnological museums. The name Amerind is a contraction of "American Indian," and this collection depicts all aspects of Native American life through thousands of artifacts of different cultures. The displays include Inuit masks, Cree tools, and sculpted effigy figures from Mexico's Casas Grandes.

The adjacent Amerind Art Gallery has a fine collection of Western art by such artists as William Leigh and Frederic Remington. The delightful pink buildings, designed in the Spanish Colonial Revival style, are also interesting.

**J. Knox Corbett House** in Tucson was designed in the 20th-century Mission Revival style by the Chicago architect David Holmes in 1906. It is characterized by white stucco walls, flat roofs, courtyards, and minimal ornamentation.

Moorish-style dome

Ornate wooden carvings

Iron grille work

Red-tiled roof

White plaster

**San Xavier del Bac Mission** is a fine example of the Baroque tradition of Spanish Colonial churches. The style saw a resurgence in the 20th century as Spanish Colonial Revival, with red-tiled roofs, ornamental terra-cotta, iron grille work, and white walls.

# ㉙ Petrified Forest National Park

Off I-40. **Tel** (928) 524-6228.
**Open** 7am–6pm daily (winter: 8am–5pm). **Closed** Dec 25.
partial. **w** nps.gov/pefo

This fossilized prehistoric forest is one of Arizona's most unusual attractions. Millions of years ago, rivers swept trees downstream into a vast swamp that once covered this whole area. Groundwater transported silica dioxide into downed timber, eventually turning it into the quartz stone logs seen today, with colored crystals preserving the shape and structure of the trees.

Running the entire length of the forest is the famous Painted Desert. This is an area of colored bands of sand and rock that change from blues to reds throughout the day as the shifting light catches the different mineral deposits.

A 28-mile (45-km) scenic road starting at the visitor center travels the length of the park. There are nine overlooks along the way, including Kachina Point, where the Painted Wilderness trailhead is located. A permit is required to camp in the wilderness area. Near the south end of the road is the fine **Rainbow Forest Museum**.

**🏛 Rainbow Forest Museum**
Off Hwy 180 (S entrance). **Tel** (928) 524-6228. **Open** 8am–5pm daily.

Eroded sandstone opening of Window Rock, near Highway 12

# ㉚ Window Rock

🏠 4,500. 🚌 🛈 Hwy 264, (928) 871-6436.

Window Rock is the capital of the Navajo Nation, the largest Native American reservation in the Southwest. The town is named for the natural arch found in the sandstone cliffs located about a mile north of the main strip on Highway 12.

The **Navajo Nation Museum** located in Window Rock is one of the largest Native American museums in the country. The huge *hogan*-shaped building houses displays that cover the history of the Ancestral Puebloans and the Navajo.

**🏛 Navajo Nation Museum**
Hwy 264 & Post Office Loop Rd, (928) 871-7941. **Open** 8am–5pm Mon, 8am–6pm Tue–Fri, 8am–5pm Sat. **Closed** major holidays.
**w** navajonationmuseum.org

# ㉛ Hopi Indian Reservation

🏠 10,000. 🛈 Hwy 264, Second Mesa, (928) 734-0044. **Open** 9am–5pm daily (extended hours in summer). **Closed** Jan 1, Thanksgiving, Dec 25. **w** hopiculturalcenter.com

Believed to be direct descendants of the Ancestral Puebloans, the Hopi Indians have lived in and cultivated this barren reservation area for almost a thousand years. They worship through the *kachina*, the living spirits of plants and animals, believed to visit the tribe during the growing season. Most Hopi villages are located on or near one of three mesas (flat-topped elevations), named First, Second, and Third Mesa. Artisans of each mesa specialize in particular crafts.

Visitors can take a guided walking tour of the impressive pueblo, **Walpi**, on the First Mesa. Inhabited in the 12th

Historic pueblo town of Walpi on First Mesa at the Hopi Indian Reservation

Ancestral Puebloan ruins of Keet Seel at the Navajo National Monument

century, it was built to be easily defended against possible Spanish or Navajo attacks. It straddles a dramatic knife-edge of rock, extending from the tip of the First Mesa. In places, Walpi is less than 100 ft (33m) wide with a drop of several hundred feet on both sides. The tour includes several stops where visitors can purchase *kachina* dolls, hand-crafted pottery, rugs, and baskets, or sample the Hopi *piki* bread. A wider range of Hopi arts and crafts are available in the galleries and stores of the Second Mesa. The Hopi Cultural Center here has a restaurant and the only hotel for miles around, as well as a museum that has an excellent collection of photographs depicting various aspects of Hopi life.

Kachina doll

On the Third Mesa, Old Oraibi pueblo, thought to have been founded in the 12th century, is fascinating because of claims that it is the oldest continually occupied human settlement in North America.

**Walpi**
*i* (928) 737-2670.
Walking Tours: 9:30am–3pm daily.
**w** experiencehopi.com

## ❷ Tuba City

🏠 17,300. *i* Tuba City Trading Post, (928) 283-5441. **Open** daily. **Closed** Jan 1, Thanksgiving, Dec 25.

Named for Tuuvi, a Hopi Indian who converted to the Mormon faith, Tuba City is best known for the 65-million-year-old dinosaur tracks found just off the main highway, 5 miles (8 km) south-west of the town. This is also the largest community in the western section of the Navajo Reservation and is a good spot from which to explore both the Navajo National Monument and the Hopi Reservation.

## ❸ Grand Canyon

*See pp530–33.*

## ❹ Navajo National Monument

**Tel** (928) 672-2700. **Open** 9am–5pm daily (extended summer hours). **Closed** Jan 1, Thanksgiving, Dec 25. 🎫 free. 🅰 **w** nps.gov/nava

Although named because of its location on the Navajo Reservation, this monument is actually known for its Ancestral Puebloan ruins. The most accessible ruin here is the beautifully preserved, 135-room pueblo of Betatakin, which fills a vast, curved niche in the cliffs of Tsegi Canyon. An easy, 1-mile (1.6-km) trail from the visitor center leads to an overlook, which provides a captivating view of Betatakin. For a closer look at these ancient houses, visitors can take the strenuous five-hour hiking tours held daily from late May to early September and on some winter weekends.

A more demanding 17-mile (27-km) hike leads to **Keet Seel**, a more impressive ruin. Only a limited number of permits to visit the ruin are issued each day. This hike requires overnight camping at a campsite with the most basic facilities. Keet Seel was a larger and more success-ful community than Betatakin. Construction began here in about 1250, but the site is thought to have been abandoned by 1300.

The Keet Seel ruins at the Navajo National Monument

# ㉝ Grand Canyon

One of the world's great natural wonders, the Grand
Canyon is an instantly recognizable symbol of the
Southwest. Running through Grand Canyon National
Park *(see pp532–3)*, it is 217 miles (349 km) long, about
4 to 18 miles (6 to 29 km) wide, and over 5,000 ft (1,500 m)
deep. It was formed over a period of six million years by
the Colorado River, whose fast-flowing waters sliced their
way through the Colorado Plateau, which includes the
gorge, most of northern Arizona, and the Four Corners
region. The plateau's geological vagaries have defined
the river's course, and exposed vast cliffs are ringed by
rocks of different color, variegated hues of limestone,
sandstone, and shale. By any standard, the canyon, with
its vast scale, is spectacular. But its special beauty is in
the ever-shifting patterns of light and shadow and the
colors of the rock, bleached white at midday, but bathed
in red and ocher at sunset.

**Mule Trip Convoy**
A popular way of exploring the
canyon's narrow trails, mule rides
must be booked in advance for
the South Rim.

**Havasu Canyon**
Since 1300 Havasu Canyon has been
home to the Havasupai Indians.
A population of around 500 Indians
lives on the Havasupai Reservation,
making a living from the tourist trade.

**Grandview Point**
At 7,400 ft (2,250 m), this is one of
the highest places on the South
Rim, the canyon's southern edge.
It is one of the stops along the
breathtaking Desert View Drive
*(see p532)*. The point is thought
to be the spot from where the
Spaniards had their first glimpse
of the canyon in 1540.

◀ Old Tuscon Studios, Tuscon, where many famous Westerns have been filmed

### North Rim

The North Rim receives roughly one-tenth the number of visitors of the South Rim. While less accessible, it is a more peaceful destination offering a sense of unexplored wilderness. Hikes include the North Kaibab Trail, a steep descent down to Phantom Ranch, the only lodge on the canyon floor.

### VISITORS' CHECKLIST

**Practical Information**

Mather Point, **Tel** (928) 638-7888. **Open** South Rim: daily; North Rim: summer only. Mule rides: South Rim: book ahead (303) 297-2757; North Rim: register at Grand Canyon Lodge (435) 679-8665. **Closed** North Rim facilities: mid-Oct–mid-May. partial. **nps.gov/grca**

**Transport**

Grand Canyon Airpt., Tusayan. Grand Canyon Railway from Williams. Flagstaff & Williams.

### Bright Angel Trail

Used by both Native Americans and early settlers, the Bright Angel Trail follows a natural route along one of the canyon's enormous fault lines. It is an appealing option for day-hikers; unlike some other trails in the area, it offers plenty of shade and several seasonal water sources.

### Yavapai Point at the South Rim

*Situated 5 miles (8 km) north of the canyon's South Entrance, along a stretch of the Rim Trail, is Yavapai Point. Its observation station offers superb views, and a viewing panel identifies several of the central canyon's landmarks.*

### How the Canyon was Formed

While the Colorado River, which changed course four million years ago, accounts for the canyon's depth, its width and formations are the work of even greater forces. Wind rushing through the canyon erodes the limestone and sandstone a few grains at a time, and rain pouring over the rim cuts deep side canyons through the softer rock. Perhaps the greatest force is ice. Water from rain and snowmelt works into cracks in the rock. When frozen, it expands, forcing the rock away from the canyon walls. Soft layers erode quickly into sloped faces, while harder rock resists erosion, leaving sheer vertical faces.

Cracks formed by water erosion

*For hotels and restaurants see pp550–55*

# Exploring Grand Canyon National Park

A World Heritage Site, Grand Canyon National Park covers 1,904 sq miles (4,930 sq km), and consists of the canyon itself, which starts where the Paria River empties into the Colorado, and stretches from Lees Ferry to Lake Mead *(see p507)*. The park has two main entrances, on the North and South Rims of the canyon. Its main roads, Hermit Road and Desert View Drive, both accessible from the south entrance, overlook the canyon. Visitors can also enter the park from the north, although this route (Hwy 67) is closed during winter. Walking trails along the North and South Rims offer staggering views but to experience the canyon at its most fascinating, the trails that head down toward the canyon floor should be explored. The Bright Angel Trail on the South Rim and the North Kaibab Trail on the North Rim descend to the canyon floor and are tough hikes involving an overnight stop.

Adobe, pueblo-style architecture of Hopi House, Grand Canyon Village

### 🏨 Grand Canyon Village

Grand Canyon National Park.
**Tel** (928) 638-7888. ♿ partial.

Grand Canyon Village has its roots in the late 19th century. The extensive building of visitor accommodations started after the Santa Fe Railroad opened a branch line here from Williams in 1901, although some hotels had been built in the late 1890s. The Fred Harvey Company constructed a clutch of well-designed, attractive buildings. The most prominent is the El Tovar Hotel *(see p551)*. Opened in 1905, it is named after Spanish explorers who reached the gorge in 1540. The Hopi House also opened in 1905 – it is a rendition of a traditional Hopi dwelling, where locals could sell their craftwork as souvenirs. It was built by Hopi craftsmen and designed by Mary E.J. Colter, an ex-schoolteacher and architect, who drew on Southwestern influences, mixing both Native American and Hispanic styles. She is responsible for many of the historic structures that now grace the South Rim, including the 1914 Lookout Studio and Hermits Rest, and the rustic 1922 Phantom Ranch on the canyon floor.

Today, Grand Canyon Village has a wide range of hotels, restaurants, and stores. It can be surprisingly easy to get lost here since the buildings are spread out and discreetly placed among wooded areas. The village is the starting point for most of the mule trips through the canyon. It is also the terminus for the Grand Canyon Railway, restored steam trains that make the 64-mile (103-km) journey from Williams.

### The South Rim

Most of the Grand Canyon's 4.4 million annual visitors come to the South Rim, since, unlike the North Rim, it is open year-round and is easily accessible along Highway 180/64 from Flagstaff *(see p520)* or Williams. **Hermit Road** and **Desert View Drive** (Hwy 64) start at Grand Canyon Village and include some of the best views of the gorge. Hermit Drive is closed to private vehicles from March to November, but there are free shuttle buses, and Desert View Drive is open all year.

From the village, Hermit Road meanders along the South Rim, extending for 8 miles (13 km). Its first viewpoint is **Trailview Overlook**, which provides an overview of the canyon and the winding course of the Bright Angel Trail. Further on, **Maricopa Point** offers especially panoramic views of the canyon but not of the Colorado River, which is more apparent from nearby **Hopi Point**. At the end of Hermit Road lies **Hermits Rest**, where a gift shop, decorated in rustic style, is located in yet another Mary Colter-designed building. The longer Desert View Drive runs in the opposite direction, and covers 26 miles (42 km). It winds for 12 miles (20 km) before reaching **Grandview Point**, where the Spaniards may have had their first glimpse of the canyon in 1540. Ten miles (16 km) farther on lie the pueblo remains of Tusayan Ruin, where there is a small museum with exhibits on Ancestral Puebloan life. The

The interior of the Hermits Rest gift store with crafts for sale lining the walls

Desert View's stone Watchtower on Desert View Drive

## California Condors

America's largest bird, the California condor, has a wingspan of over 9 ft (2.7 m). The bird was nearly extinct in the 1980s, and the last 22 condors were captured for breeding in captivity. In 1996, the first captive-bred birds were released in Northern Arizona. Today, about 70 condors fly the skies over Northern Arizona and Southern Utah. They are frequent visitors to the South Rim, though visitors should not approach or attempt to feed them.

A pair of California condors

road finally ends at the stunning overlook of **Desert View**. The Watchtower here was Colter's most fanciful creation, its upper floor decorated with early 20th-century Hopi murals.

Just east of Grand Canyon Village is **Yavapai Point** from where it is possible to see Phantom Ranch. This is the only roofed accommodation available on the canyon floor, across the Colorado River.

### The North Rim

Standing at about 8,000 ft (2,400 m), the North Rim is higher, cooler, and greener than the South Rim, with dense forests of ponderosa pine, aspen, and Douglas fir. Visitors are most likely to spot wildlife on the North Rim. Mule deer, Kaibab squirrel, and wild turkey are among the most common sights. The North Rim is reached via Highway 67, off Highway 89A, ending at **Grand Canyon Lodge**, where there are visitor services, a campground, a gas station, restaurant, and a general store. Nearby there is a National Park Service information center, which offers maps of the area. The North Rim and all its facilities are closed between mid-October and mid-May, when it is often snowed in. The North Rim is twice as far from the river as the South Rim, and the canyon really stretches out from the overlooks giving a sense of its 10-mile (16-km) width. There are about 30 miles

(45 km) of scenic roads along the North Rim as well as hiking trails to high viewpoints or down to the canyon floor (particularly the North Kaibab Trail that links to the South Rim's Bright Angel Trail).

The picturesque **Cape Royal Road** starts north of Grand Canyon Lodge and travels 23 miles (37 km) to Cape Royal on the Walhalla Plateau. From here, several famous buttes and peaks can be seen, including Wotans Throne and Vishnu Temple. There are also several short, easy walking trails around Cape Royal, along the top. A 3-mile (5-km) detour leads to **Point Imperial**, the highest point on the canyon rim, while along the way the **Vista Encantada** has delightful views and picnic tables overlooking the gorge.

Mule deer on the canyon's North Rim

### The Bright Angel Trail

This is the most popular of all Grand Canyon hiking trails.

The Bright Angel trailhead is at Grand Canyon Village on the South Rim. The trail begins near the Kolb Studio at the western end of the village. It then switches dramatically down the side of the canyon for 9 miles (13 km). The trail crosses the river over a suspension bridge, ending a little farther on at Phantom Ranch. There are two rest houses and a fully equipped campground along the way. It is not advisable to attempt the whole trip in one day. Many walk from the South Rim to one of the rest stops and then return up to the rim. Temperatures at the bottom of the canyon can reach 110°F (43°C) or higher during the summer. Day-hikers should therefore carry a quart (just under a liter) of water per person per hour for summer hiking. Carrying a first-aid kit is also recommended.

Hikers at the trailhead of the Bright Angel Trail

# ❸❺ Monument Valley

From scenic Highway 163, which crosses the border of Utah and Arizona, it is possible to see the famous buttes and mesas of Monument Valley. These ancient rocks, soaring upward from a seemingly boundless desert, have come to symbolize the American West, since they have been used as a backdrop for countless movies and TV shows. The area's visitor center sits within the boundary of Monument Valley Tribal Park, but many of the valley's spectacular rock formations and other sites are found just outside the park boundary.

**Guided Tours**
A row of kiosks at the visitor center offer Navajo-guided 4WD tours of the valley. The marketing tactics can be aggressive, but the tours offer an excellent way to see places in the park that are otherwise inaccessible.

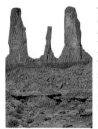

**Three Sisters**
One of several distinctive pinnacle rock formations at the valley, the closest view of the Three Sisters can be seen from John Ford's Point, and is one of the most photographed sights here.

**Art & Ruins**
Petroglyphs such as this deer can be seen on Navajo-guided tours of rock art sites, which are dotted around the valley's ancient ruins.

Left Mitten

**Monument Valley**
*Monument Valley is not really a valley. The tops of the mesas mark what was once a flat plain. Millions of years ago, this plain was cracked by upheavals within the earth. The cracks widened and eroded, leaving the formations rising from the desert floor.*

## Exploring the Valley

The awe-inspiring beauty of Monument Valley's buttes and mesas can be viewed by travelers from Highway 163. Visitors can also pay a fee to travel on a 17-mile (27-km) self-guided drive along a well-marked dirt road. (Fees are collected at the visitor center.) Alternatively, Navajo guides may be hired for hiking, horseback, or 4WD tours to fascinating and less-visited parts of the valley.

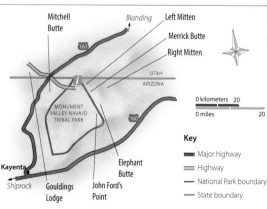

Mitchell Butte

*Blanding*

Left Mitten

Merrick Butte

Right Mitten

163

UTAH
ARIZONA

MONUMENT VALLEY NAVAJO TRIBAL PARK

160

0 kilometers 20

0 miles 20

**Key**

▬ Major highway

▭ Highway

— National Park boundary

— State boundary

Kayenta

*Shiprock*

Gouldings Lodge

John Ford's Point

Elephant Butte

### John Ford's Point

The most popular stop along the valley drive is John Ford's Point, which is said to be the film director's favorite view of the valley. Various stands offer a range of Navajo crafts. A nearby native *hogan* (Navajo dwelling) serves as a gift shop where Navajo weavers demonstrate their craft.

## VISITORS' CHECKLIST

**Practical Information**

PO Box 360289, Monument Valley, visitor center only.

**Tel** (435) 727-5870.
**Open** sunrise–sunset daily.
**Closed** Dec 25.

W navajonationparks.org

Right Mitten

Merrick Butte

**Navajo Weaver**
Navajo women are usually considered to be the finest weavers in the Southwest. One rug can take months to complete and sell for thousands of dollars. Using the natural colors of the land, the weavers often add a "spirit line" to their work to prevent their spirit being "trapped" within the rug.

## The Wild West

Romanticized in cowboy movies, the "Wild West" conjures up images of tough men herding cattle across the country before living it up in a saloon. But frontier life was far from romantic. Settlers arriving in this wilderness were caught up in a first-come first-served battle for land and wealth, fighting Native Americans and each other for land. The rugged life of the mining prospectors and ranch cowboys helped to create the idea of the American West. Today, visitors can still see former mining towns such as Bisbee or enjoy re-enacted gunfights on the streets of Tombstone (*see p525*), the site of one of the Wild West's most famous tales. In the late 19th-century, however, such survival skills as good shooting often co-existed with a kill-or-be-killed ethos. Guided trail rides, offered at many dude ranches, are a great way to explore the contemporary Wild West.

Guided trail rides, conducted to explore the Wild West

# ⚅ Canyon de Chelly National Monument

The awesome thousand-foot cliffs of the Canyon de Chelly boast of a long and eventful history of human habitation. Archaeologists have found evidence of four periods of Native culture, starting with the Basketmaker people around AD 300, followed by the Great Pueblo Builders, who created the cliff dwellings in the 12th century. They were succeeded by the Hopi, who lived here seasonally for around 300 years, taking advantage of the canyon's fertile soil. Today, the canyon is the cultural and geographic heart of the Navajo Nation, where Navajo farmers still live tending the sheep, introduced by the Spanish, and women weave rugs at outdoor looms. Pronounced "d'Shay," de Chelly is a Spanish corruption of the Native name *tsegi*, meaning rock canyon.

**Yucca House Ruin**
Perched on the mesa top, this ruin of an Ancestral Puebloan house sits in a rock hollow, precariously overhanging a sheer drop to the valley floor.

**Canyon Vegetation**
Within the canyon, cottonwood and oak trees line the river washes; the land itself is a fertile oasis of meadows, alfalfa and corn fields, and fruit orchards.

**Stone and adobe** cliff dwellings were home to the Ancestral Puebloans from the 12th to the 14th centuries and were built to face south toward the sun, with cooler areas within.

**Navajo Fortress**
This imposing rock tower was the site of a three-month siege in 1863, when a group of Navajos reached the summit via pole ladders. They were trying to escape a US government patrol led by Kit Carson (*see p538*) to settle the Navajo raids. Carson's persistence finally led them to surrender and they were marched to a camp in New Mexico.

### Hiking in the Canyon
Canyon de Chelly is a popular destination for hikers, but apart from the White House Ruins Trail, visitors can enter the canyons only with a Navajo guide.

**The pale walls** of the White House cliff drop 550 ft (160 m) to the canyon floor.

### Hogan Interior
The *hogan* is the center of Navajo family life. It is made of horizontal logs, and a smoke hole in the center provides contact with the sky, while the dirt floor gives contact with the earth. A door faces east to greet the rising sun.

## White House Ruins
*This group of rooms, tucked into a tiny hollow in the cliff, seem barely touched by time. The dwellings were originally situated above a larger pueblo, much of which has now disappeared. It is the only site within the canyon that can be visited without a Navajo guide, reached via a steep 2.5-mile (5-km) round-trip trail that winds to the canyon floor and offers magnificent views.*

## Massacre Cave

The canyon's darkest hour was in 1805, when a Spanish force under Lieutenant Antonio Narbona entered the area. The Spanish wanted to subdue the Navajo, claiming they were raiding their settlements. While some Navajo fled by climbing to the canyon rim, others took refuge in a cave high in the cliffs. The Spanish fired into the cave, and Narbona boasted that he had killed 115 Navajo including 90 warriors. Navajo accounts are different, claiming that most of the warriors were absent (probably hunting) and those killed were mostly women, children, and the elderly. The only Spanish fatality came when a Spaniard attempting to climb into the cave was attacked by a Navajo woman and both plunged over the cliff, gaining the Navajo name "Two Fell Over." The Anglo name is "Massacre Cave."

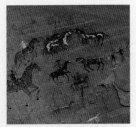

Pictograph on a canyon wall showing invading Spanish soldiers

# New Mexico

New Mexico's rich cultural heritage and unique mix of Native American, Hispanic, and Anglo American people make it a fascinating place to visit. The forested peaks of the Rocky Mountains offer ski resorts in winter and cool retreats in summer. Northern New Mexico, with its soft colors and vivid desert landscapes, has attracted generations of artists to the creative centers of Santa Fe and Taos. In the vast, wild south visitors can explore ancient Native ruins at Bandelier National Monument and the fascinating cave systems of Carlsbad Caverns.

Fajada Butte in Chaco Culture National Historical Park

## ③ Chaco Culture National Historical Park

25 miles (5 km) SE of Nageezi off US 550. **Tel** (505) 786-7014. **Open** 8am–5pm daily. **Closed** public hols. 🚻 ♿ 🅿 🆆 nps.gov/chcu

One of the Southwest's most impressive cultural sites, Chaco Canyon reflects the sophistication of the Ancestral Puebloan civilization that existed here. With its six "great houses" (pueblos that contained hundreds of rooms) and many lesser sites, the canyon was once the political, religious, and cultural center for settlements that spread across much of the Four Corners.

Visitors can access the site via a 16-mile (26-km) dirt road that is affected by flash floods in wet weather. A paved loop road in the site passes several of Chaco's highlights. The major stop is **Pueblo Bonito**, the largest of the "great houses," a D-shaped, four-story structure with more than 600 rooms, and 40 *kivas*, round, pit-like rooms used for religious ceremonies. Begun around AD 850, it was built in stages over

the course of 300 years. **Casa Riconada**, the largest religious chamber at Chaco, measuring 62 ft (19m) in diameter, lies to the southeast.

A short trail from Pueblo Bonito leads to another great house, **Chetro Ketl**, covering 3 acres (2 ha). The masonry used to build the later portions of this structure is among the most sophisticated found in any Ancestral Puebloan site. A two-hour hike northward leads to **Pueblo Alto**, built on top of the mesa at the junction of many ancient Chacoan roads.

Finely wrought stonework at Chaco Canyon

## ③ Taos

🏙 6,000. 🚌 Greyhound, Taos Bus Center, Hwy 68. 🛈 1139 Paseo del Pueblo Sur (575) 751-8800, (800) 348-0696. 🆆 taoschamber.com

The city of Taos, home to Indians for around 1,000 years, is now a vibrant artistic center. In 1898, artists Ernest Blumenschein and Bert Phillips stopped here to repair a wagon wheel and never left. In 1915 they established the Taos Society of Artists, which continues to promote the work of local artists. Some of these are exhibited at the **Harwood Museum of Art**, located in a tranquil, 19th-century adobe compound. More works by the society's artists are housed in the **Blumenschein Home and Museum**, nearby.

The tree-lined, old Spanish **Plaza** at the heart of Taos makes for a pleasant stroll. To its east is the **Kit Carson Home and Museum**. A fur trapper and soldier, Carson's remarkable life (1809–68) is the focus of this museum.

A few miles north of the town center, Taos' main street, Paseo del Pueblo Norte, leads to the **Millicent Rogers Museum**, with its brilliant collection of Native arts and crafts, and black-on-black pottery of Puebloan artist Maria Martinez. This road leads to the dramatic Rio Grande Gorge Bridge, the country's second-highest suspension bridge, built in 1965. It offers awesome views of the gorge and the surrounding stark, sweeping plateau.

**Taos Pueblo** is north of the city. It features two multistory communal adobe houses still inhabited by villagers, making it one of the oldest communities in the country.

The Hacienda Martinez (*see p545*) at **Rancho de Taos**, south of the city, is a well-preserved Spanish Colonial house with thick adobe walls and heavy gates. The 18th-century adobe church of San Francisco de Asis was often painted by Georgia O'Keeffe, one of New Mexico's best known artists.

# ❸❾ Northern Pueblos Tour

The fertile valley of the Rio Grande between Santa Fe and Taos is home to eight of the 19 Native American pueblos in New Mexico. Although geographically close, each pueblo has its own government and traditions, and many offer attractions to visitors. Nambe gives stunning views of the surrounding mountains, mesas, and high desert. San Idelfonso is famous for its fine pottery, and other villages produce handcrafted jewelry or rugs.

## Tips for Drivers

**Starting point:** Tesuque Pueblo, N of Santa Fe on Hwy 84.
**Length:** 45 miles (70 km). Local roads leading to pueblos are often dirt tracks, so allow extra time.
**Note:** Visitors are welcome, but respect their laws & etiquette (*see p548*). 🛈 Indian Pueblo Cultural Center, (505) 843-7270 (9am–5pm).
**ⓦ indianpueblo.org**

### ⑤ Santa Clara Pueblo
This small pueblo is known for its artisans and their work. As in many pueblos, it contains a number of craft shops and small studios, often run by the Native artisans themselves.

### ⑥ Puye Cliff Dwellings
Now deserted, this site contains over 700 rooms, complete with stone carvings, which were home to Native peoples until 1500.

### ⑦ Ohkay Owingeh
Declared the first capital of New Mexico in 1598, this village, once known as San Juan Pueblo, is now a center for the visual arts.

### ④ San Ildefonso Pueblo
Occupied since AD 1300, this pueblo is best known for its etched black pottery, the sales of which saved its people from the Depression of the 1930s.

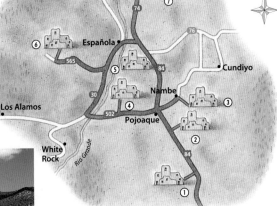

### ② Pojoaque Pueblo
The new Peoh Cultural Center and Museum here is an excellent introduction to the pueblo way of life in these small communities.

### ③ Nambe Pueblo
Set in a beautiful fertile valley, this village is bordered by a lakeside hiking trail with waterfall views and a buffalo ranch.

### ① Tesuque Pueblo
The Tewa people here have concentrated on farming and pottery-making for centuries.

0 kilometers 10

0 miles 10

### Key
▨▨ Tour route
‐‐‐ Other road

**For keys to symbols** *see back flap*

# ⑩ Santa Fe

The oldest state capital in North America, Santa Fe was founded by the Spanish conquistador Don Pedro de Peralta, who established a colony here in 1610. This colony was abandoned in 1680 after the Pueblo Revolt, but was later recaptured. When Mexico gained independence in 1821, traders and settlers from Missouri poured into the area via the Santa Fe Trail. Perched on a high plateau, this beautiful city is surrounded by mountains. Its heart, since its founding, is the central Plaza, and there is no better place to begin exploring the city. Today, it houses a Native American market under the portal of the Palace of the Governors, and the square is lined with shops, cafés, and several galleries.

**★ New Mexico Museum of Art**
Built of adobe in 1917, this museum focuses on the paintings and sculpture of Southwestern artists.

**★ Palace of the Governors**
This single-story adobe building, built in 1600, was the seat of regional government for 300 years. Now part of the New Mexico History Museum, it houses displays on the city's history.

**Key**

— Suggested route

**Original Trading Post**
sells Hispanic art, antiques, and Native American crafts.

**The Plaza**
The obelisk at the center of this main square commemorates Santa Fe's war veterans. The Plaza is lined with old Colonial buildings, including the Palace of Governors.

0 meters    100
0 yards     100

### Saint Francis Cathedral
This colorful, carved wooden statue of the Virgin stands in a side chapel that survives from the original 17th-century church on which the present cathedral was built in 1869.

## VISITORS' CHECKLIST

**Practical Information**
🏙 65,000. 🛈 201 W Marcy St. **Tel** (505) 955-6200, (800) 777-2489.
📷 Spanish Market (Jul); Santa Fe Opera Season (Jul & Aug); Indian Market (Aug); Fiestas de Santa Fe (Sep).
Ⓦ santafe.org

**Transport**
✈ Santa Fe Municipal Airport, 10 miles (16 km) SW of Santa Fe.
🚆 Lamy, 18 miles (29 km) S of city. 🚌 858 St. Michael's Drive.

## Exploring Santa Fe
This city's rich history and beautiful architecture have made it one of the country's most popular destinations. It is famous for its adobe buildings, art galleries, and the New Mexico History Museum. In addition to the Palace of the Governors and the New Mexico Museum of Art, there is the **Georgia O'Keeffe Museum**, northwest of the Plaza. This has the world's largest collection of O'Keeffe's works, including several of her best-loved paintings such as *Jimson Weed* (1932), *Purple Hills II*, and *Ghost Ranch, New Mexico* (1934).

Across the Santa Fe River, on Museum Hill, is the **Museum of International Folk Art**, with its stunning collection of folk art from all over the world. Also on Museum Hill, the **Museum of Indian Art and Culture** is dedicated to traditional Native American arts and culture. Its main exhibit, "Here, Now and Always," tells the story of the region's oldest communities, in the words of Pueblo, Navajo, and Apache people. Running parallel to the river, the gallery-lined **Canyon Road** was originally an Indian track between the Rio Grande and Pecos pueblo. To its west, on the Old Santa Fe Trail, is the **San Miguel Mission**, built in 1610. To the northwest, the 1795 **Santuario de Guadelupe**, dedicated to the Virgin of Guadelupe, patron saint of Mexican and Pueblo peoples, marked the end of Camino Real, the main trade route from Mexico. About 15 miles (24 km) south of Santa Fe, **El Rancho de las Golondrinas**, now a living history museum, was a historic stopping-off point on the Camino Real.

Museum of Contemporary Native Arts

CATHEDRAL PLACE

E SAN FRANCISCO STREET

Saint Francis Cathedral

OLD SANTA FE TRAIL

E WATER STREET

La Fonda Hotel

Girard Collection toy, Museum of International Folk Art

### Loretto Chapel
Built in Gothic style by French architects in the 1870s, the Loretto Chapel was modeled on the Sainte-Chappelle in Paris. Its elegant spiral staircase has no nails or center support, and its perfect craftsmanship is all that keeps it aloft.

🏛 **Museum of International Folk Art**
706 Camino Lejo. **Tel** (505) 476-1200.
**Open** 10am–5pm Tue–Sun.
**Closed** public hols. 📷 ♿ 🎟 🏠

# ❶ Albuquerque

🏙 580,000. ✈ 🚉 🚌 ℹ 401 2nd
St NW, (505) 842-9918, (800) 284-2282.
🌐 itsatrip.com

Occupied by Native peoples
from 1100 to 1300, the first
inhabitants of Albuquerque
were a small group of Colonial
pioneers who settled by the
Rio Grande in the wake of late
16th-century Spanish explorers.
In 1706, a band of 18 families
won formal approval for their
town from the Spanish crown
by naming the city after the
Spanish Duke of Alburquerque,
(the first "r" in the name was
later dropped). Albuquerque's
Old Town, today, still has many
original adobe buildings dating
from the 1790s, while
downtown, to its east, is much
more contemporary. Many of
the city's shops, museums, and
high-tech industries are
located here.

## Exploring Albuquerque

Dominating the historic Old
Town is the Plaza, which was
the center of Albuquerque for
over 200 years. Today, this
charming square is a pleasant
open space where both locals
and visitors relax on benches,
surrounded by lovely adobe
buildings. Opposite is the
imposing **San Felipe de Neri
Church**. Completed in 1793, this
was the city's first civic structure.
Despite many renovations, the
church retains its original adobe
walls. The nearby streets are
lined with museums, colorful
craft shops, and restaurants,
such as the Church Street Café
(see p555). Said to occupy the
oldest house in the city, this
café serves excellent New
Mexican cusine. Beyond is a

craft store, the Agape Pueblo
Pottery, which stocks
handcrafted pueblo pottery.

## 🎫 ABQ BioPark

2601 Central Ave NW. **Tel** (505) 764-
6200. **Open** 9am–5pm daily. **Closed**
Jan 1, Thanksgiving, Dec 25. 🅿 ♿
🌐 cabq.gov/biopark

The park encompasses the
Albuquerque Aquarium and the
Rio Grande Botanic Garden. The
Rio Grande Zoological Park is
located nearby. The botanic
garden occupies
10 acres (4 ha) of
woodland along the
Rio Grande and has a
wide variety of rare
plants and gardens.
   The aquarium
focuses on
the marine life
of the Rio
Grande, one of
America's
great rivers,
and features a
fascinating walk-
through eel cave
containing moray
eels. There is also an
impressive, vast floor-
to-ceiling shark tank.

## 🏛 Turquoise Museum

2107 Central Ave NW. **Tel** (505)
247-8650. **Open** for guided tours at
11am & 1pm Mon–Sat; reservation
required. **Closed** Thanksg., Dec 25. 🅿
📷 ♿

The fascinating displays in this
museum focus on consumer

San Felipe de Neri Church, at the north end
of Old Town Plaza

education, helping
visitors to judge the quality
of turquoise gemstones.
The entrance is a replica
mine tunnel that leads to
the "vault," which contains an
unsurpassed collection of rare
and varied turquoise specimens
from around the world.

## 🏛 New Mexico Museum of Natural History and Science

1801 Mountain Rd NW. **Tel** (505) 841-
2800. **Open** 9am–5pm daily.
**Closed** public hols. 🅿 ♿
🌐 nmnaturalhistory.org

This entertaining museum
has a series of interactive

Glasshouse at Rio Grande Botanic Garden, ABQ BioPark

exhibits. Visitors can stand inside a simulated live volcano or explore an ice cave. The "Evolator" is a ride through 38 million years of the region's evolution using the latest video technology. Replica dinosaurs, a state-of-the-art planetarium, and a large-screen film theater are all highly popular with children.

### 🏛 Albuquerque Museum of Art and History

2000 Mountain Rd NW. **Tel** (505) 242-4600. **Open** 9am–5pm Tue–Sun. **Closed** public hols. 🚻
**w** cabq.gov/museum

This excellent museum depicts four centuries of history in the middle of Rio Grande Valley. The well-chosen artifacts are expertly arranged for maximum impact. Exhibits focus on the Spanish Colonial period (1598–1821) and include a reconstructed 18th-century house and chapel. From March to mid-December, the museum organizes informative walking tours of the Old Town.

Sculpture garden at the Albuquerque Museum of Art and History

### 🏛 American International Rattlesnake Museum

202 San Felipe Ave NW. **Tel** (505) 242-6569. **Open** 10am–6pm Mon–Sat, 1–5pm Sun; Sep–May: 11:30am–5:30pm Mon–Fri, 10am–6pm Sat, 1–5pm Sun. **Closed** public hols. 🚻 🚻 **w** rattlesnakes.com

This animal conservation museum explains the life cycles and ecological importance of some of Earth's most misunderstood creatures. It contains the world's largest collection of different species of live rattlesnakes, including natives of North, Central, and South America. The snakes are displayed in glass tanks that simulate their natural habitat as closely as possible and are accompanied by explanatory notices suitable for both adults and children. The museum features other venomous animals such as tarantulas and the Gila monster lizard.

### 🎭 KiMo Theatre

423 Central Ave NW. **Tel** (505) 768-3522. **Open** call for program. 🚻 🚻 **w** cabq.gov/kimo

Built in 1927, the KiMo Theatre was one of many entertainment venues constructed in the city during the 1920s and '30s. The building's distinctive design was inspired by that of the nearby Native American pueblos and created a fusion of Pueblo Revival and Art Deco styles. Today, the KiMo Theatre presents an eclectic range of musical and theatrical performances.

### 🦁 Rio Grande Zoological Park

903 10th St SW. **Tel** (505) 764-6200. **Open** 9am–5pm daily (to 6pm Sat–Sun in summer). **Closed** Thanksgiving, Dec 25. 🚻 🚻

The Rio Grande Zoo forms part of the Albuquerque BioPark. The zoo is noted for its imaginative layout with enclosures designed to simulate the animals' natural habitats, including the African savanna. Among the most popular species here are lowland gorillas and white Bengal tigers.

## Sights at a Glance

0 meters 500
0 yards 500

**For keys to symbols** *see back flap*

Indian Pueblo Cultural Center courtyard

## Albuquerque: Farther Afield

New Mexico's largest city, Albuquerque, has grown to fill the valley that stretches westward from the foothills of the Manzano and Sandia Mountains and across the banks of the Rio Grande. The coming of the railroad during the 1880s brought increasing numbers of settlers and greater prosperity. Today, the best way to explore the city is by car. The major sights, including the historic Old Town *(see p542)*, are all located near highway exits.

### 🏛 Indian Pueblo Cultural Center

2401 12th St NW. **Tel** (505) 843-7270. 🚌 **Open** 9am–5pm daily. **Closed** Jan 1, Thanksgiving, Dec 25. 🅿 ♿ 📷 🖊 📷 🖼 **indianpueblo.org**

This impressive museum and cultural center is run by the 19 Indian pueblos that lie along the Rio Grande around Albuquerque and Santa Fe. It traces the Puebloan peoples' complex history and varied culture through their oral history and presents it from their viewpoint.

The building is designed to resemble the layout of a pueblo dwelling, and is set around the Puebloan Central Courtyard. This large courtyard, with its red adobe walls decorated with murals and hung chilies, emulates the layout of a Pueblo dwelling. Each weekend exuberant dance performances are held. The center also has a restaurant serving Pueblo Indian cooking, and an excellent group of gift shops offering high-quality pottery, jewelry, and other crafts.

### 🏛 University of New Mexico & Art Museum

ℹ Welcome Center, Central & Cornell, (505) 277-1989. 🖼 **unm.edu** University Art Museum: Tel (505) 277-4001. **Open** 10am–4pm Tue–Sat. **Closed** University holidays. ♿ Maxwell Museum of Anthropology: **Tel** (505) 277-4405. **Open** 10am–4pm Tue–Sat. **Closed** Sun & Mon. ♿

The campus of New Mexico's largest university (UNM) is known for its Pueblo Revival-style architecture and its museums. The **University Art Museum** has one of the state's largest fine arts collection, including paintings and sculpture by Old Masters, and other works from the 17th to the 20th centuries.

The **Maxwell Museum of Anthropology**, one of the finest of its kind in the US, emphasizes the culture of the Southwest, with an important collection of art and artifacts. The museum also has traveling exhibits on regional and international themes, as well as a permanent exhibition entitled "Ancestors," which traces human development.

Horse at Museum of Anthropology, UNM

### 🏛 Anderson-Abruzzo

International Balloon Museum: 9201 Balloon Museum Dr NE. **Tel** (505) 768-6020. **Open** 9am–5pm Tue–Sun. **Closed** major holidays. 🅿 ♿ 📷 🖼 **cabq.gov/balloon**

Named after pioneering Albuquerque balloonists Maxie Anderson and Ben Abruzzo, the museum highlights the history of ballooning. Colorful balloons and gondolas hang from the ceiling, while exhibits showcase historic gondolas and wicker baskets related to scientific and record-setting flights. Displays of memorabilia feature key events in ballooning history.

### 🏛 National Museum of Nuclear Science & History

601 Eubank Blvd SE. **Tel** (505) 245-2137. **Open** 9am–5pm daily. **Closed** Jan 1, Easter, Thanksgiving, Dec 25. 🅿 ♿ 📷 🖼 **nuclearmuseum.org**

Inside this museum, exhibits and displays tell the story of the Atomic Age and nuclear science, including the history of nuclear development, weapons, and atomic energy, as well as today's peaceful uses of nuclear technology. Outside, the Heritage Park displays aircraft, missiles, railcars, and nuclear submarines.

### 🏛 Petroglyph National Monument

ℹ 4735 Unser Blvd NW, (505) 899-0205. **Open** 8am–5pm daily. **Closed** public hols. 🅿 ♿ limited. 🖼 **nps.gov/petr**

This site, on the western outskirts of Albuquerque, was established in 1990 to preserve nearly 24,000 images carved into rock along the 17-mile (27-km) West Mesa escarpment. The earliest date back to 1,000 BC, but the most prolific period is thought to be between 1300 and 1680. The pictures range from human figures such as musicians and dancers to animals, including snakes, birds, and insects. Spirals and other geometric symbols are common, as are hands, feet, and animal tracks. The meanings of some petroglyphs have been lost over time, but others have great cultural significance to today's Puebloan population.

Hundreds of petroglyphs are accessible along Boca Negra Canyon, 2 miles (3 km) north of the park visitor center, where three trails wind past them. Visitors should not touch the petroglyphs; they are easily damaged.

# Hispanic Culture in New Mexico

The heart of Hispanic culture in the Southwest is found in New Mexico. Here, the Hispanic population, descendants of the original Spanish colonizers of the 16th century, outnumbers that of the Anglo-Americans. The Spanish introduced sheep and horses to the region, as well as bringing Catholicism with its saints' festivals and colorful church decorations. Centuries of mixing with both the Southwest's Native and Anglo cultures have also influenced every aspect of modern Hispanic society, from language and cooking to festivals and the arts. Contemporary New Mexican residents bear the Hispanic surnames of their ancestors, and speak English with a Spanish accent. Even English-speakers pepper their speech with Spanish terms.

## Spanish Influence

*The restored El Rancho de las Golondrinas (see p541) is today a living museum, centered on the hacienda, pioneered in the Southwest by Spanish colonists. In a hacienda, a large number of rooms (approximately 20) would be set around one or two courtyards, reflecting the extended family style of living favored by the Spanish.*

**Wells** were located in the middle of the main courtyard to be easily accessible.

**Adobe beehive ovens** *(hornos)* were introduced by the Spanish for baking bread. They were originally of Moorish design.

**Hacienda Martínez** *(see p538)* was built south of Taos in 1804 by Don Antonio Martínez, an early mayor of the town. It is one of the few Spanish haciendas to be preserved in more or less its original form. Today, it is open to visitors who can watch local artisans demonstrating a variety of traditional folk arts.

## Crafts

*Navajo rugs are considered a Native handicraft, but their designs also show signs of Moorish patterns brought by colonizers from Spain. Other folk art forms include artistic pottery, intricate silverwork, and carved wooden figures known as* bultos, *which combine religious beliefs and artistic expression.*

**Corn,** the region's staple food since pre-Columbian times, is used to make tortilla chips, which are served with guacamole (avocado dip).

Navajo rug

Carved wooden *bulto* of St. Joseph

## ⑫ Roswell

🏠 50,000. 🛈 912 N Main St, (575)
624-7704. **Open** 8:30am–5pm Mon–
Fri, 8:30am–4pm Sat, 9am–3pm Sun.
**w** roswellvisitorscenter.com

This small ranching town is a
byword for aliens and UFOs
since the night of July 4, 1947,
when an unidentified airborne
object crashlanded here. Jim
Ragsdale, camping nearby, later
claimed (in 1995) to have seen a
flash, a craft hurtling through
the trees, and the bodies of four
"little people," with snake-like
skin. The US Air Force issued a
statement at the time that a
flying saucer had been
recovered, and despite a denial
later on, the story caught
people's imagination.

Witnesses were allegedly
sworn to secrecy, fueling
rumors of a cover-up and alien
conspiracy theories to this day.
The **International UFO Museum
and Research Center**
features a collection of
newspaper clippings
and photographs of
the crash site, and a
film with over 400
interviews of various
people connected to
the incident.

Roswell's **Museum
and Art Center** houses
a large collection of artifacts on
the history of the American
West. The fascinating Robert H.
Goddard Collection details
11 years of experiments by
the famous rocket scientist.

Limestone columns in the Big Room at
Carlsbad Caverns

## ⑬ Carlsbad Caverns National Park

3225 National Parks Hwy, Carlsbad.
✈ to Carlsbad. 🚌 to White's City.
**Tel** (575) 785-2232, (800) 967-2283
(tour reservations). **Open** May–Aug:
8am–3:30pm daily; Sep–mid-May:
8am–2pm (Natural Entrance). Call for
last entry times. **Closed** Dec 25. 🎫
♿ partial. 🅿 **w** nps.gov/cave

Located in the state's remote
southeastern corner, this park
protects one of the world's
largest cave systems. Geological
forces carved out this complex
of chambers, and their
decorations began to
be formed around
500,000 years ago
when dripping water
deposited drops of the
crystalized mineral calcite.
Native pictographs near
the Natural Entrance
indicate that they had
been visited by Native
peoples, but it was cowboy Jim
White who brought them to
national attention in 1901.
Concrete trails and electric
lights have been laid out
through this underground

Roswell's Alien
Zone symbol

gallery of limestone caves. From
the visitor center, elevators drop
750 ft (229 m) down to the
**Big Room**. This space can also
be reached via the **Natural
Entrance Route**, which involves
a half-hour walk over a steep,
paved trail.

A self-guided tour leads to the
Big Room, 25 stories high and
8 acres (3 ha) in area, festooned
with stalagmites, stalactites,
and flowstone formations.
The adjoining ranger-led **King's
Palace Tour** takes in the
deepest cave open to the
public, 830 ft (250 m) below
ground. To its right, a paved
section serves as the popular
**Underground Lunchroom**, a
diner and souvenir shop.

The caverns' recesses are the
summer abode of almost a
million free-tailed bats. They
emerge at dusk to cross the
desert in search of food.

## ⑭ White Sands National Monument

Hwy 70. **Tel** (575) 679-2599. **Open**
9am–5pm daily (mid-Mar–Sep:
extended hours). **Closed** Dec 25.
🎫 ♿ 🅿 **w** nps.gov/whsa

The glistening dunes of the
White Sands National
Monument rise up from the
Tularosa Basin at the northern
end of the Chihuahuan Desert.
It is the world's largest gypsum
dune field, covering around

### Desert Flora and Fauna

Desert scorpion

Most of the Southwest is covered by four deserts,
yet it is not an arid wasteland. The Sonoran Desert,
with its rich array of flora and fauna, is famed for
its saguaro cactus. The climatic extremes of the
Chihuahuan Desert support hardy agaves and
coyotes. The cooler Great Basin is home to many
grasses and desert animals. The winter rain in the
Mojave Desert results in a spectacular display of
wild-flowers in spring.

**Bighorn sheep** are shy, elusive
creatures and are not easily
spotted. Now a protected species,
they are being gradually
reintroduced throughout the
desert areas.

**Prickly pear cacti** flower
in spring and are among the
largest of the many types of
cacti that flourish in the
Sonoran Desert.

*For hotels and restaurants see pp550–55*

Soaptree yucca plant in the White Sands National Monument

300 sq miles (800 sq km). Gypsum is a water soluble mineral, rarely found as sand. But here, with no drainage outlet to the sea, the sediment washed by the rain into the basin becomes trapped. As the rain evaporates, dry lakes form and strong winds blow the gypsum up into the vast fields of rippling dunes.

Visitors can explore White Sands by car on the Dunes Drive, a 16-mile (26-km) loop. Four clearly marked trails lead from points along the way, including the wheelchair-accessible Interdune Boardwalk. Year-round ranger-led walks introduce visitors to the dunes' flora and fauna. Only plants that grow quickly enough not to be buried survive, such as the hardy soaptree yucca. Most of the animals are nocturnal and include foxes, coyotes, and porcupines.

The park is surrounded by the White Sands Missile Range,

a military testing site. For safety, the park and the road leading to it (Hwy 70) may close for up to three hours when testing is underway. The **White Sands Missile Range Museum** displays many of the missiles tested here, as well as the V-2 rockets used in World War II.

## ⑮ Gila Cliff Dwellings National Monument

**Tel** (575) 536-9461. **Open** 8am–4:30pm daily. **Closed** Jan 1, Dec 25. **W** nps.gov/gicl

The Gila (pronounced hee-la) Cliff Dwellings are one of the most remote archaeological sites in the Southwest, situated among the piñon, juniper, and ponderosa evergreens of the Gila National Forest. The dwellings occupy five natural caves in the side of a sandstone bluff high above the Gila River.

Hunter-gatherers and farmers called the Tularosa Mogollon established their 40-room village here in the late 13th century. The Mimbres Mogollon people, famous for their abstract black-and-white pottery designs on hand-coiled earthenware, also lived in this area. The cliff dwellers hunted the local wildlife, including whitetail and mule deer. They probably farmed the fields alongside the Gila River, growing corn and squash. A granary still holds a dessicated reserve of tiny corn. The ruins are accessed by a 1-mile (1.6-km) round-trip hike from the footbridge crossing the Gila River's West Fork. Allow 2 hours to navigate the 40-mile (64-km) road to the site from Silver City as it winds and climbs through the mountains and canyons of the forest.

**The Joshua tree** was named by Mormons who saw the upraised arms of Joshua in its branches.

**The javelina** is a strange pig-like mammal that wanders the Chihuahuan and Sonoran Deserts in small packs.

**Yucca plants** have been gathered for centuries and have many uses: their fruit can be eaten, and the roots make shampoo.

**Golden eagles** can be seen high in the sky in daytime as they hunt for prey across the Great Basin Desert.

# Practical Information

Dotted with dramatic rock formations, canyons, ancient sites, and wild deserts, the Southwest offers visitors a range of outdoor pleasures. The cities feature superb museums, good dining, and accommodations, along with a laid-back culture. A major draw for visitors are the casinos of Las Vegas. The Southwest is a year-round destination. The high-lying areas of Arizona, New Mexico, and Utah have cold, snowy winters, making them popular for skiing, while the states' southern areas offer warm and sunny winters. But the less-crowded and milder spring and fall are the ideal seasons to visit.

## Tourist Information

Each state and major towns and cities have departments of tourism. Many of the Southwest's attractions on Indian reservation lands are managed by Native American tribal councils. For advice on these contact the local office of the **Navajo Tourism Department**.

## Personal Security

Most tourist areas in the Southwest are friendly and unthreatening, but it is wise to be cautious. Find out which parts of town are unsafe at night. Never carry too much cash, and lock your valuables in the hotel safe.

## Natural Hazards

Rapid weather changes in the Southwest often present dangerous situations. In parts of southern Utah and Arizona, sudden summer storms can cause flash floods. Visitors often underestimate the dry heat of the region's summers. Hikers must carry at least a gallon (4 liters) of drinking water per person for each day of walking.

The Southwest's wilderness harbors venomous creatures such as scorpions, snakes, and the Gila monster lizard; but it is unlikely you will be bitten if you avoid their habitats. Insect bites may hurt but are rarely fatal to adults. But, if bitten, seek medical help.

## Getting Around

Though slower than car and plane travel, trains and buses are enjoyable means of exploring the region. Visitors can take special railroad trips to enjoy some of the Southwest's most delightful scenery. The Grand Canyon Railway's diesel and steam rail trips from Williams to Grand Canyon feature packages that include Western entertainments.

Long-distance buses are the least expensive mode of travel. A bus tour is often the most convenient way of seeing both major city sights and some of the more remote scenery of the Southwest. In major cities, local bus routes cover most attractions. Taxis are also an efficient way of traveling around cities.

## Driving in the Southwest

A car is often the only means of reaching remote areas. There are car rental agencies all over the region, but it is best to arrange a fly-drive deal for cities such as Las Vegas. Pay attention to road signs especially in remote areas where they may issue warnings about local hazards. Check your route to see if a four-wheel drive (4WD) vehicle is required. Most backcountry areas now have roads that can carry conventional cars, but a 4WD is essential in some wild areas. When traveling between remote destinations, inform someone of your plans. Be wary of seasonal dangers such as flash floods in Utah's canyonlands. Carry plenty of food and water, and a cell phone as a precaution. If your vehicle breaks down, stay with it since it offers protection from the elements, and telephone for help.

## Etiquette

Dress in the Southwest is informal, practical, and dependent on the climate. Some of the region's most famous sights are located on reservation land. Visitors are welcome but must be sensitive as to what may cause offense. It is illegal to bring alcohol onto reservations – even a bottle visible in a locked car will land you in trouble. Ask before photographing anything, especially ceremonial dances or Native homes, and bear in mind that a fee may be requested. Do not wander off marked trails, as this is forbidden.

---

## The Climate of The Southwest

The weather in this region ranges from the heat of the desert to the ice and snow of the mountains. Temperatures usually vary with altitude. As a result the higher elevations in the north, especially Utah, northern Arizona, and New Mexico, experience cold, snowy winters. The southern areas, on the other hand, have mild, sunny winters and hot, dry summers. Summer temperatures in the desert often reach more than 100°F (38°C), but can drop to almost 30°F (10°C) after sunset. Except for violent summer storms, rainfall is scarce in the Southwest.

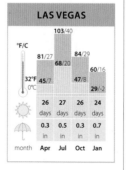

| LAS VEGAS | | | |
|---|---|---|---|
| | 103/40 | | |
| °F/C | | 84/29 | |
| | 81/27 68/20 | | 60/16 |
| 32°F 45/7 | | 47/8 | |
| 0°C | | | 29/-2 |
| 26 days | 27 days | 26 days | 24 days |
| 0.3 in | 0.5 in | 0.3 in | 0.7 in |
| month Apr | Jul | Oct | Jan |

## Outdoor Activities

With thousands of miles of rock canyons, spectacular deserts, and snowcapped peaks, the Southwest is a magnet for climbers, hikers, mountain bikers, 4WD drivers, and skiers. All national parks have well-marked trails and ranger-led hikes, focusing on the local flora, fauna, and geology.

Utah considers itself the world's mountain bike capital, and Moab is a pilgrimage site for such bikers. **Poison Spider Bicycles** sells and repairs bikes as well as runs Nichols Tours, which leads groups through wilderness areas.

The Green, San Juan, and Colorado Rivers are ideal for white-water rafting. A thrilling 6–16 day rafting trip along the Colorado River through the Grand Canyon is offered by many outfitters, including **Canyon Explorations**. Water sports, such as powerboating, jet-skiing, and fishing, are popular in the artificial lakes.

Air tours are a good option for time-restricted travelers who wish to see the remote attractions. **Red Tail Aviation of Moab** offer three-hour tours that cover Canyonlands, Lake Powell, Capitol Reef National Park, and the Grand Canyon's North Rim. However, helicopter tours of the Grand Canyon have a poor reputation for safety. Arizona's 420 golf courses make the Southwest a golfer's paradise. Scottsdale, considered America's premier golf spot, is famous for its **Boulders Resort**. The ski season runs from November to April. Utah has some of the best skiing in the region, while New Mexico's **Taos Ski Valley** includes world-class slopes.

## Entertainment

The Southwest's blend of cultures has made the region a lively center for arts and entertainment. The cities of Phoenix, Santa Fe, Tucson, and Albuquerque offer opera, ballet, classical music, and theatrical productions. The small resort towns of Sedona and Iaos, famed for their resident artists, regularly host touring productions and theater and musical shows. Most cities and major towns have a lively nightlife that includes country music, jazz, and rock as well as dinner theater and standup comedy.

The Southwest is a mecca for Western-style entertainment such as rodeo contests. Historic frontier towns such as Tombstone also stage mock gunfights. Check with the **Tombstone Visitor Center** for details. For sports fans, there are major league and college football, baseball, and basketball games.

## Gambling in Las Vegas

Despite its growing fame as the entertainment capital of the world, Las Vegas is popular mainly for its casinos. They can seem daunting at first, but with a basic understanding of the rules, most games are fairly easy. Some hotels have gaming guides on their in-house TV channels, and many casinos give free lessons at the tables. If you are winning, it is customary to tip the dealers.

## Shopping

The Southwest's exciting range of Indian, Hispanic, and Anglo-American products make shopping a cultural adventure. Native crafts, including rugs and jewelry, can be bought in reservation posts or pueblo stores.

Santa Fe is famous for its galleries selling Georgia O'Keeffe-inspired landscapes, contemporary art, and bronze cowboy sculptures.

Across the region, specialty grocery stores stock local products such as hot chili sauces and blue corn chips.

The big cities offer a choice of air-conditioned malls. The biggest concentration is in Phoenix, and its **Metrocenter Mall** is the region's largest. Las Vegas's fantasy-themed malls make shopping one of its many attractions.

## DIRECTORY

### Tourist Offices

**Arizona**
Tel (602) 364-3700, (866) 298-3795.
W arizonaguide.com

**Colorado**
Tel (800) 265-6723.
W colorado.com

**Navajo Tourism Department**
PO Box 663, Window Rock, AZ 86515.
Tel (928) 871-6436.
W discovernavajo.com

**New Mexico**
Tel (505) 827-7400, (800) 545-2070.
W newmexico.org

**Utah**
Tel (801) 538-1030.
W visitutah.com

### Mountain Biking

**Poison Spider Bicycles**
497 N Main St, Moab, UT 84532.
Tel (800) 635-1792, (435) 259-7882.

### Whitewater Rafting

**Canyon Explorations**
PO Box 310, Flagstaff, AZ 86002. Tel (928) 774-4559, (800) 654-0723.

### Air Tours

**Red Tail Aviation of Moab**
Tel (435) 259-6216.

### Skiing

**Taos Ski Valley**
PO Box 90 Taos Ski Valley, NM 87525.
Tel (866) 968-7386.

### Golf

**Boulders Resort**
34631 N Tom Darlington Dr, Carefree, AZ 85377.
Tel (866) 397-6520.

### Rodeos & Wild West Shows

**Tombstone Visitor Center**
Tel (520) 457-3929.

### Shopping

**Metrocenter Mall**
9617 Metro Pkwy, Phoenix, AZ 85051.
Tel (602) 997-8991.

# Where to Stay

## Nevada

**LAS VEGAS: Golden Nugget
Hotel & Casino** $
Historic
129 E Fremont St, 89101
**Tel** (702) 385-7111
ⓦ goldennugget.com
A favorite with both businessmen
and families, this hotel boasts
the world's largest gold nugget
and a massive shark aquarium.

**LAS VEGAS: New York
New York Hotel & Casino** $
Value
3790 Las Vegas Blvd S, 89109
**Tel** (702) 740-6969
ⓦ newyorknewyork.com
A family-friendly complex with
replicas of New York landmarks,
including the Statue of Liberty
and a Coney Island arcade.

**LAS VEGAS: Cosmopolitan
of Las Vegas** $$
Luxury
3708 Las Vegas Blvd S, 89109
**Tel** (702) 698-7000
ⓦ cosmopolitanlasvegas.com
Sleek hotel offering a casino,
a range of restaurants, several
bars, three pool areas, and an
award-winning spa.

**LAS VEGAS: Hard Rock
Hotel & Casino** $$
Resort
4455 Paradise Rd, 89109
**Tel** (702) 693-5000
ⓦ hardrockhotel.com
Famous musicians often perform
live at this hotel, which also
displays musical memorabilia
in every corner. Hip pool area.

The View Hotel, at the edge of
Monument Valley

**LAS VEGAS: MGM Grand
Hotel & Casino** $$
Luxury
3799 Las Vegas Blvd S, 89109
**Tel** (702) 891-1111
ⓦ mgmgrand.com
You'll need comfortable shoes to
get around the vast casino and
events arena at this sprawling
complex. Contemporary rooms.

**LAS VEGAS: Paris Las Vegas** $$
Luxury
3655 Las Vegas Blvd S, 89109
**Tel** (702) 946-7000
ⓦ parislv.com
This hotel offers a spa, a salon,
12 restaurants, and replicas of the
Eiffel Tower and Arc de Triomphe.

### DK Choice

**LAS VEGAS: Bellagio** $$$
Luxury
3600 Las Vegas Blvd S, 89109
**Tel** (702) 693-7111
ⓦ bellagio.com
A Tuscan-themed hotel, the
Bellagio is opulently decorated
with marble. Best known for its
prominent fountains, which
dance to music, this full-service
resort also has plenty of
shopping and dining options.
Its Gallery of Fine Art hosts
outstanding exhibitions.

**LAS VEGAS: Wynn Las Vegas** $$$
Luxury
3131 Las Vegas Blvd S, 89109
**Tel** (702) 770-7777
ⓦ wynnlasvegas.com
This opulent casino resort offers
many amenities, including a
championship golf course and a
Maserati car dealership on site.

## Utah

**BRYCE CANYON: The Lodge
at Bryce Canyon** $$
Historic
Bryce Canyon National Park, 84764
**Tel** (435) 834-8700
ⓦ brycecanyonforever.com
Built in the 1920s from sandstone
and pine, this hotel has rooms
and cabins with gas-log fireplaces.

**MOAB: The Gonzo Inn** $$
B&B
100 W 200 South St, 84532
**Tel** (435) 259-2515
ⓦ gonzoinn.com
Trendy inn with a mix of
Southwestern and retro decor.
Outdoor pool and hot tub.

**Price Guide**
Prices are based on one night's stay in
high season for a standard double room,
inclusive of service charges and taxes.

| | |
|---|---|
| $ | up to $150 |
| $$ | $150–$250 |
| $$$ | over $250 |

### DK Choice

**MOAB: Sorrell River Ranch
Resort & Spa** $$$
Luxury
Hwy 128, Mile 17, 84532
**Tel** (435) 259-4642
ⓦ sorrelriver.com
This spa resort in the gorgeous
setting of Castle Valley is a one-
stop destination for top-notch
relaxation, with a full-service
spa and Native activities such
as horseback riding. Rooms are
decorated with log furniture,
and each has a kitchenette,
sitting area, and porch with
Adirondak chairs or a swing.

### DK Choice

**MONUMENT VALLEY:
The View Hotel** $$
B&B
Hwy 163 Monument Valley
Tribal Park, 84536
**Tel** (435) 727-5555
ⓦ monumentvalleyview.com
Guests enjoy stunning views
from the Navajo-owned View
Hotel, the only hotel located
at the edge of Monument
Valley. The comfortable, well-
appointed rooms here have
private balconies that make
excellent sunrise-viewing points.
Guided tours and day trips can
be arranged.

**PARK CITY: St. Regis
Deer Valley** $$$
Luxury
2300 Deer Valley Dr E, 84060
**Tel** (435) 940-5700
ⓦ stregisdeervalley.com
High-end resort offering ski-in/
ski-out access and elegant rooms,
suites, and private residences –
some with private butler service.

**SALT LAKE CITY:
Inn on the Hill** $$
B&B
225 N State St, 84103
**Tel** (801) 328-1466
ⓦ inn-on-the-hill.com
The tasteful rooms in this inn
in a historic neighborhood
feature down bedding, jetted
tubs, and gas fireplaces.

**SALT LAKE CITY:**
**Grand America Hotel** $$$
Luxury
*555 S Main St, 84111*
**Tel** *(801) 258-6000*
W grandamerica.com
A downtown hotel offering
mountain views from most
rooms, plus Italian marble
baths and a relaxing day spa.

**ZION NATIONAL PARK:**
**Zion Lodge** $$
B&B
*Springdale, 84767*
**Tel** *(303) 297-3175*
W zionlodge.com
Cabins and rooms are
surrounded by massive
sandstone walls in a wooded
area inside Zion Canyon.

# Arizona

**BISBEE: Shady Dell** $
Historic
*1 Douglas Rd, 85603*
**Tel** *(520) 432-3567*
W theshadydell.com
Stay in a vintage trailer – a 1949
Airstream or a 1950 Spartanette –
high up in the mountains.

**FLAGSTAFF: Weatherford Hotel** $
Historic
*23 N Leroux St, 86001*
**Tel** *(928) 779-1919*
W weatherfordhotel.com
Elegant 1897 sandstone building
with a wraparound veranda. Close
to Flagstaff's Amtrak station.

**FLAGSTAFF:**
**Little America Hotel** $$
Resort
*2515 E Butler Ave, 86004*
**Tel** *(928) 779-7900*
W littleamerica.com/flagstaff
Set amid acres of pines, this hotel
has opulent rooms and suites. It
organizes fun activities and tours.

**GRAND CANYON (SOUTH RIM):**
**Bright Angel Lodge** $
Historic
*Grand Canyon Village, 86023*
**Tel** *(928) 638-2631*
W grandcanyonlodges.com
Edge-of-the-canyon cabins with
log-and-stone interiors designed
by Mary Elizabeth Colter in 1935.

**GRAND CANYON (SOUTH RIM):**
**Maswik Lodge** $
Historic
*Grand Canyon Village, 86023*
**Tel** *(928) 638-2631*
W grandcanyonlodges.com
The Maswik is a family-friendly
lodge, with two buildings that
are set amid ponderosa pines.

Lounge area in the historic Hotel Valley Ho, Scottsdale

**GRAND CANYON (SOUTH RIM):**
**El Tovar Hotel** $$
Historic
*Grand Canyon Village, 86023*
**Tel** *(928) 638-2631*
W grandcanyonlodges.com
The distinctive design at this
luxurious landmark lodge
includes natural stone and
douglas fir.

**JEROME: Ghost City Inn**
**Bed & Breakfast** $
B&B
*541 N Main St, 86331*
**Tel** *(928) 634-4678*
W ghostcityinn.com
Formerly an 1890s copper miners'
boardinghouse, this inn offers
attractively renovated rooms.

**LAKE HAVASU CITY: Heat** $$
Luxury
*1420 Mcculloch Blvd, 86403*
**Tel** *(888) 898-4328*
W heathotel.com
The contemporary rooms at this
hotel showcase its waterfront
setting. Each has a private
balcony and Internet access.

**PHOENIX: Clarendon**
**Hotel and Suites** $$
Business
*401 W Clarendon Ave, 85013*
**Tel** *(602) 252-7363*
W goclarendon.com
Located in the business district,
this hotel has a trendy interior
with cutting-edge lighting and a
French-fusion restaurant on site.

**PHOENIX: Hotel Palomar**
**Phoenix** $$$
Luxury
*2 E Jefferson St, 85004*
**Tel** *(602) 253-6633*
W hotelpalomar-phoenix.com
This contemporary and well-
connected hotel is located in
the CityScape shopping, dining,
and entertainment hub.

**PHOENIX:**
**Ritz-Carlton Hotel** $$$
Luxury
*2401 E Camelback Rd, 85016*
**Tel** *(602) 468-0700*
W ritzcarlton.com
This hotel has refined, elegant
decor and far-reaching views of
the downtown skyline, as well
as of the mountains.

**DK Choice**

**SCOTTSDALE: Hotel**
**Valley Ho** $$
Luxury
*6850 E Main St, 85251*
**Tel** *(480) 248-2000*
W HotelValleyHo.com
Built in 1956, the sophisticated
Valley Ho was once frequented
by the likes of Bogart and
Monroe. Now fully restored,
this historic property is a hip
haven, with retro-chic rooms,
a yoga and pilates studio, and
a pool. Situated on the edge
of downtown, it is a short
walk from several shops,
restaurants, and art galleries.

**SCOTTSDALE:**
**The Phoenician** $$$
Resort
*6000 E Camelback Rd, 85251*
**Tel** *(480) 941-8200*
W thephoenician.com
A world-famous resort that offers
top-notch service and amenities,
including numerous dining
options and championship golf.

**SEDONA: Cozy Cactus B&B** $$
B&B
*80 Canyon Circle Dr, 86351*
**Tel** *(928) 284-0082*
W cozycactus.com
This family-friendly property with
stunning views is attractively
furnished with Southwestern
accents. Hiking trails are nearby.

**For more information on types of hotels** *see pages 26–7*

**SEDONA:
Enchantment Resort** $$$
Resort
*525 Boynton Canyon Rd, 86336*
**Tel** *(928) 282-2900*
W enchantmentresort.com
Adobe accommodations have
typical Southwestern interiors at
this luxurious resort located
among the stunning red rocks
of Boynton Canyon.

**TOMBSTONE: Landmark
Lookout Lodge** $
B&B
*781 N Hwy 80 W, 85638*
**Tel** *(520) 457-2223*
W lookoutlodgeaz.com
The Landmark Lookout Lodge
is an inexpensive option and
a good base for visiting
Tombstone's key sights.

**TUCSON:
Hotel Congress** $
Value
*311 E Congress St, 85701*
**Tel** *(520) 622-8848*
W hotelcongress.com
This historic hotel in the heart of
downtown has vintage rooms
with retro furnishings, as well as
multiple bars and restaurants.

**TUCSON: Hacienda del Sol
Ranch Resort** $$
Resort
*5501 N Hacienda del Sol Rd,
85718*
**Tel** *(520) 299-1501*
W haciendadelsol.com
A relaxing luxury hotel, with
exquisite Spanish Colonial rooms
decorated in warm Southwestern
tones and design.

# New Mexico

## DK Choice

**ALBUQUERQUE:
Casas de Sueños** $
B&B
*310 Rio Grande Blvd SW,
87104*
**Tel** *(505) 247-4560*
W casasdesuenos.com
Translating as the "Houses of
Dreams", Casas de Sueños
once housed a 1930s artists'
colony. Today, charming
adobe-style casitas are
nestled among courtyards
and leafy gardens. Each room
is uniquely decorated, some
with kiva fireplaces or Saltillo-
tiled floors; others with patios
or Jacuzzi tubs. A full breakfast
is included and served daily in
the sunny garden studio.

Terrace dining area at Enchantment Resort, Sedona

**ALBUQUERQUE:
MCM Elegante Hotel** $
Value
*2020 Menaul Blvd NE, 87107*
**Tel** *(505) 884-2511*
W mcmelegantealbuquerque.com
An affordable option near
downtown, the MCM Elegante
has modern rooms, some with
balconies and mountain views.

**ALBUQUERQUE:
Nativo Lodge** $
Value
*6000 Pan American Freeway NE,
87109*
**Tel** *(505) 798-4300*
W nativolodge.com
This lodge near the Balloon Fiesta
Park combines Native American
culture with modern amenities.
Rooms have hand-carved murals
and Navajo-designed rugs.

**ALBUQUERQUE:
Crowne Plaza Albuquerque** $$
Luxury
*1901 University Blvd NE, 87102*
**Tel** *(505) 884-2500*
W ihg.com
Sprawling, resort-like property
with New Mexican decor and
facilities such as a pool, whirlpool,
fitness center, and sauna.

**SANTA FE: Don Gaspar Inn** $$
B&B
*623 Don Gaspar, 87505*
**Tel** *(505) 986-8664*
W dongaspar.com
Three historic buildings located
close to Santa Fe's major
attractions offer spacious rooms
and lovely gardens and courtyards.

**SANTA FE: Hotel Chimayo** $$
B&B
*125 Washington Ave, 87501*
**Tel** *(505) 988-4900*
W hotelchimayo.com
The rooms at Hotel Chimayo
feature handcrafted furniture
and fireplaces, as well as scenic
balconies or patios.

## DK Choice

**SANTA FE: La Fonda
on the Plaza** $$$
Luxury
*100 E San Francisco St, 87501*
**Tel** *(505) 982-5511*
W lafondasantafe.com
The grande dame of Santa
Fe hotels sits on the site of a
1610 adobe inn. Artworks are
everywhere – the guestroom
headboards, the blanket boxes,
and even the light switches
have been painted by the
hotel's resident artist. Modern
amenities include a swimming
pool and a state-of-the art
fitness center and spa.

**SANTA FE: The Inn of the
Five Graces** $$$
Luxury
*150 E DeVargas, 87501*
**Tel** *(505) 992-0957*
W fivegraces.com
An all-suite inn showcasing
world-class interior design.
Situated across the street from
the San Miguel Mission.

**SANTA FE: Rosewood Inn
of the Anasazi** $$$
Luxury
*113 Washington Ave, 87501*
**Tel** *(505) 988-3030*
W innoftheanasazi.com
This elegant inn is filled with
exquisite Native American
tapestries, four-poster beds,
and rustic wooden furniture.

**TAOS:
Palacio de Marquesa** $$$
Luxury
*405 Cordoba Rd, 87571*
**Tel** *(575) 758-4777*
W marquesataos.com
Atmospheric classic adobe inn
with sophisticated contemporary
interior design. Each room
honors an extraordinary
Taos woman.

# Where to Eat and Drink

## Nevada

**LAS VEGAS: The Buffet** $
American
*Golden Nugget, 129 E Fremont St, 89101*
**Tel** *(702) 385-7111*
A pleasant all-you-can-eat restaurant that hosts jovial crowds seated in comfy booths. It offers a variety of food platters and an extensive salad bar.

**LAS VEGAS: Harley Davidson Café** $
American
*3725 Las Vegas Blvd S, 89109*
**Tel** *(702) 740-4555*
This three-story motorbike heaven is instantly recognizable by the huge Heritage Softail replica and the Captain America bike from the movie *Easy Rider*. Famous for BBQ favorites such as ribs, chicken, and sausages.

**LAS VEGAS: In-N-Out Burger** $
American
*4888 Dean Martin Dr, 89103*
**Tel** *(800) 786-1000*
Wildly popular, this California-based chain provides high-quality fast food at low prices, including many varieties of burgers, fries, and shakes.

**LAS VEGAS: Pink Taco** $
Mexican
*Hard Rock Hotel, 4455 Paradise Rd, 89109*
**Tel** *(702) 693-5525*
A hip, colorful cantina-style eatery with an assortment of Mexican crafts, classic dishes, and an extensive margarita and tequila list. Friendly ambience.

**LAS VEGAS: Lotus of Siam** $$
Thai
*953 E Sahara Ave, 89104*
**Tel** *(702) 735-3033*
The chef here prepares recipes from northern Thailand that have been passed down through generations. Select from a menu of spicy stews and curries made with authentic herbs and spices.

**LAS VEGAS: Mizumi** $$$
Japanese
*Wynn Las Vegas, 3131 Las Vegas Blvd S, 89109*
**Tel** *(702) 248-3463*
The award-winning chef at Mizumi blends Japanese flavors with French techniques to create authentic *robatayaki*, teppanyaki, and sushi delights – all paired with top-quality wines and sakes.

### DK Choice

**LAS VEGAS: Picasso** $$$
New American
*Bellagio, 3600 Las Vegas Blvd S, 89109*
**Tel** *(702) 693-8865* **Closed** *Tue*
Admire the original Picasso artworks in this flower-filled room while dining on modern American fare with French and Spanish influences. Tasting menus may include sautéed foie gras with honey-roasted figs and walnuts, or roasted pigeon with wild-rice risotto. There is a big-ticket wine list, too.

**LAS VEGAS: Restaurant Guy Savoy** $$$
French
*Caesars Palace, 3570 Las Vegas Blvd S, 89109*
**Tel** *(702) 731-7286* **Closed** *Mon, Tue*
Superb French cuisine made with seasonal ingredients, in a setting that reflects chef Guy Savoy's Paris restaurant. Great wine list.

**LAS VEGAS: Top of the World** $$$
New American
*Stratosphere Tower, 2000 Las Vegas Blvd S, 89104*
**Tel** *(702) 380-7711*
Views as far as the eye can see, 833 ft (254 m) above the ground, in a slowly revolving room. House specialties include Scottish salmon with mustard and maple glaze.

## Utah

**BRYCE CANYON: The Lodge at Bryce Canyon Restaurant** $$
New American
*The Lodge at Bryce Canyon, Bryce Canyon National Park, 84764*
**Tel** *(435) 834-8760*
A rustic, elegant restaurant, nestled amid ponderosa pines.

### Price Guide

Prices are for a three-course meal for one, including half a bottle of house wine, including tax and service.

| | |
|---|---|
| $ | up to $35 |
| $$ | $35–$70 |
| $$$ | over $70 |

Large fireplaces create a relaxing, cozy atmosphere, and interesting menu items include Utah trout crusted with almonds and panko.

### DK Choice

**MOAB: Moab Diner** $
American
*189 S Main St, 84532*
**Tel** *(435) 259-4006*
From its round-the-clock breakfast menu to dinner, this sparsely decorated diner is a hit with locals and visitors alike. Don't miss the signature green-chili cheeseburger, and leave room for an ice-cream sundae or shake, available in more than a dozen flavors.

**MOAB: Sunset Grill** $$
American
*900 N Route 191 on Main St, 84532*
**Tel** *(435) 259-7146* **Closed** *Sun*
Sunset Grill is set on a hill in the former home of Charlie Steen, the discoverer of uranium. The big draws are the sunset views and fine dining. The chocolate mousse pie is a dessert specialty.

**MONUMENT VALLEY: Stagecoach Dining Room** $$
Southwestern/American
*Goulding's Lodge, 84536*
**Tel** *(435) 727-3231*
Located high on a hill, with fine panoramic views, the Stagecoach caters mainly to tourists visiting Monument Valley. The salad bar, Navajo tacos, and steaks are popular items on the menu.

The iconic Harley Davidson Café, Las Vegas

For more information on types of restaurants *see pages 28–9*

**PARK CITY: High West
Distillery & Saloon** $$
American
*703 Park Ave, 84060*
**Tel** *(435) 649-8300*
Western-inspired fare is served
in an Old Town saloon featuring
a bar made of wood from the
Trestle Bridge of 1904. The
cocktails are prepared with the
award-winning spirits made at
the on-site distillery.

**SALT LAKE CITY: Red Iguana** $
Mexican
*736 W North Temple, 84116*
**Tel** *(801) 322-1489* **Closed** *Sun*
One of the state's most
decorated eateries specializes
in a flavorful variety of smoky
mole dishes. Sit in the colorful
dining area, and enjoy fresh
dishes and well-made margaritas.

**SALT LAKE CITY:
The Copper Onion** $$
American
*111 E Broadway, 84111*
**Tel** *(801) 355-3282*
All-purpose downtown eatery
serving lunch, dinner, and drinks
to a crowd of regulars. Menu
items range from charcuterie and
cheese plates to home-made
pastas and hearty meat entrées.

**ZION NATIONAL PARK:
Red Rock Grill** $$
Southwestern
*Zion Lodge, Springdale, 84767*
**Tel** *(435) 772-7760*
Nestled among the
cottonwoods, Red Rock boasts
splendid views from its open-air
terrace. The interesting menu
includes a spicy-sweet chipotle
tilapia, and Navajo eggplant with
a tomatillo cream sauce.

# Arizona

**FLAGSTAFF: Downtown Diner** $
American
*7 E Aspen Ave, 86001*
**Tel** *(928) 774-3492*
Photos of local landscapes line
the walls at this neighborhood
favorite serving breakfasts and
coffee. The lunch menu includes
giant burgers and fresh trout.

**FLAGSTAFF: Black Bart's
Steak House** $$$
Steak House
*2760 E Butler Ave, 86004*
**Tel** *(928) 779-3142*
Named for an 1870s stagecoach
robber, this hangout offers corn-
fed steaks and fresh seafood. In
the evenings, a musical revue is
performed by the friendly staff.

**GRAND CANYON (NORTH RIM):
Grand Canyon Lodge** $$$
American
*North Rim Grand Canyon, 86052*
**Tel** *(928) 638-2611*
This beautiful, remote restaurant
offers great views of the Kaibab
Plateau, along with sophisticated
dining options. Reservations
should be made a month or two
in advance during high season.

**GRAND CANYON (SOUTH RIM):
El Tovar** $$
Southwestern
*Grand Canyon Village, 86023*
**Tel** *(928) 638-2631*
This is arguably the finest dining
option in the park. The menu at
El Tovar features a mix of classic
and Southwestern fare. Enjoy
a light meal on the veranda,
which offers lovely views.

**LAKE HAVASU CITY:
Mudshark Brewing Co.** $
American
*210 Swanson Ave, 86403*
**Tel** *(928) 453-2981*
Popular for its handcrafted
beer on tap, Mudshark offers
an eclectic menu of burgers,
sandwiches, and slow-cooked
pork chops. The wall murals
add to the lovely ambience.

**PARADISE VALLEY:
El Chorro** $$$
New American
*5550 E Lincoln Dr, 85253*
**Tel** *(480) 948-5170*
A number of classic regional
favorites can be found on a
menu that highlights fresh,
organic, and locally grown
ingredients. The relaxed Sunday
brunch features El Chorro's
legendary sticky buns.

**PHOENIX:
Matt's Big Breakfast** $
American
*825 N 1st St, 85004*
**Tel** *(602) 254-1074* **Closed** *Mon*
Head over to Matt's for top-
quality breakfast offerings made
using all grain-fed meats, free-
range eggs, and organic produce.
The decor features 1950s dinette
tables, a bright-orange counter,
and vintage artworks.

**PHOENIX:
Barrio Café** $$
Mexican
*2814 N 16th St, 85004*
**Tel** *(602) 636-0240* **Closed** *Mon*
Reliable southern Mexican
dishes and original creations are
served in three casual dining
rooms filled with wall art. The
tiny bar offers over 250 tequilas
and delicious margaritas.

Dinner at dusk at El Chorro, Paradise Valley
in the Arizona desert

## DK Choice

**PHOENIX: Pizzeria Bianco** $$
Pizzeria
*623 E Adams St, 85004*
**Tel** *(602) 258-8300* **Closed** *Sun*
A simple menu of wood-fired
pizzas and salads incorporates
a variety of local, seasonal
ingredients, such as fennel
sausage and house-smoked
mozzarella. Foodies from all
over the world flock to this
downtown venue to sample
the gourmet pizza pies that
some claim are the best in
the country.

**PHOENIX: Durant's** $$$
Steak House
*2611 N Central Ave, 85004*
**Tel** *(602) 264-5967*
Spot local celebrities dining
on a range of large appetizers,
steaks, and fresh seafood at this
bustling steak house, a Phoenix
mainstay since the 1950s.

**SCOTTSDALE: Cowboy Ciao** $$$
New American
*7133 E Stetson Dr, 85251*
**Tel** *(480) 946-3111*
Creative fare is served in
sophisticated yet casual environs.
Rare global wines are paired with
dishes such as duck confit relleno
and pastrami-style smoked ribs.

**SEDONA: El Rincon
Restaurante Mexicano** $
Mexican
*Tlaquepaque Village, 336 S Hwy 179,
86336*
**Tel** *(928) 282-4648*
Arched doorways and Spanish-
style furnishings bring the
Tlaquepaque charm indoors.
Savor Mexican dishes – from
burritos to tamales – with a
touch of Navajo influence.

### SEDONA: Barking Frog Grille $$
Southwestern
*2620 W Arizona 89A, 86336*
**Tel** *(928) 204-2000*
A varied menu features creative interpretations of all the favorites. There's a choice of three casual dining rooms, outdoor patios, and a bar. Impressive wine list.

## DK Choice
### SEDONA: Shugrue's Hillside Grill $$$
American
*Hillside Courtyard, 671 Hwy 179, 86336*
**Tel** *(928) 282-5300*
At Shugrue, guests enjoy superb steaks and seafood prepared in three ways: grilled, sautéed, or blackened. The eclectic menu incorporates seasonal, local, and organic ingredients. Gourmet breakfasts and lunches are served daily. The floor-to-ceiling windows offer beautiful views, and there is a terrace for alfresco dining as well.

### TUCSON: El Charro Café $
Mexican
*311 N Court Ave, 85701*
**Tel** *(520) 622-1922*
One of the oldest family-owned restaurants in the country. Their *carne seca* (shredded sundried Angus beef marinated in garlic and lime juice) is legendary.

### TUCSON: Café Poca Cosa $$
Mexican
*110 E Pennington St, 85701*
**Tel** *(520) 622-6400* **Closed** *Sun, Mon*
This casual-chic bistro serves inspired Mexican cuisine with a sprinkling of regional flavors. Select from a chalkboard menu that changes daily and is listed in both English and Spanish.

## New Mexico

## DK Choice
### ALBUQUERQUE: Church Street Café $
Southwestern
*2111 Church St NW, 87104*
**Tel** *(505) 247-8522*
This café is filled with Native American art and rugs. Dine inside by the kiva fireplace, or outdoors among the grapevines. On the menu is highly regarded regional fare such as *carne adovada al horno* (oven-cooked pork marinated in red chilies).

### ALBUQUERQUE: Frontier Restaurant $
Southwestern/American
*2400 Central Ave SE, 87106*
**Tel** *(505) 266-0550*
Good-value breakfasts, burritos, burgers, and legendary sweet rolls are served in a memorabilia-filled dining room. Located across from the University of New Mexico.

### ALBUQUERQUE: Garduño's $
Mexican
*2100 Louisiana Blvd, 87110*
**Tel** *(505) 880-0055*
A popular local chain serving flavorful dishes. Guacamole is prepared table-side, and burritos and enchiladas come smothered with green chilies. The hand-shaken margaritas and strolling mariachis set a festive tone.

### ALBUQUERQUE: Jennifer James 101 $$$
New American
*4615 Menaul Blvd NE, 87110*
**Tel** *(505) 884-3860* **Closed** *Sun, Mon*
Acclaimed chef Jennifer James presents a menu that goes back to basics, with high-quality recipes. The seasonal dishes are made with local, organic produce.

### SANTA FE: The Shed $
Southwestern/Mexican
*113½ E Palace Ave, 87051*
**Tel** *(505) 982-9030*
Try a chilled raspberry soup laced with rosé wine, followed by a spicy chicken dish, and end with lemon soufflé for dessert at this family-run restaurant in a 17th-century adobe hacienda.

### SANTA FE: Tomasita's $
Mexican
*500 S Guadalupe St, 87501*
**Tel** *(505) 983-5721* **Closed** *Sun*
A family-friendly local favorite, Tomasita's is housed in a train station built in 1904. No advance reservations; be prepared to wait.

### SANTA FE: Maria's New Mexican Kitchen $$
Southwestern/Mexican
*555 W Cordova Rd, 87505*
**Tel** *(505) 983-7929*
At Maria's, chicken, beef, and vegetarian dishes are served on sizzling platters with *pico de gallo* and guacamole. Diners have a choice of over 100 margaritas.

### SANTA FE: Anasazi Restaurant $$$
Southwestern/New American
*Anasazi Hotel, 113 Washington Ave, 87501*
**Tel** *(505) 988-3236*
Luxury hotel restaurant with a wood-beamed ceiling. Try such innovative dishes as almond-crusted salmon, or Berkshire pork chop with bourbon sauce.

## DK Choice
### SANTA FE: The Compound $$$
New American
*635 Canyon Rd, 87501*
**Tel** *(505) 982-4353*
The elegant menu at this restaurant, set in a historic house once known as the McComb Compound, is matched by a stylish, art-filled dining room and luxurious patio. Signature dishes include tuna tartare topped with Oestra caviar, and roasted rack of lamb with salsa verde and romesco.

### TAOS: Orlando's New Mexican Café $$
Southwestern
*1114 Don Juan Valdez Ln, 87571*
**Tel** *(575) 751-1450*
Local chili aficionados rave about the New Mexican fare here. The café is colorfully painted, and large umbrellas shade the patio. Have a beer by the fire pit on cool evenings.

Alfresco dining at Church Street Café, Albuquerque

**For more information on types of restaurants** *see pages 28–9*

# THE ROCKIES

GEORGETOWN LOOP RAILROAD

# The Rockies at a Glance

The four states of Montana, Idaho, Wyoming, and Colorado form the heart of the Rockies, the mountain range that dominates the landscape of North America. This beautiful but sparsely populated region encompasses a wealth of natural wonders such as the geysers of Wyoming's Yellowstone National Park, the varied landscapes of Montana's Glacier National Park, and the cliff dwellings of Colorado's Mesa Verde National Park. Colorado is also celebrated as the skiing capital of the United States. The area's human history lends itself to superlatives as much as the land does. Throughout the Rockies there are tangible signs of such legendary 19th-century Native Americans and cowboys as Sitting Bull and "Buffalo Bill" Cody.

IDAHO
(See pp566–69)

Kalispell
Coeur d'Alene
Great Falls
Missoula
Lewiston
Helena
Butte
Boz
Salmon
Boise
Idaho Falls
Jack
Pocatello
Twin Falls

**Coeur d'Alene** *(see p566)* in Idaho is located along Lake Coeur d'Alene. This popular vacation destination is famous for its unique floating golf green on the 14th hole.

**Sun Valley** *(see p568)*, in southern Idaho, is one of the oldest and most exclusive winter resorts in the country. Its picturesque environs also offer many recreational options.

**Yellowstone National Park** *(see pp576–7)* is perhaps one of the country's most visited parks. The highlights of this wild wonderland are the hot springs, particularly Old Faithful Geyser and its steaming plume.

◀ The Colorado & Southern Railway in Clear Creek County, Georgetown, Colorado

0 km      100
0 miles      100

**Locator Map**

Malta

Glasgow

NTANA
*p570–73)*

Glendive

s

Hardin

Broadus

Buffalo

Newcastle

Thermopolis

Riverton

Casper

WYOMING
*(See pp574–79)*

Guernsey

k

ngs

Laramie

Cheyenne

Craig

Fort Collins

Boulder

Denver

Burlington

Grand
Junction

COLORADO
*(See pp580–89)*

Colorado
Springs

ontrose

Salida

Pueblo

Lamar

Durango

Trinidad

**Billings** *(see p573)* evolved from a small frontier town
into Montana's largest city. Its cowboy heritage can be
seen at Yellowstone Art Museum.

**Denver** *(see pp580–81)*, the region's main
city, is also Colorado's state capital. This
vibrant city is also known for its
museums and parks.

**Mesa Verde National Park** *(see pp588–9)*,
one of the country's most significant
archaeological finds, preserves
the elaborate cliff dwellings of the
Ancestral Puebloan people.

# THE ROCKIES

One of the world's great outdoor regions, the Rockies offer a variety of experiences not found anywhere else. The sheer scale of the landscape is breathtaking, and words can hardly express the thrill of seeing firsthand the broad expanses of the Wyoming plains, Idaho's deep river canyons, the towering peaks of Colorado, or the rugged vastness of Montana.

The underlying geology of the Rocky Mountains is ancient, with some of the country's oldest rocks forming the highly stratified Precambrian peaks and valleys of Glacier National Park. The rest of the range is varied, with mineral-rich granite batholiths sharing space with the vast red-rock mesas of the Colorado Plateau. Evidence of volcanic activity, forming and reforming the landscape from deep beneath the surface, is also omnipresent, most prominently in Idaho's Craters of the Moon National Monument, and most famously in the geysers, mudpots, and hot springs of Yellowstone National Park in Wyoming.

This region has also been shaped by some of North America's mightiest rivers. Beside the terrifying white-water rapids of the Snake and other tumultuous rivers, the Rockies form the headwaters of many major western rivers, including the Colorado, the Missouri, the Columbia, and the Rio Grande. These rivers and their many tributaries offer some of the finest fishing in the world. Wildflowers are abundant, especially in the alpine meadows, while the dense forests are the habitat of a wide range of wildlife. Moose, elk, and bald eagles are spotted frequently along trails and roads, and the backwoods areas hold some of the nation's last wild populations of carnivores, including mountain lions, wolves, and massive grizzly bears.

## History

The history of the Rockies is as wild and larger-than-life as the land itself. From the late 18th century, intrepid "mountain men" – French-Canadian and American fur trappers – traveled throughout the Rockies, trapping beavers and other animals for their valuable skins. After the Louisiana Purchase in 1803, the fledgling country acquired control of the Rockies, and the first official American presence was established between 1803 and 1806 by explorers Meriwether Lewis and William Clark. These daring men were accompanied by a "Corps of Discovery" made up of 29 soldiers and fur trappers, and joined by

Pool along the Firehole Lake Drive, Yellowstone National Park, Wyoming

◀ Winter view of Coeur d'Alene Lake, Idaho, from the mineral ridge hiking trail the legendary Indian guide Sacagawea and her baby son. They followed the Missouri upstream from the frontier outpost of St. Louis, traveling by boat and later by foot across Montana and Idaho on an epic 5,000-mile (8,047-km) journey to the Pacific Ocean and back. Also in 1806, Zebulon Pike led an expedition to Colorado, following the Arkansas River and spotting the majestic mountain that bears his name.

These explorers' published accounts, describing the sublime landscape and its wealth of wildlife, attracted increasing numbers of trappers and hunters, and by the 1830s several commercial outposts had been established, usually at the confluence of major rivers. Their routes across what had once been seen as an impenetrable barrier slowly but surely paved the way for transcontinental travelers. By the mid-1800s, thousands of pioneers following the Oregon Trail and other routes crossed

Lewis & Clark National Historic Trail Interpretive Center, Great Falls, Montana

the Rocky Mountains, bound for the Pacific Northwest, the California gold fields, and the Mormon lands in Utah. As a result, conflicts between immigrants and Native Americans increased dramatically. In the mountains, the Nez Percé and other small tribes lived comparatively peaceful and sedentary lives, while east of the mountains were migratory bands of Plains Indians, including such diverse and often rival tribes as the Sioux, Cheyenne, Crow, Arapahoe, and Shoshone. Most of these eastern tribes were themselves recent arrivals. Living in mobile encampments of tepees, they had mastered the art of riding horses and hunting buffalo. As cowboys and ranchers moved into the rich grazing lands, some 50 million native bison were all but eradicated, and the tribes whose entire culture was based on these mighty herds came under desperate threat.

By the beginning of the 20th century, all the tribes had been contained in small reservations, far from their previous homelands. Ironically, one of the country's greatest Native American cultural repositories is in Wyoming's Buffalo Bill Historical Center, a memorial to the man who, as buffalo hunter and Indian fighter, contributed greatly to their destruction.

## Progress & Development

The first transcontinental railroad crossed southern Wyoming in the late 1860s, followed in the 1870s and 1880s by other

**KEY DATES IN HISTORY**

**1200** Ancestral Pueblo Indians abandon their cliff dwellings at Mesa Verde, Colorado

**1700–1800** French-Canadian fur trappers explore the Rockies

**1803** The US acquires much of this region through the Louisiana Purchase

**1803** The Lewis and Clark expedition begins

**1806** Zebulon Pike explores the Arkansas River in southern Colorado

**1843** The Oregon Trail is opened

**1858** Gold is discovered outside Denver

**1869** Wyoming gives women the vote

**1872** US Congress establishes the world's first national park at Yellowstone

**1876** Battle of Little Bighorn

**1915** The Lincoln Highway, the first transcontinental route from New York City to San Francisco, runs across southern Wyoming

**1951** Warren Air Force Base in Cheyenne is declared the base of operations for all US Intercontinental Ballistic Missiles (ICBMs)

**2003** Memorial commemorating the Native American victory at the Battle of Little Bighorn is dedicated at the site of the battle in Montana

**2013** Forest fire in the Colorado Springs area is the most destructive in Colorado's history

Tepees, Buffalo Bill Historical Center, Wyoming

The former silver-mining town of Wallace, near Coeur d'Alene, Idaho

railroads, such as the Northern Pacific and Great Northern. Carrying cattle to eastern markets, and bringing weapons and supplies to the Wild West, it was these railroads that actually consolidated American settlement.

The search for and discovery of valuable minerals, mainly gold, silver, and copper, was another primary impetus to settlement. Because of the region's expansive forests, the lumber industry, too, had been an economic mainstay since pioneer times, and over the previous century oil and coal deposits have been the source underlying numerous booms and busts, especially in Colorado and Wyoming.

## Tourism & the Economy

Natural resource-based industries are still active all over the Rockies, though the main economic force today is tourism. These four states contain the highest mountains, the densest forests, the wildest rivers, and the most rugged canyons in the "Lower 48" states. Consequently, the Rockies is a magical place offering sublime scenery as well as a wide variety of attractions, such as historic train rides, summer "dude ranches," and historic sites. Many places also feature music festivals,

Plains Indian pow-wows, or theatrical re-creations of Wild West shootouts.

This is also the best place to appreciate the great outdoors. Intrepid guides offer unforgettable trips such as white-water rafting or fly-fishing for trout. The proliferation of ski resorts has also added to the state's tourism potential. When gold was discovered outside Denver in 1850, several mining camps sprang up at such evocatively named places as Silverton and Cripple Creek in Colorado and "Last Chance Gulch," now Helena, Montana. Many of these erstwhile mining centers are now deluxe winter resorts, such as Crested Butte, Telluride, and Aspen in Colorado, and Idaho's Sun Valley.

Neon sign for the Cowboy Bar, Jackson, Wyoming

# Exploring the Rockies

The sheer vastness of the Rocky Mountains landscape and the relative shortness of the tourism season means that visitors need to plan well ahead. Many attractions on this 1,000-mile- (1,609-km-) long swath of mountains are on such high elevations that they are inaccessible during the long winter, with snow blocking roads from late October until June. The heavy snowfalls, however, enhance the region's phenomenal winter sports, and Denver, the main city, is a prime starting point for most visitors. Driving is the best way to explore the area, because public transportation is limited, and the national parks and most of the other attractions are far away.

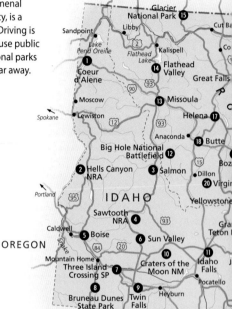

## Key

— Highway

— Major road

— Railroad

--- State border

— International border

## Sights at a Glance

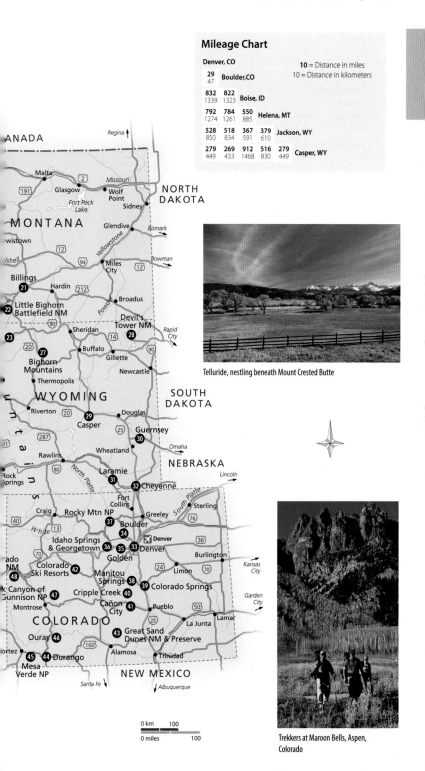

CANADA

Regina

Malta
Glasgow
Wolf Point
Sidney

Fort Peck Lake

Missouri

NORTH DAKOTA

MONTANA

Lewistown
Roundup

Glendive

Bismark

Yellowstone

Billings
21
Hardin
212

Miles City
12

Bowman

Little Bighorn Battlefield NM
22

Powder

Broadus

Devil's Tower NM

Rapid City

23
20

Sheridan
14

28

Buffalo
27
Gillette

Bighorn Mountains

Newcastle

90

Thermopolis

WYOMING

SOUTH DAKOTA

Riverton
20

29
Casper
25

Douglas

Guernsey
30

Omaha

287

Rawlins

Wheatland

NEBRASKA

Rock Springs

80

North Platte

Laramie
31

Lincoln

32 Cheyenne

South Platte

Fort Collins

Craig
40

Rocky Mtn NP

Greeley

Sterling

White
13

37
Boulder
34

76

Idaho Springs & Georgetown
70
36
35
33 Denver

36

Colorado NM
48

Golden

Burlington
24

Colorado Ski Resorts
42

Manitou Springs
38

Limon
70

Kansas City

Black Canyon of the Gunnison NP
47

Cripple Creek
40

39 Colorado Springs

Garden City

Montrose

Cañon City
41

Pueblo
50

COLORADO

La Junta

Lamar

Ouray
46
160

Great Sand Dunes NM & Preserve
43

25

Cortez
45
44 Durango

Alamosa

Trinidad

Mesa Verde NP

NEW MEXICO

Santa Fe

Albuquerque

0 km 100
0 miles 100

Telluride, nestling beneath Mount Crested Butte

Trekkers at Maroon Bells, Aspen, Colorado

# Idaho

One of the country's least populous states, Idaho has vast tracts of unexplored wilderness – remote mountain ranges, dense forests, frozen lakes, and deep river gorges. It is an ideal vacation spot for adventure sports enthusiasts, offering abundant opportunities for hiking, mountain biking, and white-water rafting. To the north lie resorts such as Coeur d'Alene; the center has the majestic Sawtooth Mountains; while the south consists mainly of cultivated fields, prompting automobile license plates in the state to declare Idaho's pride in its primary product, "Famous Potatoes."

## ❶ Coeur d'Alene

🏔 44,000. ➦ 🚌 ℹ️ 105 N First St, (208) 664-3194. 🌐 **coeurdalene.org**

A major vacation destination, Coeur d'Alene was founded in the 1870s as a US Army outpost. Its present four-star status refers to the luxury available at the town's world-famous **Coeur d'Alene Resort** *(see p592)*. Located along the shore of the beautiful Lake Coeur d'Alene, this exclusive resort is well known for its unique floating golf green on the 14th hole. On the resort's east side, the 120-acre (49-ha) **Tubbs Hill Park** is a nature preserve with hiking trails, pine forests, and great views. Lake Coeur d'Alene is also home to one of the country's largest populations of ospreys and bald eagles, which can be seen frequently in winter diving for salmon in the waters of Wolf Lodge Bay.

A century ago, Coeur d'Alene was a busy service center for the prosperous silver mines in mountains east of the lake. A number of Victorian-era towns still stand in the former mining districts, and museums and mine tours offer a glimpse

into this lost world. The town of Wallace, 52 miles (84 km) east, offers the **Sierra Silver Mine Tour**, which guides visitors through an 1890s silver mine.

🏞 **Tubbs Hill Park**
**Tel** (208) 769-2252.
**Open** 5am–11pm daily.

🚇 **Sierra Silver Mine Tour**
420 5th St, Wallace. **Tel** (208) 752-5151.
**Open** May–Sep: daily. First tour at 10am, then every half hour. 🎟 ♿
🌐 **silverminetour.org**

## ❷ Hells Canyon National Recreation Area

PO Box 907, Baker City, OR 97814.
**Tel** (541) 523-6391. 🌐 **fs.fed.us/ hellscanyon**

The deepest river gorge in North America, Hells Canyon was carved from the craggy granite of the Seven Devils Mountains by the Snake River. Over a mile (1.6 km) deep and straddling the three-state border where Idaho, Washington, and Oregon meet,

the canyon and its surroundings are now a recreational area that includes some 336 sq miles (870 sq km) of wilderness where no motor vehicles are permitted. Nearly 100 miles (161 km) of undeveloped and turbulent white-water draws kayakers, rafters, and other thrill-seekers. Hells Canyon lies downstream from Hells Canyon Dam. The main visitor center is on the Oregon *(see pp628–9)* side of the dam, while in Idaho, the best introduction to the area is from Riggins, where there are many outfitters who provide rental gear.

Kayaking, Hells Canyon

## ❸ Salmon

🏔 3,120. ℹ️ 200 Main St, (208) 756-2100. Sacajawea Center: **Tel** (208) 756-1222. **Open** Memorial Day–Sep: daily. 🌐 **salmonidaho.com**

Situated along the banks of the wild and scenic Salmon River, this was an important point along the Lewis and Clark Trail *(see p561–2)*. Essentially a supply town and resort center, Salmon makes a fine base for exploring the surrounding region. Among the activities offered are raft trips, kayaking, skiing, horseback riding, mountain biking, and snowmobiling. It is also possible to hike along parts of the legendary route that the explorers Lewis and Clark followed in the early 1800s while traveling from Illinois to find a navigable water route to the Pacific Ocean. Salmon was the birthplace of Lewis and Clark's guide, Sacajawea, and there is an interpretive center on Main Street that explores the significance of her role in their expedition.

The main highway, scenic US 93, winds along the main stream of the Salmon River, while smaller roads follow tributaries into the wild. At the hamlet of North Fork, Salmon River Road turns west from the highway, heading downstream along impassable rapids that Lewis and Clark aptly dubbed the "River of No Return."

The scenic Lake Coeur d'Alene, near the world-famous resort

The impressive Sawtooth Mountains, as seen from the shores of Redfish Lake

## ❹ Sawtooth National Recreation Area

Hwy 75, 8 miles (13 km) N of Ketchum.
ℹ️ (208) 737-3200. Campground:
**Open** year-round. ♿ 📷

This superb destination for hiking and camping encompasses 1,195 sq miles (3,096 sq km) of rivers, mountain meadows, forests, and jagged peaks of the Sawtooth Range. For visitors driving up Hwy 75 from Sun Valley (*see p568*), the best introduction to the area is at the 8,701-ft- (2,652-m-) high **Galena Summit**, where a spectacular panorama looks north over the Salmon River.

At an elevation of 6,200 ft (1,890 m), surrounded by the Sawtooth Mountains, the tiny hamlet of **Stanley** (population 75), has one of the most beautiful settings of any town in the US. The unpaved streets and wood-fronted frontier-style buildings make visitors feel like they have, at last, arrived in the Wild West, despite the fact that the glitzy resort of Sun Valley is barely an hour away to the south. Another attraction is **Redfish Lake**, 10 miles (16 km) south of Stanley, where rustic Redfish Lake Lodge is found near the foot of Mount Heyburn.

## ❺ Boise

🏛️ 205,000. ✈️ 🚌 ℹ️ 250 S 5th St, (800) 635-5240. 🅦 **boise.org**

French trappers in the 19th-century named this out-post "Boise," meaning wooded. Even today, this homespun,

slow-paced city presents a picture-postcard image of America. Locals and visitors walk, ride bicycles, or enjoy an afternoon picnic on the grass in the vast Greenbelt parkland that adjoins the Boise River in the heart of downtown.

Boise is also the state capital and the largest city in rural Idaho. Its focal point is the domed **State Capitol**, which was completed in 1920 after 15 years of construction. The building's main distinction is that it is the only US capitol to be heated by naturally occurring geothermal water. It was built of sandstone blocks quarried by inmates at the **Old Idaho Penitentiary**, 2 miles (3 km) east of the capitol.

Now open to visitors, the state penitentiary was in use from 1870 to 1970. Apart from the prison, the grounds also house a series of museums dedicated to such subjects as transportation, the uses of electricity, and mining. The city's historic center is three

blocks south of the capitol. Here a dozen late-Victorian commercial buildings have been restored and house a lively set of coffee houses, bars, restaurants, and boutiques. Boise's oldest building, completed in 1864, now houses the **Basque Museum and Cultural Center**, which traces the presence of Basque sheep-herders in Boise and across western US, and is also known for celebrating Basque culture. A cluster of museums and cultural centers lie in **Julia Davis Park**, a 40-acre (16-ha) green area that straddles the Boise River at the heart of the Greenbelt.

A 15-minute drive by car from the city is the **Peregrine Fund World Center of Prey**. One of the most successful organizations for breeding as well as studying raptors, the world center has been instrumental in recovering endangered populations of peregrine falcons in the US, a species that was nearly wiped out by lethal pesticides in the 1970s. Visitors also have the rare opportunity to see a variety of birds including eagles, condors, and falcons while enjoying a hilltop view of the surrounding sagebrush plains.

🏛️ **Peregrine Fund World Center for Birds of Prey**
5668 West Flying Hawk Lane.
**Tel** (208) 362-3716. **Open** Jun–Aug: 9am–5pm daily; Sep–May: 10am–4pm Tue–Sun. **Closed** Jan 1, Easter, Thanksgiving, Dec 25. 📷

The beautiful exterior of the Idaho State Capitol in Boise

Skaters outside Sun Valley Lodge, Sun Valley

## ❻ Sun Valley

✈ ℹ 491 Sun Valley Rd, Ketchum, (208) 726-3423. ⓦ visitsunvalley. com

Developed in the late 1930s by the Union Pacific Railroad baron Averell Harriman, Sun Valley is one of the oldest and highest-profile winter resorts in the US. The construction of the Tyrolean-style **Sun Valley Lodge** *(see p592)* and the adjacent ski area was completed in 1936, after which Harriman was inspired to invite Hollywood movie stars and other members of the glitterati to enjoy his facilities. Sun Valley's fame was thus ensured by the presence of celebrities such as Errol Flynn, Gary Cooper, Clark Gable, and Ernest Hemingway. Since then, the Olympic-quality skiing on the well-groomed slopes of the 9,151-ft (2,789-m) Bald Mountain has continued to draw an exclusive clientele during the season between November and April. The resort also commissioned the world's first ski lift.

Before the 1930s, however, the area was a mining and sheep-ranching center, based in the adjacent town of Ketchum. This town still retains many of its rugged frontier characteristics, despite the influx of multi-million-dollar vacation homes. The region's history is on view in the **Ketchum Sun Valley Heritage &**

Ski Museum. Although most visitors never stray beyond Sun Valley and Ketchum, the surrounding landscape is filled with other recreational options. Bicyclists can follow the 20-mile (32-km) **Wood River Trail**, along the old Union Pacific Railroad right-of-way. The Wood River is also a prime trout-fishing stream, while to the north, the majestic Sawtooth National Recreation Area *(see p567)* offers pristine hiking and camping country.

🏛 **Ketchum Sun Valley Heritage & Ski Museum**
180 1st Ave E. **Tel** (208) 726-8118.
**Open** noon–4pm Mon–Fri, 1–4pm Sat. ♿ ⓦ ksvhs.com

## ❼ Three Island Crossing State Park

Off I-84, Glenns Ferry Exit. ℹ Glenns Ferry, (208) 366-2394. Campground: ⓦ parksandrecreation.idaho.gov

One of the most evocative sights along the historic Oregon Trail *(see p446)* is the famous Three Islands Crossing, which provided one of the few safe places for emigrants to cross the dangerous Snake River. The ford was in use until 1869, when Gus Glenn constructed a ferry 2 miles (3 km) upstream. Not all attempts at crossing, however, were successful. Depending on the time of year and the level of the water, it sometimes proved fatal to the pioneers in the westward-bound

The Hemingway Memorial, Sun Valley

wagons. Some pioneers avoided the crossing. Instead, they would continue along the river's barren south bank before rejoining the main trail west of Boise.

Today, the park offers a campground and numerous picnic areas. At the park's Oregon Trail History and Education Center, visitors can learn about the life of the early pioneers and settlers, and about the Native Americans in this area. Displays include replicas of the Conestoga wagons used by pioneers and the original wagon ruts.

## ❽ Bruneau Dunes State Park

Hwy 78 (off State Hwy 51). **Tel** Mountain Home, (208) 366-7919. **Open** 9am–5pm daily. Campground: 🏕 ♿ ⓦ parksandrecreation.idaho.gov

Immediately south of the Snake River, at the foot of the high-desert Owyhee Mountains, a surprising sight arises from the surrounding sagebush plains. Some of the largest sand dunes in North America, the Bruneau Dunes rise to heights of nearly 500 ft (152 m). They are protected from the destructive impacts of cars, motorcycles, and dune buggies within one of Idaho's largest state parks.

A visitor center explains how these quartz and feldspar sand dunes were formed, and why they are not blown away. The reason for this phenomenon is simple: prevailing winds blow from opposite directions for roughly equal amounts of time, which keep the dunes fairly stable. There are also specimens of local wildlife on display, including a short-eared owl. A small astronomical observatory is often open to the public.

The park encompasses a variety of habitats such as marsh, prairie, and desert. Wildlife includes snakes and lizards, and birds such as owls and eagles. A few small lakes lie at the foot of the dunes where visitors can go fishing in canoes or rubber rafts. Other activities offered are camping and horseback riding.

*For hotels and restaurants see pp592–5*

The dramatic landscape of Snake River Gorge, Twin Falls

## ❾ Twin Falls

🏙 44,000. 🚌 ℹ Hwy 93, (208) 733-3974. 🇼 twinfallschamber.com

The falls for which the city was named have been diminished by dams and irrigation, but Twin Falls is still home to a splendid waterfall. Called the "Niagara of the West," the 212-ft- (65-m-) high and 1,000-ft- (305-m-) wide **Shoshone Falls** is an impressive sight, especially in spring when the water flows are at their peak.

Located 5 miles (8 km) north-east of the city, the falls are framed by the deep **Snake River Gorge**, famous for the ill-fated attempt by motorcycle daredevil Evel Knievel to leap across it in 1974. He survived, but with many injuries. The city stretches along the level plains to the south of the gorge, and is the center for potato-growing farms and cattle ranches.

## ❿ Craters of the Moon National Monument

US 20. **Tel** (208) 527-1335. 🅿 (campground only). 🇼 nps.gov/crmo

Sprawled across 83 sq miles (215 sq km) in central Idaho, the Craters of the Moon National Monument showcases one of the most extraordinary landscapes in the country. The most accessible section can be explored via the numerous short trails that lead through rippling, jagged, lava fields, strewn with cones and craters. They range from 15,000 to 2,000 years of age. The fields were formed by molten lava, which seeped out from gaps in the earth's crust over a period of 13,000 years. Despite their forbidding, blackened appearance, the lava fields harbor more than 50 species of mammals, 170 species of birds, and millions of resplendent wildflowers, which bloom in summer each year. Numerous caves and lava tubes also run beneath the surface.

The name "Craters of the Moon" was coined in the 1920s, when the monument was established. The visitor center near the entrance recounts the park's geological and natural history. Visitors can also improve their Hawaiian lava vocabulary, learning the scientific terms for sharp lava (a'a), layered lava (kipukas), and smooth lava (pa'hoe'hoe).

In the 1960s, astronauts from the *Apollo 14* space mission visited the monument to learn more about its volcanic geology, similar to that of the moon.

Camping is also available in the park during the summer, and the main loop road draws crowds of cross-country skiers during winter.

## ⓫ Idaho Falls

🏙 57,000. 🚏 🚌 ℹ 630 W Broadway, (866) 365-6943. 🇼 visitidahofalls.com

Set along the banks of the Snake River, with Wyoming's Grand Teton Mountains rising to the east, Idaho Falls is a charming and mainly agricultural city with a large Mormon population (see p511). Dominated by the towering Mormon temple, the city has a vast "Greenbelt" area where people can jog and in-line skate. Although the Idaho Falls, which lent their name to the city, have now been dammed, they still provide a scenic setting to the parkland. The **Museum of Idaho** showcases the state's history and hosts traveling exhibits. The **Idaho National Laboratory** (INL), located 50 miles (80 km) west of the city, was established in 1949 to design, build, and test nuclear reactors for military and civilian purposes. The world's first reactor, the EBR-1, was built here in 1951 and is open for viewing. On July 17, 1955, INL was the site of the world's first peaceful use of atomic power, when INL engineers sent 2,000 kilowatts (2 megawatts) of electricity to light up the nearby town of Arco.

🏛 **Museum of Idaho**
200 N Eastern Ave. **Tel** (208) 522-1400. **Open** 9am–5pm Mon–Sat (8pm Mon & Tue). 🅿 🇼 museumofidaho.org

**Idaho National Laboratory**
Hwy 20/26. **Tel** (208) 526-0050. **Open** tours by appointment only. **Closed** Jul 4. ♿ 🇼 inl.gov

Blackened volcanic cones, Craters of the Moon National Monument

# Montana

The northernmost of the Rocky Mountain states, Montana abounds in tall, rugged mountains, snowcapped peaks, lush valleys, and seemingly endless plains stretching beneath its trademark "big sky." The sheer scale and majesty of its wide open spaces and the larger-than-life character of its inhabitants, past and present, prompted Nobel Prize-winning novelist John Steinbeck to write "Montana seems to me to be what a small boy would think Texas is like from hearing Texans. Of all the states it is my favorite and my love."

Big Hole National Battlefield, surrounded by mountains

## ❼ Big Hole National Battlefield

Hwy 43 near Wisdom. **Tel** (406) 689-3155. **Open** May–Oct: 9am–5pm daily; Nov–Apr: 10am–5pm daily. **Closed** most national hols. ♿ **W** nps.gov/biho

Located near the Idaho border at an altitude of some 7,000 ft (2,134 m) in the Bitterroot Mountains, this battlefield site sits at the head of the lush Big Hole Valley, famed for its cattle ranches and trout-fishing opportunities. This serene pastoral scene is far removed from the terrible suffering experienced here on August 9, 1877. On that day, the flight north by 750 Nez Perce Indians, mostly women and children, was cut short by a surprise attack by US Army soldiers and civilian volunteers, leading to the death of nearly 100 Indians. The tribe continued their journey toward Canada, traveling another 1,500 miles (2,414 km) before finally surrendering in October, just 30 miles (48 km) short of the Canadian border.

## ❽ Missoula

🏔 67,000. ✈ 🚌 ℹ Higgins & Main, (800) 526-3465. **W** destination missoula.org

Nestling in the Rocky Mountains of western Montana, Missoula is still dependent upon traditional Montana industries, such as timber and transportation. This lively city is also home to the University of Montana.

Surrounded by wilderness, this picturesque city formed the backdrop of the book and subsequent movie *A River Runs Through It*. The city also houses the **Smokejumpers Base**, a national center for fighting forest fires in the Rockies. Exhibits explore fire-fighting techniques and equipment, and depending on the time of the year (summer is forest-fire season), guests are able to tour the airplanes and meet fire-fighters.

To the south, the Bitterroot Valley has ranches and small towns, hemmed in by a pair of towering mountain ranges.

### 🚒 Smokejumpers Base Visitor Center

Aerial Fire Depot, W of Missoula Int'l Airport, Hwy 93. **Tel** (406) 329-4934. **Open** Memorial Day–Labor Day: daily; Labor Day–Memorial Day: by appt.

## ❾ Flathead Valley

ℹ Bigfork Chamber of Commerce, 8155 Hwy 35, (406) 837-5888. Salish & Kootenai Tribal Council **Tel** (406) 675-2700. **W** bigfork.org

Most of the valley's land, which stretches between the 40-mile-(64-km-) long and 15-mile- (24-km-) wide Flathead Lake and Missoula, is part of the Flathead Indian Reservation. Since 1855 this has been home to descendants of the region's Salish, Kootenai, and Pend d'Oreille Indian tribes. In summer, communities such as Elmo and Arlee celebrate Native traditions in numerous pow-wows, which are traditional gatherings featuring rodeo competitions, craft demonstrations, and sales.

The **People's Center** in Pablo traces the history of the Flathead region from a Native American perspective. To the west, some 29 sq miles (75 sq km) of rolling ranchland were set aside in 1908 as the National Bison Range, housing bison, deer, bighorn sheep, and pronghorn.

The largest natural freshwater lake west of the Mississippi River, Flathead Lake is a deep-blue jewel at the western foot of the Rocky Mountains. Cherry orchards and towns like Bigfork line Hwy 35 on the lake's eastern shore, while to the west the busier US 93 hugs the water for over 35 miles (56 km). Rent bikes or kayaks, or take guided boat tours into the scenic lake.

### 🏛 People's Center

53253 Hwy 93, Pablo. **Tel** (406) 883-5344. **Open** 9am–5pm Mon–Fri; also 10am–5pm Sat from Memorial Day to Labor Day only. 🅿 ♿ **W** peoplescenter.org

Flathead Lake, nestling at the foot of the Rocky Mountains

*For hotels and restaurants see pp592–5*

# ⑮ Glacier National Park

North of W Glacier. ℹ (406) 888-7800.
**Open** most visitor facilities open late
May–mid-Sep. 🅿 ♿ 📷 ⛺
🌐 **nps.gov/glac**

Spreading nearly a million acres (404,690 ha) over the northern Rocky Mountains, Glacier National Park holds some of the world's most sublime scenery. With elevations ranging from 3,200 ft (975 m) along the Flathead River to summits topping 10,000 ft (3,048 m), the park contains a wide variety of landscapes. Alongside four dozen glaciers (which gave the park its name) and ancient limestone cliffs, there are lakes, waterfalls, and abundant wildlife, including moose, wolves, and bears. The flora ranges from high grassy plains to alpine tundra. In July, the park's higher altitudes are ablaze with meadows of blue gentians, yellow lilies, pink heathers, and feathery white Bear Grass.

Hiking, a popular activity in Glacier National Park

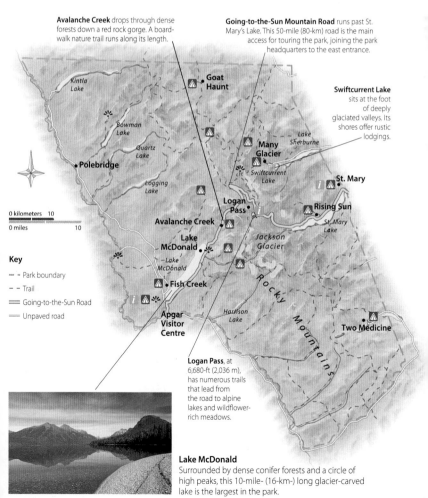

**Avalanche Creek** drops through dense forests down a red rock gorge. A board-walk nature trail runs along its length.

**Going-to-the-Sun Mountain Road** runs past St. Mary's Lake. This 50-mile (80-km) road is the main access for touring the park, joining the park headquarters to the east entrance.

**Swiftcurrent Lake** sits at the foot of deeply glaciated valleys. Its shores offer rustic lodgings.

**Logan Pass**, at 6,680-ft (2,036 m), has numerous trails that lead from the road to alpine lakes and wildflower-rich meadows.

## Key

– – Park boundary

– – Trail

▭▭ Going-to-the-Sun Road

▭▭ Unpaved road

**Lake McDonald**
Surrounded by dense conifer forests and a circle of high peaks, this 10-mile- (16-km-) long glacier-carved lake is the largest in the park.

**For keys to symbols** see back flap

## ⓰ Great Falls

🏙 59,000. ✈ 🚌 ℹ 15 Overlook Drive, (406) 771-0885. 🅦 **greatfalls mt.net**

Nestling picturesquely between the majestic Rocky Mountains to the west and Little Belt Mountains to the east, this rural city owes its name to its location along the Missouri River. As the river cuts through the city, it drops over 500 ft (152 m) in a series of rapids and five breathtaking waterfalls, first noted by explorers Lewis and Clark *(see p561–2)* in 1805.

The city is best known for its two excellent museums. One, the **Charles M. Russell Museum**, traces the history of the American West, focusing on the life and work of resident cowboy and prolific Wild West artist "Charlie" Russell, who gave the city much of its cultural flavor. His home and log cabin studio are next to the expansive museum.

On a bluff overlooking the Missouri River, 2 miles (3 km) northeast of downtown, is the **Lewis and Clark National Historic Trail Interpretive Center**, which details the epic explorations of the Corps of Discovery, the cross-country expedition led by Meriwether Lewis and William Clark from 1803 to 1806.

For 45 miles (72 km) down-stream from the center, the Missouri River runs as a "Wild and Scenic" river on one of its virgin stretches, a route paralleled by a bike trail and driving tour along US 87. The route ends at Fort Benton, historic head of navigation on the Missouri River.

🏛 **Charles M. Russell Museum**
400 13th St N. **Tel** (406) 727-8787. **Open** Jun–Sep: 9am–5pm Tue–Sun; Oct–May: 10am–5pm Wed–Sat. **Closed** Jan 1, Easter, Thanksgiving, Dec 25. 🅿 🅰 🏠 🅦 **cmrussell.org**

🏛 **Lewis and Clark National Historic Trail Interpretive Center**
4201 Giant Springs Rd. **Tel** (406) 727-8733. **Open** Memorial Day–Sep: 9am–5pm Tue–Sun; Oct–Memorial Day: 9am–5pm Tue–Sat, noon–5pm Sun. **Closed** Jan 1, Thanksgiving, Dec 25. 🅿 🅰 🅦 **fs.usda.gov/lcnf**

## ⓱ Helena

🏙 28,000. ✈ 🚌 ℹ 225 Cruse Ave, (406) 442-4120. 🅦 **helenamt.com**

The state capital, Helena makes a fine base for exploring Montana. Originally known as "Last Chance Gulch," Helena was founded as a gold-mining camp in the 1860s. Fortunately much of the wealth generated here remained, as is evident from the number of mansions built by mining millionaires. Many of these exuberantly designed Victorian-era homes have been converted into B&B inns. The centerpiece of Helena is the copper-domed **Montana State Capitol**, decorated with several fine historical murals, including one of explorers Lewis and Clark painted by Charlie Russell. A statue in the grounds portrays Helena resident Jeanette Rankin, who in 1917 was the first woman to be elected to the United States Congress.

## ⓲ Butte

🏙 34,000. ✈ 🚌 ℹ 1000 George St, (406) 723-3177, (800) 735-6814. 🅦 **buttecvb.com**

Located in the heart of the Rocky Mountains, Butte is named for the prominent conical hill, Big Butte, which guards its northwest corner. That Butte has some of the world's richest mineral reserves is evident by the extensive signs of the gold, silver, and copper mining industry that thrived here from the 1870s through the first half of the 20th century. Glimpses of Butte's multiethnic, immigrant culture are also visible in such events as the St. Patrick's Day celebration by the town's Irish Catholic population. One of Butte's many fine museums, the **World Museum of Mining** occupies the site of an early gold mine. Its superb collection of mineral specimens, mining machinery, and mementos of the town's proud industrial heritage also includes displays on Butte's leading role in the development of mine-workers' unions. Outside, some 30 historic buildings dating from 1880 to 1910 re-create an early mining camp, complete with a church, a schoolhouse, bordellos, and boardinghouses.

Sites such as the **Granite Mountain Mine Memorial** commemorate the 168 men killed in a 1917 mine disaster. High above the city, the 90-ft (27-m) statue of "Our Lady of the Rockies" stands as a

Statue of Jeanette Rankin, Montana State Capitol

Lewis and Clark National Historic Trail Interpretive Center, Great Falls

*For hotels and restaurants see pp592–5*

Exterior of the Museum of the Rockies, Bozeman

proud symbol of Butte's strength and endurance.

### 🏛 World Museum of Mining
155 Mining Museum Way, off Park St. **Tel** (406) 723-7211. **Open** Apr–Oct: 9am–6pm daily. 🅿 🚻 **W miningmuseum.org**

## ⓳ Bozeman

🏠 37,000. ✈ 🚌 🛈 2000 Commerce Way, (800) 228-4224. **W bozemancvb.com**

Situated in the heart of the Gallatin Valley, Bozeman lies in the middle of a sacred Sioux Indian hunting ground, now the state's most productive agri-cultural region. Founded in the 1860s, the city is one of the few Montana towns where the economy and history are not based on mining or railroads. Its present prominence is due mainly to the Montana State University. Established in 1893, it is the state's largest university and houses the **Museum of the Rockies**. The museum takes visitors through Earth's history, delving into everything from displays of dinosaurs unearthed in Montana Plains, to pioneer history, Indian artifacts, and Western art. A planetarium offers astronomy and laser light shows.

Downtown's tree-lined streets are pleasant to stroll through. Visitors can also learn about local history at the **Gallatin Pioneer Museum**, housed in the former jail.

### 🏛 Museum of the Rockies
600 W Kagy Blvd on the Montana State University Campus. **Tel** (406) 994-2251. **Open** May–Sep: 8am–8pm daily; Oct–Apr: 9am–5pm daily (from noon Sun). **Closed** Jan 1, Thanksg., Dec 25. 🅿 🚻

### 🏛 Gallatin Pioneer Museum
317 W Main St. **Tel** (406) 522-8122. **Open** Memorial Day–Labor Day: 10am–5pm Mon–Sat; Labor Day–Memorial Day: 11am–4pm Tue–Sat. **Closed** public hols. 🅿 🚻 **W pioneermuseum.org**

## ⓴ Virginia City

🏠 100. 🛈 300 Wallace St, (800) 829-2969. **W virginiacity.com**

Gold was discovered here in 1863 and the ensuing stampede created a boomtown. More than 100 historic buildings have been preserved, and visitors can enjoy stagecoach tours and panning for gold. On the Alder Gulch Short Line Railroad, a 1910 steam train makes the 30-minute trip to Nevada City, where the entire town is a state museum.

## ㉑ Billings

🏠 105,000. ✈ 🚌 🛈 815 S 27th St, (406) 245-4111. **W visitbillings.com**

Founded by the Northern Pacific Railroad in 1882, and now Montana's largest city, Billings was named after the railroad company's president. In just a few months, Billings grew into a bustling community of 2,000 people. Visitors can get a feel of the town's frontier days, and of Montana's cowboy traditions, from the Wild West paintings and sculptures displayed in the **Yellowstone Art Museum**, located in the old county jail. However, the most striking feature of Billings is the Rimrocks, a 400-ft- (122-m-) high sandstone wall that runs the length of the city along the Yellowstone River.

Outside the city the scenery is even more spectacular, especially along the Beartooth Highway that runs southwest toward Yellowstone National Park (see pp576–7). The 65-mile (105-km) section between Red Lodge and the Wyoming border is stunning.

### 🏛 Yellowstone Art Museum
401 N 27th St. **Tel** (406) 256-6804. **Open** 10am–5pm Mon (summer only), 10am–5pm Tue–Sun (to 8pm Thu & Fri, to 4pm Sun). **Closed** public hols. 🅿 🚻 🖥 **W artmuseum.org**

## ㉒ Little Bighorn Battlefield National Monument

Exit 510 off I-90, Hwy 212, Crow Agency. 🛈 (406) 638-2621. **W nps.gov/libi**

Located on the Crow Indian Reservation, this battlefield preserves the site of a key moment in American history, known as "Custer's Last Stand." In June 1876, the impetuous US Army Lieutenant Colonel George Armstrong Custer (see p442) led his troop of 210 soldiers of the 7th Cavalry in an attack on a large Indian encampment along the Little Bighorn River. They were quickly surrounded by more than 2,000 combined Sioux and Cheyenne Indian warriors under the leadership of legendary Chief Sitting Bull. Custer's soldiers were wiped out. A sandstone marker stands above the soldiers' mass grave, and a small museum describes the disastrous battle.

Memorial to Custer's Last Stand, Little Bighorn Battlefield

# Wyoming

The Wyoming state insignia, an image of a cowboy waving his Stetson hat while riding on the back of a bucking horse, says it all. This is classic cowboy country, a land of wide-open grasslands stretching for miles in every direction, where a half-million people inhabit an area of nearly 100,000 sq miles (260,000 sq km). For visitors, the main draws of Wyoming lie in its northwestern corner, where the twin spectacles of Yellowstone and Grand Teton National Parks attract some six million visitors annually.

Buffalo Bill Museum, Cody

## ㉓ Cody

🏙 9,000. 🚹 836 Sheridan Ave, (307) 587-2297. 🆆 **yellowstone country.org**

Cody was founded by Wild West impresario "Buffalo Bill" Cody in 1896. Long the symbol of the American West, the city maintains its frontier look and is home to two museums that document this unique era. The smaller of these is **Trail Town**, a homespun collection of artifacts and buildings assembled on the original site of Cody. One highlight here is a log cabin reputedly used as a hideout by outlaws Butch Cassidy and the Sundance Kid.

Cody's main attraction, however, is the **Buffalo Bill Museum**, a 240,000-sq-ft (22,300-sq-m) complex of galleries that traces the natural, cultural, and military history of the Wild West. It holds more than 500 weapons, a superb collection of Western art, and Plains Indians artifacts, as well as a museum on Buffalo Bill himself.

In keeping with Buffalo Bill's pursuit of public spectacle, Cody's other great attraction is the **Cody Nite Rodeo**, the nation's longest-running rodeo, held daily between late June and August.

🏛 **Buffalo Bill Museum**
720 Sheridan Ave. **Tel** (307) 587-4771. **Open** 10am–5pm daily (May–mid-Sep: 8am–6pm daily; mid-Sep–Oct: 8am–5pm daily; Dec–Feb: 10am–5pm Thu–Sun). **Closed** Jan 1, Thnksg., Dec 25. 🅿 🅱 🆆 **centerofthewest.org**

## ㉔ Yellowstone National Park

See pp576–7.

## ㉕ Jackson

🏙 10,000. 🚹 🚌 ℹ 532 N Cache St, (307) 733-3316. 🆆 **jacksonhole chamber.com**

A popular stop since the days of the fur-trapping mountain men, Jackson is perhaps Wyoming's most visited city. Located at the southern entrance to Grand Teton and Yellowstone National Parks, much of its natural beauty is giving way to ski resorts. But despite the boutiques and art galleries that surround its tree-lined central square, and the congested summer traffic, Jackson retains its Wild West vibe.

Alongside the national parks, dude ranches, and Wild West re-enactments, the main attraction is wildlife. The 39-sq-mile (101-sq-km) **National Elk Refuge**, stretching between Jackson and the Grand Teton National Park, is home to some 7,500 native elk that congregate here in winter. Its entrance lies one mile (1.6 km) northeast of Jackson. Guided tours on horse-drawn sleighs are offered between mid-December and early April. In summer, the Aerial Tram at Jackson Hole Ski Area (rated as one of the country's most challenging) lifts sightseers over 4,000 ft (1,219 m) to the top of Rendezvous Peak for a grand panorama.

🦌 **National Elk Refuge**
E Broadway at Elk Refuge Rd. **Tel** (307) 733-9212. **Open** 9am–5pm daily (8am–7pm Memorial Day–Labor Day). **Closed** Thnksg., Dec 25. 🅿 sleigh rides. 🆆 **fws.gov/refuge/national_ elk_refuge**

### Buffalo Bill

One of the most colorful Wild West figures, William Frederick Cody (1846–1917) started out as a teenage rider for the Pony Express. He then served as US Army scout during the Civil War. When the war ended in 1865, he began supplying buffalo meat to workers of the transcontinental railroad, earning himself the nickname "Buffalo Bill." Cody was the model for a series of newspaper stories and "dime novels" written by Ned Buntline. The real-life Buffalo Bill soon parlayed his credentials into worldwide fame and fortune. Star of a spectacular circus in which historical scenes were acted out by cowboys and Indians, including such figures as Chief Sitting Bull, Cody toured the world between 1883 and World War I. Despite his fortune, by 1913 he was bankrupt, and died four years later in Denver (see pp580–81).

Statue of Buffalo Bill

# ㉖ Grand Teton National Park

Moose. **ℹ** Grand Teton National Park Headquarters, (307) 739-3300. 🅿 ♿ 🚻 ⛺ **W** nps.gov/grte

The youngest peaks in the Rockies, the Grand Tetons are among the sharpest and most dramatic mountains in the world. Their silver granite peaks rise over a mile above the lush Snake River Valley of Jackson Hole, all of which has been protected within the boundaries of the 485-sq-mile (1,256-sq-km) Grand Teton National Park. There are miles of hiking trails that lead to numerous glaciers and lakes. Wildlife, such as elk, bison, and bears, abounds. In summer, kayakers and rafters float the Snake River, while powerboats and canoes take more leisurely cruises on Jackson and Jenny Lakes. In winter, all hiking trails are open to skiers who make their way through the wilderness.

The beautiful Grand Teton National Park in fall

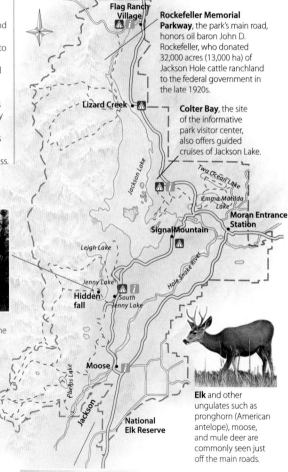

**Rockefeller Memorial Parkway**, the park's main road, honors oil baron John D. Rockefeller, who donated 32,000 acres (13,000 ha) of Jackson Hole cattle ranchland to the federal government in the late 1920s.

**Colter Bay**, the site of the informative park visitor center, also offers guided cruises of Jackson Lake.

**Jenny Lake**
The popular Jenny Lake lies at the base of the 13,770-ft (4,197-m) Grand Teton. Trails lead along forested shores to quiet beaches, with the mountains reflecting in the distance.

**Elk** and other ungulates such as pronghorn (American antelope), moose, and mule deer are commonly seen just off the main roads.

**Jackson Hole**
Frontier fur trappers referred to a large valley ringed by mountains as a "hole." This valley of the Snake River runs between the Grand Teton and Gros Ventre Mountains, upstream from Jackson.

## Key

– – Park boundary

- - Trail

═══ Major road

═══ Unpaved road

0 kilometers 10
0 miles 10

For keys to symbols *see back flap*

# ❷ Yellowstone National Park

One of the marvels of the world, and the country's oldest national park, this wild wonderland spreads across the three states of Wyoming, Montana, and Idaho. Its heart is a volcanic plateau at an average elevation of 8,000 ft (2,438 m), housing over 10,000 hot springs and geysers – more than half of the world's total. Alongside the spectacular shows of geothermal activity, it has dense forests, towering peaks, deep river canyons, and enough outdoor recreation to last a lifetime. The 175-mile (282-km) Grand Loop Road does a full circuit of the main sights. Lodging is often booked solid, so visitors should reserve in advance.

An elk crossing the road in the park

**★ Mammoth Hot Springs**
Hundreds of geothermal springs bubble up in Yellowstone, forming colored pools of boiling hot, mineral-rich water. The mineral content drapes delicate curtains of marble-like travertine over the cascading terraces of stone.

Livingston

Mammoth Hot Springs

Gardiner

Roaring M

Steamboat Gey            Norri

Madison

West Entrance            Madison

Great Fountain Geyser

Grand Prismatic Spring

Old Faithful

Lone Star Geyser            West Thum

Shoshone Lake

Approximate Caldera Boundary

MT
ID

**Grand Prismatic Spring**
The 370-ft- (113-m-) wide Grand Prismatic Spring lies close to Old Faithful. The rainbow-colored hot spring, lining the bank of the Firehole River, is one of the world's largest.

**★ Old Faithful Geyser**
Named for its precise 90-minute eruption cycle, Old Faithful is the park's icon. Its steaming plume shoots as high as 120–180 ft (36–55 m) and lasts 2 to 5 minutes. Visitors line up on the wooden boardwalk to watch it spurt nearly 8,400 gallons (31,797 liters) of water per eruption.

*For hotels and restaurants see pp592–5*

**Bison**
With over 4,500 bison, Yellowstone has the world's largest herd. They roam freely across the park, often even disrupting traffic. Despite their docile appearance, bison can be dangerous, so visitors should avoid contact with them or any other wild animal.

**VISITORS' CHECKLIST**

**Practical Information**
US 26 in Moose.
 YNP Headquarters, Mammoth Hot Springs
**Tel** (307) 344-7381.
**Open** year-round, but most facilities & roads are closed from October to May due to winter snows. The only open road is US 212, along the northern edge, between Gardiner & Cooke City, Montana.
 nps.gov/yell

Cooke City

Montana
Wyoming

Northeast Entrance

212

Red Lodge

Tower-Roosevelt

*Lamar*

Grand Canyon of
the Yellowstone

Fishing Bridge

Lake Village

Bridge Bay

East Entrance

20

Cody

*...one Lake*

*Southeast Arm*

*South Arm*

*Yellowstone R.*

0 km          10

0 miles        10

**Key**
-- Park boundary
== Major road
-- State border

★ **Grand Canyon**
Plunging 500 ft (152 m) in a pair of falls – Upper and Lower Falls – the Yellowstone River has carved this 20-mile- (32-km-) long canyon into the mineral-rich yellow and orange rhyolite rock. Many trails along its rim offer splendid vistas. "Uncle Tom's Trail" drops down a steep staircase on to a platform, offering a close-up view of the falls.

**Bears**
Bears are plentiful in the park. Black bears are the most common, and more than 600 grizzlies inhabit its wilder reaches. Most animals avoid contact with humans, and rangers advise that humans should avoid any contact with bears.

For keys to symbols *see back flap*

The Medicine Wheel on Medicine Mountain, the Bighorn Scenic Byway (US 14)

## ❷ Bighorn Mountains

Bighorn National Forest: **Tel** (307) 674-2600. **W** fs.usda.gov/bighorn

Standing at the western edge of the historic plains of the Powder River Basin, the Bighorn Mountains were named for the bighorn sheep that were once abundant here. Crowned by the 13,175-ft (4,016-m) Cloud Peak, the mountains are crossed by a pair of very scenic highways, US 16 in the south (the old Yellowstone Trail) and US 14 in the north, which divides into two forks. The northernmost section of US 14 climbs past one of the country's most enigmatic archaeological sites, the **Medicine Wheel**, an 80-ft (24-m) diameter stone circle, which is located 27 miles (43 km) east of Lovell. This ancient circle is held sacred by Native Sioux and Cheyenne Indians, and offers a vast panorama from its 10,000-ft (3,048-m) elevation.

## ❷ Devil's Tower National Monument

**i** (307) 467-5283. ⚠ **W** nps.gov/deto

Rising over 1,200 ft (366 m) above the surrounding plains, Devil's Tower is a flat-topped volcanic plug that looks like a giant tree stump. Featured in the 1977 Steven Spielberg movie *Close Encounters of the Third Kind*, this geological landmark is located in

Wyoming's northeastern corner, looming over the banks of the Belle Fourche River. Set aside as a national monument by President Theodore Roosevelt in 1906, Devil's Tower (also known as Bear's Lodge) is a sacred site of worship for many Native Americans. The rolling hills of this 2-sq-mile (5-sq-km) park are covered with pine forests, deciduous woodlands, and prairie grasslands, and abound in deer, prairie dogs, and other wildlife. The site's vertical rock walls and scenic trails are a magnet for rock climbers and hikers.

## ❷ Casper

⚠ 55,000. 🚉 **i** 139 W 2nd St, Suite 1B, (307) 234-5362. **W** visitcasper.com

Located in the heart of Wyoming, Casper has been the center of the state's large petroleum industry since 1890. Surrounded by miles of broad, flat plains, this large, busy city

grew up around the 1860s Fort Caspar, now a historical site and museum, known as the **Fort Caspar Museum**. Many of the fort buildings have been reconstructed at the point where the historic Oregon Trail *(see p446)* crossed the North Platte River, west of downtown. The museum features a variety of cultural and natural history exhibits pertaining to central Wyoming.

North and west of Casper lie miles of arid badlands, including such sites as the legendary "Hole in the Wall," where outlaws such as Butch Cassidy had hideouts. More accessible to visitors is the weirdly eroded forest of figures known as "Hell's Half Acre," located 35 miles (56 km) west of town on the south side of US 20.

### 🏛 Fort Caspar Museum
4001 Fort Caspar Rd. **Tel** (307) 235-8462. **Open** 8am–5pm Tue–Sat (May & Sep: 8am–5pm daily; Jun–Aug: 8am–6pm daily). 🅿 ♿

A view of the exterior of Fort Caspar Museum, Casper

# ⓪ Guernsey

🦌 1,150. 🛈 90 S Wyoming St (summer only).

Set along the banks of the North Platte River, this is a small town whose size belies a wealth of historical interest. Just south of town are two of the most palpable reminders of the pioneer migrations westward along the Oregon Trail. The **Oregon Trail Ruts State Historic Site** preserves a set of 4–6-ft (1–1.8-m) deep gouges carved by wagon wheels into the soft riverside sandstone. A mile south, the Register Cliff has been inscribed with the names of hundreds of explorers, fur trappers, and Oregon Trail pioneers who crossed the area in the mid-1800s.

Evocative as these sights are, Guernsey's most important historic spot is the **Fort Laramie National Historic Site**, a reconstruction of a fur-trapping and US cavalry outpost. Between its founding in the 1830s and its abandonment in 1890s, the fort was a prime point of contact between Europeans, Americans, and Native Americans. Many of the buildings have been restored, and costumed interpreters act out roles from the fort's history.

### 🏛 Fort Laramie National Historic Site

US 26. **Tel** (307) 837-2221.
**Open** dawn–dusk. **Closed** Jan 1, Thanksgiving, Dec 25. 🅿 ♿
🖥 nps.gov/fola

# ㉛ Laramie

🦌 31,000. 🚉 🚌 🛈 800 S 3rd St, (800) 445-5303. 🖥 visitlaramie.org

Home to the main state university campus, the small city of Laramie exudes an infectious youthful vitality, which is rare in other Wyoming cities. Located east of downtown at an elevation of 7,200 ft (2,195 m), the University of Wyoming is the highest college in the country. The campus is dominated by the strikingly modern **University of Wyoming Art Museum**, an art museum and library documenting Wyoming history and

culture. The town also housed Wyoming's first prison, now restored to its 1880s condition, when Butch Cassidy and other outlaws served time here. Located west of downtown, the old prison is now the centerpiece of the **Wyoming Territorial Prison State Historic Park**, which includes a re-creation of a frontier town.

The area around Laramie is rich historically and scenically. The 50-mile (80-km) stretch of the Lincoln Highway between Laramie and Cheyenne preserves part of the first transcontinental road in the US. To the west of Laramie, Hwy 130 follows the Snowy Range Scenic Byway through the beautiful Medicine Bow Mountains.

### 🏛 University of Wyoming Art Museum

22nd St & Willett Dr. **Tel** (307) 766-6622. **Open** 10am–5pm Mon–Sat (to 9pm Mon). **Closed** public hols.
♿ 🖥 uwyo.edu/artmuseum

### 🏛 Wyoming Territorial Prison State Historic Park

975 Snowy Range Rd. **Tel** (307) 745-6161. **Open** May–Oct: 8am–7pm daily.
🅿 ♿ 🖥 wyomingterritorial prison.com

# ㉜ Cheyenne

🦌 59,000. ✈ 🚉 🚌 🛈 121 W 15th St, Suite 202, (307) 778-3133.
🖥 cheyenne.org

Founded in 1867 as a US Army fort along the newly constructed Union Pacific Railroad, Cheyenne later matured from a typical Wild West town into Wyoming's state capital and the largest city in the area.

The 10-day Cheyenne Frontier Days festival, held every July, brings to life the old days with parades, Indian pow-wows, horse races, and the world's largest outdoor rodeo. Visitors can also get a sense of Cheyenne heritage at the **Cheyenne Frontier Days Old West Museum**, which displays hundreds of antique saddles and wagons, such as the historic Deadwood Stage. During the 1870s and 1880s, this coach made a three-day trip between

Statue of cowboy, Old West Museum, Cheyenne

Cheyenne and the gold mines at Deadwood in South Dakota *(see p442)*. Downtown Cheyenne features two landmark buildings – the 1917 State Capitol and the former Union Pacific Depot, an elaborate Romanesque-style structure that has been restored to its original 1886 splendor. The western edge of Cheyenne features Warren Air Force Base, the primary command center of the US arsenal of nuclear-tipped intercontinental ballistic missiles, which are known as ICBMs.

### 🏛 Cheyenne Frontier Days Old West Museum

Frontier Park on N Carey Ave. **Tel** (307) 778-7290. **Open** 10am–4pm daily. **Closed** public hols. 🅿 ♿
🖥 oldwestmuseum.org

The prison in Wyoming Territorial Park, Laramie

# Colorado

The name "Colorado" dates back to the 16th century, when Spanish explorers first used the moniker in reference to the red rock formations that skirt the Front Range of the Rocky Mountains. Over 400 years later, the term conjures images of majestic peaks and snow-clad ski slopes, with good reason. Colorado is the most mountainous state in the US, with 54 summits that measure more than 14,000 ft (4,267 m) above sea level. Officially a state since 1876, during the past century Colorado has evolved from a sparsely inhabited mining and trapping country to become the most populous business center for the Rocky Mountain region.

Denver skyline with the Rockies forming a backdrop

## ㉝ Denver

🏔 600,000. ✈ 🚉 🚌
ℹ 1600 California St. **Tel** (303) 892-1505. 🌐 **denver.org**

Founded at the junction of the Platte River and Cherry Creek as a supply base for miners in 1858, Denver's mild climate attracted settlers. Soon after, it emerged as the region's primary trade and population center, and eventually became the state capital in 1876.

In the new millennium, abundant parklands, a vibrant downtown, and a number of well-known museums define this growing city. Denver is set picturesquely at the foothills of the Rocky Mountains.

### 🏛 Civic Center Park

Between Colfax Ave & 14th Ave Pkwy, Broadway & Bannock St. History Colorado Center: 12th & Broadway. **Open** check website for opening hours. 🎫 ♿ 🌐 **coloradohistory. org** Denver Art Museum: 100 W 14th Ave Pkwy. **Tel** (720) 865-5000. **Open** 10am–5pm Tue–Thu, 10am–8pm Fri, 10am–5pm Sat & Sun. **Closed** Thanksgiving, Dec 25. 🎫 ♿ 🌐 denverartmuseum.org

The geographical, cultural, and political heart of Denver, the Civic Center Park is dominated by the gold-domed **Colorado State Capitol**. This ornate structure houses the state legislature and governor's office. To the south of the park stands the **History Colorado Center**, previously the Colorado History Museum, where exhibits focus on varied aspects of Colorado's past. Continue clockwise around the park to reach the tiled, seven-story high **Denver Art Museum**. This is one of the city's best museums and has impressive collections of both Western as well as Native American objects. Its latest addition is the ultra-modern landmark Frederic C. Hamilton Building. Finally, a block west of the park is the **Denver Mint**, one of four mints in the country, which presses more than ten billion coins in a year.

### 🏛 Molly Brown House

1340 Pennsylvania St. **Tel** (303) 832-4092. **Open** 10am–4pm Tue–Sat, noon–4pm Sun. **Closed** public hols. 🎫 📷 🌐 **mollybrown.org**

This restored mansion, now a museum, was the home of "The Unsinkable Molly Brown," so-called for her survival of the *Titanic* in 1912. Margaret Tobin Brown was a flamboyant and persistent woman whose life story exemplifies the boom-and-bust backdrop that is Colorado history. Born in 1867 in Hannibal, Missouri, she came west to the boomtown of Leadville, Colorado, in 1886, where she married a well-known mining man, J.J. Brown. When the silver market collapsed, J.J. persevered until he laid claim to one of Colorado's richest veins of gold in 1893. The couple then moved to Denver, where they lived in luxury, despite not being accepted by the city's elite. Her courageous rescue efforts during the sinking of the *Titanic* made her a national celebrity. With this came the society approval that had previously eluded her. However, she died in New York in 1932, penniless and alone. Later, in the 1960s, she was immortalized on stage and screen.

### 🏛 Larimer Square & Lower Downtown (LoDo)

Larimer Square: Larimer St between 14th & 15th Sts. ℹ (303) 685-8143. ♿ 🌐 **larimersquare.com** LoDo District: Bordered by Market & Wynkoop St. ℹ (303) 628-5428. ♿

The birthplace of Denver, Larimer Square remains a commercial and cultural hub for the city. Lying adjacent to Confluence Park, where the Platte River and Cherry Creek meet, this was the site where white settlers first set up camp. The square bustles with activity both day and night, mainly because of its many boutiques, galleries, bars, and restaurants.

After a disastrous fire in 1863, wooden structures were prohibited. As a result, red-brick Victorian architecture dominates both the square and the neighboring Lower Downtown area (nicknamed "LoDo"). Centered on Union Station, LoDo experienced a renaissance of

Larimer Square, the birthplace of Denver

orts in the 1990s, thanks to the arrival of the city's professional baseball team and their Coors Field stadium. Today, this is a favorite club-hopping district, well known for its smoky jazz joints, dance clubs, and famous microbreweries.

## City Park

Between 17th & 26th Avenues from York St to Colorado Blvd.
**Open** 24 hours daily. **Denver Zoo:** 2300 Steele St. **Tel** (303) 337-1400.
**Open** Mar–Oct: 9am–6pm daily; Nov–Feb: 10am–5pm daily.
**denverzoo.org** Denver Museum of Nature & Science: 2001 Colorado Blvd. **Tel** (303) 370-6000.
**Open** 9am–5pm daily. **Closed** Dec 25.
**dmns.org**

About 2 miles (3 km) east of downtown is Denver's largest park, which offers a wide range of activities. It has a well-stocked fishing lake, running trails, a golf course, shady picnic areas, and sports fields. The park also contains the city's two most popular attractions – the **Denver Zoo** and the **Denver Museum of Nature and Science**. The zoo is noted especially for its innovative animal habitats, which include the LEED Platinum Certified Elephant Passage, one of the world's largest bull elephant habitats. The Denver Museum of Nature and Science, on the eastern edge of the City Park, features a wide range of exhibits.

## Black American West Museum & Heritage Center

3091 California St. **Tel** (720) 242-7428.
**Open** 10am–4pm Tue–Sat.
**Closed** Jan 1, Easter, Thanksgiving, Dec 25. **blackamericanwestmuseum.com**

A hidden gem in the Five Points neighborhood, this fascinating museum is housed in a Victorian home, previously the abode of Justina Ford. In 1902 she became Denver's first female African-American doctor. The museum's founder, Paul

Black American West Museum & Heritage Center

Stewart, opened the museum in 1971 to commemorate Ford's life and to educate people about the African-American contribution to the American West. The museum's collection includes letters, photographs, and assorted memorabilia that effectively re-create the incredible stories of African-Americans in pioneer times.

## Museo de las Americas

861 Santa Fe Dr. **Tel** (303) 571-4401.
**Open** 10am–5pm Tue–Fri, noon–5pm Sat & Sun. **Closed** Jan 1, Jul 4, Thanksgiving, Dec 25.
**muse.org**

Founded in the early 1990s, the Museo de las Americas is a touchstone for Denver's sizable Hispanic population. The first such museum in the region, it relates Mexican and Latin American history, as well as offering fascinating glimpses of their artistic and cultural traditions. The permanent collections are dedicated to the pre-Columbian Aztec as well as the Colonial period. Among the exhibits on display are a replica of an Aztec Sun Stone and a wall-size mural of the Aztec metropolis Tenochtitlán.

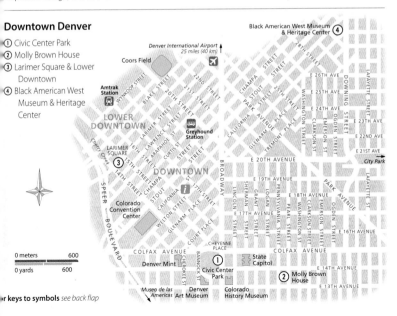

## Downtown Denver

① Civic Center Park
② Molly Brown House
③ Larimer Square & Lower Downtown
④ Black American West Museum & Heritage Center

0 meters 600
0 yards 600

The attractive University of Colorado, Boulder

## ㉞ Boulder

🏙 97,000. ✈ 🚌 🚃 ℹ 2440 Pearl St, (303) 442-2911. 🌐 **boulder coloradousa.com**

An idyllic college town set at the foot of the Rockies, Boulder is best known for its bohemian culture, liberal politics, and thriving high-tech industry. The city was founded in 1858 as a commercial hub for the miners and farmers who settled nearby. After Colorado gained statehood, the **University of Colorado** (CU) was established here, at an altitude of 5,400 ft (1,646 m). Since then, the attractive Victorian-era campus and its coinciding vibrant culture have defined Boulder, attracting intellectuals, radicals, and individualists.

Northwest of the campus, the pedestrian-only Pearl Street Mall, lined with lively restaurants, bars, and shops, is the stage for many

Cycling across Boulder Canyon, minutes from downtown Boulder

street performers. Nearby, the Hill District forms the center of Boulder's energetic nightlife and music scene. The I.M. Pei-designed **National Center for Atmospheric Research** is to the southeast. The center also features weather and climate exhibits and is a start-off point for some lovely nature trails.

West of Boulder, the jagged and forested crags of the Rockies provide a scenic backdrop to the city below. The nearby Flatiron Range, Eldorado Canyon, and Indian Peaks Wilderness Area are popular with climbers, hikers, and backpackers.

🏛 **National Center for Atmospheric Research**
1850 Table Mesa Dr. **Tel** (303) 497-1174. **Open** 8am–5pm Mon–Fri, 9am–4pm Sat & Sun. ♿ 🅿
🌐 **spark.ucar.edu**

🏞 **Indian Peaks Wilderness Area**
20 miles (32 km) W of Boulder, US Forest Service. **Tel** (303) 444-6600. **Open** 24 hours daily. 🅿

## ㉟ Golden

🏙 19,000. ✈ 🚌 ℹ 1010 Washington Ave, (303) 279-3113, (800) 590-3113. 🌐 **visitgolden.com**

Golden's history as an early nexus of trade and politics remains visible today. Its origins date to the early 1840s, when hunter Rufus Sage, one of the first Anglos to camp in this area, spotted flakes of gold in the waters of Clear Creek. His findings led to an influx of Easterners in the 1850s, and by the 1860s the city emerged

as a regional railroad hub and was declared the capital of the newly formed Colorado Territory. The original Territorial Capitol in the Loveland Building, which forms the center of downtown, dates from that period.

Golden's past is visible at the **Golden History Center** and at the impeccably restored **Astor House Museum**. Several rooms here re-create the 1867–1908 era when it served as a boardinghouse. The **Old Armory** nearby is the largest standing cobblestone building west of the Mississippi River. The 3-acre (1.2-ha) **Clear Creek History Park** houses many historic structures such as an 1876 schoolhouse. The town is also home to **Coors Brewery**, which offers tours.

The gravesite and museum of William "Buffalo Bill" Cody (see p574) overlooks the city on Lookout Mountain and there is an observation deck offering beautiful panoramic views.

🏛 **Golden History Center**
923 10th St. **Tel** (303) 278-3557. **Open** 11am–4:30pm Tue–Sat, noon–4:30pm Sun. **Closed** public hols. 🅿
🌐 **goldenhistory.org**

🏛 **Astor House Museum**
822 12th St. **Tel** (303) 278-3557. **Open** 11am–4:30pm Tue–Sat, noon–4:30pm Sun. **Closed** public hols. 🅿
🌐 **goldenhistory.org**

🏛 **Clear Creek History Park**
11th St between Arapahoe & Cheyenne St. **Tel** (303) 278-3557. **Open** daily. 🌐 **goldenhistory.org**

Cobblestone exterior of the Old Armory, near Astor House, Golden

# ⑳ Idaho Springs & Georgetown

🏛 2,000. 🚌 ℹ️ 2060 Miner St, (303) 567-4382. 🅦 visitidahosprings colorado.com

Situated within an hour's drive from downtown Denver, the well-preserved 1860s mining towns of Idaho Springs and Georgetown are best known for their unblemished Victorian architecture, stunning mountains, and some excellent museums.

Idaho Springs was founded in 1859 and quickly emerged as a mining center when the surrounding streams and mountains were found to be exceptional sources of gold. The town's mining history is traced through exhibits that include equipment, payroll records, receipts, and photographs at the **Argo Gold Mine, Mill & Museum**.

Georgetown, another mining town set up during the mid-19th-century gold rush, is 15 miles (24 km) west of Idaho Springs. It is a vision of Victorian elegance tucked into an alpine valley 8,500 ft (2,591 m) above sea level. The **Hamill House Museum**, built in 1867 and enlarged in 1879, presents the public with the opulent lifestyle of a silver-mining magnate. There's also a carriage house, cottage, log cabin, and mill. The historic 3-mile (4-km) elevated **Georgetown Loop Railroad** winds up Clear Creek Canyon and affords spectacular views of mountainous terrain.

South from Idaho Springs, summer drivers can climb up the highest road in the country. The Mount Evans Scenic Byway

Victorian architecture in downtown Georgetown

follows Highways 103 and 5 through the Pike National Forest toward the 14,264-ft- (4,347-m-) high summit of Mount Evans.

### 🏛 Argo Gold Mine, Mill & Museum

S of I-70, exit from 241A. **Tel** (303) 567- 2421. **Open** mid-Apr–mid-Oct: 9am– 6pm daily. 🅿️ 🏧
🅦 historicargotours.com

### Hamill House Museum

305 Argentine St. **Tel** (303) 569-2840. **Open** late May–Jun: noon–4pm Mon & Fri, 11am–4pm Sat & Sun; Jul & Aug: 11am–5pm daily; Sep–mid-Dec: 11am–5pm Sat & Sun. 🅿️ 🏧
🅦 historicgeorgetown.org

# ㊲ Rocky Mountain National Park

1000 US Hwy 36. **Tel** (970) 586-1206. **Open** 24 hours daily. (Trail Ridge Road closed between Nov–May). 🅿️ ♿
🄰 🅦 nps.gov/romo

This National Park offers some of the most spectacular mountain views in the United States. Established in 1915, the park

spreads across 416 sq miles (1,077 sq km) and includes 114 named peaks that measure more than 10,000 ft (3,048 m). The tallest of these, Longs Peak, is 14,255 ft (4,345 m) high. Snaking through the alpine scenery is the Continental Divide, which separates the western part of the US from the east, and where snowmelt flows down and eventually empties into the Atlantic or Pacific Oceans. Almost 150 lakes originate here, some occupying pastoral, forested settings, while others are perched on almost inaccessible shelves, high in the wilderness.

Most of the three million annual visitors to the park drive 50 miles (80 km) on **Trail Ridge Road**, a spectacular stretch of highway that showcases the park's brilliant panoramas. After leaving the resort environment of Estes Park, the road climbs to its highest point of 12,183 ft (3,713 m) near the center of the park, before descending into a scenic valley north of the small town of Grand Lake. The tundra in the park's high country is an island of arctic vegetation surrounded by plants of lower latitudes. Wildlife-watchers are likely to see elk, moose, black bear, and bighorn sheep.

Popular summer activities within the park include hiking, biking, backpacking, and fishing, while winter attracts snow-shoers and skiers. Although there are no hotels inside the park, there are five fee-based campgrounds and numerous accommodations in both Estes Park and Grand Lake.

A view of the myriad peaks from the pinnacle of Trail Ridge Road, Rocky Mountain National Park

Pikes Peak Cog Railway atop the mountain, Manitou Springs

## ❸ Manitou Springs

🏔 5,500. 🚌 ℹ️ 354 Manitou Ave,
(719) 685-5089. 🌐 **manitou
springs.org**

This charming Victorian
community attracts weekend
visitors who come to explore its
art galleries, restaurants, and
shops. A product of the Gold
Rush of the 1850s, it later
became a popular spa town
because of the natural mineral
springs found here. Manitou
(meaning "Full of Spirit" in
Native Algonquian) is one
of the largest national
historic districts in the
country. It is famous for
two attractions that
predate it by centuries:
the **Cave of the Winds**,
an impressive limestone
cavern (now with light
shows and tours) and
the **Manitou Springs
Cliff Dwellings**, dating
from 1100 to 1300.

Manitou Springs is also the
gateway to Pikes Peak. The **Pikes
Peak Cog Railway**, a historic
train that climbs to the summit
of the 14,110-ft (4,300-m)
mountain, has its depot here.

Clocktower,
Manitou Springs

### 🎯 Cave of the Winds

US 24, exit 141. **Tel** (719) 685-5444.
**Open** 10am–5pm daily (Jun–Aug:
9am–9pm). 🅿️ 📷
🌐 **caveofthewinds.com**

### 🏛 Pikes Peak Cog Railway

515 Ruxton Ave. **Tel** (719) 685-5401.
**Open** Apr–Oct: daily; Nov–Mar: limited
schedule. 🅿️ ♿ 🌐 **cograilway.com**

### 🎯 Manitou Springs Cliff Dwellings

10 Cliff Dwellings Rd. **Tel** (800) 354-9971.
**Open** daily. Mar–Nov: 9am–5pm (May–
Sep: 6pm); Dec–Feb: 10am–4pm. 🅿️ ♿
📷 🌐 **cliffdwellingsmuseum.com**

*For hotels and restaurants see pp592–5*

## ❸ Colorado Springs

🏔 415,000. ✈️ 🚌 🚉 ℹ️ 515 S
Cascade Ave, (719) 635-7506.
🌐 **visitcos.com**

Established by railroad baron
William Jackson Palmer in 1871,
Colorado Springs nestles below
Pikes Peak. The first resort town
in the western US, it was initially
nicknamed "Little London"
because of the scores of
English tourists it attracted.
The **Garden of the Gods** on
the west side of town lures
hikers and climbers with
its awe-inspiring red
sandstone formations, rife
with arches, overhangs,
stately walls, and precarious
balancing rocks. One of the
most recognizable – and
most photographed –
formations is Kissing
Camels, so named for
its resemblance to a
pair of lip-locked
dromedaries. Also
located here is the Rock Ledge
Ranch Historic Site, a preserved
ranch that dates to the 1880s.
The Italian Renaissance-style
**Broadmoor Resort** on Lake
Circle, initially opened in 1918,
epitomizes this era. In the
1950s, Colorado Springs was
chosen to be the home of the
prestigious **US Air Force
Academy** and the National
Missile Defense Headquarters
(NORAD). The latter is situated
on the city's southwestern
fringe, deep within the bomb-
proof Cheyenne Mountain.

Culturally more conservative
than Denver *(see pp580–81)*,
modern-day Colorado Springs is
one of the fastest-growing cities
in the US, with rows of houses
extending into the foothills to
the west, and the vast plains to
the east. The spirit of the Wild
West remains alive even today
at the **Pro Rodeo Hall of Fame**,
which documents the origins of
rodeo as well as the stories of
prominent American rodeo
stars through the ages. The
**Colorado Springs Pioneers
Museum** presents the area's
history in the restored 1903
El Paso County Courthouse.

### 🌳 Garden of the Gods

1805 North 30th St. **Tel** (719) 634-6666.
**Open** Memorial Day–Labor Day:
8am–7pm daily; rest of the year:
9am–5pm Fri–Sun. **Closed** Jan 1,
Thnksg, Dec 25. 🅿️ only for Rock
Ledge Ranch Historic Site (summer
only). ♿ 📷 🌐 **gardenofgods.com**

### 🏨 Broadmoor Resort

1 Lake Dr. **Tel** (719) 634-7711. **Open**
daily, can vary. Call ahead to
check. ♿ 🌐 **broadmoor.com**

### 🏛 Pro Rodeo Hall of Fame

101 Pro Rodeo Dr. **Tel** (719) 528-4764.
**Open** 9am–5pm daily (Oct–Apr:
Wed–Sun only). **Closed** Jan 1, Easter,
Thanksgiving, Dec 24, 25, 31. 🅿️ ♿
🌐 **prorodeohalloffame.com**

### 🏛 Colorado Springs Pioneers Museum

215 S Tejon St. **Tel** (719) 385-5990.
**Open** 10am–5pm Tue–Sat. ♿
🌐 **cspm.org**

Kissing Camels formations, Garden of the Gods in Colorado Springs

The magnificent view over the Royal Gorge Bridge and Park located in Cañon City

## ⑩ Cripple Creek

🏔 1,200. ℹ️ 513 E Bennett Ave, (719) 689-3315. 🆆 visitcripplecreek.com

Known as "Poverty Gulch" before a gold strike in 1890 transformed it, this is one of the best-preserved 19th-century mining towns in the entire state. The fascinating **Mollie Kathleen Gold Mine** is the best place to explore the town's mining history. Discovered by Mollie Kathleen Gortner in 1891, this gold mine on the southwest face of Pikes Peak is the country's only vertical-shaft mine that offers tours. Even though mining operations ended in 1961, gold veins are still visible on its walls.

The surrounding area is still mined for gold though mining has ceased in most other Colorado boomtowns. Gambling was legalized here in 1990, with casinos housed behind original 1896 brick façades. The historic **Butte Theater** puts on theater performances.

🎞 **Mollie Kathleen Gold Mine**
Hwy 67. **Tel** (719) 689-2466. **Open** Apr–mid-Sep: 9:45am–4pm. 🅿️ 🆑 🆆 goldminetours.com

🎭 **Butte Theater**
139 E Bennett Ave. **Tel** (719) 689-6402. 🆆 buttetheater.com

## ⑪ Cañon City

🏔 16,000. ℹ️ 403 Royal Gorge Blvd, (719) 275-2331, (800) 876-7922. 🆆 canoncity.com

Blessed with sunshine, clear skies, and spectacular scenery, Cañon City, surprisingly, is also the "Prison Capital of Colorado," a title it acquired in 1876, after it chose to house the state prison instead of the state university. Today, prisons remain a key component of the regional economy. The **Museum of Colorado Prisons** is housed in a former women's prison built in 1935. Just 12 miles

(19 km) west of the city stands the **Royal Gorge Bridge & Park**. Etched into the granite bedrock for three million years by the Arkansas River, this breathtaking gorge is over 1,000 ft (305 m) from rim to river at its deepest, but only 40 ft (12 m) wide at its base. Traversed by the world's highest suspension bridge and 12 miles (19 km) of the **Royal Gorge Route Railroad**, the park also attracts white-water rafters to the challenging stretch of the river below.

🏛 **Museum of Colorado Prisons**
201 N 1st St. **Tel** (719) 269-3015. **Open** late May–Sep: 10am–6pm daily; Oct–late May: 10am–5pm Wed–Sun. 🅿️ 🆓 🆑 🆆 prisonmuseum.org

🌉 **Royal Gorge Bridge & Park**
US Hwy 50. **Tel** (888) 333-5597. **Open** varies. 🅿️ 🆓 🆆 royalgorge bridge.com

**Royal Gorge Route Railroad**
**Tel** (888) 724-5748. **Open** late May–Oct: daily; rest of the year: call for details. 🅿️ 🆆 royalgorgeroute.com

Interior of Mollie Kathleen Gold Mine, Cripple Creek

---

### White-Water Rafting in Colorado

The best way to enjoy the pristine Colorado wilderness is to take a white-water rafting trip on the Arkansas River. The picturesque towns of Salida and nearby Buena Vista, 26 miles (42 km) to the north, are hubs for outfitters who offer guided river trips. With about 100 rafting companies in operation, this is the most intensively rafted river in the US. The Colorado River Outfitters Association (303-280-2554) is one of the best sources of information on rafting trips.

Rafting on the Arkansas River, Colorado

# ⑫ Colorado Ski Resorts

One of Colorado's most enduring symbols is of pristine white mountains dotted with skiers. The state's recreational ski industry dates to 1935 when Berthoud Pass, northwest of Denver, became the destination ski resort for pioneering skiers. As the sport's economic potential developed after World War II, many old mining towns emerged as popular ski resort towns. Today the state is undoubtedly the country's skiing capital, with more than 24 resorts. In recent years, other winter sports, such as snowboarding, have become very popular, and most ski mountains now allow snowboarders.

**Aspen**, a favorite of the rich and famous, has more than 200 different runs on four striking mountains. It developed when the Aspen Skiing Company opened its first lift in 1947. Sleek restaurants and boutiques housed behind Victorian-era storefronts complement the splendid ski terrain. Aspen also has a vibrant art and culture scene.

**Max altitude:** 11,675 ft (3,559 m)
**Geared to:** all levels
**Ski level:** 16% 61% 23%

**Steamboat Springs**, the cowboy cousin to the conservative luxury of Aspen, wears its rambunctious Western spirit as a badge of honor. It has some of the state's best snow (a dry, feathery powder), a 3,668-ft (1,118-m) vertical drop, and a total of 165 runs.

**Max altitude:** 10,564 ft (3,220 m)
**Geared to:** all levels
**Ski level:** 13% 56% 31%

Steamboat Springs
Mount Werner
(10,564 ft/3,220 m)
Pyramid Peak
(11,611 ft/3,5...)

Aspen M...
(11,210 ft/3,41...)

**Snowmass**
Snowmass Mt.
(14,092 ft/4,295 m)
Maroon Peak
(14,156 ft/4,315 m)

**Crested Butte**
Kebler Pass
(10,007 ft/3,050 m)
Crested...
(12,16... ft/...)

**Snowmass,** just a 30-minute drive from Aspen, is a complete resort in itself. Larger than all three of Aspen's ski areas combined, it has plenty of wide-open runs.

0 kilometers 50
0 miles 50

**Crested Butte** draws serious skiers to its unparalleled expert terrain. The town sits at the base of Mount Crested Butte, with a vertical drop of 2,775 ft (846 m) and 824 acres (333 ha) for "extreme" skiing.

**Montrose**
Cerro Summit
(7,958 ft/2,426 m)

Sneffels Peak
(14,150 ft/4,313 m)
Palmyra Peak
(13,319 ft/4,060 m)
**Telluride**
Red Mt. Pass
(11,018 ft/3,358 m)

**Telluride**, a former mining community, opened as a ski resort in 1971. The nearby valley was once a hideout for outlaw Butch Cassidy. The town is also known for its bohemian politics, a lively nightlife, and trails that lead to such scenic areas as Bridal Veil Falls.

**Max altitude:** 12,255 ft (3,736 m)
**Geared to:** all levels
**Ski level:** 22% 38% 40%

**Winter Park**, Colorado's oldest full-service ski resort, is linked to Denver by the Ski Train – 67 miles (108 km) of track that connect the slopes with LoDo's Union Station. The resort's five ski mountain areas offer downhill terrain for every skill level, and there are also numerous cross-country trails nearby.

**Max altitude:** 12,060 ft (3,676 m)
**Geared to:** experts

**Ski level:** 9% 21% 70%

## Ski Resorts and Companies

**Aspen Skiing Company (Aspen-Snowmass)**
**Tel** (970) 925-1220, (800) 308-6935. **Open** Dec–mid-Apr: 9am–4pm daily.
**W** **aspensnowmass.com**

**Breckenridge Ski Resort**
**Tel** (970) 453-5000. **Open** early Nov–late Apr: 8:30am–4pm daily.
**W** **breckenridge.com**

**Keystone**
**Tel** (800) 427-8308. **Open** Nov–late Apr: 8:30am–8pm most days.
**W** **keystoneresort.com**

**Steamboat Ski Corp.**
**Tel** (970) 879-6111. **Open** mid-Nov–mid-Apr: 8:30am–4pm daily.
**W** **steamboat.com**

**Telluride Ski Company**
**Tel** (800) 778-8581. **Open** late Nov–mid-Apr: 8:30am–4pm daily.
**W** **tellurideskiresort.com**

**Vail Mountain**
**Tel** (800) 404-3535, (970) 476-5601. **Open** late Nov–late Apr: 8:30am–4pm daily.
**W** **vail.snow.com**

**Winter Park**
**Tel** (970) 726-5514. **Open** mid-Nov–late Apr: 8:30am–4pm daily.
**W** **winterparkresort.com**

**Wolf Creek**
**Tel** (970) 264-5639. **Open** early Nov–early Apr: 8:30am–4pm daily.
**W** **wolfcreekski.com**

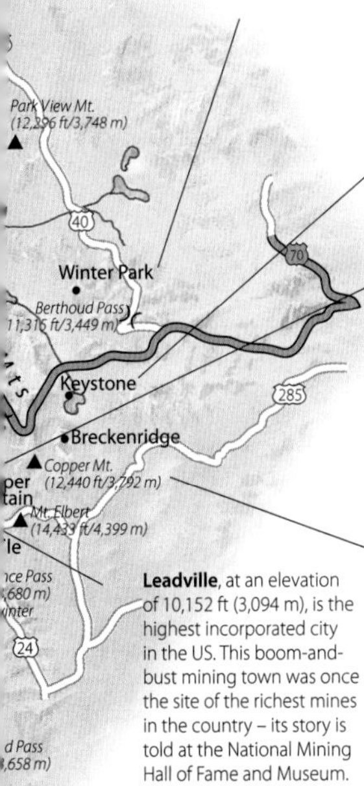

Park View Mt.
(12,296 ft/3,748 m)
40
Winter Park
Berthoud Pass
11,315 ft/3,449 m
70
Keystone
285
Breckenridge
Copper Mt.
(12,440 ft/3,792 m)
Mt. Elbert
(14,433 ft/4,399 m)
24


**Keystone,** with its 12-hour ski day, is now famous for being Colorado's best night-skiing resort. Open eight months a year, it has three ski mountains and offers a variety of activities such as snowboarding, ice-skating, sleigh rides, and indoor tennis.

**Copper Mountain** offers some of the most advanced skiing and snowboarding terrain in Colorado, as well as areas for novice and intermediate skiers. Once maligned, the re-designed village now brims with shops, bars, and restaurants.

**Leadville**, at an elevation of 10,152 ft (3,094 m), is the highest incorporated city in the US. This boom-and-bust mining town was once the site of the richest mines in the country – its story is told at the National Mining Hall of Fame and Museum. Today, it has a small, crowd-free ski resort.

**Breckenridge** boasts an interesting history, recreation facilities including ice-skating *(above)*, and nightlife. The resort is spread across four peaks on the west side of town.

**Max altitude:** 12,998 ft (3,962 m)
**Geared to:** all levels
**Ski level:** 13% 32% 55%

**Vail**, the largest single-mountain ski resort in the US, attracts skiers and snowboarders alike. The domain of Native tribes until the 1870s mining boom, the town actually developed when Vail Mountain opened to skiers in 1962. It has more than 2,000 trails and a 3,450-ft (1,052-m) vertical drop.

**Max altitude:** 11,570 ft (3,527 m)
**Geared to:** all levels
**Ski level:** 18% 29% 53%

**Key**

- Major road
- Minor road
- Good for beginners
- Good for intermediate skiers
- Good for advanced skiers
- △ Peak
- )( Pass

Great Sand Dunes National Monument & Preserve

## 🏛 Durango & Silverton Narrow Gauge Railroad & Museum

479 Main Ave. **Tel** (970) 247-2733, (888) 872-4607. **Open** early May–late Oct: daily; rest of the year: days vary. Call for details. 🅿 🅰 **W** durangotrain.com

## 🏕 San Juan National Forest

15 Burnett Court. **Tel** (970) 247-4874. **Open** 24 hrs daily. **W** fs.usda.gov/sanjuan

## ❹⑤ Mesa Verde National Park

East of Cortez via US Hwy 160.
**Tel** (970) 529-4465. **Open** 8am–5pm daily; open to 7pm in summer (cliff dwellings closed Nov 5–Apr 10).
🅿 🅰 🛖 ♿ **W** nps.gov/meve

When it was established in 1906, Mesa Verde became the first archaeological site in the US to receive national park status. Tucked into the recesses of canyon walls, the park's defining features are 600 fascinating cliff dwellings last inhabited by the indigenous Puebloan people before they abandoned them in 1300. The dwellings range from small houses to the 150-room **Cliff Palace**.

Park rangers lead tours between April and November to some of the most impressive dwellings, including Cliff Palace. Visitors can also explore several structures on their own, including the well-preserved Spruce Tree House. Square Tower House, the park's tallest ruin, can be viewed from an overlook. The **Chapin Mesa Archaeological Museum** displays a fascinating collection of items used by Puebloan people.

There are also 18 miles (29 km) of hiking trails within the park. One of them, the **Petroglyph**

## ❹③ Great Sand Dunes National Monument & Preserve

11500 Colorado Hwy 150, NE of Alamosa. **Tel** (719) 378-6399.
**Open** 24 hrs daily. 🅿 🅰 🛖
**W** nps.gov/grsa

North America's tallest sand dunes sit at the foot of the gnarled Sangre de Cristo Mountains. Their sand was carried to this scenic spot by wind, melting glaciers, and the Rio Grande River, creating a 30-sq-mile (78-sq-km) dunefield. This unusual ecosystem is home to several equally unusual animals and insects, such as a species of kangaroo rat that never drinks water, and the Great Sand Dunes tiger beetle, found nowhere else in the world.

The park has a popular campground, which fills up quickly on weekends during summer, and a mix of long and short trails. Many visitors scale the dunes, which sometimes measure up to 750 ft (229 m).

## ❹④ Durango

**Tel** 17,000. ✈ 🚌 ℹ 802 Main Avenue, (800) 525-8855, (970) 247-3500. **W** durango.org

Once described by American humorist Will Rogers as "out of the way and glad of it," Durango was established in the Animas River Valley in 1881 as a rail station for the mines in the nearby San Juan Mountains.

After the mining boom ended, Durango emerged as a major tourism center and cultural symbol of the West. This modern city is today a model of historic preservation, with late 19th-century saloons and hotels lining Main Avenue, and elegant mansions from the same era on Third Street. One thing, however, has changed – diehard mountain bikers, entrepreneurs, and artists have replaced the rugged miners.

Many visitors take a day trip on the **Durango & Silverton Narrow Gauge Railroad**. A fully functional 1882 steam engine, it follows a scenic 50-mile (80-km) journey, traveling from the valley floor to rock ledges en route to the former mining town of Silverton. Durango's other prime attraction is the great outdoors of the **San Juan National Forest**, where mountain biking is the top sport. Other popular activities are hiking, horseback riding, backpacking, rock climbing, and river rafting.

Durango & Silverton Narrow Gauge Railroad

*For hotels and restaurants see pp592–5*

Point Trail, offers visitors a chance to view ancient rock art. Camping and wildlife viewing (including foxes, mountain lions, and elk) are among the other activities. In winter, cross-country skiing and snowshoeing are popular.

### Chapin Mesa Archaeological Museum
**Tel** (970) 529-4631. **Open** 8am–5pm daily (to 7pm in summer).

Square Tower House, Mesa Verde National Park

## 46 Ouray

1,000. 1230 N Main, (970) 325-4746, (800) 228-1876.
**W** ouraycolorado.com

Nicknamed the "Switzerland of America" for its resemblance to a village in the Alps, Ouray lies 80 miles (128 km) north of Durango. It was named after the Ute chief whose people hunted in the area before gold and silver prospectors established the town in 1876. Today the entire town is listed on the National Register of Historic Places, a testament to the number of well-maintained 19th-century structures here. Two natural wonders – the massive geothermal-powered **Ouray Hot Springs Pool**, and the stunning **Box Canyon Falls**, which cascades 285 ft (87 m) down a natural cliff-side chute – are easily accessible from the town.

Ouray is also on the **San Juan Skyway**, a 236-mile (380-km) loop that includes the "Million Dollar Highway" to Silverton. Its surrounding wild-lands lure rock- and ice-climbers, four-wheel-drive enthusiasts, and other outdoors adventurers.

### Ouray Hot Springs Pool
US Hwy 550, at the northern end of Ouray. **Tel** (970) 325-7073. **Open** Memorial Day–Labor Day: 10am–10pm daily; rest of the year: noon–9pm Mon–Fri, 11am–9pm Sat & Sun. **Closed** major hols.

### Box Canyon Falls & Park
S of Ouray via US Hwy 550. **Tel** (970) 325-7080. Visitor Center: **Open** May 15–Oct 15: 8am–8pm daily. **Closed** Oct 16–May 14.

## 47 Black Canyon of the Gunnison National Park
E of Montrose via US Hwy 50. **Tel** (970) 641-2337. **Open** 24 hrs daily (North Rim Road closed late Nov–mid-Apr). **W** nps.gov/blca

Though not as vast as Arizona's Grand Canyon (see pp530–33), the Black Canyon is strikingly deep with steep sides. The canyon was created by the Gunnison River as it slowly sliced through solid stone for two million years. Its north and south rims have completely different ecosystems and are separated by a crevice 2,400 ft (732 m) at its deepest point and just 40 ft (12 m) at its narrowest point.

The **South Rim Road** meanders for about 7 miles (11 km) past several overlooks, including a fantastic vista of a multi-hued rock face known as Painted Wall, which is twice the height of New York's Empire State Building (see p83). Although the park's northern edge is more isolated, it has a campground and offers magnificent sunset views.

Climbing is a popular sport in the park, as is hiking, camping, and fishing. Among the many trails is one particularly difficult one that descends to the canyon's floor.

The park's varied wildlife includes a variety of birds such as the peregrine falcons who nest on the canyon's sheer walls. Wildcats and bears also roam the vast park.

## 48 Colorado National Monument
W of Grand Junction via I-70 or 7 miles (11 km) S of Fruita on US Hwy 340. **Tel** (970) 858-3617. **Open** 24 hrs daily. Visitors center: **Open** summer: 8am–6pm; winter: 9am–4:30pm daily. **W** nps.gov/colm

Carved by wind and water over the last 225 million years, this immense 32-sq-mile (83-sq-km) national monument has been molded into an eerie high desert landscape of spectacular canyons, and red sandstone arches. A driving tour on the 22-mile (35-km) **Rim Rock Drive** offers splendid panoramas, while numerous trails lead into the heart of the landscape. The park's two geological highlights are the incredible sandstone arches of Rattlesnake Canyon, and Miracle Rock, which is considered to be the largest balanced rock in the world.

The dramatic desert landscape of Colorado National Monument

# Practical Information

Exploring the four Rocky Mountain states requires some advance planning, simply because of the sheer size and diversity of the region's landscape. The boundaries of this mountainous region stretch from the Canadian border in the north to New Mexico in the south. To the west, the area is bordered by the plateaus and basins of the Intermontane region. The breathtaking scenery, rugged terrain, scanty resources, and sparse population of the Rockies are spread across elevations that range from under 1,000 ft (305 m) to over 14,000 ft (4,267 m) above sea level.

## Tourist Information

Travelers entering the Rocky Mountain states via an Interstate Highway are greeted with signs advertising a state "Welcome Center." These centers provide a full range of tourist information as well as clean restrooms and often free coffee. Denver's International Airport (DIA), and most of the region's other major airports and train stations have information desks with free brochures and maps. Most larger cities and smaller towns operate **Convention & Visitors Bureaus** or **Chambers of Commerce**, which provide free travel information.

## Natural Hazards

The short summers of the Rockies region are warm and glorious, but can bring sudden thunderstorms, especially in the mountains. Rock slides, bugs, and wildlife are other hazards. Elevation across the four states can vary. At higher elevations,

in areas such as Yellowstone National Park, roads may be closed by snow between late October and early June. The Interstate Highways and access routes to the region's many ski areas are kept open all year round.

The high altitude of the area means that the sun's rays are more intense so it is essential to wear sunscreen and to drink plenty of water. It is also important to be aware of altitude sickness, which can be life-threatening. Symptoms include shortness of breath, dizziness, lethargy, headache, and dehydration. Keep drinking plenty of water, limit alcohol intake, and do not hesitate to seek medical attention.

Winters are long and often bitterly cold with heavy winter and spring snows. Drivers should make sure that they possess, and know how to install, snow chains or other traction devices, which are required by law. Extra care is

required while driving on icy surfaces.

In remote areas, hikers should be prepared for all weather conditions in winter as well as summer. Carry basic emergency supplies, including food and water, and extra clothing in case the weather changes for the worse.

## Getting Around

For visitors coming from the East or West Coast, Denver is a prime starting point. Smaller regional cities throughout the Rockies have airports, such as the Missoula (MT) County International Airport. Other than organized bus tours, public transportation is limited. Denver has city buses, a light-rail system, and free shuttle buses. Having a car is essential in this region since most national parks and other sights are located at great distances from the major cities.

Seat belts are required for drivers and front-seat passengers in all four states. Child seats are compulsory for all passengers aged eight and under. Helmets are required for all motorcyclists under the age of 18.

Speed limits vary but are usually 70–75 mph (112–120 km/hr) on Interstate Highways outside the populated urban areas. Radar detectors are permitted in the entire Rocky Mountain region.

## Etiquette

Some of the region's most famous sights are located on Native American reservation land. Visitors are welcome but must be sensitive as to what may cause offense. It is illegal to bring alcohol onto reservations, and taking photographs may not be allowed.

## Festivals

Summer in the Rockies brings a deluge of outdoor events, including community and state fairs, in addition to regional and national music, and art festivals. Fireworks, bands, and festivals abound for the July 4th

## The Climate of the Rockies

Weather across the Rocky Mountain region is marked by long, snowy winters, short springs and fall, and hot summers. The main factor determining weather is elevation – temperatures are cooler and snowfalls heavier the higher you go. Visitors should be prepared for winter conditions at any time of year. Yet, months like October offer crisp days, ideal for scenic drives through the mountains when you can enjoy the fall colors of the aspens.

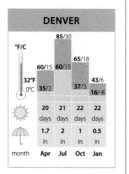

| DENVER | | | |
|---|---|---|---|
| °F/C | | 85/30 | |
| | 60/15 60/15 | 65/18 | |
| 32°F | | | 43/6 |
| 0°C | 35/2 | 37/3 | 16/-8 |
| 20 days | 21 days | 22 days | 22 days |
| 1.7 in | 2 in | 1 in | 0.5 in |
| month | Apr | Jul | Oct | Jan |

celebrations, while the region's strong Native American heritage is also celebrated with a number of pow-wows in July and August on selected reservations. Music and various cultural events, such as the ever popular **Telluride Bluegrass Festival**, the world-famous Aspen Music Festival & School (970-925-3254), and the Big Sky Arts Fesitval, take place throughout the summer months.

## Sports

The Rocky Mountain states all offer a wide variety of sports throughout the year. Denver is home to many of the region's professional teams. The **Colorado Rockies** play baseball all summer at the old-fashioned Coors Field downtown. The **Colorado Rapids** play professional soccer and the **Denver Broncos** play American football. Winter sees the **Denver Nuggets** on the basketball court. Many of the region's universities and colleges play seasonal games, often with heated regional rivalries.

One spectator sport characteristic of the Rockies is the rodeo, and many national competitions are held here. Events such as bull- and bronco-riding, calf roping, and steer wrestling showcase a cowboy's skill. Cheyenne, Wyoming, hosts the "World's Largest Outdoor Rodeo" when more than 250,000 fans flock here during **Frontier Days** at the end of July (800-227-6336). Dude ranches often offer special rodeos for guests.

## Outdoor Activities

The most popular outdoor activity is downhill skiing, which draws many participants and billions of dollars to the region's world-class resorts. Colorado has many of the biggest and most highly regarded resorts in the US, but there is also excellent skiing at Idaho's Sun Valley, Wyoming's Jackson Hole, and at smaller resorts throughout the region. Snowboarding is also popular, and cross-country skiing can be enjoyed in the stunning landscape of the region's many parks and forests. The ski season is from December to March, but many resorts are open until May or June depending on the weather.

Montana is home to such famous trout-fishing spots as the Madison and Yellowstone Rivers, while Idaho, Wyoming, and Colorado all offer excellent fly-fishing. Licenses are required, and catch-and-release is encouraged. Visitors can contact the **Montana Fish, Wildlife & Parks Department** or the **Idaho Fish & Game Department** for details.

Other popular warm-weather activities include hiking, mountain biking, and rafting. Rafting the Snake River through Grand Teton National Park is very popular, as is the wilder Salmon River in Idaho. The Colorado River Outfitters Association is one of the best sources of information on guided river-rafting trips. Lewis & Clark Trail Adventures lead white-water raft trips through miles of Idaho rivers. Snow King Ski Resort near Jackson, Wyoming also offers historical hiking and rafting trips. Bicycle and motorcycle riding is gaining as much popularity as hiking, fishing, and skiing. Open Road Bicycles in Missoula, Montana, rents bikes for a day or by the week (406-549-2453). They will also help outfit and plan trips.

## Entertainment

The ski resorts and dude ranches in the area offer evening entertainment from cabaret and local theater productions to first-run movies. However, many evenings at these resorts are spent in hot tubs, relaxing around the bar, or at in-house casinos. College towns, such as Bozeman and Missoula, Montana, have many of the amenities that the back-country lacks: good bookstores, brew pubs, museums, and events that appeal to both urban and cowboy culture.

# DIRECTORY

## Tourist Information

**Colorado**
1675 Broadway, Suite 1700 Denver, CO 80202.
**Tel** (800) 265-6723.
**W** colorado.com

**Idaho**
700 W State St, Boise.
**Tel** (208) 334-2470.
**W** visitidaho.org

**Montana**
301 S Park Ave, Helena.
**Tel** (800) 847-4868.
**W** visitmt.com

**Wyoming**
5611 High Plains Road, Cheyenne.
**Tel** (307) 777-7777.
**W** wyomingtourism.org

## Road Conditions

**Idaho**
**Tel** (888) 432-7623.

**Montana**
**Tel** (800) 226-7623.
**W** mdt511.com

## Festivals

**Colorado State Fair**
**Tel** (719) 561-8484.
**W** coloradostatefair.com

**Eastern Idaho State Fair**
**Tel** (208) 785-2480.
**W** idaho-state-fair.com

**Montana State Fair**
**Tel** (406) 727-8900. **W** montanastatefair.com

**Telluride Bluegrass Festival**
**Tel** (800) 624-2422.
**W** bluegrass.com

**Wyoming State Fair and Rodeo**
**Tel** (307) 358-2398.
**W** wystatefair.com

## Sports

**Colorado Rapids**
**Tel** (303) 727-3500.
**W** coloradorapids.com

**Colorado Rockies**
**Tel** (303) 292-0200.
**W** rockies.com

**Denver Broncos**
**Tel** (303) 649-9000.
**W** denverbroncos.com

**Denver Nuggets**
**Tel** (303) 405-1111.
**W** nba.com/nuggets

## Fishing

**Idaho Fish & Game Department**
600 S Walnut St Boise, ID 83712. **Tel** (208) 334-3700.

**Montana Fish, Wildlife & Parks Department**
1420 E 6th Ave Helena, MT 59620.
**Tel** (406) 444-2535.

# Where to Stay

## Idaho

**BOISE: Hotel 43**     $
Boutique
*981 Grove St, 83702*
**Tel** *(208) 342-4622*
**W** hotel43.com
Deluxe, artfully designed rooms offer great views of the city and the foothills at this trendy hotel close to major attractions.

**BOISE: The Grove Hotel**     $$
Luxury
*245 S Capitol Blvd, 83702*
**Tel** *(208) 333-8000*
**W** grovehotelboise.com
The area's only four-star hotel has classy, European-influenced decor and comfortable rooms. It also features a restaurant and bar overlooking downtown.

**COEUR D'ALENE:**
**Coeur d'Alene Resort**     $$
Resort
*115 S 2nd St, 83814*
**Tel** *(208) 765-4000*
**W** cdaresort.com
This deluxe lakefront resort has mountain views, spa facilities, and luxury accommodations. Activities on offer include golf facilities, parasailing, lake cruises, and more.

**KETCHUM: Knob Hill Inn**     $$$
Boutique
*960 N Main St, 83340*
**Tel** *(208) 726-8010*
**W** knobhillinn.com
The Knob Hill Inn has ski storage and a shuttle to the ski resort of Sun Valley. It boasts cozy rooms, mountain views, spa tubs, and many complimentary amenities.

Gaynor Ranch and Resort, Whitefish, in the wilderness of Montana

## DK Choice

**SUN VALLEY: Sun Valley**
**Lodge**     $$$
Luxury
*Sun Valley, 83353*
**Tel** *(208) 622-2151*
**W** sunvalley.com
A high-end hotel, located in America's original ski resort, is open year-round and offers a wide range of skiing options, as well as hiking in the summer months. Rooms are elegant and comfortable. Amenities include a glass-enclosed outdoor pool, an ice-skating rink, an elegant restaurant (Konditorei), a spa, a bowling alley, and plenty of activities for children.

## Montana

**BILLINGS: Best Western Plus**
**Clocktower Inn**     $
Motel
*2511 1st Ave N, 59101*
**Tel** *(406) 259-5511*
**W** bestwestern.com
Close to key attractions, this hotel offers clean rooms, friendly staff, and a restaurant serving hearty breakfasts and lunches.

**BOZEMAN: Fox Hollow B&B**     $$
B&B
*545 Mary Rd, 59718*
**Tel** *(406) 582-8440*
**W** bozeman-mt.com
This informal inn has inviting rooms and views of the mountains and meadows, complimentary large breakfasts, and freshly baked cookies in the evening.

**GLACIER NATIONAL PARK:**
**Glacier Park Lodge**     $$
Lodge
*US-2, E Glacier Park, 59912*
**Tel** *(406) 892-2525*
**W** glacierparkinc.com
Rooms at this century-old hotel with a huge stone fireplace in the lobby are comfortable and rustic. Closed October–Memorial Day.

**GLACIER NATIONAL PARK:**
**Lake McDonald Lodge**     $$
Lodge
*Lake McDonald, 59916*
**Tel** *(406) 888-5431*
**W** glacierparkinc.com
Rooms in the main lodge, multi-unit cottages, and a motor lodge in the woods offer rustic charm amid stunning scenery. Closed October–Memorial Day.

**Price Guide**

Prices are based on one night's stay in high season for a standard double room, inclusive of service charges and taxes.

| $ | up to $150 |
|---|---|
| $$ | $150–$250 |
| $$$ | over $250 |

## DK Choice

**WHITEFISH: Gaynor Ranch**
**and Resort**     $$$
Ranch
*1992 KM Ranch Rd, 59937*
**Tel** *(406) 862-3802*
**W** gaynorsresorts.com
This 3,000-acre (1,214-ha) retreat in the woods offers Old West hospitality. Lodging options include well-appointed cabins, with kitchens, on the ranch or in the woods. Activities include fishing, horseback riding, hiking, and skiing in the winter. Abundant wildlife can be spotted nearby.

## Wyoming

**GRAND TETON NATIONAL**
**PARK: Jackson Lake Lodge**     $$$
Lodge
*Hwy 89, 5 miles N of Moran, 83013*
**Tel** *(307) 543-2811*
**W** gtlc.com
Choose from high-end lodge rooms or basic cabins. Lovely views of Jackson Lake and the Tetons. Closed October–May.

**JACKSON: Parkway Inn**     $$
B&B
*125 N Jackson St, 83001*
**Tel** *(307) 733-3143*
**W** parkwayinn.com
Stay in well-appointed rooms and enjoy the complimentary breakfasts. Ski shuttle available.

**JACKSON: Inn on the Creek**     $$$
B&B
*295 N Millward, 83001*
**Tel** *(307) 739-1565*
**W** innonthecreek.com
Charming and romantic, the breakfasts and delicious afternoon cookies here are included.

**YELLOWSTONE NATIONAL**
**PARK: Bill Cody Ranch**     $$
Ranch
*2604 Yellowstone Hwy, 82414*
**Tel** *(307) 587-2097*
**W** billcodyranch.com
Great for families, this ranch offers breakfast, as well as trail rides. Closed October–mid-May.

**YELLOWSTONE NATIONAL PARK: Old Faithful Inn** $$
Lodge
*Old Faithful, 59758*
**Tel** *(307) 344-7311*
w yellowstonenationalpark
lodges.com
Wide-ranging accommodations are within viewing distance of Old Faithful. Closed October–May.

## Colorado

**ASPEN:**
**Aspen Mountain Lodge** $$$
B&B
*311 W Main St, 81611*
**Tel** *(970) 925-7650*
w aspenmountainlodge.com
This comfortable inn offers perks such as afternoon wine and cheese, breakfast, and ski shuttle.

### DK Choice

**ASPEN: The St. Regis** $$$
**Resort**
*315 E Dean St, 81611*
**Tel** *(970) 920-3300*
w stregisaspen.com
A grand year-round resort boasting Victorian flourishes, the St. Regis offers rooms with mountain views, Old World alpine design, and modern furnishings. The courtyards and an outdoor pool are great for relaxing. It is the perfect choice for skiers and hikers, as well as food and wine connoisseurs.

**BOULDER: Alps Boulder Canyon Inn** $$
B&B
*38619 Boulder Canyon Dr, 80302*
**Tel** *(303) 444-5445*
w alpsinn.com
Well-furnished rooms with Mission furniture and antique fireplaces. Breakfast included. Spa services.

**BOULDER: St. Julien Hotel and Spa** $$$
Luxury
*900 Walnut St, 80302*
**Tel** *(720) 406-9696*
w stjulien.com
Modern, luxurious rooms. The luminous lobby boasts a patio with views of the Flatiron Range.

**BRECKENRIDGE: The Lodge and Spa at Breckenridge** $$
Lodge
*112 Overlook Dr, 80424*
**Tel** *(970) 453-9300*
w thelodgeandspaatbreck.com
Lodgings with a rustic charm. The on-site spa has a range of services. Close to all the ski areas.

Modern, comfortable room at St. Julien Hotel and Spa, Boulder

**COLORADO SPRINGS:**
**The Mining Exchange,**
**A Wyndham Grand Hotel** $$
Historic
*8 S Nevada Ave, 80903*
**Tel** *(719) 323-2000*
w wyndham.com
Stay in comfortable, modern rooms at this sophisticated hotel in a centrally located historic building. There are business services and fine dining on-site.

**DENVER: The Holiday Chalet** $
B&B
*1820 E Colfax, 80209*
**Tel** *(303) 437-8245*
w theholidaychalet.com
In a restored Victorian mansion, this cozy inn has period decor, comfortable amenities, and an on-site library. Full breakfasts.

### DK Choice

**DENVER: The Curtis** $$
**Boutique**
*1405 Curtis St, 80202*
**Tel** *(303) 571-0300*
w thecurtis.com
This one-of-a-kind hotel is dedicated to the best of American pop culture. Each floor is themed around a different genre, such as One-Hit Wonders, Chick Flicks, and TV Mania. The rooms are spacious and comfortable, and include signature peace alarm clocks. The wake-up call from Elvis helps give a good start to the day. Superb service.

**DENVER: Warwick Hotel** $$
Luxury
*1776 Grant St, 80203*
**Tel** *(303) 861-2000*
w warwickdenver.com
An affordable luxury option in a prime location. The rooms are exceptionally large, with classic American decor. The heated rooftop pool has 360-degree views.

**DENVER: Hotel Monaco** $$$
Luxury
*1717 Champa St at 17th, 80202*
**Tel** *(303) 296-1717*
w monaco-denver.com
This stylish boutique hotel has French and Art Deco accents in the rooms, each featuring a bowl of goldfish. Complimentary evening wine hour.

**DURANGO: Strater Hotel** $
Historic
*699 Main Ave, 81301*
**Tel** *(970) 247-4431*
w strater.com
A Victorian property with antiques and period memorabilia. The on-site entertainment includes a saloon and a theater.

**SNOWMASS VILLAGE:**
**Stonebridge Inn** $$$
B&B
*300 Carriage Way, 81615*
**Tel** *(970) 923-2420*
w stonebridgeinn.com
Large rooms at this inn have exposed wood beams and modern amenities. There is also a popular on-site restaurant, Artisan. Good value in the summer.

**TELLURIDE: New Sheridan Hotel** $$
Historic
*231 W Colorado Ave, 81435*
**Tel** *(970) 728-4351*
w newsheridan.com
Charming downtown hotel with historic elegance and antique-filled rooms that are small but comfortable. The rooftop hot tubs offer mountain views.

**VAIL: Tivoli Lodge** $$$
Lodge
*386 Hanson Ranch Rd, 81657*
**Tel** *(800) 451-4756*
w tivolilodge.com
Spacious, deluxe rooms offer mountain or village views at this European-style lodge. Good value in off-season.

**For more information on types of hotels** *see pages 26–7*

# Where to Eat and Drink

## Idaho

**BOISE: Bardenay Restaurant & Distillery**                    $$
New American
*610 W Grove St, 83702*
**Tel** *(208) 426-0538*
The Northwestern-style fare here consists of regional meats and seafood – try the cider-brined pork chop or flash-fried Pacific cod. Cocktails are created from home-made spirits.

**BOISE: Cottonwood Grille**    $$$
American
*913 W River St, 83702*
**Tel** *(208) 333-9800*
This elegant restaurant with great service offers carefully prepared local fare, including fish and beef, along with decadent desserts.

**COEUR D'ALENE: Cedars Floating Restaurant**    $$$
Seafood/Steak
*1 Marina Dr, 83814*
**Tel** *(208) 664-2922*
The menu at Cedars boasts a superb list of local fish, as well as regional steaks. Stellar lake views, and simple, pleasing decor.

**KETCHUM: Sawtooth Club**    $$
American
*231 N Main St, 83340*
**Tel** *(208) 726-5233*
Overlooking the ski slopes, the menu at this popular eatery offers mesquite-grilled meats and seafood and a good wine list. The bar serves cocktails and lighter meals.

**SUN VALLEY: Gretchen's**    $$
American
*Sun Valley Lodge, 83353*
**Tel** *(208) 622-2144*
The menu at this family-friendly restaurant offers a range of meats and seafood, plus breakfasts. Closed April/May for maintenance; call ahead to check.

## Montana

### DK Choice

**BIGFORK: Bigfork Inn**    $$
New American
*604 Electric Ave, 59911*
**Tel** *(406) 837-6680*
This Swiss chalet-style restaurant is a favorite among locals. Warm professional service and live music at weekends make for a relaxed atmosphere. On the varied menu are such regional favorites as fresh salmon baked in parchment, rib-eye steak, and crispy country-inn duck.

**BOZEMAN: McKenzie River Pizza Company**    $
Pizzeria
*232 E Main St, 59715*
**Tel** *(406) 587-0055*
Choose from sourdough, natural-grain, deep-dish, or thin-crust pizza bases with classic and gourmet toppings at this friendly restaurant. There are also sandwiches, pasta dishes, and salads.

**GLACIER NATIONAL PARK: Russell's Fireside Dining Room** $$
American
*Lake McDonald Lodge, 59916*
**Tel** *(406) 888-5431*    **Closed** *late Sep–mid-May*
Decorated like a hunting lodge, Russell's serves mountain cuisine featuring wild game. Good list of Montana microbrews and wines.

**HELENA: Windbag Saloon & Grill**    $$
American
*19 S Last Chance Gulch St, 59601*
**Tel** *(406) 443-9669*    **Closed** *Sun*
Diners enjoy the old-time decor and friendly service at this charming place. Comfort food, including steaks and hamburgers, comes in large portions.

Buckhorn Exchange Steakhouse, Denver, with wild animal-themed decor

**Price Guide**

Prices are based on a three-course meal for one, with a glass of house wine, including tax and service.

| | |
|---|---|
| $ | up to $35 |
| $$ | $35–$70 |
| $$$ | over $70 |

**MISSOULA: Lolo Creek Steakhouse**    $$
Steak House
*6600 Hwy 12 W, Lolo, 59847*
**Tel** *(406) 273-2622*    **Closed** *Mon (in winter)*
The menu at this restaurant housed in a log cabin includes meats, salads, and great desserts. The Western-style sirloin, rib-eye, and New York steaks are grilled on an open-pit barbecue.

## Wyoming

### DK Choice

**BUFFALO: Bozeman Trail Steakhouse**    $$
Steak House
*675 E Hart St, 82834*
**Tel** *(307) 684-5555*
Located in a historic cowboy town, this casual, Western-themed steak house boasts a menu of delicious, certified Angus beef, elk, and bison, as well as lighter, healthier fare such as salads. Cocktails, a range of microbrews on tap, TVs, and a kids' menu make this a great choice for families.

**GRAND TETON NATIONAL PARK: Jenny Lake Lodge Dining Room**    $$$
New American
*Inner Park Rd, 83013*
**Tel** *(307) 733-4647*    **Closed** *Oct–May*
In a stunning rustic setting, the restaurant in Jenny Lake Lodge offers a memorable fine-dining experience. Dinner is a five-course gourmet affair, with delights such as elk carpaccio, venison strip loin, and decadent desserts. Reservations required. Jackets recommended.

**JACKSON: Snake River Brewing** $
New American
*265 S Millward St, 83001*
**Tel** *(307) 739-2337*
The bread and beer are made on site at this brewpub. Pulled-pork sandwiches, chipotle BBQ ribs, and the Brew House burger (two beef patties topped with bacon and cheese) are the specialties.

**For more information on types of restaurants** *see pages 28–9*

### JACKSON: Million Dollar Cowboy Steakhouse $$$
American
*25 N Cache Dr, 83001*
**Tel** *(307) 733-4790*
Attached to the Million Dollar Cowboy Bar, this rustic eatery serves traditional steaks, such as elk, with creative touches.

### YELLOWSTONE NATIONAL PARK: Old Faithful Inn Dining Room $
American
*Old Faithful Bypass, 59758*
**Tel** *(307) 545-4999* **Closed** *mid-Oct–mid-May*
This historic dining room serves classic Western entrées such as buffalo prime rib and elk tenderloin. The signature dessert is a rich chocolate caldera.

## Colorado

### ASPEN: bb's Kitchen $$
American
*525 E Cooper Ave, Ste 201, 81611*
**Tel** *(970) 429-8284*
Try monkey bread and pulled-pork Benedict for brunch at this casual restaurant. The dinner menu includes seared meats, seafood, and salads.

### DK Choice

### ASPEN: Matsuhisa $$$
Japanese
*303 E Main St, 81611*
**Tel** *(970) 544-6628*
Opened by celebrity chef Nobu Matsuhisa and housed in a historic cottage, this sushi standout has gained national recognition for its superb sushi and sashimi dishes. Enjoy cocktails and a limited menu in the lounge or outdoors. Reservations essential.

### BOULDER: Boulder Dushanbe Teahouse $
International
*1770 13th St, 80302*
**Tel** *(303) 442-4993*
The menu at this teahouse decorated by artisans from Tajikistan consists of Basque, Persian, Japanese, and Indian fare. There are over 80 kinds of tea.

### BOULDER: Frasca $$$
Italian
*1738 Pearl St, 80302*
**Tel** *(303) 442-6966* **Closed** *Sun*
Enjoy delicious home-made pastas, Colorado lamb, and fresh seafood inspired by the flavors of Friuli, Italy. The wine list includes 200 international fine wines. Reservations advised.

Artisinal Asian decor at Boulder Dushanbe Teahouse

### BRECKENRIDGE: Hearthstone Restaurant $$$
American
*130 S Ridge St, 80424*
**Tel** *(970) 453-1148* **Closed** *mid-Apr–early May*
The menu in this restaurant in an old Victorian house boasts hand-cut steaks, wild game, and seafood. There is also a long wine list and a daily happy hour.

### COLORADO SPRINGS: Blue Star $$
New American/Mediterranean
*1645 S Tejon St, 80905*
**Tel** *(719) 632-1086*
The food at this sophisticated restaurant combines the flavors of the Pacific Rim and the Mediterranean.

### DENVER: Biker Jim's Gourmet Dogs $
American
*2148 Larimer St, 80205*
**Tel** *(720) 746-9355*
Jim's tasty grilled dogs include reindeer, wild boar, rattlesnake, antelope, yak, and buffalo, all topped with Coca-Cola-soaked onions or other exotic toppings.

### DENVER: Pete's Kitchen $
Greek/American
*1962 E Colfax Ave, 80206*
**Tel** *(303) 321-3139*
Open around the clock, Pete's has everything from breakfast burritos and hash browns to late-night *gyros*. Huge portions.

### DENVER: Buckhorn Exchange $$
Steak House
*1000 Osage St, 80204*
**Tel** *(303) 534-9505*
Denver's oldest restaurant is adorned with mounted animal trophy heads and guns. Famous for its exotic game, buffalo steaks and sausages, and elk medallions.

### DK Choice

### DENVER: Steuben's $$
American
*523 E 17th Ave, 80203*
**Tel** *(303) 830-1001*
This stylish diner provides decadent, upscale takes on comfort foods from the Denver area and from around the country: mac 'n' cheese, chicken and waffles, chili burgers, and lobster rolls. Huge doors let in the breeze in the summer months, but it is warm and cozy in winter. There is a superb burger deal during happy hour.

### DENVER: Wynkoop Brewing Company $$
American
*1634 18th St, 80202*
**Tel** *(303) 297-2700*
The area's first brewpub has a fun atmosphere. Excellent ales and beers complement burgers, meatloaf, fish 'n' chips, and the daily specials.

### DURANGO: Seasons Grill $$
New American
*764 Main Ave, 81301*
**Tel** *(970) 382-9790*
The menu at this elegant bistro with an open kitchen and lovely street views is classic American, with a focus on locally grown produce. Award-winning wine list.

### TELLURIDE: Flavor Telluride $$
New American
*122 S Oak St, 81435*
**Tel** *(970) 239-6047* **Closed** *Tue (in summer)*
The simple decor at this eatery celebrates the surrounding landscape. The imaginative menu consists of seasonal soups, salads, and signature sandwiches, as well as many vegetarian dishes.

### VAIL: The Little Diner $
American
*616 W Lionshead Circle, 81657*
**Tel** *(970) 476-4279* **Closed** *Apr–May*
This legendary breakfast spot attracts crowds of locals and visitors. Pancakes, hash browns, omelets, and biscuits are served all day. At lunch, enjoy burgers, chili, and other regional offerings.

### VAIL: Sweet Basil $$$
American
*193 Gore Creek Dr 201, 81657*
**Tel** *(970) 476-0125*
Contemporary American dishes such as trout, heritage-breed pork, and lamb are served at this casual restaurant with mountain decor. Try the delicious hot sticky toffee pudding cake for dessert.

Mount Shukan reflected in Picture Lake, North Cascades National Park, Washington ▶

# THE PACIFIC NORTHWEST

# THE PACIFIC NORTHWEST

Some of North America's most rugged and spectacular terrain unfolds across the Pacific Northwest. Native cultures have lived here for thousands of years, while European settlement is as recent as the early 19th century. The region is now home to two of North America's most sophisticated cities, Portland and Seattle, surrounded by soaring mountains, dense forests, and sparkling water.

The call of the wild is what draws visitors to Oregon and Washington, the states that comprise the Pacific Northwest. This region's vast landscapes bear the imprint of the geological forces that carved deep gorges and thrust up soaring mountain peaks. Despite urban development, the wilderness areas retain a certain pristine quality, especially when one encounters the 800-year-old Sitka spruce trees in a coastal rainforest or the lava fields flanking Mount St. Helens, formed during the volcano's eruption in 1980.

The weather in this region is as varied as its topography. West of the mountains, the north Pacific Ocean currents ensure pleasant summers and wet, mild winters. On the eastern plateaus, however, temperatures dip to well below freezing in the winter, often accompanied by heavy snow, and in the summer they soar. In the central mountain region, inland deserts usually experience harsh winters with frequent road closures and dry hot summers.

## History

The region's Native peoples have lived in harmony with the land since their ancestors migrated here almost 15,000 years ago. The abundance of food and resources, west of the Cascade Mountains and along the coast, enabled many tribes to live in well-established settlements hunting and fishing. Those tribes, living in the harsher landscapes east of the mountains, pursued more nomadic lifestyles, migrating across the high-desert hunting grounds in search of bison and deer. In spring and summer, they moved up the mountain slopes to pick berries and dig roots. The lives of Native people were abruptly changed by the arrival of European traders and settlers.

Mount Rainier towering above Tacoma's Commencement Bay and its industrial tideflats, Washington

◀ The Space Needle, star of the Seattle skyline

The quest to discover the Northwest Passage – a quick ocean route linking Europe with the Far East – lured early European explorers to this region in the 16th century. The first was Spanish explorer Juan Rodriguez, who sailed from Mexico to southern Oregon in 1543. He was followed by Britain's Sir Francis Drake, who ventured as far north as the Strait of Juan de Fuca in 1592.

Britain's next major expedition was in the 1770s, when Captain James Cook, accompanied by George Vancouver and Peter Puget, sailed up the coasts of Oregon and Washington. In 1791, Vancouver and Puget also charted what is now Puget Sound in Washington. Their explorations coincided with those of an American fur trader from the East Coast, Captain Robert Gray, who discovered the Columbia River in 1792, naming it after his ship. Soon, other American vessels arrived in search of animal pelts and other bounty.

The battle to control the Pacific Northwest was waged by the British and Americans

*Portland, City of Roses*

with trade, not gunfire. The 1803–1806 Lewis and Clark expedition opened up the region to American fur traders, who were determined to wrest this very lucrative trade from the British. At that time, the dominant player was Britain's Hudson Bay Company (HBC), which continued to more or less rule the region until the middle of the 19th century. Between 1843 and 1860, thousands of American settlers migrated westward on the 2,000-mile (3,218-km) Oregon Trail. As a result, America and Britain divided the region in 1846, using the 49th parallel as the new boundary between British Columbia to the north and Oregon to the south. Oregon, which included the present-day states of Oregon, Washington, and Idaho, became a US territory two years later. In 1852, this territory was further divided into Washington and Oregon.

Those who profited least from the division of spoils were the Native peoples. Diseases had already decimated many tribes, but now those who survived were removed from their lands and moved to reservations.

## People & Politics

Nearly ten million people call the Pacific Northwest region their home. The nationwide spurt in growth of the Hispanic population in the last two decades is visible in this region as well. Hispanics, today, constitute the largest ethnic group in Oregon, representing almost 12 percent of the state's population. Hispanics form 11 percent of Washington's local

---

**KEY DATES IN HISTORY**

**1543** Spanish explorer Juan Rodriguez Cabrillo sails to the coast of southern Oregon

**1765** Robert Rogers maps the vast territory he refers to as Oregon

**1792** Merchant ship captain Robert Gray crosses the Columbia River

**1829** Oregon City is the first town west of the Rocky Mountains

**1846** US acquires Oregon and Washington

**1848** Oregon Territory established

**1851** Portland is incorporated

**1852** Washington Territory is formed

**1859** Oregon becomes 33rd state

**1865** Seattle is incorporated

**1897** Klondike Gold Rush brings prosperity to Seattle

**1889** Washington becomes 42nd state

**1905** Portland hosts World's Fair with Lewis and Clark Exposition

**1916** Boeing Air Company founded in Seattle, established by William Boeing

**1949** Seattle earthquake

**1975** Microsoft founded by Bill Gates and Paul Allen

**1980** Mount St. Helens erupts in Washington

**1995** Amazon.com launched from Seattle

Romantic interpretation of the Oregon Trail's westward trek, painted c.1904

Snowboarding at Mount Hood, Oregon

population. Native Americans have a significant presence here as well, having recovered from the decline that took place after European settlement. Many of the tribes continue to live in traditional communities, and the advent of dozens of tribal casinos has brought an income source.

Portland and Seattle are among the continent's fastest-growing cities. Though both tend to be liberal in their politics, other areas in the Pacific Northwest region remain conservative. Even so, a unique political climate has emerged. Oregonians are the first in the US to have approved assisted suicide for the terminally ill, while Washingtonians had the distinction of electing the country's first Asian-American governor. Culturally, the region has cultivated a rich tradition of excellence in the arts, sciences, public services, and creative entrepreneurship. Some of the region's best creative talents include Dale Chihuly (b. 1941), one of the world's leading glass sculpturists, rock legend Jimi Hendrix (1942–70), Matt Groening (b. 1954), creator of the popular TV show *The Simpsons*, and Linus Pauling (1901–94), winner of two Nobel Prizes, for chemistry in 1954 and peace in 1962.

Neon sign at Seattle's Pike Place Market

## Economy & Industry

In recent years, the region's economy has undergone great changes. While traditional industries such as fishing, mining, and logging struggle for survival, those based on services and technology flourish. Since the 1980s, when Bill Gates and Paul Allen, the founders of Microsoft, the world's foremost computer software company, established their headquarters in Redmond, there has been a proliferation of high-tech companies. Some 3,000 software and

e-commerce businesses operate in the Seattle area alone. Jeff Bezos, another Seattle-based entrepreneur, set up Amazon.com, the world's largest online retailer. Among the other major companies with interests here are computer industry giants Intel, Adobe, and Hewlett-Packard, the aerospace leader Boeing, which operates several plants in western Washington, and the sportswear chain Nike. Starbucks, the coffeehouse that first opened in Seattle's Pike Place Market in the 1970s, now has coffee bars all over the world.

Amid this economic transformation, one industry has done consistently well. Increasingly, tourists are spending healthy sums to enjoy what the locals have long considered their greatest resource – the Pacific Northwest's natural beauty. The region not only offers great opportunities for some of the world's finest adventure sports, such as white-water rafting, kayaking, hiking, skiing, and rock climbing, but for those who prefer more placid pastimes the opportunities for sitting next to a mountain stream, or strolling along a remote beach, are seemingly endless.

The original Seattle store in the Starbucks chain of coffeehouses, now available in more than 60 countries

# Exploring the Pacific Northwest

The Pacific Northwest, comprising Oregon and Washington, is a region of great natural beauty. Its lofty mountains, deep canyons, crystal-clear lakes, mighty rivers, and rugged shoreline offer visitors a chance to enjoy a wide range of outdoor activities. Equally alluring are its two principal cities – Portland and Seattle, with their excellent museums and vibrant cultural scene. Both cities are well-connected by air, road, and rail. However, the best way to explore the region, especially remote areas, such as Oregon's Hell Canyon and Washington's Olympic Peninsula, is by car.

The Space Needle, dominating the Seattle skyline

## Sights at a Glance

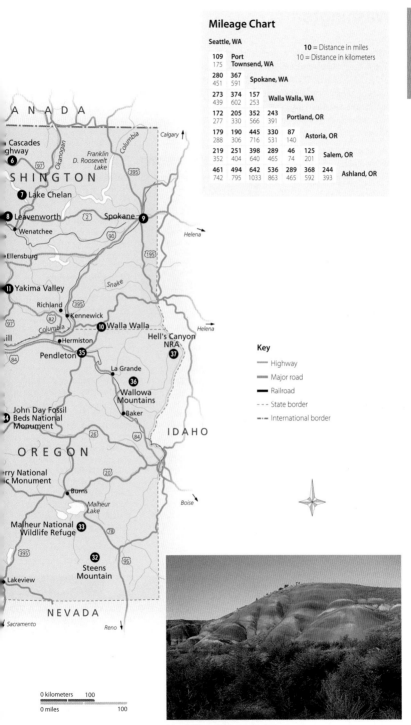

## Mileage Chart

**Seattle, WA**

**10** = Distance in miles
10 = Distance in kilometers

| | | | | | | | |
|---|---|---|---|---|---|---|---|
| **109** | **Port** | | | | | | |
| 175 | **Townsend, WA** | | | | | | |
| **280** | **367** | **Spokane, WA** | | | | | |
| 451 | 591 | | | | | | |
| **273** | **374** | **157** | **Walla Walla, WA** | | | | |
| 439 | 602 | 253 | | | | | |
| **172** | **205** | **352** | **243** | **Portland, OR** | | | |
| 277 | 330 | 566 | 391 | | | | |
| **179** | **190** | **445** | **330** | **87** | **Astoria, OR** | | |
| 288 | 306 | 716 | 531 | 140 | | | |
| **219** | **251** | **398** | **289** | **46** | **125** | **Salem, OR** | |
| 352 | 404 | 640 | 465 | 74 | 201 | | |
| **461** | **494** | **642** | **536** | **289** | **368** | **244** | **Ashland, OR** |
| 742 | 795 | 1033 | 863 | 465 | 592 | 393 | |

### Key

==== Highway
──── Major road
──── Railroad
- - - State border
-··- International border

Painted Hill in the JoÚ Day Fossil Beds, Oregon

0 kilometers 100
0 miles 100

# Washington

The only US state named for a president, Washington has an extraordinary geographical diversity within its 68,139 sq miles (176,466 sq km) of land. Of its three distinct geographic regions, the coastal Olympic Peninsula is dominated by great tracts of forest. Most of the state's largest cities are in the damp, green western region, scattered around Puget Sound. A drive through the spectacular peaks of the North Cascades takes visitors to the sunny, dry eastern part of the state.

## ❶ Seattle

🏙 608,000. ✈ 🚆 🚌 ℹ 800 Convention Place, Street Level, (206) 461-5840. 🅦 visitseattle.org

Nestled between Puget Sound and Lake Washington, with Mount Rainier in the background, Seattle has a spectacular setting. The home of Microsoft and Amazon.com, the city's growth since the Klondike Gold Rush of 1897–98 (see p723) has been vigorous. Its prime geographic location and enviable lifestyle make Seattle one of America's most attractive cities.

### 🏛 Pioneer Square

Bounded by Alaskan & Yesler Ways, 4th Ave & S King St. 🚌 15, 16, 18, 22, 56. Ⓜ Occidental Park. Klondike Gold Rush National Historical Park: 319 2nd Ave S. **Tel** (206) 220-4240. **Open** 9am–5pm daily. **Closed** Jan 1, Thanksg., Dec 25. 🅗 🅦 nps.gov/klse

Seattle's first downtown and later a decrepit skid row, Pioneer Square is now a revitalized business neighborhood and National Historic District with a thriving art and music scene. Many of its buildings were constructed in the years between the two pivotal events in Seattle's history – the Great Fire of 1889 and the Klondike Gold Rush of 1897–98. The handsome **Pioneer Building** on 1st Avenue, for instance, was completed three years after the fire.

The story of Seattle's role in the Gold Rush is told in the **Klondike Gold Rush National Historical Park** on South Jackson Street. A Seattle institution, the **Elliott Bay Book Company** nearby, occupies the site of the city's first hospital and stocks around 150,000 titles.

A display in Klondike Gold Rush National Historical Park

Opened in 1914, Seattle's first skyscraper, the terracotta **Smith Tower**, offers superb views from its wraparound observation deck.

### 🏚 Pike Place Market

Bounded by Pike & Virginia Sts, from 1st to Western Aves. **Tel** (206) 682-7453. 🚌 10, 12, 21, 22, 56. **Open** 9am–6pm daily (from 7am for fish and produce); hours may vary. **Closed** Thanksgiving, Dec 25. 🅗 🅟 🅦 pikeplacemarket.org

Said to be the soul of Seattle, Pike Place Market is known as much for its colorful personality as for its abundant local produce. Established in 1907, the country's oldest continuously operating farmers' market is now a historic district bustling with farmers, artists, and street performers. Rachel, an enormous piggy bank, stands at the main entrance to the market, whose heart is the **Main Arcade** and the adjacent **North Arcade**. Here, low counters display fresh fruit, vegetables, herbs, and flowers grown by local farmers. Shoppers get to "meet the producer," as promised by the market's signature green sign. Attractions include the Pike Place Starbucks, birthplace of the omnipresent chain, and **Pike Place Fish**, the market's best-known seafood vendor. Here, fish-flinging fishmongers are a long-standing tradition.

### 🐟 Seattle Aquarium

Pier 59, 1483 Alaskan Way. **Tel** (206) 386-4320. 🚌 10, 12, 15, 18, 21, 22, 56. 🚋 Pike. **Open** 9:30am–5pm daily. **Closed** Jun 6. 🅟 🅗 🅦 seattle aquarium.org

One of the country's top aquariums, the Seattle Aquarium showcases more than 400 species of animals, plants, and mammals indigenous to the Pacific Northwest. A highlight is the huge underwater glass dome, filled with sharks, octopus, and other Puget Sound creatures. The world's first aquarium-based salmon ladder – the fish jumping up the rungs to the maturing pond – explains the entire life cycle of the Pacific salmon. In the **Life on the Edge** exhibit, children can touch starfish and hermit crabs and examine live plankton through a high-resolution video microscope.

Pike Place Fish in Pike Place Market, which offers both fish and fun

### ⬜ Seattle Art Museum

100 University St. **Tel** (206) 654-3100.
🚌 10, 12, 125. **Open** 10am–5pm
Wed–Sun, 10am–9pm Thu. 🚇 (free
1st Thu of month, and 1st Fri of month
for seniors). 🚻 ♿ 🖊 🎦 🖼 🏛
🌐 seattleartmuseum.org

### ⬜ Benaroya Hall

200 University St. **Tel** (206) 215-4700.
🚌 125. **Open** 10am–6pm Mon–Fri,
1–6pm Sat (box office). 🖊 noon &
1pm Tue & Fri. 🚻 ♿ 🖼 🏛
🌐 seattlesymphony.org

At the entrance of the Seattle
Art Museum stands the giant
*Hammering Man*, a 48-ft (15-m)
animated steel sculpture
created as a tribute to workers.
Housed in a limestone-and-
sandstone building, the
museum has a permanent
collection that includes 23,000
objects ranging from ancient
Egyptian reliefs and wooden
African sculptures to Old Master
paintings and contemporary
American art. Traveling exhibits
are on the second floor. Also
part of the museum are the
Seattle Asian Art Museum in
Volunteer Park in Capitol Hill
*(see p606)* and the Olympic
Sculpture Park, located on

Seattle's waterfront. Across the
street, **Benaroya Hall**, home of
the Seattle Symphony, occupies
an entire city block. Of its two
performing halls, Taper
Auditorium, acclaimed for its
fine acoustics, has 2,500 seats.
The multilevel Grand Lobby,
dramatic at night when lit,
offers stunning views of the city
skyline. Benaroya Hall has some
excellent tours and an impressive
private art collection.

### 🚇 Belltown

Bounded by Denny Way, Virginia St,
Elliott Ave, & Broad St. 🚌 15, 18, 21,
22, 56. Austin A. Bell Building: 2326
1st Ave. Virginia Inn: 1937 1st Ave.
**Tel** (206) 728-1937. **Open** 11am–2am
daily. ♿ 🖊

South of the Seattle Center lies
trendy Belltown. With its broad
avenues lined with hip clubs,
chic restaurants, and eclectic
shops, it has been compared to
Manhattan's Upper West Side.
Earlier an area filled with car lots
and sailors' taverns, its identity
began to change in the 1970s,
when artists, attracted by cheap
rents and studio space, moved
in. The four-story brick **Austin A.**

The *Hammering Man* sculpture at the
entrance of Seattle Art Museum

**Bell Building** is one of the few
remaining original structures.
Commissioned in 1888 by
Austin Americus Bell, the son
of Seattle pioneer William M.
Bell, for whom Belltown is
named, it is listed on the
National Register of Historic
Places. The building now houses
pricey condominiums. The
brick-and-tile **Virginia Inn**, on
the southern boundary of
Belltown, is another historic
building. A popular watering
hole for more than a century, it
is now Seattle's hottest art bar.

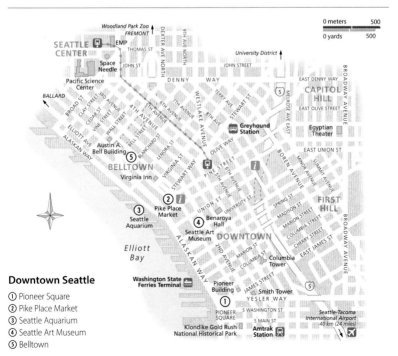

### Downtown Seattle

① Pioneer Square
② Pike Place Market
③ Seattle Aquarium
④ Seattle Art Museum
⑤ Belltown

**For keys to symbols** *see back flap*

## Seattle: Beyond Downtown

This extensive city offers plenty of opportunities for exploration and recreation. Immediately north of downtown are the prime cultural venues of Seattle Center, while to its northeast is the prominent Capitol Hill. Farther afield are the lively University District, Woodland Park Zoo, and the characterful neighborhoods of Fremont and Ballard.

### 🏛 Seattle Center

Bounded by Denny Way & 1st Ave N, Mercer & Broad Sts. 🛈 (206) 684-7200. 🚇 Seattle Center. 🚌 1, 2, 3, 4, 13, 16, 18. 🖥 seattlecenter.com Space Needle: 400 Broad St. **Tel** (206) 905-2100. **Open** check for times. ♿ 🚫 🖥 spaceneedle.com Experience Music Project/Science Fiction Museum: 325 5th Ave N. **Tel** (206) 770-2700. **Open** 10am–5pm daily (Jun–Aug to 7pm). **Closed** Thanksgiving, Dec 25. 🎭 🖂 ♿ 🎧 🚫 🖥 empmuseum.org

The proud legacy of the city's second World's Fair in 1962, this 74-acre (30-ha) urban park contains several innovative structures, cultural venues, and excellent museums. Among the most striking is the **Space Needle**. Supported by three curved steel legs, the needle's glass-enclosed tophouse features an observation deck and a revolving restaurant. At the base of the Space Needle, the exuberant Frank Gehry-designed **Experience Music Project/Science Fiction Museum (EMP)** celebrates music with rare memorabilia, interactive exhibits, and live performance space. Visitors can listen to musicians telling their

Space Needle, Seattle's best-known landmark and prime tourist attraction

own stories. Also here is the world's first museum devoted to science fiction. The museum incorporates exhibitions and a Hall of Fame, which presents respected writers, artists, publishers, and filmmakers from the world of science fiction.

The **Pacific Science Center** features six buildings of white pre-cast concrete surrounding five arches that soar over reflecting pools and fountains. Its hands-on science and math exhibits are especially appealing to children.

The center is best reached by the **Seattle Monorail**. It covers the 1.2-mile (2-km) distance between the downtown station (5th Avenue at Pine Street) and the Seattle Center in 90 seconds.

### 🏛 Capitol Hill

Bounded by Montlake Blvds E & NE, E Pike & E Madison Sts, 23rd Ave E & I-5. 🚌 3, 4, 48, 84.

Lively Capitol Hill is a colorful neighborhood where no one

blinks at spiked purple hair and multiple body piercings. Broadway, the district's major avenue, is lined with shops and ethnic restaurants. Bronze footsteps, to teach passersby the tango and fox-trot, are embedded in the sidewalk of Broadway.

While people-watching is a major source of entertainment, Capitol Hill also features two vintage movie houses: the **Egyptian Theater** on East Pine Street, and the **Harvard Exit** on East Roy Street. The hill is also home to **St. Mark's Episcopal Cathedral** on 10th Avenue Street, known for its magnificent Flentrop organ, consisting of 3,944 pipes.

### 🏛 Fremont

Bounded by N 50th St, Lake Washington Ship Canal, Stone Way Ave N, & 8th Ave NW. 🚌 26, 28.

This funky district declared itself an "artists' republic" in the 1960s, one consisting of students, artists, and bohemians attracted here by low rents. By the late 1990s, its character began to change, after a high-tech firm set up office here. However, Fremont has managed to hold on to cherished traditions, such as the Summer Solstice Parade and an outdoor film series.

Public art is a fixture of Fremont. A 13.5-ft- (4-m-) tall statue of Lenin towers above pedestrians at Fremont Place, and a 15-ft- (4.5-m-) tall Volkswagen-eating troll lurks under the north end of the Aurora Bridge. On 34th Street, sculptor Richard Beyer's *People Waiting for the Interurban* (1979) is regularly clothed by locals. The dog's face in the sculpture is modeled after an honorary mayor, with whom the artist had a dispute.

### 🏛 Museum of Flight

9404 E Marginal Way S (exit 158 from I-5). **Tel** (206) 764-5720. 🚌 154, 173, 174. **Open** 10am–5pm daily (to 9pm 1st Thu of month). **Closed** Thanksgiving, Dec 25. 🎭 🖥 🎦 🖥 museumofflight.org

As the largest air and space museum on the West Coast, this is one of Seattle's premier

The Experience Music Project building in Seattle Center

Richard Beyer's aluminum sculpture in Fremont

attractions. The focal point is the Great Gallery, a dramatic six-story steel and glass structure that holds 39 full-size aircraft. Highlights include an M-21 Blackbird – one of the fastest aircraft ever built – and a replica of the International Space Station.

Many more planes sit on the tarmac outside, and visitors can walk through Air Force One, the plane used by presidents Eisenhower, Kennedy, Johnson, and Nixon, as well as the supersonic Concorde.

Also popular are the museum's flight simulators. Visitors can experience what flight is like in a World War II fighter plane or on a hang-glider.

Nearby is the Red Barn, with exhibits on the history of human flight. A multitude of kid-friendly exhibits are available, plus a full-size control tower where visitors can listen in on air traffic from the adjacent Boeing Field.

### University District
Bounded by NE 55th St, Portage Bay, Montlake Blvd NE, & I-5. 4014 University Way NE, (206) 543-9198. 18 lines serve this district. **Open** 8am–5pm Mon–Fri. Washington Park Arboretum: 2300 Arboretum Dr E. **Tel** (206) 543-8616. Visitor Center: **Open** 9am–5pm. Grounds: **Closed** dawn–dusk. to Japanese Garden. **depts.washington.edu/uwbg**

The hub of the energetic U-District is the University of Washington, the premier institute of higher learning in the Northwest. Located on the site of the 1909 World's Fair, the lovely 693-acre (280-ha) parklike campus is home to more than 42,000 students and 218 buildings in a mix of architectural styles. Just inside the main campus entrance is the **Burke Museum of Natural History and Culture**, featuring dinosaur fossils and Northwest Native art. On the western edge of the campus sits the **Henry Art Gallery**, the first public art museum in the state. The university's main avenue **University Way Northeast**, just west of the campus, is lined with bookstores, pubs, and inexpensive restaurants. University Village, east of the campus, offers an upscale shopping and dining experience.

A must-see is the **Washington Park Arboretum**, a 230-acre (93-ha) garden and living plant museum, with 4,600 species. Its Japanese Garden has carp-filled ponds and a teahouse.

### Woodland Park Zoo
5500 Phinney Ave N. **Tel** (206) 548-2500. 5. **Open** summer: 9:30am–6pm daily; winter: 9:30am–4pm daily. **zoo.org**

Designed in 1899, this is one of the oldest zoos on the West Coast and a major Seattle attraction. The nearly 300 animal species residing at the 92-acre (37-ha) zoo are grouped together in ecosystems rather than by species, in habitats designed to resemble their natural habitats. A visitor center at the main entrance provides maps and other information, such as animal feeding times. Among the excellent naturalistic habitats are the **Elephant Forest** – with its enormous elephant pool and Thai logging camp replica – and the **Trail of Vines**, which includes the first open-forested canopy for orangutans to be created within a zoo. The **Family Farm** includes a popular petting zoo, and a Bug World exhibit featuring many species of arthropods. Indigenous North American animals can be seen in their natural habitats along the **Northern Trail**.

### Ballard
Bounded by Salmon Bay, Shilshole Bay, & Phinney Ridge. 10 lines serve this area. Hiram M. Chittenden Locks: 3015 NW 54th St. **Tel** (206) 783-7059. Grounds: **Open** 7am–9pm daily. Visitor Center: **Open** May–Sep: 10am–6pm daily; Oct–Apr: 10am–4pm Thu–Mon.

Historic bell tower in Ballard

Located in northwest Seattle, Ballard's distinct Scandinavian accent dates to its settlement by Scandinavian fishermen and loggers in 1853. At the turn of the 19th century, Ballard was a mill town, producing an impressive three million wooden shingles a day. North of the shingle mills, **Ballard Avenue** was the commercial center of this area and is now a historic district, which features a wide array of ethnic cafés and lively music clubs.

The area's Scandinavian heritage is celebrated at the annual Norwegian Constitution Day Parade on May 17, at the excellent **Nordic Heritage Museum** on Northwest 67th Street.

Located at the west end of Ballard, the **Hiram M. Chittenden Locks** allow boats to travel between saltwater Puget Sound and freshwater Lake Union and Lake Washington. Its grounds include 7 acres (3 ha) of the Carl S. English, Jr. Botanical Gardens.

# ❷ The Olympic Peninsula

Olympic National Park Headquarters:
🛈 3002 Mt Angeles Rd, 1 mile S of
Port Angeles, (360) 565-3130.
ⓦ nps.gov/olym

Bordered by the Pacific Ocean, the Strait of Juan de Fuca, and Puget Sound, Washington's Olympic Peninsula is an extraordinary piece of land. Its coastline, etched with bays and inlets, is peppered with majestic sea stacks – portions of wave-eroded headlands that remain as offshore mounds. Some of the country's most pristine mountains, beaches, and forestlands can be found in this remote region.

Sitting on the northwest tip of the peninsula, historic **Port Townsend** is known for its Victorian architecture and vibrant arts community. The 1982 movie *An Officer and a Gentleman* was filmed here. To its south, **Port Gamble**, a former logging town on the Kitsap Peninsula, has retained its original New England Victorian-style homes, country store, and church.

The centerpiece of the peninsula is the sprawling **Olympic National Park** *(see p44)*, a UNESCO biosphere reserve and World Heritage Site. Encompassing 923,000 acres (373,540 ha), this biologically diverse park is a treasure-trove of snowcapped mountain peaks, lakes, waterfalls, rivers,

The Olympic Peninsula's Lake Crescent Lodge, located on the shore of the lake

and rainforests. Running through the center of the park are the jagged, glacier-covered Olympic Mountains. With its West Peak rising to a height of 7,965 ft (2,428 m), the three-peaked Mount Olympus is the highest mountain in the range.

The park headquarters are located in **Port Angeles**, a working port town. Sitting in the rain shadow of the Olympic Mountains, Sequim (pronounced "Squim") features an elk viewing site and the Olympic Game Farm, home to endangered animals. Southwest of Sequim, **Hurricane Ridge** offers panoramic views of the Olympic Mountains, the Strait of Juan de Fuca, and Vancouver Island from its 5,230-ft- (1,594-m-) high summit. In spring, the ridge is covered with wildflowers.

To the west, is the picturesque Lake Crescent area. Trout fishing is the main draw in this 625-ft- (190-m-) deep freshwater lake, whose crystal-clear waters

also make it a favorite with divers. The historic resort **Lake Crescent Lodge**, located on the lake's southern shore, is a lovely place to stay. Farther west, the 4-mile- (6.5-km-) long **Rialto Beach** offers superb views of the Pacific Coast, with its tide pools, sea stacks, rocky islands, and the Hole in the Wall, a tunnel carved by waves into a cliff. The coastline receives the highest rainfall in the state. As a result, rainforests carpet much of the region. The **Hoh Rainforest**, with its annual rainfall of 14 ft (4 m), is a magical place, lush with Sitka spruce, Douglas fir, yew, and red cedar, draped with moss. Ancient trees here tower to nearly 300 ft (91 m) in height, and even the ferns grow taller than the hikers. Rainforests also surround the shores of Lake Quinalt. Snowcapped mountains encircle this glacial lake, which attracts fishermen and swimmers alike.

Wildlife is plentiful in the Olympic Peninsula – deer and bear abound, and the Olympic National Park has the country's largest herd of Roosevelt elk. The peninsula offers a wide range of outdoor recreation activities; among the most popular pursuits are fly- and deep-sea fishing, kayaking, whitewater rafting, mountain biking, hiking, and bird-watching. Skiing and snowshoeing are popular winter activities.

The majestic Olympic Mountains in Olympic National Park

Point Wilson Lighthouse, in Port Townsend's Fort Worden State Park

## ❸ Port Townsend

🏠 9,100. 🚢 from Keystone on Whidbey Island & from Edmonds. 🛈 2437 E Sims Way, (888) 365-6978. 🌐 jeffcountychamber.org

This seaport, a National Historic Landmark, is one of only three seaports on the National Registry. A building boom in the late 1800s left the town with several grand Victorian mansions, which now form the cornerstone of its thriving tourism industry.

Downtown's Romanesque **Jefferson County Courthouse** with its 124-ft- (38-m-) tall clock tower, is claimed to be the jewel of Port Townsend's Victorian architecture. Farther away, the old City Hall is now the **Jefferson County Historical Society**, home to the city council, as well as an excellent museum. Other famous buildings include the Ann Starrett Mansion and the Rothschild House.

The **Fire Bell Tower**, on the bluff overlooking downtown, was built to summon the town's voluntary firefighters. **Point Wilson Lighthouse**, in Fort Worden State Park, first lit in 1879, is still in operation. The fort is dotted with dozens of historic buildings and the grounds make a delightful stroll.

Port Townsend is also an excellent base from which to make whale-watching, kayaking, and cycling daytrips.

## ❹ Bellingham

🏠 81,000. ✈ 🛈 904 Potter St, (800) 487-2032. 🌐 bellingham.org

Overlooking Bellingham Bay and many of the San Juan Islands *(see pp610–11)*, this town consists of four original towns – Whatcom, Sehome, Bellingham, and Fairhaven – consolidated into a single entity in 1904. The town's historic architecture includes Old Whatcom County Courthouse on East Street, the first brick building north of San Francisco, built in 1858, and the majestic City Hall. Built in 1892 in the Victorian Second Empire style, the City Hall is now part of the **Whatcom Museum**, with historical displays from Bellingham's past. The museum's main building, the Lightcatcher, which opened in 2009 and features an iconic translucent wall, houses changing art exhibits and a kid-friendly

Tower of Bellingham's former City Hall

gallery. The downtown Art District has numerous restaurants, art galleries, and specialty shops. South of downtown, the historic Fairhaven district is an artsy enclave of Victorian buildings housing galleries, restaurants, and bookstores.

Just up the hill from downtown sits the campus of **Western Washington University**, with its famous collection of outdoor sculptures, including artworks by noted American artists Richard Serra, Mark di Suvero, and Richard Beyer.

From Bellingham's ports, passenger ferries leave for whale-watching cruises and tours to Vancouver Island and the San Juan Islands. Near the city are several waterfront parks, hiking and biking trails, and recreational areas. South of the city, Chuckanut Drive (Highway 11) is a scenic 21-mile (34-km) loop. Some 55 miles (88.5 km) east of Bellingham is the 10,778-ft- (3,285-m-) high Mount Baker, which is a popular location for skiing and snowboarding.

🏛 **Whatcom Museum**
250 Flora St. **Tel** (360) 778-8930. **Open** noon–5pm Wed–Sun (to 8pm Thu, from 10am Sat). 🎫 ♿ 📷 🌐 whatcommuseum.org

🏛 **Western Washington University**
🛈 S College Dr & College Way. **Tel** (360) 650-3000. Campus Information: **Open** mid-Jun– mid-Sep: 7:15am–4:30pm Mon–Fri, 9:30am–2:30pm Sat; mid-Sep–mid-Jun: 7:15am–8pm Mon–Fri. **Closed** public hols. ♿ 🌐 wwu.edu

Crab traps on a boat ready to set out from Bellingham Harbor

# ❺ San Juan Islands

Scattered between the Washington mainland and Vancouver Island, the San Juan archipelago consists of over 700 islands, 176 of them named. Ferries sail from Anacortes to the four largest islands – Lopez, Shaw, Orcas, and San Juan. Affectionately called "Slopez" because of its laid-back nature, Lopez's gently rolling roads, numerous stopping points, and friendly drivers make it a popular destination for cycling. Horseshoe-shaped Orcas, the hilliest island in the chain, offers breathtaking views from atop 2,409-ft (734-m) Mount Constitution. The best destination for walk-on passengers, San Juan Island is home to Friday Harbor, the largest town in the archipelago. The nationally renowned Whale Museum is located here. Primarily residential, Shaw Island has very limited visitor facilities.

**Sailboats in the Channel**
Sailors love the many harbors and good winds in the San Juan Channel.

**★ Roche Harbor**
A charming seaside village, Roche Harbor features a marina, Victorian gardens, a chapel, and the historic Hotel de Haro, built in 1886.

**Lime Kiln Point State Park**
This state park, with its picturesque lighthouse, is the only park in the country dedicated to whale-watching.

*For hotels and restaurants see pp632–5*

★ **Deer Harbor**
Sea kayakers flock to Deer Harbor and the other waters surrounding the islands of Orcas, Lopez, and San Juan.

## VISITORS' CHECKLIST

**Practical Information**
ⓘ Visitor Information
**Tel** (888) 468-3701, (360) 378-6822, (206) 464-6400.
Ⓦ wsdot.wa.gov/ferries
Ⓦ visitsanjuans.com

**Transport**
🚢 Washington State Ferries from Anacortes to Lopez, Shaw, Orcas, and San Juan Islands.

★ **Lopez**
Lopez, with its gentle slopes, is the flattest of the San Juan Islands, making it a popular destination for recreational cyclists.

★ **Friday Harbor**
The largest town in the San Juans, Friday Harbor offers a number of restaurants, inns, galleries, and shops – all within easy walking distance of the ferry dock.

### Key
▬▬ Major road
══ Minor road
- - Ferry route

For keys to symbols *see back flap*

Turquoise-colored Lake Diablo in North Cascades National Park

## ➏ North Cascades Highway

State Rte 20.

The scenic North Cascades Highway is the northernmost mountain pass route in the state of Washington. It is the 132-mile (213-km) section of Highway 20 between Winthrop in the east and I-5 to the west. Bisecting the **North Cascades National Park**, it offers access to the many wonders of this breathtakingly beautiful ecosystem of jagged snow-capped peaks, forested valleys, and cascading waterfalls. The entire route is open from mid-April to mid-October.

The road follows the Skagit River, passing Gorge Creek Falls, Lake Diablo, and Ruby Creek. Along the way, the Ross Lake Overview is an ideal spot to view the scenic lake. At 5,477 ft (1,669 m), **Washington Pass Overlook** provides heart-pounding vistas of the steep pass up Liberty Bell Mountain. A dominant feature of the park, **Mount Shuksan**, at 9,131 ft (2,783 m), is one of the state's highest mountains.

The heavily glaciated park is home to a variety of animals – bald eagles, gray wolves, and bears. Many hiking trails link the highway to the quiet town of Stehekin at the northern-most tip of Lake Chelan.

**🏞 North Cascades National Park**
**ℹ** SR 20, near milepost 120 & Newhalem, (360) 854-7200.
**w** nps.gov/noca

## ➐ Lake Chelan

**ℹ** 102 E Johnson Ave, (800) 424-3526. **w** lakechelan.com

Magnificent Lake Chelan, in the remote northwest end of the Cascades, claims the distinction of being the country's third-deepest lake, reaching 1,500 ft (457 m) at its deepest point. Fed by 27 glaciers and 59 streams, the lake, which is less than 2 miles (3 km) wide, stretches for 55 miles (89 km). In summer, it buzzes with activity – boating, fishing, snorkeling, waterskiing, and windsurfing. The resort town of **Chelan** at the southeastern end of the lake has been a popular summer vacation destination for generations of Western

Sign welcoming visitors to Lake Chelan

Washingtonians seeking the sunny, dry weather on the eastern side of the state. Basking in the rain shadow of the Cascade Mountains, the town enjoys 300 days of sunshine each year. The town's vintage **Ruby Theatre** on East Woodin Avenue is one of the oldest continuously running movie theaters in the Northwest. Chelan's other highlights are the murals on buildings, which depict the history of the Lake Chelan Valley.

About 9 miles (14 km) from downtown Chelan is the town of **Manson**, whose main attraction is the Scenic Loop Trail. It offers easy exploration of the nearby orchards and

hilly countryside. Farther north, the lakeside town of **Stehekin** can be reached by ferry.

## ➒ Leavenworth

**🏠** 2,000. **ℹ** 220 9th St, (509) 548-5807. **🚆 w** leavenworth.org

Once a logging town, Leavenworth, at the foot of the Cascade Mountains in central Washington, is now a quaint little Bavarian-style town seemingly straight out of a fairy tale. This theme was consciously developed in the 1960s to help revitalize the town and, today, every commercial building in town, Starbucks and McDonald's included, looks as though it belongs in the Alps.

The town now bustles with festivals, art shows, and summer theater productions, attracting more than a million visitors each year. Among its popular festivals are a classic Bavarian carnival held in February; Maifest, with its 16th-century costumes, maypole dances, and jousting; and Oktoberfest (*see p40*), the traditional celebration of German food, beer, and music. Teeming with Bavarian specialty shops and restaurants, the town also has the fascinating **Leavenworth Nutcracker Museum**, which showcases 5,000 nutcrackers from 38 countries, some dating back 500 years.

**🏛 Leavenworth Nutcracker Museum**
735 Front St. **Tel** (509) 548-4573. **Open** May–Oct: 2–5pm daily; Nov–Apr: 2–5pm Sat & Sun. 🚫 📷 for groups by appt. ♿

A traditional horse-drawn 13-barrel beer wagon in Leavenworth

# ❾ Spokane

 209,000. ✈ ℹ 201 W Main Ave, (888) 776-5263. **W** visitspokane.com

Washington's largest inland city, this is the Inland Northwest's commercial and cultural center. The city was rebuilt in brick and terracotta after a disastrous fire in 1889 – its many handsome buildings are reminders of that building boom.

Spokane is the smallest city to host a world's fair (Expo '74). The fair site is now the sprawling **Riverfront Park**, a 100-acre (40-ha) expanse in the heart of the city. Of the town's two museum's, the **Northwest Museum of Arts & Culture** showcases regional history, while **Campbell House** (1898) nearby is an interactive museum. Other attractions are an IMAX® Theater and a 1909 carousel. A 37-mile (60-km) trail connects the city with Riverside State Park, located 6 miles (10 km) to the northwest.

🏛 **Northwest Museum of Arts & Culture**
2316 W 1st Ave. **Tel** (509) 456-3931.
**Open** 10am–5pm Wed–Sat.
**Closed** public hols. 🚗 ♿ 🖥 📷
**W** northwestmuseum.org

# ❿ Walla Walla

🏛 31,000. ℹ 29 E Sumach St, (509) 525-0850. **W** wwvchamber.com

Located in the southeast corner of the state, Walla Walla is a green oasis in the midst of an arid landscape. The town features several National Register buildings, lovely parks, and a wealth of public art. The attractive campus of **Whitman College**, one of the nation's top-rated liberal arts colleges, is three blocks from downtown.

A popular destination for wine connoisseurs, the Walla Walla Valley has more than 35 wineries – several right in the heart of downtown. Among the town's other claims to fame are its delicious sweet Walla Walla onions and its annual Hot Air Balloon Stampede, a rally of some 35 pilots, held in May. The stampede also features live music, arts-and-crafts booths, and various events.

**Fort Walla Walla Museum**, on Myra Road, consisting of original and replica pioneer buildings, gives a historical perspective of the area. The **Whitman Mission National Historic Site**, about 7 miles (11 km) west of town, is a memorial to pioneer missionaries Marcus and Narcissa Whitman, who were massacred by Cayuse Indians. On weekends, the Living History Company honors the area's history through music and dance.

🏛 **Fort Walla Walla Museum**
755 Myra Rd. **Tel** (509) 525-7703.
**Open** 10am–5pm daily (Nov & Dec: to 4pm daily; Jan–Mar: to 4pm Mon–Fri).
🚗 ♿ (call ahead). 📷 by appt.
**W** fortwallawallamuseum.org

🏛 **Whitman Mission National Historic Site**
Hwy 12. **Tel** (509) 522-6360. **Open** Jun–Sep: 8am–6pm daily; Oct–May: 8am–4:30pm daily. **Closed** Jan 1, Thanksgiving, Dec 25. 🚗 ♿ (except Monument Hill). **W** nps.gov/whmi

# ⓫ Yakima Valley

ℹ 10 N 8th St, Yakima, (800) 221-0751. **W** visityakima.com

With its rich volcanic soil, abundance of irrigation water, and 300 days of annual sunshine, the Yakima Valley is the fifth-largest producer of fruits and vegetables in the US, and home to more than 40 regional wineries. Yakima, the valley's largest community and commercial hub, is a good base for visiting the valley's award-winning wineries.

**Grapes from Yakima Valley**

A 40-minute drive away is White Pass and Chinook Pass, where you can hike, fish or go mountain-bike riding and white-water rafting. Otherwise, soak up some native culture at the Yakama Nation Cultural Center.

# ⓬ Maryhill

🏛 100. ℹ Klickitat County Visitor Information Center, (509) 773-4395.

A remote sagebrush bluff overlooking the Columbia River is where entrepreneur Sam Hill chose to build his palatial residence. In 1907, he purchased 7,000 acres (2,833 ha) here, with the vision of creating a utopian colony for Quaker farmers. He called the community Maryhill, in honor of his daughter, Mary. The ideal community did not materialize, and Hill turned his unfinished mansion into a museum. The treasures of the **Maryhill Museum of Art** include the throne and gold coronation gown of his friend Queen Marie of Romania, 87 sculptures and drawings by Auguste Rodin, and an impressive collection of Native American art. The beautifully landscaped grounds include a picnic area.

🏛 **Maryhill Museum of Art**
35 Maryhill Museum Dr, Goldendale.
**Tel** (509) 773-3733. **Open** Mar 15–Nov 15: 10am–5pm daily. 🚗 ♿ 🖥 📷
**W** maryhillmuseum.org

Balloons over Walla Walla during the annual Hot Air Balloon Stampede

# ⑬ Mount Rainier National Park

Established in 1899, Mount Rainier National Park encompasses 337 sq miles (872 sq km), of which 97 percent is designated wilderness. Its centerpiece is Mount Rainier, an active volcano towering 14,410 ft (4,392 m) above sea level. Surrounded by old-growth forest and wildflower meadows, Mount Rainier was named in 1792 by Captain George Vancouver *(see p600)* for fellow British naval officer Peter Rainier. Designated a National Historic Landmark District in 1997, the park, which features 1920s and 1930s National Park Service rustic architecture, attracts two million visitors a year. The summer draws hikers, mountain climbers, and campers; the winter lures snowshoers and cross-country skiers.

**Mount Rainier Nisqually Glacier**
Close to the Paradise entrance, the Nisqually Glacier is one of the most visible on Mount Rainier. The glacier continues to retreat as the climate warms.

**Mount Rainier Narada Falls**
One of the more spectacular and easily accessible cascades along the Paradise River, Narada Falls is just a short, steep hike from Route 706. The falls plummet 168 ft (51 m).

0 km      4
0 miles      2

*Olympia*

Carbon River entrance

Ipsut Creek

Wonderland Trail

MOUNT RAINIER

Tahoma Vista

Cougar Rock

Narad

Westside Road

706

Nisqually entrance

Longmire

Sunshine Point

**National Park Inn**
This small, cozy inn, located in Longmire and open year-round, is a perfect spot from which to enjoy stunning views of Mount Rainier.

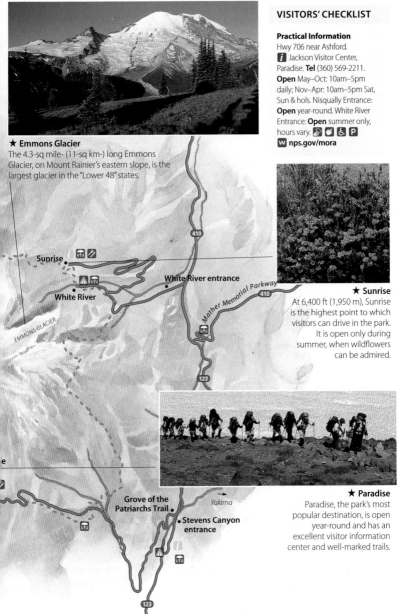

**★ Emmons Glacier**
The 4.3-sq mile- (11-sq km-) long Emmons Glacier, on Mount Rainier's eastern slope, is the largest glacier in the "Lower 48" states.

Sunrise

White River entrance

White River

EMMONS GLACIER

Mather Memorial Parkway

410

410

123

Grove of the Patriarchs Trail

Yakima

Stevens Canyon entrance

123

**★ Sunrise**
At 6,400 ft (1,950 m), Sunrise is the highest point to which visitors can drive in the park. It is open only during summer, when wildflowers can be admired.

**★ Paradise**
Paradise, the park's most popular destination, is open year-round and has an excellent visitor information center and well-marked trails.

## Getting Around

From the southwest (Highway 706), enter the park via the Nisqually gate. Open year-round, this is the primary entrance in winter. Drive 6 miles (10 km) to Longmire, where facilities include an inn and museum, and the Wilderness Information Center, open from late May to October. The 12-mile (19-km) road between Paradise and Longmire is steep; drive carefully. Carry chains when traveling by car during winter. Check the status of the roads before setting out, as conditions can change quickly and closures may be made at short notice.

**Key**

━━ Minor road
══ Dirt or four-wheel-drive road
- - Hiking trail

The modern stainless steel exterior of the Tacoma Museum of Glass

## ⑭ Tacoma

198,000. ✈ ℹ 1516 Pacific Ave, (253) 627-2836, (800) 272-2662.
w traveltacoma.com

Washington's third-largest city, located south of Seattle, Tacoma was founded as a sawmill town in the 1860s. It prospered with the arrival of the railroad in the late 1880s, becoming a major shipping port for important commodities such as lumber, coal, and grain. Many of the Pacific Northwest's railroad, timber, and shipping barons settled in Tacoma's Stadium District. This historic area, with its stately turn-of-the-20th-century mansions, is named for the French château-style **Stadium High School**, also known as the "Castle."

The undisputed star of the city's revitalized waterfront is the striking **Museum of Glass**. The 75,000-sq-ft (6,968-sq-m) landmark building showcases contemporary art, with a focus on glass. A dramatic 90-ft (37-m), metal-encased cone houses a spacious glass-blowing studio.

The stunning Chihuly Bridge of Glass serves as a pedestrian walkway linking the museum to downtown Tacoma and the innovative **Washington State History Museum**. The museum features interactive exhibits, high-tech displays, and theatrical storytelling by actors in period costume, who relate stories of the state's past history.

Sign denoting the old town of Tacoma

The 50,000-sq-ft (4,645-sq-m), stainless-steel-wrapped **Tacoma Art Museum** was designed to be a dynamic cultural center and a showpiece for the city. Its growing collection of works, from the 18th century to the present day, include a large assembly of Pacific Northwest art, European Impressionist pieces, Japanese woodblock prints, and Tacoma artist Dale Chihuly's (see p601) glassworks. In keeping with its vision of creating a place that "builds community through art," the museum's facilities include the Bill and Melinda Gates Resource Center, providing visitors with access to a range of state-of-the-art research equipment. Children of all ages can also make use of the in-house, interactive art-making studio, ArtWORKS.

Tacoma's most popular attraction is **Point Defiance Park**, ranked among the 20 largest urban parks in the US. Encompassing 700 acres (285 ha), its grounds include Fort Nisqually, the first European settlement on Puget Sound, and a major

fur-trading establishment. Also in the park are seven specialty gardens, a scenic drive, hiking and biking trails, beaches, a boat marina, and a picnic area.

Highlighting a Pacific Rim theme, the **Point Defiance Zoo and Aquarium** on Pearl Street features more than 5,000 animals. A vantage point at the park's west end offers superb views of Mount Rainier (see p614–15), Puget Sound, and the Tacoma Narrows Bridge, famous as one of the longest suspension bridges in the world.

The fishing village of **Gig Harbor**, 11 miles (17 km) south of Tacoma, has shops and restaurants that reflect the Scandinavian and Croatian heritage of its 6,500 inhabitants.

### 🏛 Museum of Glass
1801 E Dock St. **Tel** (253) 284-4750, (866) 468-7386. **Open** 10am–5pm Wed–Sat, noon–5pm Sun (Jun–Aug; daily); 10am–8pm 3rd Thu of month. **Closed** Jan 1, Thanksgiving, Dec 25.
🎨 ♿ 🖥 📷 🏛
w museumofglass.org

### 🏛 Washington State History Museum
1911 Pacific Ave. **Tel** (253) 272-3500. **Open** 10am–5pm Wed–Sun. **Closed** public hols. 🎨 ♿ 📷 for groups.
w wshs.org

## ⑮ Olympia

46,000. ℹ 103 Sid Snyder Ave, SW, (360) 704-7544.
w visitolympia.com

Named for its magnificent view of the Olympic Mountains, Washington's state capital is located at the southern tip of Puget Sound. The city's **State Capitol Campus** is dominated by the 28-story Legislative Building (the Capitol), whose 287-ft (87-m), brick-and-sandstone

The Romanesque Legislative Building on the State Capitol Campus, Olympia

dome is one of the tallest masonry domes in the world. One of the most impressive in the nation, the campus encompasses superb buildings, several fountains, and monuments. Its landscaped grounds were designed in 1928 by the Olmsted Brothers, sons of Frederick Olmsted, one of the creators of New York City's Central Park *(see p88)*.

The **State Capital Museum** provides a historical perspective of Washington's early pioneer settlements, through its collections of early photographs and documents. The **State Archives**, with its historical records and artifacts, is another institution related to the state's past. Visitors can access such unique treasures as documents from the Canwell Committee, which blacklisted suspected Communists during the 1950s *(see p60)*.

Tree-lined streets, old homes, a picturesque waterfront, and a thriving cultural community all contribute to Olympia's charm. Tucked among downtown's historic buildings are several shops, restaurants, and galleries. Within walking distance are attractions such as the lively **Olympia Farmers Market,** offering local produce, seafood, and crafts, along with dining and entertainment.

**Percival Landing**, a 1.5-mile (2.5-km) boardwalk along Budd Inlet, offers views of the Olympic Mountains, the Capitol dome, Puget Sound, and ships in port.

🏛 **State Capitol Campus**
ℹ 409 13th Ave SW, (360) 586-3460. **Closed** Jan 1, Thanksgiving, Dec 25. Legislative Building: **Open** Memorial Day–Labor Day: 8am–5pm Mon–Fri, 9am–4pm Sat–Sun; Labor Day–Memorial Day: 8am–5pm Mon–Fri. 🎦 Campus: hourly 10am–3pm daily; Temple of Justice: 8am–5pm Mon–Fri. 🚻 🅦 **ga.wa.gov/visitor**

🏛 **State Capital Museum**
211 21st Ave SW. **Tel** (360) 753-2580. **Open** 10am–4pm Sat. **Closed** public hols. 🏛 🚻 🅦 **washingtonhistory.org**

🏛 **State Archives**
1129 Washington St SE. **Tel** (360) 586-1492.

Mount St. Helens and the surrounding area after the 1980 explosion

### ⓰ Mount St. Helens National Volcanic Monument

**Tel** (360) 449-7800. 🚗 🚲 🏕
🅦 **fs.fed.us/gpnf/mshnvm**

On the morning of May 18, 1980, Mount St. Helens literally exploded. Triggered by a powerful earthquake, the peak erupted, spewing 1 cubic mile (4.17 cubic km) of rock into the air and causing the largest recorded avalanche in history. In the blink of an eye, the mountain lost 1,314 ft (400 m), and 234 sq miles (606 sq km) of forestlands were destroyed. The eruption also claimed 57 human lives and those of millions of animals and fish.

The 170-sq-mile (445-sq-km) monument was created in 1982 to allow the environment to recover naturally while encouraging research, recreation, and education. Roads and trails allow visitors to explore this fascinating region by car and foot. On the mountain's west side, Highway 504 leads to five visitor centers, which document the disaster and recovery efforts. Mount St. Helens National Volcanic Monument Visitor Center, at milepost 5, features interpretive exhibits of the mountain's history. The visitor center at Hoffstadt Bluffs, at milepost 27, gives visitors their first full view of Mount St. Helens and offers helicopter tours into the blast zone from May to September. **Johnson Ridge Observatory**, at the end of the road, offers panoramic views.

### ⓱ Fort Vancouver National Historic Site

**Tel** (360) 816-6230. **Open** Apr–Oct: 9am–5pm Mon–Sat, 10am–5pm Sun; Nov–Mar: 9am–4pm Mon–Sat, noon–4pm Sun. **Closed** Jan 1, Thanksgiving, Dec 24, 25, & 31. 🚗 🚻 partial. 🏛
🅦 **nps.gov/fova**

Between 1825 and 1849, Fort Vancouver was a major trading outpost for the Hudson's Bay Company, the British-based fur-trading organization. Located close to major tributaries and natural resources, it was the center of political and commercial activities in the Pacific Northwest during these years. In the 1830s and 1840s, the fort also provided essential supplies to settlers.

Fort Vancouver features reconstructions of nine original buildings, including the jail and fur store, all on their original sites. Guided tours and re-enactments offer a window into the fort's past. Over a million artifacts have been excavated from this site.

The three-story bastion, dating from 1845, at Fort Vancouver National Historic Site

# Oregon

Oregon is best known for its many scenic wonders – snowcapped mountains, flowing rivers, verdant forests, and desert vistas are just some of the attractions in this incredibly diverse state. This rugged landscape was first settled by pioneers who migrated along the Oregon Trail *(see p446)*. Today, the state is known not only for its scenic beauty but also for its cosmopolitan pleasures. Portlanders are eager to claim their city as one of the most sophisticated and cultured anywhere.

Evening view of the Portland skyline and the Willamette River

## ⑱ Portland

🏙 584,000. ✈ 🚗 🚌 🚊 🚉 ℹ 701 SW 6th Ave, (503) 275-8355, (877) 678-5263. 🅆 travelportland.com

Known as the City of Roses, Portland was founded in 1843, on the west bank of the Willamette River. It grew into a major port, but later, with the arrival of the railroad and decline in river trade, the city center moved inland. This area, with its steel-framed buildings, is now the city's downtown, while Old Town encompasses the former port and riverfront quarter. Portland's beautiful parks and gardens and well-preserved historic landmarks are a tribute to foresight and successful urban planning.

### 🏛 Pioneer Courthouse Square

SW Broadway & Yamhill St. **Tel** (503) 223-1613. ♿ 🅆 pioneercourthousesquare.com

This one-block, brick-paved pedestrian square, in eastern downtown, is the heart of Portland, where Portlanders gather for free lunchtime concerts, flower shows, and other events, or simply for a chance to sit and enjoy their beautiful city. Underground

spaces next to the square accommodate offices and businesses, which include the Portland Visitors Association Information Center, a coffee shop, and a branch of Powell's City of Books, a well-known store specializing in travel books.

Opposite is the **Pioneer Courthouse**, the first federal building to be built in the Pacific Northwest region. The US Court of Appeals and a US post office branch are housed here. Its octagonal tower has been a fixture of the Portland skyline from 1873. The courthouse is not open to the public.

### 🏛 South Park Blocks

Bounded by SW Salmon St & I-405, SW Park & SW 9th Aves. Oregon Historical Society: 1200 SW Park Ave. **Tel** (503) 222-1741. **Open** 10am–5pm Mon–Sat, noon–5pm Sun. **Closed** public hols. 🎫 ♿ 🏠 🅆 ohs.org Portland Art Museum: 1219 SW Park Ave. **Tel** (503) 226-2811. **Open** 10am–5pm Tue, Wed & Sat, 10am–8pm Thu & Fri, noon–5pm Sun. **Closed** public hols. 🎫 ♿ 🖥 🏠 🅆 portlandartmuseum.org

A green ribbon of elm-shaded lawns laid out by frontier businessman and legislator Daniel Lownsdale in 1852, the so-called South Park Blocks is a 12-block stretch running through the central city. Among its distinctive features are statuary and some 40 ornamental fountains. South Park Blocks is also the venue for a colorful local market, held every Saturday, where farmers sell their wares to locals and visitors alike.

The **Oregon Historical Society** to the south of the park has huge murals on its façades that depict scenes from the Lewis and Clark expedition *(see pp561–2)* and other significant moments in the state's history. On display in the galleries, which extend through three buildings, are paintings, photographs, maps, and historical documents that make this museum the largest repository of Oregon's historical artifacts.

The **Portland Art Museum**, opposite South Park Blocks in Southwest Park Avenue, is the oldest museum in the Pacific Northwest. Its sizable collection of European works, includes paintings by Picasso, van Gogh, and Monet, and sculpture by Rodin and Brancusi. Its Grand Ronde Center for Native American Art displays masks, jewelry, and totem poles created by the indigenous peoples of North America. It has undergone a program of expansion, including the renovation and restoration of the North Building, and the creation of an underground gallery linking the two main buildings.

The Saturday farmers market in South Park Blocks

Main gateway to Portland's Saturday Market

## 🏛 Governor Tom McCall Waterfront Park

Bounded by SW Harrison & NW Glisan Sts, SW Naito Pkwy & Willamette River.

Buried beneath an expressway from the 1940s to the 1970s, this 1.5-mile- (2.5-km-) long stretch of Willamette River waterfront was reclaimed and transformed into a park. Named after Tom McCall, Oregon's environmentally minded governor from 1967 to 1975, the park is now a frequently used riverside promenade and the venue for many local festivals, including the annual Rose Festival, held between May and June.

One of its most popular attractions is **Salmon Street Springs**, a fountain whose 100 jets splash water directly onto the pavement, providing relief on a hot day. Another highlight is the **Battleship Oregon Memorial**, at its southern end. Built in 1956, the memorial honors an 1893 US Navy ship. A time capsule sealed in its base in 1976 is to be opened in 2076.

**RiverPlace Marina** at the southwest end of Tom McCall Park offers many amenities including restaurants, one of the city's higher-end hotels – the RiverPlace Hotel, upscale shops, sloping lawns, riverside walks, and a large marina.

## 🏛 Old Town & Chinatown

Bounded by SW Naito Pkwy & NW Glisan St, NW 3rd Ave & SW Pine St.

Elegant brick façades and quiet streets belie Old Town's raucous, 19th-century frontier-town past. A National Historic Landmark today, this riverfront district once drew dockworkers, shipbuilders, and traders from all over the world during its heyday as a major port and the city's commercial center. Old Town is now a trendy, colorful neighborhood, especially during weekends, when vendors gather for the **Portland Saturday Market**, America's largest handicrafts bazaar. Chinatown Gate, a five-tiered, dragon-festooned gateway leads to Chinatown, formerly home to the city's many Asian immigrants, who first arrived in Portland more than 135 years ago. The neighborhood's tranquil **Lan Su Chinese Garden** is a 15th-century Ming-style walled enclave, with waterways and pavilions.

## 🏛 Pearl District

W Burnside to NW Lovejoy Sts, from NW 8th to NW 15th Aves. Portland Streetcar east- & southbound on NW Lovejoy St & 11th Ave, north- & westbound on 10th Ave & NW Northrup St. **Open** every 15 mins, 5:30am–11:30pm Mon–Fri, 7:15am–11:30pm Sat, 7:15am–10:30pm Sun.
**W** shopthepearl.com

Often called Portland's "newest" neighborhood, Pearl District actually occupies an old industrial area on the north side of Burnside Street. Many former warehouses and factories have been refurbished to house chic galleries, designer shops, design studios, clubs, cafés, restaurants, and breweries. A good time to visit Pearl District is during a First Thursday event, which takes place the first Thursday of every month. At this time, the many art galleries in the area remain open until late, usually 9pm. The district has a calendar of events, from small-dog playgroups to a regular farmers'

market held every Thursday in summer. The website has details. A quaint way to travel between Pearl District and Nob Hill, a gracious, late 19th-century neighborhood, is to take the **Portland Streetcar**. These low-slung Czech-built trams are not only a convenient way to get around but are also free within the city center.

## 🏛 Washington Park

SW Park Pl. **Tel** (503) 823-2223.
**Open** 24 hrs daily (not all sights).
🎫 to some exhibits. 📷
**W** portlandonline.com/parks

Washington Park, a popular outdoor playground, is surrounded by the city on all its sides. Its attractions include the Hoyt Arboretum, which has more than 8,000 trees and shrubs, the Japanese Garden, the International Rose Test Garden, and the popular **Oregon Zoo**, which has the largest number of elephants bred in captivity.

## 🏛 Oregon Museum of Science and Industry

1945 SE Water Ave. **Tel** (503) 797-4000. **Open** Labor Day–mid-Jun: 9:30am–5:30pm Tue–Sun; mid-Jun–Labor Day: 9:30am–7pm daily. **Closed** public hols. 🎫 ♿ 📷 of submarine. 📱 📷
**W** omsi.edu Eastbank Esplanade: bounded by Willamette River & I-5, Steel & Hawthorne Bridges.

Sign at Oregon Zoo

East of the river, the Oregon Museum of Science and Industry (OMSI) is a top US science museum. A favorite among the hundreds of interactive exhibits is the earthquake simulator, in which visitors are shaken and rattled while learning about the tectonic plates that still shift beneath Portland.

Nearby, the **Eastbank Esplanade** is a pedestrian and bicycle path following the east bank of the Willamette River. A 1,200-ft (365-m) section floats on water, while a cantilevered portion is suspended above one of the city's original commercial piers, providing unobstructed river views.

Columbia River Gorge and the Cascade Mountains

# ⑲ Columbia River Gorge

🛈 402 W 2nd St, The Dalles, (800) 984-6743. **W** crgva.org

This magnificent fir- and maple-covered river canyon cuts through the Cascade Mountains, forming a boundary between the states of Washington and Oregon. The best way to explore the area is to take the **Historic Columbia River Highway**. Blasted out of narrow cliffs, this road was designed to maximize viewing pleasure while minimizing environmental damage as much as possible. Along the route are the spectacular **Multnomah Falls**, tumbling 620 ft (186 m) in two picturesque cascades, and the cozy, rustic Timberline Lodge dating from the 1930s *(see p633)*.

# ⑳ Mount Hood

🛈 24403 E Welches Rd, Welches, (503) 622-3017. **W** mthood.org

The spectacular snow-covered peak of Mount Hood, the tallest of Oregon's Cascade peaks, rises south of the Columbia River Gorge. Home to year-round skiing and snowboarding, the valleys below are famous for their produce of apples, apricots, pears, and peaches.

The **Mount Hood Loop** is a good way to explore the area; the highest point on the loop, known as **Barlow Pass**, is so steep that at one time wagons

had to be lowered down the hillsides with ropes. The Hood River Valley offers blossoming fruit trees in season and lovely views of the majestic Mount Hood throughout the year. **Hood River**, a riverside town called the "Windsurfing Capital of the World," also offers great opportunities for sports such as mountain biking.

# ㉑ Astoria

🗺 9,500. 🛈 111 W Marine Dr., (800) 875-6807.
**W** oldoregon.com

The oldest American settlement west of the Rocky Mountains, Astoria was established when John Jacob Astor sent fur traders around Cape Horn to establish a trading post at the mouth of the Columbia River in 1811. Earlier, explorers Lewis and Clark *(see pp561–2)* spent the winter of 1805–1806 at a crude stockade near Astoria, making moccasins, preserving fish, and recording in their journals accounts of bear attacks and the almost continual rain. The stockade has since been rebuilt at Fort Clatsop National Memorial. These days, the town is a bustling port; its

old Victorian homes climb a hillside above the river. One such home, the stately **Captain George Flavel House Museum**, retains the cupola from which the captain and his wife once watched river traffic. An even better view can be enjoyed from atop the 164-step spiral staircase of the **Astoria Column**, encircled with friezes paying homage to the history of the Pacific Northwest.

The town honors its seafaring past at the **Columbia River Maritime Museum**, where riverside galleries house fishing dories as well as Native American dugout canoes and other river-oriented artifacts. The lightship *Columbia*, berthed in front, once guided ships across the treacherous area at the mouth of the river.

Astoria Column

🏛 **Captain George Flavel House Museum**
441 8th St. **Tel** (503) 325-2203.
**Open** May–Sep: 10am–5pm daily; Oct–Apr: 11am–4pm daily. **Closed** Jan 1, Thanksgiving, Dec 24–25. 🛇

🏛 **Columbia River Maritime Museum**
1792 Marine Dr. **Tel** (503) 325-2323.
**Open** 9:30am–5pm daily.
**Closed** Thanksgiving, Dec 25. 🛇 📷
**W** crmm.org

The majestic peak of Mount Hood as seen from Hood River Valley

Sea stacks rise off the weathered coast of Bandon

# ㉒ Oregon Coast

ℹ️ 137 NE 1st St, Newport, Oregon, (541) 574-2679, (888) 628-2101.
W visittheoregoncoast.com

Hundreds of miles of pristine beaches make the Oregon Coast one of the the state's best-loved tourist destinations. The developed northern part has some of Oregon's most popular resorts, while the southern part is more wild and rugged. The coast is ideal for a range of recreational activities such as driving, cycling, hiking, camping, shell-fishing, and whale- or bird-watching.

Oregon's favorite beach town, **Cannon Beach**, south of Astoria, retains a quiet charm. Haystack Rock, one of the tallest coastal monoliths in the world, towers 235 ft (72 m) above a long beach and tidal pools. **Ecola State Park**, at the beach's north end, carpets Tillamook Head, a basalt headland, with verdant forests. Viewpoints look across raging surf to Tillamook Rock Lighthouse, which was built in 1880. Nature is the main

Picturesque house on Hemlock Street, Cannon Beach

attraction along the 35-mile (56-km) **Three Capes Scenic Route**, farther south. The rocks below Cape Meares State Scenic Viewpoint and Cape Meares Lighthouse are home to one of the largest colonies of nesting seabirds in North America. The Cape Lookout State Park is a good place to spot migrating gray whales. The Oregon State Parks Association provides detailed information about the sights along this stunning route.

The **Cape Perpetua Scenic Area** has the highest viewpoint on the coast. A road ascends to the top at 800 ft (240 m), and an easy hike along the Giant Spruce Trail leads to a majestic, 500-year-old Sitka spruce. From Cape Perpetua, Highway 101 leads to Heceta Head State Park, with its ocean views – birds nest on rocks and sea lions and gray whales swim offshore. Rising high above the surf, the Heceta Head Lighthouse was first lit in 1894. Steller's sea lions inhabit the Sea Lion Caves, the only wild sea-lion rookery on the North American mainland.

The massive sand dunes of the **Oregon Dunes National Recreation Area** stretch south from Florence for 40 miles (64 km). Towering sand formations, lakes, pine forests, grasslands, and open beaches

Dune buggy, Oregon Dunes National Recreation Area

attract a variety of recreation enthusiasts. Boardwalks make it easy to enjoy stunning vistas from Oregon Dunes Overlook, about 20 miles (32 km) south of Florence, while the mile-long **Umpqua Scenic Dunes Trail**, 30 miles (48 km) south of Florence, skirts the tallest dunes.

**Bandon**, near the mouth of the Coquille River, is so small and weathered that it is difficult to imagine that it was once a major port. Craggy rock formations rise from the ocean just off the beach. These wind-sculpted shapes include Face Rock, allegedly an Indian maiden who was frozen into stone by an evil spirit. A wild landscape of dunes and sea grass can be seen at the Bullards Beach State Park, which lies across the marshy, bird-filled Coquille Estuary.

🎖 **Three Capes Scenic Route**
Oregon State Parks. **Tel** (800) 551-6949. W **oregon.gov/oprd**

🎖 **Cape Perpetua Scenic Area**
Visitor Center: **Tel** (541) 547-3289.
**Open** Spring & Fall: 10am–4pm daily; Jun–Aug: 10am–5:30pm daily; Nov–mid-Mar: 10am–4pm Thurs–Mon.
**Closed** public hols. ♿ 📷

🎖 **Oregon Dunes National Recreation Area**
ℹ️ 855 Highway Ave, Reedsport, (541) 271-6000. **Open** dawn–dusk daily. ♿ W **fs.fed.us/r6/siuslaw/recreation**

Local arts and crafts on display at the Saturday Market in Eugene

## ㉓ Salem

🏕 155,000. ℹ 1313 Mill St SE, (800) 874-7012. 🆆 travelsalem.com

Once a thriving trading and lumber port on the Willamette River, Salem became the capital of the Oregon Territory in 1851.

At the edge of Bush's Pasture Park stand **Asahel Bush House**, an 1878 home with a conservatory said to be the first greenhouse west of the Mississippi River, and the historic **Deepwood Estate**. The **Williamette Heritage Center at the Mill** preserves some of the state's earliest structures. These include the 1841 home of Jason Lee, who helped found Salem, and the Kay Woolen Mill.

Asahel Bush House, Salem

The state's history is also in evidence around the **Oregon State Capitol**. A gilded pioneer stands atop the rotunda, marble sculptures of Lewis and Clark *(see pp 561–2)* flank the entrance, and the murals inside depict Captain Robert Gray's discovery of the Columbia River *(see p600)*.

Across the street from the Capitol Building is the **Hallie Ford Museum of Art**, with its outstanding collection of 20th-century Native American basketry and paintings.

🏛 **Williamette Heritage Center at The Mill**
1313 Mill St SE. **Tel** (503) 585-7012. **Open** 10am–5pm Mon–Sat. **Closed** major hols. 🎟 🎫
🆆 williametteheritage.org

## ㉔ Eugene

🏕 156,000. ℹ 754 Olive St, (541) 484-5307, (800) 547-5445. 🆆 visitlanecounty.org

The University of Oregon brings culture and distinction to the city of Eugene, which straddles the banks of the Willamette River at the south end of the river valley. The glass-and-timber **Hult Center for the Performing Arts** is regarded as one of the best-designed performing arts complexes in the world. The **University of Oregon Museum of Natural and Cultural History** counts among its holdings some ancient shoes – a pair of sagebrush sandals dating from as early as 9500 BC.

Local artisans sell their wares at the **Saturday Market**, in downtown Park Blocks. The **Fifth Street Public Market**, an assemblage of shops and restaurants in a converted feed mill, bustles with locals and university students.

## ㉕ Madras & Warm Springs

Madras: ℹ 274 SW 4th St, (541) 475-2350. 🆆 madraschamber.com
Warm Springs: ℹ 1233 Veterans St, (541) 553-1161. 🆆 warmsprings.com

Madras is a desert ranching town surrounded by rimrock and vast tracts of wilderness recreation lands. **Crooked River National Grassland** provides endless vistas as well as fishing and rafting opportunities on two US National Wild and Scenic Rivers – the Deschutes and the Crooked – that weave through thousands of acres of juniper and sage brush. **Cove Palisades State Park** surrounds the deep waters of Lake Billy Chinook, a popular destination for boaters.

The Treaty of 1855 between the US government and the Wasco, Walla Walla, and Paiute tribes established lands for the tribes located on the 1000-sq-mile (2590-sq-km) Warm Springs Reservation in central Oregon. Today, these Confederated Tribes preserve their cultural heritage at the **Museum at Warm Springs** with a stunningly beautiful collection of basketry and beadwork, haunting historic photographs, and videotapes of tribal ceremonies. The tribes also manage a casino and a resort, where a large pool is heated by hot springs.

🏛 **Museum at Warm Springs**
2189 Hwy 26, Warm Springs. **Tel** (503) 553-3331. **Open** 9am–5pm daily. **Closed** Sun & Mon (Dec–Feb), Jan 1, Thanksgiving, Dec 25. 🎟 🎫
🆆 museumatwarmsprings.org

Swimming pool fed by hot springs at the Warm Springs Reservation resort

*For hotels and restaurants see pp632–5*

Galloping horses near Sisters, the peaks of the Three Sisters Mountains visible in the distance

## ㉖ Sisters

🚐 2,000. ℹ️ 291 E Main Ave, (541) 549-0251. 🌐 **sisterschamber.com**

This Wild-West-style ranching town is surrounded by lush pine forests, alpine meadows, and rushing streams. The peaks of the Three Sisters, each above 10,000 ft (3,000 m), rise majestically in the background.

### Environs
The McKenzie Pass climbs from Sisters to a 1-mile (1.6-km) summit amid a massive lava flow. The **Dee Wright Observatory** provides panoramic views of more than a dozen Cascade Mountain peaks, buttes, and sweeping lava fields.

### 🔭 Dee Wright Observatory
Hwy 242, 15 miles (24 km) west of Sisters. **Open** mid-Jun–Oct: dawn–dusk daily. **Closed** Oct–mid-Jun.

Bend's High Desert Museum, which showcases life in the region

## ㉗ Bend

🚐 77,000. ℹ️ 750 NW Lava Rd, (541) 382-8048, (877) 245-8484. 🌐 **visitbend.com**

Busy Bend, once a sleepy lumber town, is alluringly close to the ski slopes, lakes, streams, and many other natural attractions. While unsightly development is quickly replacing the juniper- and sage-covered grazing lands on the outskirts, the old brick business district retains its small-town charm. Drake Park is a grassy downtown retreat on both banks of the Deschutes River, and **Pilot Butte State Scenic Viewpoint**, atop a volcanic cinder cone that rises from the center of town, overlooks the High Desert and snowcapped Cascade peaks.

The **High Desert Museum** celebrates life in the rugged terrain that covers much of central and eastern Oregon. Walk-through dioramas use lighting and sound effects in authentic re-creations of Native American dwellings. A trail leads to replicas of a settler's cabin and a sawmill, and to natural habitats, including a trout stream and an aviary full of hawks and other raptors.

### 🏛️ High Desert Museum
59800 S Hwy 97. **Tel** (541) 382-4754. **Open** May–Oct: 9am–5pm daily; Nov–Apr: 10am–4pm daily. **Closed** Jan 1, Thanksgiving, Dec 25. 🌐 **highdesertmuseum.org**

### Environs
The best way to explore the magnificent South Cascades Mountains is to take the **Cascade Lakes Highway**, a 95-mile- (153-km-) long loop, starting from Bend. Southward, the route passes Lava Butte, which offers fine mountain views. Also located along the highway is Elk Lake, popular for sailing, fishing, and windsurfing. Another interesting sight is Mount Bachelor, 12 miles (20 km) west of Bend. It offers some of the best skiing and snowboarding in the region. An enormous, 45-sq-mile (117-sq-km) lava flow (Devil's Garden) lies northwest of Mount Bachelor. Astronauts used it to train on foot and in moon buggies for their historic 1969 moonwalk.

## ㉘ Newberry National Volcanic Monument

**Open** Apr–Oct: dawn–dusk daily. 🌐 **fs.fed.us/r6/centraloregon/ newberrynvm** ℹ️ Lava Lands Visitor Center, 11 miles S of Bend on US 97, (541) 593-2421.

Encompassing eerie and bleak landscapes of black lava, as well as sparkling mountain lakes, waterfalls, hemlock forests, and snow-capped peaks, the Newberry National Volcanic Monument occupies an area of 86 sq miles (220 sq km). Exhibits at the **Lava Lands Visitor Center** explain how the volcano has been built by thousands of eruptions which, seismic activity suggests, may begin again. Other exhibits here highlight central Oregon's cultural history.

At Lava River Cave, a passage extends for almost 1 mile (0.8 km) into a lava tube, through which molten lava once flowed. The Lava Cast Forest has a trail through a forest of hollow molds, formed by molten lava that created casts around the tree trunks.

A jagged outcrop at the Newberry National Volcanic Monument

# ㉙ Crater Lake National Park

Oregon's only national park surrounds Crater Lake. At 1,943 ft (592 m), this lake is the deepest in the country and the seventh deepest in the world. Its creation began about 7,700 years ago, when Mount Mazama erupted and then collapsed, forming the caldera in which the lake now sits. The rim of the crater rises to an average of 1,000 ft (300 m) above the lake. On the drive encircling the lake, 90 miles (144 km) of trails, various overlooks, and a beautiful lodge offer magnificent views.

**Key**
- ▬ Tour route
- ═ Other road

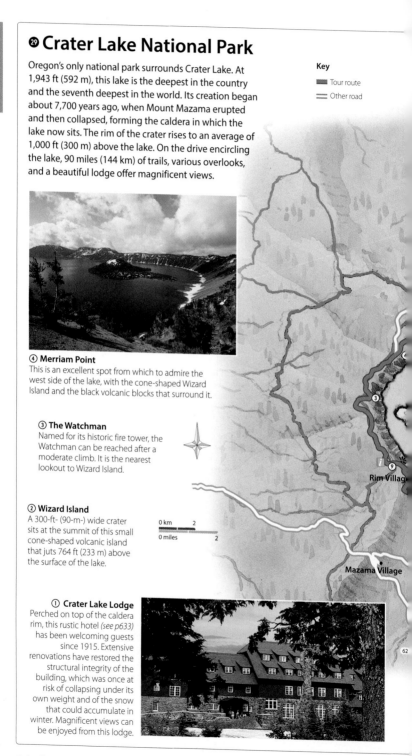

**④ Merriam Point**
This is an excellent spot from which to admire the west side of the lake, with the cone-shaped Wizard Island and the black volcanic blocks that surround it.

**③ The Watchman**
Named for its historic fire tower, the Watchman can be reached after a moderate climb. It is the nearest lookout to Wizard Island.

**② Wizard Island**
A 300-ft- (90-m-) wide crater sits at the summit of this small cone-shaped volcanic island that juts 764 ft (233 m) above the surface of the lake.

0 km          2
0 miles          2

**③**
**⑨**
**Rim Village**

**Mazama Village**

**① Crater Lake Lodge**
Perched on top of the caldera rim, this rustic hotel *(see p633)* has been welcoming guests since 1915. Extensive renovations have restored the structural integrity of the building, which was once at risk of collapsing under its own weight and of the snow that could accumulate in winter. Magnificent views can be enjoyed from this lodge.

62

### ⑤ Rim Drive
Spectacular views of the lake, the islands, and the surrounding mountains unfold at every turn of this 33-mile (53-km) circuit.

## Tips for Drivers

**Tour length:** 33 miles (53 km).
**Starting point:** Steel Information Center, on Rim Drive 4 miles (6.5 km) north of Rte 62.
**When to go:** Rim Drive is open from the end of June to mid-October, weather permitting.
**Stopping-off points:** Breakfast, lunch, and dinner are offered at Crater Lake Lodge; snacks are sold in Rim Village. Two-hour narrated boat trips (late Jun–mid-Sep: 10am–4pm daily) depart from Cleetwood Cove, at the bottom of a steep 1-mile (1.6-km) trail.

Rim Drive

Crater Lake

Phantom Ship

### ⑥ Cleetwood Trail
This 1-mile (1.6-km) strenuous trail, which drops a steep 700 ft (210 m), is the only access to the lake. In summer, a boat tour departs from the dock at the base of the trail.

### ⑦ Mount Scott
When the weather allows, views from the peak extend as far as Mount Shasta in California.

### ⑧ The Pinnacles
Pumice spires, also known as fossil fumaroles, rise from the caldera's eastern base and form this eerie landscape. Many of the spires are hollow.

### ⑨ Sinnott Memorial Overlook
Beautiful views reward the intrepid traveler who attempts the short descent to Sinnott Memorial Overlook just below the caldera rim. Here, knowledgeable park rangers give geology talks.

A park ranger with tourists in the Oregon Caves National Monument

### ㉚ Oregon Caves National Monument

ℹ 19000 Caves Hwy, Caves Junction, (541) 592-2100. **Open** Tours are organized daily late Apr–early Nov. Hours vary. **Closed** early Nov–late-Apr. 🅿 📷 🆆 nps.gov/orca

Visitors on the 70-minute guided tours of these vast underground caverns follow lighted trails past strange formations, cross underground rivers, squeeze through giant ribs of marble, and clamber up and down staircases into huge chambers hung with stalactites. Discovered in 1874 by a hunter chasing his dog into a dark hole in the side of Elijah Mountain, the caves have been formed by the steady trickling of water over hundreds of thousands of years.

### ㉛ Ashland

🅰 20,000. ℹ 110 E Main St, (541) 482-3486. 🆆 ashlandchamber.com

Every year, some 350,000 theatergoers descend on this amiable town. The major draw is the **Oregon Shakespeare Festival**, which annually presents a schedule of 11 plays by Shakespeare as well as by classical and contemporary playwrights. Theater buffs can also see props and costumes from past performances and take detailed backstage tours of the festival's three venues – Elizabethan Stage, Angus Bowmer Theatre, and the modern New Theatre.

🎭 **Oregon Shakespeare Festival**
15 S Pioneer St. **Tel** (541) 482-2111.
ℹ 🆆 osfashland.org

# ❷ Steens Mountain

Steens Mountain Loop Rd: (for 58 miles/93.5 km), starting North Loop Rd in Frenchglen. ℹ️ 484 N Broadway, Burns 97720, (541) 573-2636.
W harneycounty.com/steensmountain.html

Scenery does not get much grander than it does here on this 9,700-ft (2,910-m) mountain in southeastern Oregon. The west slope rises gradually from sagebrush country, while the eastern slope drops more steeply. Antelope, bighorn sheep, and wild horses roam gorges and alpine tundra carpeted with wildflowers; eagles and falcons soar overhead.

The **Steens Mountain Loop Road** traverses this remarkable landscape. Lovely, marsh-fringed Lily Lake, on the west side of the Warner Mountains, is slowly silting up. However, it is popular with anglers because of its trout-fishing opportunities. The nearby Donner and Blitzen River was named "Thunder and Lightning" by an army officer attempting to cross it during a thunderstorm in 1864. Kiger Gorge to the east affords views of four immense gorges scooped out from the mountainside by massive glaciers. **East Rim Viewpoint** is a full mile (1.6 km) above the alkali flats of the Alvord Desert. Sitting in the mountain's rain shadow, this desert receives a mere 6 inches (15 cm) of rain a year.

Resting mule deer in the Malheur National Wildlife Refuge

# ❸ Malheur National Wildlife Refuge

Tel (541) 493-2612. Refuge & Museum: **Open** dawn–dusk daily. **Closed** public hols. Visitor Center: **Open** 8am–4pm Mon–Thu, 8am–3pm Fri. **Closed** public hols. ♿ W fws.gov/malheur

One of the nation's largest wildlife refuges, Malheur spreads across 290 sq miles (760 sq km) of the Blitzen Valley floor. More than 320 species of birds and 58 species of mammals are found here. Sandhill cranes, tundra swans, snowy white egrets, white-faced ibis, pronghorn antelope, mule deer, and redband trout are among the most numerous of the refuge's denizens.

Spring and fall are the best times to view birds, which alight in the refuge on their annual migrations up and down the Pacific Flyway, which is a major north–south route for migrating

North American waterfowl. A small museum houses specimens of birds commonly seen in the refuge.

**Environs**
From the refuge, the 69-mile (110.5-km) **Diamond Loop National Back Country Byway** heads into sage-covered hills and red rimrock canyons. Along the route are Diamond Craters, a volcanic landscape; the Round Barn, a distinctive 19th-century structure; and Diamond, a small, poplar-shaded ranch town.

🏞️ Diamond Loop National Back Country Byway
ℹ️ 28910 Hwy 20 W, Hines, (541) 573-4400. W blm.gov/or

# ❹ John Day Fossil Beds National Monument

ℹ️ 32651 Hwy 19, 40 miles (64 km) W of John Day, (541) 987-2333.
**Open** dawn–dusk daily. Visitor Center (Sheep Rock Unit): **Open** 9am–5pm daily. **Closed** public hols between Thanksgiving & Presidents' Day.
W nps.gov/joda

Prehistoric fossil beds litter the John Day Fossil Beds National Monument, where sedimentary rocks preserve the plants and animals that flourished in jungles and savannas for 40 million years, between the extinction of the dinosaurs and the start

View of the Steens Mountain from the East Rim Viewpoint, above the alkali flats of the desolate Alvord Desert

Formations at John Day Fossil Beds National Monument's Sheep Rock unit

of the most recent Ice Age. The monument's 22 sq miles (57 sq km) comprise three units – Sheep Rock, Painted Hills, and Clarno. At all three, trails provide opportunities for the close-up observation of the fossil beds. Painted Hills presents the most dramatic landscapes – volcanic rock formations in vivid hues of red, pink, bronze, tan, and black. Clarno contains some of the oldest formations, dating back 54 million years and including some of the finest fossil plant remains on earth. At Sheep Rock, the visitor center displays many important finds from the beds.

## ㉟ Pendleton

 17,000. ℹ️ 501 S Main St, (541) 276-7411, (800) 547-8911.
**W** pendletonchamber.com

Pendleton's outsized reputation for raucous cowboys and lawless cattle rustlers is matched by the fact that it is eastern Oregon's largest town. But visitors may be disappointed to learn that these colorful days belong to the past. However, cowboy lore comes alive during the Pendleton Round-Up each September, when rodeo stunt performers and some 50,000 spectators crowd into town. Previous rodeos are honored at the entertaining **Round-Up Hall of Fame**.

The town's biggest business, the **Pendleton Woolen Mills**, is known for its warm clothing and blankets, particularly its "legendary" blankets, whose designs are a tribute to Native American tribes. The mill wove its first Indian trade blanket in 1895.

The **Pendleton Underground Tours** begin in a subterranean labyrinth of opium dens, gaming rooms, and Prohibition-era drinking establishments and include stops at a bordello and the cramped 19th-century living quarters of Chinese laborers.

The **Tamástslikt Cultural Institute** commemorates local history by displaying re-creations of historic structures, exhibits of war bonnets, and other artifacts.

### 🏛 Round-Up Hall of Fame
1114 SW Court Ave.
**Tel** (541) 278-0815. **Open** May–Sep: 10am–4pm Mon–Sat; Oct–Apr: 10am–4pm Sat. **Closed** public hols.
**W** pendletonroundup.com

### 🏛 Pendleton Woolen Mills
1307 SE Court Pl. **Tel** (541) 276-6911. Salesroom: **Open** 8am–5pm Mon–Sat, 11am–3pm Sun. **Closed** Jan 1, Thanksgiving, Dec 25. 📹 9am, 11am, 1:30pm, 3pm Mon–Fri. 📷
**W** pendleton-usa.com

A rodeo rider at the popular Pendleton Round-Up

## ㊱ Wallowa Mountains

Elkhorn Drive National Scenic Byway: (for 106 miles/171 km), starting at Baker City.

The Wallowa Mountains form a 10,000-ft- (3,050-m-) high, 40-mile- (64-km-) long wall of granite in northeastern Oregon. Driving through the region takes in some of the finest scenery in the state.

The best way to explore the Wallowa Mountains is to take the **Elkhorn Drive National Scenic Byway**, a two-lane paved road, which begins from Baker City. Nestled between the Wallowa Mountains and the Elkhorn Range, the town has some lovely downtown blocks and fine Victorian houses. Farther north, the National Historic Oregon Trail Interpretive Center displays replicas of pioneer scenes.

Wallowa Lake

Surrounded by dense wilderness, the sleepy town of **Joseph** lies to the east of the Wallowa Mountains. Named after Chief Joseph, leader of the Nez Percé peoples, Joseph is a popular destination for recreation enthusiasts and artisans. One of Joseph's main attractions is the **Wallowa County Museum**, which is devoted to Chief Joseph's famous retreat, and to the history of both Indians and settlers of the area.

The crystal-clear waters of the **Wallowa Lake** sparkle at the foot of the Wallowa Mountains. The Wallowa Lake Lodge, a log building dating from the 1920s, still provides accommodations and meals. The popular Wallowa Lake Tramway whisks riders up to the summit of Mount Howard, to enjoy spectacular views of the sparkling lake below and majestic peaks rising up.

### 🏛 Wallowa County Museum
110 S Main St, Joseph.
**Tel** (541) 432-6095. **Open** Memorial Day–late Sep: 10am–4pm daily.
**W** co.wallowa.or.us

# ⊕ Hells Canyon National Recreation Area

Some of the wildest terrain in North America clings to the sides of craggy, 9,400-ft (2,865-m) peaks at Hells Canyon before plunging to the famed basin far below. Here, the Snake River rushes through the world's deepest river-carved gorge. Visitors revel in the massive canyon walls rising 6,000 ft (1,830 m), the upland pine forests, and the delicate wildflower-covered alpine meadows – 652,000 wilderness acres (264,000 ha) in all. Much of the terrain is too rugged to cross, even on foot, making long sections of the Snake River accessible only by boat. Many visitors settle for the stunning views from several lookouts, and no one is disappointed.

Hells Canyon National Recreation Area Viewpoint

① **Buckhorn Lookout**
One of several scenic overlooks situated in the Hells Canyon area, superb views of the Wallowa-Whitman National Forest and the Imnaha River canyon are afforded from this remote spot.

② **Nee-Me-Poo Trail**
Visitors hiking along this National Historic Trail follow in the footsteps of the famous Chief Joseph and 700 Nez Percé Indians who, in 1877, embarked on an 1,800-mile (2,897-km) trek toward freedom in Canada.

⑥ **Hells Canyon Reservoir**
This 25-mile- (40-km-) long reservoir, part of a huge power-generating complex on the Snake River, is formed by Oxbow Dam to the south and Hells Canyon Dam to the north. A private road along the east shore provides access to the river.

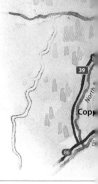

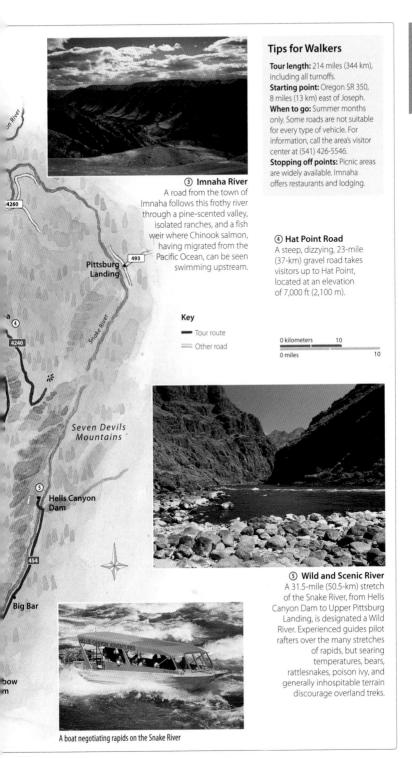

③ **Imnaha River**
A road from the town of Imnaha follows this frothy river through a pine-scented valley, isolated ranches, and a fish weir where Chinook salmon, having migrated from the Pacific Ocean, can be seen swimming upstream.

④ **Hat Point Road**
A steep, dizzying, 23-mile (37-km) gravel road takes visitors up to Hat Point, located at an elevation of 7,000 ft (2,100 m).

Pittsburg Landing

**Key**

▬ Tour route
▭ Other road

0 kilometers    10
0 miles    10

Seven Devils Mountains

Hells Canyon Dam

Big Bar

⑤ **Wild and Scenic River**
A 31.5-mile (50.5-km) stretch of the Snake River, from Hells Canyon Dam to Upper Pittsburg Landing, is designated a Wild River. Experienced guides pilot rafters over the many stretches of rapids, but searing temperatures, bears, rattlesnakes, poison ivy, and generally inhospitable terrain discourage overland treks.

A boat negotiating rapids on the Snake River

# Practical Information

The stunning scenery of the Pacific Northwest attracts visitors from around the world. Booming tourism – and, in more recent years, ecotourism – has spawned a vast network of facilities and services: internationally acclaimed restaurants and accommodations abound, and efficient transportation by air, land, and water takes travelers virtually anywhere they want to go. The peak tourist season extends from mid-May through September. Winter is also a great time to visit the region as it is ideal for skiing and other snow sports.

## Tourist Information

Maps and information about sights, events, accommodations, and tours are available free of charge from **Washington State Tourism** and the **Oregon Tourism Commission**. These agencies also provide either free reservations services for a wide range of accommodations or referrals to these services. Most Pacific Northwest communities operate visitor centers or tourism booths, offering information about local activities, lodgings, and restaurants.

## Personal Security

The Pacific Northwest prides itself on its safe cities and its welcoming attitude toward visitors. Street crime is rare, and the police are a visible presence in all major cities. However, it is wise to be careful and find out which parts of town are less safe than others. Your hotel or a tourist information center will provide information about which areas are best to stay away from. In the country, wildlife and natural dangers can be avoided by heeding local warnings and advice.

In an emergency, call 911 for the fire department, police, or an ambulance; if you are not in a major city, dial 0. The call can be placed from any phone free of charge. Hospitals are listed in phone books, and each has an emergency room that can be accessed 24 hours a day.

## Natural Hazards

Before heading out on a hike or going camping, check in with the forest service for information on the conditions in the surrounding area and recommended safety precautions. Skiers and snowboarders should always heed warning signs and stay on groomed runs.

Insects can be annoying while hiking or camping – blackflies in the spring or mosquitoes in the summer. Ticks, which can be carriers of Lyme disease, are found in dry, wooded areas. Protect yourself by using tick repellent and wear long pants, long sleeves, and socks. In case of a rash or flu-like symptoms, contact a doctor immediately.

On the beach, heed the red tide warnings that alert shellfish collectors to contamination. When camping, beware of cougars and bears. Be advised that leaving any food or garbage out will attract dangerous wildlife.

Potential safety hazards for drivers include gravel roads, which may become very slippery with rain, heavy snowfalls, black ice, and fog. To be safe, always carry a spare tire, and salt or sand in winter; also a flashlight, jumper cables, blankets, water, emergency food, and a shovel. Always carry a cell phone.

## Getting Around

Visitors to the Pacific Northwest have a wide range of transportation options. **United Airlines** offers flights to the major cities of the Pacific Northwest, while **Alaska Airlines** and its subsidiary **Horizon Airlines** fly to these and regional destinations.

Although the bus may be the slowest way of getting to the Pacific Northwest, it is probably the most economical. **Greyhound** has bus routes throughout the region; **Gray Line** offers sightseeing tours. Discounts are available for children, students, and senior citizens. The train is a good way to get to the Pacific Northwest and to travel within it. **Amtrak** offers daily services to Oregon and Washington from the Midwest and California and has daily runs between Seattle, Portland, and Eugene. **Washington State Ferries** connect 20 ports throughout Puget Sound, including Seattle.

Driving is by far the best mode of transport in the region, especially to enjoy the spectacular beauty of more remote areas. Remember to

## The Climate of the Pacific Northwest

Rain is a distinctive presence in only half the Pacific Northwest – the part west of the mountains that divide the region. The weather in this western, coastal region remains mild throughout the year, and snow is rare in all but the higher elevations. The mountains see heavy winter snowfall, much to the delight of skiers. East of the mountains, the summers are hot, dry, and sunny, and winters more severe than west of the mountains.

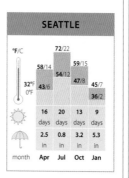

| SEATTLE | | | |
|---|---|---|---|
| | 72/22 | | |
| | 58/14 | 59/15 | |
| | 54/12 | 47/8 | |
| 32°F 43/6 | | | 45/7 |
| 0°F | | | 36/2 |
| 16 days | 20 days | 13 days | 9 days |
| 2.5 in | 0.8 in | 3.2 in | 5.3 in |
| month Apr | Jul | Oct | Jan |

tune into local television and radio news channels for regular reports on traffic and road conditions, particularly during the winter.

## Etiquette

Dress in the Pacific Northwest tends to be casual, practical, and dependent on the weather. Stricter clothing requirements apply in theaters, high-end restaurants, and other more formal places, however. A few designated beaches allow topless and nude sunbathing. The legal drinking age is 21, and smoking in public places is prohibited.

## Laws

The Seattle and Portland Police Departments are a visible presence, either on foot, bicycle, or squad car. There are also neighborhood security teams made up of citizen volunteers, which patrol on foot. Outside the metropolitan areas, there are county police and sheriff's offices to assist you.

It is illegal and insensitive to comment on or joke about bombs, guns, and terrorism in places such as airports. Drunk driving is also taken seriously; remember that open alcohol containers in a car are illegal. Narcotics users can face criminal charges and severe penalties.

## Sports & Outdoor Activities

The dramatically varied terrain and beautiful landscape of the Pacific Northwest make this the ideal region for a wide variety of outdoor activities. Both Washington and Oregon provide great conditions for adventure sports such as hang gliding and paragliding. Whitewater rafting is also popular, especially in the waters of the Cascades Range. Skiing and snowboarding are other popular activities.

For those interested in more placid pastimes, the **Oregon Department of Fish and Wildlife** or the **Washington Department of Fish and Wildlife** provide information on freshwater fishing.

One of the most exciting ways to explore the scenic Pacific Northwest is by foot. Visitor centers and the **American Hiking Society** provide information about hiking; and the **Pacific Northwest Trail Association** offers details about the beautiful 1,200-mile (1,931-km) trail, which runs from the Continental Divide to the Pacific Ocean.

In summer, the region's many beaches are ideal for relaxing and offer refreshing waters to swim in. The coasts are also a delight for bird-watchers who can catch sight of gulls, sandpipers, plovers, and ducks.

Birdwatchers can also enjoy the **Malheur National Wildlife Refuge** in Oregon. Canoeing and kayaking provide environmentally friendly ways of seeing the region's beautiful waters and abundant marine life. Washington's Puget Sound and San Juan Islands are the most popular destinations for sea kayaking, while Olympic National Park is the hot spot for canoeists. In Oregon, the Columbia River provides stretches of calmer water for paddling.

Cycling and inline skating are inexpensive ways of traveling. Bicycle Adventures offers cycling tours.

## Shopping

Downtown districts in the Pacific Northwest provide everything from luxury goods in exclusive stores to flea-market bargains. Outdoor gear manufactured by world-famous local companies such as REI are popular with tourists interested in adventure sports. Other items to shop for are antiques, books, and music from both the chain stores and independents, first-class wines (Pinot Noirs, Chardonnays, Rieslings, and dessert wines), and smoked Pacific salmon. Native American jewelry, carvings, paintings, and other handicrafts are also available throughout the region.

## DIRECTORY

### Tourist Information

**Oregon Tourism Commission**
670 Hawthorne Ave SE, Salem, OR 97301-5096.
**Tel** (503) 378-8850, (800) 547-7842.
W traveloregon.com

**Washington State Tourism**
PO Box 42500, Olympia, WA 98504-2500
**Tel** (800) 544-1800.
W experiencewa.com

### Travel

**Alaska Airlines**
**Tel** (800) 426-0333.
W alaskaair.com

**Amtrak**
**Tel** (800) 872-7245.
W amtrak.com

**Gray Line**
**Tel** In Portland: (503) 241-7373.
In Seattle: (800) 426-7532.
W grayline.com

**Greyhound**
**Tel** (800) 231-2222.
W greyhound.com

**Horizon Airlines**
**Tel** (800) 547-9308.

**United Airlines**
**Tel** (800) 241-6522.

**Washington State Ferries**
**Tel** (206) 464-6400.
W wsdot.wa.gov/ferries

### Freshwater Fishing

**Oregon Dept of Fish and Wildlife**
**Tel** (508) 947-6000, (800) 720-6339.
W dfw.state.or.us

**Washington Dept of Fish & Wildlife**
**Tel** (360) 902-2200.
W wdfw.wa.gov

### Hiking

**American Hiking Society**
**Tel** (800) 972-8608.
W americanhiking.org

**Pacific Northwest Trail Association**
**Tel** (877) 854-9415.
W pnt.org

### Bird-Watching

**Malheur National Wildlife Refuge**
**Tel** (541) 493-2612.
W fws.gov/malheur

# Where to Stay

## Washington

**BELLINGHAM:**
**Chrysalis Inn & Spa** $$
B&B
*804 10th St, 98225*
**Tel** *(360) 756-1005*
W thechrysalisinn.com
Guests enjoy the warm decor,
full-service spa, and romantic
wine bar at this hotel.

**FORKS: Kalaloch Lodge** $$
B&B
*157151 Hwy 101, 98331*
**Tel** *(866) 662-9969*
W thekalalochlodge.com
This 1953 lodge offers cabins
that are perched on a bluff
overlooking the Pacific Ocean.

**MT. RAINIER NATIONAL PARK:**
**Paradise Inn** $$
B&B
*Mount Rainier National Park, 98304*
**Tel** *(360) 569-2275*
W mtrainierguestservices.com
Built in 1916, this spacious, rustic
lodge has miles of walking trails at
its doorstep. Open May–October.

**OLYMPIA: Doubletree**
**by Hilton** $$
B&B
*415 Capitol Way, 98501*
**Tel** *(360) 570-0555*
W doubletree3.hilton.com
Large suites with flat-screen TVs.
Complimentary breakfasts.

**SEATTLE: Grand Hyatt Seattle** $$
Luxury
*721 Pine St, 98101*
**Tel** *(206) 774-1234*
W grandseattle.hyatt.com
Designed to appeal to high-tech
professionals, this hotel in a

convenient location features city
views, a range of ultra-modern
amenities, and meeting rooms.

**SEATTLE: Hotel Five** $$
Boutique
*2200 5th Ave, 98121*
**Tel** *(206) 441-9785*
W hotelfiveseattle.com
Eco-friendly lodgings feature
urban industrial art. Free bike
rentals. Dogs are welcome.

**SEATTLE: Hotel Max** $$
Boutique
*620 Stewart St, 98101*
**Tel** *(206) 728-6299*
W hotelmaxseattle.com
A 1920s-era relic dramatically
updated with striking colors and
contemporary Northwestern art.

**SEATTLE: Inn at Queen Anne** $$
Inn/B&B
*505 1st Ave N, 98109*
**Tel** *(206) 282-7357*
W innatqueenanne.com
The simply decorated rooms in
this converted 1928 apartment
building have kitchenettes.

**SEATTLE:**
**Mayflower Park Hotel** $$
Boutique
*405 Olive Way, 98101*
**Tel** *(206) 623-8700*
W mayflowerpark.com
This 1927 property is one of the
city's last independently owned
classic hotels. Good location.

### DK Choice

**SEATTLE: The**
**Edgewater Hotel** $$$
Luxury
*2411 Alaskan Way, 98121*
**Tel** *(206) 728-7000*
W edgewaterhotel.com
A waterfront hotel with
eco-friendly rooms offering
stunning views of Puget
Sound and the Olympic
Mountains. The interior feels
like a plush lodge: all rooms
feature knotty-pine furniture,
river-rock fireplaces, and
impressive bath amenities.
The excellent restaurant offers
outdoor dining. Pet friendly.

**SEATTLE: Inn at the Market** $$$
Luxury
*86 Pine St, 98101*
**Tel** *(206) 443-3600*
W innatthemarket.com
Floor-to-ceiling windows provide
spectacular views of the bay at
this hotel off Pike Place Market.

**Price Guide**

Prices are based on one night's stay in
high season for a standard double room,
inclusive of service charges and taxes.

| | |
|---|---|
| $ | up to $150 |
| $$ | $150–$250 |
| $$$ | over $250 |

**SNOQUALMIE:**
**Salish Lodge & Spa** $$
B&B
*6501 Railroad Ave, 98065*
**Tel** *(425) 888-2556*
W salishlodge.com
Set above the Snoqualmie Falls,
this inn has rooms with whirlpool
tubs, fireplaces, and feather beds.

**SPOKANE:**
**The Davenport Hotel** $$
Boutique
*10 S Post St, 99201*
**Tel** *(509) 455-8888*
W davenporthotelcollection.com
Dating back to 1914, The
Davenport has a stunningly
ornate lobby and ballroom, as
well as elegant guest rooms.

**TACOMA:**
**Hotel Murano** $$
Boutique
*1320 Broadway Plaza, 98402*
**Tel** *(253) 238-8000*
W hotelmuranotacoma.com
Hip downtown spot showcasing
glass sculpture and modern art in
its public spaces. Spacious rooms.

### DK Choice

**WALLA WALLA:**
**Inn at Abeja** $$$
Luxury
*2014 Mill Creek Rd, 99362*
**Tel** *(509) 522-1234*
W abeja.net
This meticulously restored
century-old farmstead
houses both a winery and a
sophisticated hotel. Buildings
include the original cottages,
the old carriage house, and a
barn house with immaculate
suites. Guests are encouraged
to explore the surrounding
grounds, with their gardens,
creeks, and vineyards.

**WOODINVILLE:**
**Willows Lodge** $$$
Luxury
*14580 NE 145 St, 98072*
**Tel** *(425) 424-3900*
W willowslodge.com
Willows is a sumptuous riverside
resort in Western Washington's
Wine Country, with award-
winning restaurants.

Longe area at the deluxe The Edgewater
Hotel on the waterfront, Seattle

Room at the hip Ace Hotel, Portland, featuring interesting decor

### YAKIMA: Birchfield Manor Country Inn $
Inn/B&B
*2018 Birchfield Rd, 98901*
**Tel** *(509) 452-1960*
**W** birchfieldmanor.com
Stay in antique-filled rooms in the manor house or the guest cottage at this 1910 farmhouse.

## Oregon

### ASTORIA: Hotel Elliott $
Boutique
*357 12th St, 97103*
**Tel** *(503) 325-2222*
**W** hotelelliott.com
A centrally located hotel retaining many of its original 1924 features. Luxurious rooms offer 440-count cotton sheets.

### BAKER CITY: Geiser Grand Hotel $
Luxury
*1996 Main St, 97814*
**Tel** *(541) 523-1889*
**W** geisergrand.com
A restored 1889 landmark, with a huge stained-glass skylight above the restaurant's dining room.

### BEND: Seventh Mountain Resort $$
Resort
*18575 SW Century Dr, 97702*
**Tel** *(541) 382-8711*
**W** seventhmountain.com
Stay in simple bedroom units or fully equipped suites. A good base for skiers, rafters, and anglers.

### CANNON BEACH: Stephanie Inn $$$
Inn/B&B
*2740 S Pacific St, 97110*
**Tel** *(503) 436-2221*
**W** stephanie-inn.com
This romantic oceanside inn offers rooms with fireplaces, whirlpool tubs, and lovely views.

### CRATER LAKE NATIONAL PARK: Crater Lake Lodge $$$
B&B
*565 Rim Dr, 97604*
**Tel** *(800) 774-2728*
**W** craterlakelodges.com
Built of native stone and wood, this 1915 grand lodge enjoys a spectacular location right on the rim of Crater Lake. Open May–October.

### MCMINNVILLE: McMenamins Hotel Oregon $
B&B
*310 NE Evans St, 97128*
**Tel** *(503) 472-8427*
**W** mcmenamins.com
A historic, popular stop-over for visitors to Wine Country, this inn offers a variety of comfortable rooms, some with private baths.

### MCMINNVILLE: Youngberghill Vineyards and Inn $$$
B&B
*10660 SW Youngberg Hill Rd, 97128*
**Tel** *(503) 472-2727*
**W** youngberghill.com
Overlooking picturesque rolling vineyards, this imposing Craftsman-style inn on a hill boasts an award-winning winery and a luxurious guest house.

## DK Choice

### MOUNT HOOD: Timberline Lodge $$
B&B
*27500 E Timberline Rd, 97028*
**Tel** *(800) 547-1406*
**W** timberlinelodge.com
This historic lodge's magnificent structure, famous for supplying the exterior shots in the film *The Shining*, was built in the 1930s. The lobby's massive stone fireplace is an attraction in itself. Timberline also offers a range of skiing packages, plus several award-winning dining options that lure visitors.

### NEWPORT: Sylvia Beach Hotel $
Boutique
*267 NW Cliff St, 97365*
**Tel** *(541) 265-5428*
**W** sylviabeachhotel.com
A delightfully quirky hotel housed in an old Craftsman-style building. Each room is inspired by a different author.

### PORTLAND: McMenamins Kennedy School $
B&B
*5736 NE 33rd Ave, 97211*
**Tel** *(503) 249-3983*
**W** mcmenamins.com/KennedySchool
A 1915 school transformed into a B&B, movie theater, brewery, restaurant, and more. Whimsically decorated rooms are furnished with antiques and chalkboards.

## DK Choice

### PORTLAND: Ace Hotel $$
Boutique
*1022 SW Stark St, 97205*
**Tel** *(503) 228-2277*
**W** acehotel.com/portland
The Ace is one of the hippest hotels in a city full of trendy options. After a complete overhaul, the former Clyde Hotel now offers a mix of original 1912 details and stylishly modern, eco-friendly features. Each guest room is one of a kind. Guests enjoy free bicycle rentals. Pet-friendly.

### PORTLAND: Heathman Hotel $$
Luxury
*1001 SW Broadway, 97205*
**Tel** *(503) 241-4100*
**W** portland.heathmanhotel.com
This 1927 institution is a magnet for visiting musicians and writers, featuring Old World charm, city views, and works by local artists.

### PORTLAND: McMenamins Crystal Hotel $$
Boutique
*303 SW 12th Ave, 97205*
**Tel** *(503) 972-2670*
**W** mcmenamins.com/CrystalHotel
Rooms are decorated in honor of the neighboring Crystal Ballroom at this music-themed hotel. There's a funky café and a soaking pool.

### SALEM: The Grand Hotel $$
Luxury
*201 Liberty St SE, 97301*
**Tel** *(503) 540-7800*
**W** grandhotelsalem.com
Comfortable rooms and spacious suites here appeal to business and leisure travelers alike. Eco-friendly features abound.

**For more information on types of hotels** *see pages 26–7*

# Where to Eat and Drink

## Washington

**CHELAN: Local Myth Pizza** $
Pizzeria
*122 S Emerson St, 98816*
**Tel** *(509) 682-2914* **Closed** *Sat lunch; Sun & Mon*
This hip pizzeria is busy in the summer, when both locals and tourists pack the surrounding resort. Order the thin-crust pies with gourmet toppings such as prosciutto and walnuts.

**FRIDAY HARBOR:**
**Duck Soup Inn** $$
New American
*50 Duck Soup Ln, 98250*
**Tel** *(360) 378-4878* **Closed** *lunch; Mon*
Innovative, globally influenced dishes are made with locally sourced meats, seafood, herbs, and flowers at this elegant restaurant situated by a pond.

**LEAVENWORTH:**
**Andreas Keller** $$
German
*829 Front St, 98826*
**Tel** *(509) 548-6000*
This Bavarian-style restaurant serving hearty schnitzels, *Weinkraut*, and other classics. Live accordion music adds to the fun, kid-friendly environs. There's an impressive beer list featuring Bavarian brews.

**OLYMPIA: McMenamins**
**Spar Café** $
American
*114 4th Ave E, 98501*
**Tel** *(360) 357-6444*
House classics include Olympic oyster stew at this homey 1935 café with an old-time, blue-collar feel. Ales are brewed on site.

**PORT TOWNSEND:**
**Khu Larb Thai** $$
Thai
*225 Adams St, 98368*
**Tel** *(360) 385-5023*
The menu at what was the first Thai restaurant on the Olympic Peninsula focuses on seafood and vegetarian dishes. Located in the heart of historic Downtown.

**SEATTLE: Beth's Café** $
American
*7311 Aurora Ave N, 98103*
**Tel** *(206) 782-5588*
Beth's serves large breakfasts and other greasy-spoon classics to both the early-morning and late-night crowds. Signature omelets come in 6- and 12-egg versions.

**SEATTLE: Elemental Pizza** $
Pizzeria
*2630 NE University Village St, 98105*
**Tel** *(206) 524-4930*
Savor award-winning, wood-fired pizzas – with toppings such as ghost pepper salami – and local craft brews. Desserts include a delicious ice-cream sandwich.

**SEATTLE: Salumi** $
Italian
*309 3rd Ave S, 98104*
**Tel** *(206) 621-8772* **Closed** *Sat–Mon*
This tiny Pioneer Square eatery is famous for its authentic Italian cured meats. There is also a small menu of sandwiches, soups, and pasta dishes. Open only at lunch.

**SEATTLE: The Walrus and**
**the Carpenter** $$
Seafood
*4743 Ballard Ave NW, 98107*
**Tel** *(206) 395-9227*
A nationally renowned, rustic oyster bar. The small-plates menu includes local clams and mussels, house-smoked fish, and specialty meats, plus a wide selection of craft cocktails, wine, and beer.

## DK Choice

**SEATTLE: Canlis** $$$
New American
*2576 Aurora Ave N, 98109*
**Tel** *(206) 283-3313* **Closed** *lunch; Sun*
Part of the vanguard of Seattle fine dining since 1950, Canlis offers terrific Lake Union views, fabulous seafood and steaks, and a 2,000-strong wine list, as well as lovely interiors and live music. The atmosphere is quite formal, with no jeans or casual clothing allowed.

**SEATTLE:**
**Ivar's Acres of Clams** $$$
Seafood
*1001 Alaskan Way, 98104*
**Tel** *(206) 624-6852*
Come to this venerable local institution for terrific crab, clam, oyster, and salmon dishes, as well as the classic fish 'n' chips they have been serving since 1938. Scenic water views.

**SEATTLE: Metropolitan Grill** $$$
Steak House
*820 2nd Ave, 98104*
**Tel** *(206) 624-3287* **Closed** *lunch Sat & Sun*
This luxurious steak house provides a warm, sophisticated setting for enjoying top-quality

Ivar's Acres of Clams, Seattle, a seafood restaurant with lovely water views

steaks and chops. The extensive wine list specializes in West Coast reds.

**SEATTLE:**
**Sitka & Spruce** $$$
New American
*1531 Melrose Ave, 98122*
**Tel** *(206) 324-0662*
This award-winning restaurant serves inviting small plates made with a dizzying kaleidoscope of local, seasonal ingredients. The special Mexican menu on Monday nights is good value.

**SPOKANE: Wild Sage**
**American Bistro** $$
New American
*916 W 2nd Ave, 99201*
**Tel** *(509) 456-7575* **Closed** *lunch*
An elegant bistro with three dining areas, serving quality seasonal fare. Top choices include white Cheddar fondue with local mushrooms, Brandt Farm steak, and coconut-cream layer cake.

**VANCOUVER: Hudson's**
**Bar & Grill** $$
New American
*7805 NE Greenwood Dr, 98662*
**Tel** *(360) 816-6100*
Housed in a faux-rustic, upscale lodge, Hudson's serves regional, seasonal comfort food, with an emphasis on venison, prime rib, and beef tenderloin. The wine list focuses on West Coast wineries.

**WALLA WALLA:
Brasserie Four** $$
French
*4 E Main St, 99632*
**Tel** *(509) 529-2011* **Closed** *Sun & Mon*
A diverse menu features creative pizzas and large salads, plus French-inspired fare such as fresh quiches and steamed mussels. Sunday brunch is a local favorite.

**WALLA WALLA: Whitehouse-Crawford** $$$
New American
*55 W Cherry St, 99362*
**Tel** *(509) 525-2222* **Closed** *lunch; Tue*
Housed in a converted 1904 sawmill, this elegant restaurant has helped transform the region's culinary culture. The seasonal menu draws heavily on local produce. Impressive wine list.

# Oregon

**ASTORIA: Columbian Café** $$
New American
*1114 Marine Dr, 97103*
**Tel** *(503) 325-2233* **Closed** *dinner Sun–Wed; Mon & Tue*
A local institution, this small diner with a hip ambience is popular for its specialty crêpes and hearty breakfasts. It also serves fresh, local seafood and vegetarian fare.

**CANNON BEACH:
The Irish Table** $$
Irish
*1235 S Hemlock St, 97145*
**Tel** *(503) 436-0708* **Closed** *lunch; Wed & Thu*
This homey restaurant serves Irish dishes prepared with local produce and seafood. The local wines are popular, as are the single-malt Scotches, Irish whiskeys, and freshly poured pints of imported beers.

## DK Choice

**DAYTON:
Joel Palmer House** $$
New American
*600 Ferry St, 97114*
**Tel** *(503) 864-2995* **Closed** *lunch; Sun & Mon*
A top Wine Country destination, Joel Palmer House is set in a historic antebellum mansion. The internationally inspired menu places a focus on wild, local mushrooms and truffles, and whatever else is in season. Knowledgeable servers help choose from a varied wine list that features Oregon Pinot Noir, Pinot Gris, and Chardonnay.

**HOOD RIVER: Full Sail
Brewing Company** $$
American
*506 Columbia St, 97031*
**Tel** *(541) 386-2247*
This popular brewery's pub and tasting room is an ideal spot to sample a range of award-winning craft brews. It also serves delicious sandwiches, small plates, and salads.

**MCMINNVILLE: Nick's
Italian Café** $$
New American
*521 NE 3rd St, 97128*
**Tel** *(503) 434-4471*
A Wine Country landmark, Nick's is popular for its multi-course, fixed-menu dinners. The wine list focuses on local labels.

**NEWPORT: April's at
Nye Beach** $$
Italian
*749 NW Third St, 97365*
**Tel** *(541) 265-6855* **Closed** *lunch; Mon & Tue*
Dine at this cozy café offering scenic views and fine, creatively conceived Northwest cuisine with Italian accents. There is also a well-chosen, affordable wine list and excellent desserts.

**PORTLAND: Podnah's
Pit Barbecue** $
Barbecue
*1625 NE Killingsworth St, 97211*
**Tel** *(503) 281-3700*
Come here for slow-smoked, Texas-style barbecue fare. The dining room is simple, but the tender meats keep drawing the crowds. There is a small selection of wines and microbrews, too.

**PORTLAND: Dan and
Louis Oyster Bar** $$
Seafood
*208 SW Ankeny St, 97204*
**Tel** *(503) 227-5906*
The city's oldest restaurant, this 1907 landmark offers fresh Northwest seafood, including a wide selection of oysters.

**PORTLAND: Le Pigeon** $$
New American
*738 E Burnside St, 97214*
**Tel** *(503) 546-8796* **Closed** *lunch*
Adventurous French-inspired food that has won national acclaim is served in an intimate dining room with communal tables and a chef's counter. Extensive wine list.

## DK Choice

**PORTLAND: Pok Pok** $$
Thai
*3226 SE Division St, 97202*
**Tel** *(503) 232-1387*
One of the region's most renowned restaurants, Pok Pok creates tongue-tingling northern Thai specialties, served by an informed staff. Fiery salads and spicy-sour curries provide flavors and textures rarely enjoyed in the US. The varied drinks list includes drinking vinegars and inventive cocktails. This is the bedrock of a culinary empire that has extended successfully to New York City.

**PORTLAND: Jake's
Famous Crawfish** $$$
Seafood
*401 SW 12th Ave, 97205*
**Tel** *(503) 226-1419* **Closed** *lunch; Sun*
This fish house, dating from 1892, boasts dozens of varieties of fresh fish that can be steamed, stuffed, seared, sautéed, or simply grilled. The polished paneling and old artworks create a lovely ambience.

**SALEM:
La Capitale Brasserie** $$
French
*508 State St, 97301*
**Tel** *(503) 585-1975* **Closed** *Sun*
Housed in a historic building, La Capitale focuses on local, seasonal ingredients, craft beers, and fine wines. Enjoy creative renditions of classic French dishes, and do not miss the home-made charcuterie.

Pok Pok, a highly acclaimed Thai restaurant in Portland

**For more information on types of restaurants** *see pages 28–9*

# CALIFORNIA

# California at a Glance

Situated on the Pacific Coast, California is 800 miles (1,300 km) long and 250 miles (400 km) wide, covering an area of 158,710 sq miles (411,060 sq km). An area of startling contrasts, the scorching deserts and snowcapped mountains of the south lead to the vast wilderness areas of the north. Los Angeles and San Francisco are the state's two major cities, and the state capital is Sacramento.

Crescent City
Yreka
Alturas
Eureka
Scotia
Redding
Susanville
Leggett
Chico
Mendocino
Ukiah
Yuba City
Santa Rosa
Napa
Sacramento
Stockton
San Francisco
Modesto
San Jose
Mer
Salinas
Fres
Monterey
Han
San Simeon
San Luis Obispo
Sa
Barb

**Sacramento** *(see p705)* in Gold Country is California's capital city. Its primary landmark is the California State Capitol, completed in 1874. In the old city, along the river, are many historic buildings built for the gold miners of 1849.

**Napa Valley** *(see pp700–701)*, a long sliver of land, lies in the heart of Northern California's Wine Country. Hundreds of wineries dot the entire length of the valley; most offer tours and wine tastings.

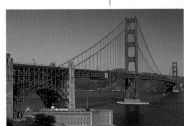

**San Francisco's** *(see pp682–99)* Golden Gate Bridge connects the city with Marin County. This famous landmark was opened in 1937.

**Santa Barbara** *(see p674)*, on the Central Coast, is a repository of the region's Spanish heritage. Its legendary mission, referred to as the "Queen of Missions," was built four years after the city was established as an important garrison in 1782.

◀ The iconic Golden Gate Bridge, San Francisco

**Yosemite National Park** *(see pp706–7)* in the High Sierras is an unforgettable wilderness of forests, alpine meadows, breathtaking waterfalls, and imposing granite rocks. The giant sequoia trees here were California's first tourist attraction.

**Locator Map**

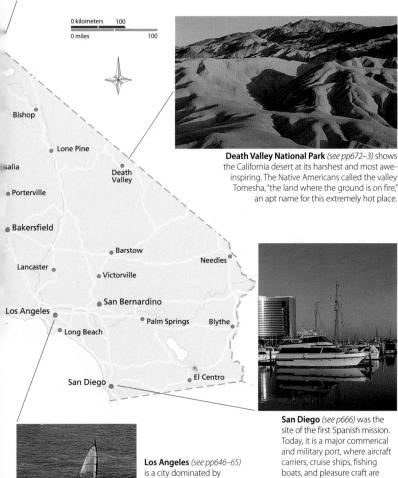

```
0 kilometers    100
0 miles              100
```

Bishop

Lone Pine

‧alia

Porterville

Death
Valley

Bakersfield

Barstow

Lancaster

Victorville

Needles

San Bernardino

Los Angeles

Palm Springs

Blythe

Long Beach

San Diego

El Centro

**Death Valley National Park** *(see pp672–3)* shows the California desert at its harshest and most awe-inspiring. The Native Americans called the valley Tomesha, "the land where the ground is on fire," an apt name for this extremely hot place.

**San Diego** *(see p666)* was the site of the first Spanish mission. Today, it is a major commerical and military port, where aircraft carriers, cruise ships, fishing boats, and pleasure craft are a common sight.

**Los Angeles** *(see pp646–65)* is a city dominated by wealth, fame, and glamor, as perceived by Hollywood. Its popular beaches along the Pacific Ocean attract more than 30 million people a year.

# CALIFORNIA

Impressive for both its size and its sway over modern culture, California symbolizes the United States' diversity and sense of prosperity. Here can be found towering forests, high mountain peaks, deserts within half a day's drive of ocean beaches, and two of the world's foremost cities, San Francisco and Los Angeles.

Perceptions of California vary so greatly that some people now joke that there are two states. The first is geographic – California is the Union's third-largest state (after Alaska and Texas). It claims some high mountain peaks such as Mount Whitney as well as the country's lowest expanse of dry land – Death Valley. Roughly one in every eight Americans is a Californian, making this the most populous of the 50 states, represented by the largest Congressional delegation.

The other California is a realm of romance, formed by flickering celluloid images. Think "California" and pictures are immediately conjured up of bikini-clad beachcombers, middle-class suburban families in sprawling ranch houses, and glamorous film stars emerging from limousines before hordes of autograph seekers. These stereotypes are perpetuated by the tourism and entertainment media, especially Hollywood. The earlier Spanish legends had glorified Califorina as exotic, while the later Gold Rush elevated it to a land of fortune and opportunity. Whatever the truth may be, such were the eulogies that created California's colorful and seductive image.

## History

Although the Spanish first "discovered" California in 1542, they colonized the area only in the 18th century. Their rule was enforced through three institutions – the mission (church), the presidio (fort), and the pueblo (town). Of these the mission was the most influential, and Franciscan friars set up 21 missions at approximately 30-mile (48-km) intervals along El Camino Real ("the Royal Road") from San Diego to Sonoma. Still, the territory remained remote until 1848 when Mexico ceded California to the US, and gold was found in the Sierra Nevada foothills. The Gold Rush of 1849 drew hordes of prospectors,

Window-shopping along Ocean Avenue, Carmel's most exclusive street

◀ A vineyard in the Sonoma Valley

known as "Forty-Niners" after the year of their arrival. The discovery of silver deposits in the western Sierras, as well as the completion of the transcontinental railroad in 1869, brought greater prosperity. But along with the changes came racial tensions, ignited by the influx of Chinese immigrants, who were brought to help build the railroad. Immigrants have since contributed to the state's cultural richness as well as its overpopulation and social tensions.

The popular Third Street Promenade, Santa Monica

On April 18, 1906, San Francisco was struck by the country's worst ever earthquake, and many believed that California's heyday was over. However, the state's subsequent revival was linked to Hollywood's lucrative film industry. Movies and the new medium of television made California the symbol of America's postwar resurgence – suddenly everybody wanted the prosperous middle-class existence they believed was common here. At the same time racial discrimination and violence persisted, state schools lacked funds, and Hollywood found itself attacked by politicians as a hotbed of Marxist Communism.

Since the 1960s, however, California has been the birthplace of some of the country's most significant social movements. The University of California at Berkeley was home to the Free Speech Movement, and Haight Ashbury in San Francisco was the mecca for "hippies." Today, Silicon Valley is a leading center of the computer industry, and many world-class high-tech firms are based here. Yet, despite progress and prosperity, California is still earthquake-prone.

## Society & Politics

If the US as a whole is a melting pot of people, California is an ethnic microcosm. It receives the highest number of immigrants (more than 200,000 every year), and its racial makeup is the nation's most diverse. The percentage of whites and African-Americans is lower than the national average, but the Asian population is more than triple the national level. Hispanics, too, account for more than a quarter of all Californians. This ethnic cocktail is most visible in such cities as San Diego, Los Angeles, and San Francisco. Population growth has inevitably disturbed the balance between rural and urban sectors. Since the 1950s, farmlands have declined as the need for housing has arisen. Today, the

### KEY DATES IN HISTORY

**1542** Spanish explorer Juan Rodríguez Cabrilho discovers California

**1769** The first mission is set up at San Diego

**1776** New presidio set up in San Francisco

**1781** Pueblo of Los Angeles founded

**1848** US annexes California. Gold discovered

**1853** Levi Strauss lands in the Bay Area and begins selling his canvas trousers

**1854** Sacramento becomes the state capital

**1869** Transcontinental railroad completed

**1891** Stanford University opens

**1893** San Andreas Fault discovered

**1906** Earthquake strikes San Francisco

**1911** *The Law of the Range* is the first film made in Hollywood

**1929** Actor Douglas Fairbanks Sr. hosts the first Academy Awards presentation

**1945** UN Charter signed in San Francisco

**1968** Senator Robert F. Kennedy assassinated

**1978** Apple Computer's first personal computer

**1984** Los Angeles hosts its second Olympics

**1992** Statewide racial riots

**2001** Energy crisis; rolling blackouts conserve electricity

**2003** Election of Arnold Schwarzenegger as 38th Governor of California

fast-expanding job markets are in the service industries and in Silicon Valley.

Most visitors usually come to see California's two main cities – San Francisco and Los Angeles. In the north and south of the state respectively, they define the opposing sides of its character. San Francisco is more compact, and prides itself on its nonconformity and open-mindedness. It has evolved into a pro-labor hotbed, with a history of activism (the Bay Area led the anti-Vietnam War movement). It also has one of the world's largest concentrations of gays and lesbians. Los Angeles, in contrast, is a sprawling city without a focal point, where illusions of wealth, fame, and glamor have created a dimensionless image of bright lights and conservative politics. The conflicting power that the two cities exert on the politics of the state and the nation explains why California may appear a little schizophrenic.

**Beat writer Jack Kerouac**

## Culture & the Arts

For most people, California's contributions to culture are Hollywood blockbusters or televised sitcoms. But another creativity reveals itself through its history of landscape painting, portraiture, and 20th-century avant-garde art. Modern artists such as John McLaughlin and Elmer Bischoff, and such pioneers of photographic art as Imogen Cunningham and Ansel Adams, have all achieved international recognition. British artist David Hockney lived here for many years, capturing the state's sun-soaked image on canvas. California is also home to some of the world's finest art museums, including the Los Angeles County Museum of Art, the San Francisco Museum of Modern Art, and the J. Paul Getty Museum. The Bay Area's Victorian architecture has always been a major tourist attraction, and visiting designers Frank Lloyd Wright and Daniel

Burnham have left their mark here as well. Recent influential architects include residents Frank Gehry and Joe Esherick.

Over the years, California has been home to scores of successful writers, including Nobel Prize-winner John Steinbeck and Beat authors Jack Kerouac and Allen Ginsberg. The tradition continues with Amy Tan *(The Joy Luck Club)*, and detective novelist Sue Grafton, among others. Pop music also plays a major role, for this is where the Beach Boys, Janis Joplin, the Grateful Dead, and the Red Hot Chili Peppers launched their careers.

Californians love to eat out, and chefs Wolfgang Puck and Alice Waters have achieved fame promoting "California cuisine" – a blend of local ingredients and Asian techniques. This, combined with a selection of world-class local wines, is proof that Californians take good care of their palates. They are generally body-conscious and frequent gyms, or participate enthusiastically in sports and a wide range of activities. Luckily, surrounded by some of the nation's most beautiful countryside and the gentlest climate, they don't have to go far to enjoy a satisfying outdoor experience.

San Francisco's cable car, a good way to get around

# Exploring California

Beyond Los Angeles and San Francisco are other interesting towns and sights to visit. Highlights include San Diego and the Death Valley National Park in the south, and Monterey, Sacramento, and the Yosemite National Park in the north. Most visitors arrive at airports in Los Angeles and San Francisco. Both cities are linked to the rest of the state by an extensive road and rail network.

Shelter Island yacht harbor in San Diego Bay

## Sights at a Glance

Giant sequoia trees in Yosemite
National Park

## Mileage Chart

**Los Angeles**

| | | | | | | | | |
|---|---|---|---|---|---|---|---|---|
| **121** 195 | San Diego | | | | | | | |
| **107** 172 | **138** 222 | Palm Springs | | | | | | |
| **95** 153 | **220** 354 | **202** 325 | Santa Barbara | | | | | |
| **320** 515 | **468** 684 | **425** 753 | **250** 402 | Monterey | | | | |
| **363** 584 | **492** 792 | **467** 752 | **272** 438 | **43** 69 | Santa Cruz | | | |
| **380** 612 | **556** 895 | **485** 781 | **337** 542 | **112** 180 | **73** 117 | San Francisco | | |
| **409** 658 | **599** 964 | **513** 826 | **380** 612 | **158** 254 | **118** 190 | **45** 72 | Sonoma | |
| **384** 618 | **504** 811 | **488** 785 | **404** 650 | **195** 314 | **156** 251 | **87** 140 | **69** 111 | Sacramento |

**10** = Distance in miles
10 = Distance in kilometers

## Key

— Freeway
— Major road
— Railroad
– – State border
▪▪▪▪ International border

# ❶ Los Angeles

Sitting in a broad, flat basin, surrounded by beaches, mountains, and deserts, the 468-sq-mile (1,200-sq-km) city of Los Angeles has a population of 3.8 million. The city's celluloid self-image, with its palm trees, shopping malls, and opulent lifestyles, has been idealized as the ultimate "American Dream." While known for its museums and galleries, it is still the fantasy worlds of Hollywood and Disneyland® that draw most people to Los Angeles.

Waterskiing, a popular activity along the south Los Angeles coastline

## Sights at a Glance

① The Getty Center
② Santa Monica
③ Venice
④ Museum of Tolerance
⑤ Westwood & UCLA
⑥ The Golden Triangle
⑦ *Sunset Boulevard pp652–3*
⑧ Mulholland Drive
⑨ Hollywood Boulevard
⑩ Hollywood Bowl
⑪ Farmers Market
⑫ Miracle Mile
⑬ Exposition Park & University of Southern California
⑭ Los Angeles Central Library
⑮ Los Angeles City Hall
⑯ Music Center
⑰ Grand Central Market
⑱ Little Tokyo
⑲ Museum of Contemporary Art
⑳ El Pueblo
㉑ Lummis Home and Garden
㉒ The Autry
㉓ Griffith Park
㉔ Hollywood Sign
㉕ Universal Studios

### Greater Los Angeles
### (see inset map)

㉖ Malibu
㉗ Pasadena
㉘ Watts Towers
㉙ Long Beach
㉚ Knott's Berry Farm®
㉛ Mission San Juan Capistrano
㉜ Newport Beach
㉝ *Disneyland® Resort pp662–3*

**For keys to symbols** *see back flap*

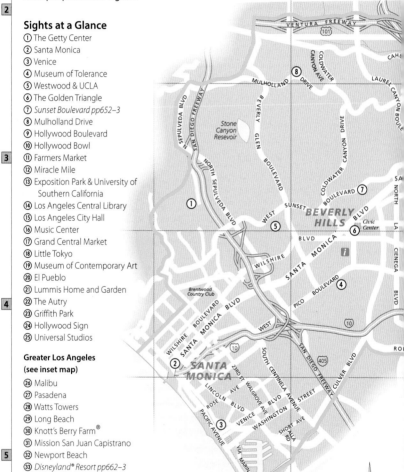

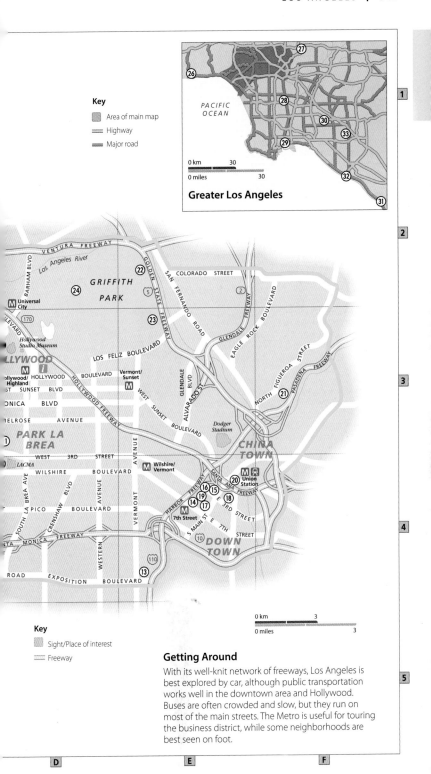

## Key

- Area of main map
- Highway
- Major road

**Greater Los Angeles**

0 km    30

0 miles    30

## Key

- Sight/Place of interest
- Freeway

### Getting Around

With its well-knit network of freeways, Los Angeles is best explored by car, although public transportation works well in the downtown area and Hollywood. Buses are often crowded and slow, but they run on most of the main streets. The Metro is useful for touring the business district, while some neighborhoods are best seen on foot.

0 km    3

0 miles    3

*Adoration of the Magi* (c.1495–1505) by Andrea Mantegna, The Getty Museum

## ① The Getty Center

**Map** B3. 1200 Getty Center Dr. **Tel** (310) 440-7300. **Open** 10am–5:30pm Tue–Fri & Sun,10am–9pm Sat. No parking reservations needed. **Closed** public hols. 🅰 📷 🚫 📷 🖥 🅦 **getty.edu**

Situated amid the untamed beauty of the Santa Monica Mountains in the Sepulveda Pass, The Getty Center holds a commanding physical and cultural position in the area. Opened in 1997, the 110-acre (45-ha) complex houses not only the Getty Museum but also the center's research, conservation, and grant programs, dedicated to art and cultural heritage.

J. Paul Getty (1892–1976) made his fortune in the oil business and became an ardent collector of art. He amassed a remarkable collection of European art works, focusing on pre-20th-century artistic move-ments, from the Renaissance to Post-Impressionism. A bold collector, Getty enjoyed the pursuit of an object almost more than the possession of it. He wanted his collection to be open to the public free of charge. His original home, the Getty Villa in Malibu, was the site of the first Getty Museum. It displays objects from ancient Greece, Rome, and Etruria.

Since Getty's death, the Trust has purchased works of the highest quality to complement the existing collection. New departments such as manuscripts and drawing have also been added.

From below, the center may look like a fortress, but once inside, the scale is intimate, with

fountains, walkways, courtyards, and niches. An electric tram brings visitors from the parking lot to the complex. The museum has a tall, airy foyer that opens onto a central courtyard. Facing this courtyard are the five two-story pavilions that feature the varied art collections. European paintings in the museum date from the 13th to the late 19th centuries and include masterpieces such as Andrea Mantegna's *Adoration of the Magi* (c.1495–1505), Rembrandt's *The Abduction of Europa* (1632), Paul Cézanne's *Still Life with Apples* (1900), and Vincent van Gogh's *Irises* (1889). The last was painted by the artist when he was in the asylum at St-Remy. The Getty's collection of sculpture contains fine examples of Baroque and Neo-Classical works, including François Girardon's *Pluto Abducting Proserpine* (c.1693–1710) and statues – *Venus*, *Juno*, and *Minerva* (1773) – by Joseph Nollekens.

The museum's photography department features works of many of the pioneers of photography, such as Louis-Jacques-Mandé Daguerre (inventor of the daguerreotypes) and William Henry Fox Talbot (the first to make prints from negatives).

Decorative arts were Getty's first love as a collector, after he rented a New York pent-house furnished with 18th-century French and English antiques. The museum holds a superb collection of ornate French furniture, decorative arts, with chandeliers wall-lights, tapestries, dating from the reign of Louis XIV to the Napoleonic era (1643–1815).

The museum traces the development of handwritten and illuminated manuscripts from the sixth to the 16th centuries, and holds an impressive collection of masterpieces from different historical periods such as

the Byzantine, Ottoman, Romanesque, Gothic, and the Renaissance.

## ② Santa Monica

**Map** B4. 🅰 90,000. ✈ 🚌 🅸 1920 Main St, (310) 393-7593. 🎪 Santa Monica Festival (May). 🅦 **santamonica.com**

With its fresh sea breezes, mild climate, and friendly streets, Santa Monica has been the star of the Los Angeles coastline since the 1890s, when trolleys linked it to the city, and beach parties became the rage. In the early days, it lived a dual life as a sleepy coastal town and the headquarters for offshore gambling ships. In the 1920s and 1930s, movie stars such as Cary Grant and Mary Pickford bought land here, creating the "Gold Coast." Following the success of the television series *Baywatch*, the popular beach and pier gained worldwide fame. But the city, perched on a high yellow cliff overlooking Santa Monica Bay, is also noted for its

**Street entertainer playing guitar**

restaurants, shopping areas, and vibrant arts scene. Lush parks dot the city's landscape, with none quite as beautiful as **Palisades Park**, on the bluff overlooking the ocean. Stretching 1.5 miles (2.5 km)

Tall palm trees lining the road in Palisades Park, Santa Monica

Santa Monica's Binoculars Building, designed by Frank Gehry

along the cliff's edge, this narrow, well-manicured park is one of the best spots to watch the sun set. For the quintessential California experience, take a walk or jog along the paths, with the ocean as a backdrop and the towering palms overhead. At the northern end, the aptly named Inspiration Point has great views of the bay, stretching from Malibu to Palos Verdes.

Inland, between Wilshire Boulevard and Broadway, is **Third Street Promenade**. Once a decaying shopping street, this boulevard has undergone a major face-lift and is now one of the liveliest places in Los Angeles. Its three pedestrian blocks are lined with shops, cafés, bookstores, and theaters. At night the mood is especially festive, with street performers entertaining visitors with music, dance, and magic tricks.

Santa Monica's other important shopping area is Main Street, which runs south toward Venice. It abounds in a wide range of shops, restaurants, and galleries. Many examples of public art are displayed along the street, such as Paul Conrad's *Chain Reaction*, a stainless-steel and copper-link chain statement against nuclear war. The Frank Gehry-designed **Binoculars Building**, shaped like a pair of binoculars, dominates the street. Main Street also features the California Heritage Museum, which has the distinction of showcasing various periods in the state's history.

Northeast of the beach, the 1908 **Santa Monica Pier** is the West Coast's oldest amusement pier, with bumper cars, roller coasters, and a giant Ferris wheel. There is also the 1922 carousel that featured in Paul Newman's 1973 film, *The Sting*. **Bergamot Station** is a large, sprawling 5.5-acre (2-ha) arts complex that stands on the site of an abandoned trolley station. The crude buildings are constructed out of aluminum siding, but with an added touch of elegant high-tech styling. More than 20 galleries display the latest in contemporary, as well as radical, art. The Santa Monica Museum of Art, within the Bergamot Station, focuses on the work of contemporary artists, particularly those who are involved in performance art.

**Santa Monica Pier**
Colorado & Ocean Aves. **Tel** (310) 458-8900, Pacific Park information (310) 266-8744. **Open** daily. Carousel: **Open** 11am–5pm Mon–Thu, 11am–10pm Sat & Sun. (310) 395-4248. **santamonicapier.org**

**Bergamot Station**
2525 Michigan Ave. **Tel** (310) 829-5854. **Open** 10am–6pm Tue–Fri, 11am–5:30pm Sat. **Closed** Sun, public hols.

## ③ Venice

**Map** B5. 2904 Washington Blvd, Suite 100, (310) 822-5425. **venicechamber.net**

Founded by tobacco tycoon Abbot Kinney, as a US version of Venice (Italy), this lively beach town was a swampland little more than 100 years ago. Hoping to spark a cultural renaissance in California, Kinney built a system of canals, and imported gondolas to punt along the waterways. Today, only a few of the original canals remain, the rest having been filled in. The best place to see the canals is on **Dell Avenue**, where old bridges, boats, and ducks grace the waterways.

However, the town is best known for the bustling, circus atmosphere of its beach. On the boardwalk during weekends, men and women whiz past on bicycles and skates, while a zany array of jugglers, acrobats, and one-man bands captivate the crowds. Muscle Beach, where Arnold Schwarzenegger used to work out, still attracts bodybuilders.

Man-made canal in Venice

### Raymond Chandler

American novelist Raymond Chandler (1888–1959) set several of his works in Santa Monica, a city that he loathed and thinly disguised as sleazy Bay City in *Farewell, My Lovely*. Corruption, vice, and the city's offshore gambling circuit of the 1920s and 1930s are well documented in his portrayal of Santa Monica. His novels, such as *The Big Sleep, The High Window, and The Long Goodbye*, depicting the dark side of LA, were made into films. A leading figure of the so-called hard-boiled school of detective writing of the period, Chandler's famous detective Philip Marlowe epitomized a tough, unsentimental point of view.

Raymond Chandler

## ④ Museum of Tolerance

**Map** C4. 9786 W Pico Blvd. **Tel** (310) 353-8403. **Open** 10am–5pm Mon–Fri & Sun (Nov–Mar: to 3:30pm Fri). **Closed** Sat, Jan 1, Thanksgiving, Dec 25, & all major Jewish hols. 🖼 ♿ 📷
**W** museumoftolerance.com

Dedicated to the promotion of respect and understanding among all people, this museum focuses on the history of racism and prejudice in the United States, and on the European Holocaust experience.

The museum tour begins in the **Tolerancenter**, where visitors are challenged to confront racism and bigotry through interactive exhibits. A computerized wall map locates more than 250 known racist groups in the US, while a 16-screen video wall depicts the 1960s Civil Rights struggle in the country. Interactive videos also pose questions of responsible citizenship and social justice. They offer footage and interviews of the 1992 LA race riots, in which 26 people were killed and 3,000 homes destroyed. The multimedia exhibit **Finding our Families, Finding Ourselves** showcases the diversity within the personal histories of several Americans, including comedian Billy Crystal and musician Carlos Santana.

The Holocaust section has a re-creation of the Wannsee Conference, in which Third Reich leaders decide "The Final Solution of the Jewish Question," right down to its implementation in a reproduced gas chamber. Some exhibits are not suitable for children under 10 years.

## ⑤ Westwood & UCLA

**Map** B4. 🚇 UCLA Campus: ℹ (310) 825-4321. **W** ucla.edu Westwood Village: ℹ LA Visitor Information Center, 685 Figueroa St, (213) 689-8822.

With its wide range of academic departments and professional schools, boasting a strength of over 35,000 students, the 419-acre (170-ha) University of California Los Angeles (UCLA) is a city within a city. The original campus was designed in 1925 to resemble the Romanesque towns of Europe. But as the university expanded, more modern architecture was favored. The disappointing mix of bland structures that resulted is redeemed by the beautiful landscaped grounds.

The four red-brick buildings that make up the **Royce Quadrangle** are the oldest on UCLA's campus. Built in the Italian Romanesque style, Royce, Kinsey, and Haines Halls and Powell Library far surpass the other buildings at UCLA in beauty.

Since it was first developed in 1928, Westwood Village, with its pleasant, pedestrian-friendly streets, has been one of the most successful shopping districts in Southern California. It remains

Entrance to UCLA at the Hammer Museum

the most densely packed movie-theater district in the US, with some theaters offering sneak previews of the latest films. South of Westwood, the **Hammer Museum** holds the art collection of oil industry businessman Armand Hammer (1899–1990). The Hammer collection includes a variety of Impressionist and Post-Impressionist works by such artists as Claude Monet, Camille Pissarro, and Vincent van Gogh. Southeast of the museum, the tranquil **Westwood Memorial Park** marks the final resting place of several celebrities such as Dean Martin, Peter Lorre, Natalie Wood, and, most famously, Marilyn Monroe.

Tucked away in a shady canyon northeast of Westwood, the serene **Mildred E. Mathias Botanical Garden** contains a wide variety of plants in its 7 acres (3 ha), with almost 4,000 rare and native species.

Farther north, UCLA's **Fowler Museum of Cultural History** holds exhibitions that focus on the prehistoric, historic, and contemporary societies of Africa, Asia, the Americas, and Oceania. The collection has 750,000 artifacts and is one of the nation's leading university museums.

🏛 **Hammer Museum**
10899 Wilshire Blvd. **Tel** (310) 443-7000. **Open** 11am–8pm Tue–Fri, 11am–5pm Sat & Sun. **Closed** Thanksgiving, Dec 25. ♿ 📷 📷
**W** hammer.ucla.edu

🏛 **Fowler Museum of Cultural History**
308 Charles E. Young Dr. **Tel** (310) 825-4361. **Open** noon–5pm Wed–Sun (until 8pm Thu). **Closed** Mon, Tue, public hols. **W** fowler.ucla.edu

Exhibition on racial prejudice at the Museum of Tolerance

# ⑥ The Golden Triangle

Map C4.

The area bordered by Santa Monica Boulevard, Wilshire Boulevard, and North Crescent Drive is the business district of Beverly Hills, known as the "Golden Triangle." The shops, restaurants, and art galleries lining the streets are some of the most luxurious in the world. Cutting through the middle is **Rodeo Drive**, one of the most celebrated shopping streets. It derives its name from El Rancho Rodeo de las Aguas ("the Ranch of the Gathering of Waters"), the name of an early Spanish land grant that included Beverly Hills. Today, Rodeo Drive's wide, tree-lined sidewalks house Italian designer boutiques and the best names in fashion, such as Gucci and Christian Dior, world-class jewelers, and many leading L.A. retailers. The place is also a prime area for celebrity-spotting.

Next to it, on Wilshire Boulevard, the cream of American department stores offer a heady mix of style and opulence. Around the corner, **2 Rodeo**, developed in 1990 as a mock-European shopping street, is one of the most expensive retail centers ever built.

At the eastern end of the Golden Triangle lies the MGM Building. Built in 1920, it was the headquarters of the newly formed Metro-Goldwyn-Mayer film studios. To the north are the beautifully manicured Beverly Gardens and the elegant **Beverly Hills Civic Center**, with

Façade of the Beverly Hills Civic Center in Los Angeles

its landmark Spanish Colonial **City Hall**. Designed in 1932 by local firm Koerner and Gage, the hall's majestic tower, capped by a tiled cupola, has now become a symbol of the European-inspired city of Beverly Hills. In 1990, architect Charles Moore linked the building to a new Civic Center by a series of pedestrianized courtyards. On the upper levels, balconies and arcaded corridors continue the Spanish Colonial theme. The modern section houses a beautiful public library as well as the local fire and police stations. Billboards are banned in the area, and a height restriction of three stories is imposed on any new buildings, leaving City Hall to dominate the skyline.

The latest addition to the Golden Triangle, the **Paley Center for Media** on North Beverly Drive, holds a collection of more than 140,000 television

Cushion on display in the Gucci boutique

and radio shows and offers a comprehensive history of broadcasting. Visitors can watch and listen to news and a collection of entertainment and sports programs from the earliest days of radio and television to the present. Pop music fans can see footage of the early Beatles or of a young Elvis Presley making his television debut, while sports enthusiasts can relive classic Olympic competitions. The museum also hosts exhibitions, seminars, and screenings on specialized topics and selected actors or directors.

North of Golden Triangle, above Sunset Boulevard *(see pp652–3)*, lie the palatial estates, the famed **Hollywood Actors' Homes** that have made Beverly Hills the symbol of success for those in the entertainment industry. When, in 1920, Mary Pickford and Douglas Fairbanks Sr. built their mansion, **Pickfair**, at the top of Summit Drive, everyone else followed – and stayed. Sunset Boulevard divides the haves from the have-nots: people who live south of it may be rich, but those who live to the north of the road are considered to be the super-rich. Houses come in almost every architectural style: some are ostentatious, others surprisingly modest. They can be toured along a 5-mile (8-km) drive, maps for which are available from street vendors. Visitors must remember that film stars' homes are private residences.

🏛 **2 Rodeo**
268 N Rodeo Dr. **Tel** (310) 247-7040.
Ⓦ **2rodeo.com**

🏛 **Beverly Hills Civic Center**
455 N Rexford Dr. **Tel** (310) 285-1000.
**Open** 7:30am–5:30pm Mon–Thu, 8am–5pm Fri. **Closed** public hols. ♿
Ⓦ **beverlyhills.org**

🏛 **Paley Center for Media**
465 N Beverly Dr. **Tel** (310) 786-1000.
**Open** noon–5pm Wed–Sun. **Closed** public hols. Ⓦ **paleycenter.org**

Mansion on exclusive Palm Drive, Beverly Hills

# ⑦ Sunset Boulevard

Sunset Boulevard has been associated with the movies since the 1920s, when it was a dirt track linking the burgeoning Hollywood studios with the hillside homes of the screen stars. Its liveliest and most historically rich stretch, Sunset Strip, is filled with restaurants, luxury hotels, and nightclubs. Once a magnet for gamblers and bootleggers, this 1.5-mile (2.4-km) stretch held famous nightclubs such as Ciro's and Mocambo – where legend says Margarita Cansino met studio boss Harry Cohen, who renamed her Rita Hayworth. While the Strip continues to be the center of L.A.'s nightlife, old "Hollywood" has become a hip, happening place with lots of nightclubs, restaurants, and shops, especially at the Hollywood & Highland Center.

A view of Sunset Strip from Crescent Heights

**The Roxy Theatre**
This trendy club stands on the site of the old Club Largo. Many famous acts have played here, from Springsteen to Nirvana.

**The Comedy Store**, a world-famous spot for stand-up comedy, occupies the site of the 1940s nightclub Ciro's.

**The Viper Room** is a popular live music club, once part-owned by Johnny Depp. In 1993 actor River Phoenix, having taken a lethal cocktail of drugs, collapsed and died on the sidewalk outside.

CLARK ST

LARRABEE ST

HORN AVE

N LA CIENEGA BLVD

Sunset Plaza

HAMMOND ST

HILLDALE ST

SAN VICENTE BLVD

HOLLOWAY DRIVE

**The Rainbow Bar & Grill**, formerly the Villa Nova, has walls lined with wine casks and gold records. Vincente Minnelli proposed to Judy Garland here and, eight years later in 1953, Marilyn Monroe met Joe DiMaggio here on a blind date.

**Sunset Plaza**
Lined with chic stores and cafés, this area is best explored on foot.

**Andaz West Hollywood**
Visiting rock stars regularly frequent this hotel. Jim Morrison stayed here when he played with The Doors at the nearby Whisky A Go Go.

*For hotels and restaurants see pp710–15*

**Sunset Tower Hotel**
Formerly the Argyle Hotel, this Art Deco landmark was an apartment complex in Hollywood's heyday, home to stars like Clark Gable.

**Chateau Marmont**
The hotel was modeled on a Loire Valley château. When it opened in 1929, it attracted actors such as Errol Flynn and Greta Garbo. Among today's regulars are Leonardo DiCaprio and Jude Law.

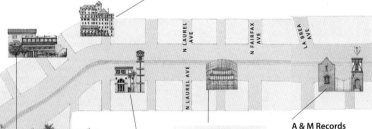

N LAUREL AVE
N LAUREL AVE
N FAIRFAX AVE
LA BREA AVE

**A & M Records**
was built by Charlie Chaplin as homes for workers at his studio.

**The Sunset Trocadero Lounge** nightclub had Nat "King" Cole as its pianist in its heyday. Only three steps remain of the old building.

**Directors' Guild of America**
This is one of the many offices on the Strip connected with the film industry.

**The Pink Taco,** formerly the Roxbury Club, is a popular Mexican restaurant. It stands on the site of the 1940s Players Club, owned by movie director Preston Sturges.

**Schwab's Pharmacy Site**
When it was open, this drugstore was a popular meeting place for film stars and columnists. Facing it, the legendary Garden of Allah apartment complex once held such residents as Scott Fitzgerald and Dorothy Parker.

**House of Blues**
This tin-roofed blues bar has been transported from Clarksdale, Mississippi. It is part-owned by the actor Dan Aykroyd, who co-starred with John Belushi in the 1980 cult movie *The Blues Brothers*.

**Billboards**
Huge billboards, handpainted by Hollywood's finest artists to promote new films or personalities, are landmark symbols of Sunset Strip.

## ⑧ Mulholland Drive

**Map** C2. Off Hwys 1 & 27, from Hollywood Fwy to Leo Carrillo State Beach.

Mulholland Drive, one of the most famous roads in Los Angeles, runs for nearly 50 miles (80 km) from north Hollywood to the Malibu Coast. As it winds along the ridge of the Santa Monica Mountains, the route offers spectacular views of Los Angeles and the San Fernando Valley.

The road was named for William Mulholland (1855–1935), who designed a series of aqueducts to channel water into Los Angeles. He oversaw the completion of Mulholland Drive in 1924.

## ⑨ Hollywood Boulevard

**Map** D3.

One of the most famous streets in the world, Hollywood Boulevard's name is still redolent with glamor. Despite its recent run-down look, many of its landmark sights retain the original appeal and charisma.

Perhaps the only pavement in the city to be cleaned six times a week, the **Walk of Fame** is set with more than 2,500 polished marble stars. Since 1960, luminaries from the worlds of film, radio, television, theater, and music have been immortalized on the boulevard and on Vine Street. However, stardom does not come easily: each personality must be sponsored and approved by the Chamber of Commerce, and pay a $30,000 installation fee.

Façade of the well-known TCL Chinese Theatre

The **TCL Chinese Theatre** on the north side of the boulevard has changed little since opening in 1927 as Grauman's Chinese Theatre, with the premiere of Cecil B. DeMille's *King of Kings*. The theater's creator, Sid Grauman, is also credited with one of Hollywood's longest-running publicity stunts: its famed autograph patio with hand- and footprints of stars. Legend has it that the custom began when silent screen star Norma Talmadge accidentally stepped on the wet cement. Grauman then invited her, along with Mary Pickford and Douglas Fairbanks Sr., to legitimately leave their imprints. Across the road stands the **Hollywood Roosevelt Hotel**, frequented by famous figures such as Marilyn Monroe, Clark Gable, and Ernest Hemingway. It was the locale of the first Academy Awards ceremony in 1929. Nearby, the restored **El Capitan Theater** was the venue for many movie openings. Neon lights draw visitors to this theater that now

MARILYN MONROE

Star in Walk of Fame

has premieres of Disney animations. To its west, **Madame Tussauds** focuses almost exclusively on Hollywood stars. The wax, lifelike figures are set up to make taking photos easy, and none are off-limits for close-up viewing. **The Hollywood Museum** features thousands of items, from the Moulin Rouge windmill to clothing worn by major stars, plus sections devoted to Marilyn Monroe, Mae West, Jean Harlow, and others.

🎦 **Walk of Fame**
ℹ️ 6541 Hollywood Blvd, (323) 461-2804, (323) 469-8311.

🎦 **TCL Chinese Theatre**
6925 Hollywood Blvd. **Tel** (323) 464-8111. **Open** daily. 🅿️ ♿
Ⓦ manntheatres.com

## ⑩ Hollywood Bowl

**Map** D3. 2301 N Highland Ave. **Tel** (323) 850-2000. **Open** late Jun–late Sep. 🅿️ ♿ Box office: **Open** 10am–6pm Tue–Sun.
Ⓦ hollywoodbowl.com

Situated in a natural amphitheater that was once revered by the Cahuenga Pass Gabrielino Indians, the 60-acre (24-ha) Hollywood Bowl is practically sacred to Angelenos. The summer home of the L.A. Philharmonic since 1922, the site attracts thousands of people on warm evenings to listen to the orchestra.

Much altered over the years, the shell-shaped stage was first designed in 1929 by Lloyd Wright, son of architect Frank

### The Rise of Hollywood

In 1887, prohibitionist Harvey Henderson Wilcox and his wife, Daeida, set up a sober, Christian community in an LA suburb and called it Hollywood. Ironically, over the next several decades the movie business with all its decadence came to replace their Utopia. The takeover started in 1913 with the filming of Cecil B. DeMille's *The Squaw Man*. Silent film stars such as Charlie Chaplin and Mary Pickford were succeeded by icons of a more glamorous Hollywood, such as Errol Flynn and Mae West. Wall Street bankers soon realized their potential and invested heavily in the film industry.

Oscar statuette

Lloyd Wright. Rumor says that material for the building was taken from the set of Douglas Fairbanks Sr's movie *Robin Hood*.

The Edmund D. Edelman Hollywood Bowl Museum explores the site's rich history through videos, old programs and posters, and memorabilia of the artists who have come here, from violinist Jascha Heifetz to the Beatles.

Hollywood Bowl, nestling in the Hollywood Hills

## ⑪ Farmers Market

**Map** D3. 6333 W 3rd St. **Tel** (323) 933-9211. **Open** 9am–9pm Mon–Fri, 9am–8pm Sat, 10am–7pm Sun. **Closed** Jan 1, Thanksgiving, Dec 25. 🚻 🅆 farmersmarketla.com

During the Great Depression in 1934, a group of farmers began selling their produce directly to the public in a field at the edge of town. Since then, Farmers Market has been a favorite meeting place for Angelenos. Bustling with stalls and shops selling everything from fresh produce to antiques and T-shirts, the market also has some of the best cafés and restaurants in the city.

## ⑫ Miracle Mile

**Map** D4. Wilshire Blvd between La Brea & Fairfax Aves. 🛈 685 S Figueroa St, (213) 689-8822; 6801 Hollywood Blvd, (323) 467-6412.

Developer A.W. Ross bought 18 acres (7.2 ha) of land along Wilshire Boulevard in 1920 and built an upscale shopping district, with wide streets meant for cars and Art Deco buildings, earning it the name "Miracle Mile." Today, dotted with grocery stores, this stretch is a

shadow of its former self. The western end of the Miracle Mile has fared better. With its five museums, including the **Los Angeles County Museum of Art** (LACMA), the area is now known as Museum Row.

The largest encyclopedic art museum west of Chicago, LACMA offers a comprehensive survey of the history of world art, with a collection of over 100,000 objects dating from the prehistoric to contemporary times. Collections include pre-Columbian stone objects, Islamic art, and a wide selection of European and American decorative arts, paintings, and sculpture. Especially impressive are its collection of scrolls and ceramics from the Far East.

Nearby, the **Page Museum at the La Brea Tar Pits** has over one million fossils discovered at the La Brea Tar Pits. The tar, formed some 42,000 years ago, entrapped and killed animals who came here to drink water. Their bones were then fossilized. For centuries the tar was used by the Native Americans, Mexicans, and Spanish to waterproof baskets and roofs. In 1906, geologists discovered the largest collection of fossils of mammals, birds, reptiles, plants, and insects from the Pleistocene Epoch ever found in one place. The only human skeleton found in the pits is that of the "La Brea Woman." A hologram changes her from a skeleton to a fully fleshed person and back again. The **Peterson Automative Museum** traces the evolution of the

Los Angeles County Museum of Art (LACMA), Miracle Mile

nation's car culture with detailed displays of vintage cars, old showrooms, and cars of film-stars, such as Rita Hayworth's 1953 Cadillac and Clark Gable's Mercedes-Benz. Its other exhibits include a 1920s garage; an opulent 1930s car showroom; and a 1950s drive-in restaurant. Farther along, the **Craft and Folk Art Museum**, houses more than 3,000 folk art and craft objects from around the world. These range from objects as diverse as 19th-century American quilts to contemporary furniture and African masks.

African mask at the Craft Museum

### 🏛 LACMA
5905 Wilshire Blvd. **Tel** (323) 857-6000. **Open** 11am–5pm Mon, Tue & Thu; 11am–8pm Fri; 10am–7pm Sat & Sun. **Closed** Wed, Thanksgiving, Dec 25. 🎟 (free 2nd Tue of month & after 5pm). 🚻 📷 📁 💻 🅆 lacma.org

### 🏛 Page Museum at the La Brea Tar Pits
5801 Wilshire Blvd. **Tel** (323) 934-7243. **Open** 9:30am–5pm daily. **Closed** Jan 1, Jul 4, Thanksgiving, Dec 25. 🎟 (free first Tue of month, except Jul & Aug). 🚻 📁 📷 🅆 tarpits.org

Model of La Brea Tar Pits in the Page Museum

## ⑬ Exposition Park & University of Southern California

**Map** E4. 🚌 DASH Shuttle C from Business District. 🚌 81. Natural History Museum of LA County: **Tel** (213) 763-3466. **W** nhm.org LA Memorial Coliseum: **Tel** (213) 747-7111. **W** lacoliseum.com University of Southern California: **Tel** (213) 740-5371. 🗐 **W** usc.edu

Located southwest of downtown, Exposition Park began life in the 1880s as an area of open-air markets, carnivals, and horseracing. By the end of the century, the district was rife with drinking, gambling, and prostitution. When Judge William Miller Bowen's Sunday-school pupils began skipping church to enjoy local temptations, he pushed for the transformation of the area into a cultural landmark that today includes three museums. The **Natural History Museum of Los Angeles County**, at the heart of the park, displays a variety of specimens and artifacts, alongside an insect zoo and a hands-on Discovery Center. A short drive southeast leads to the **California Museum of Science and Industry**, with its interactive exhibits aiming to make science accessible to all.

Farther east lies the **California African-American Museum** that is a record of Afro-American achievements in various fields. The park is also home to the **Los Angeles Memorial Coliseum**, which was the site of the 1932 and 1984 Olympics, and was also home to the University's Trojan football team. Across the street stands the 152-acre (62-ha) **University of Southern California**, which houses about 28,000 students.

Natural History Museum of Los Angeles County at Exposition Park

Rotunda of Los Angeles City Hall

## ⑭ Los Angeles Central Library

**Map** E4. 630 W 5th St. **Tel** (213) 228-7000. **Open** 10am–8pm Mon–Thu, 10am–5:30pm Fri & Sat, 1–5pm Sun. **Closed** public hols. 🗐 **W** lapl.org

Built in 1926, this civic treasure was struck by an arson attack in 1986. Seven years later, after a $213.9 million renovation program sympathetic to the original architecture, the library's capacity was doubled to more than 2.1 million books.

The original building combines Beaux Arts grandeur with Byzantine, Egyptian, and Roman architectural elements. The library also hosts prose and poetry readings, and concerts.

The **First Interstate World Center** across the street is a 73-story office block designed by I.M. Pei. At 1,017 ft (310 m), it is the tallest building in the city.

## ⑮ Los Angeles City Hall

**Map** E4. 200 N Spring St. **Tel** (213) 485-2121. **Open** 8am–5pm Mon–Fri. **Closed** public hols. 🗐 from Main St. 🗐 advance reservations required. **W** lacity.org

When it was built in 1928, sand from every county in California and water from each of the state's 21 missions was added to the City Hall's mortar. The tower of this 28-story structure

is still one of LA's most familiar landmarks. It served as the Daily Planet building in the television series *Superman*. Inside, the rotunda has a inlaid-tile dome and great acoustics. The **Los Angeles Children's Museum** across the street has some 20 hands-on activities linked by a series of ramps. Called the Discovery Maze, it was designed by Frank Gehry.

## ⑯ Music Center

**Map** E4. 135 N Grand Ave. **Tel** (213) 972-7211. 🗐 🗐 Dorothy Chandler Pavilion box office: **Open** 10am–6pm Tue–Sat. Mark Taper Forum & Ahmanson Theater box offices: **Open** noon–6pm Tue–Sun. **W** musiccenter.org

Music Center Plaza and Fountain

This performing arts complex is situated at the northern end of Bunker Hill. The Dorothy Chandler Pavilion is named after the wife of the former publisher of the *Los Angeles Times*. It is home to the Center theatre group, the Los Angeles Opera, the Los Angeles Master Chorale, and, from fall to spring, the Los Angeles Philharmonic. The Ahmanson Theater has movable walls to adjust the auditorium size, and it stages Broadway plays. The Mark Taper Forum has won almost every theatrical prize in the US. It presents first-class plays. The Walt Disney Concert Hall is the home of one of the world's leading choirs, the LA Philharmonic Master Chorale.

# ⑰ Grand Central Market

**Map** E4. 317 S Broadway. **Tel** (213) 624-2378. **Open** 9am–6pm daily. **Closed** Jan 1, Thanksgiving, Dec 25. grandcentralsquare.com

Angelenos have been coming to this vibrant indoor bazaar since 1917. Today, over 40 stallholders operate inside the marketplace, selling fruit, vegetables, meat, and herbs. The market's Latin American clientele come here to buy exotic products from their home countries, such as fresh Nogales cacti and beans from El Salvador.

Billed as the "shortest railway in the world," the adjacent **Angels Flight** funicular transported riders between Hill Street and Bunker Hill for almost 70 years. By 1969, Bunker Hill had degenerated, and the city dismantled the funicular, promising to reinstall it once the area had been redeveloped. It fulfilled that vow in 1996, some 27 years later.

**Angels Flight**
Between Grand, Hill, 3rd & 4th Sts. **Tel** (213) 626-1901. **Open** 6:45am–10pm daily. angelsflight.com

# ⑱ Little Tokyo

**Map** F4. 244 S San Pedro St, (213) 628-2725. jaccc.org

Situated southeast of the City Hall, Little Tokyo attracts more than 200,000 visitors to its Japanese markets and temples. The first Japanese settled here in 1884. Today, the heart of the area is the Japanese American Cultural and Community Center, from which cultural activities are organized. Nearby, the Japanese Village Plaza is a lively place to shop. Housed in a former Buddhist Temple, the **Japanese American National Museum** traces the history of Japanese-American life in the US.

To its east on North Central Avenue the **Geffen Contemporary at MOCA**, once an old police garage, is used as an exhibition space for the Museum of Contemporary Art (MOCA). Redesigned by Frank

Japanese American Art Museum, Little Tokyo

Gehry, the warehouse is a permanent fixture of the LA arts scene, hosting exhibition highlights from MOCA.

**Japanese American National Museum**
369 E 1st St. **Tel** (213) 625-0414. **Open** 11am–5pm Tue, Wed & Fri–Sun; noon–8pm Thu. **Closed** Jan 1, Thanksgiving, Dec 25. janm.org

# ⑲ Museum of Contemporary Art

**Map** E4. 250 S Grand Ave. **Tel** (213) 621-1745. **Open** 11am–5pm Mon, Fri, 11am–8pm Thu, 11am–6pm Sat, Sun. **Closed** some public hols. (free 5–8pm Thu). moca.org

Rated as one of the ten best works of architecture in the United States, the Museum of Contemporary Art (MOCA), designed by Japanese architect Arata Isozaki, presents an intriguing combination of pyramids, cylinders, and cubes. It holds a respectable selection

of post-1940 art, including Pop Art and Abstract Expressionist works by artists as diverse as Mark Rothko, Robert Rauschenberg, and Claes Oldenburg.

# ⑳ El Pueblo

**Map** F4. Downtown LA between N Main St & Olvera St & N Alameda St.

The oldest part of the city, El Pueblo de la Reina de Los Angeles was founded in 1781 by Felipe de Neve, the Spanish governor of California. Today, El Pueblo is a State Historic Monument, housing some of the city's oldest buildings, such as the Old Plaza Church and the Avila Adobe, the city's oldest existing house, furnished as it would have been in the 1840s. Olvera Street, preserved as a Mexican marketplace in the 1920s, abounds in shops selling colorful Mexican dresses, leather sandals, *piñatas* (clay or papier-mâché animals), and snacks like *churros*, a Spanish-Mexican fried bread. During festivals, such as the Blessing of the Animals, Cinco de Mayo (*see p38*), and the Mexican Independence Day fiesta (September 13–15), El Pueblo is ablaze with color and sound.

Nearby, the 1939 grand passenger terminal, **Union Station**, is a blend of Spanish Mission, Moorish, and Streamline Moderne architectural styles. Stars of 1940s films were photographed here. It has also been the location for several movies, such as Sydney Pollack's *The Way We Were* (1973).

The distinctive façade of Union Station, El Pueblo

## ㉑ Lummis Home and Garden

**Map** F3. 200 E Ave 43. **Tel** (323) 222-0546. **Open** noon–4pm Fri–Sun. 🚻 🅿 donation: 🆆 **socalhistory.org**

Also known as "El Alisal," Spanish for "Place of the Sycamore," this house was the home of journalist, photographer, artist, and historian Charles Fletcher Lummis (1859–1928). The structure, which Lummis built himself, displays various design elements – Native American, Mission Revival, and Arts and Crafts – revealing the influences in his life.

Today, Lummis Home is the headquarters of the Historical Society of Southern California. It exhibits Native American artifacts from the owner's collection, and its impressive interiors include a grand Art Nouveau fireplace.

The garden, originally planted with vegetables and fruit trees, now grows drought-tolerant and native Southern California plant species.

Restored interior of the 19th-century Lummis Home

## ㉒ The Autry

**Map** E3. 4700 Western Heritage Way. **Tel** (323) 667-2000. **Open** 10am–4pm Tue–Fri, 10am–5pm Sat & Sun. 🅿 🚻 Southwest Museum of the American Indian: 234 Museum Dr. **Tel** (323) 221-2164. **Open** 10am–4pm Sat. 🆆 **theautry.org**

Located in Griffith Park, the Autry National Center of the American West illustrates the experiences of the diverse

Mission Revival-style Southwest Museum of the American Indian, part of the Autry

peoples of the American West, shedding light on both the Native American and the Western perspectives. Boasting more than 500,000 artifacts, this facility also offers a fascinating roster of changing exhibitions and installations, ranging from the costumes for the film *The Lone Ranger* to pueblo pottery and Native American beadwork. The Autry also includes the collection of the Southwest Museum of the American Indian. Set atop Mount Washington and offering excellent views of downtown LA to the south, this museum displays tribal artifacts from prehistoric times to the present day, providing an excellent overview of Native American heritage.

**Sequoyah Indian relief**

## ㉓ Griffith Park

**Map** E3. 🚌 96. **Open** 6am–10pm daily. ℹ 4730 Crystal Springs Dr, (213) 485-5027. 🚻 🅿 🅿 🚻 🅿 🆆 **laparks.org**

Griffith Park is a 6-sq-mile (16-sq-km) wilderness of rugged hills, forested valleys, and green meadows in the center of LA The land was donated to the city in 1896 by Colonel Griffith J. Griffith, a Welshman who emigrated to the US in 1865 and made a fortune speculating in mining. Today, people come to Griffith Park to escape from the city crowds, visit the sights, picnic, hike, or go horseback riding. The **Griffith Observatory** is located on the southern slope

of Mount Hollywood, and commands stunning views of the LA basin below. Inside, the Hall of Science explains important scientific concepts with exhibits such as the Foucault Pendulum, demonstrating the earth's rotation. Visitors are taken on a journey through space and time, as some 9,000 stars and planets are projected onto the ceiling at the Planetarium Theater. On the roof, the Zeiss Telescope is open to the public on clear nights.

Northeast of the observatory lies the **Greek Theater**. Styled after an ancient Greek amphitheater, this open-air music venue has excellent acoustics. On summer nights, more than 6,000 people sit under the stars and enjoy popular and classical music performances. Farther north, in the hills just off Griffith Park Drive, is a 1926 merry-go-round. Adults and children can still ride on its 66 horses and listen to its giant band organ.

A short drive north leads to the 113-acre (46-ha) hilly compound of **Los Angeles Zoo**, housing more than 1,200 mammals, reptiles, and birds living in simulations of their natural habitats. Many newborn creatures can be seen in the Animal Nursery, including some from the zoo's respected breeding program for rare and endangered species. The zoo also hosts several animal shows, aimed at a young audience.

Opposite the zoo, the **Autry National Center** explores the many cultures that have shaped the American West.

View of the Griffith Observatory on Mount Hollywood, Griffith Park

*For hotels and restaurants see pp710–15*

Exhibits include a replica of a 19th-century Mexican-American ranch from Arizona. Founded by the film star Gene Autry, "the Singing Cowboy," the museum also houses a superb collection of movie and television memorabilia.

At the northwestern end of the park, **Travel Town** presents an outdoor collection of vintage trains and cars. Children and adults can climb aboard freight cars and railroad carriages, or ride on a small train. To its east, on Zoo Drive, miniature steam trains run at weekends.

### Griffith Observatory

2800 Observatory Rd. **Tel** (213) 473-0800. **Open** noon–10pm Wed–Fri, 10am–10pm Sat–Sun (reservations required). **Closed** Mon, Thanksgiving, Dec 25. Planetarium. limited. **W** griffithobs.org

## ㉔ Hollywood Sign

**Map** D2. Mount Cahuenga, above Hollywood. Hollywood Visitors Information Center, 6801 Hollywood Blvd, (323) 467-6412.

The Hollywood Sign is an internationally recognized symbol of the movie business. Set high up in the Hollywood Hills, it is now a protected historic site. Though visible for miles from many parts of Los Angeles, it is not possible for the public to reach the sign itself, since there is no legitimate trail leading up to the tall 45-ft (13-m) letters.

Erected in 1923, it originally advertised the Hollywoodland housing development of the former *Los Angeles Times* publisher Harry Chandler. The "LAND" was removed in 1949. Nearly 30 years later, donors pledged $27,000 per letter for a new sign. It has been the scene of one suicide – that of disappointed would-be actress Peg Entwhistle, who jumped off the "H" in 1932 – and numerous prank spellings, such as "HOLLYWEED," acknowledging the more lenient marijuana laws of the 1970s; and "UCLA" during a football game.

## ㉕ Universal Studios

**Map** D2. 100 Universal City Plaza, Universal City. **Tel** 1-800-UNIVERSAL. 424. **Open** Jun–Sep: 8am–10pm daily; Oct–May: 9am–7pm daily. **Closed** Thanksgiving, Dec 25. **W** universalstudioshollywood.com

Spread over 415 acres (168 ha), Universal Studios Hollywood, the world's largest working movie and television studio, opened in 1915. The theme park followed in 1964. To celebrate its 50th anniversary, the owners lavished $1.6 billion on upgrades and new attractions, including thousands of additional parking spaces and two hotels.

The famous **Studio Tour**, a behind-the-scenes view of Hollywood moviemaking that takes guests through movie sets in trams, includes **Fast & Furious – Supercharged**, a hybrid movie-thrill ride in which participants are encircled by massive movie screens, making it feel as if the trams are moving through the streets at incredible speed. Passengers also experience an earthquake, encounter King Kong and Jaws, and survive a collapsing bridge, a flash flood, and an avalanche.

Based on the movie *Despicable Me*, **Minion Mayhem** transforms riders into furry yellow Minions, launching them on an excursion through the super-villain laboratory. A water-themed play area, **Super Silly Fun Land**, is a

Jurassic Park® sign

version of the seaside carnival from *Despicable Me*.

**Silly Swirly**, billed as the park's first "real kiddie ride", is a brightly colored offering similar to Disney's Flying Dumbo attraction, but with exotic bugs instead of elephants. The TV show *The Simpsons* was the inspiration for one of the most popular motion simulator rides, and has its own themed village. In 2016, **Harry Potter and "Wizarding World"** will take the family to Hogwarts for magical adventures.

Next is **CityWalk® Promenade**, designed by architect Jon Jerde. With its assortment of shops, restaurants, bars, and theaters, Universal's CityWalk® is a prime area for visitors to buy Hollywood memorabilia. Universal's Entertainment Center and the lower portions of the studio lots offer some of the most spectacular thrill rides. Visitors become part of the wild jet-skiing in **WaterWorld®**, are terrified by monsters at the **Terminator 2®:3D™** show, and panicked in a blazing inferno in a re-creation of the final scene of the firefighting film *Backdraft*. **Jurassic Park®** recaptures the thrill of the dinosaur movie, while **Shrek 4-D™** is an animated saga based on the Oscar-winning film *Shrek*. Another ride, **Revenge of the Mummy**, takes visitors through the hair-raising labyrinths of a mummy's tomb, amid Egyptian burial chambers.

Terrifying the audience at the Terminator 2®:3D™ show, Universal Studios

# Greater Los Angeles

From the freeways, it is hard to appreciate the many treasures that lie within Los Angeles's sprawl. But a short drive beyond the central sights to nearby areas can be surprisingly rewarding. Upscale Pasadena with its delightful old town has some excellent museums and galleries. Farther south, Orange County offers visitors a wide range of attractions, from sandy beaches to cultural sites and museums. For visitors seeking family fun and roller-coaster thrills, there are the homey Knott's Berry Farm, and the fantasy kingdom of Disneyland®.

Mausoleum at Huntington, designed by John Russell Pope

## ㉖ Malibu

Malibu: **ℹ** (310) 456-2489. Malibu Lagoon State Beach: **Tel** (818) 880-0363. **Open** sunrise–sunset daily. 🏊 **&** **W** malibu.org Adamson House: **Tel** (310) 456-8432. **Open** 11am–3pm Wed–Sat. Malibu Creek State Park: **Tel** (818) 880-0350; for camp bookings (800) 444-7275. **Open** sunrise–sunset. 🏊 **W** parks.ca.gov

Twenty miles north of Santa Monica Bay, the Rancho Topanga Malibu Sequit was bought in 1887 by Frederick and May Rindge. The Rindge family fought with the state for many years to keep their property secluded. Eventually failing, they had to sell much of Malibu to film stars such as Bing Crosby and Gary Cooper. Today the **Malibu Colony** is a private, gated compound still favored by people from the entertainment industry.

A few miles east, the **Malibu Lagoon State Beach**, the largest village of Chumash people in the 16th century, is a natural preserve and bird refuge. To its east, Surfrider County Beach is considered by many to be the surfing capital of the world.

Nearby, the Spanish Colonial **Adamson House** with vivid tiles and opulent decor, houses a museum showcasing the history of Malibu.

To the north, the 16-sq-mile (40-sq-km) **Malibu Creek State Park** features forests, meadows, waterfalls, picnic areas, and hiking trails. Much of the park was owned by 20th Century Fox until 1974. *M\*A\*S\*H*, *Butch Cassidy and the Sundance Kid*, and *Tarzan* were all filmed here.

## ㉗ Pasadena

🏙 135,000. 🚌 79 from downtown. **ℹ** 300 Green St, (626) 795-9311. 🎉 Tournament of Roses Parade (Jan 1); Pasadena Spring Art Festival (mid-Apr). **W** visitpasadena.com

With the completion of the Santa Fe Railroad in 1887, wealthy people from the East Coast, along with artists and bohemians, settled in Pasadena to savor the warm winters of Southern California. This mix of creativity and wealth has resulted in a city with a splendid cultural legacy.

The historic district of **Old Town Pasadena**, at the heart of the city, underwent a recent face-lift ushering in a spate of upscale shops, restaurants, and cafés in restored historic buildings. The highlights of the area include the **Norton Simon Museum**, featuring one of the finest collections of Old Masters and Impressionist paintings in the country.

To the north, local architects Charles and Henry Greene's sprawling **Gamble House** is considered a consummate craftsman bungalow by many.

A few miles east of Old Town, opulent San Marino is home to the **Huntington Library, Art Collections, and Botanical Gardens**. Once the estate of railroad tycoon Henry E. Huntington (1850–1927), the Beaux Arts mansion holds one of the most important libraries and collections of 18th-century British and French art in the world. Rare books in the library's collection include priceless objects such as a Gutenberg bible, a Chaucer manuscript, and Benjamin Franklin's handwritten autobiography. The botanical gardens are made up of 15 theme areas: the most popular are the Desert, Japanese, and Shakespearean Gardens.

🏛 **Huntington Library, Art Collections, & Botanical Gardens**
1151 Oxford Rd. **Tel** (626) 405-2100. **Open** Jun–Aug: 10:30am–4:30pm Wed–Mon; Sep–May: noon–4:30pm Mon, Wed–Fri, 10:30am–4:30pm Sat–Sun. **Closed** public hols. 🏊 **&** 📷 📷 📖 **W** huntington.org

## ㉘ Watts Towers

1761–1765 E 107th St, Watts. **Tel** (213) 847-4646. **Open** 10am–4pm Wed–Sat, noon–4pm Sun. 🏊 (Towers). **&** Arts Center only. 📷 11am–3pm Thu, Fri; 10:30am–3pm Sat, noon–3pm Sun. **W** wattstowers.us

Watts Towers embodies the perseverance and vision of Italian folk artist Simon Rodia. Between 1921 and 1954, the

Malibu Lagoon, at the foot of the Santa Monica Mountains

*For hotels and restaurants see pp710–15*

tile-worker sculpted steel rods and pipes into a huge skeletal framework, adorning it with shells, tiles, and broken glass. He never gave a reason for building the towers and, upon finishing, deeded the land to a neighbor and left LA. The towers, standing 100 ft (30 m) at their tallest, are now a State Historic Site. Next to them, the Watts Towers Arts Center holds temporary exhibitions of work by African-American artists and also hosts art workshops.

The *Queen Mary*, Long Beach's most famous hotel

## ㉙ Long Beach

Ⓜ Metro Blue Line from downtown Los Angeles.

With palm trees and ocean as a backdrop, downtown Long Beach is a mixture of carefully restored buildings and modern glass high-rises. At its heart, **Pine Avenue**, lined with stores, cafés, and restaurants, retains the early Midwestern charm that gave the city its nickname, "Iowa by the Sea."

Along the ocean, the restaurants and shops in Shoreline Village offer views of the ocean liner *Queen Mary*. The Cunard flagship from 1930s to the 1960s, this luxury liner was converted into a troopship during World War II. It carried more than 80,000 soldiers during its wartime career. At the end of the war, it transported more than 22,000 war brides and

children to the US during "Operation Diaper." It was permanently docked for use as a hotel and tourist attraction in 1967. Today, visitors can view part of the original Engine Room, examples of the different accommodations, and an exhibition on the war years.

Nearby, the **Aquarium of the Pacific** is one of the largest aquariums in the United States. It holds 550 species in 17 major habitats, offering visitors a fascinating exploration of marine flora and fauna from the Pacific Ocean's three distinct regions: Southern California Baja; the Tropical Pacific, and the Northern Pacific.

🚢 **Queen Mary**
Pier J, 1126 Queens Hwy. **Tel** (562) 435-3511. **Open** Mon–Sat. 🅿 ♿ 🎁
Ⓦ **queenmary.com**

🐠 **Aquarium of the Pacific**
100 Aquarium Way. **Tel** (562) 590-3100. **Open** 9am–6pm daily.
**Closed** Dec 25, weekend of the Toyota Grand Prix. 🅿 ♿ 🍴 🎁
Ⓦ **aquariumofpacific.org**

## ㉚ Knott's Berry Farm®

8039 Beach Blvd, Buena Park.
**Tel** (714) 827-1776, (714) 220-5200.
🚌 29, 38, 42. **Open** hours vary per season & day. Call to verify park hours.
**Closed** Dec 25. 🅿 ♿ 🍴 🚻 🛍 🖥
Ⓦ **knotts.com**

Located in Buena Vista in Orange County, Knott's Berry Farm® has grown from a 1920s boysenberry farm to a 21st-century multi-day entertainment complex. Offering more than 165 different rides and attractions, its main charm lies in its emphasis on authenticity. The **Old West Ghost Town**, in the heart of the park, has original ghost-town buildings. America's very first theme park, Knott's offers six themed areas, dozens of live-action stages, thrill rides, shopping, and dining, as well as a full-fledged resort.

Statues of cowboys on a Ghost Town bench

Cloisters framing Mission San Juan Capistrano's central courtyard

## ㉛ Mission San Juan Capistrano

26801 Ortega Hwy. **Tel** (949) 234-1300. **Open** 8:30am–5pm daily.
**Closed** Good Fri pm, Thanksg., Dec 25.
🅿 ♿ 🍴 🎁 📷 Swallow Festival (Mar). Ⓦ **missionsjc.com**

This "Jewel of the Missions" was founded in 1776, and its chapel is the only surviving building in California where Fr. Junípero Serra preached. One of the largest in the chain, the mission was built as a self-sufficient community. Its Great Stone Church was destroyed by an earthquake in 1812, leaving a rambling complex of adobe and brick buildings. A restoration of the chapel re-creates the mission's former glory.

## ㉜ Newport Beach

Hwy 1, S from Los Angeles.

Famous for its million-dollar homes and lifestyles to match, Newport Beach has a 3-mile (5-km) stretch of wide sand and two piers along Orange County's coast. Fresh fish, caught by the historic Dory fishing fleet, is sold beside Newport Pier at the northern end of the beach. Farther inland, the coastal wetland of **Upper Newport Bay Ecological Preserve** is a refuge for wildlife and migratory birds. It also offers a bike path, fishing, and guided tours on foot and by kayak.

# ㉝ Disneyland® Resort

Disney's "Magic Kingdom®" in Anaheim is not only the top tourist attraction in California, it is part of the American Dream. Now encompassing the original Disneyland® Park, Disney's California Adventure®, Downtown Disney®, plus three enormous hotels, the Resort has become the model for theme parks around the globe. Visitors to "The Happiest Place on Earth" find fantasy, thrill rides, glittering shows, and shopping in a brightly orchestrated land of lines, fireworks, and Mickey Mouse, which is as American as apple pie.

## Exploring the Resort

Spread over 85 acres (34 ha), the original Disneyland® Park is divided into eight theme areas or "lands." Transportation around the park is provided by Disneyland Railroad and monorail. Disney's California Adventure® Park, is smaller than Disneyland® Park and can easily be covered on foot. With three theme areas, it is more suited to teenagers, as the attractions may be too intense for toddlers. At the heart of the Resort, Downtown Disney® is a lively area full of restaurants, shops, and entertainment venues.

It takes at least three days to explore the theme parks. Both parks stay open late during the peak seasons. The **Fireworks Show** in Disneyland® and in Downtown Disney® are fantastic.

## Disneyland® Park

Main Street USA is a colorful street lined with historic buildings. Central Plaza is the venue for the daily "Mickey's Soundsational Parade," featuring Disney characters and scenes from Disney's most famous movies. Guests can meet with famous Disney characters and will find ample opportunities for photographs. City Hall offers maps, dining, and entertainment schedules, while the Main Street Cinema screens early Disney silent films. There is also a large selection of shops and eateries.

Visions of the future inspire the rides in Tomorrowland, where sights change regularly to keep one step ahead of real-life technology. One of the first attractions in 1955 was **Autopia**, which has since been updated and now takes visitors on a ride into a parallel universe. **Star Tours** was redesigned in collaboration with the *Star Wars* genius George Lucas. Its fabulous use of flight-simulator technology makes it one of the park's most realistic rides. Visitors board a StarSpeeder spaceship and are transported through outer space strewn with starships, comets, and asteroids. **Space Mountain** is a Disneyland® favorite that offers a high-speed roller-coaster ride, 118 ft (36 m) above the ground. Conducted almost entirely in darkness, the ride has sudden meteoric flashes and celestial showers, and is not suitable for very young children.

The colorful architecture of cartoons comes to life in Mickey's Toontown – a three-dimensional cartoon world where all Disney's favorite animated characters reside. The most popular residences are Mickey's house and Minnie's cottage. Most of the attractions are geared toward kids from age 3 up. **Chip 'n Dale Treehouse**, a mini-roller coaster; **Goofy's Playhouse**; and a floating bumper-boat ride offer gentle thrills. **Roger Rabbit's Car Toon Spin** is the favorite. Its spinning cars take visitors on a madcap drive through a surreal cartoon world.

Fantasyland, dominated by the pink and gold towers of **Sleeping Beauty's Castle** and a replica of the **Matterhorn**, is a shrine to children's dreams. Nursery heroes such as Peter Pan and Snow White provide the themes for gentle fairy-tale rides. The historic **Matterhorn Bobsleds** offers "icy" roller-coaster rides down the slopes of a replica of Switzerland's famous peak. Bobsleds climb to its summit, then drop into a high-speed descent, passing glacier caves and waterfalls as they go. **It's a Small World** creates a Utopian vision of global harmony, with almost 300 singing-and-dancing Audio-Animatronics® dolls dressed in national costumes, brought to life using electronic impulses to control sounds and actions.

The nightly **Parade of Dreams** is a family-oriented spectacle that combines music, lights, and Disney characters. The parade down Main Street, USA features the most beloved characters. And every weekend the night skies are lit up with the "Dreams Come True" firework display. Thrill-seekers should not miss the **Big Thunder Mountain Railroad** roller-coaster ride, where a runaway train speeds through the cavernous interior of Big Thunder Mountain, narrowly escaping boulders and waterfalls.

## Tickets & Tips

Each theme park (except for Downtown Disney®) has a separate admission ticket that covers all the rides and shows, and includes a park map and schedule of events. Parking is extra, as are certain shows, food, and arcades. Multi-day tickets for three to four days and Annual Passports allow unlimited admission and access to attractions. A Fastpass lets guests obtain a voucher with a computer-assigned boarding time for specific attractions or rides. This eliminates waiting in long lines. Guests can also save time at the front gate by buying tickets in advance at any Disney store or online at www.disney.com. To help plan your day, there is updated information on show times, waiting times, and ride closures at the information board at the end of Main Street opposite the Plaza Pavillion.

Critter Country is built in a rustic style, based on the rugged American Northwest. It is home to **Splash Mountain**, one of Disneyland's most popular attractions. This watery ride in hollowed-out logs features singing characters from the 1946 film *Song of the South* such as Brer Rabbit and Brer Fox, and ends in a plummet down a steep waterfall.

The charming New Orleans Square is modeled on the French Quarter in New Orleans as it was during the city's heyday in the 19th century. Quaint wrought-iron balconies adorn buildings housing French-style shops. One of its top attractions, **Haunted Mansion**, promises "999 ghosts and ghouls," and some visitors are so familiar with its introductory commentary that they join in as they descend into its spooky world of mischievous spirits and grave-diggers. The ethereal figures, including a talking woman's head in a crystal ball, are extremely realistic. Another favorite, **Pirates of the Caribbean** provides a floating ride through a yo-ho-ho world of ruffians who have the gifts of song, dance, and heavy drinking with the use of Audio-Animatronics® *(see It's a Small World, p662).* **The Disney Gallery** shows visitors the art behind the world of Disney, and some of the original artworks and designs for Disney's elaborate projects are on display here. The exotic atmosphere in Adventureland offers dark, humid waterways lined with tropical plants. This is the smallest, but perhaps most

adventuresome, "land" in the park. The **Enchanted Tiki Room** showcases mechanical singing birds in a zany, musical romp through the tropics. Inspired by the 1982 film trilogy, the **Indiana Jones™ Adventure** sets off on a jeep-style drive through the Temple of the Forbidden Eye. Theatrical props and scenery, a realistic soundtrack, superb film images, and the sensation of a roller coaster make this the ultimate experience in Disneyland®. The safari-style **Jungle Cruise** boat ride leads visitors through a jungle full of rampant apes and bloodthirsty headhunters, accompanied by a real-life captain.

## Downtown® Disney

Located between the entrances to Disneyland® Park and Disney's California Adventure®, Downtown Disney® is a garden paradise, offering visitors some 300,000 sq ft (27,870 sq m) of innovative restaurants, shops, and entertainment venues. The fact that this area has no admission fee makes Downtown Disney® one of the more popular – but crowded – spaces. A 12-screen AMC Theatre®, ESPN Zone™, and a LEGO® Imagination Center are its top attractions. The snack shops, restaurants, vast range of retail and specialty shops, and a travel center create a total Disney experience.

## Disney's California Adventure®

The star in Anaheim is Disney's California Adventure®, lying

adjacent to Disneyland. It is divided into three "lands," each offering themed experiences that celebrate the California dream. The emphasis is on adults and older teens, but there are still plenty of rides available for all ages.

Hollywood Pictures Backlot offers a tongue-in-cheek view of the motion picture industry. The two blocks of façades and fakery give the visitor a Disney-eye view of Hollywood. The **Hyperion Theater** features staged live musical shows, and at Jim Henson's **Muppet*Vision 3-D** visitors can see Miss Piggy, Kermit, and all the lovable Muppet characters in a tribute to moviemaking. Golden State features California's topography and agriculture. The star ride is **Soarin' Over California**, a simulated hang-glider ride that portrays the beauties of California's landscape on a huge wrap-around screen. Guests can feel the wind currents and smell the scent of orange blossoms as they soar 40 ft (12 m) high. At **Flik's Fun Fair**, the 3-D experience "It's Tough to Be a Bug!" lets viewers see the world from a bug's perspective, with flying Chinese food boxes and an umbrella as a circus tent.

Considerably lower key than the thrills in the original park, Paradise Pier is the place where roller coasters, Ferris wheels, and parachute rides rule. **California Screamin'**, the giant **Mickey's Fun Wheel**, and **King Triton's Carousel** are reminiscent of seaside recreation parks as they used to be years ago.

## Shopping

The Disneyland shops, particularly those along Main Street USA, are often busy late in the day, especially at closing time. If you can, it is worth making your purchases earlier in the day and then collecting them later from the Redemption Center. Although many of the goods on sale in the theme park bear the faces of Disney characters, each of the eight lands adds its own variations to what is available. In Adventureland, for example, you can buy Indiana Jones-style clothing, while Native American Crafts are on sale in Frontierland. The Disney Gallery in New Orleans Square sells limited-edition lithographs by the Disney cartoonists. The largest of all the shops within the Magic Kingdom is the Emporium in Main Street.

# Los Angeles Practical Information

Los Angeles offers a wealth of entertainment and outdoor pleasures to its visitors. At the center of the film industry, LA dominated the world stage for most of the 20th century. It is therefore not surprising that LA sees itself as the "Entertainment Capital of the World." But the glamor of the movies is just one aspect of the city that manufactures the American Dream. This year-long vacation spot is also famous for its long beaches, mountain ranges, and some of the world's best museums.

## Tourist Information

The main branch of the **Los Angeles Convention and Visitors' Bureau** is in downtown LA, and it offers multilingual assistance. Its website has details of restaurants, coffeehouses, hotels, shops, and other attractions. There are also specialty guides available from their website. The city's two other main information centers are the **Hollywood Visitors' Information Center** and the **Beverly Hills Visitors' Bureau**. Various publications can help sift through the city's entertainment riches. The *LA Weekly* – a free paper available at bars, clubs, and corner markets across Los Angeles – has the most comprehensive entertainment and arts listings.

## Getting Around

The sprawling 467-sq-mile (1,200-sq-km-) city of Los Angeles may seem a bit daunting to navigate. The most cost-effective method of getting around is by car. A network of freeways provides a convenient, if crowded, means of traveling in the area. It is advisable to avoid the freeways during rush hours (8–9:30am and 4–6:30pm). Some freeways are busy regardless of the hour, and it can be less stressful to take one of the city's major streets. When parking, read the posted signs for limitations, and carry plenty of quarters for the parking meters. At nights, it is safer to valet-park.

Although the city is spread out, many of its districts are pedestrian-friendly. Third Street Promenade and the beach in Santa Monica are best explored on foot. Other such areas include Old Pasadena, downtown, and the Golden Triangle in Beverly Hills. Visitors should avoid walking at night unless the street is well lit and populated.

Greater Los Angeles is served by the **Metropolitan Transportation Authority (Metro)**. Bus stops display an MTA sign, and buses run on the main thoroughfares. The **DASH** shuttle provides travel within small areas, such as downtown and Hollywood, for 50 cents. Fares can be paid in exact change or with a TAP card. Visit www.taptogo.net/tap/locator for TAP retailers.

LA's growing rail subway system, the **Metro**, serves parts of the city well. It is made up of seven lines – red, blue, purple, orange, gold, silver, and green – which serve different areas. The Green Line is useful for the airport.

Other ways to get around include the somewhat expensive taxis, which have to be called by phone. Two reliable taxi companies are **Yellow Cab** and the Independent Cab Co. Visitors can also rent a limousine for a luxurious alternative. Private bus lines, such as **LA Tours**, offer package tours of the city.

## Outdoor Activities

Each year more than 30 million people visit the beaches around Los Angeles, making them the most popular vacation destinations on the West Coast. The Malibu headland, from Point Dume to Malibu Lagoon, alternates between rocky shorelines and beaches. Farther along, the shoreline becomes a long sandy strand leading to the renowned beaches of Santa Monica and Venice. Inland, the pristine and rugged terrain of the Santa Monica Mountains offer plenty of hiking trails with panoramic views of the Pacific Ocean. LA's beaches are a great natural resource and offer swimming and volleyball opportunities. The waters off the Malibu Pier and Topanga State Beach are considered to be the best for surfing.

Griffith Park offers miles of hiking trails, opportunities for horseback riding, and cycling. The best place for cyclists is the coastal bike path that runs for 25 miles (40 km) along Santa Monica Bay (bicycles are not allowed on the freeways). Bicycles and skates can be rented from **Sea Mist Rentals** (Santa Monica Pier) and at the local pizza stands (Santa Monica Beach). Sports include baseball at the famed Dodger Stadium, and college football at Pasadena's Rose Bowl. Basketball and ice hockey, at the Great Western Forum, are popular draws, as are horse racing at the Hollywood Park Racetrack and polo at the Will Rogers State Historic Park.

## Entertainment

Los Angeles's large and successful artistic community guarantees that there is always plenty to do in the city, although only small areas tend to be lively after dark.

Most visitors don't spend a lot of time seeing movies in Los Angeles, even though all the current releases and countless classics are always being shown. The movie palaces themselves, however, draw the crowds, with Mann's Chinese and El Capitan theaters on Hollywood Boulevard being the best known. Multiplexes, such as those in **Universal City** and the Beverly Center, offer state-of-the-art facilities.

Stage productions are also plentiful, with LA putting up over a 1,000 professional plays each year. Pantages in Hollywood is a leading venue for touring Broadway musicals. Housed in beautiful Mediterranean-style theaters, the **Pasadena Playhouse** and the **Geffen Playhouse** both put on new works as well as old favorites.

The city has a well-respected symphony orchestra, the LA Philharmonic, and an opera company, the **LA Opera**. In the summer there are outdoor concerts in places such as the Hollywood Bowl.

Naked ambition and unbridled youth fuel the rock clubs that line Sunset Strip. The venerable **Whiskey a Go Go** and **The Roxy** compete with relative newcomers such as the Viper Room and **1 Oak**. LA's jazz scene is exemplified by cozy joints such as **The Baked Potato**.

Whether it's house or hiphop at The Century Club, or hipster big beats at The Garage, the LA club scene runs all types of dance music. With its large gay population, West Hollywood has several discos. A current favorite is **The Factory**.

Many of LA's television and film studios offer behind-the-scenes tours as well as tickets to tapings of popular shows. In the high-tech **CBS-TV** studios, soap operas, such as *The Bold and the Beautiful*, and game shows are taped before live audiences. The popular **Warner Bros** tour is probably the truest look at modern-day filmmaking.

Most of the areas within LA have local festivals, particularly in the summer, which feature food, live music, arts, and crafts.

## Shopping

Whatever money can buy can be found in Los Angeles, from Cartier necklaces to everyday items. While indoor shopping malls are the norm for much of the US, LA's temperate climate allows for a range of pleasant outdoor alternatives. Melrose Avenue and Santa Monica's Third Street Promenade are both young, lively areas, while upscale Rodeo Drive is probably the most famous. One of the more pleasant shopping areas in LA is Old Pasadena, which has a range of unique shops in late 19th-century buildings.

LA's favorite and best known department stores are **Bloomingdales** and **Macy's**, and **Nordstrom,** which attracts hordes of customers especially in January and June during its half-price sales.

Fashion styles are casual in LA but couture clothes are available in Beverly Hills. Todd Oldham and Trina Turk are two of the hottest women's fashion labels in town, while Bernini and Mark Michaels have some of the best fashions for men.

Antique shops are centered around Melrose Place, close to Melrose Avenue, while some of LA's leading art galleries are located at Bergamot Station.

Hollywood memorabilia is on sale as well. Two good shops are Fantasies Come True and **Larry Edmund's Bookshop**. There is a selection of Latin American arts and crafts, popular in Los Angeles, at The Folk Tree.

The California fresh produce and wines have representation in LA Grand Central Market, and Farmers Market overflows with a wide range of fresh fruit and vegetables. Trader Joe's, cited as one of the finest reasons to live in Los Angeles, sells a vast array of gourmet foods and wines.

## DIRECTORY

### Tourist Offices

**Hollywood**
6801 Hollywood Blvd.
**Tel** (323) 467-6412.

**Los Angeles**
900 Exposition Blvd.
**Tel** (213) 763-3466. Ⓦ
discoverlosangeles.com

### Transportation

**LA Tours**
**Tel** (323) 460-6490.
Ⓦ latours.net

**MTA**
**Tel** (323) 466-3873.
Ⓦ metro.net

**Yellow Cab**
**Tel** (800) 200-1085,
(877) 733-3305.
Ⓦ layellowcab.com

### Cycling

**Sea Mist Rentals**
1619 Ocean Front Walk,
Santa Monica, CA 90401.
**Tel** (310) 395-7076.

### Cinemas

**Universal City Cinemas**
Universal City,
CA 91608.
**Tel** (818) 508-0588.
Ⓦ amctheatres.com

### Theaters

**Geffen Playhouse**
10886 Le Conte Ave.
**Tel** (310) 208-5454. Ⓦ
geffenplayhouse.com

**Pasadena Playhouse**
39 S El Molino Ave,
Pasadena, CA 91101.
**Tel** (626) 356-7529. `
Ⓦ pasadenaplay
house.org

### Opera

**LA Opera**
135 N Grand Ave.
**Tel** (213) 972-8001.
Ⓦ losangelesopera.
com

### Rock, Jazz, Blues, & Clubs

**1 Oak**
9039 W Sunset Blvd.
**Tel** (310) 274-5800.

**The Baked Potato**
3787 Cahuenga Blvd W,
Studio City, CA 91105.
**Tel** (818) 980-1615.

**The Factory**
652 N La Peer Dr.
**Tel** (310) 659-4551.

**The Roxy**
9009 W Sunset Blvd.
**Tel** (310) 278-9457.

**Whiskey a Go Go**
8901 W Sunset Blvd.
**Tel** (310) 652-4202.

### Studio Tours & Live Tapings

**CBS-TV**
Ⓦ tvtickets.com

**Warner Bros**
4000 Warner Blvd,
Burbank.
**Tel** (818) 977-1744.

### Shopping

**Bloomingdales**
Beverly Center,
8500 Beverly Blvd.
**Tel** (310) 360-2700.
Ⓦ bloomingdales.com

**Larry Edmund's Bookshop**
6644 Hollywood Blvd.
**Tel** (323) 463-3273.
Ⓦ larryedmunds.com

**Macy's**
8500 Beverly Blvd.
**Tel** (310) 854-6655.
Ⓦ macys.com

**Nordstrom**
10830 W Pico Blvd.
**Tel** (310) 470-6155.
Ⓦ nordstrom.com

# San Diego County

San Diego's character has always been determined by the sea. Its magnificent natural harbor attracted the Spanish as well as gold prospectors and whalers. The US Navy arrived in 1904, and today San Diego has become one of the largest military establishments in the world. Extending to the Mexican border, its coastline has 70 miles (112 km) of stunning beaches, rocky cliffs, coves, and seaside resorts, with plentiful opportunities for leisure activities.

The Gaslamp Quarter, the star of downtown San Diego

## ❷ San Diego

🏙 1,500,000. ✈ 🚆 1050 Kettner Blvd. 🚌 120 W Broadway. 🛈 1040 W Broadway, (619) 236-1212. 🎷 Wine & Food Festival (Nov). 🌐 sandiego.org

The museums and art venues of **Balboa Park** (see pp668–9) are the prime cultural attractions of San Diego, California's second-largest city. San Diego's growth as a modern city began with the waterfront development initiated by San Francisco businessman, Alonzo Horton, in the 1870s. He also designed the plan of the **Gaslamp Quarter**, which is now the centerpiece of downtown, and the best place to shop and dine. The wealth of period buildings ranges from a pie bakery to ornate offices and grand Victorian hotels. The district is particularly attractive at night, when it is illuminated by graceful gas lamps. Close by is **Horton Plaza**, an innovatively designed shopping center built in 1985.

At the western end of Broadway is the **Santa Fe Depot**, a Spanish-Colonial-style railroad station dating from 1915. The towering America Plaza houses the **Museum of** **Contemporary Art**, whose galleries display work by new artists and selections from its large permanent collection.

The promenades and piers of the **Embarcadero** waterfront pathway lead to the **Maritime Museum** and its three historic ships. Of these, the highlight is the *Star of India*, an 1863 merchantman. To the south is Broadway Pier, where visitors can take a harbor excursion.

North of downtown is **Old Town**, site of the original Spanish settlement near the San Diego River. Today, more than 20 historic buildings have been restored to form the **Old Town San Diego State Historic Park**.

The Plaza, at its center, was where parades and fiestas once took place. The old Spanish presidio and mission is now part of Presidio Park. Crowning the hill the **Junípero Serra Museum** is named after the founder of California's missions (see p680). On display are archaeological finds as well as exhibits on San Diego's successive Native American, Spanish, Mexican, and American communities.

To the west of Old Town is the **Point Loma Peninsula**, at the southern tip of which is the Cabrillo National Monument, named after the city's discoverer, Juan Rodríguez Cabrillo; his statue overlooks the Bay. Between December and March, the nearby Whale Overlook is a popular spot to watch gray whales.

The peninsula of Coronado has the city's most exclusive boutiques and hotels. The **Hotel del Coronado**, or "Del," opened in 1888 and is a lovely Victorian seaside hotel (see p710). Its guest list reads like a Who's Who of 20th-century US history, including Presidents Franklin D. Roosevelt and Bill Clinton, and film star Marilyn Monroe. It has been the setting for several films, including *Some Like It Hot*, the 1959 classic starring Marilyn Monroe, Jack Lemmon, and Tony Curtis. The Coronado Ferry ride is enchanting at dusk, when the sun's last rays illuminates the skyscrapers of downtown.

🏛 **Junípero Serra Museum**
2727 Presidio Dr. **Tel** (619) 297-3258. **Open** 10am–5pm Sat & Sun. **Closed** Dec 25. ♿

Impressive turrets and gables of the Hotel del Coronado, San Diego

## ❸ SeaWorld®

500 Sea World Dr. **Tel** (800) 380-3203.
🚌 9 (Jun–Aug), 10 (Sep–May). **Open**
daily. 🅿️ ♿ 📷 🌐 seaworld.com

San Diego's SeaWorld® covers
189 acres (60 ha) of Mission Bay.
The ride up the Skytower, a 320-
ft (98-m) column, offers splendid
views. Another fabulous ride
is the 100-ft (30-m) Bayside
Skyride, where gondola cars
make an enormous loop
over Mission Bay.

The stars of SeaWorld® are
the performing whales and
dolphins. One performance
reveals the intelligence of
dolphins and pilot whales,
while another demonstrates
the virtuosity of killer whales.
Other attractions include the
shark and otter pools, and
opportunities to feed killer
whales and seals. Children will
enjoy feeding the sea turtles
on the Animal Spotlight Tour.

SeaWorld®'s staff are devoted
to animal rescue and
rehabilitation, and run
conservation programs.

## ❹ La Jolla

🚹 32,000. 🚌 from San Diego.
ℹ️ 7966 Herschel Ave, (619) 236-1212.
🌐 lajollabythesea.com

Set amid cliffs and coves,
La Jolla is an elegant coastal
resort. Its streets are lined with
gourmet chocolatiers and
jewelers, and visitors come to
enjoy the art galleries and the
restaurants that promise a

Killer whales performing acrobatic feats for the crowd at SeaWorld®

"Mediterranean" view. The town
is home to the University of
California at San Diego and the
**Salk Institute for Biological
Studies**, founded by Dr. Jonas
Salk, who developed the polio
vaccine. The Scripps Institution
of Oceanography has the **Birch
Aquarium at Scripps Institute
of Oceanography**. It provides
an insight into the world of
oceanography. The **San Diego
Museum of Contemporary Art**
occupies a prime oceanfront
location. A companion to the
gallery in San Diego, it displays
works of post-1950 art.

## ❺ Tijuana, Mexico

Mexico. 🚈 San Diego Trolley to San
Ysidro, then bus or walk. Tourist Office:
Ave Revolución and First. **Tel** (888)
775-2417, (01152664) 685-2210.
**Open** daily.

Tijuana has gone from one
of the most visited Mexican
cities to one of the most feared.
A 2010 government crackdown

on drug cartel activity lessened
the violence briefly. However,
drug lords still reign and bring
violence and fear to the border
cities of Tijuana and Juarez.
Tourists are advised to travel
in groups, during the day and
with trusted guides.

The futuristic **Centro Cultural
Tijuana**, built on the banks
of the Tijuana River, has an
Omnimax® theater, which
screens films on Mexico. The
open-air Mexitlán rooftop
exhibition re-creates the
country's architectural
treasures in miniature.

The best shopping is in the
quiet bazaars located on the
lively Avenida Revolución.
Painted pottery, leather boots,
silver jewelry, and tequila
are some favorite buys. US
dollars and credit cards are
accepted widely.

🏛️ **Centro Cultural Tijuana**
Paseo de los Héroes and Javier Mina
Zona Rosa. **Tel** (0115266) 4687.
**Open** daily. 🅿️

The beautiful rocky shoreline of La Jolla Cove

# Balboa Park

Located in the heart of San Diego *(see p666)*, Balboa Park is one of the city's most popular attractions. Founded in 1868, its lush beauty owes much to the horticulturalist Kate Sessions, who planted trees throughout its 2 sq miles (5 sq km). In 1915, the park was the site of the Panama-California International Exposition, which celebrated the opening of the Panama Canal. Many of the Spanish Colonial-style pavilions built in that year survive along El Prado (the park's main street); the animals gathered for the exhibition formed the nucleus of the renowned San Diego Zoo. Today, Balboa Park has one of the country's richest concentrations of museums and performance spaces.

**Plaza de Panama**
This plaza was at the heart of the famous 1915 Exposition.

**★ San Diego Museum of Man**
Housed in the historic 1915 Spanish Colonial California Building, this anthropological museum traces the early history of mankind.

**San Diego Automotive Museum**
Dream cars and motorcycles from the US and Europe shine on in this nostalgic museum.

**★ San Diego Museum of Art**
This fine museum, displaying American and European works, is the main art museum in the park.

| 0 meters | | 100 |
|---|---|---|
| 0 yards | | 100 |

San Diego Zoo
entrance

★ **San Diego Zoo**
Orangutans are
among the 4,000
animals that inhabit
the enclosures
of this world-
famous zoo.

⑤

**Botanical Building**
Constructed from thin strips of redwood,
this shaded sanctuary is full of tropical
and subtropical plants.

⑥

⑦

**KEY**

① **Spreckels Organ Pavilion**

② **Pan-American Plaza**

③ **San Diego Air & Space
Museum** This A-12 Blackbird,
built in 1962, is beside a museum
devoted to flight history. Over 60
aircraft are on display here.

④ **El Prado**

⑤ **Tour bus**

⑥ **San Diego Natural
History Museum**

⑦ **Reuben H. Fleet Science Center**

**Exploring Balboa Park**
Most of the park's museums
lie along the central El Prado,
while some are located to the
south. The pleasant grounds,
shady picnic groves, and traffic-
free promenades are usually
crowded with joggers, cyclists,
and street artists.

The **San Diego Museum of
Man**, at the western end of El
Prado, is an anthropological
museum about the early history
of mankind. Exhibits cover the
cultures of ancient Egypt and the
Mayans, and Native American
crafts. Close by, the **San Diego
Museum of Art's** large and
varied collection is boosted by
special exhibitions. It displays
a vast range of European and
American art from 1300 to
the 20th century, as well some
fine exhibits from South Asia,
Japan, and China.

The **Timken Museum of Art**,
lying east of the Museum of Art,
displays a world-class collection
of European masters such as
Frans Hals, Rembrandt, and
Paul Cézanne. It also has a
collection of Russian icons.

Farther east along El Prado,
the **Natural History Museum**
features a giant-screen 3-D
theater showing five screenings
of films that focus on the
biodiversity of Southern
California and the natural world.
The main attraction at the
**Reuben H. Fleet Science Center**,
just across the plaza, is the IMAX®
cinema in the Space Theater,
where films are projected onto
an enormous domed screen.
Laser and planetarium shows
are also staged here.

Just north of the museums,
the **San Diego Zoo** is one of the
best in the world and is famous
for its conservation programs.
Spread over 100 acres (40 ha),
it houses 800 animal species in
enclosures designed to closely
resemble their natural habitat.
A 35-minute narrated bus tour
covers most of the zoo, while
the aerial Skyfari ride offers an
exciting trip across the south
of the park in gondola cars
that run 180 ft (55 m) up. There
is also a Children's Zoo. The
zoo is open in summer for
nocturnal exploration.

# The Deserts

The searing deserts of Southern California have a haunting beauty all their own, with jagged canyons, steep hills, and carpets of wildflowers in spring. At the heart of the Low Desert is Palm Springs, the region's most sought-after resort, with hotels and golf courses. The stark Joshua Tree National Park lies to the east. Farther north, the Mojave Desert is the state's greatest secret, all too often missed by visitors. Its main draw, Death Valley National Park, has some of the highest temperatures in the Western Hemisphere.

Sculpture Garden in the Palm Springs Art Museum

## ❻ Palm Springs

🏙 42,000. ✈ 🚉 Indio. 🚌 2901 N Palm Canyon Dr. ℹ 2901 N Palm Canyon Drive, (800) 347-7746, (760) 778-8418. 🎬 Palm Springs International Film Festival (early–mid-Jan). 🌐 **visitpalmsprings.com**

The largest of the desert cities, Palm Springs was first sighted in 1853 when a survey party came across a grove of palm trees surrounding a freshwater spring pool in the Coachella Valley. The first hotel was constructed in 1886, and by the turn of the century Palm Springs was a thriving health spa. Soon after, it became a fashionable winter resort for the rich and famous. Today, its population doubles each winter, when visitors come to enjoy the relaxing, outdoor lifestyle. First-class hotels such as the Marriott and Hyatt Regency abound, and a number of celebrities live here. The area around Palm Springs has numerous resort cities, such as Rancho Mirage, Indian Wells,

and La Quinta, and more than 100 luxury golf courses.

Downtown's two main shopping streets are Palm Canyon and Indian Canyon Drives; both are lined with restaurants, boutiques, and art galleries. The **Village Green Heritage Center**, in the heart of the shopping area, has a few historic buildings, including Ruddy's 1930s General Store Museum, a replica of the original, with authentic packaged goods ranging from licorice to patent medicines. The Agua Caliente Cultural Museum displays the heritage of the area's Cahuilla people.

The state-of-the-art **Oasis Water Resort** has 13 waterslides, including a 70-ft (20-m) free-fall slide. An enormous wave-action pool creates 4-ft (1.2-m-) high waves suitable for surfing and boogie boarding. The resort also has a hotel, heated spas, health clubs, and restaurants. The **Palm Springs Aerial Tramway** covers a 2.5-mile (4-km) trip via cable car, which ascends 5,900 ft (1,790 m) over spectacular scenery to the Mountain Station in the Mount San Jacinto Wilderness State Park. Visitors travel through five distinct ecosystems, ranging from desert to alpine forest, where the weather becomes icy-cold. At the top, there are 54 miles (85 km) of hiking trails, a ski center, campsites, and a cafeteria. Observation decks offer terrific views of the Coachella Valley, Palm Springs, and the San

Bernardino Mountains to the north. On a clear day, it is possible to see the Salton Sea, 50 miles (80 km) away.

The **Palm Springs Art Museum** focuses on art, natural science, and the performing arts. The galleries contain paintings from the 19th century to the present day, as well as Native American artifacts and natural history exhibits. Modern sculpture adorns the gardens.

About 5 miles (8 km) south of Palm Springs are the **Indian Canyons**, four spectacular natural palm oases, set in rocky gorges. Clustered along streams fed by mountain springs, Murray, Tahquitz, Andreas, and Palm Canyons are located on the land of the Agua Caliente Band of Cahuilla Indians. Rock art and other traces of these early inhabitants can still be seen. Palm and Andreas Canyons have many popular trails.

🚡 **Palm Springs Aerial Tramway**
Tramway Rd. **Tel** (760) 325-1391, (888) 515-8726. **Open** daily. ♿ 🌐 **pstramway.com**

## ❼ Anza-Borrego Desert State Park

🚌 Escondido. Visitor Center: **Tel** (760) 767-5311. **Open** Jun–Sep: Sat & Sun; Oct–May: daily. 🌐 **parks.ca.gov**

During the Gold Rush of 1849 (see p641–2), tens of thousands of miners passed through the Anza-Borrego Desert. Today, this former gateway to San

Oasis Water Resort in Palm Springs

Diego County is a remote and pristine park, offering an insight into the unique desert environment, with its steep ravines and rocky badlands.

The visitor center is in **Borrego Springs**, the park's only significant town. Nearby, the Palm Canyon Nature Trail leads to an oasis where endangered bighorn sheep can often be seen. From the **Box Canyon Historical Monument**, lying southwest of the visitor center, there are views of the old road once used by miners en route to the gold fields, which lay 500 miles (800 km) to the north.

The desert bursts into bloom between March and May. Cacti and desert flowers such as desert poppies and dune primroses produce a riot of color.

Much of the park, including its campsites, is accessible via the 100 miles (160 km) of roads. Four-wheel drive vehicles are recommended, however, for the 500 miles (800 km) of unsurfaced roads.

## ❽ Salton Sea State Recreation Area

🚉 Mecca. 🚌 Indio. Visitor Center: 100–225 State Park Rd, North Shore. **Tel** (760) 393-3059. **Open** daily in winter, Fri–Sun in summer. 🆆 **parks.ca.gov**

The Salton Sea was created by accident in 1905, when the Colorado River flooded and flowed into a newly dug irrigation canal leading to the Imperial Valley. By the time the flow was stemmed two years later, a 35-mile (55-km) inland sea had formed in the Salton Sink.

Despite the high salinity, saltwater game fish live here, with 10-lb (4.5-kg) orange-mouth corvina being caught regularly. Waterskiing, windsurfing, and boating are other popular activities. The area off Mecca Beach has the best spots for swimming. The adjoining marshlands are a refuge for migrating birds. On the eastern side, there are hiking trails and camp sites.

Spiny-leaved Joshua trees in Joshua Tree National Park's western half

## ❾ Joshua Tree National Park

🚌 Desert Stage Lines from Palm Springs to Twenty-Nine Palms. 🅿️ Oasis Visitors' Center: 74485 National Park Dr, Twenty-nine Palms. **Tel** (760) 367-5500. **Open** 8am–5pm daily. **Closed** Dec 25. 🆆 **nps.gov**

The Joshua Tree National Park takes its name from the Joshua trees that thrive there. The tree was named by early Mormon travelers, who saw the upraised arms of the biblical Joshua in its twisted branches. The species can grow up to 30 ft (9 m) and live for about 1,000 years.

The 1,240-sq-mile (3,200-sq-km) park, with its formations of pink and gray rocks, abandoned mines, and oases, is a climber's and hiker's paradise. A popular trail begins close to the **Oasis Visitors' Center**. South of here, the gigantic boulders in **Hidden Valley** form corrals, which were hideouts for cattle rustlers. Farther south, **Key's View** offers sweeping vistas of the valley, desert, and mountains. Close to Key's View, the **Lost Horse Mine** was the historic mine where over $270,000 in gold was extracted in its first decade of operation.

A variety of animals, which have specially adapted to this environment, thrive here. The kangaroo rat gets its food and water from seeds alone, and the jackrabbit has a coat of muted fur to camouflage it from predators such as the coyote, bobcat, and eagle.

## ❿ Mojave Desert

Barstow. 🚌 ℹ️ 831 Barstow Rd, (760) 256-8619, (888) 422-7869. 🆆 **barstowchamber.com**

Lying at an altitude of 2,000 ft (600 m), the Mojave Desert was the gateway to California for traders in the 19th century. **Barstow**, the largest town, is a stopover between LA and Las Vegas. In the 1870s, gold and silver were discovered and towns such as Calico sprang up. They were soon abandoned and became ghost towns when the mines became exhausted. Many of Calico's buildings are intact, and visitors can even take a ride in a mine train. To the west, Edwards Air Force Base is famous for its space shuttle landings. The **Red Rock Canyon State Park** nearby has red sandstone and pink volcanic rock, while the **Mitchell Caverns** have limestone formations. Northern Mojave is dominated by the **Death Valley National Park** *(see pp672–3)*.

Rock formations in the Mitchell Caverns, Mojave Desert

# ⓫ Death Valley National Park

The Native Americans called the valley Tomesha, "the land where the ground is on fire," an apt name for Death Valley, which has the highest mean temperature on earth – the highest ever recorded was 134° F (57° C) in the shade in 1913. This is a land of wrenching extremes, a sunken trough in the earth's crust that reaches the lowest point in the western hemisphere. The park stretches 140 miles (225 km) and is guarded on two sides by some of the highest mountains on the continent. Its unique landscape includes delicate rock formations, polished canyons, and burning salt flats. Although always inhospitable, it is one of the most popular tourist destinations in California.

Dante's View, taking in jagged peaks and the entire valley floor

### Exploring Death Valley National Park

Death Valley was once an insurmountable barrier to miners and emigrants. Today, it is accessible by car, and visitors can take short walks from the roads to spectacular viewpoints. The best time to visit is between October and April, when temperatures average 65° F (18° C). Avoid May to September, when the ground temperatures can exceed a searing 100° F (38° C).

There is a surprising amount of plant life, and for a few weeks each year wildflowers appear amid the rocks. An array of animals such as foxes and tortoises have evolved to survive in this harsh climate.

**Furnace Creek**, with its visitors' complex, is located in the heart of Death Valley. Millennia of winter floods have carved a gateway into the Valley through the eastern hills. The springs here are some of the desert's few freshwater sources and are thought to have saved the lives of hundreds of gold prospectors crossing the desert.

Today, the same springs make Furnace Creek a desert oasis shaded by date palms. There are a variety of restaurants and motels, and the **Death Valley Museum and Visitor Center** has exhibits and slide shows explaining the area's natural and human history. In winter, ranger programs and guided walks are available. The world's lowest golf course, lying at 214 ft (65 m) below sea level, and the 1920s Inn at Furnace Creek *(see p710)*, which runs bus tours in winter, are also located here.

On Hwy 190, close to the visitor center, the eerie ruins of the **Harmony Borax Works** can still be seen. Borax was discovered here in 1873, but mining did not begin until the 1880s, when crystallized borate compounds were taken to be purified. They were then loaded onto wagons and hauled 165 miles (265 km) to Mojave Station. Used for producing heat-resistant glass, borax is commonly used today as an ingredient in detergents. The Borax Museum has exhibits of mining tools and transport machinery used at the 19th-century refinery.

**Salt Creek**, lying near the Borax Museum, supports the hardy pupfish. Endemic to Death Valley, the pupfish can live in water almost four times as salty as the sea and can withstand temperatures of up to 111° F (44° C). The fish attract other wildlife, including great blue herons. Walkways allow visitors to explore this unique site.

Some of the Valley's most breathtaking natural features lie south of Furnace Creek. About 3 miles (5 km) south, on Hwy 178, a short hike leads into **Golden Canyon**. The mustard-colored walls after which the canyon was named, are best seen in the afternoon sun. Native Americans used the red clay at the mouth of the canyon for face paint. The layers of rock were originally horizontal, but geological activity has now tilted them to an angle of 45°. The roads are often in bad condition due to flash floods. **Zabriskie Point** offers great views of the mud hills of Golden Canyon. Made famous by Antonioni's eponymous 1960s film, the Point was named after a general manager of the Valley's borax operations.

**Dante's View** lies 5,475 ft (1,650 m) above sea level at Death Valley's southern end. Its name was inspired by

Multicolored hills of the Artist's Palette

Salt formations at the Devil's Golf Course

Dante's *Inferno*. The best time to see the view, which takes in the entire floor of Death's Valley, is in the morning.

**Badwater**, to the west, is the lowest point in the western hemisphere. It lies 282 ft (85 m) below sea level and is one of the world's hottest places. The air can reach 120° F (49° C), and as the ground temperature is 50 percent higher than the air temperature, it really is possible to fry an egg on the ground. The water here is not poisonous, but it is unpalatable, filled with sodium chloride and sulfates. In spite of the extreme conditions, Badwater is home to several species of insect and to the endangered Death Valley snail.

**Devil's Golf Course** is an expanse of salt pinnacles, located 12 miles (19 km) south of Furnace Creek, off Hwy 178. Until about 2,000 years ago, a succession of lakes covered the area. When the last lake evaporated, it left behind alternating layers of salt and gravel, some 1,000 ft (305 m) deep and covering 200 sq miles (520 sq km). The ground is 95 percent salt, and visitors can actually hear the salt expand and contract with the continual change of temperature. New salt crystals (identified by their whiter hue) continue to form. The multicolored hills known as the **Artist's Palette** are to the north. Created by mineral deposits and volcanic ash, their hues are at their most intense in the late afternoon.

Located northwest of the visitor center, the village of **Stovepipe Wells**, founded in 1926, was the valley's first resort. According to legend, a lumberjack traveling west struck water here and stayed on. An old stovepipe, similar to the ones that were used to form the walls of wells, marks the site, which is the Valley's second-largest outpost.

A walk along the 14 sq miles (36 sq km) of undulating **Sand Dunes**, north of Stovepipe Wells, is one of the greatest experiences of Death Valley. Shifting winds blow the sand into the classic crescent dune shape. Mesquite trees dot the lower dunes. A variety of wildlife feeds on the seeds of these trees, such as kangaroo rats and lizards. Among the region's other, mainly nocturnal, creatures are animals that are as diverse as the rattlesnake, the chuckwalla lizard, and the coyote.

Northern Death Valley has the 3,000-year-old **Ubehebe Crater**, where few tourists venture, despite the beauty of the landscape. This is only one of the dozen volcanic craters in the Mojave area; it is 900 yds (800 m) wide and 500 ft (150 m) deep.

East of the crater, lies the Moorish-style **Scotty's Castle**. It was commissioned by Albert Johnson at a cost of $2.4 million in 1922, and covers about 30,000 sq ft (2,800 sq m). "Death Valley Scotty," a friend of Johnson's, lived here until his death in 1948. In 1970 it was bought by the National Park Service, which gives guided tours.

**Scotty's Castle**
Hwy 267. **Tel** (760) 786-2392. Castle: **Open** daily. 🗺 🚻 Grounds: **Open** daily.

### Death Valley Scotty

Walter Scott, would-be miner, beloved charlatan, and sometime performer in Buffalo Bill's Wild West Show, liked to tell visitors that his wealth lay in a secret gold mine. That "mine" was, in fact, his friend Albert Johnson, a Chicago insurance executive, who paid for the castle where Scott lived and received visitors. Built in the 1920s by European craftsmen and Native American labor, the castle has a Moorish feel. Scott never owned the building, and Johnson paid all his bills. "He repays me in laughs," said Johnson. Although Johnson died in 1948, Scott was allowed to remain here until his death in 1954. The edifice is still known as Scotty's Castle.

The grandiose, Moorish-style Scotty's Castle

# Central Coast

California's Spanish heritage is highly visible in this pleasant coastal area. Several of the 21 missions, established by Franciscan friars in the 18th and early 19th centuries, are located here. These, as well as the Spanish Colonial capital at Monterey, preserve vestiges of the state's rich Colonial past. Besides historic sights, the rugged shoreline along the Pacific Ocean harbors beach resorts and large areas of natural beauty.

The 1929 Spanish Colonial-style County Courthouse, Santa Barbara

## ⑫ Santa Barbara

🏙 90,200. ✈ 🚉 209 State St. 🚌 1020 Chapala St. 🚏 34 W Carrillo. 🚢 Stearns Wharf. ℹ 1 Garden St, (805) 965-3021. 🎬 International Film Festival (Jan–Feb); Old Spanish Days Fiesta (Aug). ⓦ santabarbaraca.com

Santa Barbara is a Southern Californian rarity: a city with a single architectural style. Following a devastating earthquake in 1925, the entire center was rebuilt according to strict rules that dictated Mediterranean-style architecture. Santa Barbara is today a quiet administrative center with a sizable student population.

Often called the "Queen of the Missions," **Santa Barbara Mission** is the most visited in the state. The tenth mission built by the Spanish, it was founded in 1786 on the feast day of St. Barbara – four years after the colonists established a garrison here. The present structure took shape after the third adobe church on the site was destroyed by an earthquake in 1812. Its twin towers and the blend of Roman, Moorish, and Spanish styles, were the

inspiration for what came to be known as Mission Style. This is the only California mission that has been in continuous use since it was founded.

The beautifully landscaped Sacred Gardens were once a working area for Native Americans. The surrounding living quarters now display a rich collection of mission artifacts. The church's Classical façade was designed by Padre Antonio Ripoll, who was influenced by the Roman architect Vitruvius Pollio (around 27 BC). Its Neo-Classical interior has imitation marble columns, while the reredos has a painted canvas backdrop and carved wooden statues. The **County Courthouse** on Figueroa Street is still in use. In the Assembly Room are murals depicting California history. The **Museum of Art**, close by, has an outstanding collection that includes Asian and American art,

Statue of the 4th-century martyr St. Barbara

antiquities, and photographs. To its south is the **Lobero Theater**. This graceful 1924 structure stands on the site of the city's original theater. Farther east is the **Presidio**. Built in 1782, this was the last in a chain of four Spanish forts erected along the coast. Other sights include the **Paseo Nuevo**, a colorful outdoor shopping center, and the Historical Museum, housed in two adobe buildings. Among the many artifacts on display here is a statue of the 4th-century martyr St. Barbara.

🏛 **Santa Barbara Mission**
2201 Laguna St. **Tel** (805) 682-4713. 🚌 22. **Open** 9am–4:30pm daily. 🅿 donation. 🅰 🅲 ⓦ sbmission.org

🏛 **Museum of Art**
1130 State St. **Tel** (805) 963-4364. **Open** 11am–5pm Tue–Sun. 🅿 (free 5–8pm Thu). ⓦ sbma.net

## ⑬ Channel Islands National Park

🚉 Ventura. 🚌 ⛴ Island Packers, 1867 Spinnaker Dr, (805) 642-1393. Visitor Center: 1901 Spinnaker Dr, (805) 658-5730. **Open** daily. **Closed** Thanksgiving, Dec 25. ⓦ nps.gov/chis

The unpopulated volcanic islands of Santa Barbara, Anacapa, San Miguel, Santa Cruz, and Santa Rosa together comprise the Channel Islands National Park. Access is strictly monitored by park rangers, who issue landing permits from the visitor center. Camping is allowed on all the islands, but visitors must book two weeks in advance. They must also bring their own food and water, since none is available on any of the five islands. Day trips to Anacapa Island, nearest the mainland, offer an insight into this unique coastal ecosystem. All the islands' rock pools are rich in marine life, and the surrounding kelp forests provide shelter for more than 1,000 plant and animal species. The islands' many sea caves make sea kayaking an exciting experience. The snorkeling and scuba diving here are considered to be among the best on the entire Pacific Coast.

Wildlife on these islands is plentiful and includes sea lions, elephant seals, cormorants, and gulls. Depending on the time of year, visitors can spot gray whales, dolphins, and California brown pelicans on the passage across the Santa Barbara Channel.

La Purísima Concepción Mission in Lompoc Valley

# ⓴ Lompoc Valley

✈ 🚌 Lompoc. ℹ 111 S I St, Lompoc, (800 240-0999).
Ⓦ lompoc.com

One of the world's major producers of flower seed, Lompoc Valley is surrounded by hills and flower fields, and is a blaze of color between late spring and midsummer each year. Marigolds, sweet peas, asters, lobelia, larkspur, nasturtiums, and cornflowers are just some of the varieties grown here. A map of the area's flower fields is distributed by Lompoc town's Chamber of Commerce. The Civic Center Plaza, between Ocean Avenue and C Street, has a display garden where all the varieties of flowers are labeled and identified.

California's 11th mission, **La Purísima Concepción**, located 3 miles (5 km) northeast of Lompoc, was declared a State Historic Park during the 1930s. The early 19th-century buildings have now been perfectly reconstructed, and the entire complex provides a real insight into the missionary

way of life. Visitors can view the priests' living quarters, furnished with authentic pieces in the elegant residence building. The simple, narrow church is decorated with colorful stencilwork. The adjacent workshops at one time produced cloth, candles, leather goods, and furniture.

The mission's gardens also have been faithfully restored. The numerous varieties of fruit, vegetables, and herbs that are now grown here were all common in the 19th century. Visitors can also view the system that provided the mission with water.

### 🏠 La Purísima Concepción Mission
2295 Purísima Rd, Lompoc. **Tel** (805) 733-3713. **Open** 9am–5pm daily. **Closed** Jan 1, Thanksgiving, Dec 25.
🅿 Ⓦ lapurisimamission.org

# ⓯ San Luis Obispo

🏙 43,000. ✈ 🚉 🚌 ℹ 811 El Capitan Way, (805) 541-8000.
Ⓦ visitsanluisobispocounty.com

This small city, situated in a valley in the Santa Lucia Mountains, developed around

the **San Luis Obispo Mission de Tolosa**, founded on September 1, 1772, by Father Junípero Serra (see p680). Fifth in the chain of 21 missions, and also one of the wealthiest, it is still in use as a parish church. Beside the church, the mission's museum displays Chumash Indian artifacts, the padre's bed, and the mission's original altar.

In front of the church is Mission Plaza, a landscaped public square bisected by the tree-lined San Luis Creek. During the 1860s, bullfights and bearbaiting took place here; today it hosts many of the city's less bloody events.

Just west of the Plaza is the Ah Louis Store. Founded in 1874 by a Chinese cook, and railroad laborer, it became the center of a then-thriving Chinatown and served as a post office, bank, and store. The property is still owned by the Louis family, but it is now a gift shop.

### 🏠 San Luis Obispo Mission de Tolosa
751 Palm St. **Tel** (805) 781-8220. **Open** 9am–5pm Mon–Fri. **Closed** Jan 1, Easter, Thanksgiving, Dec 25.
Ⓦ missionsanluisobispo.org

## Mission Architecture

Santa Barbara Mission

The 21 missions established along El Camino Real were adaptations of Mexican Baroque architecture. Designed by friars, these provincial versions were built of adobe bricks and wood by unskilled Native Americans. Over the years they decayed or were shaken by earthquakes, but many have been carefully restored. Distinctive features include massive walls covered with white lime cement, small window openings, rounded gables, and tiered bell towers. The early 20th-century Mission Revival style is a more elegant version of the original. Today, most missions offer public tours.

# ⑯ Hearst Castle®

Perched on a hill above the village of San Simeon and set in extensive grounds, Hearst Castle® was the private playground and estate of media tycoon William Randolph Hearst. One of California's top tourist attractions, its three guest houses are superb buildings in their own right, but the highlight of the tour is the twin-towered Casa Grande® (the "Main House"). Designed by the Paris-trained architect Julia Morgan and built in stages from 1919 to 1947, its 165 rooms hold numerous artworks and epitomize the glamor of the 1930s and 1940s.

**Casa Grande®**
Casa Grande®'s "poured concrete" façade is in the Mediterranean Revival style. It is embellished with ancient architectural fragments.

**The Theater**, the walls of which are lined with damask, has 50 seats. The lamps inside are held by gilded caryatids.

★ **Billiard Room**
This room features an early 16th-century millefleurs tapestry of a stag hunt.

## William Randolph Hearst

The son of a multimillionaire, W.R. Hearst (1863–1951) was an ebullient personality who made his own fortune in magazine and newspaper publishing. He married Millicent Willson, an entertainer from New York, in 1903. On his mother's death in 1919, Hearst inherited the San Simeon property. He began to build the castle and grounds as a tribute to his mother, and then lived there with his mistress, the actress Marion Davies. The couple entertained royally at San Simeon over the next 30 years. When Hearst suffered problems with his heart in 1947, he moved to a house in Beverly Hills, where he died in 1951.

Portrait of Hearst, age 31

### ★ Gothic Study

Hearst ran his media empire from the Gothic Study. His most prized books and manuscripts were kept behind griles.

## Exploring Hearst Castle®

Visitors must take one of the six guided tours. The Grand Rooms Tour is best for first-timers. In spring and fall, evening tours feature docents or "guests" in period costume.

**Casa Grande®** was built from reinforced concrete to withstand California's earthquakes. This gilded playhouse for Hearst's many famous guests has 38 bedrooms, an Assembly Room, a Billiard Room, two pools, and a theater, where up to 50 guests could watch film premieres. Hearst himself lived in the sumptuous, third-floor Gothic Suite. The exquisite heated indoor **Roman Pool** is entirely covered with mosaics made of colored and fused-gold glass tiles.

Hearst created a veritable Garden of Eden, laying 127 acres (51 ha) of gardens. Fan palms, Italian cypresses, and huge oaks were hauled up at great expense. Four greenhouses and thousands of fruit trees supplied plants and fruit. Ancient and modern statues were collected to adorn the terraces. Among the finest are four statues of Sekhmet, the Egyptian goddess of war, dating from 1560 to 1200 BC. The 104-ft (32-m) light-veined marble **Neptune Pool** is flanked by colonnades and the façade of a Greek temple.

A great lover of the outdoors, Hearst had a covered bridle path built, so that he could ride in all weather. There was also a private zoo on Camp Hill that once had lions, bears, leopards, and pumas. Zebras, giraffes, ostriches, and even a baby elephant were free to wander the grounds. The three guesthouses – Casa del Mar, Casa del Sol, and Casa del Monte – are luxurious mansions in their own right.

Main entrance

### The Assembly Room

features a 16th-century French fireplace. Italian choir stalls line the walls, which are hung with Flemish tapestries.

### ★ Refectory

Tapestries and choir stalls cover the walls of the dining hall. Its Renaissance table has cathedral seats and is decorated with silver candlesticks.

# ⑰ Big Sur

California's wildest length of coastline was named El Pais Grande del Sur, "The Big Country to the South," by Spanish colonists at Carmel *(see p680)* in the late 18th century, and since then, Big Sur has been attracting hyperbole. The novelist Robert Louis Stevenson called Point Lobos "the greatest meeting of land and sea in the world," and the 100 miles (160 km) of breathtaking mountains, cliffs, and rocky coves still leave visitors groping for adjectives.

The scenic Highway 1 was constructed across this rugged landscape during the 1930s, but otherwise Big Sur has been preserved in its natural state. There are no large towns and very few signs of civilization in the area. Much of the shore is protected in a series of state parks that offer dense forests, scenic rivers, and crashing surf, all easily accessible within a short distance of the road.

Crashing surf and rocky cliffs, typical of the Big Sur coastline

**Point Lobos State Reserve**
This is the habitat of the Monterey cypress, the only tree to survive the region's mixture of fog and salt spray. Its branches are shaped by the strong sea winds.

**Bixby Creek Bridge**
This photogenic arched bridge was built in 1932. For many years it was the world's largest single-arch span, at 260 ft (79 m) tall and 700 ft (213 m) long. Highway 1 was named the state's first scenic highway here in 1966.

## KEY

① **Point Sur Lighthouse** sits atop a volcanic cone. It was manned until 1974 but is now automated.

② **Nepenthe** is a lovely restaurant hidden from the road by oak trees. It has long been frequented by Hollywood movie stars.

③ **The Esalen Institute** was set up in the 1960s to hold New Age seminars. Its hot springs were first frequented by Native Americans and still attract visitors.

④ **San Simeon Point** is a natural harbor that was used by William Randolph Hearst to ship in materials for his estate, Hearst Castle®, located on the inland hilltop *(see pp676–7)*.

**Andrew Molera State Park**
Opened in 1972, this park includes 10 miles (16 km) of hiking trails and 2.5 miles (4 km) of quiet, sandy beach.

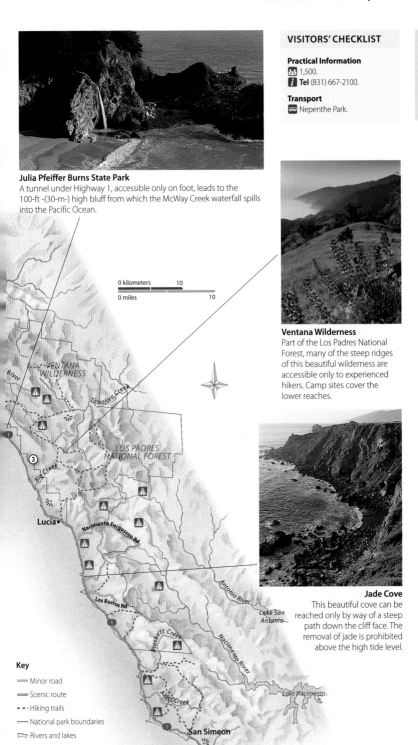

**Julia Pfeiffer Burns State Park**
A tunnel under Highway 1, accessible only on foot, leads to the
100-ft -(30-m-) high bluff from which the McWay Creek waterfall spills
into the Pacific Ocean.

**Ventana Wilderness**
Part of the Los Padres National
Forest, many of the steep ridges
of this beautiful wilderness are
accessible only to experienced
hikers. Camp sites cover the
lower reaches.

**Jade Cove**
This beautiful cove can be
reached only by way of a steep
path down the cliff face. The
removal of jade is prohibited
above the high tide level.

0 kilometers 10
0 miles 10

VENTANA
WILDERNESS

Tassajara Creek

River

LOS PADRES
NATIONAL FOREST

③

Big Creek

Lucia

Nacimiento Ferguson Rd.

Antonio River

Los Burros Rd.

Lake San
Antonio

Plaskett Creek

Nacimiento River

Alder Creek

Lake Nacimiento

San Simeon

④

**Key**

▭▭▭ Minor road

▭▭▭ Scenic route

- - - Hiking trails

—— National park boundaries

〰️ Rivers and lakes

**For keys to symbols** *see back flap*

The beautiful Gothic arch of the main altar, Carmel Mission

## ⑱ Carmel

🏙 24,000. 🚌 Monterey-Salinas Transit (MST), (831) 899-2555. 🛈 San Carlos between 5th & 6th, (800) 550-4333. 🎭 Carmel Bach Festival, Monterey (Sep–Mar). 🌐 **carmelcalifornia.org**

This wealthy resort, with its art galleries and shops, has one of the area's most spectacular beaches. Among the town's many cultural events is a Bach Festival.

A short drive from town is the **Carmel Mission**, founded in 1770 by the father of California's mission chain, Junípero Serra. The most important of the 21 missions, it served as the administrative center for the state's northern missions. Father Serra, who lived here until his death in 1784, is buried at the foot of the altar. The sarcophagus, one of the finest in the US, depicts Father Serra recumbent in death, surrounded by three mourning priests. Carmel Mission was

abandoned in 1834, and restoration work began in 1924, following the original plans. It now functions as a Catholic church. Its beautiful altar, with a Gothic arch and ornate decoration, is the only one of its kind among the 21 missions in California. The reconstructed living quarters evoke 18th-century mission life.

🏛 **Carmel Mission**
3080 Rio Rd, Carmel. **Tel** (831) 624-1271. **Open** 9:30am–5pm Mon–Sat, 10:30am–5pm Sun. **Closed** Thanksgiving, Dec 25. 🅿 ♿ 📷

## ⑲ Monterey

🏙 35,000. ✈ 🚌 Tyler, Pearl & Munras Sts, (831) 899-2555. 🛈 150 Olivier St, (888) 221-1010. 🎭 Monterey Blues Festival (Jun); Monterey Jazz Festival (Sep); Laguna Seca Races (May–Oct). 🌐 **montereyinfo.org**

The navigator Sebastián Vizcaíno landed here in 1602 and named the bay after his patron, the Count of Monterey. But it was not until the Spanish captain Gaspar de Portolá and Father Serra arrived in 1770, establishing a church and presidio, that Monterey grew into a pueblo. It served as the Spanish Colonial capital of California until the Gold Rush of 1849, when it lost its status to San Francisco. Monterey still retains its unique character as a fishing port and market town. Today, visitors come to tour its

carefully restored historic sites and attend the famous annual jazz festival in September.

In the center of town, a cluster of old buildings form the Monterey State Historic Park. The stately **Colton Hall** was where the California State Constitution was first signed in 1849. It now houses a museum commemorating the event. A short distance to the north, **Larkin House** was built in 1837 by an East Coast merchant, Thomas Larkin. Its architectural style, with two stories of adobe brick, wooden porticoes, and symmetry of plan and elevation, has become representative of the Monterey style. Farther east, **Stevenson House** is where Robert Louis Stevenson lived in 1879. It is now a museum. The Royal Presidio Chapel on Church Street was built in 1794 and is the town's oldest building. To the north are the Old Whaling Station, where mementos of the whaling industry are displayed, and the Custom House, preserved as it was in the 1830s and 1840s. Close by, **Fisherman's Wharf**, once the center of the fishing and whaling industries, is now well known for its seafood restaurants.

Street sign in Cannery Row

**Cannery Row**, a six-block harborfront street celebrated by John Steinbeck in his ribald novels *Cannery Row* and *Sweet Thursday*, was once the site of more than 20 fish-packing plants that processed fresh sardines. The canneries thrived in the early 20th century. In 1945 the sardines disappeared, and the canneries were abandoned. The buildings that remain house a collection of electic restaurants and shops. One notable building, at No. 800, is the old laboratory of "Doc" Ricketts, noted marine biologist, beer drinker, and Steinbeck's best friend. It is now a private club.

The **Monterey Bay Aquarium**, at the end of Cannery Row, is the largest in the US. More than 570 species and 350,000 specimens portray Monterey

### The 17-Mile Drive

The Monterey Peninsula has a spectacular coastline, best explored via a toll road, the 17-Mile Drive. The road offers superb views of crashing surf, coastal flora, and the Del Monte Forest. The drive begins at Spanish Bay, a popular picnicking area at the edge of Pacific Grove. Sights include the Carmel Mission; the striking Tor House, built in rock by the poet Robinson Jeffers; Lone Cypress, perhaps the most-

Spanish Bay, Pacific Grove

photographed tree in the world; and Spyglass Hill, a golf course named after a site in Robert Louis Stevenson's novel *Treasure Island*. Among the other attractions are the exclusive country clubs and championship golf courses.

Bay's rich marine environment. Among the exhibits are an enclosed kelp forest, a rock pool, and a display of live jellyfish. The Outer Bay Wing has a 1 million-gallon (4.5 million-liter) tank, which re-creates the conditions of the ocean. It contains yellowfin tuna, ocean sunfish, and barracuda. The Research Institute offers visitors a chance to watch marine scientists at work, while the Splash Zone is a hands-on aquarium for kids.

The wealthy resort of **Pacific Grove**, at the end of the peninsula, was originally founded in 1889 as a religious retreat. Today, it is best known for its quaint wooden houses, many now converted into inns, coastal parks, and the beautiful migratory monarch butterflies that arrive between October and April.

**Monterey Bay Aquarium**
886 Cannery Row. **Tel** (831) 648-4888.
**Open** daily. **Closed** Dec 25.
**w** mbayaq.org

## ⑳ Santa Cruz

252,000. 920 Pacific Ave.
1211 Ocean St, (831) 425-1234.
Santa Cruz Fungus Fair (Jan);
Clam Chowder Cook-Off (Feb).
**w** santacruzca.org

Perched at the northern tip of Monterey Bay, Santa Cruz is a lively beach town, backed by densely forested mountains. Surrounded by farmland, it evokes an agricultural rather than suburban feel. The town's cosmopolitan character is due to the presence of the large University of California campus, with its students and professors from all over the world.

Much of the downtown area was badly damaged by the Loma Prieta earthquake in 1989. It has recovered since then, and many good bookstores, art galleries, and cafés now line the streets.

The town's highlight is the waterfront, particularly the **Santa Cruz Beach Boardwalk**, the last surviving old-style amusement park on the West

Eroded archway at the Natural Bridges State Beach, Santa Cruz

Coast. Its main attraction is the Giant Dipper roller coaster, built by Arthur Looff in 1924 and now a National Historic Landmark. The car travels along the 1-mile (1.6-km) wooden track at 55 mph (88 km/h). The carousel nearby has horses and chariots hand-carved by Looff's father, craftsman Charles Looff, in 1911. The ride is accompanied by a 100-year-old pipe organ. The park also has 27 other modern rides and an Art Deco dance hall.

The **Museum of Art and History at the McPherson Center**, on Front Street, is a 20,000-sq-ft (1,858-sq-m) cultural center, which opened in 1993. The Art Gallery shows works primarily by local north-central artists, while the History Gallery displays various aspects of Santa Cruz County's past.

Standing on a hill to the northeast of town is a replica of the **Mission Santa Cruz**, founded in 1791. All traces of the original were destroyed by frequent earthquakes, and the present structure was built in 1931. It now houses a small museum. The scenic Cliff Drive along the coast takes in the

**Natural Bridges State Beach**, named for the archways that were carved into the cliffs by ocean waves. One of the original arches still remains, through which waves roll into a small sandy cove. The park also preserves a eucalyptus grove and a nature trail, which shows the stages in the life cycle of the monarch butterfly. Also along the coast is the Surfing Museum, housed in a lighthouse. The museum has artifacts from every era of Santa Cruz surfing history. Surfboards range from 1930s redwood planks to today's high-tech laminates.

East of downtown, Mystery Spot is a redwood grove, which has been drawing visitors for decades due to various strange events here. Balls roll uphill, parallel lines converge, and the laws of physics seem to be suspended. Part tourist trap, part genuine oddity, this attraction has to be seen to be believed.

**Santa Cruz Beach Boardwalk**
400 Beach St. **Tel** (831) 423-5590.
**Open** call ahead for opening times.

### Surfing in California

Surfing was originally practiced by the Hawaiian nobility as a religious ceremony; it was introduced to California by Hawaiian George Freeth in 1907. The sport evolved into a truly California pursuit with the Beach Boys' hit song "Surfin" in 1961. Films such as *Ride the Wild Surf* (1964) and *Beach Blanket Bingo* (1965) helped to establish its cultural allure, and beach parties in the style of these films were highly popular in the 1960s. Today, surf culture determines fashion as well as speech.

Surfers on fiberglass boards

# ⦿ San Francisco

San Francisco is, after New York, the second most-densely populated city in the US, with 805,000 people crowded into 47 sq miles (122 sq km). It is located at the tip of a peninsula, with the Pacific Ocean to the west and San Francisco Bay to the east. To the north, Golden Gate Bridge links it to the Marin Headlands. The Greater San Francisco area includes the cities of Oakland and Berkeley. San Francisco is a compact city, and most of the area can be explored on foot. The estimated 43 hills give many of the streets near-impossible gradients but offer superb views.

A panoramic view of San Francisco from a penthouse bar on Nob Hill

## Key

▦ Sight/Place of interest
═══ Freeway

## Getting Around

The Municipal Railway (Muni) runs San Francisco's public transportation system. Visitors can use one pass – the Muni Passport – to travel on buses, Metro streetcars (electric trams), and the three cable-car lines. Buses and streetcars serve all areas, while the high-speed BART (Bay Area Rapid Transit) rail system links the airport, suburbs, and outlying regions. Taxis are advised for traveling at night. Ferries run regularly east and north across the bay.

| 0 meters | 750 |
| 0 yards | 750 |

## Sights at a Glance

1. Financial District
2. Wells Fargo History Museum
3. Yerba Buena Center for the Arts
4. San Francisco Museum of Modern Art
5. Union Square
6. Chinatown
7. *Nob Hill p689*
8. Fisherman's Wharf
9. North Beach
10. *Alcatraz Island p691*
11. Pacific Heights
12. Asian Art Museum
13. *Mission Dolores p693*
14. Haight Ashbury
15. California Academy of Sciences
16. de Young Museum
17. Legion of Honor
18. The Presidio
19. Golden Gate Bridge

### Greater San Francisco
(*see inset map*)

20. San Jose
21. Palo Alto
22. Oakland
23. Berkeley
24. Sausalito
25. Muir Woods

Sausalito ↑

↑Alcatraz

Exploratorium

FORT MASON
(GOLDEN GATE
NATIONAL
RECREATION AREA)

MARINA BLVD

BAY STREET

**FISHERMAN'S WHARF**

MARINA

LOMBARD STREET

**MARINA**

DIVISADERO STREET

WEBSTER STREET

GOUGH STREET

VAN NESS AVENUE

FILBERT STREET

GREEN STREET

COLUMBUS AVENUE

STOCKTON STREET

SANSOME ST

THE EMBARCADERO

BROADWAY

FILBERT

GREEN

(BROADWAY TUNNEL)

TAYLOR STREET

BROADWAY

STEUART ST

**NOB HILL**

JACKSON STREET

**CHINATOWN**

CLAY STREET

**PACIFIC HEIGHTS**

CALIFORNIA

Embarcadero

CALIFORNIA STREET

BUSH STREET

BUSH STREET

TAYLOR STREET

HYDE STREET

Montgomery St

1ST STREET

GEARY ST

Powell St Cable
Car Turntable

Powell
Street

3RD STREET

HARRISON

GEARY BOULEVARD

**WESTERN ADDITION**

GOUGH STREET

MARKET ST

5TH ST

TURK

**CIVIC CENTER**

Civic
Center

GOLDEN GATE AVENUE

FULTON STREET

Van Ness

ALAMO SQUARE

STREET

FELL STREET

OAK STREET

CENTRAL FREEWAY

HAIGHT

BUENA VISTA PARK

DUBOCE AVENUE

**Greater San Francisco**

CASTRO STREET

Church

14TH STREET

MISSION STREET

DOLORES STREET

SOUTH VAN NESS AVENUE

**HAIGHT ASHBURY**

MASONIC AVE

ROOSEVELT WAY

CORONA HEIGHTS PARK

15TH

**16th St Mission**

16TH ST

17TH STREET

Castro
Street

SANCHEZ STREET

18TH STREET

19TH STREET

20TH STREET

Pacific
Ocean

San
Francisco

San
Francisco
Bay

25

24

23 Berkeley

4

24

Concord

680

80

22 Oakland

Oakland

San
Mateo

Hayward

880

92

101

84

Fremont

680

280

21 Palo
Alto

Sunnyvale

20 San Jose

1

## Key

- ▢ Area of main map
- ━ Highway
- ━ Major road
- ═ Other road
- — Railway

0 km 10
0 miles 10

**For keys to symbols** *see back flap*

# The 49-Mile Scenic Drive

Linking the city's most intriguing neighborhoods, fascinating sights, and spectacular views, the 49-Mile Scenic Drive (79 km) provides a splendid overview of San Francisco. Keeping to the well-marked route is easy: just follow the blue-and-white seagull signs. Some of these are hidden by overhanging vegetation, so you need to be alert. Set aside a whole day for this trip; there are plenty of places to stop to take photographs or admire the views.

**㉔ The Palace of Fine Arts and the Exploratorium**
The grand Neo-Classical building and its modern science museum stand near the entrance to the Presidio.

**⑤ Stow Lake**
There is a waterfall and a Chinese pavilion on the island in this picturesque lake, where you can also rent boats.

**⑧ Sutro Tower**
This distinctive orange-and-white tower is visible from all over the city.

Five-tiered pagoda in Japantown

**Key**

— 49-Mile Scenic Drive

**㉑ San Francisco National Historical Park: Maritime Museum**
This 1939 building houses a collection of nautical bric-a-brac.

**⑳ Coit Tower**
Overlooking North Beach, Telegraph Hill is topped by this tower, which has fine murals and an observation deck.

0 kilometers 2
0 miles 1

**⑱ Grace Cathedral**
This impressive cathedral, based on Notre Dame in Paris, dominates the summit of the city's steepest hill, Nob Hill.

## Finding the Sights

① The Presidio *p695*
② Fort Point *p695*
③ Legion of Honor *p694*
④ Queen Wilhelmina Tulip Garden
⑤ Stow Lake
⑥ Conservatory of Flowers
⑦ Haight Street
⑧ Sutro Tower
⑨ Twin Peaks
⑩ Mission Dolores *p693*
⑪ Ferry Building *p686*
⑫ Embarcadero Center *p686*
⑬ Civic Center

⑭ St. Mary's Cathedral
⑮ Japan Center
⑯ Union Square *p687*
⑰ Chinatown Gateway *p688*
⑱ Grace Cathedral *p689*
⑲ Cable Car Barn *p689*
⑳ Coit Tower *p690*
㉑ San Francisco National Historical Park: Maritime Museum *p690*
㉒ Fort Mason
㉓ Marina Green
㉔ Palace of Fine Arts and the Exploratorium *p692*

## Tips for Drivers

**Starting point:** Anywhere. The circuit is designed to be followed in a counterclockwise direction, starting and ending at any point.
**When to go:** Avoid driving during rush hours: 7–9am, 4–7pm. Most of the views are as spectacular by night as by day.
**Parking:** Use the parking lots that are located around the Financial District, the Civic Center, Japantown, Nob Hill, Chinatown, North Beach, and Fisherman's Wharf. Elsewhere, street parking is usually easily available.

*For hotels and restaurants see pp710–15*

Transamerica Pyramid, the tallest building on the city's skyline

## ① Financial District

**Map** F3. Between Washington & Market Sts. 🚌 1, 12, 15, 32, 42, 83. 🚋 F, J, K, L, M, N. 🚈 California St. Embarcadero Center: 🚌 1, 32, 42. 🚋 J, K, L, M, N. 🚈 California St.

San Francisco's economic engine is fueled by the Financial District, lying at the heart of downtown. The district stretches from the imposing skyscrapers and plazas of the **Embarcadero Center** to staid Montgomery Street, called the "Wall Street of the West." All the main banks, brokers, and law offices are located here.

Completed in 1981 after a decade of construction, the vast Embarcadero Center stretches from Justin Herman Plaza to Battery Street and houses a large number of commercial outlets and offices. A shopping arcade occupies the first three tiers of its four high-rise towers. The splendid foyer of the Hyatt Regency Hotel, located here, has a 17-story atrium.

North of Washington Street, the **Jackson Square Historical District** was once the heart of the business community. Renovated in the early 1950s, this area contains brick, cast-iron, and granite façades dating from Gold Rush days. From 1850 to 1910 it was known as the Barbary Coast, notorious for its brothels and squalor. Today, the buildings are used as showrooms, law offices, and antique shops; some of the best

ones can be seen in Jackson and Montgomery Streets.

Standing adjacent is a soaring San Francisco landmark, the **Transamerica Pyramid**. Capped with a spire on top of its 48 stories, it reaches 853 ft (260 m) and is the tallest building in the city. Its 3,678 windows take cleaners an entire month to wash. Designed by William Pereira, the building stands on what was earlier the site of the historic Montgomery Block, which contained many important offices. Many artists and writers took up residence in the block, including the writer Mark Twain, who often visited the Exchange Saloon, located in the building's basement. Farther south, **555 California Street** was originally the Bank of Italy, founded by A.P. Giannini in San Jose, and then the former head-quarters of Bank of America. Its 52 floors make it one of the city's tallest skyscrapers, with incredible views from the top. At the district's northeastern corner lies the **Ferry Building**, built in 1903. In the early 1930s, over 50 million passengers a year passed through here, to and from the transcontinental railroad in Oakland or homes across the bay. Its clock tower was inspired by the Moorish bell tower of Seville Cathedral in Spain. With the opening of the Bay Bridge in 1936, it began to deteriorate. A few ferries still cross to Tiburon, Sausalito, and Oakland. On the building's east side stands the Gandhi Monument (1988). Designed by K.B. Patel and sculpted by Z. Pounov and S. Lowe, it bears an inscription of Gandhi's words.

🏛 **Transamerica Pyramid**
600 Montgomery St. **Open** 8:30am–4:30pm Mon–Fri. **Closed** public hols. &

🏛 **555 California Street**
555 California St. **Open** Only the first floor is open to the public.

## ② Wells Fargo History Museum

**Map** F3. 420 Montgomery St. **Tel** (415) 396-2619. 🚌 1, 12, 15, 42. 🚋 Montgomery St. **Open** 9am–5pm Mon–Fri. **Closed** public hols. & 📷 W **wellsfargohistory.com**

Founded in 1852, Wells Fargo & Co. became the greatest banking and transportation company in the West. The company moved people, goods, gold, and mail. The Pony Express was one of their mail ventures. The museum displays splendid stagecoaches – famous for the legendary stories of their heroic drivers and the bandits who robbed them. The best-known bandit was Black Bart, who left poems at the scene of his crimes. He was later identified as the mining engineer Charles Boles. Exhibits include a simulated stagecoach ride, Pony Express mail, photographs, gold nuggets, and the imperial currency of the eccentric Joshua Norton, who proclaimed himself Emperor of the United States in 1854.

A splendid old stagecoach at the Wells Fargo Museum

## ③ Yerba Buena Center for the Arts

**Map** F3. 3rd St, between Mission & Howard Sts. **Tel** (415) 978-2700. 🚌 9, 14, 15, 30, 45, 76. 🚋 J, K, L, M, N. Center for the Arts Galleries & Forum: **Open** noon–8pm Thu–Sat, noon–6pm Sun. **Closed** public hols. 📷 (free noon–8pm 1st Tue of month). 🏷 & 📷 🖥 Children's Creativity Museum: 🛈 221 4th St (415) 820-3320. **Open** 10am–4pm Wed–Sun. **Closed** Dec 25. 📷 & 📷 W **ybca.org**

The construction of the underground Moscone Center, San Francisco's largest venue for conventions, heralded the beginning of ambitious plans for Yerba Buena Gardens, now the Yerba Buena Center for the Arts. New housing, hotels, museums, and shops have

Esplanade Gardens in the Yerba Buena Center for the Arts

sprung up. The center is situated at the heart of SoMa (South of Market), an area that has become the city's "artists' quarter," with its warehouses-turned-studios, bars, and avant-garde theaters. The **Esplanade Gardens** give visitors a chance to wander along paths or relax on benches. Close by, the Martin Luther King Jr. Memorial has words of peace in several languages. The adjacent **Center for the Arts Galleries and Forum** have visual arts galleries and a screening room featuring contemporary art and films. The **Center for the Arts Theater** presents performing arts that reflect the cultural diversity of the city. **The Children's Creativity Museum**, located at the Yerba Buena Rooftop, has an ongoing program of events involving design. The **Contemporary Jewish Museum** showcases scholarly and artistic work relating to the Jewish experience. It includes film, music, and literary readings.

## ④ San Francisco Museum of Modern Art

**Map** F3. 151 Third St. **Tel** (415) 357-4000. 🚌 5, 9, 12, 14, 15, 30, 38, 45. 🚋 J, K, L, M, N. **Closed** for expansion until 2016. Check the website for exhibits and programs throughout the city. 🎫 ♿ 🌐 **sfmoma.org**

This dramatic museum forms the nucleus of San Francisco's reputation as a leading center of modern art. Created in 1935 with the aim of displaying works by 20th-century artists, it moved into its new quarters in 1995. The focus of Swiss architect Mario Botta's Modernist building is the 125-ft (38-m) cylindrical skylight, which channels light down to the first-floor atrium court. More than 17,000 works of art are housed in its 50,000 sq ft (4,600 sq m) of gallery space, and it offers a dynamic schedule of changing exhibits from around the world.

The galleries display paintings, sculptures, architecture, design, photography, and media art, and include art of the Bay Area and California. Among the highlights are works by Dalí, Matisse, and Picasso; Diego Rivera's mural *The Flower Carrier*, a powerful irony on the human cost of luxury, painted in oil and tempera on Masonite in 1935; and Richard Shaw's sculpted figure *Melodius Double Stop* (1980) in the California Art section.

## ⑤ Union Square

**Map** E3. 🚌 2, 3, 4, 30, 38, 45. 🚋 J, K, L, M, N. 🚋 Powell–Mason, Powell–Hyde.

Union Square, lined with palm trees, is at the heart of the city's main shopping district and has a wealth of fine department stores. It was named after the pro-Union rallies held here during the Civil War of 1861–5. The original churches, gentlemen's clubs, and a synagogue were eventually overtaken by shops and offices. Some of the main stores include Macy's, Saks, and Gump's. The area also houses many antiquarian bookshops and smaller boutiques.

Victory Monument in Union Square

Union Square marks the edge of the **Theater District** and is bordered on the west side by the luxurious Westin St. Francis Hotel. At the center of the square there is a bronze statue of the Goddess of Victory, sculpted by Robert Aitken in 1903 to commemorate Admiral Dewey's victory during the Spanish–American War (1898). The former **Circle Gallery** at 140 Maiden Lane was designed by Frank Lloyd Wright as a precursor to his Guggenheim Museum in New York (*see p92*). It is now the Xanadu Art Gallery.

## California's Earthquakes

The San Andreas Fault extends some 600 miles (965 km) along California's coastline and is one of the few sites on earth where an active plate boundary occurs on land. Each year, the Pacific Plate moves 1–1.6 inches (2.5–4 cm). The terrible fire of 1906 that destroyed San Francisco was caused by an earthquake estimated at 7.8 on the Richter scale. More recently, the earthquake of October 1989, south of San Francisco, killed 62 people and caused at least $6 billion worth of damage. In 1994, the Northridge quake, magnitude 6.7, rocked Los Angeles. Scientists predict that the next major earthquake, the "Big One," will hit Southern California.

The San Andreas Fault

Oriental architecture along Grant Avenue, Chinatown

## ⑥ Chinatown

**Map** F3. 🚌 1, 2, 3, 4, 15, 30, 45.
🚋 all three lines go to Chinatown.

An estimated 25,000 Chinese migrants settled in the plaza on Stockton Street during the Gold Rush era of the 1850s (see pp641–2). Today, the district evokes the atmosphere of a bustling southern Chinese town, although the architecture and customs are distinctly American hybrids on a Cantonese theme. The sweatshops, laundries, and cramped apartment buildings that once earned this area the nickname "Golden Ghetto" have been replaced with tidy shops and refurbished residential areas. Cable cars run down two sides of the district.

The ornate Chinatown Gateway, marking the southern entrance to Chinatown, was designed by Clayton Lee as an arch over the start of the main tourist street, **Grant Avenue**. The three-arched structure was inspired by the ceremonial entrances of traditional Chinese villages. It is capped with green roof tiles and a host of propitiatory animals in glazed ceramic.

Dragon lampposts, upturned roofs, and stores selling everything from kites and cooking utensils to antiques, embroidered silks, and gems line Grant Avenue. Most of the buildings were erected after the 1906 earthquake in an Oriental Renaissance style. In the 1830s and 1840s it was the main thoroughfare of Yerba Buena, the village that preceded San Francisco. A plaque at No. 823 marks the site of the first dwelling, a canvas tent that was built in 1835.

To the east of Grant Avenue is the city's original town square, **Portsmouth Plaza**, which was laid out in 1839. In 1846, marines raised the American flag above the plaza, officially seizing the port as part of the United States. Two years later, it was here that Sam Brannan announced the discovery of gold in the Sierra Nevada Mountains (see pp706–707). It soon became the hub of the new booming city in the 1850s. Today, Portsmouth Plaza is the social hub of Chinatown. In the morning, people practice tai chi, and from noon to evening, gather to play cards.

Running parallel to Grant Avenue, **Stockton Street** is where locals shop. Boxes of the freshest vegetables, fish, and other produce spill over onto crowded sidewalks. The Kong Chow Temple, located here, features fine Cantonese wood carvings.

Chinatown's busy alleys, located between Grant Avenue and Stockton Street, echo with authentic sights and sounds of the Orient. The largest of the four narrow lanes is Waverly Place, also known as the "Street of Painted Balconies." Watch for the Tin How Temple, which is brightly decorated with hundreds of gold and red lanterns. Nearby, Ross Alley has the tiny Fortune Cookie Factory, where visitors can see how the famous San Francisco creation is made. The alleys have many old buildings as well as old-fashioned herbalist shops, displaying elk antlers, sea horses, snake wine, and other exotic wares. Numerous small restaurants, above and below street level, serve cheap and delicious food. The **Chinese Historical Society** has a range of fascinating exhibits including a ceremonial dragon costume and a "tiger fork," a triton that

Dragon's Head at the Chinese Historical Society

was wielded in one of the battles during the reign of terror known as the Tong Wars. The Tongs were rival Chinese clans who fought over the control of gambling and prostitution in the city in the late 19th century. Other artifacts, documents, and photographs illuminate the daily life of Chinese immigrants in San Francisco from the 1600s to the present day. Among these is a yearbook written in Chinese.

**🏛 Chinese Historical Society**
965 Clay St. **Tel** (415) 391-1188. 🚌 1, 30, 45. 🚋 Powell St. **Open** noon–5pm Tue–Fri, 11am–4pm Sat. **Closed** public hols. ♿ 📷 🌐 chsa.org

## Cable Cars

The cable car system was launched in 1873, with its inventor Andrew Hallidie riding in the first car. He was inspired to tackle the problem of transporting people up the city's steep slopes after seeing an accident, where a horse-drawn tram slipped down a hill.

One of the city's cable cars

His system was a success, and by 1889 cable cars were running on eight lines. Before the 1906 earthquake, over 600 cars were in use. With the advent of the internal combustion engine, however, they became obsolete, and in 1947 attempts were made to replace them with buses. After a huge public outcry, the present three lines were retained.

# ⑦ Nob Hill

**Map** E3. 🚌 1, 12, 30, 45, 83. 🚋 California St, Powell–Mason, Powell–Hyde.

Nob Hill is the highest summit of the city itself, rising 338 ft (103 m) above the bay. It is San Francisco's most celebrated hilltop, famous for its cable cars, plush hotels, and views. The steep slopes kept prominent citizens away until the opening of the California Street cable car line in 1878. The rich then flocked to build homes here, including the "Big Four" railroad barons, who were among its richest tenants. The name "Nob Hill" is thought to come from the Indian word *nabob*, meaning "chieftain". Sadly, all the grand mansions were leveled in the great earthquake and fire of 1906. The only building that survived was the home of James C. Flood, which is now the Pacific Union Club.

Nob Hill still attracts the affluent to its hotels, which recall the opulence of the Victorian era and offer fine views of the city. **Grace Cathedral** is the main Episcopal church in San Francisco. Designed by Lewis P. Hobart, this building was inspired by Notre Dame in Paris. Preparatory work began in 1928, but the cathedral was not completed until 1964. Its entrance doors are cast from molds of Ghiberti's "Doors of Paradise," made for the Baptistry in Florence.

A short distance north of Nob Hill is the **Cable Car Barn**, erected in 1909, which garages cable cars at night. It is a repair shop, museum, and power-house of the cable car system. Anchored to the ground floor are the engines and wheels that wind the cables through the system of channels and pulleys beneath the city's streets. Visitors can observe them from the mezzanine, then walk down to look under the street. The museum also houses an early cable car and the mechanisms that control individual cars.

🏛 **Grace Cathedral**
1100 California St. **Tel** (415) 749-6300. 🕐 Choral evensong: see website for schedule; Choral Eucharist: 11am Sun. 🔲 **gracecathedral.org**

🏛 **Cable Car Barn**
1201 Mason St. **Tel** (415) 474-1887. **Open** summer: 10am–6pm daily; winter: 10am–5pm daily. **Closed** Jan 1, Easter, Thanksgiving, Dec 25. ♿ mezzanine only. Video show: 🎬 🔲 **cablecarmuseum.com**

## Grace Cathedral

The interior of this Gothic-style cathedral is replete with marble and beautiful stained glass. The leaded windows were designed by Charles Connick, using the blue glass of Chartres as his inspiration. The rose window has thick faceted glass, which is illuminated from the inside at night. Other windows are by Henry Willet and Gabriel Loire, and include depictions of Albert Einstein and astronaut John Glenn. The cathedral also features a 13th-century Catalonian crucifix and a 16th-century Brussels tapestry, and is popular for its choral evensong; check website for schedule.

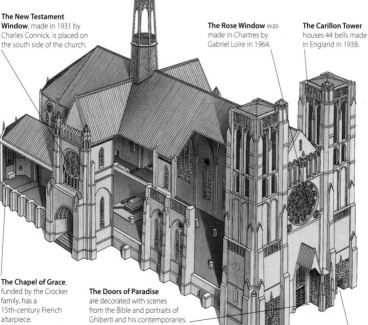

**The New Testament Window**, made in 1931 by Charles Connick, is placed on the south side of the church.

**The Rose Window** was made in Chartres by Gabriel Loire in 1964.

**The Carillon Tower** houses 44 bells made in England in 1938.

**The Chapel of Grace**, funded by the Crocker family, has a 15th-century French altarpiece.

**The Doors of Paradise** are decorated with scenes from the Bible and portraits of Ghiberti and his contemporaries.

Entrances

Shops and amusements at Pier 39, Fisherman's Wharf

## ⑧ Fisherman's Wharf

**Map** E2. Between the coastline & Beach St. 🚌 15, 19, 25, 30, 32, 39, 42, 45, 47. 🚋 Powell–Mason, Powell–Hyde.

Italian seafood restaurants have replaced fishing as the primary focus of Fisherman's Wharf. Fishermen from Genoa and Sicily first arrived here in the late 19th century and founded San Francisco's fishing industry. Since the 1950s, the area has given way to tourism, although brightly colored boats still set out to sea early each morning. The specialty here is the delicious Dungeness crab.

**Pier 39** is the Wharf's hub, with restaurants, shops, and specialty stores, set against a backdrop of stunning bay views. Refurbished in 1978 to resemble a quaint wooden fishing village, the pier is also home to groups of sea lions that bask on the docks. Docked at Pier 45 is the World War II submarine **USS** *Pampanito*, which fought several battles in the Pacific, sinking six enemy ships. Visitors can tour the torpedo room, galley, and officers' quarters. To its south on Jefferson Street is **Ripley's Believe It Or Not! Museum**, which displays the cartoonist's collection of curiosities – one of which is a cable car built of 275,000 matchsticks. Farther along Jefferson Street, **The Cannery**, earlier a fruit processing factory, now houses a mall with restaurants, museums, and shops. The **San Francisco Maritime National Historical Park** incorporates a museum on Beach Street, which displays various nautical objects, and hosts visiting exhibitions. The park also includes a large collection of old ships moored at the nearby **Hyde Street Pier**. Among the finest is the *C.A. Thayer*, a three-masted schooner built in 1895.

## ⑨ North Beach

**Map** E2. 🚌 15, 30, 39, 45. 🚋 Powell–Mason, Powell–Hyde.

South of Fisherman's Wharf is North Beach, also known as "Little Italy." Settlers from Chile, China, and Italy brought their enthusiasm for nightlife to the area, earning North Beach its vibrant reputation and attracting bohemians and writers, including the leading chronicler of the "Beat generation," Jack Kerouac.

At the junction of Broadway and Columbus Avenue, the **City Lights Bookstore**, once owned by the Beat poet Lawrence Ferlinghetti, was the first bookshop in the US to sell only paperbacks. **Vesuvio**, south of City Lights, was one of the most popular Beat bars. Welsh poet Dylan Thomas was a patron here, and it is still a favorite with poets and artists. The **Condor Club** is located on a stretch of Broadway known as The Strip, noted for its "adult entertainment." This landmark establishment was where the area's first topless show was staged in June 1964. **Caffè Trieste**, on the corner of Vallejo Street, is the oldest coffeehouse in San Francisco and a genuine Beat rendezvous since 1956. Very much a part of Italian-American culture, it offers live opera on Saturday afternoons.

**Lombard Street**, a little to the north, is renowned as "the crookedest street in the world." Banked at a natural incline of 27 degrees, this hill proved too steep for vehicles to climb. In the 1920s the section close to the summit of Russian Hill was revamped, and eight tight curves were added. There are spectacular views of San Francisco from the summit, especially at night. Close by, the **San Francisco Art Institute** is famous for its Diego Rivera Gallery, which contains an outstanding mural by the famous Mexican muralist created in 1931.

The 210-ft **Coit Tower** lies at the top of Telegraph Hill. The lobby has many Depression-era murals.

---

### San Francisco's Murals

Coit Tower's mural of Fisherman's Wharf in the 1930s

San Francisco's cosmopolitan heritage comes alive in the bright murals that decorate walls and public places in several parts of the city. Life in the metropolis is one of the major themes. The Mission District has over 200 murals showing every aspect of daily life on the walls of restaurants, banks, and schools. Many of these were painted in the 1970s, when the city and various public bodies commissioned many public works of art. One of the best is the *Carnaval Mural* on 24th Street. The city also has three major murals by Diego Rivera, the Mexican artist who revived fresco painting in the 1930s and 1940s.

Cars negotiating Lombard Street, "the crookedest street in the world"

# ⑩ Alcatraz Island

*Alcatraz* means "pelican" in Spanish and refers to the first inhabitants of this rocky, steep-sided island. In 1859, the US Army established a fort here that guarded San Francisco Bay until 1907, when it became a military prison. From 1934 to 1963 it served as a maximum-security federal penitentiary. Dubbed "The Rock" by prisoners, it housed an average of 264 of the country's most infamous criminals, who were transferred here for disobedience while serving time in prisons elsewhere in the US. Today, Alcatraz is part of the Golden Gate National Recreation Area.

**VISITORS' CHECKLIST**

**Practical Information**
**Tel** (415) 981-7625 or online for tickets & schedules. **Open** daily: first ferry 9am; last ferry 2:15pm (4:15pm in summer). **Closed** Jan 1, Dec 25. ℹ️ Night tours: (415) 981-7625. ♿ accessible in places. 📷 📷 🎞️ Film presentation: free with ticket.
🌐 alcatrazcruises.com

**Transport**
🚢 from Pier 33.

**The Cell Block** Prisoners spent between 16 and 23 hours every day alone in stark cells, equipped with only a toilet and bunk. Many cells measured 5 ft by 9 ft (1.5 m by 2.7 m).

Water tower

Prison workshops

Military morgue

Military parade ground

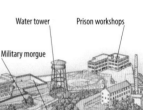

The Post Exchange

Electric maintenance shop

The Military Dorm

The Pier

**The Visitor Center** is in the barracks building behind the jetty. It houses an information center, bookstore, exhibits, and a multimedia show providing a historical overview of Alcatraz.

**Alcatraz from the ferry**
Looming ominously out of the ocean, "The Rock" promised its inmates strict discipline and constant vigilance.

**Exercise Yard**
Meals and a walk around the exercise yard were the highlights of a prisoner's day. This walled yard appeared in films that were shot here.

## Famous Inmates of Alcatraz Island

**Al Capone**
Al Capone was convicted in 1934 for income tax evasion and spent much of his five-year sentence at Alcatraz in an isolation cell. He left the prison mentally unstable.

**Robert Stroud**
Stroud spent most of his 17 years here in solitary confinement. Despite assertions to the contrary in the film *The Birdman of Alcatraz* (1962), he was forbidden from keeping birds in his cell.

**Anglin Brothers**
John and Clarence Anglin and Frank Morris chipped through the walls of their cells, hiding the holes with cardboard grates. They made a raft to escape and were never caught. Their story was dramatized in the film *Escape from Alcatraz* (1979).

**George Kelly**
George "Machine Gun" Kelly was the prison's most dangerous inmate and has the singular distinction of serving 17 years for kidnapping and extortion.

Haas-Lilienthal House in Pacific Heights, an 1886 Queen Anne mansion

## ⑪ Pacific Heights

**Map** D3. ▦ 1, 3, 12, 19, 22, 24, 27, 28, 29, 30, 42, 43, 45, 47, 49, 83. 🚋 California St.

The steep blocks between **Alta Plaza** and **Lafayette Park** are set in the heart of the exclusive Pacific Heights district. After cable cars linked it with the downtown area in the 1880s, it quickly became a desirable place to live, and many palatial Victorian houses line its quiet streets. Some date from the late 19th century, while others were built after the devastating earthquake and fire of 1906.

The **Haas-Lilienthal House**, an elaborate Queen Anne-style mansion, was built in 1886 for the merchant William Haas. Furnished in Victorian style, it is the only intact private home of the period that opens regularly as a museum. It houses the headquarters of the Architectural Heritage Foundation. The impressive **Spreckels Mansion** on Washington Street, constructed on the lines of a French Baroque palace, is now home to best-selling novelist Danielle Steele. Close by, Lafayette Park is one of San Francisco's loveliest hilltop gardens, lined with pine and eucalyptus trees. It offers excellent views of the numerous Victorian houses in the surrounding streets. Located across the street from the park, **2151 Sacramento Street** is an ornate French-style mansion, which has a plaque commemorating a visit by the famous author Sir Arthur Conan Doyle in 1923. At the center of

Pacific Heights is Alta Plaza, a landscaped urban park, where the San Franciscan elite come to relax. Set up in the 1850s, this hilltop green has tennis courts and a playground. The stone steps rising from Clay Street on the south side offer views of Haight Ashbury.

North of Pacific Heights, the streets drop steeply down to the Marina District, which was created from reclaimed land for the 1915 Panama–Pacific Exposition. The Expo's only surviving monument is the grand **Palace of Fine Arts**. This Neo-Classical building has a large rotunda with allegorical paintings on its dome. It houses the entertaining **Exploratorium Science Museum** and hosts events such as the May Film Festival.

**🏛 Haas-Lilienthal House**
2007 Franklin St. **Tel** (415) 441-3004. **Open** noon–3pm Wed & Sat, 11am–4pm Sun. 🦽 📷
🌐 sfheritage.org

## ⑫ Asian Art Museum

**Map** E4. 200 Larkin St. **Tel** (415) 581-3500. ▦ 5, 8, 19, 21, 26, 42, 47, 49. 🚋 F, J, K, L, M, N. **Open** 10am–5pm Tue–Sun (until 9pm Thu). 🦽 📷
📷 📧 🌐 asianart.org

The Asian Art Museum is located on Civic Center Plaza in a building that was the crown jewel of the Beaux Arts movement. The former Main Library, built in 1917, has undergone seismic strengthening and adaptive reuse of space to create the largest museum outside Asia devoted exclusively to Asian art. The museum's exhibits include 12,000 art objects spanning 6,000 years of history and representing over 40 Asian nations. There are also performance venues, education programs, and a hands-on discovery center. The terrace café overlooks the Civic Center and Fulton Street Mall.

The grand staircase at the Asian Art Museum

### The Sounds of 1960s San Francisco

During the late 1960s, and most notably during the 1967 "Summer of Love," young people from all over the country flocked to the

A 1960s street scene in Haight Ashbury

Haight Ashbury district. They came not just to "turn on, tune in, and drop out," but also to listen to rock bands such as Janis Joplin's Big Brother and the Holding Company, Jefferson Airplane, and the Grateful Dead, all of whom emerged out of the thriving music scene. Impresario Bill Graham put unlikely pairs such as Miles Davis and the Grateful Dead on the same bill at Fillmore Auditorium. He also brought in big-name performers such as Jimi Hendrix and The Who, making "the Haight" the focus of the rock world.

## ⑬ Mission Dolores

**Map** E4. 3321 16th St. ⬚ 22. ⬚ J. ⓘ
(415) 621-8203. **Open** 9am–4pm daily.
**Closed** Jan 1, Thanksg, Dec 25. ⬚ ⬚
⬚ ⬚ missiondolores.org

Preserved intact since it was built in 1791, Mission Dolores, after which the surrounding Mission District is named, is the oldest building in the city and an embodiment of San Francisco's Spanish Colonial roots. Founded by Father Junípero Serra as the sixth California mission, it is formally known as the Mission of San Francisco de Asis. The name Dolores reflects its proximity to Laguna de los Dolores (Lake of Our Lady of Sorrows), an ancient swamp. The building is modest by mission standards, but its 4-ft- (1.2-m-) thick walls have survived. Paintings by Native

**Figure of saint in the Mission**

Americans adorn the restored ceiling. There is a fine Baroque altar and reredos, and a display of historical documents in the small museum. Most services are held in the basilica, built adjacent to the mission in 1918. The cemetery contains graves of San Franciscan pioneers, as well as a mass grave of 5,000 Native Americans, who died in the measles epidemics of 1804 and 1826.

The altarpiece of Mission Dolores, imported from Mexico in 1780

Ceramic mural

**The statue** of Father Junípero Serra is a copy of the work of local sculptor Arthur Putnam.

**The cemetery** extended across many streets. Today, the Lourdes Grotto commemorates the forgotten dead.

Entrance and gift shop

The mission façade

## ⑭ Haight Ashbury

**Map** D4. ⬚ 6, 7, 33, 37, 43, 66, 71.
⬚ N. Lower Haight: ⬚ 6, 7, 22, 66, 71. ⬚ K, L, M.

Stretching from Buena Vista Park to Golden Gate Park, Haight Ashbury was the center of the hippie world in the 1960s. Originally a quiet, middle-class suburb – hence the dozens of elaborate Queen Anne-style houses – it changed dramatically into the mecca of a free-wheeling, bohemian community that defied social norms and conventions. In 1967, the "Summer of Love," fueled by the media, brought some 75,000 young people in search of free love, music, and drugs, and it became the focus of a worldwide youth culture. Thousands lived here, and there was even a free clinic to treat hippies without medical insurance.

Today, "the Haight" retains its radical atmosphere and has settled into being one of

the liveliest and most unconventional places in San Francisco, with an eclectic mix of people, second-hand clothing shops, renowned music and bookstores, and a variety of excellent cafés.

Buena Vista Park on its eastern fringe has a mass of knotted trees and offers magnificent views of the city. The grand (Richard) Spreckels Mansion on Buena Vista Avenue (not to be confused with the one on Washington Street) is a typical

The Red Victorian B&B in Haight Ashbury, a relic of the hippie era

late Victorian home. It was once a guest house, and its visitors included writer Jack London and journalist Ambrose Bierce. The **Red Victorian B&B**, affectionately dubbed the "Jeffrey Haight" in 1967, was a favorite among hippies. It now caters to a New Age clientele and offers rooms with transcendental themes.

Halfway between City Hall and Haight Ashbury, the **Lower Haight** marks the border of the predominantly African-American Fillmore District, which is one of the liveliest parts of the city. Unusual art galleries, boutiques, inexpensive cafés, and bars serve a largely bohemian clientele. It also has dozens of houses known as "Victorians," built from the 1850s to the 1900s, including cottages such as the Nightingale House at 201 Buchanan Street. Although safe during the day, the Lower Haight can be unnerving after dark.

## ⑮ California Academy of Sciences

**Map** C4. 55 Music Concourse Dr, Golden Gate Park. **Tel** (415) 379-8000. 🚌 44. **Open** 9:30am–5pm Mon–Sat, 11am–5pm Sun. **Closed** Thanksgiving, Dec 25. some areas. 🔣 🖥 🎞 📷 ✏
🌐 calacademy.org

Founded in 1853, California Academy of Sciences is San Francisco's oldest and most popular science museum. After 10 years of renovation, the museum reopened in 2008. Designed by Renzo Piano, the building is encased in glass walls that allow natural light to stream in. Among the building's most impressive features is a 197,000-sq-ft (18,300-sq-m) rooftop with a living tapestry of native plant species. An open-air terrace gives visitors a close-up view of the plants and is an ideal location for watching Northern California's birds, butterflies, and insects. Skylights above the larger domes open and close throughout the day, enabling sunlight to reach the exhibits below.

The **African Hall**, known for its majestic dioramas, first opened in 1934 and gives

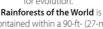
*Tyrannosaurus rex skeleton*

visitors an in-depth look into the continent's diverse eco-systems. This has been faithfully re-created in the modern building, with some surprises, including 16 dioramas show-casing mounted animals, such as lions, zebras, and baboons.

The **Altered State** exhibit explores the dangerous effects of climate change on California's natural habitats and the planet at large. **Islands of Evolution** is an exhibit exploring the remote islands of Madagascar and the Galapagos through the eyes of Academy scientists. Visitors can examine specimens collected during past exhibitions, such as Galapagos tortoise shells and Darwin's famous finches; use Wii gaming wands to collect virtual insects; and learn how islands function as living laboratories for evolution.

**Rainforests of the World** is contained within a 90-ft- (27-m-) diameter glass dome, the world's largest spherical rainforest exhibit. The rainforest is teeming with 1,600 live animals, including 250 free-flying birds and butterflies, 100 exotic reptiles and amphibians, and a cave full of bats. Each level represents a different rainforest around the world, such as Borneo, Madagascar, Costa Rica, and the Amazon.

The **Morrison Planetarium** is the world's largest all-digital planetarium, with a 75-ft- (23-m-) diameter dome projection screen re-creating the night sky. Popular shows are "Life: A Cosmic Story" and "Tour of the Universe."

The enchanting **Steinhart Aquarium**, the oldest and one of the most diverse aquariums in the US, houses over 38,000 live animals, representing more than 900 separate species.

Lifelike dioramas in the African Hall of the California Academy of Sciences

## ⑯ de Young Museum

**Map** C4. 50 Hagiwara Tea Garden Dr. **Tel** (415) 863-3330. 🚌 44. **Open** 9:30am–5:15pm Tue–Sun (until 8:45pm Fri mid-Jan–Nov). **Closed** Mon. 🎞 (free 1st Tue of month). 🔣 🛅 🖥 🎞 ✏
🌐 famsf.org

The de Young Museum was founded in 1895 and has been an integral part of Golden Gate Park for more than 100 years. In 1989 the building suffered irreparable damage from an earthquake and the old building closed to make way for a new, seismically stable one. The museum, which opened in 2005, has double the exhibition space of the old one, but returns nearly 2 acres (0.8 ha) of open space to the Park.

The de Young's permanent collection comprises American art from the 17th to the 20th centuries as well as work from nearly 30 countries. There are also special exhibitions held regularly, and outside, there's a sculpture garden and terrace, and a children's garden.

## ⑰ Legion of Honor

**Map** C4. 34th Ave & Clement, Lincoln Park. **Tel** (415) 750-3600. 🚌 18. ℹ (415) 863-3330. **Open** 9:30am–5:15pm Tue–Sun. **Closed** Mon. 🎞 (free 1st Tue of month). 🔣 🛅 🖥 🎞 ✏ 🌐 famsf.org

Inspired by the Palais de la Légion d'Honneur in Paris, Alma de Bretteville Spreckels built this museum in the 1920s to promote French art in California. Designed by the architect George Applegarth, it displays European art from the last eight centuries, with paintings by Rembrandt, Monet, and Rubens, and more than 70 sculptures by Rodin. The Achenbach Foundation, a well-known collection of graphic works, occupies a part of the gallery.

The museum's collection of European art is displayed in the galleries on the first floor. The portrait *The Impresario*

(1877), by Edgar Degas emphasizes the subject's size by making him appear too large for the frame. Claude Monet's beautiful *Waterlilies* (1914–17) is one of a series depicting the lily pond in his gardens in Giverny, near Paris. The original bronze casting of Rodin's *Le Penseur* (1904), better known as *The Thinker*, is located at the center of the colonnaded Court of Honor. It is one of the 11 castings of the statue in collections around the world.

## ⑱ The Presidio

**Map** C3. Visitor Center: 105 Montgomery St. **Tel** (415) 561-4323. **Open** 10am–4pm Thu–Sun. **Closed** public hols. ♿ Ⓦ nps.gov

To the north of Golden Gate Park, overlooking San Francisco Bay, the Presidio was established as an outpost of Spain's New World empire in 1776. For many years it was a military base, but in 1994 it became a national park, with acres of woodland full of wildlife. There are also many hiking trails, bike paths, and beaches. The coastal path is very popular.

The Presidio Museum is part of the **Mott Visitor Center** in the Main Post area. It houses artifacts relating to the Presidio's long history. Close by, the **Officers' Club** was built over the adobe remains of the original 18th-century Spanish fort, still preserved inside the building. A 19th-century cannon from the Spanish–American War lies across the adjoining parade ground.

To the north, close to the bay, is the large, grassy **Crissy Field**, which was reclaimed from marshland for the 1915 Panama-Pacific Exposition. The **Military Cemetery**, east of the visitor center, holds the remains of 15,000 US soldiers killed during various wars.

The northwestern tip of the Presidio, **Fort Point** is an impressive brick fortress that once guarded the Golden Gate

Detail of the 19th-century cannon located on the Presidio grounds

during the Civil War and also survived the 1906 earthquake. The fort was built in 1861 to protect the bay from attack, and to defend ships carrying gold from the California mines. It is a good place from which to view Golden Gate Bridge and there is also a museum displaying military uniforms and arms.

Detail, Arguello Gate

## ⑲ Golden Gate Bridge

**Map** B2. Hwy 101, Presidio. **Tel** (415) 923-2000. 🚌 2, 4, 8, 10, 18, 20, 28, 29, 50, 72, 76, 80. Pedestrians & cyclists allowed during daylight hours, east walkway only. ♿ observation area only. 📷
Ⓦ goldengatebridge.org

Named after the part of San Francisco Bay called "Golden Gate" by John Frémont in 1844, the Golden Gate Bridge opened in 1937, connecting the city with Marin County. It took just over four years to build, at a cost of $35 million. This world-famous landmark offers breathtaking views; the bridge has six lanes for vehicles, a free pedestrian walkway, and it also has a cycle lane. Each year, more than 40 million vehicles

cross it, averaging a daily count of about 118,000. It is the world's third-largest single-span bridge, stretching 1.7 miles (2.7 km). When it was built, it was the world's longest and tallest suspension structure.

Designed by engineers Joseph Strauss and Leon Moisseiff, the mammoth structure was built to withstand 100 mph (160 km/h) winds. Its south pier was sunk into the seabed, while each pier supports a steel tower, built upon a concrete fender. The original coat of paint lasted for 27 years, but since 1965 it has needed continuous painting. The two cables contain enough steel wire to circle the earth at the equator three times. The best views are seen from Marin County.

At the foot of the bridge, the **Bay Area Discovery Museum** is the only children's museum in the US to be located in a national park. It offers hands-on art, science, and environmental exhibitions, performances, special events, and cultural festivals for children aged from 6 months to 8 years.

🏛 **Bay Area Discovery Museum** 557 McReynolds Rd, Sausalito. **Tel** (415) 339-3900. **Open** 9am–5pm Tue–Sun. ♿ 🖤 📷 Ⓦ baykidsmuseum.org

The Golden Gate Bridge, with a single span of 4,200 ft (1,280 m)

# Greater San Francisco

Many of the settlements encircling San Francisco Bay were once summer retreats for the city's residents, but today they are sprawling suburbs or cities in their own right. Two popular destinations in the East Bay are Oakland's museum and Berkeley's famous university. The landmark San Francisco–Oakland Bay Bridge stretches 4.5 miles (7.2 km) and is crossed by 250,000 vehicles a day – even more than the Golden Gate. Farther south, San Jose combines the technology of Silicon Valley with fine museums and Spanish Colonial architecture. To the north is the rocky coastline of the Marin Headlands, with its abundant wildlife.

The Thinker by Auguste Rodin at the Stanford Museum of Art

## ⑳ San Jose

846,000. ✈ 🚉 65 Cahill St. 🚌 70 Almeden Blvd. 🛈 408 Almaden Blvd, (800) 726-5673, (408) 295-9600. 🎭 Festival of the Arts (Sep). 🌐 sanjose.org

The only other original Spanish Colonial town in California apart from Los Angeles, San Jose was founded in 1777 by Felipe de Neve and has become the state's third-largest city. It is now the commercial and cultural center of South Bay and the civic heart of Silicon Valley.

The **Mission Santa Clara de Asis**, on the campus of the Jesuit University of Santa Clara, is a modern replica of the adobe original, first built in 1777. Relics include bells given to the missionaries by the Spanish monarchy. The large **Rosicrucian Egyptian Museum and Planetarium** has an extensive collection of ancient Egyptian artifacts. Displays include mummies, burial tombs, and toys, some of which date to 1500 BC. There are replicas of the sarcophagus in which Tutankhamen was discovered in 1922, and the Rosetta Stone.

At the heart of San Jose, the fascinating **Tech Museum of Innovation** is crowded with hands-on exhibits, encouraging visitors to discover how technological inventions work. Here, the focus is on understanding the workings of computer hardware and software.

The **Winchester Mystery House**, on the outskirts of town, has a remarkable history. Sarah Winchester, widow and heiress of the Winchester Rifle fortune, was told by a medium that the expansion of her farmhouse would exorcise the spirits of those killed by the rifle. She kept builders working 24 hours a day, 7 days a week, for 38 years, until her death in 1922. The result is a bizarre complex of 160 rooms, including stairs that lead nowhere and windows set into floors. The total cost amounted to $5.5 million. The center of the computer industry, **Silicon Valley** covers about 100 sq miles (260 sq km) from Palo Alto to San Jose. The name refers to myriad businesses rather than a specific location. The seeds of the hardware and software industries were sown in the 1980s at Stanford University, at the Xerox Palo Alto Research Center, and in the garages of pioneers William Hewlett, David Packard, and later Steve Jobs and Stephen Wozniak, who invented the Apple personal computer.

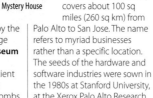

Organ, Winchester Mystery House

🏛 **Winchester Mystery House**
525 S Winchester Blvd. **Tel** (408) 247-2100. **Open** check for times.
**Closed** Dec 25. 🎟 ♿ gardens only.
📷 🎬 🖥 🌐 winchestermystery house.com

## ㉑ Palo Alto

Stanford University: **Tel** (650) 723-2560. Palo Alto Visitor Center: 400 Mitchell Lane. **Open** 9am–5pm Mon–Sat, (650) 324-3121.

Among the most pleasant of the Bay Area suburbs, Palo Alto grew up to serve Stanford University, one of the most reputed centers of education in the US. It was founded in 1891 by the railroad tycoon Leland Stanford in honor of his son, who died at the age of 16. The campus covers 8,200 acres (3,320 ha) and is larger than the downtown district of San Francisco. Designed in a mixture of Romanesque and Mission styles, its sandstone buildings are capped by red-tiled roofs. The Memorial Church is decorated with gold-leaf and tile mosaic. The **Stanford Museum of Art** holds one of the largest collections of sculptures by Auguste Rodin, including the impressive Gates of Hell.

## ㉒ Oakland

387,000. ✈ 🚉 463 11th St. 🛈 (510 839-9000). 🎭 Festival at the Lake (Jun). 🌐 visitoakland.org

At one time a small, working-class suburb of San Francisco, Oakland grew into a flourishing city when it became the West Coast terminus of the transcontinental railroad. Many of the African-Americans who worked on the railroad settled here, later followed by the Hispanics, giving Oakland a multicultural atmosphere that continues to this day. Its literary associations, including Jack London and Gertrude Stein, have also enhanced the area as a cultural center.

**Jack London Square** on the waterfront was named after author Jack London, who grew up in Oakland in the 1880s and frequently visited the area. Today, it is a bright promenade of shops, restaurants, and pleasure boats. The Jack London Museum contains books, photographs, and memorabilia. To the east is the **Oakland Museum of California**, which has undergone a $53 million renovation program. The museum is dedicated to documenting the state's art, history, and ecology, and is famous for its early oil paintings of San Francisco and Yosemite.

To the north, the two blocks of **Old Oakland** (also known as Victorian Row) attract crowds of shoppers. Northern California's only **Mormon Temple**, situated on a hilltop on the eastern edge of the city, offers great views of the Bay Area. Its central ziggurat is surrounded by four towers, all clad with white granite and capped with golden pyramids.

🏛 **Oakland Museum of California**
1000 Oak St. 🛈 (510) 318-8400. **Open** 11am–5pm Wed–Sun (until 9pm Fri). **Closed** Mon & Tue, Jan 1, Thanksgiving, Dec 25. 🎟 (free 2nd Sun). ♿ 🏛 📷 🖥 🅦 **museumca.org**

## ㉒ Berkeley

🏔 104,900. ✈ 🚌 🚉 2160 Shattuck Ave. 🛈 2030 Addison St, (800) 847-4823 🎆 Fourth of July Fireworks; Telegraph Ave Book Fair (Jul). 🅦 **visitberkeley.com**

Berkeley began to boom after the earthquake of 1906, when many San Franciscans fled their city and settled on the East Bay. It was the seat of the student uprisings against the Vietnam War in the 1960s, earning itself the nickname "Beserkeley." Many

Model of DNA at the Lawrence Hall of Science, UC Berkeley

stores still hark to the hippie era with psychedelic merchandise, but in recent years Berkeley has begun to change its profile. Stylish restaurants have emerged, as well as a reputation for fine food; it was here that the popular California cuisine was born.

Berkeley is essentially a university town. The **University of California at Berkeley's** reputation for countercultural movements sometimes eclipses its academic reputation, yet, with its student body of 30,000, it is one of the country's most prestigious institutions. Founded in 1868, it has at least ten Nobel laureates among its professors. There are many museums, cultural amenities, and noteworthy buildings to visit. The **University Art Museum** includes works by Piccasso and Cézanne among its exhibits. The main campus landmark, the 307-ft (94-m) **Sather Tower**, and the splendid **Lawrence Hall of Science** are both outstanding.

To the south, the **Telegraph Avenue** was the center of student protest in the 1960s. Today, there is a plethora of bookstores, coffeehouses, and cheap eateries. North of the University, **Shattuck Avenue**, nicknamed "Gourmet Ghetto," is known for its restaurants.

🎓 **University of California at Berkeley**
**Tel** (510) 642-5215. Berkeley Art Museum & Pacific Film Archive: **Tel** (510) 642-1412. **Open** 11am–5pm Wed–Sun (until 9pm Thu). **Closed** public hols. 🎟 ♿ 🅦 **berkeley.edu**

## ㉔ Sausalito

🏔 7,300. 🚌 🚌 🚤 🛈 777 Bridgeway Ave, 4th floor, (415) 332-0505. 🅦 **sausalito.org**

In this small town, Victorian bungalows cling to hills rising from San Francisco Bay. Bridgeway Avenue along the waterfront serves as a promenade for crowds that patronize the restaurants and shops and enjoy the views. The **Bay Model Visitor Center** is a fascinating model simulating the tides in San Francisco Bay.

🏠 **Bay Model Visitor Center**
2100 Bridgeway Ave. **Tel** (415) 332-3871. **Open** 9am–4pm Tue–Sat. **Closed** Sun & Mon, public hols.

## ㉕ Muir Woods

🚌 Mill Valley. Visitor Center: Hwy 1, Mill Valley, (415) 388-2595. **Open** 8am–5pm daily 🅦 **nps.gov**

Nestling at the foot of Mount Tamalpais is Muir Woods National Monument, one of the few remaining stands of old-growth coastal redwoods. Before the 19th-century lumber industry boom, these tall trees (the oldest is 1,000 years old) covered the Californian coastline. The woods were named in honor of John Muir, the naturalist responsible for turning Yosemite into a national park (see pp706–707). Muir Beach nearby is a wide expanse of sand.

Muir Woods, the last remaining redwood forest in the Bay Area

# San Francisco Practical Information

San Francisco occupies a compact area, making it a sightseer's dream. Its efficient transportation system has cable cars, buses, streetcars, Muni Metro, and BART lines. The city prides itself on its variety of cultural and entertainment opportunities, which make it one of the most enjoyable vacation spots in the world. The Civic Center is the main venue for classical music, opera, and ballet, while pop music – in particular, jazz and blues – is where the city really excels. There are also diverse theater companies and specialty movie houses.

## Tourist Information

Visitors planning a trip will find the *San Francisco Visitors Planning Guide*, published by the **San Francisco Convention & Visitors' Bureau**, very helpful. It is available free at the **Visitor Information Center** at Hallidie Plaza. Listings of what's on are given in the *San Francisco Chronicle* and *Examiner* newspapers. Weekly newspapers, such as the *San Francisco Weekly* or the *San Francisco Bay Guardian*, also give listings and reviews of live music, films, and nightclubs.

## Getting Around

The best way to explore San Francisco is on foot, although the hills can be strenuous. The city's main sights all lie within 15 to 20 minutes of each other. City taxis are licensed and operate 24 hours a day. **Green Cab** and Yellow Cab are good bets.

The San Francisco Municipal Railway or **Muni**, runs the city's transportation system. The Muni Passport, valid for 1, 3, or 7 days can be used for unlimited travel on Muni buses, Muni Metro streetcars, as well as San Francisco's three cable car lines. The City Pass can be used for 7 consecutive days of travel on all Muni vehicles, and includes admission to several attractions. Passes are available at the Visitor Information Center.

Buses and streetcars serve all areas. Buses stop only at designated places, every few blocks, and route numbers are printed on the buses. Muni Metro streetcars and BART trains both use the same underground terminals on Market Street. The high-speed BART trains stop at five downtown stations: Van Ness, Civic Center, Powell, Montgomery, and Embarcadero.

San Francisco's famous cable cars operate from 6:30am to 12:30am daily, at 15-minute intervals. Cars run on three routes: the popular Powell–Hyde line, the Powell–Mason line, and the California line.

Boats and passenger ferries are also a fun way to get around the city's shoreline. The Ferry Building is the terminal for the **Golden Gate Ferries**. Bay sightseeing cruises from Fisherman's Wharf are operated by the **Blue & Gold Fleet. Hornblower Dining Yachts** offer various meals on their cruises.

Other modes of travel include bicycles, which can be rented for around $25 a day or $125 a week. Details of scenic routes are available from the **Bike Hut** rental. Pedicabs and horse-drawn cabs are found on the Embarcadero. Sightseeing bus tours are also available.

## Sports & Outdoor Activities

The city has plenty of options for sports fans. The home ground of the San Francisco 49ers is Monster Park. Other football teams are supported by local colleges, UC Berkeley, and Stanford University. Two professional baseball teams play in the Bay Area: the National League San Francisco Giants (in AT&T Park) and the American League Oakland Athletics (in the McAfee Coliseum).

Golfers have a range of courses to choose from, including the municipal links in **Harding** and **Lincoln Parks**. Most of the public swimming pools are located in the suburbs; for details contact the **City of San Francisco Recreation and Parks Department** (www.parks.sfgov.org). To swim in the chilly ocean, head out to China Beach. There are tennis courts in almost all the public parks, with the largest ones in Golden Gate Park. **Claremont Hotel Club & Spa** in Berkeley offers fine courts with unlimited playing time. There are dozens of running clubs and events in all seasons. The **Golden Gate Running Club** is one of many.

## Entertainment

San Francisco offers visitors an unending variety of high-quality entertainment. It has an avid film-going community, and one of the best movie houses is the **Sundance Kabuki**, an eight-screen complex in the Japan Center, which also hosts the San Francisco **International Film Festival** each May. The main venue for first-run foreign films is the **Opera Plaza** on Van Ness Avenue. For theater goers, major shows are staged at Theater District venues, the two largest being the **Curran Theater** for Broadway shows and the Geary Theater, now home to the **American Conservatory Theater (ACT)**, both on Geary Street.

The **San Francisco Opera** season runs from September to December; tickets can cost over $100, but there is a summer season with less expensive tickets and many free outdoor concerts. The **Civic Center** complex on Van Ness Avenue offers opera, classical music, and dance. The **San Francisco Ballet** season runs from late June through May, while the Yerba Buena Center for the Arts is home to the **LINES Ballet**.

Two of the best rock clubs, **Slim's** and **Paradise Lounge**, are opposite one another in the SoMa district. Another popular place is the **Fillmore Auditorium** on Geary Boulevard, the legendary birthplace of psychedelic rock during the 1960s. Places to hear live jazz include **Yoshi's San Francisco**, and live blues is played in bars such as **The Saloon** on Grant Avenue. The annual **San Francisco Blues Festival** attracts blues bands from all over the country.

The **1015 Folsom** has some of San Francisco's best DJs. The clientele here is mainstream, but some of the most popular clubs are primarily, though rarely exclusively, gay. These include **Rawhide II** on Seventh Street.

Piano bars all have nightly live music. One of the best is the Art Deco-style **Top of the Mark** at the top of the Mark Hopkins InterContinental Hotel on Nob Hill.

San Francisco also has a number of free concerts all over the city. Watch for the **San Francisco Symphony Orchestra** in late summer at Stern Grove and Yerba Buena Gardens. The San Francisco Opera performs in Golden Gate Park in the "Opera in the Park" event. The summer Shakespeare Festival is held in the Presidio.

## Shopping

Shopping in San Francisco is a complete experience that allows a glimpse into the city's culture. The diversity of San Francisco makes buying anything here an adventure. An enormous range of goods is available, from the practical to the more eccentric, but you can take your time in choosing, since browsers are made to feel welcome, particularly in the many small specialty shops and boutiques. Guided shopping tours are available for those who want to be directed to the best shops.

For visitors who want convenience, the numerous shopping centers, such as the Embarcadero Center and Japan Center, are excellent.

Similarly, huge retail department stores such as **Macy's** and **Neiman Marcus** offer an outstanding selection of goods and services.

The city's innovative entrepreneurial spirit is evident in its specialty shops, such as the Chinese-influenced glass art at **LiuLi** or the unusual toys at **Ambassador Toys**. A mecca

for designer wear, the city is home to the famous **Levi Strauss & Co**, which has been making jeans since 1853 and offers factory tours on Tuesdays and Wednesdays to visitors. For discount designer wear, head to the trendy SoMa district.

Book lovers should head for **Green Apple Books**, or the famous Beat hideout **City Lights Bookstore**, which stays open late and is a famous San Francisco institution.

Art lovers will find something to their liking in the city's hundreds of galleries, featuring works by emerging and more established artists as well as expressions of Native American folk artists.

The city is also home to many dedicated "foodies," gastronomes whose liking for fine wine and gourmet meals have resulted in unusual and delicious grocery stores. Regular farmers' markets, held in the center of the city, abound in locally grown fruit and vegetables, while seafood and wines from **Napa Valley Winery Exchange** figure among the city's best buys.

# DIRECTORY

## Tourist Offices

**Visitor Information Center**
900 Market St.
**Tel** (415) 391-2000.
W sanfrancisco.travel

## Transportation

**BART**
W bart.gov

**Blue & Gold Fleet**
**Tel** (415) 205-8200.

**Golden Gate Ferries**
**Tel** (415) 921-5858.
W goldengateferry.org

**Green Cab**
**Tel** (415) 626-4733.
W 626greencab.com

**Muni Information**
W sfmta.com

## Film & Theater

**American Conservatory Theater (ACT)**
**Tel** (415) 749-2228.

**Sundance Kabuki**
1881 Post St. **Tel** (415) 346-3243. W sundance cinemas.com

## Opera, Classical Music & Dance

**LINES Ballet**
26 Seventh St.
**Tel** (415) 863-3040.

**San Francisco Opera**
301 Van Ness Ave.
**Tel** (415) 864-3330.
W sfopera.org

**San Francisco Symphony Orchestra**
201 Van Ness Ave.
**Tel** (415) 864-6000.
W sfsymphony.org

## Jazz

**Yoshi's San Francisco**
1330 Fillmore St.
**Tel** (415) 655-5600.

## Clubs

**1015 Folsom**
1015 Folsom St.
**Tel** (415) 264-1015.

## Sports & Outdoor Activities

**Golden Gate Running Club**
W goldengate runningclub.org

## Shopping

**Ambassador Toys**
186 W Portal Ave.
**Tel** (415) 759-8697.

**Bloomingdale's**
845 Market St.
**Tel** (415) 856-5300.

**City Lights Bookstore**
261 Columbus Ave.
**Tel** (415) 362-8193.

**Green Apple Books**
506 Clement St.
**Tel** (415) 387-2272.

**Levi Strauss & Co**
250 Valencia St.
**Tel** (415) 565-9159.

**LiuLi**
37 Yerba Buena Lane.
**Tel** (415) 979-9588.

**Macy's**
Stockton & O'Farrell Sts.
**Tel** (415) 954-6271.

**Napa Valley Winery Exchange**
415 Taylor St.
**Tel** (415) 771-2887.

**Neiman Marcus**
150 Stockton St.
**Tel** (415) 362-3900.

**Saks Fifth Avenue**
384 Post St.
**Tel** (415) 986-4758.

# The Wine Country

Born in the Sonoma Valley in 1823, when Franciscan priests planted grapes to make sacramental wines, California's wine industry was taken to new heights by the flamboyant Hungarian Count Agoston Haraszthy in 1857. Known as the "Father of California Wine," he planted European grapes in the state's first big vineyard at the revered Buena Vista Winery. Today, in addition to its superb wines and vineyards, the Wine Country is known for its mild climate, rocky landscapes, secluded beaches, redwood groves, and impressive architecture.

Vineyards in the Sonoma Valley, famous for wineries

## ㉒ Sonoma Valley

⛰ 8,600. ✈ 🚌 90 Broadway & W Napa Sts, Sonoma Plaza. 🛈 453 1st St E, (866) 996-1090. 🎭 Valley of the Moon Vintage Festival (late Sep).
🅦 sonomavalley.com

Nestling in the crescent-shaped Sonoma Valley are 6,000 acres (2,400 ha) of beautiful vineyards. At the foot of the valley lies the tiny town of Sonoma. This town has had a colorful past, as it was here, on June 14, 1846, that about 30 American farmers captured Mexican General Mariano Vallejo and his men, to protest the fact that land ownership was reserved for Mexican citizens. They seized control of Sonoma, declared California an independent republic, and flew their own flag, with a crude drawing of a grizzly bear. Although the republic was annulled 25 days later, when the United States annexed California, the Bear Flag design was adopted as the official state flag in 1911.

Sonoma's main attractions are its world-famous wineries and meticulously preserved historical sites lining the Spanish-style plaza. Many of the adobe buildings house wine shops, boutiques, and restaurants serving excellent local cuisine. East of the plaza is the restored **Mission San Francisco Solano de Sonoma**, the last of California's 21 historic Franciscan missions (founded by Father José Altimira of Spain in 1823). Today, all that survives of the original building is the corridor of his quarters. The adobe chapel was built by General Vallejo in 1840.

A short drive northward leads to the **Jack London State Historic Park**. In the early 1900s, London, the famous author of *The Call of the Wild* and *The Sea Wolf*, abandoned his hectic lifestyle to live in this tranquil 800-acre (325-ha) expanse of oaks, madrones, and redwoods. The park retains eerie ruins of London's dream home, the Wolf House, mysteriously destroyed by fire just before completion. After London's death, his widow, Charmian Kittredge, built a magnificent home on the ranch, called the House of Happy Walls. Today, the house has been made into a museum, worth a visit for its display of London memorabilia.

### 🏛 Mission San Francisco Solano de Sonoma

E Spain St. **Tel** (707) 938-9560. **Open** daily. **Closed** Jan 1, Thanksg., Dec 25. 🈲

### 🌳 Jack London Historic State Park

London Ranch Rd, Glen Ellen. **Tel** (707) 938-5216. **Open** 9am–5:30pm daily (Dec–Feb: Thu–Mon only). **Closed** Jan 1, Thanksgiving, Dec 25. 🈲 ♿ museum only. 🄲

## ㉓ Napa Valley

⛰ 115,000. ✈ 🛈 1310 Town Center Mall, Napa, (707) 226-7459. 🎭 Napa Valley Mustard Festival (Feb–Apr).
🅦 napavalley.com

Lying at the heart of California's wine industry, the 35-mile (56-km) sliver of land known as Napa Valley encompasses the towns of Yountville, Oakville, St. Helena, Rutherford, and Calistoga. More than 250 wineries are scattered across its hillsides and valleys, some dating from the early 19th century. Prominent among these is the **Mumm Napa Valley** winery, partly owned by French champagne producer G.H. Mumm, where wines are made in the classic tradition. To its north, the **Rutherford Hill Winery** features caves dug into the hillsides, for aging wines. Farther north, the modern **Clos Pegase** winery is famed for its distinctive art collection and superior wines. For a bird's-eye view of the valley, visitors can take hot-air balloon trips over the Wine Country from Yountville or a 3-hour luxury tour in the Napa Valley Wine Train, enjoying gourmet cuisine. But the best way to explore the valley is along a scenic 40-mile (64-km) drive, stopping along the way at the B&B inns in the towns of St. Helena and Calistoga. The latter is popular

Statue at Clos Pegase

for its spa treatments and good Wine Country cuisine, prepared with the freshest ingredients. A few miles north of Calistoga, the Old Faithful Geyser spouts jets of boiling mineral water 60 ft (18 m) into the sky, once every 40 minutes. To the west lies the **Petrified Forest**, home of the largest petrified trees in the world – huge redwoods which were turned to stone by a volcanic eruption that took place more than three million years ago.

**Petrified Forest**

4100 Petrified Forest Rd. **Tel** (707) 942-6667. **Open** daily. **Closed** Thanksgiving, Dec 25. limited.

The Clos Pegase winery designed by Michael Graves, Napa Valley

## ㉔ Russian River Valley

from Healdsburg. 16209 1st St, Guerneville, (707) 869-9000, (877) 644-9001. **russianriver.com**

Bisected by the Russian River and its tributaries, this valley contains many smaller valleys, dotted with vineyards, apple orchards, redwood groves, family farms, and sandy river beaches. At its hub is the town of **Healdsburg**, with a splendid Spanish-style town square lined with shops, restaurants, and cafés.

Southwest of Healdsburg lies **Guerneville**, a summer haven for San Francisco's gay population. Every September, the town hosts the famous Russian River Jazz Festival at Johnson's Beach, where visitors can take a canoe or raft down the gentle Russian River. Otters and blue herons can often be seen here.

Hikers and equestrians also flock to Guerneville to visit the 805-acre (330-ha) **Armstrong Redwoods State Natural Reserve**, one of the few

remaining old-growth redwood forests in California. Among its redwoods is a 308-ft (94-m) giant – a 1,400-year-old tree named Colonel Armstrong.

**Armstrong Redwoods State Natural Reserve**

17020 Armstrong Woods Rd, Guerneville. **Tel** (707) 869-2015. **Open** daily. **parks.ca.gov**

## ㉕ Fort Ross State Historic Park

**Tel** (707) 847-3286. from Point Arena. 19005 Coast Hwy, Jenner. **Open** 10am–4:30pm Fri–Sun & hols. **Closed** Thanksgiving, Dec 25. **fortross.org**

On a windswept headland north of Jenner stands this well-restored Russian trading outpost, founded in 1812 (the name "Ross" is a derivative of the Russian word *Rossyia*, meaning "Russia"). The Russians were the first Europeans to visit the region, serving as representatives of a Russian-American Company, established in 1799. They never tried to expand their territory in California and abandoned the fort after 30 years of peaceful trading.

Built in 1836, the house of the fort's last manager, Alexander Rotchev, is still intact. Within the wooden palisade are several other reconstructed buildings. The most impressive is the 1824 Russian Orthodox chapel. Every July, a living history day is held with costumed actors.

The town of Mendocino perched on its rocky headlands

## ㉖ Mendocino

1,200. 217 S Main St, Fort Bragg, (707) 961-6300. **mendocinocoast.com**

The founders of this fishing village came to California from New England in 1852, building their new homes to resemble those they had left behind. The Mendocino coastline is thus often referred to as "California's New England Coast." Perched on a rocky promontory above the Pacific Ocean, Mendocino retains the picturesque charm of its days as a fishing center. Its heather-covered bluffs, migrating gray whales, and stunning ocean vistas make it a popular tourist center, yet the town seems untarnished by commercialism. It is a thriving arts center with a large number of resident artists and writers. Visitors can stroll around the many exclusive boutiques, art galleries, bookshops, and cafés.

### California Wines

With over 327,000 acres (132,000 ha) of land under viticulture, California produces 90 percent of the nation's wine. Its latitude, proximity to the ocean, and sheltered valleys create a mild climate, ideal for growing grapes. Half the grapes grown here are harvested from the fertile stretch of land bordered by the Sacramento Valley to the north and San Joaquin Valley to the south. The north coast, home to most of the state's 800 wineries, accounts for less than a quarter of California's wine-growing acreage, but produces many of the country's best Sauvignon Blanc, Cabernet Sauvignon, Merlot, and Chardonnay grapes. Chardonnay and Pinot Noir grapes are the mainstays of the central coast region, which extends from the San Francisco Bay Area to Santa Barbara.

Sparkling cuvée Napa by Mumm

# Northern California

Rugged and sparsely populated, Northern California has a diverse landscape of dense forests, volcanic mountains, and arid plains. It also has the world's largest concentration of giant redwood trees, now protected by national parks. Scenic routes in the parks offer visitors a chance to view their awesome beauty. To experience the full immensity of the trees, however, it is best to walk around in these majestic groves.

Avenue of the Giants in the Humboldt Redwoods State Park

## ㉗ Humboldt Redwoods State Park

US Hwy 101. 🚌 Garberville. Visitor Center: Weott. **Tel** (707) 946-2263. **Open** Apr–Oct: 9am–5pm; Nov–Mar: 10am–4pm. **Closed** Thanksg., Dec 25. 🆆 humboldtredwoods.org

This park has the world's tallest redwood trees and the most extensive primeval redwood groves. The tallest individual specimen, the 364-ft (110-m) Dyersville Giant, was blown over by a storm in 1991. Now seen lying on its side, its size appears even more astounding.

The serpentine 33-mile (53-km) **Avenue of the Giants** runs through the 52,000-acre (21,053-ha) park. The visitor center is halfway along the road.

To the north is the town of **Scotia**, built in 1887 to house the workers of the Pacific Lumber Company's massive redwood mill. Scotia is the only complete lumber community still in existence in California. Its small museum traces the history of the town, and of the lumber industry, and offers self-guided tours.

## ㉘ Eureka

🏙 27,600. ✈ 🚌 🛈 1034 2nd St, (800) 346-3482. 🆆 redwoods.info

Founded by gold miners in 1850, Eureka was named after the state's ancient Greek motto, meaning "I have found it." Today, it is the northern coast's largest industrial center, with extensive logging and fishing operations surrounding the state-protected natural harbor. Its Old Town's many restored 19th-century buildings are now fashionable cafés, bars, and restaurants. Eureka also houses the 1885 Carson Mansion, home of the millionaire lumber baron William Carson, and now a private club. Its Gothic design is enhanced by its redwood construction, painted to resemble stone.

## ㉙ Redwood National Park

Arcata to Crescent City is 78 miles (125km). US Hwy 101 is the quickest route. 🛈 1111 Second St, Crescent City, (707) 465-7306. 🆆 nps.gov

Some of the largest original redwood forests in the world are preserved in this national park. Stretching along the coastline, the 58,000-acre (23,500-ha) park includes many smaller state parks and can be explored along a day-long drive. A two-day trip, however, allows time to walk away from the roads and experience the tranquillity of the stately groves, or spot one of the world's last remaining herds of Roosevelt elk.

The park's headquarters are in **Crescent City**, a few miles north of which lies the 9,200-acre (3,720-ha) Jedediah Smith Redwoods State Park, with the most awe-inspiring coastal redwoods. Named after the fur trapper Jedediah Smith, the first white man who walked across the US, it has excellent campground facilities. South from Crescent City, the **Trees of Mystery** grove features unusual-looking fiberglass statues of the mythical lumberjack Paul

### Redwoods & the Lumber Industry

The tallest tree on earth, the coniferous coastal redwood (Sequoia sempervirens) is unique to the northwest coast. It can live for 2,000 years and reach 350 ft (105 m), with roots that grow up to 200 ft (60 m) horizontally but only 4–6 ft (1–2 m) deep. Its fast growth and resistance to disease makes it ideal for commercial use. By the 1920s, however, logging had destroyed 90 percent of the groves. The Save the Redwoods League was formed, buying land now under state park protection. Lumber firms still own some groves, and their future remains a major environmental issue, both locally and nationally.

Redwood lumber

*For hotels and restaurants see pp710–15*

Bunyan and his faithful ox, Babe *(see p417)*. The park's main attraction is the world's tallest tree, a 368-ft (112-m) giant, standing in the **Tall Trees Grove**. Farther south is Big Lagoon, a freshwater lake stretching for 3 miles (5 km) and two other estuaries. Together, they form the **Humboldt Lagoons State Park**. The headlands at Patrick's Point State Park, at the southern end, are a good place to watch for migrating gray whales in winter.

## ⓷⓪ Weaverville

🏙 3,500. ✈️ ℹ️ 215 Main St, (800) 487-4648. 🆆 trinitycounty.com

This small rural town has changed little since it was founded by gold prospectors 150 years ago. The **Jake Jackson Museum**, in the heart of the small commercial district, traces the history of the town and its surrounding gold-mining and lumber region. Next door, the **Joss House State Historic Site** is the country's oldest and best-preserved Chinese temple. Built in 1874, it is a reminder of the many Chinese immigrants who came to the US to mine gold, and stayed on as cheap labor to build the California railroads.

North of Weaverville, the Trinity Alps rise up at the center of beautiful mountain wilderness. The mountains are popular with hikers and backpackers in summer and with cross-country skiers during the winter months.

## ⓷① Mount Shasta

🚉 Dunsmuir. 🚌 Siskiyou, Shasta. Visitor Center: 300 Pine St. **Tel** (530) 926-4865, (800) 926-4865. **Open** daily. 🆆 mtshastachamber.com

At a height of 14,162 ft (4,316 m), Mount Shasta is the second highest of the Cascade Mountains, after Mount Rainier in Washington *(see pp614–15)*. Visible more than 100 miles (160 km) away and usually covered with snow, the summit is a popular destination for adventure sports enthusiasts

Mount Shasta, towering over the town of Shasta below

such as mountaineers. At its foothills lies the picturesque town of **Shasta**, which was once one of the state's largest gold-mining camps. Today, Shasta makes a welcome base, with plenty of good places to stay.

## ⓷② Lava Beds National Monument

**Tel** (530) 667-2282. 🚌 Klamath Falls. ℹ️ **Open** daily. 🆆 nps.gov

Spreading over 46,500 acres (18,800 ha) of the Modoc Plateau, this eerie landscape of lava flows has over 200 caves and lava tubes – those cylindrical tunnels created by exposed lava turning to stone. Most of the volcanic caves lie near the visitor center, where visitors can take ranger-led or self-guided tours down into the caves. To visit any of the caves, wear sturdy shoes, carry a flashlight, and check first with the visitor center.

The park is also notable as the site of the 1872–73 Modoc War, one of the many conflicts between the US and the Native Americans. For six months a group of Modoc Indians, under the command of "Captain Jack," evaded the US Cavalry from a natural fortress of passageways along the park's northern border. The captain was eventually hanged, and the rest were forced into a reservation in what is now Oklahoma.

## ⓷③ Lassen Volcanic National Park

🚌 Chester, Red Bluff. Visitor Center: **Tel** (530) 595-4444. **Open** daily. 🆆 nps.gov

Before the eruption of Mount St. Helens in Washington in 1980 *(see p617)*, the 10,457-ft-(3,187-m-) high Lassen Peak was the last volcano to erupt on mainland US. In nearly 300 eruptions between 1914 and 1917, it laid 100,000 acres (40,500 ha) of the surrounding land to waste.

Lassen Peak is considered to be still active. Numerous areas on its flanks show clear signs of the geological processes. The boardwalk trail of Bumpass Hell (named for an early guide, who lost his leg in a boiling mudpot in 1865) leads past a series of steaming sulfurous pools of boiling water, heated by molten rock deep underground. In summer, visitors can take the winding road through the park, climbing more than 8,500 ft (2,590 m) high to Summit Lake. The road continues winding its way through the so-called Devastated Area, a bleak gray landscape, which terminates at the Manzanita Lake, and the **Loomis Museum**.

🏛 **Loomis Museum**
Lassen Park Rd, N Entrance. **Tel** (530) 595-6140. **Open** May 27–Oct 31: 9am–5pm daily.

**Sulfur springs in Lassen Volcanic National Park**

# The Gold Country

Located at the heart of California, the Gold Country was once a real-life El Dorado, where a thick vein of gold sat waiting to be discovered. Once home of the Miwok and Maidu peoples, the Gold Rush turned this quiet region into a lawless jamboree of gold miners from all over the world. But the boom went bust by 1860. A few years later, the area saw another short-lived boom, when the transcontinental railroad was constructed through the Sierra Nevada Mountains by low-paid laborers, many of whom were Chinese.

Firehouse #1 Museum, a Nevada City landmark

## 🅝 Nevada City

🏔 2,855. 🚌 🚍 ℹ 132 Main St, (530) 265-2692, (800) 655-6569, 9am–5pm Mon–Fri, 11am–4pm Sat. 🅦 nevadacitychamber.com

Located at the northern end of the Mother Lode gold fields, this picturesque city deserves its reputation as the "Queen of the Northern Mines." But the once-thriving city faded into oblivion after the Gold Rush subsided. It was resurrected as a tourist destination a century later with galleries, restaurants, and inns re-creating Gold Rush themes. The town boasts one of the region's most-photographed façades in the **Firehouse #1 Museum**, with its dainty balconies and white cupola. It is now a local history museum. Other historic buildings include the Nevada Theater, a performance venue since 1865, and the National Hotel. One of California's oldest hotels, it first opened in the mid-1850s.

*For hotels and restaurants see pp710–15*

## 🅞 Grass Valley

🏔 9,000. 🚌 ℹ 248 Mill St, (530) 273-4667, (800) 655-4667. **Open** 10am–5pm Mon–Fri, 10am–3pm Sat & Sun. 🅦 grassvalleychamber.com

One of the largest and busiest gold-mining towns, Grass Valley employed workers from the tin mines of Cornwall in England. It was their expertise that enabled local mines to stay in business long after the others had fallen quiet. At the entrance to the **Northstar Mine Powerhouse & Pelton Wheel Museum** are the giant Pelton wheel that increased production in underground mines. Also on view are a stamp mill and a Cornish pump.

Grass Valley also served the nearby **Empire Mine**, the state's richest and longest surviving gold mine. Now a state park, the mine had recovered almost six million ounces of gold when it closed in 1956. Mining equipment

and artifacts can be seen in the park and in the museum.

🏛 **Northstar Mine Powerhouse & Pelton Wheel Museum**
10933 Alison Ranch Rd. **Tel** (530) 273-4255. **Open** Sep–Apr: 10am–5pm daily; May–Aug: 9am–6pm daily.

🏛 **Empire Mine Historic State Park**
10791 E Empire St. **Tel** (530) 273-8522. **Open** daily. **Closed** Jan 1, Thanksgiving, Dec 25. 🅿 ♿ 🅲

## 🅟 Marshall Gold Discovery State Park

**Tel** (530) 622-3470. 🚌 from Placerville. **Open** 8am–sunset daily. **Closed** Jan 1, Thanksgiving, Dec 25. 🅿 ♿ 🅲 🅦 parks.ca.gov

This peaceful park protects the site where gold was first discovered in 1848. James Marshall spotted shiny flakes in the water channel of a sawmill he and other workers were building for the Swiss entrepreneur John Sutter in Coloma. Gold miners soon took over Sutter's land, leaving him penniless. Within a year, Coloma had turned into a thriving city but then declined, with news of richer deposits elsewhere.

A replica of **Sutter's Mill** stands on the original site. The park's Gold Country Museum features Native American artifacts, films, and other exhibits on the discovery of gold.

A nugget of gold set inside quartz crystal

Reconstructed Sutter's Mill, Marshall Gold Discovery State Park

# ㊲ Sacramento

🛫 🚆 🚌 30, 31, 32. ℹ️ 1002 St, (916) 442-7644, 10am–5pm daily. 🅦 **discovergold.org**

Founded by John Sutter in 1839, California's capital city preserves many historic buildings along the waterfront in Old Sacramento. Most of the structures date from the 1860s, when it became the supply point for miners. Both the transcontinental railroad and Pony Express had their western terminus here, with riverboats providing passage to San Francisco. The **California State Railroad Museum**, at the northern edge of the old town, houses some restored locomotives. A little away from the old city, the State Capitol stands in a landscaped park. To its east, Sutter's Fort is a re-creation of the town's original settlement.

🏛 **California State Railroad Museum**
125 I St. **Tel** (916) 445-2560. **Open** 10am–5pm daily. **Closed** Jan 1, Thanksgiving, Dec 25.

## California State Capitol

Designed in 1860 in grand Renaissance Revival style, this building was completed in 1874. Housing the office of the governor and the state senate chambers, the Capitol also serves as a museum of the state's political and cultural history.

**The Capitol Rotunda** was restored to its original 19th-century splendor in 1975.

**Original 1860 statuary**

**Entrance**

**The Historic Offices** on the first floor contain a few government offices restored to their turn-of-the-century appearance.

# ㊳ Highway 49

🚌 ℹ️ 542 Main St, Placerville, (530) 621-5885.

The Gold Country offers one of California's best scenic drives, through rocky ridges and flowing rivers, along Highway 49. Many of the towns it passes through, such as **Sutter Creek**, have survived unchanged since the Gold Rush. Named after John Sutter, this scenic town grew up to service the Old Eureka Mine, owned by Hetty Green, the "Richest Woman in the World." Leland Stanford, the railroad baron, made his fortune here, by investing in the town's Lincoln Mine. He used the money to become a railroad magnate and then the governor of California.

A short drive southeast leads to **Jackson**, a bustling gold-mining community that has continued to thrive as a lumber mill town since 1850. The Amador County Museum, located on a hill above the town, features a range of old mining equipment.

Northward, Highway 49 passes through **Placerville**. Once a busy supply center for the area's mining camps, the town is still a major transportation center. Of interest here are the Placerville History Museum and the El Dorado County Historical Museum, which displays a replica of a 19th-century general store, artifacts from the Chinese settlement, and other local historical exhibits.

Parrots Ferry Bridge along Highway 49

# ㊳ Columbia State Historic Park

Hwy 49. ℹ️ N255 Jackson St, (209) 588-9128. 🅦 **parks.ca.gov**

At the height of the Gold Rush, Columbia was one of the most important towns in the Gold Country. Most of the state's mining camps disintegrated once the gold ran out in the late 1850s. But Columbia was kept intact by its residents until 1945, when it was turned into a state historic park. Many of the town's buildings are preserved in their original state, like the **Wells Fargo Express Office**, and the restored **Columbia Schoolhouse**. Visitors can buy pans of sand to try panning gold.

🏛 **Wells Fargo Express Office & Columbia Schoolhouse**
**Open** 10am–4pm daily (Jun–Aug: until 6pm). **Closed** Thanksgiving, Dec 25.

# The High Sierras

Forming a towering wall at the eastern side of central California, the densely forested, 14,000-ft- (4,270-m-) high Sierra Nevada Mountains were formed 3 million years ago. Known as the High Sierras, these rugged mountains make up one of the state's most popular recreation areas, preserved by a series of national parks.

Skiing at Lake Tahoe's Alpine Meadows Resort

## ⓵ Lake Tahoe

ℹ 3066 Lake Tahoe Blvd, (530) 544-5050. 🆆 visitinglaketahoe.com

The deep, emerald waters of this beautiful lake are set within an alpine valley at the highest point of the High Sierras. For over a century, Lake Tahoe has been a year-round recreational haven, offering water sports, hiking, and camping. South Lake Tahoe, the largest town here, caters to visitors headed for Nevada's casinos. To its west, the inlet of Emerald Bay State Park is the most photographed part of the lake. To the north is the D.L. Bliss State Park with its 1903 Ehrman Mansion. The surrounding peaks are also famous for their ski resorts. The world-class Alpine Meadows and Squaw Valley are well-known because the Winter Olympics were held here in 1960.

## ⓶ Yosemite National Park

🚆 from Merced. 🚌 Yosemite Valley. 🚌 from Merced. ℹ PO Box 577, Yosemite, (209) 372-0200. **Open** daily. 🅿 ♿ 📷 🚫 🆆 nps.gov/yose

A wilderness of evergreen forests, high meadows, and sheer granite walls, the 1,170-sq-mile (3,030-sq-km) Yosemite National Park (established in 1890)

protects some of the world's most beautiful mountain terrain. Soaring cliffs, rugged canyons, valleys, gigantic trees, and waterfalls all combine to lend Yosemite its incomparable beauty. Each season offers a different experience, from the swelling waterfalls of spring to the russet colors of fall. Numerous roads, bus tours, bike paths, and hiking trails lead visitors from one awe-inspiring panoramic view to another.

Yosemite Valley is a good base from which to explore the park. **Yosemite Museum**, in the village, displays the history of the Native Miwok and Paiute people, along with works by local artists. Nearby is the **Ahwahnee Hotel** *(see p712)*. Built in 1927, this is one of the country's best-known hotels. Just to the south of the Valley Visitor Center, the tiny wooden **Yosemite Chapel** (1879) is the sole reminder of the park's Old Village, dating from the 19th century.

Standing nearly 1 mile (1.6 km) above the valley floor, the silhouette of the **Half Dome** cliff has become the symbol of Yosemite. Geologists believe that it is now three-quarters of its original size, rather than a true half. It is thought that 15,000 years ago glacial ice floes moved across the valley, scything off rock, depositing it downstream. A formidable trail leads to the 8,840-ft (2,695-m) summit, offering panoramic views of the valley. The other major cliff, **El Capitan**, standing guard at the valley's western entrance, attracts rockclimbers, who spend days on its sheer face to reach the top. But the

El Capitan, the world's largest piece of exposed granite, Yosemite National Park

great Yosemite panorama is best experienced from the 3,215-ft- (980-m-) high **Glacier Point**. It can be reached only in summer, because snow blocks the road during winter.

Among the park's most recognizable features are the cascading Yosemite waterfalls, the highest in North America. Tumbling from a height of 2,425 ft (740 m) in two great leaps, **Upper** and **Lower Yosemite Falls** are at their peak in May and June, when the snow melts. By September, however, the falls often dry up.

In summer, when the wildflowers are in full bloom, the park's striking landscape is best explored in the sub-alpine **Tuolumne Meadows** along the Tuolumne River at the Yosemite's eastern edge.

A few miles past Yosemite's southern entrance, **Mariposa Grove** features over 500 giant sequoia trees *(Sequoiadendron gigantea)*, some more than 3,000 years old.

The 1879 Yosemite Chapel, Yosemite National Park

## ❷ Eastern Sierras

Bodie State Historic Park: 🚌 from Bridgeport. 🛈 End of Hwy 270, (760) 647-6445. **Open** daily. Mono Lake: **Tel** (760) 647-3044. 🚉 Merced. 🔳 **monolake.org**

High up in the foothills of the eastern Sierras lies **Bodie State Historic Park**, the largest ghost town in California. It was named after the prospector Waterman S. Bodey, who discovered surface gold here in 1859. The town thrived in the mid-1870s but

Tufa spires rising out of Mono Lake, Eastern Sierras

declined when the gold ran out in 1882. Now protected as a state historic park, Bodie's 170 buildings have been maintained in a state of "arrested decay." The result is an experience of empty streets lined by deserted wooden buildings. The Miner's Union Hall has been converted into a visitor center and a museum.

Nearby **Mono Lake**, covering 60 sq miles (155 sq km), lies at the eastern foot of the Sierra Nevada Mountains and presents an eerie sight of limestone towers rising from the water. Set between two volcanic islands, the lake has no natural outlet, but evaporation and water diversion to Los Angeles, through aqueducts, have caused it to shrink to one-fifth of its size. The lake's water has turned brackish and alkaline, putting the local wildlife and ecosystem in grave danger. In recent years, Mono Lake has been the subject of much environmental debate.

## ❸ Sequoia & Kings Canyon National Parks

Ash Mountain, Three Rivers. **Tel** (559) 565-3135. **Open** daily. 🅿️ 🅰️ call ahead. 🏠 📷 summer only. 🔳 **nps.gov/seki**

These twin national parks preserve lush green forests, magnificent glacier-carved canyons, and granite peaks. America's deepest canyon, the south fork of the Kings River, cuts a depth of 8,200 ft (2,500 m) through Kings Canyon. Roads serve the western

side of the parks; the rest is accessible only to hikers or rented pack-trains of horses or mules.

The parks embrace 34 separate groves of the sequoia tree, the earth's largest living species. **Giant Forest**, at the southern end of Sequoia National Park, is one of the world's largest groves of living sequoias. A 3-mile (5-km) trail from here leads to Moro Rock, a granite monolith affording a 360-degree view of the High Sierras and the Central Valley. To its east lies the marshy Crescent Meadow, bordered by sequoias. Another short trail leads to **Tharp's Log**, a hollowed-out sequoia, home to Hale Tharp, a 19th-century farmer who was introduced to the area by Native Americans.

North of Giant Forest is the world's largest living tree, the 275-ft (84-m) **General Sherman's Tree**. It still grows 0.4 inches (1 cm) every ten years and is rivaled by the third-largest sequoia, **General Grant Tree**, in Kings Canyon Park. This park also features the Big Stump Trail, lined with tall stumps, left by loggers in the 1880s.

Along the eastern boundary of Sequoia is the 14,496-ft (4,420-m) **Mount Whitney**, one of the highest peaks on the US mainland. A steep trail leads from Whitney Portal Road to the summit, offering a panorama over the High Sierras. The mountain, named in honor of geologist Josiah Whitney, was first climbed in 1873. The lovely green alpine meadows around it are ideal for backpacking in the summer months.

# Practical Information

California is a vibrant and diverse vacation destination. The spirit of the state can be felt in the busy cities of San Francisco, Los Angeles, and San Diego as much as in the quiet wilderness of the Sierra Nevada Mountains. At the center of the film industry, Los Angeles prides itself as the entertainment capital of the world. All over the state visitors' needs are well tended. The state's major tourist spots see a rush of visitors from mid-April to September. But the winter months are equally popular, either for the warm climate of the south or the ski slopes of Lake Tahoe.

## Tourist Information

Advance information can be obtained from the **California Division of Tourism** or the nearest US Consulate. Local Visitors' and Convention Bureaus supply maps, guides, event listings, and discount passes for public transportation and tourist destinations.

## Personal Security

San Francisco is one of the safest large cities in the US. Problems are more visible in Los Angeles, although the notorious gangs of the city generally do not bother visitors. Still, as in every big city, visitors can be victims of petty thefts or car crime. Although police patrol regularly in the tourist areas, it is good to be cautious. Safety rules for pedestrians are strictly observed – jaywalking, or crossing the road anywhere except at an intersection, can result in a fine.

## Natural Hazards

In the event of an earthquake, it is most important not to panic. Most injuries occur from falling material. Stand in a doorway, or crouch under a table. In a car, slow down and pull over.

When hiking in the wilderness, be wary of occasionally dangerous wildlife. Also be careful of rapid climatic changes in deserts, where temperatures can drop to below freezing points at high elevations. The Pacific Ocean can often be rough, with a strong undertow.

## Getting Around

Although often more time-consuming, traveling by train, bus, and ferry is an inexpensive way of getting around the state. Within the major cities of San Francisco, Los Angeles, and San Diego, the public transportation network serves parts of the city very well, with shuttle buses, trams, Metro trains, ferries, taxis, and cable cars.

The network of Amtrak railroad lines and connecting bus services serves the state's populous areas. Guided bus tours are a convenient way of sightseeing. Express boat services provide a fast link from Los Angeles to Santa Catalina Island, while others sail more leisurely across San Francisco Bay. Most ferries carry foot passengers and bicycles.

## Driving in California

Driving is the best way to travel around the state. It is best to arrange a fly-drive package before leaving for California. Find out exactly what is included and whether any extra payments may arise when the car is returned. These additions – which may include collision damage waiver, drop-off charges, and rental tax – can double the original fee. Litigation is common in California, so it is best to be fully insured.

In the US, cars are driven on the right side of the road. Seat belts are compulsory. The maximum highway speed limit is generally 65 mph (104 km/h) In cities, the speed limits are restricted as marked and may vary within a few miles. These controls are rigorously enforced by the Highway Patrol. Drunk driving is a serious offense and carries very heavy penalties. You can turn right on red at traffic lights if you first make a full stop, and there is nothing coming the other way. The first vehicle to reach a stop-sign junction has the right of way. It is against the law to use a cell phone while driving unless it is "hands-free."

Parking in Californian cities is strictly controlled and can be somewhat expensive. In remote areas, drivers should be wary of wildlife that may stray onto the roads.

## Outdoor Activities

California is practically synonymous with the great outdoors. The deserts, redwood forests, alpine meadows,

## The Climate of California

Apart from the extremes of the north and the deserts, the state's climate is neither oppressive in summer nor too cold in winter. The Northern Coastal Range is temperate, although wet in winter. To the east, rain turns to snow on the Sierra Nevada Mountains. Central California and the Central Valley have a Mediterranean climate, characterized by seasonal changes in rainfall – a dry summer and a rainy winter – but only moderate changes in temperature. The weather becomes drier and warmer toward the south with soaring temperatures in the desert in summer.

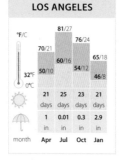

**LOS ANGELES**

| °F/C | Apr | Jul | Oct | Jan |
|---|---|---|---|---|
| | | 81/27 | | |
| | 70/21 | | 76/24 | |
| | | 60/16 | | 65/18 |
| | 50/10 | | 54/12 | |
| 32°F | | | | 46/8 |
| 0°C | | | | |
| days | 21 days | 25 days | 23 days | 21 days |
| in | 1 in | 0.01 in | 0.3 in | 2.9 in |
| month | Apr | Jul | Oct | Jan |

mountains, lakes, and white beaches all welcome visitors. The state has a culture rich with physical activity, and wilderness is never far from any city.

With more than 250 places classified as state parks, wilderness areas, or historic sites, California is a hikers' and campers' paradise. For camping, reserve a site with **State Park Reservations** or **Yosemite Reservations**. There are more than 1 million miles (1.6 million km) of trails in California, the longest being the Pacific Crest Trail, stretching from Canada to Mexico. The **Sierra Club** organizes guided outings and provides detailed maps. Many state parks also allow cyclists on their hiking trails. Outfitters such as **Backroads** lead groups of cyclists on tours.

Equestrians find a wide variety of riding trails here. California's 900-mile (1,450-km) coastline offers various beaches. Some have rough waves and rocky shores; others, with white sand, arching waves, and warm water, are ideal for surfing. The best beaches include the **Leo Carrillo State Beach** in Orange County, **Windansea Beach** in La Jolla, and **Corona del Mar** in Newport.

The lakes, rivers, and beaches of California offer a variety of water sports, from slow cruises on houseboats to parasailing and white-water rafting. Most outfitters that offer river rafting also provide kayak and canoe trips. For more information, contact **American River Touring Association**. The rivers and coastline are feeding grounds for migrating birds. In autumn, ducks, geese, and other shorebirds can be spotted here. The state is also an angler's haven. The rivers and streams of the Sierra Nevada Mountains have plenty of trout. Bass fishing in California's lakes and reservoirs is plentiful throughout the year.

From December through April, gray whales travel 7,000 miles (11,260 km) from the California coast to Mexico. Ocean cruises offer views of the impressive mammals.

California's great outdoors list also includes island hopping. Five volcanic islands off the coast of Southern California form the Channel Islands National Park, ideal for hiking, exploring rock pools, and spotting whales and dolphins. **Island Packers** is only one of the many outfits that offer island tours.

California is famed for its special interest vacations, the most popular being the tours of the state's missions along El Camino Real. Resident writers often give readings at international events such as the **Santa Barbara Writers' Conference**. Institutes such as **Tante Marie's Cooking School** provide lodging, cooking classes, shopping tours, and visits to the Wine Country.

## Shopping

A major player in the global economy, California is known for its casual clothing as well as the best in cutting-edge fashion. It is the largest producer of children's clothing in the US, with Sara's Prints and **Levi Strauss** being among the best. It is equally famous for its sportswear and swimwear, designed by names such as **C&C California**.

Fresh fruit, nuts, and vegetables from the San Joaquin Valley feeds the entire nation. The fine wines of Napa and Sonoma Valleys are available in wineries across the state. Some, such as **Viansa Winery** and **Sebastiani Vineyards**, also sell a range of wine-related products.

Aside from the shopping districts of LA and San Francisco, the state's smaller towns offer a wide range of merchandise and local produce in roadside food stands, wineries, antique shops, and flea markets, where prices tend to be cheaper than in cities.

## DIRECTORY

### Tourist Offices

**California Division of Tourism**
Tel (877) 225-4367.
W visitcalifornia.com

### Special Interest Vacations

**Santa Barbara Writers' Conference**
PO Box 6627, Santa Barbara, CA 93160.
Tel (805) 568-1516.
W sbwriters.com

**Tante Marie's Cooking School**
271 Francsico St, SF, CA 94133. Tel (415) 788-6699.
W tantemarie.com

### Camping

**State Park Reservations**
Tel (800) 444-7275.
W parks.ca.gov

**Yosemite Reservations**
Tel (801) 559-4884.
W yosemitepark.com

### Hiking

**Sierra Club**
Tel (916) 557-1100.
W sierraclubcalifornia.org

### Mountain Biking

**Backroads**
801 Cedar St, Berkeley.
Tel (800) 462-2848.
W backroads.com

### White-Water Rafting & Kayaking

**American River Touring Association**
24000 Casa Loma Rd, Groveland, CA 95321.
Tel (800) 323-2782.
W arta.org

### Island Hopping

**Island Packers**
1691 Spinnaker Dr, Ventura, CA 93001.
Tel (805) 642-1393.
W islandpackers.com.

### Shopping

**C&C California**
W candccalifornia.com

**Original Levi's Store**
300 Post St, San Francisco, CA 94108.
Tel (415) 501-0100.
W levi.com

### Wineries

**Sebastiani Vineyards**
389 Fourth St E, Sonoma, CA 95476.
Tel (800) 888-5532, (707) 933-3230.
W sebastiani.com

**Viansa Winery**
25200 Arnold Dr, Sonoma, CA 95476. Tel (800) 995-4740. W viansa.com

# Where to Stay

## Los Angeles

**BEVERLY HILLS:**
**Hotel Avalon**                    **$$$**
Boutique                    Map C4
*9400 W Olympic Blvd, 90212*
**Tel** *(310) 277-5221*
ⓦ avalonbeverlyhills.com
A splendid mid-20th-century
hotel with friendly service.
The award-winning restaurant
has poolside dining.

**DOWNTOWN:**
**Figueroa Hotel**                    **$$**
Value                    Map E4
*939 S Figueroa St, 90015*
**Tel** *(213) 627-8971*
ⓦ figueroahotel.com
This quirky hotel combines
elements of Southern California,
Mexico, and Northern Africa for
an eclectic effect.

**HOLLYWOOD: Hollywood**
**Orchid Suites**                    **$$**
Value                    Map C3
*1753 Orchid Ave, 90028*
**Tel** *(323) 874-9678*
ⓦ orchidsuites.com
Located directly behind the
famed Chinese Theatre, this
converted apartment-hotel has
neat rooms and free breakfasts.

**HOLLYWOOD:**
**The Standard Hotel**                    **$$$**
Boutique                    Map C3
*8300 Sunset Blvd, 90069*
**Tel** *(323) 650-9090*
ⓦ standardhotels.com/hollywood
Boasting a prime location on the
hip Sunset Strip, The Standard
offers modestly appointed
rooms, but with plenty of flair.

Exotic decor in the lobby of Figueroa Hotel
in downtown Los Angeles

**SANTA MONICA: Best**
**Western Gateway Hotel**                    **$$**
Value                    Map B4
*1920 Santa Monica Blvd, 90404*
**Tel** *(310) 829-9100*
ⓦ gatewayhotel.com
A budget option with basic yet
comfortable rooms. A beach
shuttle service is a welcome
extra. Multilingual staff.

### DK Choice

**VENICE: Hotel Erwin**                    **$$$**
Boutique                    Map B5
*1697 Pacific Ave, 90291*
**Tel** *(310) 452-1111*
ⓦ hotelerwin.com
The charming Hotel Erwin's
rooms are filled with art and
modern features such as luxury
beds, HD TVs, and desks with
ergonomic chairs. Enjoy views
of the ocean and boardwalk
from private balconies and the
open-air rooftop bar.

### DK Choice

**WEST HOLLYWOOD:**
**Andaz West Hollywood**                    **$$$**
Boutique
*8401 Sunset Blvd, 90069*
**Tel** *(323) 656-1234*
ⓦ andaz.com
Infused with an ambience of
simple luxury, the Andaz offers
stylish and comfortable rooms.
Experience impeccable service
and an ideal location with easy
access to some of LA's most
noteworthy restaurants,
shops, and nightclubs.

## San Diego County

**CORONADO: Hotel**
**del Coronado**                    **$$$**
Historic
*1500 Orange Ave, 92118*
**Tel** *(619) 435-6611*
ⓦ hoteldel.com
Situated on the beach, this
iconic Victorian resort features
modern rooms and cottages
with plenty of amenities.

**SAN DIEGO: Catamaran**                    **$$**
Value
*3999 Mission Blvd, 92109*
**Tel** *(858) 488-1081*
ⓦ catamaranresort.com
A casually elegant resort adjacent
to the Mission Bay and Pacific
shoreline. Guests can relax in
the tropical outdoor pool.

**SAN DIEGO: Omni Hotel**                    **$$**
Modern
*675 L St, 92101*
**Tel** *(619) 231-6664*
ⓦ omnihotels.com
Sleek rooms with modern
amenities offer great views of the
San Diego Bay and downtown.
Well-equipped business center.

**SAN DIEGO: Paradise Point**                    **$$**
Luxury
*1404 Vacation Rd, 92109*
**Tel** *(858) 274-4630*
ⓦ paradisepoint.com
Comfortable bungalow-style
rooms are scattered across a
44-acre (18-ha) island. There is
also an award-winning spa.

### DK Choice

**SAN DIEGO: The US Grant $$$**
Historic
*326 Broadway, 92101*
**Tel** *(619) 232-3121*
ⓦ usgrant.net
A landmark since 1910, this
hotel is in a prime spot for
visiting major attractions. The
rooms have a period feel but
are equipped with all sorts of
modern, luxurious amenities,
offering a timeless and
elegant experience.

## The Deserts

**DEATH VALLEY: Inn at**
**Furnace Creek**                    **$$$**
Luxury
*Hwy 190, 92328*
**Tel** *(760) 786-2345*
ⓦ furnacecreekresort.com
This gorgeous property offers
sumptuously appointed rooms. A
spring-fed pool, horseback riding,
golf, and tennis are on site.

**MOJAVE: Best Western Plus**
**Desert Winds**                    **$**
Value
*16200 Sierra Hwy Mojave, 93501*
**Tel** *(661) 824-3601*
ⓦ bestwestern.com
Clean and comfortable rooms are
offered at this friendly, chain
hotel. An outdoor pool is on site,
and hiking trails are nearby.

## DK Choice

**PALM SPRINGS: Ace
Hotel & Swim Club** $
Boutique
*701 E Palm Canyon Dr, 92264*
**Tel** *(760) 325-9900*
**w** acehotel.com
This trendy hotel is a popular
hipster hangout. The rooms are
decorated with contemporary
Americana and furnished with
comfortable beds and all
amenities. Take a dip in the
pool or enjoy a massage in
a Mongolian yurt.

**PALM SPRINGS: Desert
Riviera Hotel** $
Value
*610 E Palm Canyon Dr, 92264*
**Tel** *(760) 327-5314*
**w** desertrivierahotel.com
Manicured gardens and
panoramic views of the
mountains can be enjoyed at
this renovated 1950s hotel.

# Central Coast

**ANAHEIM: Disney®'s
Grand Californian Hotel** $$$
Luxury
*1600 S Disneyland Dr, 92802*
**Tel** *(714) 956-6425*
**w** disneyland.disney.go.com
This magnificent hotel inside
Disney's California Adventure
Park features pools and a spa,
as well as a kids' club.

## DK Choice

**LAGUNA BEACH: Surf
and Sand Resort** $$$
Luxury
*1555 S Coast Hwy, 92651*
**Tel** *(877) 741-5908*
**w** surfandsandresort.com
A top-rated California resort
located on prime beachfront
property. Each welcoming
guest room and suite features
modern luxury and views of
the ocean. Excellent facilities,
including pools, a spa, and a
restaurant, make this a popular
getaway destination.

**SAN LUIS OBISPO:
Garden Street Inn** $$
B&B
*1212 Garden St, 93401*
**Tel** *(805) 545-9802*
**w** gardenstreetinn.com
Housed in a restored Victorian
building, this inn has rooms
furnished with antiques; some
have fireplaces and Jacuzzis.

Four Seasons The Biltmore, Santa Barbara

**SANTA BARBARA:
Hotel Santa Barbara** $$
Historic
*533 State St, 93101*
**Tel** *(805) 957-9300*
**w** hotelsantabarbara.com
This charming 1926 property,
with tidy, well-equipped rooms,
is located five blocks away from
the beach.

**SANTA BARBARA:
Four Seasons The Biltmore** $$$
Luxury
*1260 Channel Dr, 93108*
**Tel** *(805) 969-2261*
**w** fourseasons.com
Exquisite attention to detail can
be enjoyed at this Spanish
Colonial-style hotel with opulent
rooms and secluded cottages.

# San Francisco

## DK Choice

**BERKELEY:
Berkeley City Club** $$
Historic
*2315 Durant Ave, 94704*
**Tel** *(510) 848-7800*
**w** berkeleycityclubhotel.com
Built in 1929, the Berkeley City
Club boasts charming, if small,
guest rooms and elegant
public spaces. Take a dip in
the gorgeous indoor pool or
make use of the superb fitness
center. The on-site club hosts
performances and lectures.

**CHINATOWN AND NOB HILL:
Hotel Triton** $
Boutique
*342 Grant Ave, 94108*
**Tel** *(415) 394-0500*
**w** hoteltriton.com
Whimsical, eclectic, Chagall-like
decor can be seen throughout
this friendly inn with smallish,

colorful rooms – some eco-
oriented, some suitable for the
solo traveler.

**CHINATOWN AND NOB HILL:
The Fairmont** $$$
Luxury
*950 Mason St, 94108*
**Tel** *(415) 772-5000*
**w** fairmont.com/san-francisco
A century-old Nob Hill hotel, The
Fairmont welcomes guests with a
dazzling, gilded lobby. It also has
a nightclub and three renowned
restaurants and lounges.

**DOWNTOWN:
Taj Campton Place** $$$
Luxury
*340 Stockton St, 94108*
**Tel** *(415) 781-5555*
**w** tajhotels.com
Sumptuous rooms have leather-
topped desks and padded
hangers. Guests enjoy 24-hour
room service, a Michelin-starred
restaurant, and a cozy bar.

**FISHERMAN'S WHARF AND
NORTH BEACH: Best
Western Tuscan Inn** $$
Value
*425 North Point St, 94133*
**Tel** *(415) 561-1100*
**w** tuscaninn.com
Steps from the waterfront, this
hotel has spacious and colorful
rooms, some with fireplaces. A
leafy courtyard and an Italian
restaurant are on site.

**HAIGHT ASHBURY AND THE
MISSION: The Red Victorian
Bed, Breakfast & Art** $
B&B
*1665 Haight St, 94117*
**Tel** *(415) 864-1978*
**w** redvic.com
Each room is a different hippie
haven at this B&B in a bright-red
building, a leftover from the
Summer of Love. Some rooms
have shared bathrooms. No TV.

For more information on types of hotels *see pages 26–7*

**OAKLAND: Waterfront Plaza Hotel** $$
Value
*10 Washington St, 94607*
**Tel** *(800) 729-3638*
W jdvhotels.com
Rooms have a nautical theme; some have balconies, fireplaces, and bay views. There is also a fitness center, a pool, and sauna.

**PACIFIC HEIGHTS: Inn at the Presidio** $$
Boutique
*42 Moraga Ave, 94129*
**Tel** *(415) 800-7356*
W innatthepresidio.com
In the former officers' quarters, this inn has lovely rooms with views of the Golden Gate Bridge.

**SAUSALITO: Hotel Sausalito** $$
Boutique
*16 El Portal, 94965*
**Tel** *(415) 332–0700*
W hotelsausalito.com
A 1915 Mission Revival-style landmark near the San Francisco ferry, with armoires, wrought-iron beds, and a small patio.

## The Wine Country

**HEALDSBURG: Camellia Inn** $$
B&B
*211 North St, 95448*
**Tel** *(707) 433-8182*
W camelliainn.com
This 1869 Italianate Victorian house, surrounded by lush gardens, has romantic rooms and a beautiful swimming pool.

**MENDOCINO: The Stanford Inn by the Sea** $$
Boutique
*Hwy 1 & Comptche-Ukiah Rd, 95460*
**Tel** *(707) 937-5615*
W stanfordinn.com
Rooms and suites have private ocean-view decks. Spa services, an indoor pool, and a restaurant are on site. Surrounded by gardens.

**NAPA: La Residence** $$$
B&B
*4066 Howard Lane, 94558*
**Tel** *(707) 253–0337*
W laresidence.com
In a 19th-century mansion amid pretty gardens, this romantic B&B offers a complimentary breakfast and evening wine reception.

**SONOMA: The Inn at Ramekins** $$
B&B
*450 West Spain St, 95476*
**Tel** *(707) 933-0450*
W ramekins.com
A few blocks from the plaza, this inn is situated above a renowned

Homey cottage interior of Sutter Creek Inn, Sutter Greek

cooking school. It has spacious rooms with countryside views and French antiques.

## Northern California

**BIG SUR: Deetjen's Big Sur Inn** $$
Historic
*48865 Hwy 1, 93920*
**Tel** *(831) 667-2377*
W deetjens.com
A tranquil forest retreat with cozy, eclectic rooms, pretty gardens, and an excellent restaurant.

### DK Choice

**CARMEL: Pine Inn** $$
B&B
*Ocean Ave & Monte Verde, 93921*
**Tel** *(831) 624-3851*
W pineinn.com
Conveniently located near boutiques, galleries, and the beach, this iconic inn offers elegant rooms and suites equipped with all modern comforts. The on-site restaurant is popular with the locals.

**EUREKA: Carter House Inns** $$$
Historic
*301 L St, 95501*
**Tel** *(707) 444-8062*
W carterhouse.com
This complex of five historic buildings houses plush rooms and suites. A Michelin-starred restaurant is on site.

**SANTA CRUZ: Sea and Sand Inn** $$
Value
*201 West Cliff Dr, 95060*
**Tel** *(831) 427 3400*
W santacruzmotels.com
Every room has an ocean view at this inn situated on a clifftop near

the beach. Suites and studios are also available. A delicious Continental breakfast is included in the price. .

## The Gold Country

**GRASS VALLEY: Holbrooke Hotel and Restaurant** $
Historic
*212 W Main St, 95945*
**Tel** *(530) 273-1353*
W holbrooke.com
Established in 1851 to cater to Gold Rush pioneers, this hotel offers modern facilities while still retaining its Old West charm.

**SACRAMENTO: Sheraton Grand Sacramento** $$
Value
*1230 J St, 95814*
**Tel** *(916) 447-1700*
W starwoodhotels.com
The generously sized rooms have modern decor at this downtown hotel in a charming old red-brick building.

**SUTTER CREEK: Sutter Creek Inn** $$
B&B
*75 Main St, 95685*
**Tel** *(209) 267-5606*
W suttercreekinn.com
This country-style 1859 inn has private cottages with fireplaces. Shaded gardens are laced with walkways and hammocks.

## The High Sierras

**YOSEMITE NATIONAL PARK: Cedar Lodge** $
Value
*9966 Hwy 140, 95318*
**Tel** *(209) 379-2612*
W nationalparkreservations.com
Cedar Lodge offers a wide range of rooms, from standard to 14-person suites. Located close to Yosemite National Park.

### DK Choice

**YOSEMITE NATIONAL PARK: The Ahwahnee Hotel** $$$
Historic
*Yosemite Valley, 95389*
**Tel** *(559) 253-5636*
W yosemitepark.com
This justly famous lodge opened in 1927. A variety of accommodations and warm hospitality make it a top choice for a stay in the national park. It also features a beautiful solarium and a great restaurant.

# Where to Eat and Drink

## Los Angeles

### BEVERLY HILLS: The Bazaar $$$
Spanish                  Map C4
*SLS Hotel at Beverly Hills,*
*465 S La Cienega Blvd, 90048*
**Tel** *(310) 246-5567*
Chef José Andrés's gourmet fare
lures foodies here from all over
the world. Guests have a number
of areas to choose from: striking
dining rooms, a breezy
Mediterranean-style terrace,
or a welcoming patisserie.

### DOWNTOWN: Hae Jang Chon
Korean BBQ Restaurant       $
Korean                   Map E4
*3821 W 6th St, 90020*
**Tel** *(213) 389-8777*
Head to this eatery in the
city's bustling Koreatown for
authentic fare. Dutiful servers
explain the traditional menu's
various intricacies. Exceptionally
popular for celebrations.

### DOWNTOWN: Philippe
The Original                  $
Delicatessen/Café        Map E4
*1001 N Alameda St, 90012*
**Tel** *(213) 628-3781*
Founded in 1908, this is one
of LA's oldest restaurants – and
the self-proclaimed birthplace
of the French dip sandwich –
Philippe serves beef, lamb,
pork, and turkey versions.

### HOLLYWOOD: Pink's
Famous Hot Dogs               $
Hot Dogs                 Map C3
*709 N La Brea Ave, 90038*
**Tel** *(323) 931-4223*
This legendary hot-dog stand is
where Orson Welles once ate
18 frankfurters. The classic chili
dog is a crowd favorite. Specialty
dogs are named for celebrities.

### DK Choice

**HOLLYWOOD: Musso and
Frank Grill            $$$**
Steak House            Map C3
*6667 Hollywood Blvd, 90028*
**Tel** *(323) 467-7788*   **Closed** *Sun
& Mon*
Hollywood's oldest restaurant,
Musso and Frank never seems
to go out of style. Featuring
classic mahogany and leather
decor, it draws a crowd of both
tourists and locals, who head
to the bar for expertly made
martinis. Old-school favorites
include chicken pot pie, liver
and onions, and juicy steaks.

### MIDTOWN: Pizzeria Mozza   $$
Pizza/Italian            Map D3
*641 N Highland Ave, 90036*
**Tel** *(323) 297-0101*
Come here for creative pizzas
served straight from the stone
oven, located within sight of
the diners. The Italian wines
on offer are modestly priced.
Its sister restaurant Osteria
Mozza is located next door.

### DK Choice

**SANTA MONICA:
JiRaffe                 $$$**
New American           Map B4
*502 Santa Monica Blvd, 90401*
**Tel** *(310) 917-6671*   **Closed** *Sun*
The rustic California/French
cooking at this casually chic
restaurant is among the best in
town. Produce comes directly
from local farms and farmers'
markets. House favorites include
purple Peruvian gnocchi with
rock shrimp, and pan-roasted
New Zealand rack of lamb. Well-
made classic cocktails and a
varied wine list ensure there
is something for everyone.

## San Diego County

### CORONADO:
1500 Ocean                  $$$
Mediterranean
*Hotel del Coronado, 1500 Orange
Ave, 92118*
**Tel** *(619) 522-8490*   **Closed** *lunch;
Sun & Mon*
The farm-to-table cuisine at the
Hotel Del's signature beachfront
restaurant makes use of coastal
ingredients. Cocktails incorporate
fresh herbs. Extensive wine list.

### DK Choice

**LA JOLLA:
California Modern       $$$**
New American
*1250 Prospect St, 92037*
**Tel** *(858) 454-4244*   **Closed** *lunch*
This hip restaurant with refined
service has a menu that boasts
cleverly conceived seafood
dishes made using local
ingredients. An extensive list
of wines and cocktails
complements the inventive
cuisine. Gorgeous views of the
ocean and modern design make
this an indulgent dining choice.

### SAN DIEGO: Hodad's        $
Burgers
*5010 Newport Ave, 92107*
**Tel** *(619) 224-4623*
This beachside joint has served
huge burgers to hungry surfers
for decades. Hefty patties stacked
high with fresh toppings are
accompanied by a basket of
"frings" – fries and rings.

### SAN DIEGO: Karl Strauss
Brewing Company               $
American
*1157 Columbia St, 92101*
**Tel** *(619) 234-2773*
A downtown microbrewery
offering pub fare and a wide
assortment of hand-crafted
beers on tap. Menu favorites
include meat loaf, burgers,
salads, and wings.

Pink's Famous Hot Dogs, Hollywood

**For more information on types of restaurants** *see pages 28–9*

# The Deserts

## DK Choice

**DEATH VALLEY: Inn at Furnace Creek Dining Room** $$$
New American
*Furnace Creek Resort, Hwy 190, 92328*
**Tel** *(760) 786-3385*
In an adobe-and-stone building, this upscale restaurant offers gorgeous views. The food combines Southwestern and Pacific Rim influences. While dishes such as cactus salad and rattlesnake empanadas reflect the desert environment, simpler (and vegetarian) options are also available. Afternoon tea in the lobby is a tradition. The restaurant may be closed in the summer; call ahead.

**PALM SPRINGS: Melvyn's Restaurant** $$
American
*200 W Ramon Rd, 92260*
**Tel** *(760) 325-2323*
In the historic Ingleside Inn, Melvyn's has been a special-occasion restaurant since 1975. The menu of classics is well regarded, and many dishes are prepared table-side. Enjoy a drink in the piano lounge.

# Central Coast

**ANAHEIM: Napa Rose** $$$
New American
*Disney's Grand Californian Hotel, 1600 S Disneyland Dr, 92803*
**Tel** *(714) 781-3463*     **Closed** *lunch*
The gourmet dishes at Napa Rose feature farm-fresh ingredients that encapsulate the flavors of California Wine Country. World-renowned vintage wines complement the food.

**ORANGE: The Hobbit** $$$
Continental/French
*2932 E Chapman Ave, 92669*
**Tel** *(714) 997-1972*     **Closed** *lunch; Mon & Tue*
Seven-course, prix-fixe "feasts" begin in the wine cellar and include an "intermission" during which guests may tour the kitchen. Book ahead for a unique dining experience.

**SAN LUIS OBISPO: Cioppinot Seafood Grill** $$$
Italian
*1051 Nipomo St, 93401*
**Tel** *(805) 547-1111*     **Closed** *lunch*
Family-owned seafood grill and oyster bar. The wine list focuses on white and red Pinots from around the globe, and the no-corkage fee appeals to wine lovers. Warm, friendly service.

**SANTA BARBARA: La Super-Rica Taqueria** $
Mexican
*622 N Milpas St, 93103*
**Tel** *(805) 963-4940*     **Closed** *Wed*
A roadside shack with devoted customers who wait in line for simple Mexican fare. Try the tacos, made from freshly grilled tortillas and filled with marinated pork, beef, chicken, chorizo, and more.

## DK Choice

**SANTA BARBARA: Bouchon** $$$
French/New American
*9 W Victoria St, 93101*
**Tel** *(805) 730-1160*     **Closed** *lunch*
A classy bistro with a warm vibe. Favorites include bourbon- and maple-glazed duck and buffalo tartare. Try the warm chocolate molten lava cake for dessert. Servers explain the menu's intricacies while offering wine-pairing advice. Couples will enjoy the romantic atmosphere.

# San Francisco

**BERKELEY: Skates on the Bay** $$
Seafood
*100 Seawall Dr, 94710*
**Tel** *(510) 549-1900*
Fresh Pacific seafood, from oysters to salmon and sushi, plus steaks, chicken, burgers, and pasta dishes are on the menu. There are lovely bay and harbor views, and a lively cocktail bar scene.

**CHINATOWN AND NOB HILL: Great Eastern** $
Chinese
*649 Jackson St, 94133*
**Tel** *(415) 986-2500*
One of the top Mandarin-style seafood restaurants in town, with tanks of live cod, crab, prawns, and more. Also on the menu are Peking duck, dim sum, and savory clay pots.

**DOWNTOWN: Tadich Grill** $$
American
*240 California St, 94111*
**Tel** *(415) 391-1849*     **Closed** *Sun*
Choose from seafood dishes, crab cocktails, and pot roast at this restaurant with an Old San Francisco vibe, cozy booths and staff that have been here for decades. Good martinis.

## DK Choice

**DOWNTOWN: The Slanted Door** $$$
Vietnamese
*One Ferry Building #3, 94111*
**Tel** *(415) 861-8032*
Nationally acclaimed, this restaurant on the bayfront serves everything from traditional street food to dishes with a French twist. Sip on signature cocktails while trying caramelized shrimp, cellophane crab noodles, chicken clay pot, lemongrass tofu, and many veggie dishes. Book well ahead.

**HAIGHT ASHBURY AND THE MISSION: Kate's Kitchen** $
American
*471 Haight St, 94117*
**Tel** *(415) 626-3984*
This friendly spot is famous for French toast, biscuits and gravy, bacon-cheddar cornmeal pancakes, home-made chicken soup, and other comfort food.

**OAKLAND: Bay Wolf** $$
Seafood
*3853 Piedmont Ave, 94611*
**Tel** *(510) 655-6004*
An adopter of the Slow Food and kitchen garden trends, Bay Wolf is

Chic interior of Bouchon, Santa Barbara

housed in a revamped Victorian house. Come for rustic duck dishes, Mediterranean seafood specialties, cassoulet, gnocchi, risotto, and fried chicken.

**PACIFIC HEIGHTS:**
**Swan Oyster Depot** $$
Seafood
*1517 Polk St, 94109*
**Tel** *(415) 673-1101*
Since 1912, this eatery has been serving excellent clam chowder, oysters, cracked crab, lobster, and fresh seafood. Beer and wine are available. Cash only.

# The Wine Country

## DK Choice

**GEYSERVILLE: Rustic**
**Francis's Favorites** $$$
Italian
*300 Via Archimedes, 95441*
**Tel** *(707) 857-1485*
On the Francis Ford Coppola Winery, this restaurant offers family favorites such as Mrs. Scorsese's lemon chicken, habit-forming ribs, and Florentine steak. Diners can eat at the movie-memorabilia-surrounded bar, around the swimming pool, indoors by the Argentine-style *parrilla*, or on the terrace with views of the vineyard.

**HEALDSBURG: Jimtown Store** $
American
*6706 Hwy 128, 95448*
**Tel** *(707) 433-1212*
A general store and antiques shop, plus gourmet deli and café. Feast on chili, grilled cheese, deli sandwiches, home-made chocolate cake, and other snacks. Also offers packed picnic lunches.

**NAPA:**
**Bistro Don Giovanni** $$$
Italian
*4110 Howard Ln, 94558*
**Tel** *(707) 224-3300*
Come here for pastas, *fritto misto*, wood-oven pizzas, local seafood, roasted half-chicken, and Bostini trifle. Bar as well as patio seating.

**SONOMA: The Girl and**
**the Fig** $$$
French
*110 W Spain St, 95476*
**Tel** *(707) 938-3634*
Enjoy French cuisine in art-filled dining rooms or on the patio. The menu has artisanal cheeses and charcuterie, tartares, *steak-frites*, and creative veggie dishes. Sip on local wine at the antique bar.

Elegantly served dish at the acclaimed Restaurant 301, Eureka

# Northern California

**CARMEL: Pacific's Edge** $$$
California Coastal
*120 Highlands Dr, 93923*
**Tel** *(831) 622-5445*
Try beef, lamb, and seafood dishes, or opt for the chef's tasting menu or bar menu at this elegant venue with ocean views in the Highlands Inn. Award-winning wine list.

## DK Choice

**EUREKA: Restaurant 301** $$$
Californian
*301 L St, 95501*
**Tel** *(707) 444-8062*
This is an award-winning foodie mecca in an elegant Victorian building. The daily-changing menu includes organic vegetables from the kitchen gardens, local seafood, poultry, and meats. Oenophiles make pilgrimages here for the winemaker dinners and vintages from the 3,400-bottle list.

**MENDOCINO: Ravens'**
**Restaurant** $$
Vegetarian
*44850 Comptche Ukiah Rd, 95460*
**Tel** *(707) 937-5615*
This vegetarian-friendly eatery on the coast serves soups, pizzas, pastas, and grilled veggies. Come early and visit the organic gardens.

**MONTEREY: Old**
**Fisherman's Grotto** $$
Seafood
*39 Fishermans Wharf, 93940*
**Tel** *(831) 375-4604*
A beloved family-run spot with stunning views of the harbor. The menu includes fresh seafood, as well as steaks, pasta dishes, and delicious home-made desserts.

**SANTA CRUZ: Crow's Nest** $
Seafood
*2218 E Cliff Dr, 95062*
**Tel** *(831) 476-4560*
An icon since 1969, this eatery serves seafood specialties as well as pasta, steaks, and chops. The upstairs bar has a more casual atmosphere. Great harbor views.

# The Gold Country

**GRASS VALLEY: Swiss**
**House Restaurant** $
German
*535 Mill St, 95945*
**Tel** *(530) 273-8272* **Closed** *Mon–Wed*
Swiss House is popular for its German and Swiss specialties. On the menu are soups, *sauerbraten*, *jaegerschnitzel*, and bratwurst, along with breads and pastries. Quick and friendly service.

## DK Choice

**SACRAMENTO:**
**Chando's Tacos** $
Mexican
*863 Arden Way, 95815*
**Tel** *(916) 641-8226*
This brightly colored roadside stand is considered one of Sacramento's best eateries. The tacos, in particular, are exceptional. All of the meats – such as *adobado* and *carnitas* – are perfectly spiced, grilled, and tucked into fresh-made tortillas. The *tortas* are also a hit.

# The High Sierras

**MAMMOTH LAKES: The**
**Restaurant at Convict Lake** $$
American/French
*1 Convict Lake Rd, 93546*
**Tel** *(760) 934-3803*
Enjoy perfectly cooked local meats and fish, paired with an excellent wine list, in this beautiful alpine setting. There is also a delicious brunch on offer.

**YOSEMITE NATIONAL PARK:**
**Wawona Dining Room** $$
American
*Wawona Hotel, 8308 Wawona Rd, 95389*
**Tel** *(209) 375-1425* **Closed** *Dec 1–19, Jan 2–Apr 10*
Wawona is popular for its seasonal specialties and traditional favorites. Flavorful steaks and trout are highlights. Sit outdoors or in the Victorian dining room.

**For more information on types of restaurants** *see pages 28–9*

# ALASKA &
# HAWAI‘I

# ALASKA

For most visitors, familiar images of Alaska include pristine waterways, towering snowcapped peaks, glaciers calving to form icebergs, and massive grizzly bears feasting on salmon. All this and much more can still be found here on North America's "Last Frontier," where less than one percent of the state's 375 million acres (150 million ha) shows any sign of human habitation.

Situated at the top of the North American continent and separated from the rest of the country by Canada, Alaska is more than twice the size of Texas, the next largest state. Alaska can be divided into three regions, both geographically and for the purpose of travel. Southeast Alaska, commonly called the Inside Passage, is a long, narrow stretch of islands and channels sandwiched between the Pacific Ocean and Canada's Coast Mountains. Picture-postcard coastal towns, including the state capital Juneau, are linked conveniently by an efficient state-run ferry system.

The bulk of Alaska's landmass, however, lies in the continent's extreme northwest corner, closer to Russia than the "Lower 48" states. The modern city of Anchorage is a good base for exploring the Kenai Peninsula and Denali National Park, or as a jumping-off point for more adventurous destinations such as Kodiak Island and the Alaska Peninsula. To the west of the mainland, the windswept volcanic archipelago of the Aleutian Islands stretches 1,200 miles (1,932 km) west into the Bering Sea.

**Russian doll on sale in Juneau**

### History

Alaska's southeast corner is 500 miles (805 km) from the rest of the US, but its farthest reaches a mere 50 miles (80 km) from Russia. As a result, the state's history reflects its role as a bridge and buffer between these two powerful nations. Human history here goes back much farther, since Alaska was the point of entry for some of the first people to set foot in North America, when they crossed a land bridge over the Bering Strait 13,000 to 30,000 years ago. While some groups continued their migrations southward, a few remained for millennia, hunting and fishing until the arrival of Western Europeans. The original Alaskans' descendants today include the island-dwelling Aleut, the coastal Tlingit, the Athabascans of the interior, and the Eskimos of Arctic and western Alaska.

The first non-Native settlements were outposts built by Russian fur traders in the late 18th century. Although their far-flung colony stretched as far south as California, it declined as trappers decimated once-huge populations of seals and sea otters.

A panoramic view of North America's highest peak, Mount McKinley in Denali National Park

◀ Makapu'u Beach, with a view of Turtle and Rabbit Islands, O'ahu, Hawai'i

A brown bear fishing for salmon at Brooks Camp, Katmai National Park, Alaska Peninsula

Seen as a liability, Alaska was sold by Russia in 1867 to the US Secretary of State William Seward. The purchase was popularly considered a waste of money and dubbed "Seward's Folly"; however, doubts vanished when the first of many deposits of gold was found near Juneau. More mineral discoveries, including gold in 1898 at distant Nome, as well as vast quantities of copper, and oil at Prudhoe Bay, have all proved the wisdom of Seward's purchase.

## Alaska Today

Alaska is home to 710,000 people. Of the population, 14 percent are of Native descent, while the remainder come from diverse backgrounds (only 34 percent of the total are born in the state). It has a population density of just one person per square mile (compared to over 1,000 in New Jersey).

Alaska's economy depends upon oil from the North Slope, but government jobs, seafood processing, and tourism are also important. Anchorage is a major international hub for air cargo shipments. Over time, there has been a growing awareness about preserving and protecting Alaska's unique wilderness from the commercial pressures arising from the state's natural wealth. The vast majority of Alaska is owned by the government, and much of this is protected in national parks and other undeveloped areas stretching from Glacier Bay to the Gates of the Arctic.

### KEY DATES IN HISTORY

**13,000–30,000 years ago** Migratory peoples cross from present-day Siberia into Alaska

**1741** Working for the tsar of Russia, Danish explorer Vitus Bering and his crew are the first Europeans to visit Alaska

**1867** To ease an economic recession, the tsar of Russia sells Alaska to the US for $7.2 million

**1880** Gold is discovered near Juneau

**1897** The Klondike Gold Rush hits Skagway

**1912** Alaska becomes a US Territory

**1942** US Army builds the 1,442-mile (2,322-km) Alaska Highway as an overland link

**1959** Alaska becomes the 49th state

**1964** Good Friday earthquake destroys much of Anchorage

**1968** Oil discovered at Prudhoe Bay

**1977** Trans-Alaska pipeline completed

**1989** *Exxon Valdez* runs aground on Bligh Reef, spilling 11 million gallons (50 million liters) of oil into Prince William Sound

**2000 onwards** Global warming is causing dramatic changes in Alaska, particularly in the Arctic. Climate changes will have major impacts on the state's people, animals, and plants

Visitors at Aialik Glacier, one of the main attractions at Kenai Fjords National Park

# Exploring Alaska

A vast wilderness of virgin rivers, towering mountain peaks, abundant wildlife, and calving glaciers, Alaska is by far the largest state in the United States. Its sheer size means that travel takes up a fair proportion of a visitor's time. However, the state has an excellent transportation and tourism infrastructure, which caters to 1.5 million visitors each year, most of whom arrive during the brief summer season from late May to early September. Good roads connect Anchorage, Fairbanks, and other cities, but much of Southeast Alaska – including the capital city of Juneau – are inaccessible by road. Ferries, planes, and cruise ships connect coastal towns, while remote bush villages are accessed only by air.

King Salmon Antler's Inn, outside Katmai NP, Alaska Peninsula

## Sights at a Glance

1. Ketchikan
2. Sitka
3. Juneau
4. Glacier Bay National Park
5. Skagway
6. Anchorage
7. Valdez
8. Seward
9. Homer
10. Kodiak Island
11. Alaska Peninsula
12. Aleutian Islands
13. Nome
14. Fairbanks
15. Wrangell-St. Elias National Park
16. *Denali National Park pp728–9*

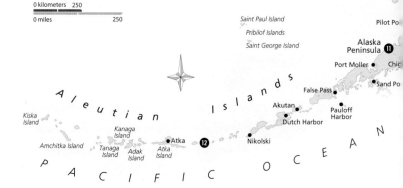

## Key

— Major road
‥‥ International border

## MILEAGE CHART

| | | | | | | |
|---|---|---|---|---|---|---|
| *Skagway* | | | | | **10** = Distance in miles | |
| **833** | *Anchorage* | | | | 10 = Distance in kilometers | |
| 1340 | | | | | | |
| **757** | **307** | *Valdez* | | | | |
| 1218 | 494 | | | | | |
| **960** | **127** | **429** | *Seward* | | | |
| 1544 | 205 | 690 | | | | |
| **1055** | **236** | **531** | **180** | *Homer* | | |
| 1697 | 379 | 854 | 289 | | | |
| **712** | **429** | **362** | **484** | **582** | *Fairbanks* | |
| 1145 | 690 | 582 | 779 | 936 | | |
| **833** | **237** | **504** | **364** | **473** | **121** | *Denali NP* |
| 1340 | 382 | 811 | 585 | 761 | 195 | |

ARCTIC OCEAN
ow
Teshekpuk Lake
Deadhorse
Kaktovik
olville Umiat ⑪
Range
Arctic Village
Chandalar
L A S K A
Beaver
Hughes
Circle ⑥
Yukon
Yukon
Ruby
Fairbanks ⑭ North Pole
Eagle
Anderson
Delta Junction ②
Tok
Denali National Park ⑯ Cantankell Paxson
③ Susitna
Curry Gakona ①
Whitehorse
Farewell Tazlina Lake
Talkeetna ④
Wrangell-St. Elias National Park ⑮
McCarthy
C A N A D A
me lage Palmer
Anchorage ⑥ Valdez ⑦
Whitehorse
Anchorage
Cordova
Port Nikiski ⑨
Katalla Yakutat
Skagway ⑤
Lake Clark
⑧ Seward
Glacier Bay National Park ④ Haines
Newhalen Homer ⑨
Pelican
Juneau ③
English Bay
Petersburg
mna ake Gulf of Alaska
Sitka ②
Port Alexander
Wrangell
Hyder
nek
Kodiak Island Kodiak ⑩
Ketchikan ①
Akhiok Old Harbor
Hydaburg

Aialik Glacier near Seward, with seals on icebergs in the foreground

Floatplanes docked on Kodiak Island, Gulf of Alaska

# ❶ Ketkikan

🏔 7,400. ✈ 🚢 2 miles (3 km) S of downtown. ℹ 131 Front Street, (907) 225-6166, (800) 770-3300. 🆆 visit-ketchikan.com

Strung out along the waters of the Tongass Narrows and backed by forested hills, Ketchikan is the first stop along the Inside Passage for Alaska-bound cruise ships and ferries. All kinds of watercraft, floatplanes, and kayakers jostle for space along the crowded waterfront. Cruise ships dock outside downtown, providing passengers with easy access to local attractions such as the **Creek Street** precinct. Formerly the heart of a red-light district, the street is lined with colorfully restored wooden houses built on pilings over the water and linked by a boardwalk.

Even for those who are not planning a trip into the wilderness, the **Southeast Alaska Discovery Center** is definitely worth a visit. Exhibits here relate the human and natural history of the southeast region of Alaska, and also include a fabulous re-creation of a rainforest. Ketchikan's **Totem Heritage Center** displays an incredible collection of more than 30 original totem poles, many more than a century old.

Lying to the north of the city, Tongass Avenue runs along the waterfront all the way to the **Totem Bight State Historical Park**. From here, a trail leads past huge totem poles to a reconstruction of a Native clan house.

🏕 **Southeast Alaska Discovery Center**
50 Main Street. **Tel** (907) 228-6220.
**Open** May–Sep: 8am–5pm Mon–Fri, 8am–4pm Sat–Sun; Oct–Apr: 10am–4pm Thu–Sat. 🐾 ♿

# ❷ Sitka

🏔 9,000. ✈ 🚢 7 miles (11 km) N of downtown. ℹ 303 Lincoln St, (907) 747-5940, (800) 557-4852. 🎏 Alaska Day (Oct 18). 🆆 sitka.org

Founded by Russian entrepreneur Alexander Baranof in 1799, Sitka was the capital of Russian America until Alaska was sold to the United States in 1867. Even now, a strong Russian influence survives here. The center of town is dominated by **St. Michael's Cathedral**, a Russian Orthodox cathedral that was rebuilt after the original 1848 structure burned down in 1966. It preserves many Russian artifacts, including the Sitka Madonna, supposedly blessed with healing powers. Beyond St. Michael's is **Sitka National Historical Park**, the site of a fierce week-long battle between the Russians and local Tlingit tribe in 1804.

Totem pole, Sitka

The area is sprinkled with totem poles, and its shores are gently lapped by the waters of Sitka Sound. Native workers display their craft skills at a cultural center throughout the warm summer. The park is also a good place to view the town's natural setting. Islands dot the Sound, and the snowcapped volcano Mount Edgecumbe – often compared to Japan's Mount Fuji – sits majestically on the horizon.

The Russian-style St. Michael's Cathedral, Sitka

The **Alaska Raptor Center**, across Indian River from the park, rehabilitates bald eagles, owls, and falcons. Visitors are free to walk or join a guided tour. Sitka also has a network of hiking and biking trails.

🏕 **Alaska Raptor Center**
1000 Raptor Way. **Tel** (907) 747-8662, (800) 693-9425. **Open** May–Sep: 8am–4pm daily. **Closed** Oct–Apr. 🗒 ♿ 🆆 alaskaraptor.org

# ❸ Juneau

🏔 31,000. ✈ 🚢 Auke Bay, 14 miles (22 km) NW of downtown, (907) 465-3940. ℹ Centennial Hall Visitor Center, 101 Egan Dr, (907) 586-2201, (888) 581-2201.
🆆 traveljuneau.com

Juneau is possibly the most spectacularly located capital city in the US. It is also the most remote, with no road access to the outside world or even to the rest of Alaska. With its large resident population, as well as over one million visitors who arrive during the short summer (late May–early Sep), Juneau is the busy hub of the Inside Passage. Sandwiched between steep-sided forested peaks and the Gastineau Channel, the heart of the city is an intriguing mix of modern high-rise buildings and historic gems such as the **Red Dog Saloon**, and the **Alaskan Hotel**. The best way to appreciate the town's wonderful location is by taking the tramway up **Mount Roberts**, from where the panorama extends across

Ketchikan's Creek Street, with restored buildings linked by a boardwalk

*For hotels and restaurants see pp744–7*

Gastineau Channel. The downtown **Alaska State Museum** holds a fine collection of Russian artifacts as well as Native crafts such as Eskimo masks. Its natural history section exhibits a re-creation of a bald eagle's nest. Located at the northern end of the city, 13 miles (21 km) from downtown, **Mendenhall Glacier** is an impressive attraction. A part of the massive Juneau Icefield, this slowly retreating 1.5-mile- (2.4-km-) wide glacier is calving icebergs into Mendenhall Lake. A lakeside visitor center offers interpretive panels describing the forces behind glacial movement. This is the starting point for hiking trails that provide close-up views of the glacier. Rafting is also offered.

🏛 **Alaska State Museum**
395 Whittier St. **Tel** (907) 465-2901.
**Closed** for restoration until April 2016.
🅰 ♿ 🆆 **museums.state.ak.us**

📷 **Mendenhall Glacier**
Off Mendenhall Loop Rd. **Tel** (907)
789- 6640. **Open** May–Sep: 8am–
7:30pm daily; Oct–Apr: 10am–4pm
Thu–Sun. 🅰 ♿

## ❹ Glacier Bay National Park

↗ ⛴ from Juneau. ℹ (907) 697-
2230. 🆆 nps.gov/glba
Glacier Bay Lodge & Tours: Departures:
Jun–early Sep: 7am–3:30pm daily.
**Tel** (907) 264-4600, (888) 229-8687.
🆆 visitglacierbay.com

Glacier Bay has changed greatly since the British explorer Captain George Vancouver *(see p600)* found his way through Icy Strait in 1794. During the ensuing 200 years, the glaciers have retreated almost 100 miles

The scenic White Pass & Yukon Route Railroad near Skagway

(160 km), creating a magnificent waterway indented by long bays and protected by the 5,156-sq-mile (13,354-sq-km) national park. Six glaciers reach the sea and break up into massive chunks of ice, which float into a bay inhabited by humpback whales, porpoises, and seals.

Most visitors to Glacier Bay arrive aboard cruise ships. Travelers can also come by way of the hamlet of Gustavus from Juneau, making the short overland trip to Bartlett Cove and Glacier Bay Lodge *(see p744)* by shuttle bus. From Bartlett Cove, it is 40 miles (64 km) to the nearest glacier in a high-speed catamaran. An onboard park naturalist describes the bay's natural history.

## ❺ Skagway

🚠 800. ↗ 🚌 ⛴ SW end of
Broadway. ℹ Broadway at 2nd Ave,
(907) 983-2854. 🆆 skagway.com

The final northbound stop for travelers on the Inside Passage is this little tourist town surrounded by towering peaks. In 1897, thousands of fortune seekers heading for the Klondike goldfields arrived

here only to be faced with an almost insurmountable obstacle – the 33-mile (53 km) **Chilkoot Trail**. This trail traversed a harrowing 45-degree slope nicknamed the "Golden Staircase" over the White Pass to the headwaters of the Yukon River. In the following years, Skagway became a lawless outpost, unofficially ruled by the notorious businessman "Soapy" Smith, who died in a famous shoot-out with a local surveyor outside the City Hall.

Today, Skagway's fortunes rely largely on promoting its colorful history. The whole of the downtown district is protected as the **Klondike Gold Rush National Historic Park**, encompassing false-fronted buildings, old-time saloons, as well as the distinctive Arctic Brotherhood Hall, whose interesting façade is decorated with over 8,000 pieces of driftwood. The **White Pass & Yukon Route Railroad**, which was originally built over the White Pass as an alternative to the Chilkoot Trail, now operates purely for tourists on a scenic three-hour-long round-trip to the pass and back.

### Alaska Marine Highway

Logo, Alaska Marine Highway

The state-operated ferry service links towns that are inaccessible by road throughout southeast and south central Alaska, extending service as far south as Prince Rupert (British Columbia) and Bellingham (Washington). En route, visitors pass magnificent fjords, towering glaciers, and virgin forests. The comfortable and well-equipped vessels carry vehicles, and feature cabins, dining areas, and onboard naturalists. It is possible to even pitch tents on the outer deck. Bookings should be made well in advance *(see p742)*.

Clan house in the Alaska Native Heritage Center, Anchorage

## ❻ Anchorage

🏙 292,000. ✈ 🚌 🚐
ℹ 4th Ave at F St, (907) 274-3531.
🎪 Alaska State Fair (late Aug).
🌐 anchorage.net

Lying between Cook Inlet and the Chugach Mountains, Anchorage is Alaska's largest city. Although this coastal urban sprawl is often described as being un-Alaskan, it is still worth spending a little time in this northern metropolis. It also serves as Alaska's financial and transportation hub. Most of downtown was destroyed by the 1964 Good Friday earthquake (see p719), when the north side of 4th Avenue sank 10 ft (3 m). Interpretive displays at **Earthquake Park**, west of downtown toward the airport, tell the story of the Big One.

One of Alaska's finest museums, the **Anchorage Museum** houses exhibits on Alaskan history, science, and Native culture, along with some of the state's finest art, and the Imaginarium Discovery Center. At the **Alaska Native Heritage Center**, costumed actors provide visitors with a glimpse of Native culture through dance. An entire section has been dedicated to a re-created Native village set beside a pond. Located 50 miles (80 km) southeast of the city, **Portage Glacier** is steadily retreating and is now out of sight from the visitor center. A tour boat plies the lake close to the glacier. The **Iditarod Trail Sled Dog Race** takes place in March.

🏛 **Anchorage Museum**
121 W 7th Ave. **Tel** (907) 929-9200.
**Open** May–Sep: 9am–6pm daily; Oct–Apr: 10am–6pm Tue–Sat, noon–6pm Sun. 🍴 ♿
🌐 anchoragemuseum.org

🏛 **Alaska Native Heritage Center**
8800 Heritage Center Dr. **Tel** (907) 330-8000, (800) 315-6608. **Open** early May–early Sep: 9am–5pm daily. **Closed** late Sep–early May. ♿
🌐 alaskanative.net

## ❼ Valdez

🏙 4,000. ✈ 🚐 downtown.
ℹ 104 Chenega St, (907) 835-4636.
🌐 valdezalaska.org
Stan Stephens Glacier & Wildlife Cruises departures: mid-May–mid-Sep: daily, (907) 835-4731, (866) 867-1297. ♿ limited.
🌐 stanstephenscruises.com

The picturesque town of Valdez nestles below snowcapped peaks along an arm of Prince William Sound, a vast bay encompassing islands, glaciers, and icy waters teeming with wildlife. This is North America's northernmost ice-free port. The **Trans-Alaska Pipeline**, which runs above ground for 800 miles (1,288 km) across the state from Prudhoe Bay on the Arctic Ocean, ends here, from where it is transferred to oil tankers. The *Exxon Valdez* ran aground in 1989, spilling millions of gallons of oil into the Sound. A huge cleanup effort has attempted to restore the Sound, and although there are no obvious signs of the spill today, its adverse effect on birds, fish, and marine mammals persists. A cruise of the Sound passes the **Columbia Glacier**, which is more than 3 miles (4.8 km) wide at its 250-ft- (75-m-) high face, and continuously calves icebergs into the sea. Check with the vistor center for summer tours. The town's **Valdez Museum** explores the Native culture, the importance of oil for the local economy, the *Exxon Valdez* oil spill, and the 1964 Good Friday earthquake, whose epicenter lay less than 60 miles (97 km) from Valdez.

Bronze sculpture, Valdez Museum

🏛 **Valdez Museum**
217 Egan Dr. **Tel** (907) 835-2764.
**Open** mid-May–mid-Sep: 9am–5pm daily; mid-Sep–mid-May: noon–5pm Mon–Sat. 🍴 ♿
🌐 valdezmuseum.org

Re-creation of a traditional miner's cabin, Valdez Museum

The magnificent Exit Glacier in the Kenai Fjords National Park, north of Seward

## ❾ Seward

🗺 3,200. 🛫 🚇 🚌 🚢 downtown.
ℹ 3rd St, (907) 224-8051.
🌐 seward.com

One of the only large towns on the Kenai Peninsula, Seward is a charming fishing port at the head of Resurrection Bay, surrounded by the snow-capped Kenai Mountains. One of its main attractions is the **Alaska SeaLife Center**, which exhibits the marine life of the surrounding ocean. The centerpiece is a string of three huge aquariums holding colorful puffins, seals, and sea lions. Smaller tanks provide a home for crabs and octopuses, while a "touch tank" encourages a hands-on approach to exploring sessile life along the tidal zone.

Seward is bordered by the **Kenai Fjords National Park**, a 906-sq-mile (2,347-sq-km) glaciated coastal wilderness. From the gigantic Hardy Icefield, glaciers radiate in all directions, eight of which are "tidewater glaciers" extending to sea level. Seward's downtown dock is the departure point for boat trips along the park's coastline. These day cruises also provide excellent opportunities for viewing whales, seals, sea lions, porpoises, and large concentrations of photogenic puffins perched on rocky outcrops. The park's most accessible glacier is Exit Glacier, located off the highway, 4 miles (6.4 km) north of Seward. From the end of the access road, a short trail leads through a forest of stunted trees, emerging at a deep-blue river of ice within the valley it carved.

🍽 **Alaska SeaLife Center**
Railway Ave. **Tel** (907) 224-6300, (800) 224-2525. **Open** Sep–late May: 10am–5pm daily; late May–Aug: 9am–9pm Mon–Thu, 8am–9pm Fri–Sun. **Closed** Thanksg., Dec 25.
📷 ♿ 🌐 alaskasealife.org

🍽 **Kenai Fjords National Park**
Park 🅿 ♿ Visitor Center: **Tel** (907) 422-0500. ◐ late May–early Sep: 8:30am–7pm daily; winter: 9am–5pm Mon–Fri. 🌐 nps.gov/kefj

## ❾ Homer

🗺 5,000. 🛫 🚢 Homer Spit.
ℹ 201 Sterling Hwy, (907) 235-7740.
🌐 homeralaska.org Islands and Ocean Center: 95 Sterling Hwy, (907) 235-6961.

At the end of the Sterling Highway lies Homer, a delightful little hamlet by the water. It was discovered by Homer Pennock, a gold-prospector who arrived here in 1896. Today, this town has become a popular destination for visitors. Its main focus is **Homer Spit**, a 4-mile (6.4-km) finger of land that juts into Kachemak Bay, with the rugged Kenai Mountains glistening across the water. A busy road traverses the entire Spit, passing beaches, a colorful collection of fishing boats, fishing-supply stores, and lively restaurants. Known as the "Halibut Capital of the World," fishing is its main attraction. Charter operators and their boats line the Spit; day trips include tackle and bait as well as instruction. Those who manage to hook a halibut or salmon can arrange to have it frozen and shipped home. The **Fishing Hole** on the Spit is a man-made water hole stocked with salmon for an easy catch.

The magnificent wilderness of the **Kachemak Bay State Park**, on the bay's opposite shore, can be explored through a number of hiking trails. The best known of these leads the visitor to the Grewingk Glacier.

Fishermen with a halibut "weigh-in" on Homer Spit

The northern end of Kodiak Island, covered with thick spruce forests

## ⑩ Kodiak Island

🏔 14,000. ✈ 🚢 downtown. ℹ 100 Marine Way, (800) 789-4782, (907) 486-4782. 🌐 **kodiak.org**

The second-largest island in the United States, Kodiak extends for 100 miles (160 km) across the Gulf of Alaska. Most of the island is an inaccessible stretch of wilderness protected by the 2,969-sq-mile (7,690-sq-km) **Kodiak National Wildlife Refuge**. Kodiak Island is famous as the habitat of about 2,500 Kodiak bears – the world's largest brown bear – some of which stand 10 ft (3 m) tall and weigh up to 1,500 lb (675 kg). The visitor center provides details on charter flights to the best viewing spots.

Most of the island's residents live in the town of Kodiak, home of the country's largest Coast Guard station and its third-largest fishing fleet. North America's oldest Russian building, a storehouse dating to 1808, is now the excellent **Baranov Museum**. A repository of Kodiak's history, the museum's highlights include a superb samovar (urn) collection, Aleut kayaks, and photographs of the town after it was hit by a tsunami (massive tidal wave), triggered by the 1964 Good Friday earthquake (see p719). To explore the local fishing

industry, follow Shelikof Street past the harbor to the canneries.

🏛 **Baranov Museum**
101 Marine Way. **Tel** (907) 486-5920. **Open** Jun–Aug: 10am–4pm Mon–Sat; Sep–May: 10am–3pm Tue–Sat. 📷 🌐 **baranovmuseum.org**

## ⑪ Alaska Peninsula

✈ ℹ King Salmon Airport, (907) 246-4250.

Dominated by the Alaska Range, this remote part of the state attracts visitors for its intriguing wilderness and wildlife-viewing opportunities. In 1912, the second-largest blast in recorded history occurred when the peninsula's Mount Novarupta erupted, covering a 400-sq-mile (1,036-sq-km) area with ash and pumice up to a height of 700 ft (210 m). The blast was heard as far away

Samovar, Baranov Museum

as Seattle, and the ash that erupted stayed in the atmosphere for an entire year.

The 6,250-sq-mile (16,187-sq-km) **Katmai National Park** encompasses the area where the volcano was most active. A remnant is the Valley of 10,000 Smokes, where gases and ash continue to spew across a lunar-like landscape.

Adjacent to Katmai, photographers from around the world gather at the **McNeil River State Game Sanctuary** to photograph brown bears catching salmon as they struggle up to McNeil River Falls. Access to the falls is by air taxi from King Salmon or Homer (see p725).

🐾 **Katmai National Park**
(907) 246-3305. 🌐 **nps.gov/katm**

🐾 **McNeil River State Game Sanctuary**
**Open** Best viewing: Jul–mid-Aug. 📷 Permit required: from Department of Fish & Game, (907) 267-2182. 🌐 **adfg.alaska.gov**

A brown bear at Katmai National Park, Alaska Peninsula

## ⑫ Aleutian Islands

🏔 9,000. ✈ ⛴ Unalaska. ℹ
Unalaska Dutch Harbor Convention
and Visitors' Bureau, (907) 581-2612,
(877) 581-2612. 🌐 **unalaska.info**

Beyond the Alaska Peninsula,
the summits of the Aleutian
Range have created a string of
islands that extend 1,200 miles
(1,932 km) into the Pacific
Ocean. Originally settled by
hardy Aleut seal hunters, the
islands were occupied for more
than a year by the Japanese
during World War II. Today,
over half the archipelago's
population live in the town of
**Unalaska**, which is set around
a picturesque Dutch Harbor.
This town is North America's
number one seafood
producer. The catch
includes crab, halibut,
cod, and pollock. Its
harbor is lined with
fishing boats, container
cranes, and processing
plants, all catering
to this industry. The
**Russian Orthodox
Church of the Holy
Ascension**, built
in 1827, dominates
the foreshore.

Caribou at the Ice Museum,
Fairbanks

## ⑬ Nome

🏔 3,000. ✈ ℹ 301 Front St, (907)
443-6555, (800) 478-1901.
🌐 **visitnomealaska.com**

Few would argue with
the local catchphrase that
"there's no place like Nome."
Perched on the edge of the
Bering Sea, closer to Russia
than to Anchorage, the town
was named after an early
cartographer marked this
location as "Name?" on a
map. Later another
mapmaker misread the
annotation as "Nome."
    Although Nome is now a
shadow of its former self, it is
still a fascinating and popular
destination. Friendly staff at
the tourist information office
obligingly indicate historic
relics such as the **Last Train
to Nowhere**, and the rusting
hulks of dredges that have
long since been abandoned.

There are many hiking trails
stretching across the treeless
tundra. Panning for gold
along the beach is another
unique activity.

## ⑭ Fairbanks

🏔 35,000. ✈ 🚌 ℹ 101 Dunkel St,
(907) 456-5774, (800) 327-5774.
🌐 **explorefairbanks.com**

Surrounded by subarctic
wilderness, Fairbanks is Alaska's
second-largest city and has one
of the largest populations at
this latitude anywhere in the
world. Located just 150 miles
(241 km) south of the Arctic
Circle, the sun barely dips
below the horizon at the
time of the summer
solstice (Jun 21). The
long hours of darkness
through winter make it
a good place to view
the aurora borealis,
or northern lights,
a phenomenon of
dazzling sheets of
light produced in the
sky by electron and
proton particles of
the solar wind.
Fairbanks is also known for its
extremes in temperature, which
often soar well above 90° F
(32° C) in summer, but dip
below -60° F (-15° C) in winter.
The downtown **Morris
Thompson Cultural & Visitor
Center** has information and
excellent exhibits on regional
history. The University of Alaska
Museum of the North focuses
on natural history and art. At

The old mining town of McCarthy in
Wrangell-St. Elias National Park

View of the aurora borealis, or northern
lights, Alaska

**Pioneer Park**, historic buildings
collected from around the state
re-create a Gold Rush-era town
on the banks of the Chena River.
Each summer evening, Pioneer
Park plays host to a musical
revue, with dancers who are
dressed in period costume.

🏛 **Pioneer Park**
Airport Way. **Tel** (907) 459-1087. **Open**
daily. Gold Rush Town: **Open** late
May–early Sep: noon–8pm daily. ♿

🏛 **Morris Thompson Cultural &
Visitor Center**
101 Dunkel St. **Tel** (907) 459-3700.
**Open** daily.

## ⑮ Wrangell-St. Elias
## National Park

✈ McCarthy. 🚌 to McCarthy.
ℹ Wrangell-St. Elias National Park
Visitors' Center, Mile 106.5 Richardson
Highway; (907) 822-7476. Ranger
stations at Chitina and Slana. 🅿 💻
📷 ♿ 🌐 nps.gov/wrst

The largest National Park
in the US – six times the size
of Yellowstone. Wrangell-St.
Elias National Park is a
20,000-sq-mile (52,500-sq-km)
wilderness sprawling across
the southeast corner of the
Alaskan mainland. Dominated
by the volcanic Wrangell
Mountains and the glaciated
St. Elias Range, the park has
nine of the 16 highest
mountains in the US.
Designated a UNESCO World
Heritage Site in 1992, the park
contains historic mining sites,
such as the town of McCarthy.

# ⑯ Denali National Park

Alaska's top attraction, Denali National Park encompasses 9,375 sq miles (24,281 sq km). The 20,320-ft- (6,194-m-) high Mount McKinley, North America's highest peak, dominates the landscape, rising 10,000 ft (3,048 m) above the surrounding peaks. The park is home to abundant wildlife, including grizzly bears, moose, and caribou, and wildflowers explode with color across the tundra in July. Only one road penetrates Denali, traversing varied landscapes that include lowlands and high mountain passes. Several hiking trails can be enjoyed in the vicinity of the visitor center. Other activities include sled dog demonstrations, rafting on the Nenana River, and flight-seeing around Mount McKinley.

**The Alaska Railroad**
Many travelers opt for rail travel when it comes to visiting Denali.

**★ Wonder Lake**
Near the end of the park road, Wonder Lake affords one of the finest views of Mount McKinley.

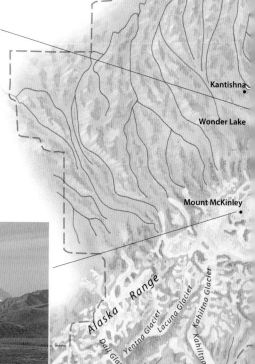

Kantishna

Wonder Lake

Mount McKinley

Alaska Range

Dahl Glacier

Yentna Glacier

Lacuna Glacier

Kahiltna Glacier

Kahiltna Glacier

0 kilometers 20
0 miles 20

**★ Mount McKinley**
View of the snow-clad Mount McKinley from Park Road, en route to Wonder Lake. Originally called Denali, "the Great One," by Athabascan Natives, many Alaskans still continue to refer to Mount McKinley by its old name.

★ **White-Water Rafting**
Thrills and spills abound on the Nenana River, which flows along the eastern boundary of the national park.

## VISITORS' CHECKLIST

**Practical Information**
W nps.gov/dena
W reservedenali.com
Park: Open daily. Visitor Center:
Open mid-May–mid-Sep:
8am–6pm daily.
Tel (907) 683-2294.
Park shuttle buses: Reserve seats
in advance. Some buses return
from the Eielson Visitor Center,
which has great views of
Mount McKinley; others continue
to Wonder Lake 25 miles (40 km)
from the peak. The 90-m/150-km
round-trip takes 13 hours.
Departures: mid-May–mid-Sep:
daily from 6am to 2pm at
regular intervals. Check website
for schedule.
Tel (907) 272-7275,
(866) 761-6629.

*Fairbanks*

Santuary
River
Teklanika
River
Savage
River
Riley
Creek
Igloo Creek

**Toklat**

Alaska Range

**Eielson Visitor
Center**

Cantwell

Idrow Glacier

Eldridge Glacier

Alaska Railroad

Parks Highway

Nenana River

Ruth Glacier

↓ *Anchorage*

Tourists on a park shuttle bus trip

## Wildlife Viewing

One of the major attractions in Alaska is wildlife viewing, and Denali National Park provides great opportunities to see a wide variety of the state's largest and most impressive animals. Grizzly bears, moose, Dall sheep, and caribou are routinely sighted by visitors from the park shuttle buses, with drivers stopping to allow viewing and photography. The park is also home to wolves, and while they are not as commonly sighted as many other mammals, spotting these magnificent creatures in the wild is a memorable experience for visitors.

Grizzly bear feeding
on berries

Moose wading in water

Caribou are a
common sight

### Key

- – Park boundary
— Alaska railroad
═ Major road
═ Unpaved road

For keys to symbols *see back flap*

# HAWAI'I

A tropical island paradise of golden sand beaches, waterfalls, and lush forests, the Aloha State attracts more than 6 million visitors a year. An isolated archipelago in the middle of the Pacific Ocean, the islands' exotic landscape and luxurious hospitality offer a wealth of experiences from volcanic eruptions and world-class surfing to glimpses of the fascinating cultural heritage of Polynesia.

Located in the middle of the Pacific Ocean, 2,500 miles (4,000 km) southwest of Los Angeles, the Hawaiian Islands are volcanic in origin. In fact, the islands are still evolving, as is evident from the lava flows on the slopes of 13,796-ft (4,205-m) Mount Kīlauea on the island of Hawai'i or the "Big Island."

The next largest island, Maui, was formed by the dormant volcano Haleakalā. This, the fastest-growing of the islands, still retains some significant history, especially in the former whaling port of Lahaina. The next island along in the chain, Moloka'i, is well off the tourist trail. Formerly a pineapple ranching center, Moloka'i is famous for the towering cliffs that line its northern coast. Lāna'i, another small island, is also offshore from Maui.

The most popular and developed island is O'ahu, where three-quarters of the population lives and most of the visitors congregate. The center of O'ahu is Honolulu, the state capital and only big city. Across the ocean from O'ahu sits magical Kaua'i, known as the "Garden Isle" for its verdant rainforests, kept moist by more than 400 inches (10 m) of annual rainfall.

Polynesian dance, a popular attraction

## History

Hawai'i's historical connections to the US mainland are both distant and contentious. Originally colonized by Polynesians, Hawai'i was a group of independent kingdoms when it was discovered by English sailor Captain James Cook in 1778. Initially welcomed by the natives, Cook was killed by them a year later. Other explorers followed, bringing new, often fatal diseases.

By the end of the 18th century, however, the islands had been united into a respected monarchy under the revered monarch, King Kamehameha the Great (ruled 1795–1819).

During the early 19th century, European traders introduced fundamental changes. Christianity was introduced by Puritan missionaries from Boston in 1820, while economically, forestry and whaling gained importance. These proved destabilizing to Native culture, and by the 1880s, white American entrepreneurs, mainly sugar cane and pineapple farmers, acquired control, and the monarchy was overthrown in 1893. After a series of highly complicated political maneuvers, Hawai'i became part of the US in 1898. Much later, in 1993, the US issued a formal apology to the people of Hawai'i for its leading role in the "illegal overthrow of the Kingdom of Hawai'i."

Powerful American plantation owners dominated the first half of the 1900s, and all attempts to unionize the low-paid, mostly Japanese labor force were firmly

The summit of Maui's Mount Haleakalā

Canoeing and swimming, some of the most popular water activities in Hawai'i

squelched. Ironically, it took the threat of invasion to make the feudal institutions democratic. On December 7, 1941, Japan attacked Pearl Harbor, instigating America's entry into World War II, and changing Hawai'i forever.

## Hawai'i Today

Located midway between mainland US and the Far East, Hawai'i has a diverse population. Of its 1.3 million residents, roughly one-third are non-Asian, one-third are of Japanese descent, and the rest a wide-ranging mix of Filipinos, Chinese, Koreans, and Samoans. Only a few thousand full-blooded indigenous Hawaiians survive today, but the native spirit of "Aloha," a Hawaiian word that simultaneously means hello, goodbye, welcome, and love, is still alive.

The introduction of air travel in 1959 brought Hawai'i within easy reach of the West Coast. As tourism became the chief industry, resort developments proliferated, signaling a new era for the island economy. At the same time, a resurgence in Native culture, language, and crafts has softened the harsher edges of the commercial development, so that no matter where you go in the islands, their Polynesian roots are clearly visible.

Cyclist on a scenic bike ride, away from the crowded beach Waikīkī

### KEY DATES IN HISTORY

**AD 400** Polynesians migrate to the Hawaiian Islands from the Marquesas Islands

**1778** James Cook is the first European to the islands, which he names the Sandwich Islands after his benefactor, the Earl of Sandwich

**1795** Reign of Kamehameha begins

**1893** With the support of the US Navy, American businessmen overthrow the Kingdom of Hawai'i, declaring an independent republic

**1898** Hawai'i is annexed as a US Territory

**1941** Japanese bombers attack Pearl Harbor on December 7

**1959** Hawai'i becomes the 50th state

**1983** Mount Kīlauea begins its present eruption

**1993** US government issues a formal apology on the 100th anniversary of the overthrow of the Kingdom of Hawai'i

**1996** Citizens vote to convene on the issue of sovereignty

# Exploring Hawai'i

The world's most isolated archipelago, Hawai'i lies 2,500 miles (4,000 km) from the West Coast. The five main islands – O'ahu, Moloka'i, Maui, Hawai'i, and Kaua'i – stretch across over 500 miles (805 km) of the Pacific Ocean. Most of Hawai'i's six million annual visitors arrive by air in Honolulu, the state capital, and travel from one island to another is mainly by inter-island flights. A handful of ferry services and some luxury cruises also link the islands. The most reliable way to explore individual islands is by car, as public transportation is minimal, except on O'ahu.

A secluded swimming spot on the rocky coast of the Ke'anae Peninsula

## Sights at a Glance

### O'ahu
1 Honolulu
2 Byodo-In Temple
3 Hawai'i's Plantation Village
4 North Shore

### Moloka'i & Maui
5 Kaunakakai
6 Kalaupapa National Historical Park
7 Lahaina
8 Haleakalā National Park
9 Hāna

### Hawai'i
10 *Hawai'i Volcanoes National Park p738*
11 Hilo
12 Pu'uhonua O Hōnaunau National Historical Park

### Kaua'i
13 Līhu'e
14 Kīlauea Point
15 Waimea Canyon & Kōke'e State Park
16 Kalalau Trail

Windsurfers in action at Ho'okipa Beach County Park, near the beach town of Pā'ia on Maui's north shore

Dramatic Honomanū Bay with its clear blue waters, surrounded by lushly forested cliffs

**Key**

Highway

Major road

PACIFIC
OCEAN

Kalaupapa
NHP
**6**
MOLOKA'I
**5**
Kaunakakai
(450)

Lahaina
**7**
Pā'ia
Wailua
MAUI
(30)
Pukalani
Lāna'i City
Kīhei
LĀNA'I
**8**
Mānele
Bay
Haleakalā
NP
**9** Hāna
(37)
Kaho'olawe

'Alenuihāhā Channel

Honoka'a
Laupāhoehoe
Waimea
Mauna Kea
4205m
Wailea
Keāhole-Kona
Kailua
Hilo
**11** Kea'au
Kahalu'u
Mauna Loa
4169m
Mountain
View
Captain Cook
Hawai'i
**10**
Pu'uhonua O Hōnaunau
National Historical Park
**12**
Volcanoes NP
(130)
Pāhoa
(11)
HAWAI'I
Pāhala
0 kilometers    50
0 miles         50
Nā'ālehu

# O'ahu

The third largest island in the archipelago, with an area of 600 sq miles (1,550 sq km), O'ahu is Hawai'i's most visited and most populous island. Three-quarters of the state's 1.3 million residents live here, most of them in the Greater Honolulu area. Outside the urban areas, with their cultural attractions, O'ahu offers spectacular scenery, with lush plantations, tropical beaches, and a surfers' paradise on the North Shore.

Statue of King Kamehameha, his hand extended in welcome

## ❶ Honolulu

🚩 905,000. 🛈 O'ahu VB, (808) 524-0722. 🌐 visit-oahu.com; HVCB (Hawai'i Visitors and Convention Bureau), (808) 923-1811, (800) 464-2924. 🌐 gohawaii.com

Hawai'i's capital city has two focal points – the historic and business district of downtown Honolulu, and the world famous resort of Waikīkī, 3 miles (5 km) to its east. The downtown area, which first gained prominence as a trading port in the early 19th century, today manages to squeeze together towering skyscrapers, a royal palace, Japanese shrines, New England-style missionary houses, a bustling Chinatown, strip joints, and fish markets in a relatively small and compact area.

Dominating downtown's Capitol District is the magnificent Victorian-style **'Iolani Palace**, completed in 1882. The only royal palace in the US, it was designed and first lived in by King David Kalākaua, followed by his sister Queen Lili'uokalani, who reigned for only two years before the monarchy was overthrown in 1893 *(see p730)*. The site of frequent community events, the palace has luxurious interiors and a *koa*-wood staircase.

To its south is the New England-style **Kawaiaha'o Church**, constructed of coral blocks. It was built in 1842, by which time American missionaries had gained many influential local converts to Christianity. The upper gallery has portraits of Hawaiian monarchs, most of whom were baptized, married, and crowned here. Adjacent to the church is

'Iolani Palace crest

the **Mission Houses Museum**, which contains the oldest timber-frame house in Hawai'i, built in 1821 by the New England missionary Reverend Hiram Bingham. Housed in three buildings, the museum has a printing house and lovingly preserved interiors.

Nearby is the bronze **Statue of King Kamehameha**, Hawai'i's most revered monarch, who ruled from 1795 to 1819 *(see p730)*. The statue, with its feathered cloak and an arm extended in welcome, is one of Hawai'i's most famous sights.

North of the Capitol District is **Chinatown**, with two marble lions guarding its entrance. The area is an exotic neighborhood of open-air markets, *lei* (flower garland) stands, eateries, and herbal medicine shops. Hawai'i's first Chinese arrived on merchant ships in 1789, followed in 1852 by larger numbers who came to work on O'ahu's sugar plantations. Chinatown's buildings include the Art Deco **Hawai'i Theatre** and the state's oldest Japanese Shinto shrine,

the **Izumo Taisha Shrine**, built in 1923. At Honolulu Harbor, the fascinating **Hawai'i Maritime Center** displays antique canoes and exhibits tracing the exploits of Polynesian navigators. Moored next to it are the *Hōkūle'a*, a modern replica of an ancient Polynesian canoe with sails, and the restored 1878 *Falls of Clyde*, the world's last surviving full-rigged four-masted sailing ship.

**Waikīkī**, originally a place of taro patches and fish ponds, now has one of the world's famous beaches – a sliver of people-packed sand against the backdrop of **Diamond Head** crater. Waikīkī bustles with some 65,000 tourists a day who flock here to sunbathe on the golden sand, swim in the sheltered water, and surf the gentle waves. The sandy beach stretches for 2.5 miles (4 km), from the Hilton Hawaiian Village to Diamond Head. The streets and shopping malls are packed with beachwear vendors, honeymooners, Japanese matrons, and boys carrying surfboards. Conspicuous amid the glass and concrete skyscrapers are two stately

The Waikīkī Beach front, lined with high-rise hotels

old hotels – the coral pink **Royal Hawaiian Hotel** and the Colonial-style **Moana Hotel**, Waikīkī's oldest.

Several interesting sights are also located in Greater Honolulu. Considered the world's finest museum of Polynesian culture, **Bishop Museum** was created by American businessman Charles Bishop to preserve royal heirlooms left by his wife, a Hawaiian princess. Its priceless exhibits include fabulous ceremonial feather standards, rare *tamate* costumes made of shredded fiber, sacred images, and a *hale* (traditional house) thatched with *pili* grass.

The **National Memorial Cemetery of the Pacific**, located in Punchbowl, the crater of an extinct volcano, has over 33,000 graves. Among those buried here are victims of Pearl Harbor and those killed in the Korean and Vietnam wars.

**Pearl Harbor**, a place of pilgrimage for many visitors, houses warships, military museums, and memorials. Most significant among these is the **USS *Arizona* Memorial**, which stands perched above the ship of the same name that was sunk during the Japanese bombing on December 7, 1941. Some of the volunteer guides that you will meet here happen to be survivors of that fateful attack, which killed more than 2,000 US officers and men, and destroyed 18 battleships, bringing the United States into World War II *(see p731)*.

**Hawai'i Maritime Center**
Pier 7, Honolulu Harbor. **Tel** (808) 599-3810. 19, 20. **Open** 9am–5pm Wed–Mon. **Closed** Dec 25.
**W** bishopmuseum.org

**Bishop Museum**
1525 Bernice St. **Tel** (808) 847-3511. 2. **Open** 9am–5pm Wed–Mon. **Closed** Dec 25. Craft demonstrations, music & dance recitals: daily.
**W** bishopmuseum.org

**Pearl Harbor**
7 miles (11 km) NW of downtown Honolulu. 20, 42. USS *Arizona* Memorial: 1 Arizona Memorial Drive. **Tel** (808) 422-0561. **Open** 7am–5pm daily. **Closed** Jan 1, Thanksgiving, Dec 25. **W** nps.gov/usar

## ❷ Byodo-In Temple

47-200 Kahekili Hwy (Hwy 83), Kāne'ohe. **Tel** (808) 239-8811. on Kahekili Hwy (Hwy 83), then 10-min walk. **Open** 9am–5pm daily. **Closed** Dec 25. **W** byodo-in.com

This replica of a 900-year-old Japanese temple in a tranquil and secluded spot is O'ahu's hidden treasure, its bright red walls framed against the backdrop of fluted green cliffs. A curved vermilion footbridge and a three-ton bell lead to the Byodo-In Temple, which houses a beautiful 9-ft (3-m) Buddha. Sunset here is a magical experience, with the cliffs giving off pink and mauve hues.

## ❸ Hawai'i's Plantation Village

94-695 Waipahu St, Waipahu. **Tel** (808) 677-0110. 43. **Open** Tours on the hour, 10am–2pm Mon–Sat. **Closed** public hols. **W** hawaiiplantationvillage.org

This three-million dollar restored village portrays a hundred years of sugar plantation culture, from 1840 to 1943. It also contains various re-created buildings from the major ethnic groups that worked in the plantations – Korean, Puerto Rican, and Japanese homes – as well as a Shinto shrine. Personal objects placed in the houses give the impression that the occupants have just left, soon to return. The small on-site museum runs informative walking tours for visitors.

## ❹ North Shore

2,500. HVCB, Oahu, (877) 525-6248. O-Bon Buddhist Festival (Jul or Aug). **W** gohawaii.com

The hub for the North Shore surfing community is **Hale'iwa**. The town's picturesque harbor is flanked by well-appointed public beaches. **Ali'i Beach** is famous for big waves and surfing contests. The adjacent **Hale'iwa Beach Park** is one of the few North Shore spots where it is usually quite safe to swim in winter. At the enchanting annual O-Bon Festival, thousands of floating lanterns are released into the ocean here.

Sign for Hale'iwa, O'ahu's surf town

Another popular North Shore spot is **Waimea Valley**. The valley is a botanical paradise, with 36 gardens, thousands of rare tropical plants, and 30 species of birds. There are no longer the commercial shows that Waimea Valley was once famous for, such as hula, and cliff-diving. Instead, the center provides an important educational resource and is a beautiful and unspoilt environment. Visitors can tour the valley, but bring binoculars as the park has great opportunities for bird-watchers. Afterwards, swim or snorkel at the Waimea Beach Park across the street from the center.

**Waimea Valley**
59-864 Kamehameha Hwy (Hwy 83), Waimea. **Tel** (808) 638-7766. **Open** 9am–5pm Mon–Fri. **Closed** Jan 1, Thanksgiving, Dec 25.

The enchanting Byodo-In Temple, a Buddhist shrine

# Moloka'i & Maui

The small island of Moloka'i, between O'ahu and Maui, is much less developed for tourism than its neighbors. The gentle pace of life, and the spectacular scenery of its flower-decked south coast and of the Kalaupapa National Historical Park, backed by the world's highest sea cliffs, enchant most visitors. Maui, Hawai'i's second-largest island, offers lively resorts with a range of water sports, as well as lush plantations and the awesome grandeur of the Haleakalā Volcano.

Moloka'i's isolated Kalaupapa Peninsula, backed by towering cliffs

## ❺ Kaunakakai

🏠 2,700. 🛈 Ala Malama St & Kamehameha V Hwy (Hwy 450), (800) 464-2924. 🎭 Ka Moloka'i Makahiki (cultural festival, late Jan).
🌐 **gohawaii.com**

Moloka'i's main town, Kaunakakai, was built in the 19th century as a port for the local sugar and pineapple plantations. Today, commercial agriculture has all but disappeared from the island, and Kaunakakai looks its age. The main street, with its wooden boardwalk, is lined with false-fronted stores. A short distance from the town center, local fishermen throng **Kaunakakai Harbor**, its long stone jetty jutting out into the ocean. About 2 miles (3 km) west of town is the **Kapuāiwa Coconut Grove**, whose 1,000 soaring trees are a majestic sight, silhouetted against the setting sun.

### Environs
East of Kaunakakai begins the **Kamehameha V Highway**, which is among the most beautiful coastal drives in

Hawai'i. The 27-mile (44-km) highway takes in ancient sites, picturesque churches, pristine beaches, and sleepy villages tucked away amid tropical flowers and luxuriant rainforests. The road finally twists to a halt at the stunningly beautiful **Hālawa Valley** which, with its soaring walls, lush vegetation, idyllic beaches, and shimmering waterfalls, is Moloka'i's most scenic spot.

## ❻ Kalaupapa National Historical Park

Reached by foot or mule on Kalaupapa Trail: trailhead on Hwy 470, 3 miles (5 km) N of Kualapu'u, between the mule stables & Kalaupapa Overlook. 🚻 🅿️ 🖼️ compulsory. Father Damien Tours, (808) 567-6171. Book well in advance. Visitors must be 16 years of age or older. For Moloka'i Mule Ride, (808) 567-6088, book in advance.
🌐 **muleride.com**

The isolated Kalaupapa Peninsula, sealed off from the rest of Moloka'i by a mighty wall of cliffs, is home to the

**Kalaupapa National Historical Park**. In 1865, when the imported disease of leprosy seemed to threaten the survival of the Hawaiian people, the peninsula was designated a leper colony, and those afflicted were exiled here. The park now serves as a memorial. The main settlement was at the village of Kalaupapa, on the western side of the peninsula. The last patients arrived in 1969, when the policy of enforced isolation ended. Kalaupapa's small population today includes a few aging patients who chose to live out their lives here.

South of the village is the **Kalaupapa Trail**, a favorite with hikers and mule riders who enjoy stupendous views during the 2-mile (3-km) trip. At the center of the peninsula is the **Kauhakō Crater**, with an 800-ft (245-m) deep lake.

On the peninsula's eastern shore is **St. Philomena Church**, in the original leprosy settlement of Kalawao. Shipped out from Honolulu in 1872, the church was later modified by the Belgian priest Father Damien (1840–89), who dedicated his life to caring for the leprosy patients. Father Damien succumbed to leprosy in 1889 and has been beatified by the Pope. His right hand is interred in the church. From the peninsula's eastern side, small islands poke out of the waters of the ocean, next to staggering 2000-ft (600-m) cliffs – the tallest sea cliffs in the world.

St. Philomena Church, where Father Damien's hand is buried

*For hotels and restaurants see pp744–7*

Locals demonstrating their courage at Keka'a Point, Kā'anapali

# ❼ Lahaina

🏠 9,100. 🚢 Lahaina Harbor. ℹ 648 Wharf St, (808) 667-9175. 🎭 A Taste of Lahaina (food festival, mid-Sep); Halloween Mardi Gras of the Pacific (Oct 31). 🌐 visitlahaina.com

One of Maui's most popular attractions, this small harbor town was the capital of the Kingdom of Hawai'i until 1845 and a major center of the whaling trade. The area around Front Street has a wealth of well-restored historic sites, evocative of Lahaina's past. Among them is the **Baldwin Home**, Maui's oldest Western-style dwelling, dating from the 1830s, with original furnishings and artifacts. Nearby is the **Chinese Wo Hing Temple**, built in 1912. A favorite landmark is Lahaina's first hotel, the charming 1901 **Pioneer Inn**, still a tourist mecca and hotel.

Docked in the harbor, beside the lighthouse, is the *Carthaginian II*, a 1920s German schooner transformed to look like the kind of small freighter that brought cargo and people to the islands in the 1800s. It has a fascinating museum in the hold, devoted to whales and the whale trade.

Just 6 miles (10 km) north of Lahaina is Maui's biggest resort, **Kā'anapali**, its long white beach lined with hotels. **Pu'u Keka'a**, better known as Black Rock, towers above the beach and overlooks one of Maui's best snorkeling spots. Vintage steam locomotives make the short and scenic trip here from Lahaina. A 20-minute drive north of Kā'anapali is Maui's other major resort, **Kapalua**, with its exquisite crescent bays, blue waters, luxury hotels, golf courses, and beautiful pineapple plantations.

# ❽ Haleakalā National Park

Haleakalā Crater Road (Hwy 378). **Open** 24 hrs daily. 🚵 🚙 Park Headquarters: **Tel** (808) 572-4400. **Open** 8am–4pm daily. ♿ Visitor Center: **Open** 6:30am–3:30pm daily. ♿ 🌐 nps.gov/hale Cabins: 🌐 fhnp.org/wcr (for reservations).

The landmass of East Maui is really the top of an enormous volcano that begins more than 3 miles (5 km) below sea level. Haleakalā last spewed molten lava some 200 years ago and is still considered to be active, although not currently erupting. Its summit depression is 7.5 miles (12 km) long and 2.5 miles (4 km) wide. This natural wonder is preserved as part of the national park. The 2-hour drive to the 10,023-ft (3,055-m) **Pu'u 'Ula'ula Summit**, the highest point in Maui, offers a breathtaking view of the entire volcano, with its cinder cones and brightly colored ashes.

The best way to appreciate Haleakalā's scale and varied terrain is to descend 3,000 ft (900 m) into the volcano. The 10-mile (16-km) **Sliding Sands Trail** takes you from the visitor center through scenery that ranges from barren cinder desert to alpine shrubland. Also worth exploring is the **Silversword Loop** where one of the world's rarest plants, the Haleakalā Silversword, thrives. It takes up to 50 years to flower, when it raises a spectacular spike of purplish flowers.

# ❾ Hāna

🏠 700. 🚌 ℹ MVB, Wailuku, (808) 244-3530. 🎭 East Maui Taro Festival (Mar/Apr). 🌐 hanamaui.com

Often called Hawai'i's most Hawaiian town, Hāna continues to lag lazily behind modernity. Its perfect round bay and dreamy climate have made it a prized settlement since ancient times. **Ka'uiki Head**, the large cinder cone on the right flank of the bay, served as a natural fortification.

The **Hāna Cultural Center** presents a *kauhale* (residential compound) in the precontact style once unique to this area and exhibits artifacts that give a sense of local history. **Wānanalua Church**, constructed from blocks of coral in 1838, was built by missionaries on top of an existing *heiau* (temple), thus symbolizing the triumph of Christianity over paganism.

The scenic **Hāna Belt Road** twists along the coast to Pā'ia, with views of waterfalls, gulches choked with vegetation, taro fields, botanical gardens, rocky cliffs, and the dramatic Honomanū Bay with its black sand beach.

Pu'u 'Ula'ula Summit in Haleakalā National Park, Maui's highest point

# Hawai'i

Spreading over 4,035 sq miles (10,450 sq km), the island of Hawai'i, also known as the Big Island, is more than twice the size of all the other islands combined. Its natural wonders include the earth's most massive mountain, Mauna Loa, which rises over 30,000 ft (9,150 m) from the ocean floor, and Kīlauea, the most active volcano on earth, both of which form part of the Hawai'i Volcanoes National Park. Equally fascinating are the island's well-preserved cultural sites within the Pu'uhonua O Hōnaunau National Historical Park.

## ❿ Hawai'i Volcanoes National Park

Hawai'i Belt Road (Hwy 11). **Open** 24 hours daily. 🅿️ ⚠️ Kīlauea Visitor Center: **Tel** (808) 985-6000. **Open** 7:45am–5pm daily. ♿ Jaggar Museum: **Tel** (808) 985-6049. **Open** 8:30am–8:30pm daily. ♿ Volcano Art Center: **Tel** (808) 967-7565, (866) 967-7565. **Open** 9am–5pm daily. **Closed** Dec 25. ♿ 🎁 Volcano House Hotel: **Tel** (808) 967-7321. ♿ 🅿️ 🌐 nps.gov/havo

Encompassing about a quarter of a million acres, this national park includes the 13,677-ft (4,169-m) summit of Mauna Loa, 150 miles (240 km) of hiking trails, and vast tracts of wilderness that preserve some of the world's rarest species of flora and fauna. But it is Kīlauea Caldera and the lava flows of its furious East Rift Zone that draw most visitors. Two roads – **Crater Rim Drive**, which loops around the caldera, and **Chain of Craters Road**, which descends through the recent outpourings – form a gigantic drive-through museum. The present eruption started in 1983 and produces slow-moving lava, which poses no threat to visitors. However, you should stay out of closed areas; no one knows how long the flow will continue or where it will next erupt.

Lava fountains spewing from Kīlauea during the 1983 eruption

**Key**

▰▰▰ Major road

▭▭▭ Minor road

•–• Hiking trail

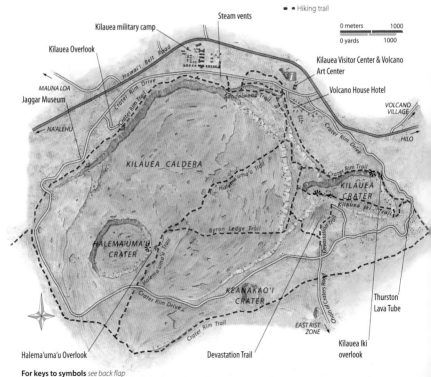

Thurston Lava Tube, formed by the hardening of a lava stream

East of the park, the **Kīlauea Iki Overlook** gives a view of the crater, which in 1959 filled with bubbling lava, shooting fire fountains 1,900 ft (580 m) into the air. Across the road from the crater, at the eastern edge of the park, lies the Thurston Lava Tube. This huge tunnel was left behind when a subterranean river of lava drained away. An easy trail runs through the tube and a grove of giant ferns. Nearby, the short Devastation Trail features ghostly remains of a rainforest, wiped out by ash falling from Kīlauea Iki's 1959 eruption. Farther west, the Halema'uma'u Overlook affords views of the once boiling lake of lava. The crater below still steams with sulfurous fumes. This is the home of Pele, the fiery-tempered volcano goddess, who migrated from Kahiki (Tahiti) seeking a dry place for her eternal fires.

## ⓫ Hilo

🗺 45,000. ✈ 🚌 Kamehameha Ave, near Mamo St, (808) 961-8744. 🛈 BIVB, 250 Keawe St, (808) 961-5797. 🎭 Merrie Monarch Festival (Mar or Apr). 🌐 **gohawaii.com/bigisland**

Although it is the state's second city, "rainy old Hilo" is a contrast to sunny, urban Honolulu. The city's progress has been checked by nature – rain falls 278 days of the year, and two destructive tsunamis pounded Hilo in 1946 and 1960. The city has since retreated from the sea, turning the waterfront area into enormous parks, while the rain has made it a natural garden, full of orchids and anthuriums. Hilo's population is largely Japanese and Filipino in ancestry.

The downtown business district, with its restored buildings, is worth exploring on foot. The **Lyman Museum and Mission House** vividly evokes a bygone era – it is preserved as it was in the 1830s, with Victorian furnishings and artifacts.

On the Waiākea Peninsula, jutting into Hilo Bay, is the 30-acre (12-ha) **Lili'uokalani Gardens**, landscaped in Japanese style, while east of downtown are the 80-ft (24-m) high **Rainbow Falls**. The morning sun, filtering through the mist of the waterfall, often creates beautiful rainbows.

The east side of Hilo Bay offers fine snorkeling and swimming at the **James Kealoha Beach Park**; and at the **Richardson Ocean Park**.

## ⓬ Pu'uhonua O Hōnaunau National Historical Park

Hwy 160, off Hawai'i Belt Rd (Hwy 11). **Tel** (808) 328-2326. **Open** 7am–8pm daily. 🅿 ♿ Visitor Center: **Open** 8:45am–4:30pm. Daily orientation talks. 🌐 **nps.gov/puho**

From the 11th century on, social interactions were regulated by the *kapu* (taboo) system, and even minor infractions, such as stepping on a chief's shadow, were punished by violent death. Lawbreakers could, however, escape punishment by reaching a *pu'uhonua* (place of refuge). The greatest of these was at **Hōnaunau**, a 6-acre (2-ha) temple compound dating from the 16th century, which offered absolution to all those who could swim or run past the chief's warriors. The sanctuary was stripped of power in 1819, after the fall of the *kapu* system. Now partly restored, it provides a glimpse into precontact Hawai'i.

Located on a peninsula of black lava, whose jagged shoreline made it difficult for *kapu*-breakers to approach from the sea, the *pu'uhonua's* focal point is the 1650 **Hale O Keawe Heiau**, the temple that once held the bones and therefore the *mana* (sacred power) of great chiefs. Outside it stand Ki'i – wooden images of gods. As impressive is the great drystone wall, 10 ft (3 m) high and 17 ft (5 m) wide. Built around 1550, it separated the *pu'uhonua* from the palace area inland.

---

### Professor Jaggar (1871–1953)

Thomas A. Jaggar was a pioneer in the young science of volcanology. A professor of geology at Massachusetts Institute of Technology, he founded the Hawaiian Volcano Observatory at Kīlauea Caldera in 1912. Four years later, he and Honolulu publisher Lorrin Thurston persuaded Congress to preserve the area as a national park. Professor Jaggar developed techniques for collecting volcanic gases and measuring ground tilt, seismic activity, and lava temperatures. The work he initiated has made Kīlauea one of the world's best understood volcanoes.

Professor Jaggar on a boat trip

The Hale O Keawe Heiau, a place of spiritual power

*For hotels and restaurants see pp744–7*

# Kaua'i

Wind and water have had six million years to transform Kaua'i, the oldest of the major Hawaiian islands, into a stunning array of pleated cliffs and yawning chasms, cloaked with a mantle of emerald-green vegetation. Also known as the "Garden Island," Kaua'i is Hawai'i's most beautiful and irresistible destination. Its highlights include Kīlauea Point's glorious beaches, the dramatic Waimea Canyon, and the soaring cliffs of the Kalalau Trail on the Nā Pali Coast. You can drive anywhere in Kaua'i in three hours or less.

The shady *koa*-wood veranda at Grove Farm Homestead

## ⑬ Līhu'e

🏨 5,900. ✈ 🚌 Rice St, (808) 241-6410. ℹ KVB, 4334 Rice St, Suite 101, (800) 262-1400, (808) 245-3971. 🎭 Kaua'i-Tahiti Fete (mid-Aug). 🆆 **gohawaii.com**

Although Līhu'e happens to be the administrative and business center of Kaua'i, it is actually little more than a plantation village. It was built in the 19th century to serve the Līhu'e Sugar Mill, whose rusting machinery still dominates the downtown area. Līhu'e's oceanfront district, with the beautiful Kalapakī Beach, is especially appealing, and the outskirts of town offer such delights as grand plantation mansions and a stunning waterfall.

Within the town, **Kaua'i Museum** displays a splendid collection of traditional artifacts, including huge *koa*-wood bowls, royal feather standards, and old weapons. It also has exhibits on the island's history and geology. The imposing **Grove Farm Homestead** on Nāwiliwili Road is an early

20th-century mansion, paneled in dark, heavy *koa* wood. A guided tour, which must be reserved in advance, covers the rather formal house, the cramped servants' quarters, and the beautifully scented orchard.

**Kalapakī Beach**, with gently sloping beautiful white sands and sheltered inshore waters, is the safest beach in the area and especially suitable for families with small children. On its far side, the scenic palm-fringed **Nāwiliwili Beach County Park** is ideal for picnics.

The grand 1930s house known as **Kilohana Plantation**, 1.5 miles (2.5 km) west of Līhu'e, resembles an English country estate. Visitors can tour the house, which has a restaurant and some shops, and explore the cane fields in old-fashioned horse-drawn carriages. The mansion commands superb views of the Kilohana mountain inland.

## Environs

Just 5 miles (8 km) north of Līhu'e, a winding road through cane fields leads to the twin cascades of the 80-ft (24-m) **Wailua Falls**. They are best viewed from the roadside parking lot, as the path down the hillside can be slippery. **Menehune Fish Pond** 1.5 miles (2.5 km) south, is located in idyllic pastoral landscape. With its ancient stonemasonry, the pond was used to fatten mullet for the royal table.

## ⑭ Kīlauea Point

Kīlauea Road, off Kūhiō Hwy (Hwy 56), 10 miles (16 km) NW of Anahola. 🚌 Kīlauea. ℹ KVB, Līhu'e, (808) 245-3971. 🆆 **kauaidiscovery.com**

The northernmost spot on the Hawaiian archipelago, Kīlauea Point is a rocky promontory pounded by mighty waves. The windswept clifftop has been set aside as the **Kīlauea Point National Wildlife Refuge**, where bird-watchers can spot frigatebirds, Laysan albatrosses, and many other species. A short walk beyond the visitor center leads to the red and white **Kīlauea Lighthouse**, erected in 1913. Approaching the tip of the headland, there are splendid views westward to the fabled **Nā Pali** cliffs. Half a mile (800 m) west of the Kīlauea turnoff on Kalihiwai Road, a red dirt track

The twin cascades of Wailua Falls near Līhu'e

The Pu'u O Kila Lookout, with views of the Kalalau Valley

leads to the vast but little-visited shelf of glorious yellow sand known as **Secret Beach**. The ocean can be rough for swimming here, but it is a beautiful place to walk, with its dramatic views of the lighthouse and a glorious waterfall at the far end.

🦋 **Kīlauea Point National Wildlife Refuge** Kīlauea Point. **Tel** (808) 828-1413. **Open** 10am– 4pm Mon–Fri. **Closed** Jan 1, Thanksg., Dec 25. 🅿️ ♿

### ⑮ Waimea Canyon & Kōke'e State Park

Kōke'e Road (Hwy 550). **Tel** Kaua'i Division of State Parks, (808) 587-0400. Kōke'e State Park: **Open** daily. Kōke'e Museum: **Tel** (808) 335-9975. 🅿️ donation. **Open** 10am–4pm daily. 🆆 kokee.org 🏠 Kōke'e Lodge: **Tel** (808) 335-6061. 🅿️ Cabins available for rent. 🆆 thelodgeatkokee.net

No visitor should leave Kaua'i without taking in the rugged grandeur of Waimea Canyon and the breathtaking views from Kōke'e State Park. Waimea Canyon, known as the "Grand Canyon of the Pacific," was created by an earthquake that almost split Kaua'i in two. The gorge, now 3,000 ft (915 m) deep, is still eroding as landslides and the Waimea River continue to carry away tons of soil. Of the several lookouts dotted along the rim, the **Waimea Canyon Lookout**,

despite being the lowest of the lookouts, offers the best canyon views. The more adventurous can take hiking trails to explore in greater depth. The **Kukui Trail** heads sharply down into the canyon as far as the Waimea River – a relatively easy and rewarding trip. At the North End of Waimea Canyon is **Kōke'e State Park**, laced through with more hiking trails. From the park's **Pu'u O Kila Lookout**, the majestic amphitheater of the Kalalau Valley opens out; another view is from the nearby **Kalalau Lookout**. A highlight of the park is the **Alaka'i Swamp**, a bowl-like depression drenched by nearly 42 ft (13 m) of rain every year. Part rainforest, part bog, the area boasts some of Hawai'i's rarest birds, such as the *'i'iwi* or honeycreeper, and the tiny yellow *'anianiau*. Information, hiking advice, and maps are all available at the Kōke'e State Park headquarters.

**KILAUEA LIGHTHOUSE** Official marker

### ⑯ Kalalau Trail

Visitors must obtain permission in advance from the State Parks office. Na Pali Coast State Parks office: 3060 'Eiwa St, Lihu'e, HI 96766, (808) 274-3444. 🆆 hawaiistateparks.org

The precipitous cliffs of the Nā Pali Coast make it impossible for the road to continue west of Kē'ē Beach on Kauai's north shore. But hardy hikers can follow the narrow Kalalau Trail for another 11 miles (18 km) to isolated Kalalau Valley. One of the most dramatic hikes in the world, it covers a landscape of almost primeval vastness and splendor. While this is not an expedition to undertake lightly, a half-day round-trip to Hanakāpī'ai Valley is within most capabilities and is an unforgettable experience.

The trail begins at the end of **Kūhiō Highway**, climbing steeply to **Makana Peak** and affording spectacular views of the rugged coastline. It continues on to **Ke Ahu A Laka**, which was once Hawai'i's most celebrated school for *hula* dancing. The next stop is **Hanakāpī'ai Valley** where in summer a pristine sandy beach replaces the pebbles found at the valley mouth in winter. Wading and swimming here are unsafe, due to dangerous rip currents.

The more challenging part of the trail continues through an abandoned coffee plantation to the **Hanakāpī'ai Falls**, and then to **Pā Ma Wa'a**, an 800-ft (240-m) cliff, which is the highest point on the trail. The trail then dips into several hanging valleys where the streams have still to cut their way down to sea level, before reaching the beautiful campsite at **Hanakoa Valley**, set amid the ruins of ancient taro terraces. For the last 5 miles (8 km), the trail clings perilously to a sandstone cliff. The magical view of **Kalalau Valley** is the trail's reward. Note that there is no food or safe drinking water en route.

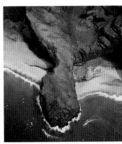

The soaring, pleated cliffs of the Nā Pali Coast, Kalalau Trail

# Alaska Practical Information

Traveling around the largest state in the US requires a great deal of advance planning. From endless snowfields, towering mountains, majestic rainforests, sweeping tundra, active volcanoes, and the spectacular northern lights to some of the world's most abundant wildlife preserves, Alaska has much to offer its visitors. Although traveling in Alaska is more expensive than in other parts of the country, visitors on a small budget can also have a memorable trip.

## Tourist Information

The best source of travel information is the very comprehensive Alaska Vacation Planner, published by the **Alaska Travel Industry Association** (ATIA). The ATIA is run jointly by the state and various travel businesses. Many regional tourism councils also publish brochures on travel in their areas.

## Getting Around

Visitors have a number of transportation options. **Alaska Airlines** flights link larger cities and towns, while smaller "bush" planes take visitors to more remote areas. The state-run **Alaska Railroad** connects Fairbanks, Anchorage, Seward, and Denali National Park. The main intercity bus service, **Alaska Direct Bus Line**, has year-round service.

A government-operated ferry service, the **Alaska Marine Highway System**, links towns throughout southeast, south central, and the Alaska peninsula, with service extending as far south as Bellingham, Washington.

The large, comfortable, and well-equipped ships carry hundreds of vehicles and feature cabins, multiple dining areas, and onboard naturalists. The pace is relaxed and the atmosphere is very casual; some travelers even sleep under the stars on the outer deck. Book well in advance for this popular ferry service. However, driving within Alaska involves long distances; be especially careful of collisions with moose and other wildlife.

## Natural Hazards

Most travelers visit Alaska in the milder summer season between late May and early-September. Even so, bring a jacket and warm clothes for chilly nights. Summer also brings the worst of Alaska's insects, mainly mosquitoes and blackflies. Backcountry travelers also need to take precautions in bear country. **Park Service** or **Forest Service** rangers can provide safety tips.

## Festivals

There are a number of special events taking place in Alaska at different times of the year. Starting in March, the famous **Iditarod Trail Sled Dog Race** runs between Anchorage and Nome. April sees the **Alaska Folk Festival** held in Juneau. The **Alaska State Fair** (August) in Palmer is famous for its pumpkins and cabbages, which grow to world-record sizes under the state's 24-hour sunshine. On October 18th, the **Alaska Day Celebration**, the day Alaska was bought from Russia by the US, livens up the Colonial town of Sitka.

## Outdoor Activities

The vast majority of Alaska is set aside as public land, making the state a paradise for hikers, fishermen, and other outdoor enthusiasts. Trekking, mountain climbing, skiing, rafting, kayaking, and whale-watching are some of the activities that visitors can enjoy here. Most tourist offices provide information and details of outdoor pursuits that Alaska has to offer.

## The Climate of Alaska

Although situated near the Arctic Circle, weather patterns vary a great deal in Alaska. Winters are cold and dark, but summer with its warm weather and long days is the prime season for visitors. In the state's northern tier, the sun does not set for two months of the year, and there is daylight for as many as 22 hours each day in June at Fairbanks. July is the rainiest month. Most coastal cruises take place in the summer.

**ANCHORAGE**

| | Apr | Jul | Oct | Jan |
|---|---|---|---|---|
| °F/C | 44/7 | 65/18 | 43/6 | |
| | 27/-3 | 49/9 | 29/-2 | 19/-7 |
| | | | | 5/-15 |
| days | 15 | 13 | 11 | 10 |
| in | 0.7 | 1.8 | 2 | 0.8 |

32°F / 0°C

month

# Hawai'i Practical Information

Tourism is Hawai'i's most important industry. From the bright lights of Waikīkī and Honolulu to the remote waterfalls of Maui's Hāna district, the islands offer something to suit all budgets. The cost of living in Hawai'i is about 40 percent higher than that in the rest of the US; even so, Hawai'i is a year-round destination. However, visitors will enjoy better prices in the off-season, between April and December.

## Tourist Information

Visitor information desks at all airports provide maps and guides, and all major hotels have a guest services desk. All islands have a branch of the **Hawai'i Visitors' and Convention Bureau** (HVCB), or some other visitors' bureau.

## Getting Around

Driving is the best way to get around, since public transportation is limited. Seat belts are mandatory, and children under three must sit in approved car seats. Distances between gas stations can be long, so keep the tank at least half full. Always check the weather – many roads wash out during or after heavy rains.

Allow plenty of time for any trip. The locals move at a leisurely pace, seldom using horns. On narrow roads, pull over to let cars pass.

## Natural Hazards

Visitors should be aware of certain potential dangers that the sun and the ocean pose to health. Thus, wear a hat and sunglasses, use sunblock cream, and drink plenty of fluids as a protection against the harsh sun.

Ask the lifeguard about ocean conditions, as some beaches can be safe in summer but very dangerous in winter. Swim facing away from the beach, as sudden rogue waves can sweep you out to sea. If you get carried out by a rip current, try to swim with it until it dissipates. Always check for rocks and corals below the surface, and wear protective foot gear. If you cut yourself on coral, clean the cut thoroughly with antiseptic. If you step on a sea urchin, or are stung by a jellyfish, immerse the wound in hot water to relieve the pain. Although shark encounters are rare, it's best that you check with the lifeguard before swimming.

## Outdoor Activities

Hawai'i offers a plethora of outdoor activities, many focused on the ocean, such as surfing, swimming, fishing, scuba diving, and snorkeling. In addition, sports enthusiasts have a variety of opportunities such as horseback riding, hiking, and playing golf on some of the world's best courses.

## Entertainment

Music and dance are as important to Hawaiians as the air they breathe. Most islands offer extravagant Polynesian shows, with *lū'au*-style meals, and music and dance from other Pacific islands such as Tahiti and Fiji. You can dance the night away in nightclubs in Honolulu and Maui, but also be prepared for earlier nights in other parts of the state.

## Festivals

A diverse range of festivals and events take place all through the year. The onset of summer sees **Lei Day**, with everyone donning flowered garlands. The **King Kamehameha Day** honors the chief who united the islands. All summer long, there are cultural, music, and food festivals, as well as sports events, from rodeos to canoe races and the grueling **Ironman Triathlon**. Summer draws to a close with the grand **Aloha Week Festivals**.

Winters offer sports and cultural events such as the **Triple Crown of Surfing**, and the **Merrie Monarch Festival** which culminates with the "Olympics" of *hula*.

## DIRECTORY

### Tourist Information

**Hawai'i Visitors & Convention Bureau**
**Tel** (800) 464-2924.
Ⓦ **gohawaii.com**

### Snorkeling

**Snorkel Bob's**
700 Kapahulu Ave, Honolulu, O'ahu. **Tel** (800) 262-7725.
Ⓦ **snorkelbob.com**

### Scuba Diving

**Bubbles Below**
PO Box 157, Eleele, Kaua'i.
**Tel** (808) 332-7333.
Ⓦ **bubblesbelowkauai.com**

## The Climate of Hawai'i

Hawai'i has two distinct seasons, summer and winter. May to October is hot and dry, while November through April is cooler and wetter. Happily for visitors, there are very few days when Hawai'i's beaches do not beckon. Sudden rains or storms mean the onset of winter, as do the big waves that surfers eagerly await. However, Hawai'i is not all sunshine, and residents in the cooler upcountry areas spend Christmas Eve gathered around the fireplace.

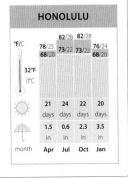

**HONOLULU**

| °F/C | Apr | Jul | Oct | Jan |
|---|---|---|---|---|
| high | 78/25 | 82/28 | 82/28 | 76/24 |
| low | 68/20 | 73/22 | 73/22 | 68/20 |
| sun (days) | 21 | 24 | 22 | 20 |
| rain (in) | 1.5 | 0.6 | 2.3 | 3.5 |

32°F
0°C

month  Apr  Jul  Oct  Jan

# Where to Stay

## Alaska

### ANCHORAGE: Dimond
### Center Hotel                    $
Value
*700 E Dimond Blvd, 99515*
**Tel** *(907) 770-5000*
W dimondcenterhotel.com
Spacious rooms feature deluxe
beds and bathrooms with jetted
tubs. Complimentary breakfast
buffet and free airport shuttle.

### ANCHORAGE: Inlet Tower
### Hotel and Suites               $
Boutique
*1200 L St, 99501*
**Tel** *(907) 276-0110*
W inlettower.com
Inviting hotel with tastefully
appointed rooms and suites, and
views of the surrounding hills.

### ANCHORAGE:
### Hotel Captain Cook           $$$
Luxury
*939 W 5th Ave, 99501*
**Tel** *(907) 276-6000*
W captaincook.com
Luxurious rooms have great
views of the Cook Inlet and the
Chugach Mountains. Athletic
club and four restaurants on site.

### DENALI NATIONAL PARK: Denali
### Mountain Morning Hostel       $
Value
*Mile 224.5 Parks Hwy, 99755*
**Tel** *(907) 683-7503*
W hostelalaska.com
Quiet dorms and cabins on the
banks of a creek just south of the
park. Open May–mid-September.

### FAIRBANKS: Minnie Street
### B&B                            $$
B&B
*345 Minnie St, 99701*
**Tel** *(907) 456-1802*
W minniestreetbandb.com
Some of the suites at this upscale
B&B have kitchens and jetted

tubs; the premium suites have
Jacuzzis. Centrally located, close
to the Chena River.

### FAIRBANKS: River's
### Edge Resort                   $$
Resort
*4200 Boat St, 99709*
**Tel** *(907) 474-0286*
W riversedge.net
This RV park on the Chena River
offers full hookups, lodges, and
tent camping, as well as fully
equipped cottages.

## DK Choice

### GLACIER BAY NATIONAL
### PARK: Glacier Bay Lodge      $$
Resort
*179 Bartlett Cove Rd, 99826*
**Tel** *(907) 264-4600*
W visitglacierbay.com
Surrounded by large rainforest
trees, on the shores of Bartlett
Cove, this is the only lodging
option in the famed Glacier Bay
National Park. Rooms are cozy
and comfortable. The lodge's
sitting area, with a roaring fire, is
an inviting retreat after a day of
cruising past glaciers. Open only
during the summer months.

### HOMER: Land's End Resort     $
Resort
*4786 Homer Spit Rd, 99603*
**Tel** *(907) 235-0400*
W lands-end-resort.com
Located on Homer Spit, this
resort has a jetted lap pool,
sauna, and outdoor hot tub.

### JUNEAU: Historic
### Silverbow Inn                 $$
B&B
*120 2nd St, 99801*
**Tel** *(907) 586-4146*
W silverbowinn.com
This friendly little boutique inn
has an on-site bakery famous for
its bagels and great brunches.

| Price Guide |
| --- |
| Prices are based on one night's stay in high season for a standard double room, inclusive of service charges and taxes. |

| | |
| --- | --- |
| $ | up to $150 |
| $$ | $150–$250 |
| $$$ | over $250 |

### KETCHIKAN: Gilmore Hotel     $
Historic
*326 Front St, 99901*
**Tel** *(907) 225-9423*
W gilmorehotel.com
Built in 1927, this hotel has a retro
vibe and views of the Tongass
Narrows. Popular restaurant.

### KODIAK: Best Western
### Kodiak Inn                    $
Value
*236 W Rezanof Dr, 99615*
**Tel** *(907) 486-5712*
W kodiakinn.com
This hotel caters mainly to
business travelers and anglers,
even providing freezers for fish
caught by guests. Complimentary
Continental breakfasts.

### SEWARD: Seward
### Windsong Lodge               $$
Resort
*Mile 0.5 Herman Leirer/Exit Glacier
Rd, 99664*
**Tel** *(907) 224-7116*
W sewardwindsong.com
In the middle of the Resurrection
River Valley, this well-appointed
lodge caters to those visiting
Kenai Fjords National Park.

### SITKA: Sitka Hotel           $
Value
*118 Lincoln St, 99835*
**Tel** *(907) 747-3288*
W sitkahotel.net
A well-maintained hotel in the
heart of town. Budget rooms
have shared bathrooms. Kids
under 12 can stay for free.

### SKAGWAY: Skagway Inn        $$
Historic
*7th & Broadway, 99840*
**Tel** *(907) 983-2289*
W skagwayinn.com
Formerly a brothel, this 1897
Victorian-style inn has period
furnishings and a garden.

### VALDEZ: Best Western
### Valdez Harbor Inn            $
Value
*100 Harbor Dr, 99686*
**Tel** *(907) 835-3434*
W valdezharborinn.com
The finest hotel in town has a
business center, fitness room,
and hot tubs in some rooms.

Land's End Resort, Homer, with panoramic views of Kachemak Bay and the Kenai Mountains

# Hawai'i

### HĀNA: Travaasa Hana $$$
Resort
5031 Hāna Hwy, Maui, 96713
Tel (888) 820-1043
W travaasa.com/hana
This full-service spa offers activities such as snorkeling, garland-making, and throw-net fishing. The cottages provide great views.

### HILO: Uncle Billy's Hilo Bay Hotel $
Value
87 Banyan Dr, Hawai'i, 96720
Tel (808) 935-0861
W unclebilly.com
All rooms feature private porches at this hotel on Hilo Bay. Some rooms have kitchenettes.

### KĀ'ANAPALI: Kā'anapali Beach Hotel $$
Resort
2525 Kā'anapali Pkwy, Maui, 96761
Tel (808) 661-0011
W kbhmaui.com
Beachfront rooms and suites here have island-style furnishings. Guests enjoy Hawaiian cultural activities and a tropical garden.

### KAPOLEI: Aulani, A Disney Resort & Spa $$$
Resort
92-1185 Ali'lnui Dr, O'ahu, 96707
Tel (808) 674-6200
W resorts.disney.go.com
Mickey, Minnie, and Co. are on vacation alongside guests at this resort. There are several pools and many child-friendly activities.

### LAHAINA: Lahaina Inn $
Historic
127 Lahainaluna Rd, Maui, 96761
Tel (808) 661-0577
W lahainainn.com
Rooms and parlor suites at this small boutique hotel are decorated with authentic Victorian furnishings.

### LAHAINA: Best Western Pioneer Inn $$
Historic
658 Wharf St, Maui, 96761
Tel (808) 667-5708
W pioneerinnmaui.com
This inn, which dates back to 1910, is located in scenic Lahaina Harbor. Rooms have all modern amenities.

### LAHAINA: Lahaina Shores Beach Resort $$$
Luxury
475 Front St, Maui, 96761
Tel (808) 661-4835
W lahainashores.com
Beachfront lodgings in one-bedroom, studio, and penthouse

Bar at the Kā'anapali Beach Hotel, set in a tropical garden

suites have full kitchens, porches, and ocean or mountain views.

### LĪHU'E: Kaua'i Marriott Resort $$$
Resort
3610 Rice St, Kaua'i, 96766
Tel (808) 245-5050
W marriott.com
A pool, two championship golf courses, and several restaurants can be found at this resort on a white-sand beach near the airport

### PRINCEVILLE: Hanalei Bay Resort & Suites $$
Resort
5380 Honoiki Rd, Kaua'i, 76722
Tel (808) 826-6522
W hanaleibayresort.com
This bright and airy hotel has tropical furnishings, lagoon pools, and sports facilities.

### VOLCANO VILLAGE: Kīlauea Lodge $$
B&B
Old Volcano Rd, Hawai'i, 96785
Tel (808) 967-7366
W kilauealodge.com
Originally built as a YMCA camp in 1938, this hotel is just a mile away from Hawai'i Volcanoes National Park. On-site restaurant.

### WAIKĪKĪ: Holiday Inn Waikīkī Beachcomber $$
Value
2300 Kalākaua Ave, O'ahu, 96815
Tel (808) 922-4646
W waikikibeachcomberresort.com
Just across the street from the beach, this hotel has numerous dining and entertainment options on site.

### WAIKĪKĪ: Lotus Honolulu $$
Luxury
2885 Kalakaua Ave, O'ahu, 96815
Tel (808) 922-1700
W lotushonoluluhotel.com
This deluxe haven, located between Diamond Head and

Waikīkī Beach, boasts a unique blend of island leisure and sleek style. Amenities on offer include morning yoga classes and an evening wine hour.

### WAIKĪKĪ: Outrigger Reef on the Beach $$
Resort
2169 Kālia Rd, O'ahu, 96815
Tel (808) 923-3111
W outriggerreef-onthebeach.com
Nightly Hawaiian entertainment, a lively swimming pool, and an oceanside spa, as well as three on-site restaurants and complimentary Internet access are offered at this resort located near Fort DeRussy.

## DK Choice

### WAIKĪKĪ: Halekulani $$$
Luxury
2199 Kālia Rd, O'ahu, 96815
Tel (808) 923-2311
W halekulani.com
The island's most luxurious option, Halekulani is located right on the beach. It offers excellent service and amenities throughout, including a spa, manicured tropical grounds, tasteful yet simple decor, and a signature "orchid pool." There is also superb cuisine at La Mer. The multilingual staff cater to the guests' every whim.

### WAIMEA: Aston Waimea Plantation Cottages $$$
Luxury
9400 Kaumuali'i Hwy, Kaua'i, 96796
Tel (808) 338-1625
W astonhotels.com
Individual plantation cottages with fully equipped kitchens and all modern amenities are set in a seaside coconut grove at the gateway to Waimea Canyon.

For more information on types of hotels see pages 26–7

# Where to Eat and Drink

## Alaska

**ANCHORAGE: Moose's Tooth Pub and Pizzeria** $
Pizza/American
*3300 Old Seward Hwy, 99503*
**Tel** *(907) 258-2537*
A casual and trendy restaurant serving gourmet pizzas, sandwiches, and soups prepared with seasonal ingredients. It also has a good range of local brews.

**ANCHORAGE: Glacier Brewhouse** $$
American
*737 W 5th Ave, 99501*
**Tel** *(907) 274-2739*
This well-known eatery has a casual ambience, warmed up by roaring fireplaces. Wild Alaskan seafood and rotisserie-roasted meats are the highlights of the vast menu. The handcrafted ales and stouts are extremely popular.

### DK Choice

**ANCHORAGE: Marx Bros Café** $$$
New American
*627 W 3rd Ave, 99501*
**Tel** *(907) 278-2133* **Closed** *Mon*
Hailed by many as the state's best restaurant, Marx Bros Café is a tiny place famous for its innovative seasonal menu, which always features fresh Alaskan seafood. The delectable made-at-your-table Caesar salad is a must-have. The restaurant boasts a notable wine list, as well as a selection of delicious desserts. Reservations are essential.

**DENALI VILLAGE: McKinley Creekside Café** $$
American
*Mile 224 George Parks Hwy, 99755*
**Tel** *(907) 745-7116*
A popular café located along the quiet Carlo Creek, 13 miles (21 km) south of the entrance to Denali National Park. The varied menu includes dishes such as halibut tacos and grilled rib-eye steaks. Open only during the summer.

**FAIRBANKS: LemonGrass** $
Thai
*388 Old Chena Pump Rd, 99709*
**Tel** *(907) 456-2200*
LemonGrass offers authentic Thai cuisine made with ingredients imported from Asia. Ask the friendly staff to adjust spice levels to your personal preference.

Authentic Thai dish at LemonGrass, Fairbanks

**FAIRBANKS: The Pump House** $$
American
*Mile 1.3 Chena Pump Rd, 99708*
**Tel** *(907) 479-8452*
This vast restaurant hugging the banks of the Chena River is located in a historic setting that evokes the Gold Rush of the 1890s. Savor well-prepared Alaskan seafood. The Sunday brunches are especially popular.

**HAINES: Mountain Market and Café** $
American
*151 3rd Ave, 99827*
**Tel** *(907) 766-3340*
A good option for a light lunch or a healthy breakfast, with superb wraps, sandwiches, home-made soups, and croissants. Behind the café is a health-food store.

**HOMER: Homestead Restaurant** $$$
New American
*Mile 8.2 E End Rd, 99603*
**Tel** *(907) 235-8723*
This acclaimed eatery specializes in fusion cuisine made with local ingredients. Housed in a rustic cabin adorned with Alaskan fine art, it overlooks the stunning Kachemak Bay glaciers.

**JUNEAU: Hangar on the Wharf** $$
American/International
*2 Marine Way, 99801*
**Tel** *(907) 586-5018*
Set in a waterfront location with a sunny deck, Hangar is often noisy and packed with locals and tourists alike. The extensive menu includes salads, wraps, steaks, burgers, and Alaskan seafood.

**Price Guide**
For a three-course meal for one, a glass of house wine, and all unavoidable extra charges including tax.

| | |
|---|---|
| $ | up to $35 |
| $$ | $35–$70 |
| $$$ | over $70 |

**JUNEAU: Tracy's King Crab Shack** $$
Seafood
*356 S Franklin St, 99802*
**Tel** *(907) 723-1811*
Popular for its Alaskan crab varieties, this restaurant serves King, snow, and Dungeness crabs in various styles, with garlic rolls and butter on the side.

**KETCHIKAN: Ketchikan Coffee Company** $
Café
*211 Stedman St, 99901*
**Tel** *(907) 247-2326*
This bright café is housed in the historic New York Hotel, just steps from Creek Street. Enjoy fresh bagels, panini sandwiches, eggs Florentine, and steaming lattes.

**KODIAK: The Old Power House Restaurant** $$
Sushi/Japanese
*516 E Marine Way, 99615*
**Tel** *(907) 481-1088* **Closed** *Sun & Mon*
A popular eatery serving freshly rolled sushi. The lengthy menu also includes Japanese fish, meat, and vegetarian dishes.

**SEWARD: Ray's Waterfront** $$$
American/Seafood
*1316 4th Ave, 99664*
**Tel** *(907) 224-5632* **Closed** *Oct–mid-Apr*
This famous restaurant serves delicious local fish. House specials include cedar-planked salmon and nut-encrusted halibut.

**SITKA: Ludvig's Bistro** $$
Mediterranean
*256 Katlian St, 99835*
**Tel** *(907) 966-3663* **Closed** *Sun; Oct–mid-Feb*
This cozy bistro is renowned for its excellent Mediterranean cuisine made with local seafood and organic ingredients.

**SKAGWAY: Red Onion Saloon** $
American
*205 Broadway, 99840*
**Tel** *(907) 983-2222* **Closed** *Nov–Mar*
Formerly the town's bordello, this historic site is now a lively hangout offering pub grub such as sandwiches and creative pizzas, along with local beers and live entertainment.

# Hawai'i

### HALE'IWA: Coffee Gallery $
Café
*66-250 Kamehameha V Hwy,*
*North Shore Marketplace, O'ahu,*
*96712*
**Tel** *(808) 637-5355*
Popular with surfers and local
residents, this laid-back café
serves legendary breakfasts,
including huge omelets with
surf-lingo names. The espresso
bar boasts a large selection of
gourmet coffees.

### HĀNA: Dining Room at
### Travaasa Hotel $$$
Hawaiian/New American
*5031 Hāna Hwy, Maui, 96713*
**Tel** *(808) 359-2401*
In a lovely tropical setting, this
upscale restaurant serves Pacific
Rim cuisine made with fruits and
vegetables sourced from a nearby
farm, plus the freshest fish.

### HILO: Café Pesto $$
Hawaiian
*308 Kamehameha Ave, Hawai'i,*
*96721*
**Tel** *(808) 969-6640*
The menu at this casual café
features regional cuisine, such as
island fish, as well as organic
salads, pasta dishes, and pizzas.

### HONOLULU:
### Ono Hawaiian Foods $
Hawaiian
*726 Kapahulu Ave, O'ahu, 96816*
**Tel** *(808) 737-2275* **Closed** *Sun*
Always packed with regulars, this
restaurant serves delicious local
classics such as *poi* (taro paste),
*laulau* (leaf-wrapped meat or fish
bundles), and *lomi-lomi* salmon.
Combos come with authentic
sides: raw onion and Hawaiian salt.

### HONOLULU: Nico's Pier 38 $$
Seafood
*1133 N Nimitz Hwy, O'ahu, 96817*
**Tel** *(808) 540-1377*
This large eatery with an outdoor
deck offers gourmet Hawaiian
lunches and dinners made with
fish sourced from the neighboring Honolulu Fish Auction.

### KAHUKU:
### Giovanni's Shrimp Truck $
Seafood
*56-505 Kamehameha Hwy, O'ahu,*
*96731*
**Tel** *(808) 293-1839*
Order at the counter and enjoy
steaming plates of garlic shrimp
scampi on the covered patio
at what is probably the most
popular of North Shore's
many shrimp trucks.

### KAUNAKAKAI: Kanemitsu's
### Bakery $
Café/Bakery
*79 Ala Malama St, Moloka'i, 96748*
**Tel** *(808) 553-5855*
A friendly bakery offering an
array of goods, including the
famous Molokai sweet bread. In
the adjoining coffee shop, local-
style breakfasts and lunches are
served in booths or ordered to go.

### LAHAINA: Sansei Seafood
### Restaurant & Sushi Bar $$
Sushi/Japanese
*Kapalua Resort, 600 Office Rd, Maui,*
*96761*
**Tel** *(808) 669-6286*
Modern Asian cuisine is served
by friendly staff in a lively setting.
A lengthy list of sakes and
creative cocktails complements
the inventive dishes.

### LAHAINA: Longhi's $$$
Italian
*888 Front St, Maui, 96761*
**Tel** *(808) 667-2288*
One of the island's most
acclaimed restaurants, Longhi's
serves well-prepared Italian fare.
Extensive wine list.

### LĪHU'E: Hamura Saimin Stand $
Hawaiian/Asian
*2956 Kress St, Kaua'i, 96766*
**Tel** *(808) 245-3271*
Frequented by foodies, Hamura
offers steaming bowls of saimin,
a noodle soup made with
wontons, vegetables, pork,
and a range of condiments.

### LĪHU'E: Tip Top Café $
Café/Bakery
*3173 Akahi St, Kaua'i, 96766*
**Tel** *(808) 245-2333* **Closed** *Mon*
Filled with 1950s-style booths
and colorful orchids on every
table, Tip Top has been a local
favorite since 1916 for fare such
as macadamia nut pancakes and
oxtail soup.

### WAIKĪKĪ: Duke's Waikiki $$
American
*Outrigger Waikiki on the Beach,*
*2335 Kalākaua Ave, O'ahu, 96815*
**Tel** *(808) 922-2268*
Named after Hawaiian surfing
champion Duke Kahanamoku,
this beachfront eatery is popular
for its live Hawaiian music.
It serves steaks and seafood
dishes, as well as lighter fare.

### WAIKĪKĪ: Side Street Inn $$
Hawaiian
*1225 Hopaka St, O'ahu, 96814*
**Tel** *(808) 591-0253*
A favorite of off-duty chefs and
foodies looking for late-night bites.
Favorites include ahi *poke* (raw
fish salad) and fried pork chops.
Karaoke and big-screen TVs.

### DK Choice

### WAIKĪKĪ: Chef Mavro $$$
New American
*1969 South King St, O'ahu, 96826*
**Tel** *(808) 944-4714* **Closed** *Mon*
French-born chef George
Mavrothalassitis has become
an island staple by applying
both modern and classic
techniques to an endless
assortment of fresh, local
ingredients. Diners enjoy
an excellent gourmet tasting
menu and an impressive,
though pricey, wine list in
an elegant dining room.

### WAIKĪKĪ:
### La Mer at Halekulani $$$
French
*2199 Kālia Rd, O'ahu, 96815*
**Tel** *(808) 923-2311*
Located in one of the island's
most luxurious hotels, this high-
end restaurant offers modern
French cuisine executed impeccably and served by an expert
staff. Award-winning wine list
and romantic beach views.

Sansei Seafood Restaurant & Sushi Bar, serving Asian food, in Lahaina

**For more information on types of restaurants** *see pages 28–9*

# General Index

# Acknowledgments

## DK London

### Revisions Team
Emma Anacootee, Emily Anderson, Brigitte Arora, Lydia Baillie, Claire Baranowski, Sherry Collins, Jo Cowen, Caroline Elliker, Nicola Erdpresser, Caroline Evans, Madeline Farbman, Emer FitzGerald, Rhiannon Furbear, Jacky Jackson, Maite Lantaron, Jude Ledger/Pure Content, Hayley Maher, Pamela Marmito, Alison McGill, Sam Merrell, George Nimmo, Catherine Palmi, Susie Peachey, Rada Radojicic, Marisa Renzullo, Ellen Root, Locamata Sahoo, Sands Publishing Solutions, Jaynan Spengler, Stuti Tiwari, Ros Walford, Conrad Van Dyk.

### Proofreaders & Indexers
Glenda Fernandes, Susanne Hillen, Helen Peters, Nikky Twyman.

### Factcheckers
Mary Bergin, D. Clancy, Jerry Dean, Paul Franklin, Patricia Harris, Joseph Hayes, Lyn Kidder, David Lyon, Jill Metzler, Nancy Mikula, Carolyn Patten, Don Pitcher, Alice Powers, Mike Rogers, AnneLise Sorensen.

### Senior DTP Designer
Jason Little.

### Senior Cartographic Editor
Casper Morris.

### DK Picture Library
Mark Dennis.

### Production Controllers
Sarah Dodd, Melanie Dowland, Mary Slater.

### Managing Art Editor
Jane Ewart.

### Publishing Manager
Helen Townsend.

### Publisher
Douglas Amrine.

Dorling Kindersley would like to thank the following people whose contributions and assistance have made the preparation of this book possible.

### Additional Contributors
Ruth & Eric Bailey, Bob Barnes, Jyl Benson, Mary Bergin, Eleanor Berman, Jeremy Black, Lester Brooks, Patricia Brooks, Tom Bross, Susan Burke, Rebecca Carman, Richard Cawthorne, Brett Cook, Donna Dailey, Jackie Finch, Bonita Halm, Michelle de Larrabeiti, David Dick, Susan Farewell, Rebecca Poole Forée, Paul Franklin, Donald S. Frazier, Bonnie Friedman, Jennifer Greenhill-Taylor, Rita Goldman, Eric Grossman, Patricia Harris, Ross Hassig, Carolyn Heller, Pierre Home-Douglas, Lorraine Johnson, Penney Kome, Esther Labi, Philip Lee, Helga Loverseed, David Lyon, Clemence McLaren, Guy Mansell, Fred Mawer, Nancy Mikula, Melissa Miller, Kendrick Oliver, Barry Parr, Carolyn Patten, Ellen Payne, J. Kingston Pierce, Don Pitcher, Alice L. Powers, Jennifer Quasha, George Raudzens, Juliette Rogers, John Ryan, Alex Salkever, Litta W. Sanderson, Kem Sawyer, AnneLise Sorensen, Emma Stanford, Brett Steel, Arvin Steinberg, Phyllis Steinberg, Nigel Tisdall, Brian Ward, Greg Ward, John Wilcock, Ian Williams, Marilyn Wood, Paul Wood, Stanley Young.

### Additional Illustrators
Ricardo Almazan, Ricardo Almazan Jr, Arcana Studios, Robert Ashby, William Band, Gilles Beauchemin, Richard Bonson, Joanne Cameron, Stephen Conlin, Gary Cross, Richard Draper, Dean Entwhistle, Eugene Fleurey, Chris Forsey, Martin Gagnon, Vincent Gagnon, Stephen Gyapay, Stéphane Jorisch, Patrick Jougla, Nick Lipscombe, Claire Littlejohn, Luc Normandin, Lee Peters, Mel Pickering, Robbie Polley, Kevin Robinson, Hamish Simpson, Mike Taylor, Pat Thorne, Chris Orr & Associates, Jean-François Vachon, John Woodcock.

### Additional Photographers
Max Alexander, Peter Anderson, Jaime Baldovinos, Alan Briere, Demetrio Carrasco, Philippe Dewet, Philip Dowell, Neil Fletcher, Bruce Forster, Steven Greaves, Patricia Harris, John Heseltine, Ed Homonylo, Philip C. Jackson, Eliot Kaufman, Alan Keohane, Dave King, Andrew Leyerle, Neil Lukas, David Lyons, Norman McGrath, Andrew McKinney, Tim Mann, Gunter Marx, Neil Mersh, Howard Millard, Michael Moran, Sue Oldfield, Scot Pitts, Rob Reichenfeld, Julio Rochon, Rough Guides/Greg Ward, Kim Sayer, Neil Setchfield, Mike Severns, Chris Stevens, Clive Streeter, Giles Stokoe, Scott Suchman, Matthew Ward, Stephen Whitehorne, Linda Whitwam, Francesca Yorke.

### Photographic & Artwork Reference
Madeline Farbman; Emily Hovland; Independence National Historic Park: Phil Sheridan; National Park Service: Tom Patterson; Philadelphia Convention & Visitors Bureau: Danielle Cohn, Ellen Kornfield, Marissa Philip, San Antonio Convention & Visitors Bureau: Angela McClendon; M&A Design: Ajay Sethi, Mugdha Sethi; AirPhoto USA: Brian Garcia, Shannon Kelley.

### Photography Permissions
Dorling Kindersley would like to thank the following for their assistance and kind permission to photograph at their establishments (the establishments are listed in chapter order):

Old Merchant's House, East Village, NY; American Museum of Natural History, NY; Museum of American Folk Art, NY; Studio Museum in Harlem, NY; The Cloisters, NY; Columbia University, NY; Rockefeller Group, NY; Massachusetts State House, Boston; Nichols House Museum, Boston; Trinity Church, Boston; Museum of Fine Arts, Boston; Sackler Museum, Boston; New England Aquarium, Boston; Salem Witch Museum, MS;

Plimoth Plantation, MS; Mark Twain House, CT; Florence Griswold Museum, CT; Currier Gallery of Art, Manchester; National Air and Space Museum, Washington, DC; National Museum of Natural History, Washington, DC; National Museum of African Art, Washington, DC; National Museum of American History, Washington, DC; Kenmore House, VA; Library of Congress, Washington, DC; South Carolina State Museum, SC; Stone Mountain Park, GA; Shaker Village of Pleasant Hill, Harrodsburg, KY; Graceland, TN; Historic New Orleans Voodoo Museum, New Orleans, LA; Nottoway Plantation, LA; National Voting Rights Museum and Institute, Selma, AL; Elvis Presley Park, Tupelo CVB; Spertus Museum of Jewish Studies, Chicago; Field Museum, Chicago; Oriental Institute Museum, Chicago; Museum of Broadcast Communications, Chicago; University of Notre Dame, IN; Eiteljorg Museum, IN; Franklin Park Conservatory and Botanical Gardens, OH; Detroit Metro CVB, MI; The Detroit Institute of Arts, MI; Circus World Museum, Baraboo, WI; Walker Art Center, MN; The Mammoth Site of Hot Springs, South Dakota Inc., SD; The Nelson Atkins Museum of Art, MO; City Manager, Vince Capell, St. Joseph, MO; Woolaroc Ranch Museum, OK; Oral Roberts University, OK; Cowboy Artists of America Museum, Kerville,TX; Museum of Indian Arts and Culture, Santa Fe; Millicent Rogers Museum, Taos, NM; Las Vegas Natural History Museum; Cedar City Museum, UT; Museum of Northern Arizona, Flagstaff, AZ; Phoenix Museum of History, Phoenix, AZ; Hopi Learning Center, AZ; New Mexico Museum of Natural History and Science, Albuquerque, NM; Albuquerque Museum of Art and History, Albuquerque; Maxwell Museum of Anthropology, Albuquerque, NM; Hubbell Trading Post, NM; Odyssey Maritime Discovery Center, WA; Seattle Art Museum, WA; National Park Service, OR; Museum of Tolerance, Los Angeles, CA; Balboa Park, San Diego; Hearst Castle, San Simeon; Huntington Library, San Marino; Knotts Berry Farm, Buena Park; Museum of Contemporary Art, LA; *Queen Mary*, Long Beach; Sacramento State Capitol; San Diego Aerospace Museum; San Diego Automotive Museum; San Diego Museum of Art; San Diego Zoological Society; Santa Barbara Mission, CA; Wells Fargo History Museum, San Francisco, CA; San Francisco History Center, San Francisco Public Library, CA; University of California, Berkeley; University of California, LA; Winchester Mystery House, San Jose; Valdez Museum, Valdez, AK; Baranof Museum, Kodiak Island, AK; Ice Museum, Fairbanks, AK; as well as all the other churches, museums, hotels, restaurants, shops, galleries and sights too numerous to thank individually.

## Picture Credits

a = above; b = below/bottom; c = center; f = far; l = left; r = right; t = top.

Works of art have been reproduced with the permission of the following copyright holders:

**Courtesy Commonwealth of Massachusetts Art Commission**: *Civil War Army Nurses Memorial* Bela Pratt, 1911, 144tr; Stained-glass window, Main Stair Hall, 1900/
details: *Magna Carta seal 43, Seal of the Commonwealth* (pre-1898) 144cl; *Return of the Colours to the Custody of the Commonwealth,* December 22, 1986, mural by Edward Simmons 1902: 145cbl. © Denman Fink: Detail from *Law Guides Florida's Progress,* 1940, 287tl; **Historic New Orleans Voodoo Museum**: *Marie Laveau* by Charles M. Gandolfo, 346br; **Courtesy Florence Griswold Museum**: *The Harpist, A Portrait of Miss Florence Griswold,* by Alphonse Jongers, 1903, 165br; © Georg John Lober: *Hans Christian Anderson,* 1956, 88bl. **Millicent Rogers Museum**: 499tl; **Henry Moore Foundation**: *Reclining Figure: Hand* (1979), the work illustrated on page 86bl has been reproduced by permission of the Henry Moore Foundation; **Sackler Museum,** Cambridge, Boston: 155tc; **Courtesy Kenneth Treister Holocaust Memorial**: © Kenneth Treister, *A Sculpture of Love and Anguish,* 1990, 293cl. **Courtesy The Seattle Arts Commission** © Jonathan Borofsky: *Hammering Man,* 1988, 605tr. © Victor Arnautoff, *City Life,* Coit Tower, 1934, 690bl. **Collection of Spertus Museum**: *Flame of Hope* by Leonardo Nierman, 1995, 390crb.

The publisher would like to thank the following individuals, companies and picture libraries for permission to reproduce their photographs:

**1661 Inn and Hotel Manisses:** Malcolm Greenaway 185tr; **4Corners:** SIME/Antonino Bartuccio 36-7; SIME/Estock 336.

**Ace Hotel,** Portland: 633tl; **Aiden Marketing:** 235tr **Al Forno:** 188br; **Alamy Images:** Aurora Photos/Cary Anderson 744bl; Daniel Borzynski 403bc; Gary Crabbe / Enlightened Images 679cra; Ian G Dagnall 503tr; dbimages 280tl; Patrick Eden 505bl; Greg Balfour Evans 713br; Andre Jenny 238tr; Mervyn Rees 433b; **The African American Museum in Philadelphia:** 110cla; **Albuquerque Convention & Visitors Bureau www.ItsATrip.org:** 543tr **Atlanta–Fulton Public Library Foundation, Inc. Courtesy The Atlanta History Center:** 262cr; **Audubon Aquarium of the Americas:** 350bl; **AWL Images:** Walter Bibikow 466-7; Alan Copson 487t; Danita Delimont Stock 168-9, 428-9, 432, 528-9, 556-7, 598; Michele Falzone 716-7.

© **Richard Beyer:** *People Waiting for the Interurban* 607tl; **Beach Bistro:** 331bc; **Bell Tower Hotel:** 422bl; **The Biltmore Hotel:** 326bl; **Blue Point Grill:** 427br; **Bouchon Bistro:** 714bl; **Boulder Dushanbe Teahouse:** 595tc; **Brasa:** 426tr; **The Brooklyn Museum of Art:** 97bc; **Buckhorn Exchange Steakhouse Denver:** O'Hara 594bl.

**Caesars Entertainment:** 503br; © **Carnegie Museum of Art, Pittsburgh:** W. Cody 118bc; **Carolina Inn,** Chapel Hill: 276bc; **Caroline's Restaurant:** 465br; **The Catbird Seat:** Strategic Hospitality LLC 281bl; **Chateau on the Lake:** 461tl; **El Chorro:** 554tr; **Church Street Cafe:** 555br; **City Tavern Restaurant:** 127tr; **The Class Act:** 464ca; **Clumsy Butcher:** 491br; **Commander's Palace:** 372tr; **Bruce Coleman, London:** Raimund Cramm GDT 303br; **Colorado Historical Society**: William Henry Jackson Collection: *Westward HO!* 1904, 600bl; **Convention and**

Visitors Association of Lane County, OR: 622tl; **Corbis**: 42br, 44br, 48tr, 48cl, 49br, 57b, 59t, 63ca, 105tl, 105b, 133b, 174br, 193tl, 392bl, 676bc, 727tr; 738cla, 739bl; AFP 63br; James L. Amos 67tl; Craig Aurness 208tl, 676tr (Hearst Castle, CA Park Service); 680tl; Dave Bartruff 111br; Tom Bean 45tl, 51br, 519br, 727bc; Nathan Benn 66cl; Corbis-Bettman 38br, 53b, 54br, 55t, 56tl, 60tl, 63tl, 63tc, 63tr, 70cl, 100bl, 104bl, 197bl, 229cl, 229bc, 230cla, 338tl, 347br, 391crb, 419cla, 446cla, 503bl, 641ca, 649br; Richard Bickel 118cr; Kristi J. Black 677tl;Steve Chenn 112bl; Jerry Cooke 102cr, 245b; Richard A. Cooke 119b, 192bl, 225b; Lake County Museum 511br; Richard Cummins 40bc, 113tc, 117tr, 337b, 479tc; Jeff Curtes 587bl; Corcoran Gallery of Art, Washington, D.C.; 2003: *Washington Before Yorktown*, 1824-25, by Rembrandt Peale, 52; *George Washington*, 1796, by Gilbert Stuart, 62cla; Dennis Degnan 115tl; Hulton–Deutsch Collection 146cr; Jay Dickman 223br; Henry Dittz 653br; Duomo 39br; Sandy Felsenthal 478tr; Peter Finger 100tr, 101tr; Kevin Fleming 193cr, 196t, 229tr, 230br, 231br, 405br; Owen Franken 39cl; Michael Freeman 202c; Raymond Gehman 519tc; Mark E. Gibson 198br; Tod A. Gipstein 193br; Farell Grehan 107br, 173bl; Bob Gomes 39tr; The Solomon R. Guggenheim Foundation, NY: (*Man with Arms Crossed*, 1895-1900, by Cézanne, photo by Francis G. Mayer) 92tr; Liz Haymans 585br; Robert Holmes 114bc; Dave G. Houser 700cla; George H. H. Huey 495ca; Swim Ink 58ca; Woolfgang Kaehler 44cl; Catherine Karnow 111tc; Steve Kaufman 571tr; Layne Kennedy 119tr, 419tr; Bob Krist 13tc, 71bl, 108tr, 113cl, 132, 676clb, 677bl; Owaki-Kulla 351bl; Robert Landau 103tl, 658br; Larry Lee 42tr; Danny Lehman 45tr; George D. Lepp 49tr; Jean-Pierre Lescourret 8-9; Craig Lovell 42cl; Georgia Lowell 694bl; James Marshall 509bc; Francis G. Mayer 54tl, 70tr, 91tl, 104crb; Buddy Mays 101cr, 469br; Joe McDonald 75b; Kelly-Mooney Photography 41tl 106br, 107tl, 203c; David Muench 43tl, 66bl, 102bc, 116cla, 192tr, 222br, 223cla, 224cla, 228tr, 519crb, 741tl; Marc Muench 586tr, 587tl, 587cr; Walley McNamee 63crb; © National Portrait Gallery, Smithsonian Institution, Washington, DC, acquired as a gift to the nation through the generosity of the Donald W. Reynolds Foundation, 2003; 207br (*Lansdowne portrait of George Washington*, 1796, by Gilbert Stuart, 60tl) by Archivo Iconografico, S. A.); Richard T. Nowitz 114tl, 195b, 224br, 225tl; Douglas Peebles 43bl, 586cl; The Phillips Collection, Washington, D.C.: (*The Luncheon of the Boating Party*, 1881, by Pierre Auguste Renoir (1841-1919), photo by Francis G. Mayer) 214tl; Charles Philip 45bl; Philadelphia Museum of Arts: 115crb; Neil Preston 271bl; Carl & Ann Purcell 104tc; Roger Ressmeyer 286br, 617tr; Jim Richardson 43cr; Bill Ross 48bl, 73br; Paul A. Souders 228b; Kevin Schafer 66tr; Alan Schein 67br, 102tl, 118tl; Phil Schermeister 376cb, 508bc; Flip Schulke 61tr; Michael T. Sedam 44tr, 599b, 736cla; Leif Skoogfors 112cla, 117bl; Lee Snider 71ca, 101bl, 106clb, 110tr, 111cr, 111cb, 116br, 203cl, 222tl, 231tl; Joseph Sohm; ChromoSohm Inc. 49tl, 51tl, 221cra; 480b; Ted Spiegel 67cb; Mark L Stephenson 41crb, 741br; Frank Trapper 659c; Underwood & Underwood 103bl, 266cla, 379b; Ron Watts 42bl, 43tr, 72tr, 103br; David H. Wells 115b; Stuart Westmorland 596-7; Nick Wheeler

657tc; Oscar White 63cb; Michael S. Yamashita 106cla, 419b; Bo Zaunders 475tl; **Currier Museum of Art:** 176crb. **Deveny:** Adrienne Battistella 350tr; **Dreamstime.com:** Brandon Alms 332-3; Hasan Can Balcioglu 638; Andrey Bayda 68; Jay Beiler 10cl; Gary Blakeley 12tc; Jeff Coleman 553br; Shelley Coleman 374-5; Jerry Coli 206cr; Brett Critchley 284; Daveallenphoto 240-1; Sydney Deem 11tl; Songquan Deng 190-1, 496; Prochasson Frederic 636-7; Jorg Hackemann 282-3; Heysues23 244; Svitlana Imnadze 17br; Wangkun Jia 194; Wangkun Jia 138tr; Kguzel 2-3; Leerobin 128-9; Mike Little 15br; Lunamarina 13br, 492-3; Michigannut 378; Mkjoot 352-3; Luciano Mortula 1; Sean Pavone 78tc; Daniil Peshkov 67cra; Photoquest 16bl, 507tl; Jorge Salcedo 12br; Shutterfree, Llc/R. Gino Santa Maria 15tl; Snehitdesign 64-5; Peter Spirer 94cla; Tupungato 14bl; Wollertz 560; Robert Zehetmayer 11bl.

**Edgewater Hotel,** Seattle: 632bl; **Emeril's:** 371br; **Empire State Building Company L.L.C.:** The Empire State Building design is a registered trademark and is used with permission by ESBC 83bl; **Enchantment Group:** 552tr.

**Figueroa Hotel:** 710bl; **Firehouse Brewing Company:** 463bc; **The Floridian:** 329bl; **Four Seasons Resort The Biltmore Santa Barbara:** 711tr; **Paul Franklin:** 533tr; **The Frick Collection:** *Lady Meux* by James Abbot McNeill Whistler, 1881, 90bl.

**Gaynor Ranch and Resort:** 592bl; **Getty Images:** AFP/Mark Ralston 601br; Obama Transition Office/Pete Souza 63cr; Redferns/David Refern 59bc; © **J Paul Getty Trust:** *Adoration of the Magi*, 1495-1505, by Andrea Mantegna, 648tl; **Grand Bohemian** 327tl; **The Grand Hotel Mackinack Island:** Don Johnston 423tl; **Granger Collection, New York:** 62ca, 62clb, 62bl, 62bc, 62br, 63bl; **Grapevine Public Relations:** 425br.

**Courtesy of Harley Davidson Motor Company:** 117br; **Heard Museum Collection:** 522ca; **Hells Canyon Adventures:** 629crb, 629bl; **Hemingway's Hyatt Regency Resort:** 330tr; **Henry Ford Museum & Greenfield Village:** 407tr; **Hilton Hotels & Resorts:** 462tr; **Historic New Orleans Collection:** 349cb; **Historic New Orleans Voodoo Museum:** *Portrait of Marie Laveau* 346br; **Hotel Valley Ho:** 551tr; **The Hotel Hershey:** 124bl; **Husk:** Courtesy of NDG 279br;

**The Jefferson Hotel:** 236tr; **Jessop's Tavern:** 239br.

**Ka'anapali Beach Hotel:** 745tr; **Kapalua Resort:** 747br; **The Kessler Collection:** 328tl.

**L'Espalier Restaurant:** 187bc; **Las Vegas News Bureau:** 504tr; **LemonGrass:** 746tc; **Lincoln Park Zoo,** Chicago: 394cl; **The London NYC:** 122tr; **Louisiana Office of Tourism (CRT):** 357crb.

**Mandarin Oriental, New York:** George Apostolidis 123tl; **Mary Evans Picture Library:** 475bl; **Masterfile:** Bill Brooks 50tr; Gail Mooney 45crb; Randy Lincks 51cr;

MGM Resorts: 504c; Museum of Fine Arts, Boston: HU–MFA Expedition *Shawabtis of Taharka* 153tl; Egypt Exploration Fund *Inner Coffin of Nes-mut-aat-neru* 153cl; Ruth & Carl J. Shapiro Colonnade and Vault *John Singer Sargent Murals* 153br; Museum of International Folk Art, a unit of the Museum of New Mexico: Girard Foundation Collection, Photo Michel Monteaux *Toy Horse* Bangladesh, Indian. C. 1960. 541cb.

© 2003 Board of Trustees, National Gallery of Art, Washington, DC: *The Alba Madonna*, 1510, by Raphael (Raffaello Sanzio of Urbino, 1483–1520), Andrew W. Melon Collection: 205tl; NHPA: David Middleton 547br; National Museum of American History/Smithsonian Institution: 204ca; National Museum of American Jewish History: Collection of Congregation Mikveh Israel: 110clb; National Park Service, OR: 625tr; The Nature Conservancy: Rich Franco Photography 313b; Nelson-Atkins Museum of Art, Kansas City, Missouri: *Shuttlecocks* by Claes Oldenburg and Coosje van Bruggen, 1994: 453tl; New Orleans Hotel Collection: 368br; New Orleans Metropolitan Convention & Visitors Bureau: Ann Purcell 342bl; Carl Purcell 344ttl.; The New Tropicana Las Vegas: 502bl;

Omni Hotels: 184bc, 186tl.

Pedro E. Guerrero © 2002, Talesin Preservation Inc.: 413tl; © Courtesy of the Pennsylvania Academy of Fine Arts; Philadelphia: Joseph E. Temple Fund, 2003: *The Fox Hunt*, 1893, by Winslow Homer 113br.; Peter Luger Steakhouse: 126br; Pok Pok: David Reamer 635br; Provenance Hotels: Hotel Preston 278tc; Pure Food and Wine: 125tc.

Restaurant 301: 715tc; Ritz-Carlton: 369tr, 424tl; Riviera Hotel & Casino: 505crb; Robert Harding Picture Library: Ruth Tomlinson 17tl; The Ronald Grant Archive: 654bl.

San Francisco History Center, San Francisco Public Library, CA: 691br; Mae Scanlan: 206tl;

Shack Up Inn: 370tl; John G. Shedd Aquarium, Chicago: © Edward G. Lines 391tr; Sleep Inn & Suites: 234br; St Julien Hotel and Spa, Boulder: B Public Relations 593tr; Stonehurst Place, Atlanta: Prairie Dog Media 277tr; Superstock: 312tl.; Sutter Creek Inn: 712tc;

Terra Galleria Photography: 612tl; ThinkFoodGroup: 237br.

© 2011 Universal Orlando® Resort. All Rights Reserved: 308–9 all; Universal Studios Hollywood: 659br.

The View Hotel and Restaurant: Rebecca S. Ortega, Two World's Photography 550bl; Viewfinders: Bruce Forster 611cra, 625ca, 625bl, 627bc, 628c; Trevor Graves 601tl; Rich Iwasaki 608tc; Pefley 610tr; Bob Poole 620br; Greg Vaughn 608b, 611tl, 616br, 620cra, 621t, 621crb, 623br, 624cla, 624br, 626b, 628bl, 629tl.

Walla Walla Chamber of Commerce: 613bl; Walker Art Center, Minneapolis: *Spoonbridge and Cherry* by Claes Oldenburg and Coosje van Bruggen, 1987-1988, Gift of Frederick R. Weisman in honor of his parents, William and Mary Weisman, 1988: 414tr; White Horse Tavern: 189tr; © White House Historical Association (White House Collection): 210cla, 210bc, 211tc, 211cr, 211bl (653, 579, 656, 140, 663) Bruce White 199tr (3074); Wintzell's: 373br; Wyndham Hotel Group: 460bl, 490tc; Words and Pictures: 342bl, 344ttl.; World Pictures: 639b.

Back Endpaper: Corbis: Tom Bean Lbl; Jan Butchofsky-Houser Rcr; Charles Krebs Ltl; Owaki-Kulla Lcl; Robert Landau Lcrb; Lester Lefkowitz Rtc.

Jacket
Front and spine t: AWL Images: Michele Falzone.

All other images © Dorling Kindersley. For further information see **www.dkimages.com**

---

### Special Editions of DK Travel Guides

DK Travel Guides can be purchased in bulk quantities at discounted prices for use in promotions or as premiums. We are also able to offer special editions and personalized jackets, corporate imprints, and excerpts from all of our books, tailored specifically to meet your own needs.

To find out more, please contact:
*in the United States* **SpecialSales@dk.com**
*in the UK* **TravelSpecialSales@uk.dk.com**
*in Canada DK Special Sales at* **general@tourmaline.ca**
*in Australia* **business.development@pearson.com.au**